Psychology Today

AN INTRODUCTION

Psychology Today -

Consultants and Reviewers

Chapter Consultants

Jonathan Baron, University of Pennsylvania
Chapter 11, Intelligence

Randy Blake, Vanderbilt University
Chapter 4, Sensation and the Senses, and Chapter 5, Perception

Judith Harackiewicz, University of Wisconsin at Madison
Chapter 17, Personality

Kenneth D. Kallio, State University of New York at Geneseo
Chapter 10, Language

Arnold Leiman, University of California at Berkeley
Chapter 3, The Brain and Behavior

James Meindl, State University of New York at Buffalo
Chapter 23, Industrial/Organizational Psychology

Robert Valois, University of Texas at Austin
Chapter 14, Sexuality and Love

Specialist Reviewers

Anthony Ahrens, American University
Jonathan Baron, University of Pennsylvania
Helen Crawford, Virginia Polytechnic Institute
Mike Dixon, Concordia University
Susan Fiske, University of Massachusetts at Amherst
Eric Golanty, University of California at Davis
David J. Hill, University of Virginia
Terrence Hines, Pace University
Earl Hunt, University of Washington
Kenneth D. Kallio, State University of New York at Geneseo

Mary M. Kralj, Human Resources Research Organization
Lois E. Layne, Western Kentucky University
Peter J. McDonald, North Georgia College
Doug Mook, University of Virginia
Gregory L. Murphy, Brown University
Darren Newtson, University of Virginia
Phillip R. Shaver, State University of New York at Buffalo

"Core" Reviewers

Arthur L. Blumenthal, University of Massachusetts, Harbor Campus
David C. Devonis, University of Redlands
Mark Garrison, Kentucky State University
Bernard S. Gorman, Nassau Community College
John Vitkus, Barnard College

General Reviewers

Ronald Baenninger, Temple University
Gordon A. Barr, Hunter College
Carol J. Barz, Mid Michigan Community College
Daniel Cervone, University of Chicago
George A. Cicala, University of Delaware
Sue Donaldson, University of Southern Indiana
Linda M. Douglas, Coastal Carolina Community College
Paul M. Evans, Washington State University
William Rick Fry, Youngstown State University
Adrienne Gans, New York University
Peter Hanford, Indiana University—Purdue University at Indianapolis
Lewis O. Harvey, Jr., University of Colorado at Boulder
Myra D. Heinrich, Mesa State College
Chris Jazwinski, St. Cloud State University
James Luginbuhl, North Carolina State University
Lois McDermott, University of Washington
James Nairne, University of Texas at Arlington
Stuart Taylor, Kent State University
Jean Volckmann, Pasadena City College
Charlene Wages, Francis Marion College
Benjamin Wallace, Cleveland State University

Seventh Edition

Psychology Today

AN INTRODUCTION

Richard R. Bootzin
University of Arizona

Gordon H. Bower
Stanford University

Jennifer Crocker
State University of New York at Buffalo

Elizabeth Hall

McGraw-Hill, Inc.

New York   St. Louis   San Francisco   Auckland   Bogotá   Caracas
Hamburg   Lisbon   London   Madrid   Mexico   Milan   Montreal
New Delhi   Paris   San Juan   São Paulo   Singapore
Sydney   Tokyo   Toronto

PSYCHOLOGY TODAY: *An Introduction*

1 2 3 4 5 6 7 8 9 0   VNH   VNH   9 5 4 3 2 1 0

ISBN 0-07-006539-X

This book was set in Stempel Garamond by York Graphic Services, Inc.
The editors were Christopher Rogers, Cele Gardner, and Sheila H. Gillams;
the cover and interior design were done by Armen Kojoyian;
the production supervisors were Stacey Alexander and Janelle S. Travers.
Cover illustration by Jim Finlayson.
Von Hoffmann Press, Inc., was printer and binder.

Library of Congress Cataloging-in-Publication Data

Psychology today: an introduction / Richard R. Bootzin . . . [et al.].
   —7th ed.
         p.   cm.
   Includes bibliographical references and indexes.
   ISBN 0-07-006539-X
   1. Psychology.   I. Bootzin, Richard R., (date).
BF121.P85   1991
150—dc20   90-36651

Richard R. Bootzin is a specialist in personality and abnormal psychology, and a prominent researcher in the areas of sleep and sleep disorders, principles of behavior change, and mental health evaluation. Dr. Bootzin received his Bachelor's degree from the University of Wisconsin at Madison and his Ph.D. from Purdue University in 1968. From 1968 through 1986, he was a faculty member at Northwestern University, serving as Chairman of the Psychology Department from 1980 to 1986. Since 1987, he has been Professor of Psychology and Director of the Graduate Program in Clinical Psychology at the University of Arizona.

Dr. Bootzin is a fellow of the American Psychological Association (APA), a member of the American Psychological Society (APS), a member of the Forum on Research Management of the Federation of Behavioral, Psychological, and Cognitive Sciences, and a member of the Executive Board of the Council of University Directors of Clinical Psychology. He has served as a reviewer for more than twenty-five journals, including the *Journal of Abnormal Psychology*, the *Journal of Consulting and Clinical Psychology*, the *Archives of General Psychiatry*, and the *Journal of Personality and Social Psychology*. He has published five books and more than seventy-five scientific papers. He is coauthor of *Abnormal Psychology: Current Perspectives*, 5th edition, published in 1988 by McGraw-Hill.

Gordon H. Bower is a cognitive psychologist who specializes in studies of human learning and memory. His work includes research on the influence of imagery and organizational factors on the storage, retrieval, and forgetting of memorized material. Dr. Bower received his Bachelor's degree from Western Reserve University, and his Ph.D. from Yale University in 1959. He holds a distinguished chair professorship in Stanford University's Psychology Department where he has remained his entire academic career. Earlier he served as Chairman of the Department and then as Associate Dean of the School.

Dr. Bower has received many honors including election to the National Academy of Sciences, the Society of Experimental Psychologists, the American Academy of Arts and Sciences, and is a fellow of the American Psychological Association and the American Psychological Society. Over the years he has been elected to the Presidency of the Psychonomic Society, the Cognitive Science Society, the Society of Experimental Psychologists, APA's Division of Experimental Psychologists, the Western Psychological Association, and the Board of Directors of APS. His honors include the Distinguished Scientific Contributions Award of APA and the Warren Medal from SEP. Dr. Bower has published six books and over 150 scientific papers. He has served on the editorial board for many professional journals (currently *Cognitive Science* and the *Annual Review of Psychology*); and he edits an annual volume of research on learning and motivation.

Jennifer Crocker received her Bachelor's degree from Michigan State University, and her Ph.D. in Social Psychology from Harvard University in 1979. From 1979 to 1985 she served as Assistant Professor at Northwestern University and at the University of Minnesota. In August 1985 she became an Associate Professor of Psychology at the State University of New York at Buffalo. She was promoted to Full Professor in August 1989. She currently serves as Associate Chair of the Psychology Department.

Dr. Crocker's research concerns stereotyping and prejudice, and the effects of social stigma on self-esteem. She has received major grants from the National Science Foundation to support her research on these topics, and has published over thirty journal articles and chapters in books. She received the 1988 Gordon Allport Intergroup Relations Prize from Division 9 of the American Psychological Association for the best paper on intergroup relations.

Dr. Crocker is Associate Editor of *Personality and Social Psychology Bulletin*, and has served on several editorial boards, including *Journal of Personality and Social Psychology, Psychological Bulletin, Social Cognition,* and *Journal of Consumer Research*. She has also served as a reviewer for over fifteen psychology journals, and served as a grant review panel member for the National Science Foundation. She was elected to the Executive Committee of the Society for Experimental Social Psychology (SESP), and is currently the secretary-treasurer of that organization. She has been elected Chair of the Executive Committee of SESP effective October 1990.

Elizabeth Hall is a science writer and consultant in the human sciences to Casa Editrice Giunti Barbera, an Italian publishing firm. She is coauthor of *Seasons of Life,* the companion book to the 1990 PBS television series on human development, as well as coauthor of *Developmental Psychology Today,* 5th edition, of *Child Psychology Today,* 2d edition, and of *Sexuality* (all published by McGraw-Hill), and of *Adult Development and Aging*. A former managing editor of *Psychology Today,* Ms. Hall was with that magazine from its inception in 1967 until she left in 1976 to found *Human Nature,* a magazine about the human sciences, as its editor-in-chief. She continues to contribute to *Psychology Today,* and some of her magazine conversations with prominent psychologists have been collected as *Growing and Changing: What the Experts Say* (1987). Of her many books for children, two—*Why We Do What We Do: A Look at Psychology* and *From Pigeons to People: A Look at Behavior Shaping*—received Honorable Mention in the American Psychological Foundation's National Media Awards.

Contents in Brief

CONTENTS

Psychology Today has long been recognized as one of the most up-to-date and comprehensive introductory psychology textbooks on the market. In keeping with that tradition, we have updated the text throughout for this new edition, incorporating the latest theories and most recent work in the various areas of psychology. We have, however, departed from past practices in an important way: we have decided that it is possible to be comprehensive without being ency-clopedic. Accordingly, we have consolidated the text into five fewer chapters than in previous editions, and we have integrated its concepts and themes so as to reflect the integration that is taking place in the field itself. We have also presented the material in a way that encourages students to think critically about what they have read, so that they identify connections between concepts and understand and evaluate the research from which these concepts were derived.

The process begins in Chapter 1, where we present an overview of the origins of psychology, the emergence of the theoretical perspectives that have come to dominate the field, and the major areas of professional specialization in psychol-ogy today. This foundation prepares the student for the chapter's exploration of five enduring psychological themes that reflect the interaction of forces outside and within individuals: heredity and environment, biological continuity and human uniqueness, conscious and unconscious experience, individual differences and universal principles, and the individual and society. In subsequent chapters, these themes frequently emerge as principles by which the work of psychologists, regardless of differences in theoretical perspectives, can be integrated. Thus, for example, the spectrum of viewpoints on the nature/nurture issue is covered where appropriate throughout the book, with special emphasis in the chapters on intelli-gence and development. We believe that this thematic unity lends the text a greater degree of coherence and clarity.

Three features are used to stimulate critical thinking. First, we describe major studies in detail so that students can assess their validity and relevance. Second, Mark Garrison of Kentucky State University has provided two types of questions at the end of each chapter: concept-review questions, which require students to articulate the main ideas; and critical-thinking questions, which ask students to analyze and integrate theories, studies, or perspectives discussed in the chapter. Third, John Vitkus of Barnard College has written seven critical-thinking essays, which are published in the Study Guide that accompanies the textbook. Each essay focuses on a single issue that is central to the corresponding unit of the book. The essay describes one or more studies that have explored some aspect of the issue, offers a critical analysis of that research, and sums up the research findings.

NEW ORGANIZATION AND CONSOLIDATION

We have reduced the number of chapters in this edition from twenty-eight to twenty-three and have reorganized the material as follows:

- The discussion of biological perspectives on behavior is presented where rele-vant in various chapters, rather than in a separate chapter.
- Human development through the life span is discussed in two chapters instead of three.

- Psychoanalytic theories of personality are combined with humanistic, behavioristic, and trait theories in a single chapter.
- The various theoretical perspectives on abnormality are not discussed in a separate chapter, but are incorporated into the chapter on psychological disorders.
- The sixth edition's two chapters on attitudes and interpersonal perception are consolidated into one chapter.
- There is now a separate chapter on intelligence, which presents the latest research on the nature of intelligence and incorporates an updated discussion of IQ testing.
- The use of statistics in psychological research is now presented in an appendix at the back of the book.

With this reorganization and consolidation, we believe, the sequence of chapters becomes more logical and organic. It serves our goal of integration, leading student readers smoothly through the various recurrent themes as they apply to the biological bases of behavior (Chapters 3–6), to cognitive processes (Chapters 7–14), to the development and psychological adjustment of the individual (Chapters 15–20), and finally to the behavior of individuals in the social context (Chapters 21–23).

PEDAGOGICAL AIDS

Each chapter contains one or more boxed features on an aspect of "Psychology Today and Tomorrow." The topic may be classic or recent research in an area that pertains to the chapter or the very latest work in an area that points the way toward psychology's future.

Each chapter begins with an outline of its contents, to help orient readers to the chapter's topic and coverage. Each chapter is followed by a summary in bulleted-list form (easier to use than a narrative, paragraph-style summary); an alphabetical list of the key terms that are introduced in the chapter; and the concept-review and critical-thinking questions described above.

A running glossary of key terms now appears in the text margins, in addition to the alphabetical glossary at the back of the book.

DESIGN AND ILLUSTRATIONS

The book has been completely redesigned. The text is printed in a single column, which is visually more "open" and accessible to student readers than the two-column format of previous editions.

This edition contains more than 250 photographs—many more than in any past edition, and the vast majority of them in full color. New tables and diagrams have been selected for their value in elucidating the text.

ANCILLARIES

A full range of ancillary materials is available, integrated with the text and with one another by Mark Garrison via the Instructor's Manual. The ancillaries include:

- Instructor's Manual, by Paul Rosenfeld and Mark Garrison. Contains outlines of the text chapters accompanied by detailed suggestions for using the other ancillaries, answers to the end-of-chapter concept-review and critical-thinking questions, and answers to the questions that follow the seven critical-thinking essays that appear in the Study Guide.

- Computerized Instructor's Manual (for IBM and Apple).
- Study Guide, by Daniel Paulk and Mark Garrison. Now includes comprehensive critical-thinking essays, questions, and exercises.
- Computerized Study Guide.
- Test File, by Wendy Dunn of Coe College.
- Computerized test systems (for IBM 3½ and 5¼, Apple, and Macintosh).
- Overhead transparencies.
- Slide Set. A "library of films and videos" to select from. Adopters may choose one free video per 100 books purchased from McGraw-Hill.
- Additional software: *PsychWorld*, 2d ed. (for IBM 3½ and 5¼ and Apple); *Mac Laboratory*, 2d ed. (for Macintosh); *Computer Activities for Psychology*, 4th ed. (*CAPS IV*, for IBM and Apple); *Report Card* (a computerized grade-management program, for IBM and Apple); *Experiments and Personal Applications in Psychology* (for IBM and Apple); and *Statistical Computation Program for Students* (for IBM and Apple).

These improvements and innovations make this the best edition yet of *Psychology Today*. Students can embark on their introduction to psychology with full confidence that they will find the experience enjoyable and rewarding. It is our hope that instructors will find this new edition a valuable review of past research integrated with the newest research and ideas in the field of psychology.

ACKNOWLEDGMENTS

We would like to thank the many consultants and reviewers who assisted us on this revision. We are indebted to the consultants who supervised the preparation of both new and revised chapters outside our areas of expertise. Our thanks also go to the specialists who carefully reviewed and helped fine-tune specific chapters. We are grateful to the "core" reviewers who advised us on the revision of the entire text. And, of course, we are deeply appreciative of the time and effort our general reviewers gave to the various chapters. Because their contributions were invaluable to us, we have featured the names of these consultants and reviewers on page ii of the book.

We are indebted to Dr. Robert B. Zajonc of the University of Michigan for his work on previous editions. Our special thanks go to Betty Gatewood, Jinny Joyner, and Mary Marshall, who helped us write some of the chapters.

Richard R. Bootzin
Gordon H. Bower
Jennifer Crocker
Elizabeth Hall

PART ONE

About
Psychology

...*Understanding Psychology: An Introduction*

Psychology today is a science. This statement is widely accepted by psychologists. Yet for many people—psychologists and nonpsychologists alike—psychology is a "problematic science" (Woodward and Ash, 1982). In what sense, then, is psychology a science, and why does this assertion cause problems?

If you tell your friends that you are going to study chemistry—or biology, astronomy, or physics—they know right away that you are going to focus on a science and that you are likely to become a scientist, a fairly clear-cut role. But if you tell them you are going to study psychology, they may very well respond, "Oh, are you going to analyze us?" Your becoming a scientist is probably not the first thing that comes to their minds.

Of course, you are not going to ask your friends to lie down on a couch and reveal their most intimate thoughts and feelings. But you will analyze them—and yourself in the bargain, although in a broader sense than even you might guess.

WHAT IS PSYCHOLOGY?

Scientific study is a particular form of analysis. It is the search for regularity, form, and order in nature. The focus of the science of psychology is the human being, a notoriously complex subject. A human being is at once a biological organism, a social organism, and an organism with a mind. (The word *psychology* comes from the Greek root *psyche*, meaning breath, soul, and/or mind.) The first two elements—biological and social—are relatively straightforward and measurable; but the third element, the mind, is neither. The mind is precisely what makes psychology unique *and* problematical. The mind is a factor at some level of every psychological question. Psychologists today take the mind seriously.

In asking, How do we remember? we might turn first to biology, studying the structure and function of the brain, and then try to define the relationship between the biological facts and the behaviors we observe. But if we did not remember and forget in the first place, we could not even ask the question, How do we remember? Remembering and forgetting are the very activities that have helped us build and define *mind*. Thus, the biological facts do not quite suffice for a complete description of the mental processes of remembering and forgetting. By the same token, in asking, Why do humans make war? we might investigate the biological possibility that, like other species, humans have an inbuilt aggressiveness, which finds its outlet in war. From a social point of view, we might analyze the influence of persuasive leaders on groups, the role of prejudice, the effect of class structure, the history of the state, and the behavior of mobs. But if we could not imagine war or its alternative; if we did not have such things "in mind"; if there were no possibility that an explanation of war would affect human choices and actions—then, again, we would not be asking the question in the first place.

Some psychologists have tried to avoid speaking about the mind or any internal states or events (thoughts and feelings). They have maintained that it is more scientific to investigate only that which can be externally observed and measured. The mysterious mind does not satisfy this requirement. However, such an extreme position is far less common now than it once was. That is because psychology today is much more convinced that inner states and events are important, if not essential, subjects of study and can indeed be reliably observed, at least indirectly. Nevertheless, this notion of the "mysterious mind" has contributed to the problematic aspects of psychology as a science. Psychology can be seen as attempting to explain and predict what may appear inexplicable and unpredictable. It is true that the ultimate questions—How do people think? What is feeling? Why do people make the choices they do?—have not been answered. But all sciences have aims that have not yet been realized. And psychologists have explained a great deal in their field's relatively brief history. Much of what they have discovered is described in this book.

Another reason that psychology can be seen as a problematic science has to do with control. A science's essential abilities to explain and predict also imply an ability to control. For instance, because a biochemical explanation of a disease leads to an ability to diagnose and treat it—to *control* it to some degree—

biochemistry may be applied to medicine. Moreover, although all sciences have a theoretical and an applied side, psychology has perhaps more difficulty than most in keeping its theory and its practice separate. Popular conceptions and expectations about psychology play a role here: people expect all psychologists to be therapists, counselors, and healers ("Are you going to analyze me?") rather than scientific researchers. Also, we live in a technological society that is anxious to apply science to life. Because psychologists are affected by people's expectations and by societal values and demands, they may believe that they *can* explain and also alter and control human thought and behavior. Public skepticism of psychology is an inevitable reaction to such beliefs. As the applications of psychology become more and more wide-ranging, new issues continually arise: Who shall be helped? Who *can* be helped? Which treatment is most effective, and which can we afford? So here, in the conflict between belief in psychology's power and skepticism about that power, we see again the field's problematic aspect.

Psychology draws on techniques from the physical, biological, and social sciences. It addresses issues inherited, as you will see shortly, from the long tradition of philosophical investigations of the mind. And it forges its own techniques for studying internal events. In these ways, psychology is capable of asking questions at multiple levels about virtually all human behavior. Taken together, the varied questions, potential answers, problems, levels, and points of view about human nature, and about the very nature of scientific inquiry, make up psychology—a rich, diverse, fascinating, and surprisingly young field.

A Working Definition

The very richness of psychology makes it hard to define concisely. As you might guess, psychologists have disagreed among themselves about what psychology is, what the goals of psychology should be, and what methods psychologists should use to understand human nature. There are two important points to consider in defining psychology. First, psychology aims at a comprehensive account of human activity. Some find this comprehensiveness unwieldy. But we can also think of psychology's multiple approaches and aspects as forming a complicated system made up of many parts. We cannot always expect to see all the parts at once, but this does not mean that we should not try to do so, or that we should not try to understand each part. Second, because psychology is a science it adheres to a common scientific method that emphasizes strict definitions, clearly defined procedures, and reproducible results. Psychologists are **empiricists**: they believe in verifying phenomena by experiment and experience. They wish to be able to discuss human behavior in terms that can be unambiguously defined. Generally, they wish to be able to "break up" behavior into component parts, each of which can be measured and related to the other parts.

Taking account of these two crucial points, in this text we define **psychology** as the scientific study of mental processes and behavior, and we emphasize those parts of psychology in which research reaches or approaches this ideal. But it should be realized that the science of psychology is only beginning to understand some aspects of human behavior, and that any science in its formative stages often contains much theoretical speculation, not-yet-analyzed descriptive material, and tentative experimentation.

EMPIRICIST   scientist who believes in verifying phenomena by experiment and experience

PSYCHOLOGY   the scientific study of mental processes and behavior

An Old Tradition, a New Science

Although psychology is generally considered to be a younger science than the other physical and social sciences, the initiation of the field is not clear-cut. Certainly the accepted date of the founding of the first psychology laboratory is 1879. But it is also true that the modern concept of science and the scientific method is not terribly old, either: the study of natural phenomena under controlled condi-

Wilhelm Wundt.

INTROSPECTION   a technique in which subjects report their own conscious experience in response to various stimuli

STRUCTURALISM   an attempt to analyze the structure of the conscious mind by breaking it down into its component elements

tions dates from around 1840. Yet questions about the mind and human behavior have been asked for centuries, as have what today would be called biological and social-science questions. In the wide-ranging works of the great Greek philosopher, Aristotle (384–322 B.C.), for example, we find precursors of evolutionary theory as well as a formulation of the workings of the mind. Aristotle observed his own thoughts and asked other people about theirs, and he concluded that memory results from the association of ideas of objects, events, and people—a theory that was strongly held through the nineteenth century and that persists in modified forms today. In the writings of Aristotle's teacher, Plato (427–347 B.C), we find a highly developed social theory, which is still analyzed by students of political science, as well as the rudiments of a theory of emotion. Other classical works also dealt with such topics. In short, psychology's roots run deep in philosophy and the history of thought.

The investigation of the biological aspects of what is now psychology also began centuries ago. Theories about the brain and nervous system began to develop in the seventeenth century, when French philosopher René Descartes (1596–1650) distinguished the physical brain, sense organs, and nerves from the soul, paving the way for the eventual separation of psychology from philosophy. Descartes also proposed a detailed model of human responses to physical stimuli. By 1750, laboratories devoted specifically to the study of the nervous system were well established. The study of the sense organs also began fairly early and was particularly important to the development of psychology as we know it today. During the nineteenth century, more and more sensations and simple reactions were found to exhibit reliable, measurable relations to the physical stimuli that produced them.

These findings, coupled with the growing body of research in the same period on the structures and functions of the brain and nerves, gave direct impetus to the founders of modern psychology, including Wilhelm Wundt (1832–1920), a physicist by training and a philosopher by temperament and interest. In 1874, Wundt published an influential book, *Physiologische Psychologie* (*Physiological Psychology*), whose title sums up one of the central ideas on which psychology was founded: psychological phenomena have at least some physical—and therefore measurable—basis. With funds from the University of Leipzig, Germany, Wundt established the first psychological laboratory in that city in 1879. There he studied a variety of phenomena, including reaction time to stimuli, consciousness and attention, and the dimensions of emotion. His best-known technique was **introspection**, in which subjects were trained to report their own conscious experience while reacting to a variety of sensory stimuli. By this method Wundt hoped to discover the principles of "mental chemistry"—principles by which the mind combined sensations to form ideas. His emphasis on careful measurement, experimental procedures, and statistical analysis of data has had a lasting impact on psychology as a science. His interest in mind and consciousness is also still very much apparent.

Several of Wundt's students brought to the United States elements of the new study of consciousness and the desire to emulate it. British-born Edward Titchener (1867–1927), arriving in the United States in 1892, had particularly strong ideas about the proper subject matter and methods of psychology. He remained true to one specific aspect of Wundt's approach, the introspective analysis of conscious experience. Because Wundt and Titchener attempted to analyze the structure of the conscious mind by breaking it down into its component elements, their approach became known as **structuralism**.

A returning American, James Cattell (1860–1944), brought back a different aspect of the German approach: an emphasis on the external measurement of the speed of reactions. Cattell attempted to use reaction-time measurements and statistical analysis to study intelligence and personality; his efforts led to important developments in both those areas (see Chapters 11 and 17).

However, one tremendously influential American figure did *not* study with Wundt and, in fact, criticized the entire German approach. This was William James (1842–1910), who was trained in medicine and physiology and had a deep interest in moral philosophy. In 1889 James became the first professor of psychology in the United States. James also was interested in consciousness and the mind, but in a very different way from Wundt and Titchener. He viewed consciousness as a constantly flowing stream—indeed, he is responsible for the phrase "stream of consciousness," now associated with so many major twentieth-century works of literature. Influenced by Darwin's then-new theory of evolution, James described consciousness as a function that had evolved so that humans could make reasoned, moral choices among various ideas. In other words, James considered this ability to make moral choices one of the most highly evolved human adaptations. This is a tenet of his *Principles of Psychology*, published in 1890 and considered one of the classic works in the field. James's concern with adaptive functions and his interest in emotions, the self-concept, and a host of other topics have direct ties with many current psychological theories. In part to distinguish it from structuralism, James's "school" of thought became known as **functionalism**, because it emphasized the adaptiveness of human thought and behavior.

Both structuralism and functionalism fell out of favor in American psychology after the early years of the twentieth century. The study of the mind, of consciousness as such, became less and less the focus of psychological study as more and more rats and pigeons found their way into psychology labs. Indeed, after 1910 or so, American psychologists repudiated any concern with unobservable mental processes and turned instead to a view of psychology as the study of organisms in environments. Observable, measurable behavior was deemed the only appropriate focus of research. Until relatively recently, then, most American psychologists believed that humans were basically reactive organisms and that behavior was for the most part, if not entirely, the result of external forces acting on the organism. Learning was *the* topic, because learning summed up the effects of the environment. All or most behavior, it was argued, had to be learned. (Note that this topic, although undeniably still important, now occupies only one chapter in this text, Chapter 7.) The most readily observable and controllable organisms, like rats and pigeons, could be used for lab study and the findings applied to humans, since all organisms must adhere to the same principles of learning. These popular, strongly entrenched beliefs formed the basis of what we know as *behaviorism*, which we discuss in more detail in the next section. Behaviorism as a separate approach or school is now itself somewhat out of favor, for psychology has again taken up mental processes, though in a new and different light.

Before we discuss the major perspectives in psychology today, a few other historical points should be made. First, the two world wars played a central role in putting psychology "on the map" (Samelson, 1979). Psychologists devised tests to classify recruits, assisted in the design of more efficient weaponry, and provided psychological counseling to returning veterans. So in a sense, these two devastating wars brought one of the three elements of psychology, social processes, into the lab and helped weave it into the overall fabric of the field.

Second, we have up to this point emphasized developments in the United States after Wundt. However, since 1900, several important influences from European cultures have penetrated American psychology. Among these are the psychologies of Freud, of Piaget, and of the Gestalt school. These tended to preserve the idea of consciousness and were less insistent on the rigid view of science that characterized much of American psychology in the twentieth century. In addition, European existentialist philosophy contributed to the development of the humanistic approach in the United States. Psychology as it stands today owes much of its continuing interest in problems of thought, personality, consciousness, education and child development, social behavior, morality, and treatment applications to this intercontinental exchange of ideas.

Psychology today studies many topics that would have been familiar to Wundt and James and appears to place consciousness and choice in a more prominent position in its theories about human behavior. As technologies of measurement have been refined, especially those that enable us to see how the brain functions, the idea that mental processes, as well as more directly observable biobehavioral and social ones, can be measured continues to spread. The experimental studies described throughout this text represent the development to date of the long and ongoing extension of the scientific method through psychology.

FUNCTIONALISM   a school of thought associated with William James that emphasizes the adaptiveness of human thought and behavior

Ivan Pavlov and his staff with the apparatus used to study classical conditioning in dogs.

PERSPECTIVES IN PSYCHOLOGY TODAY

Psychology today continues to support a variety of viewpoints or perspectives, five of which predominate. Each of these five perspectives provides a somewhat different approach to analyzing behavior. Each asks characteristic questions, makes certain assumptions, and relies on particular methods of research. Although the different perspectives may conflict sharply with one another on specific points and interpretations, in a broad sense we can see them as complementary. Each perspective contributes unique and useful explanations that together help us understand as fully as possible our complex behavior as human beings.

The Behavioral Perspective

BEHAVIORISM a psychological school that focuses on observable, measurable behavior and asserts that learning is the key factor in human psychology

John B. Watson.

We have already looked briefly at **behaviorism**, the perspective concerned with the principles governing observable activity. As noted, behaviorism arose after the first decade of this century. In 1913 American psychologist John B. Watson (1878–1958), already well known for his pioneering experimental studies of animal behavior, published a paper that can be considered the first manifesto of behaviorism. In this paper Watson argued that the method of introspection, on which Wundt and Titchener had relied so heavily, could not form the basis of a scientific psychology, because results varied from laboratory to laboratory, from subject to subject, and even from one time period to another within the same subject. Thus, consciousness could never be studied scientifically; instead, Watson asserted, psychologists should study only what they could directly observe and therefore reliably measure.

Watson was greatly influenced by the work of Russian physiologist Ivan Pavlov (1849–1936), who received the Nobel prize in 1904 for his work on digestive secretions. Pavlov was part of a school of Russian neurophysiologists who relied on a strictly objective, experimental approach. He conducted a series of studies in which dogs evidently learned to salivate at the sound of a metronome or a bell. In one experiment (1927), Pavlov set a metronome ticking each time he gave a dog some meat powder. At first the dog salivated—a biologically determined response, or reflex—the moment it saw the food. After the procedure was repeated several times, the dog salivated each time it heard the metronome, even if no food appeared. The implications of this research for the study of behavior were far-reaching, because they suggested a mechanism by which learning occurs. This process became known as **classical conditioning**. Watson claimed that classical conditioning could explain human behavior; neutral stimuli become associated with nonneutral, "natural" stimuli that elicit responses, and these responses make up behavior. Thus, behavior is the result of conditioning.

This approach can indeed explain many of our learned responses, especially emotional responses to otherwise neutral stimuli like money, foods that have once made us sick, and even, say, studying psychology. But this simple learning principle cannot explain behavior that appears either to be under the control of multiple stimuli or to be the result of a purpose or plan. To account for complex behaviors, including those that appeared to involve consciousness, psychologists who followed Watson devised a variety of explanations. One group, led by B. F. Skinner (b. 1904), proposed that complex sequences of behavior might be explained without reference to consciousness by a version of conditioning called **operant conditioning**. This form of learning operates according to two basic principles. First, behavior is emitted more or less at random by organisms. Second, some of these random actions result in something that either "rewards" or "punishes" the organism. What occurs then, said Skinner, is "selection of behavior by its consequences" (1953). There is a direct parallel between the principle of natural selection in evolution and the way in which, according to the operant conditioning model, complex behavior evolves. From both points of view, whatever helps the organism survive is "reinforced" and whatever is reinforced survives—whether it is a genetic trait or a pattern of behavior.

Whereas Watson's approach might be considered a stimulus–response, or an "S → R," approach, Skinner's system might be called an "R → S" form of learning: a response must be made by the organism *before* a stimulus is applied. Neither Watson nor Skinner had much to say about what went on between "R" and "S," whichever came first. They have been called "empty organism" theorists because they did not propose anything like a brain or mind intervening between an action and either its antecedent or its result. This form of behaviorism has also been called "radical," since it cuts to the root (*radix*) of the problem of consciousness and mind by denying it (or at least ignoring it). At first, radical behaviorism was greeted enthusiastically in America because of its practicality, but recently it has lost much of its early appeal. It stimulated a great deal of opposition, both within psychology and in the society at large, after publication of Skinner's *Walden Two* (1948), a widely read novel that described a benign utopia based on principles of operant conditioning. Many critics claimed the kind of social control the book (and, by extension, operant conditioning) proposed limited freedom of choice and conscience and was therefore morally dangerous.

Behaviorists—all of whom based their theories on observation of simpler organisms—also began to discover behaviors in animals that appeared to call for an explanation that involves more than simple connection or for one that describes the evolution of a pattern of multiple connections. In this regard, some behaviorists adopted the formula S → O → R, in which an organism O stands between stimulus and response; into this O succeeding generations have put expectation, memory, and forms of thought. Moreover, even behaviorists could not ignore the realities of human language, memory, and choice, and much of the early experimentation that led to the modern cognitive approach was done by psychologists in the behavioral tradition. The modern theoretical descendants of radical behaviorism have vastly increased the amount of attention they give to the inner organism so that "cognitive" and "behavioral" are often found together in psychological theory today.

Classical conditioning and operant conditioning (which are described in detail in Chapter 7) have proved to be powerful tools for psychologists to use in both explaining and controlling behavior. They have been used successfully to eliminate unreasonable fears and phobias and to help people quit smoking, lose weight, and learn new skills. Behavioral principles have become increasingly popular in education and form the basis of modern programs of computerized instruction. Perhaps behaviorism has been most influential in its emphasis on objective, observable verification of findings.

CLASSICAL CONDITIONING a learning mechanism by which neutral stimuli (such as a bell) become associated with stimuli that "naturally" elicit responses (such as food)

OPERANT CONDITIONING a learning mechanism by which a random behavior performed by an organism results in reward or punishment, after which the behavior increases or decreases

B. F. Skinner.

Computerized instruction is a widespread application of the behavioral perspective in daily life. Students advance through the learning program as each correct response is reinforced.

The Cognitive Perspective

COGNITIVE PERSPECTIVE a psychological school that focuses on the process of thinking and knowing—cognition

The **cognitive perspective** focuses on the processes of thinking and knowing—cognition—and can be considered both the oldest and the newest approach in psychology. The types of phenomena investigated by Wundt and described by James—attention, memory, and thought—are among the topics studied by cognitive psychology today. For much of this century, as you have seen, leading psychologists tended to explain human behavior by analogies to simpler organisms—such as rats, pigeons, and dogs—and mental processes were kept in the distant background. Now the situation has turned almost completely around. Most psychologies now have the word "cognitive" attached to them—we find "cognitive social psychology" (Chapter 22), "cognitive neuropsychology," even "cognitive behavior therapy" (Chapter 19).

What distinguishes a cognitive approach from other approaches is its emphasis on people's *internal* states. Cognitive psychologists believe that these internal mental events—thoughts, images, memories, feelings, decisions, and emotions—are real, and that they are important parts of any explanation of behavior.

A simple example of the cognitive approach can be seen by considering how a cognitive psychologist might look at different reactions to the same situation. For instance, suppose that a softball team has lost an important game. A cognitive psychologist would be interested in how each team member's cognitive appraisal of the situation influenced his or her emotional reaction to the defeat. One player might become angry because she felt that the officials had been unfair. Another player, convinced that his team could have won the game with a little more effort, might become determined to play better for the rest of the season. (We discuss the connection between appraisals and emotions in Chapter 12.)

Another simple example can be found in a straightforward and typical verbal test of memory. Suppose you are given a list of words—"shoe," "sandwich," "fruit," "blouse," "pants," "potato," "soup," and "skirt." After you have looked at the list, you are asked to perform some action such as counting backward from 100 by threes; finally you are asked to remember the list. It generally occurs that, when remembering, you are likely to rearrange the words so that you recall the articles of clothing together and the foods together. Such a seemingly simple test has helped psychologists understand that we tend to *categorize* objects we encounter and to organize them in memory with respect to those categories.

These have turned out to be basic principles of human memory. In addition, many other methods for obtaining behavioral measures of cognitive processes are available, such as looking at the time it takes to make judgments about stimuli— usually calibrated in milliseconds (thousandths of a second). We look at these methods and their results in Chapters 8 and 9.

Cognitive psychology has gone far in demonstrating that the mind is, at least in part, a beautifully organized system within the human organism, with its own regularities and predictabilities. Indeed, the continuing discoveries of regular patterns of thinking, remembering, and decision making by the rigorous methods of science have added new strengths to psychologists' belief in the reality of the mind.

The invention and rapid development of computers have played an important role in the current prominence of cognitive psychology. Since the 1950s, the new—and over the years increasingly sophisticated—technology has spurred researchers to try to create computer programs that think and make decisions like humans, but with the advantages of never being subject to fatigue, inattention, or emotional unpredictability. To help them reach such goals, scientists in the field of *artificial intelligence* have turned to cognitive psychology to understand how human decision making actually works. This has spurred psychologists to learn more and more about human perception, thinking, and language. In turn, cognitive psychologists have learned about human cognition from the *differences* between computers and people, especially in the types of mistakes computers have tended to make. For example, early attempts to program computers to generate new sentences yielded some very impressive results, but also some amusing errors. One computer programmed with information on current events generated the statement, "Castro throws eggs at China" (Abelson, 1976). This was a logical inference from the computer's program, but it violates our everyday common sense. Such studies have revealed an important element of human memory and decision making: our dependence on our memory's vast store of diverse and extensive practical knowledge.

Since those studies were conducted, enormous strides have been made. Computers can now be programmed with large amounts of knowledge and a greatly expanded ability to make logical inferences (see Chapters 8 and 9). More sophisticated and more flexible language programs are also being devised (see Chapter 10). All in all, the cross-fertilization between artificial intelligence and cognitive psychology has proved tremendously fruitful and has expanded both fields.

Like any other perspective, cognitive psychology has received criticism. Some have argued that because cognitive psychologists, no matter how objective their methods, still study the unobservable, it remains difficult to relate cognitive events closely or definitively with observable behavior. Also, some have feared that because of the predominance of the cognitive approach, processes like emotion, motivation, and even straightforward action—what humans actually *do* rather than think or know—may be neglected. However, developments in these areas should calm such fears. Research into the relationship between emotion and cognition has yielded important findings, which are discussed in Chapter 12. Computerized control of robotic limbs, like computer simulation of human thought, has passed beyond its primitive stages and promises to become ever more sophisticated. Finally, in the late twentieth century, we are steadily drawing closer to an ability to "see" and to understand at least some of the intricate workings of the brain where all these processes take place. That is, we are coming closer to the ideal of observing the unobservable and discovering the links that hold together so many divergent aspects of human behavior.

The Physiological Perspective

As you have seen, the **physiological perspective**, which is concerned with the biological processes that underlie behavior, is both old and new. In one sense, we could say it is at least as old as Hippocrates (c. 460–c. 377 B.C.), the Greek "father of medicine." Certainly Wundt, often called the father of modern psychology,

PHYSIOLOGICAL PERSPECTIVE
a psychological school that is concerned with the biological processes that underlie behavior

held that the newly emerging science *must* be based on a solid understanding of anatomy and physiology. Many today, as we indicated earlier, believe strongly that the research done by physiological psychologists will eventually reveal the underpinnings of all other aspects of psychology. For example, when one looks at images of the brain produced by a PET scan or by nuclear magnetic imaging, or when one considers the successes of drug treatments for often crippling cases of depression, this belief seems quite well founded.

Physiological psychologists work on the assumption that every psychological event—a thought, a mood, a fleeting feeling, or a decision to act—is associated with some biochemical event or set of events. Biochemistry is the basis for all communication between and among nerve cells and hormones. This is true whether we are talking about communication between individual brain cells or among complex networks of such cells; about messages sent from the brain to nerve cells in, say, the stomach or the skin; or about instructions to various organs and glands to release hormones into the bloodstream.

Physiological psychologists, also known as behavioral neuroscientists, are highly trained in biochemistry and general physiology; they come closest to the popular image of the scientist. They may study snails or rats or crabs, hoping to discover in these simpler organisms the basic principles of nervous system function. Some concentrate only on isolated cells or organs. And some work with medical researchers. Most psychologists from other perspectives realize at some level that their colleagues in the physiological area are working on the absolute basics of mental processes and behavior. Nevertheless, they sometimes find the physiological explanations of psychological phenomena somewhat remote, even abstract. Despite this, of course, physiological research moves steadily forward, developing technologies that make the microprocesses of the nervous system visible. Although physiological psychology has been criticized for reductionist tendencies, it has contributed greatly to our understanding of human behavior in general and of psychological problems and their treatment in particular. If, when you begin reading the chapter on the brain (Chapter 3), the material on visual processing (Chapter 4), or the discussion of drug effects (Chapter 6), you are troubled by a feeling that "this is not psychology"—rest assured that it is, and that as students of psychology today we must all become accustomed to the possibility that what we thought was unexplainable may have a physical basis. We must learn to relate the physical to the mental and back again, no matter how strange the relationship seems at first.

The Psychodynamic Perspective

Many of the popular images of psychology, including the one brought up at the beginning of this chapter (lying on a couch being "analyzed"), are drawn directly from a particular psychological viewpoint—the psychodynamic perspective. This perspective is based on the monumental work of Sigmund Freud (1856–1939), one of the most original thinkers of modern times, whose ideas have permeated Western culture. Indeed, the popular association of psychology with the couch, analysis, and revelation of deep and troubling secrets reveals the degree to which Freud's ideas, and the very figure of the man himself, have pervaded so many aspects of our lives. The **psychodynamic perspective** is concerned primarily with unconscious inner forces, impulses, and conflicts that are believed to influence behavior. This is in sharp contrast, for example, with behaviorism, which was gaining a strong foothold in the United States at around the same time Freud was developing and refining his theories.

Freud, a Viennese neurologist, formed his conviction that behavior was the result of inner and unconscious conflicts as he worked with patients who showed paralysis or other physical problems that had no discernible physical cause. Freud hypothesized that these "hysterical" symptoms had their roots in now forgotten but deeply troubling childhood experiences.

At first, Freud treated his patients with hypnosis. Later on, he developed the technique of **free association**, in which patients were asked to relax and describe

PSYCHODYNAMIC PERSPECTIVE a psychological school that is concerned with unconscious inner forces, impulses, and conflicts that are believed to influence behavior

FREE ASSOCIATION a psychodynamic technique in which patients are asked to relax and describe everything that comes to mind

everything that came to mind. He believed that every thought, image, or feeling, no matter how fleeting or seemingly trivial, must be connected in some psychologically meaningful way with the original source of a patient's complaint. Thus, free association would lead inevitably to the patient's unconscious, and the buried or *repressed* thoughts and feelings could be unearthed. The *unconscious*, according to Freud, was the repository of all the thoughts, feelings, images, conflicts, and memories of which we are not normally aware, but which exert great power over us. Another important technique for plumbing the unconscious was the interpretation of dreams, which Freud (1900) called "the royal road to the unconscious." The goal of Freud's techniques was to bring early traumatic experiences and the resulting emotional conflicts into consciousness, where they could be expressed and dealt with directly.

On the basis of his work with his patients, Freud developed a major theory of personality (discussed more fully in Chapter 17) that encompassed (1) the unconscious; (2) a universal (that is, applicable to all people) personality structure made up of three often-conflicting aspects called the *id*, the *ego*, and the *superego*; and (3) distinct stages of childhood development. The theory emphasized the role of childhood experience and the centrality of sexual and aggressive impulses, which Freud believed to be present from early childhood. To fit into society (even to have created culture in the first place), humans must learn in childhood to control these impulses and to express them in socially acceptable forms. The effort to do this inevitably arouses some conflicts, one's early experience may either minimize or aggravate these impulses, but in either case, the unacceptable wishes and urges are pushed out of conscious awareness to reduce the child's anxiety over them. The urges and conflicts—the sources of anxiety—remain in the unconscious, however, where they continue to influence everyday behavior.

Today, the psychodynamic perspective actually encompasses a range of viewpoints, from strict adherence to Freudian theory and practice to loose applications of certain ideas about treatment. A number of Freud's followers reworked his theories in their own terms, and others who have followed *them* have made additional revisions.

The psychodynamic perspective has been severely criticized over the years on a number of grounds. Many have found Freud's essential view of human nature too deterministic. This criticism is in part a reaction to the Freudian assumption that all behavior reflects unconscious wishes and conflicts; if this is so, such critics argue, then behavior must be largely outside an individual's control. (Compare this to the criticism leveled at the behaviorists, who were also considered deterministic because they emphasized controlling forces from outside the person.) Other critics note that, by definition, the unconscious is nothing if not unobservable; so how can its very existence be validated? This has been a major stumbling block for anyone who wishes to test Freudian theory objectively. Another criticism is that the work of Freud and his followers is based not on research but almost entirely on case histories of individual patients and theoretical interpretations of these histories. Perhaps, say some, the theories themselves are distorted because the subjects were troubled and not necessarily healthy or "normal" people. And some critics have simply been put off by the pessimism they find inherent in the theories. For all these reasons, then, the psychodynamic perspective is less popular among psychologists than it once was. Nevertheless, the methods of Freud and his followers are still widely used. Freud's overall contribution to psychology—even in sparking and fueling debate—has been incalculable.

The Humanistic Perspective

The **humanistic perspective**, called the "third force" in the field of psychology, was born in the 1950s. This new perspective rejected what was seen as the bleak determinism in both the psychodynamic and the behavioral perspectives (the "first" and "second" forces). It rejected both environmental stimuli and internal, biologically based impulses as the primary controlling forces of our lives. Instead, humanists emphasized subjective experience and the total human being, the indi-

HUMANISTIC PERSPECTIVE a psychological school that emphasizes subjective experience and the total human being, the individual's freedom of choice, and an inherent potential for growth

vidual's freedom of choice, and an inherent potential for substantial growth.

Abraham Maslow (1908–1970), one of the most prominent humanists, theorized that people are motivated not just by basic, biologically dictated needs like those for food, drink, and shelter but also by uniquely human needs for love and acceptance, self-esteem, and creativity. Maslow formulated this range of needs as a hierarchy. He believed that when the most basic needs are satisfied, people move "up" the hierarchy to seek love, knowledge, and ultimately self-fulfillment. His theory of motivation is discussed in more detail in Chapter 13.

Carl Rogers (1902–1987), another American humanist, made particularly important contributions to psychotherapy. In his "client-centered" therapy, as he called it (he believed "patient" was too negative a term), the person seeking help could be enabled to change and grow if the therapist provided a kind of mirror to the person's own self-description and offered unconditional acceptance. Central to Rogers's view was the assumption that if given the opportunity, individuals would see themselves in a more positive light and therefore behave in more healthful, positive ways. His ideas are taken up in Chapter 19.

Humanistic psychology has tended to be more theoretical than experimental. Its greatest influence has been on psychotherapy, particularly therapy aimed at helping those who are basically healthy lead richer, more fulfilling lives. The humanistic approach has also been important to the rest of the field as a kind of balance to other views, a reminder of individual uniqueness and human potential. In addition, the humanistic emphasis on consideration of the whole person—subjective as well as objective experiences—helps offset the field's insistence on objectivity above all.

Figure 1.1 diagrams the basic relationship between the five major perspectives that we have just discussed and the various professional areas of specialization within psychology, the topic to which we now turn.

Figure 1.1 The major psychological perspectives used in various areas of specialization. This graph indicates, very broadly, which of the five main psychological perspectives are used most frequently by psychologists working in the areas of specialization discussed in the text.

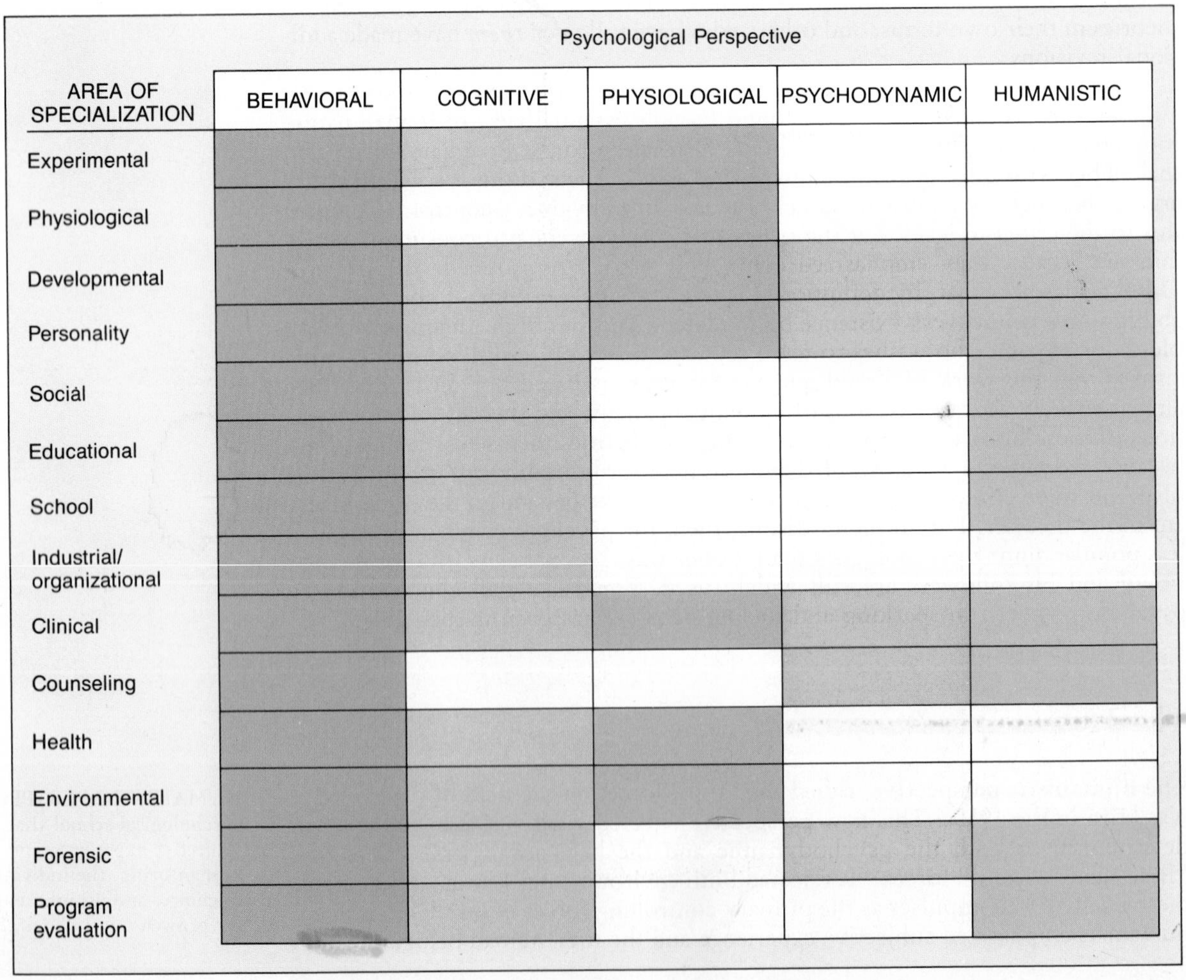

AREA OF SPECIALIZATION	Psychological Perspective				
	BEHAVIORAL	COGNITIVE	PHYSIOLOGICAL	PSYCHODYNAMIC	HUMANISTIC
Experimental	■	■	■		
Physiological	■		■		
Developmental	■	■	■	■	■
Personality	■	■	■	■	■
Social	■	■		■	■
Educational	■	■		■	■
School	■	■		■	■
Industrial/organizational	■	■		■	■
Clinical	■	■	■	■	■
Counseling	■			■	■
Health	■	■	■	■	■
Environmental	■	■	■		
Forensic	■	■		■	■
Program evaluation	■	■			■

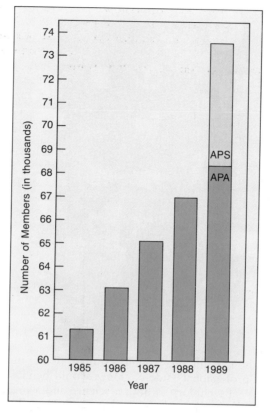

Figure 1.2 Membership in American Psychological Association (APA), 1985–1989, and American Psychological Society (APS), 1988–1989.

THEORY AND PRACTICE: THE DIVERSE PROFESSIONS WITHIN PSYCHOLOGY TODAY

Before 1988, one could point to the American Psychological Association (APA) (founded in 1892) as the main professional organization of psychologists. In 1988 that organization, which had experienced a long period of internal dissent, split in two, with some styling themselves "scientists" and some—the majority—calling themselves "practitioners." Some (but not all) of the "scientists" founded a new organization, the American Psychological Society (APS). Recent membership figures for the two organizations are given in Figure 1.2. Each side has defended the division by claiming that science and practice, by definition, have little in common and that scientific knowledge in psychology is still too tentative to form the basis for responsible social practice. Of course, in complex modern psychology, there probably are no "pure" science and no "pure" application that can be cleanly separated from each other. The split may be just one of the growing pains that an expanding field with diverse aims necessarily experiences.

However, the recent split does dramatize the problems involved in separating theory and practice, as well as the difficulty of classifying psychologists today simply on the basis of their membership in a single organized body. It was certainly easier in 1892, when the APA had fewer than 50 members! By 1988, before the split, the APA had grown to almost 67,000 members. It is important to note that this figure is only a rough approximation of the number of people in the United States who are involved in psychology or psychology-related activities. It does not include many psychologists with specialized interests who have left the more generalist APA over the past twenty-five years. It does not include psychiatrists or social workers, or the large number of mental-health professionals who work in association with clinical psychologists. It does not include the volunteers who staff hotlines. Nor does it include all the people who deliver casual advice. Some have claimed that a great amount of psychological activity is carried on by ordinary citizens: police, pastors and rabbis, family, and friends. A more realistic,

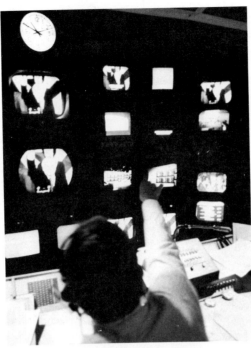

Experimental psychologists have shown that the ability to divide our attention among several different stimuli—as in this television control room—is a skill that can be learned.

though still very rough, estimate of the number of people involved in just the "professional" side of things would be closer to 135,000.

Psychology is both a science and a profession. The two are not necessarily exclusive, regardless of what the APA–APS split implies. The scientific activities of psychology are usually carried out in colleges and universities. Currently, the number of research and teaching psychologists in these settings is approximately 28,000. The vast majority hold a doctorate, or Ph.D. ("Doctor of Philosophy"), which represents about five to seven years of specialized professional training beyond the undergraduate level. Some are primarily teachers; others are involved mainly in research activities. We discuss the research specialties first, then shift our focus to some of the more application-oriented subfields. Remember, however, that the boundary between the research and the applied fields is inexact.

Major Areas of Specialization

Research Specialties

Both experimental and physiological psychologists are trained to do laboratory research. **Experimental psychologists** study sensation, perception, learning, memory, problem solving, communication, emotion, and motivation—certainly a diverse group of processes. (Bear in mind that experiments are also done by other types of psychologists who study other types of processes.) Researchers in the fields of **physiological psychology** and, more specifically, **neuropsychology** attempt to untangle the connections between the nervous and endocrine systems and behavior. Psychologists who specialize in **psychopharmacology** study the relationship between drugs and behavior. In the work of all these specialists, animal studies often play a large role.

Most experimental psychologists work in academic settings, where the freedom of inquiry allows basic research to flourish. In addition, many experimental psychologists today receive special training in mathematics and computer sciences and work in the rapidly growing computer industry. Psychopharmacologists are often employed by pharmaceutical companies to assess the psychological effects of drugs.

Developmental psychologists study psychological change throughout life. Every psychological concept—learning, memory, motivation, perception, personality, thinking, and so on—can be examined in terms of changes over a lifetime. Some developmental psychologists specialize in studying the capabilities of

EXPERIMENTAL PSYCHOLOGY the laboratory study of sensation, perception, learning, memory, problem solving, communication, emotion, and motivation

PHYSIOLOGICAL PSYCHOLOGY/ NEUROPSYCHOLOGY the branch of psychology that studies the connection between the nervous and endocrine systems and behavior

PSYCHOPHARMACOLOGY the study of the relationship between drugs and behavior

Developmental psychologists are increasingly interested in the behavioral changes that take place in old age. Here a psychologist interviews an elderly couple.

the newborn infant. Others concern themselves with the development of these capabilities through childhood, and still others focus on changes through adulthood and into old age. At one time, most developmental psychologists concentrated on infancy and childhood, but the past decade has seen the rapid growth of *life-span developmental psychology*, which focuses on age-related behavioral change from birth to death. This expanded perspective, which sees development as a lifelong process, has been in part a response to stepped-up interest in the developmental tasks connected with aging. And this, in turn, is due to the growing number of older people in the population as, thanks to medical and health advances, more and more people live longer.

Developmental psychologists work in a wide variety of settings: as consultants to children's television programs; in federal programs such as Head Start; in private practice; in institutions, where they may do psychotherapy with emotionally disturbed children; in industry, where they may try to determine how an employee's attitude toward work alters with age; and in schools, where they may work with children who have learning problems. Most of them, however, work in university settings and conduct research.

Personality psychologists study individual differences in behavior, the sources and consequences of such differences, and the degree of consistency of characteristics within the individual across situations and over time. This combination of differences among individuals and consistency within individuals creates what we call personality.

Most personality psychologists work in academic settings. However, some who specialize in the assessment of personality work in psychiatric hospitals, where they diagnose patients, or in industry, where they assist in personnel selection.

Social psychologists are concerned with the ways in which our thoughts, feelings, and behavior are influenced by other people and by society as a whole. They study such topics as prejudice, attitudes and attitude change, why people like or love others, aggression, social conflict, and behavior in groups. The work of social psychology reflects two broad themes: first, the ways in which behavior is influenced by the situations that people find themselves in, and especially by what others do or say; second, the ways in which people think about and understand their social milieus and relationships, including their attitudes and their perceptions of others.

Social psychologists generally work in academic settings, but not always in psychology departments. Some social psychologists who are interested in group

DEVELOPMENTAL PSYCHOLOGY the study of psychological change throughout life

PERSONALITY PSYCHOLOGY the study of individual differences in behavior, the sources and consequences of such differences, and the degree of consistency of characteristics within the individual across situations and over time

SOCIAL PSYCHOLOGY the branch of psychology concerned with the ways in which our thoughts, feelings, and behavior are influenced by other people and by society as a whole

processes and decision making can be found in business and industry. The rising interest in applying social psychology to concrete social problems has attracted social psychologists to politics, law, and medicine.

Applied Specialties

As noted, by and large the professional specialties just discussed are those most frequently found in universities. There are a variety of other specialties in which university-based research is an important component but which are by nature very strongly involved in the delivery of psychological services in the country at large.

Educational psychologists investigate all the psychological aspects of the learning process. At just one professional conference, for example, educational psychologists presented research on gender differences in mathematical ability, teachers' effects on students' behavior, identification of gifted children, and attention problems in learning-disabled children.

Most educational psychologists work in colleges or universities, where they conduct research and train both teachers and psychologists. But a few work in schools, developing curricula, materials, and procedures; others can be found in government agencies, business, and the military.

The work of school psychologists differs considerably from that of educational psychologists. Most **school psychologists** work in elementary and secondary schools, where they assess students' learning or emotional problems and devise programs to help parents and teachers help the children. School psychologists also administer personality, intelligence, and achievement tests in the schools.

Industrial and organizational psychologists study the relationships between people and their jobs. They investigate such topics as employee morale, job-related stress, the qualities that make a good boss, job enrichment, and flexible working hours. **Human factors psychologists** help create designs for machinery and work environments that are convenient, comfortable, efficient, and appropriate for humans.

The majority of organizational and industrial psychologists work in business or industry, in government agencies, or as consultants to business or government. Some of these psychologists practice **personnel psychology**: they screen job applicants, evaluate job performance, and recommend employees for promotion. Others specialize in **consumer psychology**, studying consumer preferences, buying habits, and responses to advertising.

EDUCATIONAL PSYCHOLOGY the study of all psychological aspects of the learning process

SCHOOL PSYCHOLOGY the approach to psychology concerned with testing children in elementary and secondary schools and devising programs to train teachers and parents to help students with emotional or learning problems

INDUSTRIAL AND ORGANIZATIONAL PSYCHOLOGY the branch of psychology that studies the relationship between people and their jobs

HUMAN FACTORS PSYCHOLOGY the branch of psychology that helps create designs for machinery and work environments that are comfortable, efficient, and appropriate for people

PERSONNEL PSYCHOLOGY the branch of psychology that involves plans for screening job applicants and evaluating job performance

CONSUMER PSYCHOLOGY the branch of psychology that studies consumers' preferences, buying habits, and responses to advertising

Industrial psychologists would be interested in knowing how a "country club" office setting affects workers' behavior and attitudes.

Counseling psychologists offer personal and career guidance to students.

Clinical psychologists study, diagnose, and treat behavior disorders. The number of clinicians practicing in the United States may be upward of 50,000. About half of all clinical psychologists work in hospitals or clinics or have private practices. In most states, clinical psychologists must be licensed; licensing requires a Ph.D. or its equivalent plus an internship under the supervision of a licensed therapist. Clinical psychologists are to be distinguished from **psychiatrists**, who attend four years of medical school and then complete residencies in psychiatry. Some psychiatrists—not all—have a more physiological perspective than psychologists. The only consistent difference between psychiatrists and clinical psychologists is that psychiatrists may legally prescribe drugs for treatment and psychologists may not. This difference has led to a good deal of friction between clinical psychologists and psychiatrists: with the exception of prescribing drugs, clinical psychologists clearly perform every service that psychiatrists do. Clinical psychologists believe that since this is true, they should be granted the same privileges as psychiatrists with an M.D. Several recent lawsuits have arisen out of this situation. There has also been a movement to award a degree—the Psy.D. (Doctor of Psychology) degree—that would indicate the special status of clinical psychologists with training in psychiatric practice.

Counseling psychology is a subfield of clinical psychology that deals with less severe behavioral disorders and emotional problems. Counseling psychology departments are often found in schools of education. In addition, many counseling psychologists work as guidance counselors in high schools and colleges, where they help students deal with social and emotional adjustment problems and academic or career choices. Counseling psychologists also come under many states' licensing requirements for psychologists, as do other familiar and not-so-familiar kinds of counselors—family and marriage counselors and pastoral counselors, to name two.

CLINICAL PSYCHOLOGY the branch of psychology involving the study, diagnosis, and treatment of mental and behavior disorders

PSYCHIATRIST doctor of medicine who specializes in the treatment of behavior disorders

COUNSELING PSYCHOLOGY the subfield of clinical psychology that deals with less severe behavioral disorders and emotional problems

The Field Expands

As the field of psychology develops and our knowledge of human behavior broadens, psychology is applied to new areas of human life. Some psychologists have begun to specialize in **health psychology**, or **behavioral medicine**, investigating how people stay physically healthy, why they become ill, and how they react to illness. Health psychology seeks to understand the relationship between the mind and the individual's physical condition. Among the relevant issues in this area are

HEALTH PSYCHOLOGY/BEHAVIORAL MEDICINE the branch of psychology that deals with behavioral factors in health and illness

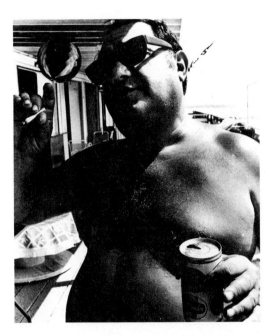

Identifying the psychological factors that lead some people to overeat or drink too much is one concern of health psychologists.

individual's attitudes toward health, the role of emotional stress in disease, the design of community education campaigns, the role of social support in treatment, and, perhaps most important overall, prevention of disease.

Another relatively new area of specialization is **environmental psychology**, the study of the relationship between people and their physical settings. Of course we can modify our environment in a number of ways, but we are also modified by the environment. Environmental psychologists investigate this complex relationship, studying such problems as the effects on city dwellers of crowding, noise, and perception of danger. Some environmental psychologists explore the effects that building design has on social interaction or the quality of life.

A third emerging field is that of **forensic psychology**, whose practitioners apply psychological principles to law enforcement and court procedures. Forensic psychologists can be found in academic settings, researching the psychological implications of eyewitness and expert testimony (see Chapter 8), jury selection, and jury decision making. Many other forensic psychologists work in applied areas—in community mental health centers and in police departments, for example, training officers to handle family quarrels, crowds, suicide threats, and hostage crises. Some forensic psychologists work in prisons, where they provide counseling to inmates.

A fourth new area of specialization is **program evaluation**, in which psychologists work with economists, political scientists, and sociologists to evaluate the effectiveness and cost of a range of government programs aimed at alleviating social problems. The increasing need to make every dollar count is bringing psychologists into program evaluations relating to health care, employment, transportation, energy conservation, and criminal rehabilitation.

In addition to all the areas of specialization that we have mentioned—and our list was by no means complete—there are a number of psychologists who have formal positions in the academic community or in applied areas, but who also serve as consultants in various settings, including education, the government, and the military. **Consulting**—the providing of expert advice, usually for a fee—is a widespread phenomenon in modern American commercial society. This is yet more evidence of the influence that research and scientific expertise has in our lives. Consulting can be a very efficient means of bringing psychological knowledge to public policy and to daily life. Often, too, consultants conduct research on very specific topics dictated by the needs of the corporation, foundation, or government bureau that hires them. For example, much of what we know today about vision might not have been discovered if the U.S. Army had not called J. J. Gibson from his academic post in 1941 and set him to work training pilots. (Gibson's pioneering studies are described in Chapter 5.)

ENVIRONMENTAL PSYCHOLOGY the study of the relationship between people and their physical settings

FORENSIC PSYCHOLOGY the application of psychological principles to law enforcement and court procedures

PROGRAM EVALUATION the cooperation of psychologists, economists, political scientists, and sociologists to evaluate the effectiveness and cost of government social programs

CONSULTING the providing of expert advice, usually for a fee

Remember also that a large number of people study and read psychology simply because it is interesting. Psychology includes all of us. This text presents the views of the main fields of academic research and gives some indication of how these views are translated into practice. But in light of the much larger number of psychologists who work in applied settings, it would be a good idea to ask, as you go along, how what you are learning about psychology might be put to use.

PSYCHOLOGY AND CRITICAL THINKING

Using Psychology To Understand Critical Thinking

Psychology is uniquely valuable as a route to develop the skills involved in critical thinking. Unlike some other fields (such as law, history, or philosophy), for the most part psychological theories and the policies they engender are based on the findings of methodologically sound empirical research studies that employ commonly accepted procedures which can be evaluated openly and critically. In this way we can separate the good research from the bad—the factual from the merely plausible. As scientific research becomes more influential in forming public policy, our ability to understand and evaluate it becomes more important.

What makes psychology particularly suitable for the development of critical thinking is that much of the research in psychology is accessible to introductory students (Winter, 1984). Students at all levels are able to analyze the procedures and conclusions of important past research. This analysis is good preparation for the evaluation of research findings they come across later in life, whether in psychology or in some other discipline. According to David Winter, the two most important contributions that psychology makes to a general education are to gain an understanding of behavior and to gain an understanding of *"the nature, uses, and dangers of research"* (p. 85; italics in original).

Using Critical Thinking To Understand Psychology

Not only will psychology help you develop critical analysis skills, but your critical thinking will help you better understand psychology. The next twenty-two chapters will cover a diverse array of topics, ranging from how our nerves transmit messages to how we become unique individuals and social beings. The findings reported in this text come from scientific studies conducted in laboratories and field settings around the world. To know if these studies are reliable or if researchers' inferences are valid, we must *critically evaluate* the research evidence we are given (see the accompanying box).

A critical thinking essay covers each of the seven parts of this text in the Study Guide. The first essay introduces the methods of critical thinking. The other six examine research evidence on different aspects of controversial issues in psychology: What do dreams mean? What are the sources of creativity? Do women really have a motive to avoid success? What are the effects of divorce on children? Can a positive attitude help to cure cancer? Does absence make the heart grow fonder—or go wander? As we will see, no study is—or can be—perfect. But by critically analyzing evidence gathered in different studies, often from disparate perspectives, we are better able to determine whether a researcher's conclusions are valid. Thus, critical thinking not only helps us understand what different studies say but also helps us understand what they really mean.

PSYCHOLOGY TODAY AND TOMORROW

The Psychological Consequences of Abortion: Critical Thinking about Research on a Sensitive Issue

Abortion is a topic about which feelings run strong. Following the Supreme Court's 1989 decision in *Webster* v. *Reproductive Health Services*, which allowed states to restrict access to abortion, debate on the issue intensified. Although most of those who oppose abortion have done so with the argument that the fetus is a person and that abortion is therefore murder, others have suggested that abortion also harms women. Specifically, it has been argued that women often experience a *post-abortion syndrome* involving guilt and depression, which sometimes does not emerge until years after the abortion.

The existence of a post-abortion syndrome has been disputed by critics, who have claimed that reports of long-term psychological problems involving many women are not based on scientific data. Instead, they say, these reports are based on clinical experiences with the relatively small number of women who seek therapy or counseling after their abortions. In addition, such reports rely mostly on the clinical impressions of a few therapists, who may or may not be objective sources of information about their clients' problems.

Most researchers who have studied abortion have concluded that most women cope well with it and have few, if any, psychological aftereffects. Women who do have problems are more likely than others to fear that they "can't cope" with the abortion, to blame themselves or their partner or both for the abortion, to be ambivalent about being pregnant, and to have little social support from their partner, family, or friends (Major, 1989). For most women, however, the abortion seems to be a relief; they bounce back from the experience comparatively quickly, as from any other stressful experience, and do not report significant distress or depression afterward (Adler et al., 1989). However, few studies that have as- sessed women's reactions to abortion have involved follow-up interviews with women more than a year after the abortion took place. There- fore, claims that women experience negative emo- tions long after their abortions cannot yet be evaluated.

If further research is needed to see whether abortion might have long-term psychological con- sequences, what might this involve? First, con- sider the situation of women who have unwanted pregnancies. They have three choices: have an abortion, give the baby up for adoption, or keep it. Each of these options may have negative psy- chological consequences. The woman who chooses abortion may feel guilty or depressed, but the woman who gives up a newborn baby may have even stronger emotional reactions. As for the woman who bears a child she does not want, she may suffer economically, socially, and educationally (most women who have abortions are young and unmarried), or in other ways from the stress of caring for a child she did not plan to have. A meaningful study of the aftermath of abortion would need to compare groups of women who have chosen these various alterna- tives. Second, such a study would also face the challenge of most research in psychology: proving that event A actually is the cause of event B. For example, if women who have abortions are found years later to be more depressed, to feel more guilty, or otherwise be more psychologically troubled than other women, how do we know that the abortion experience is responsible? Other sources of stress (job, marriage, lack of marriage, divorce, family conflicts—just to name a few) would have to be ruled out. (Adler et al., 1989). Very little scientific research of this kind has been conducted, yet it is necessary before we can un- derstand and critically evaluate claims about the psychological consequences of abortion.

Evaluating the Quality of Psychological Research

Although it is rare for any research study to be absolutely conclusive, clearly some studies are more scientifically sound than others. As citizens, consumers, and decision makers, it is important for us to be able to evaluate the quality of the research that is presented to us.

Winter (1984) outlines two general points to keep in mind when evaluating research: First, all experimental research studies are laboratory facsimiles of real-life phenomena. The laboratory model should accurately reflect the vital aspects of the actual research question. Second, characteristics not found in the real-life phenomenon are often present in the laboratory model. These characteristics should not contaminate or otherwise bias the results. These criteria should be met before we accept any research finding as meaningful.

Understanding how to evaluate the quality of psychological research will not only give you a better understanding of psychology, it will also give you an appreciation for some of the findings of research from other fields. In medicine, for example, the AIDS epidemic has sparked an explosion of research over the past few years. Let's say you read a study reporting the effectiveness of a new anti-AIDS drug. Having evaluated the quality of psychological research, you will be able to ask crucial questions that are important in weighing the merits or limitations of this medical study on AIDS. Who were the subjects? How were they chosen? Were control groups used? How was the effect of the drug measured? By knowing these facts, among others, you will be better able to evaluate the study as a whole.

Analyzing Complex Problems from Divergent Viewpoints

Because of its diverse nature and the open way in which its research findings are tested and criticized, the field of psychology offers students a unique opportunity to explore different approaches to any of a number of topics. As we have seen in this chapter, psychology offers a variety of frameworks, perspectives, and theoretical approaches. The number of theoretically important issues is virtually limitless, and each issue can be looked at in any of several ways. The better able you are to make sense of different perspectives on a particular problem, the better able you will be to comprehend it and ultimately to reach appropriate conclusions about it.

Take a relatively simple question: How does a tennis player make a serve? This problem can be approached in terms of the player's neurons (Which nerves are firing to control the eyes and motor movements?), perceptions (How does the player see the ball and feel the racket?), prior learning (How well has the player learned this skill?), motivations (How great is the player's desire to win?), development (Is the player physically and emotionally mature?), personality (How competitive is the player?), and social context (Is the crowd on the player's side?)— to name but a few possibilities.

Not only do psychologists look at problems from different levels of complexity, they often interpret the same process in entirely different ways. In analyzing the tennis player's motivation, for example, a behavioral psychologist might focus on the player's anticipation of reinforcers like prize money or social approval, whereas a psychodynamic psychologist might interpret the player's motives as stemming from underlying conflicts, such as a sublimation of repressed hostility. As you read this book's discussions of the different areas of psychology, keep in mind that for each study, the researcher had just one perspective in mind. Other perspectives could be applied to the same problem.

ENDURING THEMES IN PSYCHOLOGY TODAY

As you study this text, you will find that certain thematic issues recur from chapter to chapter. In the past, these thematic issues have often been set up as controversies such as "nature vs. nurture." But bear in mind that taken together, the two "opposing" aspects of any issue represent a whole spectrum of viewpoints, not merely two opposing sides. Usually the end result is one of integration, compromise, and degree. For example, the question is not "Are we products of our heredity or our experiences?" but rather "To what extent does our heredity control our behavior, and to what extent do our experiences shape our lives?"

Let's summarize some major thematic issues, pertaining to events both outside and within organisms, that will be touched on again and again in the following chapters.

Nature and Nurture

How does the system of heredity and environment function? How shall we define the role of each in our lives? These are deep and nagging issues for many psychologists, in a number of areas. Let us consider some examples of how this theme applies to particular topics.

Standardized tests have revealed both racial differences in IQ and sex differences in mathematical ability. Are these results due to genetic differences, environmental differences, or a combination of the two? Do whites achieve higher average scores on IQ tests because many of them are "smarter" than most blacks (nature) or because the questions on IQ tests reflect white middle-class culture (nurture)? Are most girls born without much ability or interest in mathematics (nature), or does society perhaps discourage them from doing well in math—or even from taking advanced math at all (nurture)? Psychologists who have argued for nature in either case have been branded racists or chauvinists, while those who have argued for nurture have been seen as biased as a result of their liberal political agenda. Any answers to these sensitive questions, which may very well form the basis of policy, have political and social repercussions. If you are in any doubt about the need for critical thinking when faced with these issues, turn to Chapter 11, on intelligence, and read more about this topic.

The nature–nurture interaction will also play a role in our study of development over the life span (Chapters 15 and 16). What makes parents behave as they do with their newborn? Are they acting or reacting? Does the infant elicit particular responses because of some inborn "nature"? You will find that at the very outset of life, a complex feedback system is set in motion between child and parents. (You could even argue that it begins earlier, at conception—or perhaps at the time of the parents' own birth!) Gender issues also show up in early develop-

The interplay of nature and nurture begins at birth. Psychologists explore how babies' inborn, hereditary makeup is affected by their parents' treatment of them, by education, and by the other social and environmental influences they encounter.

ment. Do mothers and fathers treat babies differently? Do parents treat daughters differently from sons? If so, is it because of a daughter's and a son's inherent difference, or because of the parents' own projected expectations for girls and boys?

Biological Continuity and Human Uniqueness

There are two indisputable facts about humans: we are members of the animal kingdom, and we also have traits and abilities that separate us from all other animals. We must analyze ourselves from both points of view. How do we integrate the two? You already know, for example, that strict behaviorists might emphasize the behavior principles we share with other animals; humanists might emphasize our uniquely human potential. (See Chapters 7, 13, and 19.) Are these approaches necessarily mutually exclusive? Between them, innumerable possibilities exist.

What makes the findings of any animal research study pertinent to the human condition? How do we know when and where to apply such findings? How far beyond the basic principles of animal learning or aggression or altruism or brain function must we go in order to explain how a first-grader learns to read, why people go to war or sacrifice themselves for others, or why they lose control of their feelings or limbs? Is language a gift only humans possess? How can we go about investigating this question if we can't talk to other animals? (This is not nearly as silly a question as it may sound.) These, too, are some of the points that will crop up in various parts of the book.

Conscious and Unconscious Experience

We have already brought up Freud's notion of the unconscious, its major role in his theories, and its vulnerability to criticism from a strictly scientific, evaluative point of view. (Chapters 17, 18, and 19 go into greater detail on all this.) But between Freud's notion and, say, the behaviorists' utter discounting of anything unobservable lies a range of intriguing possibilities. Indeed, some psychologists have preferred to conceptualize consciousness as a continuum rather than a set of compartments. Even the definition of consciousness is not an easy one to pin down. What sort of state are we in when we are asleep? hypnotized? tipsy? (See Chapter 6.) Whether or not Freud was right about the unconscious, there may be instances in which perceptual and cognitive processes *do* occur with little or no awareness (see Chapters 5 and 9). How would such processes affect what we *are* aware of? What are the implications for how much control we actually have over our own thoughts, feelings, and actions? And if there are less-than-conscious processes, how can we hope to describe them consciously?

Individual Differences and Universal Principles

Once more, we must take account of two self-evident truths: we are all somewhat alike, and we are all somewhat different. We have all been told on the one hand, "Each of us is special and utterly unique," and on the other, "We're all in the same boat." Our goal here, of course, is not a glib statement of the obvious but a comprehensive explanation of behavior. In order to reach that, we must focus sometimes on differences and sometimes on similarities and, at the same time, try to weave them together.

In cognitive development, to give one example, some researchers have focused on clear-cut stages by which all children proceed to mental maturity. Others have attempted to track individual differences in information processing. Both approaches are important. We will also ask, among other questions, Can intelligence be defined simply as an individual difference (Chapter 11)? Why do some people strive endlessly for career success or a perfect golf swing while others simply give up (Chapter 13)? Why are personalities so divergent? Are there given "types" into which all individuals, no matter how "different," can be categorized (Chapter 17)?

The Individual and Society

The relationship between the individual and society is, as you know, a theme not just in psychology but in literature and the other arts as well. It provides another double viewpoint: we function both as individuals and as members of a society, with each role influencing the other. Sometimes the roles are in conflict; sometimes they are harmonious. We can try to explain behavior in terms of internal factors such as personality and genetics, or external influences such as the social context of the behavior. What determines each of these situations? What purposes does a mob mentality serve? Are fads and social trends illustrations of passivity and conformity? Other animals live in groups and communities; how are human societies similar to and different from theirs? How do we define ourselves in relation to other people and others in relation to us? What kinds of social demands foster individual decisions, and to what extent? Can people learn to work together in harmony, and if so, how? Why are some attempts at persuasion successful while others are not? What governs prejudice? To what degree is morality an individual issue, and to what degree is it a social one? Questions about group behaviors, attitudes, and the concept of the self are specifically addressed in Chapters 21 and 22. But the larger issues touched on here are implied and relevant in the discussion of all manner of topics. Questions about that strange and familiar creature, the human being, are always there for the asking, and the effort to answer them is part of our study of psychology today.

SUMMARY

What Is Psychology?

- Psychology is the scientific study of mental processes and behavior.
- Although modern psychology dates from the nineteenth century, the study of mental phenomena goes back at least to the Greeks.
- Wilhelm Wundt (1832–1920), a founder of modern psychology, published *Physiological Psychology* in 1874 and established the first psychology laboratory in 1879.
- Edward Titchener (1867–1927), together with Wundt, made the first attempts to study the mind by analyzing its component elements (structuralism).
- William James (1842–1910), the first professor of psychology in the United States, emphasized the adaptiveness of human thought and behavior (functionalism).
- Behaviorism, an early-twentieth-century school within psychology, focused on observable, measurable behavior and asserted that learning was the key factor in human psychology.

Perspectives in Psychology Today

- The behavioral perspective in psychology, initiated by the American John B. Watson, is based on the notion that only observable behavior can be studied scientifically. Ivan Pavlov (1849–1936) identified the learning mechanism known

as classical conditioning. B. F. Skinner (b. 1904) identified the learning mechanism known as operant conditioning.
- The cognitive perspective in psychology focuses on the processes of thinking and knowing—cognition. Cognitive psychology emphasizes people's internal mental states.
- The physiological perspective in psychology is concerned with the biological processes that underlie mental processes and behavior.
- The psychodynamic perspective in psychology is concerned with unconscious inner forces, impulses, and conflicts that are believed to influence behavior. Sigmund Freud (1856–1939), the originator of the psychodynamic perspective, believed that psychological symptoms had their roots in repressed childhood experiences, which must be unearthed during treatment.
- The humanistic perspective in psychology, which developed as a reaction to the determinism of behavioral and psychodynamic theories, emphasizes people's subjective experience, individual freedom of choice, and potential for growth.

Theory and Practice: The Diverse Professions within Psychology Today

- Psychology is both a science and a profession.
- Experimental and physiological psychologists are trained to do laboratory research.

■ Psychologists can specialize in various fields that focus on behavior (neuropsychology, psychopharmacology, and personality and developmental psychology).

■ Social, educational, industrial/organizational, and human factors psychologists investigate how we interact with other people in particular facets of society.

■ Clinical psychologists study, diagnose, and treat mental and behavior disorders. Counseling psychology is a subfield of clinical psychology dealing with less severe behavioral disorders and emotional problems.

■ In program evaluation, psychologists work with economists, political scientists, and sociologists to evaluate the effectiveness and cost of government programs meant to alleviate social problems.

Psychology and Critical Thinking

■ By critically evaluating research, we are able to determine whether information is useful, relevant, and factual.

■ Some scientific studies are sounder than others, and it is important to distinguish among them.

■ All experimental studies are analogues of real-life phenomena and may not represent them without bias.

Enduring Themes in Psychology Today

■ The relative importance of nature and nurture—heredity and environment—continues to be debated in psychology.

■ The distinction between human beings and the animal kingdom and the existence of varying states of consciousness are still matters of interest.

■ Whether we function as individuals or are influenced by our social roles, by persuasion, or by the acts of others is a matter of continuing interest in psychology.

KEY TERMS

behaviorism
classical conditioning
clinical psychology
cognitive perspective
consulting
consumer psychology
counseling psychology
developmental psychology
educational psychology
empiricists
environmental psychology
experimental psychology

forensic psychology
free association
functionalism
health psychology/behavioral medicine
human factors psychology
humanistic perspective
industrial and organizational
   psychology
introspection
operant conditioning
personality psychology

personnel psychology
physiological perspective
physiological psychology/
   neuropsychology
program evaluation
psychiatrists
psychodynamic perspective
psychopharmacology
psychology
school psychology
social psychology
structuralism

CONCEPT REVIEW

1. Summarize the working definition of *psychology* given in the chapter. What are the subjects, aims, and goals of the science of psychology?

2. Who were the key early contributors to the scientific approach to psychology? How did they help change psychology from a philosophical to a scientific endeavor?

3. Identify the five contemporary psychological approaches outlined in the chapter, and describe them in enough detail to distinguish them from one another.

4. What are the main criticisms of each of the five approaches?

5. What are the singular contributions of Watson, Skinner, Freud, Maslow, and Rogers?

6. What is the APA? What is its most significant challenge today?

7. Describe the major areas of specialization in psychology. Of the various disciplines in these areas, who would be considered "practitioners" and who would be considered "scientists"?

8. Describe the process of critical thinking as it applies to the science of psychology.

9. Describe each of the enduring themes of concern that are presented in the chapter.

CRITICAL THINKING

1. The enduring themes presented at the end of the chapter are quite similar to themes one might find in biology, sociology, political science, and philosophy. Use the working definition of *psychology* to distinguish the interest of psychological, scientific inquiry from the broader and more general interests that all these disciplines share. Describe what makes the psychological approach different from these others.

2. How would proponents of each of the five perspectives presented in the chapter define, analyze, and interpret the enduring themes in psychology? As you consider each of the themes, consider whether any of these perspectives would lead to scientific disagreements with the other perspectives.

...*The Methods of Psychology*

Explain the concept of cognitive dissonance, cite a prominent study that illustrates it, and give several examples of the concept from daily life.

You are taking a psychology test in your classroom, and this question has you stumped. Suddenly, while you are staring at the edge of the blackboard where your professor usually stands, the answer pops into your mind. You visualize the professor writing on the board and almost hear the words of explanation. Then you also recall the relevant section of the text—all by association with that particular spot in the room. When the test is over, you wonder whether you would have recalled that answer if you had been in another classroom: Could it be easier to remember something when you are in the same place where you originally learned it? This seems plausible, but is it really true?

Psychologists have studied just this question and many others about human memory. In this chapter, we explore *how* they have done so; we examine *what* they have learned about memory in Chapter 8 of this book. The important issue at the moment is how psychologists, or any other scientists, go about doing research.

THE SCIENTIFIC METHOD

Scientific research involves carefully following a set of procedures known as the **scientific method.** The scientific method consists of three basic steps. The first step is that a researcher *observes* something of interest in the natural world. In the case of psychologists, that something is an aspect of how people or other organisms think, feel, or act. In most cases researchers make conscious observations, but often their observations are serendipitous—they occur just by chance. The earliest antidepressant drug, for example, was found by accident when it was first used to treat tuberculosis. Although it did not improve the state of patients' lungs, it did seem to make them more cheerful and optimistic. This discovery raised an important scientific question: Could the drug be used to relieve the symptoms of depression?

The second step in the scientific method is to formulate a **hypothesis,** a testable prediction or proposition that attempts to explain some observed phenomenon. *Testable* is a key word in this definition. A hypothesis must be carefully stated to ensure its testability—to ensure that it is capable of being supported or disproved. Consider this hypothesis: Maria is unhappy because she is depressed. In this case the meaning of "depression" is not clear. If we simply mean being unhappy, as the term is commonly used, then we do not have a useful hypothesis to test. Unhappiness and depression are synonymous; one cannot explain the other. If, however, by "depression" we mean something more technical (perhaps a certain chemical state in the brain), then this definition must be specified precisely. With the meaning of "depression" left unclear, the hypothesis is untestable. We have no idea what kind of evidence to gather to support or refute it.

Another kind of hypothesis that is difficult to test is one that refers to something that is not directly observable. For example, Freud proposed that every boy goes through an Oedipal conflict in which he sees his father as a rival for the sexual affections of his mother. Freud held that this conflict (which we discuss in more detail in Chapter 17) takes place in the boy's unconscious, outside of his awareness. As a result, it cannot be observed directly, even by the boy himself. This makes it hard to gather concrete evidence that will support or disprove the hypothesis. If we see a young boy making sexual overtures toward his mother, how do we know that an Oedipal conflict is at work? Conversely, if there are no signs of seductiveness toward the mother, perhaps the boy is just repressing his unconscious urge. Most modern-day psychologists are careful to specify the observable consequences of hypothesized unobservable phenomena.

Once they have a testable hypothesis, scientists proceed to the third step in the scientific method: collecting data that support or refute what the hypothesis proposes. Let us look at some of the ways in which scientists have gathered data about how the brain is organized.

SCIENTIFIC METHOD a set of procedures that scientists follow in conducting their research, consisting of (1) observing a phenomenon of scientific interest, (2) formulating a hypothesis about it, and (3) collecting data for or against what the hypothesis proposes

HYPOTHESIS a testable prediction or proposition that attempts to explain some observed phenomenon

The scientific method requires the gathering of data in an objective, systematic way. In sleep research, for example, sensors tell the researcher when the subject is likely to be dreaming; he does not have to rely on only the subject's reports of whether or not she dreamed, which may not be accurate.

In 1864, a German doctor who was dressing a soldier's head wound observed that when he touched the surface of the brain on one side of the head, muscles on the *other* side of the body twitched. He hypothesized that areas of the brain on one side of the body are linked to body parts on the opposite side. To test this hypothesis, he exposed the surface of a dog's brain and stimulated it with weak electric current. Sure enough, when one side of the brain was stimulated, muscles on the opposite side of the body contracted (Restak, 1984).

Some forty years later another scientist, John Hughlings Jackson, expanded our knowledge of brain organization. Jackson's wife was an epileptic, and he noticed that her seizures were always confined to specific parts of her body. The tremors moved up her hand to the wrist, elbow, shoulder, and face; then they passed down the leg on the same side of the body. Jackson hypothesized that small areas of the brain controlled specific muscles of the body. As abnormal activity spread through some of these brain regions, it caused contraction of the muscles to which those regions were linked. Jackson further hypothesized that the areas of the brain controlling neighboring parts of the body were relatively close together. For instance, the brain region that controlled the hand should be much closer to the one that controlled the wrist than to the one that controlled the leg.

Jackson's hypotheses were tested in the 1950s and 1960s by neurosurgeon Wilder Penfield (Penfield and Rasmussen, 1950). Penfield stimulated the brains of patients in preparing them for surgery to stop severe epileptic seizures. As he applied painless bursts of weak electric current to small brain regions, the patient moved a finger, a wrist, a leg, and so on. It turned out that Jackson had been right: the closer together body parts are, the closer together are the brain areas controlling the movement of those parts. Using the data he gathered, Penfield developed a map of the brain's motor areas (the areas related to movement) that is still accepted today.

Hypothesis forming and data collection are highly interrelated. A hypothesis *guides* the collection of data. It tells researchers which kinds of evidence must be gathered to support or disprove what a hypothesis claims. For example, if specific brain regions are indeed linked to specific parts of the body, as Jackson hypothesized, stimulating a given brain region must cause effects in the connected body part. At the same time, research findings *feed* hypotheses. They provide a continually growing body of data for hypotheses to explain.

Once they have accumulated a mass of data in testing a hypothesis, researchers must consolidate their observations into manageable and meaningful form.

Scientists use theories to explain natural phenomena. Astronomers, for example, can explain the "diamond ring" effect created by this total solar eclipse with a set of statements about the movements of the earth and moon.

THEORY an attempt to fit all the currently known facts about a subject into an integrated and logical whole

They do this by employing a variety of statistical techniques, which are discussed in the Appendix at the back of this book.

As more and more data about a particular topic accumulate, scientists build **theories**—attempts to fit all the currently known facts into a logical whole. A theory is broader than a hypothesis. While a hypothesis is a testable proposition about a single phenomenon, a theory tries to integrate and explain many different research findings. For instance, scientists have developed overall theories of brain organization and function that incorporate the large number of facts we have learned about the brain. Such theories, in turn, help generate new hypotheses to be tested, which, in turn, lead to new studies and the acquisition of new knowledge. This new knowledge often helps researchers elaborate and refine their theories, and so their scientific understanding grows.

THE RESEARCH METHODS OF PSYCHOLOGY

The scientific method is a set of general procedures that all researchers, regardless of their discipline, are expected to follow if their findings are to be accepted as valid. Biologists, geologists, chemists, physicists, psychologists, and all other kinds of scientists make observations, formulate hypotheses, and gather and analyze data. But the specific methods that scientists use to carry out these procedures may vary from one discipline to another. In psychology, research methods are of three basic types: *descriptive methods* (which enable researchers to observe interesting aspects of behavior and generate hypotheses about them), the *correlational method* (which allows psychologists to determine whether different aspects of behavior are related), and the *experimental method* (which is a means of gathering evidence that a cause-and-effect relationship exists). Although in this chapter we talk about each of these methods in a separate section, please bear in mind that they are often used together to study a particular problem. Different research methods are complementary. Each adds its own kinds of insights into the what and why of human behavior.

Descriptive Methods: Discovering What Subjects Think and Do

By accurately describing the full range of human behavior, psychologists acquire a broad base of information from which to generate hypotheses. There are three methods for describing behavior: naturalistic observation, the survey, and the case study. **Naturalistic observation** involves observing subjects in their natural environments (without any interference on the part of the researcher) and carefully recording what those subjects say and do. This method tries to see how subjects respond to everyday situations, not how they react when they know they are being studied or when they are placed in a setting that the researcher has created. A **survey** involves asking people a carefully prepared set of questions about their attitudes, beliefs, feelings, or behaviors. The researcher then tabulates the answers to get a picture of the various ways in which these people think and act. Finally, a **case study** looks in depth at the thoughts, feelings, and actions of a particular individual of interest to psychologists. For instance, people with rare mental disorders, or those exposed to unusual environmental conditions, are often selected as subjects for case studies. The case study offers researchers highly detailed information about a person's emotions, motivations, and thoughts—information that would be hard to obtain in any other way. Let us look more closely at each of these descriptive methods.

Naturalistic Observation

Naturalistic observation involves observing subjects in their natural, everyday environments. The researchers watch from a distance (often hidden from the subjects' view) and carefully record what they see and hear. They do not involve themselves with the subjects' activities. They simply observe the normal flow of behavior and the subjects' responses to situations as they naturally arise.

Jane Goodall (1986) used naturalistic observation to study chimpanzees in the wild. For years, she observed a group of chimps in their African habitat. She watched their courting rituals, their child-rearing practices, their squabbles, and their efforts to dominate one another. Until Goodall saw the chimps making and using simple tools—stripping the leaves from twigs and using the twigs to "fish" termites out of their nests, for example—scientists had assumed that toolmaking was a uniquely human skill.

In the study of human behavior naturalistic observation is generally used to see how people normally react to matters that arise in their everyday environments. The researchers are precise and systematic in recording their observations. For instance, they may make a checklist of possible responses and mark off each response as it occurs. Or they may observe each subject for a specified period and record all the activities in which that person engages during that time. Videotape is tremendously valuable in naturalistic observation for it can be analyzed frame by frame to find minute changes in behavior.

In a typical observational study, researchers watched children at nursery schools for youngsters from abusive and stress-ridden homes (Main and George, 1985). They wondered whether the experience of being abused would diminish a child's concern for others in distress. They found that abused toddlers not only failed to respond sympathetically to the distress of other children, but also became

The one-way window is an aid to naturalistic observation. The little girl sees only a mirror, so her behavior is not affected by the researcher's presence.

fearful or angry when another youngster was upset. Sometimes they even threatened or attacked the other child. These fascinating findings could have been learned only through naturalistic observation, for researchers cannot ethically cause distress in toddlers simply for the sake of seeing how abused peers respond.

But *why* did the abused youngsters become angry or fearful when other children were distressed? Naturalistic observation cannot answer this question; it can only allow the reaction to be noted. Perhaps the abused youngsters were so emotionally numbed that they could feel no sympathy for others. Or perhaps they had learned by watching their own parents or caregivers that indifference or anger is the "appropriate" response when a child is upset. Fear on the part of the abused youngsters might be explained if they expected that a child's crying would bring harsh punishment from adults—punishment that might extend to *all* youngsters present, not just the one distressed. All these explanations are plausible, but naturalistic observation cannot tell us which ones, if any, are correct.

The Survey

A survey is a way of obtaining descriptions of human behavior drawn from more people than direct observation usually allows. Survey researchers ask subjects carefully prepared sets of questions about their attitudes, beliefs, and characteristic ways of acting. In writing these questions, the researchers try to avoid vague or biased wording. Vaguely worded questions can cause confusion about what is being asked, and biased questions can invalidate answers by prompting subjects to respond as the researchers want them to.

SAMPLE a representative selection of members of a defined population

When a group is very large, it is usually impossible to survey all the members, so researchers pick a **sample** that is representative of the group. A sample is considered representative if its essential characteristics match those of the group. Researchers can then make inferences about the group as a whole based on what they learn about the sample. The best way to create a representative sample is to choose it through **randomization**—that is, in such a way that each person in the group has an equal chance of being chosen (say, by drawing lots).

RANDOMIZATION a method of assigning people to a group in such a way that each person has an equal chance of being chosen

But the best-laid plans for choosing a representative sample can sometimes go awry. Suppose that some of the respondents chosen refuse to participate or answer only some of the questions. In a survey on the prevalence of fears and phobias among women, for example, 16 percent refused to answer (Costello, 1982). Were these women more or less likely to have fears and phobias than the women who did participate? There is no way of knowing. The representativeness of any sample is threatened when less than 100 percent respond.

Another problem arises when respondents feel compelled to answer questions in "socially desirable" ways. For example, many people surveyed on a delicate topic, such as safer sex, may give what they think are the "approved" answers, even though they do not really apply to themselves. People who carry the AIDS virus, for instance, may feel compelled to say that they always use condoms, even though they sometimes do not. The pressure to answer in socially desirable ways threatens to invalidate a survey. Providing respondents with anonymity reduces but does not eliminate the social desirability bias.

A well-planned and carefully conducted survey can provide valuable information about trends in buying habits and many other kinds of behavior.

The Case Study

In contrast to the survey, which is a relatively extensive study of a large group of people, the case study is usually an intensive investigation of an individual or small group. The subject typically has some unique characteristic that can contribute to the understanding of human behavior. The researcher uses both in-depth interviews and observation, sometimes over the course of months or years.

Some comprehensive theories of human thought, emotion, or behavior have been based largely on case studies. For instance, Sigmund Freud based his theory of personality development (discussed in Chapter 17) on intensive case studies of his patients. Later Swiss psychologist Jean Piaget formulated a theory of intellectual development that began with meticulous observation of his own three children, almost from the moment of birth (see Chapters 15 and 16).

A case study can sometimes serve as an "extreme test" to help confirm some widely accepted principle. Consider the study of a child known as Genie. From the time she was an infant, Genie was severely abused by her father and neglected by her mother. By day, the father harnessed her to a chair in an attic room. By night, he caged her in a crib. Whenever Genie made a noise, her father beat her with a large piece of wood. No one ever talked to Genie; the father made only barking and growling sounds at her. This situation continued until Genie was thirteen, when her mother finally got her out of the house and into the hands of people who would care for her. It was only then that anyone tried to teach Genie to speak. Although she did make some progress with language after a great deal of training, her speech was never normal (Curtiss, 1977). This case study is an extreme test of the view that a critical period for language development exists early in life, a period during which the brain is especially "prepared" to acquire language.

The Correlational Method: Exploring Relationships and Making Predictions

Sometimes researchers want to explore how various factors are related to one another—that is, whether or not these factors are *correlated*. Is major surgery correlated with the onset of depression? Is being a first-born child correlated with high academic achievement? Is being a member of a certain ethnic group correlated with having certain personality traits? **Correlational research** investigates such possible relationships. It determines whether certain factors occur together at a rate significantly higher than would be expected to happen by chance. These factors are called variables. In science, a **variable** is any measurable or observable factor that can differ in either amount or form from one instance of it to another.

Correlational research often deals with variables that are beyond a researcher's power to control. Examples are age, gender, and race. This method is also useful for studying variables that cannot ethically be imposed on people just for the sake of science (drug addiction, for instance, or emotional abuse). Instead, researchers find naturally occurring instances of such factors and explore what other phenomena regularly accompany them. Are drug addicts usually young,

CORRELATIONAL RESEARCH studies that investigate the relationships between variables to determine whether they occur together at a rate significantly higher than would be expected to happen by chance

VARIABLE any measurable or observable factor that can differ in either amount or form from one instance of it to another

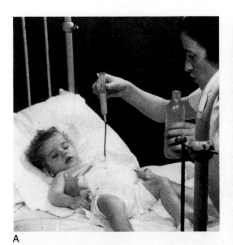

A   B   C

A long-term case study of a girl called Monica provided valuable insights into the influence of early experiences on later behavior. Monica was born with a malformation of the esophagus that required her to be fed by gastric fistula until she was two years old. She was not held in a caregiver's arms for feeding during this entire period. As a young girl, Monica fed her dolls without holding them. Later, as a mother, Monica did not hold her own babies in her arms while feeding them. [G. L. Engel, F. Reichsman, V. T. Harway, and D. W. Hess (1985). Monica: Infant-feeding behavior of a mother gastric fistula-fed as an infant: A 30-year longitudinal study of enduring effects, in E. J. Anthony and G. H. Pollock (eds.), *Parental influences in health and disease.* Boston: Little Brown. Courtesy Dr. George Engel.]

and are they more likely to be male than female? Is child abuse more likely to occur among certain socioeconomic groups than among others?

In correlational research, the degree of relationship between two variables is statistically calculated and called the **correlation coefficient.** A correlation coefficient is expressed by a number ranging from −1 to +1. When two variables are completely unrelated (having major surgery is unassociated with the chances of being depressed), the correlation coefficient is 0. When two variables are found to change in the same direction (for instance, people who have major surgery also tend to suffer depression), we say there is a *positive* relationship between them, and the correlation coefficient is a positive number between 0 and +1. The stronger the relationship, the closer to +1 the correlation coefficient will be. (If *all* people who have major surgery also suffer depression and all people who do *not* have major surgery do *not* suffer depression, the correlation coefficient is the maximum positive number, +1.) If one variable increases as the other decreases, we say there is a *negative* correlation, and the correlation coefficient is a negative number between 0 and −1. Here we say the variables are *inversely* related: more of one is associated with less of the other (having major surgery is related to a *reduced* incidence of depression).

When two variables are found to be correlated, it is often very tempting to assume that one has *caused* the other. For instance, going through a divorce is generally related to an increased incidence of seeking psychiatric help (Bloom, Asher, and White, 1978). Does this mean that divorce causes emotional problems? The connection may seem likely, even logical; but in fact this conclusion is unwarranted. We cannot determine cause and effect from correlational findings alone. Perhaps emotional problems lead to divorce rather than the other way around. Or perhaps some third variable related to both divorce and emotional problems is causing the observed correlation. Financial hardship, for example, could produce both marital discord *and* emotional disorders. Thus, the simple fact that two factors tend to occur together does not tell us *how* they are related or whether there is any cause and effect.

Sometimes it is possible to gain insights into causality by conducting what is called a longitudinal study. In a **longitudinal study,** the same group of people is followed over time. A researcher might select a sample of married couples, for example, and assess their economic situations, their marital satisfaction, and their emotional health over, say, ten years. If the incidence of both divorce and emotional problems increases whenever economic conditions decline, there is reason to believe that financial hardship is a third variable contributing to a link between divorce and emotional disorders.

CORRELATION COEFFICIENT a statistical calculation stating the degree of relationship between two variables in terms of a number between −1 and +1

LONGITUDINAL STUDY a study that follows the same group of subjects over a period of time

Correlational research explores the relationship between one variable, such as educational level attained, and another, such as gender, race, or age.

Longitudinal research is very laborious and time-consuming. An alternative way of collecting somewhat similar kinds of data is to conduct what is called a cross-sectional study. In a **cross-sectional study,** subjects are divided into subgroups on the basis of some variable, then each subgroup is assessed regarding one or more other variables. In this case, subjects would be divided into subgroups on the basis of their financial situations, and their marital satisfaction and emotional health would then be assessed. If those in the worst financial situations also had the highest divorce rate and the highest incidence of emotional disorders, there would be reason to believe that financial hardship *may* be contributing to both these other problems. We say *may* be contributing because this study gathers correlational data at only a single point in time. We do not get to see which factor arises first and which ones follow after, so we are not really able to infer cause and effect.

Despite the limitations of correlational research, it is still very valuable. First, it allows us to make predictions. We can predict, for example, that a person going through a divorce is more likely than a happily married one to seek psychiatric help. Or we can predict that a bad-tempered child is more likely than a cheerful one to become an irritable, moody adult (see the accompanying box). The stronger the correlations, the more likely these predictions are to be right. Second, correlational data often allow us to make educated guesses about what the causes of something *might* be. For instance, scientists knew for years that a correlation existed between cigarette smoking and lung cancer, and they had a strong suspicion that smoking might cause this disease. They did not yet have evidence to support their suspicion, however. To get it they had to conduct experiments.

The Experimental Method: Establishing Cause and Effect

An **experiment** is a research method designed to control the factors that might affect a variable under study, thus allowing scientists to establish cause and effect. To determine the cause-and-effect relationship between smoking and lung cancer, for instance, scientists performed an experiment. Two groups of animals were treated identically in all respects, except that one group was exposed to repeated doses of cigarette smoke. When the "smokers" contracted lung cancer more often than the nonsmokers did, the researchers finally had evidence that smoking *causes* cancer.

Experiments must meet three requirements in order to demonstrate causality. First, if one event is the cause of another, the two must vary together—that is, when one changes, the other must change too. This requirement is called **covariation of events.** Second, a **time-order relationship** must be established: the presumed cause must occur *before* the presumed effect. Third, all plausible alternative causes, known as **confounding variables,** must be ruled out. We must be able to say that, in this situation, only one cause is likely. Descriptive and correlational studies may tell us something about the covariation of events, and possibly about a time-order relationship as well. Sometimes they may even rule out a few possible causes. Neither sort, however, is designed to rule out *all* confounding variables. This last, most stringent requirement for showing causality is the province of experiments. In an experiment, researchers are able to control most extraneous influences and so demonstrate quite clearly that A causes B. To understand how this is done, let us look at how an experiment is structured.

The Structure of an Experiment

An experiment explores the relationship between two variables: the independent variable and the dependent variable. The **independent variable** is the factor that the researcher deliberately manipulates in order to see its effects. Changes in this variable do not depend on what the subjects in the study do, which is why it is called "independent." Exposure to cigarette smoke is the independent variable in

CROSS-SECTIONAL STUDY a study in which subjects are divided into subgroups on the basis of some variable, then each subgroup is assessed regarding one or more other variables

EXPERIMENT a method of collecting data in which researchers actively control the factors that may affect the variable under study

COVARIATION OF EVENTS a state in which two events vary together so that as one changes, the other also changes (a condition for causality)

TIME-ORDER RELATIONSHIP a relationship in which one factor precedes a second one in time and therefore may possibly have caused the second

intervening variable

CONFOUNDING VARIABLE a factor that is one possible cause of a phenomenon and that interferes with the accurate measurement of the causal factor under study in an experiment

INDEPENDENT VARIABLE the factor in a research study that is manipulated by the experimenter to determine its effects

PSYCHOLOGY TODAY AND TOMORROW

What Happens to Bad-Tempered Boys: A Correlational Study

What happens to boys who have a history of temper tantrums? Does their childish bad temper affect their behavior as adults? A correlational study that followed schoolchildren for thirty years of their lives has indicated that bad-tempered boys tend to become moody, irritable men whose marriages fail and who experience frequent bouts of unemployment (Caspi, Elder, and Bem, 1987).

How did the researchers establish these correlations? The longitudinal study began with boys eight to ten years old. Those considered "bad-tempered" by their mothers often had explosive outbursts in which they bit, kicked, struck, swore, screamed, shouted, and threw things. The researchers followed the lives of these and other boys well into manhood. Thirty years after the study began, researchers rated the adult personalities of their subjects and discovered a strong relationship between temper tantrums in middle childhood and irritability and moodiness in mid-

dle adulthood. The ill-tempered men were twice as likely to be divorced as the other men in the study, and their work history was erratic. They tended to change jobs often, to have frequent periods of unemployment, and to suffer declines in socioeconomic status. More than half held jobs that were lower in status than those their fathers had held at the same age. In a world that demands interpersonal skills for occupational success, bad temper seems to be associated with downward economic mobility.

Although we cannot say that throwing temper tantrums in childhood *causes* difficulty in later life, we can say that school-age children who find it impossible to control their tempers also seem to have difficulty with social relationships as adults, both at home and on the job. And we might safely predict that bad-tempered boys will be likely to have future marital and occupational problems.

DEPENDENT VARIABLE the factor expected to change when the independent variable changes

experiments on the effects of smoking. It is the factor that the researcher intentionally manipulates in order to see whether animals are more or less likely to contract lung cancer. The factor that is expected to change when the independent variable changes is called the **dependent variable.** (It is "dependent" on what happens to the subjects.) In experiments on the effects of smoking, the incidence of lung cancer is the dependent variable.

In order to conduct a fair test of a hypothesis using the experimental method, researchers must make sure that the independent variable is the only likely cause of the results they get. They do this by means of three control techniques: (1) controlling the independent variable so that it differs significantly for each group of subjects; (2) controlling the other conditions of the experiment to make sure they are constant for all the subjects; and (3) controlling the assignment of subjects to groups so that each group gets roughly the same "mix" of people. To explain each of these techniques, let us look at an experiment designed to test the hypothesis proposed at the beginning of this chapter: the hypothesis that the environment in which information is first learned can later provide cues that help students retrieve that material from memory.

OPERATIONALIZING A HYPOTHESIS restating a hypothesis so as to specifically suggest a way of testing it

You, the researcher, would begin by restating the hypothesis so as to suggest a specific way of testing it. This is called **operationalizing a hypothesis.** For instance, we could operationalize our hypothesis in this manner: students who take an exam in a different room from the one in which they were taught get lower marks than students who are tested in their original classroom.

You would then design the experiment. In this case, the dependent variable is the students' test performance, which, according to your hypothesis, depends on the room in which they are tested. This makes the testing room the independent variable, the factor that you are going to manipulate. When you test one group of subjects in a *different* room from the one they originally learned in, you are creating what is called the **experimental condition**—a change in the independent variable so as to permit a test of your hypothesis.

EXPERIMENTAL CONDITION the condition in an experiment in which the independent variable is manipulated in order to test its effects

Every experiment also has a **control group** of subjects, a group exposed to all the same factors as the experimental subjects *except* the experimental condition. In this case, the control subjects would take the exam in their original classroom, *not* in a different one. This is known as the **control condition.** Control groups and conditions are essential in order to provide a point of comparison against which to assess the experimental group's behavior.

Eliminating Confounding Variables

Control subjects do not experience the experimental condition, but they do experience all the other conditions to which the experimental subjects are exposed. They are taught the same material by the same instructor in the same manner, and they are given the same exam. Although the rooms in which the exam is taken are different for the two groups, the two rooms are similar in obvious ways that might affect test performance, such as lighting, temperature, and noise level. These similarities help eliminate confounding variables.

One way to help ensure that no confounding variable is overlooked is to use a procedure called **counterbalancing.** In this case, you would teach half your experimental subjects in room A and test them in room B, while you would teach the other half in room B and test them in room A. Similarly, your control subjects would be split between the two environments; each half would stay in the same room: half would both learn and be tested in room A, the other half in room B. This procedure ensures that any influence unique to one room or the other is distributed evenly across the two groups. Thus, even if you have overlooked a confounding variable related to the rooms, it will still be controlled for in your experiment.

What about confounding variables that your subjects might introduce? For instance, how can you make sure that all the smartest students do not end up in one group? And how can you guarantee that one group or the other does not have a disproportionate number of people with low motivation? The answer is to assign subjects to groups at random (by drawing their names out of a hat, for example). Random assignment helps ensure that, by the luck of the draw, a roughly equivalent "mix" of subjects will end up in each group. This is especially likely when the number of subjects is large.

With a small number of subjects, however, random assignment may not be sufficient to ensure that the members of your two groups are similar in all important ways. This is because the smaller the group, the more any one person's characteristics may affect, or skew, the overall group performance. For example, if your experimental group consists of only four people and one has a very high academic aptitude, that exceptional person may unduly raise the average test score of the group as a whole. To avoid this problem, you must first match the students on the basis of their academic skills and *then* randomly assign the matched pairs to your two groups. This ensures that students in each group will have roughly equivalent academic ability. The "amount" of measurable aptitude is spread evenly over both groups.

Eliminating Biases

Sometimes researchers unwittingly introduce their own biases into an experiment. These biases are called **experimenter effects.** Experimenter effects can creep in whenever a researcher has specific expectations about the outcome of a study. In your study, for instance, you expect that the experimental subjects will score lower than the controls because they are tested in a different room from the one in which they originally learned. To help ensure that these expectations do not influence your results, you have to follow certain procedures. For example, you cannot be both the person who assigns the subjects to groups *and* the one who grades their tests. Why? If you are the grader and know what conditions each student has been exposed to, your expectations about their performance could influence your scoring.

Expectations on the part of subjects can also bias an experiment. If the stu-

CONTROL GROUP the group of subjects in an experiment who are exposed to all the same factors as the experimental subjects *except* the experimental condition

CONTROL CONDITION the condition in an experiment that remains unchanged (is not manipulated) and that serves as a point of comparison for the experimental condition

COUNTERBALANCING a procedure for eliminating the effect of confounding variables by making sure that they are evenly distributed across the experimental and control conditions

EXPERIMENTER EFFECT a bias that the experimenter unwittingly introduces into a study

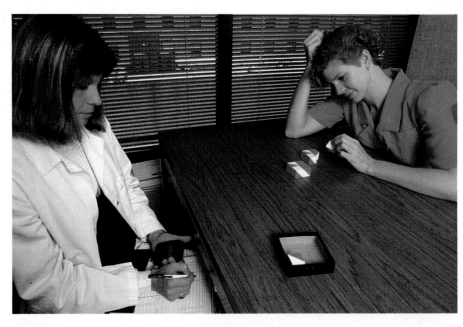

Objective measurements are crucial to the reliability and validity of an experiment's findings. In testing this woman's aptitude for visual and spatial organization, the researcher times her carefully so that the results can be compared with the performance of others who took the same test in the same amount of time.

dents in your study are aware of the hypothesis you are testing, their behavior may be affected. Those assigned to the experimental group may slacken their efforts on the assumption that they will not perform well, or they may work harder than they normally would in order to overcome the hypothesized effect. When certain characteristics of the research setting seem to suggest or even "demand" a particular response from subjects, we say that **demand characteristics** are at work.

To eliminate both kinds of bias, experimenters often use a **double-blind procedure,** in which neither the experimenter nor the subjects know who is assigned to which condition, experimental or control. Double-blind procedures are commonly used in research on the effects of drugs. Here expectations can have significant effects on how subjects react to a drug or on how experimenters interpret a reaction.

Measurement and Replication

Even when a double-blind procedure, counterbalancing, and other safeguards are used, the results of an experiment can still be faulty if measurements are not precise. Researchers' impressions of how subjects respond are never enough because impressions tend to be vague and unreliable. Instead, researchers must *measure* the phenomenon they are interested in, and they must measure objectively (in a manner based on facts, not personal bias). Usually, this involves using some countable unit of measure, such as grams consumed, minutes elapsed, or test scores achieved.

Objective measurement helps ensure that other researchers can repeat an experiment that is of interest to them. Such **replication** of studies is essential in science, for the more often a research finding can be replicated, the more confidence we can have in it. If many different scientists carefully repeat a study and get essentially the same results, it becomes increasingly unlikely that those results are biased or happened just by chance.

DEMAND CHARACTERISTIC a bias in the research setting that seems to suggest or "demand" a particular response from subjects

DOUBLE-BLIND PROCEDURE method of avoiding bias in an experiment in which neither the experimenter nor the subjects know who is in the experimental group and who is in the control group

REPLICATION repetition of a scientific study; if its findings are accurate, any study should be able to be replicated

Ecological Validity

Some researchers complain that experiments—particularly those conducted in laboratory settings—are so contrived that the results have little relationship to daily life. Psychological research, they say, must have **ecological validity**: it must focus on processes that occur in real-life environments. To the extent that laboratory settings are unnatural and artificial, people in them may act in ways they would not otherwise act.

These critics, however, may be expecting too much from the experimental method. The purpose of experiments is to test hypotheses by separating the various strands of influence on behavior. Pulling apart these interrelated strands may be artificial, but it is also the principal advantage of the experimental method. Moreover, psychologists who conduct experiments are not necessarily seeking to make generalizations about what people do in daily life. Many are trying to discover how people respond under certain conditions, even if those conditions do not usually prevail. This approach can help them identify major influences on behavior (Mook, 1983). Thus, despite its limitations, the experiment remains the best method scientists have for investigating cause and effect.

ECOLOGICAL VALIDITY a characteristic possessed by studies in which the subjects behave as they would in real-life environments

ETHICAL ISSUES AND PRINCIPLES

No matter which research method a psychologist uses, ethics are a matter of the utmost concern. Psychologists are obligated to try to find answers to important questions, but they are also obligated to protect those who participate in their research. Some studies simply cannot be conducted for ethical reasons. For instance, it would clearly be unethical to deprive infants of human contact in order to determine whether early exposure to language is needed for the normal development of speech. This deprivation would cause irreparable harm, as we saw in the case of Genie. With many other procedures, however, the ethical considerations are not so clear-cut. What guidelines do psychologists follow to ensure that their research is ethically sound?

The Ethics of Human Research

Proposed research involving human subjects is generally reviewed by a panel of scientists and laypersons. This panel determines whether the intended study sufficiently protects subjects from possible harm and allows them to participate voluntarily and with prior knowledge of what the study will entail (a condition referred to as "informed consent"). Such a review is required by most universities for all research conducted at those institutions and by the U.S. government for research funded by federal grants.

To help psychologists design studies that meet ethical standards, the American Psychological Association (APA) has drawn up a code of ethics to guide research involving human subjects (1981). This code includes guidelines regarding subjects' rights to privacy, voluntary participation, informed consent, and freedom from harm.

1. The *right to privacy* is a fundamental one for people who participate in research. Their thoughts and feelings should not be revealed without their permission. Researchers must also keep all personal information about subjects private, and they must report their findings in such a way that the identities of the participants cannot be determined. This is usually done by reporting data anonymously (without reference to specific individuals), or by assigning code numbers to subjects and referring to them in that way.

2. People who serve as subjects in psychological studies must also be allowed *voluntary participation*. They must be free to decide whether or not they want to take part. And even after they have agreed to take part in a research project,

In response to public protest, some cosmetics companies have stopped using the painful Draize test, which uses rabbits to determine the safety of various ingredients.

they must be allowed to drop out at any stage in the study without reprisals or any kind of pressure to stay.

3. In order to meet ethical standards, voluntary participation must entail *informed consent*. Prospective subjects must be told in advance what the study requires them to do and whether or not they run any risks by participating. Of course the researchers should not divulge the hypothesis they are testing, for such prior knowledge could bias the results. But the subjects should be told enough about the study to make an intelligent decision about taking part.

4. Finally, *no lasting harm* should come to subjects from participating in a study. In fact, many psychologists believe that no effects of any kind, bad *or* good, should linger after a study is over and contact between the researcher and the subjects has ended.

If subjects participate in a study that seems to violate these ethical guidelines, they can lodge a complaint with the researcher's department, university, or affiliated institution, or with the APA's Committee on Scientific and Professional Ethics, which investigates all such complaints. If charges are substantiated, the psychologist is suspended or expelled from the APA and is likely to be fired (Hare-Mustin and Hall, 1981).

The Ethics of Animal Research

Some people wonder whether animal research can reveal anything about human beings. Animals are so different from humans, they argue, what is the point of studying them in order to understand ourselves better? This skepticism is unwarranted. Animal studies *can* provide valuable insights into the workings of the human body and human behavior. After all, we share with other mammals a large number of anatomical features, physiological processes, and even patterns of behavior, some of which may be inborn. So there is much to be learned about ourselves from research on other species.

But why bother studying other species when humans could be studied directly? One important reason is the level of control that animal research affords. Using animal subjects, researchers can control the environment in ways that are often impossible with human beings. Animal researchers can also control the heredity of their subjects. Strains of experimental mice and rats have been pure-bred over generations in order to minimize variations in genetic make-up like those that exist in humans. These pure-bred strains are extremely useful for exploring, among other things, the differential contributions of heredity and environment to individual variations in behavior. Finally, researchers have more options for investigating the biology of behavior in animals than in humans. For instance, methods of probing the brain that are acceptable with mice or rabbits are often prohibited with human beings. For all these reasons, much important research is based on studies of animal subjects.

Although scientists sometimes use procedures with animals that would be unethical with people, there are stringent standards that govern the treatment of research animals. State and federal regulations specify procedures and standards for animal care—housing, feeding, and cleaning. And ethical standards prohibit researchers from inflicting unnecessary pain. To determine what is necessary and what is not, researchers must, in every case, carefully weigh the goals of the experiment and its importance to human knowledge against the potential harm to the animals involved. Thus, humane treatment of animals is today a central concern in scientific research.

SUMMARY

The Scientific Method

- Scientific knowledge begins with a discovery, which can come about through accident, a hunch, or a sudden insight.
- A scientist's proposed explanations for his or her findings are known as hypotheses. They must be stated in such a way that they can be tested.
- Hypotheses are generated and evaluated by three main types of research methods: descriptive studies, correlational research, and experiments.

Descriptive Methods

- Naturalistic observations of behavior are made in natural settings without any interference by the researcher.
- The survey is a method for exploring people's characteristics, attitudes, opinions, or behaviors by asking a number of people in a group the same questions. When the group is large, the survey must be made of a sample that is representative of the group as a whole. Representativeness is assured by choosing the members of the sample at random.
- The case study is an intensive investigation of a single person or a select group.

The Correlational Method

- Correlational research is used to explore relationships between variables. It determines whether variables occur together at a rate significantly higher than would be expected to happen by chance.
- The degree of relationship between two variables is a statistical calculation called the correlation coefficient. The strength of the relationship can range from -1 (completely negatively correlated) to $+1$ (completely positively correlated).
- Correlational research allows us to make predictions about behavior that have a good chance of being accurate, but it does not permit us to make assumptions about the cause of behavior. Just because two variables have a systematic relationship does not mean that one causes the other.

The Experimental Method

- Cause and effect are established through the experiment, a research method that scientists use to control the factors that might affect a behavior under study.
- The factor that the researcher manipulates in an experiment is called the independent variable. The factor that the researcher looks at to measure the effect of the independent variable is called the dependent variable.
- The only possible cause for any obtained outcome in an experiment should be the independent variable. The experimenter ensures this by assigning subjects randomly to balanced experimental and control conditions and holding all factors for both conditions constant, except for the independent variable.
- Biases that researchers unwittingly introduce into their experiments are known as experimenter effects. When subjects feel that the research setting seems to "demand" a particular response, demand characteristics are said to be operating, and these too can bias an experiment.
- A researcher can help control biases by using a double-blind procedure in which neither the experimenter nor the subject knows which subjects are assigned to the experimental condition and which to the control condition.
- Accurate measurement of the results of an experiment and the ability to replicate its procedures and findings are also important requirements of the experimental method.

Ethical Issues and Principles

- Psychologists must find answers to important scientific questions, but they must also protect the animals and people they use in their research. Sometimes these obligations conflict, raising ethical issues.
- In research with human beings, researchers should be guided by principles drawn up by the American Psychological Association. These principles state that subjects have the right to privacy and confidentiality; the subjects must participate voluntarily and give informed consent; and no lasting harm should come from participating in the study.
- Animals play an important role in scientific research partly because of the level of control they afford. While researchers may use procedures with animals that it would be unethical to use with people, stringent standards govern the treatment of animal subjects. The importance of the research is weighed against the potential harm to the animals involved.

KEY TERMS

case study	dependent variable	naturalistic observation
confounding variable	double-blind procedure	operationalizing a hypothesis
control condition	ecological validity	randomization
control group	experiment	replication
correlation coefficient	experimental condition	sample
correlational research	experimenter effects	scientific method
counterbalancing	hypothesis	survey
covariation of events	independent variable	theory
cross-sectional study	longitudinal study	time-order relationship
demand characteristics		variable

CONCEPT REVIEW

1. Outline the three steps of the scientific method as presented in the chapter. What is the goal of a researcher who uses the scientific method?

2. Define *theory*. Do theories always have a scientific basis?

3. Identify and distinguish the three types of descriptive research. Which type requires a sample population?

4. What are the advantages and disadvantages of using the descriptive approach?

5. What kind of relationship between variables does the correlational method allow researchers to claim? How is the relationship calculated and then expressed?

6. Distinguish between a longitudinal study and a cross-sectional study. What are the advantages of each? Why would a researcher use one rather than the other?

7. What are the three requirements for establishing a cause-and-effect relationship? Why are descriptive and correlational methods unable to meet all three requirements?

8. Describe the components of an experimental study. How are control conditions used to eliminate confounding variables? How are they used to eliminate experimenter effects?

9. Why is replication of an experiment so important to scientific research?

10. What conditions must be met in order for a scientific study involving human subjects to be considered ethical? What about studies involving animal subjects?

CRITICAL THINKING

1. Psychologists today are interested in a number of sensitive social issues like Acquired Immune Deficiency Syndrome (AIDS), drug abuse and addiction, and sexual abuse of children. Outline a study that would improve our understanding of one such problem. Identify all the components of your study. What steps would you take to ensure the fair and ethical treatment of your subjects?

2. Design an experiment to test the relationship between sugar intake and student performance on examinations. Describe how the hypothesis is formed and then operationalized. What methods can be used to ensure that your proposed test of your hypothesis will not be biased by conditions of the experiment?

PART TWO

Biology, Perception, and Awareness

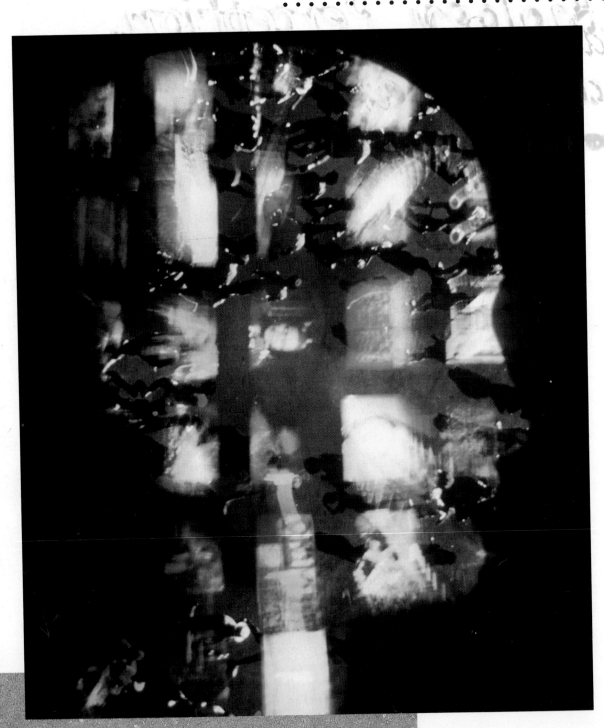

...The Brain and Behavior

"Did I remove the gallbladder?" the surgeon asked the nurse not long after he had finished the procedure. The nurse looked puzzled, but respectfully answered that the gallbladder was indeed out. A few minutes later the doctor asked again: "Did I remove the gallbladder, nurse?" Apparently, he could recall nothing about what was occurring during the operation. Despite this, his hands moved deftly, stitching up the surgical wound, skillfully completing a task that he had done many times before (from Klawans, 1988). How could the surgeon remember how to perform this medical technique and yet have no idea of what he had just said or done?

The answer lies in a brain disorder called transient global amnesia, in which the victim temporarily loses the ability to store new information, even though he or she retains old knowledge perfectly. Usually, the person is aware that something odd is happening and feels bewildered by it. Force of will alone cannot reverse the condition, however; a few minutes or hours must pass before normal memory returns. Interestingly, transient global amnesia is often triggered by intense exertion—a Sunday morning jog, for instance, or a sexual orgasm. The cause is probably a reduction in blood flow to regions of the brain involved in the process of remembering new experiences.

The vital importance of the brain to human thought, feeling, and behavior is the reason that we devote most of a chapter to it in an introductory psychology text. Trying to understand behavior without studying the brain is like trying to understand how a car works without looking under the hood. You would never see the mechanisms that lie beneath the surface.

In recent years the study of the brain has involved many approaches. Researchers have looked at the brain's anatomy and dissected its interconnected parts. They have studied humans and animals with brain damage to see what abilities they have lost. They have probed single brain cells and explored the brain's biochemistry. They have even developed sophisticated techniques for watching a living brain at work. All the knowledge acquired has created a golden age in brain research. Although we do not yet fully understand how a thought, an emotion, or a memory arises, the biological basis of these brain activities is gradually becoming clearer.

In this chapter, we begin by taking an overall look at the human nervous system, of which the brain is a major part. We explore the nervous system's subdivisions and the roles that each performs. We then turn to the nervous system's basic unit, the nerve cell. The process by which nerve cells send and receive messages is a complex and fascinating one. Next, we examine the brain in some detail, focusing on the functions of its many interconnected parts. We also consider how the two sides of the brain are specialized to perform somewhat different tasks. We go on to discuss how scientists have learned what they currently know about the brain, including a survey of the latest research techniques. Finally, we take a look at the nervous system's partner: the endocrine system of glands and hormones, which also affects behavior.

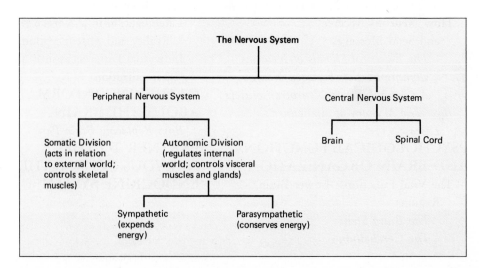

Figure 3.1 Diagram of the relationships among the parts of the nervous system.

AN OVERALL VIEW OF THE NERVOUS SYSTEM

The human nervous system is made up of billions of nerve cells, each of which can produce and transmit electrical signals. To help understand something so complex, scientists divide the nervous system into two interconnected parts: the **central nervous system,** which consists of the brain and the spinal cord, and the **peripheral nervous system,** which is made up of all the nerve cells outside the skull and backbone. See Figure 3.1 for a schematic of the nervous system.

CENTRAL NERVOUS SYSTEM the brain and the spinal cord

PERIPHERAL NERVOUS SYSTEM the relay system of nerve cells outside the skull and backbone connecting the central nervous system and all parts of the body; contains ganglia and nerves

The Central Nervous System

The **brain** is the master control center for all human activities—from remembering what you have just said or done, to learning how to program a computer, to feeling embarrassed when you've done something foolish, to enjoying the warmth of the summer sun, to solving a crossword puzzle. The brain, in short, is the basis of what we call the *mind*—the seat of all our thoughts, memories, and feelings. The brain gives each of us both self-awareness and a distinctive personality. If you had a heart transplant, you would still be the same person, even though you had someone else's heart beating inside you. But if medical technology permitted someone else's brain to be placed inside your skull, you would no longer be "you."

BRAIN the master control center for all human activities

    The **spinal cord** is the brain's link to the peripheral nervous system. It receives information from the skin and muscles and transmits it to the brain. At the same time, it routes commands coming down from the brain to the appropriate muscles and glands of the body. But do not conclude that the spinal cord is nothing more than a relay station. The spinal cord is an information-processing system in its own right, fully capable of analyzing certain kinds of data and initiating commands for **reflex responses** (immediate, involuntary actions by the nervous system). For instance, the orders for the reflex of quickly jerking back your hand after you touch a hot surface come from your spinal cord.

SPINAL CORD the column of neurons that serves as a link between the brain and the peripheral nervous system and as an information-processing system for reflex responses

REFLEX RESPONSE an immediate, involuntary action by the nervous system

The Peripheral Nervous System

The peripheral nervous system contains two elements: ganglia and nerves (see Figure 3.2). **Ganglia** are collections of nerve-cell bodies. Many are located just outside the vertebrae that form the backbone, or spinal column. Others are located close to the internal organs with which the nervous system connects. **Nerves** are pathways containing bundles of fibers that look something like tiny telephone cables. These bundles transmit sensations and other kinds of information through the ganglia to the central nervous system, and they also carry the central nervous system's commands to the body's muscles and some of its glands. Scientists have classified the nerves of the peripheral nervous system according to their function. Some are part of a subdivision called the *somatic system*, while others are part of a subdivision called the *autonomic system*.

GANGLIA collections of nerve-cell bodies

NERVES pathways containing bundles of fibers that transmit sensations and other kinds of information to the central nervous system, as well as commands to muscles and glands

The Somatic System

The **somatic system** both transmits sensations from the outside world to the spinal cord and/or brain and relays the central nervous system's orders to contract the body's skeletal muscles (the muscles attached to bones), thus generating movements. Consider what happens inside your body if you touch a hot pan on the stove. Electrical signals begin in your fingers and travel along somatic nerves to your spinal cord. From there, the signals are passed on to the brain, which registers that something hot has been touched. Then, before you even have time to be

SOMATIC SYSTEM the subdivision of the peripheral nervous system that transmits sensations from the outside world to the spinal cord and/or brain and relays the central nervous system's orders to contract the body's skeletal muscles

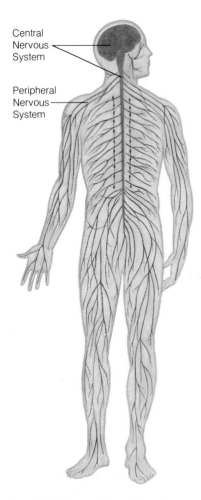

Central Nervous System

Peripheral Nervous System

Figure 3.2 The central nervous system (CNS) and the peripheral nervous system (PNS) in the human body. Both of these systems are made up of billions of nerve cells, or neurons, each of which is capable of transmitting a train of chemical-electrical signals in one direction. In the CNS, these neurons form an immensely complex network that organizes, stores, and redirects vast quantities of information. In the PNS, neurons in every pathway carry information either from receptors (such as the sense organs) toward the CNS or away from the CNS to effectors (in the muscles, for example). There is a close match between information going to the CNS and information coming from it. Every muscle, for example, not only receives directions from the CNS to contract or relax but also sends back information about its present state of contraction or relaxation.

aware of a burning feeling, your hand is usually pulled back from the heat. The command to pull back is issued by your spinal cord, which sends electrical signals back out through somatic nerves to your arm. This reflex response by the spinal cord helps ensure your physical safety because of its rapid speed. However, the brain can override a spinal cord reflex. For instance, if you voluntarily tense your leg muscles before a doctor taps you on the knee, your brain can prevent the reflexive jerk of your leg.

The Autonomic System

The **autonomic system** affects heart rate, certain glandular secretions, and the activities of smooth muscles. Smooth muscles, which form part of the walls of the blood vessels, the intestines, the stomach, and many other internal organs, derive their name from their appearance. While skeletal muscles have a ridged surface, smooth muscles look slick and smooth even when magnified.

The autonomic system itself has two divisions: the sympathetic and the parasympathetic. Each supplies nerves to the heart, to some of the body's glands, and to most of the smooth muscles, but the two divisions tend to dominate in different situations and to have opposite effects (see Figure 3.3). In emergencies and stressful situations, when vigorous action is needed, the **sympathetic division** dominates. It prepares the body to fight or to flee by increasing the heart rate, blood pressure, and blood-sugar level and by slowing down digestion. In relaxed situations, in contrast, the **parasympathetic division** exerts control. It enhances digestion and conserves energy by slowing down the heart rate and the blood flow to the skeletal muscles.

It was once believed that the autonomic nervous system operates automatically, with no possibility of voluntary modification. We now know, however, that this belief is incorrect. Through a procedure called *biofeedback training*, people can learn to regulate autonomic responses. Biofeedback training uses electronic sensors of body temperature, pulse rate, blood pressure, and so forth to give a person continual information about the activities of his or her autonomic nervous system. The person then learns, through trial and error, to gain some control over these physiological responses. For instance, a paraplegic who cannot maintain normal blood pressure when in an upright position would be urged to imagine blood pressure rising and to try to keep it elevated. A tone or light would signal when the person's efforts were successful. Using this method, some paraplegics learn to regulate blood pressure well enough to be able to walk using crutches and braces without feeling faint.

THE NERVOUS SYSTEM'S BASIC UNITS: NEURONS

The human nervous system contains billions of nerve cells, each capable of producing and transmitting electrical signals. These nerve cells, or **neurons**, as they are more technically called, are linked to one another to form elaborate circuits that make the circuits of even the most complex computer seem simple by comparison. The secrets of how we learn and remember, feel emotions, perceive the world around us, walk, talk, and do countless other things are all related to the basic properties of neurons and how they are connected to one another.

Neurons are not the only cells in the nervous system. In some areas they are greatly outnumbered by smaller, surrounding **glial cells,** which keep the neurons functioning by supplying them with nutrients, clearing away their wastes, helping to separate them from other neurons, and giving them a structural and chemical foundation in which to grow and organize themselves. Certain glial cells form a fatty covering, known as a **myelin sheath,** around part of some neurons. A myelin sheath helps increase the speed at which electrical signals can be sent down a neuron. Although glial cells are important, they are not the heart of the nervous system. That role is played by the neurons, which we now look at in detail.

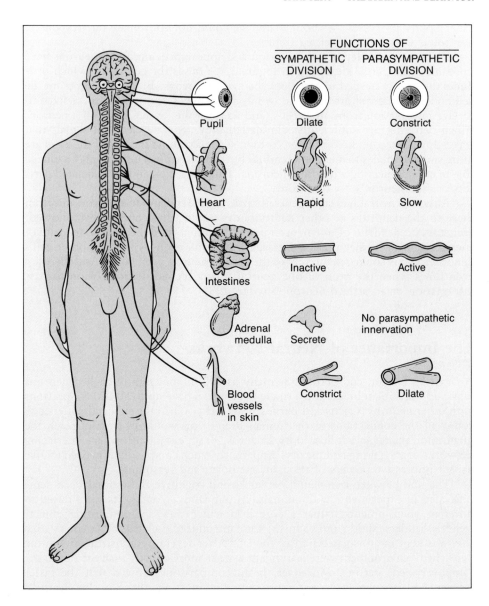

FUNCTIONS OF

	SYMPATHETIC DIVISION	PARASYMPATHETIC DIVISION
Pupil	Dilate	Constrict
Heart	Rapid	Slow
Intestines	Inactive	Active
Adrenal medulla	Secrete	No parasympathetic innervation
Blood vessels in skin	Constrict	Dilate

Figure 3.3 The autonomic nervous system has a sympathetic and a parasympathetic division. The two divisions tend to operate in different kinds of situations and in opposite ways.

AUTONOMIC SYSTEM the subdivision of the peripheral nervous system that affects heart rate, certain glandular secretions, and the activities of smooth muscles

SYMPATHETIC DIVISION the part of the autonomic system that prepares the body for stressful situations by increasing heart rate, blood pressure, and blood-sugar level and by slowing down digestion

PARASYMPATHETIC DIVISION the part of the autonomic system that exerts control in relaxed situations, enhancing digestion and conserving energy by slowing down the heart rate and the blood flow to the skeletal muscles

NEURONS specialized nerve cells that connect motor and receptor cells and transmit information throughout the body

GLIAL CELLS cells that keep neurons functioning by supplying them with nutrients, clearing away their wastes, helping to separate them from other neurons, and giving them a structural and chemical foundation in which to grow and organize themselves

MYELIN SHEATH a fatty covering made of glial cells around part of some neurons, which helps increase the speed of electrical signals

SENSORY NEURONS neurons that receive and transmit information about the outside world, initiating the process of sensations

MOTOR NEURONS neurons that connect to the body's skeletal muscles and carry signals that cause those muscles to contract, producing movement

INTERNEURONS neurons that connect one neuron to another, thus integrating brain activities and other bodily processes

The Structure of Neurons

When neurons are classified according to their shapes and sizes, there are some 200 different kinds in the human nervous system (Rosenzweig and Leiman, 1989). The specific structure of a neuron determines some of the tasks it performs. Neurons are also categorized into three types according to their functions. Some nerve cells receive and transmit information about what is happening in the outside world. These **sensory neurons** are stimulated by receptor cells in the sense organs, which respond to particular kinds of changes in the environment (such as changes in light, heat, and pressure). Once stimulated, sensory neurons transmit signals to other neurons, thus beginning the complex process of creating our awareness of sights, sounds, tastes, smells, and skin sensations. Other neurons are the **motor neurons,** which connect to the body's skeletal muscles and carry signals that cause those muscles to contract, producing movement. Your leg can kick a football, your fingers can strum a guitar, and your lips and tongue can move to read this sentence aloud partly because of the activities of motor neurons. **Interneurons,** the third type, are the most numerous in the human body. Their function is to connect one neuron to another—a sensory neuron and a motor neuron, for example, or two other interneurons. Interneurons integrate brain activities and

CELL BODY   the part of a neuron that produces the energy needed to carry on its work

DENDRITES   short fibers branching out from the cell body, which form the "input zone" of a neuron

AXON   a nerve fiber between the dendrites and the terminal buttons, part of the "output zone" of a neuron

TERMINAL BUTTON   small structure at the end of a branch of the axon, part of the "output zone" of a neuron

other bodily processes. Without them, we could not coordinate our responses, nor could we perceive, feel, or think.

Despite their differences in function and appearance, almost all neurons have the same basic parts, illustrated in Figure 3.4. One is the **cell body,** which produces the energy needed to carry out the neuron's work. Branching out from the cell body are many short fibers known as **dendrites.** Dendrites are specialized to receive information from other cells, and so form the "input zone" of a neuron. When dendrites are sufficiently stimulated, they generate electrical signals that travel down a second kind of fiber, known as the **axon.** At the end of the axon are more small branches that end in **terminal buttons.** Terminal buttons play a crucial role in communicating with other neurons. Thus, the axon and its associated parts serve as the neuron's "output zone."

Although neural messages generally pass from dendrites to the axon and from there to the dendrites of other neurons, this route is not necessarily followed. Sometimes a dendrite of one neuron passes information directly to a dendrite of another neuron. Other times a message leaving an axon bypasses another cell's dendrites and is conveyed directly to the second neuron's cell body. And there are even times when the axon of one neuron uses a second neuron's axon to pass information on to a third neuron (Snyder, 1984).

The Importance of Neural Networks

At least 50 billion, and perhaps as many as 100 billion, tightly packed neurons make up the human brain, and a single neuron can have up to 80,000 connections with other neurons (Curtis and Barnes, 1989). If you had the skill and patience to count all the connections in the human brain, you would eventually reach the quadrillion mark—a 1 followed by 15 zeros. Brain circuits, then, are interlacing networks of staggering complexity. Apparently, such complexity is needed to give us our impressive powers of thought, memory, and reasoning.

The link between rich neural networks and cognitive abilities has been demonstrated in experiments with animals. In one study, young rats were raised in different environments: either a cage into which new and interesting objects (wheels, ladders, slides, and so forth) were introduced each day or an empty cage that was kept in an isolated part of the lab. After several months, the rats in the "enriched" environment were learning new tasks more quickly than the rats in the "impoverished" setting. Moreover, brain comparisons showed that the faster learners had larger neurons and more neural connections than the slow learners did (Rosenzweig et al., 1972). Apparently, environmental stimulation can expand neural networks in the brain and enhance learning ability (Diamond, 1988).

Whenever we talk about the brain's role in behavior, in this chapter and later ones, the concept of neural networks will come up again and again. There are many factors that determine the kinds of connections that neurons make, some of them genetic, others environmental. But regardless of the reasons that neural connections form, the end result is a nervous system with incredibly elaborate circuitry. Complex networks formed by thousands upon thousands of interconnected neurons underlie the human abilities to think, speak, reason, perceive, learn and remember, feel emotion, and have awareness of ourselves. Later in this chapter we will survey the major parts of the brain involved in these important processes.

How Neurons Receive and Send Messages

The Electrical Signals of Neurons

IONS   tiny, electrically charged particles inside the membrane of neurons, which supply the electric charge

Like all other living cells, neurons have an electric charge inside their membrane, a charge that is supplied by tiny particles called **ions.** The membrane of a neuron allows some ions to pass through it more easily than others. For instance, when a

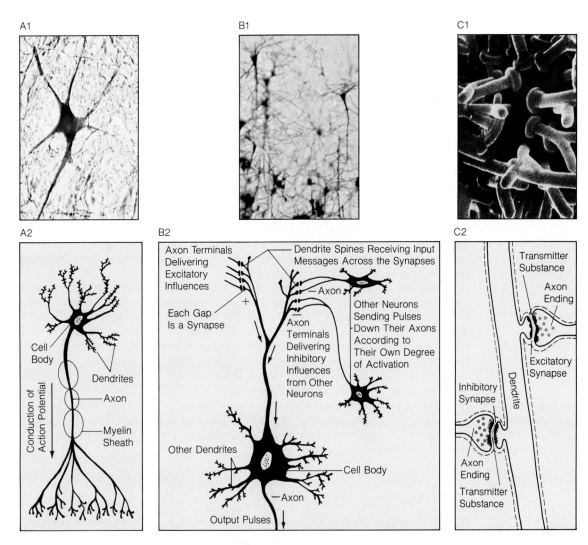

Figure 3.4 The fundamental structures in the nervous system. (Al and A2) A photomicrograph and a diagram of the parts of a single neuron. The dendrites are the receiving end of the neuron; the axon is the sending end. An action potential is transmitted along the axon of a neuron only when its dendrites have been sufficiently excited within a brief span of time. (B1) A photomicrograph of neurons connecting with one another in the cerebral cortex. (B2) A diagram of a typical neuron, representing it as a device that adds up excitatory and inhibitory influences and responds accordingly with a firing rate of so many pulses per second. (C1 and C2) An electron micrograph and a diagram of the structures at the synapse. Note the correspondence between the axon endings and the small protrusions on the dendrites in B2 and C2. When an action potential reaches the end of the axon of a neuron, small amounts of transmitter substances are released from storage areas and cross the synapse to the dendrites of another neuron. The substances from some neurons are excitatory in their effect; the substances from others are inhibitory. If the receiving neuron gets sufficient excitation (and not too much inhibition), it in turn fires.

neuron is inactive (said to be in its resting state), positively charged sodium ions outside the neuron do not pass readily through the membrane, but rather tend to stay outside it; those that manage to leak in are actively "pumped" out. In contrast, positively charged potassium ions inside the neuron do move readily through the membrane, so they tend to move to the outside, leaving behind them negatively charged ions. A point of equilibrium is reached when potassium ions stop migrating outward. At this point, the inactive neuron has a slightly more negative charge inside its membrane than outside it. This is called the cell's **resting potential.**

The resting potential of a neuron is usually short-lived. Soon the neuron is stimulated by another neuron, and this stimulation may trigger an electrical response in the first neuron's axon. The response involves a change in the axon's

RESTING POTENTIAL a more negative charge inside a neuron's membrane than exists outside the membrane at equilibrium

ACTION POTENTIAL   a sudden change in electric charges inside and outside a neuron that makes the inside of the cell more positive than the outside

NERVE IMPULSE   a spreading action potential along a neuron

ALL-OR-NOTHING LAW   the rule that a neuron either fires in response to stimulation or it does not

ELECTROENCEPHALOGRAPH   an instrument that records fluctuations in electric voltage in the brain

SYNAPTIC CLEFT   a tiny gap between the terminal buttons of one neuron and those of another

NEUROTRANSMITTER   chemical messenger that travels across the synaptic cleft from one neuron to another

SYNAPTIC VESICLE   small spherical container that stores neurotransmitters; located inside terminal buttons

membrane at the point of stimulation. Suddenly, the membrane in that area becomes permeable to positively charged sodium ions—that is, it readily allows sodium ions to pass through it. So sodium ions rush inside the membrane, making the cell interior's charge more positive than the exterior's. This sudden change in electric charges inside and outside the axon is called the **action potential.** An action potential lasts for only a millisecond or less. In a self-correcting process, the membrane stops letting sodium ions rush in, and those that have already come inside are actively pumped out. At the same time, positively charged potassium ions also flow out until the resting potential is restored.

Once an action potential is triggered, it spreads down the length of the axon the way an explosion travels down a row of dynamite sticks, with the heat from one explosion setting off the next. In the neuron, the area of the axon next to the point at which the action potential began is stimulated to produce another action potential. It too undergoes a sudden permeability to sodium ions, an inrush of those ions, and a reversal in relative electric charges inside and outside the cell membrane. The next point on the axon follows suit, and so on again until the tip of the axon is reached. This spreading action potential is called a **nerve impulse,** and the neuron involved is said to be "firing."

Once an action potential is generated, there is no way to stop it. It continues until it reaches the axon's tip. Because the action potential is continually regenerated as it passes down the axon, the signal is as strong at the terminal buttons as it is farther up the axon. Moreover, every time a neuron fires, the action potential is the same; its intensity never varies. Under what is known as the **all-or-nothing law,** either a neuron fires in response to stimulation, or it does not.

Scientists are able to look in on the firing of large groups of neurons in the brain by using an **electroencephalograph** (EEG), which records fluctuations in electric voltage from outside the skull. These fluctuations are created as groups of neurons fire and then return to the resting state. As the fluctuations occur, they cause a pen to trace the underlying "brain waves" on rolling graph paper. A typical EEG readout is shown below.

Communication between Neurons

We mentioned earlier that an action potential is triggered when a neuron is stimulated by another neuron. But what form does this stimulation take? How does one neuron "talk" to another? The answer lies in a process of chemical communication. When an action potential reaches an axon's terminal buttons, it can usually go no farther, for terminal buttons are separated from other neurons by a tiny gap called a **synaptic cleft.** Neurons communicate via chemical messengers, known as **neurotransmitters,** that travel across these gaps. Neurotransmitters are stored in small, spherical containers, called **synaptic vesicles,** which are located inside each terminal button. An action potential, upon arriving at a terminal button, stimulates release of the neurotransmitter within that button's synaptic vesicles. The

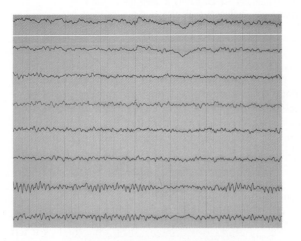

Researchers study records of brain waves by measuring their amplitude (the height of the wave as it appears on the EEG) and their frequency (the number of waves that appear per second). Voltages recorded from the scalp are tiny—just a few thousandths of a volt; they must be amplified to be studied. A normal human EEG pattern is shown here. The top five tracings are a record of beta waves; the bottom three are alpha waves.

neurotransmitter flows across the synaptic cleft to the neuron on the other side, which has specialized sites for receiving it, usually located on its dendrites (see Figure 3.4C2). The entire area where this important communication process occurs (including the first neuron's terminal button, the tiny synaptic cleft, and the second neuron's receptor sites) is called a **synapse.**

The molecules that form receptor sites on a neuron's dendrites have very specific shapes and sizes. So do the molecules that make up the various kinds of neurotransmitters found in the nervous system. Each neurotransmitter molecule released from a certain synaptic vesicle fits into neighboring receptor-site molecules like a key fits into locks. Only when this exact fit between transmitter and receptor occurs will the receiving neuron be chemically stimulated (see Figure 3.4B). Such chemical stimulation, of course, does not last forever. Neurotransmitter molecules bind to receptor sites only briefly before they are diffused away, are broken down by other chemicals, or are reabsorbed by the terminal buttons and stored for future use.

On the receiving side of a synapse after neurotransmitter molecules temporarily bind to receptor sites, the resulting chemical stimulation produces an electrical reaction in the receiving dendrite. This reaction, which is often called a **postsynaptic potential,** can be either excitatory or inhibitory, depending on the particular receptor sites involved. If it is excitatory, the neuron's membrane is altered in such a way that an action potential is more likely to be triggered. (The membrane may temporarily become more permeable than normal to sodium ions, making it easier for an inrush of these ions to occur.) If the reaction is inhibitory, in contrast, the neuron's membrane is temporarily altered in such a way that an action potential is less likely. (The membrane may become more permeable to an outflow of potassium ions, so that an even greater inrush of sodium ions is required in order to make the interior of the cell slightly positive in charge relative to the exterior.)

Of course, a single neuron does not receive just one or even a few messages at a time; it receives hundreds, perhaps thousands. Some are excitatory, while others are inhibitory. With so much incoming information of different kinds, what determines whether or not the neuron's axon will fire? The answer depends on the net amount of excitation the neuron gets. If there are more excitatory signals overall at any given moment, and if those signals are strong enough, the axon will fire. If inhibitory signals predominate, the axon will not fire (see Figure 3.4C).

The intensity of the neuron's overall excitation determines the *rate* at which the axon fires. If the initial stimulus is very strong (the band is playing very loudly, the sunlight is very bright, or the milk is extremely sour), a highly excitatory response will occur in the affected dendrites, and the neuron's axon, in turn, will fire at a high rate—about 200 times per second, and in some cases as many as 900 times. This rapid rate of firing affects the neurons with which the first neuron forms synapses. The more rapidly an axon fires, the more packets of neurotransmitters flood into the synaptic cleft, and the greater the effect on the receiving neuron.

A Closer Look at Neurotransmitters

Research on neurotransmitters is at the forefront of modern neuroscience (McGeer, Eccles, and McGeer, 1987). It has provided essential keys to the intricate biochemistry of the nervous system and how it affects behavior. Scientists are not yet certain how many neurotransmitters exist. The list of possible ones includes some fifty different chemicals. Whether all of these will turn out to be genuine neurotransmitters remains to be seen. Some may be neuromodulators, which alter the effects of neurotransmitters. Others may serve functions that are still unknown. Therefore, we will focus here on chemicals that have been definitely identified as neurotransmitters and thoroughly researched.

One of the first neurotransmitters to be identified was **acetylcholine (ACh),** which plays important roles in both the central and peripheral nervous systems. Motor neurons leading from the spinal cord use ACh to convey messages to the body's muscles. Many toxic substances are deadly to humans and other animals because they affect the synapses of these neurons. For instance, the poison known

SYNAPSE the area between neurons where communication occurs, including the first neuron's terminal button, the synaptic cleft, and the second neuron's receptor sites

POSTSYNAPTIC POTENTIAL an electrical reaction, either excitatory or inhibitory, in a receiving dendrite, which follows chemical stimulation

ACETYLCHOLINE (ACh) a neurotransmitter that plays important roles in both the peripheral and central nervous systems, conveying messages to muscles and affecting learning and memory

EPINEPHRINE a catecholamine neurotransmitter that boosts alertness, arousal, and readiness to act

NOREPINEPHRINE a catecholamine neurotransmitter that is involved with learning, memory, and emotion

DOPAMINE a catecholamine neurotransmitter that is involved with fine control of the skeletal muscles

SEROTONIN a neurotransmitter that is involved in mood and emotion

GABA (GAMMA AMINO-BUTYRIC ACID) a neurotransmitter that seems to be the central nervous system's main inhibitory transmitter

NEUROPEPTIDES a class of brain chemicals that seem to function as neurotransmitters

ENDOGENOUS OPIOIDS neuropeptide chemicals: opium-like substances that occur naturally in the body, reducing pain

as *curare,* in which some South American Indians dip the tips of their hunting arrows, causes paralysis and death by blocking acetylcholine receptors. The victims suffocate when their respiratory muscles stop working. Botulism, an often fatal disease spread by a bacterium in spoiled food, causes paralysis and death by interfering with ACh in another way: it prevents terminal buttons from releasing the transmitter. What happens when there is an *over*supply of acetylcholine in motor synapses? Ask someone familiar with the plant toxin physostigmine: it blocks the action of enzymes that break down ACh, so excessive amounts can cause muscles to go into painful spasms. ACh is also found in parts of the brain, including areas that have to do with learning and memory. Alzheimer's disease, which is characterized by severe memory loss, involves a dramatic deficiency of acetylcholine. When its victims die, the supply of ACh in affected brain regions has been found to be reduced by up to 90 percent (Coyle, Price, and DeLong, 1983; Edelman, Gall, and Cowan, 1987). (Alzheimer's disease is discussed further in the accompanying box.)

The catecholamines are a class of important neurotransmitters consisting of epinephrine, norepinephrine, and dopamine. This trio plays essential roles in both the sympathetic nervous system and the brain. When you are under stress, for instance, neurons in a lower region of your brain release the catecholamine **epinephrine,** which has the effect of boosting your alertness, arousal, and readiness to act. The catecholamine **norepinephrine** also seems to be involved in learning, memory, and emotion. Low levels of it leave a person feeling depressed, which is why drugs that increase norepinephrine are sometimes used to treat depression. In contrast, excessive amounts of norepinephrine are associated with a state of hyperelation, to the point where the person may feel anxious and out of control. The catecholamine **dopamine** is involved with fine control of the skeletal muscles. Gradual destruction of brain pathways that employ it leads to the development of Parkinson's disease, a chronic, often progressive condition that involves tremors of the limbs and head. Patients who receive L-dopa, a drug that the brain transforms into dopamine, often find that their symptoms of Parkinson's disease subside.

People who suffer from severe depression are sometimes treated with drugs that increase the amounts of other transmitters in the brain, including one called **serotonin,** which is involved in mood and emotion. Neurons that produce serotonin originate mainly in an area at the base of the brain, but they project from there into many higher brain regions. Among other things, serotonin helps moderate emotions, which is probably why increased levels of it can help relieve depression. Another important neurotransmitter is gamma amino-butyric acid, called **GABA** for short. Neurons that release GABA have been found in both the brain and the spinal cord. GABA seems to be the central nervous system's main inhibitory neurotransmitter. It plays a key role in restraining a variety of motivational and emotional behaviors, from eating to aggression. Some tranquilizers, such as Valium, work by enhancing the activity of GABA. Interestingly, GABA has more synapses in the brain than does any other neurotransmitter (McGeer, Eccles, and McGeer, 1987).

The discovery of a whole new class of brain chemicals, called **neuropeptides,** has further expanded the list of possible neurotransmitters. Among the neuropeptides are chemicals known as **endogenous opioids**—opium-like substances that occur naturally in the body. The existence of these chemicals was deduced when it was found that opiate drugs (such as heroin) bind to receptor sites in the brain, receptors located on certain neurons involved in the experiences of mood and pain. Since it seemed unlikely that people have receptors specifically designed for addictive drugs, researchers concluded that our brains must have natural substances with molecules similar in size and shape to those of narcotics. Further study revealed that these endogenous opioids are heavily concentrated in the nervous system pathways that carry messages about pain, where they inhibit those signals. Opiate drugs seem to relieve pain by mimicking the action of endogenous opioids. Severe pain can also be reduced by electrically stimulating brain areas that contain endogenous opioids, thereby triggering their release (Fields, 1985). The Chinese medical technique of acupuncture may work by likewise triggering the action of endogenous opioids (Carlson, 1981).

PSYCHOLOGY TODAY AND TOMORROW

The Mystery of Alzheimer's Disease

Alzheimer's disease is a progressive brain disorder that is particularly common among the elderly, although it strikes middle-aged adults as well. The first sign of Alzheimer's is a slight memory loss, which usually is not enough to cause serious day-to-day problems. As the disease progresses, however, severe memory impairment sets in, accompanied by marked deterioration of personality, attention, and judgment. Because there is currently no cure for Alzheimer's, and because our elderly population is growing, this disorder is increasingly becoming a public health concern. By the turn of the century it will be the most costly health problem we have.

Certain abnormal changes in the brain accompany the behavioral symptoms of Alzheimer's disease. Within neurons of the cortex and hippocampus, researchers find twisted clumps of fibrils, called neurofibrillary tangles. There are also so-called senile plaques—patches of hardened debris arising from degenerating axon terminals. In addition, the brains of advanced Alzheimer's patients contain very little acetylcholine, primarily because many neurons in a major area where this neurotransmitter is produced have died (Hyman et al., 1984).

Alzheimer's disease may often be partly genetic in origin. Scientists have discovered that a defective gene on human chromosome number 21 is responsible for at least 10 percent of Alzheimer's cases (St. George-Hyslop et al., 1987). Another nearby gene on the same chromosome triggers production of a special protein found at the core of the brain-cell plaques and in the neurofibrillary tangles (Goldgaber et al., 1987). Most likely, additional genes and chromosomes are also involved in this disorder.

Environmental factors may also play a role in Alzheimer's disease. Some researchers think that certain cases may be triggered by the action of an unusual virus (Price, Whitehouse, and Struble, 1985). Others suspect that as a person ages, wear and tear may take its toll on the brain. The result is deterioration in brain function, as occurs in Alzheimer's disease. The fact that Alzheimer's disease strikes as many as 20 to 25 percent of those who live to be over 90 years old lends some support to this theory. Another possibility is that exposure to certain neurotoxins sometimes starts the disease. Such toxins might have a delayed action, or might have to accumulate for many years before having damaging effects. This would explain why Alzheimer's disease occurs mainly in older people. Researchers are currently exploring all these avenues in order to unravel the mystery of Alzheimer's disease.

Recent research has toppled some previous assumptions about neurotransmitters. For instance, until a few years ago, scientists assumed that each neuron released only a single kind of transmitter. We now know that most neurons contain two or even three different neurotransmitters (Snyder, 1984). Some of these work by stimulating neighboring neurons, while others work by modifying the effects of other neurotransmitters. Our understanding of how different neurotransmitters integrate their messages is still in its early stages, but new knowledge is rapidly being gained. And the more we learn, the clearer it becomes just how incredibly complex the biochemistry of the human nervous system is.

PSYCHOLOGICAL FUNCTIONS AND BRAIN ORGANIZATION

Your brain serves several different functions that together make you both alive and human. First, your brain regulates your vital bodily activities, such as breathing, circulation, and digestion. Second, your brain receives information about the outside world through your sense organs and in response issues commands to move various parts of your body. Third, the brain produces the emotions you feel; it enables you to experience anger and shame or surprise and happiness.

Air traffic controllers and people in other stressful occupations tend to have high levels of the neurotransmitter epinephrine, which enhances alertness.

Fourth, your brain is your machinery for learning, thinking, and planning; it stores past experiences and uses them to determine how to act in a given situation. In the following sections, we look at the various parts of the brain that are primarily involved in carrying out each of these functions.

But before we explore psychological functions and brain organization, it will help if we give you an overview of how the brain works. Most behaviors involve a complex integration of activity in many brain regions. Even the simplest action, such as touching two fingers together, activates circuits in numerous parts of the brain, all of which are closely coordinated. Yet researchers have long known that damage to specific areas of the brain causes specific behavior disorders. This suggests that different brain regions are involved in different behaviors. The parts of the brain that enable you to see a sunset, for example, are not the same as those that allow you to solve a mathematical equation or plan your career. Different abilities, in other words, are localized in different brain areas, even though no one area alone is responsible for a complex behavior. The brain works by integrating the activities of its many different parts, each of which controls a limited set of functions. With this in mind, let us turn first to the brain regions involved in keeping a person alive.

The Vital Functions: Lower Brain Regions

The brain activities that keep us alive continue even when we are unconscious. If a person is in a coma, the heart can still keep beating and the lungs can still keep drawing air. What parts of the brain control these vital physiological functions?

The Brain Stem

BRAIN STEM the oldest part of the brain, located at the base of the skull, which regulates the basic bodily functions

MEDULLA the part of the brain stem that helps regulate many autonomic activities, such as circulation and breathing

PONS the part of the brain stem that integrates the movements of the body's right and left sides

At the uppermost part of the spinal cord, diagrammed in Figure 3.5, right at the base of the skull, is an area called the **brain stem.** In evolutionary terms, this is the oldest part of the brain. It contains several specialized regions that play roles in regulating some of our most basic bodily functions. For instance, at the base of the brain stem is the **medulla,** which helps regulate many autonomous activities, such as circulation and breathing. The medulla is also involved in the control of chewing, salivation, and facial movements. Above the medulla, but still within the brain stem, is an area called the **pons** (Latin for "bridge"). Neural fibers from the two sides of the body cross over here. The pons integrates the movements of the body's right and left sides, helping to coordinate them. The pons is also important in controlling sleep.

A latticework of neurons, the **reticular activating system,** extends through the center of the brain stem. The reticular activating system plays a critical role in keeping us alert and aroused. It also helps focus our attention, perhaps by selectively blocking incoming sensory stimuli. Sleeping pills and anesthetics work by suppressing the activity of this brain region. Not surprisingly, serious damage to the reticular activating system can cause a permanent coma.

RETICULAR ACTIVATING SYSTEM a latticework of neurons through the center of the brain stem that plays a critical role in keeping us alert and aroused and enabling us to focus our attention

The Cerebellum

If we regard the higher brain regions as a large computer system, we can think of the **cerebellum,** which is perched on the back of the brain, as a much smaller computer component. The cerebellum is involved in posture, movement, balance, and fine motor control. It monitors the continuous inflow of information about muscle tension and body position. Then, if necessary, it modifies the motor commands from higher brain regions to keep the body's actions smooth and balanced. Dancers, basketball players, and gymnasts depend heavily on the cerebellum. The typical test for drunkenness—close both eyes, stretch out an arm, and touch a finger to your nose—is a test of the cerebellum's functioning. Damage to the cerebellum can cause a lack of coordination that resembles the movements of a person who has had too much to drink.

CEREBELLUM the part of the brain that is involved with posture, movement, balance, and fine motor control

Motivation and Emotion: Central Brain Structures

Above the brain stem and deeply embedded in the central mass of the brain lie two regions that play key roles in motivation and emotion. One is called the *hypothalamus,* the other the *limbic system.* Damage to these brain regions can cause dramatic changes in behavior that vary depending on exactly where the damage occurs. For instance, damage to a certain area of the limbic system can cause a docile animal to have fits of rage, while damage to a nearby part of this region can produce fear in an animal that before was ferocious. Similarly, there is an area of the hypothalamus that when damaged promotes voracious eating, and another that when injured causes loss of appetite. Let us look more closely at these important parts of the brain to see what other feelings and behaviors they control.

The Hypothalamus

Despite being only the size of your fingertip, the **hypothalamus** is a tremendously important part of the brain. It makes us feel urges that keep us and our species alive—namely, hunger, thirst, and sexual desire. For instance, the hypothalamus monitors the levels of sugar, water, and salt in the blood and responds when any drops too far. The result? We feel hungry or thirsty, and we eat or drink until normal levels of these elements are restored. In this way, the body's internal environment is kept in a relatively stable state known as **homeostasis.**

Another example of the hypothalamus's homeostatic functions is the regulation of body temperature. When your internal temperature begins to get too hot or too cold, the hypothalamus acts as a thermostat. Certain cells in the hypothalamus trigger physiological reactions that cool you off or warm you up. For example, the reddening of your face on a hot summer day is caused by the dilation of blood vessels in the skin, which, in turn, is produced by a chain of internal events set off by the hypothalamus. These dilated blood vessels are one way in which your body loses excess heat and maintains a temperature close to 98.6 degrees Fahrenheit.

The hypothalamus is also important in controlling the body's **circadian rhythms,** behavioral and physiological cycles that occur over a roughly 24-hour period (the daily activity–rest cycle, for instance, or the daily rise and fall of body temperature). A small region of the hypothalamus, called the **suprachiasmatic nucleus,** is one of the master "pacemakers" for regulating circadian rhythms.

HYPOTHALAMUS a structure in the center of the brain that controls hunger, thirst, and sexual desire; regulates body temperature; controls circadian rhythms; and is involved in emotion

HOMEOSTASIS a relatively stable state of the body's internal environment

CIRCADIAN RHYTHM a behavioral and physiological cycle that occurs over a roughly 24-hour period

SUPRACHIASMATIC NUCLEUS a region of the hypothalamus that is one of the master pacemakers for regulating circadian rhythms

Figure 3.5 The structures composing the central core of the brain. The structures represented in this figure are the first to receive incoming information, and they regulate the most fundamental processes of the body. The reticular formation, which controls the most general responses of the brain to sensory input, is located in the area that connects the brain to the spinal cord and to the rest of the nervous system. The thalamus has a central location in the brain, and the hypothalamus is very close to the pituitary gland, which controls the activity of the other endocrine glands.

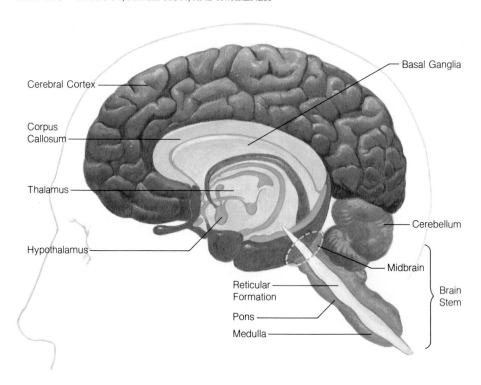

Damage to the suprachiasmatic nucleus interferes with these daily cycles (Moore and Eichler, 1972; Stephan and Zucker, 1972). We discuss circadian rhythms in more detail in Chapter 6, on consciousness.

The hypothalamus plays a role in emotion, too, and in the body's responses to stress, which we say more about in Chapter 12, on emotion. To summarize briefly, certain hypothalamic regions connect to ganglia of the sympathetic nervous system. Recall that the sympathetic system controls the body's reactions to emergency situations, when quick or forceful action is needed. Thus, the hypothalamus triggers the pounding heartbeat, the rapid breathing, and the heightened emotion you feel when something excites or threatens you. The hypothalamus also affects activities of the body's glands, a topic we take up at the end of this chapter.

The Limbic System

LIMBIC SYSTEM a part of the brain that helps control emotions and species-typical behaviors such as mating and fighting

Bordering the brain stem is an important set of structures called the **limbic system** (see Figure 3.6). Parts of the limbic system originally evolved to analyze odors, but over millions of years this region of the brain has come to have many other functions. In particular, it helps control emotions and species-typical behaviors, such as mating and fighting. The limbic system interacts closely with the hypothalamus.

AMYGDALA a part of the limbic system that is involved in regulating fear, anger, and aggression as well as memory

One structure of the limbic system, the **amygdala,** is involved in regulating fear, anger, and aggression. For instance, stimulation of one area of the amygdala makes an animal run away in fright; if the same area is damaged, however, the animal shows no fear, even in the presence of a natural predator. Other parts of the amygdala affect an animal's tendency to attack rather than to flee when threatened. Stimulation of these areas can cause ferociousness and rage. But if the same cells are damaged, even the fiercest of animals becomes docile. Interestingly, the amygdala also plays a role in memory.

HIPPOCAMPUS a part of the limbic system that is involved in memory and emotion

Like the amygdala, a second limbic-system structure, the **hippocampus,** is involved in memory and emotion as well. This close tie between emotion and memory in the brain may help explain why we usually recall emotionally charged experiences more readily than nonemotional ones. The importance of the hippocampus to memory was discovered forty years ago when H.M., a patient with

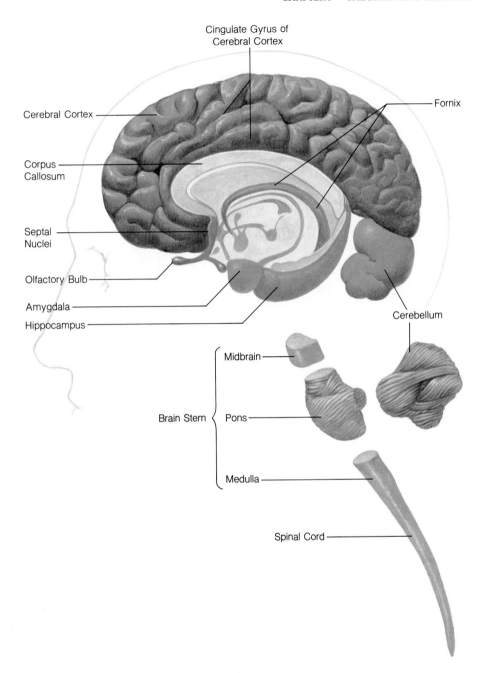

Cingulate Gyrus of
Cerebral Cortex

Cerebral Cortex

Corpus
Callosum

Septal
Nuclei

Olfactory Bulb

Amygdala

Hippocampus

Fornix

Cerebellum

Midbrain

Brain Stem

Pons

Medulla

Spinal Cord

Figure 3.6 The limbic system. Structures within this system play a significant role in a variety of emotional behaviors. Damage to various regions of the limbic system may cause wild animals to become tame, or tame animals to become vicious. Other limbic lesions may radically alter sexual and feeding behavior. The olfactory bulb (responsible for the sense of smell) is closely associated with other limbic structures, suggesting the importance of this sense to several limbic system functions.

severe epilepsy, underwent radical brain surgery to reduce his seizures (Milner, Corkin, and Teuber, 1968). Much of the hippocampus on both sides of the brain was removed. When H.M. recovered, his doctors discovered that his ability to form new memories was drastically impaired. H.M. could remember things that happened before the surgery, and he could talk intelligently about whatever was taking place at the present moment. But within a few minutes he had no recollection of what he had just said or done. He constantly felt as if he were "waking from a dream"; his experiences simply drifted away, beyond his power to retain them. As you will see later, the hippocampus and amygdala seem to work in tandem with higher parts of the brain to make memory possible.

A third structure in the limbic system, the **septum,** has regions that seem to help restrain aggression and, at the same time, act as major pleasure centers. When cells in these areas are destroyed, rats become highly aggressive; animals without such damage will work for hours to have these areas stimulated with mild electric current (Olds and Milner, 1954). The stimulation is apparently so pleasurable that hungry rats will pass up food in order to experience it. Similar pleasure networks

SEPTUM a part of the limbic system that is involved in pleasure and the restraint of aggression

Figure 3.7 A view of the left hemisphere of the brain. The diagram shows the two major fissures and the four lobes of the cerebral cortex. Colored regions identify parts of the cortex involved in speech, hearing, vision, sensory, and motor function. Also indicated schematically are the locations of the internal structures of the brain—the central core and the limbic system. For a closer look at these structures, see Figure 3.6.

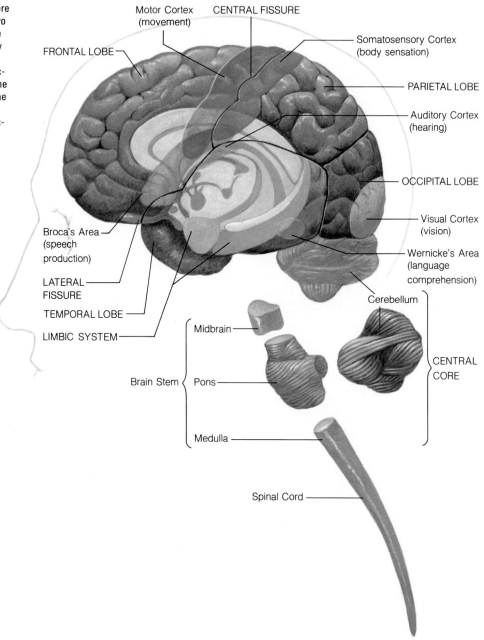

exist in the human brain. Epileptic patients who receive stimulation of these circuits report feeling "drunk," "happy," and "great." Some liken the feeling to that of being on the verge of a sexual orgasm (Heath, 1972). In humans, pleasure centers are located in several parts of the brain, but those in the septum seem to generate the most pleasurable sensations.

Other Brain Functions: The Cerebral Hemispheres and Cortex

CEREBRAL HEMISPHERES the two halves, right and left, of the cerebrum

CEREBRUM the cerebral cortex and the tissue beneath it (divided into left and right cerebral hemispheres); the part of the brain that allows us to plan, learn, and reason

CORPUS CALLOSUM a wide band of nerve fibers connecting the cerebral hemispheres

Crowning the brain stem are two large structures known as the **cerebral hemispheres,** one on the left side, the other on the right. The limbic system forms the lower border of these hemispheres, which together are called the **cerebrum.** The two hemispheres are connected by a wide band of neural fibers, the **corpus callosum.** Each region of the left hemisphere is linked to the same region of the right hemisphere via this connecting bridge. Thus, the two sides of the brain are always in close communication.

Emotion and memory are closely linked in the brain's limbic system, which is one reason extremely emotional experiences are easier to remember than emotionally neutral ones.

The cerebral hemispheres contain the **thalamus,** a pair of egg-shaped structures that link the higher brain regions with the other parts of the nervous system and play a major role in integrating the brain's activities. The thalamus serves as a kind of relay station, where information is sorted before being sent on its way. For instance, certain parts of the thalamus relay data from receptors in the sensory organs to the higher brain. Like postal clerks who receive and handle bags of incoming mail, these areas sort the incoming messages and direct them to their proper destinations. The thalamus also processes outgoing information from various parts of the cerebral hemispheres and helps coordinate it.

The part of the cerebrum most vital to our ability to think and reason is its outer covering, called the **cortex.** Compared with the cortices of many other animals, the human cerebral cortex is enormous. Our ancestors survived by inventing tools, weapons, and defenses both to outwit stronger predators and to adapt to changing climates. For this they needed the reasoning powers that a large cortex provides. But how to fit all this cortical tissue into a human-sized skull? Nature solved the problem by folding the cortex, much as you would crumple a sheet of paper. This folding, which gives the outside of our brains a highly convoluted appearance, greatly increases the size of the cortex. Thus, despite being only 1.5 to 4 mm thick, the human cortex contains billions of neurons.

Two deep crevices (or fissures) on the surface of each cerebral hemisphere divide the cortex into separate regions, called **lobes.** Each side of the brain has the same four lobes: the frontal (at the front of the brain), the parietal (the upper posterior region), the temporal (behind the temples), and the occipital (at the rear of the brain). Within each lobe, cortical tissue is highly organized. For one thing, there are six distinct layers of cells in the cortex, and the cells in each layer are distinguished by either size or structure. The layers of the cortex also differ in thickness, depending on the lobe. For instance, in the parts of the cortex that process sensory data, the fourth cortical layer is particularly thick. This is because the many incoming axons from sensory areas of the thalamus terminate predominately in that layer.

In addition to being organized into layers, the cortex also has columns of neurons that run from surface to base. These columns act as information-processing units. All the cells in a given column tend to serve the same function. For example, in the parts of the cortex that process sensory information from the skin, one column of neurons might respond to a light touch on the tip of the left index

THALAMUS a pair of egg-shaped structures that link the higher brain regions with the other parts of the nervous system and help integrate the brain's activities

CORTEX the outer layer of the cerebrum; the part of the brain most vital to our ability to think and reason

LOBES regions of the cerebral cortex: frontal, parietal, temporal, and occipital

finger, while neighboring columns respond to a light touch at other points on the same hand. All these touch-sensitive columns of cells are organized into a band that stretches across a certain cortical region. Adjacent bands of neural columns respond selectively to other skin sensations, such as heat, cold, and pressure. We say more about neural columns in the cortex in Chapter 4, on sensation.

As our discussion of cortical structure has already implied, different parts of the cortex serve different functions, just as different lower-brain regions do. The various cortical areas do not work independently, however. Many parts of the cortex are always involved in any complex behavior. Their activities are smoothly and efficiently coordinated to permit human thought and action.

You can see how localized regions are integrated into larger neural circuits as we discuss some of the functions that the cerebral hemispheres and cortex carry out. First, there are the motor and sensory functions—the abilities to move our bodies and to detect stimuli. The major brain regions responsible for these functions are the cortex's **motor and sensory areas.** In addition, the cerebral hemispheres carry out "higher" psychological functions, such as learning, remembering, planning, reasoning, and perceiving the meaning of things. These higher brain functions are largely conducted in regions of the cortex that are *not* devoted to motor or sensory tasks. Such regions, which compose about three-fourths of the cortex, are known as **association areas.**

MOTOR AND SENSORY AREAS
parts of the brain that are responsible, respectively, for movement and the detection of stimuli

ASSOCIATION AREAS parts of the brain that are responsible for the higher psychological functions, such as learning, remembering, planning, reasoning, and perceiving meaning

Motor and Sensory Functions

Our voluntary movements are regulated by the motor areas of the cortex, which occupy the posterior portion of each frontal lobe, near the top of the brain. Much of this motor cortex is devoted to controlling parts of the body that are capable of very precise movements. For instance, a relatively large portion is devoted to controlling the hands and fingers, which in humans are very dexterous. Damage to areas of the motor cortex results in difficulty in moving the body parts to which those areas are linked. If the injured cortex is on the left side of the brain, the affected body parts will be on the right side of the body, and vice versa. The left motor cortex, in other words, controls movement of the body's right side, while the right motor cortex controls movement of the body's left side. This pattern of brain organization is called **contralateral control.**

CONTRALATERAL CONTROL
the pattern of brain organization whereby the left side of the cortex controls the right side of the body, and vice versa

Contralateral control occurs in the sensory areas of the cortex as well. Thus, a touch to your left fingertips registers on the right side of your brain, while a sound picked up by your right ear first travels to your left hemisphere. The wiring between your eyes and your brain follows the same pattern, but with an added complexity, which we describe in detail in Chapter 4, on sensation. Briefly, images that fall in the left visual field (of *either* eye) are sent to the right side of the

Much of the motor cortex of the brain's frontal lobes is involved in controlling precise, complex bodily movements.

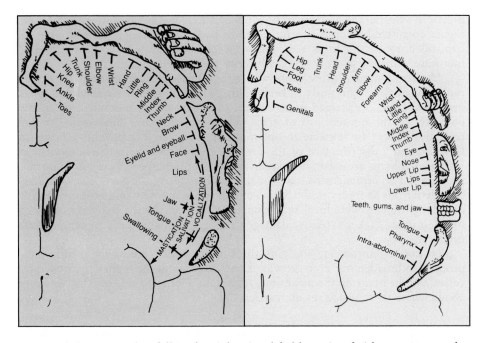

Figure 3.8 Both A and B represent the right hemisphere of the brain, which controls the voluntary muscles on the left side of the body. (A) A diagram representing the location and amount of cortical space devoted to the motor capacities of various body parts. Areas of the body capable of the most complex and precise movements take up the largest quantities of space in the motor cortex. For example, the eyelid and eyeball (capable of many precise movements) have a larger representation than the face. (B) A diagram representing the location and amount of cortical space devoted to the sensory capacities of various body parts. In the sensory realm, those organs capable of the highest sensitivity have the largest representations in the somatosensory cortex. Relatively direct linkages connect sensory areas to homologous motor areas. (Penfield and Rasmussen, 1950.)

brain, while images that fall in the right visual field (again of either eye) go to the brain's left side. This arrangement allows each hemisphere to see the area in which the hand that it controls normally operates.

Several areas of the brain receive sensory input. One, the **somatosensory cortex,** lies along the forward edges of the parietal lobes, right next to the motor cortex. The somatosensory cortex is the major receiving area for skin sensations. The more sensitive a particular part of the body is to touch, pressure, and so forth, the larger is the area devoted to it in the somatosensory cortex. This is illustrated in Figure 3.8, which also shows a stylized map of the motor cortex. The close proximity of the somatosensory cortex and the motor cortex allows for rapid feedback between the two as we move through the world and manipulate objects.

A different area of the cortex is the primary region for receiving and initially analyzing visual information. This is the **visual cortex,** located at the back of the brain in each occipital lobe. Damage to the visual cortex often produces blind areas in the visual field. People with such injuries may be able to distinguish light, dark, and movement in the affected parts of the visual field, but they cannot distinguish the shape of objects whose images fall there.

The initial perception of sounds is carried out in the upper part of the temporal lobes, just above the ears. From each ear, auditory signals travel through several relay stations, including the thalamus, until they arrive at the **auditory cortex,** which responds with a flurry of activity. Certain spots on the auditory cortex respond to sounds with specific pitches. For instance, the musical scale is represented in a more or less orderly fashion along the auditory cortex, with low notes at one end, high notes at the other, and middle notes in between (Woolsey, 1961). Not surprisingly, electrical stimulation of the auditory cortex (or stimulation through epileptic activity) can produce the hallucination of sounds. The person may hear buzzing noises, gunshots, or trickling water when no such stimuli exist in the outside world (Hecaen and Albert, 1978).

SOMATOSENSORY CORTEX the area along the forward edges of the parietal lobes that is the major area for receiving skin sensations

VISUAL CORTEX the area in the occipital lobes that is the primary region for receiving and analyzing visual information

AUDITORY CORTEX the area in the upper part of the temporal lobes that is responsible for receiving and analyzing sounds

Higher Cognitive Functions

Tell me, where is fancy bred?
Is't in the heart, or in the head?

Shakespeare, *Merchant of Venice*

We now know that fancy—our likes and dislikes; our ideas, opinions, and values— is a product of the head, not the heart. But neuroscientists cannot always say precisely where in the head such thoughts occur. This is because in most cases our higher cognitive functions (learning, remembering, reasoning, and planning) are controlled not by one brain area, but by several areas at once, all of which communicate with one another and with other parts of the brain.

Much of what we know about where the complex brain functions are carried out has come from the study of brain-damaged patients. It is assumed that whatever tasks a brain-damaged person cannot perform must be controlled, at least partially, by the injured area or areas. We must emphasize the words "at least partially." There are few one-to-one matchups between a complex psychological function and a discrete area of the brain. Researchers believe that a number of interrelated brain areas handle similar or overlapping aspects of these important processes. This arrangement has probably been adaptive for our species. Imagine how disastrous an injury to the brain could be if the ability to either learn, reason, or solve problems were localized in one small region. As the brain is now organized, it usually takes extensive damage to completely wipe out a higher cognitive function.

Newer techniques for studying the brain, which we describe a little later, promise to broaden our ever-growing knowledge about the higher cognitive processes and the brain. In the meantime, let us take a look at some of what we know about where these processes are carried out.

MEMORY We have already indicated that the hippocampus, a part of the limbic system that lies in the temporal lobes, is involved in the formation of long-term memories. H.M., the epileptic patient who had had much of his hippocampus surgically removed, could not remember new experiences only minutes after they had happened. The neighboring amygdala also plays a role in memory, as do parts of the temporal-lobe cortex that lie above these two limbic structures. Interestingly, the temporal lobes on either side of the brain each serve somewhat different memory functions. When the left temporal lobe is damaged, verbal memory (recall of stories, names, lists of words, and the like) is affected. When the right temporal lobe is damaged, recall of nonverbal information (pictures, faces, or tunes, for example) is impaired (Kolb and Whishaw, 1985). This asymmetry of function occurs in many parts of the cerebral hemispheres that are involved in higher cognitive processes. We discuss it in more detail later in this chapter.

In addition to forming long-term memories, which endure over days, months, or years, people also have a short-term memory bank for holding information they are actively using at the moment. In H.M., this short-term (or working) memory was not impaired, for he could carry on a conversation and remember people while he was talking to them. This suggests that the areas of the brain responsible for short-term memory are not exactly the same as those that carry out long-term storage and recall. Precisely where short-term memory circuits are found is not yet clear, but posterior portions of the parietal lobes seem to be somehow involved. People with damage to these areas on the left side of the brain often have trouble repeating a short string of numbers or words that they have just heard. People with damage to the same regions on the right side of the brain may also have short-term memory impairment, but for *non*verbal information, such as where things are located in space (Kolb and Whishaw, 1985).

PERCEPTION Perception is the process by which the brain interprets sensory information and gives meaning to it. For instance, when your eyes focus on a car approaching you, sensory signals travel to the visual cortex at the back of your occipital lobes, where they register the colors, shapes, and movements that make up this stimulus. What you *perceive*, however, is much more than just colors, shapes, and movements. You perceive that this object is an automobile, located at a certain distance from you, and traveling at a certain speed. In fact, you may perceive all this even though you encounter the car at night and actually see only its two headlights. Perception, then, is the process of making sense of sensory data. As such, it is quite a complex brain function.

Perception does not take place in the parts of the brain that initially receive sensory signals. These initial receiving areas (called *primary* sensory cortex) simply register the basic stimuli involved. Thus, the primary visual cortex registers the basic elements of sights (line, color, and movement), the primary auditory cortex registers the basic elements of sounds (volume, pitch, and timbre), and the primary somatosensory cortex registers the basic elements of skin sensations (pressure, temperature, and pain). From these initial receiving areas, neural signals are passed on to the other regions of the cortex where the perceptual processes take place. Here the information is synthesized, interpreted, and coordinated with data received through the body's other sensory systems.

The study of brain-damaged patients has helped researchers learn where in the brain the areas of perceptual processing lie. Various parts of three lobes of the cortex seem to be involved: the occipital, the temporal, and the parietal. For instance, people with damage to certain anterior parts of the right occipital lobe, extending into posterior areas of the right temporal region, often have trouble recognizing drawings. It is as if they cannot synthesize the content of the picture into an identifiable whole. If similar damage occurs on the left side of the brain, the person may have trouble naming or using objects. One such patient, when given a needle to thread, became bewildered by the task. He simply could not grasp what these objects were for, even though they seemed familiar to him (Luria, 1976). Difficulty identifying everyday sounds is another perceptual disorder, which seems to arise from damage to areas in the mid-temporal lobes. Either the person may confuse one sound with another (mistake a telephone's ring for a dog's bark, for instance), or all nonverbal sounds may seem identical. Similar problems can arise with damage to perceptual processing areas of the somatosensory system. For example, injury to posterior portions of the parietal lobes can result in the inability to recognize objects by touch. A person may reach into a pocket and feel a set of keys but have no idea what the object is. Disorders like these show that understanding the world involves far more than simply seeing, hearing, and touching. Higher brain regions must analyze sensory data and perceive them as meaningful (Ellis and Young, 1988).

PLANNING, COORDINATING, AND EXECUTING COMPLEX BEHAVIORS Some years ago a famous neuroscientist, Karl Lashley, asked how we managed to put together chains of complex behaviors with such speed and efficiency. An accomplished musician, for instance, can play a rapid series of notes without a single error, and an accomplished tennis player can run and return a volley with impressive smoothness and grace. How, asked Lashley, does the brain coordinate such intricate sets of actions? He surmised that the answer must lie somewhere in the cortex, but he was not sure where. Today, researchers believe that this important brain function is largely carried out in the frontal lobes. When patients with certain kinds of frontal-lobe damage are asked to copy a series of arm or facial movements, they tend to perform the movements correctly but in the wrong order (Kolb and Milner, 1981).

Certain parts of the frontal lobes may also play a major role in our ability to make plans, set priorities, stick to a task, and monitor our progress. The *prefrontal* cortex (just behind the forehead) seems especially crucial to these functions. People with prefrontal damage tend to be easily distracted, to lack persistence, and to have trouble pursuing long-range goals. For instance, a dinner-party hostess with damage to both prefrontal regions might serve dessert before the main course or go to the kitchen for a basket of rolls and end up doing the dishes, completely forgetting the guests at the table.

Interestingly, the frontal lobes, which have important links to the limbic system, exert a kind of "executive" control over emotions, too. Data from cases of severe frontal-lobe damage indicate that these lobes monitor emotions, making sure they are appropriate to the situation. Damage to the right frontal lobe can result in a loss of emotional restraint: the person becomes brash, tactless, and disrespectful, sometimes exhibiting the grossest kind of rudeness. In contrast, damage to the left frontal lobe can result in symptoms of depression: the patient becomes withdrawn, apathetic, and indifferent to people and things. Although these effects seem quite opposite, notice that they both involve a loss of the abilities to modulate emotions and adapt them to circumstances.

HEMISPHERIC SPECIALIZATION

Throughout the previous sections we have mentioned that the two sides of the brain have areas that process different kinds of information and perform different tasks. This asymmetry of function is known as **brain lateralization** or **hemispheric specialization.** Some of the earliest evidence that the two cerebral hemispheres are not functionally identical came in the early 1860s when a French surgeon, Paul Broca, studied patients who had great difficulty speaking because of brain damage. Upon their deaths, autopsies revealed that they all had injury to a lower posterior part of the *left* frontal lobe. This region became known as *Broca's area,* and the slow, labored speech characteristic of damage to it became known as *Broca's aphasia* ("aphasia" is a general term meaning a language disorder caused by brain damage). In 1874, Carl Wernicke discovered that damage to a part of the left temporal lobe causes difficulty in understanding words and arranging sounds into meaningful speech. This left brain region became known as *Wernicke's area,* and the symptoms of injury to it were called *Wernicke's aphasia.* Thus, over the years, evidence grew that the left hemisphere has specialized regions involved in speaking and language comprehension that the right hemisphere may not have.

Split-Brain Research

If the left brain is specialized for controlling language, among other things, what is the right brain specialized for? Much of the answer has come from studies of "split-brain" patients conducted by Nobel prize–winning psychologist Roger Sperry and his colleagues. The term *split-brain patient* refers to someone whose corpus callosum (the fibers that connect the two sides of the brain) has been severed in order to relieve debilitating epileptic seizures. Such seizures arise when epileptic activity (a random firing of neurons) spreads back and forth from one hemisphere to the other. When the corpus callosum is cut, the epileptic activity is

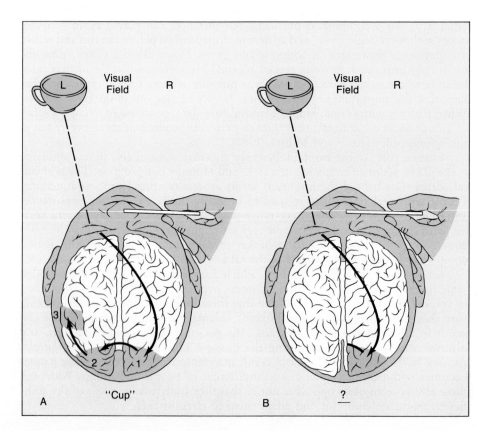

Figure 3.9 Testing of a split-brain patient (right) compared with a normal subject (left). Words projected to the left visual field activate the right visual cortex (1). In normals (A), right-visual-cortex activation excites corpus callosum fibers, which transmit verbal information to the left hemisphere (2) where analysis and production of language takes place (3). In split-brain patients (B), the severing of callosal connections prevents language production in response to left-visual-field stimuli.

confined to the side of the brain where it starts, and the severity of seizures is thus greatly reduced. Upon recovering from the surgery, split-brain patients behave normally. This is because in everyday situations each hemisphere uses its sensory systems to tell, indirectly, what the other hemisphere is doing and can help it out as needed. Through special techniques in the laboratory, however, it is possible to isolate one side of a split brain from the other. This affords an excellent opportunity to discover the special skills that each side of the brain possesses.

Consider the following split-brain experiment illustrated in Figure 3.9. The patient sits in front of a screen on which researchers flash pictures to either the right or the left visual field. (Remember that images to the right visual field go to the left hemisphere, while images to the left visual field go to the right hemisphere.) Suppose that a picture of a cup is flashed to the right visual field and thus to the left brain. When asked what she saw, the patient readily answers "cup" because the left hemisphere is proficient at speech. When the same picture is flashed to the left visual field, however, the patient reports a blank screen. This is because the right hemisphere, which received the image, is incapable of talking. So the left hemisphere, which saw nothing, speaks up to fill the silence.

How do we know that the right hemisphere is not blind to visual stimuli? We know by the fact that when given the chance to answer in another way, the right hemisphere is perfectly capable of identifying what it sees. For example, after seeing a cup, it can guide the left hand to pick out a cup from among a group of objects. It can also respond emotionally to what it sees, even though it cannot give a verbal description. For instance, when a picture of a nude person was flashed to the right hemisphere of one split-brain woman, she giggled and blushed even while her left hemisphere reported seeing nothing.

The study of split-brain patients has greatly expanded our knowledge of hemispheric specialization, particularly the special abilities of the right hemisphere, about which we previously knew little. Perceiving spatial relationships, processing visual imagery, recognizing faces, and processing music are all done more efficiently by the right hemisphere than by the left. The right hemisphere also deals better with such nonspeech sounds as coughing, laughing, and crying. Thus, the right hemisphere's abilities tend to complement those of the left.

Lateralization in a Normal Brain: Reality and Misconceptions

Even when the corpus callosum is intact, the two sides of the brain are still somewhat specialized. For example, if words are flashed to the left hemisphere of a normal person, he or she will read them a little faster than if they are flashed to the right hemisphere. Most likely this difference in processing time occurs because the right brain must pass verbal information to the left brain for help with analysis. This passage of information across the corpus callosum slows down the speed of processing. The same thing happens when faces to be recognized are flashed to the left hemisphere. The data are sent to the right hemisphere for help with identification, so the processing time is a little longer than if the faces are flashed directly to the right brain (Springer and Deutsch, 1989).

Some writers have claimed that the right and left brains have different styles of thinking. The left brain is said to be more logical and analytical, and the right brain is said to be more emotional and intuitive. This distinction can be misleading, however. For one thing, both sides of the brain have analytical abilities, as evidenced by the fact that some of the tasks the right brain excels at involve logic and reasoning (reproducing geometric patterns, for instance). Second, both hemispheres seem to be involved in emotion, although they may play different roles. For example, when the right hemisphere is anesthetized (in preparation for a medical procedure), people tend to become euphoric, sometimes to the point of mania, whereas inactivation of the left hemisphere tends to produce depression (Kinsbourne and Hiscock, 1983). Similarly, left-hemisphere stroke patients are more likely to feel despondent than are right-hemisphere ones, even when in both cases the brain damage is equally extensive (Robinson et al., 1984). Such findings suggest that the left and right hemispheres may play special roles in mediating opposite kinds of emotions (Tucker, 1981).

Thus, it is best not to think of the two sides of the brain as radically different from each other, each totally unable to handle the other's tasks. The right hemisphere, for example, does have some language ability. It understands many words, even though it processes them very slowly. Similarly, the left hemisphere does have some ability to perform tasks for which the right hemisphere is specialized, even though it does so much less efficiently than the right. A stylized representation is drawn in Figure 3.10.

It is also a mistake to think of the brain as having a rigid division of labor, with one hemisphere always totally dominating the other at certain tasks. In fact, some tasks that are normally considered the province of one side of the brain may, through training or experience, gradually become handled mainly by the other. For example, most people process music primarily in the right hemisphere, but trained musicians, who extensively analyze the structure of music, process it in the left hemisphere as well. Similarly, most people process the dots and dashes of the Morse code in the right hemisphere, but skilled users of the code, who think of it as a language, process it mainly in the left hemisphere (Kinsbourne and Hiscock, 1983). The brain's division of labor, in short, is often quite flexible. Much depends on how a person perceives the cognitive demands of a task.

Individual Differences in Brain Lateralization

To make matters even more complex, not everyone's brain is lateralized in the same manner. For instance, about 30 percent of left-handed people do not have their speech localized in the left hemisphere. For half of this group, speech is localized in the right hemisphere, while for the other half both hemispheres seem to have relatively equal speech capabilities (Springer and Deutsch, 1989). In addition, the brains of many left-handers appear more flexible than those of right-handers, more capable of transferring tasks from one hemisphere to another. For

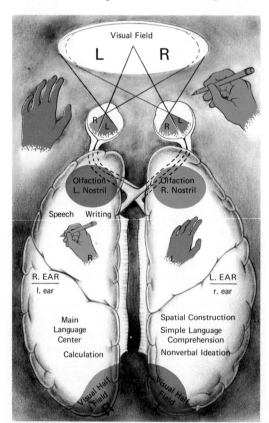

Figure 3.10 This drawing, though greatly simplified, suggests the sensory input and the types of information processing handled by the left and right cortical hemispheres of the brain.

example, among people who have difficulty speaking after suffering a stroke, the left-handers have a much better chance of recovering than the right-handers do (Luria, 1970). This advantage applies to more than just the 15 percent of left-handers with speech represented bilaterally in the brain. For some reason, many other left-handers seem better able than their right-handed peers to shift the control of language from damaged brain regions to undamaged ones in the opposite hemisphere.

Does a left-handed pattern of brain organization cause cognitive deficits of any kind? Apparently not. Although a higher than average incidence of left-handedness occurs in people who are mentally retarded or who have reading disorders, it is not because the left-handed brain is "wired" in some defective way. Instead, most of these disorders are probably cases in which brain damage at birth has caused both a reversal in handedness and cognitive deficits. When researchers study the normal population, they generally find quite similar cognitive performances among left-handed people and right-handed ones. What differences *are* discovered are usually quite small, and sometimes even in favor of the left-handed group (lefties, for instance, have sometimes been found to have better artistic abilities) (Mebert and Michel, 1980). Thus, aside from the small annoyances that left-handers suffer living in a right-handed world, there is no reason to think of left-handedness as a disadvantage.

A similar conclusion can be drawn on the basis of what we know about the differences in brain organization between men and women. The female brain, on the average, seems to be organized more bilaterally than the male brain is. For instance, compared with men, women generally suffer less visuospatial impairment when the right brain is damaged and a smaller loss of language ability when damage to the left brain occurs (McGlone, 1978). This suggests that in many women certain visuospatial and verbal functions are carried out in *both* hemispheres. In support of this theory, it was recently found that parts of the corpus callosum tend to be larger in women than in men (Witelson, in press, reported in Goleman, 1989). Since neural fibers in the corpus callosum link the left and right sides of the brain, larger ones would facilitate the greater interhemispheric communication that a more bilateral pattern of brain organization would entail.

What significance do the brain differences between men and women have for cognitive abilities? It is interesting that, in general, women are better than men at certain verbal tasks. As children, girls usually begin to talk earlier than boys do, and later in life women tend to be more verbally fluent than men. Men, in contrast, tend to have an edge over women in visuospatial skills. For instance, they are usually better at imagining how a geometric shape will look when it is rotated,

Left-handedness is sometimes an inconvenience, but it is not necessarily a sign of cognitive deficiencies or of a strict division of labor between the brain's hemispheres.

Gender differences in brain organization mean that men generally have better visuospatial skills than women.

and they also tend to outperform women at tasks like drawing maps. Could these small but reliable differences in skills be related to differences in brain organization? If they are, the relationship is not easy to unravel. If a more bilateral brain organization gives women a verbal advantage, why doesn't it also give them an edge in visuospatial skills? Of course, degree of brain lateralization may affect performance on different tasks differently, but why this would be so is not yet clear. More research needs to be done in order to determine just what is the significance of male–female differences in brain organization.

GATHERING INFORMATION ABOUT THE BRAIN

The study of the brain has been going on for many decades, and over the years important new research methods have been developed. No one method alone can give all the answers to the many questions we have about how the brain works. But together, the available methods are rapidly providing insights into this organ, which for centuries has defied human understanding.

The oldest technique for studying the brain is to observe the behavioral effects of damage to different brain regions. For instance, the functions of Broca's and Wernicke's areas were deduced over 100 years ago by studying the brains of people who had suffered various language disorders after strokes or severe injuries to the head. Of course, scientists cannot control the extent or location of naturally occurring brain injuries. That is why many researchers have turned to making various types of lesions in the brains of experimental animals and then observing what behavioral changes those injuries create.

It is not always easy to interpret the effects of a brain lesion, however. If an animal has trouble learning new information after a lesion is made, we do not know whether the lesion has affected the motivation to learn or the learning process itself. And if the learning is affected, we do not know whether the storage of new information or its later retrieval is impaired. It may also be difficult to tell whether the lesioned area affects these abilities directly or indirectly. Perhaps neural circuits passing through the lesion connect with major learning centers elsewhere. Of course, researchers are continually developing more sophisticated methods for assessing brain damage and its consequences. Today, there is a rich array of tools for evaluating injury to human as well as animal brains.

In addition to exploring the effects of brain damage, researchers study the brain by using a variety of electrical techniques. One approach is to stimulate neurons with mild electric current in order to see what feelings or behaviors are

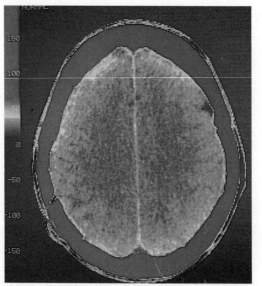

In a CT scan, a narrow beam of x-rays is passed through the brain from a number of angles. The multiple x-ray pictures that result are fed into a computer that has been programmed with a knowledge of projective geometry. With this knowledge, the computer can reconstruct pictures of single cross sections. When neuroscientists suspect brain damage, they can easily obtain a number of cross sections of the affected area. Shown here is a CT scan of a normal brain.

produced. This approach has contributed greatly to our understanding of how motor and sensory areas of the cortex are organized. It has also helped build our knowledge of the limbic system and other structures deep within the brain. But as with the lesion method, interpretation can be a problem. For instance, neurosurgeon Wilder Penfield stimulated different parts of the cerebral hemispheres in order to locate the abnormal regions in his epileptic patients. He found that stimulation to certain areas seemed to provoke the recall of long-forgotten things (Penfield, 1969). Were these areas central to long-term memory retrieval? Perhaps not. Some researchers believe that the experiences these patients had as a result of brain stimulation were more imaginary perceptions that true memories (Loftus and Loftus, 1980; Halgren, 1982). We must therefore avoid jumping to conclusions about brain organization from stimulation studies alone.

Another electrophysiological approach to studying the brain is to record the electrical activity of neurons as a person is engaged in some task. Such recordings can be made from outside the skull by placing electrodes on the scalp. When a computer is used to analyze the mass of electrical data, it can pick out patterns of activity in various brain regions. For instance, using this technique, scientists can tell that a high note stimulates one part of the auditory cortex, a low note another, and a middle note an area in between. This technique also provides a look at the electrical activity related to complex psychological processes, such as making a decision or being surprised by something. Apparently, different kinds of mental events are accompanied by their own distinctive electrical patterns.

In addition to looking at overall patterns of electrical activity in the brain, researchers can record the activity of single brain neurons. To do so, they use microelectrodes carefully implanted in the brains of experimental animals. This single cell recording technique has revealed many details about nerve-cell activities. For instance, it has taught us a great deal about how neurons in the visual cortex respond. Some react only to the visual image of lines of a particular width, positioned at a certain angle in a certain part of the visual field. Others react only to moving lines, not stationary ones, and the lines must be travelling in a certain direction. Still others respond to a line's width, angle, position, or direction, and its length as well. We say more about such stimulus-specific neurons in Chapter 4, on sensation and the senses.

The latest research methods actually provide us with visual images of a living human brain at work. For instance, with the technique called the **CT scan (computerized axial tomogram)**, an x-ray source is moved in a circular path around the head, and small amounts of x-radiation are passed through the skull to detectors on the opposite side. Pictures are taken from many different angles to provide a cross-sectional look at the brain. The procedure is shown in the photograph on page 72. An even more detailed look at the brain is possible with the technique called **MRI (magnetic resonance imaging)**. MRI generates pictures of a living brain by measuring the effects of magnetic fields on the arrangement of certain brain molecules. When these effects are analyzed by computer, the result is a very detailed cross-sectional view of the brain. The image is so detailed that physicians can detect many brain disorders that are hard to see in a CT scan.

A look at the metabolic activity of a living brain is the prized accomplishment of the **PET scan (positron emission tomogram)**. This technique involves inject-

CT SCAN (COMPUTERIZED AXIAL TOMOGRAM) a technique in which an x-ray is moved around the head, resulting in a cross-sectional look at the brain

MRI (MAGNETIC RESONANCE IMAGING) a technique involving measurement of the effects of magnetic fields on brain molecules, producing a detailed cross-sectional image of the brain

PET SCAN (POSITRON EMISSION TOMOGRAM) a technique involving injection of radioactive substances into the brain, yielding a vivid computerized picture of the metabolic activity of the living brain

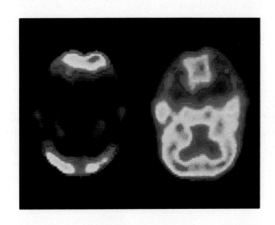

To do a PET scan, researchers inject radioactive glucose into the body and trace the brain's uptake of this substance. More active brain sites take up glucose faster: as the radioactive ions decay, their presence can be translated to create maps of the brain. The scan on the left indicates Alzheimer's disease in a seventy-three-year-old patient; the one on the right shows the normal brain of a person of seventy-two.

PSYCHOLOGY TODAY AND TOMORROW

Replacing Brain Parts

It seems as if what was science fiction just a few years ago is today's research achievement. Who would have dreamed that "worn out" parts of the brain could be replaced? Well, the time for this accomplishment has arrived. We are rapidly entering the era of brain-tissue transplants.

A startling series of studies involving animal subjects has given reason for hope that brain-tissue transplants can effectively replace neurons damaged through trauma or disease. Transplantation of appropriate embryonic or fetal brain tissue into the brains of adult rats can correct motor deficits caused by experimental lesions (Brundin and Björklund, 1987). Similarly, transplantation of dopamine-containing cells into the brains of apes and monkeys with chemically induced Parkinson's disease can alleviate the characteristic limb and head tremors (Sladek et al., 1987).

These successes with animal subjects have led to controversial experiments in which brain-tissue transplants have been tried in humans with Parkinson's disease. The brains of some patients in advanced stages of the disease have been implanted with dopamine-containing cells from their own adrenal glands. Scientists in Mexico who conducted this procedure reported dramatic successes, but follow-up observations in the United States have been more varied. At the Society for Neuroscience Meeting in 1988, a group of researchers from Spain reported excellent results when they transplanted human fetal brain tissue into the brains of patients with Parkinson's disease (Lopez-Lozano et al., 1989). Films of the patients showed striking improvement of the major symptoms of the disorder. Some who had been completely bedridden before the operation could get up and walk several months after the transplant.

Another brain disorder that researchers think may benefit from transplantation techniques is Alzheimer's disease, with its severe mental impairment, including memory loss. Some animal studies have shown that transplants into brain

regions involved in this disorder (especially those with acetylcholine-containing cells) can reverse some of the symptoms. Successes like these have given new hope to people disabled with various degenerative diseases that strike the central nervous system.

Of course, brain-tissue transplants do raise ethical issues, especially when tissue from aborted human fetuses is used. Some people fear that fetuses will sometimes be produced for the sole purpose of supplying tissue for these operations. The moral questions that surround brain tissue transplants are bound to increase in number and in scope as these procedures become more common and more successful.

Dr. John R. Sladek, Jr., with tissue slides used in his research on brain-cell transplants.

ing radioactive substances that are selectively taken up by brain cells. For instance, when a radioactive form of sugar is injected, it is taken up in greater amounts by the more active neuron in the brain. Radiation detectors outside the skull can locate the regions where the sugar is concentrated, and this information can be turned into a vivid computerized picture of the living brain at work. PET scans are becoming important in the early diagnosis of Alzheimer's disease (see the box, above). In addition, PET scans allow us to see which cells are activated when someone performs a complex cognitive task.

PARTNER TO THE NERVOUS SYSTEM: THE ENDOCRINE SYSTEM

As electrical signals race through the nervous system, orchestrating a person's thoughts, feelings, and actions, the bloodstream is coursing with chemical messengers: **hormones** from glands that all together, compose the **endocrine system.** These hormones soon reach receptor sites on specific "target" tissues, where they trigger a wide range of physiological activities. Hormones affect physical growth, emotional responses, sexual functions, metabolic rate, the supply of sugar and various ions in the bloodstream, and the body's water balance.

Hormones and neurotransmitters have many things in common. Some, in fact, are chemically the same. Norepinephrine, for example, is both a neurotransmitter and a hormone. As a neurotransmitter it affects learning, memory, and mood in the brain, as well as blood pressure in the sympathetic nervous system. As a hormone (secreted by the adrenal glands), it stimulates the heartbeat and increases the strength of muscular contractions in the limbs (Hadley, 1984). Like neurotransmitters, hormones work in a lock-and-key manner: the hormone molecules fit exactly into receptor sites on target cells.

Neural signals can travel from one area to another in a fraction of a second; hormones take more time to reach their destinations because they are carried by the circulating blood. However, split-second speed is not essential for the functions that hormones regulate. What is needed is a comprehensive, economical way to affect cells throughout the body. This relatively slow but thorough kind of action is complemented by the fact that the effects of hormones tend to persist for substantial amounts of time. When a neuron is no longer stimulated, it immediately ceases to fire and returns to the resting state, after which it has no further action until stimulated again. Hormones, in contrast, usually have more sustained influences. The responses they trigger typically outlive the relatively brief period during which the hormone binds to receptors.

The endocrine system and the nervous system are partners in controlling the body. Sometimes the activities of the two overlap, as in reactions to emergencies and stress. The nervous system, however, is the "senior partner." It ultimately controls the hormone secretions of the endocrine glands, largely via hormones sent from the hypothalamus. These hypothalamic hormones travel to the **pituitary gland** (sometimes called the "master gland"), which lies at the base of the brain. There they regulate the output of the pituitary's hormones, which in turn affect the activities of organs and glands throughout the body. The brain then monitors the levels of hormones and other substances in the blood and adjusts its messages to the pituitary whenever these levels mount too high or drop too low. Thus, the complex feedback loops between the nervous system and the endocrine system keep important bodily functions from getting out of control.

A good example of this interaction between the nervous and endocrine systems can be seen in the area of sexual development and reproductive functions. When a child reaches the preteen years, something triggers the hypothalamus to stimulate the pituitary gland to release hormones that initiate puberty. As a result of these hormones, the sex glands develop and begin releasing sperm or egg cells. Sexual reproduction is now possible. At the same time, hormones stimulate the body to take on the physical appearance of a mature adult. Not surprisingly, damage to the hypothalamus can disrupt normal sexuality and sex characteristics. For instance, when one man suffered damage to neurons in the hypothalamus that are normally involved in stimulating production of male hormones, he lost interest in sex, his chest and facial hair disappeared, and his sperm count dropped steadily. Without the necessary orders from the hypothalamus, his pituitary failed to pass along the "produce male hormones" message. To correct the condition, physicians installed a pump that automatically administered tiny doses of the missing hypothalamic hormone. The patient's male hormone production resumed, his sperm count climbed to normal, and his other masculine traits returned. He grew a beard, and his wife became pregnant (Bloom, Lazerson, and Hofstadter, 1985). Without knowledge of the interplay between the nervous and endocrine systems, doctors could never have brought about this cure.

HORMONES chemical substances released from glands that control a wide range of physiological activities

ENDOCRINE SYSTEM the collection of glands that release hormones

PITUITARY GLAND a structure located at the base of the brain that regulates the actions of other endocrine glands

SUMMARY

An Overall View of the Nervous System

- The nervous system is divided into the central nervous system (brain and spinal cord) and the peripheral nervous system (all the nerve cells outside the skull and backbone).
- The brain is the master control center for all human activities. The spinal cord is the brain's link to the peripheral nervous system.
- The peripheral nervous system is made up of ganglia (collections of nerve-cell bodies) and nerves (pathways containing bundles of fibers that transmit sensations and other kinds of information).
- The peripheral nervous system has two divisions: the somatic system, which transmits sensations from the outside world and relays orders to the skeletal muscles, and the autonomic system, which governs involuntary body activities such as heart rate and digestion.
- The autonomic system has two divisions: the sympathetic, which prepares the body to fight or to flee, and the parasympathetic, which exerts control in relaxed situations.

The Nervous System's Basic Units: Neurons

- The basic unit of the nervous system is the neuron, or nerve cell.
- Glial cells surround nerve cells and keep neurons functioning by providing them with nutrients, removing their wastes, and giving them a structural foundation. Certain glial cells form a myelin sheath, a fatty covering around part of some neurons.
- There are some 200 different kinds of neurons in the human nervous system, including sensory neurons, motor neurons, and interneurons.
- The neuron's main parts are the cell body, the dendrites, the axon, and the terminal buttons.
- Complex networks of thousands of interconnected neurons underlie the human abilities to think, speak, reason, perceive, learn, remember, feel emotion, and have awareness.
- A nerve impulse is passed when a neuron's resting potential is changed electrically to its action potential. A neuron fires either completely or not at all, and is thus said to act according to the all-or-nothing law.
- Neurons communicate with other neurons by releasing chemical substances known as neurotransmitters across the synaptic cleft. Among the most important neurotransmitters are acetylcholine, epinephrine, norepinephrine, dopamine, serotonin, and GABA.

Psychological Functions and Brain Organization

- The lower brain structures control the body's vital functions. The brain stem contains the medulla, the pons, and the reticular activating system. The cerebellum is involved in posture, movement, balance, and fine motor control.
- The central brain structures are involved in motivation and emotion. The hypothalamus regulates hunger, thirst, sexual desire, body temperature, and circadian rhythms. The limbic system includes the amygdala, the hippocampus, and the septum. The amygdala is involved in regulating fear, anger, and aggression; the hippocampus in emotion and memory; and the septum in sensations of pleasure.
- Within the cerebrum, or the upper brain, is the thalamus, which links higher brain regions with other parts of the nervous system and helps integrate the brain's activities. The outer part of the cerebrum, the cortex, is vital to our ability to think and reason.
- Each side of the brain has four lobes, the frontal, parietal, temporal, and occipital.
- Voluntary movements are regulated by the motor areas of the cortex at the rear of the frontal lobes.
- Sensory information (especially skin sensations) is processed by the somatosensory cortex at the front of the parietal lobes.
- The visual cortex, in the occipital lobes, receives visual information.
- Sounds are registered in the auditory cortex in the upper part of the temporal lobes.
- The various brain areas coordinate in the performance of higher cognitive functions, such as memory, perception, planning, and reasoning.

Hemispheric Specialization

- Research with split-brain patients has revealed that the two sides of the brain process different kinds of information and perform different tasks, a phenomenon known as brain lateralization or hemispheric specialization.
- In most people, the left side of the brain is specialized for language and the right side for visual and spatial perception and the processing of music and nonspeech sounds.
- Even though the two sides of the brain are specialized, their functions overlap somewhat, and there are individual differences in the pattern of lateralization.

Gathering Information about the Brain

- The oldest technique for studying the brain is to observe the behavioral effects of damage to different brain regions.
- Researchers also study the brain by using a variety of electrical techniques.
- Visual images of the brain at work are provided by the CT scan (computerized axial tomography), MRI (magnetic resonance imaging), and the PET scan (positron emission tomography).

Partner to the Nervous System: The Endocrine System

- The endocrine system comprises the glands that secrete the chemical messengers known as hormones.
- The endocrine system and the nervous system are partners in controlling the body.

KEY TERMS

acetylcholine
action potential
all-or-nothing law
amygdala
association areas
auditory cortex
autonomic system
axon
brain
brain lateralization/hemispheric
  specialization
brain stem
CT scan
cell body
central nervous system
cerebellum
cerebral hemispheres
cerebrum
circadian rhythms
contralateral control
corpus callosum
cortex
dendrites
dopamine
electroencephalograph

endocrine system
endogenous opioids
epinephrine
GABA
ganglia
glial cells
hippocampus
homeostasis
hormones
hypothalamus
interneurons
ions
limbic system
lobes
medulla
motor and sensory areas
motor neurons
MRI
myelin sheath
nerve impulse
nerves
neurons
neuropeptides
neurotransmitters

norepinephrine
parasympathetic division
peripheral nervous system
PET scan
pituitary gland
pons
postsynaptic potential
reflex responses
resting potential
reticular activating system
sensory neurons
septum
serotonin
somatic system
somatosensory cortex
spinal cord
suprachiasmatic nucleus
sympathetic division
synapse
synaptic cleft
synaptic vesicles
terminal buttons
thalamus
visual cortex

CONCEPT REVIEW

1.   What role in behavior does the brain play that makes understanding it and its parts so important?

2.   Outline the divisions of the nervous system and identify its major parts.

3.   Identify the parts of the neuron and describe their functions. What is the relationship of the glial cell to the neuron?

4.   Describe the resting and action potentials of neurons. Name several neurotransmitters and describe how they contribute to the communication of the neuron's signal. Is the signal always an excitation of the receiving neuron?

5.   What are the known effects of neurotransmitters? How are drugs sometimes used to alter neurotransmitter function?

6.   Describe the components of the brain stem and the cerebellum. What are the functions of the various regions of the brain? Which region keeps us alert and aroused?

7.   Which of the subcortical structures controls motivation? Which controls emotion? Which controls the body's internal environment?

8.   Locate the areas of the brain responsible for sensory input and motor output. What effect does *contralateral control* have on these areas?

9.   Identify the brain regions responsible for each of the higher functions. Why do these regions appear to be less localized?

10.   How has split-brain research supported the concepts of hemispheric specialization? What does information from split-brain studies suggest about normal brain lateralization? Are these patterns true for all individuals?

11.   Describe the techniques and equipment used to study and map the brain. What are the different physiological structures or processes observed with the CT scan, MRI, and the PET scan?

12.   Describe how the endocrine system works, how it is different from the nervous system, and what role hormones play in behavior.

CRITICAL THINKING

1.   In Chapter 2 we discussed ethical standards for the treatment of human and animal subjects. Does the intense interest in individuals with brain-function deficits or individuals who have undergone the split-brain operation in any way compromise these ethical standards? What ethical considerations are involved in the transplantation of neural tissues from human

fetuses, animals, or other available donors?

2.   To many students, the material in this chapter seems more appropriate to a biology or anatomy course. What aspects of the study of the brain place it within the domain of psychology as a science, as defined in Chapter 1?

Sensation and the Senses

Toni, a healthy baby girl, is stretched out on her stomach. She lies quite still, smiling to herself. She is not asleep, not even drowsy, yet she does not move. Twenty minutes later, she is still prone, still smiling, still pressed silently to the carpet. This is strange behavior for a healthy nine-month-old, but Toni is different from other babies in a very important way: she has been blind since birth. She lives in unbroken darkness. She cannot see the stuffed animal and rattle that lie within inches of her hand. Unless she touches them accidentally, they are not there for her.

Toni recognizes her mother's voice, and responds to it with joyful smiles. But most of the intermittent sounds she hears have no meaning for her. The jangling of keys, the thud of a bouncing ball, the squeak of a teddy bear—all are meaningless noises. She will not reach for a rattle that is shaken next to her. A sighted baby would begin reaching for the rattle at five months, but for Toni, sound is not a signal that something is "out there." That is why Toni does not creep, although she has good control of her body and can support her weight on her hands and knees. Because she cannot see, she has no reason to move forward; because she does not connect sound and object, she has no reason to reach out toward the source of noise. Deprived of visual stimulation, blind babies like Toni are slow to make sense of the world (Fraiberg, 1977).

Without sight, there is nothing to lure babies into reaching, grasping, creeping, walking, or exploring the world. Without sight, they cannot see smiling faces or loving expressions that help kindle emotional bonds. They take longer to develop motor skills, emotional attachments, language, and even a sense of self. The experience of babies like Toni demonstrates how the senses forge a vital link between the internal and external worlds.

OUR SENSES AND THE WORLD

Our senses bring in a continual stream of information about the world around us. As we deal with the environment, we use this information almost without thinking. We drive a car automatically, perhaps carrying on a conversation as we speed along. Yet driving depends on our *seeing* changes in the road or the traffic ahead, *feeling* our hands on the steering wheel and our foot on the accelerator or brake, and *hearing* the sounds of other cars. As our only links to external reality, the senses are the starting point for learning, thinking, remembering, communicating, and problem solving—in short, for all psychological processes.

The richness of sensory information can fool us into thinking that *all* of reality is available to us through our senses, but our sensory experience is selective. Each of the specialized sensory systems—seeing, hearing, feeling, smelling, tasting—gathers information that humans must have to get along in the world, accentuating the kind of information that is needed and suppressing what is not essential to survival. If we slept by day and roved at night, for instance, we might be color-blind but have a more acute hearing system, like many nocturnal animals.

How do sensory systems go about their business of bringing the outside world "inside"? One way to imagine their function is to think of each system as a communication channel that receives a complex set of signals, breaks them down, then reassembles them into a meaningful form. The process is complex but extremely rapid. When you attend a rock concert, you recognize the lead singer as a human figure on the stage. Before you did this, the light rays that hit your eyes projected a flat, two-dimensional, inverted pattern of colored blotches onto the back of your retina. These sensations were broken down into a cascade of neural signals carrying coded information about patches of light and dark, angles and curves, and movement. Within the brain, you reconstructed the three-dimensional scene before you, guided by your expectations and knowledge about rock concerts, and you transformed the array of sensory data into a costumed figure moving against a background of other band members. This chain of events, from sensation to perception, is known as *sensory information processing,* as illustrated in Figure 4.1.

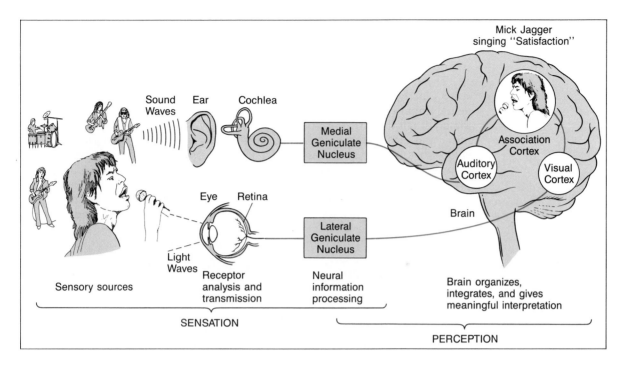

Figure 4.1 Sensory information processing is a sequence of events, proceeding from left to right in this diagram, in which sensory information is processed into our perception of the sensory stimulus—in this case, a performance by the Rolling Stones.

The chain is a single continuous process, but psychologists have traditionally broken it into two parts in order to study it: the process of sensation and the process of perception. This text follows the traditional division. **Sensation,** which we look at in this chapter, refers to the early and middle stages of the chain. It includes the activation of sensory receptors by patterns of physical energy and the processing and transmission of these signals to higher centers in the brain. In the following chapter we study **perception,** the final link in the unbroken chain. Perception refers to the brain's organization and interpretation of the signals to produce a mental representation of the original stimuli.

Our sensory systems gather information about the world through the various forms of stimulus energy they can detect. Through evolution, our sensory systems have adapted so that they respond best to particular kinds of stimulation: our eyes respond to light energy, our ears to sound energy, our skin to mechanical pressure, and so on.

Each sense organ has a large number of specialized structures called *receptor cells* that are designed to detect a particular form of energy. These cells also function as filters, or screens, for incoming information. They select some raw stimuli for processing and reject others, thus reducing the load that our sensory systems must deal with at any one time.

These sensory receptor cells are part of the nervous system, so they operate and communicate in the same manner as other cells in the nervous system—through the language of neural signals. Each kind of sensory receptor picks up a specific form of energy from the outside and, through a conversion process known as **transduction,** converts the energy into neural activity. For example, visual receptors transduce light energy and auditory receptors transduce sound energy.

After external stimuli are transduced at the receptor level, the signals are relayed to lower (subcortical) brain areas, where neural signals from several sources in the same sensory system may be fused. From here the signals are sent on to higher brain centers, specifically to the primary sensory cortex for that particular sense, where further analysis of the information takes place. The brain

SENSATION the activation of sensory receptors and the processing and transmission of these signals to higher centers in the brain

PERCEPTION the organization and interpretation of sensory signals to produce a mental representation of the original stimuli

TRANSDUCTION the conversion of sensory stimuli into neural activity

reassembles and reconstructs the converging neural information it receives about a particular object or event in the physical world, even filling in missing details by association or inference. In this way, the cortex develops a representation, in strictly neural terms, of what we have seen, heard, touched, smelled, and tasted.

The receptor apparatus for each sense is highly specialized, yet each system sends exactly the same kind of information to the brain: the electrical signals of neural impulses. Why, then, don't we "hear" lights or "see" sounds? How does the brain tell the difference between electrical impulses that signal the sounds of music and those that signal the sight of the rock singer? Psychologists have concluded that tissue in each sensory cortex can interpret signals in only one particular way. Any electrical stimulation of the visual cortex, no matter what its source, produces a visual experience, and any stimulation of the auditory cortex produces a hallucinated sound. Perhaps if the neural pathways were rerouted so that visual sensations from the eye were sent to the auditory cortex, we would indeed "see" sounds (Sekuler and Blake, 1985).

No matter what kind of energy a sensory system responds to, all systems function in the same general way. And so we begin our study of sensation by examining the basic principles they share. We then explore the five classic senses: sight, hearing, touch, smell, and taste. The main emphasis is on sight and hearing because research has concentrated on them and because these senses give human beings most of their knowledge about the world. In conclusion, we look at two senses that you may not have thought about, but that enable you to move about without losing your balance: the vestibular and kinesthetic senses.

BASIC PRINCIPLES OF SENSORY SYSTEMS

Most sensory systems respond discriminatingly to four different aspects of sensation. First, sensations obviously differ in *quality*. Tastes can be salty, bitter, sweet, or sour; sounds can vary in pitch and complexity. This suggests that a separate class of receptor cells within each system is specialized to detect each distinct quality.

Second, sensations differ in *quantity*, or intensity. Thus tones vary in loudness, and lights vary in brightness. A sensation's quantity seems to be signaled primarily by the rate of firing of the system's receptor cells.

Third, sensations differ in *timing*; each starts at a particular moment and continues for a measurable period. A sound begins and then dies away, as does a touch or an odor. Sensations may even change their properties over time: a light may dim, or an odor may become less distinct.

Fourth and finally, some sensations carry information about *location*; they tell where in space the signal came from. For example, you may determine from the buzzing that a mosquito is near the left side of your face, and so you expect to feel it land on your left cheek, where your sense of touch can locate it. By localizing a stimulus source, you know where to direct your actions (swatting the mosquito, walking toward the smell of grilling hamburgers, or getting out of the way of an oncoming car).

How does the brain represent these sensations so that you can differentiate them? That is, how does it receive visual stimuli so that you can tell the difference between a scarlet sweater and one that is magenta, or taste stimuli so that you can distinguish Pepsi from Coke? The answer is that the brain recognizes patterns of stimuli across the sensory receptors as features of sensations (Erickson, 1984).

Sensory Thresholds and Signal Detection

Sensory systems can be characterized by their sensitivity, or differential responsiveness, to natural variations in stimulation. At every moment we are bathed in a sea of sensory energies. Some of them, such as x-rays, magnetic forces, ultraviolet rays, and high-frequency sound waves, do not stimulate our sensory receptors.

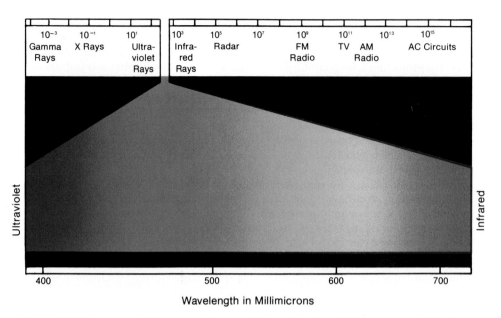

| 10⁻³ | 10⁻¹ | 10¹ | | 10³ | 10⁵ | 10⁷ | 10⁹ | 10¹¹ | 10¹³ | 10¹⁵ |

Figure 4.2   The spectrum of electromagnetic energy. The small portion of this spectrum to which the human eye is sensitive is shown expanded at the bottom. The top scale on the large spectrum is a logarithmic scale of wavelength: each step on the scale corresponds to a tenfold increase in the wavelength of the electromagnetic radiation.

(See Figure 4.2 for a scale of electromagnetic energy.) Researchers are interested in discovering the widest range of energies that human beings can detect. Think of a set of human sensory receptors as a smoke detector. Your safety may depend on this detector's sensitivity. If it went off only after flames shot up and began to spread, it would be useless. You want something that will react to very small amounts of smoke. You also want it to discriminate between smoke and other substances. For instance, you wouldn't want it to react to steam from a shower. Psychologists examining a sensory system ask the same sort of questions you would if you were shopping for—or, better yet, designing—a smoke detector.

The Absolute Threshold

In determining human limits of sensitivity, researchers focus on a primary question: What is the weakest stimulus that our senses can reliably detect? This limit is called the **absolute threshold.**

ABSOLUTE THRESHOLD   the weakest stimulus a person can detect half the time

Figure 4.3   Under ideal conditions a specific point would exist at which the intensity of a stimulus was great enough for a person to detect it. Below that point, the person would never detect the stimulus, while above that point he or she would always perceive it. This ideal threshold of sensation is depicted by the red line on the graph. Such ideal conditions never prevail because of intrinsic variability in the stimulus and a person's sensory apparatus. The ability to detect a stimulus is influenced by such factors as fatigue or alertness, motivation, and expectations concerning the signal. As shown by the blue curve on the graph, sometimes low-intensity stimuli are perceived and sometimes not. For comparisons, most psychologists arbitrarily define the absolute threshold as the weakest stimulus that a person can detect 50 percent of the time.

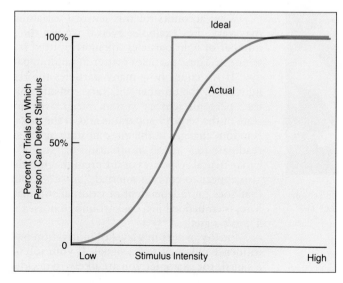

Researchers can determine a person's absolute threshold for a light, a sound, or an odor by testing that individual repeatedly with very weak stimuli. For example, to measure your absolute threshold for a spot of light, a researcher might start by projecting a very faint light spot on a screen, so faint that it is impossible for you to see. Then the researcher would gradually increase the light's intensity until you said that you could see it. Or the researcher might project a clearly visible spot of light, then gradually decrease its intensity until you said that you could no longer see it. To build up confidence in the test results, the researcher would repeat these procedures a number of times. By convention, the lowest intensity at which you reported seeing the light *half the time* is considered your absolute threshold (see Figure 4.3).

When conditions are ideal, our absolute threshold is quite low, with only minute amounts of stimulation required to produce sensations. For example, your nose can detect one drop of perfume in a three-room apartment. Your tongue can taste a teaspoon of sugar dissolved in two gallons of water. And on a clear, dark night, your eyes can detect the light of a candle burning thirty miles away (Galanter, 1962).

The Difference Threshold

Another type of threshold is also important. Suppose a piano tuner is getting a grand piano ready for a concert of classical music. Unless the piano is well tuned, the music it produces will sound discordant. The tuner is trying to adjust each string so that he can sense no difference between the note a string actually sounds and the "correct" note it is supposed to sound. Such sensitivity is measured by the **difference threshold,** or **just noticeable difference (jnd).** The jnd refers to the smallest change in a stimulus that produces a noticeable change in sensation.

In the laboratory, your visual jnd can be measured by a procedure similar to that used for the absolute threshold. A researcher would begin with two equal light spots and then gradually increase the difference between them until you said that one spot looked brighter to you than the other. This technique makes it possible to identify the smallest increase in light intensity that a person can detect. Similar methods are used with other kinds of stimuli.

Sensory Variability

Even under ideal conditions, our responses to stimuli are not consistent. Tested with the same weak stimulus, we may detect it at one moment but fail to do so a few minutes or an hour later. EEGs (electroencephalographs), which record fluctuations of electrical activity at the skull, show that the same weak stimulus can evoke different sensory responses at different times (Hillyard and Hansen, 1986).

What accounts for this sensory variability? First, the physical stimulus itself may vary. For example, even if we use the same flash of light on each test, the number of light particles (quanta) emitted from the bulb varies from one flash to the next. These particles scatter in random paths, and only some of them reach the eye. If we count how many particles the retinal receptors capture from a given light flash, the number will vary considerably from one test to the next. Second, each person's sensory system varies over time. Random changes in the internal state of the sensory apparatus and in the person's sensory system varies over time. Random changes in the internal state of the sensory apparatus and in the person's readiness (e.g., level of attention or fatigue) cause the same physical stimulus to evoke neural responses of different magnitudes at different times. Sensory systems also appear to contain internal "noise"—spontaneous, random firing of neurons that goes on independent of external stimulation. Any stimulus, or signal, therefore, is embedded in a background of noise that can make it difficult to distinguish a weak signal.

Finally, a person's level of motivation may wax and wane, which can strongly influence judgments of a signal. If your job or your survival depends on detecting a signal, for example, you are likely to decide that it is there even when you are in

DIFFERENCE THRESHOLD, OR JUST NOTICEABLE DIFFERENCE (JND) the smallest change in a stimulus that produces a change in sensation

A piano tuner's work depends on sensitivity to the just noticeable difference between musical notes.

doubt. Such heightened motivation might explain the tragic incident of July 1988 in which radar operators on the U.S.S. *Vincennes* in the Persian Gulf concluded that an approaching airplane was a hostile military aircraft—a judgment that led to the captain's decision to shoot down an Iranian Airbus carrying civilians.

Detecting extremely weak signals is not easy, and people can pick them up only if they set a very low standard for deciding that they have detected a signal. When people in experiments are trying hard to detect such signals, they occasionally think they have heard (or seen) a signal when none has occurred. They have been fooled by a "catch trial," in which the experimenter merely pretends that a signal has been presented. What they have actually reported is their detection of noise in the sensory system. Such errors are called *false alarms*. Clearly, someone who turns in lots of false alarms on catch trials is not very trustworthy (or "discriminating") in telling whether a signal actually was present. Such a performance lowers our assessment of that person's sensory ability. Several factors are known to increase a person's tendency to give false alarms. For example, if you strongly expect a signal, or if it is profitable to detect all signals and not too costly to turn in false alarms, then when you are unsure you will probably guess that there was a signal. Although the strategy produces extra false alarms on catch trials, it also increases your likelihood of reporting weak signals. In an attempt to solve the false-alarm problem, researchers developed modern signal detection theory, which provides a way to estimate a person's actual sensitivity to signals (Green and Swets, 1966; Luce and Krumhansel, 1988). His or her score is "corrected" by taking into account the tendency to turn in false alarms.

The basic approach of signal detection theory has been applied in many areas of psychology. Whether the task is answering true/false questions, recognizing words in a memory study, identifying a suspect in a police lineup, distinguishing real from counterfeit money, or judging the moral behavior of a friend, the same approach can be brought to bear. All cases can be analyzed along signal detection lines. The central problem in all these cases is one of matching: Does the test item match the conception in your memory? In all of these situations, many extraneous factors may bias your judgment. To cancel out these biases psychologists routinely use the signal detection model to correct raw scores and inaccuracies—to correct, in other words, for extraneous influences (Sekuler and Blake, 1985).

Sensory Scaling

Human sensory systems do not register changes in intensity in a straightforward manner, as mechanical meters do. Thus, when a person hears two trumpets playing together, they do not sound twice as loud as one trumpet; two teaspoons of sugar in a cup of water do not taste twice as sweet as one teaspoon.

Weber's Law

This phenomenon of gauging the intensity of sensations was investigated by Ernst Weber (1795–1878). Weber found that the jnd was not constant, but varied in a consistent way for each sense. To account for the disparity between actual changes in the intensity of a stimulus and changes in a person's experience of that stimulus, he proposed what became known as **Weber's law.** The law states that for each sensory system a specific, characteristic ratio exists between the intensity of the original stimulus and the increase in intensity that causes a jnd in sensation. In other words, the jnd is a constant proportion of the intensity (or magnitude) of the original stimulus. That is why people notice small changes in a weak stimulus but require much larger changes to notice any difference in a strong stimulus. If you are a hiker, you may have experienced this. You are just able to notice a difference in weight if someone adds one-fifth of a pound of chocolate to your ten-pound backpack. But if the backpack already weighs fifty pounds, someone would have to add a pound of chocolate before you noticed any increase. That is because the jnd ratio in the human sensory system that assesses weight is about one to fifty.

WEBER'S LAW the law stating that the increase in stimulus intensity needed to produce a second stimulus that is a just noticeably different is proportional to the intensity of the first stimulus

TABLE 4.1	Some Common Difference Thresholds

To be experienced by the average person as a just noticeable difference,

two	⎡ solutions ⎤	must vary in	⎡ saltiness ⎤	by	⎡ 8% ⎤
	lights		intensity		8%
	objects		weight		2%
	sounds		intensity		5%
	⎣ sounds ⎦		⎣ frequency ⎦		⎣ 0.3% ⎦

Source: Adapted from R. Teghtsoonian (1971), On the exponents of Stevens's law and the constant in Ekman's law, *Psychology Review, 78,* pp. 71–80.

Other systems have their own ratios, some of which are shown in Table 4.1. Vision is the most efficient sense, with a brightness ratio of one to sixty. Most people experience light from a 102-watt bulb as just noticeably brighter than light from a 100-watt bulb. The human auditory system is less sensitive than vision, with a ratio of one to ten for detecting changes in the intensity of a tone. Taste is our least sensitive system. The differences in ratios suggest that some senses have been more important than others in the evolution of our species.

Direct Magnitude Estimation

When we talk about detecting intensity, we are really referring to our private experience, as opposed to physical changes in magnitude. Weber's law describes our sensitivity to the differences between two stimuli. But what if we were asked to judge the intensity of one stimulus? How reliable would we be? This is a test much like your judgment of the distance to an onrushing car, and it is just as subjective. Yet psychologist S. S. Stevens (1957) found a simple relationship between the physical intensity of a stimulus and our perception of it. Stevens would select a standard stimulus and assign it a number—say, a standard sound labeled 100. He would then ask subjects to rate stimuli on their magnitude by assigning numbers relative to that standard. For example, after hearing the standard tone (100), subjects who thought that the new tone seemed twice as loud as the standard would assign the new tone a number twice as large as that of the standard (200). Using this direct approach, Stevens found that people's ratings of intensity were reliable and that the subjective experience and the actual physical intensity were related in a regular way. These principles are referred to as *Stevens's power law.*

Sensory Adaptation

You have probably had the experience of walking from a sunny sidewalk into a dimly lit theater and discovering that you were unable to see which seats were occupied. As your eyes adjusted to the darkness, the temporary blindness passed, and you began to distinguish the seats and the people in them. If you went back outside, you would be blinded by the sunlight, but you would readjust quickly. In both cases, you get used to the prevailing amount of light. This change of sensitivity in response to a constant, unchanging level of stimulation is called **adaptation.**

ADAPTATION a change in sensitivity in response to a constant, unchanging level of stimulation

All sensory systems display adaptation. Some senses, like sight, smell, and touch, adapt quickly; others, like the sensation of pain, adapt very slowly. Our sensory systems seem geared to react to change, which is a potent source of information. By adapting to a source of constant stimulation, a sensory system becomes more prepared to detect and react to any changes, even very small ones, in that stimulation. Adaptation is closely related to Weber's law for noticing differences in stimulus intensity. For example, when our eyes are adapted to relative darkness, where the intensity of overall stimulation is low, small variations in light may be significant and we are extremely sensitive to small changes. But in brilliant sunlight, small variations in intensity are unimportant and our eyes do not notice them.

When only part of a sensory system adapts, you may find that sensations are distorted. This commonly happens when the foot you have been using to test the bath water tells you that the temperature is fine, but the rest of your body protests it is too hot when you climb in. You can experience an odd version of this distortion by placing one of your hands in a pan of icy water and the other in a pan of very hot water. Wait a few minutes to give your hands a chance to adapt, then thrust both hands into a pan of tepid water. The initial sensation will be bizarre, because the contradictory messages sent by your two hands will make the water feel hot and cold at the same time.

One of the main points about adaptation, as this experiment demonstrates, is that our perception of any new stimulus is related to the intensity and quality of the stimuli immediately preceding it. Baseball hitters rely on this persisting adaptation when they swing a very heavy bat (or several bats) just before going to the plate. Their regulation-weight bat now feels much lighter and they can swing it faster. Adaptation helps provide a context for changes in the environment—another instance of the ways in which we are equipped to make sense of the world.

VISION

The early Greeks erroneously believed that we see because the eye projected light beams out to objects, and these beams carried copies of those objects back to the mind. Now, of course, we know that it is the sun and other light sources that illuminate objects, not the eye. The Greeks were partly right, though, because the eye does receive images of objects in our environment, images created by patterns of light reflected from the surfaces of those objects. Those images are focused on the back of the eye, where they stimulate specialized receptor cells, called *photoreceptors*, which convert the light energy into neural impulses. This process of sensory transduction, in turn, triggers a chain of events that culminates in our visual impressions of the world. As you will learn, neural impulses flow into ever more

The human visual system adapts quickly to sudden differences in light.

specialized regions of the brain, each of which processes information about certain aspects of the visual scene (Livingstone, 1988). Let us begin our discussion of seeing by examining the nature of light, the messenger that conveys to our eyes the descriptions of objects and events in our environment.

Light: The Stimulus for Vision

Light is a kind of energy that is transmitted in a wavelike form. What we actually see as visible light is only a small part of a much larger range of energy called the *electromagnetic spectrum.* Included in this broad spectrum are radio waves, infra-red waves, ultraviolet waves and gamma rays; none of these portions of the spectrum are visible, and their presence can be measured only with special instruments. The energy waves that make up the electromagnetic spectrum are defined in terms of their wavelengths, expressed in units termed *nanometers* (abbreviated *nm;* 1 nm equals one billionth of a meter). Visible light ranges from just below 400 to about 780 nm. It is no accident that the human eye evolved sensitivity to this range of wavelengths: longer wavelengths of light would not be reflected very effectively from many objects, and shorter wavelengths of light would be difficult for the eye to focus.

The Structure of the Eye

CORNEA the curved, transparent surface at the front of the eye that helps focus light rays

PUPIL the opening in the center of the eye through which light waves enter the eye chamber

IRIS the ring of muscle around the pupil that controls the amount of light reaching the receptors; the pigmented portion of the eye

LENS the transparent structure behind the iris that focuses light waves on to the retina

ACCOMMODATION a reflexive change in the lens of the eye to bring into sharp focus objects at different distances

RETINA the surface at the back of the eye where rods and cones are located

Light arriving at the eye first strikes the **cornea,** the curved, transparent surface at the front of the eye that helps focus light rays. Just behind the cornea is the **pupil,** the black circular area that forms a hole through which light enters the chamber of the eye. The margins of the pupil are formed by the **iris,** a ring of muscle whose pigmentation gives the eye its characteristic color. This ring of muscle can contract and relax, changing the size of the pupil and thereby controlling the amount of light reaching the receptors located at the back of the eye. In darkness, your pupil widens to a diameter of almost 9 mm, while in bright light it squeezes down to less than 2 mm. Your pupils tend to be larger (more dilated) when you are aroused, which explains why some poker players wear dark glasses to shield their excitement when they have a winning hand. (These structures are illustrated in Figure 4.4.)

Light passing through the pupil is further focused by the **lens,** a transparent structure resembling a lentil or bean, whose shape is varied by muscles attached to it. These reflexive changes in the shape of the lens, in a process called **accommodation,** control the sharpness of the image formed on the surface at the back of the eye, the **retina.** Accommodation occurs any time you switch your gaze to an object at a different distance. When focusing up close (such as on the pages of this book), the lens assumes a more circular shape. In many people the lens and the cornea cannot achieve the proper degree of focus; these individuals must wear glasses or contact lenses to obtain clear vision. Once focused by the lens, light travels through the *vitreous humor,* a thick, transparent fluid with the consistency of egg white. Occasionally, small pieces of harmless debris from inside the eye will float about in this fluid; when you look at a bright surface such as the sky, you may see these so-called floaters in the periphery of your visual field.

To work most effectively, the eyes need to move within the head. For instance, as you read this sentence, your eyes are moving together from left to right across the page. Other times you may need to hold your gaze steady while you scrutinize an object such as a photograph. Your control over eye position is accomplished by the coordinated activity of six muscles attached to different parts of each eye. These muscles allow you to direct your gaze in a variety of directions, and they also can keep your eyes fixed on a moving object such as a tennis ball.

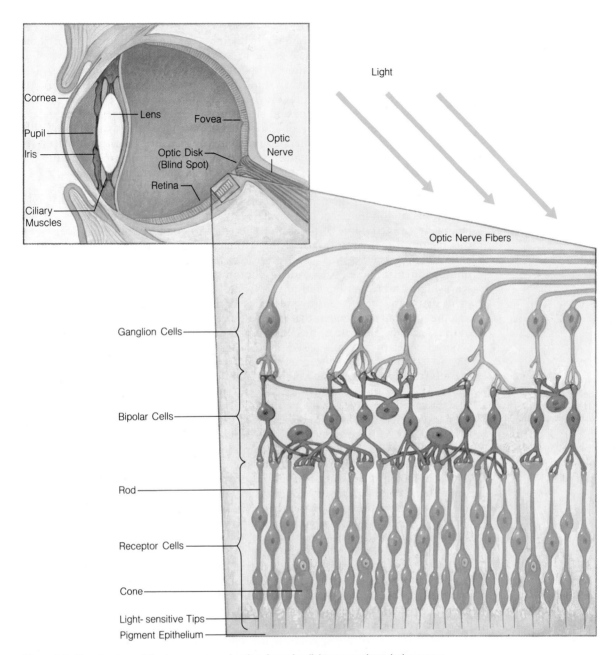

Figure 4.4 The structure of the human eye and retina. Incoming light passes through the cornea, pupil, and lens and hits the retina. As the inset shows, light filters through several layers of retinal cells before hitting the receptor cells (rods and cones) at the back of the eyeball and pointed away from the incoming light. The rods and cones register the presence of light and pass an electrical potential back to the adjacent bipolar cells. The bipolar cells relay the impulses to the ganglion cells, the axons of which form the fibers of the optic nerve, which transmits the impulses to the brain.

Sending the Signal to the Brain

Once focused light arrives at the retina, the nervous system takes over. Located in one layer of the retina is a matrix of photoreceptors, totaling about 130 million in each eye. These are specialized cells that convert light energy into neural signals. The conversion starts when light is absorbed by molecules of light-sensitive chemicals known as **photopigments.** This absorption changes the electrical properties of the receptor (Schnapf and Bailer, 1987), and this change generates a neural

PHOTOPIGMENT a light-sensitive chemical within photoreceptors whose response transduces light to a neural signal

RODS the photoreceptors (receptor cells) in the eye that are specialized for vision in dim light; convey information about brightness but not about color

CONES photoreceptors (receptor cells) in the eye that are specialized for vision in bright light; convey information about color and fine details

FOVEA the center of the retina that lies almost directly opposite the pupil; contains only cones

GANGLION CELLS neurons in the retina that do the final processing of signals within the eye

OPTIC NERVE the nerve, formed by the axons of the ganglion cells, that carries visual signals from the retina to the brain

OPTIC DISK the area in the retina where the optic nerve leaves the eye, causing a blind spot in vision

impulse in another set of retinal cells in very close proximity to the photoreceptors. These complex events—ranging from light striking the photoreceptor to the generation of a neural impulse—occur in less than one-thousandth of a second.

Your eye contains two distinct types of photoreceptors, rods and cones. The **rods** are specialized for dim-light vision; they convey information about brightness but not about color. The **cones** operate under daylight conditions; they convey information about color and are also responsible for signaling fine details in a scene. Having two types of photoreceptors in your eye is somewhat like owning two cameras: one camera contains highly sensitive black-and-white film (the rods), while the other contains a less sensitive, high-resolution color film (the cones). In the case of your eye, it is the level of light that determines which type of "film" your eye will use.

All rods contain the same kind of photopigment, called *rhodopsin*. Under conditions of dim illumination, we are best at detecting light composed of wavelengths from the middle of the visible spectrum, around 510 nm. Wavelengths in this region of the spectrum cause the strongest response in the rhodopsin molecules. Unlike the rods, a cone photoreceptor can contain any one of three photopigments. Some cones contain photopigment that is maximally sensitive to wavelengths near the blue end of the visible spectrum; others contain photopigment that is maximally sensitive to wavelengths near the middle of the spectrum; and the rest contain pigment that is most sensitive to wavelengths near the red end of the spectrum. Because of their differential sensitivity to wavelength, these three types of cones provide the basis for color vision, as you will learn in a moment.

Rods and cones also differ in their total numbers and in their distribution over the retina. The eye contains roughly 120 million rods but only about 10 million cones. The bulk of these cones are concentrated near the very center of the retina, an area called the **fovea** that lies almost directly opposite the pupil. When you stare at yourself in a mirror, you are looking at yourself with the cones in your fovea. Because cones are so sparsely distributed in the periphery (the outer edges) of the retina, your color vision is much poorer in your peripheral visual field. To confirm this, try the following simple experiment: dump a box of crayons onto a table and look at them out of the corner of your eye, noting how difficult it is to identify the colors. Rods, in comparison, are numerous everywhere within the eye *except* within the fovea, where there are none. Next time you are outdoors on a cloudless night, note how you can see very dim stars if you look slightly to the side of them. When you stare to the side, the star is imaged on an area of the retina containing a wealth of light-sensitive rods. But when you try to look directly at a dim star, you image it on your rod-free fovea and it disappears from sight.

Neural messages registered by the photoreceptors are passed through several intermediary neural links to the **ganglion cells,** neurons in the retina that do the final processing of signals within the eye. The axons of the ganglion cells form the **optic nerve,** which carries visual signals from the retina to the brain; it exits the eye through a small passage called the **optic disk.** The optic disk contains no

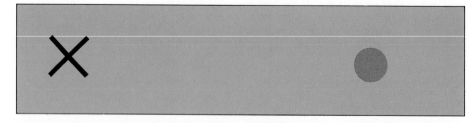

Figure 4.5 Although you are never normally aware of it, the blind spot is literally blind. To demonstrate this fact to yourself, hold this figure at arm's length, cover your left eye, and focus on the center of the X. Slowly move the figure toward you, staring continuously at the X. At some point, you will no longer be able to see the red spot. This is the point at which the red spot's image has fallen on the blind spot in your right eye. The red spot will reappear if you move the figure even closer. Now cover your right eye and try to use the same procedure to find your left eye's blind spot. What happens? Turn the book upside down and try again. Blind spots are not ordinarily noticed because they are off center, so that one eye fills in much of what the other is missing. In addition, the continual movement of the eyes shifts the area of the blind spot, enabling the brain to fill in the missing information.

photoreceptors, thus creating a small blind spot in the visual field of each eye. You can experience this blind spot by following the instructions in Figure 4.5.

The optic nerves from each eye merge at a point near the base of the brain called the **optic chiasm.** Here the axons are rerouted so that signals from the right visual field are carried to the left hemisphere of the brain and signals from the left visual field are carried to the right hemisphere. (We mentioned this crossover of visual signals in Chapter 3.) A small minority of these rerouted axons project to subcortical structures that control visual reflexes such as pupillary constriction. Most of the ganglion cell axons, however, are channeled to the **lateral geniculate nucleus (LGN),** a six-layered grouping of cell bodies in the thalamus. Three of these layers receive input from ganglion cell axons originating in the left eye, and the other three layers receive input from the right-eye axons (see Figure 4.6). Exactly what role the LGN plays in visual processing is not certain, but it appears that arousal and attention may exert an influence at the LGN (Koch, 1987).

Axons from LGN cells project up to the *occipital cortex,* the portion of the brain located near the back of the head. The occipital cortex is subdivided into several distinct processing areas, each apparently responsible for processing particular types of visual information (Livingstone, 1988). The occipital cortex, in turn, projects to other lobes of the brain as well as back to the LGN.

With this overview of the visual system in mind, consider what these different stages of visual processing actually accomplish.

OPTIC CHIASM the junction within the brain where the optic nerves converge and axons are rerouted so that signals from each half of the visual field are carried to the opposite side of the visual cortex

LATERAL GENICULATE NUCLEUS (LGN) a six-layered grouping of cell bodies in the thalamus that accept signals from ganglion cells and send them on to the visual cortex

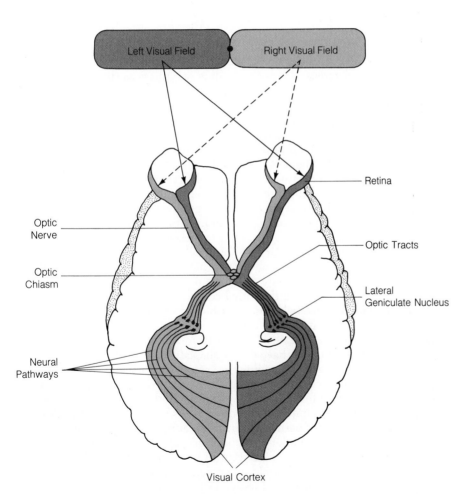

Figure 4.6 Pathways for the transmission of visual information from the left and right eyes to the visual cortex. Light from the left visual field—the area on the left side of the fixation point at which you are looking directly—hits the right side of each eye's retina; light from the right visual field strikes the left sides of the retinas. Neural impulses from the right sides of the retinas travel to the left hemisphere of the brain, and vice versa.

Visual Information Processing

Recall how vision is initiated at the first level of the retina: each photoreceptor (rod or cone) signals the amount of light falling within its tiny domain. At the level of the photoreceptors, then, the image consists of many millions of points of light. Yet we do not see tiny points of light—we see people, furniture, trees, and a host of other objects. What transpires between the photoreceptors and conscious perception to transform those points of light into objects? As you will learn in this section, neurons at one level of the visual system collect and recombine inputs from cells at the previous level. At each level, the process of recombination is designed to extract some details about the visual world, such as the orientation of a line, the size of a bar, or the direction in which an object is moving. Psychologists sometimes refer to these extracted details as *visual features,* and the process of extracting these features is termed *feature analysis.* Here is how feature analysis is thought to work.

RECEPTIVE FIELD the area in the retina from which a neuron gathers sensory information

To begin, you must understand the concept of the **receptive field.** This refers to that region of space within the visual field where the neural activity of a cell can be influenced. (Remember from Chapter 2 that all information within the nervous system is conveyed by means of neural impulses.) Every visually activated neuron, whether in the retina or in the brain, has a receptive field, and as a rule the size of an individual receptive field is quite small in comparison to the overall size of the entire visual field. In nearly all cases, receptive fields contain ON regions and OFF regions. A cell responds vigorously when light falling in the ON portion of its field is considerably brighter than light falling in its OFF region. The layout of these ON and OFF regions of the receptive fields becomes more complex at higher and higher stages in processing. You can think of the ON and OFF portions of a cell's receptive field as forming a template whose size and shape dictate what kind of visual feature will activate that cell. To illustrate this concept, let us start with the ganglion cells, a very early stage in the chain.

Retinal ganglion cells come in two varieties, both with donut-shaped receptive fields. In some ganglion cells, a circular ON region is surrounded by a larger OFF region; in others, the OFF region is in the center and the ON region constitutes the surround (see Figure 4.7). Now suppose that the entire receptive field is exposed to a uniform field of light. The ON and OFF regions would cancel each other, and the cell would not fire. However, if the cell is centered on a spot, a restricted region of brightness bordering a region of darkness, the cell would respond with vigor. These donut-shaped receptive fields, in other words, are designed to detect discontinuities in brightness, not the overall level of light. A brightness discontinuity in the image usually corresponds to the presence of an edge in the environment, and edges form the boundaries of objects. So you can see how at even this early stage of processing, the visual system has transformed the points of light from the photoreceptors into more meaningful messages about the presence and location of edges. And because the retina contains over a million ganglion cells, each with its own receptive field, the distribution of edges over the entire visual field can be represented in the train of impulses within the optic nerve.

Cells in the LGN receive their inputs from the ganglion cells, so it is not surprising that LGN cells also have donut-shaped receptive fields. However, the boundaries between ON and OFF regions are sharpened at the LGN, and some of those cells require a particular color of light within the ON and OFF region. Things change even more once information is transmitted to the next level of processing, the visual cortex in the occipital lobe. Cortical cells respond to edges, but only if those edges are oriented in a particular direction. Some cells, for example, respond only to vertical edges, while others respond only to horizontal. Among the millions of cortical cells, all orientations seem to be represented. Working together, these orientation-sensitive cells could unambiguously register the pattern of contours throughout the visual field (Frisby, 1980).

Cells in the visual cortex can also signal information about whether an edge is moving and, if so, in which direction (see Figure 4.8). Some cells have receptive fields that trigger a response only when the edge is located a given distance from the eyes; these cells may play a role in depth perception (Hubel and Livingstone, 1988). And at higher stages of visual processing, cells respond to even more com-

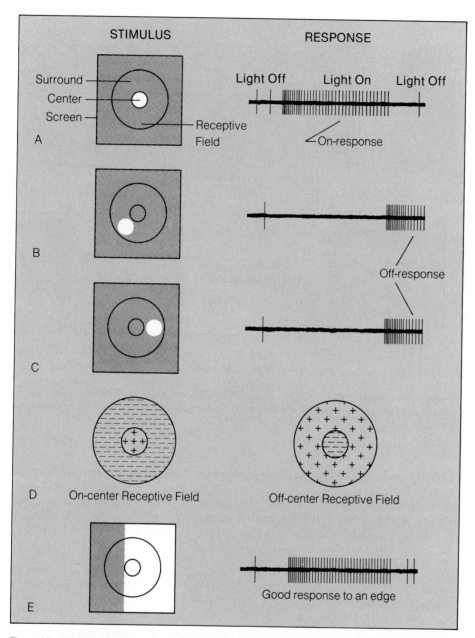

Figure 4.7 Single cell recordings of responses to light stimuli made by a cat's retinal ganglion cell. (A) The basic recording technique involves shining a spot of light (the stimulus) on a screen in a position that corresponds to the center of the cell's receptive field, which in this case causes the cell to emit a vigorous burst of impulses (represented by the cluster of vertical lines under "Light On"). (B and C) Shining the spot of light anywhere on the receptive field's periphery, or surround, inhibits the cell's activity. Only when the light is switched *off* does the cell respond with a burst of impulses. Because of this pattern of firing, this type of cell is described as an ON-center/OFF-surround cell. (D) The center and surround areas of a receptive field are concentric and thus can be plotted by exploring the receptive field with a spot of light. The cell at left has an ON-center receptive field, firing in response to a light shone on its center, as indicated by the plus signs; the cell at right has an OFF-center receptive field. (E) Retinal ganglion cells vary in their responses to edges as well as to light. Here a dark edge is shown falling on the receptive field in such a way that the entire center is receiving a high light intensity while the inhibitory surround is only partly covered. The center responds strongly when it detects the edge because relatively little inhibition is generated from the surround. (Adapted from Frisby, 1980.)

plex combinations of features, such as a mouth, a nose, and eyes in the configuration of a face (Perrett, Mistlin and Chitty, 1987). Evidently our visual perception depends on the pattern of activity within networks of these feature-detecting neurons. It is thought that different visual areas of the brain may handle particular aspects of visual perception, a kind of modular approach to seeing (Livingstone,

RECEPTIVE FIELD

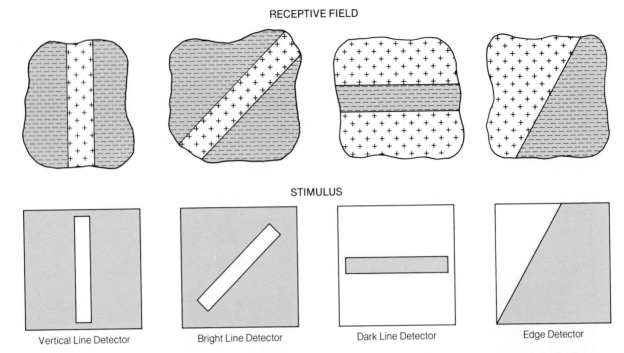

STIMULUS

Vertical Line Detector   Bright Line Detector   Dark Line Detector   Edge Detector

Figure 4.8 Receptive fields of nerve cells in the visual cortex vary in their responses to stimuli presented at different orientations. As these examples show, some cortical cells respond most vigorously to vertical lines, others to oblique lines, and so on. (Plus signs indicate a receptive-field region that emits an ON response to the specific stimulus; minus signs indicate an OFF response.) (After Hubel and Wiesel, 1962.)

1988). This leaves unanswered the question of how these different qualities of perception are blended into the unitary visual scene that we experience. In Chapter 5 we discuss some of the principles that seem to govern the combination of features. For now, though, let us look at a couple of basic visual capacities that can be related to the operations of our visual systems: visual acuity and color vision.

Visual Acuity

Earlier we examined the sensitivity of sensory systems in general. A natural question to ask about sensitivity in the visual system is how well it can *resolve*, or distinguish, the different parts of an image. When the eye detects a dual cassette deck, does it see a fuzzy black mass, or are the edges sharp and clear? Are the controls clearly visible? Is the lettering on them visible and distinct?

Sharpness of eyesight, or the eye's ability to resolve lines and shapes, is known as **acuity.** Your acuity is measured by the fineness or thinness of lines or shapes you can see distinctly and clearly. A familiar test of acuity is the letter chart used by eye doctors and motor vehicle bureaus.

The key to the ability to see letters is sensitivity to contrasts and edges. The light and dark sides of a contour (such as a printed letter) give rise to different retinal signals, which are perceived as an edge.

Acuity is determined by the size of the letters you can distinguish at a distance of 20 feet. People with normal 20/20 vision can read letters of a standard size at a distance of 20 feet. If at 20 feet you can read only letters that people with normal vision see at 30 feet, you have 20/30 vision. Even normal acuity is not good enough for some occupations. Most successful hitters in major-league baseball probably have 20/10 vision or better, so that they can rapidly detect the flight of a pitched ball.

ACUITY sharpness of eyesight; the eye's ability to resolve (distinguish) lines and shapes

Our acuity is partially determined by the distribution of cones in the retina. Cones in some areas of the retina share ganglion cells, but each cone near the fovea has its own donut-shaped ganglion cell. This region is also densely packed with cones, so that light hitting the area stimulates more cones (and more ganglion cells), making acuity best near the fovea.

Acuity is generally best among the young; in fact, most normal teenagers have better than 20/20 vision. As Figure 4.9 indicates, acuity declines with age, so that "normal" vision in a sixty-year-old is about 20/25. Some of this decline can be traced to the reduced size of the pupil in older people, which means that less light reaches their retinas (Sekuler and Blake, 1985).

Reduced light is not the only factor that interferes with acuity. If the eyeball is abnormally elongated or shortened, the image does not focus sharply on the retina at all distances, even though the lens has accommodated as well as it can. Although both conditions are common at all ages, they may also develop with aging. Glasses, which act as corrective lenses, can solve these problems by altering the path of incoming light rays so that the image is sharply focused on the retina.

The abnormally long eyeball is an especially common visual problem that is known as **myopia,** or nearsightedness. In myopia, the image focuses in front of the retina, so that distant objects appear blurred. Myopia has several causes. One major factor is genetics: among certain ethnic groups, such as Orientals, myopia is very common. For example, 80 percent of adults of Chinese descent living in Hawaii were found to be myopic (Baldwin, 1981). Another factor in myopia is sustained work at close range. As you might expect, studies have shown that the incidence of myopia in college students rises steadily (Young, 1981). Apparently, constant reading, which requires continual near accommodation, slowly degrades their eyes' ability to accommodate to distant sights. Students who develop myopia can take some comfort from the fact that myopia correlates with high grades.

High visual acuity is crucial to success as a major-league hitter.

Color Vision

We live in a many-splendored world of color; the human visual system can distinguish about 200 different colors (Coren, Porac, and Ward, 1984). Earlier we learned that cones are responsible for color vision, but that there are only three types of cones in the retina. Obviously, there are too few cone types to have one for every color we can distinguish. So the question is, how do we manage to see so many colors? Researchers have proposed two major theories of color vision. Both theories assume that color vision begins when light of different wavelengths is absorbed to differing degrees by the photopigments in the three kinds of cones. The colors we experience are determined by the blend or mixture of the basic cone types plus dark–light information from the rods. Other factors, such as the light's intensity, the way it is reflected from a surface, and the color of surrounding objects, affect the way the cones respond to light waves, and so influence our perception of color.

MYOPIA nearsightedness; a condition in which light waves are focused in front of the retina, blurring vision for distant objects

Figure 4.9 Normal visual acuity is 20/20, which means that a person standing 20 feet away can read the same letters on an eye chart that the average healthy person can read at 20 feet. Acuity is 20/50 if a person must be 20 feet away in order to read what the average person can read at 50 feet. Visual acuity is better than 20/20 in most adolescents, but it tends to decline with age. (Owsley, Sekuler, and Siemsen, 1983.)

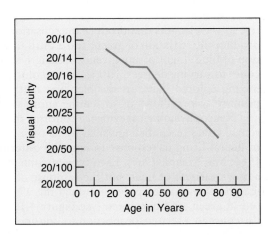

The human eye can detect about 200 colors, plus subtle differences in the shade of a single color.

Trichromatic Theory and Color Mixtures

Do you remember painting at an easel in grade school? You quickly found that when you mixed red and blue paint you got purple, that blue and yellow gave you green, and that mixing all three **primary colors** of paint (red, blue, and yellow) turned your paint into a muddy brownish-black mess. Mixing *lights* of different colors, however, produces entirely different effects from mixing paints, as you can see in the accompanying photographs. With lights, as with paints, any shade on the spectrum can be produced by mixing three primary colors, but with lights the primary colors are blue, green, and red. Combining a pure red light with a pure green light produces yellow, and mixing the primary light colors produces pure white. Why the difference? When paints are mixed, we are actually *subtracting* light wavelengths, because each pigment absorbs particular wavelengths of the light spectrum. The paint color we see is created by the wavelengths that are *not* absorbed, but that are reflected to the eye. (When all primary paint colors are mixed, we see black, because the entire spectrum has been absorbed.) When we mix lights, none of the light is absorbed—it is all reflected. We are *adding* light wavelengths; in fact, mixing colored lights is known as *additive color mixing*.

These principles form the basis of the trichromatic theory of color vision. It was first proposed in the early nineteenth century by Thomas Young and was elaborated about fifty years later by Hermann von Helmholtz, so it has come to be known as the **Young-Helmholtz trichromatic theory.** The theory was based on experimental observations of additive color mixing and good guesswork. Young and Helmholtz proposed what recent evidence supports: that color vision relies on the combined responses of three types of receptors, one primarily sensitive to wavelengths that produce the sensation of red, another to wavelengths that produce the sensation of green, and a third to wavelengths that produce the sensation of blue. Light of any given wavelength stimulates each of these three types of cones to varying degrees. Just as all the colors of the spectrum can be produced by mixing colored light, so the blending of the receptors' responses to the three primary colors allows us to see the entire visible spectrum.

Neurophysiological evidence confirms the existence of three different types of retinal cones, each distinguished by its own photopigment and by a different rate of neural firing in response to lights of differing wavelengths (Brown and Wald, 1964; MacNichol, 1964). Each type of cone responds at least minimally to almost any wavelength of light, but the response of each cone *peaks* at a different wavelength. One of these peaks occurs at the wavelength that normally appears blue, one at green, and one at red (see Figure 4.10). Light of any wavelength activates the cones in a relative proportion to one another, producing our color experience

PRIMARY COLORS the three basic colors whose mixing can produce the entire color spectrum

YOUNG-HELMHOLTZ TRICHRO- MATIC THEORY the theory that color vision depends on the combined responses of three types of cones, each most sensitive to light waves of different frequencies

Figure 4.10 Light-absorption curves of the three types of cones. One group of cones is maximally sensitive to short-wavelength (around 435 nm), another to medium-wavelength (535 nm), and a third to long-wavelength (565 nm) light. (A nanometer is a billionth of a meter.) The trichromatic theory holds that the perceived color of a light depends on the *relative* intensity of activity caused by that light in the three types of cones.

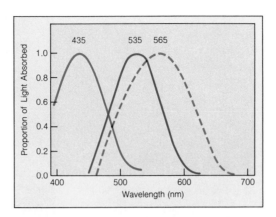

(Bowmaker and Dartnell, 1980). For example, a light of 500 nm evokes a 10 percent response from the blue-sensitive cones, a 50 percent response from the red-sensitive cones, and a 75 percent response from the green-sensitive cones. The brain interprets the pattern, and we see bluish-green.

Additional support for the trichromatic theory comes from studies of color-blindness. People who lack one or more of the photopigments have predictable forms of colorblindness. People without the pigment that is most sensitive to the longest wavelengths (in the red range) cannot distinguish red from green. The same red-green deficiency affects people who lack the photopigment that responds best to medium wavelengths (those in the green range). Both these groups of people are called *dichromats*. (Tests for dichromatic colorblindness are shown in Figure 4.11.) People who are totally color-blind are called *monochromats*. They see the world in shades of gray, as if they were watching a black-and-white movie. They can't see the color associated with the wavelength to which their single photopigment responds because the brain's interpretation of color depends on the pattern of responses from at least two photopigments. A single pigment acting alone supplies no information about wavelength, only information about how much light has been absorbed.

Some aspects of color vision are not explained by the trichromatic theory. Although dichromats confuse red and green, they can see yellow. But according

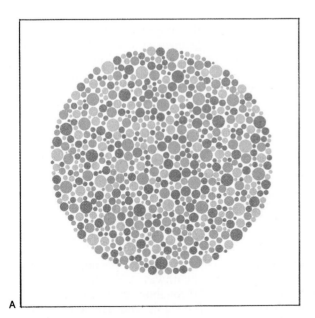

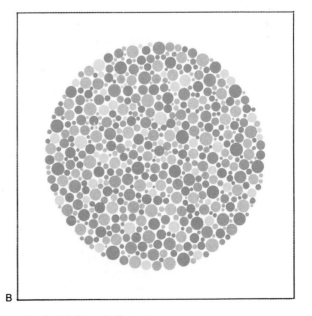

Figure 4.11 These two figures are used to test for dichromatic (red-green) color blindness. In A, normal subjects will see the number 8 and those with red-green deficiencies the number 3. In B, normal subjects can read the number 16, but most people with red-green deficiencies cannot.

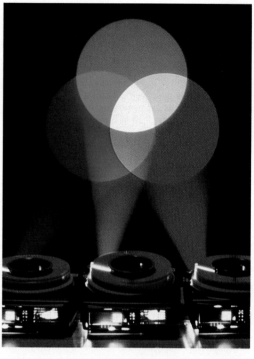

(Left) Subtractive color mixing by superimposing blue, yellow, and red filters in a beam of white light. When all three are placed over each other, black results. (Right) Additive color mixing by superimposing blue, green, and red lights. Note that when all three are present in equal amounts, white results.

to the theory, our perception of yellow comes when red *and* green photopigments are stimulated at the same time. Also, if we can see reddish-yellow, bluish-green, and yellow-green, why can't we see reddish-green (or bluish-yellow), instead of gray or white, when those colors are combined? Finally, the theory does not tell us why we see some colors (such as yellow) as "pure," with no hint of their component colors, but see other colors as blends of recognizable components.

Opponent-Process Theory

COMPLEMENTARY COLORS
pairs of colors that can be mixed to produce gray or white (in the case of lights) or gray or black (in the case of paints)

Hoping to solve such puzzles, Ewald Hering (1878), a nineteenth-century German physiologist, turned to the notion of complementary colors. **Complementary colors** are found opposite each other on the color wheel in Figure 4.12. Green, for example, is the complement of reddish-purple, and yellow is the complement of violet-blue. When mixed, two complementary colors produce gray or white.

Hering proposed that yellow was not a mixture of red and green, but a fourth primary color, and that the chemical process that allowed us to see color took place in the cones and was based on the antagonistic pairing of complementary colors—red with green and blue with yellow. According to Hering's **opponent-process theory,** the same photopigment works in opposing directions with each color of the pair, so that stimulation of one color cancels out the other. In this way we see either red *or* green (and blue *or* yellow) (Schneider and Tarshis, 1986). When both sides of the opposing pair are stimulated, they cancel each other out and, instead of seeing reddish-green (or bluish-yellow), we see a colorless gray or white.

OPPONENT-PROCESS THEORY
the theory of color vision that proposes the antagonistic pairing of complementary colors (red with green and blue with yellow) and the same photopigment working in opposing directions with each color of the pair, so that stimulation of one color cancels out the other

Later research supported Hering's general idea, but moved the opponent process from the cones to higher points in the visual pathway. Cells that operate by the opponent-process principle have been found throughout the visual pathways, including the LGN and the visual cortex (DeValois and DeValois, 1975; DeMonasterio, 1978; Boynton, 1979).

Psychologists Leo Hurvich and Dorothea Jameson (1957) theorized that opponent cells analyze signals received from cones and pass on their color analysis to the brain. If red cones pass many signals to a red-green opponent cell, it reports a

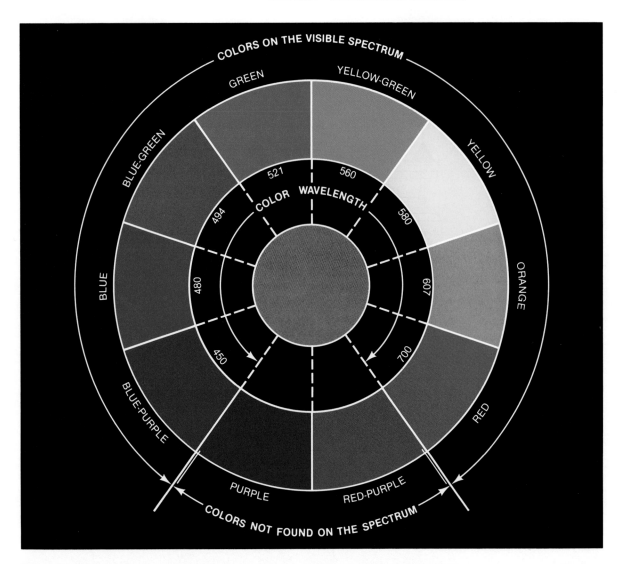

Figure 4.12 The color wheel. Any two colors that are opposite each other are complementary; that is, combining them (in the proper proportions) produces gray or white. The numbers of the "spokes" of the wheel are wavelengths, expressed in nanometers (billionths of a meter). Spectral colors are shown in their natural order, but not at uniform intervals by wavelength because of space limitations. The nonspectral reds and purples are also shown.

"red" sensation; if most signals come from green cones, the cell reports a "green" sensation. When two types of cells are stimulated (the red side of a red-green cell and the blue side of a yellow-blue cell), the brain will perceive the sensation as "purple" (see Figure 4.13).

The opponent-process theory also explains the curious experience of colored **afterimages**—sensory impressions that persist after the removal of a stimulus. You can see an afterimage simply by staring intently for 45 seconds at the lower right-hand star of the flag in Figure 4.14, then transferring your gaze to a white area, such as a blank sheet of paper. You should see the flag in its correct colors. What has happened? As you gazed at the colored flag, the opponent cells that increase firing in response to green adapted to the steady green stimulation; after a while they began to respond less vigorously. White stimulated all cells equally. When you shifted your gaze to the white paper, the cells that increase their activity in response to red responded more vigorously than the adapted green cells. And so you see red stripes. The afterimage of the blue field is a similar response to the adaptation of cells stimulated by blue's complement, yellow. And you see white stars and stripes because of the adaptation of cells stimulated by white's complement, black.

AFTERIMAGE a sensory impression that persists after removal of a stimulus

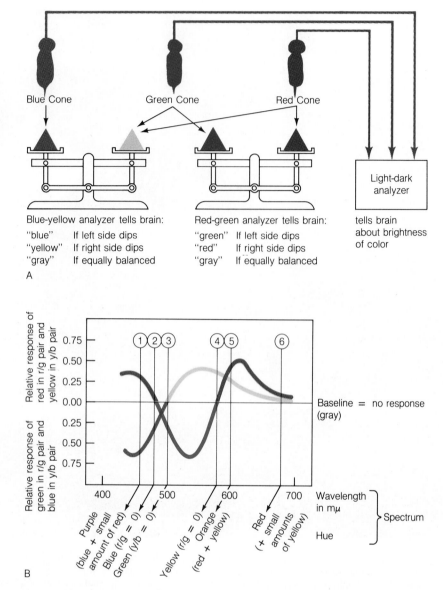

Figure 4.13 The interaction of the trichromatic and opponent-process aspects of color vision. Part A of the figure shows one way in which the three types of cones might give information to color opponent cells. The "blue" cone is actually sensitive to both blue and yellow. The blue-yellow and red-green analyzer cells each produce a moderate output called the "baseline" output when it is not stimulated, or if its two kinds of input are equal. If the blue-yellow analyzer's left side dips—if it produces an output much below baseline (due to a predominance of input from the blue cones)—while the red-green analyzer's right side dips—if it produces an output somewhat above baseline (due to receiving greater input from the red cone than from the green cone)—the result will be a mixture of red and blue that the brain will perceive as purple.

This example can be visualized more easily in part B, where it is shown as line 1. This shows the output of the blue-yellow and the red-green color opponent analyzer cells, both of which are taken into account by the brain in perceiving the color of any given patch of light. The other numbered lines show how we see other colors, according to the opponent-process theory of color vision. For example, line 4 shows that when the red-green analyzer is at baseline (which means gray to the brain) and the blue-yellow analyzer responds at above baseline, we see yellow. (After Hochberg, 1978.)

HEARING

Briefly, hearing begins when pressure changes in the atmosphere, caused by a sound source, generate vibrations among air molecules. These sound waves of compressed and expanded molecules travel through the air until they strike the eardrum. The compressions and expansions rapidly push and pull the eardrum, and it vibrates in response, triggering our sensation of hearing.

Sound Waves: The Stimulus for Hearing

We can hear differences in sound because sound waves vary in their frequency and amplitude. The **frequency** of a sound wave is expressed in a unit known as a *hertz (Hz)* (named after its discoverer, German physicist Heinrich Rudolph Hertz), which indicates the number of compression and expansion cycles that occur within 1 second. The **pitch** of a sound—the subjective interpretation of its frequency—depends on its frequency: the higher the frequency, the higher the pitch. Most speech and music are complex mixtures of many frequencies, but a few simple examples will give you an idea of the range of common sounds. The pitch of the human voice ranges from 120 Hz to about 1100 Hz, middle C on a piano is 256 Hz, and the highest note on a piano is 4100 Hz. Young adults can hear sounds with frequencies as low as 20 Hz and as high as 20,000 Hz. Figure 4.15 diagrams the hearing range of several species.

The other physical attribute of a sound wave is its **amplitude,** or intensity, which can be thought of as the height of the wave, where pressure is greatest. Amplitude is usually expressed in *decibels (dB)*. Perceived loudness nearly doubles whenever the physical intensity of a sound increases by 10 dB (Stevens, 1957). Among common sounds, a whisper is generally about 20 dB, normal speech is about 60 dB, and the roar of a subway train is about 90 dB. Thus, normal speech seems sixteen times (not three times) louder than a whisper, and a subway train seems eight times louder than normal speech. We experience sounds above 120 dB as painful, which explains why listening to an amplified rock band (130 dB) is unpleasant to many people and dangerous to the ears.

Extremely loud music can be painful and may cause hearing damage.

FREQUENCY   the number of sound waves, or compression and expansion cycles, that occur within 1 second; expressed in a unit known as a hertz (Hz); the basis of pitch

PITCH   the subjective interpretation of a sound's frequency as high or low

AMPLITUDE   the intensity of a sound wave as determined by wave height; usually expressed in decibels (dB)

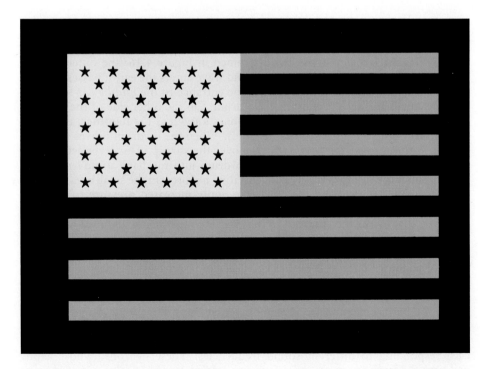

Figure 4.14   The text explains how this drawing can be used to demonstrate the phenomenon of afterimage—a sensory impression that persists after removal of the stimulus that originally caused it. The afterimage will show the flag in its "proper" red, white, and blue colors, thus demonstrating that color opposites are somehow paired in the brain.

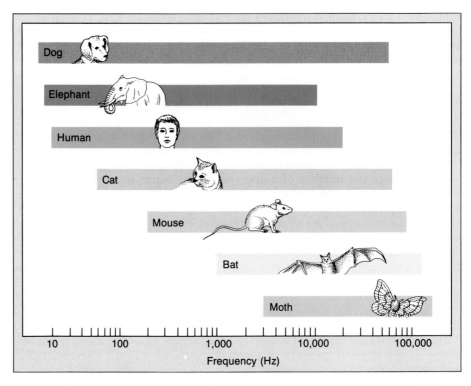

Figure 4.15 The range of sound frequencies audible to six species of mammals and one species of insect. (Hefner and Hefner, 1983.)

EARDRUM the oval membrane that separates the outer and middle ear; it vibrates when struck by a sound wave

OSSICLES a series of bones in the middle ear which convert changes in sound pressure into mechanical movement

HAMMER one of the ossicles in the middle ear

ANVIL one of the ossicles in the middle ear

STIRRUP one of the ossicles in the middle ear

OVAL WINDOW the flexible membrane that divides the middle ear from the inner ear

COCHLEA a spiral, fluid-filled chamber in the inner ear

ROUND WINDOW the membrane at the base of the cochlea

HAIR CELLS sensory receptors attached to the basilar membrane, the semicircular canals, and the olfactory epithelium

BASILAR MEMBRANE the thin sheet of tissue in the cochlea to which are attached hair cells that are sensory receptors for sound

The Structure of the Ear

The ear has three major divisions, diagrammed in Figure 4.16: the outer ear, the middle ear, and the inner ear. When a sound wave enters the ear, it passes through the *outer ear* and strikes a membrane at the entrance to the *middle ear* known as the **eardrum,** causing it to vibrate like a drum. On the other side of the eardrum are the **ossicles,** a series of delicate little bones known as the **hammer,** the **anvil,** and the **stirrup** (so named for their shapes). When the eardrum moves the hammer, it in turn moves the anvil, which moves the stirrup. This lever action converts changes in sound pressure at the eardrum into mechanical movements. It also amplifies the sound wave by concentrating its force on the small area at the tip of the stirrup. This enables the stirrup to apply increased pressure to the **oval window,** a flexible membrane on the side of the **cochlea** (a spiral, fluid-filled chamber) that marks the entrance to the *inner ear.* Just below the oval window is a second membrane on the cochlea, called the **round window,** which can be deflected outward (by cochlear fluid) as the oval window is deflected inward. As the oval window vibrates, it pushes cochlear fluid over rows of sensory receptors called **hair cells,** bending the hairs in a crosswise motion. The bending of hair cells generates the neural signal that begins the hearing process. Hair cells are embedded in the **basilar membrane,** a membrane that runs like a long tongue through the cochlea.

Individual neurons are attached to different portions of the basilar membrane, each responding to different sound frequencies. These neurons, whose axons make up the auditory nerve, pass auditory information through a series of relay stations to the auditory cortex, located in the temporal lobe of the brain. As with vision, increasingly complex analyses of the signal seem to be carried out as it is relayed to higher brain structures.

Auditory Information Processing

How does your ear encode neural impulses so that you "hear" a sound's pitch and loudness? Attempts to understand this process have focused on responses to simple tones. We know that a tone's loudness is registered through the total number of auditory nerve fibers that fire, as well as through the activation of certain cells by the vigorous bending of hair cells. Yet we still do not fully understand how the brain discriminates pitch. How does it distinguish a high tone from a low one, or tell the difference between F sharp and C? Two distinct mechanisms appear to be involved, one described by place theory, the other by frequency and volley theories.

Place Theory of Pitch

According to the **place theory** of pitch, the specific location (or place) on the basilar membrane that is most disturbed by a sound wave (and so produces the most intense stimulation of its cells) signals the frequency of that sound to the brain. A version of this theory was first advanced by the same von Helmholtz who proposed the trichromatic theory of color vision. Nearly a century later it was supported by Georg von Bekesy (1956), who won a Nobel prize for his research. Von Bekesy discovered that the entire basilar membrane does not always vibrate uniformly to waves of a given frequency. Instead, high-frequency waves

PLACE THEORY   the theory that pitch is signaled to the brain by the vibration of particular areas of the basilar membrane

Figure 4.16   Anatomy of the ear. (A) Cross section showing the outer, middle, and inner ear. Sound waves pass through the auditory canal and are transformed into mechanical vibrations by the eardrum. The three small bones amplify this motion and transmit it to the oval window of the cochlea, which is depicted in (B). The motion of the oval window sends pressure waves through the fluid in the cochlea in the directions shown by the arrows.
(C) Closeup cross section of the organ of Corti, within the cochlea. Waves in the cochlear fluid cause the basilar membrane to vibrate, which in turn disturbs the hair cells, the receptor cells of hearing.

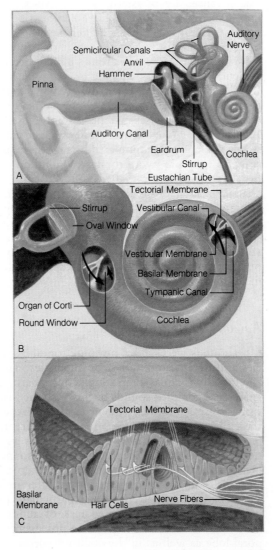

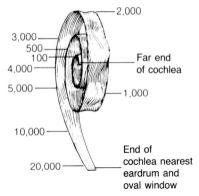

Figure 4.17 The place theory. This diagram shows the basilar membrane as removed from the cochlea. It depicts sound waves traveling down the basilar membrane and indicates the points at which the waves are largest for a number of different frequencies. Because greater displacement produces more stimulation of receptor cells at that site, the brain could use the location of the most rapidly firing receptors as a code for the frequency of the sound.

FREQUENCY THEORY the theory that pitch is signaled to the brain by the frequency of the basilar membrane's vibration as a unit

VOLLEY THEORY a revision of the frequency theory that assumes that neurons vibrate in volleys instead of in unison to send signals about pitch to the brain

vibrate the region near the oval window most intensely, and intermediate frequencies cause the greatest vibration farther along the basilar membrane. Low frequencies do cause the whole membrane to vibrate uniformly (see Figure 4.17).

Place theory has been supported by several kinds of data. First, in elderly patients who no longer can hear certain high-frequency tones, groups of damaged receptors have been found along the specific portions of the basilar membrane predicted by place theory (Crowe, Guild, and Polvogt, 1934). Second, nerve fibers from different regions of the basilar membrane have been found to be connected to neural relay stations that are "tuned" to respond most vigorously to pure tones in a narrow band of frequencies (Whitfield, 1968; Liberman, 1982). Signals appear to be sent from a given location on the basilar membrane only when that location is most activated by a sound wave of a particular frequency. Third, it has been discovered that mild electrical stimulation of small groups of neurons at the basilar membrane causes a person to experience different pitches, depending on the area that is stimulated (Simmons et al., 1965). Despite these supporting observations, place theory is not the whole story; it cannot explain the perception of low-frequency sounds, because sounds below 1000 Hz activate such a broad area of the basilar membrane that firing comes from no specific "place" (Sekuler and Blake, 1985).

Frequency and Volley Theories of Pitch

The second major theory of pitch discrimination, known as **frequency theory**, was advanced by physicist William Rutherford, who proposed that the entire basilar membrane vibrates like a banjo string and the auditory nerve relays these impulses to the cortex. The higher the tone, the faster the membrane vibrates and the more nerve impulses are sent along the auditory nerve in a specified time. According to this theory, a tone's pitch is determined by the frequency per second of neural impulses sent to the brain.

When researchers tested frequency theory, however, a major problem appeared. Recordings from the auditory nerve indicated that, as the theory predicted, neural impulses matched sound frequency—but only up to tones of about 1000 Hz. Individual neurons can conduct only about 1000 impulses per second, so when a neuron is stimulated by higher frequencies, it cannot increase its rate of firing to keep pace with the faster vibration. Frequency theory had to be modified. Its modification, called **volley theory,** attempts to solve the problem by assuming that neurons activated by a tone do not fire in unison, but in a staggered fashion. For example, two adjacent cells firing out of phase at 1000 Hz would produce a volley of pulses at 2000 Hz (Sekuler and Blake, 1985).

Contemporary researchers subscribe to a combination of place theory and volley theory. Place theory best explains high-frequency sounds, and volley theory best describes low-frequency sounds. As for sounds in the middle range, both mechanisms seem to be involved.

Auditory Pattern Analysis

Most sounds we hear are not pure tones, but combinations of different frequencies at different amplitudes, or intensities. The brain's task is to analyze sounds and identify them as a rap song, a dog's bark, or a politician's plea for votes. The analysis of complex sounds begins with the firing of auditory nerve fibers (axons) that correspond to the frequencies mixed in the complete sound. As we have seen, these fibers are tuned to respond to a different, small range of frequencies. At its favored frequency, a fiber responds to a very soft sound, but it can respond to nearby frequencies as the intensity of the sound increases. More selective analysis occurs at substations along the auditory nerve. Thus, the auditory cortex receives a profile of different frequencies and different intensities. These sound spectrums are recognized as patterns—as a particular voice or a particular musical instrument. The most sophisticated task of auditory identification is understanding speech, which seems to depend on processing in the association areas of the temporal lobe as well as in the auditory cortex.

PSYCHOLOGY TODAY AND TOMORROW

Helping the Deaf Hear

Efforts to bring sound into the silent world of the deaf once focused on amplifying the intensity of sounds. It was hoped that causing an increase in the vibrations of hair cells would translate into increased stimulation of the auditory nerve. But some researchers have tackled the problem of deafness by bypassing the damaged or destroyed hair cells and transmitting electrical impulses directly to the nerve fibers (Feigenbaum, 1987). The result has been the cochlear implant, in which an array of electrodes is threaded into the cochlea and connected to a small receiver-stimulator implanted behind the ear. Sounds picked up by the receiver are processed by a pocket-sized computer, which, relying on the frequency theory of pitch, separates sound information into its components and applies them directly to specific points on the basilar membrane. The implant delivers information about tone, tempo, and intensity.

Profoundly deaf adults whose auditory systems still function beyond the cochlea seem most likely to benefit from these devices (Feigenbaum, 1987). After lengthy training, patients with implants find that they can detect most environmental sounds, such as a knock on the door, footsteps, running water, barking dogs, ringing telephones, whistling tea kettles, and crumpling paper. They can also hear environmental sounds that warn them of danger, such as a car horn or a shout. A substantial minority regain enough hearing to use the telephone, although the majority still cannot decipher the sounds of human speech without reading lips. But even for these patients, lip-reading ability improves. In one study, lip-reading accuracy improved from 53 percent without the assistance of the implant to 83 percent with it (Brown, Dowell, and Clark, 1987).

People who have been deaf from birth cannot use cochlear implants successfully, possibly because the structures in the temporal cortex that usually process speech have been coopted for other functions in the congenitally deaf. Their best hope seems to be some kind of device based on the sense of touch. One such device is the "tickle belt," developed by psychologists Carl Sherman and Barbara Franklin (Thompson, 1984). Small rectangular transducers that respond to various sound frequencies are mounted on a belt worn next to the skin. The transducers change sounds into brief bursts of electricity, which the wearer senses as vibrations. High frequencies are felt at one end of the belt and low frequencies at the other; a word is felt as a pattern of stimulation moving across the belt. Of course, this sort of device requires the wearer to associate speech sounds with tactile sensations, which entails a great deal of training.

Another device that depends on touch is the "electrotactile speech processor," in which an array of electrodes is held between the fingers and a larger electrode is attached to a wristband (Blamey, 1987). The speech processor is based on principles similar to those used in cochlear implants, but instead of stimulating specific places on the basilar membrane, the hand device stimulates specific places on the fingers. Both the tickle belt and the speech processor are still in the experimental stage.

THE SKIN SENSES: TOUCH

Our skin is a pliable shield that keeps out bacteria, holds in body fluids, wards off harmful sun rays, and regulates the temperature of the body core. At various depths within the skin are a number of receptors that connect with neurons to inform the brain about environmental stimulation. These receptors transmit information about three different kinds of skin sensations: temperature, pressure, and pain. But not all such receptors are in the skin: receptors for pressure and pain are also found in the muscles and in the internal organs.

The different skin sensations do not appear to have their own specialized receptors. Although specific nerve endings in the skin appear to transmit only one kind of sensory stimulus, microscopic examination has revealed no consistent relationship between the structure of these nerve endings and the type of sensory stimulus they transmit. Yet stimulation of some receptors around the roots of hairs seems to be followed by the sensation of pressure on the skin, while different receptors seem to respond to pressure within muscles and internal organs.

Temperature

If your skin is touched by a metal rod that is at skin temperature (usually 32° Centigrade), you will experience neither warmth nor cold. This temperature is called *physiological zero*. At temperatures above physiological zero, you will feel warmth, and at temperatures lower than that point you will feel cold.

But you cannot feel both warmth and cold at every point on your skin. If an area of skin about the size of your little fingernail is stimulated with pinpricks, you will feel a cold sensation at about six spots and a warm sensation at one or two different spots. The separate identity of warm and cold receptors is generally accepted: stimulating a cold spot with a warm stimulus sometimes yields a cold sensation—a phenomenon known as *paradoxical cold*.

These bathers' skin receptors are transmitting a sensation of warmth—but only as long as they stay in the heated water.

Pressure

Pressure-sensitive receptors in the skin are more responsive to changes in pressure than to steady states. Once the skin has been displaced to accommodate a source of pressure, adaptation occurs, and any sensation of pressure rapidly disappears. If we did not adapt, we would be constantly aware of the gentle pressure of our clothes, eyeglasses, and jewelry.

Sensitivity to touch varies enormously over different portions of the body. Our fingers and lips, for example, are exquisitely sensitive to any degree of pressure, but portions of the back are relatively insensitive. This variation is reflected in the disproportionately large area of the brain's sensory cortex that is devoted to the fingers and mouth, as we saw in Chapter 3 (see Figure 3.8).

The sensitivity of touch receptors in human fingers is exploited by blind people who learn to read Braille, a code in which each letter of the alphabet corresponds to a specific combination of tiny raised dots (see Figure 4.18). By moving the fingers over the dots, a skilled Braille reader can read at the rate of about fifty words per minute.

Pain

Pain is a puzzle with many pieces. There are many different kinds of pain: acute pains (a pinprick or cut), chronic-periodic pains (angina, migraine headache, menstrual cramps), chronic-intractable-benign pains (incurable but not worsening lower-back pain), and chronic-progressive pains (arthritis or an inoperable growing tumor). People's descriptions of pain are varied—shooting, scalding, splitting, throbbing, cramping, bright, sharp, or dull. Solving the puzzle of pain has been difficult because of its very nature: ethical considerations prevent researchers from doing much more than experiment with mild pain stimuli such as moderate heat or cold and pinpricks.

Pain has a physiological component, which is tied up with specific nerves, brain structures, and neurotransmitters; it also has a subjective component, which varies with the person's attitudes and fears, the context of the painful stimulus, and the strategies that are used to cope with it. The physiological component is relatively easy to describe. Pain receptors are found in the skin, corneas of the eyes, deep muscles, organs, and joints. These receptors are stimulated by punctures, cuts, scrapes, twists, extreme cold or heat, and some chemical substances. Most pain receptors are not specific; they can respond to several types of noxious stimuli. Most receptors relay their messages along sensory fibers to the spinal cord. If you step on a tack, prick your finger, or burn your hand, a message

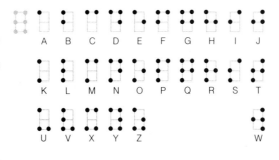

Figure 4.18 The Braille alphabet. Each combination of dots corresponds to one letter of the alphabet. Based on the Braille cell at the upper left, the first ten letters are formed by distinct arrangements of the top four dots; the next ten letters are made by adding a dot to the lower left; the remaining letters, U to Z, are made by adding a dot to the lower right corner. W is an exception. When printed, the dots are raised slightly above the surface of the page so that blind readers can detect the patterns with their fingertips.

immediately goes into and back out from the spinal cord, telling you to jerk your hand or foot away from the source of pain. Because these reflexes are based in the spinal cord, you remove your hand or foot before your brain has become fully aware of the pain.

Pain signals from the dorsal spine are sent to the brain along two pathways: a fast pathway, which goes by way of the thalamus to the sensorimotor cortex; and a slow pathway, which projects through the reticular formation and limbic system to the prefrontal cortex. The fast pathway functions as a sensory information channel; it carries messages that allow you to determine where the pain is, how serious the injury might be, and how to react to it. The slow pathway sends information about the emotional aspect of the experience; messages that travel along it signal the feeling of pain and arouse your emotional system. Your final perception of pain is a fusion of these two qualities.

With time, we adapt to minor pain. However, we show little adaptation to intense pain. Because pain tells us that something is amiss, it is fortunate that we do not adapt to it immediately. Consider the situation of those few people who are born without the ability to feel pain. Such people may experience severe burns, broken bones, or even a ruptured appendix without feeling the pain signals that would alert them either to protect themselves against further injury or to seek medical attention.

Neurotransmitters are intimately involved in the transmission and experience of pain. A neurotransmitter called *substance P* (for pain) has been found in the dorsal spinal cord of primates. It appears to play a major role in transmitting pain messages from the peripheral pain receptors to the central nervous system. The presence of substance P may result in the persistence of pain for some time after the noxious stimulus has stopped. Luckily, the dorsal spine and the central nervous system seem to produce natural painkillers—the endorphins discussed in Chapter 3. Endorphin-containing neurons are scattered throughout the spinal cord and along the slow pain pathways in the reticular formation and the limbic system. When pain pathways are stimulated, these neurons eventually respond by releasing endorphins and the pain begins to diminish. Electrical stimulation through electrodes implanted in the reticular formation releases endorphins; this procedure has been used on an experimental basis to help people with intractable pain who have been unable to obtain relief through other methods.

Our bodies not only deal with actual pain by releasing endorphins; they also release these natural painkillers to prepare for *anticipated* pain. Research has shown that when animals hear a tone that has regularly signaled an impending electric shock, their bodies release endorphins. People tested in similar circumstances have decreased their sensitivity to pain that follows a signal (Bloom, Lazerson, and Hofstadter, 1985).

Certain treatments that reduce pain may act by stimulating the release of endorphins. For example, acupuncture, in which tiny needles are inserted into specific skin areas, relieves the anguish of pain. Acupuncture may work by causing the release of endorphins (Carlson, 1986). For instance, when a patient is first given naloxone, a drug that blocks the synaptic action of endorphins (and morphine), acupuncture fails to relieve pain. Endorphins may also be responsible for the relief from pain that follows the administration of a placebo—an inert "sugar pill." Because tablet medicines have been associated with real pain relief in the past, the brain is fooled into releasing endorphins when a placebo is taken.

PSYCHOLOGY TODAY AND TOMORROW

Can You Recognize the Scent of Spruce?

When you step into the house and are greeted by the smell of evergreens, no one needs to tell you that the Christmas tree has been brought home. But if you are sitting in the college library trying to conjure up that exciting aroma, it will elude your best efforts.

Why are odors so central to our memories, but so elusive when we strive to recall them? Psychologist Trygg Engen (1987) believes that it is nearly impossible to recall odors because of the way we store olfactory memories. Familiar odors are not stored according to their names but as part of the situation in which we have encountered them. The more important the situation seems to us, the more enduring the memory.

For that reason, it is difficult to recognize odors that have been stripped of all context. When brought into the laboratory, most people can name correctly no more than a half-dozen extremely common odors (such as coffee). A less common odor may seem familiar, but they are unable to name it. When the experimenter provides the correct name (such as cloves, chocolate, or lemon), subjects recognize the odor immediately and seem surprised at their inability to pull its name from memory.

In exploring this puzzle, Engen discovered that we do know something about most familiar odors, even if we cannot name them. Unable to identify "lemon," subjects tend to use related odor words ("fruity"), some object associated with the odor ("Pledge dusting spray"), or a related sensation ("bitter"). Apparently, we store our memories of odors according to their similarity to other odors or to the context in which we encounter them. When we try to name a familiar odor, we come up with some personal experience we have had with the odor. For example, some people responded to the scent of Johnson's baby powder with "baby oil." And perhaps because some people use baby oil when tanning, one person called it "suntan lotion."

This muddling of our memory for odors showed clearly when Engen gave subjects a multiple-choice test of odors. When the alternatives were completely unrelated to the test odor (pizza, turpentine, grape, and clove as possible choices for the odor of grape), nearly everyone named the odor correctly. But when the alternatives were related (melon, plum, grape, and strawberry as possible choices for the odor of grape), only about half the answers were correct.

SMELL

Our sense of smell is extremely sensitive, possibly 10,000 times more sensitive than our sense of taste. You may be surprised to learn that smell, as well as taste, plays a vital role in our enjoyment of food. Try a simple experiment. First grate a raw potato, a pear, and an apple to make their texture similar. Then pinch your nostrils shut with one hand and taste them, one at a time. Can you tell the difference between them? Most people find it impossible. The intimate involvement of our sense of smell with our sense of taste explains why food loses its appeal when we have a bad cold.

OLFACTION   the sense of smell

We consider the sense of smell, or **olfaction,** to be one of our "minor" sensory abilities, but it often is central to our experiences, especially to the awakening of distant memories. The aroma of a certain perfume may evoke memories of your grandmother; the scent of a crushed spruce twig may bring back memories of a previous Christmas (see the accompanying box).

Smell also serves a vital function in our lives: it warns us of possible danger, such as a gas leak, fire, or spoiled food. Odors also enhance human pleasure. Our use of perfumes, deodorants, and fragrant flowers shows the premium we place on pleasant aromas, and our bulging spice cupboards testify to the importance of odor in our enjoyment of food. Manufacturers and dealers are aware that artificially created odors can boost sales. Plastic briefcases may be sprayed with a "real leather" smell, and used cars get a liberal application of "new car" smell.

Some animals communicate by means of odors. They release **pheromones,** chemicals that trigger some reaction in other animals of that species. Since pheromones travel on air currents, they can communicate over great distances. They move slowly and leave a lingering message. One major purpose of pheromone production is to attract members of the other sex. Sex-attractant pheromones have been found in many species, including crabs, spiders, moths, fish, amphibians, reptiles, and monkeys (Wilson, 1975).

Despite its sensitivity, olfaction shows marked sensory adaptation over time; within several minutes of exposure to an odor, our ability to detect it drops to 30 percent of our initial sensitivity (Halpern, 1983). For this reason, a constant foul odor soon fades from our consciousness, as does a pleasant floral perfume dabbed on ourselves or the person next to us.

About 8 percent of the population have an impaired sense of smell as a result of head injury, influenza, asthma, endocrine disorder, or cancer (Bloom, 1984). For these individuals, the pleasures of eating have vanished. Wine tastes like vinegar; ice cream is simply a cold paste; garlic and pepper taste the same. About 25 percent of people who lose their sense of smell also lose interest in sex, apparently because odors played some role in their sexual arousal.

The receptors for olfaction lie in the **olfactory epithelium,** a patch of tissue located high in each nasal passage and connected to the base of the brain. The olfactory epithelium is packed with millions of receptor cells that are sensitive to molecules of odorous substances that are given off in vapors. The receptor cells convert this biochemical reaction into neural impulses. Unlike some other sensory receptors, olfactory cells are constantly being replaced. Approximately every four to five weeks, you have a completely new set of receptor cells at work in your nose.

The exact physical basis of odor sensations remains a mystery. Most of the odors that we smell are organic compounds (compounds that contain carbon), but how olfactory cells convey specific messages to the brain is still uncertain. Scientists have found many substances with similar chemical structures whose odors seem quite different to people. So we cannot say why people can smell some substances and not others, or why certain groups of odors smell alike; nor can we predict the odor of a new chemical compound from its molecular structure.

Another puzzle that no one has been able to explain is the fact that women seem to be more sensitive to odors than men are (Cain, 1982; Doty et al., 1985). Some researchers have suggested that hormonal differences may affect sensory receptors and other levels of the perceptual system, because there is evidence that women's sensitivity to odors changes over the menstrual cycle. Others believe that there may be no gender difference in the recognition of odors, but that women's greater verbal ability may make it easier for them to come up with an odor's name (Engen, 1987).

PHEROMONE a chemical whose odor, on emission by an animal, triggers a behavioral reaction in other animals of the same species

OLFACTORY EPITHELIUM the patch of tissue in the nose that contains receptor cells for odors

TASTE

When wine tasters sample a new vintage, they swirl the wine in the glass, then sniff the released odor before they taste it. Wine tasters are highly aware of the fact we mentioned earlier, that odor contributes a great deal to the taste and flavor of food. Descriptions of how food "tastes" include its odor, which circulates from the back of the mouth up to the olfactory receptors. How important is odor to the sensation of taste? In one study, researchers asked people to taste and identify various solutions, such as coffee and dill pickle juice (Mozel et al., 1969). When they were allowed to smell the solution, their labeling was highly accurate, but when they could not smell the solution, their ability to identify it dropped dramatically. Even such strong substances as garlic, coffee, and chocolate were virtually impossible to detect by taste alone. Odor is so closely linked to our taste perceptions that when the odor of a substance is intensified, we say that its *taste* has been enhanced.

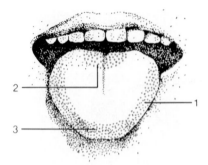

Figure 4.19 If you map your own taste buds, you can discover which parts of your tongue are sensitive to different tastes. You will need four glasses, half-filled with water. Into the first, stir a teaspoon of salt; the second, a teaspoon of sugar; the third, two teaspoons of lemon juice or vinegar; the fourth, a half-teaspoon of epsom salts. Label each glass, but hide the labels from yourself and move the glasses around so that you cannot tell which glass contains which solution. Using a fresh cotton swab for each glass, dab the solution on various spots around your tongue. You can use a mirror to keep track of your dabbing. Note on the map where you can taste each solution. Between each application of the swab, rinse your mouth out with fresh water. Your taste map should be marked "sour" in the area labeled 1, "bitter" in area 2; "sweet" in area 3; "salty" should be located fairly evenly across the entire surface. (After McBain and Johnson, 1962.)

TASTE BUDS sensory receptors for taste stimuli

Taste (gustation) itself is a more restricted sense than olfaction. We can detect and identify an odor from a distance, but the chemical substances in the food we eat must be dissolved in saliva and then come in contact with receptors on our tongue. We can identify and discriminate hundreds of odors, but when odor and other sensory qualities, such as texture, are eliminated, we can experience only four basic taste sensations: sweet, sour, salty, and bitter. Yet our taste experiences are not as impoverished as that limitation would seem to indicate. The gourmet chef and the wine taster will argue that a huge range of taste sensations can be created by mixing and blending these primary tastes in various combinations (Bartoshuk, 1980; Erickson, 1984).

The context of a taste is also important. The taste of most substances varies, depending on what you had in your mouth just before eating them. Water will taste sweet if you swish your tongue in strong coffee for about 30 seconds before sipping the water. But if you sip very salty water for about 30 seconds, tap water will then taste bitter or sour. You have probably noted that orange juice tastes very sour if you drink it just after brushing your teeth with toothpaste. Taste interactions may explain why former smokers say that food tastes much better and its flavors are more intense than when they smoked.

People differ in their sensitivity to various tastes. Can you drink very strong coffee without sugar or cream? If you can, you probably are relatively insensitive to the chemical phenylthiocarbamide (PCT). Researchers have discovered that about a third of us can barely detect this chemical, which other Americans find extremely bitter (Bartoshuk, 1979). Nontasters of PCT are also unable to taste the bitter edge of other substances, such as saccharin, which was once used in all diet sodas. The insensitivity to bitter tastes seems to be inherited. This phenomenon reminds us that not all people experience the world in the same way.

Different areas of the tongue are especially sensitive to each of the four basic taste qualities, as shown in Figure 4.19. Other areas of the tongue can detect all four qualities when a solution is strong, but the primary areas are sensitive to these qualities even in a weak solution. The specific sensation of each taste results from stimulation of the 10,000 **taste buds** on the surface of the human tongue, which contain receptor cells for taste stimuli.

Taste buds send taste information to the brain through the fibers of three different cranial nerves. Their use of these pathways is the reason that a visit to the dentist may temporarily spoil your sense of taste. The novocaine injected into

The taste of coffee can be subtly altered by adjusting the blend of the various types of beans used.

your gums deadens the nerve fibers that carry taste sensations as well as those that signal pain.

Taste is a more complicated process than the taste map in Figure 4.19 indicates. Most taste buds respond to at least two of the four basic taste stimuli (McCutcheon and Saunders, 1972). Each nerve fiber is probably more sensitive to one kind of taste than to another and responds differently, depending on the nature of a substance and its strength. Each area of the tongue contains all kinds of taste buds, but their density differs from one area to the next. Since taste buds respond differently to different taste stimuli, the pattern of responses across a group of taste receptors helps the brain identify a specific taste. Robert Erickson (1984) believes that taste is produced by a principle similar to that used by the visual system to produce color. Just as the spectrum of color becomes visible through the proportional responding of only three different photopigments, so the enormous variety of tastes becomes perceptible through the proportional responding of four different taste receptors. The taste of apple pie, for example, is signaled by a particular profile of proportional activity across the receptor neurons. Tastes that are subjectively similar stimulate similar profiles of activity and are processed similarly in the brain. This "distributed coding" hypothesis explains how a given solution tastes nearly the same whether it is placed on the front or the back of the tongue. Distributed coding helps the brain decide when two tastes are equivalent, even though they stimulate somewhat different groups of cells.

THE VESTIBULAR SENSE

Our **vestibular sense** is the sense of balance. The vestibular sense organ lies in the inner ear, buried in the bone above and to the rear of the cochlea. Its major structures are three fluid-filled **semicircular canals,** which lie at right angles to one another (look back at Figure 4.16). Any movement of the head causes the fluid in these canals to slosh against and bend the endings of the receptor hair cells, which are similar to those in the cochlea. The hair cells send their signals down the vestibular nerve, which goes to the brain.

Vestibular responses are stimulated by spinning about, walking more rapidly or running, falling, and tilting the body or head. The direction of the head's movement sets up a distinct pattern of stimulation in the semicircular canals. The speed of movement is translated into appropriately coded neural messages. Vestibular stimuli interact with eye-movement systems. For example, spinning rapidly in a circle can cause vestibular nystagmus, an uncontrollable, rapid back-and-forth motion of the eyes.

Unusual vestibular stimulation can cause motion sickness. It is most likely to develop when the body bobs rhythmically up and down on a boat in rough seas or an airplane in turbulent air. In one study, more than half the people who took a simulated ride on 7-foot waves coming at the rate of twenty-two waves per minute became "seasick" within 20 minutes (Wendt, 1951). The symptoms of motion sickness may include dizziness, "cold sweat," vertigo, and nausea, often accompanied by vomiting. You can help prevent motion sickness by keeping your head fixed even if your body is moving (which is why experienced sailors advise keeping your eyes fixed on the horizon). It also helps to move yourself actively through the gyrations of your vehicle rather than being moved passively by it (which is why drivers, who can anticipate the car's motion and move with it, are less likely than passengers to become sick).

THE KINESTHETIC SENSE

Kinesthesis is the sense that gives us information about our body movements and position. Receptor cells for the kinesthetic sense are in nerve endings within and near the muscles, the tendons, and the more than 100 body joints. Nerve endings

VESTIBULAR SENSE the sense of balance

SEMICIRCULAR CANALS three fluid-filled canals in the inner ear that make up the vestibular organ

KINESTHESIS the sense that provides information about body movement and position

in the joints are especially important in sensing bodily movements; which receptors respond depends on the direction and angle of movement. Together, the various kinesthetic receptors give us the feedback we need to regulate our posture and our active body movements. The kinesthetic sense cooperates with the vestibular and visual senses to maintain balance and equilibrium. As you walk along, your head never stops moving, yet you see a steady, solid world. Your vision remains steady because receptors in the semicircular canals signal your eye muscles to move in conjunction with your head, but in the opposite direction, so as to cancel out the variations produced by your head movements.

The cooperation of the visual, kinesthetic, and vestibular senses can be disrupted by a situation that our bodies have not evolved to meet: space travel. Motion sickness has plagued the space program, with four out of every ten astronauts becoming sick during space-shuttle missions. The motion sickness that follows weightlessness is somewhat different from motion sickness suffered on earth. Both the vestibular and kinesthetic systems are probably involved in space sickness (Chaikin, 1984). In space, the brain receives conflicting messages from both systems. Without the pull of gravity, receptors in the semicircular canals can no longer tell up from down, and muscle receptors can no longer report body position. The loss of information from these ever-present senses makes the experience of weightlessness strange and disturbing. Astronauts who become sick generally vomit, but they do not report the cold sweat and nausea that commonly accompany motion sickness on earth. Research in space indicates that when gravity is removed, the normal involuntary muscle action (peristalsis) of the digestive system stops. Perhaps the digestive system plays a larger part in space sickness than either the vestibular or the kinesthetic sense (Chaikin, 1984).

Now that we have reviewed the structures and processes of sensation—the means by which we obtain information about the outside world—we turn in Chapter 5 to perception. Perception is the process by which we integrate and interpret sensory stimuli.

SUMMARY

Our Senses and the World

■ We bring in information about the world around us through a chain of events known as sensory information processing. The first part of this process is sensation, the activation of sensory receptors by physical stimuli and the transmission of neural signals to the brain. The second part is perception, the final mental representation of the original stimuli as organized by the brain.

■ Each sensory system has receptor cells designed to detect a particular form of energy and to filter incoming information. They convert the energy stimuli into neural activity through the process of transduction.

Basic Principles of Sensory Systems

■ Sensations can vary in four ways: quality, quantity, timing, and the information they carry about location.

■ One characteristic of a receptor is its sensitivity to stimulation. The weakest stimulus that our senses can reliably detect half the time is called the absolute threshold. The smallest change in a stimulus that produces a noticeable change in sensation is known as the difference threshold, or just noticeable difference. Weber's law states that the just noticeable difference increases with the intensity of the stimulus and varies across senses.

■ Stevens's power law states that our evaluation of the intensity of a stimulus increases with the actual physical intensity of the stimulus raised to the power varies for each sensory system.

■ Adaptation allows us to react quickly to any change of stimulus once our senses are exposed to a constant, unchanging level of stimulation.

Sight

■ Light waves are the stimulus for vision. Light enters the eye through the cornea and pupil and is focused by the lens onto the back of the eye, the retina.

■ Two types of receptor cells on the retina transduce the light rays into neural signals. The rods signal information about brightness but not color. The cones are responsible for sharpness of vision and color vision.

■ Sharpness of vision is known as acuity, or the ability to resolve (distinguish) lines or shapes. Acuity tends to decline with age.

■ Color vision begins when light of different wavelengths is absorbed to differing degrees by photopigments in three types of cones. The blend or mixture of the cone types plus dark/light information from the rods determine our color experience.

■ The Young-Helmholtz trichromatic theory proposes that

color vision relies on three types of cones, each with its own photopigment, responding selectively to different wavelengths. The opponent-process theory uses the notion of complementary colors to describe a mechanism of color vision in which cells are excited by one color but inhibited by its complement.

Hearing

- Sound waves are the stimuli for hearing. The frequency of a sound wave (the number of waves passing a given point in a given time) determines the pitch of sound. The amplitude, or intensity, of a sound wave determines the loudness of a sound.
- A sound wave travels through the outer ear and strikes the eardrum. This vibration sets in motion the ossicles, which, in turn, vibrate the oval window at the entrance to the inner ear (the cochlea). This vibration pushes cochlear fluid over rows of receptors called hair cells. As these cells bend, they generate neural signals that are sent to the brain through a series of relay stations.
- Two theories attempt to explain how we hear the pitch of a tone. According to place theory, the site of highly stimulated receptors signals a sound's pitch; this best explains high-frequency sounds. According to frequency theory, modified as volley theory, the frequency of neural impulses signals pitch; this best explains low-frequency sounds.

The Skin Senses: Touch

- Receptors in the skin are sensitive to three different kinds of skin sensations: temperature, pressure, and pain. The receptors are connected to neurons that relay sensory information to the brain.

- Neurotransmitters are involved in the transmission and experience of pain. The body releases endorphins (natural painkillers) in response to pain and in anticipation of it.

Smell

- The sense of smell is extremely sensitive, yet can quickly adapt to constant odors. Hair cells projecting from the olfactory epithelium respond to the molecules in odorous vapors by transmitting neural messages.
- The sense of smell enables us to enjoy the taste of food, warns of possible dangers, and allows animals to communicate.

Taste

- Taste is related to smell, but is far more restricted. Receptors on the human tongue can experience only sweet, sour, salty, and bitter tastes.
- The pattern of responses across a group of taste receptors helps the brain identify a specific taste.

The Vestibular Sense

- The vestibular sense contributes to balance.
- Its major sense organ consists of the semicircular canals of the inner ear.

The Kinesthetic Sense

- Kinesthesis, the sense of body movement and position, cooperates with the vestibular and visual senses to maintain balance and equilibrium.
- Receptor cells for this sense are located in nerve endings in and near joints, muscles, and tendons.

KEY TERMS

absolute threshold	ganglion cells	photopigment
accommodation	hair cells	pitch
acuity	hammer	place theory
adaptation	iris	primary colors
afterimage	kinesthesis	pupil
amplitude	lateral geniculate nucleus (LGN)	receptive field
anvil	lens	retina
basilar membrane	myopia	rods
cochlea	olfaction	round window
complementary colors	olfactory epithelium	semicircular canals
cones	opponent-process theory	sensation
cornea	optic chiasm	stirrup
difference threshold/just noticeable difference (jnd)	optic disk	taste buds
	optic nerve	transduction
eardrum	ossicles	vestibular sense
fovea	oval window	volley theory
frequency	perception	Weber's law
frequency theory	pheromone	Young-Helmholtz trichromatic theory

CONCEPT REVIEW

1. This chapter describes the act of bringing the outside world inside as a continuous process. Define *sensation* and locate it in this process. What components of the nervous system are involved in this "sensory information processing"?

2. Distinguish *absolute threshold* from *difference threshold.* How is the concept of sensory variability related to these two kinds of thresholds?

3. Referring to Table 4.1, can you think of some examples from everyday experience that illustrate Weber's law?

4. What does the process of adaptation suggest about the importance of change in sensory processes? In what way is sensory adaptation related to Weber's law?

5. Describe the important structural components of the eye. How do these components work together to send visual signals to the brain?

6. As the physical stimulus is translated into an electrochemical process, highly specific cells respond only to select stimuli. What is this process called, and how does it work?

7. Distinguish the trichromatic theory of color vision from the opponent-process theory of color vision. How does color-blindness support these two theories?

8. Describe the structure of the ear and the way physical stimuli are translated into sensory signals.

9. Distinguish the place theory of pitch from the volley theory of pitch. How might these two theories work together to explain the different sounds we hear?

10. The sensation of touch is a combination of inputs from several sensory registers. What are these different types of stimulation, and how are they processed?

11. What is the physiological basis for the experience of pain?

12. How are smell and taste related? Describe the mechanisms of the senses of smell and taste.

13. Identify the roles of the vestibulary and kinesthetic senses. Explain motion and space sickness.

CRITICAL THINKING

1. Most of this chapter is devoted to discussions of vision and hearing. Assuming that the amount of attention given to these two senses reflects their relative importance, explain why they may be so important for the understanding of human behavior. What is life like without either of these two senses? Without both?

2. Just like Chapter 3, The Brain and Behavior, the material in this chapter seems to many to be more appropriate for a biology or anatomy course. How would you explain the psychological importance of understanding sensation to someone unfamiliar with psychology?

Perception

... Perception

Take a moment to look around the room. What do you see? Now close your eyes and listen. What do you hear? Finally, sniff deeply, paying attention to any odors. What do you smell? This simple exercise tells you a lot about perception. When you looked, you sensed colors, edges, boundaries, and contrasts, but you perceived objects—perhaps a desk, a reading lamp, a vase of flowers, a half-eaten piece of cake, or a dog on the lawn outside the window. When you listened, you sensed pitches and frequencies, but you perceived events—music from the radio, the whirring of a fan, or the barking of the dog. When you sniffed, you sensed invisible vapors in the air, but you perceived objects—the scent of carnations or the aroma of chocolate from the neglected cake. The first lesson, then, is that *we sense stimuli but we perceive objects and events.*

In each case, you made no conscious attempt to transform the information picked up by your sensory receptors. The task was completed in a twinkling—automatically. By the time perception became conscious, the interpretations had already been made. Thus the second lesson is that *perception is usually effortless.*

When you perceived the barking dog, you integrated the sight of the dog's moving jaws with the sounds coming from the dog's throat. So the third lesson is that *perception integrates the information picked up by all the senses.* Psychologists say that perception is *multimodal,* with each sense reflecting a different mode of gathering information. The multimodal nature of perception is underscored when two information modes contradict each other—as when you watch a foreign film that has been dubbed in English. The movements of the actors' mouths and the projected dialogue are clearly out of sync—sometimes so badly that it interferes with your enjoyment of the movie.

The effortless, multimodal process of **perception** can be defined as the brain's attempt to describe objects and events in the world, based on sensory input and knowledge. By combining information provided by the senses with knowledge derived from past experience, the brain creates representations of objects and events. Perception is actually part of the continuum of information processing by the central nervous system. The continuum begins with sensation, which blends into perception, which blends into attention, which blends into working memory, which blends into thought. Thus, it is often difficult to define the precise point at which one process leaves off and the next begins.

PERCEPTION   the brain's attempt to describe objects and events in the world, based on sensory input and knowledge

THE ACTIVE BUT SELECTIVE NATURE OF PERCEPTION

Perception is an active process, which means that we often must act in order to perceive. By turning our heads, we orient our eyes and ears toward a moving car. We manipulate an object with our hands to determine its shape. We sniff a steak before eating it. According to J. J. Gibson (1966), movements and changes in the orientation of our sense organs are necessary if we are to perceive anything. Gibson demonstrated the importance of this activity with a simple demonstration called "the great cookie-cutter experiment" (Gibson, 1962; Harre, 1983). Taking metal cookie cutters of various shapes (circle, star, heart, half-moon), Gibson pressed them one at a time onto a blindfolded subject's passive palm. In this condition, the subjects could identify only 29 percent of the cookie cutters' shapes. But when the cookie cutters were gently rotated on the palm, the subjects could identify 72 percent of the shapes, and when subjects were allowed to explore the cookie cutters with their fingers, they identified 95 percent of them. Active exploration allows the changing sensations on the skin to transmit information about the unchanging properties of the cookie cutters, such as their angles and the ratio of their sides.

In our explorations of the world, we use attention in two ways. We can concentrate on an object or event by overtly orienting our sense organs toward it. When we want to inspect an object, we usually turn our eyes and heads to look directly at it. That's because we see things best when they are straight ahead—directly in front of the fovea, where (as we saw in Chapter 4) the cones responsible

In some situations, such as street fairs, all our sensory systems are bombarded by stimuli; but our perception is selective—we can direct our attention toward any stimulus we choose.

for sharp vision are so densely packed that their fibers connect with a majority of the information-interpreting neurons in the visual cortex. We also move our heads when trying to detect the source of an odor, sniffing as we try to locate the dead mouse whose stench threatens to drive us out of the house.

We can also direct our attention by covertly focusing on some part of the environment. For instance, when your attention is focused on an object in the periphery of vision, your response to the object's movements quickens, even though your gaze is directed straight ahead (Posner and Presti, 1987). You can also listen selectively: at a loud party, you can pick out one particular conversation and follow it, shutting out the rest of the din about you; and at a concert, you can focus on a single section of instruments—the flutes or the cellos—picking out and following their voices in the blended music.

Paying attention to specific objects and events helps us negotiate our environment. With our ears and eyes, we can explore things at a distance and decide whether the object ahead is friend or foe, whether we should move closer or get away fast, or whether we should answer a call or remain discreetly silent. In this way, perception guides our behavior, because what we perceive determines what we do next. There is, in other words, a constant interplay between action and perception: actions form our perceptions, and perception guides our actions.

In perceiving, the brain actively constructs meaning. To comprehend what's "out there," the brain applies built-in assumptions, based on knowledge of the physical world. If there are gaps in the sensory information, the brain fills them in. A compelling instance of this phenomenon is the series of geometric designs in Figure 5.1, in which the brain perceives triangles that do not exist. The lines are *perceptually* present but *physically* absent. These nonexistent lines, which are known as *subjective contours,* appear naturally as the result of the brain's automatic attempts to enhance and complete the details of an image (Kanisza, 1976). This is something the brain probably does all the time when perceiving an object whose actual edges are partially obscured, or when low contrast and inadequate lighting limit the information that reaches our senses (Parks, 1986). The completion process is a regular part of perception, one that we share with other species. Monkeys and cats perceive subjective contours in figures similar to those in Figure 5.1, with cells in the visual cortex that respond to actual corners and edges responding to the illusory contours as if they were real (von der Heydt, Peterhans, and Baumgartner, 1984; Bravo, Blake, and Morrison, 1988).

As the brain makes inferences, it strives for constancy. This task is more complicated than it seems, because each object's exact retinal image continually varies in size, shape, color, and brightness. Yet we perceive objects as having

Figure 5.1 Subjective contours. The brain seeks to tie the components of an incomplete picture together by creating the perception of contours that complete the picture. (A) The subjective contours form a white triangle in the middle of this visual image. (B) In this case, the outline of a center triangle is perceived once again, but this time the triangle appears black as the result of the background color. C and D illustrate the fact that subjective contours may be curved as well as straight. (After Kanisza, 1976.)

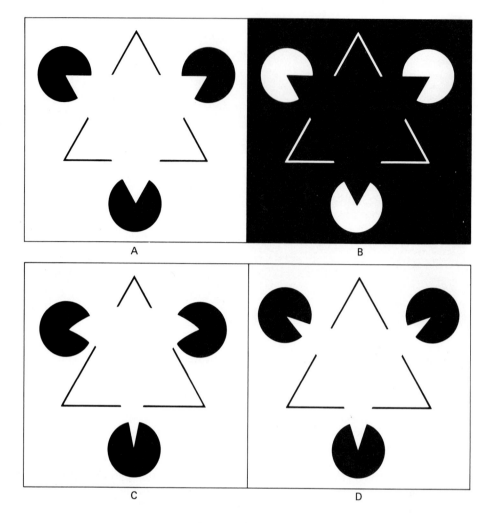

PERCEPTUAL CONSTANCY the tendency for an object's size, shape, color, and brightness to remain constant despite changes in the retinal image

stable properties despite variations in the retinal image, a process known as **perceptual constancy.** An opening and closing door continues to appear rectangular even though its actual image on the retina becomes a trapezoid as the door swings on its hinge (shape constancy). The grass looks green whether the sun is shining directly on it or whether it is in the shadow of a bush (color constancy). A piece of paper on your desk retains its brightness even though you dim the room light (brightness constancy). In maintaining constancy, the brain transcends the information picked up at the retina. This keeps the environment stable and allows us to recognize objects no matter how conditions change.

Perceptual constancy tells us that the brain does not arrive at absolute judgments; instead, perception is relative. Our impressions of objects are influenced by context. Thus, the brightness of the sheet of paper is not based on the amount of light reflected from it, but instead on the amount of light reflected from its surface relative to the amount reflected from adjacent areas. This means that when the surrounding context changes, your perception of brightness changes. Thus, when we see a gray spot against a light background, it appears darker than when the same spot appears against a dark background. This phenomenon is called *brightness contrast,* and it may be a function of the ON/OFF retinal fields described in Chapter 4.

Such examples lead to a question. Is the world actually as we perceive it? The answer has to be no. Our perceptions are inaccurate, both because our sensory systems limit the amount of information we can gather from the environment and because the brain augments sensory information with its own biases and assumptions. The world is full of information that falls outside the range of our senses. Dogs hear high-frequency sounds where we detect only unbroken silence. Cats see objects that to us remain obscured in darkness. Moths smell odors that escape our noses. Honeybees "see" polarized light. Bats and dolphins use sonar to detect objects, by bouncing sound waves off them. Fish can sense the earth's magnetic field and use it as a navigation aid.

Our perceptions also change over the life span. Infants, young adults, and older people perceive the world differently. Newborns see a world of flat, fuzzy, indistinct objects and cannot see small objects at all. Older adults are unable to see close objects clearly and cannot hear many of the high-pitched sounds that once were clearly audible to them.

ENDURING ISSUES IN PERCEPTION

Since the world is not exactly as it appears, studying perception is not a straight-forward matching of neural events to objects in the world. Perception is both a biological and a psychological process, and researchers are still trying to resolve some of the basic questions that surround it. One issue centers on the relative roles of nature and nurture in perception, asking how much we have to learn to be able to perceive. A second issue is whether our perceptions are built up from parts or whether we see patterns. A third is whether illusions tell us anything useful about human perceptual systems. A fourth has to do with the effect of knowledge on perception.

The Role of Learning

How much of what we perceive is innate and how much is the result of learning? Do infants enter the world in a "blooming, buzzing confusion," as psychologist William James (1890) proposed, assailed by a chaotic jumble of light and shadow, sounds, odors, and touches, or do they perceive objects and events from the moment of birth? Philosophers have argued this question for centuries, and twentieth-century psychologists have addressed it more practically by conducting experiments. For instance, rats were raised in darkness and then brought out into the light to see whether they could judge distances (Lashley and Russell, 1934). They could; on their first day in full light, the rats adjusted their jumping accurately, whether they had to leap 2 feet or more than 3 to reach their food. Other psychologists looked at blind people who had suddenly recovered their sight. A man who was given sight by a corneal transplant at the age of fifty-two said that at

Unlike bats, humans do not possess a sonar system for echolocation—a reminder that our perception of the world is determined by the capabilities and limitations of our sensory systems.

first he saw only a blur, but within a few days he was able to see relatively well. Yet his depth vision was terrible; he thought that stepping from a second-story window to the ground was a simple feat (Gregory and Wallace, 1963). None of these studies have resolved the issue, but babies probably have less to learn than James believed. As we will see later in this chapter, newborns' senses are all functional, and some degree of perceptual ability is probably innate.

Parts versus the Whole

In identifying an object, does the perceptual system build up its description from simple sensations, or do you perceive an entire form? As we noted in Chapter 1, nineteenth-century structuralists believed in the "building-block" process and sought to identify the elementary sensations that were its blocks. Using introspection, subjects would examine an object, perhaps an apple, and report all the sensations they experienced: color, curvature, glossiness, volume, and firmness. Since parts of the apple would be in shadow, there would be more than one variety of color and glossiness to report. Introspection proved an impractical tool, however, because it was both unwieldy and unreliable. Before long, the list of simple sensations exceeded 40,000 (Boring, 1942). Even worse, two people who looked at the same object could not agree on the list of sensations. Although the method was discarded, the basic position was not. Later, we explore modern views of the building-block process, which is called *feature analysis*. (We introduced feature analysis in the section on visual information processing in Chapter 4.)

At the same time that structuralists were decomposing objects into elementary sensations, members of the **Gestalt school** of psychology were arguing for the

GESTALT SCHOOL psychologists who believe that a meaningful overall pattern *(gestalt)* is perceived before its parts are recognized

This engraving by William Hogarth demonstrates the usefulness of illusions in the study of perception. The artist's amusing use of false perspectives shows how we rely on depth cues to determine the relative location of objects.

opposite position, that we perceive entire forms before we perceive their parts. When we look at a triangle, they said, we do not see three separate lines, but a meaningful pattern, or *gestalt* (after the German word for "form" or "shape"). In perceiving a simple triangle—or any other object—the brain follows innate rules in organizing sensory data. Gestalt psychologists took as their motto the saying, "The whole is greater than the sum of its parts." They insisted that trying to understand the perception of forms by focusing on elementary sensations was as useless as trying to understand how the printed word conveys information by analyzing the specks of ink covering a page. Gestalt psychologists did identify the properties of figures that lead the brain to identify various forms, but Gestalt theory was based on a theory of brain function that proved to be wrong (Sekuler and Blake, 1985). As we will see, modern versions of form perception adhere to the view that the brain works with units much larger than elementary sensations.

Perceptual Illusions

The place of illusion, or misperceived reality, in the study of perception has been equally hard to establish. Looking over this chapter, you might assume that the examples of perceptual illusions scattered through textbooks are there only to add a bit of entertainment and keep you reading. Gibson (1966) might have agreed with you, for he contended that illusions were simply laboratory curiosities that occur when people are given limited stimulus information. Perceptual errors, he maintained, tell us nothing about the normal processes of perception. But other psychologists (Gregory, 1977) have found that illusions are helpful tools for studying perception, because they demonstrate important perceptual processes that go unnoticed under ordinary conditions. Instances in which perceptual constancies or depth cues mislead us actually throw the normal functioning of these phenomena into bold relief. By setting up illusion-producing situations, we can learn how people process perceptual information and precisely what kind of information the system must have for error-free operation.

Bottom-Up versus Top-Down Processing

To ask whether perception is a bottom-up or a top-down process is to ask about the role of knowledge in perception. Bottom-up processing begins at the lowest level of the information-processing continuum: the sensory system takes in patterned stimuli and passes them along through successively higher stages of pro-

Figure 5.2 A stable differentiation of the elements of this picture into figure and ground is difficult at first, and would probably be impossible if you had no previous knowledge of or experience with Dalmatian dogs. The knowledge that there is a Dalmatian dog in this picture, however, makes it possible to differentiate one set of spots as figure and the other spots as undifferentiated ground.

cessing until the brain finally concludes, "That's a dog." Information flows only from the bottom (the sensory receptors) to the brain. Top-down processing begins at the high end of the continuum: the perceiver's expectations and context play a role from the very beginning, so that information flows downward as well. When we look at an object, our experience leads us to make hypotheses and assumptions about what we see, hear, touch, and taste.

In the nineteenth century, top-down processing was powerfully championed by the same Hermann von Helmholtz who developed the Young-Helmholtz trichromatic theory of color vision (Chapter 4). Helmholtz insisted that all perception involves unconscious inferences that can be based only on experience—or, as Helmholtz described it, "the unconscious processes of association of ideas going on in the dark background of our memory" (1925, p. 26). Many twentieth-century psychologists have also stressed the importance of inference in perception (Gregory, 1977; Rock, 1983); Figure 5.2 provides a convincing demonstration. When you first look at the picture, it seems formless. Once you see the collection of dark and light patches on the right as a dog, it becomes difficult for you to look at this picture again and *not* see the dog.

We also use top-down processing to interpret ambiguous sounds or to distinguish words, relying on their context. The same sound can be perceived as a heartbeat or a bouncing ball; a clattering sound may be interpreted in one context as horses on cobbled streets and in another as booted soldiers clambering up stone steps. When people speak rapidly, it is difficult for us to divide their continuous stream of speech into separate words unless we know the topic of conversation. A given sound sequence may be segmented differently and heard as different messages, depending on the context of the conversation. For instance, part of the sequence "Have you see the *nu-dis-pla*?" will be heard as "nudist play" or "new display," depending on whether you are talking about a nudist camp or a recent exhibit at the museum.

Top-down processing also explains an auditory illusion discovered by Richard Warren (1970). If you play a tape of normal speech but replace a single syllable with a brief cough, buzz, or noise of equal loudness and duration, people will not notice the replacement. Even when they are told to listen for the substitution, they have great difficulty picking it out of the speech stream. We apparently become so caught up in the utterance as a whole that the intruding sound is simply assimilated into the overall pattern. When the tape is played backward and cannot be understood as speech, people have no trouble picking out the cough or buzz.

Another instance of top-down processing comes when our goals and desires direct our attention and therefore our perception. For example, restaurant signs are noticed by hungry travelers who might ignore them if they were not hungry. Ambiguous stimuli are also interpreted in line with our preoccupations and anxieties. In one experiment, mothers were tested for word-recognition thresholds a few hours before their children were to have their tonsils removed (Parkinson and Rachman, 1981). The mothers listened to a set of words spoken softly while fairly loud music played in the background. The mothers had no trouble identifying words that related to surgery, like "operation," "pain," "bleeding," and "infection." But they failed to identify similar-sounding words that had no connection with surgery, such as "operatic," "pine," "breeding," and "inflection." These examples illustrate that thinking about a concept makes its verbal label—and the concepts and labels associated with it—more readily available. And so the mental context creates a **perceptual set**—a readiness to interpret stimuli in a specific way on the basis of expectations, experience, or psychological state. Perceptual set is adaptive; it enables us to respond quickly and appropriately to stimuli that are related to our current concerns. In the chapters on memory and thinking (8 and 9) we see how perceptual set affects broad areas of our lives.

Despite the prevalence of top-down processing, the role of knowledge in perception is limited. For instance, no matter how familiar we are with a perceptual illusion, it can continue to deceive us. Try as we may to see the figure as we *know* it to be, the perceptual error persists. This indicates that the information provided by the senses can override the information that comes down from the top. In modern theories of bottom-up processing, the brain builds up a perception, grouping together clusters of features into larger structures, and applies its knowledge about the world relatively late in the process.

PERCEPTUAL SET a readiness to interpret stimuli in a specific way on the basis of expectations, experience, or psychological state

FUNCTIONS OF PERCEPTION

These four issues run through most discussions of what perception does and how it does it. One way to trace their influence is to look at the functions of perception. For one thing, perception tells you where an object is in relation to yourself. For another, it tells you whether the object is moving, and in what direction. Finally, it tells you what the object is. Let us look at each of these functions in turn.

Where Is It?—Location

In deciding where an object is, we rely primarily on our **distance senses,** vision and hearing, which can pick up information about objects that are too far away to touch. Distance senses serve us much as radar serves a ship at sea, letting us explore objects in our environment without coming into direct contact with them. As we noted earlier, this ability to explore at a distance allows us to think about how we will deal with remote objects before they are upon us. Without our distance senses, we would go through life reacting reflexively to objects that we could perceive only when they were within reach.

DISTANCE SENSES vision and hearing; senses that can pick up information from objects too far away to touch

Attention

Locating an object often involves focusing our attention on it, picking it out from all the other stimuli that surround us. Information from our other senses or from images in the periphery of the visual field alerts us to the object's existence. The first stage of attending is automatic; it involves distinguishing the object from its background on the basis of color, shape, texture, distance, or motion. A flash of silver on a dusty path, a looming image, a bird lighting on a branch, suddenly seem to "pop out" from the background. The second stage is more deliberate and involves a conscious allocation of attention to some part of the scene (Wise and Desimone, 1988). Now we are moving higher on the processing continuum, tapping our memory to identify the object and preparing ourselves to respond to it.

Depth Perception

Once an object catches our attention, we rely on depth perception to determine how far away it is. **Depth perception** is a twofold task, for with it we can determine either absolute or relative distance. *Absolute distance* refers to the distance between you and the object. It is the sort of depth perception you use in deciding how far it is from you to the building across the street. *Relative distance* refers to the distance between two objects or between two parts of the same object. It is the sort of depth perception you use to decide whether one object is closer to you than another. We seem to be much better at determining relative distance than we are at judging absolute distance (Sekuler and Blake, 1985).

Depth perception relies on several kinds of information. Although we use these sources of information without conscious effort, most psychologists refer to them as "depth cues."

DEPTH PERCEPTION the ability to recognize distances between objects (relative distance) and from the observer to objects (absolute distance)

BINOCULAR DEPTH CUES Depth information that requires the cooperation of both eyes is known as *binocular information* (*bi* meaning "two" and *ocular* meaning "eye"). When objects are no more than 15 meters (about 50 feet) away, your eye muscles provide a source of binocular information known as **convergence,** which refers to the eyes' movement inward as they focus on objects close to the viewer. If you first focus on your finger at arm's length, then move it up to your nose, you may be able to feel the tension created in the eye muscles as they work together to rotate the eyes inward. This slight muscular tension gives information about distance.

CONVERGENCE the eyes' movement inward as they focus on objects close to the viewer

PSYCHOLOGY TODAY AND TOMORROW

Seeing without Seeing

On the television screen attractive young people cavort in the surf, accompanied by the upbeat sounds of a commercial. Throughout the commercial the words "Drink Ziggy Cola" flash on the screen, but each exposure is so brief that the viewer's eye does not detect it. Will sales of Ziggy Cola increase beyond expectation? If they do, advertisers may decide that they have made effective use of *subliminal perception* (*sub*, "below"; *limen*, threshold). In subliminal perception, sensory information is registered by the relevant sensory system, but there is no conscious experience of the stimulus. The information may be a sight, a sound, or an odor.

Psychologists have had a running debate about the validity of subliminal perception and about attempts to demonstrate it. Direct tests of subliminal perception—asking subjects to report the meanings of words flashed but not seen—have not settled the matter (Holender, 1986). Indirect tests, in which subjects decide whether a string of letters spells a real word—"doctor" versus "soctor," for example—have been more promising (Fowler et al., 1981; Marcel, 1983). In these studies, the time needed to make such decisions is shortened if the target word is immediately preceded by a subliminally presented word that is related in meaning to the target word. "Nurse," for example, may be flashed before the string of letters making up "doctor." (This is called *priming* and is a version of perceptual set.)

In theory, subliminal perception of a word activates associated words in our mental dictionary, so that a conscious decision gets a boost from a related subliminal stimulus. This effect occurs even though subjects insist that they had no idea whether anything was shown in the flash that preceded the target word. Yet the increase in speed and accuracy that follows subliminal priming is often nearly as large as that produced in other experiments by above-threshold priming words.

Despite these demonstrations, critics object to the concept of subliminal perception at a more basic level, as related to signal detection theory (see Chapter 4). If, as signal detection theory indicates, there is no absolute threshold, but only a convenient, statistically defined fiction, then it makes no sense to talk about "subliminal perception," or perception below a (nonexistent) threshold. Different indicators are simply more sensitive (priming) or less sensitive (awareness) to variations in the intensity or duration of a stimulus. In addition, subjects' reports of awareness, by which thresholds are measured, are not necessarily valid. Such reports are vague and easily biased, and they often turn out to be false alarms.

Other investigators have been less willing to dismiss the subliminal concept and have focused on the difference in effect between stimuli above and below the threshold of reported awareness (Balota, 1983; Cheesman and Marikle, 1986). This work suggests that subliminal perception may exist and that perceptual processes follow different rules, depending on whether they are conscious or unconscious.

But what about advertising that uses "subliminal" techniques? Can such hidden persuasion manipulate your buying habits? The evidence is solidly against such claims. Subliminal effects are usually weak and transitory. Nor is there any convincing evidence that subliminal suggestions (recorded repeatedly in audiotapes of music or ocean waves) have any effect in persuading people to give up smoking, drinking, or eating sweets or to develop more powerful, dynamic personalities. The most effective agents of persuasion and behavior change remain the above-threshold appeals to self-esteem and social values that have been used since the beginning of recorded history.

STEREOPSIS the perception of depth based on binocular disparity

A second source of binocular information arises from human anatomy. Because our eyes are set some distance apart, the retinal images formed on the two eyes are slightly different. This difference, known as *binocular disparity,* provides potent information for judging relative distance. The brain essentially receives "stereo" images and fuses them together, creating a particular and vivid form of depth perception called **stereopsis.** The amount of disparity between the images provides essential information on the relative positions of objects in the environment. You can discover binocular disparity by holding a finger close to you and lining it up with an object some distance away—a window or the corner of a room. Then look at the finger with one eye at a time. Your finger will seem to shift position in relation to the background or distant object. When you look at your finger with both eyes, the brain is reconciling that shift and aligning the two different images.

MONOCULAR DEPTH CUES   Our three-dimensional world is not solely the product of binocular information. If one eye is covered, we can rely on *monocular information*, which does not require the cooperation of both eyes. Airplane pilots and at least one professional baseball player have successfully managed their work with the use of only one eye (Regan, Beverley, and Cynader, 1979). If you close one eye, you still perceive depth, sometimes with the same vividness and precision that binocular information provides.

The monocular source of information that gives the same sharp three-dimensional effect as stereopsis is called *motion parallax* (Rogers and Graham, 1982). You have often experienced it. When you move your body or head through the environment, objects closer to you appear to move faster (relative to your own motion) than distant objects. That is why, as you drive along an open highway, the trees and telegraph poles along the road seem to whiz by, but distant mountains appear motionless. In this case, motion parallax arises because as *you* move, images of closer objects move across the retina more rapidly than do those of distant objects. When you are stationary, the effect can be created by the motion of objects in the environment. For example, if you look at leaves on a tree with one eye closed, they form a confusing array. But when they flutter in the breeze, groups of leaves stand out and depth becomes apparent (Sekuler and Blake, 1985).

Other monocular cues provide depth information when we are stationary. Artists were aware of such sources of depth information long before psychologists began to study them. The "discovery" of perspective, in which painters reproduce changes in the appearance of objects as they recede from the viewer, is considered one of the landmarks of art history. The techniques artists use to achieve the impression of depth mimic monocular sources of information in the world. Many of these techniques are illustrated in the Perugino painting reproduced here.

Size is one effective cue to depth, because as the distance between you and an object increases, the size of the image on your retina gets smaller. In the painting, the figures in the foreground are considerably larger than those farther "back," which makes them seem much closer. This comparative cue for depth and distance is called *relative size*. But size provides no depth information unless you already know something about the size of the object. When you have some notion of the object's actual size, the visual system's perpetual striving for constancy helps you out. *Size constancy* refers to the visual system's habit of automatically taking into account any information you have about an object's distance and translating the perceived size into the object's real size.

This Renaissance painting, *Delivery of the Keys* by Il Perugino (1446–1524), uses relatively sophisticated monocular cues to show depth. Linear perspective is illustrated by the lines of the pavement, which converge from front to back. Relative size is illustrated by the difference in size of the background and foreground figures. Interposition is illustrated by the kneeling man's blockage of the woman behind him. Texture gradient is illustrated by the atmospheric haze that makes distant trees and buildings less sharply defined than the figures in the foreground.

Figure 5.3 The moon looks larger on the horizon than higher in the sky.

For a striking demonstration of size constancy, look at the photographs below. Which woman is larger? In the left photograph, the women seem roughly equal in size, even though the retinal image cast by the woman in the foreground is three times as large as the image cast by the more distant woman. You see them as the same size because other monocular cues in the photograph (which we explore shortly) tell you that the second woman is seated farther from the camera. In the right photograph, the woman in the background has been cut out and placed next to the woman in the foreground. Now the disparity is obvious—and startling (Boring, 1964).

Sometimes size constancy breaks down and our perception seems to play tricks on us. The well-known "moon illusion" is one of these perceptual "tricks" (see Figure 5.3). As the moon rises on the horizon, it appears enormous. But once it has moved higher into the sky, it seems comparatively small—even though there is no real difference in the size of the retinal image. If you looked at the moon in both positions through a tube, its size would be the same in both situations. Size constancy fails us here. So does our knowledge and perception of the world, reminding us once again of the limits of top-down processing (Greene, 1986). The illusion arises because of our literal-minded perceptual logic. Generally, we assume that the horizon is distant and that objects overhead are closer to us. From experience, we know that a flight of geese overhead grows smaller as it approaches the horizon, and we also know that when two objects are at different

A
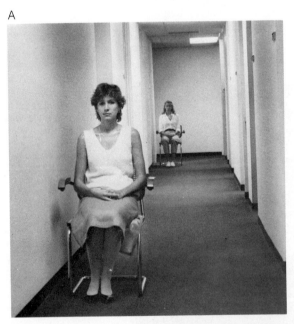

B
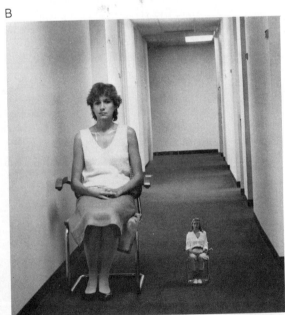

Because we expect two adult women to be roughly equal in size, we attribute the apparent difference between the women in photo A to the distance between them. In photo B, the woman in the background now appears next to the larger woman, and their size difference is obvious.

distances from us but create the same-sized retinal image, then the distant object must be larger.

The moon illusion would not "work" if there were any information about depth at the zenith. When the moon is rising, the silhouetted landscape in front of it provides information about relative size and distance. But when the moon is overhead, we have no human-scale objects for comparison, nothing to go on but the size of the retinal image. And so the moon appears relatively small in the huge sky. Because of size constancy, we unconsciously scale things according to their perceived distance, and we underestimate the distance between us and the zenith. Perceived size depends on perceived distance, accurate or not.

Perspective provides a wealth of information about distance. *Linear perspective* refers to the apparent convergence of parallel lines as they recede in the distance. In the painting above, Perugino applies perspective by making the plaza's parallel lines appear to converge as they extend toward the horizon. The receding lines of the corridor provided linear perspective in the earlier photograph of the two women. Another aspect of perspective is *texture gradient*, an important source of depth information that goes hand in hand with relative size. As objects recede from us, their texture is gradually altered, as it is in the photograph at the right. The stones near the camera appear larger and coarser, while the stones farther back appear smaller and finer. Texture gradient not only tells us about surface distance; it gives us information about slant, about the sizes of objects located on the surfaces, and—when there is a sudden discontinuity in texture—about bends or corners in the surface (Gibson, 1950). A final type of perspective, called *aerial perspective*, refers to the haziness of distant objects, a feature that is created by the light-scattering particles of dirt and water in the atmosphere. The more distant an object, the more particles between it and the viewer. To provide aerial perspective, Perugino has made the figures in the foreground of his painting more distinct, their features, clothes, and forms more defined, than the figures, buildings, and landscape in the background.

A final source of depth information is *occlusion*, in which one object partially obscures another. The visual system perceives the occluded object as farther away than the object in front of it. In Perugino's painting, the kneeling man in the foreground partially blocks our view of the woman behind him, creating the impression that she is farther away. Occlusion also is responsible for the perception of a subjective triangle in Figure 5.1; we assume that the corners of the triangle are obscuring parts of the circles.

An example of texture gradient as a cue to depth perception.

Illusions of Depth

Many illusions are created by our natural tendency to view two-dimensional scenes as projections of three-dimensional reality: we automatically infer a third dimension. Look, for example, at Figure 5.4A, known as the Müller-Lyer illusion. The vertical lines appear to be of different lengths, but if you measure them with a ruler, you will find that they are identical. Some psychologists believe that the illusion fools us because the arrows are interpreted as corners, and so they seem to indicate "walls" coming toward us ("longer" line) and going away from us ("shorter" line) (Figure 5.4B). Because both lines project the same-sized image onto the retina, the line interpreted as closer (or pointing *at* us) is perceived as smaller, in accordance with the principle of size constancy (Gregory, 1970).

Linear perspective cues to depth create a related effect. In the Ponzo illusion (Figure 5.4C), the converging lines are interpreted as parallel lines extending away from the observer, just as the converging lines of the plaza are interpreted in the Perugino painting. This interpretation makes the same-sized horizontal bar in the "distance" larger. Figure 5.4D demonstrates the same illusion using railroad tracks. Once again, we have been tricked by size constancy.

Striking visual illusions have been created by building models using these principles. In the Ames room, shown in Figure 5.5, size constancy combines with perceived distance to fool the visual system, just as it does in the moon illusion. The dramatic disparity in the two women's perceived size is the result of misleading depth information, created by a distorted room whose construction relies on

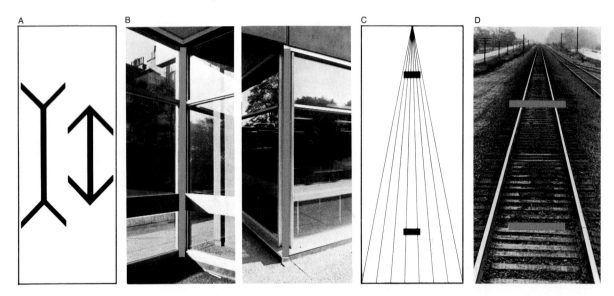

Figure 5.4 Two famous illusions and possible explanations for how they work. The vertical lines of the figures in the Müller-Lyer illusion (A) are identical in length, but they do not appear to be. An explanation for this illusion, suggested in B, is that the arrow markings on the lines in A cause them to be perceived as three-dimensional objects that have corners. The corners seem to induce a size-constancy effect: the vertical line that appears to be distant is perceived as larger. The horizontal lines in the Ponzo illusion (C) are also identical in length. As the photograph in D suggests, this figure, too, could easily be perceived as three-dimensional, and again size constancy would cause the apparently more distant "object" to be scaled up in apparent size relative to the "nearer object." (After Gregory, 1970.)

perspective and size for its effect (Ames, 1951). The back wall of the room is actually farther away on the left side than on the right, but the height of the ceiling and the size of the window frames have been designed to mislead us. To viewers of the three-dimensional room, the illusion works only if they view it through a peephole (using one eye eliminates binocular disparity) and do not move around (eliminating motion parallax).

Illusions are not simply laboratory curiosities; they can influence our everyday behavior. An illusion we often experience, but pay little attention to, is known as the *vista paradox*. Objects seen through a frame—such as a window or a windshield—appear larger and closer when the viewer is several feet away than they do when the viewer is close to the frame (Walker, Rupich, and Powell, 1989). You can experience the vista paradox by looking across the room through a window that opens onto distant buildings or trees. Then walk toward the window and notice how the objects seem to shrink. The vista paradox may help account for the anxiety of back-seat drivers: approaching cars and obstacles may appear closer and more threatening to a person in the back seat of a car than they do to the driver.

Auditory Localization

Hearing plays a large role in helping us locate objects by sound. It is something that we do effortlessly and automatically, and it is an ability that we are born with. Hearing is somewhat similar to seeing. The brain takes input from two major sensory sources—this time, ears instead of eyes—and, on the basis of slight differences in the input, calculates where the object is located. That is why having two ears is essential for the localization of sound: differences in how and when a sound reaches the two ears enable the brain to compute the location of its source. (See Figure 5.6.)

Without puzzling over it, we know that the sobbing child is down the hall to the right or that the ominous crash in the underbrush is back of us and on our left. We know this because our brain uses the differences in sound intensity and arrival time to locate a sound's source; neurons in the auditory system may be specialized

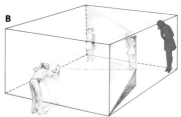

Figure 5.5 The Ames room. The illusion is produced by trapezoidal windows that run parallel to the sloping floor, making the room look rectangular (A). In B the actual construction of the room is compared with the way the room is perceived. The brain infers that both women standing against the back wall are at the same distance from the eye and interprets the difference between the size of their images as a real difference in size.

to pick up these subtle differences (Carr and Konishi, 1988; Manley, Koppl, and Konishi, 1988). Sounds from either side arrive at the nearer ear before they reach the farther, and though the time difference is less than a millisecond, the brain can detect it. Sounds also seem slightly louder at the nearer ear. Sounds that come from straight ahead or directly behind are the most difficult to place, since they arrive at both ears simultaneously. In such cases, rotating your head may create enough difference in arrival time to help your auditory system place the sound.

Time differences help us most in locating the source of low-frequency sounds, and intensity differences help most in locating the source of high-frequency sounds. The capacity to hear any frequency depends on the condition of the receptors (hair cells) in the basilar membrane of the inner ear. A sound of excessive intensity may cause the vibrating cochlear fluids to tear out the hair cells, leading to irreversible hearing loss in that frequency range.

Is It Moving?—Movement

Once we locate an object, we have to decide whether or not it is moving and, if so, in what direction. The survival of our prehistoric ancestors depended on catching moving prey and avoiding their own predators. The ability to perceive motion is just as important today. Imagine driving a car down a highway without being able to judge the speed of cars and which way they were going. When brain damage destroys motion perception, the unlucky victim lives in a world filled with frustration and danger. Consider the strange, motionless world of a woman who, though her vision is normal in other respects, cannot perceive movement:

She had difficulty, for example, in pouring tea or coffee into a cup because the fluid appeared to be frozen, like a glacier. In addition, she could not stop pouring at the right time since she was unable to perceive the movement in the cup (or pot) when the fluid rose. . . . In a room where more than two other people were walking she felt very insecure and unwell, and usually left the room immediately, because people were suddenly here or there but she had not seen them moving. . . . She could not cross the street because of her inability to judge the speed of a car, but she could identify the car itself without difficulty. "When I'm looking at the car first, it seems far away. But then, when I want to cross the road, suddenly the car is very near." (Zihl, von Cramon, and Mai, 1983, p. 315)

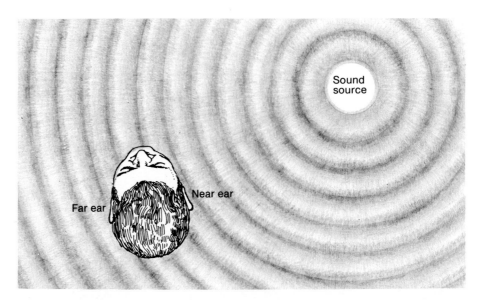

Figure 5.6 Auditory localization. Human beings perceive the direction of a sound source by comparing the times at which the sound reaches each of their two ears. You can demonstrate sound auditory localization by blindfolding a seated friend, then tiptoeing around the chair, staying about four feet from your friend and snapping your fingers from time to time. Ask your friend to point directly toward the sound source, which you vary by changing your direction occasionally so the sound does not progress in a smooth circle. Your friend is likely to pinpoint the sounds to each side but may confuse sounds directly ahead with those directly behind. This confusion is due to the fact that sounds coming from straight ahead or behind arrive at both ears simultaneously. Now have your friend block one ear by putting cotton smeared with Vaseline in it and repeat the experiment. Your friend is likely to be much less accurate at localizing sounds when only one ear can be relied on. (After Lindsay and Norman, 1972.)

This bizarre visual disorder, caused by damage to a specific region of the brain, implies that different aspects of visual perception—color, form, and motion—are handled by specialized processing areas of the brain (Livingstone and Hubel, 1988). When information from one brain area is not available, an odd perceptual disorder is created.

Motion Perception

Any creature soon learns to distinguish between changes in the visual world that are caused by movements in the world and changes that are caused by the creature's own movements. We know when we are in motion, so we relate the movements of our own bodies to the resulting changes in what we see. When we look from one side of a room to another, what we see changes constantly, but we know that those changes result from the movement of our eyes and not the movement of the room.

We know this because the clues that tell us when it is the *object* that is actually moving are missing. When an object moves against a fixed background, we can judge that the movement is in the object and not in ourselves because the object covers and uncovers successive parts of the background in a continuous direction. You can tell that your friend is running to the right in pursuit of a Frisbee because she successively blocks the background in a line from left to right. Once again, perception is relative—this time, relative to the background. The more structured or complex the background, the easier it is to perceive movement. It is, in fact, extremely difficult to "track" an object or spot moving against a dark or neutral, undifferentiated background—for example, a pinpoint of light on a dark TV screen in a darkened room.

Our ears can tell us about motion, too. If you stand on a street corner and close your eyes, information in the auditory stream used to localize the sound also indicates where a moving source of sound is going.

Illusions of Motion

Our ability to perceive motion is just as fallible as our ability to perceive distance. We sometimes perceive motion when nothing is moving. Even when we know the motion is an illusion, the objects—or ourselves—still seem to move. Top-down processing apparently is powerless against any kind of illusion.

Perhaps the most familiar illusion of motion is **apparent motion,** which is created by a rapid succession of motionless images. The brain, filling in the gaps between one image and the next, interprets the succession of images as continuous motion. One such illusion, the **phi phenomenon,** is responsible for your perception that lights are rushing in ceaseless circles around a beckoning sign, as in Figure 5.7. The phi phenomenon, first described by Gestalt psychologist Max Wertheimer (1923), provides the basis for TV and motion pictures. A film is nothing but a series of still photographs in which portions of objects change position in small, separate steps. But the film is shot and projected at the speed of twenty-four frames per second, so that we perceive smooth, continuous motion. Early film cameras shot only about sixteen frames each second; when modern projectors run these films at twenty-four frames per second, the action seems jerky.

Induced motion is an illusion created by relative motion: when objects near a stationary object move, we are tricked into seeing movement in the stationary object. On windy nights, for example, the moon appears to be racing through the clouds, when it is actually the clouds that are being blown across the moon's face. Some researchers believe that induced motion is related to neural activity in motion-sensitive cells in part of the brain's visual cortex (Allman, Miezin, and McGuinness, 1985).

Another form of illusory movement is the **motion aftereffect.** After staring at movement in one direction, we tend to see movement in the opposite direction. When a train stops, a passenger looking out the window sees the stationary scenery outside appear to move slowly backward. This effect is the result of sensory adaptation (Hammond, Mouat, and Smith, 1985). Sensitivity to movement in one direction has been dulled by adaptation, but sensitivity to movement in the other direction is not affected. Do you recall the complementary-color afterimage in Chapter 4, when a green, black, and yellow American flag produced an afterimage of red, white, and blue? Motion aftereffect is based on the same principle.

Motion aftereffects are not confined to vision; researchers have discovered a similar, though weaker, illusion with sounds (Grantham and Wightman, 1979; Grantham, 1989). When sound moves steadily in one direction for a time, we hear a stationary tone of the same frequency as moving in the opposite direction. As in the case of vision, the aftereffect seems at least partly based on adaptation to the sound's direction by neurons that are sensitive to moving sound sources.

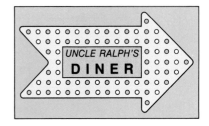

Figure 5.7 Electrical signs like this one illustrate the phi phenomenon. The vertical rows of lightbulbs blink on and off alternately from left to right, giving the impression that the lights are moving in the direction of the arrow.

APPARENT MOTION   the perception of motion from a rapid succession of motionless images

PHI PHENOMENON   the apparent motion caused by still lights flashing rapidly in sequence

INDUCED MOTION   the illusion that a stationary object is moving, created when objects near it move

MOTION AFTEREFFECT   the illusion that a stationary object is moving, created by prolonged viewing of motion in the opposite direction

WHAT IS IT?—FORM

We now know how far away the object is, and we know that it is moving toward us. But how does the brain interpret this moving source of stimulation as a dog and not as a human or a horse? Theories of form perception differ on exactly how the process works; as we noted at the beginning of this chapter, one of the enduring issues in the study of perception is whether we perceive forms by analyzing a scene into its parts (feature analysis) or by immediately interpreting entire organized patterns (Gestalt view).

Feature Analysis

If form perception involves breaking down a pattern into its parts, what are the parts? We learned in Chapter 4 that cells in the visual system respond selectively to contrast, width, edges, angles, lines, and their motion; therefore, the proposal that we perceive form by analyzing an object into such features seems to make

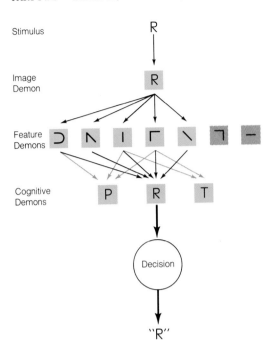

Stimulus

Image Demon

Feature Demons

Cognitive Demons

Decision

"R"

Figure 5.8 The process by which a feature analysis system recognizes the letter R.

FEATURE ANALYSIS the theory that we perceive a form on the basis of a relatively small collection of features, which can be combined, rotated, and expanded

sense. According to **feature analysis,** the visual system constructs our perception of a form on the basis of a relatively small collection of features. Each of these features can be combined, rotated, or expanded to form the objects that we see in the world.

Suppose we are trying to identify printed letters (see Figure 5.8). According to the feature-analysis theory, the visual system decomposes letters into corners, angles, intersections, arcs, and lines at various angles and orientations. A look at the alphabet shows that letters in printed text are indeed made up of distinctive features whose presence or absence characterizes each letter (or set of letters). For each letter, then, the brain notes the distinctive features, compares them with features stored in memory, and places the stimulus-letter in the appropriate category—the "feature list" that provides the best match with the stimulus.

Modern versions of feature analysis have grown out of computer models of pattern recognition (e.g., McClelland and Rumelhart, 1981), but they rely on what has been discovered about the neurophysiology of vision (summarized in Chapter 4). These theories go beyond the simple recognition of features—although the identification of elementary features like lines, intersections, and corners is a first step in the perceptual process. In addition to identifying features, the brain notes their location, orientation, contrast, and fuzziness. The next step consists of finding structures within the mass of features; this is done by grouping the features into clusters. The nature of the clusters is determined by assumptions that are built into the brain—assumptions that resemble the Gestalt principles of perception. At this level of processing, some cells may be "pretuned" to certain combinations of features. For instance, researchers have found cells in the temporal lobe that fire at the sight of faces, with some "face neurons" most responsive to the distances between various facial features (Perrett, Mistlin, and Chitty, 1987; Yamane, Kaji, and Kawano, 1988).

Grouping features produces what David Marr (1982) calls the *primal sketch* of the object. The primal sketch is a structural description of an object's form—rather like a cartoon. We have little difficulty recognizing a familiar face in a caricature, perhaps because such an exaggerated drawing resembles a primal sketch (Frisby, 1980). Once the structural description has been produced, it is matched against stored descriptions and we perceive an object instead of patterned stimulation.

The Gestalt View of Form Perception

The Gestalt psychologists, led by Max Wertheimer, Kurt Koffka, and Wolfgang Kohler, had a very different view of form perception. They maintained that we first take in the unified whole, the "global picture," or gestalt, and then understand the parts. The context gives the individual elements meaning. Because we tend to absorb meaning through context and in whole chunks—a sentence, paragraph, painting, or figure against its background—we can fill in misssing information. We can also compensate for or overlook mistakes, like the misspelling in the preceding sentence.

In the Gestalt view, our perception of form is controlled by the brain's organizing principles. The idea of organizing principles recently reemerged, with the realization that without some preconceived notion of possibilities, the brain would have so much work to do that it would be unable to derive objects from sensation (Marr, 1982). Today, scientists speak of evolved constraints that the brain applies in deriving descriptions of objects. These constraints, which are the brain's assumptions about stimuli, simplify its solutions to the otherwise intractable problem of perceiving the world.

Let's consider the three basic organizing principles in the Gestalt view.

THE FIGURE–GROUND DISTINCTION   One of the brain's organizing tendencies is to make figures stand out from their settings. This organizational principle is called the **figure–ground distinction**. No matter what we look at, whether it is a landscape or a printed page, we automatically divide the scene before us into *figures*, the dominant object or objects, and *ground*, the background against which the objects appear. The figure stands out from the ground like a word on a page; it seems to be more solid and well defined, and it seems to lie in front of a uniform background.

Camouflage, which can fool even the experienced eye, works by blurring this distinction between figure and ground. Either the target figure is hidden among other figures so that it is difficult to isolate, or else it is blended into the background so that it is hard to identify. We are familiar with the use of camouflage by hunters and the military, who usually try to blend into the background. Camouflage in nature relies on both principles. When perched on a branch, for example, some insects are virtually impossible to distinguish from a twig or a leaf; other animals are colored or patterned so that they blend into the general background. In both cases, it is hard for predators to detect the camouflaged animals.

GROUPING   Faced with many stimulus elements, said the Gestalt psychologists (Wertheimer, 1923), we invariably group them according to several innate principles of organization. This way of organizing stimuli determines what pattern we perceive. Using simple dot patterns, Figure 5.9 illustrates these basic principles.

- Part A shows no stable distinguishing organization. Because it is composed of dots of equal size spaced equally across the field, we perceive only an undifferentiated blob.

- Part B demonstrates the rule of *proximity*. Because some dots have been moved closer together, we perceive a series of four parallel lines. When the members of a marching band spell out the school's name on the football field, we see the rule of proximity at work.

- Part C demonstrates the rule of *continuity*. Because the dots now form a single, continuous curve, we perceive them as grouped together. Simply changing a few dots of Part B has caused the principle of continuity to overrule the principle of proximity.

- Part D demonstrates the rule of *similarity*. Because some of the dots are now similar to one another (but different from the rest), we perceive a cross standing out from the original pattern of dots. Back at the football game, when the rooting section suddenly flashes its colored cards and the figure of the team mascot appears, we have witnessed the rule of similarity.

Caricatures use exaggeration to call our attention to the features by which we recognize celebrities.

FIGURE–GROUND DISTINCTION
the tendency to perceive a scene as a solid, well-defined object (figure) standing out from a less distinct background (ground)

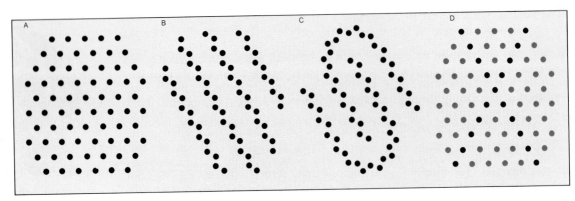

Figure 5.9 A demonstration of some of the Gestalt principles of grouping. The pattern of equally spaced identical dots in A is not easily organized. It is seen either as an undifferentiated field or as a set of unstable overlapping patterns. In B a stable perception of parallel lines emerges because of the *proximity* of some dots to others. When some of these lines are made *continuous* with one another in C, dots that are physically quite distant from one another are seen as belonging to a single curved line. In D a very stable organization emerges suddenly because some of the dots have been made *similar* to one another and different from the rest.

Continuity reflects the brain's tendency toward regularity, consistency, and wholeness. We tend to see one continuous pattern rather than several disjointed figures close together. It is this principle that enables the brain to fill in gaps at the edge of figures, as happens when one object partly obstructs our view of another. Look at Figure 5.10. Why do we perceive a whole board resting behind a block rather than two disconnected pieces on either side? Largely because the Gestalt principle of continuity suggests that we mentally extend the edges of the board to fill in the gaps caused by the obstructing block. Once again, despite the physical incompleteness of the board, the brain registers two complete shapes.

Gestalt grouping principles govern our visual perception in extremely important ways. Without them, we would be unable to read. When the trained eye of the reader encounters the printed words "Every good boy does fine," it uses the spaces between words to group the letters into words, the spaces between letters within each word to segregate the letters, and the features of a letter to distinguish the letters. All these cues can be disrupted simply by altering the usual spacing between letters and words and the size of the letters, as in

eVe   R   yGo   O   dB   oY

AMBIGUOUS FIGURE a figure that can be interpreted in at least two ways, because there is just as much information for one perception as for the other

Such physical changes in printing completely disrupt the flow of normal reading, which depends heavily on automatic processing of the gestalts for each word.

The rules of grouping apply to hearing, too. When we listen to a Bach fugue, we can hear two or more simultaneous melodies, each with a highly distinctive quality. Much of our enjoyment of the composition lies in its creative use of counterpoint. In a symphony or choir, we can hear different melodic, harmonic, or rhythmic lines from the different sections. We do this by using grouping principles, primarily continuity and similarity. Sometimes we group the notes of a melody according to their proximity in time, but more often we automatically group notes of similar timbre, so that we hear several continuous lines at once.

PERCEPTUAL AMBIGUITY Gestalt principles relating to the brain's reliance on natural constraints are responsible for the existence of **ambiguous figures**—figures that can be interpreted in at least two different ways. In these figures, there is an equal amount of information to produce either figure. The brain satisfies both perceptions, but it must do so without violating a general principle that it has incorporated: the principle that only one object can occupy the same space at the same time. And so we can see only one interpretation at a time.

Usually, we resolve the ambiguity by choosing the most likely possibility, using context as our guide. For example, the two lines at the top of Figure 5.11 are

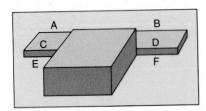

Figure 5.10 Even though our view of the board is partially obstructed by the block, the principle of continuity enables us to see the board as a whole, rather than as two disconnected segments. Our brain fills in the gaps created by the block by extending edge A into B, C into D, and E into F.

ambiguous stimuli. Placed in the sentence "Fido is drunk," the lines are interpreted as the word "is." Yet when the same lines are placed in the number 14,157,393, they become the numbers 1 and 5.

Look at Figure 5.12. Do you see a white vase against a black background? Or a pair of silhouetted profiles against a white background? Both possibilities are equally likely. This type of sensory ambiguity is called *figure–ground reversal*, for obvious reasons. Deciding which part of the picture is figure and which is ground depends on which interpretation you focus on. And what you focus on depends on expectations. If you are told beforehand to look at the vase in the picture, that will be the first configuration you see. Then, as you stare at the picture, the two interpretations tend to switch back and forth. Without cues or expectations to direct attention, figure and ground alternate.

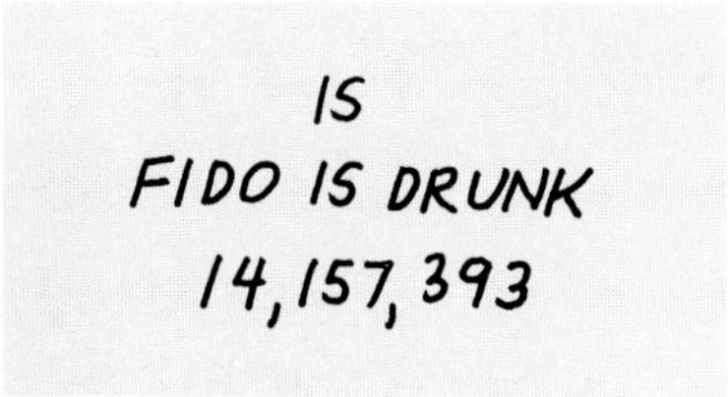

IS
FIDO IS DRUNK
14,157,393

Figure 5.11 The stimulus above the handwriting can be interpreted as either 15 or IS, depending on its context.

LIFE-SPAN CHANGES IN PERCEPTION

As we have looked at the process of perception, we have largely ignored the fact that the world can look, sound, feel, smell, and taste differently to different people. Some people are color-blind, some cannot hear, and some cannot see. In this chapter and the preceding one, we have seen how the world changes for people with some sensory or perceptual deficit, whether inborn or the result of later damage. It is even impossible to know whether two people with normal perception perceive the same object in the same way. When Shakespeare's Juliet said, "A rose by any other name would smell as sweet," she had no way of knowing whether a rose smelled the same to Romeo as it did to her—or whether its redness appeared the same to both of them.

Some differences in perception are the result not of deficit, damage, or normal individual variations, but of the developmental process. Perception changes in predictable ways from a baby's first day on earth until that same individual draws a final breath as an adult of eighty-five.

The Sensory World of the Infant

Babies come into the world with their senses functioning: they can see, hear, feel, smell, and taste. But what do they perceive? Some of the newborn's sensory systems are developed further than others. The newborn's senses of touch, smell, and taste are more acute than the senses of sight and hearing. That is because the more complex a sense, the longer it takes for the specialized sensory area of the brain to develop. Because newborns cannot move around, they do not need exquisitely tuned distance senses. It does not matter, in other words, whether they can see very well or respond quickly to sounds. Someone else has to take care of their needs while their distance senses are developing. Limited in their motor development, newborns need only their near senses—touch, smell, and taste—to contribute to their own survival.

Sight, although functional, is probably the least developed sense in newborns (Gottlieb, 1983) (see the accompanying box). Most of what newborns see is blurry, although they probably see most clearly at distances of about 8 to 10 inches. Their vision is poor in part because they have trouble changing focus, or accommodating, and converging both eyes on the same object (Banks and Salapatek, 1983). As a result, they probably see mostly misaligned objects in a two-dimensional world: they have poor depth perception. And while newborns see color, it is nothing like the full spectrum available to adults.

Despite these limitations, newborns *can* see a great deal. They seem organized to acquire information through their eyes. When awake, they keep moving their eyes, looking about them even in the dark. They can perceive and follow slow movement. They prefer looking at some things rather than others, and they find patterns more interesting than solid colors (Fantz, 1963). Once newborns locate a potentially interesting sight, they generally do not scan the entire shape, but con-

Figure 5.12 This drawing is a classic demonstration of figure-ground ambiguity. What you perceive as figure and as ground depends on a number of factors, including your expectation.

PSYCHOLOGY TODAY AND TOMORROW

Finding Out What Babies Look At

How do we know that newborn babies would rather look at patterns than at solid colors, or that they look at the sides or corners of objects instead of squarely at them? Until about twenty-five years ago, no one knew what babies liked to look at—or even if newborns could see at all. Then William Kessen, Philip Salapatek, and Marshall Haith developed a way to find out. Behind a target, they placed infrared marker lights that reflected in the baby's cornea. By photographing the lights several times each second, they could plot the baby's eye movements, then match the eye movements with positions on the target.

With technological advances, the corneal reflection technique has become more sophisticated. Today researchers use television cameras and a computer that enable practically continuous monitoring of the baby's gaze and an automatic computation of eye movements and locations. In the illustration opposite, you can see the recording system used by Louise Hainline and Elizabeth Lemerise (1987). In this setup, the experimenter holds the baby upright against his or her shoulder, gently supporting the baby's head. The baby looks at a projection screen through a beam splitter, a device that transmits both visible light and reflected infrared light. Behind the screen is a slide projector, which throws the stimulus (a triangle, a circle, or a square) onto the screen. A "face" camera provides the researcher holding the baby with a clear view of the baby's face on a TV monitor. The "eye" camera provides a close-up of the baby's eye, showing the corneal reflections; it sends the picture to two monitors, one viewed by the researcher holding the baby and the other viewed by the researcher operating the equipment. The "scene" camera sends a picture of the stimulus to the researcher operating the equipment. Both the eye and the scene cameras are connected to a digital minicomputer, which calculates the position of the eye about sixty times each second and sends the information to a storage device. Later the computer analyzes the record, distinguishing between eye movements and fixation of gaze and noting what section of the visual field the infant looked at.

Despite the efficiency of this device, it is still extremely difficult to obtain information from infants about the sights they prefer. Thirty-two infants tested by Hainline and Lemerise in one experiment could not be used at all because they fell asleep, cried, or moved about too much, or their eyes would not photograph well (the eye was too small or the pupil too dim). Ten other babies could not be used because either the equipment failed or one of the researchers made an error. Another thirty-three infants completed part of the experiment, but not all of it. Thus, the researchers had to test one hundred and eleven babies in order to find thirty-six who could complete the experiment.

centrate on a side or a corner, where contrast is highest and which is thus the richest source of information (Bornstein, 1984).

Early experiences can have a profound effect on the development of vision. Some aspects of perception develop only when an individual is raised in a normal visual environment. Abnormal visual experience in the first year can have serious effects on some aspects of vision (Banks and Salapatek, 1983). For example, unless babies have an opportunity to use both eyes in a coordinated fashion during infancy, they never develop stereopsis but must rely on monocular sources of depth information (Banks et al., 1975; Hohmann and Creutzfeldt, 1975).

All normal newborns hear, and some can hear very well. But their hearing, like their vision, is not fully developed. Any sound must be 10 to 20 dB louder than the adult threshold before they can detect it (Aslin, Pisoni, and Jusczyk, 1983). However, newborns can distinguish their mother's voice from that of another woman. In one study, three-day-old infants were given a choice between hearing their own mother reading a story and hearing another woman reading the same story. By the way in which they sucked on a nipple that was attached to electronic equipment, newborns could control the tapes on which the stories were recorded. Sucking when a tone sounded kept their mother's voice reading the stories; sucking after the tone kept the story going in the other woman's voice. Most of the babies quickly adapted their sucking patterns so that they could hear their mother's voice (DeCasper and Fifer, 1980).

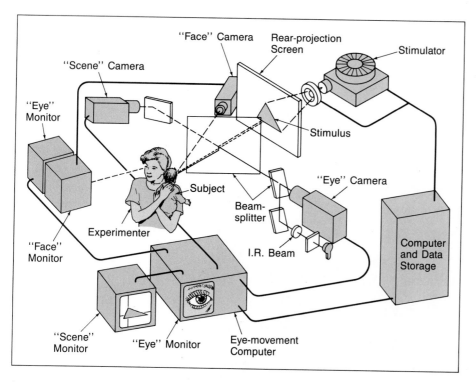

A schematic representation of an eye movement recording system designed for use with infants. [From L. Hainline and E. Lemerise (1987), Infants' scanning of geometric forms varying in size, *Journal of Experimental Child Psychology, 33,* 241.]

Some aspects of hearing follow a pattern of disappearance and reappearance. Most newborns seem able to localize sounds. When researchers shake a bottle filled with popcorn, newborns slowly turn their heads toward the source of the rattling sound. By three months, babies make no attempt to look in the direction of the sound; a month later, however, they again search for its source (Field et al., 1980). Some researchers believe that early hearing is a reflexive response, controlled by the lower brain, but when the auditory system develops and the cortex takes over, hearing and the baby's response become a voluntary, coordinated movement. As we see in Chapter 15, this is a common developmental pattern.

Compared with the sense of sight and hearing, a newborn's sense of taste and smell are highly developed. Babies only 2 hours old respond to bitter fluid by opening their mouths and arching their tongues—a sort of rudimentary gag reflex. Sour liquids cause them to purse their lips. For both unpleasant tastes, they screw up their eyes and wrinkle their noses. But when they are given sweet liquids, newborns relax and suck eagerly (Rosenstein and Oster, 1988). These responses are so consistent that they are probably reflexive, not learned.

Newborns are also sensitive to strong odors and, as with taste, seem to distinguish between "pleasant" and "unpleasant." They screw up their faces and arch their tongues in disgust when they smell rotten eggs or concentrated shrimp. In response to the aroma of butter, bananas, vanilla, chocolate, strawberry, or honey, they lick and suck eagerly (Steiner, 1979). By the time they are ten days old, babies' sense of smell is so keen that breast-fed babies can distinguish the scent of their own mother from that of another woman—and they prefer their mother's odor (Cernoch and Porter, 1985).

Perceptual abilities develop rapidly, and by the second half of the first year babies' vision and hearing are acute. They perceive depth, perceptual constancies are operating, and their visual system appears to follow Gestalt organizing principles. Yet their perceptions of objects and events often differ from those of older children and adults because they have little control over their attention and lack the information required to infer the usefulness, pleasure, or danger inherent in many of the things they perceive (E. Gibson and Spelke, 1983).

Most people experience a loss of visual acuity in middle age.

The Aging Senses

Most older adults live in a world of diminished perceptions—a world in which it is always twilight, conversations are difficult to follow, food loses some of its savor, and the scent of flowers and perfume has faded. Sensory systems age slowly, beginning in the forties, and by the time people reach their seventies or eighties, the losses may be so great as to interfere with daily life.

As the lens of the eye thickens and becomes less flexible, accommodation becomes extremely difficult, and most people develop *presbyopia*, or farsightedness. Middle-aged adults whose vision has been perfect may find that they need reading glasses, and those who have always worn glasses graduate to bifocals. By the mid-fifties, the lens of the eye has accumulated so much yellow pigment that blues and greens may start to look alike (Weale, 1982). Once people are past the age of sixty-five, they may find that getting about at night has become a major problem. So much less light enters their pupils that stepping into darkness is like putting on a pair of dark welder's goggles. Their eyes adjust so slowly to changes in light intensities that they may find night driving hazardous.

Hearing presents its own problems. As they age, most people undergo some hearing loss as a result of the degeneration of hair cells, the loss of auditory neurons, the stiffening of moving bones in the inner ear, or the stiffening of the basilar membrane. Many older people find it especially difficult to discriminate sounds that fall in the high-frequency range, a condition known as *presbycusis*, which literally means "old hearing." Hearing aids are often ineffectual because most amplify all sounds equally, including those in the background; thus, when an older person turns up a hearing aid to catch the high-pitched sounds of speech, lower-pitched sounds from music or machinery may become distracting, even painful. The problem is widespread: 75 percent of people past their mid-seventies have noticeable hearing problems (Olsho, Harkins, and Lenhardt, 1985).

The sharpness of smell deteriorates markedly, beginning in the mid-fifties. Odors must be from two to twelve times as concentrated for people older than seventy to detect them as for younger people. Once an odor is detected, older people often have trouble identifying it. The proportion of older adults with major smell dysfunction rises from 25 percent between the ages of sixty-five and eighty to 50 percent after the age of eighty (Sekuler and Blake, 1987).

Taste also declines, much more than tests of sensory ability would indicate. Because the number of papillae (small bumps on the tongue that contain the taste buds) begins to decline starting about the age of forty, researchers have assumed that taste deteriorates because older people have fewer taste buds than young adults. But it has recently been discovered that fewer than half of the papillae contain taste buds and that there is no decline in actual taste-bud concentration with aging. Instead, there are wide individual differences in the numbers of taste buds at every age, with some young adults showing much smaller concentrations than other adults in their nineties (Miller, 1988). Nevertheless, taste *perception* weakens with age. Sour, salt, and bitter liquids must be stronger before older people can detect the taste, although there seems to be no change in the threshold for sweet tastes (Spitzer, 1988). Because, as we saw in Chapter 4, odor plays such an important role in the perception of taste, flavors seem weak to older people and their ability to identify tastes declines. To them, a cup of coffee that has just been brewed from freshly ground beans may taste no different from a stale cup of coffee that has been sitting on a warmer all day. And herbs and spices may have to be lavished on food before the dish tastes "good" to older adults.

No one is certain just how much of this sensory loss is the result of "normal" aging. In every study, researchers find a few older people whose sensory systems are as acute as those of the average young person. Years of life in the noisy environment of a technological world contribute to hearing loss. Unsuspected factors may also be involved. Researchers have found, for example, that prescribed medications are responsible for part of the reduction in taste sensitivity among the elderly (Spitzer, 1988).

Whatever a person's age—infant, young adult, or elder—perception does a remarkably able job of placing the individual in touch with reality, even if the reality is created by the senses and the brain. Apparently, perception's rendition of that reality is reasonably accurate, because most of us navigate successfully within our complex environment most of the time.

SUMMARY

The Active but Selective Nature of Perception

- We sense stimuli, but we perceive objects and events.
- Perception is usually effortless.
- Perception integrates the information picked up by all the senses.
- We often must act in order to perceive.
- In perceiving, the brain actively constructs meaning.
- Perceptual constancy indicates that perception is relative, not absolute.

Enduring Issues in Perception

- One enduring issue in perception has to do with the role of experience: how much of perception is innate and how much is learned?
- A second enduring issue is whether the perceptual system builds up its descriptions from simple sensations (feature analysis) or whether it perceives an entire form (Gestalt view).
- A third enduring issue is whether illusions demonstrate important perceptual processes or whether they are simply curiosities.
- A fourth enduring issue is whether perception is a bottom-up or a top-down process—what the effect of knowledge is on perception.

Where Is It?—Location

- Locating an object begins by focusing attention on it.
- Depth perception can determine an object's absolute or relative distance. Depth can be perceived through either binocular or monocular sources of information.
- Size is one effective cue to depth, and perspective provides a wealth of information about distance.
- Among the illusions of depth are the Müller-Lyer illusion, the Ponzo illusion, and the Ames room.
- Differences in sound intensity and arrival time also help us locate objects.

Is It Moving?—Motion

- An object's motion is detected by the object's covering and uncovering successive parts of the background in a continuous direction.
- The brain continues to perceive illusions even when the nature of the illusion is known.
- Among the illusions of motion are apparent motion, induced motion, and the motion aftereffect.

What Is It?—Form

- According to modern views of feature analysis, the visual system identifies features, notes their characteristics, and groups them into clusters, producing a primal sketch.

- According to the Gestalt view, we perceive the unified whole before we identify its parts.
- The brain's organizing tendencies, first noted by Gestalt psychologists, include figure–ground distinction, as well as such grouping principles as proximity, similarity, and continuity.
- Gestalt principles are responsible for the existence of ambiguous figures.

Life-Span Changes in Perception

- Perception changes in predictable ways over the life span.
- Newborns' distance senses are not as well developed as their near senses of touch, smell, and taste.
- Some aspects of perception can develop only when individuals are raised in a normal visual environment.
- Sensory systems begin aging during the forties, and the losses may become severe by the time people reach their seventies or eighties.

KEY TERMS

ambiguous figures
apparent motion
convergence
depth perception
distance senses

feature analysis
figure–ground distinction
Gestalt school
induced motion
motion aftereffect

perception
perceptual constancy
perceptual set
phi phenomenon
stereopsis

CONCEPT REVIEW

1. The chapter begins by emphasizing that "we sense stimuli, but we perceive objects and events." What are the characteristics of perception that distinguish it from sensation?

2. How do the various illusions studied by perceptual psychologists contribute to our understanding of perception?

3. Describe several examples of both top-down and bottom-up processing. In what way is top-down processing equivalent to perception of wholes and bottom-up processing equivalent to perception of parts?

4. Explain how binocular disparity provides information enabling the perceiver to see depth and three dimensions. List and define the other kinds of binocular and monocular depth perception.

5. Which of the visual means of perceiving distance is most similar to the means of auditory location described in this chapter?

6. The phi phenomenon, an illusion of apparent motion, is very important for Gestalt psychologists. What aspect of the phenomenon would make it so meaningful to them?

7. Describe the activities or steps in feature analysis that would lead to the perception of a particular object, such as this book. Where does the "primal sketch" fit into the process?

8. Give some examples in which the perception of a figure–ground relationship is important for the perception of an object or event.

9. Look at the ambiguous pictures in Figures 5.9 and 5.10. Identify all the Gestalt organizing principles that you can find in these illustrations.

10. Which of the senses are well developed in humans at birth? Why would these be so well developed but not the others?

11. Describe how the priming of a word supports the concept of subliminal perception.

CRITICAL THINKING

1. The chapter suggests that several of our perceptual mechanisms improve during early childhood. However, the relative nature of many visual perceptions, especially the perceptions related to Gestalt principles and the effects of illusions, suggest that the world is not as we perceive it. What purpose do the selective and active roles of perception play in the way we interpret the world around us? How does experience affect our interpretation?

2. Neither the feature analysis approach nor the Gestalt approach provides a complete understanding of how perception works. What possible solutions to this "part versus whole" controversy are suggested by the various concepts discussed in the chapter?

Consciousness

.. *Consciousness*

One day in 1962 Canadian neurologist Wilder Penfield flew to Moscow to examine a new patient, Nobel prize–winning physicist Lev Landau. Six weeks earlier Landau had suffered severe head injuries in an automobile accident, and he was still unconscious. His limbs were paralyzed, his eyes were unfocused, and he seemed unable to see or understand anything. When Penfield recommended a minor diagnostic operation, Landau's estranged wife came to Moscow and visited her husband for the first time since the accident. As she told her unconscious husband about the proposed operation, Landau's eyes focused on her. Suddenly he appeared to see, hear, and understand. Her voice had roused him, and although he could not speak or move, he had regained consciousness. A hemorrhage deep within his brain was blocking the passage of nerve impulses, but it allowed messages to pass between the brain stem and the uninjured cortex. Consciousness and understanding were present, although motor control and the ability to lay down new memories were lost (Penfield, 1979). As the hemorrhage was gradually absorbed, Landau began to recover, but he never remembered his meeting with Penfield or anything that happened to him in the months after the accident.

What do we mean when we say that someone "regained consciousness"? We usually have no trouble distinguishing a conscious state from an unconscious or comatose one. Landau's behavior, for example, tells us that consciousness is somehow separate from the processes that control our limbs and muscles, store memories, and keep us breathing and our hearts beating. But that only tells us what consciousness is *not*. What is consciousness?

Although the word did not exist in English before the seventeenth century, today we use "consciousness" in so many ways that it is difficult to settle on a satisfactory definition. For example, "consciousness" can mean being awake as opposed to being asleep. It can mean being aware of something in the environment, as when you become conscious of someone's presence. It can mean deliberately choosing a course of action as opposed to being driven by hidden motives, as when you make a conscious decision. To one modern observer (Minsky, 1986), consciousness resembles the menu list that flashes on a computer screen each time you want to invoke another routine. To William James (1892), it meant the unattended flow of perceptions, deliberate thoughts, memories, associations, and preoccupations—often called the "stream of consciousness." In this stream, a succession of images and ideas rise almost involuntarily to the surface, where we become aware of them (Oatley, 1988). The term can also refer to our reflections on the stream of consciousness—to being "conscious" of "consciousness." Finally, the term "consciousness" can refer to alterations in its state—that is, to changes in awareness produced through fantasy and daydreaming, sleeping and dreaming, meditation, hypnosis, or psychoactive drugs.

In each of these meanings, consciousness is directed toward a different object, but in every case it involves the awareness of some mental process. And so "consciousness" is often defined as "awareness" (Natsoulas, 1978). This definition suggests the enormous role that consciousness plays in our lives. Consciousness allows us to attend to stimuli and to act upon them. It enables us to exert some control over our actions and experience and to choose among possible ways of thinking and behaving. This definition of consciousness is not universally accepted, however, primarily because it is still too narrow. In some states of consciousness, for instance, information may be processed without much awareness on the part of the person involved. When we include such states, the definition of **consciousness** broadens to include *all mental experiences, whether or not we are aware of them.*

CONSCIOUSNESS   all mental experiences, whether or not we are aware of them

THE NATURE OF CONSCIOUSNESS

Not all languages have a word for consciousness, yet all languages have words for four separate phenomena related to consciousness: (1) wakefulness (as opposed to sleep); (2) bodily sensations such as itching and pain; (3) perceptions obtained through hearing, sight, and the other senses; and (4) deliberating, pondering, desiring, and believing (Wilkes, 1988). The collection of awarenesses that we call "consciousness" may also include varieties that depend on different physiological mechanisms.

Conscious Awareness: Subjective and Objective

Traditionally, consciousness has been regarded as a private world, accessible mainly through introspection. For this reason, many psychologists once rejected consciousness as a topic for scientific study. Modern advances in research and theory, however, have restored researchers' interest in the study of consciousness. As knowledge about attention, perception, memory, thought, emotion, and other areas of mental experience accumulated, it became possible to study consciousness in new ways. By examining the physiological activities that accompany changes in awareness, such as those produced by dreaming, meditation, or drugs, psychologists have learned more about the workings of consciousness. New instruments and new methodologies have produced objective, verifiable findings about the varieties of consciousness.

As a result, consciousness is now considered both subjective *and* objective. *Subjective consciousness* refers to our personal experience of the world—that is, to the way things seem to us (Dennett, 1988). It includes the way a sunset looks or the way a waterfall sounds and feels. Yet, our awareness is not an awareness of the world itself but of our perceptions of it. As we saw in Chapter 5, we experience an integrated world, and the brain's integration of our perceptions produces the "unity of consciousness" (Marcel, 1983). Another aspect of subjective consciousness is awareness of the self. Without self-awareness, we could not deal effectively with the world. We are not born with self-awareness, and in Chapter 15 we will trace its gradual emergence in toddlers and its connection with cognitive development and social experience.

Many scientists protest that the study of subjective consciousness is outside the scope of science, yet the fact remains that humans can do a reasonably good job of communicating their subjective experiences. For example, even though patients may have no prior experience with a particular disorder, their answers to such questions as whether a pain is sharp or dull can give physicians a reliable basis for diagnosing various ailments (Marcel, 1988). Thus, although it is difficult to

Problem-solving ability is an indication of the objective aspects of consciousness—those whose existence can be verified by others.

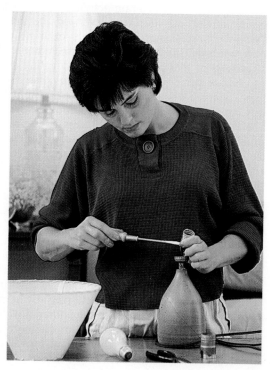

study the subjective aspects of consciousness, without such study we are unlikely to ever understand the relationship between brain and behavior.

Objective consciousness refers to those aspects which can be verified by others. We can study various processes of consciousness, such as attention, perception, and memory (Bisiach, 1988). We can infer consciousness from an organism's ability to solve problems. We can obtain objective evidence of consciousness by measuring the physiological changes that accompany changes in awareness, such as brain waves and eye movement. Responses from signal-detection tests (see Chapter 4), which indicate awareness of stimuli, have also been used to study consciousness.

An important feature of consciousness is that we have some control over it. We can deliberately focus on anything we choose—an object's color, shape, identity, or function; the fact that we are categorizing objects in a certain way; the sounds made by a particular instrument that we pick out from the orchestra; even theories that attempt to explain just what consciousness is. As we saw in Chapter 5, such selectivity is crucial to our everyday functioning. So many sensations, feelings, thoughts, and memories are accessible at any given moment that attending to all of them would overwhelm us. By screening out most of the information that is available to us, we can be conscious only of those things we wish to attend to. This aspect of consciousness—attention—is an important area of cognitive research. In the remaining chapters in this unit, we will examine its role in determining what we understand, what we learn, and how much of it we remember.

The Brain and Consciousness

For centuries, it has been believed that consciousness and brain activity are closely connected. Neuroscientific evidence has supported this notion for nearly half a century. For example, stimulation of parts of the cerebral cortex in patients who are undergoing brain surgery produces conscious, though dreamlike, visual and auditory experiences (Penfield and Rasmussen, 1950). Yet, despite evidence indicating the close connection between consciousness and physiological brain activity, the exact nature of that connection has yet to be determined. Many neuroscientists (e.g., Rose, 1973) have argued that the distinction between consciousness and brain activity is purely semantic. Consciousness, they say, is nothing more than the sum total of brain activity. This explanation makes consciousness and brain activity two different levels of the same phenomenon. If so, when we "study" consciousness, we merely examine the same psychological event at a different level, shifting our analysis from neurophysiological activity to subjective awareness of that activity.

Nobel prize–winning psychobiologist Roger Sperry (1977) challenges this view. Sperry, whose research focused on split-brain patients like those discussed in Chapter 3, maintains that consciousness has a role in directing brain activity, but also that brain activity is necessary for consciousness to emerge. We might think of consciousness as an emergent property of brain activity in the way that ice is an emergent property of water. The proposal that consciousness somehow emerges from brain activity is appealing because it echoes our instinctive feeling that there is something unique, immediate, and willful about consciousness (Rey, 1983). Even if we accept Sperry's proposal, however, we still do not know exactly what kind of brain activity is necessary for consciousness or how complex a brain must be before consciousness emerges. As we saw in Chapter 3, neurons work similarly in all creatures with a nervous system, and as we will see in Chapter 7, animals and people learn in a similar fashion. Do animals also have mental experiences? Are they aware of a stream of consciousness? Earlier we saw that there is more than one kind of consciousness. What sort of consciousness might a chimpanzee have? a dog? a fish? Referring to the selective nature of consciousness, James (1890) wrote: "Other minds, other worlds, from the same monotonous and inexpressive chaos! My world is but one in a million, alike embedded and alike real to those who may abstract them. How different must be the world in the 'consciousness' of ants, cuttle fish, or crab!"

Attempts to probe the relationship between brain activity and consciousness have gone far beyond direct stimulation of the cortex, with some startling results. The research with split-brain patients described in Chapter 3 indicates that cognitive activity can occur outside conscious awareness. Recall that in one study, researchers flashed a picture of a nude woman to a patient's right hemisphere. The patient said she saw nothing, but blushed and giggled, covering her mouth with her hand. When the woman was asked why she had laughed, she seemed confused and could not explain. Her right brain had seen the nude picture and reacted to it, but her verbal left brain had seen nothing (Gazzaniga, 1967). With another split-brain patient, Michael Gazzaniga (1985) flashed the picture of a chicken claw to the left hemisphere and the picture of a snow scene to the right. Asked to point to pictures in front of him that went with what he had just seen, the man pointed to a chicken with his right hand (left hemisphere) and a snow shovel with the left (right hemisphere). Faced with such evidence of cognitive activity outside awareness, we try to explain the situation to ourselves. Asked why he pointed to those particular pictures, the man justified his response in terms of what the verbal left hemisphere had seen: "Oh, that's easy. The chicken claw goes with the chicken and you need a shovel to clean out the chicken shed." Gazzaniga explains his findings by hypothesizing that many mental systems coexist within our brains in a sort of confederation. Consciousness emerges from the verbal left brain's attempts to explain the actions of our multitude of mental systems, and it is this inference-making capacity that is a uniquely human aspect of consciousness.

Other Levels of Consciousness

Consciousness appears to operate on a number of different levels, many of them outside our subjective awareness. In some circumstances, as when we walk in our sleep, we can carry out complex activities without remembering or being aware of our actions. In other circumstances, as when we perform well-learned activities, our actions are almost automatic. When we first learn to drive a car, for example, we are highly conscious of performing each task. As our driving skill improves, many of these processes—such as monitoring the traffic, adjusting the speed, or indicating a turn—become automatic. This transformation from focused awareness of each action to unawareness is typical of most skills we learn through extensive practice, such as typing or riding a bicycle. Operating at an automatic level frees consciousness to pay attention to more immediate claims on attention. When driving has become automatic, we can carry on a conversation while we operate a car; when typing has become automatic, we can attend to *what* we are typing instead of the mechanics of operating a typewriter.

When a function becomes automatic, the change is so significant that if we *try* to focus our awareness on some aspect of a well-learned skill, we may blunder—type the wrong letter or fall off the bicycle. This automatic aspect of consciousness also explains why it is difficult to teach someone else a skill: it is hard to realize what the learner needs to be told.

Although psychologists do not agree on just how these levels of consciousness should be categorized, we can use Sigmund Freud's terminology and speak of them as being subconscious, preconscious, and unconscious. Activities carried on at the *subconscious* level take place entirely outside subjective awareness. Information (memories and thoughts) that we are not thinking about at the moment but that could be voluntarily brought to awareness occupy the *preconscious*. Thoughts and images that we keep submerged, perhaps because they are painful or produce psychological conflict, reside in the *unconscious*.

Once we have learned a skill, it becomes automatic. We can do it without thinking about it, and thinking about it may interfere with our ability to do it.

Subconscious Processes

Some cognitive processes are **subconscious:** stimuli are monitored but not registered in subjective awareness. Although we cannot actively attend to all the stimuli around us, there is evidence that, at some level, we receive and record much of

SUBCONSCIOUS the area of mental processes in which stimuli are monitored but are not registered in subjective awareness

the information that we seem to ignore. In Chapter 5 we pointed out that it is possible to listen to a conversation at a crowded party, ignoring the clinking glasses, background music, and voices that surround us; this *cocktail party phenomenon* is an act of selective attention. During this attending, however, the brain receives and records the background sounds.

Support for the proposal that the brain picks up unattended information comes from experiments in **dichotic listening.** Subjects wear a set of earphones through which they hear two simultaneous, but different, messages, one in each ear. When asked to repeat aloud the message received by one ear, most people can do so about as well as they can when there is no competing message being transmitted to the other ear (Cherry, 1953). Afterward, they have no memory of the second, unattended message; they cannot even say whether it was meaningful or nonsensical. But the studies show that they hear the second message at a subconscious level. They can say, for example, whether the "unheard" message was spoken by a man or a woman or both. Moreover, if the person's name is inserted into the "unheard" message, he or she immediately becomes conscious of it.

The unattended message registers firmly enough in the subconscious to influence a person's subsequent behavior, even though the person is not aware of having heard it. For example, if the unattended message consists of words for members of various categories ("cardinal," "daisy," "poodle"), and the person is later asked to name a member from the category "bird," he or she would be likely to say "cardinal"—even though there is no recollection of having heard the word. Such a memory, which influences performance although it is not consciously recalled, is known as an **implicit memory** (Schacter, 1978). A growing body of evidence indicates that in some types of amnesia implicit memory continues even though the person is no longer able deliberately to recall any recent events (Schacter, 1978). Apparently, a considerable amount of complex cognitive processing occurs in the subconscious.

Another example of cognitive activity at the subconscious level is *blind sight*. This phenomenon appears in people whose eyes are intact but who have suffered damage to the visual cortex or to the pathways between the cortex and the lateral geniculate nucleus in the thalamus (see Chapter 4). They cannot see at all, but they can "guess" the direction of light flashes (Poeppel, Held, and Frost, 1973). They can even point accurately toward objects (Weiskrantz et al., 1974). Although these people are blind, they continue to process visual stimuli even though they lack direct awareness of them. Blind sight indicates that the visual cortex controls our awareness of sight but that it does not control all the functions of vision (Marcel, 1983). Other evidence of subconscious cognitive activity comes from studies of subliminal perception, which we mentioned in Chapter 5.

Preconscious Processes

A different kind of nonconscious awareness involves information that we are not thinking of at the moment, but that we can produce if we choose to do so. Such memories are **preconscious.** At the moment you are reading this text and thinking about psychology, but if someone asks you what you did last summer, or what other courses you are taking, or what your phone number is, the information would quickly enter your consciousness so that you could answer them. Preconscious memories encompass your entire store of general knowledge, from the multiplication tables, your vocabulary, and your family history to everything you know about chemistry, computers, finance, and literature, for example. Preconscious memories also include all your personal knowledge: memories of incidents that have happened to you or that you have witnessed.

Unconscious Processes

Preconscious memories are there when we need them. Their accessibility distinguishes them from another sort of information that we possess but cannot easily retrieve: material that is said to be in the **unconscious.** Not all psychologists

DICHOTIC LISTENING   a process of selective attention, exemplified by a person hearing two simultaneous, but different, messages, one in each ear, and attending to only one, remaining unaware of the other

IMPLICIT MEMORY   a memory that results from unattended stimulation; it influences performance even though it cannot be consciously recalled

PRECONSCIOUS   the area of mental processes that is not in alert awareness but that may be recalled at will; all personal knowledge

UNCONSCIOUS   the area of mental processes that is not available to the conscious mind, but whose contents may slip out in disguised form

accept the notion of an unconscious, as we will see in later chapters, but the basic concept is important to explore. Freud was not the first to propose the idea of the unconscious, but it is a cornerstone of his theory of personality, and it remains basic to modern psychoanalysis (see Chapter 17). In Freud's view, the motivation behind some of our feelings, thoughts, and actions is buried in the unconscious. Try as we may, we cannot readily bring this material from the unconscious into consciousness, but some of its contents do slip out in disguised form—in dreams, in slips of the tongue, and in psychological and physical symptoms.

NATURAL STATES OF CONSCIOUSNESS

What do all these variations tell us about consciousness? Consciousness is flexible, multilayered, and multifaceted. It is naturally stimulated daily (by fantasy, sleep, or dreams), and it can deliberately be altered (by meditation, hypnosis, or psychoactive drugs). Although such a broad concept is very difficult to grasp, we will be unable to understand ourselves or human nature until we have understood the phenomenon of consciousness. A century ago, James (1890) stressed the existence of a variety of states of consciousness outside our awareness and their importance:

> *Our normal waking consciousness, rational consciousness as we call it, is but one special type of consciousness, whilst all about it, parted from it by the filmiest of screens, there lie potential forms of consciousness entirely different. We may go through life without suspecting their existence; but apply the requisite stimulus, and at a touch they are there in all their completeness, definite types of mentality which probably somewhere have their field of application and adaptation. No account of the universe in its totality can be final which leaves these other forms of consciousness quite disregarded. How to regard them is the question—for they may determine attitudes though they cannot furnish formulas, and open a region though they fail to give a map. At any rate, they forbid a premature closing of our accounts with reality.*

Fantasy and Daydreaming

One uniquely human aspect of consciousness is the capacity to create alternative realities (Coan, 1988). Through fantasy, we escape the realities of everyday life in play—often creatively. Besides having a role in the arts, creative fantasy is basic to science; many advances have followed from insights that scientists have obtained while playfully imagining alternative realities.

These alternative realities are part of daily life, yet we do not usually think of them as alternative levels of consciousness. Between our normal waking consciousness and sleep (which we explore in the next section) lie various states of consciousness that are based on imagination and graded degrees of removal from reality. When we fantasize, we tune out the external world and shift our attention inward.

Daydreams are a familiar form of fantasy. As you sit on the bus in the midst of city traffic, you may envision lying on a sunny beach or holding a conversation in which you win an argument with your boss. All of us have daydreams, although there are strong individual differences in the types of fantasies we have. Some people's daydreams are mostly positive; others tend to be unpleasant or troublesome (Segal, Huba, and Singer, 1980). These persistent differences in the tone of daydreams may reflect differences in customary activities, attitudes, emotions, and moods. Daydreams seem to come in cycles; most people have some sort of daydream every 90 to 100 minutes. These cycles appear to occur whether people record their thoughts under strict experimental supervision or merely go about their daily routines (Kripke and Sonnenshein, 1978). As we will see in the next section, night dreams follow a similar cycle.

REALISTIC FANTASY daydreams that resemble waking thought; they occur in a state of consciousness in which awareness is removed from the outer world

AUTISTIC FANTASY daydreams that lack any connection with reality; they occur in a state of consciousness removed from the normal waking state

REVERIE the state of consciousness filled with unrelated images that are not under the conscious control of the fantasizer

HYPNOGOGIC IMAGE an image produced in the state of consciousness that exists as a person is falling asleep

HYPNOPOMPIC IMAGE an image produced in the state of consciousness that exists as a person is waking up

Some daydreams, called **realistic fantasy,** are closely connected to realistic situations. They generally take a narrative form and may be problem-oriented, like an imaginary argument with your boss. Other daydreams, called **autistic fantasy,** lack any connection with reality. Daydreams of living several hundred years in the future or traveling to another galaxy are autistic fantasies.

Other types of fantasy have even less connection with reality. **Reverie** consists of unrelated images, scenes, or memories and is not under the control of the fantasizer. Reverie can be overwhelming in people who have been deprived of sleep, then awakened abruptly (Dinges, 1989). When this happens, a person is often extremely confused by uncontrolled thoughts and images that flood into consciousness. People who are on call for emergencies throughout the night may find that reverie interferes with their performance just after they are awakened.

Between waking and sleep lie other forms of brief fantasy—vivid, dreamlike images and intense sounds. These images are as uncontrollable as reverie. When the images occur as we are falling asleep, they are called **hypnogogic images.** ("Hypno" refers to sleep.) When the images occur during the transition between sleep and waking, they are called **hypnopompic images.**

Some researchers have suggested that these states of consciousness (awake alertness, realistic fantasy, autistic fantasy, reverie, hypnogogic and hypnopompic images, and sleep) exist on a continuum. None is sharply defined; one state merges into the next (Martindale, 1981). Others believe that the key factor is the level of cortical arousal, which, as we saw in Chapter 3, is controlled by the reticular activating system—the "watchdog" of consciousness. In this view, the various states of consciousness form a broad spectrum, ranging from very low to very high arousal levels (Fischer, 1971). Decreased arousal leads to relaxation and tranquility; increasingly higher levels of arousal are associated with creativity, irrational behavior, and ecstasy in that order.

Sleep and Dreams

Sleep is a radically altered form of consciousness. Although our awareness of the outside world is reduced during sleep, it is not eliminated entirely. We frequently change our sleeping positions without waking up, and we are apparently aware of the edge of the bed, since few of us fall onto the floor while asleep. We also seem to monitor the environment and process some meaningful information. That is why we sleep through meaningless sounds but wake if we are called by name (Oswald, 1962) and how a mother can sleep soundly through a thunderstorm but wake at her baby's cry.

CIRCADIAN RHYTHM any cycle that occurs on a daily basis (circadian = about a day)

Sleep is a regularly occurring state of consciousness that works on a **circadian rhythm.** ("Circadian," from the Latin *circa dies,* means "about a day.") Sleep is part of a daily biological rhythm that takes the form of a 24-hour sleep/wake cycle. Body temperature, hormone secretion, alertness, and other physiological functions also follow circadian rhythms, but usually we are unaware of them. Alertness, for example, tends to be highest during the day and lowest at night, when people ordinarily are sleeping. This rhythm is so pronounced that when people must work on night shifts, they tend to have difficulty sleeping during the day and are drowsy on the job. They also tend to become less productive and more accident-prone. Most people eventually adjust to the reversal in their sleep/wake cycle, but the adjustment takes some time. It did not surprise researchers to discover that the major accident at the Three-Mile Island nuclear plant near Philadelphia occurred at 4 A.M. with a crew who had been working on the night shift for only a few days (Moore-Ede, Sulzman, and Fuller, 1982).

The cause of the sleep and behavior problems associated with night work can be found in the body's response to a change in its natural rhythm. The body protests at being asked to sleep at a time when it is "set" to be alert. Jet lag is another example of the body's negative reaction to a disruption in its circadian rhythm. The effects of jet lag are less noticeable when we travel west across time zones than when we travel east. Westward travel is easier on the system because the body's natural sleep/wake rhythm is actually about an hour longer than the

The disruption of biological rhythms known as jet lag results from east–west travel across time zones. Passengers flying north–south do not experience this fatigue and disorientation.

24-hour cycle (Moore-Ede, Sulzman, and Fuller, 1982). A trip from New York to California extends the day in the same direction as the body's underlying rhythm. When we fly east, our body is forced to stay alert at a time when we are normally sound asleep. We know that jet lag is caused by travel across time zones because when we stay in the same time zone—flying from Canada to South America, for example—jet lag does not occur. The disparity between our 25-hour biological rhythm and society's 24-hour day may help explain why we tend to extend social activities, TV watching, or studying into our usual sleep time. It is easier to stay up later than to wake up earlier. Daylight and regular schedules of meals, work, and social interaction tend to maintain the circadian rhythm at the shorter schedule.

The Stages of Sleep

Much of what we know about sleep has come from sleep experiments, which typically involve attaching electrodes in the form of small disks to a volunteer subject's scalp and face and connecting them to a device that records brain waves (EEGs), eye movements, and changes in muscle tension while the subject sleeps overnight in the laboratory. This recording of physiological activity during sleep is known as **polysomnography.**

POLYSOMNOGRAPHY recordings of physiological activity (brain waves, eye movements, muscle tension) during sleep

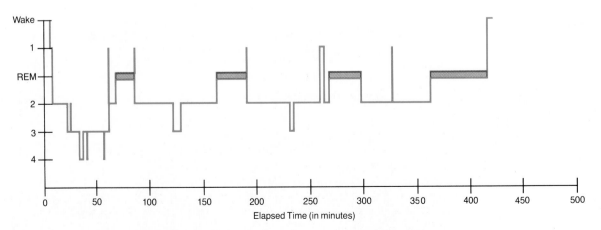

Figure 6.1 The kinds of sleep and their durations, as measured from midnight on, during a normal night's sleep of a twenty-five-year-old male. The horizontal axis indicates minutes elapsed. The vertical axis indicates types of sleep. Shaded bars represent periods of rapid eye movement (REM) sleep.

REM (RAPID EYE MOVEMENT) SLEEP   the state of sleep that is characterized by rapid eye movements and contradictory physiological characteristics; most dreams occur in this state

NREM (OR NON-REM) SLEEP   the state of sleep, divided into four stages, in which there is no rapid eye movement

ULTRADIAN RHYTHM   any cycle that occurs more frequently than once each day (ultradian = "faster than a day")

Such studies have revealed two major sleep states: **REM (rapid eye movement) sleep,** so named because the sleeper's eyes move back and forth beneath closed eyelids; and **NREM sleep** (pronounced "non-REM"), in which the eyes do not move. The sleeper begins by progressing through four stages of NREM sleep, from light sleep to deepest sleep, then goes back through each stage to light sleep (see Figure 6.1). At this point, instead of repeating the NREM cycle, the sleeper enters the REM state. Most dreams occur during REM sleep, and the state has proved basic to an understanding of sleep and dreams. From the REM state, the sleeper again enters NREM sleep, at which point another cycle begins.

This pattern of sleep follows one of the body's short rhythmical cycles, called **ultradian rhythm,** from the Latin *ultra dies* ("faster than a day"). The sleep cycle repeats itself throughout the hours of sleep in an ultradian rhythm lasting about 90 minutes.

What happens to the body as we progress through these successive stages of sleep? Each sleep stage is dominated by certain brain-wave frequencies, measured in cycles per second (Hz), as are sound waves. When we are awake and alert, with our eyes open, *beta waves*, which are rapid, low-amplitude waves, dominate the EEG. As we relax with our eyes closed, beta waves are replaced by slower alpha waves, which indicate a resting mind and body. At this point we are still awake. As we begin to fall asleep, we enter stage 1, signaled by a change in the pattern of brain waves (see Figure 6.2). Alpha waves drop out and are replaced by even slower theta waves. Stage 2 sleep is indicated by bursts of high-frequency waves called sleep spindles. As sleep becomes progressively deeper (in stages 3 and 4), slow delta waves dominate the EEG. In stage 3, from 20 to 50 percent of brain waves are delta; in stage 4, more than 50 percent are delta.

When a person is in deep sleep (stage 4), muscles relax and heart rate and respiration are slow and regular. Because it is difficult to rouse someone from deep sleep, we know little about the nature of consciousness during this stage. By the time a person is awake, it is difficult to tell whether whatever is recalled from sleep actually took place during stage 4 or during the awakening period. Yet we know that the brain is active during stage 4, because sleep disturbances such as sleepwalking, sleep talking, and night terrors occur during this stage. (See the accompanying box for a discussion of several sleep disorders, including night terrors.)

Although most of us sleep through the general stimuli that surround us, not all sleepers are able to do so. Sometimes this inability to remain asleep is so pronounced that a form of **insomnia,** or chronic sleeplessness, develops. Insomniacs often complain that they get little sleep, yet when they are brought into a sleep laboratory their EEGs show normal sleep patterns. When aroused during stage 2 sleep, insomniacs are more likely than sound sleepers to say that they were awake when called (Borkovec, Lane, and VanOot, 1981). They can give detailed accounts of their thoughts during sleep and sometimes accurately describe any sounds that occurred while they were sleeping (Engle-Friedman, Baker, and

INSOMNIA   the inability to sleep; chronic sleeplessness

Figure 6.2 Records of the electrical activity of the brain (EEG) in a person in various stages of sleep and in the relaxed waking state known as "alpha." Note that in the deeper stages of sleep the high-frequency, small-amplitude waves give way to lower-frequency, large-amplitude waves. This change is thought to reflect the fact that the neurons in the brain are all firing at about the same level and in about the same pattern. Note also that the EEG pattern in REM sleep is very similar to stage 1.

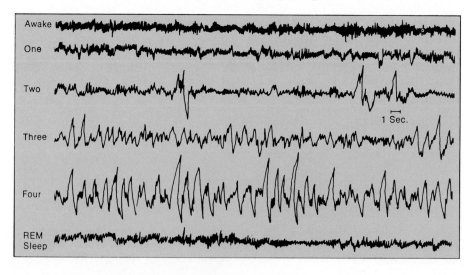

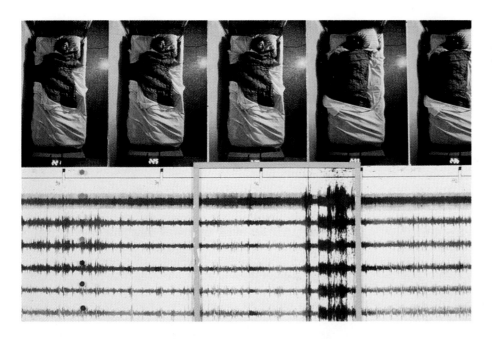

In recent years monitoring of volunteer sleepers has revealed a great deal about the changes in physiological activity that take place during the various stages of sleep.

Bootzin, 1985). Thus, it appears that some insomniacs have trouble shutting external stimuli out of their sleeping consciousness.

Under certain conditions the environmental events that we monitor during sleep may find their way into our dreams. Studies have found that sounds and changes in temperature or pressure do not initiate a return to REM sleep or to the beginning of a dream. But if a sleeper is already in a REM period, stimuli from the environment may be incorporated into the dream's content. When water was sprayed on the faces of some volunteer sleepers, they reported more dreams involving water than did sleepers who were undisturbed (Dement and Wolpert, 1958).

Why We Sleep

We spend more time in sleep than in any other single activity. No one knows for sure exactly why we—and all other animals—need to sleep so long, or to sleep at all, but several explanations have been advanced.

Evolutionary explanations ask what adaptive value sleep might have. Some researchers believe that sleep is not directly related to survival but instead is the way species occupy time that is left over after activities related to survival are completed (Meddis, 1977). Sleep patterns of various species indicate that animals sleep when they are safe and face no pressing survival need. In this view, we sleep because there are no demands on our alertness.

Other sleep researchers view the connection between sleep and survival somewhat differently. They propose that our early ancestors were in extreme danger during the hours of darkness, when they could not see possible predators or environmental hazards. By sleeping during the night, they were better able to stay out of harm's way (Webb, 1975). This suggestion is supported by animal hibernation; species that hibernate do so in winter, when food supplies are scarce and exposure to weather might threaten life. Hibernation depresses metabolism, heart rate, breathing, and brain activity, greatly reducing the need for energy.

Sleep deprivation studies tend to support the view that sleep also serves a restorative function. When deprived of any form of sleep, whether REM or one of the NREM stages, people become tired or irritable. They feel sleepy, fall asleep quickly when allowed to, and are hard to wake. After periods of deprivation, both slow-wave sleep (stages 3 and 4) and REM sleep increase, as if in compensation. Some researchers believe that the nature of our fatigue determines our need for a particular sleep stage. For example, after heavy physical activity, we need extra

PSYCHOLOGY TODAY AND TOMORROW

Sleep Disorders

For most of us, the worst sleep-related problem is being awakened by our alarm clock so that we can get to work or school on time. We may occasionally have trouble sleeping—on the night before an exam or an important job interview, or when we have eaten or drunk too much. But we rarely think of sleep as a problem. People with sleep disorders, however, often find their worries about sleep dominating their lives. The major sleep disorders are insomnia, sleep apnea, narcolepsy, and night terrors.

People who suffer from *insomnia* either have trouble falling asleep or else waken during the night and can't get back to sleep. As noted in the text, most insomniacs get more sleep than they realize. The problem is that either they dream that they are awake or spend most of the night in lighter stage 1 or stage 2 sleep. For example, one volunteer who reported that he averaged less than five hours of sleep each night slept more than seven hours when tested in a sleep laboratory (Mitler et al., 1975).

Some insomniacs can obtain relief by learning ways to relax, avoiding daytime naps, and using the bedroom only for sleeping (or for sexual activity), not for eating, watching TV, or reading (Bootzin and Engle-Friedman, 1987). Insomniacs are instructed to go to bed only when sleepy; to get up and go into another room if sleep does not come; and to get out of bed at the same time every morning no matter how little sleep they got during the night. These instructions aim at establishing a consistent sleep rhythm and arranging the environment so that the bed is strongly associated with sleep—and sleep only.

Some cases of insomnia are caused by another sleep disorder known as *sleep apnea*, in which the person actually stops breathing for ten seconds or more; this happens repeatedly during the night. The breath stoppage awakens the sleeper, who takes a deep breath and immediately goes back to sleep. This may happen dozens of times each night—sometimes as many as several hundred times. Most people who suffer from sleep apnea are awake so briefly that they are not aware of their night-time breathing difficulties. However, they may be troubled by sleepiness during the day. Other sufferers stay awake but are unaware of what awoke them; they attribute their wakefulness to ordinary insomnia (Mitler et al., 1975). Sometimes the breathing problem is caused by an obstruction in the airway. If so, the removal of tonsils or adenoids may end the apnea—especially among children. In severe cases, adults may wear a mask to bed that provides continuous positive air pressure to the airways, keeping them open.

Not all sleep disorders involve lack of sleep; sometimes people sleep too much. Those who suffer from *narcolepsy* have frequent "sleep attacks"—irresistible urges to sleep. Sleep attacks last from five to thirty minutes and occur during boring activities such as driving long distances or listening to a lecture in a stuffy room. Many narcoleptics also have brief episodes of *cataplexy*, during which they suddenly lose muscle tone and cannot move, although they remain aware of what is going on around them. These episodes are often brought on by emotional excitement. Many narcoleptics also experience *hypnogogic imagery*, frightening dreamlike images, as they fall asleep.

Narcolepsy appears to be a disturbance of REM sleep. Instead of entering REM sleep after passing through NREM stages, narcoleptics often begin the night with REM sleep. The symptoms of cataplexy and hypnogogic imagery also appear to be REM phenomena occurring at the wrong time. Medication can help to control the symptoms of narcolepsy. Stimulants can reduce the frequency of sleep attacks, and medication that suppresses REM sleep can reduce the frequency of cataplexy and hypnogogic imagery.

The most dramatic sleep disorder is the *night terror*, which is a brief, vague, and terrifying sleep disturbance. Night terrors bear little resemblance to the familiar nightmare. Night terrors are a disturbance of stage 4 sleep and generally occur within the first two hours of sleep; nightmares occur much later in the night, during REM sleep. Night terrors are characterized by sudden sharp changes in the autonomic nervous system—increased pulse, respiration, skin resistance, and perspiration; nightmares produce more gradual autonomic changes. Finally, the person who has a night terror is aware only of the frightening emotion, but reports little content. In contrast, the person who has a nightmare can often describe its frightening content in detail.

Night terrors are most common among children between three and eight years old and generally disappear by adolescence. Unless the night terrors are severe, there is no need to treat them. Daytime naps and earlier bedtimes, which seem to reduce the pressure for the slow-wave sleep of stage 4, may lessen night terrors (Bootzin and Chambers, 1990). When these remedies fail and the terrors are severe, supervised treatment with Valium, which is believed to suppress slow-wave sleep, may be effective.

William Shakespeare's *Macbeth* provides a classic summary of the reasons we need sleep: "Sleep that knits up the raveled sleeve of care, / The death of each day's life, sore labor's bath, / Balm of hurt minds, great nature's second course, / Chief nourisher in life's feast."

slow-wave sleep. This proposal is supported by a study of long-distance runners, who showed a dramatic increase in stage 3 and 4 sleep after a 92-mile marathon (Shapiro et al., 1981).

How long can people survive without any sleep at all? Although most of us sleep from 6 to 8 hours each night, there are documented cases of individuals who never slept more than 2 hours a night and showed no obvious harmful effects (Meddis, 1977). The record for sleeplessness is held by Randy Gardiner, a sleep-experiment subject who stayed awake for 11 days (Dement, 1974). On the eleventh day, he was still alert and won every pinball game he played with the sleep researcher who was monitoring him. The only ill effect that Gardiner experienced was transient mild hallucinations. On the basis of his performance, some researchers have speculated that sleep may not be necessary after all. Yet it is possible that people who go for days without sleeping actually fall into frequent microsleeps—sleep periods that last only a few seconds. Studies with animals indicate that if animals are continuously deprived of sleep, they die (Rechtschaffen et al., 1983). Although the mechanisms of sleep are not completely understood, it appears that sleep may have both restorative and evolutionary functions.

The Function of REM Sleep

Because REM sleep is such a unique state of consciousness, investigators have speculated that it may have a special function. In a test of this proposition, researchers deliberately deprived volunteers of the opportunity to dream (Dement, 1974). For several consecutive nights, sleepers were awakened each time they entered a REM period. After a few nights it became increasingly difficult to arouse the sleepers as a REM stage began. The longer the sleepers were denied REM sleep, the more often REM sleep appeared. When, on the fifth night, the sleepers were allowed to stay in REM sleep, they experienced a "REM rebound," spending twice as much time in REM sleep as they normally would.

Indirect evidence from developmental studies indicate that REM sleep may help maintain the brain's responsiveness. Some researchers suggest that REM sleep stimulates the growth and maintenance of neural tissue, thereby preparing sensory and motor areas to handle the next day's load of environmental stimulation (Anders and Roffwarg, 1973). Logically, the need for neural growth should be greatest in newborns and should decrease with age—and this is precisely the REM pattern that appears (Roffwarg, Muzio, and Dement, 1966). Newborns

Figure 6.3 Sleep patterns change with age. REM sleep as a percentage of total sleep tends to decrease as we get older. (Roffwarg, Muzio, and Dement, 1966.)

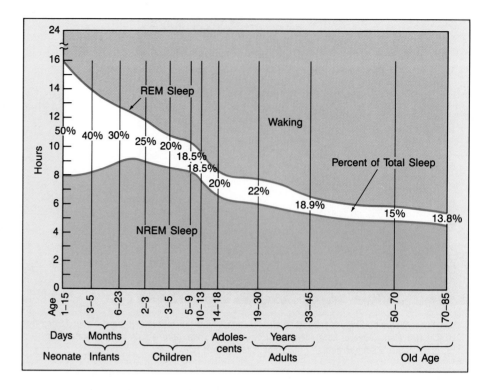

spend about half their sleeping time in REM sleep, infants under two years 30 to 40 percent, and adolescents and adults about 20 to 25 percent (see Figure 6.3). As people reach their seventies, there is a slight additional decrease in REM sleep (Williams, Karacan, and Hursch, 1974). REM sleep apparently fills some psychological or physiological function—or both—but the precise nature of that function remains unclear.

The average person goes through four or five episodes of REM sleep each night, entering a REM state about every 90 minutes. The physiological characteristics of this state of consciousness are so contradictory that the REM state is often called *paradoxical sleep.* Although the person in REM sleep is obviously not awake, the EEG pattern shows more arousal than would be expected from a sleeper: heartbeat and breathing are irregular and highly varied; blood pressure increases; signs of sexual arousal appear. These physiological signs resemble those of a person who is awake and highly excited. PET scans, which make the brain's metabolism visible, support this impression. Brain metabolism during REM sleep is much closer to metabolism in the waking state than is metabolism in NREM sleep (Franck et al., 1987). Yet by other measures a person is more deeply asleep in REM than in NREM. Despite the aroused physical activity of REM sleep, major body muscles lose their tone and become limp. This drop in muscle tone, which makes it impossible to move the muscles, apparently works to prevent sleepers from injuring themselves or others by acting out their dreams.

Loss of muscle control during REM sleep apparently is controlled by a specific part of the brain stem. When this part of a cat's brain is removed, the animal no longer lies still during episodes of REM sleep. Instead it leaps about, shows rage or fear, or plays with its paws as if a mouse were between them (Jouvet, 1975). After a stroke or some other neurological disorder, some people—usually older adults—no longer lose muscle tone during REM sleep. Like the cats, these people move and even throw themselves around the bedroom during REM sleep (Schenck, et al., 1986). One man, for example, developed wild sleep movements after a localized brain hemorrhage. During a taped interview, he described one incident that occurred during a dream:

> *Somebody was after me and I figured my only escape was to jump through a window, so I got up and I jumped . . . and I hit the wall and the dent is still in there like a soup bowl. (Schenck et al., 1986, p. 300)*

Fear of injury led him to tie a rope around his waist and fasten it securely to the bed. But he frequently got loose and continued his escapades, sometimes injuring himself. All-night sleep recordings confirmed that his activities occurred during the REM state. Physicians successfully controlled his REM disorder with anticonvulsant sleep medication.

Researchers first suspected that REM sleep was associated with dreaming when they observed sleepers' eyes moving back and forth as though the sleepers were watching something behind their closed eyelids. And indeed, subjects awakened during REM periods reported dreams with vivid visual imagery at least 80 percent of the time (Webb, 1973; Dement, 1974). Sleepers awakened during a NREM period rarely reported storylike dreams; instead they reported mental activity that took the form of persistent ideas or fleeting images (Hobson, 1988).

Dreaming

Dreams are the content of consciousness during REM sleep. Just as everyone spends time in REM sleep, everyone dreams—even those of us who claim we never do. It took specialized sleep research to verify the universality of dreams, but long before there was scientific evidence, dreams were a topic of interest. In the earliest written records, dreams have been linked to religion, to prophecy, to the fortunes of individuals, and to the destiny of cultures. The belief that dreams *mean* something is found in virtually every society.

Sigmund Freud (1900/1955) maintained that dreams are symbolic expressions of repressed desires stored in the unconscious. He also believed that dreams have two distinct layers of content—one plainly evident and the other hidden. The **manifest content** is the dream's surface meaning and consists of an interweaving of daily events, memories, and sensations during sleep. This manifest content disguises the dreamer's unconscious wishes, which are the dream's **latent content.**

Over the past thirty-five years, research conducted in sleep laboratories has persuaded many psychologists to reject Freud's explanation. Some researchers hold that dreams are simply the predictable result of a physiological process (Hobson and McCarley, 1977; Hobson, 1988). In this view, which is known as the *activation-synthesis hypothesis,* during REM sleep the cortex is activated by random stimulation. The dream that results is the brain's attempt to interpret the random electrical messages it receives.

A related explanation of dreams was put forth by Francis Crick (who shared the Nobel prize for his work on DNA) and Graeme Mitchison (1983). They agree with Hobson and McCarley that dreaming is a random pattern of neural firing in the cortex, which occurs when cortical neurons are stimulated by nonspecific signals sent from the brain stem. In addition, they propose that this firing helps weaken unimportant neural connections made during the day, thus preparing neurons to deal with fresh information the next day. According to Crick and Mitchison, the brain routinely goes through this process in order to avoid becoming overloaded. In essence, inappropriate information is "unlearned" or erased from the cortex, leaving room for new material to be absorbed. In this view, dreaming prevents the brain from overloading its cortical networks—a situation that can result in such abnormal behavior as inappropriate fantasies, obsessive repetitions, and hallucinations. Although this theory is intriguing, it has not yet been tested.

Later, Martin Seligman and Amy Yellen (1987) extended the cognitive aspects of the random-firing explanation. They agree that dreams consist of random visual images created by nonspecific signals and emotional activation—which, in turn, may be affected by the previous day's experiences. They propose that dreams represent an attempt to integrate these disparate images and emotions, but the process is not unique to sleep. It is the same as the steps we take during our waking hours to integrate our perceptions of the world. Some people seem to do a more efficient job of this than others, these researchers found—a discovery that may help explain individual differences in the types of dreams people report.

In their study, Seligman and Yellen compared the degree of integration in dreaming and in active thinking. Students first recorded at least three of their

MANIFEST CONTENT the surface meaning of dreams, consisting of interwoven daily events, memories, and sensations during sleep

LATENT CONTENT a dreamer's unconscious wishes, which influence the content of a dream, where they appear in symbolic form

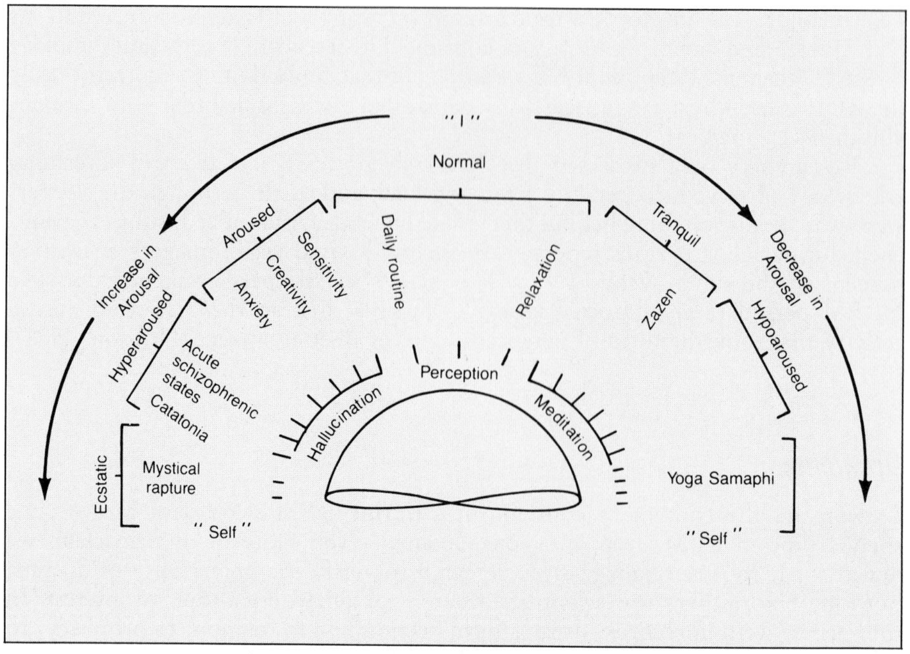

Figure 6.4 Most altered states of consciousness can be classified according to how much they increase or decrease the arousal of the brain's cortex. Thus, altered states can be arranged on a continuum from those associated with very high arousal to those associated with very low. (After Fischer, 1971.)

dreams; later they were asked to write narrations for a series of seven unrelated slides. Some students integrated the slides into a story with a tightly knit plot, while others produced a text with little or no integration. The results of this exercise showed consistent individual differences: those with coherent dreams wrote coherent stories for the slides and those with unconnected dreams wrote unconnected responses to the slides. Apparently, people who are good at integrating disparate images while awake are also good at integrating the disparate images of dreams.

Other aspects of dreaming make it appear that physiological explanations cannot completely explain dreams. Dreams often seem to concern themselves with our daily activities and problems. Studies with volunteers in sleep laboratories indicate that the four or five dream periods of a typical night are related and often deal with the same theme or problem (Cartwright, 1977). The first dream of the night is closest to reality; the middle dreams are the most distorted and fantastic; the final dream often returns to the problem and attempts to work out a solution. Whether the solution carries over into waking consciousness is not known, but the pattern suggests that dreams may have a problem-solving function. Some researchers are exploring this idea. In one study, women who are going through the stress of divorce are being taught to pay more attention to their dreams in the hope of increasing their problem-solving ability (Cartwright, 1989).

Whatever their explanation for the mechanism behind dreaming, all these researchers have focused on the brain's attempt to integrate or understand internal stimulation. Earlier we saw that the unified consciousness of our waking state is the result of the same process. Apparently, the waking brain is compelled to explain its various internal activities. The sleeping brain seems to be similarly motivated. On some level dreams seem to be an attempt to understand experience—whether physiological processes or the day's events.

Exploring how dreams are created is one way to explain them; another is to try to become aware of them while they are in progress. Some people report having **lucid dreams,** ones in which they realize that they are dreaming. At one sleep lab, researchers attempted to work out a method by which dreamers could notify investigators when a lucid dream began (La Berge et al., 1981). Prearranged signals included fist clenches or a specified sequence of eye movements (which were recorded on graphs of eye movements). Sometimes the attempts were successful.

From time to time lucid dreamers report that once they become aware that they are dreaming, they are able to change the course of the dream. Lucid dreams are evidence of consciousness during sleep, and people can sometimes train them-

LUCID DREAM a dream in which a person is aware that he or she is dreaming

Figure 6.5 To meditate, it is necessary to empty the mind of distracting thoughts by focusing on a simple pattern or thought that will not lead to distractions. In some forms of meditation the meditator concentrates on a visual pattern such as the mandala shown here, which continually returns the gaze to its center.

selves to reach this level of awareness during the REM state. An effective treatment for people troubled by nightmares is to help them become aware of the experience as a dream. If the person can realize during the nightmare that he or she is dreaming, the nightmare suddenly becomes more controllable and thus less frightening (Halliday, 1988).

ALTERED STATES OF CONSCIOUSNESS

Members of virtually every society known to us have attempted to alter consciousness deliberately, generally for either religious or recreational purposes. Meditation, hypnosis, and psychoactive drugs are commonly used methods for leaving the state of waking consciousness. Figure 6.4 correlates shifts of consciousness with the increase or decrease of cortical arousal.

Meditation

Meditation is a method of refocusing attention in order to enter inner consciousness. The aim of meditation can be the establishment of a relaxed, tranquil state of mind or the achievement of a heightened state of spirituality. In one type of meditation, known as *the path of concentration,* the meditating person directs attention away from the external world, focusing on a specific object such as a short prayer, a mantra, a picture, or a candle flame (see Figure 6.5). The path of concentration is used in yoga, transcendental meditation, and Sufism. In another type of meditation, known as *the path of mindfulness,* the person focuses on observing the actions of the mind itself. Buddhism uses both approaches (Goleman, 1977).

Meditation has always played a significant role in religion. In Eastern religions, meditation generally becomes part of a comprehensive philosophy of life. Using meditation, the individual progresses systematically through different levels of consciousness, each seen as superior to normal waking consciousness (Paranjpe, 1984). The highest goal of the meditator is to enter a state of consciousness in which experiences of self and world are subsumed within a more comprehensive perspective and personal goals and identity lose all importance. In this state, the meditator's consciousness has been absorbed into a consciousness of life that transcends individual existence. In the West, meditation is often used pragmatically to produce a relaxed state that allows a person to handle stress more effectively (see Chapter 20).

MEDITATION a method of refocusing attention through "concentration" or "mindfulness" to produce relaxation or a heightened state of spirituality

In many Western countries, meditation has become a popular technique for coping with stress.

Franz Mesmer treats a patient in Paris.

Hypnosis

Hypnosis is a social interaction in which the responses of one person (the subject) to the suggestions of another person (the hypnotist) result in altered perceptions, memories, and voluntary actions (Kihlstrom, 1985). This is very different from the popular concept of hypnosis, in which the hypnotist controls the action of the subject, who is compelled to do the hypnotist's bidding.

To anyone who has watched a demonstration of hypnosis, the state of a hypnotized person resembles that of a sleepwalker—someone who has lost touch with waking awareness but who can stand, move, see, hear, and talk. Yet the sleepwalker and the hypnotized person differ in dramatic ways. For one thing, their physiology differs. During sleep, oxygen consumption gradually decreases, but during hypnosis it remains unchanged. The sleepwalker's EEG shows the slow brain waves of stage 3 or stage 4 sleep, but the hypnotized subject's brain waves are those of an awake person. For another thing, the sleepwalker and the hypnotized person behave differently. Sleepwalkers seem unaware that other people are around, and they will not follow instructions; hypnotized people are aware of others and will follow most instructions. Finally, memory functions differently. On waking, sleepwalkers cannot recall their wanderings; on emerging from hypnosis, hypnotic subjects remember the details of the experience unless they have been instructed to forget.

Although hypnosis is named after Hypnos, the Greek god of sleep, hypnosis is obviously not sleep. Yet, after years of research, psychologists still cannot say exactly what hypnosis is. Many psychologists doubt that hypnosis should be considered a separate state of consciousness.

An early version of hypnosis, known as "mesmerism," was used by Franz (or Friedrich) Anton Mesmer (1733–1815) to treat patients with psychological disorders. Mesmer, an Austrian physician, believed that the shiftings of a magnetic fluid within the body was responsible for the health or sickness of mind and body. In order to readjust his patients' magnetic fluid, Mesmer placed them in an artificially induced, sleeplike state in which they were highly susceptible to suggestion. Many of Mesmer's patients improved, in a demonstration of the power of suggestion in curing mental disorders. After Mesmer's death, mesmerism developed into the technique of hypnosis and was used by a number of French physicians to treat psychological disorders. As a young physician, Sigmund Freud (1856–1939) encountered the technique when he studied with the famous French neurologist Jean-Martin Charcot (1825–1893). Back in Vienna, working with a physician named Josef Breuer (1842–1925), Freud used hypnosis to enable patients to discuss their problems freely. Freud and Breuer believed that while they were in a hypnotic state patients could express unconscious conflicts that were inaccessible to waking consciousness. Although Freud later discarded the technique, as we will see in Chapter 19, its use set him on the path that would lead to the development of psychoanalysis.

Hypnotic Susceptibility

Not everyone can be hypnotized. About 10 percent of the population do not respond at all to the hypnotist's suggestions. The rest can be hypnotized to some degree—if they want to be and if they trust the hypnotist. Only about 10 to 15 percent of people are highly hypnotizable, and once they are hypnotized, their experience is strikingly different from that of people who show only a slight susceptibility (see Table 6.1). Such individual differences are highly stable; they remain the same from week to week and from year to year (Kihlstrom, 1985).

Psychologists measure a person's hypnotic susceptibility with standardized tests such as the Stanford Hypnotic Susceptibility Scale (Weitzenhoffer and E. R. Hilgard, 1959). In this test, the subject is hypnotized; then the hypnotist offers a series of suggestions, such as "Your left arm will become rigid." Those who are unable to bend their arm more than 2 inches and who respond similarly to an ordered series of suggestions are considered highly susceptible to hypnosis. Such people tend to have highly developed imaginative capacities. Many developed their fantasy skills in childhood, when they daydreamed frequently and typically had an imaginary playmate (J. R. Hilgard, 1979).

What Happens in Hypnosis

"I want you to relax." In the familiar process used to hypnotize a person, the hypnotist begins by slowly persuading the subject to relax and lose interest in

TABLE 6.1   Subjective Reports Based On an Inquiry Following Attempted Hypnosis

INQUIRY	Affirmative Replies to Inquiry as Related to Hypnotic Susceptibility (Percent)*			
	HIGH (N = 48)	*MEDIUM* (N = 49)	*LOW* (N = 45)	*SLIGHTLY SUSCEPTIBLE* (N = 17)
Were you able to tell when you were hypnotized?	65	60	47	31
Any similarity to sleep?	80	77	68	50
Disinclination to act:				
to speak?	89	79	68	31
to move?	87	77	64	50
to think?	55	48	32	12
Feeling of compulsion?	48	52	20	6
Changes in size or appearance of parts of your body?	46	40	26	0
Other feelings of changes:				
of floating?	43	42	25	12
of blacking out?	28	19	7	6
of dizziness?	19	31	14	0
of spinning?	7	17	0	6
of one or more of the prior four feelings?	60	60	39	25

*Based on an inquiry following the taking of one of the two forms of the Stanford Profile Scales of Hypnotic Susceptibility, after having scored at least 4 on SHSS-A; the insusceptible are not included.

Source: From E. R. Hilgard (1977), *Divided consciousness: Multiple controls in human thought and action.* New York: Wiley-Interscience, Table 10, p. 164.

external distractions. The hypnotist then suggests something easy, such as "Your left arm will rise." After the subject complies with a few easy suggestions, the hypnotist proceeds to more difficult ones.

Once in hypnosis, highly susceptible people respond to many suggestions. Some responses occur during hypnosis, but they can also be carried out in waking consciousness after the hypnotic session has ended. These latter are called **post-hypnotic suggestions**. Often these are simple acts, such as "Tug your left earlobe three times," but many people have relied on posthypnotic suggestion to try to lose weight, stop smoking, relax, control pain, or change their behavior in other ways (Dengrove and Dengrove, 1987; Hilgard and Hilgard, 1983). In addition, in response to suggestion, some hypnotized people experience **posthypnotic amnesia**. If the hypnotist tells subjects to forget certain events that happened during hypnosis, the events seem wiped from memory when they return to waking consciousness. But at a prearranged signal from the hypnotist (a clap of the hands, a specific word or phrase) the memory returns.

Is there any validity in the claim that hypnotized people can be regressed to their childhood? In a typical instance of age regression, a hypnotized person is told that she is attending her own sixth birthday party. The woman begins to talk and behave like a six-year-old, and she gives a lengthy and impressive account of the party—complete with cake, candles, presents, guests, and surroundings. She seems convinced that the report is accurate, yet it can almost always be shown that the subject has combined incidents from several parties and invented missing details. In one study, people who were regressed to the ages of ten, seven, and four talked about their teachers and their classmates, describing them all with great conviction. But when the school records were checked, many of the children described had not been members of the class, and the hypnotized subjects provided no more accurate details than members of an unhypnotized control group (Orne, 1979). Perhaps in age regression highly susceptible subjects are trying so hard to please the hypnotist that they simply invent missing information in order to fill out their account.

Does hypnosis actually relieve pain? It has been used successfully to anesthetize patients during surgery and to lessen the severity and incidence of migraine headaches. Hypnosis has enabled people to go through other ordinarily painful experiences without reporting pain. In one instance, a thirteen-year-old boy had suffered extensive second- and third-degree burns on his left leg. Whenever his dressing was changed, he cried, writhed, and had to be held down. After being hypnotized, he was able to remain calm while the surgeon removed dead tissue and dressed his leg (Graham, 1986). The value of hypnosis in the treatment of severe pain appears to be unique (Wadden and Anderson, 1982), yet how it manages to alleviate pain is unclear.

Is Hypnosis an Altered State?

Hypnotic subjects firmly believe they are in an altered state, yet they show no specific physiological changes that distinguish their hypnotic trance from normal waking consciousness. What evidence indicates that hypnosis is an altered state? According to Ernest Hilgard (1977), hypnosis is a state we can all recognize but cannot measure. Hypnotized people show typical changes in behavior: increased suggestibility; enhanced imagery and imagination, including visual memories from early childhood; uncritical compliance with the hypnotist's instructions; avoidance of initiative; and the uncritical acceptance of distortions of reality.

Researchers who reject the notion that hypnosis is an altered state of consciousness contend that all of these changes can be induced outside hypnosis. But what about the strange feats that sometimes occur in the hypnotic state? For example, hypnotists often tell subjects that their bodies have become rigid, then have them balance their head on one chair and their feet on another. As they become human planks suspended between the two chairs, someone stands on their chests. Despite its seeming difficulty, anyone (hypnotized or not) can accomplish this feat. If unhypnotized people are motivated and assured that they can perform the task, they can carry out many of the bizarre acts associated with hypnosis (Barber, 1976; Barber, Spanos, and Chaves, 1974).

POSTHYPNOTIC SUGGESTION suggestion of the hypnotist that a hypnotized person carries out after hypnosis

POSTHYPNOTIC AMNESIA a hypnotized person's inability to remember events after hypnosis in response to hypnotic suggestion

Psychologists' inability to agree as to whether hypnosis is actually a separate state of consciousness has produced two very different explanations of the hypnotic condition. Those who consider it an altered state explain it in terms of **dissociation theory**: during hypnosis, consciousness splits into several more or less independent systems, each one unaware of what the others think or feel. For example, the hypnotized person reports no pain because the system that registers pain has become dissociated from the system that controls consciousness. This is apparently what happened in the case of the badly burned thirteen-year-old. According to the theory, dissociation may also occur outside of hypnosis. People who suddenly develop amnesia and cannot remember past experiences have dissociated these memories from waking consciousness. The psychological disorder called multiple personality, in which several clearly defined personalities seem to inhabit the same body, is an example of extreme dissociation, as we will see in Chapter 18.

Another version of this theory, proposed by Ernest Hilgard (1978), is known as neodissociation theory. **Neodissociation theory** builds on the idea that the mind contains many parallel mental processes and that they may not share information or emotions. During hypnosis (or any altered state) the process that controls consciousness shifts. But Hilgard believes that during hypnosis the dissociated level of consciousness continues to register, process, and store information that is blocked from the awareness of the hypnotized subject. He calls this dissociated level "the hidden observer." Studies have supported the existence of this dissociated awareness. For example, in pain studies, Hilgard has asked the hidden observer to record the level of perceived pain by pressing a key while the hypnotized subject gives a verbal report. This method of response shows that although the hypnotized person feels no pain, his or her hidden observer is aware of it. Hilgard's theory that thought is affected by multiple mental systems is in accord with information from split-brain studies (in which the two hemispheres received different information and produce contradictory responses) and with what we know about the mind's various levels of awareness.

Researchers who maintain that hypnosis is not a separate state of consciousness explain its effects in terms of **role enactment theory**. They contend that hypnosis is simply an extreme example of role playing, in which the subject behaves "as if" hypnotized. Like an actor playing a role, the hypnotized subject takes the part of a hypnotized person, behaving as he or she expects such a person to behave and as he or she thinks the hypnotist expects (Sarbin and Coe, 1972). People are not actually regressed to childhood, for example, but simply play the role of a young child (see Figure 6.6). In this view, social and psychological factors, not some alteration in the subject's conscious state, are responsible for the apparent effects of hypnosis. Even posthypnotic amnesia and pain relief have been explained this way (Spanos, 1986). Subjects *expect* to forget and do; they *expect* their pain to be reduced and find that it is. Yet it is hard to explain the badly burned thirteen-year-old's response to hypnosis in terms of role enactment theory. He had little interest in playing the role of a hypnotized person and little reason to play act. No matter which explanation of hypnosis turns out to be correct, the changes people undergo in hypnosis indicate that we have the capacity to induce altered states of consciousness by cognitive means.

Psychoactive Drugs

Certain drugs can alter our state of consciousness by interacting with the central nervous system to affect mood, perception, and behavior. Such drugs, known as **psychoactive drugs**, change the chemistry of the brain, and each psychoactive drug induces a distinctive state of consciousness. Among the psychoactive drugs are such commonplace substances as nicotine and the caffeine in coffee, tea, and many soft drinks, as well as powerful substances such as marijuana, cocaine, amphetamines, alcohol, valium, heroin, LSD, all of which sharply alter consciousness. (The mechanisms and problems involved in abuse of these and other drugs are discussed in Chapter 18.)

DISSOCIATION THEORY the view that during hypnosis, consciousness splits into independent systems, each unaware of what the others think or feel

NEODISSOCIATION THEORY a variation of dissociation theory that maintains the dissociated systems continue to pass information back and forth, even though the information does not register in awareness

ROLE ENACTMENT THEORY the view that hypnosis is not an altered state, but an extreme example of role playing

PSYCHOACTIVE DRUG any drug that interacts with the central nervous system by changing brain chemistry to affect mood, perception, or behavior, thus altering consciousness

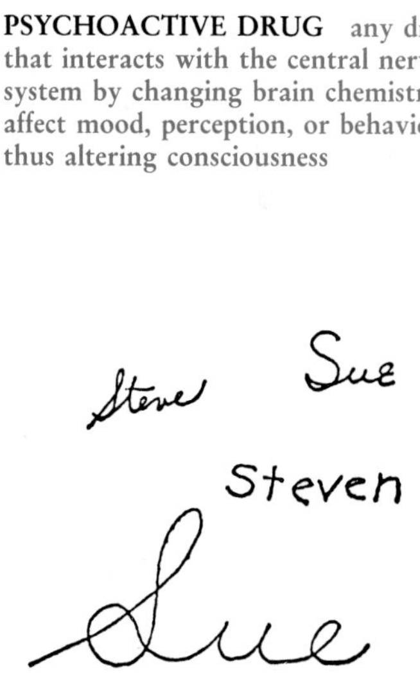

Steve   Sue

Steven

Sue

Figure 6.6 Signatures obtained from hypnotized subjects with eyes closed under "normal" and "regression" conditions. In the "regression" condition each subject was asked to return to the second grade. Were the subjects temporarily reentering their past, or were they instead acting out an imagined second-grade self? A definitive answer to this question has not yet been found. (Hilgard, 1965.)

Marijuana

Marijuana has a long history of use in Eastern societies. Some cultures that forbid the use of alcohol regard marijuana as an accepted psychoactive drug. Since the 1960s, marijuana has become so common in the United States that among Americans older than twelve, more than one out of three have tried it. Its use peaked in 1978 and 1979, and since that time its popularity has been decreasing slowly (Kozel and Adams, 1986).

The consciousness-altering agent in marijuana is tetrahydrocannabinol (THC), a complex molecule that occurs naturally in Indian hemp, or cannabis (*Cannabis sativa indica*). The plant can be dried to produce marijuana; and the resin exuded by the flowers of the female plants can be used to make hashish, a gummy powder that is up to ten times more concentrated than marijuana.

We know almost nothing about marijuana's effects on brain chemistry. Its behavioral effects are unpredictable and depend in good part on the setting in which a person uses the drug. Despite this variability, regular users tend to agree about marijuana's effects. Sensory experiences are heightened: objects are more distinct and their colors take on subtle shades; musical notes sound purer and the rhythm stands out; food tastes better and familiar tastes take on new qualities; smells are richer; sexual pleasure is intensified. Worries disappear and there is a sense of profound well-being, even euphoria. Especially among first-time users, everything seems hilarious—the world is a "cosmic joke" (Naranjo, 1986). Time becomes distorted and may even seem to stop. Perhaps for this reason many users say they become totally absorbed in their drug experience—perceptually, imaginatively, and cognitively (Fabian and Fishkin, 1981).

Marijuana may also have negative effects on consciousness: it can heighten unpleasant emotions. If a user is anxious or depressed, the drug may intensify the mood to the point of acute anxiety and paranoia. The person may become convinced that he or she is ill, dying, or going insane. This effect is most likely to befall an inexperienced user who takes an extremely heavy dose and is unprepared for its effects (Grinspoon, 1977).

Studies have shown that reaction time, attention, time estimation, motor coordination, and driving skills are generally impaired by marijuana. Yet the experienced user appears to be able to "come down" when necessary to carry out a task (Grinspoon, 1977). Perhaps the most consistent finding is that marijuana interferes with some aspects of memory. While on a marijuana high, users may be unable to recall information from memory, to store information for later recall, or to remember information presented only a few seconds earlier.

Marijuana does not appear to have permanent effects on cognition. In a study of ten Americans who had been extremely heavy users for seven years, no long-term cognitive effects were found (Schaeffer, Andrysiak, and Ungerleider, 1981). The users' IQ scores, taken as a measure of their intellectual functioning, were virtually identical with their IQ scores on tests taken fifteen to twenty years earlier. In other respects, however, long-term use may be damaging (Institute of Medicine, 1982). First, heavy, prolonged marijuana use may harm the lungs, leading to lung cancer. Second, marijuana seems to have a mild, temporary effect on the body's immune system, so that users might be more susceptible to infection. Third, some heavy users develop an amotivational syndrome, characterized by apathy, loss of ambition, and difficulty in concentrating. But there is some indication that the syndrome is primarily an accentuation of preexisting behavior patterns (Maugh, 1982).

Stimulants

STIMULANT any drug that stimulates the central nervous system by changing brain chemistry to speed physiological and mental activity

As their name suggests, **stimulants** act to stimulate the central nervous system. Depending on the dosage, they can also significantly increase heart rate, blood pressure, and muscle tension. The heart contracts more strongly, blood vessels constrict, and bronchial tubes and the pupils of the eyes dilate, and the adrenal glands go into action (Combs, Hales, and Williams, 1980). The major stimulants used to alter consciousness are nicotine, caffeine, cocaine, and amphetamines.

MILD STIMULANTS: NICOTINE AND CAFFEINE The most common method of nicotine use is cigarette, cigar, and pipe smoking. Studies indicate that smoking neither calms smokers nor elevates their moods (Schachter, 1978). On tests of performance, smokers do no better than nonsmokers, but when they stop smoking and their blood nicotine level sags, they perform much worse than nonsmokers. The primary reason for continued smoking may be the avoidance of withdrawal symptoms. Smokers become so dependent on nicotine that many people find smoking extremely difficult to give up. The major psychological effects of nicotine are felt during withdrawal. They include irritability, headaches, anxiety, tension, restlessness, and an inability to concentrate.

Caffeine, another central nervous system stimulant, is found in tea, soft drinks, chocolate, and cocoa, but the most common source is coffee. Unlike many recreational drugs, caffeine is associated with more energized work. Since it increases alertness and speeds reaction time, most users feel that it improves their daily performance. But more than 250 mg (the caffeine content of about two cups of coffee) may cause restlessness, irritability, muscle twitching, an irregular heartbeat, and sleep disturbance. Abrupt withdrawal from caffeine is often followed by headaches and depression.

Once regarded by many people as a recreational stimulant, cocaine is now recognized as a hazardous, potentially lethal substance.

INTENSE STIMULANTS: COCAINE AND AMPHETAMINES Cocaine is the most powerful known natural stimulant. One study found that 40 percent of twenty-seven-year-olds have tried it at some time in their lives (Kozel and Adams, 1986). About 8 minutes after cocaine is snorted, it produces a rush of euphoria that lasts for about 20 minutes. When it is smoked in the form of crack (rock-like pieces of concentrated cocaine), it produces an immediate, much more intense rush that wears off within a few minutes. Cocaine users claim that the drug improves attention, reaction time, memory, and speed on simple mental tasks. They find it helpful for work that requires alertness and a free flow of associations. Yet because of their euphoria, people who have taken cocaine often overestimate both their own capacities and the quality of their work. The burst of energy that characterizes the cocaine high is generally followed by physical exhaustion, anxiety, and depression when the drug wears off (Resnick, Kestenbaum, and Schwartz, 1977).

Large doses of cocaine may be followed by hallucinations. In severe cases, users have the sensation that bugs are crawling beneath their skin. This effect is probably caused by a drug-induced hyperactivity of nerves in the skin. Because cocaine blocks the reuptake of dopamine and norepinephrine, large doses can trigger symptoms similar to those of paranoid schizophrenia (see Chapters 3 and 18). Massive injections of cocaine may cause headaches, hyperventilation, nausea, convulsions, coma, and death. The deaths of basketball star Len Bias and comedian John Belushi provided widely publicized demonstrations of the lethal possibilities of cocaine overdose. Long-term use of cocaine can produce serious, permanent damage. Perhaps the most widely known effect of snorting cocaine is irreversible damage to the mucous membranes of the nasal septum, the membrane separating the nostrils; less well known is an increased susceptibility to heart attacks (Kozel and Adams, 1986).

Amphetamines, collectively known as "speed," are synthetic stimulants. Among the most common are Benzedrine, Dexedrine, and Methedrine. In moderate doses amphetamines produce feelings of euphoria and energy, increased alertness, and heightened reaction time and physical coordination. But they can also interfere with concentration, and their use is often accompanied by anxiety and irritability. When taken in massive doses, the drugs can cause "amphetamine psychosis," a condition with symptoms that strongly resemble those of paranoid schizophrenia (see Chapter 18). Amphetamine psychosis is characterized by fear and paranoid delusions, and it may include the compulsive repetition of trivial behavior. For example, one adolescent sufferer spent hours counting cornflakes (Snyder, 1979). As we saw in Chapter 3, amphetamines both promote the release of norepinephrine and dopamine into the synapses and prevent their reuptake, so that the levels of the two transmitters in the brain rise dramatically.

DEPRESSANT any drug that retards the action of the central nervous system by changing brain chemistry to slow physiological and mental activity

SYNERGISTIC combined action of drugs, in which the effect of two together is greater than the sum of the two drugs

Depressants

Depressants act on the central nervous system to reduce pain, tension, and anxiety, to relax and disinhibit behavior, and to slow intellectual and motor reactions. In small doses they produce intoxication and euphoria, but they also decrease alertness and motor coordination and slow reaction time. Large doses produce slurred speech, unsteadiness, and even loss of consciousness. The major depressants are alcohol, hypnotics such as barbiturates, tranquilizers such as Librium or Valium, and narcotics like heroin and morphine. When taken together, depressants are **synergistic**—that is, the effect of the two depressants is greater than the sum of each of the two drugs' effects. For example, if alcohol is drunk with a barbiturate, the effect is four times (not twice) as great as that of either of the drugs taken alone (Combs, Hales, and Williams, 1980).

ALCOHOL As people drink, the alcohol level of their blood rises, and effects of alcohol on behavior are related to the amount of alcohol in the bloodstream (see Table 6.2). In all fifty states, a blood alcohol level of 0.10 percent (that is, 0.10 milligrams of alcohol per 100 milliliters of blood) or more is considered evidence of intoxication.

At the level of brain chemistry, alcohol apparently affects several neurotransmitters in various ways in different parts of the brain. Researchers cannot explain all of alcohol's effects, but it seems to increase the supply of acetylcholine, decrease the supply of norepinephrine, and increase the tendency of neural receptor sites to lock onto GABA, another neurotransmitter. As we saw in Chapter 3, decreased levels of norepinephrine tend to make us feel depressed, while high levels of GABA inhibit neural firing.

Apart from the changes in brain chemistry, a drinker's expectations may determine many of the behavioral changes that accompany drinking. In fact, a drinker's expectations seem to have a more powerful effect on the release of inhi-

TABLE 6.2 Relationships among Sex, Weight, Oral Alcohol Consumption, and Blood Alcohol Level

ABSOLUTE ALCOHOL (OUNCES)	BEVERAGE INTAKE IN 1 HOUR	Blood Alcohol Levels (Milligrams of Alcohol per 100 Milliliters of Blood)					
		FEMALE (100 LBS.)	MALE (100 LBS.)	FEMALE (150 LBS.)	MALE (150 LBS.)	FEMALE (200 LBS.)	MALE (200 LBS.)
½	1 oz. spirits* 1 glass wine 1 can beer	0.045	0.037	0.03	0.025	0.022	0.019
1	2 oz. spirits 2 glasses wine 2 cans beer	0.09	0.075	0.06	0.05	0.045	0.037
2	4 oz. spirits 4 glasses wine 4 cans beer	0.18	0.15	0.12	0.10	0.09	0.07
3	6 oz. spirits 6 glasses wine 6 cans beer	0.27	0.22	0.18	0.15	0.13	0.11
4	8 oz. spirits 8 glasses wine 8 cans beer	0.36	0.30	0.24	0.20	0.18	0.15
5	10 oz. spirits 10 glasses wine 10 cans beer	0.45	0.37	0.30	0.25	0.22	0.18

*100-proof spirits.

Source: O. S. Ray (1983), *Drugs, society, and human behavior,* 3d ed. St. Louis: Mosby Company.

bitions than the amount of alcohol actually consumed. This is especially true with regard to sexual arousal, which seems primarily the result of expectations, not of alcohol itself (Hull and Bond, 1986). We *expect* a drink or two to ease social interactions, loosen our sexual inhibitions, and make us aggressive; and, indeed, many people find that alcohol has those effects. Research indicates that we respond in this manner primarily because we expect to, so that our beliefs about alcohol's effects both maintain such behavior and excuse it (Critchlow, 1986).

Some other effects of alcohol, however, such as poor motor coordination and sluggish reaction time, do not depend on our expectations. Because so many people drive after drinking, these effects can be dangerous, and the practice is responsible for the majority of fatal traffic accidents. For example, among 440 young men who were killed in traffic accidents in California, 70 percent had alcohol in their bloodstream at the time of the accident (Williams et al., 1985).

Long-term effects of alcohol on memory and information processing seem to depend on how much alcohol is usually consumed on single occasions, not on the total amount consumed over the years. People whose drinking patterns show heavy inebriation on widely separated occasions are more likely to show intellectual impairment than people who drink the same amount of alcohol but over longer periods of time (Parker and Noble, 1977). Apparently the brain can handle a drink each day better than it can handle seven drinks on one day followed by six days of abstinence. Sometimes drinkers have memory blackouts; that is, after they have sobered up they cannot remember what happened the night before. Drinkers are most likely to black out if they drink alcohol quickly, are extremely tired when they begin drinking, or take another depressant along with the alcohol (Loftus, 1980).

HYPNOTICS AND TRANQUILIZERS **Hypnotics,** or sleep-inducing drugs, are often taken to relieve insomnia. A class of powerful depressants are called barbiturates, and they are usually prescribed as sleeping pills (such as Nembutal and Seconal). Barbiturates, like other depressants, slow the arousal centers in the reticular activating system, thus inducing sleep. The chronic use of barbiturates is known to have many risks. The major hazard is the rapid development of tolerance, so that the user needs increasingly larger (and potentially lethal) doses to get the original sleep-inducing effect. Barbiturates are also strongly synergistic. Taken with alcohol, for example, the effect can be fatal. For this reason, most prescriptions for hypnotics are now written for nonbarbiturates, such as tranquilizers.

Minor tranquilizers and nonbarbiturate sedatives are used to treat symptoms of anxiety and stress as well as insomnia. Some of the more familiar tranquilizers are Tranxene, Librium, and Valium. The most frequently prescribed nonbarbiturate sedatives are Dalmane, Restoril, and Halcion. Tranquilizers and hypnotics have a number of negative side effects. Because they are central nervous system depressants, they can aggravate respiratory and cardiac disorders and can produce mild depression, impaired motor and intellectual functioning, and daytime sleepiness (Bootzin and Engle-Freidman, 1987).

Tranquilizers and barbiturates have similar effects on brain chemistry. Both, like alcohol, increase the amount of GABA that locks onto neural receptor sites and inhibits neural firing. Although tranquilizers combine with other depressants, they are less likely than barbiturates to be fatal when taken with alcohol or other depressants.

Ironically, chronic use of any of these hypnotics eventually makes insomnia worse. These depressants block REM sleep; as a result, when the insomniac tries to sleep without the drug, *REM rebound* occurs. The lengthy periods of REM lead to fitful sleep, filled with restless dreaming and nightmares. With this disrupted sleep pattern, the insomniac can neither sleep well with the drug nor feel able to sleep without it (Bootzin and Engle-Friedman, 1987).

NARCOTICS Narcotics can relieve pain and anxiety, as well as induce relaxation and reverie; many also produce a temporary state of euphoria. They appear to work on the spinal cord, the limbic system, and the cortex, where they mimic the action of neurotransmitters such as endorphins that are connected with pleasure and relief from pain (Schneider and Tarshis, 1986).

HYPNOTIC any depressant drug that induces sleep

Heroin is a highly addictive depressant that disrupts almost every aspect of the user's life.

Among illegal narcotics, heroin, a substance derived from the opium poppy, is the most widely used. Users either inject heroin directly beneath the skin (called *skin-popping*) or into the vein (*mainlining*). Mainlining brings an immediate rush of euphoria that lasts up to 15 minutes. Either method produces a state of satisfaction and well-being in which negative feelings of guilt, tension, and anxiety disappear. With regular use, the user becomes addicted to the drug and also requires increasingly larger doses. The addict's life becomes centered on obtaining money to buy more heroin in order to stave off the craving, anxiety, nausea, and other symptoms of withdrawal from the drug.

Methadone, a synthetic narcotic, is widely used in treatment programs for heroin addicts, because it satisfies the craving for heroin without producing a strong euphoria. Although users also become dependent on methadone, many addicts are able to live functional, productive lives while maintained on methadone.

Hallucinogens

HALLUCINOGEN any drug with the ability to produce hallucinations

The **hallucinogens**, which produce hallucinations, include LSD, mescaline, peyote, and psilocybin. As far as we can tell, hallucinogens have been used to alter consciousness since the beginning of recorded history (Schultes, 1976). Because some people believe that these drugs contain the potential for an expansion of human consciousness, they are sometimes called *psychedelic*, or *mind-manifesting*.

Natural hallucinogens are found in many common plants, including belladonna, henbane, mandrake, datura (Jimson weed), morning glory, peyote cactus, and some wild mushrooms. Synthetic hallucinogens include phencyclidine (PCP) and lysergic acid diethylamide (LSD). We know little about the precise effect of some hallucinogens, although all are known to interfere with information processing.

Mescaline, which comes from the peyote cactus, produces vivid hallucinations. Its effects were carefully described by British writer Aldous Huxley (1979), who believed that mescaline opened "the doors of perception." Huxley found that his visual perceptions were intensified while he was under the drug's influence.

One of the synthetic hallucinogens, PCP, or angel dust, may be taken by mouth, smoked along with marijuana, snorted, or injected. In low doses it produces hallucinations, but in large doses it can cause stupor, coma, or death. Even in low doses PCP has proved dangerous because the hallucinations sometimes lead the user to harm himself or herself or others.

The major hallucinogen, LSD, is one of the most powerful drugs known. Extensive studies have indicated that it is 4000 times stronger than mescaline. After taking an average dose (100 to 300 μg), the user embarks on a consciousness-altering "trip" that lasts from 6 to 14 hours.

An LSD trip is unpredictable because the setting in which the drug is taken and the user's initial mood, beliefs, and expectations have a powerful influence on the total experience. The drug affects mood, and the user may experience a series of intense mood changes. LSD may also have profound effects on visual and auditory perception. For most people, at first the hallucinations take the shape of simple geometric forms. These abstractions soon change to kaleidoscopic images and eventually to dreamlike, often bizarre scenes (Siegel, 1977). Perception may become so distorted that familiar objects are unrecognizable. A wall, for example, may seem to pulsate, breathe, or even melt. Sensory impressions may cross over (a state called *synesthesia*), with the user claiming to "see" sounds and "hear" sights. The self may seem to split into one being who observes and another who feels. Time may seem to speed up or stretch out interminably.

Some people may find the LSD experience mystical and feel that it has given them a harmonious, unified sense of consciousness. Other people find it a nightmare, because LSD can also produce extremely unpleasant side effects. The most unsettling are panic reactions, which can be terrifying. Panic usually develops among users who try to shake off the sensations produced by the drug but discover that it is impossible to do so. When the panic is severe, medical attention may be required. Another unpredictable aspect of LSD is the possibility of *flashbacks*—sudden recurrences of the perceptual distortions and other effects of the drug months or years after a dose was last taken.

We know more about LSD's effect on brain chemistry than that of some other hallucinogens, but we are still not certain exactly how these effects are connected with behavior. LSD's hallucinogenic power apparently comes from its resemblance to serotonin, a neurotransmitter that plays an important role in the regulation of sleep and emotions. LSD blocks the effect of serotonin on brain tissue, perhaps by mimicking the neurotransmitter at the neural receptors. Low levels of serotonin have been associated with severe depression and with insomnia, and serotonin has also been linked with heightened sensory states (Schneider and Tarshis, 1986).

Psychologists' attempts to study consciousness indicate that the mind is much more complicated than our waking experience would indicate. Consciousness is somehow different from information processing, because the various cognitive functions, such as perception, memory, and problem solving, can take place outside of our awareness (Kihlstrom, 1987). There seem to be several levels to consciousness, although researchers disagree as to whether the levels exist horizontally (in higher and lower depths) or vertically (as parallel processes) (E. Hilgard, 1978). Gazzaniga (1985, 1988), who is convinced that the levels are parallel, believes that we often have access to the products of these other states, but not to the processes themselves. More goes on outside our awareness than we once realized, but only when new methods of studying consciousness were developed did we begin to realize how much of our potential may reside in altered states of consciousness.

SUMMARY

The Nature of Consciousness

- Consciousness is both subjective and objective.
- Subjective consciousness includes one's personal experience of a unified world and self-awareness.
- Objective consciousness includes aspects of consciousness that can be verified by others.
- Some neuroscientists regard consciousness as the sum total of brain activity; others believe brain activity is necessary for consciousness to emerge.
- In addition to normal awake alertness, the levels of consciousness include automatic, practiced operations, the subconscious, the preconscious, and the unconscious.

Natural States of Consciousness

- Fantasy is a natural state of consciousness that includes daydreams (realistic or autistic fantasy), reverie, and hypnogogic and hypnopompic images.
- Sleep is a radically altered state of consciousness in which the body selectively monitors the environment.
- The ultradian sleep cycle, which lasts about 90 minutes, contains two major sleep states: REM and NREM sleep, with NREM sleep progressing through four stages.
- Sleep may have both evolutionary and restorative functions. Although the precise function of REM sleep is unclear, such sleep may stimulate the growth and maintenance of neural tissue.
- Dreams are the content of consciousness during REM sleep.
- Freud believed that dreams came from the unconscious and reflected repressed desires.

- Many researchers today regard dreams as either (1) the predictable result of a physiological process, in which the mind tries to explain the random stimulation it receives; (2) an "unlearning" process, in which inappropriate responses are erased to protect the brain from overload; (3) a nocturnal version of the same process that integrates perceptions during waking hours; or (4) a problem-solving activity.

Altered States of Consciousness

- Meditation, which can produce relaxation or heightened spirituality, refocuses attention to enter inner consciousness.
- Hypnosis is different from sleep, both physiologically and behaviorally.
- Hypnotized people are highly suggestible and may respond with altered perceptions, memories, or voluntary actions after hypnosis.
- Generally, people highly susceptible to hypnosis tend to have highly developed imaginative capacities.
- According to dissociation theory, hypnosis is an altered state, in which consciousness is split; according to role enactment theory, hypnosis is simply an extreme example of role-playing.
- Psychoactive drugs alter consciousness by interacting with the central nervous system to change mood, perception, and behavior. They affect the brain's chemistry.
- Marijuana seems to enhance sensory stimuli and heighten both pleasant and unpleasant sensations; it impairs reaction time and motor coordination and interferes with some aspects of memory.

- Stimulants in small doses (including nicotine, caffeine, cocaine, and amphetamines) increase alertness and speed reaction time.
- Large doses of intense stimulants, such as cocaine and amphetamines, produce feelings of euphoria beside symptoms of paranoid schizophrenia and sometimes death. Withdrawal results in irritability, anxiety, and depression.
- Depressants (including alcohol, hypnotics, tranquilizers, and narcotics) slow activity in the central nervous system, reducing pain, tension, and anxiety. In small doses they release inhibitions and produce euphoria, but in large doses they result in unsteadiness and unconsciousness, and sometimes death.
- Hallucinogens such as mescaline, PCP, and LSD, produce hallucinations and profound mood changes.

KEY TERMS

autistic fantasy
circadian rhythm
cocktail party phenomenon
consciousness
depressant
dichotic listening
dissociation theory
hallucinogen
hypnogogic image
hypnopompic image
hypnosis
hypnotic

implicit memory
insomnia
latent content
lucid dream
manifest content
meditation
neodissociation theory
NREM (or non-REM) sleep
polysomnography
posthypnotic amnesia
posthypnotic suggestion

preconscious
psychoactive drug
realistic fantasy
REM (rapid eye movement) sleep
reverie
role enactment theory
stimulant
subconscious
synergistic
ultradian rhythm
unconscious

CONCEPT REVIEW

1. Define *consciousness*. What are the four separate phenomena related to consciousness?

2. Describe the evidence for identifying brain processes and consciousness. Why is evidence from split-brain patients so important for understanding consciousness?

3. In addition to conscious awareness, the chapter identifies three other levels of consciousness. Name and describe these levels. What are some examples of behavior that illustrate conscious activity at each level?

4. What is the importance of our ability to fantasize—that is, to create alternate forms of reality? Give some examples of fantasy and daydreaming.

5. Outline the stages of sleep. What occurs in each stage?

6. REM sleep is perhaps the most thoroughly investigated aspect of sleep. What is its importance, and what theories attempt to explain its relationship to dreaming?

7. Describe the various theories regarding the functions of dreaming.

8. Define *altered states of consciousness*. Is meditation a true altered state? Why or why not?

9. What is hypnotic susceptibility? How do the different theories of hypnosis account for how hypnosis works? Describe the evidence both for and against hypnosis as an altered state.

10. What effects must a drug have in order to be classified as psychoactive? Name the classes of psychoactive drugs and describe the effects of each.

CRITICAL THINKING

1. How would each of the five perspectives in psychology that are described in Chapter 1 account for consciousness?

2. Dreams and hypnosis are two of the more intriguing phenomena in psychology because they touch upon highly personal aspects of our lives. Describe the similarities between these two phenomena and the similarities (if any) between theories that account for their occurrence. How does the scientific approach to dreams and hypnosis challenge your personal views about them?

PART THREE

Learning, Thinking, and Communicating

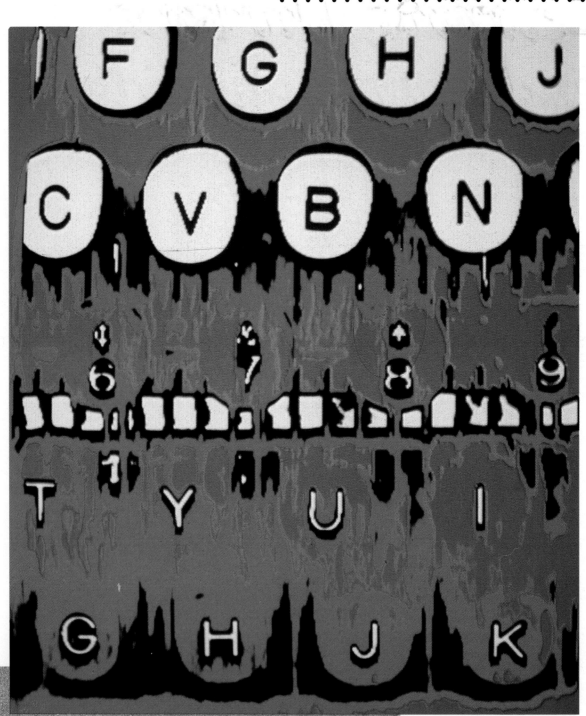

... *Learning*

For most of us the topic of learning brings to mind a classroom, whether elementary, high school, or college; books like this one or an early reader; lectures, biology labs, or the three Rs; practice in long division or library research on the forest peoples of Africa. But learning encompasses far more than formal education. Indeed, it permeates every aspect of life, and not just human life at that. To a greater or a lesser degree, all animals learn. Simple invertebrates live largely by genetically programmed reflexes, which prepare them to behave in given ways. But the more complex an organism, the less it depends on innate responses and the more it must rely on learning in order to adapt rapidly and appropriately to changing conditions. This means that the more capable of learning an organism is, the more adaptable it is and the more environments it can inhabit—as with humans, who populate the globe.

Though traditionally they are studied separately, the topics addressed in this unit's chapters are intimately related. The link between learning and memory is obvious; cognition and language both presuppose learning and memory; and intelligence is typically assessed by measuring our learning, memory, thinking, and language abilities. No matter what area of psychology we consider, learning plays a central role. Learning even seems to have a physiological effect: for example, animals raised in enriched environments—which promote exploration—tend to have more synaptic connections in their brains and are prepared to learn more readily than others (Rosenzweig and Leiman, 1989).

Outside the schoolroom or the lecture hall, we can find innumerable instances of learning going on. If you get a stomach ache after eating oysters for the first time, you probably will not particularly want to go near them again: you have "learned" by simple association that, as far as you are concerned, oysters are linked with stomach upset. An abused child learns that withdrawal or abuse of others is an acceptable way, or perhaps the only way, to deal with fear, anger, or frustration. Many of us learn what later in life appear to be inappropriate, unhealthy, or destructive behaviors and emotional reactions—overeating, worrying about achievement, excessive shyness—and some of us will have to spend time at some point learning more appropriate behaviors, through psychotherapy, others' guidance, or self-scrutiny. All through life we observe other people at school, in offices, at parties, at theaters, at funerals, or in street fights and take in how the society around us expects us to behave in those situations. With help an autistic child, so painfully removed from normal life, can learn to play, to relate to people, and to speak. Chimpanzees and dolphins are taught to understand human commands and to communicate back to humans. Whether or not they have learned what humans consider a language (a topic we take up in Chapter 10), it is clear that the chimps and dolphins have learned a limited form of communication.

Psychology's exploration of learning in both animals and humans has, among other things, given us insights into daily life; has enhanced formal education in a number of ways, from computer-assisted learning to reward systems that motivate children to set goals in writing term papers; and has formed the basis of therapies that help to free people with phobias from their terrors.

WHAT IS LEARNING? DEFINITIONS AND PERSPECTIVES

Learning comes about through experience. In fact, we can think of learning as the process that underlies the nurture side of the nature–nurture interaction. But is it an outward change in actual behavior, or an inward change in knowledge, or both?

Historically, as we saw in Chapter 1, behaviorists and cognitive psychologists have answered this question differently. Behaviorists have thought of learning as changes in observable behavior caused by environmental events. This goes along with behaviorism's central tenet: learning is to be characterized *only* in terms of the organism's history of external events and responses to those events; in this view, future behavior can be brought about by controlling the environmental events that produce the learning of that kind of behavior.

Cognitive psychologists are more likely to describe learning in terms of changes in internal mental processes and knowledge. In this view, overt behavior *(performance)* is the result of processes that include perceiving stimuli, retrieving appropriate knowledge, anticipating events, and behaving accordingly (see Mackintosh, 1983; Pearce, 1987; Roitblat, 1987). Thus, performance is considered only one indicator of an organism's knowledge brought about by learning. Although a cognitive view of learning has been available since the days of Edward Tolman (1932), it was overshadowed for decades by the behaviorist framework. Over the past few years, however, an increasing number of learning researchers have adopted the cognitive perspective. Despite disagreements over the appropriate theory, the fundamental facts and principles of learning have been established with contributions from many types of psychologists and approaches.

How then can we define learning so that the different approaches can be accommodated, at least to some degree? We can state that **learning** refers to a long-lasting change in an organism's disposition to behave in certain ways as a result of experience. This definition excludes any changes caused by maturation or by temporary states like fatigue, illness, or drug use. The stipulation that learning involves a *disposition* allows for the possibility that what is learned is not necessarily exhibited in behavior: for instance, a liar is clearly *not* revealing what he or she has learned. Defining learning as a "change in disposition to behave" also makes clear that, for the most part, we cannot observe learning directly. Instead, learning must be *inferred* from performance.

In order to encompass the broad range of learning, psychologists have divided it into several types, each of which we will consider in this chapter. There is habituation, a simple type of learning that we will cover quite briefly; associative learning, or the learning of temporal (and/or causal) sequences, which includes the two kinds of conditioning, classical and instrumental, and covers such diverse topics as punishment and skill learning; spatial learning, focusing on our understanding of the location of objects in space and our own orientation in the physical environment; and observational learning, an area that illustrates the coming together of the behavioral and cognitive points of view.

LEARNING   a long-lasting change in an organism's disposition to behave in certain ways as a result of experience

HABITUATION

Habituation is the simplest form of learning; it refers to an organism becoming familiar with a particular stimulus. Habituation occurs when there is a decrease in the strength of a response after a stimulus has been presented consistently, either in one prolonged stretch or briefly and repeatedly. Before habituation, each time an organism encounters a new or unexpected object, there is a "surprise reaction," known as the **orienting reflex** (Sokolov, 1963). The reflex is one of physiological arousal (a topic we look at closely in Chapter 12). In humans the eyebrows lift slightly, the eyes widen, the heart beats faster, the muscles become slightly tense, the skin resistance drops, and a recording of brain waves would show a typical arousal pattern. After habituation, the same object causes no such reflex.

Habituation appears in even the simplest organisms. For example, when a sea snail's gill is touched, the gill withdraws reflexively; if the touch is repeated, after about the tenth prod the snail habituates and stops withdrawing the gill (Kandel, 1979). The same mechanism appears in us. The first time a young child sees the family's new dog, for instance, she may squeal loudly with delight or pull away in fear. Eventually, with daily exposure, the novelty wears off, the child establishes a dependable relationship with the dog, and she no longer reacts to the dog as a novel surprise.

Like sensory adaptation, which we described in Chapter 4, habituation is an adaptive physiological process that allows an organism's attention to shift to more important or threatening information. Whereas sensory adaptation might be defined as neuron fatigue, habituation can be compared to becoming a little bored.

HABITUATION   a simple form of learning in which the response to a stimulus decreases after lengthy or repeated presentation; similar to "boredom"

ORIENTING REFLEX   a physiological reaction of "surprise" or arousal to a novel stimulus

Habituation—familiarity—is the basis for a small child's relationship with the family pet.

As in other cases of boredom, as soon as a prominent feature of the stimulus changes, the organism once again reacts with a full orienting reflex; however, habituation to this "revised" stimulus will be much quicker this time. An organism's ability to detect changes in a familiar stimulus indicates that the brain continues to monitor habituated stimuli at a low level and will react with full attention if some change occurs.

Habituation has often been used successfully to do research on learning in very young infants, because no "instructions" are required. Babies will look at any new visual stimulus; as the stimulus is repeated, however, they eventually habituate and spend less time gazing at it (Olson, 1984). Any significant change in the stimulus causes babies to orient toward it once more. Used in this way, habituation studies allow researchers to infer which changes babies notice and consider significant.

Habituation studies have been used to show that infants can learn to categorize visual patterns by ten months of age. Psychologists Barbara Younger and Leslie Cohen (1985) showed ten-month-old infants about a dozen drawings of fictitious animals that paired different features, such as feet, tails, and heads, with certain body shapes. After seeing the initial stimuli for some time, the infants when tested spent little time looking at (were "bored" by) drawings of new animals that maintained familiar pairings, but looked a lot at (were "surprised" by) drawings that violated the familiar pairings of the initial stimuli. The surprise caused by the unfamiliar pairings indicates that the babies had learned—become habituated to—and remembered the "normal" pairings. They could also, it seemed, categorize patterns at this surprisingly young age (Strauss, 1979; Younger and Cohen, 1983).

CLASSICAL CONDITIONING

ASSOCIATIVE LEARNING
learning a correlation between two events

The ability to grasp temporal (time) sequences—winter follows fall, night follows day, B follows A, pain follows touching a hot stove, a class begins after the ringing of a bell—is a central feature of learning. Both classical and instrumental conditioning are types of **associative learning**—that is, both involve association of temporal sequences. Association of one external event with another in a temporal sequence, so that the first event becomes a signal for the second, is the core of classical conditioning.* As we mentioned in Chapter 2, classical conditioning was first systematically studied by Ivan Pavlov early in this century.

Pavlov's Dogs and What They Taught Us

CLASSICAL CONDITIONING the form of learning in which two stimuli are associated so that the first evokes the response that normally follows the second; also called Pavlovian conditioning

Pavlov (1927), a Russian physiologist who won the Nobel prize in 1909 for his work on digestion, noticed that the dogs in his laboratory salivated not only when they ate food but also as soon as it was placed in front of them, before they had taken a bite. By experimenting, Pavlov discovered that if he regularly rang a bell just before he let the dogs eat, they eventually began salivating each time the bell sounded, as though they had learned to anticipate the food (see Figure 7.1).

Pavlov's experimental arrangement is called **classical conditioning** (sometimes called *Pavlovian*, or *respondent, conditioning*); the organism learns to associate two specific kinds of stimuli in a temporal series—in this case, first the bell, then food. Pavlov's dogs indicated their learning by several specific changes in behavior. Each ring of the bell set off a number of actions typical of dogs about to be fed: excitement, a run to the food bowl, ducking the head into the bowl, tail

---

* Of course, temporal sequences suggest causation between events—but not necessarily, as we saw from the discussion of correlation (a type of association) and causation in Chapter 2. We can *infer,* on the basis of certain kinds of evidence, that the first event causes the second. Conditioning is a primitive way for organisms to learn important causal regularities in their environment.

Figure 7.1 The apparatus used in early studies of classical conditioning. Saliva dropping from a tube inserted into the dog's cheek strikes a lightly balanced arm, and the resulting motion is transmitted hydraulically to a pen that traces a record on a slowly revolving drum. Pavlov's discovery of conditioned salivation was an accidental by-product of his researches into the activity of the digestive system.

wagging, chomping, lip smacking, and salivation. From this pattern of behaviors, Pavlov chose to record only one: salivation. This is important, because this particular response is reflexive—a dog has no voluntary control over salivation. Thus, what Pavlov decided to investigate was how the dogs learned through association to make a reflexive, involuntary response to a previously neutral stimulus, the bell.

Through conditioning, an insignificant stimulus (the bell) became highly significant to the hungry dogs (see Figure 7.2). In Pavlov's terminology, the food, which normally caused the dogs to salivate, was called the **unconditioned stimulus (UCS).** Salivation in response to food was called the **unconditioned response (UCR)** because it happened as an innate reflex, without conditioning; it did *not* have to be learned. During conditioning, a neutral stimulus, or **conditioned stimulus (CS),** was repeatedly paired with the UCS. In the case of Pavlov's dogs, the bell (CS) was rung just *before* presentation of the food (UCS) that normally evoked the salivation (UCR). Eventually, after repeated pairings, the dogs responded to the CS, the bell, in somewhat the same way they responded to the UCS, the food. This response (salivation) to the CS, which occurs in anticipation of the UCS (the food), was termed the **conditioned response (CR).**

You might be interested to know that college students have been conditioned by a very similar method; after a sound was repeatedly paired with eating potato chips and salted peanuts, the students came to salivate in response to the sound alone (Razran, 1939). In fact, since Pavlov conducted his experiments, researchers have discovered that all sorts of organisms can be conditioned to respond to all sorts of stimuli—such as lights, visual patterns, sounds, whistles, touches, tastes, odors, even internal bodily sensations—by associating them with various UCS's—such as heat, water, electric shock, puffs of air, and drugs that induce nausea or euphoria (Bykov, 1927; Pavlov, 1927; Bower and Hilgard, 1981).

Many of our emotional reactions may be the result of classical conditioning. In particular, seemingly irrational fears are likely to have been conditioned. Early evidence for this statement came from a famous experiment performed by behaviorists John Watson and Rosalie Raynor (1920), in which an eleven-month-old baby named Albert was conditioned to fear a tame white rat. Before the conditioning, Albert enjoyed playing with the rat. One day, as Albert began to touch the rat, Watson hit a steel bar with a metal hammer just behind the baby. Albert's reaction to the loud noise was a fearful startle (the UCR), which then became associated with the rat (the CS). Later, when the rat (without any loud noise) was presented, Albert reacted with fear (the CR), crying and trying to get away from it. He also showed a similar fear when he encountered other formerly neutral objects that resembled the rat—a rabbit, a fur coat, cotton balls, and a white-

UNCONDITIONED STIMULUS (UCS) a stimulus that evokes a response innately, not dependent upon prior learning

UNCONDITIONED RESPONSE (UCR) an unlearned or innate response to a stimulus

CONDITIONED STIMULUS (CS) a formerly neutral stimulus that, through association, evokes a response normally evoked by the UCS in classical conditioning

CONDITIONED RESPONSE (CR) a response that, through association, is evoked by the CS in anticipation of the UCS in classical conditioning

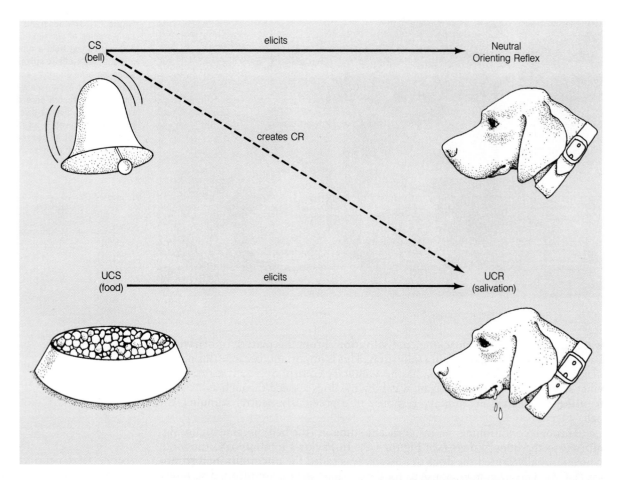

Figure 7.2 The creation of a conditioned response (CR). At first, the ringing bell (CS) elicits only a neutral orienting reflex. Then the bell is paired with food, which elicits an innate, or unconditioned, reflex of salivation (UCR). With repeated pairings, the CS comes to elicit salivation when presented by itself: the subject's expectation of the food, created by the ringing of the bell, causes salivation.

bearded Santa Claus mask. (This experiment was later widely criticized on ethical grounds.) In the same way, a car accident can teach one to fear driving or to fear cars in general; from a bad fall from a horse, one can learn fear of horses. And horror films rely to some degree on the ability of stock conditioned stimuli—like the dark, windy night, the creaking door, eerie music, and the howl of a wolf—to provoke the conditioned response, fear.

Other emotional reactions—like anger, disgust, and sexual attraction and arousal—may also be classically conditioned. Boxers, for example, deliberately use visualizations that arouse anger and trigger their sympathetic nervous systems so that they can be "psyched up" and ready to fight when they enter the ring. And sexual fantasies and pornography are full of conditioned stimuli—all those movements, sounds, words, objects, perhaps even a type of music that we have learned to associate with arousal and that can thus often arouse us on their own.

Classical conditioning can also be used to "unlearn" or reverse habits, fears, and other reactions. One example is the behavior therapy used routinely to cure bedwetting (Mowrer and Mowrer, 1938; Azrin and Foxx, 1974). The child sleeps on a special pad that sounds a loud buzzer the moment it detects a drop of urine. The buzzer wakes the child, who then goes to the bathroom. Pressure from the child's full bladder comes to be associated with the buzzer (the UCS), which awakens the child from sleep (the CR), so that the child soon wakes simply to the cue of a full bladder, *before* wetting the bed. Even though bladder pressure occurs naturally, it is the CS here because originally it does *not* wake the child. The buzzer is the UCS because the child does not have to learn to wake up when the buzzer sounds; it directly causes awakening.

Principles of Classical Conditioning

Classical conditioning has been intensively studied as an elementary example of associative learning. Although results vary to some extent, depending on the species studied and the exact stimuli and responses used, many regularities hold across studies and species: acquisition, second-order conditioning, extinction, recovery, reconditioning, generalization, and discrimination. We will examine these regularities in different phases of a classical-conditioning experiment.

Acquisition

The process by which an organism learns an association in classical conditioning is known as **acquisition,** and it follows a typical learning curve like the one shown in Figure 7.3. The conditioned stimulus (CS) and unconditioned stimulus (UCS) are paired; the experimenter waits a short time, then presents the CS–UCS pairing again. Each pairing is called a trial. As the CS and the UCS are repeatedly paired, the animal's (or person's) response to the CS generally becomes stronger and quicker, as the subject's anticipation of the UCS becomes stronger. Generally, conditioning proceeds most efficiently when the UCS follows the CS after a very brief interval. The optimal interval for conditioning varies depending on the species, the responses involved, and the time lapses between trials, but it usually ranges from one-fourth of a second to 20 seconds (Mackintosh, 1983). (Longer intervals may be less effective simply because the organism is likely to attend to other stimuli before the UCS occurs.) As we will see a little later, however, there are exceptions and limitations to these general rules for acquisition of conditioned responses.

ACQUISITION the process by which an association is learned in classical, or operant, conditioning

Second-Order Conditioning and Social Attitudes

Once a conditioned stimulus has been established, it may in turn serve as an unconditioned stimulus for other neutral stimuli. A well-conditioned CS can be paired with a new neutral stimulus, which eventually becomes associated with the

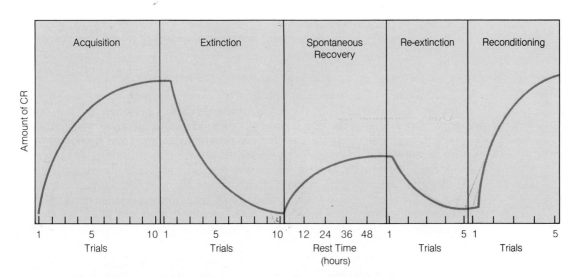

Figure 7.3 The process of classical conditioning, showing the *acquisition* of a conditioned response when the UCS and CS are repeatedly paired; the *extinction* of the conditioned response when the CS is consistently repeated without the UCS; the *spontaneous recovery* of an extinguished conditioned response when the subject is returned to the experimental situation after a rest of several hours; the *reextinction* of the response when the CS is again presented but is not paired with the UCS; and the rapid recovery of the conditioned response, or *reconditioning*, when the CS is again paired with the UCS.

SECOND-ORDER CONDITION-ING the form of learning in which a conditioned stimulus becomes associated with a second neutral stimulus that precedes it, which then evokes the conditioned response itself

EXTINCTION the gradual decline and disappearance of a conditioned response when it no longer is reinforced

SPONTANEOUS RECOVERY the reappearance of an extinguished response upon returning to the familiar situation and the conditioned stimulus

same conditioned response (CR) as the initial CS. For example, if Pavlov's bell, to which a dog is already conditioned, is repeatedly paired with a *second* neutral stimulus (say a flashing light), the second stimulus becomes associated with the first (the bell), and the new CS (the light) soon begins to elicit the CR (salivation) by itself. This sort of chain reaction is known as **second-order conditioning.**

Psychologist Arthur Staats (1967; 1968) has proposed that second-order conditioning may underlie the formation of some social attitudes and prejudices. Staats has suggested that when we hear the names of ethnic, racial, or religious groups consistently paired with either pleasant or unpleasant words, we come to associate the emotional meaning of the words with the groups. In one study (Staats and Staats, 1958), college students repeated words spoken by the researcher as they watched the names of national groups flashed on a screen. Some groups were always associated with pleasant words (Dutch = gift, sacred, happy), others with unpleasant words (Swedish = bitter, ugly, failure). When the students later rated the nationalities, their ratings mirrored the emotional quality of the words that had been associated with them. According to Staats (1967; 1968), we may very well hear people of a particular ethnic group called dirty, disgusting, criminal, lazy, or stupid and form a negative attitude toward that group without ever having met any member of it. The formation of attitudes is undoubtedly more complicated than this, as we see in Chapter 21. Nevertheless, second-order conditioning of emotional reactions probably does play some role in attitude formation.

Extinction, Recovery, and Reconditioning

Learning is by definition adaptive. If conditions change, learned responses should change as well if they are to remain adaptive. If an unconditioned stimulus no longer follows the conditioned stimulus—as when the dog no longer is fed after the bell rings—the organism's conditioned response gradually becomes weaker and eventually is *extinguished*. This process is known as **extinction** (see Figure 7.3).

Extinction has to do with dissociating two stimuli—with experiencing one stimuli *without* the other and with breaking their temporal sequence. Psychologists often tell of a door-to-door salesman who rang a customer's doorbell when the kitchen happened to be filled with escaped gas. The spark from the doorbell ignited the gas and the house blew up. Afterward, whenever the salesman pressed a doorbell, he felt a sinking, clammy fear. But he persisted and eventually, after he had pressed many doorbells without blowing up another house, his fear was extinguished.

The process of extinction is often used by behavior therapists to help people overcome *phobias,* or irrational fears, such as the fear of flying or of snakes and spiders (Wolpe, 1958; Rachman, 1978). One extinction technique is known as *systematic desensitization.* In the safety of the therapist's presence, the person is exposed repeatedly to the feared object or situation or to pictures or mental images of it, beginning with the least anxiety-provoking element and working up to more fearful ones. If whatever the person fears (snakebite, disaster, or even the panic itself) repeatedly fails to occur, the fear will be gradually extinguished.

Another extinction technique often used in therapy for phobias is called *flooding:* the phobic person is encouraged to remain in the presence of the feared stimulus despite the overwhelming flood of terror (Wilson and O'Leary, 1980). For example, a man with an intense fear of spiders might be required to sit still as spiders crawl on him. Although he feels terrified, the terror and arousal soon "fatigue" and begin to wane. At this point the person is experiencing the spiders without having much fear, so the extinction process begins. (Systematic desensitization, flooding, and other therapies based on extinction are discussed in more detail in Chapter 19.)

If, several hours or days after a CR has been extinguished, an organism is returned to the experimental situation and is again exposed to the CS, the CR will reappear, though not as strongly as it once did. This recurrence of the CR after a lapse of time is called **spontaneous recovery.** For example, suppose we have extinguished Pavlov's dog's conditioned salivation by ringing the bell again and

Principles of classical conditioning explain why the pairing of cigarettes and coffee make it harder for a person to give up either one.

again without feeding the dog until the animal no longer salivates at the sound of the bell. The next day we bring the dog back into the lab and ring the bell again: the dog will salivate somewhat. Spontaneous recovery is a bit like forgetting, but in reverse: the animal forgets that it has just learned to stop anticipating food when the bell sounds.

As Figure 7.3 shows, the longer the rest interval between the end of the extinction period and the next test of the CS, the stronger the initial recovery of the CR. But after another period of extinction and a lapse of time, the next spontaneous recovery will be weaker than the initial reappearance. With repeated reextinction periods, the CR will eventually be completely eliminated. The organism—dog, rat, or human—apparently learns that one event will *not* follow another. However, after complete extinction, if the UCS is once again paired with the old CS, the extinguished response will be quickly *relearned*. This relearning of a conditioned then extinguished response is called **reconditioning.**

Spontaneous recovery and the ease of reconditioning provide eloquent testimony to the strong, long-lasting effects of classical conditioning. They can also present problems for recovering drug addicts and smokers. Many smokers, for example, learn to crave a cigarette whenever they drink coffee because of the repeated social pairings of cigarettes and coffee. For several weeks after having stopped smoking, a recovering smoker may drink a cup of coffee and again feel the old urge for a cigarette—a case of spontaneous recovery (Guthrie, 1952; O'Leary and Wilson, 1975). If the smoker gives in and has a cigarette with the coffee, rapid reconditioning is likely: the ex-smoker can quickly become a habitual smoker again, as many smokers will testify.

RECONDITIONING   the relearning of a conditioned then extinguished response

Generalization and Discrimination

Once an organism has been conditioned to respond to a specific stimulus, other similar stimuli or situations may elicit the same response. This process is called **stimulus generalization.** Stimulus generalization is adaptive because under normal circumstances no two situations or stimuli are exactly alike. Without generalization, to cite an extreme example, a pedestrian who has learned to get out of the way of a Ford might stand still and be run over by a Buick. Stimulus generalization may sound close to second-order conditioning, but there is an important difference. In second-order conditioning a second CS regularly precedes and becomes associated with the initial CS, and the two are typically very different; generalization is based on transfer of an association between similar stimuli. Gen-

STIMULUS GENERALIZATION the tendency for a conditioned response to be evoked by similar stimuli or situations

eralization allows us to transfer what we have learned in one situation to another that is like it in some way.

Generalization is as common among human beings as it is in all other species. If you have an extremely warm relationship with an aunt, for example, you may find that your affection extends to people who resemble her. You may begin your acquaintance with such people already expecting to like them simply because they look like your aunt.

To be adaptable, an organism must have some way not only of recognizing similarities among stimuli but also of perceiving differences—of distinguishing among stimuli. These opposing processes, generalization and discrimination, allow an organism to adjust and fine-tune its responses to the world. **Discrimination** is the process by which an organism learns to distinguish among stimuli and to respond differently to each. A dog quickly learns to discriminate its owner's whistle (which is followed by dinner, an unconditioned stimulus) from the whistles of others who don't feed it. When its owner whistles (conditioned stimulus) the dog runs to its food dish; when a stranger whistles, the dog learns to ignore the sound. In discrimination training, the UCS is regularly presented after one particular (conditioned) stimulus but not after presentation of other, similar stimuli. As you can see, discrimination training mixes conditioning and extinction trials in alternation. The organism learns to respond only to the stimulus paired with the UCS and not to any similar stimuli.

DISCRIMINATION the process by which an organism learns to distinguish among stimuli and to respond differently to each

Critical Factors in Classical Conditioning

Over the years, researchers have attempted to identify as specifically as possible which factors affect conditioning and in what ways. What is the optimal situation for conditioning? Under what circumstances will an organism learn a response quickly? Under what circumstance is a response likely to be weak? to be strong? When is an organism *not* likely to learn?

As stated earlier, in general, a conditioned response is likely to be strong when the CS precedes the UCS and the interval between them is quite brief. Other conditions that affect the strength of the CR are the strengths of the CS and the UCS and the similarity between the two stimuli (Mackintosh, 1983). Researchers have further narrowed down optimal conditions and have proposed more detailed explanations of how and why conditioning occurs.

Information Value of the Conditioned Stimulus

Researchers once believed that conditioning was a simple, mechanical—almost inevitable—result of pairing a neutral conditioned stimulus with an unconditioned stimulus. They have now concluded, however, that it is not enough simply to pair a CS with a UCS. Indeed, in some cases they have found that a more cognitive orientation was needed to explain the results of experiments in conditioning.

One of the important findings is that the conditioned stimulus must have *information value:* it must communicate relevant information. The CS must serve as a signal or predictor of the unconditioned stimulus; but for that to happen, the *absence* of the CS must also predict the absence of the UCS (Kamin, 1969; Wagner, 1969). This factor became clear in a classic experiment by Robert Rescorla (1968), who found that conditioning was strongest when both of two conditions prevailed: the CS consistently preceded the UCS, *and* the UCS seldom occurred without the CS. Rescorla placed dogs in a restraining box, where they received a brief, mild shock every few minutes. Some dogs always heard a tone (CS) before they received the shock (UCS). Other dogs received the paired tone and shock just as often as dogs in the first group, but they also received shocks that were not preceded by the tone. When there was a high correlation between tone and shock (that is, when the tone was usually followed by a shock and shocks seldom if ever occurred without the signal of the tone), dogs quickly learned to associate the two. But when the correlation was low (that is, when the shock came nearly as often *without* the tone preceding it as with the tone preceding it), dogs gave little evidence of associating the tone and the shock. For these dogs, the tone was *not* informative enough; it did not enable them to predict when they would be shocked. Rescorla hypothesized that when a CS and a UCS are highly correlated, so that they are either both present or both absent, the organism *infers* a causal relationship from the consistent temporal relationship between the two stimuli.

Further experiments have shown that a correlation between a neutral stimulus and UCS, by itself, may not always lead to conditioning. In addition, the neutral stimulus must be a better predictor of the UCS than are other stimuli that are also present. If another stimulus presented along with the neutral stimulus already predicts the UCS, then the organism will not become conditioned to the neutral stimulus unless it adds information and enhances the predictability of the UCS's occurrence, amount, or quality.

This requirement that the neutral stimulus provide *new* information was first demonstrated by Leon Kamin (1969). Kamin first conditioned rats to associate a loud noise with a shock. Then he added a new, simultaneous stimulus to the noise: each time the noise was presented, a light went on over the rats' heads. Both stimuli ended several seconds later with an electric shock.

Did the rats learn to fear the light? After all, the light was now as highly correlated with the shock as was the noise. But Kamin discovered that, when tested with the light by itself, without any accompanying noise, the rats showed practically no fear. They had failed to associate the light with the shock. In contrast, Kamin's control group of rats experienced *only* the second phase of the experiment—simultaneous light-and-noise paired with shock. This group *did* become conditioned to *both* stimuli; either light or noise alone evoked the response.

In Kamin's experimental group, then, the initially conditioned noise had evidently *blocked* conditioning to the light. The process by which an organism fails to become conditioned to a second stimulus presented simultaneously with the initial CS thus became known as **blocking.** And what causes blocking? Here again, the most plausible explanation in the case of the first group of rats is that light provided no additional predictive information to that provided by the noise (Kamin, 1969; Rescorla and Wagner, 1972). When more than one cue signals a UCS, the more predictive cue tends to overshadow or even cancel out the less predictive one and comes to control the organism's expectations of the UCS. If a second stimulus is completely redundant with the first CS, it is in effect useless; because it adds no new information, conditioning to it is blocked.

BLOCKING the process by which an organism fails to become conditioned to a second redundant stimulus presented simultaneously with an initially, more valid CS

Biological Constraints on Conditioning

Certain biological limitations to and requirements for conditioning have also been found. Genetic factors play a role, since species seem to be genetically prepared to make some kinds of associations more readily than others. Biological preparedness to make certain types of associations apparently accounts for conditioning that occurs despite a lapse of hours between the CS and UCS. This is an exception to the general rule that the CS–UCS interval must be brief.

The idea of genetic preparedness was suggested by a series of classic experiments by John Garcia and his associates (Garcia and Koelling, 1966; Garcia, Ervin, and Koelling, 1966). In one of Garcia's experiments, thirsty rats were allowed to drink water from two different spouts. One spout delivered saccharine-sweetened water ("tasty water"). The other spout delivered plain water, with each lick on the spout setting off a clicking noise and a flashing light ("noisy-bright water"). The tasty water and the noisy-bright water both served as potential conditioned stimuli for a later unconditioned reaction.

After both drinking spouts were removed, some of the animals received shocks delivered through the wire floor of the cage; the others were given a heavy dose of x-rays that made them feel nauseated. The researchers wondered whether the rats would connect their fear or nausea (UCR) to the water, and if so, which kind of water (CS) would be associated with it. A few days later, the animals were given another chance to drink from the two spouts. Rats who had been shocked avoided the noisy-bright water but eagerly drank the tasty water; those who had been sick avoided the tasty water (their CR) but eagerly drank the noisy-bright water. The stimulus selected by an animal as a conditioned signal depended on the type of UCR—on whether the animal had been shocked externally or made sick internally.

According to Garcia, a rat's brain is programmed to connect taste with subsequent illness and to connect externally caused pain with sights or sounds. Such connections have probably been essential to the species' evolutionary survival. Rats forage at night and thus rely on taste and odor to identify safe, palatable food; sight and sound are more likely to identify potentially dangerous conditions or objects. Apparently, the sick rats in Garcia's study scanned their memories of food and drink and selected the unfamiliar taste of sweet water as the likely cause of their nausea. Rats can learn to associate illness with sights and sounds, but they make the association slowly and only after considerable training (Masur, 1986). The association between illness and an unfamiliar taste can develop after a single experience. Thus, what a species finds easy to learn may depend on the history of that species' adaptations in its typical environment (Masur, 1986).

In Garcia's later experiments, rats connected the novel taste of sweet water with their illness even when the delay between drinking the water (CS) and becoming sick (UCS) was as long as 24 hours (Revusky and Garcia, 1970). Such results refute the idea that conditioning could occur only when the delay between the CS and the UCS was brief. But the animal must be biologically prepared to make the necessary association. If, for example, the CS and UCS are not naturally connected, as with food or water and shock, animals may not make the association unless the UCS follows the CS within a matter of seconds (Klein, 1987).

Such taste-aversion conditioning has been put to practical use in preventing wolves and coyotes from killing lambs grazing on pastures in the American West. Farmers put out dead lambs poisoned with lithium chloride, which causes nausea and vomiting. After eating this prepared bait, coyotes develop an aversion to lambs, refusing not only to eat lamb meat but also to kill lambs. They retch and run away whenever a lamb comes near them (Gustavson et al., 1974; Garcia, Rusiniak, and Brett, 1977).

The conditioning of taste aversions in humans produces results similar to those Garcia found in rats. In one experiment children with cancer ate Mapletoff, a distinctively flavored ice cream, just before they received chemotherapy—a treatment which often causes nausea. Several months later, three-fourths of the children rejected the Mapletoff flavor, but among young cancer patients who had not received chemotherapy after eating ice cream, half preferred Mapletoff to another flavor (Bernstein, 1978). Similar taste aversions developed when the experiment was repeated with adult cancer patients (Bernstein and Webster, 1980).

Behavior therapists have used taste aversion to treat alcoholism. The alcoholic patient takes a nausea-inducing drug, with the dose timed so that illness and vomiting closely follow the drinking of alcohol. Thus, a drink results in immediate nausea, and the alcoholic is conditioned to avoid alcohol. About half the patients who go through this program, which involves four to six sessions, remain abstinent for at least four years (Nathan, 1976).

Physiological Aspects of Conditioning

Recently researchers have discovered that they can condition internal physiological responses like those of the immune system, which protects us from infection by manufacturing antibodies and white blood cells. In a now classic experiment, Robert Ader and Nicholas Cohen (1981) placed rats in a distinctive cage where they drank saccharine water before being injected with a mild poison that suppressed the immune system. After the animals' immune system had recovered, Ader and Cohen placed them back into the cage where they had drunk the sweetened water. Although the rats got no more of the poison, their immune responses again became suppressed. Using a similar procedure, other researchers have used the smell of camphor to stimulate the production of immune cells in mice, after first conditioning the mice to associate the odor with a UCS that increased the reactivity of their immune system (Eppinger and Horton, 1985). Such studies show that, contrary to traditional belief, psychological processes can influence the immune system, causing it to become either more or less responsive. This sort of research can help us understand how emotional stress, depression, and loneliness can depress our immune systems, causing health to deteriorate and increasing our vulnerability to illness and death (Justice, 1988).

What actually happens in the nervous system when classical conditioning takes place? Some studies indicate that the neural basis of most simple associative learning may be an increase in the efficiency of existing neural pathways (Hebb, 1949; Hawkins and Kandel, 1984; Hawkins and Bower, 1989). Others suggest that learning may also lead to the establishment of entirely new connections— either excitatory or inhibitory (see Chapter 3). If experience can alter the efficiency of synaptic chains or establish new connections, then a complex network of many synapses provides an organism with rich resources for learning about its environment and establishing effective ways of dealing with it.

INSTRUMENTAL CONDITIONING

In classical conditioning we learn the temporal relationship of two events—events we do not control. Pavlov's dog did not control the appearance of the food after the bell; it merely observed that consistent sequence of events. In contrast, in **instrumental conditioning** (also called **operant conditioning**) we learn an association between our own response and what follows it, its consequences. In this form of conditioning, our response *operates on* the environment and is *instrumental* in producing or affecting the consequences. To get a snack, we open the refrigerator door. To get an A on an exam, we study for the test. We also learn to avoid behavior that brings unpleasant consequences and to act in ways that forestall unpleasant consequences: to avoid disapproval, we do not smoke in church; to avoid having our bike stolen, we lock it. These responses do not occur automatically; we carry out such instrumental responses because the consequences either are rewarding or prevent unpleasantness.

Around the turn of the century, Edward Thorndike began to study instrumental conditioning in animals. In a classic experiment, Thorndike (1898) confined a cat inside a wooden "puzzle" box and observed what happened when the cat tried to escape—which it did, vigorously. Eventually, in thrashing about, the cat happened to trip the latch that opened the box's door. On successive trials, the cat tripped the latch more and more quickly, until it could open the door and escape as soon as it was placed in the box. According to Thorndike, through trial and error the cat had learned the "correct" response, which brought it the satisfaction of escape. The cat's escape served as a reward that strengthened or "stamped

INSTRUMENTAL CONDITIONING the form of learning in which a voluntary response is strengthened or diminished by its consequences; also called operant conditioning

OPERANT CONDITIONING see instrumental conditioning

A principle of instrumental conditioning holds that applause after a speech provides positive reinforcement for the speaker's behavior, making it more likely that the next speech will also be effective.

LAW OF EFFECT the proposal that a response that produces an annoying or a satisfying outcome will weaken or strengthen, respectively, that response's connection to the situation

in" the correct response; other responses, which brought no reward, were eventually "stamped out."

Thorndike (1911) summed up the results of his experiments in his famous **law of effect,** which proposed that responses which are closely followed by satisfaction will be more firmly connected with the situation, while those which are closely followed by discomfort will have their connections to that situation weakened. What determines whether a particular outcome is "satisfying" or "annoying"? Thorndike (1913) had an answer:

> By a satisfying state of affairs is meant one which the animal does nothing to avoid, often doing things which maintain or renew it. By an annoying state of affairs is meant one which the animal does nothing to preserve, often doing things which put an end to it. (p. 2)

Principles of Instrumental Conditioning

During the 1930s, B. F. Skinner (1938; 1953; 1974) began studying the learning process in animals, and the results of his studies led him to believe that most human and animal learning could be explained by the principles of instrumental conditioning. In a series of painstaking experiments, which culminated in the publication of *The Behavior of Organisms* (1938), he established the basic principles of instrumental conditioning (reinforcement, acquisitions, extinction, recovery, generalization, and discrimination), then went on to show how patterns of reward, which he called *schedules of reinforcement,* determined the organism's performance. See Table 7.1 for a comparison between classical and instrumental conditioning.

Consequences and Reinforcement

POSITIVE REINFORCEMENT strengthening a response by rewarding it

In instrumental conditioning, consequences of behavior are classified according to their effects on subsequent behavior. When a consequence increases the likelihood or strength of repetition of the behavior that precedes it, the process is called **positive reinforcement.** Positive reinforcers are often pleasant rewards like food, a drink, a bonus, or applause. A teacher may use systematic praise and attention to reinforce peaceful, socially appropriate classroom behavior in problem children (Kazdin, 1975). But as the law of effect implies, there is no way to tell in advance whether a given outcome will be reinforcing. That judgment depends solely on the outcome's effect on a person's subsequent behavior. For example, when a child who acts up in class is often scolded by the teacher or sent to the principal's office, the attention may positively reinforce and increase later misbehavior because it helps the child impress his or her classmates; what the teacher thought would be a negative outcome actually was a positive reinforcer for the child.

TABLE 7.1 Comparing Classical and Instrumental Conditioning

CLASSICAL CONDITIONING	INSTRUMENTAL CONDITIONING
Similarities	
Acquisition, extinction, spontaneous recovery, reconditioning, generalization, and discrimination	
Differences	
Association between conditioned stimulus and unconditioned stimulus	Association between response and reinforcing consequence
Unconditioned stimulus does not depend on subject's response	Consequence occurs only when subject makes a critical response
Response is usually involuntary	Response is usually voluntary
Conditioned response often resembles unconditioned response (or is a part of it)	Response is often arbitrary and usually does not resemble the customary reaction to the reinforcer

TABLE 7.2 Consequences in Instrumental Conditioning and Typical Emotional Reactions

EMOTIONAL TONE OF STIMULUS	Response Causes Stimulus To Be	
	PRESENTED	*REMOVED*
Pleasant	Reward—joy	Penalty—frustration
Unpleasant	Punishment—fear	Reward—relief

When a stimulus, usually aversive or unpleasant, is removed after a response, and the *removal* strengthens that response, the process is called **negative reinforcement.** When Thorndike's cat opened the box, its action was negatively reinforced by its escape from the box and the relief from its aversive confinement. If a parent stops nagging you when you finally clean up your room, your relief negatively reinforces your tendency to clean your room.

If you think about these examples, you will realize that negative reinforcement is not the same as punishment. Punishment has a very specific meaning in instrumental conditioning. When the consequence of any behavior suppresses or decreases the frequency of that behavior, the process is known as **punishment.** Punishment can involve the presentation of an aversive stimulus like shocks, excessively bright lights, or loud noises for a rat or a spanking for a child who has misbehaved. Punishment can also involve the removal of a pleasant state of affairs— for example, removing a thirsty rat's water bowl, sending a naughty child to bed without supper, or withdrawing privileges. Table 7.2 summarizes the types of reinforcement and punishment.

NEGATIVE REINFORCEMENT strengthening a response that leads to removal of an aversive stimulus

PUNISHMENT weakening or suppressing a response by producing an aversive consequence

Acquisition, Extinction, and Recovery

When a hungry rat is placed into an operant conditioning chamber (generally known as a *Skinner box*), it explores until—by chance, just like Thorndike's cat—it presses a small switch or lever that causes a food pellet to drop into a nearby cup. The rat eats the pellet and begins to acquire an association between its lever pressing and getting food. Each time the rat presses the lever, gets a food pellet, and eats it, it seems to learn a little more about the connection between its action and the arrival of food. It begins to press the lever more and more often. Soon the animal is pressing and eating steadily until it is full. Placed in a similar chamber, a pigeon will learn to peck at a lighted plastic disk mounted on the chamber wall to get food.

Over thousands of experiments, researchers have found that almost every organism can learn to increase almost any behavior of which it is capable in order

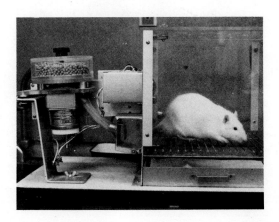

A rat in an operant-conditioning chamber.

PSYCHOLOGY TODAY AND TOMORROW

Tacit Knowledge: What Makes a Decision "Feel Right"?

Have you ever disliked someone but couldn't say why? How do you decide whether people are warm or cold, kind or cruel, capable or incompetent? If you try to put your criteria for such judgments into words, you will find that you can't stipulate your rules—if you have any rules at all. Psychologists call such standards *tacit knowledge;* you can demonstrate your knowledge by the way you judge performance, but you have no direct access to whatever rules guide your judgment. Another name for tacit knowledge is *intuitive knowledge,* which refers to judgments people make because they "just feel right."

Tacit knowledge often involves associations between features of different stimuli. For example, you may dislike an older man who in some particular way resembles a difficult relative you once knew but be unaware that this association controls your negative reaction.

In a study of tacit knowledge, Pawel Lewicki (1986a; 1986b) asked people to judge the character of six women on the basis of their photographs (see below). As the subjects looked at photographs A through F, a researcher described the women in photos A, D, and F as (among other things) "kind, warm, and friendly" and the women in photos B, C, and E as "capable, intelligent, and competent." After a few minutes, the subjects looked at four new photographs (photos 1, 2, 3, and 4) and decided, using their own standards, whether each woman seemed "kind" and, separately, whether she seemed "capable." Try judging these four photographs yourself.

Most subjects decided that women 1 and 4 were more kind than capable and that women 2 and 3 were more capable than kind. If you judged them this way, you relied on the same tacit knowledge that guided the subjects: hair length, the only feature shared by the women in each group. Like A, D, and F, 1 and 4 have long hair; like B, C, and E, 2 and 3 have short hair. Yet none of the subjects were aware of the standard they had tacitly learned. When asked to explain their judgments, they talked about a friendly smile, soft-looking eyes, a round face—everything except hair length. And when asked to describe the women in the photographs, they rarely mentioned hair length. The subjects in this experiment learned arbitrary correlations between a personality trait and a stimulus feature they apparently did not consciously notice. Yet this feature controlled their "intuitive judgments." Lewicki showed that the correlation was arbitrary; for new subjects, the lettering of the sample pictures was reversed; these new subjects judged short-haired women as "kind" and long-haired women as "capable."

A   B   C   1   2

D   E   F   3   4

In a number of such experiments, Lewicki has demonstrated that we learn complex things without being aware of what we are learning—or even that we are learning. The subjects, highly verbal adults, were unable to describe the associations they had made, even though these associations were controlling their behavior. We have seen that infants learn nonverbally; a ten-month-old can recognize and sort visual patterns without being able to tell us about it (Younger and Cohen, 1983; 1985). Lewicki has shown that adults, too, often make complex discriminations nonverbally. Lewicki's study reveals a dissociation between what a person learns and her or his verbal description of it.

No cognitive theorist has yet responded specifically to Lewicki's work. But cognitive views on the matter have been put forward clearly by Dulany and colleagues (Dulany, Carlson, and Dewey, 1984), who argued that no adult human learning takes place without some kind of awareness: we must at least be aware of the cues or rules that we are applying as we learn. The evidence of nonconscious learning, which Lewicki (1986b) has found across many situations and different sorts of content, is at least mildly embarrassing to cognitivists—although we can expect that responses will be forthcoming. In the meantime, the topic of nonconscious learning could be seen as resurrecting the old behavioral–cognitive debate. After all, Lewicki's findings do seem to support the behaviorist claim that learning, human and otherwise, is automatic and can go on independently of awareness (see Skinner, 1974).

to obtain some desired consequence. How rapidly an animal is conditioned depends on several factors, including the likelihood that the desired response (and not others) will be followed by the reinforcer; the elapsed time between the response and the arrival of the reinforcer; the size of the reward (whether it's worth the effort); and the animal's need for the reinforcer (a hungry animal will work harder for food). Rats, pigeons, and other animals trained in Skinner boxes have taught us some very important principles of learning, which in many cases apply to humans. Indeed, Skinner has devoted much of his own writing to applications of behavioral learning principles to education and social issues.

Extinction of an instrumental response usually occurs when reinforcement is withdrawn—just as you stop using a broken light switch or stop going to the refrigerator for food when you learn that it's empty. Technically, instrumental extinction is defined as a gradual weakening of the instrumental response because it no longer is followed by positive reinforcement. In the case of rats, the stronger the initial conditioning, the greater the resistance to extinction. As we will see, the schedule of reinforcement determines how persistent the response will be during extinction, as well as the conditions for its recovery.

Generalization and Discrimination

Generalization has been studied intensively among many animals. For example, a pigeon trained to peck a red plastic disk to get food will "generalize" this behavior to pecking an orange disk. Generalization is also common in our own lives. A young child who has just learned to call the family dog "doggie" may generalize that name and start applying it to cats and squirrels. If you learn to operate one kind of VCR, you will probably generalize your behavior and have no trouble with an unfamiliar model. An adult who customarily drives a sports car with a stick shift often generalizes and tries to depress the nonexistent clutch pedal when driving a car with automatic transmission. As for the reverse process, *discrimination*, we quickly learn to distinguish our own car from others, our house key from our car key, our own dog from the dog next door. We also make social discriminations: we know when the boss is feeling good and when he or she is in a foul mood, and we adjust our behavior accordingly.

Cognitive Interpretations of Instrumental Conditioning

More recent cognitive interpretations of conditioning have led to an *expectancy* view of instrumental learning and the consequences, whether rewarding or punishing, that it involves. This view holds that an organism's anticipation of a re-

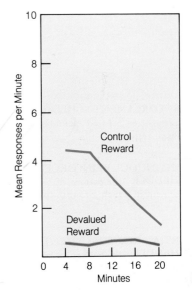

Figure 7.4 After rats had been conditioned to associate sweetened water with nausea, they readily stopped pulling a chain, which formerly had been rewarded by this sweetened water. These results (discussed in more detail in the text) support the view that expectations about the outcome influence an organism's response in instrumental conditioning. (From Colwill and Rescorla, 1985.)

warding outcome guides and motivates its instrumental responses (Dickinson, 1980; Mackintosh, 1983). Early learning theorists, including Thorndike (1911), Clark Hull (1943), and Edwin Guthrie (1935) maintained that organisms simply learned to make a certain response to a stimulus but that this did *not* mean that the organisms "knew" or anticipated that their response would produce a given outcome. In everyday terms, the behaviorists were saying, in effect, that the organism had no idea what was going to follow its response. The situation was supposed to trigger a mechanical response; they supposed it was almost as automatic as the reflexive salivation of Pavlov's dogs.

Some cognitive research, however, has indicated that organisms *do* learn to expect specific consequences of their actions, just as Rescorla's and Kamin's work in classical conditioning showed that organisms can learn to expect and to predict stimuli. The same kind of learned expectations of reward have been found in instrumental conditioning, and they control performance of the response.

Ruth Colwill and Robert Rescorla (1985) trained rats to press a lever to get food pellets and to pull a chain to get sweet water. After the rats had learned these responses, they were classically conditioned in another situation to associate nausea with the drinking of sugar water (through the same nausea-conditioning methods Garcia used so successfully). Afterward, when given another opportunity to press the lever and pull the chain, rats pressed the lever as often as before, but their chain-pulling declined dramatically (see Figure 7.4). Apparently, the rats had learned to *expect* dry food to follow their lever pressing and sweet water to follow their chain pulling. When a rat considered pulling the chain, it apparently anticipated the now-nauseating sugar water, and so rejected that response. Such research has convinced many psychologists that conditioning is best thought of as the acquisition of knowledge about the relationship between events (Mackintosh, 1983). This might also include tacit knowledge (see the accompanying box).

Aspects of Reinforcement

The heart of Thorndike's law of effect is that responses are positively reinforced when they are followed by "satisfying" events. But how consistently must the reinforcer follow the response? And what sort of pattern of reinforcement is most effective?

Schedules of Reinforcement

REINFORCEMENT SCHEDULE pattern of reward that maintains conditioned response

CONTINUOUS REINFORCEMENT SCHEDULE the pattern of reinforcement in which a reward follows each response

PARTIAL REINFORCEMENT SCHEDULE the pattern of reinforcement in which only some responses are rewarded

FIXED-RATIO SCHEDULE the pattern of reinforcement in which a reward comes after a specific number of responses

Reinforcement schedules are simply patterns of reward that maintain conditioned responses (Skinner, 1938; Ferster and Skinner, 1957). Over the years, psychologists have learned a great deal about the effects of various kinds of schedules.

An animal that receives a reward for each press of a lever is on a **continuous reinforcement schedule:** a reward follows each response. Yet the lives of animals in the wild and our own lives provide few examples of continuous schedules. Sometimes we drop coins in a vending machine and get neither a can of soda nor our money back; sometimes our telephone call is not answered; many of our basketball shots miss the hoop.

A **partial reinforcement schedule** rewards only some responses. Partial reinforcement schedules can be based either on numbers of responses, on the lapse of time since the last reinforcement, or on both. In a **fixed-ratio schedule,** rewards come after a specific number of responses. A hungry animal on a fixed-ratio schedule presses a bar at a rapid rate, and for a good reason: the faster it works, the more quickly it gets fed. Similar fixed-ratio schedules are occasionally used with humans who work for piece-rate wages, as when fruit pickers are paid by the number of boxes they fill with fruit rather than by the hour or day. On a **fixed-interval schedule,** rewards come for the first response that is made after a specified time has elapsed. An animal on this schedule tends to stop after it gets a reward, waiting until near the time that it estimates a reward is due before it responds again. When you are not wearing a watch and are waiting for a train, you may keep looking up the track for it; you are operating on a fixed-interval schedule.

Fly fishing may be said to work on a variable-interval schedule of reinforcement: Not every cast results in a catch, but the occasional, unpredictable catch is enough to encourage the fisherman to keep trying.

Not all partial schedules of reinforcement are based on a fixed relationship between behavior and reward. Once a response has been established through frequent reinforcement, it can be maintained with progressively fewer and less regularly scheduled rewards. The organism continues to respond, seemingly because the next response might be rewarded. Animals on a **variable-ratio schedule** are rewarded after a random number of responses since the last reward. If the schedule calls for an average of ten responses, rewards might come after six, then fourteen, then two, then eighteen responses, in a random order. A fly-fisherman casting for trout and a hitchhiker signaling each passing car for a ride are both operating on a variable-ratio schedule. In a **variable-interval schedule,** organisms are rewarded for their first response after a variable period of time has elapsed since the last reward. On such a schedule, rewards may follow the first response after 2 minutes, then 30 seconds, then 6 minutes, then 10 seconds, and so on. When you telephone and get a busy signal, your wait before redialing is like a variable-interval schedule. The longer you wait, the more likely it is that the person has completed the earlier conversation, leaving the phone free to receive your call. On either variable schedule, animals and humans respond more or less steadily, presumably because they realize, in expectancy terms, that there is always a chance that the next response will bring a reward.

Behavior that has been maintained on a variable schedule is quite resistant to extinction, probably because the animal has difficulty discriminating whether rewards have stopped appearing or whether they are just being presented at highly irregular intervals. In most cases, organisms keep responding for at least the longest interval or the largest ratio that separated rewards in their training schedule. The variable-ratio schedule is what makes the slot machine such a compelling attraction. Similar variable schedules of payoffs dominate enterprises that involve risk, such as investing in the stock market, prospecting for gold, or betting at the racetrack. Because decisions in these fields lead to a wide range of possible outcomes, superstitious beliefs about how to identify a "good bet" may develop when a decision is coincidentally reinforced (see the accompanying box).

FIXED-INTERVAL SCHEDULE a pattern of reinforcement in which a reward comes for the first response that is made after a specified time has elapsed

VARIABLE-RATIO SCHEDULE the pattern of reinforcement in which rewards come for the first response after a random number of responses since the last reward

VARIABLE-INTERVAL SCHEDULE the pattern of reinforcement in which rewards come for the first response after a random period of time since the last reward

Primary and Secondary Reinforcers

Over the years, psychologists have offered various hypotheses about what "satisfying" (or reinforcing) events might have in common. Hull (1943) proposed that

PSYCHOLOGY TODAY AND TOMORROW

How We Learn Superstitions

A batter steps up to the plate. He taps his foot three times with the bat, then taps the plate once and tugs his cap. Each time he comes to bat, he goes through the same ritual, certain it will bring him good luck. Is conditioning responsible for his superstition? Yes and no. More likely, the actions of his ritual were, by chance, followed once or twice by a base hit or a home run, which was a big reinforcer. The association was a coincidence, but the player apparently believed that his actions actually *caused* the reinforcement.

This learning of a coincidental association leads to superstitious behavior, which, once established, is often difficult to extinguish. In the case of batters, most hit safely about a quarter of the time. This percentage functions as a variable-ratio schedule, which provides enough reinforcement to maintain the superstition that their ritual helps them get a hit. Similar "superstitions" appeared in pigeons when Skinner (1948a) fed them at very close intervals (about every 15 seconds) no matter what they were doing. The reward reinforced *whatever* they were doing at the moment. If the same behavior was accidentally rewarded several times in a row, the pigeons developed it into a stereotyped behavior pattern, as though they believed it caused food to appear. Most of the patterns consisted of behavior that pigeons naturally show when foraging for food, such as pecking at the wall or floor of the cage and turning in circles near the food dispenser.

Not all psychologists have interpreted the pigeons' behavior as superstition. Researchers who replicated Skinner's experiment concluded that the pigeons had simply learned the fixed-interval schedule of reinforcement for food-foraging responses (Staddon and Simmelhag, 1971). But no matter what interpretation we give to the pigeons' behavior, it seems clear that coincidental reinforcement *can* establish behavior patterns (Schwartz, 1984).

Researchers have attempted to discover whether humans form superstitious beliefs and rituals in a similar manner (e.g., Catania and Cutts, 1963). In an especially clear demonstration, college students sat before a panel containing a circle of sixteen buttons around a score-keeping counter (Wright, 1960). Their job was to figure out whether there was some rule for punching the correct button or sequence of buttons that would earn them points on the counter. In fact, there was no rule; the researcher awarded points on a variable-ratio schedule that had nothing to do with which buttons were punched. Yet within a few dozen trials, nearly every student had become trapped in a superstition. The rituals of some students were quite elaborate—for instance, pressing the buttons around the circle clockwise, then counterclockwise, then repeating that sequence but skipping one button, then repeating it but skipping two, and so on. Few subjects realized that there was no relationship between their actions and their scores. Many were quite confident of their own hypothesis—which brings up another point.

Experiments like this one shed some light on people's shortcomings in evaluating hypotheses. The students tended to concentrate on *confirming* hypotheses rather than disconfirming them. They rarely tried out other patterns to see if they would work just as well as their favored pattern. In addition, they discounted disconfirming evidence—as baseball players do when their rituals work only occasionally. In Chapter 9, we look at how this human tendency to seek only confirmation functions as a cognitive bias, and in Chapter 21, we see how the same tendency affects our beliefs about other people.

PRIMARY REINFORCER a stimulus that reduces some basic drive or need

SECONDARY REINFORCER a formerly neutral stimulus that does not reduce any primary need and that has acquired reinforcing power by becoming associated with a primary reinforcer

effective reinforcers consist of any stimuli or events that reduce basic drives or needs. This hypothesis recognizes the reinforcing power of **primary reinforcers,** such as food for a hungry animal, water for a thirsty animal, oxygen, escape from pain, and so on. Although Hull's assumption that anything that reduced needs would be a reinforcer was correct, his view was limited because it did not explain the wide array of reinforcing events that are not primary need reducers.

A reinforcer that is learned and that does not reduce primary needs is known as a **secondary reinforcer.** It derives its power by becoming associated with primary reinforcers through classical conditioning. For example, a hungry animal that has consistently heard a click just before food drops into its cup will press the level for some time just to hear the click, the secondary reinforcer.

Praise, approval, and applause work for us in similar fashion, although some might argue that we have innate needs for love and approval. Note that the click plays a role similar to that of the CS in classical conditioning. This gives rise to the speculation that for animals, secondary reinforcers are established by a process related to classical conditioning. Psychologists have also proposed that this process explains why money has become such a powerful secondary reinforcer among humans. We are willing to work for money, because we know it can eventually be exchanged for primary reinforcers, such as food and shelter, as well as pleasurable commodities (which are also secondary reinforcers). In general, a secondary reinforcer like money retains its reinforcing power only as long as it can be exchanged for primary rewards. When it can no longer buy primary reinforcers, as in times of very high inflation, it becomes worthless and no one will work for it. This situation developed in Germany during the hyperinflation of the early 1920s—when a pound of butter cost 1 million Deutschemarks, for instance, money had lost its value. People refused to accept payment in Deutschemarks and would work only for the primary reinforcers of goods and services.

There are some important exceptions to this general rule. A secondary reinforcer's power *can* remain intact even though it is rarely if ever actually exchanged for a primary reinforcer. Think, for example, of the miser, who hoards money for its own sake and never exchanges it for anything else (unless one considers that the mere fantasies of what the money *could buy* are tangible enough to substitute for the real thing). Similarly, emblems of social power and prestige—like luxury cars, fur coats, and designer clothes—are often sought after for themselves. The instrumental means apparently may become ends (primary reinforcers) in themselves.

In schools and psychiatric hospitals, secondary reinforcers may be used successfully to motivate desired positive behaviors. In these settings, the reinforcers may be tokens—chips, stars, cards, checkmarks, whatever—that are awarded when the desired behavior is performed. These tokens can then be exchanged for primary rewards and privileges. Such a system is called a **token economy** (Ayllon and Azrin, 1968). In classrooms, for instance, tokens might be offered for exhibiting positive social behavior, completing homework, obeying quiet rules, or producing outlines or term papers; the tokens might be exchangeable for candy, school supplies, toys, extra play time, games, chances to listen to records, or free reading time. In hospitals, tokens might be awarded for social interaction, personal hygiene, taking medication, or any other positive rather than withdrawn or destructive behavior; and tokens might be exchanged for day or weekend passes, movie or concert expeditions, television time, time alone—or whatever the staff has determined that the patient or patients want to have or do.

TOKEN ECONOMY   a training system in which desired behaviors are rewarded with symbolic tokens exchangeable for primary rewards and/or privileges

The determination of what individuals find reinforcing, particularly what activities the individual wants to engage in, can be quite important in treatment, in education, in child rearing, and even in individual goal setting. A withdrawn patient who loves music might be coaxed into some interaction if it meant an hour alone listening to music; he or she might find the interaction reinforcing enough to continue it later. A child might read her history assignment if she can watch an extra half-hour of TV after homework; an adolescent might be more willing to mow the lawn if he can then go with his friends to a rock concert. And you might find it easier to study for a solid 2 hours if you promise yourself some fun afterward, whether it is a visit with a friend, a walk or run outside, or coffee and dessert at the local pastry shop.

David Premack (1959; 1965) recognized the high reinforcing value of pleasurable activities and stated it as a general principle, which is actually a broadening of Thorndike's law of effect. The **Premack principle** states that any activity an organism finds more preferable (usually one the organism engages in freely) can be used to reinforce a less preferable activity. Teachers use the principle regularly when they use the promise of play activities as rewards in order to strengthen academic activities such as paying attention in class and studying the lesson, and even in order to maintain classroom discipline ("If you all sit quietly at your desks for the next hour, you may go out for recess"). The Premack principle implies that the search for some basic ingredient shared by all reinforcers is futile. There is none. Instead, what is reinforcing is always a relative value—some thing or activity that is rated more pleasurable as compared to something else.

PREMACK PRINCIPLE   more preferred activities can be used to reinforce less preferred ones

Aversive Conditioning

Negative reinforcement and punishment are often considered together as types of **aversive conditioning:** learning based on escaping or avoiding unpleasant (aversive) stimuli. Negative reinforcement occurs in both *escape learning* and *avoidance learning.* As we explore these kinds of learning, it is important to recall the difference between negative reinforcement and punishment: negative reinforcement *strengthens* a response that *removes* an aversive stimulus; punishment *weakens* a response that *produces* an aversive stimulus.

Escape and Avoidance Learning

In **escape learning,** the organism's response ends an unpleasant stimulus, enabling it to escape from an aversive situation. Escape learning occurs readily, and we can find it in many daily activities. When you step out into the bright noonday sun, for instance, you put on your sunglasses to remove the glare. When you have a headache, you take an aspirin to relieve it.

Escape learning may rescue some adolescents with scoliosis from the uncomfortable and disfiguring braces used to bring their curved, *S*-shaped spines back into alignment. Psychologists have developed a lightweight device that promises to do the job (Dworkin et al., in press). Worn under the clothing, it monitors the spine, and whenever the wearer slumps and lets the spine sag back into a curve, an attached buzzer makes an unpleasant noise. The adolescent escapes from the noise by straightening the spine.

In **avoidance learning,** a neutral signal precedes a noxious event; the organism associates the signal with the event and learns a response that allows it to turn off the signal and avoid the event. For instance, a rat can learn to avoid a shock by performing some response after hearing a buzzer that normally signals the shock. The rat can learn, say, to rotate a small wheel in its Skinner box at the sound of the buzzer, which it has learned to fear through classical conditioning, by associating sound and shock (Mowrer, 1960). Rotating the wheel turns off the buzzer and prevents the shock. The wheel turning is reinforced by avoidance of the shock and more immediately by the removal of the fear-producing buzzer (the CS). Fear reduction serves as a negative reinforcement (Miller, 1951; Mowrer, 1960; Bolles, 1970). The absence of the buzzer has come to represent relative safety in the box.

Avoidance underlies many of our own activities. We pay our bills on time to avoid late charges; we carry an umbrella to avoid getting wet when it rains; we use a potholder to avoid a burn when taking a casserole out of the oven. And on a broader scale, a chemical company will, it is hoped, clean up its toxic wastes to avoid a fine. Notice the similarity between avoidance conditioning and punishment: we can say that people learn to avoid those activities which lead to punishment.

Punishment: Use with Care

Punishment, as we have seen, involves any unpleasant event (such as shock or denial of privileges) that follows a response and *weakens* it. If a rat receives a painful electric shock each time it presses a lever, it will soon stop pressing the lever. Life is full of aversive or painful consequences that serve as punishments: parents spank children, students get failing grades, lawbreakers are fined or jailed. Thus, both as individuals and as a society, we seem to regard punishment as a useful means of controlling behavior. Our environment provides many "natural" punishments that effectively suppress specific behavior. A child has to touch a hot stove only once. After slipping and falling on an icy sidewalk, anyone walks more carefully.

Sometimes punishment involves denying or removing some pleasant or desired object or event. A small girl who misbehaves is not allowed to watch her favorite television program. Teachers often use "time out"—placing an unruly child in temporary isolation to control disruptive behavior (Kazdin, 1975). Misbehaving teenagers are "grounded" by their parents. Hockey players are treated in a similar fashion; they are sent to the penalty box for fighting.

A word of warning is in order: unless it is used wisely, punishment can produce unwanted consequences. The association between punishment and a particular act can generalize, so that when the undesirable behavior disappears, desirable behavior also vanishes. For example, a child who is regularly and severely punished for aggression may stop fighting but may also become passive, giving up assertiveness along with aggression (Bandura, 1969; 1986). When punishment takes the form of harsh criticism, it can have very negative emotional consequences, lowering self-esteem and eroding any sense of competence. In addition, punishment may lead, by association, to intense dislike and to the avoidance of whoever administered the punishment as well as avoidance of the situation in which it occurred. For this reason, children who are frequently punished by their teachers may come to dislike school—and perhaps even drop out in order to avoid it (Bandura, 1986).

Although punishment clearly tells people what *not* to do, it gives no hint as to what they should do. It suppresses inappropriate behavior without establishing an *appropriate* response in its place. For this reason punishment is probably most effective when used in conjunction with positive reinforcement for a specific alternative behavior (Bandura, 1969). Such a combination effectively ended a retarded boy's painful attacks on other children in an institution (Martin and Pear, 1978). Each time Ricky bit another child, the staff made him wear a catcher's mask for 10 minutes. The mask made it impossible for him to bite. Because Ricky disliked the face mask, he soon stopped his attacks. The staff also began rewarding Ricky with attention and approval whenever he played constructively with others for a certain length of time without biting. In another instance, a six-year-old autistic girl responded to the combination of punishment and reward by stopping her bizarre climbing, which had led to several serious injuries (Risley, 1968). Each time she started to climb the furniture, the experimenter gave her a mild shock on the leg. During the same session, he rewarded her with food whenever she sat down quietly or made eye contact with him. She learned not only what not to do but also what sort of behavior was acceptable.

Our society's laws are enforced solely by punishing lawbreakers, whether by fine or imprisonment. The high rate of recidivism, or repeat offenses, testifies to the ineffectiveness of these sentences. In recent years, the courts have been experimenting with a type of punishment that provides built-in guidance. Known as *restitutive sanctions*, it requires transgressors to undo whatever damage they did, either by performing community service or by compensating their victims through a work program. Someone who vandalized property, for example, must clean up the site and repair the damage. Restitutive sanctions seem relatively effective. As long as the sentence is not vindictive and does not greatly exceed the damage done, such restitution apparently avoids the negative effects of punishment (Bandura, 1986).

The effectiveness of imprisonment as a punishment for wrongdoing is still being hotly debated.

SKILL LEARNING: CHAINING AND SHAPING

The instrumental conditioning studies that we have looked at thus far involve fairly simple acts, but behavior in daily life is usually complex. A complicated skill like playing tennis or typing a letter is based on repeated practice of a series of coordinated acts. The learning of a series of movements making up a skill can be speeded by a process known as **shaping,** in which an organism is reinforced for ever-closer approximations of a desired behavior. Shaping generally refers to the teaching of a complex series of skilled movements, but even a simple movement or action can also be conceived of as parts that can be shaped. For example, you could use shaping to teach a rat a simple activity like pressing a lever for food; this would considerably speed up the process of learning as it did for Skinner in his lab. You could chain the activity, or break it down into smaller units of behavior—

SHAPING the process by which an organism is reinforced for ever-closer approximations of a desired behavior

Performing animals are trained through
shaping, the one-by-one, gradual learning
of small units of a complex behavior.

moving near the lever, approaching the food cup, touching the lever, and so on.
After teaching the animal to eat pellets from the food cup when it heard the food
dispenser click, you would begin to reinforce the animal for any orientation or
approach toward the lever. As the rat's behavior moved closer to the target behavior—pressing the lever—you would initially reinforce it but would then advance the requirement, withholding reinforcement until the next step was accomplished and the rat made an even closer approximation to the target behavior. This
type of training is routine in psychology labs, because it speeds up learning. It
means that researchers do not have to wait until the actual full response desired
(say, lever pressing) occurs naturally.

Note that if a well-established chain of responses in a series is broken at any
point (say, a plexiglass shield is placed in front of the lever), the responses in the
chain up to that point will be extinguished. But if the organism is then given an
opportunity to complete the chain (the plexiglass shield is removed), the organism
will complete it (the rat will go to the lever and press it for food).

Through the shaping procedure, animals can learn extremely complex behaviors by stringing together small units learned one at a time. By such training,
pigeons have learned to play Ping-Pong and to tap out simple tunes on a toy piano
(Skinner, 1951). Dolphins have learned to "hula" while balancing on their tails
(Pryor, 1975). Lions have learned to ride horseback (Hall, 1983). Trainers have
taught sea lions to locate and recover antisubmarine rockets so that recorded
information on each rocket's performance can be evaluated by the U.S. Navy
(Monagan, 1983). Dolphins have been trained to identify submerged mines that
might damage ships at sea, as well as to detect enemy divers, then clamp a signaling device on them before alerting Navy guards (Holing, 1988).

Shaping works well for humans, whether we are learning to play basketball,
to cast a fishing line, or to play the piano—all chains of highly coordinated perceptual-motor responses. Shaping is an effective way to teach children such skills
as printing letters of the alphabet, dressing themselves, making their beds, and
using the toilet. For example, two psychologists (Azrin and Foxx, 1974) devised a
way to toilet-train young children by reinforcing each step in the sequence of
walking toward the potty chair, lowering their pants, sitting down, and urinating.
The training was so effective that it was completed in one or two sessions.

The most efficient reinforcement when learning complex skills is immediate
feedback—information as to whether a response is right or wrong, closer to or
further from the ideal form. Being reinforced with praise for closer approximations is effective, but we learn far more rapidly if we are also told the exact nature

FEEDBACK information about the
most recent performance that is used
to adjust succeeding performances

Practicing in front of a mirror gives a dancer the immediate feedback he needs to correct his movements.

of our errors. For some skills the behavior itself produces direct feedback: the golfer can see where his putt has gone relative to the cup, and the tennis player can see where her serve has landed relative to the spot she was aiming for. In other cases, the learner may get feedback through verbal descriptions from a coach or through watching his or her own performance in a mirror or on videotape. The Monday video replay of the Sunday game gives professional football players feedback on their tackling, blocking, and passing. In the same way, intellectual skills like calculating math proofs and programming computers can be learned much more quickly with a tutor than in a conventional classroom: the tutor provides immediate and specific feedback and correction, thus minimizing a novice's wasted efforts (Anderson et al., 1984).

Once we have acquired the rudiments of a complex skill, our performance improves with practice. Improvement is rapid at first and then slows down: we must practice for increasingly greater periods to produce noticeable improvements (Anderson, 1981; Newell and Rosenbloom, 1981). As practice continues, execution becomes smoother and more rapid (Anderson, 1985). Many psychologists believe that skilled motions are speeded up because the learner condenses a large series of small perceptual-motor units into a few larger "chunks" (e.g., Newell and Rosenbloom, 1981; Anderson, 1982). The skill then can become automatic, in the sense that performance requires little attention and is maintained despite distraction or stress. In fact, at this point, if we attempted to analyze our skill and focus awareness on it, our performance might be disrupted. In Chapter 8 we look at human memory for skills and discuss further how this kind of learning becomes efficient and combines with other types of learning.

SPATIAL LEARNING AND COGNITIVE MAPS

Both classical and instrumental conditioning involve learning about the temporal order of events: the CS precedes the UCS, or the instrumental response precedes the reward. Another, rather different form of learning has also been important to the survival of our species: **spatial learning**, which refers to learning where things are located in the environment.

SPATIAL LEARNING the form of learning where things are located in the environment

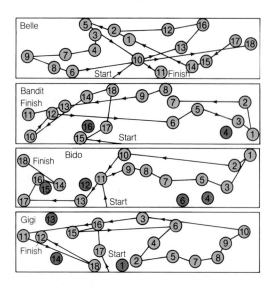

Figure 7.5 These maps show four chimps' performance in finding food that they had seen hidden in a familiar one-acre enclosure. The numbers indicate the sequence in which each chimp saw the food being hidden, while the arrows indicate the sequence in which each chimp found the caches of food. Numbered circles not touched by the start-to-finish line indicate food that was not found. (Menzel, 1973.)

COGNITIVE MAP an integrated internal representation of the way objects and landmarks are arranged in the environment

Recall how you first learned about your college campus. You walked its streets, noting the landmarks—the parks, statues, prominent buildings, and so on. Gradually, you built up a working knowledge of the campus layout. Some 40 years ago, Tolman (1948) explained spatial learning by proposing that, while exploring the environment, organisms construct a **cognitive map,** or an internal representation of the way objects and landmarks are arranged in their environment. A cognitive map integrates into one "picture" a large set of spatial relationships among sensory landmarks, such as buildings and objects.

This kind of spatial learning contrasts in important ways with the temporal-sequence learning that we have been investigating. First, organisms learn spatial relationships between landmarks without any explicit reinforcement or punishment. This is true even for rats. In a classic demonstration (Tolman and Honzik, 1930), hungry rats were allowed to explore a complex maze for nearly 2 weeks, but without receiving any food rewards there. Then one day the rats found and ate food at the far end of the maze. On the very next trial, the rats quickly threaded their way through the maze, going straight to the food. The researchers concluded that during their earlier explorations, the rats had been learning a cognitive map of the maze, but that this learning was "latent"; it was not displayed earlier because the rats had no reason to dash directly through the maze. Once the rats had food as an incentive to express their learning, they did so.

A second contrast between temporal-sequence and spatial learning is that in spatial learning the organism puts together a large number of relationships, then draws out or infers conclusions from them. If you know that the pharmacy is east of the grocery store and that the grocery store is east of the restaurant, you infer that the pharmacy is east of the restaurant. Organisms learn a cognitive map of an environment by exploring it, noting the landmarks along their route (a temporal sequence of stimuli); then they integrate the various routes into a map that permits them to move through the territory in novel ways—reversing their usual route, using short cuts, and taking alternative routes when a familiar one is blocked. So spatial learning is marked by integration and flexibility.

Tolman's idea, unpopular when first proposed, is now backed by a wealth of evidence and is well accepted. Cognitive maps of varying levels of detail seem to be learned and relied on not only by humans but also by other primates (see Figure 7.5), by birds, and by insects like the honeybee (Menzel, 1973; 1978; Gould, 1984).

When humans enter a new environment, they develop isolated route maps (from home to school; from school to pizzeria; from home to laundromat). Lacking an overall map of the various reference points, they would probably get lost if they tried to take a short cut. As they become familiar with the area, however, their cognitive maps expand to cover a wider area and to relate various locations to one another (Anderson, 1985). Still, most cognitive maps are highly simplified and filled with errors (B. Tversky, 1981; Moar, 1983).

Recently, researchers have been analyzing the abilities of various organisms to construct cognitive maps from partial information. They have discovered that human beings tends to make regular kinds of distortion. People seem to simplify their internal representations of city streets into a grid of parallel and perpendicular lines, no matter how winding the roads actually are (Moar, 1983). When they draw maps, people enlarge familiar areas near their homes and shrink unfamiliar areas that lie farther away. And although we tend to think of cognitive maps as visual, even people who are blind construct internal maps of their environment. So do people whose eyes are covered when they are in a new location. In one study (Levine, Jankovic, and Palij, 1982), people who walked blindfolded along a five-point route (from point A to point E), were able to move directly from any point to any other on command. They were equally accurate whether they were asked to repeat the practiced route ("A to B"), its reverse ("B to A"), a forward short cut ("B to E"), or a reverse short cut ("D to A"). Indeed, research on cognitive mapping is revealing the extraordinary ability of the human brain to construct internal representations of reality—which we explore further in the next chapter, on memory.

OBSERVATIONAL LEARNING AND SOCIAL COGNITIVE THEORY

The types of learning that we have been investigating all involve direct experience. But direct experience can be an extremely inefficient way to learn some things. Think about a world in which punishment for our errors gradually shaped us into drivers or surgeons. The costs to other drivers or to patients as we "learned from our mistakes" would be intolerable. Although this is an extreme example, it makes the point: our knowledge is not limited to what we can learn from doing or responding, acting or reacting; we need not depend on trial and error. We can learn by watching others, a process that is known, quite logically, as **observational learning.**

In observational learning, we observe and then imitate the behavior of others. Other people serve as our **models:** by watching them, we can learn complete patterns of behavior instead of laboriously acquiring each step bit by bit. A model can show us how to behave in new ways, how to stop behaving in a certain way, or how to behave in ways that have previously been forbidden. We may even learn to behave in an old way we had forgotten but recall as we watch the model's performance (Bandura, 1986). And we don't have to imitate this behavior immediately; we can store it in memory (how to perform a new dance step, how a friend gets dates, how to replace a worn light switch) and imitate it after weeks, months, or even years have passed. Many of us imitate parents, teachers, or friends, and some of us imitate prestigious people we will never meet—movie stars, fictional characters, or athletes.

Observational learning and modeling are central concepts of **social cognitive theory,** an approach that combines learning theory with a concern for human thought processes. According to Albert Bandura (1977; 1986), the theory's principal proponent, learning is not simply a matter of connecting a response to a stimulus. Instead, we select from the stimuli we encounter, organizing them into mental representations of temporal and causal sequences. We infer the regularities with which particular consequences follow certain responses. We form expectations that, in certain situations, specific responses will be followed by specific consequences.

In this view, learning and behavior depend on information provided by stimuli, people's interpretations of those stimuli, and on the expectancies the interpretations arouse. Bandura also emphasizes that people regulate their own behavior by setting goals to motivate and reward themselves. In other words, we tend to be self-motivators and self-reinforcers. In social cognitive theory, the consequences

Observational learning in a garden: father serves as the model in his daughter's acquisition of a new skill.

OBSERVATIONAL LEARNING the form of learning by watching others and noting the consequences of their behavior

MODEL a person from whom behavior is learned by observation

SOCIAL COGNITIVE THEORY the view that learning involves the application of cognitive processes, including observational learning, expectancies, and self-regulating processes

Prominent people can play a role in the type of observational learning through which we become familiar with our culture's priorities and social issues. First Lady Barbara Bush has called attention to the importance of encouraging children to read.

of models' actions play a significant role in determining our behavior, partly because these consequences influence the way we interpret others' actions. We tend to imitate those whose behavior is rewarded rather than those who are punished or are not rewarded.

Through observational learning, we learn much more than *specific* behavioral responses. This form of learning is one of the chief ways we come to know our culture in general; it allows us to acquire abstract values, attitudes, and social styles, as well as ways of behaving. Observation plays a large part in the way children learn, or at least refine, moral standards (Bandura, 1986). Research indicates that adults' actions often seem to speak louder than their words. In one study (Ormiston, 1972), when children watched models who preached high standards but practiced lower ones, the children adopted the model's lower standards for themselves.

Classic Studies in Observational Learning and Antisocial Behavior

Children's aggressive behavior seems especially susceptible to the power of observational learning. In a classic study by Bandura and his colleagues (Bandura, Ross, and Ross, 1963), children watched an adult beat up a large, inflated Bobo doll. When these children were later frustrated by not being allowed to play with attractive toys, they were much more likely to pound, punch, kick, and toss the Bobo doll than were children who had not seen the aggressive model. They were also more likely to "shoot" dolls, "kill" animals, and smash toy automobiles. Simply watching an aggressive model increased aggressive behavior. These children's aggression increased whether they had seen aggression in live human beings, people on film, or cartoon characters. Researchers have found that the consequences of an aggressive model's behavior are also extremely important. In another study (Bandura, 1965), children who watched filmed models go unpunished for their physical aggression were quick to imitate them, but children who watched aggressive models being punished were hesitant to act aggressively themselves. The implications of this research for children who watch a great deal of television—where violence is frequently portrayed—are disturbing and have been investigated by a number of psychologists. We explore the long-term effects of televised aggression in Chapters 15 and 22.

An Analysis of Observational Learning

Bandura (1986) has proposed that observational learning consists of four subprocesses: attention, retention, motor reproduction, and motivation. *Attention* paid to the model depends on such factors as the model's attractiveness, engaging personal qualities, prestige, age, race, sex, religious beliefs, political attitudes, and general similarity to the viewer. We *retain* modeled behavior by creating internal images or linguistic descriptions of the model's actions. (In the next two chapters, we explore the nature and use of mental representations.) Then we must *reproduce* the model's movements or mental steps. Here, as described earlier, motor skills are important, as are feedback and practice. Practice, by the way, need not always be physical. Skills that involve complex cognitive activity (such as mental addition of numbers) or a complex sequence of movements (a gymnastic routine) often improve sharply if we rehearse them mentally (Feltz and Landers, 1983).

Finally, our *motivation* to imitate any act depends in good part on the consequences that befall the model and on how the outcome corresponds to our own needs. The more the outcome corresponds to our needs, and the more the model has been rewarded as part of that outcome, the more likely we are to imitate the behavior. We are especially motivated to reproduce a modeled behavior in those situations in which we can expect to be rewarded as the model was.

Understanding appropriate situations for given behavior is part of our cultural heritage. Social learning, or *socialization* as it is called by developmental psychologists, has to do with learning *what* is appropriate *when,* according to social traditions and values. After all, we are cultural beings and as such are the result of the way our learning mechanisms operate within our particular environment of home, community, and nation.

At one time, as you have seen, there was considerable debate over how active or passive the process of learning was. Today, there is general acceptance that in all learning, even in classical conditioning, cognitive and biological elements are involved: here again the nature–nurture issue comes in. Mental operations as part of learning (whether conscious or not) are more or less assumed to take place. Humans and, indeed, other animals are no longer considered blank slates for experience to write upon; we are involved in our responses, which of course become part of our experience too. This chapter has presented the fundamentals of learning, the groundwork for what follows. The next few chapters will focus on how we store and call upon our experience, and how we apply it to our lives.

SUMMARY

What Is Learning? Definitions and Perspectives

- Behaviorists see learning as an external change in behavior; cognitive psychologists view it as an internal change in knowledge.
- Learning is a long-lasting change in an organism's disposition to behave in certain ways as a result of experience.
- Learning cannot be observed directly; it must be inferred from performance.
- Organisms can learn through personal experience, observation, or language.

Habituation

- Habituation is the simplest form of learning.
- It follows an initial orienting reflex and refers to that an organism becoming familiar with a particular stimulus.

Classical Conditioning

- Classical conditioning is the learning of a temporal sequence of two stimuli.
- During classical conditioning, a conditioned stimulus (CS) is repeatedly paired with an unconditioned stimulus (UCS) which evokes an unconditioned response (UCR). Eventually the CS comes to evoke a conditioned response (CR).

- Many of our emotional reactions, particularly irrational fears, are the result of classical conditioning. Classical conditioning can be used to "unlearn" or reverse habits, fears, and other emotional reactions.
- A CS may be used to condition its response to a second stimulus which regularly precedes it, in a process called second-order conditioning. Second-order conditioning of emotional reactions probably plays a role in attitude formation.
- A CR may be extinguished when the UCS no longer follows the CS—the two stimuli have become dissociated. Once a CR has been extinguished, it may be relearned through reconditioning.
- The principles of spontaneous recovery and reconditioning illustrate why it is so difficult for people to completely eliminate their addictions.
- An organism may generalize a CR to a specific CS to other similar stimuli; it may also distinguish between—discriminate among—similar stimuli and respond differently to each.

Instrumental Conditioning

- In operant, or instrumental, conditioning an organism learns to associate a response with the consequences of that response. The organism's response *operates* on the environment and is *instrumental* in producing rewards and punishments.

- Positive reinforcement and negative reinforcement both increase the strength of a response. Punishment suppresses or weakens a response.
- The rapidity of instrumental conditioning depends on the likelihood of a reinforcer being present, how quickly it is delivered, the size of the reward, and the organism's need for the reinforcer.
- When reinforcement is withdrawn, the instrumental response is usually extinguished.
- Primary reinforcers—such as food—are effective because they reduce basic needs or drives. Secondary reinforcers—such as money—are effective because they have become associated with primary reinforcers.
- Escape learning uses negative reinforcement to teach an organism a response that removes an aversive stimulus. Avoidance learning uses punishment to teach an organism a response that avoids an aversive stimulus.
- Punishment may produce unwanted consequences. It may suppress inappropriate behavior without establishing an appropriate response in its place.

Skill Learning: Chaining and Shaping

- Shaping speeds the learning of complex behavior by reinforcing ever closer approximations of a desired behavior through a chain of simpler responses.

- The most efficient reinforcer when learning complex skills is immediate feedback. After the rudiments of a complex skill are learned, performance is improved by practice.

Spatial Learning and Cognitive Maps

- Learning where things are located is important to the survival of most species.
- Organisms construct cognitive maps to represent their environment without explicit reward or punishment. They also infer conclusions from a large number of relationships.
- Spatial learning is marked by integration and flexibility.

Observational Learning and Social Cognitive Theory

- In observational learning, people observe and imitate other people, who serve as models of behavior.
- Observational learning allows us to acquire abstract values, attitudes, and social styles, as well as ways of behaving.
- Observational learning consists of four subprocesses: attention, retention, motor reproduction, and motivation.

KEY TERMS

acquisition	fixed-ratio schedule	punishment
associative learning	habituation	reconditioning
aversive conditioning	instrumental conditioning	reinforcement schedules
avoidance learning	law of effect	secondary reinforcer
blocking	learning	second-order conditioning
classical conditioning	model	shaping
cognitive map	negative reinforcement	social cognitive theory
conditioned response (CR)	observational learning	spatial learning
conditioned stimulus (CS)	operant conditioning	spontaneous recovery
continuous reinforcement schedule	orienting reflex	stimulus generalization
discrimination	partial reinforcement schedule	token economy
escape learning	positive reinforcement	unconditioned response (UCR)
extinction	Premack principle	unconditioned stimulus (UCS)
feedback	primary reinforcer	variable-interval schedule
fixed-interval schedule		variable-ratio schedule

CONCEPT REVIEW

1. Define *learning*, specifying what the definition includes and what it excludes. How are habituation and the orienting reflex related to learning?

2. Describe how Ivan Pavlov's experiments with reflexive behavior in dogs led to his development of the basic concepts of classical conditioning. What are those basic concepts?

3. The chapter names seven principles of classical conditioning. What are they, and how do they effect the basic stimulus–response relationship?

4. Describe John Garcia's classic experiment using radiation and electric shock. What other phenomena illustrate similar constraints on classical conditioning?

5. How does instrumental conditioning differ from classical conditioning? Explain how events like recovery, extinction, generalization, and discrimination would be described by each conditioning methodology.

6. Give an example from everyday life of each of the schedules of reinforcement. In which of these do you find primary reinforcers and in which do you find secondary reinforcers?

7.   Distinguish escape and avoidance techniques from punishment techniques. Do the two kinds of techniques have different goals?

8.   What is the difference between temporal-sequence learning and spatial learning?

9.   Define *observational learning*. How is it different from the other two types of conditioning presented in the chapter?

10.   Name and define the four subprocesses that Albert Bandura suggests constitute observational learning.

CRITICAL THINKING

1.   Learning has a number of qualities that make the concept particularly appropriate subject matter for experimental study. What aspects of learning make it so appropriate, and how would the various criteria of experimental design be met by studies of learning processes?

2.   In what ways does being a student place you in a token economy? In what ways is student life *not* a token economy?

Memory

... *Memory*

Yes, yes. . . . This was a series you gave me once when we were in your apartment. . . . You were sitting at the table and I in the rocking chair. . . . You were wearing a gray suit and you looked at me like this. . . . Now then, I can see you saying . . . .

And with that the Russian newspaper reporter, known to psychologists as S, flawlessly repeated a list of fifty unrelated words, one of many such series he had previously heard. The words came tumbling out with no hesitation, all in the proper order and never confused with words from other lists. S found the task no harder than you would find it to recall what you had for breakfast this morning. And if S's feat of memory sounds impressive already, consider this: he had memorized the list in a mere 3 minutes some *fifteen* years before and had never repeated it since (Luria, 1968).

How did S do it? His method is not as difficult as you might think. He used his powers of visual imagery to associate each word with a mental picture, and then he associated each mental picture with a place in a familiar series of places (such as the buildings along a familiar street). Later, by "visiting" each place in his imagination, he could rekindle his memory of the mental pictures and, in turn, the related words. Notice how S converted the memory task into a set of simple stimulus-response associations. Each familiar place is a stimulus that evokes a picture in response, and each picture is then a stimulus that prompts recall of a certain word.

Reading this chapter will not make you a memory whiz like S, but it will give you tips on how to improve your powers of recall. It will also give you a great deal of interesting information about how memory works. We begin by presenting an overview of memory in which we discuss three basic stages in the memory process, as well as alternative models of memory that researchers have proposed. Next we turn to several different types of memory: sensory, short-term, and long-term. These three work together to provide our impressive memory capabilities. Finally, we take a look at ways that people modify their memory performance, including the use of drugs and of memory aids called mnemonics.

AN OVERVIEW OF MEMORY

You are walking home when suddenly, without warning, a white car darts out from a side street and cuts across the road. There is a screech of brakes and a red car, which was in the oncoming traffic, swerves sharply to avoid a collision. The red car skids out of control and crashes into a lamppost. The white car stops for a moment and then speeds away. A few seconds later, the door of the red car opens and a shaken but uninjured driver steps out. "Did you see that?" he asks you angrily. "That stupid woman pulled out without looking. She could have killed me!" Within a few minutes a police officer arrives and starts to ask you questions about the accident. You are surprised to discover that though you had been right there and had watched the whole incident, you have trouble answering some of the questions. The officer is very patient as you try to dredge up the facts, but some things you are simply not sure of and others seem completely lost. (Based on Smyth et al., 1987.)

Often, you are most aware of your memory when it fails you, when for one reason or another you simply cannot remember something. At these times it becomes clear how much you depend on **memory**, the cognitive process of preserving information for use now or in the future. Without memory you would live only in the present. A scene like the one described above would register in your senses, but an instant later you have trouble describing what you had just seen or heard. In fact, without memory you would not be able to speak at all. Your knowledge of words and how they can be meaningfully strung together is part of the vast network of information that human memory holds.

MEMORY the cognitive process of preserving current information for later use

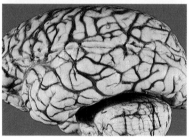

Basically, computers are attempts to reproduce the human memory-storage system. The earliest computers (*left*) were room-size and not very efficient or flexible. Today's personal computers (*top right*) are extremely compact and highly sophisticated. However, the original model, the human brain (*bottom right*), remains the fastest and most complex human memory system of all.

Stages in Remembering

The process of memory can be thought of as having three stages: *acquisition, retention,* and *retrieval.* **Acquisition** involves attending to a stimulus and encoding it into memory. When you attended to the car accident, your memory system acquired information about it. But that information first had to be "encoded"— translated into a form that your memory system could use. To understand encoding, consider how a VCR works. It translates TV pictures into a pattern of magnetized spots on a special tape. The magnetized spots are a code that tells the machine what colors to turn on at each point on the screen. In much the same way, your brain has electrochemical codes for representing all your thoughts and perceptions.

Retention is the stage of memory in which information is stored. You stored many facts about the car accident you witnessed, and you retained them long enough to report them to the police officer. Some facts, like the colors of the two cars, seem to have become firmly fixed in your mind with little or no effort. But retention is not necessarily an automatic process; often we must consciously work at getting information stored. Even then, new information can sometimes cloud or distort the old. For example, did you really see a woman driving the white car? Or did the other driver's mention of a woman influence your recall?

The third stage of memory is **retrieval,** the process by which information is taken out of storage for use. Sometimes retrieval seems effortless, as when you vividly remember the red car swerving and crashing into the post. Other times, retrieval is a slow, deliberate process in which you actively search for a fact. Did the white car stop at the stop sign before pulling out into traffic? You must concentrate hard on reviewing the scene before you can give an answer.

ACQUISITION attending to a stimulus and encoding it into memory

RETENTION the preservation of stored information over an interval

RETRIEVAL the process by which information is taken out of storage for use

But try as you may, you cannot remember everything about what happened. Such failure to remember can occur at any of the three stages in the memory process. You can fail to remember because you do not pay attention or store the material in the first place (acquisition failure), because the information has faded or been overwritten (retention failure), or because you cannot recall it when needed (retrieval failure). In the first two cases, the information is permanently forgotten; in the third, forgetting may be only temporary.

Memory Models

After you look up a phone number and make your call, the number you dialed usually fades from memory very quickly. In contrast, your recollection of the house in which you grew up is something you feel you will never forget. In order to account for such differences in the duration of memory, some psychologists offer a three-store model of memory: sensory, short-term, and long-term (Atkinson and Shiffrin, 1968).

SENSORY MEMORY the momentary lingering of sensory data after stimulation has ceased

Sensory memory is the momentary lingering of sensory data after stimulation has ceased. Sensory memory can involve any of the five senses—a sight, a sound, a touch, a taste, or a smell. Apparently, sensory memory is based upon a brief persistence of neural activity after a stimulus is removed (Coltheart, 1980). Thus, as you watched the white car speeding away from the accident, you may briefly have had the feeling that you saw the license plate, even though seconds later you could not recall the numbers. The sight of this object probably entered your visual sensory storage, which holds information for only an instant before it fades away.

SHORT-TERM MEMORY the holding bin for information that a person has actively in mind; also called working memory

Short-term memory is also referred to as *working memory*. It is the holding bin for information that a person has actively in mind. That information is not just a set of unprocessed sensory data; it is information that has been analyzed and given meaning. For instance, what you are reading now and temporarily storing in short-term memory are meaningful words, not just black squiggles on a page. But short-term memory can hold only a limited amount of data at any one time, and those data fade quite quickly if not attended to.

Flavors, like information from the other senses, are registered in sensory memory.

Long-term memory, in contrast, can hold *unlimited* information for an indefinite period of time. It is a vast library of facts, images, and knowledge that we have stored away, outside immediate awareness, for possible future use. Everything you recall about the accident you witnessed, or any other event in your life, plus all the abstract knowledge you have accumulated over the years, is being held in your long-term memory files.

This three-store model of memory is illustrated in Figure 8.1. It shows information flowing from the environment, to sensory memory (a different sensory register for each of the senses), and from there to short-term memory if the information is attended to. While it is in short-term memory, the information may be used to guide a response. For instance, your answers to the police officer's questions about the accident were guided by information that you held in short-term storage. In order to analyze the data that get put into short-term storage, you draw upon knowledge held in long-term memory. For example, the sight of the red car swerving had meaning to you because you had amassed a permanent knowledge of cars and the hazards of driving. At the same time that information flows from long-term to short-term storage, it may also flow from short-term to long-term memory. For instance, if you realize the importance of getting the white car's license number, you may consciously try to record it into short-term and then long-term storage. The arrows in Figure 8.1 show all the directions in which information flows through the three-store memory model.

Short-term memory is particularly important in this model, for it is here that a person exercises some control over the flow of information. For instance, using short-term memory you can consciously rehearse data in order to keep it active (mentally repeating a license number, for example), or you can deliberately code new information in a way that will make it easy to store and retrieve (perhaps associating the license number AP-168 with a friend's birthday: April 1, 1968). Figure 8.1 lists some other control processes that take place in short-term memory, which is also called "working" memory.

One drawback to the three-store memory model is the danger that the idea of a three-part structure will be taken too literally. We do not really have three separate storage compartments in the brain where different kinds of memories are held. Instead, the model is just a convenient way of summarizing some of the facts we know about memory. Moreover, not all psychologists endorse this model. Some believe that human memory is more accurately represented as a single, vast interconnected network (Cowan, 1988). When a part of this network becomes activated above a certain threshold level, the ideas or images associated with it enter conscious awareness. This unitary model of memory avoids making memory seem more compartmentalized than it actually is. Short-term recall of old

LONG-TERM MEMORY a system of unlimited capacity holding our knowledge and long-retained memories that are forgotten only very slowly

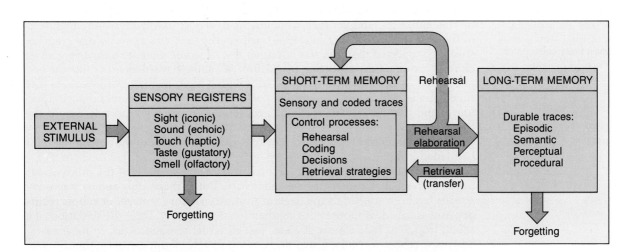

Figure 8.1 This two-store model of memory shows the flow of information into short-term memory and its transfer into long-term memory. Rehearsal is a process that both transfers information from short-term to long-term memory and refreshes the recirculated trace in short-term memory. (Adapted from Atkinson and Shiffrin, 1971.)

information simply involves activating portions of long-term memory networks in the brain. By the same token, when new information enters consciousness, it creates circuits of neural activity with the potential for forming new long-term memory traces.

Whether or not newly created neural circuits go on to become permanent may depend on how the information involved is processed (Craik and Lockhart, 1972). *Shallow processing* (focusing on merely the physical, "surface" properties of a stimulus) is not usually associated with long-lasting recall. In contrast, *deep processing* (in which a stimulus is given meaning and related to other things) is associated with much more permanent memory traces. This "levels of processing" view of memory, as it is called, is another attempt to overcome the limitations of the three-store memory model. It views new information as analyzed more or less deeply in a unitary memory system, and the level of processing, in turn, determines how well things are stored and recalled.

Even though the three-store model of memory has critics, it is still widely used, especially in introductory psychology courses. It is a valuable framework for describing many of the findings that researchers have made about memory. That is why we use it to organize much of the rest of this chapter. But keep in mind that alternatives to it, which psychologists are currently debating, do exist.

SENSORY MEMORY

Although psychologists believe that, as we noted earlier, we have a sensory register for each of our senses, they disagree about the nature of this form of memory. It now appears that sensory memory has two phases (Coltheart, 1980; Yeomans and Irwin, 1985; Cowan, 1988). The first is a brief lingering of a sensation, a fleeting "snapshot" that for an instant takes in all the sensory stimuli present. This sensory lingering fades very quickly, however—often in just a few hundred milliseconds. Slightly longer lasting is the second phase of sensory storage, which entails a very vivid recollection of what the stimuli just encountered were. Here long-term memory is accessed to begin identifying the stimuli's physical features. This is a rapid, automatic, and fairly superficial kind of identification, but the stimuli are nevertheless processed to some degree.

Visual sensory storage, which is often referred to as **iconic memory,** has been studied quite extensively. At first, researchers were uncertain just how much information iconic memory could hold. To find out, they tried briefly flashing sets of unrelated items (like the letters shown in Figure 8.2) and asking people to report how many they had seen. Most people had the feeling that they had "taken in" the entire set, and yet they were unable to report having seen more than four or five things. George Sperling (1960), who at the time was a psychology graduate student, suspected that this was not a fair test of iconic memory's capacity. So he cleverly modified the reporting procedure. When he flashed an array like the one in Figure 8.2, he immediately followed it with a high, medium, or low tone. The tone signaled which line (top, middle, or bottom) the subject should report. Sperling found that, using this method, people had no trouble reporting *any* of the three lines. Apparently, the entire array *did* briefly enter sensory storage, but by the time a person had reported four or five items, the image of the remaining items had faded away.

Iconic memory is just one type of sensory storage. Each of the other senses has its own sensory register, as we said before. But of these, only auditory sensory storage has been studied to any degree. Auditory sensory storage, or **echoic memory** as it is called, is more enduring than iconic memory. True, the sensation of a sound begins to fade almost at once, just as visual sensations do. In most cases, however, echoic memory traces do not completely disappear until about 4 seconds after a sound has ceased (Darwin, Turvey, and Crowder, 1972). This relatively long duration of echoic memory is very helpful in comprehending spoken language. It gives us ample time to start the process of determining the meaning of the words we hear.

Figure 8.2 When exposed to this array of unrelated letters for a brief period, people typically recall no more than four or five of them. But if subjects are signaled immediately after the exposure to recall just one of the lines, they can always recall all four letters correctly. This evidence suggests that people "read" the information from some sort of complete sensory image of the stimulus, which fades in the time it takes to say the names of the letters in the image.

ICONIC MEMORY   storage of visual sensory information

ECHOIC MEMORY   storage of auditory sensory information

SHORT-TERM MEMORY

A good way to understand what is meant by short-term memory is to consciously use it. For instance, say aloud the letters *E, K, L,* and *Z* several times in a row. Soon you can repeat them without looking at this page; they are *actively* in your mind. These letters are now being held in short-term storage.

This short-term holding bin for information serves a number of purposes. First, short-term memory functions as our conscious awareness. It allows us to *know* that we are perceiving and mentally "working" on things. Second, short-term memory enables us to combine the many bits of data we get from our senses into an integrated picture of the world. For example, we do not see separate "snapshots," but rather a smooth-flowing "movie" of what is going on around us. It is short-term memory that gives us this integrated view. Third, short-term memory serves as a temporary scratch pad to hold information while we are thinking and solving problems. You can multiply 3 times 5 and then subtract 2 times 6 because short-term memory stores the intermediate result (15) while you are doing the remaining steps (minus 12 equals 3). Fourth, short-term memory holds our current intentions and the strategies we plan to follow. As a result, it enables us to carry out complex sequences of behaviors all leading toward some ultimate goal. Given all these important functions of short-term memory, our mental abilities would be greatly impaired if we lacked such a storage system (Baddeley, 1984).

Entering Sensory Information into Short-Term Memory

Selective Attention

Selective attention acts as a filter for entering information into short-term storage. We can't possibly attend to all the stimuli that bombard us at any given time, so we ignore many of them and focus only on those that seem important. Unattended-to stimuli register very weakly in short-term storage, or do not register there at all.

You can demonstrate selective attention for yourself by trying to draw from memory the "heads" side of a penny. This is an object you have seen thousands of times, and yet you have probably never attended to all of its details. Instead, you have selectively attended to its features, focusing mainly on its size and color. This is all you need to identify a penny in a handful of coins. Figure 8.3 shows other students' attempts to draw a penny from memory (Nickerson and Adams, 1979). More than likely, your own attempt will be no more accurate, because of selective attention.

What guides selective attention? What kinds of things do we focus on? Large, loud, strikingly colorful, or otherwise intense stimuli usually get noticed. So do things that are unexpected or that depart from the ordinary. A man walking a dog would probably just blend into the scenery, but a man walking a lion would attract many stares. Things that arouse emotions also capture attention, as do things that are personally relevant to us. An environmentalist, for instance, would notice signs of air and water pollution more readily than someone who has no interest in this topic (Kahneman, 1973; Shiffrin, 1988).

Encoding

Once information is attended to, it must be encoded in order to be placed in short-term storage. Encoding, as we have seen, involves translating data into forms that the memory system can use. These forms represent the objects we perceive and the thoughts we have.

Suppose you look at an eye doctor's chart and see a *K* in the top row. You first

Figure 8.3 When student subjects were asked to draw the "heads" side of a penny from memory, selective attention caused them to produce results like those shown here. (After Nickerson and Adams, 1979.)

encode it into short-term memory using a visual (nonverbal) representation. If you close your eyes you are able to "see" the *K* in your mind; it is as if you are looking at a picture of it. Animals who lack language depend entirely on this kind of representation to encode stimuli in short-term storage. They, like us, form short-term **memory traces** of how objects appear—how they look, sound, smell, taste, and feel. The memory trace is believed to form a physiological change in the brain that decays as time passes.

Humans, of course, also form verbal memory traces. They name the things that they perceive or that they think about and use these verbal labels as codes in short-term storage. In the case of perceiving a *K*, you would enter a second representation (the word "kay") into short-term memory alongside your visual trace. You would then have two different short-term memory traces active at the same time—one visual, the other verbal.

These two different representations are not equally enduring, however. The visual (or other sensory) representation is more fragile than the verbal one (Posner

MEMORY TRACE the physiological changes assumed to occur in the brain when recording information about an event; as time passes, the trace decays

et al., 1969). Within a few seconds, the details of the visual trace will fade, and you will be left with only the sketchy outline of a *K*. Eventually, even this sketchy outline will disappear, and you will have only verbal knowledge of what you have just seen.

The use of both sensory and verbal representations in short-term memory has been demonstrated in the laboratory (Posner et al., 1969; Kroll et al., 1970; Parks et al., 1972). In one study, people were shown letters one at a time and later asked to recall them (Murray, 1967). Ordinarily, most of the errors they made were based on similarity in sound (mistaking *Z* for *C*, for instance, or *V* for *B*), which suggests that they had formed verbal memory traces. However, when the same people were prevented from naming the letters as they were shown (by requiring them to keep repeating some irrelevant word), recall errors become based on appearance, not on sound (*F* might be mistaken for *E*, for instance, or *O* for *Q*). Apparently, when prevented from forming verbal memory traces, people can still rely on sensory representations to encode things in short-term storage.

Retention and Rehearsal

As sensory representations fade, they must be renewed or replaced if people are to remember things long enough to use them. Verbal representations are extremely important for keeping information "active" in short-term storage. For instance, if you wanted to keep a string of five letters actively in your mind, you would not just picture them to yourself, you would silently repeat their names. This silent repetition is called **rehearsal.** Rehearsal "refreshes" a stimulus, reactivating it before it can fade. Rehearsal helps us retain what we want to retain. Of course, some things are easier to keep in mind than others. You can retain the color of something without rehearsing it, just as it is easy to remember where an object is located in space. But you must often "work" to hold strings of unrelated numbers or letters, just as it sometimes requires effort to remember people's names.

Researchers have conducted experiments to find out how fast numbers, letters, word lists, and the like fade from short-term storage when they are *not* rehearsed. For instance, they have asked people to read aloud three consonants (such as *CPQ*) and then to count backward by threes before trying to recall them (Peterson and Peterson, 1959). The mental arithmetic prevents rehearsal of the consonants and displaces them in short-term storage. Usually, recollection of the letters fades within 20 seconds (see Figure 8.4).

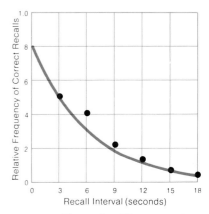

Figure 8.4 The results of Peterson and Peterson's experiment to measure the length of time that short-term memory lasts without the aid of rehearsal. Subjects were shown a three-consonant combination (*CPQ*, for example) that they were to remember; immediately after they saw it, they began to count backward by threes from some number supplied by the experimenter. The longer the experimenter let them count before asking them to recall the letter combination, the less likely the subjects were to recall it correctly.

REHEARSAL the silent repetition or reviewing of material in order to remember it

Just as actors need rehearsal to remember their lines and movements in a play, in daily life we need to rehearse the sensory information that we receive if we want to remember it.

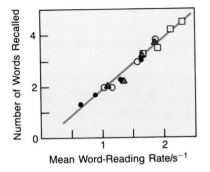

- ● 8 year olds
- ○ 10 year olds
- ▲ 12 year olds
- □ Adults

Figure 8.5 This graph shows the relationship between number of words recalled and rate at which they are read aloud in four age groups. From left to right the data points for each group correspond to words of four, three, two, and one syllables. (Hitch and Halliday, 1983, p. 328; after Nicolson, 1981.)

CHUNK   the larger clusters of information that we can recognize as a familiar pattern

CHUNKING   the process by which the brain organizes incoming data into chunks

The Limited Capacity of Short-Term Memory

An important property of short-term memory is its limited capacity. You can keep active in it the representations of only a few perceptions or ideas at any one time. To add more information to short-term storage, you must often make room by dropping some of what is already there.

Researchers have tried to measure the capacity of short-term storage by presenting people with lists of unrelated items and seeing how many they can retain. In a classic paper, psychologist George Miller argued that the capacity of short-term memory is approximately seven, plus or minus two—that is, short-term memory can hold somewhere between five and nine items (Miller, 1956). These items can vary greatly in size, however. They might be single letters (such as P-D-M-R-T-V-B), or they might be groups of letters that form meaningful words (penny-door-man-river-tugboat-vapor-balloon). They could even be whole phrases or sentences, as long as they are familiar ("A penny saved is a penny earned" would count as one item for most people). During short-term memory encoding, the brain organizes incoming information into the largest possible clusters that it can recognize as familiar patterns. These clusters are called **chunks,** and the process of organizing data in this way is called **chunking.**

Subsequently, researchers have found that the capacity of short-term memory is not quite as constant as Miller and others once believed. It varies depending on the time needed to rehearse the chunks that a person is trying to remember. The more time it takes to rehearse a series of items, the fewer of those items short-term memory can hold. Apparently, when the rehearsal process is long, we tend to forget the items at the beginning of a series before we reach the end (Baddeley, 1976; Baddeley, Thomson, and Buchanan, 1975). As you might expect, people who speak very rapidly have larger short-term memory spans than do those who speak slowly. Rapid speech presumably allows rehearsal and retention of more items in a given period of time. This speech-rate hypothesis can also help explain the increase in memory span that occurs during childhood (Nicolson, 1981; Hitch and Halliday, 1983). As children learn to talk more fluently, they can rehearse items more quickly and so perform better on tests of memory span (see Figure 8.5).

But even for the most rapid-fire speaker there is a limit to how much material can be rehearsed before it starts to fade from short-term storage. That limit is not too far from the upper end of the memory span that Miller identified (seven plus two, or nine items held in short-term memory at any one time). How, then, can we explain people who have phenomenal powers of short-term recall—people who can look at a set of many, many items and remember it flawlessly? The answer lies in their clever use of chunking strategies. Through chunking, a long string of items can be grouped into a much smaller number of clusters, a number well within the bounds of normal short-term storage. Chunking, then, is very important because it helps stretch the limited capacity of short-term memory.

Effective chunking can give experts an edge when it comes to remembering things in their own areas of knowledge. Master chess players, for instance, can reproduce an entire chessboard after just a 5-second look at the arrangement of pieces (Chase and Simon, 1973). Believe it or not, the capacity of a chess master's short-term memory is not larger than anyone else's. The advantage comes simply from the ability to identify larger chunks. "Knight attacking king protected by rook in upper file" is just one item to remember for a chess master, but many items for a nonplayer of chess. The clusters of pieces that a chess master chunks must be meaningful ones, however. When chess pieces are arranged in a random pattern that is unlikely to appear in an actual game, chess masters are no better at reproducing the board than nonplayers are.

By learning to chunk effectively, most people can perform substantially better on short-term memory tasks. For instance, one average college student, identified by researchers as S. F., devised a chunking scheme for encoding numbers into short-term storage that was based on his vast knowledge of running (Ericsson, Chase, and Falloon, 1980; Chase and Ericsson, 1982). S. F. encoded the numbers he was given into running times for various races. The number 3492, for example, he encoded as "3 minutes and 49 point 2 seconds, a near world-record mile time."

S. F. worked with psychologists to improve his memory performance over a period of a year and a half, during which he added several other chunking techniques to help him when his running-time strategy was inadequate. He encoded some numbers as dates, for instance. Given the digits 1, 9, 4, and 4, he might encode them as the year 1944 and tag them with the label: "near the end of World War II." After 230 hours of practice, S. F. could hold in short-term storage up to eighty-four separate digits using his chunking techniques.

Yet this student's phenomenal memory for numbers did not spill over into other aspects of his life. For instance, S. F.'s short-term memory capacity for random strings of letters or words remained at about seven items, just like everyone else's. His learning had been limited to number-encoding strategies, which did not transfer to other kinds of information. Memory ability, it seems, is usually domain-specific. It is best in the areas with which a person is most familiar, for these allow the most effective chunking strategies.

Retrieval from Short-Term Memory

Does it make sense to talk about retrieval from short-term storage? After all, the contents of short-term memory are the things we have actively in mind. Since they are immediately available to us, why would we have to "retrieve" them? The answer seems to be that short-term memory is rather like a blackboard: people must search the board in order to "focus" on some specific item.

The need for retrieval from short-term storage has been shown in numerous studies. In one of them, Saul Sternberg (1966) showed that it takes time to find an item in short-term memory, and the more items that are active, the longer it takes to retrieve one. Sternberg asked people to memorize and keep in mind from one to six random digits. Then he gave them another digit and asked them to indicate whether or not it was one of the original set. The more digits the people were keeping active, the longer it took them to decide whether the new digit was included among the old ones. Presumably, they had to mentally "scan" all of the digits in order to respond.

Forgetting from Short-Term Memory

Nothing stays in short-term storage indefinitely. Information there is constantly being discarded. We forget things from short-term memory for two reasons: *displacement* and *decay*. **Displacement** is the drawing away of our attention from things we are currently focusing on in order to attend to and rehearse new information. At some point the new information will probably replace the old, because short-term memory has such limited storage capacity. Displacement works together with **decay,** the degeneration of short-term memory traces due to the passage of time. As we turn our attention to new information and ignore the old, the old memory traces immediately begin to decay. Unless we switch our attention back to them, they will soon completely fade away.

Theoretically, information could be lost from short-term storage due to decay alone, even if no new material arrives to displace it. Judy Reitman (1974) conducted a study that attempted to find out if decay in the absence of displacement would indeed lead to forgetting. She presented subjects with three words to recall after a brief waiting period. During that time, the subjects were exposed to a continuous noise and were asked to listen for a faint tone that might sound at any moment. This tone-detection task presumably prevented rehearsal of the three words, thus giving them a chance to decay. Reitman found that the short-term memory traces did decay somewhat even though no new lists of words displaced them. But such decay was a minor factor in forgetting. Displacement by similar new material was a far more important cause.

DISPLACEMENT newly arriving information displaces or bumps out of short-term memory traces of previous information

DECAY the degeneration of short-term memory traces due to the passage of time

LONG-TERM MEMORY

Memory would be very limited if we lacked a system for the long-term storage of information. Anything we perceived would simply fade away moments after we shifted our attention from it. Nothing we ever looked at, heard, felt, smelled, or tasted would ever seem familiar to us. Life would be a steady stream of new experiences. In short, we would be incapable of learning.

Transferring Information from Short-Term to Long-Term Storage

The three-store memory model proposes that to retain information indefinitely, we transfer it from short-term to long-term storage. This transfer process depends on several factors. One is how long the information has been rehearsed: the longer the rehearsal, the more likely the transfer. But sometimes we rehearse information for a substantial amount of time and yet forget it completely once we stop rehearsing. Why didn't this information get transferred to long-term memory?

The answer is that there are two kinds of rehearsal, one much more effective than the other for promoting long-term retention. One is a "mindless" repetition of the material to be remembered without thinking about its meaning. Such unthinking, rote repetition is called **maintenance rehearsal.** Although maintenance rehearsal can keep information active in short-term memory, it seldom gets it transferred to long-term storage. In one study, for instance, subjects had to remember strings of five digits after rapidly repeating pairs of words a number of times (Glenberg and Bradley, 1979). They believed that the word repetition was merely a distractor task to make recall of the numbers harder. At the end of the session, however, they were surprised with a memory test of all the word pairs they had spoken. Because they had repeated these words in an unthinking, "maintenance" fashion, the subjects remembered less than 1 percent of them.

The other kind of rehearsal is much more successful for transferring information to long-term storage. In **elaborative rehearsal,** as psychologists call it, we expand on the meaning of information, draw inferences about it, and relate it to other things. Suppose, for instance, you had to remember that flight 1225 leaves at 5:03. You might associate the flight number, 1225, with December 25, Christmas Day. To remember the departure time, you could picture the face of a clock with the small hand on the 5 and the big hand a little past 12. Notice that when you elaborate the information in this manner you retrieve facts from long-term storage (facts about dates, holidays, and clocks) and link them to the new facts in short-term memory. Then, when asked what plane you are taking and when it leaves, you can think of Christmas Day and picture a clock to help bring the answers to mind. The more associations you build while the flight and time are still in short-term storage, the more resistant to forgetting this information will be.

The Structure of Semantic Memory: Networks and Schemas

Why is forming associations so helpful in remembering information? The answer lies in how *semantic memory* is organized. **Semantic memory** is the portion of our knowledge base that has to do with the meaning of things and the relationships among them. Much of semantic memory consists of general concepts, such as "dog," "white," "bark," "friendly," and so forth. Semantic memory also includes specific examples of concepts. "Fido" and "Rover," for instance, are specific examples of dogs. Finally, semantic memory includes knowledge of the many interconnections among concepts and examples. You might know, for example, that Fido is a dog, is white, can bark, and is not very friendly. Since each concept has associations with many others, semantic memory contains huge networks of

MAINTENANCE REHEARSAL the unthinking, rote repetition of material to be remembered

ELABORATIVE REHEARSAL reviewing material by expanding on its meaning, drawing inferences about it, and relating it to other things

SEMANTIC MEMORY the collection of knowledge about words, concepts, and meanings we hold in long-term memory

interconnected links (see Figure 8.6). Whenever a certain concept is activated—that is, brought into awareness—the activation spreads along the concept's links so that soon other, related concepts also come to mind (Anderson and Bower, 1973). Thus, if you are searching for a particular piece of information, activation of an associated concept can help you retrieve it.

As they build upon simple relations among concepts, people create increasingly complex networks of knowledge. We store large clusters of interrelated concepts regarding people and objects (human anatomy, for instance, or automobile engines), as well as events and procedures (what the Fourth of July is like or how to fix a leaky faucet). These large clusters of interrelated concepts, which provide us with general concepts of people, objects, events, and procedures, are called **schemas.**

Your long-term memory has many hundreds, even thousands, of schemas. Consider your schema of shopping at a grocery store. This schema describes in general terms a complex procedure in which you make out a list, go to the store, take a shopping cart, walk up and down the aisles selecting the items you want, and finally go to the check-out counter, unload your purchases, and give the money for them to the cashier. Such procedural schemas, or general understandings of the various elements that routines entail, are also called **scripts.** A script, in essence, is the outline of a little drama with a set plot and prescribed roles for the various actors involved (Schank and Abelson, 1977). Scripts help us enormously in making our way through the world. Because you have a general notion of what a grocery store is like, you know how to behave there even when you enter a store that you have never been in before (Schank, 1982; Schank and Childers, 1984).

You create your scripts and other types of schemas by experiencing many instances of a similar object or event and abstracting from them the common elements. Think of all the times you have gone grocery shopping. The first time, long ago, was a special event, and you probably remembered it as such. But as you went shopping again and again, the specialness started to fade. Soon the details of each trip blurred together and you ended up remembering mostly the basic steps in the process—that is, the schema.

Once formed, schemas help you record new experiences. Suppose you hear that your friend John got a part-time job at the Super Store, a new supermarket. You add such facts to memory partly by creating new relationships between existing concepts and schemas. For instance, you can take your schema "has a job" and record in memory that this relationship holds between two familiar concepts, John and the Super Store. Here you are storing new knowledge by arranging the old in new ways. What if you don't know the Super Store? In that case, you must enter a new name (the Super Store) into memory, and record it as an instance of a supermarket. Now suppose you go to the Super Store and discover that it differs from a conventional supermarket in that it also has a bakery, a pharmacy, a bookstore, and a flower shop. You still keep the Super Store as an instance of your schema "supermarket," but with a few variations added. Notice the efficiency of these approaches to storing new information. You do not approach each new experience as if it were entirely novel, unrelated to anything you know. Instead, you form associations between new experiences and old information, thus saving yourself cognitive effort.

A script is a procedural schema that enables us to perform our day-to-day routines without devoting much effort to thinking about how we are supposed to behave in each situation. Thus, grocery shopping is a routine activity for most of us because the same pattern of behavior is required each time we shop.

SCHEMA large cluster of interrelated concepts that encodes general knowledge of people, objects, events, and procedures

SCRIPT procedural schema, or general understandings of the various elements that a routine entails

Figure 8.6 The associative connections in memory between the idea of "canary" and some of its properties. Concepts or ideas are shown within circles and relations are represented by arrows. This diagram is very much simplified; in reality, memory contains many thousands of such concepts and connections in a complex network.

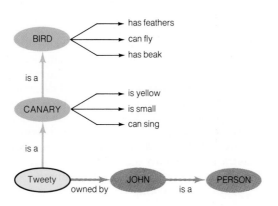

Another advantage of relating new information to existing schemas is that it puts the new information into a meaningful context, which makes it easier to learn and retain. Studies have demonstrated this effect (Bransford, 1979; Ross and Bower, 1981). For instance, when people are instructed to learn seemingly unrelated words ("ropes, lights, canvas, bell"), they learn them slowly. But when a schema that provides a meaningful framework is suggested to them ("boxing ring"), learning occurs much faster. Schemas also have a powerful effect on the ability to understand and remember simple sentences. Consider these:

The notes were sour because the seams split.
The voyage was delayed because the bottle did not break.
The haystack saved him because the cloth ripped.

If these sentences are puzzling to you, it is because you are having trouble relating them to your schemas. Without appropriate schemas, you are likely to forget the words quickly, even if you do manage to memorize them for a while. But when given the right schemas—bagpipe, ship christening, parachutist—your confusion changes to insight. Now the sentences are easy to understand and recall (Bransford and Johnson, 1973). The same effect occurs when you try to memorize seemingly meaningless sketches, such as those in Figure 8.7. You will remember far more of these "droodles" if you give them interpretations—that is, if you store them in relation to schemas.

Storing new information in relation to schemas has yet another benefit. It allows you to make *inferences* about the new facts. When you hear, for instance, that John has a part-time job in a supermarket, you infer that he is either stocking shelves or working at the check-out counter. You know this because your schema of supermarkets tells you that these are the kinds of tasks part-time workers in such stores perform. By making such inferences, you can actually build a mental image of what John does at his job. You can act much like a director, staging your own "internal play," based on whatever facts you receive (sometimes sketchy) and supplemented with information from your schemas (Johnson-Laird, 1983; Norman, 1988).

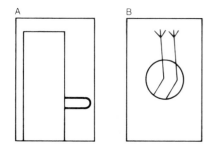

Figure 8.7 "Droodles." (A) A midget playing a trombone in a telephone booth. (B) An early bird who caught a very strong worm. (After Bower, Karlin, and Dueck, 1975.)

Inferences and Memory Distortions

There is, however, a risk to making inferences based on schemas. With the passage of time, it can be hard to remember what you actually perceived or were told and what you inferred. For instance, if you are told that Helen's alarm clock didn't work this morning, you may infer that she must have overslept, even though she did not. This inference occurs because oversleeping is part of your schema about what happens after an alarm clock fails to work. Later, when relating this information to a friend, you may believe that oversleeping had been mentioned and report it that way. In other words, your inference has blended with the fact you learned, and you can no longer separate the two. Schemas, then, can often be useful for filling in missing details, but in some cases those details are incorrect. You will see how disastrous incorrect inferences can be when we discuss stereotypes in Chapter 21.

Our tendency to blur the distinction between what we are told and what we infer is often exploited by advertisers. For instance, an ad might say: "Get through this winter without cold symptoms. Take Eradicold caplets." We infer that Eradicold prevents colds, even though no medication has ever been proven to do this. Can the makers of Eradicold therefore be prosecuted for false advertising? Technically, they cannot, because the ad does not explicitly assert that the caplets prevent colds. Most consumers, however, assume that it does, and they don't realize that this assumption is of their own making. When psychologist Richard Harris (1982) tested people's memories about such ads, 85 percent believed that the ads explicitly mentioned the inferences that the ad writers had encouraged but stopped short of explicitly claiming.

The way that long-term memory works makes us prone to other kinds of

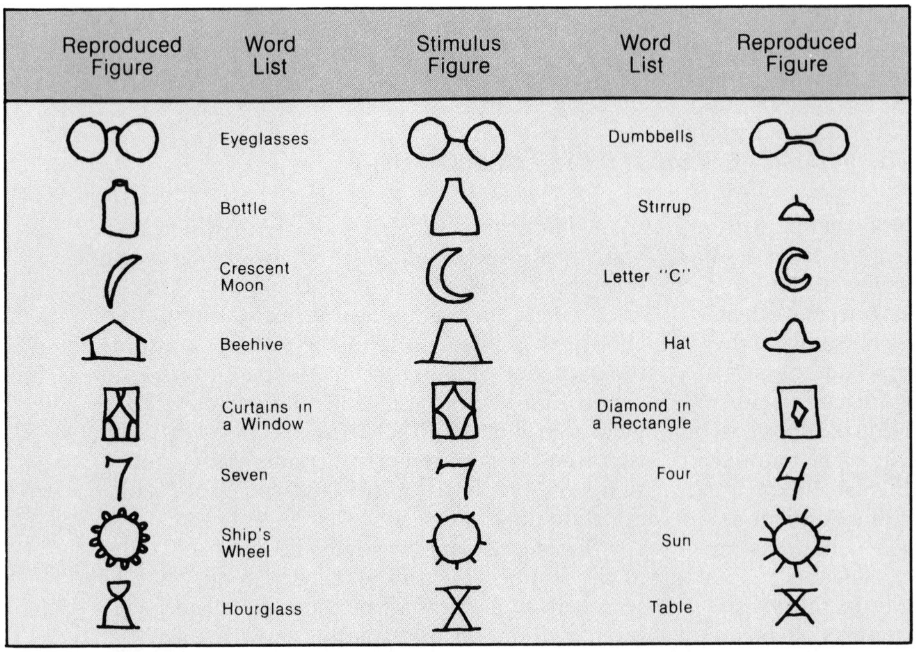

Reproduced Figure	Word List	Stimulus Figure	Word List	Reproduced Figure
	Eyeglasses		Dumbbells	
	Bottle		Stirrup	
	Crescent Moon		Letter "C"	
	Beehive		Hat	
	Curtains in a Window		Diamond in a Rectangle	
	Seven		Four	
	Ship's Wheel		Sun	
	Hourglass		Table	

Figure 8.8 Carmichael, Hogan, and Walter designed an experiment to study the influence of schematic encoding on memory. Subjects were shown the line patterns in the middle column of this figure, and these stimuli were described as drawings of various objects. Later, when the subjects were asked to reproduce from memory the patterns they had seen, they made the drawings shown in the right and left columns. You can see how the schemas used to encode the patterns influenced their drawings from memory. (After Carmichael, Hogan, and Walter, 1932.)

memory distortions. For instance, when we encode something as an example of a schema with a few variations noted, we may forget most of those variations. As a result, our memory of the particular object or event becomes distorted in the direction of the general schema. This tendency was shown in a classic experiment conducted by Leonard Carmichael and his associates (1932). They showed people the outline drawings in Figure 8.8 accompanied by the label for one or another schema (e.g., "eyeglasses" or "dumbbells"). When the subjects later reproduced the drawings from memory, their sketches were distorted to resemble whichever schema label they had been given. Apparently, the original figures were encoded in terms of a schema plus a correction to that schema ("eyeglasses but with a straight wire across"). When it came time to reproduce the figures, however, the corrections were often forgotten.

Perceptual Memory and Sensory Coding

Up to now we have focused on memory for verbal information—that is, on semantic memory. But this slights the importance of memory for sensory information, called **perceptual memory.** When we see, hear, feel, smell, or taste something new, we build perceptual schemas about it: visual or iconic schemas (how it looks), acoustic or echoic schemas (how it sounds), haptic schemas (how it feels), olfactory schemas (how it smells), and gustatory schemas (how it tastes) (Kosslyn, 1980; Rumelhart and Norman, 1988). Thus, when a little girl learns the concept of "orange," she associates the word "orange" with the object's sensory features—its bright orange color; its round, ball-like shape; its smooth, glossy texture; its pungent aroma; and its sweet, juicy taste. In short, she links more concrete perceptual schemas to her abstract semantic knowledge.

Perceptual schemas allow us to re-create sensory experiences—to "relive" them in our minds, so to speak. Visual schemas are particularly impressive in this regard. Not only can we generate an image from a visual memory code, we can also perform operations on it once it is active in short-term storage. For instance, we can rotate the image, scan across it, zoom in on a part of it, and enlarge or diminish it (Kosslyn, 1980). We will explore these abilities to re-create, manipulate, and think in images in Chapter 9, on cognition.

Memory for each sense follows its own laws of acquisition and forgetting. For example, smells seem harder to learn than pictures; but once encoded into long-term storage, smells are easier to remember. Engen and Ross (1973; Engen, 1987)

PERCEPTUAL MEMORY storage of sensory information

PSYCHOLOGY TODAY AND TOMORROW

Memory and Eyewitness Testimony

In the accident described at the beginning of this chapter, a white car darted out from a side street and caused a red car to swerve into a lamppost. A police officer questioned you and other witnesses about what you had seen. Suppose the officer asked if the woman driving had stopped at the corner before pulling out. You clearly remember that the white car had only slowed down at the corner, not come to a full stop, and you tell the officer this. You also thought that a *man* was driving, but both the officer and the accident victim have said otherwise. Will their comments on this point influence your later recollection?

Some psychologists who study memory have tried to answer this important question. If memory can in fact be changed by subsequent information, we have reason to be concerned about the accuracy of eyewitness testimony. People who witness accidents or crimes often talk at length to others (police officers, lawyers, fellow witnesses) about what they saw. Could things they hear in these conversations distort their memories?

Psychologist Elizabeth Loftus and her coworkers have conducted a large number of studies which they contend show how easily memories can be distorted by later misinformation. In one such study (Loftus, Miller, and Burns, 1978), people saw thirty color slides that depicted an accident in which a red car stopped at an intersection before turning right and hitting a pedestrian. Half the people saw a slide in which there was a stop sign on the corner; the rest saw a slide showing a yield sign in the same place. Afterward, everyone answered a series of questions about the accident; one of the questions assumed the existence of a sign. Half the people who saw a stop sign heard a question that presupposed a yield sign, and half the people who saw a yield sign heard a question that presupposed a stop sign. The rest heard a question consistent with the slide they had seen.

When everyone was later shown both slides of the stopped car and asked which one they had seen before, 41 percent of those who had been given *inconsistent* information chose the wrong slide. In contrast, only 25 percent of those who had heard *consistent* information made the same mistake. It was as if some of the people who had been given misinformation unconsciously altered their memory of the accident.

Not all psychologists agree that experiments like these necessarily show that memories have been distorted. Michael McCloskey and Maria Zaragoza (1985) argue that these same results can occur even if subsequent misinformation has *no* effect on people's ability to remember what they originally saw. How could this be, when erroneous recollections are so much more frequent in the misinformed group?

demonstrated this by having some people smell and try to remember four dozen common odors (camphor, lemon, and so on), while others memorized the pictures of four dozen objects that have distinctive odors (a mothball, a lemon, and so forth). A month later, those exposed to the smells remembered more of them than did those exposed to the pictures.

Despite such differences, all sensory memory codes adhere to one basic rule: the more similarly two stimuli are encoded, the more we tend to confuse them and the more one memory interferes with the other. For instance, if you hear rather than see a list of words, your memory of that list will suffer more if you later *hear* another list than if you *see* one (Hall, 1989). What's more, if the two lists you hear are very similar in content, memory of the first will be impaired more.

Conversely, when sensory stimuli to be remembered each have distinctive features, recollection of them is usually clear and strong. Our memory for pictures with distinctive features is especially good. In one study, college students who looked at more than 2500 pictures of distinctive nature scenes could pick them out from others a few days later, even though they had seen each picture for only 10 seconds (Haber and Standing, 1969). We build up visual schemas of pictures such as these by fixating very quickly on the most distinctive and informative areas (Loftus, 1972). The same process is involved when we form a schema of someone's face: we focus on distinctive features and their relationship to one another. Later, we can usually recognize the face as familiar by matching it with the schema we have stored in memory. Of course, if distinctive features are miss-

McCloskey and Zaragoza argue that there are undoubtedly some subjects who remember what sign was mentioned in the critical question, even though they don't remember what sign was shown in the critical slide. What effect would this have on their behavior? Clearly, it would not impair the performance of those in the group that gets *consistent* information. These subjects would still choose the correct slide in the memory test. Subjects who get *inconsistent* information, however, would not fare so well. With only the misleading information in the question to go on, they would choose the wrong slide *all* of the time. Also impaired would be subjects in the inconsistent-information group who remembered both the sign mentioned in the critical question *and* the sign shown in the critical slide. The two are inconsistent, so which is right? Many, McCloskey and Zaragoza say, will assume that the *mis*information must be right. These subjects reason that the researchers wrote the questions, and they must know what the slides showed. Mc-

Closkey and Zaragoza believe that the combination of these two factors can explain why the misinformed group does so poorly in Loftus's experiments. In their view, original memories are *not* distorted nor does misinformation cause more loss of the original information. When subjects do forget the original information, they are more likely to guess the wrong answer when they have been misinformed.

There is little disagreement that "misinformation effect" occurs (Loftus, Schooler, and Wagenaar, 1985). Just by suggesting that a certain thing was present in a scene, eyewitnesses can be induced to report that they did in fact see it. This widely publicized finding has made us more aware that even an eyewitness who earnestly wants to tell the truth may become confused about exactly what the truth is.

The critical slides used by Loftus, Miller, and Burns (1978) to test the accuracy of recollection. Half the subjects saw the photo with the stop sign and half the photo with the yield sign.

ing (glasses and a mustache, for instance), our pattern recognition may break down. The face no longer "fits" our schema; it seems unfamiliar to us (Davies, Ellis, and Shepherd, 1981). Such a breakdown in pattern recognition is one reason eyewitnesses sometimes misidentify suspects. (Other reasons for eyewitness errors are discussed in the accompanying box.)

Interestingly, the memory of an image with distinctive features seems to be more enduring than the memory of its verbal label. Allan Paivio (1971) argues that this is why we remember words for concrete objects better than we remember words for abstract ideas ("technology" or "democracy," for example). Because we can form images of concrete words, we create for them *two* memory traces: a verbal one and a visual one. Abstract words, in contrast, cannot be pictured, so for them we have only our verbal memory trace.

Not surprisingly, when we deliberately visualize verbal information, our memory of it improves. Gordon Bower demonstrated this by having people form mental images of meaningful relationships between 100 pairs of nouns (Bower, 1972; Bower and Winzenz, 1970). For "dog/cigar," for instance, people imagined a dog smoking a cigar; for "chair/canary" they imagined a canary sitting in a chair. At the end of the session, these subjects were given a surprise memory test. They remembered more than twice as many of the pairs of nouns as did people who had verbally rehearsed the words but hadn't pictured them. This was true

PSYCHOLOGY TODAY AND TOMORROW

The Body's Own Memory Enhancers

Why can't you remember where you parked your car at school last Thursday, yet you would remember perfectly if another car had smashed your headlights? Why is it that you can't recall what you had for lunch two weeks ago, but the memory would be permanently etched in your mind if the food had made you violently sick? Psychologist Paul Gold (1987) asks these questions in his search for answers locked away in the physiology of the brain. Gold reasons that it would make sense for evolution to give us a biological mechanism for making sure that important experiences were not easily forgotten. But what could that biological mechanism be? What processes within the body might help us learn information potentially important to survival?

Those processes seem to be related to a heightened state of physiological arousal. When arousal is elevated (up to a certain point), learning is facilitated (Yerkes and Dodson, 1908). But what specific physiological changes underlie this relationship? Likely possibilities include changes in hormones associated with arousal.

One such hormone is adrenaline, also called epinephrine. Adrenaline is not the only hormone suspected of affecting memory, but it is one that researchers have widely studied because its levels and actions are easy to measure. The adrenal glands release adrenaline into the blood whenever an organism becomes aroused. For example, when rats are given an electric shock upon entering a darkened room, adrenaline pours into their bloodstreams as they try to escape. Significantly, the greater the shock and the more adrenaline (up to a certain level), the better the rats remember to avoid the same room again. A similarly strong and enduring avoidance can be induced by giving rats an adrenaline injection after exposure to an electric shock that is too weak to stimulate much adrenaline release. Apparently, having adrenaline in the blood right after learning somehow enhances the memory formation process (McGaugh, 1983; Sternberg et al., 1985).

And yet the adrenaline cannot be acting *directly* on the brain, for this hormone does not readily pass from the blood into brain cells. How, then, could adrenaline affect memory? One possibility is that an increased level of adrenaline triggers the release of some other substance that *does* pass into the brain. This other substance may be blood glucose (or sugar), which rises significantly in response to increased adrenaline output. Experiments show that an injection of glucose right after training enhances memory of the events just experienced (Gold, 1986). This glucose effect occurs even when drugs that block the action of adrenaline are also given (Gold et al., 1986).

If glucose is indeed an intermediary in the connection between adrenaline and memory enhancement, can it be used to improve memory? Gold and his colleagues have tried to find out by giving elderly people doses of glucose prior to memory tests (Hall et al., unpublished). Their preliminary findings suggest that memory performance does in fact improve. Interestingly, too, their elderly subjects with poor memories tended to be those whose bodies were poor at regulating blood glucose. This is not to say that eating lots of sugar is a cure for a poor memory. But by learning more about the role that glucose plays in the process of remembering, we may come one step closer to discovering agents that could someday help alleviate memory disorders.

even though the subjects who engaged in verbal rehearsal were *expecting* a memory test. Visualization of verbal material aids memory because it is a form of elaborative rehearsal, which we talked about earlier. When we form a mental image and link it to a word, this association can later be used to help retrieve the information. We will say more about the value of visual imagery later, but first let's look in general at the process of memory retrieval.

Retrieval from Long-Term Memory

Long-term memory is useless unless we can retrieve the stored information when we want it. Sometimes, as when we read, retrieval is rapid, almost automatic. As soon as we see each word on the page, our memory of it clicks in. The written words are providing good **retrieval cues,** stimuli that aid or trigger retrieval. In much the same way, a mental image of a dog smoking a cigar is a good retrieval cue for the nouns this image represents. Other times, however, retrieval is not so easy. We have to search our memory files and struggle to find information. And then there are occasions when, no matter how hard we try, facts we thought we once had learned now elude us. What has happened when we can't quite retrieve data from memory? Is there an effective way to come up with the missing information? These are some of the questions that researchers who study memory retrieval ask.

Most retrieval tasks involve either *recognition* or *recall*. **Recognition** is the process of identifying a piece of information as familiar. A multiple-choice test is an example of *pair recognition*, where you select which of several alternatives is associated with a given item (the question). Even easier is *single-item recognition*, where you simply identify an item as one you already have in memory ("That's the dog I saw bite the mailman"). **Recall** is a more difficult process than recognition because it involves retrieving stored information from memory without the benefit of having that information currently before you. *Free recall* is especially difficult because no retrieval cues are given—as, for example, when you are asked to name all the state capitals. In contrast, if you are asked, "What is the capital of Nevada?" you are being given a *cued recall* test. The word "Nevada" serves as a retrieval cue that can lead you to the answer, "Carson City."

RETRIEVAL CUE stimulus that triggers the retrieval of memories

RECOGNITION the process of identifying a piece of information as familiar

RECALL the process of retrieving stored information from memory without having that information present

Retrieving What You Can't Remember: Relearning

When you can't recall something you thought you knew, when you can't even recognize it, the connections in your memory network have probably become so weak that they no longer respond to cues. Yet the information may still be present. If it is, you can quickly relearn it. With just a small amount of review, weak associations can often regain their original strength. The more thoroughly you learned something the first time, the more quickly you will be able to relearn it later. For instance, if you study French in school and then don't use it for a number of years, you will tend to forget it. But if you spend a summer in France, the "forgotten" language will quickly return.

Retrieval and Priming

Retrieval can be speeded by **priming,** in which either an item to be remembered or something associated with it is presented several seconds or minutes before memory is tested. The *prime* serves as a preparatory cue, activating concepts or readying their retrieval. For example, you will recognize a picture more easily if you have just recently seen it, even though the picture in the test is fragmented or flashed so briefly that it is difficult to make out (see Figure 8.9). Priming improves our ability to identify pictures or words even when we can't consciously recall having seen them (Jacoby and Dallas, 1981; Jacoby, 1983). The effect of priming does gradually fade, however, so the test must occur before too much time has elapsed.

Priming is also effective when the prime is not the same as the test item but is associated with it. We examined this sort of priming in the discussion of subliminal perception in Chapter 5. If you are given strings of letters and asked to decide which are real words, you will need less time to decide about "purple" if you were previously primed with "green." Similarly, if you recently saw the word "baby," it is likely to pop into mind as soon as you are asked to free-associate to the word "cry." This is true even though you have forgotten ever seeing "baby" (Shimamura and Squire, 1986). This kind of priming works because activation of the prime prepares concepts that are linked to it in memory to be similarly activated.

PRIMING the facilitation in processing a given item caused by presenting it, or a related item, in an earlier series

TIP-OF-THE-TONGUE PHENOME-NON the experience of knowing that we know something, being able to retrieve part of it, but experiencing difficulty retrieving the complete memory

METAMEMORY the knowledge of what our memories contain and how our own memory works in different situations

METACOGNITION the knowledge about and ability to monitor our own cognitive processes

Figure 8.9 A test for priming involves presenting first the most fragmented version of the picture or word (the top version in each series shown here), and then increasingly complete versions until the subject identifies the item. If the subject has been "primed" by being shown the intact item beforehand, he or she is likely to be able to identify the item sooner, in an early fragmented version, during testing. (Warrington and Weiskrantz, 1968.)

When we cannot remember information that we want or need, such as a foreign language, we must relearn it. However, relearning is fairly rapid because it is built on our forgotten knowledge, which comes back fairly quickly with re-exposure to the language.

Almost Remembering: The Tip-of-the-Tongue Phenomenon

Sometimes we are certain that we know something, but we have great trouble pulling it out of storage. This experience is known as the **tip-of-the-tongue phenomenon.** The frustration involved has been likened to that of being on the brink of a sneeze. When the missing information—or the sneeze—finally comes, we feel greatly relieved.

Experiments have shown that when a word is "on the tip of our tongue," we have some information about it, some clues to its identity. We may know how many syllables it has and approximately what it sounds like. On the basis of this fragmentary information we can confidently reject incorrect guesses at the target word (Brown and McNeill, 1966).

The tip-of-the-tongue phenomenon illustrates the fact that we may "know we know something" without being able to retrieve it. Knowledge of what our memories contain and how best to use the information is known as **metamemory** (Flavell, 1985). Metamemory, in turn, is an aspect of **metacognition,** our knowledge about and ability to monitor our own cognitive processes. We return to the topics of metamemory and metacognition when we explore cognitive development in Chapter 15.

Retrieval as Problem Solving

The tip-of-the-tongue phenomenon is not always quickly resolved. Sometimes a prolonged search is needed to get missing information out of memory. If you have ever had trouble finding your class notes, recalling the name of an old acquaintance, or remembering a message you had promised to deliver, you know how long, drawn-out, and frustrating a memory search can be. Such prolonged searches are a form of problem solving, a process we discuss in detail in Chapter 9.

Michael Williams and James Hollan (1981) studied the problem-solving aspects of retrieval by asking adults to think aloud as they tried to recall the names of former high school classmates. At first the names came quickly, then more and more slowly, making the task increasingly difficult. The subjects used several strategies to bring names to mind. One was to imagine school settings (a home room, the glee club, a class play, and so forth) and to try to match these visual memories with names. A second was to match names to visual memories of yearbook photos. A third was to think of first names beginning with a certain letter and to use those names as possible retrieval cues. In these ways, the subjects approached the task as a complex problem to solve.

Forgetting from Long-Term Memory

Sometimes even the longest memory search is unsuccessful, and we must finally acknowledge that we have forgotten something. Forgetting, in fact, is a very common occurrence. We forget the details of a movie we saw 6 months ago and what we had for dinner last Tuesday night. We forget that this coming Saturday is an old friend's birthday and that we promised to send an acquaintance a magazine article we enjoyed. What accounts for such memory lapses? Some may be caused by lack of appropriate cues for retrieval, while others may be caused by interference from similar memories we have acquired. Some may be due simply to memory fading with time, while others may be prompted by a desire to forget unpleasant information. Occasionally, too, memory failures can be traced to organic causes. Let's take a closer look at each of these reasons for forgetting.

Retrieval Failure: The Absence of Cues

If you try to recall your childhood, cueing yourself with thoughts of where you lived, what your room looked like, your childhood friends, your elementary school, your toys, your pets, and so forth, you will find you can retrieve memories that you believed were permanently lost. Apparently, some things appear to be forgotten because we can't find the right cues to retrieve them. When such a cue is found (an odor, a song, a taste, or whatever) it may unexpectedly trigger vivid recollection. A successful retrieval cue corresponds to how you have stored material in your conceptual network. A particular song, for example, might be linked to a certain person, who in turn is linked to other people you have known and places you have been. Once again association is the key, since memory is a web of associations. Strongly associated items are readily cued. One memory serves as a cue to another, or to many others.

We get effective retrieval cues from the *context* in which we first learned the information. Memories are therefore easiest to retrieve if the retrieval situation is the same as or similar to the one in which we originally learned. This principle, known as **encoding specificity,** is based on a series of experiments by Endel Tulving and his associates (Tulving and Psotka, 1971; Tulving and Thomson, 1973). These researchers found that the more the retrieval situation differs from the learning one, the poorer our memory is.

Encoding specificity explains why walking into your old third-grade classroom, seeing the desks and blackboard, and smelling the odor of chalk can bring

ENCODING SPECIFICITY the principle that a memory is easiest to retrieve if the retrieval situation is the same as or similar to the one in which we originally learned

Retrieval cues are powerful aids to memory. Just hearing a certain song on the radio can bring back vivid memories of our senior prom.

back a host of memories from your elementary school days—your teacher, your classmates, a science lesson you had, a spelling test you once had trouble with, and so forth. All these items are associated in your memory, so perceiving the features of the room can activate the others. Encoding specificity also explains why, when you come home from the supermarket, the first thing you think of as you enter the kitchen is the jar of mustard you forgot to buy. The kitchen, where you were when you realized you were out of mustard, is linked with mustard in your mind, and so it triggers recall.

The encoding specificity principle is much the same idea as stimulus control and generalization, which we discussed in Chapter 7, on learning. When you encounter a certain stimulus that has been associated with a reward, you tend to perform the behavior that has delivered the reward in the past. The more closely a new stimulus resembles the one originally present in the learning situation, the more likely you are to give the learned response. Encoding specificity goes beyond this process, however, because it deals with more than just the physical surroundings associated with what we learn. Our thoughts and sensations at the time we learn information are also linked in memory and can later serve as retrieval cues.

The ability of context to provide retrieval cues has practical implications. If a final exam is given in a different room from the one in which the course was taken, most students will perform more poorly than they would have if tested in their regular classroom. Studies consistently show that memory for material learned in the laboratory drops about 10 to 15 percent if testing is moved to a new location (Spear, 1978; Smith, Glenberg, and Bjork, 1978). A study of underwater divers provided a novel demonstration of this context effect. Half the members of an underwater diving club learned a list of words on land, while the other half learned the list under 30 feet of water. Later, those who had learned the list underwater recalled more words when again underwater, while those who had learned it ashore recalled more when tested ashore (Godden and Baddeley, 1975).

Even changes in verbal context can affect memory. In one study, for instance, subjects were asked to learn the right-hand words in word pairs such as "train/black" and "whiskey/water" (Tulving and Thomson, 1973). Then they were given a different list of words and asked to jot down whatever other words they associated with each one (for example, given the word "white" a subject might jot down "horse, hat, black, snow"). Next the subjects were asked to circle any word that they had written which was also on the original list (circling the word "black," for instance). Surprisingly, most failed to recognize many of the words they had learned earlier. Yet when cued with the left-hand words in the original word pairs ("train," "whiskey," and so forth) their memories improved dramatically. Apparently, the change in verbal context had a sizable effect. It was actually harder for subjects to recognize words that were right before their eyes than it was to recall those same words when given cues from the learning context.

Decay: The Effects of Time

The idea that forgetting is caused by lack of retrieval cues rests on the assumption that most of what we learn remains stored away in memory and that all we need to bring it into consciousness are the right cues. Not everyone agrees with this assumption, however. Some believe that memories decay with the passage of time. Eventually, a memory trace may become so weak and faded that any attempt to retrieve it will fail, no matter what cue we use.

The sort of forgetting that decay theory predicts appeared among a group of adults who were asked to recognize the names of television programs that had aired for not more than one season during the past 15 years (Squire and Slater, 1975). With the passage of time, subjects gradually forgot more and more of the old TV shows (see Figure 8.10). Memories of street names and campus landmarks from a person's college years show a similar gradual loss over time (Bahrick, 1983). As you might expect, the stronger the initial learning, the more resistent to decay memories are. For instance, among English-speaking people who had stud-

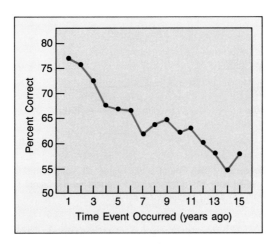

Figure 8.10 Gradual forgetting by decay. A test of remote memory was administered annually for eight years to groups of approximately 25 persons (total of 205 persons). The multiple-choice test asked subjects to recognize the names of television programs that had broadcast for no more than one season during the past fifteen years. The test results show that forgetting occurs gradually over the years, linking some support to the decay theory of forgetting. (Squire, 1987, p. 36.)

ied Spanish, those who had taken more courses and gotten better grades remembered more of this second language when researchers tested them years later (Bahrick and Karis, 1982).

Interference and Forgetting

The idea that memories decay with time fits our experiences. The memory of last week's football game, for instance, is usually stronger and more detailed than the memory of a game from last season. It is as if the older memory has gradually faded. But decay theory cannot explain all, or even most, instances of forgetting. A person with Alzheimer's disease may readily recall events from childhood but not remember what happened yesterday. Moreover, some memories never seem to fade, despite long intervals between retrievals. For example, an adult who has not been on ice skates for many years can usually demonstrate the skill to a grandchild. These facts are difficult to explain if we assume that decay is inevitable and the primary cause of forgetting.

Another way of explaining our gradual loss of memories is through **interference,** the blurring of one memory by others that are similar to it. For instance, maybe we have lost our memory of last year's football game because of interference from all the other games we have seen. If last year's game had been the only one we had ever witnessed, our memory of it might have remained much clearer.

Research suggests that interference is indeed a major cause of forgetting (Anderson, 1983). If you were to learn an association between two words, for example, you would tend to forget it if you later learned to associate the first word with a different second word (McGeoch, 1942). You can test this finding for yourself by having two groups of people memorize a list of dating couples, such as list A in Figure 8.11. One of these groups would then also learn the dating pairs in list B, which links each man with a new partner. Those who memorized both lists would remember fewer women from list A than would those who memorized list A only. The second list of couples apparently interferes with retrieval of the first list. This is called **retroactive interference** because the information on list B has moved in a backward ("retro") direction to blur the information on list A.

Interference can work in the other direction as well: list A can interfere with recall of list B. For instance, if subjects who had learned both lists in our example were later tested for their memory of the women on list B, they would remember fewer names than would those who had memorized list B alone. This is called **proactive interference** because the information on the first list learned has moved in a forward ("pro") direction to inhibit recall of the names on the second list. Not surprisingly, the greater the similarity between two batches of information, the greater the interference (Crouse, 1971). If list B in our example had paired each man with his favorite food (instead of with another girlfriend), interference between lists A and B would be much less likely.

INTERFERENCE the blurring of one memory by others that are similar to it and which compete with its retrieval

RETROACTIVE INTERFERENCE the blurring of previously learned information by competing information learned subsequently

PROACTIVE INTERFERENCE the blurring of newly learned information by previously learned, competing information

List A		List B		Final Test: Recall List A	
Cue	Response	Cue	Response	Cue	Response
Bill ⟶	Sally	Bill ⟶	Evelyn	Bill ⟶	?
Jim ⟶	Linda	Jim ⟶	Karen	Jim ⟶	?
Harry ⟶	Julia	Harry ⟶	Margaret	Harry ⟶	?

Figure 8.11 Two lists of paired words used to illustrate interference in forgetting. Those who have learned both lists are likely not to remember the paired response for list A because of interference from the paired response for list B.

When interference occurs, retrieval of the desired information is not necessarily blocked completely. People may be able to remember some of it, or even all of it, if given sufficient cues. For instance, in studies where a second list of word pairs interferes with recall of a previous list learned, subjects are able to *recognize* much of the first list when given a multiple-choice test (Postman and Stark, 1969; Anderson, 1981). But such recognition takes longer than it does when no interference is involved.

Motivated Forgetting

Sometimes we forget not because of interference, decay, or the absence of appropriate retrieval cues, but because we don't *want* to remember. For example, people whose childhoods were marked by sexual abuse often blot out the memory of those traumatic events. Too painful to think about, the memories are said to be *repressed*. Sigmund Freud argued that repressed memories are pushed back into the unconscious, where they can still affect a person's feelings and behaviors, but no longer cause such overwhelming distress. Although some psychotherapists report that their clients do harbor unconscious, repressed memories, it has been hard to obtain experimental evidence of this (Hilgard and Bower, 1975; Erdelyi and Goldberg, 1979). Nevertheless, uncovering repressed memories and moving beyond them to promote psychological healing remains an important part of Freudian psychotherapy, as you will see in Chapter 19.

Blotting out painful memories need not occur in the way that Freud proposed. It may result from much more conscious and deliberate processes. For instance, people may deliberately try not to think about unpleasant experiences. They consciously avoid "reliving" these events, which is another way of saying they don't rehearse them. The result is formation of weak memory traces and poor retention. In addition, we sometimes deny to ourselves that some unpleasant thing has happened, or we tell ourselves that it really wasn't as bad as it was. With repetition, such denial becomes well learned and automatic, and the unwanted memories are forgotten.

A similar process occurs when we "rewrite" our recollections to put ourselves in a more favorable light. For instance, we tend to remember that we accomplished more than we actually did, that we received better grades, had more insightful opinions, held more important jobs, had a more successful marriage, raised more intelligent children, and so forth. In one study, 1800 men were asked to state their current incomes; ten years later, when they were asked to recall these earlier incomes, three out of four remembered their income as higher than it actually had been (Loftus, 1980). Such self-serving memories are rarely deliberate attempts to deceive. Instead, they are unconscious reconstructions of the past that bolster self-esteem (Greenwald, 1981). The motivation to maintain self-esteem is discussed in detail in Chapter 13.

Organically Caused Amnesia

Most forgetting is "normal." It is the kind that we *expect* to happen, the kind that we complain about but don't find alarming. Sometimes, however, people suffer

Injury-related amnesia is especially common among boxers.

more severe memory deficits, serious enough to be considered abnormal and termed **amnesia.** Usually, amnesia has an organic cause, such as a major injury to the head. Boxers are especially susceptible to injury-related amnesia. It is also common among football players, despite their protective helmets.

Some people with accident-related amnesia are temporarily unable to recall old information and prior events. They are said to be suffering from **retrograde amnesia,** because the memory loss pertains to things that are backward ("retro") in time. The extent of the problem varies depending on the damage sustained. A person may forget everything that happened minutes, hours, days, or even years before the accident. Usually, these memories are not lost completely; they are just temporarily inaccessible. The condition is, in effect, a kind of retrieval failure that lasts until the brain recovers (Russell and Nathan, 1946). The first memories may begin to return within minutes after the accident, or, in the case of more serious injury, within several weeks. Memories from the distant past usually return first and more recent ones later. Sometimes memories of events that occurred just seconds before the injury are never recovered, probably because they didn't have a chance to become fixed in long-term storage.

People who have suffered a brain concussion often have a headache and complain of feeling disoriented and confused. They can answer simple questions and have a moderately good short-term memory span, but they have great difficulty laying down *new* long-term memories. This condition is known as **anterograde amnesia** ("antero" meaning forward in time). Apparently, new information does not get transferred to long-term memory, or if it does, the traces are so weak that memories can't be activated (Squire, 1987). To add to their problems, people with anterograde amnesia may also have some trouble retrieving facts from long-term memory—that is, they may have some retrograde amnesia as well (Kinsbourne and Wood, 1975). Here, too, how long their memory impairment lasts depends on the severity of the injury.

Head injuries are not the only cause of amnesia. Carbon monoxide poisoning can cause temporary memory loss, as can electroconvulsive shock treatment. Destruction of areas in the hippocampus or the temporal lobes of the brain can result in severe and permanent amnesia of the anterograde type. (Remember the case of H. M. discussed in Chapter 3.) People with a long history of alcoholism may develop a similar memory disorder, known as *Korsakoff's syndrome.* Korsakoff's syndrome is not directly caused by alcohol consumption, but rather by a deficiency of vitamin B_{12}, which is common in severe alcoholics because they usually

AMNESIA   the loss of memory serious enough to be considered abnormal

RETROGRADE AMNESIA   the loss of memory for experiences leading up to a brain injury or trauma

ANTEROGRADE AMNESIA   the loss of the ability to lay down new long-term memories just after a brain injury or trauma

eat a poor diet. The deficiency produces degeneration of cells near the hippocampus, and anterograde amnesia results. Finally, destruction of cells in and near the hippocampus, accompanied by a depletion of the neurotransmitter acetylcholine, seems responsible for the debilitating memory loss suffered by people with Alzheimer's disease (see Chapter 3).

MODIFYING OUR MEMORY CAPABILITIES

People often alter their memory capabilities, making themselves more or less able to learn and remember things. In this section we take a look at two factors that affect memory. One is the use of drugs, the other the use of mnemonic systems.

Drugs and Memory

Drugs have a direct effect on memory. Commonly abused psychoactive drugs, while in the body, can greatly reduce the ability to learn. Alcohol, Valium, cocaine, and marijuana all impair short-term memory, perhaps because they make it difficult to concentrate (Wolkowitz, Tinklenberg, and Weingartner, 1985). These drugs also interfere with the transfer of information to long-term memory.

Do any drugs improve memory? Caffeine and amphetamines may keep us awake, allowing us to study longer, but because they also slow the rate at which we learn, we may not profit much from them. Since the neurotransmitter acetylcholine appears to be essential to the formation of new memories (as we saw in Chapter 3), drugs like physostigmine and arecoline, which enhance that transmitter's activities, may also enhance memory. These drugs have produced slight memory improvements in older patients with Alzheimer's disease, but so far the effects have been short-term and too small to be of much practical value (Davis et al., 1982). The drug tacrine (THA) inhibits an enzyme that destroys acetylcholine, and researchers have begun a nationwide test to evaluate its effects on memory loss in Alzheimer's patients (Hostetler, 1987). They hope that THA will improve memory by increasing acetylcholine levels in the brain.

STATE-DEPENDENT MEMORY
storage of information that is more easily retrieved when a person is in the same physiological state as when he or she learned the information

Some drugs can also promote an interesting condition known as **state-dependent memory.** Here information is more easily retrieved when a person is in the same physiological state as when he or she learned the information. In the case of drug use and state-dependent memory, information that is learned under the influence of a drug is difficult to recall when someone returns to a drug-free condition. But once the person is under the influence of the drug again, the "forgotten" facts can be retrieved. As you may have recognized, state-dependent memory is another example of encoding specificity. When something is learned, it is linked by association to cues in the environment, in this case a cue in our internal environment—an altered psychological state. Then later that same state provides a cue for retrieving the data. Without the cue, the data are hard to recall.

Mnemonic Systems

MNEMONIC SYSTEM   strategy deliberately designed to help people remember particular kinds of material

Any of us can improve our ability to remember by adopting **mnemonic systems** (also called mnemonic techniques, or simply mnemonics). These are strategies deliberately designed to help people remember. Mnemonic systems have been known for thousands of years and were practiced by ancient Greek orators. (The Greek word *mnemonikos* means memory; Mnemosyne was the ancient Greek muse of memory.) Mnemonic systems organize information so that it can be easily stored and retrieved. They use imagery, association, and meaning, the brain's basic tools, as well as schemas already stored in memory.

Mnemonic systems do not take the work out of learning. At first, some of them may even take more time than rote memorization. But people who learn to

Practice is necessary to develop our memory for physical skills as well as for facts.

use mnemonics gain two advantages in the long run. First, they can memorize lists of facts more efficiently, freeing their minds for tasks that involve thought and creativity. Second, because they are good at remembering facts, they can develop a strong base of information to draw on when reasoning and solving problems (Higbee, 1977; Bellezza, 1982).

"One Picture Is Worth a Thousand Words"

Many popular mnemonic systems involve the use of imagery. These methods work particularly well when several images are woven into a meaningful, integrated scene (Bower and Winzenz, 1970; Bower, 1972). For example, you might remember the pair of words "gorilla/piccolo" by imagining a gorilla playing a piccolo. Images need not be as bizarre as this to aid memory; ordinary scenes work just as well. Thus, if you wanted to remember the word pair "man/computer," it would be just as effective to picture a man working at a computer as it would be to picture a man with a computer screen for a head.

Unfortunately, imagery doesn't work as well when the words to remember are abstract ones. It is harder to think of an image to represent an abstract concept; and even when you do, the image can usually stand for a number of other things (Paivio, 1971). If asked to remember the word pair "memory/democracy," for instance, you might picture a finger with a string tied around it and an American flag at its top. Later, however, when you conjure up this image again, you may get confused about the words you were to recall. Was it "memory," "reminder," or "recollection"? "Democracy," "freedom," or "republic"?

Let's look at some examples of mnemonic systems that involve the use of imagery.

METHOD OF LOCI S, the Russian newspaper reporter with the incredible memory whom we mentioned at the start of this chapter, used a mnemonic system based on visual imagery known as the **method of loci**. This system employs a series of *loci* (Latin for places) that are firmly fixed in memory—like places along a route to go home. To remember a list of words, you create a mental image for each of the words and "place" each image in one of your loci. Then to recall the list, you take a "walk" past your loci and see what images they contain.

METHOD OF LOCI a mnemonic system based on visual imagery involving a series of loci (places) that are firmly fixed in memory

PEG-WORD SYSTEM a mnemonic system involving the memorization of a list of simple words to use as memory pegs

PEG-WORD SYSTEM A similar mnemonic device is the **peg-word system,** which requires you to memorize ten or more simple words. Once memorized, these words act as pegs upon which a series of items to be remembered can be hung. Below are ten peg words made easier to remember because each rhymes with its number:

One is bun.
Two is shoe.
Three is tree.
Four is door.
Five is hive.
Six is sticks.
Seven is heaven.
Eight is gate.
Nine is wine.
Ten is hen.

Each item on a list to be recalled is visualized as interacting with the corresponding peg word. Suppose you want to remember a shopping list—tomato soup, potatoes, spaghetti, pickles. Imagine tomato soup being poured over a bun, a potato resting inside a shoe, strands of spaghetti hanging over a tree limb, and pickles sticking like knives into a door. Once you are in the market, you run through the peg words and retrieve the related images (Bower, 1978). This method, like the method of loci, is effective because it gives you a device for systematically storing information and later generating retrieval cues for it.

KEY-WORD SYSTEM a mnemonic system based on associating an unfamiliar item to its translation by using a similar-sounding keyword in a visual image

KEY-WORD SYSTEM Imagery is also the basis of the **key-word system,** which is useful for learning foreign vocabulary. To remember a foreign word, think of an English word that is similar in sound and imagine it associated with an image of the foreign word's meaning. For example, if you want to remember *pato* (pronounced "pot-o"), the Spanish word for duck, you could imagine a pot (which sounds a bit like *pato*) sitting on a duck's head. Later, when you hear or see the word *pato,* it will suggest to you the English word "pot," which in turn will cue the pot/duck image and enable you to recall "duck." Similarly, to learn the french word *peau* (pronounced "poe"), which means skin, you might imagine Edgar Allan Poe's "Masque of the Red Death," a story involving a mysterious disease where the skin bleeds spontaneously. Students who use the key-word method learn almost twice as many words in the same study time as do students who use rote memorization (Atkinson, 1975). The system works best when an instructor suggests the key words and leaves the students to create their own images.

Organizing Information into Hierarchies

Chunking, described earlier in the chapter, can be a mnemonic technique as well. Information is easier to learn when we chunk it into meaningful categories and then relate the chunks to one another. Thus, outlining an essay or a chapter you have just read helps you recall its contents because the outline organizes the information into a hierarchy of categories, each of which serves as a retrieval cue for the others.

The mnemonic power of hierarchical organization was demonstrated in a study in which people tried to remember a large number of words (Bower et al., 1969). The 112 words could be divided into four major categories, each composed of about 28 words. Some people were given the words arranged in four hierarchically organized diagrams, one of which is shown in Figure 8.12. Others saw four groupings of the same words, but each grouping was a jumbled collection of words from all four categories. When tested later, the subjects who had been given the organized diagrams recalled 65 percent of the words, whereas the subjects who

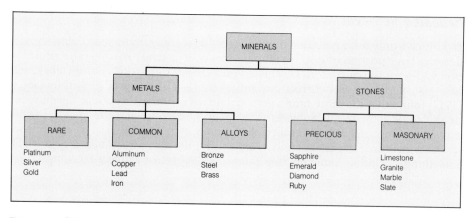

Figure 8.12 This diagram organizes minerals in a hierarchy, allowing the category labels at each node to serve as retrieval cues. (After Bower et al., 1969.)

had been given the disorganized lists remembered only 19 percent. The diagrams aided memory because each category in them served as a retrieval cue for subordinate categories. By following the diagram in memory, the subjects were able to "unpack" the hierarchy level by level.

Organizing information in other ways can be a help to memory, too. For instance, look at the two ways of presenting medication instructions shown in Figure 8.13. The list format makes it hard to remember when the various drugs should be taken. This is partly because the information is given in three different ways—number of pills per day, general time of day to take them, and hours elapsed between doses. The matrix format, in contrast, is much easier to learn and remember. All the information is now related to four specific times of day for taking pills—breakfast, lunch, dinner, and bedtime. Not only does this organization make the data less confusing and therefore easier to encode into memory, but it also establishes daily events as reminders of when medication is needed. Psychologist Ruth Day (1988) found that people who are given medication instructions in this matrix format (compared with the traditional list format) are much better at answering simple questions about them (questions such as "How many Quinaglute do you take per day?" and "When do you take Zantac?") Day believes that a matrix chart is especially valuable to elderly people who take many medications, some of which are essential to their health.

List Format	
Inderal	– 1 tablet 3 times a day
Lanoxin	– 1 tablet every a.m.
Carafate	– 1 tablet before meals and at bedtime
Zantac	– 1 tablet every 12 hours (twice a day)
Quinaglute	– 1 tablet 4 times a day
Coumadin	– 1 tablet a day

Matrix Format	Breakfast	Lunch	Dinner	Bedtime
Lanoxin	✓			
Inderal	✓	✓	✓	
Quinaglute	✓	✓	✓	✓
Carafate	✓	✓	✓	✓
Zantac		✓		✓
Coumadin				✓

A   B

Figure 8.13 Organization of data into related categories can enhance memory. (A) At left is a list of unrelated medication instructions that a doctor gave a patient. (B) At right, the same information has been reorganized into a matrix format, in which each dosage is related to one or more of four specific times of day. The matrix format makes the instructions much easier to remember. (Day, 1988.)

Repeated Retrieval

If you have only a limited time to study (see the accompanying box), you should devote a large portion of it to recitation—that is, to actively recalling the information you want to remember. This gives you a chance to try out your memory, see how you perform, and correct any mistakes. In a classic study, Arthur Gates (1917) found that the more time a person devoted to active recitation, the more he or she could later recall. Subjects who spent 80 percent of a designated period actively testing themselves recalled three times as much material as those who spent all their time in passive study. Apparently, the best way to become skilled at something, including remembering things, is to *practice* actively recalling.

PSYCHOLOGY TODAY AND TOMORROW

The PQ4R Method of Remembering What You Study

College students sometimes complain that mnemonic techniques like the method of loci and the peg-word system aren't always suited to learning their course material. This is because learning what is contained in a college textbook involves more than just memorizing lists of words or concepts. How, then, can students improve their recollection of what they read? One approach that makes study time extremely effective is called the *PQ4R method* (Thomas and Robinson, 1972). The term "PQ4R" comes from the six steps involved: preview, question, read, reflect, recite, and review.

When you study a textbook chapter, begin with a *preview* of the chapter's topics. Read the summary first. Identify the major sections, then visualize the chapter's organization, making an outline that organizes the content into a hierarchy. On the basis of your preview of the chapter, make up *questions* about the material. As you *read* each major section, perform the next three steps.

First, *reflect* on the material as you read it. Try to see how it relates to information presented earlier in the book and to your other knowledge. When the book lays out general principles or conclusions, try to think of examples that illustrate them. Reflection forces you to elaborate on the material and relate it to your schemas, which improves memory.

Second, once you have completed a section, *recite* the answers to the questions you created for it. Actively formulating answers is much more effective than just reading carefully. The questions serve as retrieval cues for the major points of each section. If you have trouble recalling any information, reread that portion of the text.

Finally, mentally *review* the entire chapter. This step amounts to a repetition of the section-by-section reviews. Can you recall the major facts and concepts in the chapter? Can you answer your questions for each section? Reviewing gives you practice in active retrieval.

SUMMARY

An Overview of Memory

■ The process of memory—preserving information for use now or in the future—has three stages: acquisition, retention, and retrieval.
■ Acquisition of memory involves attending to a stimulus and encoding it into memory. Retention refers to the preservation of stored information over time. Retrieval is the process by which information is taken out of storage for use.
■ Sensory memory is the momentary lingering of sensory data after stimulation has ceased. Short-term memory is information that a person has actively in mind. Long-term memory is a limitless repository of facts, images, and knowledge stored away for possible future use. The three-store model of memory is a convenient metaphor; some scientists believe memory is a single, vast interconnected network.

Sensory Memory

■ Iconic memory is visual sensory storage; echoic memory is auditory sensory storage.
■ Each sense has its own sensory register.

Short-Term Memory

- Short-term memory enables us to combine bits of data into an integrated picture of the world.
- Selective attention acts as a filter for entering information into short-term storage; it allows us to ignore extraneous stimuli and to focus only on those that seem important.
- As sensory representations (both visual and verbal) fade, they must be renewed or replaced if they are to remain in memory. Silent repetition, or rehearsal, refreshes a stimulus and reactivates it before it can fade.
- Short-term memory has a limited capacity; it can contain only a few perceptions or ideas at a time.
- During short-term memory encoding, the brain organizes information into chunks (the largest possible clusters it can recognize as familiar patterns), a process known as chunking.
- Information is constantly being discarded from short-term memory by displacement (moving our attention to new material) and decay (the fading of short-term memory traces due to the passage of time).

Long-Term Memory

- Semantic (verbal) memory is the portion of our knowledge base that has to do with the meaning of things and the relationships among them; it contains huge networks of interconnected concepts.
- In semantic memory we store schemas (large clusters of interrelated concepts, providing us with general concepts of people, objects, events, and procedures) and scripts (procedural schemas of the various elements that routines entail).
- Schemas enable us to integrate new information with what we already know and to make inferences about new facts but also to draw incorrect inferences, making us prone to certain kinds of memory distortions.
- Perceptual memory is memory for sensory information such as faces, places, and scenes.
- Long-term memory is useless unless we can retrieve the stored information when we need it.
- Retrieval cues are stimuli that trigger our retrieval of data from memory.
- Recognition is the process of identifying information as familiar. Recall is the process of retrieving stored information from memory without having it currently before you.
- Retrieval can be speeded by priming, in which either an item to be remembered or something associated with it is presented some time before memory is tested.
- We get effective retrieval cues from the context in which we first learned information; memories are easiest to retrieve if the retrieval situation is similar to the one in which we originally learned.
- Our gradual loss of memories over time may be due to a process of decay or to interference—the blurring of one memory by others that are similar to it.
- Memory retention may also be affected by the emotions, as when painful experiences are repressed or consciously excluded from the mind, or when we cast our recollections in a way more favorable to ourselves.
- Amnesia is memory loss serious enough to be considered abnormal; usually it has an organic cause.

Modifying Our Memory Capabilities

- The transfer of information to long-term memory is usually reduced when people are in a drugged state.
- Memory can be increased by a number of mnemonic devices: imagery, method of loci, the peg-word system, the key-word system, and arranging items into hierarchies.

KEY TERMS

acquisition
amnesia
anterograde amnesia
chunk
chunking
decay
displacement
echoic memory
elaborative rehearsal
encoding specificity
iconic memory
interference
key-word system
long-term memory

maintenance rehearsal
memory
memory trace
metacognition
metamemory
method of loci
mnemonic systems
peg-word system
perceptual memory
priming
proactive interference
recall
recognition

rehearsal
retention
retrieval
retrieval cues
retroactive interference
retrograde amnesia
schemas
scripts
semantic memory
sensory memory
short-term memory
state-dependent memory
tip-of-the-tongue phenomenon

CONCEPT REVIEW

1. Name and describe the three stages of memory. How do these three stages relate to the components of the three-store model of memory?

2. Define *sensory memory*. What kind of evidence confirms the existence and nature of sensory memory?

3. How do the concepts of selective attention and encoding control the entry of information into short-term memory?

4. George Miller's concept of the limited capacity of short-term memory has been a focus of attention since it was introduced. How then can we explain the remarkable feats of memory that can be achieved?

5. Distinguish between the decay and displacement processes by which items in short-term memory are forgotten.

6. Give examples of the two kinds of rehearsal and their effectiveness in making permanent memories. How might the more effective rehearsal strategy achieve its results?

7. Describe the role of schemas in making inferences and distortions, and in forming perceptual long-term memories.

8. Define *retrieval*. What processes may be involved in retrieval of memories from the long-term store?

9. Distinguish among the five different causes of forgetting presented in the chapter.

10. Explain state-dependent memory. What are the disadvantages of memorizing something while in an altered state?

11. Describe each of the mnemonic systems discussed in the chapter. Which of the earlier rehearsal concepts are most like these systems?

CRITICAL THINKING

1. In our daily lives we determine whether or not we have learned something by our ability to recall it. This common-sense connection between memory and learning confirms a close relationship between the two concepts in psychology. What similarities and differences do you see in the way the concepts, of learning versus memory, are investigated and understood by psychologists?

2. Several factors may contribute to the distortion of memory, including leading questions, self-serving schemas, drugs, and moods. Which of the research methods presented in Chapter 2 might be most susceptible to memory distortions? Explain your reasons for this analysis and steps that can be taken to avoid these hazards.

Cognition

... *Cognition*

A student director begins blocking the first scene of a new college play. She knows where the stage props and furnishings will be located and now must decide where to place the actors and how they should move as they listen to others and deliver their own lines. As the student director ponders her problem, she takes small stickers labeled with the names of the actors and attaches them to a large map of the stage. Going through the scene, she moves the stickers around the model stage set, abiding by certain rules in their placement. Some of her rules are obvious: the actor who is speaking must be near any prop to be picked up. Some are less obvious: actors should pick up props with their "upstage" hand, so that their actions will be visible to the audience. Working under such constraints, the director devises a plan that solves her problem, arranging the scene to produce an effective dramatic impact.

WHAT IS COGNITION?

COGNITION all the ways of using one's store of knowledge in order to plan something in the imagination, usually in the hope of solving a problem

The director is putting to work the processes and tools of **cognition,** a term that includes all the ways of using the store of knowledge that each of us possesses (Bandura, 1986). The director recognizes that she has a problem to solve. There are constraints on any possible solution, and any solution must achieve certain goals—dramatic, thematic, and physical. There are also standards, however vague, for evaluating the product of her plan and whether she has fulfilled her goals. The director's model stage set and stickers are *symbols* of real objects and people moved around in a representation of the problem situation.

Cognition encompasses an enormous range of mental activities: symbolizing reality, reasoning, pondering, reflecting, calculating, judging, visualizing, imagining, devising, inventing, and inferring. The list goes on and on. Most of these activities require us to *plan* something in our *imagination,* usually in the hope of *solving a problem,* whether it's deciding which subject to major in, selecting the foods for a healthy weight-loss plan, or devising a new hypothesis to test in the psychology lab. Modern theories of cognition agree that when people think, they use models, symbols, and rules much as the student director does. The model of the problem situation and the symbols that represent it may be external, as with the director and her stickers, a diagram of an engine, or long division written on paper; or the symbols may be internal, in inner speech or "in the mind's eye," as when you think about how to rearrange your furniture.

Reflect for a moment on the director's act of thinking. Her thoughts, the materials of cognition, consist of ideas, concepts, images, or schemas. She has images and schemas concerning what the characters look like, how they act, and how quickly or slowly the dramatic action should progress. These ideas are built out of simpler concepts: stage, sets, actors, and all the other elements of theater.

Working with this material, the director carries out certain processes or operations. She mentally simulates the scenes, visualizing the sequence of actions in each one. To do this, she draws on scripts and schemas, supplied by her memory, of experiences in the world and the theater. Mental simulation is one of the crowning achievements of the human brain. By substituting symbolic actions for external events, we can try out solutions and deduce their consequences without having to carry them out (Bandura, 1986). Without symbolic thought, for example, architects designing a skyscraper would have to erect one building after another until by chance they hit upon the sort of structure that would not collapse under the weight of seventy stories. Without mental simulation, we could not compare two possible courses of action, forecast probable outcomes, or act with foresight and intelligence.

Perception, learning, and memory are all components of thought. Without them, we would have no **concepts,** the general mental categories into which we group our knowledge about the world. Concepts and images are the symbols of external reality that are both the content and the tools of thought. Accordingly, before we study the nature of thought, we need to understand how we learn concepts and use them to classify the world.

CONCEPTS the ideas underlying categories for grouping items according to their shared properties

Concepts and Categories

The brain is a sophisticated pattern-recognizing machine. It is also an economical one. It tries to identify each new object as resembling a familiar object already stored in memory. In previous chapters we have seen this tendency in the way the brain identifies perceptual patterns; learns through habituation, conditioning, and observation; and recognizes old information in memory. The mind reduces its labor by grouping similar objects and events into concepts, according to their similarity and familiarity. Red, yellow, and green apples, for example, are all instances of the concept "apple." By recognizing instances, the mind seeks and provides meaning in a fairly efficient manner.

How Do We Learn Concepts?

As a father pushes the shopping cart down the produce aisle at the local supermarket, his two-year-old points a stubby finger at the display of oranges and says, "What's that?" The father says, "That's an orange. Orange." The child considers the reply, then points at the grapefruit and says, "Orange." The father, intent on his grocery list, looks up and says, "No, Jessica. That's a grapefruit." By noting instances of the concept "orange" and comparing them with noninstances, like grapefruit, lemons, and tangerines, Jessica eventually draws out the pertinent features and establishes the concept "orange." Along the way, Jessica encounters a tangerine—an object that is similar to the concept yet differs from it in important ways. The tangerine is a close noninstance of the concept "orange." Such related noninstances are important in concept learning: they enable a child to distinguish one concept from another and to see the connection between similar concepts. As the child compares the noninstance with the instance, she infers the essential features of an orange. At the same time, she also forms another concept— that of "tangerine." So a concept is learned in part by distinguishing it from closely related others.

As Jessica learns about oranges, the instances and noninstances she encounters teach her which features to exclude and which to include in her mental representation of the concept. She notices that the same cluster of features is usually present: shape, texture, smell, and taste. These features are stored as part of her perceptual schema of an orange, and she quickly learns that the presence of one feature (the orange's distinctive smell) allows her to infer the presence of other

Sesame Street has performed a valuable service in teaching basic concepts to millions of children.

features (its taste and texture). These perceptual features of the orange, along with all the other information she picks up about the concept "orange" ("grows on a tree"; "can be made into juice") are stored among the propositions in her semantic memory.

Children's earliest concepts are formed around the natural kinds of objects that appear in their environment: earth, sky, stone, tree, bird, baby, domestic animals, woman, man, water. As children grow older, they learn many concepts in a more abstract fashion—through the words that symbolize them. This linguistic learning is accomplished with the help of formal teaching by schools or, in traditional societies, by elders. But formal vocabulary instruction accounts for only a small part of our concept learning. We learn many of our concepts through *inference,* deriving conclusions by reasoning from the evidence—which is one of the brain's favorite ways of working. We infer the meaning of new concepts by using contextual clues, whether in a text we are reading or in conversation (Sternberg and Powell, 1983; Just and Carpenter, 1987). To take a simple example, if you read, "At dawn, the *blen* arose on the horizon and shone brightly," you would be able to infer from the clues in the sentence that *blen* probably means something like *sun* (Sternberg, 1987). The statement tells us that the *blen* is a physical object whose "arising" occurs at a specific time and place, and that it has a property of "shining brightly."

Fuzzy Categories and Prototypes

Some concepts are *well-defined:* they have neat, logical properties. Many mathematical concepts such as "square root" and "prime number" are well-defined; so are a few natural concepts like "man" and "woman." For these concepts, an instance is either clearly a member of a category or clearly not a member. But for most concepts, this sharp division does not exist. When we look at our everyday concepts, they turn out, by and large, to be vague and fuzzy, with wavering boundaries. Even the everyday category "chair" suffers from fuzziness. You may try to define "chair" by listing the necessary and sufficient features: legs, a flat surface (the seat), and a backrest. This definition will not work because a bean-bag seat is technically a chair, and so are a canvas sling, a stool, and an orange crate. Perhaps the critical feature of a chair is not its physical attributes but its function: chairs are things people sit on. That's not good enough either, because there are doll's chairs and chairs under marble statues, neither of which real people can sit on. Perhaps a chair is simply anything that can physically support something else. But even that will not do, for now the category includes bridge supports, pier supports, poles for birdhouses, and so on. It begins to look as if we cannot identify the necessary and sufficient conditions that qualify objects as chairs. The concept of chair is fuzzy—yet each of us knows a chair when we see it.

Most of our everyday categories are similarly fuzzy. In order to classify instances, we note how much they resemble, or are *typical* of, other members of the category. Children usually learn the typical instances of a category first; and when adults judge category membership, they are fastest at judging typical instances (Rosch, 1973). When we think about a category, it is the typical instances that first come to mind. If asked to list the members of a category such as "bird," we generally begin with the most typical, like robin or sparrow, and we tend to put penguins, ostriches, or kiwi birds near the end of the list, if we recall them at all (Battig and Montague, 1969). People generally agree on just how typical various instances are. In the continental United States, for instance, there's little argument that "orange" and "apple" are good examples of "fruit" but "pomegranate" and "guava" are not.

Typicality seems to be based on *family resemblance.* The more closely an instance (an apple) resembles other category members (fruits), the more typical of the category we say the instance is (Rosch and Mervis, 1977). Family resemblance is determined by a member's features—the more features an instances shares with other members of the category, the more typical it seems.

The family-resemblance idea suggests that for each category, we have a most typical example—a best instance or most representative member—called a **proto-**

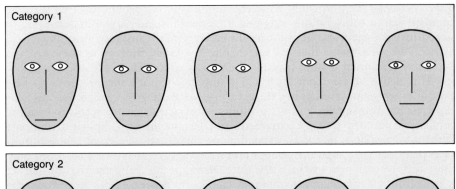

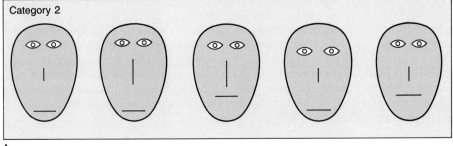

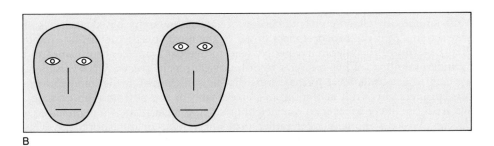

Figure 9.1 In an experiment that tested the ability to categorize prototypes, subjects first learned to sort ten drawings of faces into the two categories shown in A. Then, when they looked at the two prototypical faces shown in B, most subjects had no trouble assigning each of them to the appropriate category. (After Reed, 1972.)

type. We decide how to classify things in the world by comparing them to prototypes. This comparison can be seen as a sort of feature-matching process that works for abstract as well as for concrete concepts. We compare the peacock at the zoo to our prototype of "bird," the pomegranate at the grocery to our prototype of "fruit," and last night's meal to our prototype of "dinner."

A prototype may be either the single most typical example (such as "robin" for "bird"—at least in temperate Western cultures), or it may be the most memorable or noteworthy example, whether or not it is typical (such as "New York" for "city"). Or it may be a composite of the most typical features of all members of a category, a sort of average culled from our experience. Researchers have shown that, in any case, people have little trouble extracting the prototypical features of a new concept. In one study, after learning to sort the ten faces in Figure 9.1A into two categories, nine out of ten people could look at the two prototypical faces in Figure 9.1B and correctly decide in which category each belonged (Reed, 1972; Anderson, 1985).

A Challenge to Prototype Theory

Recently, some psychologists have challenged the notion of the prototype and the way we use it. They have proposed new *instance-storage* theories that take an opposite view of concept building. These theories assume that there is *no* prototype and that no abstraction, no averaging, and no generalization go on when we learn a new concept. Instead, they assume that we store fairly detailed representations of the instances and noninstances that we encounter (Smith and Medin, 1981; Jacoby and Brooks, 1984; Hintzman, 1986; Estes, 1986). When we see a new instance, it reminds us, not of the "most typical" member, but of the instance stored in memory that it most closely resembles. According to prototype theories,

PROTOTYPE the most typical example—a best instance or most representative member—of a category

if we encounter a 5 foot-high winged creature walking around on two legs, we compare it to a robin before assigning it to the bird category. But according to stored-instance theories, we compare the creature to the instance most like it—an ostrich. We then assign the new instance to the same category as the ostrich, a decision determined by the features the two creatures share (Nosofsky, 1987).

This debate is far from settled. The instance-storage theory seems to best explain experimental studies in which students learn categories based only on their experiencing of instances, but the prototype-abstraction theory seems to be more compatible with the way we acquire verbal concepts through explicit definitions. Perhaps we use both methods, depending on the situation. Recent research indicates that if we first learn the *general properties* of a category, we will record only those features of a new instance that differ from the general properties or that set it apart from other category members (Clapper and Bower, 1988). If we know the general properties of a dachshund, we need to store only a few bits of information about a friend's peculiar dachshund with a bald tail. We note first that it is a dachshund (with all the attributes of the species) and second that it has a bald tail, its individual peculiarity. In most cases, we probably select and store in memory whatever information is most useful for identifying an object as an instance of some category (Glass and Holyoak, 1986).

Concept Hierarchies

Most families of related concepts fall into a natural hierarchy based on levels of abstraction, from the broadest class down to the most specific details (see Table 9.1). In terms of this hierarchy, people tend to overuse some concept names and to underuse others. When we refer to ordinary objects in everyday conversation, we tend to use **basic level terms,** terms that lie somewhere in the middle of the concept hierarchy—not at the top (superordinate) or the bottom (subordinate). We are more likely to refer to our neighbor's pet as a cat than as a mammal or a Persian. We talk about our car rather than our vehicle or our sports car. This tendency is so persistent that adults almost invariably choose the basic level when naming objects for toddlers.

We seem to zero in on this intermediate level because it conveys the most discriminating information in the most economical fashion, it is the easiest level to retrieve from memory, and it is thus most efficient. In a revealing study, Eleanor Rosch and her associates (1976) discovered that when people were asked to list the distinguishing features of categories at a high level of the hierarchy, such as "furniture," they listed only a few features. But when they moved from the superordinate level to the basic level ("chair"), they supplied a lengthy list of features. For items at the lowest, or subordinate, level ("bar stool"), people came up with only a few more features than they had already provided at the basic level. The basic level turns out to be a useful compromise: it has so many features that go together that the category is easy to pick out from others, but it is comprehensive enough to encompass many instances. Once again, the mind seizes on the most efficient means of understanding the world.

Symbolic Imagery

Often we think in images—mental pictures of objects, people, and scenes. If someone asks you to think of your neighbor's cat, a picture of the cat seems to pop into your head, almost as if a videotape were running on a screen inside your skull. Yet mental images have some peculiarities that are nothing like videotapes. Basically, images are not fully developed pictures. For one thing, they are often sketchy, vague, and incomplete. You can visualize a zebra but probably are not able to count its stripes; and although you may think you can readily visualize a long word, in fact you can read its letters forward much faster than you can read them backward. For another thing, images are often missing whole parts of the visualized object. Finally, and oddly enough, we can often see behind the image, or at least we can imagine looking at its hidden parts.

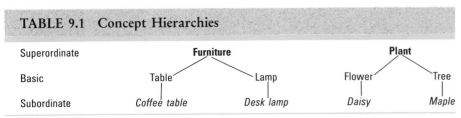

TABLE 9.1   Concept Hierarchies

Superordinate	**Furniture**		**Plant**	
Basic	Table	Lamp	Flower	Tree
Subordinate	*Coffee table*	*Desk lamp*	*Daisy*	*Maple*

Source: Rosch et al. (1976), Basic objects in natural categories, *Cognitive Psychology, 8*, 382–439.

For decades, psychologists have been struggling to understand mental images and the way we use them in thinking. The most comprehensive theory has been formulated by Stephen Kosslyn (1980; 1985; 1987), who explains mental images with an analogy drawn from computer science. He proposes that the mind has something like a visual graphics program that converts perceptual schemas stored in long-term memory into something like a computer display—the inner screen of our working, or short-term, memory. The brain builds the mental image from lines, angles, curves, and so on, just as it builds perceptions from similar patterns in the way we described in Chapter 5. And like a graphics program, the brain can move mental images around, alter their size, zoom in on parts, and rotate them.

Characteristics of Mental Images

In many experiments, researchers have identified some of the characteristics of mental images (Kosslyn, 1980; 1985). First, it takes us more time to generate complex images than simple ones. Second, we can "see" and verify details much faster when we have conjured up a large visual image of an object than when we have visualized it in miniature. Third, when we scan a mental image, we go through a process that is analogous to the way we move our eyes steadily along a path from one location to another. The farther apart two features are on the map in Figure 9.2, the longer it takes us to notice the second one—to move our focus from a first feature and verify the presence of a second (Kosslyn, 1983). Fourth, we can juxtapose parts of images to discover new and unsuspected relationships. For example, people have no trouble visualizing simple parts (lines, circles, letters, and angles) and mentally combining them to produce complex novel patterns (Finke and Slayton, 1988) (see Figure 9.3).

Physiological Aspects of Symbolic Imagery

There is some evidence, as studies of mental imagery imply, that perceiving an object and producing a mental image are functionally equivalent. When judging the similarity of the shapes of the fifty states, for example, our judgments tend to be the same whether we look at outline drawings of the states or simply recall and compare their shapes as they are named (Shepard and Chipman, 1970; Shepard, 1978). Moreover, we seem to use the same brain structures to produce visual images that we use to see the world. Researchers have found that imagery (imagining the neighbor's cat) interferes with visual perception (looking for locations on a map), and vice versa (Farah, 1985). Within those structures, however, the visual subsystem that encodes and interprets patterns may be distinct from the subsystem that generates images. Other studies have shown that some brain-damaged people can recognize objects but find it difficult, if not impossible, to generate mental images (Farah, Levine, and Calvanio, 1987).

We saw in Chapter 3 that visual imagery and the recognition of faces are both considered special abilities of the brain's right hemisphere, but there is evidence that one aspect of visual imagery may be primarily a left-hemisphere function. For example, J. W., a split-brain patient, could draw overall, general shapes using only his left hand, which is controlled by the right hemisphere, but he could not generate complex images, such as those made up of many parts. Yet with his right

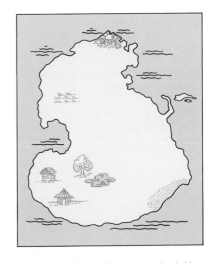

Figure 9.2 After subjects memorized this map, they were asked to hold an image of the entire map in mind as they mentally focused on one of its seven features—hut, well, tree, lake, beach, rock, and patch of grass—and then "looked" for a second one. The farther apart two features actually were on the map, the longer it took subjects to "scan" the mentally depicted distance between them. (Kosslyn, 1983.)

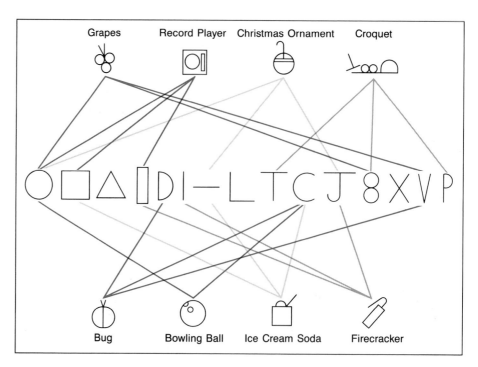

Figure 9.3   In an experiment on creative visual synthesis in mental imagery, subjects worked with the array of shapes shown in the center. They were asked to rearrange these parts mentally, combining them into familiar patterns. Some of the more creative patterns they recognized in various combinations of shapes are shown in the top and bottom rows. (Finke and Slayton, 1988.)

hand, which is controlled by the left hemisphere, he handled the complex-image task smoothly and efficiently (Kosslyn et al., 1985). Apparently, the left hemisphere does a better job than the right of interpreting relationships, arranging parts, and filling in intricate details, whether with language or with images (Kosslyn, 1987).

REASONING

REASONING   logical thought; the ability to think logically

Reasoning, the ability to think logically, is considered one of the highest forms of human thought. Traditionally, many philosophers have assumed that whenever we tried to think our way through problems, we followed certain inborn logical rules. They believed that the laws of logic were the universal laws of thought. But once psychologists began examining people's thought processes as they "reasoned," it became increasingly clear that we frequently fail to apply logical principles and often end up drawing less than logical conclusions.

Two major forms of logical reasoning have traditionally been distinguished: *deduction* and *induction*. People normally use both types, either alternately or together.

Deductive Reasoning

DEDUCTIVE REASONING   a form of logical reasoning in which we draw out the implications of some assumptions

In **deductive reasoning,** we draw out the implications of some assumptions: we conclude that certain consequences must be true if we grant that certain initial things are true. One basic method of formal deductive reasoning, which dates back to Aristotle, is the syllogism (Adams, 1984). A **syllogism** begins with two assumptions, known as *premises,* and ends with a conclusion that *must* be true if the premises are true.

Premise 1:	All astronauts are intelligent.
Premise 2:	Sally Ride is an astronaut.
Conclusion:	Therefore, Sally Ride is intelligent.

We often use syllogisms in our daily life, even though we usually run through the premises so fast that we're hardly aware of the process. You're supposed to meet Cathy for lunch. You think, "Cathy is always late for appointments. Cathy and I have a lunch appointment today. Cathy will be late today." And so you take your time getting to the restaurant.

In classical logic, the premises and conclusion in a syllogism can take one of four forms. The four possible statement forms are as follows: *All* As are Bs; *No* As are Bs; *Some* As are Bs; *Some* As are *not* Bs. The premises usually relate A to B and B to C, and the conclusion asserts some relation of A to C. Since there are four forms in each of the three statements, there are sixty-four (4 × 4 × 4) different syllogism forms, but only some of them produce valid conclusions. Examples of valid syllogisms are:

All As are Bs.	Some As are Bs.
All Bs are Cs.	No Bs are Cs.
Therefore, all As are Cs.	Therefore, some As are not Cs.

Researchers have found that some syllogism forms are much harder to recognize as valid or invalid than others, so they may mislead people into reaching erroneous conclusions. Note, too, that the validity of an argument is completely unrelated to its truth or falsity. A valid argument merely draws out the implications of premises that are assumed to be true.

Even when we are trying hard to be logical, we may misinterpret a premise and draw the wrong conclusion (Adams, 1984). One trap that is easy to stumble into is the **atmosphere effect,** in which certain terms in the premises—"all," "no," "some," and "not"—are carried over to the conclusion. They seem to push us toward a conclusion that contains the same term:

Some lawyers are in Congress.
Some Republicans are in Congress.
Therefore, some lawyers are Republicans.

We are tempted to accept the conclusion, because we know that some lawyers are indeed Republicans, but it does not follow logically from these premises. The hazards of the atmosphere effect become clearer when we look at an identical syllogism:

Some women are astronauts.
Some men are astronauts.
Therefore, some women are men.

Another logical pitfall is the **conversion error,** in which we "convert" the premise and erroneously assume that its reverse is also true. For example, we might reverse the premise "All New Yorkers are Easterners" and conclude, "All Easterners are New Yorkers." Before you smile at such a silly judgment, consider the following conversion error, which is a type of error frequently made:

All communists wanted the United States to stop the war in Vietnam.
Alex wanted to stop the war in Vietnam.
Therefore, Alex was a communist.

Deducing from these premises that Alex was a communist is as erroneous as deducing that all Easterners are New Yorkers.

When we try to reason logically, we apparently don't follow the laws of logic, as philosophers once supposed. Instead, we set up a **mental model** of the problem, using either abstract symbols or imagery. We may imagine a little stage play, in which sets of actors are introduced to represent the premises. As we watch this

SYLLOGISM   one method of deductive reasoning, in which two premises (if true) lead to a correct conclusion

ATMOSPHERE EFFECT   in deductive reasoning, an error in which the presence of terms like "some" and "all" in the premises leads to invalid conclusions containing the same words

CONVERSION ERROR   in deductive reasoning, an error in which the converse of a true statement is assumed to be true

MENTAL MODEL   the use of abstract symbols or imagery to represent and reason about a problem

Aristotle (384–322 B.C.) was the Greek philosopher who formulated the syllogism, the basis for deductive reasoning.

internal drama, we try to read off the conclusion (Johnson-Laird, 1983). Given the premise "All chefs are bakers," we could visualize several figures wearing chefs' hats and carrying a cake. The second premise, "All bakers have mustaches," leads us to put a mustache on each baker. The conclusion is perceptually obvious: "All chefs have mustaches." (If the second premise had been "Some bakers have mustaches," we would have put a mustache on only some of the figures, and our conclusion would have been, "Some chefs have mustaches.") We go astray in solving logical problems when the premises require us to keep track of too many alternative models (Johnson-Laird and Steedman, 1978). In such cases, either our working memory becomes overloaded or we simply omit (ignore) one of the models (the people who wanted to stop the war who were not communists) and come up with the wrong answer.

Other kinds of mistakes are likely in deductive reasoning. A false assumption in one of the premises of a syllogism can lead us to jump to a conclusion that is factually incorrect because our reasoning is invalid (Rips, 1983; Braine, Reiser, and Rumain, 1984). Consider the following:

■ If members of ethnic group A are less intelligent than members of ethnic group B, As will have lower average scores than Bs on IQ tests.

■ Members of ethnic group A do have lower average scores on IQ tests.

■ Therefore, members of ethnic group A are less intelligent than members of group B.

This conclusion is erroneous because the first premise falsely assumes that inferior intelligence is the only possible cause of group A's lower IQ scores. In fact, however, any number of other factors may be involved—cultural differences, test biases, poor schooling, poor motivation, and discrimination (Halpern, 1984). Our mistakes in logic can have serious consequences for social policies. (We will return to this issue in Chapter 11, on intelligence.)

Even if we all used perfect logic all the time, the world would still be full of strife and disagreement. Disagreement would not disappear unless everyone accepted the same factual or moral premises. As we have seen, logic simply allows the premises to dictate the conclusion. Consider the debate about surrogate motherhood. Whether you believe the practice should be outlawed depends on the premises you hold regarding such issues as a woman's control over her body, the importance of honoring a contract, the importance of the natural mother–child

Disagreements over issues such as abortion rights arise from different factual or moral premises.

bond, the money paid to the surrogate mother, the situation of poor women who volunteer to become surrogates, and artificial insemination. The inability to agree on premises explains why people of good will can reason logically and still disagree over presidential candidates, abortion, capital punishment, atomic weapons, and a host of other issues. Logic and morality do not necessarily go hand in hand.

Inductive Reasoning

The logic of **inductive reasoning** moves in the opposite direction from that of deductive reasoning. In *de*ductive reasoning, the conclusion is *de*rived from general rules; in *in*ductive reasoning, the general rule is *in*ferred from specific cases. We note several cases and try to figure out a rule that explains them all, concluding that some generalization is true on the basis of experience. The conclusion that a dropped pebble will fall to the ground because that has always happened in the past is an induction. But inductions are not necessarily correct. If the first five Jamaicans you meet as you walk down the street in Kingston speak English, you might infer that all natives of Kingston speak English—yet this is not logically required and may even be false. Another example of inductive reasoning is little Jessica's discovery of the concept "orange," which required her to infer general properties of the concept, such as "Oranges are round," from specific instances.

Inductive reasoning is basic to the way we learn. The close relationship between induction and intelligence is reflected in the fact that IQ tests include many questions that require inductive reasoning. This type of reasoning is also central to the scientific method, which we explored in Chapter 2. It's the sort of reasoning that researchers use when formulating hypotheses to explain results; they then test those hypotheses. Such testing is crucial to the process. Scientists constantly test their generalizations and assumptions against reality—against specific cases. To understand your private world as fully as possible, you must do the same. If you had talked with a sixth native of Kingston, you might have discovered someone who spoke only French, which would have invalidated your assumption about *all* natives. Or consider the following situation: A man drank bourbon and soda on Monday, and became drunk. The same thing happened after he drank Scotch and soda on Tuesday, and again after he drank rum and soda on Wednesday. He concluded that he should give up soda because it was the common element in all the concoctions that made him drunk. He has confused correlation with causation. If he has sense enough to try drinking soda by itself or mixed with fruit juice, he will quickly see that soda was not the culprit.

Inductive generalizations allow us to make sense of the world. Once we get our beliefs in order, we are reluctant to upset them, so we tend to avoid testing our generalizations. We avoid exposing ourselves to communications that try to persuade us that our political or religious beliefs are mistaken. This reluctance may arise because we find contradictions of our attitudes or beliefs distressing—a human tendency we will return to in Chapter 21. We use several devices to avoid overturning our generalizations. Sometimes we engage in *wishful thinking*: we want our belief to be true, so we ignore or discount opposing evidence and exaggerate favorable evidence. Sometimes we are guilty of *overconfidence*: we expect our judgment to be accurate more often than experience proves it to be. Even scientists sometimes place too much confidence in their own intuitions and are surprised when their experiments are less successful than they expected. And sometimes we are guilty of *perseverance*: even when the original evidence for our generalization is discredited, we nonetheless cling to our general belief because it is comfortable, familiar, and we can think of no better one.

Frequently, when we do decide to test a general belief, we go about it unproductively, choosing examples that can only confirm it and avoiding the harder tests that might disprove it. This is another form of mistaken reasoning, called **confirmation bias.** In a classic study, people were presented with a number series like 2-4-6 and were asked to figure out the rule the experimenter had in mind governing the series. The subjects were to do this by generating and checking their

INDUCTIVE REASONING a form of logical reasoning in which we infer a general rule from specific cases; it can produce probabilities, but not certainty

CONFIRMATION BIAS in inductive reasoning, an error in which a generalization is tested by using only examples that can confirm it rather than seeking those that might disprove it

own series (Wason, 1960, 1968). Each time the subjects generated a sample series, the researcher told them whether it conformed to the researchers' rule. Then, after subjects stated what rule they had used to generate the series, they were told whether their rule was the one the researcher had in mind. Time after time, subjects came up with a three-number series that conformed to the rule, but they persisted in guessing a far more specific rule than the experimenter had in mind. The problem was that when testing the rule they came up with, they generated only examples that would confirm their hypothesis. They rarely generated series that were inconsistent with their rule. For example, if they hypothesized that the rule was "Add 2, beginning with even numbers," they came up with series like 10-12-14. While such series conformed to the researcher's rule, their own rules were far more specific than they had to be. If the subjects had tried a series like 8-10-11 or 15-18-19, which would have violated their rule, they would have discovered that these series also conformed to the researcher's rule. The actual rule, which few subjects discovered, was extremely simple: form a series of any three numbers in ascending order.

From this study, we can induce a helpful lesson: we would probably be wrong less often if we looked for examples that would *dis*confirm our generalizations. It takes only one disconfirmation (a white crow) to disprove a generalization (all crows are black). But even if all our examples seem to support a generalization, we can never be certain that our inductive generalizations are correct. With this in mind, we would do well to remain more or less tentative about our inductive generalizations, stating our confidence in them in terms of probability. For example, we might say, "There's about a 95 percent chance that this car will need fewer repairs than that car." Far too often, we have to make decisions when information is limited and conditions are uncertain—a situation that we take up in the next section.

DECISION MAKING AND JUDGMENTS

Many of our decisions force us to weigh the costs and benefits of several courses of action and the probability of various future events. The solution to such problems is often unclear. Sometimes we are uncertain because we do not have enough

A major decision such as choosing a house to buy requires us to consider many alternatives and to estimate the probability of many future events.

knowledge to be aware of all the options: in looking for a job, for instance, we may not know the entire range of occupations that we might consider. Sometimes we are uncertain because the decision can be affected by events beyond our control: on the verge of buying a house, we might be concerned whether mortgage interest rates are going to rise or fall. Sometimes we are uncertain because our own preferences are not clear: we may not know whether we want to marry a particular person—or to marry at all. In all these cases, we are faced with choices that may bear heavily on our future, yet the outcomes depend on events that we cannot predict with any precision. Policymakers, government officials, diplomats, and business executives also face decisions whose outcomes may affect millions of people.

Decision-Making Heuristics

At times like these the human mind uses its own practical logic, based on experience. Faced with an uncertain situation, most of us come up with an answer based on **heuristics,** quick and intuitively sensible mental rules of thumb that allow us to assess probabilities. When used in many of life's everyday situations, heuristics lead us to workable solutions. But it is easy to find cases in which heuristics lead us astray. Two common heuristics that people often use are representativeness and availability.

HEURISTICS   quick and intuitively sensible mental rules-of-thumb that allow us to reason and make judgments

Representativeness

When we are trying to estimate the probability of some event, we are often betrayed by our reliance on **representativeness,** a heuristic in which our decision is based on how closely the event resembles a prototype or stereotype. In order to see how it works, read this description of Tom W., then decide whether he is more likely to be a computer science major or a humanities major.

REPRESENTATIVENESS   a heuristic that judges probability according to the resemblance of an event to a prototype

> *Tom W. is of high intelligence, although lacking in true creativity. He has a need for order and clarity, and for neat and tidy systems in which every detail finds its appropriate place. His writing is rather dull and mechanical, occasionally enlivened by somewhat corny puns and by flashes of imagination of the sci-fi type. He has a strong drive for competence. He seems to have little feeling and little sympathy for other people, and does not enjoy interacting with others. Self-centered, he nonetheless has a deep moral sense. (Kahneman and Tversky, 1973, p. 138)*

Chances are that you decide Tom is a computer science major. When Daniel Kahneman and Amos Tversky (1973) presented this profile to groups of university students, 95 percent of the students placed Tom in computer science. Tom certainly resembles the stereotypical computer science major, so the decision seems reasonable. But what if Tom is part of a classroom of 100 people and you know that 80 of them are majoring in the humanities and 20 in computer science? The odds that Tom is a computer science major should now be considerably less than 95 percent—say, about 30 percent to 40 percent. Yet that information had virtually no effect on the university students' judgment: they still believed Tom was almost certainly majoring in computer science. The students relied on representativeness, comparing Tom to their stereotypes of computer scientists and humanities majors, then choosing the stereotype he more closely resembled. Most significantly, they virtually ignored the important information that only 20 percent of the people in the room were computer science majors. In such situations, the salience of the person's resemblance to the stereotype of computer science majors leads subjects to ignore the statistics about population proportions. People seem to assume that stereotypes are accurate and that a person's resemblance to the stereotype is far more decisive than is more abstract statistical information.

The representativeness heuristic may mislead us into thinking that an athlete who scores on several consecutive attempts will be "hot" for the rest of the game—or even for the rest of the season. In fact, however, each shot is statistically independent of all the others.

AVAILABILITY a heuristic that relies on how easily relevant events are remembered

The representativeness heuristic also traps us when we try to judge whether a probability process is random or lawful; our bias is to see a purposeful plan behind any series or pattern. When judging the toss of a coin, we commit the "gambler's fallacy" (Jarvik, 1951). If we toss a coin ten times and it lands heads up each time, we believe that the odds of the next toss turning up tails are overwhelming. We fail to realize that each toss is independent of the last. On any toss of a fair coin, the chances are 50 percent that it will come up heads and 50 percent that it will be tails. The same fallacy causes gamblers to lose money at roulette. There is no "law of averages" at work, making it likely that, after a run of other numbers, our lucky number will come up soon. A similar superstition is behind the belief that a basketball player who suddenly begins to score one basket after another has a "hot hand." When the hit-and-miss sequences of NBA players are analyzed, the probability of various sequences are what would be expected if the probability of success of each shot was unrelated to the success of the player's previous shot (Tversky, Vallone, and Gilovich, 1984).

Availability

Most of us probably worry more about being murdered than about dying of diabetes, yet statistically we are twice as likely to die of diabetes as we are to be slain. In one study, researchers asked people to estimate how many people in the United States die each year from various causes (Lichtenstein et al., 1978). Whether they asked college students or members of the League of Women Voters, the response was the same: people greatly overestimated deaths due to dramatic or scary causes (plane crashes, murders, tornadoes, floods, and traffic accidents) and greatly underestimated deaths due to illness (asthma, diabetes, stomach cancer, and stroke). People make these mistakes because they use the **availability** heuristic, in which the likelihood of any event is estimated on the basis of how easily the memory of similar events springs to mind—in other words, on how available such events are in memory. We assume that the easier it is to generate lots of examples, the more examples of that type there must be. For example, people nearly always judge that there are more seven-letter words ending in "-ing" and in "-ly" than seven-letter words ending in "-_n_" and in "-l_." It is much easier to retrieve the "-ing" and the "-ly" words, so we persist in this judgment even though it is clear that every word that ends in "-ing" also ends in "-_n_." The set of "-_n_" words also contains words ending in "-_ne," "-_nt," "-_ns," and so on, so it must be larger than the "-ing" set (Tversky and Kahneman, 1982).

When therapists are making decisions about mental patients, they can be betrayed by the availability heuristic. Faced with a deeply depressed man, for example, a therapist has to decide how likely it is that this patient will attempt suicide. In such a situation, the therapist is unlikely to look at the statistical probability, based on all previous instances of depressed patients. Instead, the therapist is likely to recall earlier depressed patients who were suicidal. In this case, availability leads to an overestimation of the probability that this patient will attempt suicide (Glass and Holyoak, 1986).

The availability heuristic also leads to erroneous judgments when rare events (such as a mugging) are sensationalized by the media or made especially memorable in some other way (as when you are mugged yourself). The media do not report the hundreds of thousands of successful airplane flights, but they give extensive publicity to the flights that crash. Availability may explain why hundreds of tourists cancelled European tours during the months after terrorists murdered passengers waiting at the ticket counter in the Rome airport a few years ago. Such events stick out in our minds and thus appear far more likely to happen than they actually are.

Availability biases can distort beliefs in ways that are dangerous for all of us. Government leaders make many decisions based on judgments of risks: How safe are nuclear plants? Is recombinant-DNA research likely to introduce a new killer virus into our midst? Should AIDS patients be quarantined? Does cigarette smoking in public places materially affect the health of nonsmokers? Will the Russians abide by the INF missile treaty? Public opinion often influences such decisions,

The availability heuristic may cause people to change their behavior unnecessarily. The massive publicity given to plane crashes like the one in Sioux City, Iowa, in 1989 makes available more information about the danger of air travel than about its safety; as a result, people may avoid flying.

whether directly, through voting, or indirectly, through polls or lobbying. Thus, the public's perception of the risks involved in any given situation may make a difference in the outcome.

We are all familiar with the baseball fan who berates the manager for not changing pitchers when it was "obvious" that the next ball would be hit out of the park or the political pundit who explains *after* an election why the outcome should have been expected by everyone. When the availability heuristic works in this way, it's known as **hindsight** (Fischhoff, 1975). Looking back on events, we convince ourselves that the outcome was inevitable. In one study, people were given descriptions of two possible, but opposing, outcomes to an experiment and asked to estimate the probability of each result (Slovic and Fischhoff, 1977). Those who were tipped off as to the actual outcome gave it a much higher probability of occurring than did people who had no inkling of what actually happened.

Our moods and emotions may affect our judgment by influencing what is available to us in memory (Bower, 1983; Johnson and Tversky, 1983). When we are happy, we tend to view the world through rose-colored glasses, overestimating the likelihood of positive events and underestimating the likelihood of negative events. But when we are depressed or anxious, we become pessimists, downgrading the likelihood of positive events and raising the likelihood of negative events. Because of its effect on availability, mood may alter our diligence in studying, our performance on the job, our love life, or our tennis scores. When we are happy, we expect to do well on challenging tasks, whether they are romantic, assertive, intellectual, or athletic. But when we are sad, we expect to do poorly (see Figure 9.4B). Our estimates of our ability change with our mood, because when we are happy we remember more of our past successes and when we are sad, we remember more of our failures (Kavanaugh and Bower, 1985).

Another example of availability's pervasive influence on our judgment is the **conjunction fallacy,** which refers to our tendency to overestimate the likelihood of a connection between two events. The probability of two events occurring in a row (on the same morning, the newspaper isn't delivered and the car won't start) is always at most equal to (and usually less than) the probability of either one occurring separately. Probability theory also tells us that the likelihood of both events occurring together can be no greater than the chances of the first (say .03) times the chances of the second (say .008)—or .00024. But experiments show that we violate this rule, sometimes because of availability and sometimes because of representativeness (Tversky and Kahneman, 1983).

Conjunction fallacies caused by representativeness are probably as common

HINDSIGHT a bias in judgment, based on availability, in which a possible outcome is afterward seen as having been very probable

CONJUNCTION FALLACY judging the joint probability of two events to be greater than the probability of the less-likely one

as those caused by availability. They often arise when we assess other people, as in the following sketch:

> *Linda is 31 years old, single, outspoken, and bright. She majored in philosophy. As a student she was deeply concerned with issues of discrimination and social justice, and also participated in anti-nuclear demonstrations. (Tversky and Kahneman, 1983, p. 197)*

The students were asked how likely is it that Linda is an elementary-school teacher? an active feminist? a bank teller? a bank teller *and* an active feminist? Eighty-five percent of those who took this test believed that Linda was more likely to be both a bank teller *and* an active feminist than to be just a bank teller. But statistically this has to be a fallacy. What led so many people into this fallacy? Our picture of Linda is very similar to our *stereotype* of a feminist, and that makes the resemblance of Linda to a "feminist bank teller" greater than her resemblance to our idea of a "bank teller." So most people decided that the conjunction ("feminist bank teller") was more likely than the statistically more probable ("bank teller"). By confusing probability with similarity judgments, they violated the most basic rule of probability theory: the probability of a conjunction of events or features is always equal to or less than the probability of the less frequent event.

Judgmental Comparisons: Anchoring and Framing

Most of our judgments are based on a comparison to some standard. The trouble is that the standards are always shifting, and we do not necessarily shift along with them. Once we have set on a standard, it "anchors" our comparison, and we find it difficult to move farther. If you ask a stock-market analyst to predict the Dow-Jones high for the current year after being told last year's *high*, the expert will come up with a higher figure than she would have if you had mentioned the Dow-Jones *low* for the previous year (Tversky and Kahneman, 1973). Like the stock-market analyst, we become focused on the starting point (or "anchor") and do not adjust sufficiently to arrive at an unbiased judgment. This tendency is known as **anchoring**, which means making a judgment that is biased by the effect of the starting point from which the decision is made, and it influences many of our financial decisions. If you see a sticker price of $500 on a VCR and are told by the salesclerk that you can have it at the special price of $350, you feel that you are getting a bargain. Anchored at $500, you never stop to ask why the "regular price" is so exorbitant.

When we are trying to decide on a course of action, the way the choice is framed can determine our psychological bookkeeping and hence our decision. **Framing**, which refers to the way the problem is presented or the question is worded, can lead us to think of an action in terms of either gains or losses. And most of us hate losses even more than we like gains. When asked to judge whether to start a new business, we are likely to give the go-ahead if told that we have an 80 percent chance of success but to back off if told that we have a 20 percent chance of failure. We have been given the same information in both instances, but the second focuses our attention on the loss that might be involved.

In a classic example, Amos Tversky and Daniel Kahneman (1981) asked people to imagine that the outbreak of an unusual disease was expected to kill 600 people. Two programs to limit the disease's effects were proposed: Program A would save 200 lives; with Program B, there was a one-third probability that all 600 people would be saved and a two-thirds probability that no one would be saved. Both of these options are framed in terms of *saving* lives, and most people chose Program A. But when the program was presented to other people, now framed in terms of *losing* lives, the picture changed. Told that Program A would lead to the death of 400 people but Program B offered a one-third probability that no one would die and a two-thirds probability that 600 people would die, most people chose Program B. When options were framed this way, subjects were willing to take the very same risk that was avoided when the choice was framed in

ANCHORING making a judgment that is biased by the effect of the starting point from which a decision is made

FRAMING presenting a problem so that outcomes are described as gains or losses from a presumed reference point

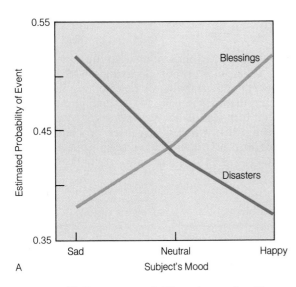
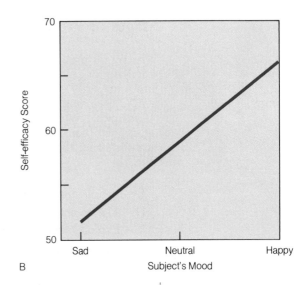

Figure 9.4 (A) The average probability estimates of positive events ("blessings") and of negative events ("disasters") for subjects in a happy, neutral, or sad mood. (Data from Wright and Bower, unpublished.) (B) The average self-efficacy score, or prediction of performance skill across diverse activities, for subjects who were feeling sad, neutral, or happy about themselves. (Data from Kavanagh and Bower, 1985.)

terms of gains. The certainty of 400 deaths seemed worse than the risk of 600 deaths; but the certainty of saving 200 lives seemed preferable to the risk of saving no one. The researchers concluded that, in decisions involving risk, people generally evaluate the negative impact of potential losses as far greater than the positive impact of potential gains. (See the accompanying box for more on decision making.)

The implications of framing extend into the voting booth, and some researchers believe that it explains the electorate's tendency to vote for incumbents when the economic situation is good and for challengers when the economy appears to be deteriorating (Quattrone and Tverksy, 1988). Because incumbents are familiar, they are usually seen as less risky than challengers, so the less risky candidate fares best when conditions are good. But risky candidates profit from hard times even when the public rates them as no better than the incumbent.

PROBLEM SOLVING

Every day we solve hundreds of small problems, and in the process we learn routine actions for handling those that recur. The solutions become automatic, and we no longer consider ourselves to be "solving problems." Only when an established routine fails do we begin to think again about familiar problems. Getting to school poses no problem unless your car or bike breaks down and the buses are on strike. Fixing dinner is no challenge unless a power failure turns off all your appliances.

These problems are everyday puzzles, but others, such as repairing a stereo, require expertise. Problems differ in many ways. Some are **well-defined**: there is an accepted procedure for determining whether a proposed solution is correct. Thus, math and logic problems are well-defined, since you can prove whether you have found the solution. Other problems are **ill-defined**: there is no universally accepted method for determining the "correct" answer. Ill-defined problems include devising an efficient study schedule, formulating a plan to save money for a vacation, designing a house, and writing a novel. There are many more or less acceptable solutions to each of these problems, but they vary according to the individual's tastes.

WELL-DEFINED PROBLEM a problem with a clear structure and accepted rules for solution

ILL-DEFINED PROBLEM a problem with no agreed-on rules or form for solution

Stages of Problem Solving

Whether the problem is well- or ill-defined, we follow somewhat the same steps in searching for a solution. According to one view, problem solving can be analyzed into four partly overlapping stages: (1) understanding or representing the problem; (2) planning a solution; (3) carrying out the plan; (4) evaluating the results (Glass and Holyoak, 1986). A similar formulation has been put forth by psychologists John Bransford and Barry Stein (1984), who add an earlier, problem-identification stage; their five stages of problem solving are known collectively as IDEAL:

I = Identify that a problem exists and what it is.
D = Define and represent the problem.
E = Explore possible strategies.
A = Act on a selected strategy.
L = Look back and evaluate the results.

The name IDEAL, made from the initial letters of each stage, forms a handy mnemonic that may help you remember the entire process.

I = Identify the Problem

Problem-solving activities aren't triggered unless someone *identifies* the existence of a problem. We all know that necessity is the mother of invention. That popular saying simply means that every inventor begins by noticing a need and then designs a gadget to solve it. Every tool, every appliance, every piece of furniture, and every article of clothing represents a problem identified and then solved by some inventor. Most of us learn to put up with many of life's little frustrations, but inventors can turn them into opportunities. The person who designed the magnetic case for spare keys had probably been locked out of a house or car, but after jimmying the lock or breaking a window went on to invent a marketable solution (Bransford and Stein, 1984). Every advance in human thought and science depends on the identification of a problem whose solution is then worked out. Not until poor sanitation was identified as a major health problem did cities around the world begin to build sewers. Not until the long-term consequences of deforestation were recognized was there an effort in Third World countries to

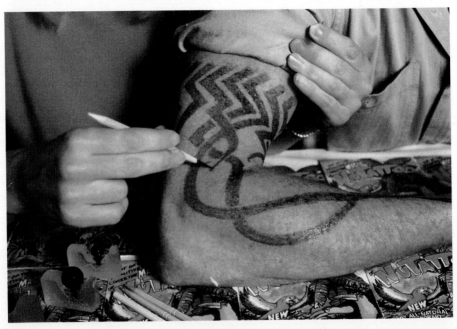

A number of problems with conventional tattoos have been identified, including the risk of infection from the needles used and that tattoos are permanent. The ingenious solution: the temporary tattoo, which does not puncture the skin and fades away after about two weeks.

PSYCHOLOGY TODAY AND TOMORROW

How To Make Better Decisions

After exploring the pitfalls of decision making, you may feel that good decisions are impossible. Yet major decisions must be made—about jobs, mates, children, where to live, what to do with your money, or how to make money in the first place. You discover whether a decision is good or bad only after you make it and begin to see its consequences. Sometimes you may never know whether your choice was the right one. If you decide to remain single, you can only guess what your life would have been like if you had married.

There is no way to guarantee good decisions, but a useful procedure exists that can increase your chances of doing somewhat better. This procedure uses a worksheet, which defines the problem, lists possible solutions, assesses the considerations that enter into each solution, and then provides a weighted evaluation of each option you can use to guide your choice (Halpern, 1984). It's too time-consuming to use when the question is where to go for dinner or which TV program to watch, but the worksheet can be invaluable when you're trying to decide on your college major, your career, your summer job, or even which used car you should buy.

Suppose you are trying to decide which summer job to accept. You've been offered three: a job behind the counter at McDonald's, a job filing and doing word processing at an insurance agency, and a job working on a crew for a local landscape architect. You decide what considerations (attributes) are important to you: salary, interest in the work, and working conditions. Next you *weight* each attribute in terms of its relative importance to you (for example, less important = 1; somewhat important = 2). Then, on a scale of 1 to 10 (1 = least), you estimate how well each job satisfies each consideration. After filling in the columns, you add them up. This is the simple sum. Finally, you multiply each satisfaction figure by its importance, then add the products to get the weighted sum.

If one of the jobs rates highest on all three dimensions, or if one rates worst, your decision is easy. But when rankings of the alternatives differ across dimensions, as they usually do, you have to decide how to weight the various dimensions themselves. Is your interest in the job only half as important to you as salary or working conditions? Are working conditions as important to you as salary? Say that before you weight the scores, the insurance company looks like your best bet. The poor working conditions on the landscape crew (hard labor in the summer sun) may explain why the salary is so good, just as the quiet, air-conditioned insurance office with no pressure and plenty of coffee breaks explains why the salary there is so low. But if your weightings are correct, you would go to work on the landscape crew with the conviction that you made the most nearly rational decision you could.

Studies of college students indicate that those who used the worksheet method to select a college felt less hassled by the decision and were happier about their choices than students who had used other methods (Mann, 1972). Patients who used the worksheet method to make decisions about elective surgery reported similar benefits (Janis and Mann, 1977). The worksheet gives people the feeling that their decision was made as reasonably as possible. The benefits of this method are not in the choices themselves, but in the way it allows people to perceive the choices and reduce their later worry and regret at not having made a careful decision.

Worksheet on Choosing a Summer Job

		Alternative Summer Jobs		
ATTRIBUTES	IMPORTANCE OF ATTRIBUTE	MCDONALD'S	INSURANCE AGENCY	LANDSCAPE CREW
Salary	2	4	2	7
Interest	1	3	6	3
Working conditions	2	6	7	4
Simple sum		13	15	14
Weighted sum		23	24	25

Rating: 1 = least; 10 = most.

Figure 9.5 An invention for reducing grease spatters.

make cooking stoves that burned wood more efficiently. In science and in business, in politics and government, problem finders are as important as problem solvers. Management consultants are paid enormous sums by corporations to observe company operations and point out problems that are reducing productivity and profits.

D = Define and Represent the Problem

Once a problem is identified, it is important to define it carefully and try to represent its essential features. A given problem may be defined in several ways, and each way suggests a different path to a solution. Suppose you identify as a problem the fat that splatters whenever bacon is fried (Bransford and Stein, 1984). If you define the problem as a consequence of too much heat, your solution would call for a way to cook bacon at a lower temperature. Another person might define the problem as one of reducing the chances of painful burns. The solution would call for protecting the cook's hands and arms, perhaps with heat-resistant gloves. A third person might define the problem as one of preventing the flying grease from spattering the area around the burner. That solution led to the device pictured in Figure 9.5, a screened lid that can be purchased in most housewares departments. The screen keeps hot fat in but lets steam out. The way in which the problem was defined determined the type of solution.

The way you represent a problem also can determine how easily you solve it. Visualization, either mental or on paper, often helps. One useful technique is to diagram the problem. Try working out the following problem in your head:

> There are three separate boxes of equal size. Inside each box are two separate, small boxes. Inside each small box are four even smaller boxes. How many boxes are there altogether?

If you did the multiplication in your head, you probably came up with the wrong answer ($3 \times 2 \times 4 = 24$). Most people do. But if you draw the boxes as small rectangles or circles, you immediately see that there are twenty-four of the smallest boxes, six medium-sized boxes, and three large boxes, for a total of thirty-three. See Figure 9.6 for another example.

Another sort of representation that helps you keep track of the possibilities in a problem is the logic table. Try it with a simple reasoning problem:

> Janet, Barbara, and Elaine are a homemaker, lawyer, and physicist, although not necessarily in that order. (1) Janet lives next door to the homemaker. (2) Barbara is the physicist's best friend. (3) Elaine once wanted to be a lawyer, but decided against it. (4) Janet has seen Barbara within the last two days, but has not seen the physicist. What is the occupation of each woman? (Sternberg, 1986).

This problem becomes easy to solve with a systematic representation like the logical table presented in Table 9.2. Every numbered sentence in the paragraph above excludes one or more of the possible pairings of woman and occupation. The cells in the table are filled in with the numbers of the statements that rule out various possibilities. The cells that are left blank reveal which woman has which occupation.

E = Explore Possible Strategies

A general rule is to avoid impulsive answers and to explore possible options systematically—breaking the problem into simpler, solvable parts; solving each of them; then combining the answers. The advantage of this technique becomes clear if you are asked, "What day follows the day before yesterday if two days from now will be Sunday?" Take it a step at a time. If two days from now is Sunday, today is Friday. The day before yesterday is Wednesday; the day following that is Thursday. You have your answers without any struggling or head-scratching.

TABLE 9.2   Logic Table for Problem Solving

	LAWYER	HOMEMAKER	PHYSICIST
JANET		No (1)	No (4)
BARBARA	Infer No (from 1 and 4)		No (2 and 4)
ELAINE	No (3)	Infer No (from 1, 2, and 4)	

MEANS–END ANALYSIS   Not all problems can be broken down so easily. Sometimes it is difficult to distinguish the subparts and the order in which they should be tackled. A technique known as **means–end analysis** is designed to do just that (Newell and Simon, 1972). In this heuristic strategy, the overall problem is broken down into subgoals that can be achieved by solving smaller problems. Each subgoal you reach brings you closer to the solution of the overall problem. Suppose the problem is to get to the airport. An airport bus will take you there, but first you must catch it. Where do you do that? At the bus stop. The next subgoal is to get to the bus stop. How do you do that? Walk to it. But suppose you reach the bus stop only to find that the buses are on strike. Then you have to begin problem solving again, searching for an alternate means of transportation such as calling a friend who has a car.

MEANS–END ANALYSIS   breaking a problem into subgoals that can be reached by solving smaller problems

PROBLEM-SOLVING AS SEARCH   Another way to look at the strategies involved in problem solving is to reformulate the problem as one involving search.

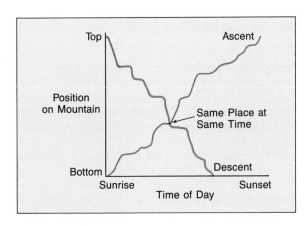

Figure 9.6   The importance of representation: The Buddhist monk problem. The way we represent a problem can affect the ease with which we solve it. Consider the following problem:

> One morning, exactly at sunrise, a Buddhist monk began to climb a tall mountain. A narrow path, no more than a foot or two wide, spiraled around the mountain to a glittering temple at the summit. The monk ascended at varying rates of speed, stopping many times along the way to rest and eat dried fruit he carried with him. He reached the temple shortly before sunset. After several days of fasting and meditation he began his journey back along the same path, starting at sunrise and again walking at variable speeds, with many pauses along the way. His average speed descending was, of course, greater than his average climbing speed. Show that there is a spot along the path that the monk will occupy on both trips at precisely the same time of day.

If you represent this problem verbally or mathematically, you may conclude that it is highly unlikely that the monk would find himself at a given spot at the same time on two different days. But if you represent the problem *visually*, a simple proof emerges that such a spot must exist. Simply visualize a second monk who begins to ascend the mountain at the same time that the first monk starts his descent. It then becomes obvious that, regardless of their speed, the two monks must meet at some spot along the trail at the same time of day. An abstract visual representation of the problem, like the one below, makes it even easier to "see" the solution. (Problem from Duncker, 1945; solution diagram from Glass and Holyoak, 1986, p. 375.)

You want to reach a goal, and a range of moves and methods exist that can get you from your present place to your goal (or subgoal). Thus, when you went from your home to the bus stop, your method was "walking." If you considered all the possible moves you might make at each step in your solution, you could generate an enormous number of possible plans, each leading to further steps. Finding a solution requires you to search efficiently the "tree" of possible options that you have generated. If you are working on a complex problem or immersed in a complex game (chess, checkers, jigsaw puzzles), you could not possibly explore all the options by trial and error. But through means–end analysis, you can reduce the number of useless searches.

WORKING BACKWARD *solving a problem by working backward from the goal*

WORKING BACKWARD An especially effective version of means–end analysis is **working backward** from your goal. The mazes that appear in the Sunday comics page are easy to solve if you merely work backward from the endpoint, because that way you have fewer options than with the forward path, which is full of dead ends (see Figure 9.7). You often work backward when solving such familiar problems as what time to leave the house in order to make an 8 o'clock movie. You calculate that you want to be at the ticket line by 7:40, that it takes 10 minutes to find a parking space, 10 minutes to walk to the theater from your car, and 20 minutes to drive to the theater from your home. You have no trouble deciding that you should leave at 7 o'clock. And when you make your calculations, you'll probably take into account potential obstacles—how popular the movie is, whether it is a weeknight or a weekend, probable traffic conditions, and the like.

Some problems turn out to be far easier when worked backward. When worked forward, from day 1, the following problem is a prescription for insanity: "Water lilies on a certain lake double in area every 24 hours. From the time the first water lily appears until the lake is completely covered takes 60 days. On what day is it one-fourth covered?" Worked backward, this problem can be solved in seconds: day 58. (On day 59, the lake is half-covered—¼ covered × 2 in 24 hours = ½ covered—so the lake must be one-fourth covered on day 58.)

ANALOGY *a parallel or correspondence between two different systems whose parts are similar in some way*

ANALOGY Sometimes the solution to another problem will suggest a way to solve a problem that, on the face of it, seems quite different. This kind of solution requires you to find an **analogy**, a parallel or correspondence between two different systems whose parts are similar in some way. A familiar analogy in physics texts is that drawn between the flow of electricity through a circuit and the flow of water through pipes in a house.

To see how the technique works, read the following problems and determine the analogy between them.

You are a doctor with a patient who has a malignant stomach tumor. You cannot operate, but unless you can destroy the tumor, the patient will die. A kind of ray, at sufficiently high intensity, can destroy the tumor. But at this level the rays will also destroy the healthy tissue in their path. At intensities low enough to spare the healthy tissue, the rays have no effect on the tumor. How can you use the rays to destroy the tumor without injuring the healthy tissue?

A small country is under the control of a dictator, who rules the country from a strong fortress. The fortress is situated in the middle of the country, surrounded by farms and villages. Roads radiate outward from the fortress like spokes on a wheel. You are a general who has vowed to capture the fortress and free the country. You have a large army massed at the border of the country and are certain that if you could attack the fortress at once, you could capture it. Your troops are poised at the head of one of the roads, ready to attack. Then a spy brings you disturbing news. The dictator has planted mines on each of the roads, and they will explode when any large force of men tries to cross. If any of the mines are detonated, the road will be impassable and the dictator will destroy many villages in retaliation. A full-scale

Figure 9.7 Working backward is a
good strategy when there are
fewer paths from the goal than
from the start. (Halpern, 1984.)

*attack on the fortress seems impossible. However, small bodies of men can
pass over the roads safely, because the dictator has to be able to move his
troops and workers. Can you mount a successful attack on the fortress? (Gick
and Holyoak, 1980, p. 351)*

The analogy is between sending many small groups of men along the different
roads to arrive at the same time and sending several small doses of radiation
through the body, focusing on the tumor from different angles, so that only the
tumor receives a concentrated, lethal dose. Students who solved one problem
were often able to solve the analogous problem, especially when some clue or hint
reminded them of the analogy (Gick and Holyoak, 1980).

Analogies often serve as the inspiration for inventions. Cyrus McCormick got
his idea for the grain reaper by drawing an analogy between stalks of wheat and
human hair. Noting the function of the barber's hair clipper, McCormick thought
that a similar, larger clipper might work on wheat stalks. His larger clipper became the mechanical wheat harvester.

There is no single standard by which a work of art can be judged, but training and experience help artists learn how to assess objectively the quality of their own and others' work.

A and L = Act and Look at Your Results

Once the plan is selected, you follow it, then check to see how it's progressing. These two problem stages are so closely related that they cannot be discussed separately, and in fact they sum up the scientific method of experimentation. If the problem was well-defined, you are likely to know soon whether your answer is correct. Sometimes, however, verification may be difficult—as when a computer programmer must "debug" a program, checking to see whether it is error-free under all conditions.

With ill-defined problems, which have no strict criteria for good solutions, evaluating proposed solutions may be the most difficult part of the problem. But with training, evaluation techniques can be learned. During their formal education, for example, artists, musicians, and scientists learn to judge the quality of work in their own profession and, by extension, the objective quality of their own work. Novices, even though they may be able to produce some original ideas at all levels of quality, cannot tell the good ideas from the bad ones (Johnson, Parrott, and Stratton, 1968).

Obstacles to Problem Solving

Obstacles continually get in the way of our attempts to solve problems. To see just how easily they can defeat us, try these simple word problems:

1. An airplane crashes on the U.S.–Canadian border. In what country are the survivors buried?

2. In the Thompson family, there are five brothers; each brother has one sister. If you count Mrs. Thompson, how many females are there in the Thompson family?

3. The black socks and blue socks in a drawer are mixed in a ratio of 4 to 5. Because it is dark, you cannot see the colors of the socks. How many socks do you have to take out of the drawer to be assured of having a pair of the same color?

Some people cannot answer the first two questions because they read carelessly and act on some preconception of the question. In question 1, "survivors" will not be buried anywhere; they are the ones left alive. In question 2, there are only two females: Mrs. Thompson and her only daughter, who is the "one sister" all the brothers have. The fact that there are five brothers is irrelevant. In question 3, the problem statement (the frame) can mislead us so that we focus on the wrong information (the 4 to 5 ratio). If you pick out any three socks, you are guaranteed

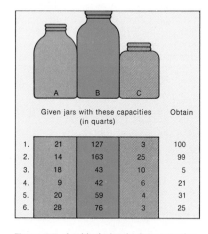

	Given jars with these capacities (in quarts)			Obtain
	A	B	C	
1.	21	127	3	100
2.	14	163	25	99
3.	18	43	10	5
4.	9	42	6	21
5.	20	59	4	31
6.	28	76	3	25

Figure 9.8 Luchins' classic demonstration of fixation in problem solving. In each of the problems in this series you must work out how you could measure out the quantities of liquid indicated on the right by using jars with the capacities shown on the left. Try the series yourself before reading on. After solving the first five problems, nearly two-thirds of Luchins' subjects were unable to solve the sixth. The sixth problem actually requires a simpler strategy than the first five, and it would be easily solved were it not for the fixation established by the first five.

that two will match in color. We are misled by our experience with problems in which such information has been relevant. In this case, drawing an analogy to a ratio problem would mislead us.

Fixation

Using an inappropriate strategy in the effort to solve a problem is often the result of **fixation**—literally, getting stuck on an ineffective approach and finding ourselves unable to move beyond it. In many cases, we apply the inappropriate tactic automatically and are not even aware that we need to see the problem in a new way. Sometimes fixation is referred to as **mental set** or *negative set,* both indicating our persistence in applying strategies that have worked in the past but are not appropriate to the situation at hand.

Before reading on, try the "water-jug" problem in Figure 9.8. The first five problems in the figure can be solved in the same way. Fill the largest jar (jar B), then from it fill the middle-sized jar (jar A) once and the smallest jar (jar C) twice. This method can be stated in a simple formula: B − A − 2C. But this solution does not work on the sixth problem.

In a series of classic studies (Luchins, 1946), most people who began with problem 6 solved it readily. People who solved the other five problems *before* they attempted problem 6 found it extremely difficult. Two-thirds of these people persisted in using the B − A − 2C formula, although it wouldn't work on problem 6, and they ignored the easy, one-step solution. Their fixation was so strong that many gave up, while others staunchly maintained that the formula worked, insisting that 76 − 28 − 2(3) must equal 25.

Two traditional examples of perceptual fixation are the nine-dot square problem and the six-match problem shown in Figure 9.9. Try to solve them before finishing this paragraph. The dot-problem task is to connect all the dots by drawing four straight lines without lifting the pencil from the paper. Most people perceive the nine dots as a square; they assume that the pencil lines must be drawn within the boundaries of the square. But even when people are told that the solution requires going outside the square, 80 percent of them still cannot solve it. The six-match problem has a similar obstacle: people assume that the triangles of the solution must all lie in the plane of the paper. (See Figure 9.11 for the solutions.)

A more specific type of fixation, called **functional fixedness,** refers to people's inability to use a familiar object to perform an unfamiliar function. In a classic test of functional fixedness, a person is shown into a room where a candle, tacks, and a box of matches lie on a table (see Figure 9.10). The problem is to mount the candle on the wall so that it burns properly, using any of the objects on the table. Because the matches are in their original box, most people think of the box as only a container and become fixed on this familiar function (Duncker, 1945). How would you solve this problem? (See Figure 9.12 for the solution.)

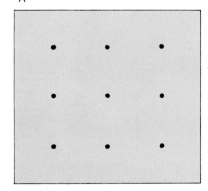
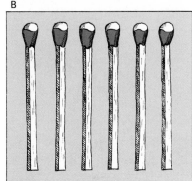

Figure 9.9 Two mind-teasers designed by Martin Scheerer (1963). (A) Nine dots are arranged in a square. The problem is to connect them by drawing four continuous straight lines without lifting pencil from paper. (B) Six matches must be assembled to form four congruent equilateral triangles each side of which is equal to the length of the matches. (If you don't have matches, any six objects equal in length will do.) Check your answers with those given in Figure 9.11.

FIXATION the tendency to apply automatically an inappropriate strategy to a new problem, then rigidly cling to that approach

MENTAL SET the tendency to repeat a representation of an object and its function that worked in other situations

FUNCTIONAL FIXEDNESS the inability to use a familiar object for an unfamiliar function

Figure 9.10 A problem used by K. Duncker to demonstrate functional fixedness. He gave subjects the materials shown and asked them to mount a candle on a wall so that it could be used to give light. Try to solve the problem yourself. (The use of the term "functional fixedness" gives you a clue to the solution of the problem that Duncker's subjects did not have.) The solution is given in Figure 9.12.

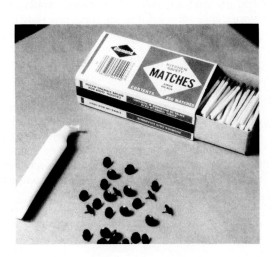

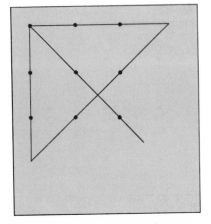

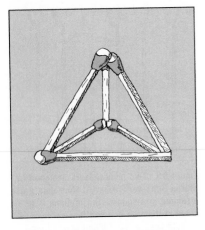

Figure 9.11 Solutions to the mind-teasers in Figure 9.9. The principal impediment in both of these problems is perceptual fixation. (A) The dot problem is solved by extending the lines beyond the dots; most people assume that they must stay within the perceived square structure. (B) The match problem is solved by building a three-dimensional pyramid; most people assume that the matches must lie flat, as they were first perceived.

ARTIFICIAL INTELLIGENCE (AI)
the science that develops computer programs that behave intelligently

Isolation of Knowledge

In fixation, we cannot solve a problem because we transfer an incorrect mental set; we see a similarity between problems that is inappropriate or maladaptive. In other cases, we fail to solve a problem because we do not realize that something we already know is relevant to the solution. We simply do not see the connection unless we're hit over the head with it, as we saw in the discussion of analogies. The key to the solution seems to sit unused in memory, because for some reason the problem fails to remind us of the relevant clue.

Just how stubbornly such clues can elude us became clear when researchers gave people needed information, only to find that they didn't use it (Perfetto, Bransford, and Franks, 1983). First, people rated the truth of a number of sentences such as "A minister marries several people each week." Three minutes after reading the list of sentences, they were asked to solve word puzzles, whose solution had been hinted at by the earlier sentences. For example, one puzzle read: "A man who lived in a small town in the United States married twenty different women. All are still living and he has never divorced any of them. Yet he has broken no law. Can you explain?" Those who had read the sentences could solve no more puzzles than people who were given the word puzzles cold. But those who were told that the earlier sentences contained clues to the word puzzles solved three times as many. Their alertness to the connection between the two situations allowed them to recognize the relevant clues and retrieve the crucial information from memory.

Computers as Problem Solvers

Theorists and researchers in the field of **artificial intelligence (AI)**, the science that develops computer programs that behave intelligently, use the analogy between the computer and the human mind as a way of understanding human problem solving. By making computers "think" like humans, researchers hope to understand how we solve problems, why—and how—we fail, and how we can improve our success rate. To this end, they have written computer programs that solve, and fail to solve, problems by using the strategies and steps used by humans. The programs apply these thinking abilities to broad, theoretical problems as well as to specific, practical problems, from diagnosing diseases to authorizing credit-card charges.

Programs that explore the theoretical basis of human thought are known as *general problem solvers.* When these were first designed, researchers believed that reasoning was a general skill that relied on several powerful strategies like means–end analysis. The earliest project in this area, spearheaded by Allen Newell and Nobel prizewinner Herbert Simon (1972), was written to enable the computer to solve well-defined problems in logic and mathematics or to play games like chess or checkers. Such problem-solving programs present the computer with the problem, the goal, the rules of the game, strategies like means–end analysis, and a set of inference rules for moving from one state to another. These are all well-defined problems that can be formulated as a heuristic search through a set of states, looking for a path to the goal state. More recent versions of general problem solvers are more flexible and more powerful than the early ones. Their greater power makes them better chess players and much cleverer at making inferences (Johnson, 1986; Waldrop, 1987).

Many AI workers now believe that problem solving is not a general skill that can be applied to any kind of problem. Studies of human expertise suggest that experts' superior performance is based on their large fund of knowledge about their specialty, including its typical problems and specific techniques for solving them. From these findings, researchers have developed *expert systems:* computer programs that are designed to make decisions and solve problems in a specific domain.

Scientists who build expert systems incorporate knowledge about a given domain in the form of a semantic network of concepts, or schemas (see Chapter

PSYCHOLOGY TODAY AND TOMORROW

Expert Systems in Business: Deciding When To Extend Credit

When the American Express credit-card division installed an expert system, the company had no idea that the new computer program would save them millions of dollars each year (Feigenbaum, McCorduck, and Nii, 1988). Authorizer's Assistant is an expert system that helps account advisers decide whether to approve a customer's request for a charge, and it works in the following manner. When a merchant wipes your credit card through the reader, the card numbers are flashed to Phoenix, Arizona (or to London if you are in Europe), where a big computer looks up the number and determines the status of your account—whether the card has been stolen or whether the account is badly delinquent, for instance. If the answer to the request for credit is obvious, the expert system handles it alone, passing or rejecting about a third of the requests without any human intervention.

If the amount is extremely large or the account's status is questionable, a human authorizer, or account adviser, gets the request posted on a computer screen along with a screenful of pertinent facts about the customer. The program acts as a smart consultant, telling the authorizer whether extending further credit would be wise—and why. Using a chain of inference-drawing rules, it analyzes past activity on the account. It notes whether an account is overdue because of simple failure to pay or because the card holder has been traveling extensively and has not been home to receive the bill. It takes the type of charge into account (hotel, restaurant, or merchandise). If it decides that the current charges are too far out of the account's usual pattern, it will warn the account adviser to beware of fraud.

Authorizer's Assistant enables decisions to be made faster and more accurately. It has cut the time for making difficult decisions by 20 percent, and it has increased American Express's income. By relying on the expert system, authorizers have been able to reduce the refusal rate on questionable charges by one-third—an outcome that brings in more revenue and makes more customers happy. Despite the decrease in refusals, only half as many of the authorized charges become delinquent. Since introducing the system, American Express has saved an estimated $27 million each year in account advisers' time and in bad account charges.

---

8), and a set of knowledge rules. Some rules are designed to draw inferences; others tell the computer to take a particular action if it detects a particular pattern of data. For instance, when a medical program diagnoses a patient's disease, it starts with the patient's reported symptoms, then reasons through a complex chain of rules. These rules take a specific form, known as "if-then": "If symptoms X and Y appear, then guess the patient has disease Z." The program then presents several likely diagnoses, ranked in order of their probability, and recommends a treatment for each diagnosis (Feigenbaum, 1977; Clancy, 1983). Some of these programs are notable because they include the sort of tacit, "intuitive," hard-to-verbalize knowledge that underlies the expert's skill. In tests, MYCIN, an early expert system that diagnosed and prescribed treatment for blood infections, meningitis, and similar ailments, performed as well as nationally recognized specialists in the field (Shortliffe, 1976; Waterman, 1986).

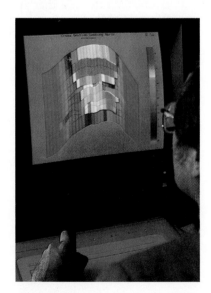

Using specialized programs known as *expert systems*, computers can point to correct solutions for problems in specific areas, such as the best method to use in extracting oil from a particular oil field.

Although expert systems are now used in medicine, engineering, geology, law, manufacturing, and business (see the accompanying box), even their developers admit that they cannot accurately reflect all aspects of a human expert's thought. For one thing, medical computers may know hundreds of symptoms but have no understanding of anatomy, physiology, or the underlying disease process. And so the computer sometimes appears stupid, as when it decides to ask for the blood pressure of a patient who has died. The computer also lacks all the additional information that human diagnosticians have about the patient in front of them, information that spurs hunches or qualifies the results of tests and the interpretation of symptoms (Dreyfus and Dreyfus, 1986). The accompanying box illustrates recent advances in problem-solving computer programs.

PSYCHOLOGY TODAY AND TOMORROW

The Super Expert Problem Solver

Allen Newell, one of the originators of the first general problem-solving computer, has turned AI research in a new direction. With John Laird and Paul Rosenbloom, Newell (1986) has merged general problem solving with expert systems and thrown in a dash of learning ability. SOAR, the new problem-solving program, uses the approach of the general problem solver but also has the knowledge rules of the expert system. SOAR goes even further. Expert systems can apply only one rule at a time, but SOAR can apply its rules in parallel, then examine all the recommendations and choose the best course of action. And it can learn. An expert system stops functioning when it gets a problem that is not covered by its rules. But when SOAR reaches an impasse, it figures out a sequence of moves that will get around it, then stores in its memory a description of the problem situation and the successful way of resolving it. In effect, SOAR writes a new knowledge rule for itself. The next time it meets the same impasse, it pulls out the rule and applies it (see the diagram below). Its ability to learn can turn SOAR from a novice to an expert in very little time (Waldrop, 1988a; 1988b).

Like humans, SOAR sometimes makes mistakes, drawing a wrong conclusion and writing an erroneous rule, and that presents a problem. When SOAR creates an incorrect rule, it has no way to erase it from memory. A current focus of

research is finding a way for SOAR to recognize errors. Once it can do that, the program will be powerful enough to reformulate its strategies so that it can avoid the incorrect rule in the future, even though it will still be in its memory.

Newell, who believes that all cognition involves some form of problem solving, hopes that SOAR will develop into a way of explaining all human cognition. Skeptics say that our knowledge of human cognition is still far too fragmentary to allow us to think in terms of a single, integrated set of information-processing mechanisms that can explain every aspect of human thought. They note, too, that SOAR lacks an important human element—it has no way to deal with emotion and consciousness (Waldrop, 1988b).

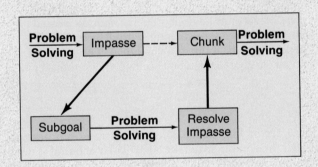

Human Expertise

When researchers in the field of AI began to rely on the thinking of experts to devise problem-solving programs, the computer's ability to make critical decisions expanded enormously and we began to learn more about the strengths and weaknesses of human thought. Researchers have discovered that human experts and novices approach problems in a very different manner, and they are now beginning to discover why this is so.

Every field, from auto mechanics to music, has its experts, who quickly solve problems in their own field that baffle novices. No matter what the field, to become an expert takes about ten years of concentrated application; during those years, the expert builds up an enormous store of specialized knowledge (Mayer, 1987). This knowledge gives experts their power. They outshine novices because they look at problems in a different fashion. Many of the problems that stump the novice are so common that the expert either recognizes the pattern or has already stored the solution in memory, so that no problem-solving thought is necessary. In the case of chess experts, the master player can recognize about 50,000 different patterns on the chessboard, with each pattern forming a single chunk in memory

(Simon and Gilmartin, 1973). (We discussed chunking in Chapter 8.) The chess expert also knows what to do when one of those patterns appears. She or he draws on the pertinent inferential rule that is stored away: for example, if chess pattern X, then move queen to square Y. The recognized pattern acts as a retrieval cue, and the expert merely has to retrieve the answer from memory, without having to reason through the move (Anderson, 1985). Thus, for the expert, not much problem-solving thought is necessary; or, perhaps more accurately, problem solving has become automatic. By contrast, the novice has to think through a host of possible moves and figure out what the responses of the other player might be. Short-term memory gets overloaded and the novice loses track of what he or she is doing.

Their deep fund of relevant knowledge also changes the way experts tackle problems whose answers they do not have on tap (Anderson, 1985). Experts represent problems in a particular way, in terms of implicit principles instead of surface features. Whereas novices represent a physics problem in terms of a spinning top or inclined planes, the expert represents the first in terms of conservation of energy and the second in terms of Newton's second law of motion. This speeds the expert's performance, because the principles are keyed to the relevant equations needed to find the solution. Experts also search for a solution differently. In the fields of geometry and physics, for example, they work forward, reasoning from the elements given in the problem, while the novice works backward from the goal set up by the problem (Anderson, 1985).

Figure 9.12 The solution to the problem depicted in Figure 9.10. Functional fixedness prevents most people from using the matchbox as a candleholder and using the thumbtacks to fasten the box to the wall.

Creativity and Problem Solving

Creativity enters the realm of problem solving when we produce a solution that is entirely new to us. This is true not just in everyday life but also in the arts, entertainment, the sciences, and technology. Some psychologists believe that creative achievements are neither romantic nor mysterious; instead, they result when highly motivated experts solve ill-defined problems, using the cognitive processes available to all of us. For example, the artist before the canvas may be solving a

A large fund of specialized knowledge acquired over the years makes it easier for experts in any field to solve problems by recognizing underlying patterns with which they are thoroughly familiar.

dual problem: how to express some feeling about his or her own life and how to produce a painting that will move others in a similar fashion (Weisberg, 1986).

All of us have some degree of creativity, and it can be encouraged or stifled. Yet too often when we try to solve a problem, we are unable to come up with the new ideas that would point the way to a solution. Computer scientist Roger Schank (1988) believes that the rules and ready answers of daily life tend to make us depend on somebody else's solution to a problem and, by keeping us from asking questions, effectively reduce our creativity. In this view, we become mired in our scripts. Scripts give us rules for almost every situation we encounter, so we can go about our business efficiently without looking for new solutions or simply wondering about the world—why magnets attract metal, how airplanes fly, what your cat is thinking, or why waiters get tipped. Yet such playful thought is closely related to creativity and the production of imaginative ideas, even though we seem to leave it behind when we emerge from childhood. One way to regain a creative approach to problem solving is to learn to question our assumptions.

Identifying Implicit Assumptions

Some researchers believe that we can improve our ability to detect the assumptions we make about the world and so increase our own creativity. Suppose you are stumped by a problem; you have been working on it for a long time and are getting nowhere. If you can identify your implicit assumptions about the problem or the form of its solution, you might break through the block to creativity. The difference an assumption can make shows clearly in the following example:

> *A man has four chains, each three links long. He wants to join the four chains into a single, closed necklace. It costs 2 cents to open a link and 3 cents to close it. The man had his chains joined into a continuous loop for only 15 cents. How did he do it? (Wickelgren, 1974)*

Try to solve the problem, representing it on a piece of paper. The diagram in Figure 9.13 may give you some ideas.

Many people bog down on the "cheap necklace" problem because they assume that they should work only with the chains' end links. But if you take apart all three links in one of the chains, the solution suddenly becomes obvious. Many scientific discoveries arise from questioning hidden assumptions. Astronomers tried for centuries to fit the data on planetary motion into the Ptolemaic hypothesis, which assumed that all heavenly bodies revolved around the earth. They put the planets through all sorts of eccentric loops in order to make their observed motion concur with the culture's assumptions. Once Copernicus questioned that assumption and placed the sun, instead of the earth, at the center of the universe, the data fell into line and the universe's heliocentric nature became obvious. But it wasn't easy to get society to accept this new view. Some years later, Galileo had to recant the sun-centered view of the universe before a council of the Catholic Church, which found the notion heretical. People, as well as societies, can be-

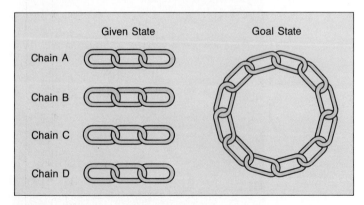

Figure 9.13

come so emotionally attached to their assumptions that they find it almost impossible to free themselves from their mental straitjackets.

The lesson we can learn from the Church's attachment to its earth-centered solar system is to search our own ideas for inconsistencies. If you generate an idea that seems plausible, try to think up an alternative that is also plausible but is inconsistent with your first idea (Bransford and Stein, 1984). Then examine the contexts in which both ideas seem plausible, and you just might discover the implicit assumptions behind your first idea.

Generating Novel Ideas

Most people are more creative than they realize. Researchers have discovered that people are not good at predicting their own success on problems that require creative solutions (Metcalfe, 1986). In our discussion of visual images, we saw how people can put together simple forms in their imagination, mentally playing with objects until they create novel patterns that they had no idea would appear (Finke and Slayton, 1988; see Figure 9.3).

Creative problem solving is the basis for technological advances. Here an agricultural researcher is examining pine shoots that have been cloned rather than grown from seeds.

If you can manage to increase the flow of novel ideas, you can improve your own creativity. First, stop worrying about failure. Shut off your critical sense, release your inhibitions, and let your imagination play freely with images and ideas. The immediate goal is lots of ideas, no matter how implausible or silly they may seem. Evaluation can come later, after you have generated all those ideas. In fact, too much evaluation, too early, can impede creativity. Studies have shown that college students who show little creativity tend to be highly critical of their own attempts and of the tasks themselves (Meichenbaum and Cameron, 1974). Such "uncreative" students have learned to increase their novel ideas by deliberately changing their thoughts and feelings. After observing a model, they practiced talking out loud in a positive fashion while they worked, saying such things as:

> *I want to think of something no one else will think of—something unique. I'll be freewheeling, no hangups. I don't care what anyone thinks. I'll just suspend judgment. I'm not sure what I'll come up with; it will be a surprise. The ideas can just flow through me. (Meichenbaum and Cameron, 1974, p. 278)*

With time, spoken statements became unspoken, almost automatic, thought patterns. Students who took such training not only showed significant increases in original thought, compared with a control group, but they also tended to view their own lives in a more creative fashion. Many reported applying creativity techniques to their personal and academic problems.

Another way to increase the number of ideas is to get a group of people thinking about a problem in a noncritical atmosphere. In this process, known as **brainstorming,** people think up unusual products or novel solutions, saying whatever comes to mind without fear of criticism or ridicule from the others (Osborn, 1963). The advantage to thinking in a group is that people tend to take differing perspectives, to start from different assumptions, and to put forward ideas that stimulate others to think along new lines. As researchers have found, novel solutions to problems are often produced when new information pushes the problem solver in a different direction (Weisberg, 1986).

One more strategy for generating ideas is **fractionation,** in which an idea is broken down into its parts and each part is examined for new possibilities and new properties (de Bono, 1967). Take the example of a simple brick. If asked to think of uses for a brick, most people think of it as a heavy rectangular object: a building block, a door stop, bookshelf support, a pavement for a walk or terrace, an edging for a flower bed, and the like. But if you fractionate the brick, you consider in turn each of the object's properties (red, porous, heavy, retains heat, can be held in one hand), then use these properties to trigger new uses. Why not crush it into tiny pellets and use it as a colorful groundcover in a garden? Why not warm it in the oven and put it in a bed to warm the sheets on a cold night? Such solutions

BRAINSTORMING a creative technique in which a group of people suggest unusual products or novel solutions in a situation free from criticism or ridicule

FRACTIONATION a creative technique in which an idea is broken down into parts and the parts are examined for new possibilities or properties

represent the ability to put together things we know in a new and different way, an outlook on which creativity thrives. Finding new solutions to old problems is just as creative as finding a solution to a problem that has never been solved before (Glass and Holyoak, 1986).

Becoming an IDEAL problem solver requires more than learning the five stages of the problem-solving process. As we have seen, obstacles to problem solving are incorporated into our mental processes, and expertise enhances the ability to solve problems in any area. Some schools have begun to teach problem-solving courses, in which children learn the various problem-solving skills detailed in this chapter and practice using them. The programs focus less on correct answers than on the thinking processes involved; in effect, they are courses in **metacognition**—knowledge about cognition and an understanding of the ways in which we can control our thought processes. Yet the role of expertise in problem solving suggests that teaching such skills in isolation may not be the best answer. In fact, the available evidence suggests that students may not transfer the specific skills learned in these courses to problems they encounter in their science, math, and history classes (Mayer, 1987).

METACOGNITION the knowledge about cognition and an understanding of the ways in which we can control our thought processes

The realization that thinking skills are learned within a particular context, whether it's chess or physics or menu planning, has led some psychologists to recommend that appropriate problem-solving strategies be incorporated into the teaching of various subjects. This view prompted Scott Paris and his associates (Paris, Cross, and Lipson, 1984; Paris and Jacobs, 1984) to draw on the metacognitive skills of "expert readers" to enhance children's reading comprehension. They taught the children such reading strategies as skimming, rereading, paraphrasing, making inferences, and checking to see if they understood what they had read. The children responded with increased reading comprehension. Like the expert-reader program, successful strategies help students analyze their own methods of solving problems and the way they learn (Bransford et al., 1986).

SUMMARY

What Is Cognition?

- Cognition allows us to solve problems by substituting symbolic actions for external events.
- Concepts and images, the symbols of external reality, are both the content and the tools of thought.
- Most everyday concepts are fuzzy, often consisting of a prototype surrounded by less typical examples.
- In instance-storage theories a concept is represented by detailed memories of instances and noninstances.
- Mental images may be formed by generating images from perceptual schemas; inspecting visual images involves processes similar to those involved in inspecting perceptual scenes.

Reasoning

- Reasoning tasks can be divided into deduction and induction.
- In reasoning with syllogisms, people are often misled by atmosphere effects or conversion errors.
- Although inductive reasoning can produce only statistical generalizations, it is the basis for most of our learning and allows us to form concepts.

Decision Making and Judgments

- Our judgment of events often rely on the heuristics of representativeness and availability, which occasionally lead to errors.
- Errors due to hindsight or conjunction fallacies can be explained by the availability heuristic.
- Judgments can be biased by the anchoring or framing of the problem.

Problem Solving

- Problems can be either well-defined or ill-defined.
- The problem-solving process goes through five IDEAL stages: identifying the problem; defining and representing it; exploring possible strategies; acting on a strategy; looking back and evaluating the results.
- Among the obstacles to problem solving are fixation, functional fixedness, and the isolation of knowledge.
- Workers in artificial intelligence try to simulate human problem solving by writing computer programs that use solution strategies similar to those used by humans.
- Some of these programs are general problem solvers; others are expert systems for specific problems.
- Because of their enormous fund of knowledge, human experts have automatic solutions for many problems in their fields; they approach other problems in a different fashion from novices.
- Most people can become more creative if they learn to identify their implicit assumptions and develop nonevaluative ways of thinking that permit the flow of novel ideas.

KEY TERMS

analogy
anchoring
artificial intelligence (AI)
atmosphere effect
availability
basic level terms
brainstorming
cognition
concepts
confirmation bias

conjunction fallacy
conversion error
deductive reasoning
fixation
fractionation
framing
functional fixedness
heuristics
hindsight
ill-defined problem

inductive reasoning
means–end analysis
mental model
metacognition
prototype
reasoning
representativeness
syllogism
well-defined problem
working backward

CONCEPT REVIEW

1.   Define *cognition*. Why does it include such a wide range of phenomena?

2.   How do concepts and categories develop? How do we learn new concepts? Distinguish symbol from concept.

3.   What is the primary distinction between the prototype approach to concept formation and the best-instance approach? In which situations does each have more explanatory power?

4.   Use an example from your own experience to explain the difference between deductive and inductive reasoning. Identify some of the errors made in both. Which of these two kinds of reasoning is used more frequently in science? Why?

5.   Describe the main types of heuristic reasoning used in everyday decision making. How do anchoring and framing affect the process?

6.   Describe the components of the "IDEAL" approach to problem solving. How is problem solving different from decision making?

7.   Distinguish among the four strategies for problem solving: means–ends analysis, search, working backward, and analogy. Can these be used together?

8.   Describe the obstacles to problem solving presented in the chapter. Where are these kinds of problems most likely to occur in your own learning process?

9.   Explain the idea of an expert system. How is it related to human experts?

10.   Summarize the two main views of creativity given in the chapter.

CRITICAL THINKING

1.   On the basis of what has been presented in Chapters 7 to 9 on learning, memory, and cognition, analyze the proposition that computers will someday be able to think as well as humans. Be sure to consider the types of evidence that will verify or falsify this proposition (a good analysis should be able to examine both options and lead to a judgment in favor of one).

2.   There are many views of creativity. Give your own definition of creativity. If your definition were to be studied scientifically, what are the measurable results or characteristics of creative performance that would support your view? Propose an experiment or a test that would utilize these objective components.

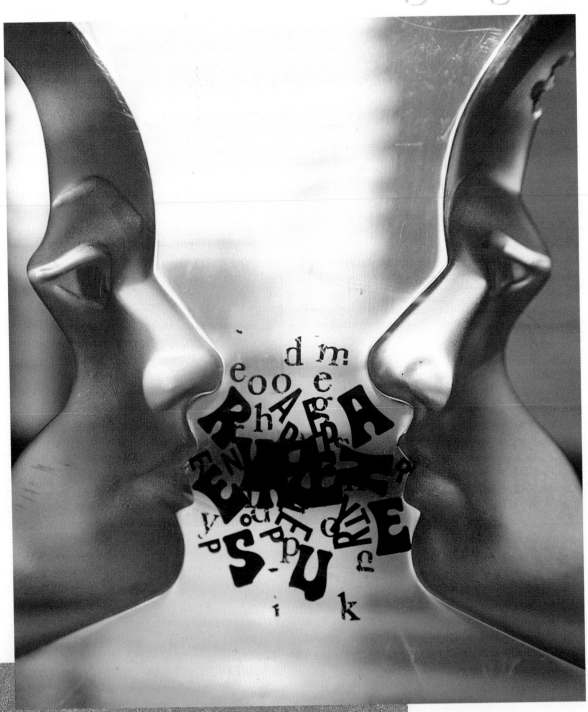

....Language

David Ford's aphasia made asking a simple question a nightmare and explaining his thoughts a near impossibility. Ford, a thirty-nine-year-old Coast Guard radio operator, had suffered a stroke 3 months before, and his brain's left hemisphere was damaged. He was alert and attentive, but talking presented a formidable problem.

> *"I'm a sig . . . no . . . man . . . uh, well . . . again." The words came out slowly, each syllable a separate explosion that erupted only after a protracted struggle.*
> *Psychologist Howard Gardner tried again. "Were you in the Coast Guard?"*
> *"No, er, yes, yes . . . ship . . . Massachu . . . chusetts . . . Coastguard . . . years." Twice he raised his hands, indicating with his fingers nineteen years. Asked why he was in the hospital, the Coast Guard veteran pointed to his paralyzed right arm. "Arm no good."*
> *Then to his mouth. "Speech . . . can't say . . . talk, you see."*
> *"What happened to make you lose your speech?"*
> *"Head, fall, Jesus Christ, me, no good, str, str . . . oh Jesus . . . stroke."*
> *"And what have you been doing in the hospital?"*
> *"Yes, sure. Me go, er, uh, P.T. [physical therapy] nine o'cot . . . speech . . . two times . . . read . . . wr . . . ripe, er, rike, er write . . . practice . . . get-ting better" (Gardner, 1974).*

Most of us take speech in daily life for granted, rarely stopping to think how central it is to human experience. For most of us, too, reading and writing are "second nature"; we routinely gather information and seek pleasure from the written word and express our needs, desires, and thoughts (as well as grocery lists, bills, and phone messages) through writing. We don't usually pause to consider that reading and writing, like speech, are essential to human civilization. Often it is only when speech (as in David Ford's case), comprehension, reading, or writing become impaired that the significance of language—be it in mundane matters or in the realms of creative art—becomes abundantly clear.

Certainly, the language that we learn so easily and effortlessly before we start school represents one of the highest achievements of human cognition—even though the precise relationship between language and other aspects of cognition is not terribly clear. Many researchers have been convinced that if we could analyze the workings of language in all its richness and complexity, we might indeed at last understand the human mind (Chomsky, 1975). In this chapter we will first cover the basics of language structure and then investigate how we put this structure to work—how we use and understand both spoken and written language.

UNIVERSAL FEATURES OF HUMAN LANGUAGE

The first time you hear a foreign language, it is a meaningless clatter. The sounds are different, the words—once you begin to pick them out of the rush of sound—seem bizarre, and the rules that govern their combination appear unfathomable. But no matter whether the language is Urdu or French, Catalan or Russian, it shares certain features with every other human language. All human languages have the properties of expressive power, productivity, and displacement.

EXPRESSIVE POWER a language's ability to communicate virtually anything

Expressive power refers to a language's ability to communicate almost any situation, any feeling, any internal state, any idea, any thought, or any slice of time. This is in contrast to nonhuman communication systems. The communication systems of other species are limited to fixed signals that serve a survival function—protection from predators, searching for food, protection of territorial rites, and mating. Examples of these include the calls of monkeys to signal the presence of predators, the dance of bees to signal the location of food, and the songs of birds to attract mates. Human language is not limited to messages that concern our immediate survival. We can, for example, use language to explore and discuss language itself or any other scholarly topic. Language is a medium we use to express thoughts we want to communicate to others or to ourselves. Languages do differ to some degree in their expressivity: some ideas and emotional or perceptual nuances can be more directly expressed in some languages than in others. In fact, some linguists maintain that such differences in language make for different ways of perceiving and understanding the world. It is also possible that languages reflect differences in perception and values, and we address this issue later in the chapter. However language and thought are related, it is clear that all human languages exhibit an extraordinary degree of expressive power.

Productivity grows out of the rule-governed nature of language. With a fairly large but nonetheless limited set of words (50,000 or so), we have the potential to produce an infinite number of sentences. What gives language its productive power is the set of rules called **grammar,** which governs how elements, such as words and phrases, can be combined to form sentences. In other words, these rules permit us to combine words into an unlimited number of acceptable sentences. Thus, when we learn a language, we do not simply learn a set of sentences to speak in particular situations. If that were so, then we would be limited to speaking and understanding only those sentences we had been trained to speak or understand. But every day, each of us utters and understands sentences that have never been said before, by anyone. Consider the following example:

> An army ant named Chelsea moved to the United States with millions of her relatives.

Linguists argue that our ability to speak and comprehend novel sentences such as this is one reflection of our knowledge of the grammar of our native language. That we can judge the preceding example to be an acceptable sentence and the following *not* to be is also a reflection of our grammatical knowledge:

> An ant Chelsea to United States millions her army named moved the with of relatives.

As should be obvious, the two examples use the same words, but only the first is a sentence, because it conforms to the rules of grammar for English.

PRODUCTIVITY   the ability to produce an infinite number of sentences

GRAMMAR   the rules governing sentence formation

Language makes it possible for humans to pass knowledge, stories, and traditions from one generation of a society to another.

American Sign Language has all the features of a true language—expressive power, productivity, and displacement.

DISPLACEMENT the ability to refer to anything not actually present, like past and future

Displacement, or the ability to talk about something that is not present, is the aspect of language that makes civilization possible. It allows us to describe the past and the future, the absent and the lost, the possible and the imaginary. Without it language would be limited to places, people, and events in our immediate vicinity. We would be mired in a world of "here and now." By transcending the immediate present, we can transmit knowledge from generation to generation. Individuals do not have to experience an event directly to learn about it; they can benefit from the past experiences of others.

These critical features are found in all human languages, and not merely those that use the spoken word. They appear in written languages, in Braille, and in the silent, gestural languages of the deaf. With a small number of hand gestures, configurations, movements, and positions, American Sign Language can express almost any thought, as discussed in the box on page 280.

LINGUISTIC STRUCTURE

LINGUISTICS the study of language knowledge and structure

Speakers of a language know the rules of their language even though they may not be able to state them. As already indicated, this knowledge is implicit in the human language user's ability to produce novel sentences and to judge that some strings of words are sentences while others are not. The discipline of **linguistics** has as its goal the description of this knowledge. Language knowledge is thought to be organized into several components: a sound component, a syntactic component, and a semantic component. The sound and syntactic components each have their own productive sets of rules that operate on a specifiable type of element. The semantic component addresses how meaning is obtained from sentences.

The Organization of Sound: Phonological Rules

PHONOLOGICAL RULES rules governing the combination of phonemes to make words

PHONEMES speech sounds; the basic unit of sound in a language

The component of language that contains our knowledge of sound is known as the *phonological component.* The rules in this component are called **phonological rules,** and they are applied to **phonemes,** the basic unit of sound. Languages differ in terms of the number of phonemes they use and in their phonological rules. For example, English contains approximately forty phonemes (Akmajian, Demers, and Harnish, 1984). Phonemes are identified by their ability to signal differences in meaning. The sounds /b/ and /p/ are very similar (slashes are the conventional designation for phonemes). In fact, they differ in only one way. A buzz, called *voicing*, is produced by vibration of the vocal cords and appears in /b/ but not in /p/. All other aspects of the pronunciation of these two sounds are the same. But notice that in English "big" and "pig" have different meanings. The only acoustic difference between these two words appears in the first sound. Because this difference in sound makes a difference in meaning, /b/ and /p/ are said to be different phonemes. (Of course, "big" and "pig" each contain two other phonemes, /I/ and /g/.)

The phonological rules of a language determine how phonemes can be combined. Some combinations of phonemes will not conform to the phonological rules and will be very difficult for native speakers to pronounce or to accept as a possible word in their language. Other combinations will conform to the rules and will be considered acceptable. For example, in English we have a rule that constrains how we construct plural forms of nouns. Consider that the final phoneme in "cats" is different from the final phoneme in "dogs" (/s/ versus /z/). This occurs because there is a rule that requires that the pluralizing phoneme have the same voicing quality as the final phoneme of the root word (Akmajian, Demers, and Harnish, 1984). That is, since the /g/ in "dog" is voiced, so must the pluralizing phoneme be voiced (/z/). Rules such as this permit us to pronounce or understand alternative forms of the same root word without ever having heard them before. Indeed, even very young children seem to be aware of these phonological rules, as is illustrated by the *wug test* (Berko, 1958). In this test children are shown a series of pictures of novel characters or items. A child might be shown a picture such as the one in Figure 10.1 and told that "This is a wug." Then the child is shown a picture of two of the same and told, "Now there is another one. There are two of them. There are two ____." The child responds by filling in the blank with the plural form of "wug." The wug test shows that even very young children can respond in accord with the phonological rules of English.

This is a wug.

Now there is another one.
There are two of them.
There are two _____.

Figure 10.1 A test used to assess children's knowledge of pluralization rules. (Berko, 1958.)

The Organization of Sentences: Syntax

The second component of the grammar of a language is called the *syntactic component*. The rules of this component, called **syntax**, determine how the basic units of meaning in a language, called **morphemes**, can be combined to form sentences. Morphemes are not necessarily the same as words. Morphemes are of two basic types: free and bound. Free morphemes are generally words and can stand alone, such as "dog," "idea," and "red." Bound morphemes are common prefixes and suffixes that also carry meaning but must be attached to a free morpheme, such as the *un* in "unusual," the plural *s* in "dogs" or the *ed* in "jumped." The rules of syntax determine how morphemes are to be combined and sequenced to produce sentences. For the sake of convenience, we will describe the syntactic component as if the rules operated only on words, not on parts of words as well.

It is important to keep in mind when examining the issue of syntax that although these are the rules that describe sentences, they are not restricted to describing just those sentences that English grammar texts say are correct forms for our language. One point that linguists want to make is that even our seemingly sloppy, casual language is highly rule-governed. For example, many young speakers of English insert the word "like" at various points in sentences such as "Pete is, like, the best baseball player in town" or "We intended to leave for the concert at, like, 8 o'clock." But even this use of "like" is like rule-governed because "like" cannot appear between just any two words in a sentence; it can appear only at certain points. This is evident in the ungrammatical "Pete, like, is the best baseball player in town" (Ross and Cooper, 1979).

One of the central principles of contemporary linguistics is that syntactic rules are of two kinds: phrase-structure rules and transformation rules (Chomsky, 1957, 1965, 1975). **Phrase-structure rules** are those that describe the ways in

SYNTAX the rules governing the combination of words and roots into phrases and sentences

MORPHEMES the basic units of meaning in a language—words, suffixes and prefixes

PHRASE-STRUCTURE RULES rules governing the hierarchical organization of words in a sentence

Talking with the Hands

American Sign Language (ASL), the manual-visual language used by deaf people in the United States, is a full-fledged linguistic system in which the hands and arms communicate by means of location of hands, hand shape, movement, and the orientation of the palm (Tartter, 1986). There are about twenty-five locations, forty-five ways of shaping the hand, ten distinct movements, and ten ways of orienting the palm. The signs of ASL may or may not have an exact English equivalent, but anything said in one language can be translated into the other. Speakers of ASL sometimes supplement their "speech" by finger spelling words, but finger spelling is used primarily for proper names, for borrowed words from English, or to "talk" with someone who is not fluent in ASL.

Signers can refer to other times and other places, and they can combine individual signs into a unlimited number of statements. At one time, linguists assumed that ASL was an incomplete language that lacked function words, but as more linguists became fluent in the language, it became clear that function words and syntax are present, although not based on any English equivalent. One example is raised eyebrows to indicate a subordinate clause. Another example is the location of the hand in relation to the face to indicate gender: the sign for "girl" (mother, grandmother, or lady) is produced with the hand touching the cheek; the similar sign for "boy" (father, grandfather, or gentleman) is produced at the forehead. Other markers can change a sign from a verb to a

noun, note whether an action is a single or a habitual occurrence, indicate plural, signify past or future, make clear that the sign is being used in a metaphorical sense, or indicate that the signer is coining a new term (Klima and Bellugi, 1979).

Signed poetry draws heavily on the fluidity and grace of ASL. To communicate a poem, signers balance the movement of their hands and maintain the flow of movement between signs. They may also superimpose a special design on the way they make the individual signs or in a pattern of timing and rhythm. In one instance, Bernard Bragg, a member of the National Theater of the Deaf, chose to sign e. e. cummings':

> *since feeling is first*
> *who pays any attention*
> *to the syntax of things*
> *will never wholly kiss you.*

Instead of signing a literal translation of the first line, Bragg changed "since" to "because," "first" to "foremost" (the actual sign was "mostest"— "most" plus the sign indicating a superlative) and "itself" instead of the "true" he would have signed for "is" in a literal rendition. These changes produced balance, substituted sweeping for intricate motions, and turned the line into a repetition of handshapes that is analogous to the alliterative repetition of sound in spoken poetry (Klima and Bellugi, 1979). The growing tradition of signed poetry shows how poetic imagination can triumph over the loss of sound.

Signed poem from Klima and Belugi, 1979. Reprinted by permission.

| Green | deep | below | Green | high | above |

| White | clouds | and | quiet | hour |

| Slow | Hot | Heavy | on | hands |

which words are grouped hierarchically to form a sentence, and the ways in which the various elements of a sentence relate to one another. These rules are stated as a set of *rewrite operations* which involve breaking a possible sentence into its constituents—first types of phrases, then types of words. The simplest sentences, of course, consist only of subject (noun) and verb, such as "I am" or "She walks." Most sentences combine two broad types of phrases, a noun phrase plus a verb phrase. Table 10.1 provides a simplified set of phrase-structure rules describing a small part of English syntax. The arrows in the table mean "can be rewritten as." Thus, the first rule, S $\longrightarrow$ NP + VP, states that a sentence is made up of a noun phrase and a verb phrase in that order. Each of these phrases can be broken down and rewritten: NP can be rewritten as Article + Adjective + Noun; VP can be rewritten as Verb + NP. (Notice that to develop the full structure of the VP, one also has to apply the rule for the NP.) Once constituents are completely broken down, words can be inserted according to *lexical insertion rules*. Under these rules appropriate lexical items or words are selected to fill the abstract roles of noun, verb, and so forth. You should now be able to see how even a small vocabulary can be used to produce a very large number of sentences. In fact, the grammar described in Table 10.1 generates 14,400 unique and grammatical seven-word sentences.

The hierarchical structure of the constituents of a particular sentence can be clearly exhibited in a **phrase-structure tree.** Such a tree is illustrated in Figure 10.2 for the sentence "The hungry fox chased the fat rabbit." At the top of the tree is the *S* symbol that began the rewrite operation. *S* is broken down into two subnodes labeled *NP* and *VP*, and these nodes are in turn broken down into their subnodes. This "decomposition" process corresponds exactly to the rewrite operations of the phrase-structure rules described above and shown in Table 10.1. The phrase-structure tree has the advantage of revealing at a glance the hierarchical structure of sentences.

By examining the hierarchical phrase structure of sentences, we can begin to understand why some sentences are ambiguous, or unclear in their meaning. **Ambiguity** occurs whenever a sentence has more than one plausible interpretation. One source of ambiguity, called *lexical ambiguity,* results when a word in a sentence has more than one meaning (as in "Mary went to the bank," where "bank" could mean "financial institution" or "river's edge"). But syntax may also contribute to ambiguity. *Structural ambiguity* occurs when a sentence can be mapped into two different phrase-structure trees. Consider the sentence "The father of the girl and the boy left." This sentence could be said to have either a single subject (the girl's and the boy's father, one person) or a compound subject (the girl's father and the boy). Thus, two different but equally acceptable phrase-structure trees are shown for this sentence in Figure 10.3. The first corresponds to a reading of the sentence in which only one person left (the father), and the second corresponds to a reading in which two people left (the father and the boy) (Akmajian, Demers, and Harnish, 1984). (Note that the phrase-structure rules shown in Table 10.1 are not adequate to account for the more complex subject in this example; this is an illustration of how little of the structure of English sentences this small set of rules can explain.)

Now that you have a sense of what phrase-structure rules are, you can begin to see what transformation rules do. **Transformation rules** operate on what is called the deep structure of a sentence to turn it into its surface structure. The **surface structure** of a sentence is the actual sequence of words that one hears or produces. In contrast, the **deep structure** is an abstract representation of the grammatical relations of the subject to the verb and the verb to the objects (direct and indirect).

Not all sentences (surface structures) present these grammatical relations in a direct way. For example, consider the following two sentences:

John is easy to please.
John is eager to please.

Both seem to have the same surface structure and would produce identical phrase-structure trees, yet there is something quite different about them. We can see what

PHRASE-STRUCTURE TREE the graphic representation of phrase structure

AMBIGUITY unclearness in meaning that occurs when two or more plausible interpretations of a sentence exist

TRANSFORMATION RULES rules governing the changing of deep structures into surface structures

SURFACE STRUCTURE the actual sequence of words in a sentence

DEEP STRUCTURE a representation that exhibits the basic grammatical relations between subjects, verbs, and direct and indirect objects

TABLE 10.1   A Simple Phrase-Structure Grammar

PHRASE-STRUCTURE REWRITE RULES	LEXICAL INSERTION RULES
Sentence (S) ⟶ Noun Phrase (NP) + Verb Phrase (VP)	N ⟶ fox, rabbit, cat, dog, rat, goat
NP ⟶ Article + Adjective + Noun	V ⟶ chased, bumped, kissed, punched
VP ⟶ Verb + NP	Article ⟶ a, an, the
	Adjective ⟶ hungry, fat, thin, tall, short

is different when we attempt to recast them in the same way. We can turn the first one into "It is easy to please John," but we cannot turn the second one into "It is eager to please John." This is because the deep structures of the two are very different. In the first, John is really the direct object of the infinitive "to please," and that is why "It is easy to please John," which means the same as "John is easy to please," is also grammatical. In the second sentence, "John" is really the deep-structure subject of the infinitive—that is, "John" will be the cause of pleasing someone. Because of some other requirements on syntax, we cannot say "It is eager to please John," so "John" is forced to the front of the sentence, producing "John is eager to please." The movement of "John" from its deep-structure position of subject or object is accomplished by a transformation rule. It is because of the differences in sentences such as these that linguists have argued for the existence of deep structure in addition to the surface-structure representation. The addition of transformation rules and deep structure to the theory helps to explain people's intuitions about grammatical relations that could not be addressed simply by examining the surface structures of sentences.

It should be noted that the theory of syntax we have been discussing does not fully explain how we produce and understand speech. Chomsky argued that the three components of linguistic knowledge—phonological, syntactic, and semantic—constitute the **language competence** of the speaker. This is the knowledge that forms the basis of our ability to make certain linguistic judgments. Our language competence allows us, for example, to recognize that "toasted frozen the Susan waffle" is not a sentence but that "Susan toasted the frozen waffle" is. Our ability to produce and understand sentences has its foundation in our language competence, but this competence must be implemented by a **performance system,** an information processor that constructs mental representations of sentences. The performance system includes perceptual mechanisms, working memory, long-term memory, and perhaps even processors that specialize in constructing linguistic representations of speech.

The competence-performance distinction describes the very real discrepancy between our powerful syntactic ability and the limited capacity we have to comprehend or produce sentences beyond a certain length. One feature of syntax is called **recursion,** which permits us to embed sentences within sentences or phrases within phrases. For example, we could take a sentence like "The rat ate the cheese" and embed within it another sentence such as "The cat chased the rat" to produce the sentence "The rat that the cat chased ate the cheese." This operation

LANGUAGE COMPETENCE grammatical knowledge that forms the basis of our ability to make linguistic judgments

PERFORMANCE SYSTEM language processes, including memory, engaged when we design and use spoken and written language

RECURSION embedding sentences within sentences and phrases within phrases

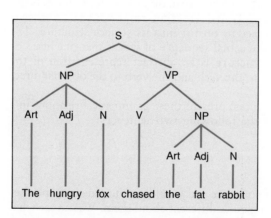

Figure 10.2 A phrase-structure tree for a sample sentence. Each node, or fork, of the tree is a syntactic constituent that expands into the nodes below it.

of embedding could, in principle, go on forever, but our understanding could not. After only one or two embeddings such sentences become very difficult to understand: "The rat that the cat that the dog bit chased ate the cheese." The limitation on our ability to understand this sentence is due not to our language competence but to limits of our working memory and language-specific processing strategies (Frazier and Fodor, 1978). Performance is also limited by temporary factors such as fatigue, anxiety, and drugs. Thus, a complete study of language must encompass not only language competence but also the information-processing or performance system that implements our competence. The question of language processing will be taken up later in the chapter.

Meaning and Grammar: More Than the Sum of the Parts

The third component of a grammar is called the *semantic component,* which provides interpretations for sentences generated by the syntactic component. Semantics is the study of meaning, and **semantic** applies to anything having to do with meaning or with differences in meaning. There are two aspects of meaning that can be analyzed: word (or morpheme) meaning and sentence meaning, or the ways in which sentence meaning is related to the meanings of words.

In general, those who study *word meaning* find it useful to distinguish between sense and reference. The **sense** of a word is simply its definition—a description of the (abstract) concept that it represents or points to. A definition may be in

SEMANTIC   having to do with meaning

SENSE   a definition of a word

Figure 10.3   Two phrase-structure trees for the same sentence.

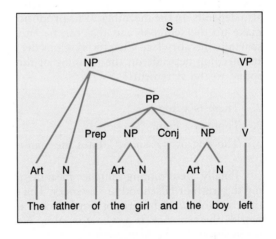

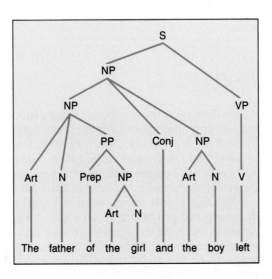

REFERENCE   an indication of the external object or thing a word points to or represents

one of two forms: a rule that admits no exceptions (a "triangle" is a two-dimensional, three-sided figure) or a family resemblance structure with fuzzy borders (a "house" is a dwelling that may be made of brick, wood, dried mud, or other materials and may take any of a wide variety of shapes). (As you saw in Chapter 9, there are competing theories about how concept knowledge is organized in memory.) A word's **reference** indicates the sense in which the word points to a tangible object in the external world. (The objects themselves are called *referents*.) There are things in the world, for example, to which we can appropriately apply the label "cat." Note that two different words may have the same referent but quite different senses. "Neighbor" and "thief" may both be applied to the same individual (the referent), but the two words have obviously different senses. Likewise, a term may have no referents at all in the real world and still have a sense—for example, "Lilliputian," an adjective derived from the invented land of tiny people, Lilliput, in Jonathan Swift's novel *Gulliver's Travels* (Devitt and Sterelny, 1987).

To distinguish between word meaning and *sentence meaning*, we can apply the Gestalt principle of perception—the whole is different from the sum of the parts (see Chapter 5). That is, a whole sentence means something rather different from the meanings of the individual words simply added up. Compare the following simple sentences:

> Dog bites man.
> Man bites dog.

Both sentences consist of the same words, but each has a distinct meaning.

PROPOSITIONS   basic conceptual units that make up a sentence and that can be either true or false

Sentence meaning is governed, first, by the order of the words (which comes under syntactic structure) and their syntactic relations. The meaning of a sentence also depends on the meanings of its **propositions**—the basic conceptual units that make up the sentence and that can be either true or false. They are stored in semantic memory (see Chapter 8). Consider again the sentence "Dog bites man." Its meaning depends on the meaning of three distinct ideas that roughly correspond to the statements:

1. There is a dog.
2. There is a man.
3. The dog of statement 1 bites the man of statement 2.

Finally, determining sentence meaning must at some point involve determining the truth or falsehood of sentences. The truth of any one sentence depends on the truth of *all* of its propositions. If any of the propositions is not true in the world, the sentence as a whole is false. We will have much more to say about propositions in the next sections.

DESIGNING AND USING SPEECH IN DAILY LIFE

PSYCHOLINGUISTICS   the study of the mental processes involved in how we use and understand language

As we have seen, the discipline of linguistics is primarily concerned with explaining our intuitions about language—our language competence. **Psycholinguistics**, in contrast, is primarily concerned with describing the mental processes involved in using and understanding language—the performance system. For clarity, we will discuss the design and use of language in this section and will consider language comprehension separately in the next section.

Without visible effort, we move quickly through the complex processes of designing and producing an utterance—from choosing the idea we want to get across to choosing the exact words and expressing them as a series of sounds in a series of sentences. Although we are hardly aware of it, we tailor our choice of words to fit our goals, our audience, and the social situation.

A speech act involves a physical and social setting, and its meaning may be influenced by the tone of voice, gestures, and facial expressions that accompany the spoken words.

Deciding What to Say

We choose what to say in order to achieve certain goals. We arrange our words to have a particular effect on the listener—to persuade, warn, pledge, command, intimidate, inform, request, plead, and so on. An utterance is as much an instrumental act as is opening a door, and for this reason utterances can be viewed as **speech acts** (Searle, 1969). Speech acts are performed "properly" only when certain logical conditions prevail. For example, I can properly request information from you only if there is reason to believe that you have the information and I do not, that you are willing to share it with me, and that you would not do so unless I asked. If any of these conditions are violated, then the request is likely to have overtones of humor or sarcasm, as when a prisoner asks a guard to borrow the keys to the cell, or one derelict asks another to lend him $10,000.

A speech act is made in a physical and social context, which includes the setting (a courtroom, an automobile, the dinner table, or a football game), the relationship of the people involved (friends, parent and child, strangers, or co-workers), and the content of whatever conversation has preceded the utterance. This physical and social context constrains (limits) what you say and what words you use to say it. It also limits the number of alternatives your listener must consider in order to figure out what you have said. A general principle guides these choices: "Unless I stipulate otherwise, I can refer only to items that are within our shared knowledge." These items, such as mutual surroundings, friends, beliefs, and recent topics of conversation, make up the **common ground** between speaker and listener (H. H. Clark, 1984).

When referring to something in our surroundings, I have to construct an expression that enables you to identify it within our common ground. For example, if three men of various ages are sitting at a nearby table, I can specify one of them by saying "the oldest man," but if that same man and two women are at the table, I might pick him out by simply saying "the man." Our choice of words is also constrained by past topics in our conversation. After I refer to John as "the older man," that phrase has a specific referent and is temporarily locked up for other uses; I cannot use "the older man" to refer to someone other than John unless I specify that I am doing so.

SPEECH ACT utterance designed to have some effect, such as a promise, a bet, a request

COMMON GROUND the knowledge and context shared by discourse participants

The Cooperative Principle

Making use of common ground is one example of the operation of a more general
agreement that holds between speaker and listener called the **cooperative principle.** Speaker and listener cooperate on the mechanics of speech—using a common language, following the rules of sentence structure and pronunciation, and
speaking loudly and clearly enough to be heard. They cooperate by referring only
to concepts in the common ground, unless they explicitly introduce some new
concept into that ground. And they cooperate on more subtle conventions: in
general, the listener assumes that the speaker is trying to be informative, truthful,
clear, brief, and relevant (Grice, 1975). Even speech between enemies follows
these rules—except, perhaps, the rule of truthfulness. Consider the assumption of
informativeness: If you are told that Ned has fourteen children, you believe that
Ned has *only* fourteen children and not more. Ned could have twenty children
and the statement that he has fourteen children would still be true, but it would
violate the cooperative principle by being, for practical purposes, uninformative
(Levinson, 1983). Again, informativeness can often explain our choice of words to
identify objects. For example, when all the ducks in a pond are white, it does not
make much sense to refer to a specific one as "the white duck." Instead, you
might say something like "It's the dirty one on the left."

Information value plays an important role not only in human conversation
but also in our understanding of concepts and in classical conditioning of humans
and other species. Recall, for example, that what we tend to remember and to
focus on is the instance or representative from the basic level of a concept—
"chair," rather than the more general "furniture" or the more specific "bentwood
rocker." The basic level is that which offers the most information most efficiently.
And the information value of a stimulus determines its learning in classical conditioning.

Indirect Speech

English playwright Oscar Wilde poked fun at people in polite society for their
habit of not saying what they mean:

Jack: *Charming day it has been, Miss Fairfax.*
Gwendolen: *Pray don't talk to me about the weather, Mr. Worthing. When-
ever people talk to me about the weather, I always feel quite certain that they
mean something else. And that makes me so nervous.*
Jack: *I do mean something else.*
Gwendolen: *I thought so. I am never wrong.*

One of the most interesting aspects of speech acts is the amount of implication, indirectness, and innuendo (indirect suggestiveness) that we manage to work
in. We often mean something quite different from the literal meanings of our
sentences. Take a simple example: If you wanted your friend to answer the door
for you, you might say, "Would you mind getting the door?" A literal response
to a literal interpretation of your question might be "Yes" or "No." But normally, you would simply expect your friend to comply with your implied request
to answer the knock or doorbell. Such a request is called an *indirect speech act*
because the literal meaning of the sentence is not the speaker's intended meaning,
but the intention is clear, usually by convention (another element of the cooperative principle). As in the manners Oscar Wilde satirized, we often use indirect
speech as a means of maintaining a degree of politeness.

Again, indirect requests highlight an important distinction—that between the
speaker's meaning and the *linguistic meaning* (that is, the literal meaning) of an
utterance (Clark, 1985). The speaker's meaning can be determined only by drawing inferences based on the context of the utterance and by assuming the cooperative principle to be in effect. In fact, given these ground rules, a speaker's meaning
can seem quite opaque and metaphorical and still be interpretable. Metaphors are
not just figures of speech confined to literature; we often use them in everyday
conversation. They often crop up in proverbs and sayings, some of which are part

For a variety of reasons, politicians frequently want to appear communicative without actually imparting much substantive information.

of a given culture's common ground—for instance, "Let sleeping dogs lie." Or consider the indirect request, "You make a better door than you do a window." The literal meaning of this assertion does not make much sense, but in the proper context it can be interpreted as a request for the listener to move out of the way so that the speaker's view is no longer blocked.

Planning a speech act is an exercise in problem solving. The problems vary, but the solution almost always involves choosing the form that will have the desired effect on the listener. If the general goal is communication, then we must apply our knowledge of the common ground we share with our listener and follow the cooperative principle. Sometimes it seems that the goal is *non*communication—as when a political leader wants to give the impression of providing information but intends in fact to say little of substance. Even in a case like this, however, in order to accomplish these goals, speakers (or writers) must adhere to certain rules. They must, for instance, imply to listeners (or readers) that they are on common ground, that they *are* being informative. The desired effect of propaganda or "disinformation" on listeners and readers may be to persuade them that certain "facts" are true or to stir angry emotions; but this desired effect is still the guiding force of word choice and sentence form.

We are all solving communication problems perhaps hundreds of times a day, usually without much effort or agonizing. Planning what to write, whether a letter, a term paper, or a short story, is very much the same as planning a speech act, except that the planning is often more deliberate and perhaps for that reason more effortful and time-consuming.

Slips and What They Tell Us

When speaking, we occasionally say something we did not intend. For example, former President Ronald Reagan in his speech before the 1988 Republican National Convention said, "Facts are stupid things—stubborn things, I should say." Sigmund Freud (1914) believed that such speech errors, or **slips of the tongue,** result from anxiety-provoking unconscious thoughts that interfere with our speech processing. Accordingly, these errors are sometimes called *Freudian slips.* Was Freud correct in asserting that speech errors reflect unconscious motives, or do they result from some other, more strictly linguistic cause (or both)?

To test the Freudian hypothesis, investigators have attempted to induce slips of the tongue. In one study, men were asked to read aloud word pairs that were flashed on a screen. Those who were tested by an attractive, provocatively dressed woman tended to make such slips as "fast passion" for "past fashion" and "nice legs" for "lice negs" (Motley, 1980, 1987). Those tested by a male researcher

SLIP OF THE TONGUE a speech error in which we say something we did not intend to say

made many fewer sexually loaded slips. In a second experiment, male subjects with higher measured levels of sexual anxiety produced more sex-related slips than did those with lower sexual anxiety.

However, before concluding that Freud was essentially correct about the cause of speech errors, we might consider the fact that most speech errors are fairly mundane. We tend to notice those speech errors that have embarrassing consequences; but few of our everyday speech errors are actually embarrassing or reveal some hidden truth about ourselves. Speech errors can be classified in a variety of ways. If someone says, "Bake my bike" instead of "Take my bike," the error is one of **anticipation,** the commonest form of slip. The /b/ was scheduled to appear later in the phrase but had already been called up from memory and was available when the speaker began the planned three-word phrase. Other kinds of slips include **perseverations,** in which a sound is erroneously repeated ("pulled a pantrum" for "pulled a tantrum") and **reversals,** in which sounds are exchanged ("food the peech" for "feed the pooch"). Such reversals are called *spoonerisms,* after William Spooner, a nineteenth-century English clergyman famous for probably deliberate reversals that produced rather silly sequences, such as "insanitary specter" for "sanitary inspector" and "You have tasted the whole worm" for "You have wasted the whole term." In addition to varying by type, speech errors differ in the size of the speech unit that slips (Shattuck-Hufnagel, 1979). Sometimes only a phoneme slips, as in "a but-gusting meal." Larger units include slips of morphemes ("naming a wear tag"), slips of words ("Any guys, you time"), and syntactic slips ("No, I'm don't" for "No, I don't" or "I'm not"). When embarrassing Freudian slips are analyzed along with other samples of speech errors according to categories like anticipations, perseverations, reversals, and size of affected speech unit, then it seems that the processes leading to all kinds of errors are basically the same (Ellis, 1980).

In general, psychologists now tend to believe that most slips occur as a result of a breakdown in speech planning. The **speech plan** begins with the selection of a syntactic structure, proceeds with the insertion of morphemes into this structure, and ends with a translation of these morphemes into phonetic segments that can be articulated (Fromkin, 1973). Occasionally, linguistic units at any one of these levels "slip," either in relation to one another or in relation to competing thoughts, words, and so forth that are not planned. As you might guess, these slips occur most often when our attention is divided or our concentration is broken—in other words, when we are distracted by anxiety or befuddled by fatigue. Thus, slips of the tongue may be more appropriately and more scientifically explained as faulty processing in the speech planning system, rather than as the intrusion of unconscious wishes or desires into speech. However, it is quite plausible for Freudian psychologists and others to argue that the competing thoughts and images that intrude unplanned into our speech when, say, anxiety or fatigue is present may indeed have something to do with unconscious desires or conflicts. Nevertheless, this argument is quite difficult to demonstrate adequately.

UNDERSTANDING LANGUAGE

A professor goes through a number of mental processes in order to plan and deliver the lectures you attend. What processes must you, in turn, go through in order to comprehend the lectures? Once the speaker has done his or her part in communication, what must the listener do to achieve understanding?

Understanding both spoken and written language involves at least three activities: recognizing patterns (i.e., sound/word) and word meanings; identifying the propositions represented by these patterns; and relating these propositions to known *schemas*—that is, to our own stored knowledge of the world (see Chapter 8). Taken together, these interrelated processes are called discourse. **Discourse** is any connected series of statements in written or in spoken form. Psychologists consider it the natural form in which human language occurs. By integrating discourse with a schema, we can construct a *mental model* of the speaker's or writer's meaning (Johnson-Laird, 1983; Perrig and Kintsch, 1985). The mental

ANTICIPATION   a slip that inserts a later phoneme earlier than planned

PERSEVERATION   a slip in which a sound is repeated

REVERSAL   a slip in which sounds are exchanged between words

SPEECH PLAN   the entire plan of utterance, including syntactic choices, insertion of morphemes, and translation of morphemes into sound segments

DISCOURSE   any connected series of statements, either written or spoken

model, which we discussed in Chapter 9, contains the information gleaned directly from the discourse plus all the inferences about that information contained in our schemas.

Although the same basic processes are at work in both listening and reading, we can consider the pattern-recognition/word-identification aspects separately for each activity. Then we can explore the construction and use of mental models in understanding both spoken and written discourse.

Identifying Words in Speech: What Did You Say?

Listeners pick up words from a relatively complex stream of sound. Speech is usually just one of several sources of sound impinging on our auditory sense. So listeners must first of all filter out all the extraneous sounds. Next they must segment the speech stream into units that can be identified as words so that the process of constructing meaning can begin. This act of identifying words is known as the **segmentation problem** (Cole and Jakimik, 1980). It is considered a "problem" because it is not necessarily an easy task: after all, most words are not spoken with distinct pauses between them. Consider that the phrase *new display*, if spoken at normal speed, could also be heard as *nudists play*, depending on where one believes the second word begins.

Of course, the listener is helped in the process of segmentation by a variety of clues. Once a word has been identified, the listener knows automatically where that word ends and the next begins. In addition, knowledge of the phonological rules aids the listener. These rules, as you already know, specify how phonemes can be combined within words. Knowing that a certain sequence of phonemes cannot occur within a word provides an indication that one is crossing a word boundary. For example, in English a voiced and an unvoiced consonant phoneme, such as /b/ and /p/, cannot occur adjacently within a word. Thus, if such a sequence is heard, the listener knows that a word boundary has been crossed. Schematic knowledge also helps the listener. For example, one young child looked for tiny boards in his bowl of ice cream after having been told it was "Borden's ice cream." Not recognizing Borden's as a trade name, he segmented the speech in the only way that made sense to him—board in ice cream. In fact, this sort of misinterpretation occurs often in children; other examples include "Gladly, the cross-eyed bear" for "Gladly the cross I'd bear. . . ."

Once the beginning of a word has been identified, the process of recognizing the word can begin. One popular theory of word recognition proposes that once the first two or three phonemes of a word have been heard, all the words beginning with those phonemes are activated in the listener's *lexicon,* or mental dictionary, a part of long-term memory. Word candidates are eliminated as they fail to match the incoming phonemes. This continues until all word candidates but one are ruled out (Marslen-Wilson and Welsh, 1978; Marslen-Wilson, 1987). This theory explains the observation that we often identify a word well before we have heard all its phonemes. That is, we identify a word at the point at which it becomes phonetically unique. Also, we often do not notice a mispronunciation in a word if it occurs late in the word: it seems that once a word has been identified, sometimes before all its phonemes are heard, the rest of the incoming acoustic properties are dropped from memory, and only the mental representation activated by the stimulus is available. Finally, this process of elimination theory can explain why a word that shares its beginning with many other words takes longer to recognize than a word with an uncommon beginning: the point at which the word becomes phonetically unique is likely to occur later in the word (Cole and Jakimik, 1980).

After a word is identified, we can then "look up," or activate, its meaning in our lexicon. Of course, many words have more than one meaning (for instance, river "bank" and savings "bank"). Experiments show that when we hear such a word, we often retrieve all its meanings for a fleeting moment, even though we may not be conscious of doing so. As the context makes the speaker's meaning clear, the unwanted meanings slip from working memory (Seidenberg et al.,

SEGMENTATION PROBLEM   the problem of identifying words within a stream of speech sounds

1982). Sometimes the context leads us astray, so that we choose the wrong mean- ing and have to back up and search for a different one. The early part of the sentence "The punch at the party gave Betty a concussion" leads us to focus on *drink* as the meaning of punch; when we hear the last word, we realize that can't be right, so we have to go back and reprocess the sentence (Tartter, 1986).

Recognizing Words in Written Text

When we read, our goal is the same as when we listen—to construct a mental model of the discourse (the text) in written material. As in listening, the first crucial step toward this goal involves pattern recognition—matching the input (printed words) to internal representations of words in the lexicon. Pattern recog- nition for written words is known as **decoding.**

DECODING pattern recognition for written words

Obviously, however, there are some major differences in word identification between listening and reading. In listening, as we saw, segmenting the speech stream is the major problem involved in activating the correct word representa- tions. In reading, word boundaries are clearly marked by spaces, but we are faced with other problems, primarily having to do with the relation of written symbols to pronunciation. First, in English and many other languages there is no intrinsic relationship between the forms of letters and the sounds the letters represent. That is, the pairing of sounds with letters is completely arbitrary. Second, the letter-to- sound correspondence rules are very complicated, especially in English. Com- pare, for example, the pronunciation and spelling of "rough," "though," and "through" or "have" and "gave." Words that follow the same spelling pattern are often pronounced very differently. How much of an obstacle to word identifica- tion are these arbitrary and complex relations between visual symbol and sound?

It turns out that we do not always have to rely on sound to decode written words. We decode in two possible ways: by sounding out a word's individual letters or letter groups, going from spelling to sound, and "hearing" the word; or by immediately recognizing the whole-word image, associating the full pronunci- ation with the whole word as one chunk (recall from Chapter 8 that chunking enlarges the capacity of short-term memory). Children seem to learn reading and are generally taught reading with both these decoding methods, although often the earliest formal lessons focus on sounding out words. Psychological theories of reading skills assume that adult readers can use either decoding route, or both (Coltheart, 1980; Funnell, 1983; Henderson, 1985; Taraban and McClelland, 1987). Evidence to date suggests that both decoding methods may occur simulta- neously, as if in a race to see which can identify the word first. In skilled readers, the whole-word process usually wins. Only occasionally, when the skilled reader encounters an unfamiliar word, does sounding out win the race (Just and Carpen- ter, 1987). Thus, by chunking, the skilled reader can process and keep track of more text from moment to moment than the poor reader can. This obviously allows for comprehension of longer, more recursive, and more complex sen- tences.

You can demonstrate for yourself some of the evidence used to support the claim that we recognize at least some words without sounding out each letter. Try quickly counting the number of *t*s in the text presented in Table 10.2. Stop reading now and try it. Did you find twenty-two *t*s? Most people miss several, and usu- ally these are the ones that occur in the word "the." The reason we miss these *t*s is that we tend to recognize such words as wholes. "The" is so common and identified so automatically, we don't even think of it as containing individual letters (Healy, 1976).

Of course, there is more to reading than simply decoding the printed words. One experimental approach that has provided some interesting data on reading is the study of gaze duration, or *fixation*. While they read, subjects' eye movements are monitored by a computer system. This method can tell the investigator exactly how long the reader fixated any word in the text, the order in which words were fixated, and which words were not fixated at all. Research using this method has revealed that college students typically fixate about 80 percent of the content

Children's first efforts in learning to read usually involve sounding out the letters and syllables in each word. They gradually move on to the second method of decoding written text, recognizing each word as a whole.

words (nouns, verbs, adjectives) in a text, but only about 50 percent of the function words (articles, prepositions, conjunctions). The average fixation for a word is around 250 msec (¼ sec), but it varies over a wide range, depending on such factors as the length of the word (in letters) and the frequency with which the word appears. Shorter words and more frequently appearing words are very rapidly processed compared to longer and less frequent words (Just and Carpenter, 1987).

An interesting and important point gleaned from reading and fixation research is that we fixate words longer than it actually takes simply to decode them. This demonstrates that decoding is not enough to provide us with the full meaning of what we read; processing written text involves more than pattern recognition. The more difficult the text at any given moment, the greater the processing demands and the longer the fixations; as processing demands decline, fixations pick up speed (Daneman and Carpenter, 1980). We can surmise, then, that the reader as she or he decodes is also constructing a mental model of the discourse. We can also say that reading speed is determined not solely by speed of decoding but also by the total time needed to extract meaning from the text (Just and Carpenter, 1987)— the time needed, in other words, to build an adequate and adaptable mental model. (See the accompanying boxes on speed reading and on dyslexia.)

TABLE 10.2 Letter Search Task

Go through the following passage once, *counting each instance of the letter* t.

Then he was afraid and went; but he was quite faint, and shivered and shook, and his knees and legs trembled. And a high wind blew over the land, and the clouds flew, and towards evening all grew dark, and the leaves fell from the trees, and the water rose and roared as if it were boiling, and splashed upon the shore; and in the distance he saw ships which were firing guns in their sore need, pitching and tossing on the waves.

Excerpt taken from the story "The Fisherman and His Wife," in R. Adams, ed., *Grimm's Fairy Tales.* London: Routledge & Kegan Paul, 1981.

PSYCHOLOGY TODAY AND TOMORROW

Speed Reading

Wouldn't it be wonderful if you could triple or even quadruple your reading speed and maintain a high level of comprehension? Think of the time you would save on studying. Advocates of speed reading think such improvements are possible with training. They often cite the success of famous people who were speed readers, such as John F. Kennedy, as support for the benefits of speed reading. What does the scientific evidence reveal about the efficacy of speed reading?

Early research on speed reading was poorly designed (Just and Carpenter, 1987). Several studies verified that speed readers made fewer fixations on each page, often skipping lines and even entire sections of pages. Often in these studies comprehension was not investigated, and when it was, improper control methods were used. For example, one study showed that a comprehension test used in an earlier study of speed reading could be answered almost as well by individuals who had never read the passage on which the test was based (Carver, 1971).

To study speed reading, Just, Carpenter, and Masson (reported in Just and Carpenter, 1987) compared the reading performance and comprehension of three groups on two passages, one from *Reader's Digest* and a second from *Scientific American*. A group of normal readers (i.e., those instructed to read at their normal rate) read the two passages at a rate of 240 words per minute (WPM), a group of trained speed readers (all recent graduates of an Evelyn Wood Reading Dynamics course) read at a rate of 700 WPM, and a group of normal readers asked to skim rapidly read at a rate of about 600 WPM. On comprehension tests that measured memory for the gist and for the details of the two passages, the normal readers scored substantially higher than either the speed readers or the skimmers. The only test on which the speed reader's comprehension exceeded that of the untrained skimmers was the one that tested for the gist of the relatively easy *Reader's Digest* passage.

The Meaning Is the Message: Getting the Gist

As we noted in the first section of this chapter, linguists have been primarily concerned with the syntactic properties of language and therefore have focused on the sentence as the basic unit of analysis. Psychologists, however, have been more concerned with underlying meaning and how people grasp it and thus have tended to focus on the proposition as the basic vehicle for meaning. Although the syntactic properties of sentences are clearly important to the meaning of any discourse, over and over again psychologists have found that what people remember from discourse is not the syntactic structures of the sentences but the gist of the message—the essence derived from the interconnection of propositions.

In one famous study of recognition memory, Sachs (1967) had subjects listen to stories that each contained a designated target sentence. At various intervals—either 0, 80, or 160 syllables—after the target sentence, the subjects heard a sentence and were asked if it was identical to the target sentence in the story. For example, one story's target sentence was "He sent a letter about it to Galileo, the great Italian scientist." There were four possible forms of the test sentence. One was identical to the target, two were syntactic rewordings of the target that preserved its meaning (e.g., "A letter about it was sent to Galileo, the great Italian scientist"—a different surface structure from the target sentence)—and the fourth test sentence introduced a semantic change (e.g., "Galileo, the great Italian scientist, sent him a letter about it"). Sachs found that at 0 syllables after the target's presentation, subjects were very accurate in recognizing the exact sentence wording. At 80 and 160 syllables, subjects no longer recognized the exact wording but were quite good at rejecting the semantically altered sentence. What this study, along with several others, shows is that what we tend to remember is the gist of the message, unless we are explicitly instructed to remember the exact wording. (However, once we have memorized exact wording, say of a poem or song, it hangs on tenaciously.)

To get a more complete picture of the differences between normal readers and speed readers, Just, Carpenter, and Masson examined the eye-fixation patterns of all three groups while reading the two passages. The researchers found that speed readers tended to fixate only half the words that normal readers fixate. Speed readers also spent less time on each fixation (about 100 msec less) than did normal readers, but this did not prove a particularly effective feat. Despite their training, speed readers did not do a better job at fixating only the "important" words in the text.

What these findings suggest is that speed readers are not processing as many of the details of the text. Indeed, a careful analysis of speed readers' comprehension results bears this out. Although the speed readers generally did much less well on detail comprehension than the normal readers, examination of the speed reader's knowledge for details showed big differences between knowledge of details they had fixated and thus presumably processed and those they had *not* fixated or processed. When speed readers *had* fixated the words needed to answer a detail question, they were right 20 percent of the time, but when they had *not* fixated crucial words, they were right only 3 percent of the time. Thus, because speed readers process fewer of the words, they are much more likely to miss important details provided in the text.

The major advantage for speed readers over the skimmers was that their comprehension of the gist of the text did not decline as much as the skimmers' did when their somewhat faster reading rate was taken into consideration. Thus, training in speed reading may enhance one's ability to quickly glean the major ideas from a text.

In sum, speed reading instruction does not seem to dramatically alter how long one fixates the words of a text. Nor can this instruction increase how many words we see in a single fixation. Rather, "speed" readers gain their greater reading speed simply by reading fewer of the words in a text. This may not pose problems when one already knows the material being presented, or when one is only reading to obtain the a very general idea, but it is of little use when one needs to know the details as well as the general ideas. This latter situation is the one college students are most likely to face. There may not be any shortcuts on the difficult path of acquiring knowledge.

But how do we get at the gist of the message in order to remember it? Understanding and remembering a discourse involves, in part, the extraction of its propositions. Psychologists have found that describing the content of a discourse in terms of propositions is one step in mapping the comprehension process. As we saw in Chapter 8, propositions express relationships among concepts. Recall that propositions are *not* the same as sentences; a single sentence may contain several propositions. Consider the following discourse:

The old actor approached the podium. The audience rose and applauded him enthusiastically.

Each of these sentences contains several propositions. The first sentence contains the following propositions:

1. There was an actor.
2. There was a podium.
3. The actor was old.
4. The actor moved toward the podium.

The propositions of the second sentence are:

1. There was an audience.
2. The audience stood.
3. The audience applauded.
4. The applause was enthusiastic.
5. The applause was directed at the actor.

Note that although these propositions are presented here as simple, declarative sentences, they may be quite abstract and independent of any syntactic form in our minds.

PSYCHOLOGY TODAY AND TOMORROW

What Is Dyslexia?

Poor readers are often said to suffer from dyslexia, but the diagnosis depends on how we define the term. Some researchers classify all people who read at least 30 months below their grade level as dyslexic, but that wide definition includes reading disabilities that may be caused by poor schooling, sensory deficits, or low IQ. Many researchers define *dyslexia* narrowly, as severe reading problems in people who have normal IQs and no other noncognitive disability that might account for their difficulty (Just and Carpenter, 1987; Vellutino, 1987).

Dyslexic college students read more slowly than typical students; they mispronounce many words, especially proper names and words encountered infrequently, and glean less information from what they have read (Just and Carpenter, 1984). When reading silently, dyslexics' eye fixations are twice as long as those of typical students, and they keep looking back at material they have already read. They also have trouble spelling, making three times as many spelling errors as typical students.

Some researchers believe that the source of such problems is primarily a failure to master the relationship between printed letters and their sounds. Although they can match two written or two spoken words, dyslexics have enormous difficulty relating printed words to spoken words. The best explanation for dyslexics' failure to master the print/sound connection seems to be that they are extremely slow at retrieving verbal information from long-term memory (Just and Carpenter, 1987). Whether they are searching for representations of phonemes, syllables, morphemes, or words, they take an inordinate amount of time to find them. This slowness creates a bottleneck that overloads their working memory, which then prevents them from devoting enough working memory to the process of comprehension. Researchers also believe that problems in storing and retrieving the names of printed words can easily lead to such errors as calling *was* "saw" and to other reversal problems that once led researchers to suspect that dyslexics had some sort of visual deficit (Vellutino, 1987).

Understanding even a simple discourse also involves connecting all the propositions to one another, identifying the most important propositions, and organizing them accordingly. Connections are made not only among propositions from the same sentence, but also among propositions in the different sentences. In our example, the pronoun "him" in the second sentence serves to connect the propositions of the second sentence to those in the first.

Some propositions receive more connections than others. Typically, the highly connected propositions are the most central: they contain the essence of the discourse. Propositions with fewer connections usually concern less essential details. As you recall from Chapter 8, the more connections a proposition has, the more elaborated it is, and thus the more likely it is to be remembered—to be activated in long-term memory and brought into working memory. A large number of connections (or a high degree of elaboration) ensures easier access because there simply are more handles, more ways "in" to the memory. Further, the more times a proposition is activated and brought into working memory—in other words, the more it is *rehearsed*—the better our chances of recalling it again (Kintsch and Van Dijk, 1978). Thus, our memory processes serve to increase our recall for the main ideas but not necessarily for the details of a discourse.

Go back for a moment to our brief sample discourse about the old actor, this time with the idea in mind that it is about George Burns. You might guess that Burns is being recognized by the audience for his acting accomplishments; perhaps he is receiving an Oscar or some other award. But suppose you are told now that the actor is Ronald Reagan. Your interpretation of the discourse is likely to be completely different: perhaps Reagan is about to give a political or fund-raising speech. The point is that your interpretation of a discourse depends very heavily on what aspects of your prior knowledge are activated.

As you know, not only do we make connections among the various propositions of a discourse, but we also relate these propositions to those that make up the schemas in our long-term memory. The prior knowledge stored in our sche-

mas forms part of the common ground between the writer/speaker and reader/
listener. The discourse does not need to repeat this information. Indeed, repeating
it would actually violate the cooperative principle by providing *too much* information. Instead, we elaborate new information with information from and inferences
based on prior knowledge. Out of all this taken together, we construct a complete
mental model.

To see how important activating schemas are to discourse comprehension, try
to make sense out of the following paragraph:

> *The procedure is actually quite simple. First you arrange items in different
> groups. Of course, one pile may be sufficient depending on how much there is
> to do. If you have to go somewhere else due to lack of facilities, that is the
> next step. Otherwise, you are pretty well set. It is important not to overdo
> things. That is, it is better to do too few things at once than too many. In the
> short run this may not seem important, but complications can easily arise. A
> mistake can be expensive as well. At first the whole procedure will seem
> complicated. Soon, however, it will become just another facet of life. It is
> difficult to foresee any end to the necessity for this task in the immediate
> future, but then one never can tell. After the procedure is completed, one
> arranges the materials in different groups again. Then they can be put in their
> appropriate places. Eventually they will be used once more and the whole
> cycle will then have to be repeated. However, that is part of life. (Bransford
> and Johnson, 1973)*

People who read this passage as part of an experiment found it practically incomprehensible. When asked to recall it, they did poorly. Yet when other people were
given only a single short clue before reading it, they readily understood the passage and later recalled substantially more of it. The clue was "washing clothes."
This thematic clue activated the appropriate schema in memory, providing a common ground between writer and reader.

Without the clue, what makes the passage so difficult to understand? Certainly, each sentence in the passage is grammatical and sensible, yet the overall
impression is one of fuzziness and incoherence. Why? First, many of the words
("items," "facilities," "things") are vague and general, so they provide no clues to
specific referents. Second, we cannot figure out the relationships among the objects and activities without already knowing or being able to infer these referents—
that is, without knowing what objects and activities are being talked about. We
cannot easily build a mental model of the situation unless we have this kind of
information. But once our schema about "laundry" or "washing clothes" is activated, it provides particular referents for each vague term in the passage. We know
that *items* means "articles of clothing," that *facilities* means "washing machines,"
and so on. (This is, incidentally, why a good title or subhead helps readers: it
serves to activate the appropriate schema or schemas for interpreting the propositions of the text that follows. Titles and subheads, in other words, provide useful
clues for readers, giving them a head start on interpretation.)

Activation of appropriate schemas is just as important in conversation as it is
in reading, and speakers design their utterances accordingly. Within an utterance,
there is usually some component that represents "old" (or *given*) information,
which the listener uses to activate the appropriate representations in memory. The
listener simply adds or connects any *new* information the speaker is providing to
the old. If someone tells you, "It was your mother who called yesterday about the
Sunday picnic," you clearly already know that you had a phone call and that a
picnic is planned; the speaker is merely providing whatever new information is
available. This implicit agreement between speaker and listener to deal with new
information in such a way that it can be easily linked with old is known as the
given-new contract (Haviland and Clark, 1974) and is derived from the cooperative principle discussed earlier. It is a means of streamlining communication.

In sum, understanding language involves a complex series of mental processes
that begins with the decoding of either auditory or visual input, continues with
the extraction of the propositions represented by groups of those words, and ends
with a mental model that reflects the integration of the propositions of the discourse with our own prior knowledge.

GIVEN-NEW CONTRACT an implicit agreement between speaker and
listener to represent new information
so it can be efficiently linked with old

LANGUAGE AND THOUGHT

In George Orwell's futuristic novel *Nineteen Eighty-Four* (1949) the government sharply reduces vocabulary in the belief that subversive thought is impossible when there are no words to express it. Was Orwell right? Today, for example, many people believe that our language affects the way we think about women, and this conviction has led to conscious efforts to eliminate sexist language. The substitution of "sales representative" for "salesman" and "firefighter" for "fireman" is one sort of change. Another is the attempt to eliminate the use of "lady" (as in "lady doctor") and "girl" (for any female who is beyond adolescence) on the grounds that the words perpetuate the view of women as frivolous and childish. Similar motives underlie attempts to remove pejorative terms for ethnic groups from the language.

LINGUISTIC DETERMINISM the theory that language determines how we perceive and understand the world

Linguistic determinism, the idea that language determines thought, was eloquently expounded by Benjamin Lee Whorf (1940/1956) some fifty years ago. When children acquire a language, Whorf believed, they simultaneously acquire a world view, because what their language allows them to talk about determines the way in which they perceive the world. From this Whorf concluded that people speaking different languages must therefore think about the world differently. For example, English has a single word for snow, but Eskimos—who live in an environment where snow is extremely important—have more than twenty distinct words for different types of snow. If language determines our perception, the Eskimo who looks out on a fresh snowfall perceives the white substance differently—in perhaps more subtle variations—than does an English-speaking American. In the next section we consider this issue by first examining evidence on how language influences the way we categorize the world; then we look at evidence on how language influences our images and memories of the world.

Language and Perceptual Categories

Whether we label an object as blue or green depends on how we categorize the color spectrum. Although light varies continuously in wavelength (as you saw in Chapter 4), our perceptual experience of hue forms only a few major categories: red, green, blue, and so on. Linguistic determinism proposes that the categories into which we divide the color spectrum is determined by our language. In other

The importance of snow in the lives of Eskimos has given rise to more than twenty words for it in their language. The question of whether such examples mean that our language determines how we perceive the world is still being debated.

words, individuals speaking languages that each have different color-naming conventions may perceive and categorize the color spectrum differently.

Evidence from some very clever experiments by Eleanor Rosch (formerly Heider) does not seem to support the view that language determines the way in which we perceive colors. She compared two groups of people: native English-speaking Americans and the Dani of New Guinea, whose two color terms refer to differences in brightness (*mola* for light and *mili* for dark) rather than differences in hue, as in English (red, blue, green, yellow and so on). Before her study, it had been established that some colors are perceived as **focal colors**—shades at the center of a group of colors all given the same label (for example, red is a focal color and brick-red is a nonfocal color). Focal colors are most likely to be labeled by a single word (blue, green, or yellow) and nonfocal by a compound word (blue-green or orange-yellow).

In one of Rosch's experiments, both groups were tested on their memory for specific color chips (Heider, 1972). Each group looked at a color chip for 5 seconds; after 30 seconds they were presented with an array similar to that shown in Figure 10.4, from which they were to select the same color as the color chip they had just seen. The Americans showed much better memory for both focal and nonfocal colors than the Dani.

At first this might seem to support linguistic determinism by suggesting that a more elaborate color-labeling system in one's language allows for better color memory. However, there are actually other differences between the Dani and the Americans that may explain the memory-test results. For one thing, the Dani may place much less emphasis on developing memory skill in their society. For another thing, both the Americans and the Dani were much better at remembering the focal colors than the nonfocal colors (Heider, 1972). Since for the Dani language codability is the same for focal and nonfocal colors, their better memory for the focal colors cannot be attributed to language codability. In another experiment, Rosch examined which shades were most easily confused in a color-memory task and found that the Americans and the Dani made similar confusions (Heider and Olivier, 1972). It appears, then, that despite having only two color terms in their language, the Dani perceived similar color categories with similar hues to those perceived by the Americans.

Other research by anthropologists has shown that although languages differ in the number of basic color terms they have, speakers of different languages tend to agree on which hues are focal. That is, although one language may have only six color terms and another may have eleven, speakers of both languages are likely to select the same hue as the best example of the color red (Berlin and Kay, 1969). Furthermore, color terms make their appearance in languages in generally the same order (see Figure 10.5). This order is easier to understand if we think about it in terms of the history of languages. The first two color terms to enter a language are the equivalents of black and white—the most fundamental perceptual distinction. The next color term to enter a language is red, followed by yellow, green, and blue; then brown; and finally purple, pink, orange, and gray. A language with only three color terms would presumably assign all the colors that English speak-

FOCAL COLOR the basic colors, like red, blue, or brown; the ideal or best-example color within the range of a given color term

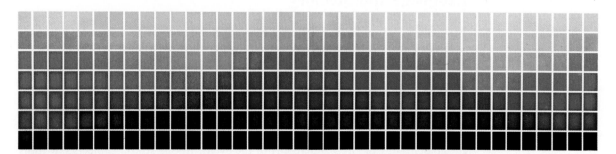

Figure 10.4 This array of color chips is used in color-naming experiments like that of Brown and Lenneberg (1954). See how closely you and a friend agree on which chips correspond to "pure blue" and "pure red" versus "teal blue" and "brick red." People usually agree more closely on the names of focal colors.

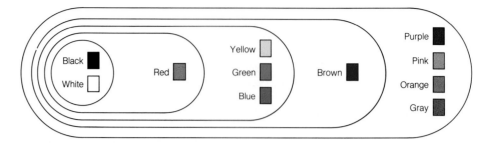

Figure 10.5 This diagram illustrates the logical relations among color names in different languages, with the names arranged from left to right in order of use. If a language had only three color terms, they would correspond to English black, white, and focal red; all other colors that English speakers distinguish (toward the right in the figure) would be assigned one of those three labels. If a language had six color terms, these would correspond to the English terms toward the left—black, white, and red, as before, plus yellow, green, and blue—with the other color terms toward the right being assigned one of those six labels. Color terms tend to be introduced into a language in historical sequence from left to right.

ers distinguish to the categories black, white, or red; a six-term language would add yellow, green, and blue (Berlin and Kay, 1969). These findings suggest that color categorization is determined by some universal property of color sensation, not by language. The universal characteristic that probably determines these cultural similarities is the structure of the visual system (Au, 1988).

Language, then, does not determine what we can perceive, but it does apparently label and encode those differences that are significant for a given social and cultural group. Subtle qualities of snow may be important for Eskimos, for example, but those of us who live in more temperate climates need only one term to designate it. When an aspect of the environment becomes important, words are added to the language to enhance communication: consider the very special vocabulary that skiers have developed to talk about different snow conditions.

Thus, it seems that there are some aspects of perception and thought that are universal, are biologically determined, and are therefore relatively unaffected by language differences. Note, as further evidence for this, that the first concepts children learn the world over are virtually the same, as you saw in Chapter 9: an infant in Nepal is likely to categorize the world in a very similar way to the two-year-old in Toronto. (And in Chapter 12 you will learn that there seem to be both universal, biologically based emotions and other, more culturally influenced emotions.) Then there are aspects of cognition that are determined at least in part by culture, are affected in some way by cultural differences, and are therefore more intertwined with linguistic differences. It is also likely that memory may be heavily influenced by language and culture, and we explore this idea in the next section.

Language and Memory

Language may not determine how we perceive and categorize the world, but there is considerable evidence that language influences how we remember the world. As we saw in Chapter 8, the way we label something influences the way we remember it; an ambiguous figure labeled "eyeglasses" will be remembered differently than the *same* figure labeled "dumbbell" (Carmichael, Hogan, and Walter, 1932). We encode at least some memories verbally and often use the verbal label to get at those memories later.

Experiments on eyewitness memory show how the wording of questions about an event can affect our report of the event. In one study, subjects saw films of automobile accidents. Afterward, they were asked to provide an estimate of how fast the cars were traveling with one of two questions: "About how fast were the cars going when they *hit* each other?" or "About how fast were the cars going

Figure 10.6 Parts of the human vocal apparatus. Air expelled from the lungs vibrates the vocal cords, which can stretch or contract to produce high or low frequencies (pitches). The vibrating cords cause the column of air in the pharynx and oral cavity to vibrate like the air in a pipe organ. By moving the tongue, velum, and lips, we can alter the nature of the sound produced. For example, pressing the tongue against the hard palate so the sound is forced up through the nasal cavity produces the nasal sounds *n, m,* and *ng.* (Clark and Clark, 1977.)

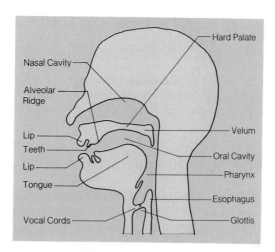

when they *smashed into* each other?" The group given the "smashed" question gave significantly higher reports of the speed of the cars than the group given the "hit" question. Even more interesting was the finding that, a week later, those asked the "smashed" question were also more likely to report having seen broken glass at the accident scene than members of the "hit" group, even though no broken glass was visible in the film (Loftus and Palmer, 1974).

In another experiment, which we discussed in detail in Chapter 8, subjects saw a stop sign at an intersection; one group was later asked a question that assumed they had seen a yield sign instead. These subjects were more likely to say they had indeed seen a yield sign than those in another group who were neither reminded of the stop sign nor told it was a yield sign (Loftus, Miller, and Burns, 1978). According to Au (1988), these effects may reveal the cooperative principle at work. According to this principle, if listeners assume that the speaker is being cooperative, then they also expect the speaker to be truthful. In the case of the stop sign/yield sign study, the witnesses might not have remembered a stop sign at all, but when subtly "reminded" of a yield sign, they might simply have added that information to their memory of the event, without even considering that the speaker might have been trying to deceive them (see also McCloskey and Zaragoza, 1985, for a similar explanation). This explanation fits with the findings of Dodd and Bradshaw (1980), whose subjects saw a sequence of slides depicting an automobile accident and afterward read a description of the event that introduced misleading information. Later memory tests showed that subjects were more likely to accept the misleading information if they were told that the written description was based on an interview with a neutral bystander than if told it was based on an interview with the driver of the car, who had clearly been at fault. The subjects evidently and understandably assumed that both the neutral bystander and the writer of the description based on the bystander's testimony were obliged to be truthful and informative. Thus, the specific wording of utterances or texts, by providing false cues, can have a significant impact on the content of our memory.

In a sense, these eyewitness-testimony studies illustrate cases in which details (which we tend not to hang onto as easily if not explicitly told to do so) and exact wording (usually part of the surface structure, which we are also less likely to hold onto) are very important and may trip us up. After all, differences between stop and yield signs, between 3 A.M. and 4 A.M., and between speeds of 30 and 50 miles per hour can make or break a lawsuit in court. Our memory may be tripped up in such cases not only because of our tendency to remember more of the big picture than the exact details but also because of our assumptions about what we read or hear, which we make on the basis of the cooperative principle. At the same time, our memory may be quite vulnerable to how exact the wording is in recall tests, since words serve as cues for recall.

BIOLOGICAL FOUNDATIONS OF LANGUAGE

Our ability to use spoken language is closely related to our biological structure. The human vocal organs, breathing apparatus, auditory system, and brain are highly specialized for spoken communication (see Figure 10.6).

Our Speech Apparatus

What sets our speech apparatus apart from that of chimpanzees or gorillas? Our teeth grow upright and close together, and the top and bottom teeth meet; this allows us to articulate such sounds as *s*, *f*, *y*, *sh*, and *th*. The human mouth is small and oval and can be opened and shut rapidly; our lips contain many highly developed and interlaced muscles. Together, the mouth and lips enable us to create additional phonemes (such as /p/ and /b/) by the way we shape them. In addition, our tongue is thick, short, and flexible, which enables us to change the shape of the vocal cavity so that we can produce a wide range of vowel sounds. Our simple larynx lets air move freely up and out through the mouth without interference; our vocal cords within the larynx have a wide range of possible positions (Aitchison, 1976).

When we speak, our lungs expel air through the throat and mouth; the vocal cords vibrate like violin strings to create sound in the larynx and throat, which act like a pipe organ; and the tongue, palate, lips, teeth, and facial muscles work together to pronounce vowels and consonants. Stop a moment, put your hand on your throat, and read this sentence aloud. Feel how these structures move flexibly and how your windpipe resonates.

Brain Specialization

For most people, language functions appear to be controlled primarily by the left hemisphere of the brain, while the right hemisphere primarily controls processing of nonspeech sounds, music, and spatial patterns. This division of labor is called **lateralization.** Evidence for lateralization comes from several sources.

As we saw in Chapter 3, damage to sections of the left hemisphere of the brain can cause various forms of **aphasia,** a disruption in the ability to produce or understand language, while damage to corresponding areas of the right hemisphere do not disrupt language functioning. **Expressive aphasia** (otherwise known as Broca's aphasia), which is a disruption of the ability to produce coherent speech, is caused by damage to part of the left frontal lobe of the brain. The difficulties shown by David Ford, described at the beginning of this chapter, are characteristic of expressive aphasia. In general, the speech of affected individuals is halting and limited to content words (nouns, verbs); few or no function words (articles, prepositions, conjunctions) are uttered, and speech is generally ungrammatical. In addition, these aphasics seem to have lost command of at least some aspects of syntax needed to comprehend speech. For example, expressive aphasics usually can correctly understand sentences whose content words limit possible interpretations, such as "The apple that the boy is eating is red." But when syntactic relations must be grasped for comprehension, aphasics behave as if they were randomly linking nouns to predicates. In "The girl the boy is chasing is tall," for example, half the time aphasics would say the girl is tall and half the time they would say it is the boy who is tall (Caramazza and Zurif, 1976).

Receptive aphasia (otherwise known as Wernicke's aphasia) is a condition in which the ability to comprehend spoken and written language is seriously disrupted, as is the ability to generate coherent speech. This condition stems from damage to a portion of the left temporal lobe of the brain. In general, receptive aphasics do not seem to understand what is said to them and also seem to have

BRAIN LATERALIZATION different capabilities developed in the right versus left hemispheres of the brain

APHASIA a disruption in the ability to produce or understand language

EXPRESSIVE APHASIA a condition in which the ability to produce coherent speech is impaired

RECEPTIVE APHASIA a condition in which the ability to comprehend speech and to generate coherent speech is impaired

difficulty monitoring their own speech. Their speech is very fluent but often makes no sense. The following sample of speech was taken from a conversation with a person suffering from receptive aphasia:

Examiner: *Do you like it here in Kansas City?*
Aphasic: *Yes, I am.*
Examiner: *I'd like to have you tell me something about your problem.*
Aphasic: *I can't hill all of my way. I can't talk all of the things I do, and part of the part I can go all right, but I can't tell from the other people. I usually most of my things. I know what can I talk and know what they are but I can't always come back even though I know they should be in, and I know something eely I should know what I'm doing. (Akmajian, Demers, and Harnish, 1984)*

Other evidence for lateralization comes from dichotic listening tasks (see Chapter 6), in which people listen to two different sound signals at the same time. If a word is spoken to one ear and a different word to the other, people usually report the word spoken to the right ear more accurately. The explanation is that although the left hemisphere receives signals from both ears, as does the right hemisphere, the signal from the opposite side, the right ear, dominates the channel (Kimura, 1967). Thus, for a word presented to the left ear to be reported, it must first travel its dominant path to the right hemisphere, then cross the corpus callosum to enter the left hemisphere. The greater processing needed for words presented to the left ear accounts for the increased number of errors. When the sounds in dichotic listening tasks are not words but musical chords, bird calls, or car horns, people usually report hearing the sound directed to their left ear (right hemisphere) more accurately, thus demonstrating some of the right hemisphere's more specialized functions.

Dichotic listening studies of split-brain patients reveal analogous patterns. These patients will report only the word presented to the right ear under these circumstances. Of course, in split-brain patients the connection between the two hemispheres no longer exists, so a word presented to the left ear in a dichotic listening task cannot be reported at all.

Signs of lateralization have also been detected in newborn infants. When babies hear passages of speech or consonant-vowel sounds, recordings of their brain waves show more activity in the left hemisphere than in the right. And when babies hear musical chords or bursts of sound, their brain-wave recordings show greater activity in the right hemisphere (Molfese and Molfese, 1979; 1980). Such studies suggest that special left-hemisphere mechanisms for analyzing speech may serve as the foundation for learning language.

Yet the immature human brain seems to have a limited degree of flexibility. If an infant's left hemisphere is injured, the right hemisphere is still capable of some language functioning. Very young children whose left hemispheres have been surgically removed to prevent debilitating seizures appear to develop close to normal language abilities (Smith and Sugar, 1975). Children whose left hemispheres had been removed before they were five months old had almost normal language when tested at nine and ten years old (Dennis and Whitaker, 1976). The language deficits they did show seemed to involve mostly syntax. For example, they exhibited difficulty in comprehending passive sentences and in applying language rules, such as those for forming the past tense of regular verbs by adding *ed* (as in "jumped"), to nonsense words (Dennis, 1983). Apparently, the syntactic aspects of language develop quite slowly if children have only a right hemisphere.

Language and Nonhumans

We have outlined the biological foundations of human language, in the voice apparatus and in the specialization of the brain. It should be noted that some eminent linguists, such as Noam Chomsky (1975), have postulated that humans

Washoe, a chimpanzee, was taught to communicate in sign language. Eventually she was able to learn more than a hundred signs, but she never mastered grammar.

have an innate capacity to learn language, an inborn knowledge of its general rules. Given these points, is the human species *uniquely* suited to language? Does language actually separate us from other species? Or is there some continuity, some kind of link through language abilities, with other species? Are we limited to our definition of language by our own use of it? Does our definition of language in itself perhaps limit language capacity to humans? One way to explore these questions is to examine the results of attempts to teach a human kind of language to nonhumans, particularly to large-brained mammals like apes and dolphins.

Consider this glimpse at the evidence: When Washoe, a five-year-old chimpanzee trained in American Sign Language, wanted to go outdoors, she stood at the door and signed, "Open out." When she wanted an apple, she stood in front of the refrigerator and signed "Food open hurry" (Gardner and Gardner, 1969; 1975). Was Washoe demonstrating knowledge of a human language? This question is at the center of an ongoing controversy in psycholinguistics.

That other animal species communicate is not at issue. Many species have communication systems: bees dance on the floor of a hive to tell other workers where nectar has been found (Brines and Gould, 1979), seagulls use distinct cries to communicate the location of food or the presence of danger, and howler monkeys have twenty distinct calls—including a signal to other males that a certain territory is occupied (Altmann, 1973). But such animal signaling systems are fairly simple and inflexible. An animal's cry is like a knee-jerk reaction to a specific emotional stimulus. A vervet monkey's loud "Rraup!" whenever it spots a leopard is much like the "Ouch!" that escapes your lips when you bang a shin on a sharp corner. This is quite different from your ability to discuss where you were headed when you walked into the furniture.

Some researchers have reasoned that if other species in a rich training environment could learn to use language—to create new sentence constructions and follow syntactic rules—then a number of philosophical and psychological questions are raised. We might, for instance, need to reassess our relation to the animal world. We would have another thread to weave into the language/cognition connection. However, great care must be taken in drawing conclusions about demonstrations of apparently successful training. Some people in the past have mistakenly interpreted an animal's behavior as evidence for knowledge of language. This type of mistake has been named the **"Clever Hans" phenomenon** after a famous case (Sebeok and Umliker-Sebeok, 1980).

At the turn of the century, a German named van Osten exhibited a highly intelligent horse now known as Clever Hans who could answer questions by

"CLEVER HANS" PHENOMENON attributing more understanding to an animal than is warranted; Clever Hans was a horse who responded to his trainer's subtle cues, not to the sense of linguistic requests

tapping his foot or moving his head. The horse could apparently count, do simple arithmetic, tell time, and read German. However, careful investigation revealed that the horse was reading the questioner's body language. From posture, facial expression, and the like, the horse could tell when the questioner expected him to start tapping and when he had tapped long enough. What is most interesting about this case is that van Osten himself was apparently unaware that the horse was merely responding to these subtle cues. Thus, researchers who have attempted to teach a language to a nonhuman species must demonstrate through painstaking procedures that the animal's behavior is not due to subtle prompting from the researcher or trainer or to some nonlanguage skill on the part of the animal.

Chimpanzees lack the vocal apparatus for speech, so Beatrice and Allen Gardner (1969; 1975) used American Sign Language in Washoe's language lessons. After four years, Washoe had learned to use 132 signs in appropriate situations. As soon as she had learned ten signs, she began to use them in combination. However, unlike human children, Washoe paid little attention to word order and seemed to lack a grasp of syntax (Klima and Bellugi, 1973). Lana, another chimp, learned to type simple messages in learned symbols on a computer-controlled keyboard (Rumbaugh, 1977). She not only produced rudimentary sentencelike sequences but also "read" what her trainers wrote on the screen and responded appropriately to their questions and commands.

For a while it appeared that chimpanzees were well on their way to language. Then Herbert Terrace (1979) analyzed videotaped conversations with Nim Chimpsky, the chimpanzee from his own lab. Nim had learned 125 signs and regularly combined them in utterances. But he was producing a grab bag of every sign that could apply to a situation, and his long, repetitive utterances were no more complex (syntactically or semantically) than his shorter remarks. For example, Nim's longest utterance was "Give orange me give eat orange me eat orange give me eat orange give me you." Unlike a young child's sentences, which convey more and more information as they get longer, Nim's longer strings conveyed no more information than his shorter strings. More importantly, in most cases Nim turned out to be either imitating his teacher or responding to the teacher's prompting. When Terrace examined films of other "talking" primates, he found a similar pattern of imitative signing. Thus, many of the early attempts to teach language to nonhuman primates may not have adequately ruled out the "Clever Hans" phenomenon as an explanation.

Although Terrace's criticisms were questioned by Washoe's trainers (Gardner, 1981), Sue Savage-Rumbaugh and her colleagues (1980), who had worked with Lana, had already come to similar conclusions. They decided that Lana—and other "talking" chimpanzees—had gone no further in acquiring language than the average nine-month-old child. But neither Terrace nor Lana's instructors had said that chimpanzees *could* not learn language, only that they *had* not.

This debate on the language competence of chimpanzees has centered on two issues. The first issue concerns whether nonhuman animals are able to use signs as symbols: do they have the ability to understand that a sign refers to objects and can even be used to "talk" about the objects when they are not present? The second issue concerns whether nonhuman animals are able to master a system of rules by which sentences are constructed—that is, a grammar.

With regard to the first issue, researchers found that chimpanzees seemed to use signs primarily to get rewards; like pigeons pecking keys to get corn, they may have learned only that a certain act (making the sign) in a specific situation produced a particular reward. This meant that although the apes were associating specific gestures with specific objects, they had not learned that the signs "named" the objects and could be used to refer to them.

After three years of intensive training, however, Savage-Rumbaugh and her colleagues (1983) finally taught two chimpanzees the referential connection on which language is based. The researchers then went on to work with pygmy chimpanzees, a species that is more intelligent than the common chimpanzee (Savage-Rumbaugh et al., 1986). Their pupil was Matata, a wild-caught pygmy chimpanzee who brought her six-month-old baby, Kanzi, along to her lessons. The baby played in the lab while the mother learned symbols. To the researchers' surprise, Kanzi eventually began using the symbols on his own. Like a human child, he had learned that the graphic symbols (somewhat similar to the ones Lana had used) could be used to refer to absent objects. He had apparently learned the referential function of language by watching and imitating his mother and the trainers. Kanzi's little sister, Mulika, also spontaneously learned to use symbols in a referential manner. The two pygmy chimpanzees took another giant step: they apparently imagined interaction between others and then used symbols to get it started ("Bill chase Patty; Liz tickle Bill").

With regard to the second issue, few of the attempts to teach chimpanzees a language has provided compelling evidence that a nonhuman can grasp a simple grammatical system. Recently reported research with dolphins, however, may demonstrate that these animals are capable of some grammatical understanding. At the University of Hawaii, several female bottlenosed dolphins have shown that they "understand" a variety of sentences conveyed through one of two languages (Herman, Richards, and Wolz, 1984; Herman, 1987). One is a visual language consisting of hand and arm signals, and the other is an acoustic language consisting of whistlelike sounds. The dolphins first learned a small set of signals for simple actions, which the trainers taught them using shaping techniques (Chapter 7) with reinforcements of fish and the trainer's approval. As they learned the set of actions, the dolphins also learned signs for categories of objects, such as balls, hoops, pipes, and baskets. The objects in each category varied from day to day in color, size, and exact shape, so the dolphins were learning to recognize a variety of instances for each concept. The dolphins also learned modifiers (signs for "on your left," "on your right," "surface of water," and "submerged") as well as to reply "yes" or "no" by pressing the appropriate panel.

All commands were constructed from a simple phrase-structure grammar, which could be used to generate sentences up to five "words" long. These five-word sentences made possible a very large number of combinations of signs, so the researchers were able to train the dolphins on a subset of sentences and to test the dolphins' understanding of sentences to which they had never been exposed. The dolphins showed evidence of an ability to respond correctly to novel sentences. For example, after a dolphin learned "Hoop fetch surfboard" (which told the dolphin to swim to the hoop and take it to the surfboard), it was able to understand "Hoop on surfboard" (which told it to get the hoop and put it on the surfboard). They usually carried out such actions quickly and without error, despite the presence of distracting objects and other dolphins moving about in the tank. Such findings demonstrate a grasp of syntax.

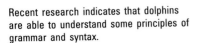

Recent research indicates that dolphins are able to understand some principles of grammar and syntax.

The dolphins have also shown some grasp, although far from perfect, of semantically reversible sentences. Consider the sentence "Hoop fetch pipe," which means "take the hoop to the pipe." The opposite action of taking the pipe to the hoop could be requested with "Pipe fetch hoop." The dolphins rarely made errors in reversing their interpretations of such sentences, indicating that they had grasped the significance of word order in these reversible sentences.

The researchers who worked with the dolphins were careful to design the tests to eliminate the Clever Hans phenomenon. To make certain that the dolphins were responding to language and not to contextual cues, the "speaker" wore opaque goggles to eliminate gaze cues; an observer who had not seen the signal categorized the dolphin's behavior on each trial and shouted what would have been the appropriate command. The signals, the dolphin's performance, and the observer's interpretation of it were all recorded by a third person.

Clearly, attempts to teach language to nonhumans have produced some impressive results, revealing glimmers—albeit controversial ones—of the central characteristics of human language: expressiveness, productivity, and displacement. Computers, too, have been "taught" some verbal basics, and recent programs have shown great advances (see Chapter 9). But many psychologists would have us consider with what effort such results have been obtained and compare it to the relative ease with which infants and young children acquire the complexities of language (language acquisition is discussed in Chapter 15). Nevertheless, the effort to train dolphins and chimps and to program computers to use human-type language has paid off in a number of ways. Artificial intelligence and chimpanzees' sign language may seem far removed from one another, but psychologists have learned a great deal from both.

Perhaps, after all, we must consider language a centrally human ability. Language is so integral an aspect of human life that to imagine living or thinking without it seems almost "unthinkable." So much of human knowledge is acquired and stored through language, and pushed forward because of it, that it is hardly surprising that language is seen as the crowning glory of the human intellect.

SUMMARY

Universal Features of Human Language

- Every human language has three basic properties: expressive power, productivity, and displacement. In every language there is an infinite number of possible sentences.

Linguistic Structure

- Linguistics studies language knowledge, which is made up of sound, syntactic, and semantic components.
- The sound component contains knowledge of phonological rules, which govern the combination of phonemes. These rules allow us to pronounce and understand alternate forms of the same root.
- The syntactic component contains knowledge of syntax, the rules for combining morphemes, both free and bound, into sentences.
- Phrase-structure rules govern the interrelation of word groups within a sentence. Through rewrite operations, these rules allow for the hierarchical breakdown of phrases into component parts and the insertion of words to construct sentences. Ambiguity occurs whenever a sentence has more than one plausible interpretation.
- Transformation rules govern the relation of a sentence's surface structure to its deep structure.

- The semantic component covers both word and sentence meaning. Word meaning involves both the sense and the reference of a word. Sentence meaning is governed by word order, the syntactic relations of the words, the meanings of the propositions, and the truth or falsehood of all the propositions.

Designing and Using Speech in Daily Life

- Language competence is to be distinguished from language performance. Linguistics concentrates on competence, whereas psycholinguistics focuses on performance—on putting our knowledge of language to work in order to communicate.
- A speech act is governed by the goal of the speaker and the entire context of the communication—physical, social, verbal, and cognitive. This entire context forms the common ground between speaker and listener.
- Speaker and listener are able to participate in a dialogue by adhering to the cooperative principle, according to which it is assumed that the speaker will be informative, truthful, clear, brief, and relevant.
- Indirect speech highlights the distinction between literal meaning and the speaker's actual intention. The speaker's meaning can generally be determined by drawing inferences.

■ Slips of the tongue are probably the result of faulty processing in the speech planning system, although Freud argued that they revealed unconscious wishes or conflicts.

Understanding Language

■ To understand a discourse, we must construct a mental model of it, by extracting information and integrating it with our own schemas.
■ To understand speech, the listener must segment the flow of sound into words, with the help of phonological rules and inference.
■ After a word is identified, its meaning (or meanings) is activated and retrieved; unwanted multiple meanings are eliminated based on the verbal context.
■ We decode words in written text either by sounding out the words or by recognizing words as whole chunks, or by some combination. Eye fixation research shows that processing written text involves more than decoding; we must extract the propositions, connect them to one another, and elaborate them by connecting them to our prior knowledge (i.e., by integrating them with our own schemas). We tend to remember the gist of a discourse rather than the exact wording (unless we are explicitly instructed otherwise).
■ The importance of activating appropriate schemas cannot be overestimated.

Language and Thought

■ Whorf's theory of linguistic determinism proposes that our language determines the way we perceive and understand the world. This theory has not held up in tests of color categorization in people from widely divergent cultures.
■ Language does seem to reflect differences in culture.
■ Language also influences memory, in part because we encode at least some memories verbally. Eyewitness testimony studies have shown that we may be quite responsive to verbal cues, which affect the content of what we recall.

Biological Foundations of Language

■ Our voice apparatus is specially adapted for speech.
■ The left hemisphere of the brain appears to be primarily responsible for language functions, as evidenced in aphasic patients and dichotic listening studies.
■ The attempt to teach humanlike language to nonhumans springs from basic questions about our continuity with other species and about the complex interrelationship between cognition and language.
■ Such attempts have caused some controversy over chimpanzees' competence in human language. Some have claimed that, thus far, chimps taught language have not learned displacement and do not apply grammatical rules. More recent work with pygmy chimps and with dolphins has produced some indications of referential use of language and displacement in chimps and a grasp of a simple grammatical system in dolphins.

KEY TERMS

ambiguity	given-new contract	psycholinguistics
anticipation	grammar	receptive aphasia
aphasia	language competence	recursion
brain lateralization	linguistic determinism	reference
"Clever Hans" phenomenon	linguistics	reversal
common ground	morphemes	transformation rules
cooperative principle	performance system	segmentation problem
decoding	perseveration	semantic
deep structure	phonemes	sense
discourse	phonological rules	slips of the tongue
displacement	phrase-structure rules	speech acts
expressive power	phrase-structure tree	speech plan
expressive aphasia	productivity	surface structure
focal colors	propositions	syntax

CONCEPT REVIEW

1. Describe the three universal features of human language.

2. Identify the major components of phonology and syntax. What is the difference between phonemes and morphemes? Between deep structure and surface structure?

3. Distinguish between word meaning and sentence meaning in semantics. Do transformation rules affect the meaning of either sentences or individual words?

4. What defines a speech act? Explain the role of common ground and the cooperative principle in communication.

5. In what ways can a slip of the tongue also be an indirect speech act?

6. Identify the three processes that the chapter suggests are involved in discourse. What is the definition of *discourse?*

7. What are the differences in recognizing spoken and written words? Do we need to read or hear the entire word before we are able to identify it? Why or why not?

8. How do schemas govern the way we interpret or identify the propositions contained in communicated language? In

order to understand discourse, must we understand all the propositions?

9. Explain what is meant by linguistic determinism. What is the evidence from memory experiments that supports the concept of linguistic determinism?

10. What is an aphasia? What do aphasias confirm about brain lateralization? Give an example of each type of aphasia discussed in the chapter.

11. Describe the competing views regarding nonhuman communication. Identify the most compelling evidence for each point of view.

CRITICAL THINKING

1. Identify the concepts and processes that learning, memory, cognition, and language have in common. Does each of these areas treat its common concepts and processes identically?

2. Just as we may question the viability of artificial intelligence, we may use the problem of communication to test whether computers will ever have "a mind of their own." Use the three universal features of human language as criteria to test the assumptions about artificial intelligence. What must computers be able to do in order to meet all three criteria?

Intelligence and
Intelligence Testing

CHAPTER 11

Intelligence and Intelligence Testing

WHAT IS INTELLIGENCE?

Most of us have a pretty clear idea of what intelligence is. We readily classify people as "smart" or "dense." Most of us would agree that intelligence has something to do with the capacity to profit from experience and to adapt to relatively new situations (Sternberg, 1985). When we try to define the nature of intelligence more precisely and to measure it, however, these intuitive concepts prove inadequate. Even experts on the topic have not moved much beyond such intuitions. This uncertainty has generated impassioned controversy over intelligence tests, which, as we shall see, are useful but far from perfect.

This chapter considers intelligence to be a set of abilities: the ability to learn quickly, the ability to solve difficult problems, the ability to perform tasks quickly and accurately, and so on. An ability allows a person to achieve a higher criterion of performance than someone else who lacks that ability. So intelligence has to do with individual differences in abilities.

INTELLIGENCE   general abilities that help people achieve their goals

We do not count all abilities as stemming from intelligence, however. To narrow our working definition a bit, we can say that the abilities that constitute **intelligence** are *generally useful* in helping people achieve their goals, no matter what their goals may be (Baron, 1985). Playing the piano, for instance, does not demonstrate intelligence: some people simply do not care whether they can play the piano or not. However, if learning to play the piano is your goal, you will be helped by being able to learn quickly and to perform tasks quickly and accurately—helped, in other words, by intelligence.

This definition, however, says nothing about what the abilities that constitute intelligence are, or about whether there is one basic ability underlying everything or several different abilities. It also says nothing about whether each ability is general across situations: a person who is good at learning to play the piano might or might not be good at learning Spanish. These are matters for the scientific study of intelligence to determine. We look at some of the aspects of that study in this chapter.

To understand what psychologists know about intelligence, we must turn to the history of attempts to define intelligence and measure it. Our thinking is still influenced by these early attempts. After discussing this history and the types of modern tests, we shall discuss the question of how such tests are validated—how we know that they measure what they are supposed to measure. Part of the answer to this question concerns the use of tests for prediction and classification: selection for colleges and jobs, classification of children as retarded or gifted, and evaluation of environmental effects. Therefore, in discussing this question, we will be led to ask also about the nature of retardation and giftedness. In the final section of the chapter, we look at the determinants of intelligence as measured by tests: genetic, environmental, and educational. This will also bring up the controversial nature of racial differences in tested intelligence.

THE MEASUREMENT OF INTELLIGENCE

History: The Invention of the IQ Test

From the outset, the scientific study of intelligence has been tied to the measurement of intelligence (Fancher, 1986). Sir Francis Galton (1822–1911), a cousin of Charles Darwin, was interested in the measurement of intelligence because he hoped to increase it through selective breeding of human beings, which he called **eugenics.** If we had a good intelligence test, Galton reasoned, we could use it to pick out people who ought to be encouraged to reproduce (for example, by giving them prizes for having large families). In a few generations, the overall level of intelligence would increase.

EUGENICS   the selective breeding of humans

In his own work, Galton did little more than simply measure and tabulate individual differences in a variety of mental functions, such as reaction time and memory span. (In the memory-span test, the subject is read a list of digits at a measured pace; the "span" is the number of digits that the subject can repeat back immediately without error.) Galton's ideas caught hold, however, and were pursued by others.

James McKeen Cattell (1860–1944) was an American who followed Galton in gathering data on mental-test performance, including speed of color naming and judgment of the duration of a 10-second time interval. One of his students, Clark Wissler (1901), found that scores on such tests failed to correlate with class standing among Columbia University undergraduates. That is, students who did well on such tests received no better grades than students who did less well on the same tests. Wissler took only a few measurements from each subject, and it is likely that his failure to find a correlation was partly the result of inadequate measurements. Charles Spearman (1904) found that simple tests, using more measurements for each subject, *did* correlate with teacher ratings of children's intelligence; however, Wissler had already convinced most workers that tests based on such simple processes were useless.

Psychologist Alfred Binet (1857–1911) had a specific problem to solve, and he solved it by inventing the first modern intelligence test (Binet and Simon, 1905). After compulsory schooling was instituted in France, officials and teachers noticed that many children seemed mentally incapable of doing the work. Binet was a member of a commission charged by the government with making recommendations about how to educate such apparently retarded children. Binet and his colleague Théopile Simon put together a test—made up partly from other tests previously used by Binet to study intellectual development—for the purpose of distinguishing what we now call mild retardation from other possible causes of school failure. Binet hoped that the test could be used to select children who would benefit from special remedial instruction. As we shall see later, this hope has been realized, although Binet did not live to see it.

Binet and Simon tried to make up items that would measure higher-level abilities, such as memory, judgment, the ability to maintain a *set* for a task (that is, a state of readiness to do the task as required), the ability to follow instructions, and the ability to check one's own answers. Their criterion for a good test item was that it be able to distinguish older children from younger children; they thus assumed that intelligence, or at least its measurable products, increases with age. The test Binet and Simon arrived at included such items as identifying body parts, the memory-span test (again), rhyming, interpreting pictures, comparing the meanings of words, filling in missing words in a story, and answering questions about relative lengths of straight lines. Each item took less than a minute to administer, and all items could be scored relatively objectively, with very little judgment required by the tester.

The items were grouped so that the average child of a given age would pass most items in the group of items for that age and fail most in the group for the next higher age. Intelligence was therefore expressed in terms of level of development in comparison to the typical age at which a test would be passed (much as we now classify children by grade in reading and arithmetic). In other words, a child of eight who could answer most of the items in the test for eight-year-olds would be said to have the **mental age** of eight. An eight-year-old who could not answer most of the items for eight-year-olds but could answer most of the items for seven-year-olds would have a mental age of seven, and so on. Binet recommended that a child who was two "mental" years behind his or her actual age be considered as subnormal.

In 1912 German psychologist William Stern noticed that Binet's two-year standard led to higher percentages of children being classified as subnormal as the children got older. Moreover, children diagnosed as retarded fell further behind as they got older. He found, however, that the percentage of subnormal children stayed about the same if he looked at the *ratio* between the child's mental age and chronological age instead of at the difference between the two. Lewis Terman, at Stanford University in 1916, decided to multiply this ratio by 100 to get a simple way of expressing a child's performance, which he called the **intelligence quotient,** or **IQ.** The IQ was therefore the ratio of mental age to chronological age, multiplied by 100:

MENTAL AGE a measurement of intelligence based on average abilities for a given age group

INTELLIGENCE QUOTIENT (IQ) the ratio of mental age to chronological age multiplied by 100

$$IQ = \frac{\text{mental age}}{\text{chronological age}} \times 100$$

Children who performed at their mental age would thus have an IQ of 100. Above-average IQs are those above 100, and IQs of less than 100 are below average.

Modern Tests

Most of our current intelligence tests are descendants of Binet's test and the concepts behind it. Like Binet's test, they are designed to provide as much information as possible in a short time. They consist of short problems or questions that are easily scored. They do not include other things that would seem to have just as much to do with intelligence: they do not, for example, give subjects a chance to learn and use a body of new knowledge, for that would take too long. Nor do they ask for judgments or decisions about complex social situations or moral dilemmas, for those answers would be too difficult to score. Still, as we shall see, the tests have been quite useful.

Paraphrased Wechslerlike Questions

General Information
1. How many wings does a bird have?
2. How many nickels make a dime?
3. What is steam made of?
4. Who wrote "Paradise Lost"?
5. What is pepper?

General Comprehension
1. What should you do if you see someone forget his book when he leaves his seat in a restaurant?
2. What is the advantage of keeping money in a bank?
3. Why is copper often used in electrical wires?

Arithmetic
1. Sam had three pieces of candy and Joe gave him four more. How many pieces of candy did Sam have altogether?
2. Three men divided eighteen golf balls equally among themselves. How many golf balls did each man receive?
3. If two apples cost 15¢, what will be the cost of a dozen apples?

Similarities
1. In what way are a lion and a tiger alike?
2. In what way are a saw and a hammer alike?
3. In what way are an hour and a week alike?
4. In what way are a circle and a triangle alike?

Vocabulary
This test consists simply of asking, "What is a _____?" or "What does _____ mean?" The words cover a wide range of difficulty or familiarity.

A

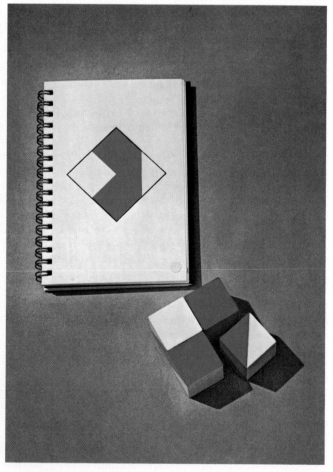

B

Figure 11.1 These test items are similar to those included in the various Wechsler intelligence scales. (A) A sampling of questions from five of the verbal subtests. (B) A problem in block design, one of the performance subtests in which the subject is asked to arrange the blocks to match a pattern on a card. *Opposite page:* (C) Another example of a performance subtest, in which the subject is required to put together puzzle pieces to form an object such as a duck. (D) A performance subtest in which the subject is asked to encode digits using a series of symbols. (Reproduced by permission of The Psychological Corporation, New York.)

The Stanford-Binet Test

Terman (1916; Terman and Merrill, 1973) improved Binet's test by gathering more data on the ages at which items are typically first solved, thus allowing for more accurate grouping of items. Terman's test has been revised over the years to improve its accuracy and to eliminate items that were noticeably unfair to certain ethnic groups. It is called the **Stanford-Binet test,** and it is still one of the most widely used tests of intelligence in the United States. The current version is made up of various subtests, grouped by age. Some of these subtests evaluate verbal ability; others assess nonverbal abilities. The nonverbal subtests, known as **performance tests,** include such tasks as picture completion, paper cutting, and maze tracing.

The Stanford-Binet test is administered to an individual child by a highly trained examiner who carefully carries out the standardized instructions. The examiner begins by making sure the child being tested feels comfortable and is motivated to do his or her best. The first items presented establish a proper starting level, usually on the basis of answers to a few items from the vocabulary subtest. The examiner will probably start with questions that can be answered by a slightly younger child, so that a ten-year-old first gets questions designed for a nine-year-old. If the ten-year-old misses some of the items for nine-year-olds, the examiner drops back to the eight-year-old level. The aim is to find the child's *basal mental age,* which is the age for which she or he can answer all test items. Once the basal age is established, the tester moves on to the next year, and so on. The testing continues until the child encounters a level at which she or he can answer none of the items.

STANFORD-BINET TEST the modified, widely used version of Binet's original test

PERFORMANCE TEST an intelligence subtest that measures nonverbal abilities

C

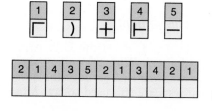

D

So that they can be scored objectively, group intelligence tests are typically multiple choice, with only one correct answer possible for each item.

The Wechsler Scales

During the 1930s, David Wechsler became dissatisfied with the Stanford-Binet test because it was a poor measure for adults; after all, it had been developed for children. To overcome these problems Wechsler developed a test for adult performance and verbal ability. This test eventually became the **Wechsler Adult Intelligence Scale (WAIS);** the revised version, published in 1981, is known as the WAIS-R. Wechsler also developed the **Wechsler Intelligence Scale for Children (WISC),** for ages six through sixteen, which he revised in 1974 as the WISC-R. In the 1960s, he developed the **Wechsler Preschool and Primary Scale of Intelligence (WPPSI),** to be used with children from four to six and one-half years old. It is similar in form to the WISC, although some easier items have been added to it.

WECHSLER ADULT INTELLIGENCE SCALE (WAIS-R) an individual IQ test for adults

WECHSLER INTELLIGENCE SCALE FOR CHILDREN (WISC-R) an individual IQ test for children aged 6 to 16

WECHSLER PRESCHOOL AND PRIMARY SCALE OF INTELLIGENCE (WPPSI) an individual IQ test for children aged 4 to 6½

The WAIS-R, the WISC-R, and the WPPSI are among the most frequently used individual intelligence tests today. They all consist of subtests of similar items, such as block design (see Figure 11.1). Unlike the Stanford-Binet, which yields only a single IQ score, the Wechsler subtests generate separate IQ scores for verbal and performance abilities. This method of scoring helps the examiner determine specific intellectual strengths and weaknesses. It also encourages educators to treat intelligence as a number of related abilities rather than as a single general ability.

The Wechsler and the Binet tests are individual intelligence tests, designed to be administered to one person at a time. The examiner can note whether the person is trying to do his or her best. Because this can have a major effect on the final score, an individually administered test is essential whenever a major decision is to be made, such as determining whether a child is retarded. Individual tests can also be used to gather information about the way people think as well as about their IQ.

Group Tests: Intelligence, Aptitude, and Achievement

Group intelligence tests have existed since World War I, when the U.S. Army Alpha and Beta tests were developed to classify draftees. With 1.5 million army candidates to be evaluated, individual IQ testing was financially out of the question. Revised versions of these paper-and-pencil tests are still used today. Most group tests use multiple-choice items, which can be scored by a computer. This eliminates the subjectivity that can affect interaction with an examiner during an individual test. And the mass administration of tests to hundred of thousands of people has also allowed test developers to *standardize* their tests on huge sample groups (Anastasi, 1988)—that is, to gather information about the average performance, variability, and usefulness of each item. (We discuss standardization in detail a little later in the chapter.)

Because group tests are both convenient and inexpensive, their use has become common. Schools, businesses, employment offices, and the military rely on them for routine testing. Individual tests are reserved for cases in which an individual requires extensive study.

Test publishers make a distinction among three types of group tests: intelligence tests, aptitude tests, and achievement tests. **Intelligence** (or **ability**) **tests** are supposed to measure relatively stable abilities that help in the achievement of practically any goal. **Aptitude tests** are supposed to measure stable abilities required for the achievement of a particular goal. For example, the College Entrance Examination Board's Scholastic Aptitude Test (SAT), a direct descendant of the Army Alpha Test, is designed to measure "aptitude for college studies," not school achievement or general ability. Aptitude tests have also been devised to select pilots, dentists, and police. **Achievement tests** are supposed to measure learning in a particular field, such as mathematics or history. They are not supposed to measure stable abilities, and their scores should improve after study of a particular subject. Achievement tests depend on specific knowledge. A person who has never studied (or spoken) German, for instance, would surely not do well on the German Advanced Placement portion of the Graduate Record Examination.

Intelligence tests contain items that should be meaningful even to someone who has not been to school. Most IQ tests include no mathematics beyond the simplest arithmetic, for example. But aptitude tests fall somewhere between achievement and intelligence tests. Academic success in college *does* depend somewhat on achievement—on the acquisition of certain knowledge in high school, such as knowledge of high school mathematics, of history, and of the sort of vocabulary and grammar used in academic textbooks. Inclusion of items testing this knowledge is not "unfair" when the test is used for college selection, because the knowledge tested is truly relevant to performance in college. In the same way, the distinction between ability (IQ) tests and aptitude tests is not sharp. IQ tests also depend on learning, such as the learning of vocabulary and the meaning of proverbs, that people in a given culture have had a chance to acquire. People who learn these things well are likely to be good learners in general. For those who

INTELLIGENCE (ABILITY) TEST test measuring stable, general abilities

APTITUDE TEST test measuring stable abilities for reaching specific goals; test for predicting future performance

ACHIEVEMENT TEST test measuring learning in a given field

Toddlers can readily grasp new and often quite advanced knowledge; yet IQ scores at this age do not necessarily predict adult IQ scores.

have attended high school, the SAT is essentially another IQ test: it contains items that they have had a chance to learn; and it correlates with IQ tests about as well as different IQ tests correlate with one another.

IQ Tests for Toddlers and Infants?

How early can IQ be measured? Attempts have been made to design IQ tests for infants and toddlers based on the same principles as the Binet test, measuring rate of development in terms of milestones such as reaching for a ring held out in front of the infant (3 months), ringing a bell purposefully (9.9 months), making a tower out of two cubes (13.5 months), naming three objects (21.5 months), and copying a circle (34.6 months) (Bayley, 1933). The scores of these tests, however, do not correlate with scores of IQ tests given years later to the same children (Wohlwill, 1980). Apparently, rate of development in infancy is a poor predictor of later abilities. Scores for toddlers do a bit better at predicting adult scores, but still not nearly as well as tests given later in childhood (Bayley, 1949, 1955).

Recent research suggests that later IQ scores *can* be predicted from infant tests based on different principles. Fagan (1985) summarizes several studies in which recognition memory of infants as young as two months was measured. Individually, infants were shown a face or an abstract design. Later, the same infants were shown two faces or two designs. Infants tend to look at the face or design that they have *not* seen before, showing that they remember what they have seen and prefer to look at something new. Measures of the size of this effect predict IQ scores on tests given several years later. Similarly, babies only a few months old who quickly lose interest in an object (habituation, a concept we discussed in Chapter 7) and then show immediate interest in new items seem destined to score above average on preschool tests (Bornstein and Sigman, 1986).

ATTEMPTS TO DESCRIBE INTELLIGENCE

IQ tests were developed, then, without an adequate theory of intelligence. None of the scientific questions about the nature of the important abilities, their number, or their generality was answered—nor did Binet, Weschsler, and the others really *attempt* to answer these questions. Until recently, much of the scientific study of intelligence has been based on analysis of the tests themselves.

To a great extent, this research has been based on *correlations*. Recall from Chapter 2 that a correlation is measured by the *correlation coefficient* (usually represented by the letter *r*), a number that ranges between +1 and −1. (The correlation coefficient is also sometimes called simply a *correlation*, for short.) A correlation of +1 indicates a perfect positive linear relationship between the two measures, so that one measure can be perfectly predicted from the other without error. For instance, weight in inches is perfectly correlated with height in centimeters, so *r* = +1 for these two measures. A correlation of 0 indicates no relationship. Thus, the correlation between height and the time of day at which a person was born is probably about 0. An example of a perfect negative correlation (*r* = −1) is that between one's height and the distance of one's head from a 10-foot ceiling. (Correlations are discussed in greater detail in the Appendix to this book.)

Factor Analysis

The g Factor

The study of intelligence has concerned itself largely with correlations between tests or between test items. Spearman in his 1904 paper noted the correlation between tests and teacher ratings; he also found that all the different tests and measures he looked at correlated with one another. Ability to discriminate pitches of tones had a correlation of about .31 with ability to discriminate weights; sensory discrimination in general had a correlation of about .38 with teacher-rated intelligence; and so on. (A correlation of .38 indicates a modest but real relationship.)

Spearman proposed that such correlations are the result of a single component which he called the **general intelligence factor,** or **g factor.** The tests are correlated with one another because they are all correlated with g. The g factor cannot be measured directly by any single kind of test item, but the average of a number of different test items—such as those included in an IQ test—can come close.

Spearman's idea was the beginning of **factor analysis,** a statistical technique now used throughout the social and natural sciences. Factor analysis accounts for patterns of correlations by postulating an underlying quantity or "factor" that is itself correlated with the quantities that are measured. Spearman's theory had one main factor, the g factor (although he called it a "two-factor" theory because he postulated another factor specific to *each* of the tests he used). We can represent the g factor's correlation with examples of three other quantities as follows:

g factor——Tone discrimination
\Weight discrimination
\Teacher ratings

GENERAL INTELLIGENCE FACTOR (G FACTOR) a basic component underlying all types of intellectual abilities and explaining correlations among all kinds of intelligence measures

FACTOR ANALYSIS a statistical technique for formulating correlations between assorted variables and one common factor

Group Factors

When Spearman and others applied the new technique of factor analysis to tests of the Binet type, the g factor was still found; that is, every kind of item correlated with every other item. There seemed to be other factors, too. When the effect of the g factor was removed, *groups* of items correlated with one another.

The Wechsler tests provide a good example of this effect. Items measuring knowledge of general information, ability to explain similarities, and vocabulary correlate with one another after g is removed, as do items measuring ability to do block puzzles, to assemble objects, and to encode digits. These correlations can be explained by "group" factors, factors that characterize groups of tests. For example, the first correlations mentioned above can be accounted for by a factor that we might call "verbal comprehension"; the second group might be accounted for by a "perceptual speed" factor. Names such as these do not come from any theory but simply from examination of the list of items that seem to correlate more highly with each other than can be explained by g alone. These various relationships may be diagrammed as follows:

g factor——Verbal comprehension——General knowledge
\Explanation of similarities
\Vocabulary
Perceptual speed——Block-puzzle solving
(group factors) \Object assembly
\Digit encoding

Fluid versus Crystallized Intelligence

Raymond Cattell (1963) proposed a different kind of distinction between test items—those that measure "fluid" intelligence and those that measure "crystallized" intelligence. According to Cattell, **fluid intelligence**—the ability to learn and perform—is measured by tests of speed, energy, and quick adaptation to new situations—for example, tests of memory span, ability to copy symbols, and ability to solve abstract problems. **Crystallized intelligence**—acquired knowledge—is measured by tests of vocabulary, social reasoning, and problem solving.

Cattell and others (Horn, 1986) have found group factors that correspond to these different kinds of intelligence, but the best evidence for the distinction comes from studies of the effects of age. Scores on fluid tests decline with age after adolescence, whereas scores on crystallized intelligence tests continue to increase

FLUID INTELLIGENCE the ability to learn and perform, which declines with age

CRYSTALLIZED INTELLIGENCE acquired knowledge, which does not decline with age

throughout the life span. Although the total score remains approximately the same after adolescence, on the average, this must be seen as a coincidence. If more of the crystallized items were used, IQ would increase with age; if fewer, IQ would decrease. We do not have a principle for deciding on the appropriate combination.

Cattell suggests that fluid intelligence represents *abilities* useful in learning and performance, whereas crystallized intelligence measures *knowledge*—what has actually been learned. Therefore, crystallized intelligence is in part the result of earlier fluid intelligence. People with large vocabularies at age sixty-five are likely to have been good at learning words when they were young, even though they may no longer be so good at it. Interestingly, performance on fluid items, but not on crystallized items, is improved by administration of stimulant drugs (Gupta, 1977).

Because fluid intelligence affects crystallized intelligence, the two are correlated, so we could still suppose that there is some sort of *g* factor underlying everything—perhaps something like mental energy that is reflected in the fluid items themselves. Similarly, even in the Wechsler tests, which separate verbal from nonverbal items, every kind of item correlates with every other kind. People who do well at the block-design subtest tend to have larger vocabularies. Thus, we can still maintain the idea that there is one major ability underlying all of intelligence.

We must remember, however, that these results are based on IQ tests themselves. As we noted earlier, some sorts of measures are not included on IQ tests because they would involve subjective scoring or because they take too long to administer. Whether or not there is actually a *g* factor, we still have no theory of intelligence that tells us that these more complex items *should not* be on the tests. Their exclusion has been a matter of convenience.

Creativity and Expertise

Do IQ test items correlate with other sorts of abilities *not* included on IQ tests—creativity or manual skills, for example? If they do, the evidence for an underlying *g* factor—a single source of all the abilities that help us achieve our goals—would be stronger. However, the evidence is mixed.

As you have seen, IQ tests correlate highly with school grades and other measures of school performance. But in other cases, correlations are low. Take the

This boy, who was the subject of a *60 Minutes* profile, is an idiot savant—mentally retarded except for a great talent at the piano.

PSYCHOLOGY TODAY AND TOMORROW

Gardner's "Frames of Mind"

A theory of *multiple intelligences* has been proposed by Howard Gardner (1984). Assuming that there is no single core of "intelligence," Gardner gives equal weight to seven types, each independent of all the others, but all interacting to produce a person's intellectual capabilities. These seven intelligences are linguistic, logical-mathematical, spatial, musical, bodily-kinesthetic (skill in using the body), intrapersonal (knowledge of the self), and interpersonal (knowledge of others).

According to Gardner, each "intelligence" is localized in certain brain areas, so that it can be impaired by damage to one part of the brain. For example, linguistic intelligence is impaired by damage to the speech areas (see Chapters 3 and 10). Gardner cites histories of child prodigies in several of the intelligences, and he argues that their development is similar. Early discovery of an "innate" talent is followed by intense concentration on the development of that talent over many years. For example, composer Igor Stravinsky's talent was recognized at the age of two, when he sang from memory a song he had heard some women sing on their way home from working in the fields (Gardner, 1984, p. 121).

Cultures differ in the intelligences they emphasize. "Western" culture emphasizes linguistic and logical-mathematical intelligence. In Microne-sia, where navigating the open sea without chart or compass is a highly rated ability, success depends on spatial intelligence and bodily-kinesthetic intelligence, as well as an impressive linguistic memory.

In some ways, Gardner's theory resembles those of factor analysts, for they, too, have postulated different kinds of intelligence, such as verbal and spatial. But Gardner does not intend his theory as an explanation of correlations among test items. It is, rather, a broader look at the nature of human abilities and their development. If we accept the goal-oriented definition of intelligence given at the beginning of this chapter, Gardner's theory is not about intelligence at all, for some of the abilities in question (e.g., bodily-kinesthetic) are of no interest to people with certain goals (say, a mathematician). Gardner is concerned with *differences* in the goals that people seek in different cultural environments. The more traditional theory of intelligence is concerned with the similarities.

Gardner suggests that his theory could serve as a basis for identifying talented children at an early age and encouraging the development of their talent. This idea has not yet been tried or evaluated, though you might keep it in mind when you read this chapter's section on giftedness.

---

case of creativity. Wallach (1976) points out that real-world measures of creativity (such as ratings by critics and number of awards, poems published, or inventions patented) do not correlate highly with measures of academic performance or with IQ. The best way to predict future creativity in a field is to look for past creativity in the same field. Of course, creativity can sometimes depend on education, which, in turn, does require the kinds of abilities measured on IQ tests. A person with an IQ of 90 or below is unlikely to become a creative scientist; scientists these days have to go to graduate school. But some apparently creative artists have had such low IQs that they spent their lives in institutions for the retarded (Hill, 1978). Such people, gifted in a specific area but otherwise retarded, are often known as *idiot savants*.

Idiot savants have what other creative people have: passionate devotion to their art, which builds expertise (Perkins, 1981). Indeed, it seems that one of the more effective ways to discuss creativity, or at least creative output, is in terms of expertise, a topic we considered in Chapter 9. Creative expertise is typically built up over many years of practice. Hayes (1985) found, for example, that it takes composers about 10 or 15 years to "hit their stride" as measured by the number of recordings of their works in the Schwann record catalog. It doesn't matter much when they start. Mozart was doing well as an adolescent because he was little more than a toddler when he started composing. (See the accompanying box on a theory that might be useful in identifying talented children.)

Is expertise related closely to IQ? Not necessarily, according to a recent study that looked at another skill built up over many years without formal education—handicapping racehorses (Liker and Ceci, 1977; see also Reagan, 1977; Ceci and Liker, 1986a,b; Detterman and Spry, 1988; and Ceci and Liker, 1988). At all race tracks, bets are paid on the basis of odds calculated by handicappers. To figure a horse's chances of winning its race, the handicapper has to consider many factors, including the horse's earnings, speed, position, and racing moves; the track's size and condition; and the jockey's skill.

Ceci and Liker studied ardent harness-racing fans who had been going to the track at least twice a week for the last eight years. "Some men had attended races nearly every day of their adult lives, with occasional absences due to illnesses, marriage of children, and so forth" (Ceci and Liker, 1986b, p. 124). Ceci and Liker gave these men a standard intelligence test, then had them handicap the horses in ten regular races before the track released the odds. After the races, Ceci and Liker used the results to divide the men into "experts" (who had done at least as well as the track's professional handicappers) and "nonexperts." They could find no correlation between IQ scores and the ability to handicap horses. One expert picked the top horse in all ten races and the top three horses (in the correct order) in five of them. He was a construction worker with a below-average IQ score of 85. One nonexpert picked only three winners and the top three horses only once. He was a lawyer with an IQ score of 118, higher than average. All subjects had an enormous store of knowledge about harness racing. So, as important as background information is, it wasn't simply knowledge that divided the expert from the nonexpert. The difference lay in the way the men reasoned: expert handicappers consistently reasoned in a complex manner, weighing all variables. Nonexperts rarely did this. Thus we cannot consider the expert handicappers "highly intelligent" according to IQ tests. But would you say that they had some specific kind of intelligence? How do we distinguish expertise, and its relation to complex reasoning, from intelligence?

A Triarchic View of Intelligence

COMPONENTIAL INTELLIGENCE
in Sternberg's theory, the ability to process information

EXPERIENTIAL INTELLIGENCE
in Sternberg's theory, the ability to learn from experience and carry out familiar tasks efficiently

CONTEXTUAL INTELLIGENCE
in Sternberg's theory, the ability to adapt to the world; practical intelligence

Robert Sternberg (1985a; b) has found a way to describe intelligence that accounts for a number of the elements we just looked at, as well as for IQ scores. Sternberg proposes that there is no single factor that underlies all intelligence, nor is there a splintered set of diverse factors; he maintains there are three different types of human intelligence. In Sternberg's triarchic view, **componential intelligence** involves most of the abilities discussed in Chapter 8, on memory: planning and monitoring one's own actions (this is similar to the concept of metacognition); encoding information into schemas on the basis of inferences and comparisons of new information with existing information; and decision making and the execution of plans. **Experiential intelligence** involves the ability to learn from experience. Experiential intelligence is hard at work when we face either very new situations or very familiar ones. In the familiar situations, it is our experiential intelligence that helps us carry out tasks "automatically"—reading, typing, or driving—by making whatever information processing is involved quick and highly efficient. This aspect of intelligence, then, is very similar to the concept of procedural memory (Chapter 8). Finally, **contextual intelligence** enables us to succeed in the real world—to adapt to our specific environment, or context. The expertise of the handicappers in the Ceci and Liker study cited above was, Sternberg might say, based on contextual intelligence—intelligence useful to the handicappers for achieving specific goals in a specific context, the horse race. In other words, contextual intelligence is what we might call practical intelligence.

Sternberg's triarchic formulation is quite appealing in its broadness and in its recognition of practical abilities and skills that exist outside of the schoolroom. However, there has been as yet no major response to or evaluation of his ideas.

The evidence that we have looked at on creative output and unschooled abilities does not support the existence of a *g* factor. (Nor does Sternberg's theory seem to.) It is quite possible that the *g* factor is a statistical feature of IQ tests,

Expertise—thorough knowledge of a certain subject—applies to physical as well as mental abilities.

resulting from a lack of variety in the selection of tasks, rather than a real entity. Most IQ test items are short tasks that require some general knowledge, but not of specific school subjects, and that can be timed and easily scored for quality. There is no reason for use of such items other than tradition and convenience. (See Baron, 1985, pp. 38–39, for other criticisms of the *g* factor.)

HOW GOOD ARE INTELLIGENCE TESTS?

A good test has two properties: reliability and validity. **Reliability** refers to how well the test measures whatever it measures, and **validity** refers to how well the test measures what it is supposed to measure. In the case of IQ tests, we do not fully understand what they are supposed to measure, so we must turn to practical criteria of validity: How well do IQ tests predict what they are supposed to predict? How useful are they?

Intelligence tests must meet the same standards as any other psychological test. Psychological tests are objective, standardized measures of a sample of behavior that provide a systematic basis for making inferences about people (London and Bray, 1980; Anastasi, 1988). Unless a test is reliable and valid, it cannot measure behavior accurately, and unless it has been standardized, there is no way to determine the meaning of an individual's score.

RELIABILITY   measuring consistently

VALIDITY   measuring what a test purports to measure

The Properties of a Good Test

Reliability

A test is reliable if it measures something consistently. A yardstick produces the same measurements whether it is used today or tomorrow and whether it is used by a dressmaker or a carpenter. Like a yardstick, a psychological test is reliable only if it yields the same results with repeated measurements.

There are several ways to determine reliability, and the nature of the test determines which is most appropriate. We can use the test's internal consistency, its ability to produce the same results on retests, or its ability to produce the same results regardless of who scores it.

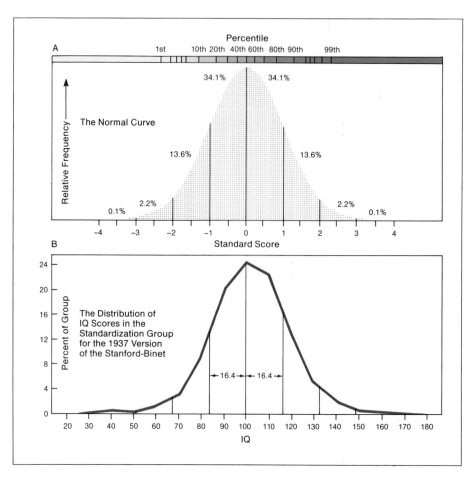

Figure 11.2 The theoretical normal curve (A) and a practical application of it (B). The curves show the proportions of a group or population that fall at various points on a scale. The theoretical curve is useful because it has precise mathematical characteristics from which such relative measures as standard and percentile scores can be calculated. A standard score describes the position of an individual's score in terms of the variance of the group's scores. A percentile score describes the position of an individual's score in terms of the percentage of scores in the group that his or her score exceeds. A single standard score unit corresponds to about 16.4 IQ points on the 1937 Stanford-Binet Test. Knowing this correspondence and knowing the average IQ (approximately 100), one can convert any IQ into a standard score or a percentile score by reading the theoretical curve. (Bottom graph after Terman and Merrill, 1973.)

INTERNAL CONSISTENCY RELIABILITY the extent to which different parts of a test produce the same results

A test's **internal consistency reliability** refers to the extent to which different parts of the test produce the same results. When a test uses many items to measure a certain characteristic, such as anxiety, internal consistency is extremely important. Internal consistency can be measured by randomly dividing the test in half and comparing people's scores on the two halves. On an internally consistent test, the scores will be highly correlated. In contrast, merely comparing scores on the first thirty questions with those on the second thirty doesn't tell us whether the test is reliable, because boredom, fatigue, or practice can begin to affect the way people answer different parts of a test. A division of questions at random throughout the test, or a comparsion between odd- and even-numbered questions, works better.

TEST-RETEST RELIABILITY the extent to which repeated administrations of a test to the same people produce the same results

Test-retest reliability is the extent to which repeated administrations of the test to the same people produce the same results. This sort of reliability is important if the test measures a relatively stable characteristic, such as intelligence. When test-retest reliability is high, such temporary influences as stress, illness, or distraction will not affect scores very much. Test-retest reliability is usually measured with different but equivalent forms of the same test, like the different forms of the Scholastic Aptitude Test. (If exactly the same form of the test were used, the subject could simply remember the answers from one time to the next.)

Interjudge reliability is the extent to which a test produces the same result when scored by different judges. This sort of reliability is extremely important when a person's answers must be interpreted. Unless two appropriately trained raters can arrive at similar scores on a subjectively scored test, a person's score will depend more on the scorer than on the answers. Tests that are in special need of interjudge reliability include those that involve psychiatric diagnoses, essay examinations, and ratings of observed behavior. Group IQ tests, of course, have perfect interjudge reliability, because the "judges" are computers. For individual IQ tests, interjudge reliability among trained scorers has been found to be extremely high.

INTERJUDGE RELIABILITY the extent to which a test produces the same results when scored by different judges

Validity

A test is valid when it measures what it attempts to measure, and the purpose of the test will determine how its validity is established. A test with **content validity** covers a representative sample of whatever it is measuring; in other words, it covers the given subject or topic adequately. Unless the Advanced Placement portion of the Graduate Record Examination (GRE) has content validity, it cannot assess your knowledge of the given field. Suppose you took the GRE in English literature and found that all the questions were about French or Spanish poetry. The test would lack content validity. The content validity of IQ tests cannot be determined until we have a theory that tells us what kind of content ought to be included.

CONTENT VALIDITY covering a representative sample of whatever is being measured

If the purpose of a test is to predict future performance, it must have **predictive validity.** Scores on the test must be related to future performance. If people who make low scores on a test screening prospective firefighters do as well at preventing and fighting fires as those who make high scores, the test lacks predictive validity and is obviously worthless for selecting personnel.

PREDICTIVE VALIDITY a positive correlation between test scores and future performance

Tests are also considered good predictors when they have **concurrent validity**—when scores on the test correlate highly with other measures or standards. Simple tests that have concurrent validity are especially useful when they can be substituted for time-consuming, expensive tests, as when a quickly answered paper-and-pencil test of depression correlates highly with a lengthy interview by trained clinicians.

CONCURRENT VALIDITY a positive correlation between test scores and other measures

Finally, a test with **construct validity** must measure just the theoretical construct that it claims to measure (Anastasi, 1988). Psychological constructs are complex ideas formed from a number of simpler ideas. They include intelligence, anxiety, shyness, leadership, mechanical ability, fatigue, and anger. A test with construct validity is a valid measure of the theoretical aspects related to the construct.

CONSTRUCT VALIDITY measuring aspects of the theoretical construct that a test focuses on

One way to assess construct validity is to show, first, *convergent validity*—the test correlates with measures that, according to theory, ought to tap the same construct—and, second, *discriminant validity*—the test does *not* correlate with measures that ought not to tap the same construct. For example, scores on a test of shyness should correlate with the number of parties a person attends, talkativeness in groups, and ratings of shyness obtained from parents and friends. But shyness scores should not correlate highly with measures of other constructs, such as intelligence—*unless* a theory of intelligence includes social abilities (a "social intelligence").

If a test is valid, it must be reliable. But reliable tests are not always valid. Astrological horoscopes are highly reliable; they all produce the same prediction for the same person. (They often produce the same predictions for *different* people!) But horoscopes are not valid because they neither describe personally nor predict future events accurately. If head size were used as an indicator of intelligence, it would be a *reliable* measurement (in that using the same tape measure in the same way always produces the same head measurement); but it would not be a highly *valid* indicator of intelligence because there is not much relationship between head size and academic success or scores on intelligence tests. However, head size is both a reliable and a valid indicator of hat size.

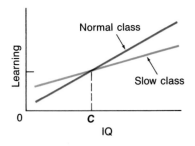

Figure 11.3 The validity of IQ tests has been supported by evidence that beyond a certain cutoff point (*C*), students in slower classes do better than students in regular classes—an indication that IQ tests are useful in identifying students who can benefit from special education.

NORM   frequency with which particular score is made and which serves as standard of comparison for test takers

STANDARDIZATION GROUP   a representative sample of test takers whose scores become norms

PERCENTILE SYSTEM   a method for comparing test scores to norms by dividing scores into 100 equal parts (or percentiles); shows the proportion of norms above and below any individual score

STANDARD SCORE SYSTEM   a method for comparing test scores to norms by converting scores using the standard deviation and plotting them around the mean

Standardization

Test scores tell us little about a person unless we know about the scores of others who have taken the test. If you correctly answer 53 of 88 questions on a test in your psychology course, you do not know whether you have done well or poorly unless you know how other people in the class have done. If you find out that most students had no more than 44 correct answers, you know that you have done well. Before tests are put into general use, testers establish **norms,** which show the frequency with which particular scores on the test are made. Norms are established by giving the test to a large and well-defined sample group of people, called a **standardization group.** Each person to take the test is then compared to the members of the standardization group. Separate norms can be used for different groups. Physical fitness tests have different norms for males and females; most intelligence tests have different norms for various age groups. But the normative, or standardization, group must actually represent the population with which the individual test taker is to be compared.

The two most common methods of making this comparison are the percentile system and the standard score system. The **percentile system** divides a group of scores into 100 equal-sized parts. Since each part, or percentile, contains $\frac{1}{100}$ of the scores, a percentile number shows the proportions of the standardization group that are above and below any one individual's score. For example, a score at the eightieth percentile would be higher than the scores of 79 percent of the people who took the test and lower than the scores of 19 percent.

The **standard score system** is more complex. Standard scores represent points on a bell-shaped curve that reflects the normal pattern of distribution on almost any test. As Figure 11.3 shows, in a normal distribution the majority of people's scores fall within a narrow range somewhere in the middle of the distribution. The farther a score is from the middle, the smaller the number of people who obtain it. (The normal curve of distribution is discussed further in the Appendix at the back of the book.)

On most intelligence tests, raw scores of people within the same age group are converted to standard scores with a mean of 100 and a *standard deviation* of 15 (see the Appendix). As a result, about 68 percent of the population achieve scores between 85 and 115; more than 99.7 percent achieve scores between 55 and 145. These scores are called IQ scores, but they no longer represent the ratio between mental and chronological ages. Instead they are *deviation IQs,* showing how far a person's score deviates from the mean of his or her own age group. Stern's idea that IQ be defined in terms of rate of development could no longer work when tests were developed for adults, because (as we noted earlier) raw test scores do not increase with age after adolescence. Thus, the Wechsler scales use deviation IQs to determine scores.

Unless the standardization group represents the current population taking the test, information about a score's relative standing will be inaccurate. On some tests performance has improved over the years. The reason seems to be that the scores of current test takers are being compared to the old standardization group—the group that took the test years or decades earlier. As a result, most of the people who take the test now get "above-average" scores. Some school systems have found outdated tests of academic achievement quite helpful, though misleading, in convincing parents that district schools are doing a good job.

The Uses of Ability Tests

How can we validate ability (IQ) tests? What are they supposed to do? They are potentially good for many different things. Perhaps, in time, different tests will be developed for different purposes. Their original purpose is still the one for which they are most often used: educational selection, or the assignment of students to different programs, curricular tracks, schools, and colleges. A related function is the use of ability tests for job selection. IQ tests have other purposes as well. Some of these functions involve the measurement of aspects of intelligence that can be learned: tests are sometimes used to evaluate the effects of education or of educational experiments. Other functions involve the measurement of aspects of intelligence that are not learned—those aspects that depend, for example, on genetics or on the condition of the brain (tests are sometimes used in clinical diagnosis). Let us examine some of these functions of IQ tests.

Job Selection

IQ-type tests correlate with income (Jencks et al., 1972). This effect is partly, but not entirely, a result of the fact that the abilities tested are needed for advanced education, which, in turn, is required for many high-income occupations. However, these correlations are small, because income is affected by many factors, both internal (such as the desire to be rich, a motivation in which people differ) and external (such as sheer luck and circumstance).

Ability tests, such as civil service examinations and the Armed Forces Qualification Test, are often used to select people for jobs, on the assumption that such tests have predictive power. These tests are, like the SAT, essentially IQ tests, and they actually do predict job performance extremely well, whether performance is measured by supervisor ratings or by worker output. A review of hundreds of studies on the predictive power of ability tests (Hunter and Hunter, 1984) reports that these tests predict job performance about as well as they predict grades: the mean correlation between aptitude and performance is about .5. The only other measure that predicts job performance this well is a test based on a work sample, and this gauge is valid only when the subjects have had some experience in the job they will be doing. (The use of high school grades to predict college grades can be seen as a kind of work-sample test, and in this case we have seen that the work sample is a slightly better predictor than the aptitude test.)

The use of ability tests is often controversial because they may work against certain ethnic groups—in the United States, blacks and Hispanics—who tend, on the average, to score lower on them. If companies hire on the basis of ability tests, such groups may receive far less than a proportionate share of desirable jobs. Is this fair? Psychological research can go only so far in answering this question, for it depends on what is considered fair, and this is a moral issue. What the research tells us is that ability tests do equally well at prediction for different ethnic and racial groups (Hunter and Hunter, 1984). That is, the tests have about the same .5 correlation between aptitude measures and performance no matter what group is tested.

A test has predictive validity if its scores are related to future performance on the job. A test for prospective firefighters, for example, should include the kind of physical feats that firefighters sometimes have to perform.

Nevertheless, there are many factors other than ability or aptitude that can affect both test scores *and* job performance. These include impoverished or enriched background, fatigue, motivation and ambition, and different cultural values. If all these factors are at work, of what value are ability tests in job selection? At the moment, these tests are the best available predictors of performance; but their predictions are clearly not perfect. A moral and social-policy issue thus arises. Any test used for job selection that has a less than perfect predictive validity has the potential to create two types of injustice: a certain proportion of applicants will be unfairly rejected for employment, and a certain proportion will be hired who will fail on the job.

Academic Prediction

The SAT is highly reliable, and its validity is high enough to make it a useful predictor of college grades; the correlation between total SAT score and freshman grade-point average (GPA) was .39 in one major study (the National Longitudal Study; see Crouse and Trusheim, 1988). High school class rank did slightly better at predicting freshman GPA ($r = .41$), and when SAT scores and high school records were combined in the best possible way, the correlation of this combination with GPA rose to .46. (See the accompanying box on coaching to improve SAT scores.) The improvement from .41 to .46 was small because SAT scores also correlate with high school class rank, so once we know a student's class rank, the test does not add that much information. When achievement test scores are considered as well as high school class rank, the SAT becomes essentially useless (Crouse and Trusheim, 1988, ch. 8). However, regardless of its practical utility, the SAT is a valid test of ability, because it correlates with things it ought to correlate with. IQ tests in general do a good job of predicting grades at any level of schooling.

Diagnosis of Mental Retardation

The use of the SAT for college admissions and tracking is just one of many applications of IQ-type tests for educational selection. Another use is the one Binet focused on: the selection of children for removal from regular school classes on grounds of mental retardation.

Approximately 5.6 to 6.7 million people in the United States are classified as mentally retarded. Such a large pool of individuals represents a serious social problem, because **mental retardation** involves a decreased ability to function in the world as well as decreased intellectual performance. These twin aspects define mental retardation. In the words of the American Association on Mental Deficiency: "Mental retardation refers to significantly subaverage general intellectual functioning existing concurrently with deficits in adaptive behavior and manifested during the developmental period." (1977, p. 11)

Mental retardation is described in terms of four levels—mild, moderate, severe, and profound—with an individual's level of retardation determined by estimates of his or her deficits in adaptive behavior and scores on standard intelligence tests. Each level of retardation blends into the next, so clear boundaries between the categories do not exist.

More than 90 percent of the retarded have **mild retardation.** Their IQs, based on Stanford-Binet scores, range from 50 to 69. Although they develop much more slowly than normal children, mildly retarded people are fairly independent by adolescence and most of them can hold undemanding jobs, marry, and have children. People with **moderate retardation** have IQs between 35 and 49. Although they can take care of themselves, they must live in supervised group homes. They rarely marry or become parents. People with **severe retardation** have IQs between 20 and 34. They require considerable supervision, but they can learn to care for some of their physical needs, and they can be trained to perform simple tasks in sheltered workshops or to do household chores. People with **profound retardation** have IQs below 20. Many remain in institutions, but they can sometimes

MENTAL RETARDATION significantly below-average intellectual functioning combined with impaired ability to function in the world

MILD RETARDATION retardation within an IQ range of 50–69

MODERATE RETARDATION retardation within an IQ range of 35–49

SEVERE RETARDATION retardation within an IQ range of 20–34

PROFOUND RETARDATION retardation based on a below-20 IQ

PSYCHOLOGY TODAY AND TOMORROW

Does Coaching Raise SAT Scores?

Is there any point in taking a special course to try to raise your scores on the SAT? Many high schools offer courses aimed at improving students' performance on this vital test, and more than 150 independent firms will coach you for a fee. You can even buy computer software to help you prepare for the SAT. Is this money and effort well spent, or are students wasting their money and are high schools squandering valuable time on worthless courses?

Coaching does increase scores, but only to a limited degree. The average student can expect to gain 14 points on the verbal SAT and 15 points on the math SAT. How helpful is a 29-point jump? It means you answered about three more questions correctly than if you hadn't taken the course (Kulik, Bangert-Drowns, and Kulik, 1984). That sort of boost is so slight as to have little effect on college-admission decisions.

If the rise in scores is so small, how can coaching schools make such extravagant claims in their ads? The reason is the lack of a control group. Most high school students show an improved score over time, because they are continu-

ally learning—in school, at their part-time jobs, while reading, while watching TV, while pursuing a hobby. And simply taking the preliminary SAT test gives students a small boost by familiarizing them with the actual exam. In a typical study, forty-five students who took a commercial coaching course (ten 3-hour sessions) were matched against forty-five students who had no coaching at all. Both groups tested higher on the second SAT than on the first, but the coached students' extra gain was only 8.4 on the verbal SAT and 9.4 on the math SAT (Messick and Jungeblut, 1981).

What if you study hard and really apply yourself in your coaching sessions? You may well increase your score more than 30 points on both parts of the SAT, but such large increases take as much time and effort as full-time schooling (Messick and Jungeblut, 1981). The kind of coaching you receive also makes a difference. Practice in taking the test and instruction in strategies meant to make you "test wise" are both helpful. So is training in the sort of logical reasoning and problem-solving skills we explored in Chapter 9 on thinking.

carry out a few tasks under close supervision. Some cannot speak, although they may understand simple communication.

The various levels of retardation do not have different causes; the labels are used merely for descriptive convenience, as a kind of professional shorthand. The major causes of mental retardation are genetic abnormalities, brain damage, and environmental deprivation. The most common of the genetic abnormalities is **Down syndrome,** caused by the presence of an extra chromosome. Besides retardation, symptoms of this disorder include heart abnormalities (giving Down syndrome patients a shortened life expectancy) and altered facial appearance, which struck some early observers as similar to mongoloid racial characteristics (although this is not true in fact) and gave rise to the original, now obsolete name for the disorder—mongolism. Down syndrome can be detected by medical tests performed early in pregnancy. Parents who discover that their child will have this condition can choose abortion.

DOWN SYNDROME a disorder caused by the presence of an extra chromosome and characterized by retardation

Retardation can also result from any factors that impair intelligence in general: subtle brain damage caused by drugs or alcohol consumed by the mother during pregnancy, inadequate nutrition during the mother's pregnancy, inadequate nutrition in childhood, toxic agents such as lead, infections, other diseases, and inadequate social stimulations as a result of parental neglect or other circumstance. (We shall discuss these factors later.) It is difficult to say which of the nongenetic causes of retardation is more common, as they often occur together. It is clear, however, that a great deal of nongenetic retardation is preventable through appropriate societal intervention.

Retardation in intellectual tasks—those tasks on which IQ tests focus—seems to be somewhat separate from retardation in adaptive behavior. In the United States blacks tend to score lower on IQ tests than whites *on the average* (with some blacks scoring higher than the majority of whites, and some whites scoring

Many mentally retarded people are capable of learning useful work skills.

lower than the majority of blacks). We'll discuss this finding in more detail later in the chapter. It has led some observers to conclude that blacks and whites differ in the more "academic" abilities that IQ tests cover. However, Jane Mercer (1973) noted that the blacks classified as retarded, usually largely on the basis of IQ tests, did not seem as impaired as the white retardates in nonacademic school areas. She developed an Adaptive Behavior Scale based on a standard interview. This scale was constructed in the same way as the Stanford-Binet test, with items keyed to each age, but the items on Mercer's test attempted to measure adaptation: Does the individual help put away toys? button clothing without help? Can he or she go on errands outside the home? sing a few songs? take down a phone message? write letters? go to the movies? visit friends? read the newspaper? participate in sports? (The later examples are for adolescents and adults.) Black retardates were found to be more advanced on this scale than white retardates. More generally, blacks and whites differ less in the kind of adaptation measured by Mercer's test than in IQ.

Whatever the cause or level of retardation, it is clear that retardates, even mild retardates, do not learn well in regular classrooms. Interestingly, their learning *improves* when they are put in classes that move at a slower, more deliberate pace. Nonretarded children in such classes simply learn more slowly (Snow and Yalow, 1982).

These findings provide an example of an *aptitude–treatment interaction* (Snow and Yalow, 1982), illustrated in Figure 11.3. The horizontal axis shows IQ. The vertical axis shows the amount of learning in two different kinds of classes, a normal class and a slow class. (The amount of learning has been measured in different ways in different studies, but the general result is the same.) Notice that when the IQ is below a certain cutoff point, C, students do *better* in the slower class than in the normal class. This kind of result—which has been found many times—is strong evidence for the validity of IQ tests in their original purpose. It shows that the IQ test can tell us which children can benefit from which kind of education. Moreover, the IQ test is essentially the *only* test that has been repeatedly shown to be useful for the purpose of educational assignment (Snow and Yalow, 1982).

Identification of Gifted Children

A truly gifted person is one who does things that few others can do: compose beautiful music, discover a cure for a disease, make peace between long-standing enemies, invent a useful new product, prove a mathematical theorem that has eluded proof for centuries, and the like. More informally, children are called gifted when they can do things that most children of their age cannot do. Mozart was a "gifted" child because he played the harpsichord very well and wrote good music for a child. (As we noted earlier, his music got better over time.) Many professional tennis players today were excellent tennis players even when they were young children.

In recent years, the term "gifted" has been used loosely as an educational classification, by which bright and generally cooperative children are singled out for special treatment in schools. The IQ test usually plays a role in such selection: most school districts in the United States require a certain minimum score (135 or 140) for admission into programs for "gifted" children. How useful is the IQ test in such selection? Is it valid at the high end as well as the low end? Can we use it to select children for special encouragement?

Before the twentieth century, a number of well-known gifted children who had grown up to be gifted adults—including Mozart, composer Felix Mendelssohn, and philosopher John Stuart Mill—gave the impression that gifted children *did* grow up to be gifted adults. In other words, it was assumed that special treatment and education of gifted children paid off in the "gifts" that these children grew up to offer society. However, early in this century, this conventional wisdom about treatment of the gifted was challenged by a well-publicized case, that of William James Sidis (1898–1944) (Montour, 1977). Sidis's parents were ambitious medical psychologists with strong theories about education. Their son, named after the Harvard philosopher and psychologist William James, could read before the age of three, studied medical anatomy at six, and devised a new table of logarithms at eight. He was educated largely by his father. At eleven, as a special student at Harvard, he presented a lecture on "four-dimensional bodies" to the Harvard Mathematics Club, an event that intensified the publicity he was receiving. At sixteen, Sidis began to fall apart emotionally and was thenceforth unable to work productively at anything like the level expected of him. He spent his remaining years doing low-level jobs and staying out of the public eye.

Sidis's story created a popular stereotype of the gifted child as someone who finds it difficult to adjust to the real world, and a popular belief that it is possible to be *too* intelligent. Close examination of Sidis's life history, however, turns up many possible antecedents to his breakdown, particularly the emotional coldness of his parents and the public scrutiny under which he lived. Examination of other gifted children shows that such children can generally live happy and productive adult lives, almost always making good use of their intellectual gifts (Montour, 1977).

In 1921, Lewis Terman (the same one who adapted the Binet test, and a former gifted child himself) selected 1000 children with IQs of at least 150. These children were followed and tested periodically for more than sixty years (Terman and Oden, 1947; Terman and Oden, 1959; Oden, 1968; Sears, 1977). Many of Terman's subjects achieved national recognition in their professions, but none was considered a creative genius (Wallach, 1985). Their average income was more than four times the national average, and most were satisfied with the way their lives turned out. The rates of subjects' delinquency, criminality, alcoholism, drug dependency, and severe mental illness were lower than in the general population. And they were less likely to commit suicide or to die accidentally.

However, the relationships found by Terman may not have been entirely the result of high IQs. His sample came from a pool of children nominated by their teachers, who may have been influenced by the children's emotional stability as well as their IQs. And Terman did not select a comparison (control) group matched in relevant aspects of family background, such as parental education, which could also explain some of the results. Still, they do give us some reason to think that people with very high IQs are not especially neurotic or crazy.

But high IQ is not enough for true giftedness. Genius also usually requires a basis of knowledge that can come only from practice and instruction. The child prodigy develops expertise while most children are playing in the sandbox. Whether their field is chess, music, math, or literature, child prodigies who have come to psychologists' attention have usually had intensive training, as well as supportive families (Feldman, 1986).

Psychologists' recognition that giftedness will not bloom without focused instruction is the reason for the existence of the Center for the Advancement of Academically Talented Youth at Johns Hopkins University (Stanley, 1983). Talent is detected by administering the SAT to seventh-graders, who receive counseling and summer instruction in advanced math, chemistry, physics, and languages at a college level. In general, these young people seem to fare well. They don't all grow up to be Nobel prize winners. (Very few people do.) But most of them make use of their talents (e.g., by going to graduate school).

A good example is Colin Camerer, whose giftedness was picked up by the SAT when he was twelve, and who had earned a Ph.D. and become an assistant professor in Northwestern University's Graduate School of Management at the age of twenty-one—about the time he would have normally received a B.A. During the year Camerer spent in high school, he was on the varsity wrestling team; while in college, he was on the varsity golf team and worked on the school paper. Now he is a member of the Decision Sciences Department in the Wharton School of Economics, University of Pennsylvania, and he is becoming well known for his work in experimental economics. On the side, he owns a record company. Camerer had task commitment and encouraging parents as well as talent, and, like Terman's subjects, his personal development did not seem to suffer.

We come back to the IQ test. Can it select students who will benefit from more advanced instruction? The answer seems to be yes. High-IQ students do better when instruction is fast paced and somewhat self-directed than they do in ordinary instruction, whereas normal-IQ students do worse (Snow and Yalow, 1982). These results argue for acceleration of high-IQ students and provide further validation of IQ tests by showing yet another aptitude–treatment interaction.

Many school districts use IQ tests as a criterion for admission into special classes that provide "enrichment," as opposed to acceleration: special projects and small discussion groups. The question of whether average-IQ students benefit from such enrichment as well as high-IQ students has not been addressed. Nor is it clear whether the IQ test does better than teacher recommendations or grades in predicting who will benefit from accelerated classes.

Gifted children, like this eleven-year-old college student, need training and family support to develop their expertise.

THE DETERMINANTS OF INTELLIGENCE: HEREDITY, ENVIRONMENT, AND EDUCATION

How is intelligence determined? To what extent is it affected by genetic inheritance, by environmental effects such as nutrition and disease, and by education? This is of course a nature/nurture sort of issue.

To a large extent, psychologists have tried to answer these questions by studying the determinants of IQ scores. As we consider the evidence, we should remember that IQ test results are *not* the same as intelligence itself. Intelligence is a set of many different abilities, some learned, some innate, some measured well by the tests, and some measured poorly if at all. Certainly, *some* of the abilities that constitute intelligence—such as mental energy or mental speed—are unlikely to show any effects from education, whereas other abilities might well show such effects (Baron, 1985). The abilities measured by IQ tests are important, but they may be more (or less) affected by heredity, environment, or education than other abilities.

The Heritability of IQ

To determine the genetic influence, we seek the heritability of IQ. **Heritability** is a numerical estimate of the relative contribution that heredity makes to differences among people in a single trait (such as IQ or height). Thus, heritability refers to the extent to which differences among people can be explained by genetic factors. Heritability can theoretically run from 0 (differences totally caused by environment) to 1 (totally caused by genes).

Notice that heritability refers to *individual* differences; it quantifies the variation in environment and genes from person to person. If everyone were raised in the same environment, heritability would be 1 (because environment could not explain the observed differences), and if everyone were an identical twin of everyone else, with the same genetic inheritance, heritability would be 0 (because genetic inheritance could not explain the observed differences).

Note, too, that heritability is an estimate of the *relative* contribution of heredity. If the variation in the measured population's environment is low, then heritability will be high—but environmental factors can still have an enormous effect on the trait being measured. Conversely, if the subjects' environment varies widely, the heritability index will decrease, even though the genetic contribution to the trait remains the same. In short, heritability is *not* a zero-sum game, in

HERITABILITY a numerical estimate of the relative contribution that heredity makes to differences among individuals in a single trait

TABLE 11.1 Correlation of IQ Scores of Relatives and Nonrelatives

RELATIONSHIP	CORRELATION (r)
Genetically identical:	
Identical twins reared together	.87
Identical twins reared apart	.75
Genetically related (first-degree):	
Fraternal twins reared together	.53
Nontwin siblings reared together	.49
Nontwin siblings reared apart	.40
Parent–child living together	.50
Parent–child separated by adoption	.45
Genetically unrelated:	
Unrelated children reared together	.23
Adoptive parent–adoptive child	.20
Unrelated persons reared apart	−.01

Source: R. Plomin and J. C. DeFries (1980), Genetics and intelligence: Recent data, *Intelligence, 4,* 15–24.

which the higher the genetic contribution to a trait, the lower the environmental contribution, or vice versa.

The evidence that IQ scores are somewhat inherited (heritability above 0) comes from the study of correlations between IQ scores of people who are related to one another in different ways. In several studies done before 1980, the correlations between IQs of various relatives were as shown in Table 11.1 (Plomin and DeFries, 1980). The correlation between identical twins reared together (.87) should be compared to the correlation of IQ scores on the same test taken twice, which is also about .87. When heredity is the same and when environment is as similar as it is for twins raised together, IQ scores are about as similar as they can be.

Certain comparisons in the table suggest a role for heredity, with some qualifications. First, identical twins reared apart have a higher correlation (.75) than nontwin siblings reared apart (.40), and this correlation is much higher than that of unrelated persons reared apart (−.01). However, even when identical twins are separated at birth and raised apart, many aspects of their environment tend to be more similar than they are for random pairs of unrelated children, so these comparisons could exaggerate the effect of heredity. (See the accompanying box for other facts about the similarity of identical twins reared apart.) Second, identical twins reared together have a higher correlation (.87) than fraternal twins reared together (.53). But again, it is possible that the environments of identical twins are *more* similar than those of fraternal twins, so environmental effects could account for some of the correlation. It is also the case that prenatal environmental influences like toxins or disease can affect one twin more than the other, which would lower the correlation (Baily and Horn, 1986).

Other comparisons in the table suggest a role for environment. Identical twins and nontwin siblings reared together have higher correlations than identical twins and nontwin siblings reared apart; unrelated children reared together have a correlation greater than unrelated persons reared apart; and adoptive parents and adoptive children likewise show a positive correlation (.20).

A third influence on IQ test scores is the *interaction* between heredity and environment (Plomin and DeFries, 1980). Is it possible to isolate heredity from all the environmental influences in order to generalize about the heritability of IQ? A very rough guess, accepted by many workers in this area, is .5, indicating that heredity and environment contribute about equally to IQ (Plomin, 1985). But there is plenty of room for disagreement in both directions.

Some of the highest estimates of IQ heritability have come from the early data of Sir Cyril Burt, a noted English psychologist (1966; see Fancher, 1986). At the beginning of his research on IQ, Burt apparently collected some data on twins reared apart, and he claimed that he continued to collect data on new pairs of twins throughout his long career. Leon Kamin, however, discovered that at least the later data were fraudulent. Kamin (1974) and Arthur Jensen (1978) found twenty instances in which Burt reported exactly the same correlation coefficients, to the third decimal place, despite large changes in the reported size of his sample. The chances of an identical correlation arising from different sets of data are one in many millions. Moreover, it strains belief to imagine that such identities could result from mere carelessness. Other evidence indicates that Burt became so convinced that his hereditarian views were correct that he felt his fabrications were justified (Fancher, 1986). Behavior of this sort undermines the entire structure of science. But Burt was widely respected, and many people, including Jensen, who helped expose Burt's fraud, have continued to believe that the heritability of IQ is higher than more recent (and more reliable) data have indicated.

IQ and Racial Differences

In the United States, blacks score lower on IQ tests than whites on the average, as has been noted, and Jews and Asian-Americans score higher than white gentiles (Loehlin, Lindzey, and Spuler, 1975), although there is much variation within each group. Similar differences have been found between other ethnic and racial

PSYCHOLOGY TODAY AND TOMORROW

Resemblances between Identical Twins Raised Apart

Jim Springer and Jim Lewis were identical twins separated at the age of five weeks. Each was adopted by a different family, and they grew up in different towns. Until they were thirty-nine years old, neither knew of the other's existence. When the twins were brought together for study, psychologists found that their pulse, blood pressure, and sleep and brain-wave patterns were not just similar but *identical*. When the two men took personality tests, it was as if the same person had taken the test twice (Holden, 1980; Jackson, 1980). Their lives had also followed similar patterns. Both drove Chevrolets, worked part-time as deputy sheriffs, chewed their fingernails, chain-smoked, drank the same brand of beer, disliked baseball, enjoyed stock-car racing, and crossed their legs in the same way. Both liked mechanical drawing and carpentry, and both had hated spelling but liked math in school. Each had been married twice (first to a Linda, then to a Betty), and each had a son—one named James Allan, the other James Alan. Each owned a dog named Toy.

Although some of these similarities are doubtless coincidental, Bouchard (1981) has found many such similarities between identical twins raised apart, far too many to be explained by coincidence alone. Tastes, personality, and habits, as well as IQ scores, are affected by inheritance. Of course, our genes play a far smaller role in determining our beliefs, attitudes, and particular skills and knowledge.

Jim Lewis (left) and Jim Springer (right).

groups. For example, in Hawaii, children of "white," Chinese, Japanese, and Korean descent scored highest on the average, and children of Filipino, Hawaiian, Portuguese, and Puerto Rican descent (in that order) scored progressively lower. These average group differences persisted over the period from 1924 to 1938, even though scores for all groups rose substantially over this period (probably as a result of improvements in education)(Smith, 1942). Today, Japanese children, whose average IQ is between 108 and 115, outscore American children by almost as many points as American whites outscore American blacks (Lynn, 1982).

The origin of group differences has puzzled people since the time of Galton, when most writers assumed that these differences were hereditary. Many modern writers have argued that the study of racial differences is in itself immoral, because simply asking the question in public—regardless of the answer—encourages racial prejudice (see Block and Dworkin, 1974). Others (e.g., Jensen, 1981) have argued that we can best deal with problems of group differences in education and social class by trying to understand the origin of these differences. The other side counters that the existence of "facts" in this field is an illusion because of the difficulties of achieving any sort of certainty. Let us examine some of these difficulties.

Focusing on the black–white difference of about 15 points in average IQ scores, Arthur Jensen (1969, 1981) has argued that the difference is likely to be at least partly genetic. Blacks and whites also differ, on average, in many environmental areas, including levels of medical care, nutrition, and motivation as well as economic and social status (Jencks et al., 1972), but Jensen argued that such environmental differences between groups in the United States were too small to account entirely for the IQ difference, given what he took to be the high heritability of IQ. (As we have seen, however, he was somewhat misled in this regard by Burt's data.) In addition, Jensen pointed out, environmental deprivation does not always lead to lower IQ: Native Americans (or Indians) were more disadvantaged than blacks on every measure, yet their ability test scores were substantially higher on the average than those of blacks (Jensen, 1969, pp. 85–86).

Still, even the comparison of Native Americans and blacks might overlook subtle cultural factors, such as type of parental attention, or medical factors such as premature birth. It is also possible the American Indians may have genetically higher IQs than blacks, even though whites may not.

More direct evidence than Jensen's suggests that black–white differences are largely caused by environmental factors rather than genetic factors. When poor black children were adopted by white middle-class couples of above-average intelligence, the children's IQ scores averaged 106—above the national average for whites on the test used and about 15 points above the average IQ of black children reared in their own homes in the same part of the country (Scarr and Weinberg, 1976; Moore, 1986). Sandra Scarr (1981) found *no* connection between the degree of African ancestry (as determined by blood analysis and skin color) and IQ scores. On IQ tests, blacks with a high degree of African ancestry did as well, on the average, as blacks with only a trace. Black children with IQs over 140 were found to be identical to other black children in the proportion of African ancestry (Witty and Jenkins, 1936; most blacks in the United States do not have purely African ancestry). Finally, Eyferth (1961) studied illegitimate children, born in Germany between 1945 and 1953, whose fathers were U.S. soldiers and whose mothers were German women. These children, raised in Germany, did not differ in IQ scores as a function of whether their father was black or white.

A recent cross-cultural study (Ogbu, 1986) has found that patterns of group IQ and school achievement among minority groups worldwide—whether the subordinate group is black, European, or Asian—are similar to the patterns observed for blacks in the United States. These findings point to subordinate status, rather than race or ethnic group per se, as a factor in racial differences in IQ.

In sum, although IQ scores seem to be affected by genetic inheritance, there is no good evidence that racial differences in scores are due to genetic differences between the races. It may be impossible, for all practical purposes, even to test this hypothesis. It is clear, however, that environment as well as heredity affects IQ, and environment probably plays a large role in individual differences and group differences of all sorts.

Environment and IQ

The effect of severe malnutrition on IQ is especially devastating during gestation and infancy, when it can disturb brain growth, thus affecting connections between neurons and the development of neurotransmitters (Parmelee and Sigman, 1983). Chronic malnourishment, even when it is not severe, increases the risk of disease, and it makes children listless and decreases their motivation. Hungry children simply have no energy to play or to explore the environment, and as we will see in Chapter 15, play and exploration are how children learn about the world. Whatever the mechanism, malnutrition has lasting effects on IQ scores (Birch et al., 1971; Winick et al., 1975; Stoch et al., 1982).

Poisons in the environment can also affect intelligence (Phil and Parkes, 1977). Lead and other heavy metals can cause brain damage in young children, which results in sharp decreases in IQ scores and difficulty in focusing attention (Needleman et al., 1990). At one time, urban air was filled with lead particles from leaded gasoline, but since lead has been removed from most gasoline, levels of this toxin in the air have been significantly reduced. Lead paint is no longer made, but lead is still common in paint chips that peel from the walls in many older slum dwellings, and very young children often eat these chips.

The level of cognitive stimulation within the home is another important factor. Children from homes full of books, magazines, and interesting toys tend to have higher IQ and achievement test scores in the first grade than do children from homes without such stimulation (Bradley and Caldwell, 1984). Even the way parents interact with their children can hamper or boost the development of intelligence. Researchers have discovered that the techniques a parent uses to teach

Cognitive stimulation provided at home can enhance the development of intelligence.

her preschooler a simple task correlate with the child's achievement scores at the age of twelve (Hess and McDevitt, 1984). Children whose parents use direct control, telling them exactly how to perform the tasks, do much less well in school than do children whose parents encourage them to think about the problem and then to apply their own ideas.

The makeup of the family may be yet another factor related to differences in test scores. Data collected from several countries show that the more older brothers and sisters a child has, the lower his or her IQ is likely to be (Zajonc, 1983). The relationship is not simply a late twentieth-century development. Records for more than 12,000 Americans born between 1894 and 1964 showed that no matter which birth year was examined, the more brothers and sisters a person had, the lower was his or her score on a verbal test, a score that correlates highly with WAIS scores (Van Court and Bean, 1985). The explanation for this may be that when a child's principal companions are other children—who are, of course, intellectually immature—he or she is exposed to low levels of vocabulary and intellectual stimulation and observes mostly immature ways of meeting intellectual demands.

In addition, the past two decades have seen certain shifts in IQ scores that cannot be explained by heredity but must, it seems, result from environmental influences. The first of these shifts is an increase in IQ scores not only in the United States and Canada but in twelve other countries studied—a number of Western European nations, as well as Norway, East Germany, New Zealand, Australia, and Japan (Flynn, 1987). It is interesting to note that at the same time, SAT scores in the United States have decreased. Flynn (1987) has explained this apparent contradiction by concluding that specific abilities like problem solving, which are measured by IQ tests, have increased, largely due to the spread of mass communication, but that the SATs pick up changes in achievement, which may be more vulnerable to educational quality, content, and methods. As you may know, there have been many complaints recently about achievement levels in U.S. schools, particularly in comparison to those of other nations like Japan.

In a second IQ shift, the gap between males and females in relative verbal and mathematical abilities, as measured by IQ tests, has begun to close. Females no longer show an advantage over males on language ability tests (Feingold, 1988; Hyde and Linn, 1988). And males no longer show an advantage over females in perceptual and mathematical abilities on some tests like the PSATs (Feingold, 1988). Even though the very best scorers on mathematical abilities still tend to be male, it is quite likely, given the trend, that this discrepancy may eventually disappear. Certainly, then, social influences can be seen at work here, since no strong genetic influence could make itself felt over the course of just a generation or two.

Education and Intelligence

Is the standard IQ test sensitive to the effects of education? The answer seems to be yes, if we look at extreme manipulations of education, such as the difference between going to school and not going to school. People who grow up in cultures without Western-style schooling perform poorly on IQ tests and similar tasks, even when efforts are made to exclude tasks that the subject might not have done in school. These cultural differences are due to schooling itself, and not to other aspects of the cultures in question. For example, Wagner (1974, 1978) found that rural Mexican children and both rural and urban children in Morocco showed no improvement with age in a memory task similar to the one used by Galton and Binet, unless the subjects had attended school. (The subjects had to remember the order in which the experimenter pointed to a series of pictures.) The schooled subjects showed the same age trends that had been found in other studies in the United States, trends of the sort usually explained in terms of increasing use of rehearsal as a way of remembering the items. Sharp, Cole, and Lave (1979) found that the number of years of schooling, in contrast to age, was also a main determinant of performance on most of the subtests of Thurstone's Test of Primary Mental Abilities (a kind of IQ test) and on a set of problems from Raven's Progressive Matrices (another IQ test). Stevenson and colleagues (1978) reached similar conclusions with still other tests.

Within cultures that have universal schooling, it is difficult to determine definitively whether differences in the quality of schooling affect IQ scores. We can, however, look at the effects of special educational experiments designed to increase intelligence. Such experiments have a long history. Binet himself developed and partially implemented a program of "mental orthopedics" for those diagnosed by his test as lagging behind. This program included exercises intended to increase attention span—such as maintaining a "frozen" physical position for progressively longer periods—and to increase response speed. Binet's program was one of the first attempts to increase intelligence—to "teach children how to learn"—before asking them to do the real thing. The effectiveness of the program was never evaluated.

More recently, in Venezuela, Luis Alberto Machado (1980) was appointed (at his own request) minister of state for the development of human intelligence during the Campins administration (1979–1984). He initiated several programs, including an experimental course designed to increase intelligence (Adams, 1986), which led to an almost 50 percent increase in the rate of increase in test scores over the school year (Herrnstein et al., 1986).

The IQ test itself, however, is *not* specifically designed to measure the effects of such interventions. To design such specific measures, again, we need a theory of teachable intelligence. Baron (1985, 1988), in attempting to provide such a theory, has argued that education to increase intelligence should try to encourage *actively open-minded thinking*. Actively open-minded thinkers consider alternatives to their own favorite ideas, in hopes of improving them. They do not dismiss evidence simply because they don't like its implications. When making decisions, they pay attention to goals that their favorite option subverts as well as goals that it serves. They are not lawyers trying to defend their initial ideas, but detectives in search of the truth or the best decision. That is, they look for *disconfirming* evidence as well as confirmations, just as we discussed in Chapter 9. Indeed, we are talking here about the same kind of creativity and avoidance of obstacles in problem solving covered in that chapter—notions that are also presented in the critical-thinking essays in the Study Guide, for actively open-minded thinking is much like critical thinking and has the same goals.

A study by Perkins, Faraday, and Bushey (in press) shows how a theory of open-minded thinking (or critical thinking) can be used to design an intervention program as well as a test of its effectiveness. These researchers taught high school students to think in an actively open-minded way through a sixteen-session course that emphasized searching thoroughly for arguments on both sides of an issue. Students were taught that the arguments they consider when thinking about a controversial issue should be *true* (to be the best of the thinker's knowledge), *relevant* to the issue, and *complete*—that is, all important relevant arguments

The *juku*, or "cramming school," provides Japanese children with summertime and after-school coaching to help them improve their grades and their entrance exam scores for high schools and universities. Partly as a result of their culture's strong emphasis on formal education, students in Japan tend to score higher on achievement tests than do students in Western industrial nations.

should be considered. Controversial issues were discussed in class, and students were encouraged to generate and evaluate (for truth and relevance) arguments on both sides, especially the side with which they disagreed.

Before and after the course, students were tested by asking them to write down their thoughts on such difficult and timely issues as, "Would providing more money for public schools significantly improve the quality of teaching and learning?" and "Would a ban on selling and owning handguns significantly reduce violent crime?" Two issues were used at the beginning of the course, and another two were used at the end. To ensure that the issues themselves did not account for the change, each issue was used for some students at the beginning and for an equal number of students at the end.

The course nearly doubled the *number* of arguments that students offered on the *other* side from their own. The rated quality (truth and relevance) of these arguments increased as well. These gains were not simply the result of greater thoroughness in general: the course did not increase the number or quality of arguments on the student's own side. The effect was truly a matter of increased open-mindedness.

Such a change in students' thinking would increase the likelihood of arriving at a balanced view of any issue, regardless of its nature. A program such as the one described would, in theory, help make students more effective at achieving their goals—unless their goal was simply to have been right all along, which is, in any case, unachievable. And since our definition of intelligence has to do with abilities that help people achieve their goals, we could say that such a program should therefore increase intelligence. It remains to be shown that courses like this one can lead to lasting and general improvement and that such improvement will really help people achieve their goals. (For a general review of attempts to teach thinking, see Nickerson, 1989.)

This chapter has concerned itself largely with the determinants of IQ scores, which are essentially the same as scores on other ability tests, such as the SAT. We must remember that IQ tests measure a great many general abilities that help us achieve our goals, but they measure some abilities better than others and may not measure other abilities at all. We still lack a good description of the full range of these abilities, both those that depend on the condition of our nervous system and those that we learn.

Despite these reservations, the IQ test serves as a good summary measure of a composite of a set of important abilities, just as the gross national product serves as a summary of many, though not all, important characteristics of the economic well-being of nations. Research on the determinants of IQ scores can thus inform us about the determinants of abilities in general. We have learned that various abilities are affected by genetic inheritance, environmental factors that affect the condition of the brain, and learning. IQ scores will continue to serve as indices for measuring effects of national and international trends in nutrition and medical care. IQ tests, however, probably do less well in picking up abilities connected with actively open-minded and critical thinking. We may need new experimentation on developing these abilities and new tests—based on new, more comprehensive theories—in order to evaluate education adequately and to understand what quality in education really means in terms of intelligence.

SUMMARY

What Is Intelligence?

■ As precisely as it can currently be defined, intelligence consists of general abilities that help people achieve their goals.
■ Most of our knowledge about intelligence is based on attempts to measure it with tests.

The Measurement of Intelligence

■ Alfred Binet, commissioned in the early twentieth century by the French government to find a way to select and educate slower-learning schoolchildren, invented the first modern intelligence test. The Binet-Simon test grouped items according to age. Scoring was based on the concept of mental age.
■ William Stern found that, according to Binet's system, more and more children would be classified as subnormal as they grew. To correct this, Stern focused instead on the ratio of mental to chronological age. Lewis Terman multiplied this ratio by 100, thus setting the formula for the intelligence quotient, or IQ.
■ Terman's version of Binet's test is known as the Stanford-Binet and is still widely used.
■ The Wechsler scales, which include tests for adults and children and have separate scores for verbal and performance abilities, are also extensively used today.
■ Group intelligence tests were first used by the U.S. Army during World War I. There are three types of group tests: intelligence (or ability), aptitude, and achievement. The distinction between aptitude tests and the two other types is somewhat blurred.

Attempts To Describe Intelligence

■ Charles Spearman proposed that the correlations among different intelligence measurements were the result of a single, general factor, g, that underlies all intellectual abilities. (This was the basis of the statistical technique called factor analysis.)
■ Raymond Cattell proposed that fluid intelligence may represent learning abilities, whereas crystallized intelligence may represent actual knowledge acquired. The first declines with age; the second probably increases.
■ IQ scores do not correlate particularly well with artistic success, measures of creativity, or types of manual or other expertise.
■ Robert Sternberg described three types of intelligence: componential, or major information-processing and metacognitive abilities; experiential, or abilities learned from experience that allow us to carry out familiar tasks easily; and contextual, or practical intelligence.

How Good Are Intelligence Tests?

■ A good test must be both reliable and valid. A reliable test provides consistent measurement; a valid test measures what it purports to measure. If a test is valid, it must also be reliable.
■ Standardized tests are given first to a representative standardization group, whose scores are used to establish norms. Scores of current test takers are then compared to the norms, either by the percentile or the standard score system.
■ Ability tests can be somewhat helpful in predicting job performance, although other, not necessarily quantifiable factors may also be involved.
■ Scores on ability tests like the SAT correlate quite well with academic performance.
■ Ability tests are useful (and were originally designed) for diagnosing different levels of mental retardation. The major causes of retardation are genetic abnormalities, brain damage, and environmental deprivation. Retarded students learn more readily in specialized slower classes.
■ IQ tests can be useful in selecting students who would benefit from advanced instruction.

The Determinants of Intelligence: Heredity, Environment and Education

■ The heritability of IQ is an estimate of the genetic contribution to individual differences in IQ scores.
■ Evidence that some proportion of IQ scores are affected by heredity comes from studies of twins. But it is now thought that environment contributes almost equally to IQ.
■ Some psychologists, notably Arthur Jensen, have argued that the generally slightly lower IQ scores of blacks in comparison to those of whites was at least partly genetic. More recent direct evidence suggests environmental causes may account for this difference.
■ Severe malnutrition, environmental toxins, and cognitive deprivation (lack of stimulation) seem to affect intelligence and IQ scores negatively. Birth order may also influence scores.
■ Standardized IQ tests are sensitive to extreme differences in education. But they are less useful in assessing differences in educational quality within a single culture.
■ Nor are IQ tests helpful in measuring educational interventions. But some intelligence-boosting programs, such as those designed to develop open-minded, critical thinking, seem quite successful if analyzed from a perspective that identifies such thinking with intelligence.

KEY TERMS

achievement tests
aptitude tests
componential intelligence
concurrent validity
construct validity
content validity
contextual intelligence
crystallized intelligence
Down syndrome
eugenics
experiential intelligence
factor analysis
fluid intelligence
general intelligence factor (g factor)

heritability
interjudge reliability
intelligence
intelligence (ability) tests
intelligence quotient (IQ)
internal consistency reliability
mental age
mental retardation
mild retardation
moderate retardation
norms
percentile system
performance test
predictive validity

profound retardation
reliability
severe retardation
standard score system
standardization group
Stanford-Binet test
test-retest reliability
Wechsler Adult Intelligence Scale
(WAIS)
Wechsler Intelligence Scale for
Children (WISC)
Wechsler Preschool and Primary Scale
of Intelligence (WPPSI)
validity

CONCEPT REVIEW

1. What is the general definition of intelligence given in the introduction to the chapter? What conditions and limitations must be incorporated in this definition?

2. What were the goals of the earlier investigators of intelligence—Galton, Cattell, Binet, and Stern?

3. Describe the four modern intelligence tests presented in the chapter. What are the unique features or applications of each?

4. Explain factor analysis and the *correlation coefficient.*

5. What is the evidence supporting the existence of a *g* factor, of fluid intelligence, and of crystallized intelligence? Is there a correlation between fluid intelligence and creativity?

6. Describe the three components of the triarchic theory of intelligence. How does Sternberg support this theory?

7. Define *reliability, validity,* and *standardization.* How is each of these criteria applied to the evaluation of an IQ test?

8. How effective are IQ tests in the four areas in which they are generally used? Which test is most reliable? Which is least reliable?

9. Identify the IQ score levels that categorize mental retardation and giftedness. What are the shortcomings of this kind of classification?

10. Summarize the various explanations for the causes of racial differences in IQ.

11. What is the evidence for the heritability of intelligence? What is the evidence for the role of the environment in intelligence? Can education or practice improve performance on intelligence tests?

CRITICAL THINKING

1. The use of intelligence test data to classify individuals—whether the scores are used to identify giftedness, predict school performance, account for racial differences, or whatever—inevitably involves some form of stigma. What are the ethical considerations for psychologists who conduct such tests and for the people who use the test scores?

2. The evidence for heritability of intelligence is based on studies of twins and is quite convincing. What other areas of psychology could benefit from similar studies of twins? What kinds of limitations might develop when these kinds of studies are undertaken?

Emotion and Motivation

....*Emotion*

My parents and I had arrived at a shopping mall. Dad was parking the car, and I started to cross over to the mall. All of a sudden, a car squealed around the corner without stopping for the stop sign and almost hit my mother. I felt I wanted to kill the driver because he was inconsiderate and broke the law, almost killing my mother. My face got red, my voice deepened, my breathing quickened, and I began to shake. I blew up quickly, without worrying about the consequences. I made an obscene gesture at the driver and shouted after his car that he should come back and fight. About twenty minutes later I felt embarrassed for having been so crude in a public place, where there were a bunch of older women, a few couples, and a group of my peers. When I think about the incident, though, my blood still quickens and I again have the feeling of wanting to kill the idiot. (Adapted from Shaver and Schwartz, in press)

It is easy to sympathize with this young man's anger, and even if we cannot approve of his outburst, we understand it. Anger is an emotion everyone has felt and many have acted on. Often, the action is followed by regret.

We expect such emotional incidents to lead to hasty, ill-considered action, because popular conceptions of emotions portray them as undesirable, out of control, and irrational. They affect our judgment. We are "swept away" by passion or anger, "overcome" by grief, "delirious" with joy. Among the ancient Romans, Horace wrote that anger was "a little madness"; Seneca counseled that "the first blows of anger are heavy, but if it [anger] waits, it will think again." Even the words "emotion" and "passion" suggest that they overtake us, that we submit to them. "Emotion" comes from the Latin for "to move," and "passion" from the Latin for "submission." Until recently, scientific theories ran close to these long-standing popular views, presenting emotions as arbitrary, irrational, and unpredictable. They were seen as the remnants of our evolutionary heritage, reactions that we highly evolved human beings had to overcome with reason.

Within the last ten to fifteen years, scientific views of emotion have begun to change. New theories and research have led to surprising insights and revealed some regularities in emotions (Frijda, 1988). A new consensus on the process of emotions is emerging; this model is diagrammed in Figure 12.1 and forms the basis for this chapter's discussion of emotion (Shaver et al., 1987). We explore the often-contradictory theories that have been proposed to account for our emotional experiences. We discuss the various components of emotion—its physical, cognitive, and behavioral or expressive aspects—and their interrelationship. We take an in-depth look at one emotion, happiness. Finally, we explore similarities and differences among emotions across cultures.

WHAT IS EMOTION?

AROUSAL physical excitement; the physiological changes that are part of emotion

It is difficult to define an emotion, in part because our emotional experience is so varied and complex. There are hundreds of emotion words in the English language, from "abashed" to "xenophobia." Do all these terms mean that there are actually hundreds of emotions? Psychologists have tried to sort out this profusion of emotion terms by identifying a few underlying dimensions of emotional experience. Virtually all accounts of emotion agree that emotions can be classified along two broad dimensions—degree of pleasantness and degree of physical excitement, or **arousal** (Osgood, 1955; Block, 1957; Averill, 1975; Daly, Lancee, and Polivy, 1983; Russell, 1983). Some emotions—such as fear—are clearly negative or unpleasant, and others—such as joy—are just as clearly positive or pleasant. Some emotions—such as anger and joy—involve high levels of activity, excitement, or physiological arousal, whereas others—such as sadness—involve decreased energy and low levels of arousal.

Although researchers agree that pleasantness and arousal are two important dimensions of the emotional experience, they have not agreed about other dimensions (Smith and Ellsworth, 1985). Yet it is clear that emotions are more complex than a two-dimensional model suggests. Consider, for example, anger and fear.

Shared emotions hold relationships together, and, on a larger scale, emotions like patriotism can help to hold a nation together. On Memorial Day, veterans are honored for the sacrifices they made for their country.

Both of these emotions are negative and both are high in arousal, yet they are quite distinct emotional experiences.

Another way to make sense of the variety of emotion terms is to identify which emotions are *basic*, in the sense that they share some kind of underlying biological foundation or are universal, and which are *subordinate*, or variations on the basic emotions. The majority of emotion researchers agree that the list of basic emotions is limited to five or six: the positive emotions of love, joy, and possibly, surprise; and the negative emotions of anger, fear, and sadness. These emotions appear in most scientific theories of emotions, and they also seem to organize the way all people talk and think about emotions. Yet even here, there is some disagreement. Some researchers consider disgust a basic negative emotion (Ekman, 1984); some think surprise is a reflex rather than an emotion (Ekman, 1984; Fehr and Russell, 1984); and others strike love from the list (Shaver and Schwartz, in press).

Given this lack of agreement and the complexity of the issue, how are we to define emotion, which we must do, at least provisionally, in order to study it? We can say that an **emotion** is a pattern of responses to an event that is relevant to the goals or needs of the organism. The responses include physiological arousal, impulses to action, thoughts and expression of all these. According to this definition, individuals who do not have needs, goals, or concerns cannot experience emotions (Frijda, 1988). The needs or goals may be as fundamental as food, shelter, and survival, or they may be as complex as the yearning for love, an ambition to win a Nobel prize, or a will to build self-respect. (The significance of needs and goals is a topic we explore further in Chapter 13, when we consider motivation in more

EMOTION the pattern of responses to an event relevant to needs or goals, including bodily changes, impulses to act, thoughts, and expression

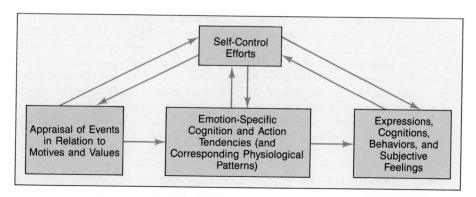

Figure 12.1 A dynamic model of the emotion process. (Adapted from Shaver et al., 1987, p. 1080.)

detail.) As we shall see, each component of an emotion plays an important role in our subjective experience of it. We will also see that different theorists have rather different ideas about the relative importance of the three components.

AROUSAL

Suppose you are crossing a street when the sudden loud blast of a car horn startles you. Your body responds with a series of changes:

1. Heart rate increases, sometimes more than doubling.
2. Movement in the gastrointestinal tract nearly stops as blood vessels leading to the stomach and intestine constrict. At the same time, vessels leading to the larger skeletal muscles expand, diverting blood to where it may be needed for fighting or (as in this case) fleeing.
3. The endocrine glands stimulate the liver to release sugar into the bloodstream, so that needed energy can be supplied to skeletal muscles.
4. Breathing deepens and becomes rapid. The *bronchioles* (small divisions of the bronchi, the air passages that lead into the lungs) expand, and mucus secretion in the bronchi decreases. These changes increase the supply of oxygen in the bloodstream, which helps to burn the sugar being sent to the skeletal muscles.
5. The pupils of the eye dilate, and visual acuity increases.
6. The salivary glands may stop working, causing dryness of the mouth, while the sweat glands increase their activity, resulting in a decrease in the **galvanic skin response**, or **GSR**, the measure of the skin's resistance to electrical conduction.
7. The muscles just beneath the surface of the skin contract, causing hairs to stand erect, a condition called "goose bumps." (Lang, Rice, and Sternbach, 1972)

GALVANIC SKIN RESPONSE (GSR) the measure of the skin's resistance to electrical conduction; a measure of arousal

All of these changes together constitute arousal.

These changes are the result of complex processes in the brain, involving neurotransmitters and hormonal pathways (see Chapter 3). Strong emotions are associated with the activation of the autonomic nervous system (ANS). As noted in Chapter 3, the ANS controls glands and visceral muscles. The sympathetic division of the ANS is in control during an emergency or when we are under stress. It prepares us for action (such as leaping out of the way of an oncoming car) by responding in ways that promote energy expenditure. Most of the internal changes that accompany emotions involving arousal, such as intense fear or anger, are associated with action of the sympathetic division. In contrast, the parasympathetic division, because it promotes energy conservation, dominates when we are relaxed. Thus, after you leap to safety and the car passes, the opposing effects of the parasympathetic division reassert themselves. Heartbeat, respiration, glandular secretions, and muscular tension return to normal, and the physiological experience of the emotion subsides.

Psychologists have disagreed about the precise role of arousal in emotional experiences. The controversy revolves around three questions: (1) Does emotion cause physiological changes, do physiological changes cause emotion, or is the relationship between them more complex? (2) A related question concerns time sequence: does arousal occur before, at the same time as, or after the other elements of the emotional experience? (3) Is there a unique pattern of physiological response associated with each emotion, or is a single physiological response (or a few unique patterns) associated with all emotional experiences? Our language suggests that each emotion is associated with specific physiological changes. We say that fright knots the stomach, that anger causes a pounding in the temples, that we blush with shame.

The theories of emotion popular in the late nineteenth century held that events in the environment trigger a psychological state—the emotion—which, in turn, gives rise to a physiological state—arousal. According to this view, arousal

In a situation of fear or threat, our sympathetic nervous system is activated; our heart pounds, our stomach constricts, and our breathing becomes rapid. These bodily changes prepare us to cope with danger.

was likely to be a consequence of emotions but was not the cause or even the main component of the emotion. Thus, this view suggested that a distinct physiological response was *not* associated with each emotion. (It did not, however, really tell us *what* emotion was.)

The James-Lange Theory

The influential American philosopher and psychologist William James disagreed with this popular view. He proposed that each emotional state produces a unique pattern of bodily changes and that these changes cause the emotion we experience. According to James, the emotional experience consists of our perception of these bodily changes. He argued:

> *My theory, on the contrary, is that* the bodily changes follow directly the perception of the exciting fact, and that our feeling of the same changes as they occur IS the emotion. *Common-sense says, we lose our fortune, are sorry and weep; we meet a bear, are frightened and run; we are insulted by a rival, are angry and strike. The hypothesis here to be defended says that this order of sequence is incorrect . . . and that the more rational statement is that we feel sorry because we cry, angry because we strike, afraid because we tremble. . . . Without the bodily states following on the perception, the latter would be purely cognitive in form, pale, colorless, destitute of emotional warmth. We might then see the bear and judge it best to run, receive the insult and deem it right to strike, but we should not actually feel* afraid or angry. (James, 1890; emphasis in original)

According to James, then, our perception of a stimulus triggers a pattern of changes in the body—visceral or "gut" reactions. Awareness of these reactions is the emotional experience.

Writing at about the same time as James, a Dane named Carl Lange proposed a similar theory that specifically emphasized changes in blood pressure. Ever since, the view that emotion is simply the perception of bodily changes has been called the **James-Lange theory** of emotion (Lange and James, 1922).

JAMES-LANGE THEORY the theory that emotion is the perception of bodily changes

Cannon's Critique

The James-Lange theory stimulated a great deal of research, much of it designed to disprove the theory's claims. In 1927, American physiologist Walter B. Cannon presented a powerful critique of the theory. He contended that emotions appear

The sympathetic division of the autonomic nervous system contributes to Boris Becker's intense emotional reaction to winning at Wimbledon.

too swiftly to be the result of bodily reactions. We see a bridge collapsing and immediately feel panic; we see an old friend and instantaneously feel joy. Yet some of the visceral reactions associated with emotion, such as increased heart rate, gastrointestinal changes, and sweating, are relatively slow to develop. How could these slow-acting physiological changes be the cause of sudden emotion? Cannon argued that when an emotional event occurs, two things happen *simultaneously*: the thalamus is stimulated, and the ANS and the cortex are activated.

Today, scientists are reasonably certain that it is not the thalamus but the hypothalamus and the limbic system that are involved, in addition to the ANS and, ultimately, the cortex. Cannon's critique is nevertheless very important, because he realized that *both* physiology and cognition (i.e., the involvement of the cortex) are central to the experience of emotion.

Another point: the James-Lange theory assumed that each emotion is accompanied by a unique physiological response, and we identify which emotion we are experiencing from the particular pattern of bodily sensations. Cannon's own research, as well as that of others, was unable to identify such distinct patterns of physiological responses associated with particular emotional states. Rather, the research suggested that a general increase in arousal is associated with many different emotional experiences.

Schachter's Two-Factor Theory

TWO-FACTOR THEORY the theory that emotion consists of arousal and cognitive interpretation of the arousal

A different view of the connection between physiological changes and emotional experience led Stanley Schachter to propose a **two-factor theory** of emotion. Schachter contended that emotions have two components: physiological arousal *plus* a cognitive interpretation of that arousal. According to Schachter, when an emotional event occurs, we become physiologically aroused, and then (not simultaneously, as Cannon proposed) we interpret the meaning of that arousal on the basis of cues in the situation. For example, we see a fire, become aroused, and infer that we feel fear because we see other people running from the fire. Schachter's theory shares with the James-Lange theory the idea that emotions follow from physiological arousal, and it shares with Cannon's view the position that there is a general arousal associated with all emotions rather than specific physiological responses for specific emotions. The novel aspect of Schachter's theory was its emphasis on the cognitive interpretation of arousal.

In experiments that explored this theory, subjects received what they thought was a vitamin injection (Schachter and Singer, 1962). The subjects had been told that they were participating in a study to assess the effects of vitamins on vision. The injection was actually adrenaline, which produces physiological arousal, and the real purpose of the study was to see whether people would experience different emotions when given different cues for interpreting the arousal. Subjects in one group were told that the "vitamin" produced certain side effects, such as heart palpitations and tremors. (These are the arousal symptoms actually produced by adrenaline.) With this cue, these subjects were expected to interpret their arousal as an effect of the vitamin and, in line with Schachter's theory, were not expected to experience the arousal as emotion. Subjects in two other groups either were told that the "vitamin" produced itching and headache (symptoms *not* associated with adrenaline) or were given no information about any possible side effects of the injection. Thus, subjects in these two groups were offered no explanations for the arousal actually caused by the injection and were expected to interpret the arousal according to whatever emotional cues were present.

While waiting for the vision test, each subject sat in a room with a confederate of the experimenters. Sometimes this person acted in a slap-happy, frivolous manner, throwing paper airplanes, laughing, and playing with a hula hoop. At other times, the confederate acted annoyed and angry, finally tearing up a questionnaire he was supposed to fill out. Schachter and Singer predicted that subjects who were told that the vitamin produced arousal would not experience any emotional response in this situation, but that subjects in the other two groups, who did not have an explanation for their arousal, would feel angry in the presence of the angry confederate and euphoric in the presence of the euphoric confederate. The results confirmed their predictions (see Figure 12.2), supporting Schachter's view that emotions consist of two factors: arousal and a cognitive interpretation of that arousal.

If Schachter's theory is correct, our emotions are fairly malleable. That is, given the proper set of cues, a person in a state of arousal could be induced to experience any emotion. But this malleability depends on the assumption by both Schachter and Cannon that one physiological state of arousal is associated with *all* emotions. Suppose Schachter had wanted to make his subjects feel sad. He might have given them an injection of adrenaline to arouse them, then let them see another person cry. Would arousal in conjunction with a sadness cue actually produce sadness? The language we use to talk about sadness suggests that it would not. We regard sadness as a "down" feeling of low arousal, not an "up" feeling of high arousal. So does each emotional state have its own emotional profile? This may depend on how we categorize emotions, and how specific we get.

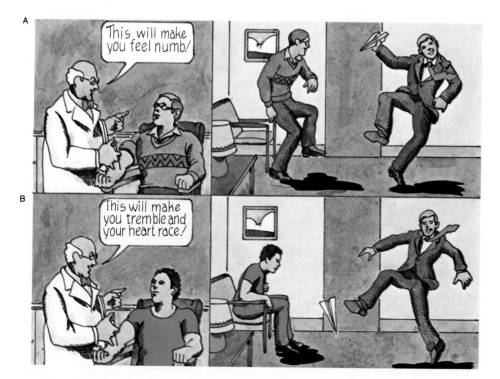

Figure 12.2 Two of the conditions in Schachter and Singer's experiment on emotion. (A) A subject is misled about the effects he should expect from the adrenaline injection he is receiving. Placed with a companion who joyfully flies paper airplanes around the waiting room, he attributes his state of arousal to a similar mood in himself and joins in. (B) A subject is told exactly what to expect from the injection. Although placed in the same situation as the first subject, he recognizes his physical sensations as the product of the injection and is unmoved by the euphoria of the experimenter's confederate.

Evidence does suggest that sadness is, indeed, associated with a particular physiological state, different from anger or euphoria. Several drugs produce the emotion of depression but not other emotions, without any labeling or interpretation on the part of the individual. These chemical depressants affect internal physiological responses (heart rate, muscle tone, and blood pressure all decrease), behavior (movements become sluggish and facial muscles droop in a sad expression), and subjective feelings (the individual feels unhappy, hopeless, and unmotivated). Many drugs prescribed for patients with hypertension produce depression as a side effect; in this case, the physiological symptoms alone seem to cause the emotional experience of depression.

Other distinctions among the physiological states accompanying different emotions have also been identified. Anger is generally associated with an increase in gastric activity, whereas fear is associated with an inhibition of gastric function (Wolff and Wolff, 1947). Recently, scientists have begun to agree that different regions of the brain are involved in different emotional experiences (Panksepp, 1982). However, it does not seem, according to current evidence, that every specific emotion has its own particular pattern of physiological arousal. It may be that the differences in physiological states accompanying emotion occur along slightly more general lines—that increased arousal, for example, with perhaps differing degrees of individual physiological responses, is paired with certain basic emotions, and decreased arousal with certain others. The next section examines an approach that is very different from Schachter's, and which points to the level of complexity in the arousal–emotion relationship that we have just suggested.

Ekman's Differentiation of Arousal States

Paul Ekman and his colleagues (Ekman, Levenson, and Friesen, 1983) have identified five major problems that may have prevented earlier researchers from pinning down the arousal–emotion relationship:

1. Most studies have compared only two or three emotional states, such as fear and anger, a procedure that might have obscured differences that would have been found if a broader range of emotions had been considered.
2. Most researchers have not made certain that subjects were experiencing *only* the intended emotion. If subjects were embarrassed by their participation in a study or frustrated by the tedious procedure, the measures used would have picked up a mixture of emotions.
3. Researchers have rarely, if ever, measured a wide range of physiological indicators of emotion. By depending on just one or two measures, they may have missed those on which emotions differ.
4. Most researchers have not monitored physiological states throughout the study. Because they took measures only before and after the emotion was induced, they may have missed fleeting instances of the emotion they were trying to track.
5. Most researchers have used only a single task to elicit whatever emotions they were measuring, and their failures may have been connected with the nature of the task they selected.

Ekman and his colleagues tried to design a single study that would correct all of these shortcomings. They studied six emotions: anger, fear, sadness, joy, surprise, and disgust. Their subjects were scientists studying the face and actors; these groups were selected because they were unlikely to feel embarrassed or frustrated by experimental techniques and to muddle the study with unintended emotions. The researchers used five physiological measures of emotion instead of one, monitored physiological states continuously, and relied on two tasks instead of just one to elicit emotions.

In one task, subjects evoked each of the six emotions by reliving emotional experiences from their past. In the second, subjects created emotional expressions by manipulating particular facial muscles as instructed by the researchers. (As we shall see in the next section, this task in itself can result in emotional experiences.) Ekman and his associates found several highly significant differences among emotional states: they discovered that they could distinguish negative emotions from positive emotions, and they uncovered particular patterns of heart rate, skin temperature, and GSR associated with anger, fear, and sadness. However, they could not distinguish the positive emotions—joy and surprise—from each other. Ekman's study is particularly important because it marks the first time that researchers have been able to detect specific physiological patterns associated with particular emotions—at least negative ones.

Ekman's results suggest that emotions are not as malleable as Schachter's findings indicated. How can we reconcile the two studies? Two points suggest how this might be done. First, Schachter proposed that we first feel an undifferentiated arousal, then label it on the basis of cognitive cues, and finally experience an emotion. In the normal course of events, the cognitive cues for a particular emotion are present *before* we are aroused—and may even cause the arousal. For example, seeing a fire both causes us to become aroused and provides a cue about why we are aroused. By injecting subjects with adrenaline, Schachter short-circuited the usual sequence in which emotions follow from the perception of an event (Shaver and Klinnert, 1982). Indeed, other researchers have found it difficult to replicate Schachter and Singer's results, which suggests that their theory applies only under very special conditions (Marshall and Zimbardo, 1979; Maslach, 1979; Reisenzein, 1983).

Second, Ekman's study shows that emotional states are differentiated by a fairly complex pattern of physiological indicators. Injections with adrenaline may *approximately* mimic emotional states that are associated with increased heartbeat but *precisely* mimic none. As a result, people who are injected with adrenaline and do not know that they have been artificially aroused may be in a malleable emotional state because they have some, but not all, of the physiological correlates of several states. Physiologically, they may be *sort of* angry, *sort of* fearful, and so on; their ambiguous physiological state may lead them to interpret their arousal in terms of the most likely available clue.

Arousal as an Emotion Intensifier

Although the sequence that Schachter suggested—arousal followed by a cognitive cue, followed by an inference about one's emotion—is probably not the usual sequence of events in emotional experiences, his results are consistent with a somewhat different role for arousal in emotions: *arousal intensifies our emotional state*. By injecting subjects with adrenaline or having them do vigorous exercise to increase their level of arousal, researchers can observe the effects of arousal on emotions. In one experiment, subjects who had been injected with adrenaline laughed more and harder while watching a slapstick comedy film than did people in a control group who received injections of salt water—a placebo that causes no physiological change. What is more, people who were injected with chlorpromazine, a drug that inhibits physiological arousal, laughed less than the control group (Schachter and Wheeler, 1962). In a similar study, people behaved more aggressively toward a person they disliked after they had been physiologically aroused by exercise (Zillman, 1971).

As a consequence of this intensifying effect of arousal on emotions, the arousal that is part of one emotional reaction can intensify a subsequent, and different, emotional reaction (Zillman, 1971). Under special circumstances, researchers were able to induce a transfer of fearful arousal to sexual arousal (Dutton and Aron, 1974). In this study, fear was induced in a group of men by having them cross a deep, rocky gorge on an unsteady bridge that swayed in the wind. As they stepped from the bridge, an attractive woman (a confederate of the experimenter) approached and asked them, as part of a project, to tell a brief story in response to an ambiguous picture of a woman. The stories these men wrote contained more sexual imagery than stories told by men in a control group who met the same woman after crossing a solid bridge spanning a shallow stream. The men who crossed the unsteady bridge were also more likely to telephone the attractive confederate later to "learn more about the project." The arousal that accompanied their fear transferred to sexual arousal upon meeting the attractive woman.

Arousal and the Impulse to Act

Arousal seems to be closely related to another component of emotional experiences—the impulse to act. In the emotional incident that opened this chapter, a striking feature of the young man's experience was his impulse to act: "I felt I wanted to kill the driver." Impulses to "do something" may be the most conspicuous part of an emotional incident, even if the impulse is not translated into action. Angry people often clench their fists and make aggressive, threatening gestures; when people are afraid, they have an impulse to flee; when they are sad, they have an urge to withdraw and become inactive; when they are joyful, they have an impulse toward physical affection or generosity; when they are in love, they have a compelling desire to spend time with the loved one (Shaver et al., 1987).

The physiological states associated with particular emotions are consistent with, and probably related to, the tendencies to action that also accompany those emotions. Indeed, the impulse to act may be *why* we become aroused during an emotional experience. Recall that strong emotions are associated with activation of the autonomic nervous system, which functions to prepare us physiologically for action. When we are angry and want to strike out, the particular physiological accompaniments to anger prepare us for such aggressive action. When we are sad and feel the urge to withdraw, the specific physiological responses that accompany sadness inhibit activity. It is possible that our evolution has built in the physiological responses so that we may act as the situation demands, at least as far as physical survival goes.

Nico Frijda (1986; 1988) believes that the impulse to act may indeed be the central aspect of emotional experience (see also Arnold, 1960; Plutchik, 1980; Ekman, 1984; Roseman, 1984; Scherer, 1984). Frijda, along with many other emotion researchers, believes that emotions are primarily adaptive— that is, they serve an important function for the organism by organizing behavioral reactions to events. For example, when we discover that our goals are unjustly blocked, we feel anger, which involves the urge to strike out. By striking out, we may be able to remove the obstacle to our goals. Fear arises when we find ourselves in danger, and our impulse is to flee. By fleeing, we may escape the danger. Emotions appear to be useful; they prepare us to act in ways that are helpful for achieving our goals and for surviving. In terms of evolution, emotional responses represent an improvement over innate releasing mechanisms and fixed action patterns (which we discuss further in Chapter 13) by providing a measure of flexibility. That is, emotions *prepare* an organism to act and provide the *tendency* toward a particular action, yet they leave the organism free to modulate its active response according to the situation and its own current needs and expectations (Smith and Ellsworth, 1987).

Frijda (1988) further points out that a given impulse to act seems to take temporary *control precedence* over other impulses and actions. It is as if we are directed to attend and respond (to narrow our focus) to only one stimulus or set of stimuli, which thus takes priority over anything else for the moment. This again illustrates the adaptiveness of emotion: our emotions can communicate to us what is most important in a given situation.

Frijda's (and others') functional view of emotion as an adaptive response with survival value goes back to Charles Darwin, who proposed the idea in his classic work *The Expression of the Emotions in Man and Animals* (1872/1967). As the title indicates, Darwin was much concerned with the continuity between humans and other animal species as evidenced by similarities of emotional expression. In the next section, you will see that there is also some continuity in expression among humans of all races and all areas of the world. Some aspects of emotion do seem to be universal and are therefore probably influenced to some degree by genetics and evolution.

Note that the tendency toward action is closely tied to emotional expression. Indeed, the impulse to act is often visible, whether in clenched fists or a slack posture; and we are all able to "read" action impulses in other people's facial, bodily, and vocal expressions. From an evolutionary standpoint this makes good sense, as you will see shortly.

Notice too that the functional view of emotion, far from characterizing emotion as irrational, in a sense emphasizes the rational and predictable nature of emotion. Emotion serves a very clear purpose—such as protection from harm or furtherance of needs—in the given situation. "Watch out!" it says. "You're about to be hurt or humiliated!" or "Here's your chance to get what you want!" Your impulse to act is guided in this way. This does not mean that in a broader context, a given emotion and the action it inspires will look rational—it may not. Emotion is functional in terms of the very specific situation and our interpretation of that situation. In short, emotion functions "locally," not broadly.

At the beginning of the chapter, we noted that those who saw emotion as irrational tended also to see it as an evolutionary vestige, linking us to "lower" animals. But now you can see that an evolutionary perspective does not necessarily mean "irrational" at all.

EXPRESSIVE BEHAVIOR

Every day, in countless situations, we convey our emotions to others and respond to their emotions. Emotions can be seen as part of the communication system, an aspect of our social existence. The facial expression of your friend as you describe your problems may betray sympathy, annoyance, impatience, or indifference. The decision to continue or cut short your tale of woe will probably depend on the nonverbal reactions you detect. Often we convey our emotions to those around us with body language—shrugs, slumps, winces, yawns, laughter, grunts, and more.

When our emotions run strong, they are obvious in our behavior. Emotionally expressive behavior is so transparent that actors in silent movies could convey a range of emotions without a word. When the villain bared his teeth and clenched his fists, the audience assumed that he was angry. When the heroine furrowed her brow and wrung her hands, the audience assumed that she was worried. Or think of Charlie Chaplin's Little Tramp. Without words, Chaplin conveys the gamut of emotions. Happiness? He does a little dance. Despair? His shoulders slump, the corners of his mouth turn down, and he seems to shrink physically. All of us learn to recognize such broad nonverbal cues very early in life.

Our voice also provides many clues to our emotional states. It can make plain to those around us whether we are angry or affectionate. The message comes through even if we are talking to someone who does not speak our language. The emotional qualities of speech are more important than we realize—often more important than the verbal content. "You are a real friend" has an entirely different meaning when uttered with feelings of gratitude and when spoken with sarcasm (Scherer, 1982).

The most widely studied aspect of emotional communication is facial expression. The face is a very important instrument of communication. If we cannot see another's face, we often find it quite difficult to interpret her or his remarks. We have an impressive capacity to express subtly different emotions through facial expressions. Facial expressions of surprise, for example, can be conveyed with many different overtones. There are various qualities of surprise (questioning, dumbfounded, startled, and dazed) as well as various intensities (slight, moderate, or extreme) (Ekman and Friesen, 1975). Often our expression conveys a blend of diverse emotions such as surprise and joy, anger and fear, amusement and annoyance. (See the accompanying box on cues to lying, for example.)

PSYCHOLOGY TODAY AND TOMORROW

How Our Emotions Can Make It Harder for Us To Lie

People lie for any number of reasons—to avoid getting into trouble for their actions, to avoid hurting another person's feelings, to ingratiate themselves with someone they want to impress. Who can lie successfully—and when?

Apparently, most people can lie successfully when they don't care whether or not their lie is successful. But when the substance of the lie concerns their feelings, their true emotions often leak through and betray the falsehood. We express our emotions through several channels: verbal, visual, and vocal. It is relatively easy to control the verbal aspects of our emotional expression, but the nonverbal aspects are likely to trip us up (Ekman, 1981).

The more motivated we are to lie successfully, the less successful we may be, because clues to our deception in the nonverbal channels become more obvious. The more we care about lying successfully, the more emotion we experience—usually some form of fear. We may fear that our lie will be detected; we may be anxious about the other person's opinion of us, especially when we want to be liked and accepted; we may worry about hurting the other person unnecessarily. The more we care, the harder we try to control our channels of expression. The visual and vocal channels are especially difficult to control, however, so the heightened motivation (and the greater degree of fear) allows more clues to leak through these nonverbal channels.

This seemed to describe the difficulty college students had when trying to lie for an experiment conducted by social psychologist Bella DePaulo (DePaulo, Stone, and Lassiter, 1985). With the goal of making a favorable impression, the students expressed opinions on controversial issues to another student. Motivation made all the difference. When the students' motivation to lie successfully was low (when the other person was the same gender or was unattractive, or when the disagreement was faked), they generally came across as sincere. But when students were highly motivated to lie successfully (when the other person was of the other gender or was highly attractive, or when the disagreement was real), their lies became relatively easy to detect. It was not their words that gave them away. When the other student had only a typed transcript of their remarks, he or she was unable to detect the falsehood. But when nonverbal channels were available, the students were generally perceived as insincere.

A sex difference appeared unexpectedly among the findings: women were generally less successful liars than men. In fact, the men seemed nearly as sincere when lying as they did when telling the truth. Women's lies were easier to catch, especially when the lie was shown on a soundless videotape—which presented only nonverbal, visual information.

It's not clear why women should find it so difficult to lie successfully, but there are two possible explanations. First, women are generally better than men at expressing emotions with their tone of voice, their facial expressions, and their body language. They may spontaneously express what they feel more plainly than men do and as a result may be at a loss when trying to disguise their emotions. Second, women may have a stronger motive to gain the approval of others. As the chapter text explains, our emotions are elicited by our appraisals of events in relation to our motives and values, or underlying concerns, so these concerns direct our emotional experiences to some degree. Accordingly, if women's underlying concerns are primarily interpersonal, their desire for approval increases their motivation to lie, and to lie successfully—which heightens their emotion to the point where it can no longer be disguised.

The Evolutionary Theory of Emotional Expression

Charles Darwin asserted that many human patterns of emotional expression have a genetic basis, handed down through generations because they had survival value. Since there are no fossils of behavior, such conjectures obviously cannot be proved, but the possible evolutionary significance of some expressions is easy to see. Raising the eyebrows in surprise or fear increases our visual acuity; raising the upper lip in rage bares teeth and readies us to bite. Other animals also bare their teeth as a threat or when preparing to fight, giving their enemies a warning that may in itself prevent a violent and damaging encounter (see Figure 12.3). Darwin believed that baring the teeth served a similar function among our ancestors; the expression communicated a threat. (We may not fully bare our teeth much any-

more, because we have developed other, but analogous, forms of threats.) A threat warns enemies of the impulse to act—in this case, to fight. What could be the purpose of visible fear? Researchers believe that a threatened animal's expression of fear signals danger to kin or to the animal's companions, preparing them as well as the threatened individual to flee if necessary.

If the expression of emotion has an evolutionary, genetic basis, then it should be similar across a variety of cultures. Consistent with Darwin's view, people from widely diverse cultures use highly similar postures, gestures, and facial expressions to convey comparable emotional states. When people in different societies were asked to identify the emotions expressed in a series of photographs (see Figure 12.4), they consistently recognized anger, fear, disgust, surprise, and happiness, regardless of the culture in which they lived (Ekman and Friesen, 1971). Even members of New Guinea tribes, who had little previous contact with Westerners and their characteristic emotional expressions, promptly labeled these basic emotions and, as shown in Figure 12.5, had little trouble in displaying them (Ekman, 1980). The role of prominent facial features in emotional expression across cultures has been precisely described for most of the basic emotions. We convey these emotions by the positions of the muscles in brow and forehead, eyelids, and lower face (see Table 12.1). In Figure 12.6, you can see the differences in brow and forehead formation for surprise, fear, and anger.

Further evidence for a biological, hereditary basis of emotional expression comes from studies of infants, which show that the capacity for emotional expression develops very early—or is present at birth. In one study, infants as young as two months were observed during inoculations against childhood diseases. The infants all showed distinctive facial patterns that could be readily recognized as responses to pain (Izard, et al., 1983). Some researchers believe that *all* the basic emotions may be present in the newborn, but they appear only in response to biological needs like food and protection (Campos et al., 1983). Although the first truly social smile appears at about two months, some researchers have found that infants as young as forty-two minutes will imitate emotional expressions quite accurately, sticking out their tongues or opening their mouths in response to an adult's actions (Meltzoff and Moore, 1983; Haviland and Lelwica, 1987). Whether these responses are true imitations has been much debated. Nevertheless, that basic emotional expressions have been observed repeatedly on the faces of infants certainly suggests that emotional expression is not merely the result of learning (see Figure 12.7).

Photograph Judged						
Judgment	Happiness	Disgust	Surprise	Sadness	Anger	Fear
Culture			**Percent Who Agreed with Judgment**			
99 Americans	97	92	95	84	67	85
40 Brazilians	95	97	87	59	90	67
119 Chileans	95	92	93	88	94	68
168 Argentinians	98	92	95	78	90	54
29 Japanese	100	90	100	62	90	66

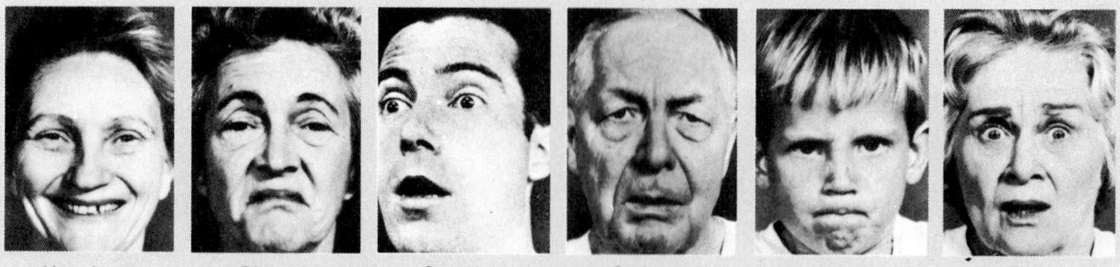

Figure 12.4 As this table indicates, there is a great deal of agreement among the members of different cultures about the meaning of facial expressions. This suggests that we are biologically programmed to produce the emotions conveyed by certain facial expressions. (After Ekman, Friesen, and Ellsworth, 1972.)

The Facial Feedback Hypothesis

The term *emotional expression* implies that the major role of emotional facial action is to manifest (or express) our internal states. Reversing this common-sense view, the **facial feedback hypothesis** holds that our subjective experience of emotion comes from an awareness of our facial expressions (Tomkins, 1962, 1963; Gellhorn, 1964; Izard, 1971). That is, we feel angry because we scowl or happy because we smile—not the other way around. This view dates back at least to William James (1884), who argued that emotion is the perception of changes in our bodily states which follow emotional events. Although other researchers interpreted this to mean the perception of visceral and organic components of bodily changes, James himself believed that changes in facial muscles also played a role in the experience of emotion. "Smooth the brow, brighten the eye, contract the dorsal rather than the ventral aspect of the frame, and speak in a major key, pass the genial compliment, and your heart must be frigid indeed if it does not gradually thaw!" James wrote (1884, p. 1078).

Researchers have typically tested the facial feedback hypothesis in two ways. In one type of study, subjects are induced to experience an emotion by watching a film that elicits emotion or by simply thinking about emotional experiences. These studies have shown that increased facial expression of emotion *is* related to both increased subjective experience of emotion and increased physiological arousal. However, although these studies are consistent with the facial feedback hypothesis, they are correlational and cannot test whether the facial expression of an emotion actually *causes* a person to experience that emotion (Adelman and Zajonc, 1989).

The causal role of facial expression has been tested by actually inducing people to smile, frown, or look sad and then measuring their physiological arousal and their subjective experience. In one study (Laird, 1974), electrodes were attached to subjects' faces, supposedly to monitor the minute electrical activity of facial muscles while the subjects watched cartoons. Subjects were told that any movement of their facial muscles would disturb recordings from the electrodes.

FACIAL FEEDBACK HYPOTHESIS the proposal that our subjective emotional experience is the result of facial expressions—that is, that the expression creates the emotion

VASCULAR THEORY the theory that facial expressions cause emotions because facial muscles alter patterns of blood flow to the brain

Figure 12.5 Video frames of attempts to pose emotion by subjects from the Fore of New Guinea. (Copyright © 1972 by Paul Ekman.)

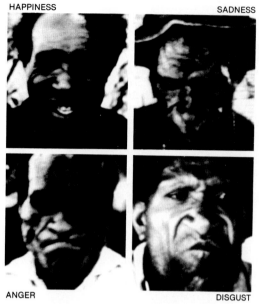

HAPPINESS

SADNESS

ANGER

DISGUST

Each subject was instructed to extend some muscles and contract others and then to hold the muscles in that position while watching and rating the cartoons. The subjects did not know that the instructions had led them to produce an emotional expression, such as a smile or a frown. Subjects who were smiling rated the cartoons as funnier than did those who were frowning as they watched.

A number of studies using this kind of approach have supported the facial feedback hypothesis (Laird and Crosby, 1974; Rhodewalt and Comer, 1979; McArthur, Solomon, and Jaffe, 1980; Rutledge and Hupka, 1985; Strack, Martin, and Stepper, 1988). Although there have been exceptions (e.g., Tourangeau and Ellsworth, 1979), most of these studies have found that inducing subjects to hold a facial expression that is consistent with an emotional cue increases the experienced emotion, while inducing subjects to hold a facial expression that is not consistent with the cue decreases the emotional experience. Other researchers have shown that, even in the absence of emotional cues, inducing subjects to arrange their facial muscles in ways that are similar to facial emotional expressions can initiate the subjective feeling of emotion (Zajonc, Murphy, and Inglehart, 1988) and the physiological correlates of emotion (Ekman, Levenson, and Friesen, 1985; Strack et al., 1988), although, again, not all studies have been consistent.

The Vascular Theory of Emotional Expression

Although most of the research on the facial feedback theory of emotional expression supports the theory, one troubling question remains unanswered. *How* do facial muscles cause us to experience emotions? Recently, Robert Zajonc (1985; Adelman and Zajonc, 1989) has revived an old theory—the **vascular theory** of emotional expression, which claims that manipulating facial muscles affects our experience of emotion by altering patterns of blood flow to the brain.

In 1907 a little-known French physician, Israel Waynbaum, offered a revolutionary theory of emotional expression that until recently was completely ignored. Waynbaum questioned the idea that facial gestures are expressive and that their primary function is to display an individual's internal state. Instead, he proposed, facial gestures may serve a regulatory function, controlling blood flow to the face and therefore to the brain.

Since the brain requires a stable blood flow, and since both brain and face get their blood from the same artery (which separates at the neck into an internal and a facial branch), Waynbaum reasoned that perhaps the muscles act as tourniquets on the veins and arteries. The muscles might press against the bony structure of the face, allowing more or less blood to reach the brain. Along with this suggestion, Waynbaum noted that all expressive acts—blushing, weeping, sobbing, and

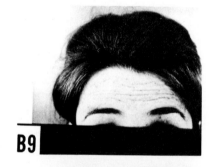

B9

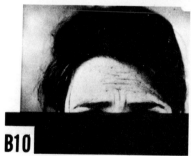

B10

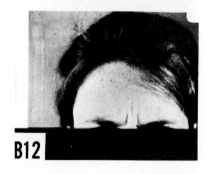

B12

Figure 12.6 Examples of the Facial Affect Scoring Technique (FAST) scoring definitions: the brows-forehead items for surprise (B9), fear (B10), and anger (B12). (Copyright © 1972 by Paul Ekman.)

TABLE 12.1   Appearance of the Face for Six Emotions

	BROWS-FOREHEAD	EYES-LIDS	LOWER FACE
Surprise	Raised curved eyebrows; long horizontal forehead wrinkles	Wide-open eyes with sclera showing above and often below the iris; signs of skin stretched above the eyelids and to a lesser extent below	Dropped-open mouth; no stretch or tension in the corners of the lips, but lips parted; opening of the mouth may vary
Fear	Raised and drawn-together brows; flattened raised appearance rather than curved; short horizontal and/or short vertical forehead wrinkles	Eyes opened, tension apparent in lower lids, which are raised more than in surprise; sclera may show above but not below iris; hard stare quality	Mouth corners drawn back, but not up or down; lips stretched; mouth may or may not be open
Anger	Brows pulled down and inward, appear to thrust forward; strong vertical, sometimes curved forehead wrinkles centered above the eyes	No sclera shows in eyes; upper lids appear lowered, tense and squared; lower lids also tensed and raised, may produce an arched appearance under eye; lid tightening may be sufficient to appear squinting	Either the lips tightly pressed together or an open, squared mouth with lips raised and/or forward; teeth may or may not show
Disgust	Brows drawn down but not together, short vertical creases may be shown in forehead and nose, horizontal and/or vertical wrinkles on bridge of nose and sides of upper nose	Lower eyelids pushed up and raised, but not tensed	Deep nasolabial fold and raising of cheeks; mouth either open with upper lip raised and lower lip forward and/or out, or closed with upper lip pushed up by raised lower lip; tongue may be visible forward in mouth near the lips, or closed with outer corners pulled slightly down
Sadness	Brows drawn together with inner corners raised and outer corners lowered or level, or brows drawn down in the middle and slightly raised at inner corners; forehead shows small horizontal or lateral curved and short vertical wrinkles in center area, or shows bulge of muscular contraction above center of brow area	Eyes either glazed with drooping upper lids and lax lower lids, or upper lids are tense and pulled up at inner corner, down at outer corner with or without lower lids tensed; eyes may be looking downward or eyes may show tears	Mouth either open with partially stretched, trembling lips, or closed with outer corners pulled slightly down
Happiness	No distinctive brow-forehead appearance	Eyes may be relaxed or neutral in appearance, or lower lids may be pushed up by lower face action, bagging the lower lids and causing eyes to be narrowed; with the latter, crow's feet apparent, reaching from outer corner of eyes toward the hairline	Outer corners of lips raised, usually also drawn back; may or may not have pronounced nasolabial fold; may or may not have opening of lips and appearance of teeth

Source: Ekman, P. (1972). Universals and cultural differences in facial expression of emotion. In J. K. Cole (ed.), *Nebraska Symposium on Motivation.* Lincoln: University of Nebraska Press. Copyright © 1972 by Paul Ekman.

laughing—are intimately connected with the circulatory process. Blushing allows blood to rush to the face; tears are supplied by the lachrymal artery, which branches off from the artery that supplies the brain; sobbing activates the diaphragm and modulates oxygen intake, as does laughing heartily. As we have seen, emotional excitement produces circulatory imbalances. Facial gestures might help counteract these disturbances, restoring balance to the cerebral blood flow.

When a person smiles, Waynbaum suggested, the major zygomatic muscle (which runs diagonally across the cheek to the corner of the mouth) presses on branches of the facial artery and, together with the action of the corrugator muscles (near the eyebrow), momentarily increases blood flow to the brain. This action is beneficial, Waynbaum claimed, and it *causes* a positive subjective feeling. Generally, he argued, a sudden small surge of blood to the brain is positive, and a similar sudden drop of blood flow leads to a depressed feeling. The functions of these relatively small, short-lived changes in cerebral blood flow are mainly restorative. In Waynbaum's view, we do not smile because we feel good; we feel good because we smile. (Note the similarity to the James-Lange theory.)

When Waynbaum constructed this theory in 1907, scientists knew little about the physiology of the vascular system. However, his basic idea does organize the disparate facts about emotional expression in a reasonable manner. Today, draw-

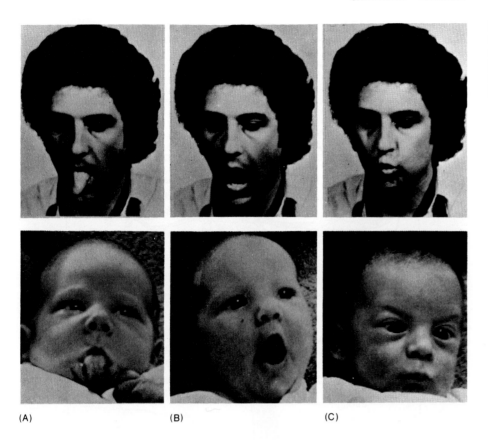

Figure 12.7 Sample photographs from videotape recordings of two- to three-week-old infants imitating (A) tongue protrusion, (B) mouth opening, and (C) lip protrusion demonstrated by an adult experimenter. (From Meltzoff and Moore, 1983.)

(A)   (B)   (C)

ing on current physiological knowledge, we can adjust Waynbaum's theory in a way that agrees with his overall position. Perhaps, for example, changes in our subjective state are not due mainly to the cerebral blood flow itself. Instead, they may be due to sudden changes in the metabolic processes of the brain or to changes in brain temperature (caused, perhaps, by sudden action of the facial muscles on the returning blood supply). By relating changes in facial muscles to changes in the blood supply to the brain, the vascular theory of emotional expression might explain *how* facial feedback affects emotional experience (Adelman and Zajonc, 1989; see also Zajonc, Murphy, and Inglehart, 1989). Most psychologists remain very skeptical about this theory, however, and await further data and evaluation. (See Figure 12.8.)

APPRAISAL

We have seen that there appears to be a biological, evolutionary basis for emotions. Yet this does not mean that emotions function in humans in exactly the same way that they function in other species. Indeed, humans have more highly evolved cognitive abilities than other species, and it seems likely that, as in other behaviors, this cognitive capacity plays an important role in the human emotional experience.

At the beginning of this chapter, we defined an emotion as a response to an event that is relevant to the organism's needs, goals, or concerns. In other species and in infants, these emotional responses appear to be innate, with particular emotions following reflexively from particular eliciting events. Of course, infants and other animals cannot tell us what they are feeling, so we can only infer their emotional state from their behavior and expressions. For example, infants appear to become angry when their arms are held to prevent them from moving freely, and they soon develop the ability to express what appears to be joy when they are reunited with their mothers (Izard et al., 1983).

Among older children and adults, however, it is not the events themselves that appear to elicit the emotional response, but the person's **appraisal**, or cogni-

APPRAISAL the cognitive interpretation of an event in terms of an individual's needs and desires; a central aspect of emotion

Figure 12.8 According to the vascular theory of emotion, as facial muscles relax or tighten in a smile or a frown, the blood's temperature and flow patterns change. Thus, preliminary findings indicate, the flow of warm blood to the brain is associated with unpleasant emotions and cooler blood with pleasant feelings. Further research is needed to determine whether facial feedback does affect emotional states. (Robert Zajonc; adapted from *The New York Times,* July 18, 1989.)

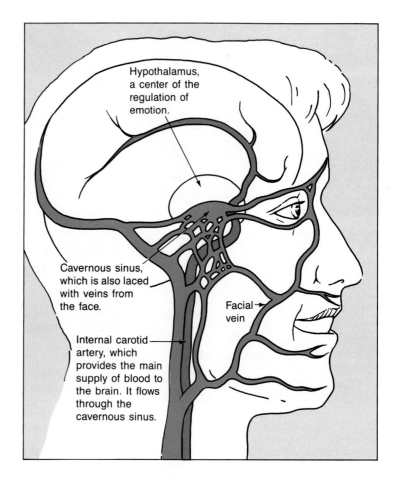

tive interpretation, of an event with respect to his or her needs, goals, wishes, or concerns (Arnold, 1960; Ekman, 1980; Plutchik, 1980; Lazarus, 1982; Scherer, 1982; Mandler, 1984; Roseman, 1984; Frijda, 1986; Smith and Ellsworth, 1987). The transition from the simple, reflexive response in infants to cognitive mediation of responses in older children fits in well with the general course of cognitive development (see Chapter 15). Brain maturation, especially the eventual control of many responses by the cortex, may be responsible. In any case, appraisal becomes central fairly early in human life.

In a classic study that demonstrated the importance of appraisal, researchers purposefully influenced people's interpretation of an emotion-arousing film (Lazarus and Alfert, 1964). The film was an explicit portrayal of a tribal puberty rite for boys, in which the underside of the penis was slit open. Some people saw a silent version of the film and interpreted what they were seeing as a "real" infliction of pain. Others heard a special "denial" sound track, which explained that the participants were actors and that the incision was causing no pain. People who heard this sound track reacted far less strongly than people who saw the silent version of the film, as evidenced by recordings of the GSR. People who heard the sound track *before* they saw the film had the lowest GSR of all, perhaps because their appraisal had already been constructed before the film began, so that their expectations were altered (see Figure 12.9).

The Process of Appraisal

The most fundamental type of appraisal, and probably the first one made, is whether the event is good or bad for you (Lazarus, Kanner, and Folkman, 1980; Scherer, 1984). Does it further your wishes, values, and goals; does it interfere

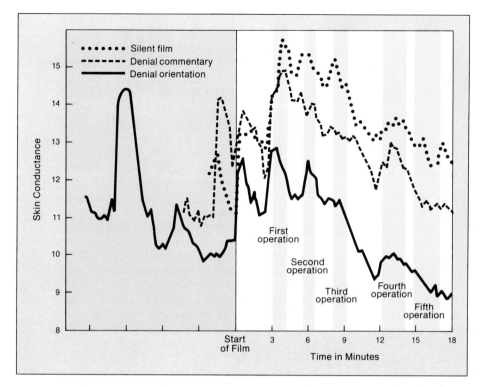

Figure 12.9 The results of an experiment on emotion and cognition by Lazarus and Alfert. They used an anthropological film about puberty rites involving subincision (the cutting open of the urethra along the underside of the penis) as the emotion-provoking stimulus. Changes in galvanic skin response (GSR) were measured as an index of anxiety. All the subjects saw the film. One group (denial commentary) heard a sound track with the film saying that the people in the film were actors and the operations were causing no pain. Another group (denial orientation) heard the same sound track before they were shown the film. A third group (silent film) heard no commentary at all. (After Lazarus and Alfert, 1964.)

with them; or is it of no concern? Depending on the appraisal, the same event can produce a positive emotion in one person and a negative emotion in another. A grade of C on an exam may be appraised as a success by a student who has been struggling with schoolwork or as a failure by a student who has been maintaining an A average. This fundamental appraisal of an event as good or bad with respect to one's needs or goals may explain why the distinction between positive and negative emotions, described earlier, emerges so clearly in studies of the dimensions underlying emotional experience.

Beyond the more general positive/negative distinction, just which emotion is felt also depends on the form of the appraisal (Lazarus, Kanner, and Folkman, 1980; Roseman, 1984; Weiner, 1985; Smith and Ellsworth, 1987). It appears that specific appraisals may automatically trigger certain emotions, although the crucial aspects of these appraisals have yet to be determined. In any case, people seem to agree about which types of appraisal elicit which basic emotions (Shaver et al., 1987; Shaver and Schwartz, in press).

Most people believe that an event appraised or judged as causing loss of power or status, violating an expectation, interrupting an activity aimed at some goal, or causing or threatening pain leads to anger. However, to unleash the anger, the event or situation must also be judged as illegitimate, wrong, unfair, or contrary to what ought to be (de Rivera, 1981; Shaver et al., 1987; Smith and Ellsworth, 1987). In the episode described at the beginning of this chapter, for example, the young man was especially infuriated because in his judgment the driver had been in the wrong. People also agree that an event appraised as posing a threat of social rejection, failure, loss of control, physical harm or death, or being left alone or in the dark triggers fear. On the positive side, people agree that when they see themselves as successful or accepted, when they believe they have achieved what they desired, when they receive a wonderful surprise, or when they find their expectations exceeded, they experience *joy*.

PSYCHOLOGY TODAY AND TOMORROW

Do Men and Women Live in Different Emotional Worlds?

Are women really more emotional than men? Are men by contrast "uptight," repressed, unfeeling, or at least more limited in emotional expression? Certainly, many people believe this. In order to find a way to answer these questions scientifically, Virginia O'Leary and Devorah Smith (1988) sought to determine whether or not men and women interpret emotions differently. Do men and women, for example, assign different causes to emotion in general and to individual emotions in particular? Do they attribute some emotions to men and others to women?

For their study, O'Leary and Smith randomly selected twelve male and twelve female university students in the northeastern United States. The subjects were presented with ten emotions: interest, fear, disgust, happiness, surprise, distress, anger, shame, contempt, and sadness. The subjects were asked to come up with explanations for each of these emotions in an anonymous person, X. They were also asked how they would know, in real life, what X might be feeling: what cues would they go by? Finally, for each emotion, the subjects were asked whether they thought X was a man or a woman.

O'Leary and Smith did find some significant and interesting differences in men's and women's attributions of emotions, and these different attributions fit in with certain culture-based gender stereotypes. Males are generally expected to be more focused on the outside world of politics, business, sports, and the like. In the O'Leary and Smith study, male subjects were indeed more likely to attribute emotion to external—that is, situational—causes. And the women? Think for a moment about our stereotypes for women. In general, they are expected to be concerned primarily with the "inner life" of love and family relationships, but (in compensation, some would argue, for having less influence in the wider world) they are allowed greater freedom to delve into emotions and the inner self. True to these expectations, female subjects in the study tended to attribute emotion primarily to relational causes (such as interactions with others) and secondarily to internal causes (such as moods). (As we saw in the other box in this chapter, this underlying concern with interpersonal relationships may also

contribute to women's greater difficulty in lying convincingly.)

This basic difference in male and female attributions was particularly apparent when O'Leary and Smith's subjects addressed anger and fear. Both sexes attributed anger to relational causes, but women did so to a greater extent than men. In the case of fear, both sexes turned to internal explanations—that is, to explanations based on disposition, mood, personal desires, or needs. But women relied more heavily on internal explanations than men did.

Do men and women go a step beyond such gender differences in attributions and think of emotions as characteristically either male or female? Here, we might expect cultural stereotypes—for example, anger is male, fear is female—to lead to consistent sex-typing of individual emotions. But the researchers found that men were more likely to sex-type emotions: men tended to describe *all* the emotions tested as characteristically male. Women, in contrast, seemed less willing to label *any* emotion as strictly male or female. Some have theorized (see O'Leary and Hansen, 1985) that men tend to generalize their own emotional perspectives to everyone else, including women.

Finally, O'Leary and Smith found that their male subjects were more likely to regard most of the emotions studied as subject to self-control. The only exceptions were anger and fear, which the men did not see as potentially controllable while the women did. If men attribute emotions primarily to external factors, think of emotions as "male," and assert the possibility of personal control over most emotions, it seems that men believe they can control external forces to some extent.

O'Leary and Smith's study indicates that men and women do inhabit different emotional worlds. If the sexes attribute emotions differently, they are also likely to respond to emotion differently. As the researchers point out, however, this does not mean that men and women have different capacities for emotion and its expression. It merely shows that they tend to use (or choose not to use) their capacities differently, in different situations. (See also Deaux, 1985.)

Young children cannot offer a cognitive appraisal of their emotional states, but sometimes such an interpretation is not needed.

Other evidence that certain appraisals trigger certain emotions comes from researchers' ability to predict emotional responses to real events, such as reactions to midterm grades, on the basis of people's appraisals (Smith and Ellsworth, 1987). If we know that someone appraises an event as negative, unfair, and caused by another person, we can predict with some certainty that the person will feel anger. Knowing who was in control of the situation seems especially important in the case of negative events. Given the same unpleasant event, we tend to feel angry if we perceive it as caused by another person, guilty if we perceive it as caused by ourselves, or sad if we perceive it as unavoidable and controlled by circumstances (Smith and Ellsworth, 1987).

Unconscious Appraisal

The entire appraisal process can take place without our being aware of it. We may not even be aware of the goals or wishes that have made the event a matter of concern to us. As we saw in the discussions of the unconscious (Chapter 6),

The same ostrich that looks tame and even comical wandering around in a zoo becomes a menacing creature when running loose on a city street. This bird escaped from a truck en route to a zoo and scattered passersby for twenty minutes until it was captured.

subliminal perception (Chapter 5), and priming (Chapter 8), some cognitive processing can occur "automatically," without conscious awareness. Indeed, the operation of goals and appraisals outside of awareness may account for some of the apparent mystery and irrationality of emotions. For example, you may have an immediate and at first puzzling emotional response to someone you meet for the first time. Perhaps this new person reminds you of someone else whom you strongly like or dislike, but you do not consciously note the resemblance (or you notice only one aspect of resemblance and "automatically" infer the rest). Or perhaps you are responding merely to physical attractiveness or unattractiveness, without being aware that you are thinking about appearance at all and without being able to say what it is that makes this person attractive or unattractive to you.

This process of "unconscious" appraisal is not at all unusual. Particularly in social situations, we are constantly and more or less unconsciously monitoring what is going on at various levels. We are in fact processing the other person's emotional responses the whole time. For instance, as you talk to your friend Alicia, you begin to have a vague sense that she is irritated, does not approve of your activity, and will seek some way of thwarting you if she can. It may not be until much later, when you stop to consider *why* your conversation with Alicia made you defensive or angry (this will depend on another appraisal—how you stand generally in relation to Alicia; Roseman, 1984) that you may realize all the emotional information you were actually taking in. Without this kind of analysis, you may never quite understand why you reacted the way you did.

Cognitive Control of Emotions

Thus, we are not always aware of our goals, our standards, our values, our expectations, or their influence over our appraisals and reactions. But to some extent (and sometimes with help) we can *make* ourselves aware. Once we are aware, we are freer to alter desires and goals that seem destructive, impractical, or unrealistic.

Many people turn to religious and spiritual organizations and many kinds of psychological interventions for help in achieving exactly this sort of control. Religious belief can give the believer some control over emotion, especially negative emotion, by placing it in a larger context and thus giving it meaning and, in some

Religious belief can help us achieve a sense of control over our negative emotions by giving them meaning in a larger context.

cases, offering reward in the afterlife for suffering in this world. Awareness of emotions, thoughts, and goals, along with cognitive control over them, are also central to most psychotherapies. In particular, the cognitive approach to therapy, which will be discussed in Chapter 19, is based on the notion that maladaptive behavior and emotions (such as depression and anxiety) are direct results of ingrained but inappropriate thought patterns. The point of cognitive therapies is to alter the thoughts themselves in order to adjust the consequent emotions (Beck, 1967).

Apart from therapy, however, we can also exercise some cognitive control over our more ordinary emotions. Emotions involve goals and desires, so we can alter our emotional responses by reevaluating and altering our goals. Emotions also involve appraisals of events and situations, which we can reevaluate and alter, thereby modifying our emotional reactions.

Suppose you have your heart set on attending graduate school at University A but are accepted only by University B. Because this event interferes with your *goal* of attending University A, you are likely to feel disappointment, sadness, or perhaps anger if you believe the decision is unfair. However, you can decide to take another hard look at the goals themselves. After you investigate the graduate program at University B in greater detail, you may find that the program is actually better suited to your needs. This means you have much less cause for disappointment or anger. You may even end up feeling quite pleased. By changing your goals, you gain control over your feelings. Thus, the common-sense advice to look for the silver lining in every cloud (or for the good in every situation) has real psychological merit.

Alternatively, you can alter your *appraisal* of what University A's rejection of your application means with respect to your goals (Lazarus, Kanner, and Folkman, 1980). Initially you may regard the rejection as a loss; you think you will never have the chance to attend University A, and you feel depressed. Then it may occur to you this need not be a permanent loss; after all, the rejection is only for this year's admissions, and you can reapply the following year. You may decide to improve your standardized test scores, seek additional letters of recommendation, or obtain relevant work experience. In this way, you change your appraisal from one of loss to one of challenge and consequently improve your emotional state (Folkman, 1984).

There is yet another way to look at the same situation. Suppose you initially regard your admission to graduate school as a judgment of your intellectual worth. In this case, any rejection is devastating and bound to make you feel dejected and unhappy. If you can alter that appraisal, however, you can to some extent control the power that such an event has over your feelings. Some initial disappointment may be inevitable in this situation, but it need not cast a pall over your future life.

A word of warning: cognitive control is not necessarily as simple as it may sound. For example, a cognitive response to an emotion can sometimes trigger another emotion. If you are angry but realize that anger is inappropriate or dangerous in a given situation, this realization may trigger sadness or fear instead. Active suppression of an emotion—based on cognitive appraisal such as "Anger will get me into trouble in this situation" might be regarded as yet another form of cognitive control. But this can enmesh us in a discussion of unconscious versus conscious functioning and any number of complex speculations that are difficult to evaluate. (We discuss some of the consequences of suppressing emotion in Chapter 18.) The main point to remember here is that thought and feeling are so intertwined that they are almost inseparable.

HAPPINESS: AN IN-DEPTH LOOK AT ONE EMOTION

For centuries, philosophers have regarded happiness, an extended form of joy, as the greatest human good. "The pursuit of happiness" is enshrined in the Declaration of Independence, along with life and liberty, as an inalienable right. Most of

A family camping trip provides the kind of change of scene that can make us happy by prompting a positive appraisal of the way our lives are going.

us would like to be happy, if only we knew how. What makes people happy? Can we control how happy we are?

Objective Determinants of Happiness

Try to list the things that would make you happy. The list compiled by the French philosopher Jean Jacques Rousseau consisted of a good bank account, a good cook, and a good digestion (Diener, 1984). Your own list might include getting your college degree, making a lot of money, and staying healthy. Although these objective circumstances seem related to happiness, they account for surprisingly little of the differences in happiness among people. (Most of us know at least one person who has everything he or she ever wanted, but is still not happy.) In fact, health, wealth, age, gender, employment, and education—objective circumstances of any type—cannot account for much of the difference.

If we return to some of the basic points made earlier, we can see why this may be so. First, emotions follow from events that involve *change*. A steady state of affairs, even though it is extremely positive, is unlikely to trigger the emotion of happiness. It is possible for a constant to produce feelings of contentment, if we stop and reflect upon our lives and see clearly that we have some of the things we want and that these can make us feel good for the moment. In other words, such a cognitive appraisal of our situation triggers, or retriggers, contentment. We must make the appraisal in order to feel the emotion. And according to our definition of emotion, this feeling will not last unless it is constantly renewed.

Second, almost all theories of happiness, from the observations of the ancient Greeks to the most modern views, have recognized the importance of goals and wishes to feelings of happiness (Diener, 1984). Thus, objective circumstances should relate to happiness only if those circumstances are relevant to our goals. A person who cares about very little or who has very narrow interests in life has fewer chances to be happy—but is also less likely to encounter events that bring unhappiness.

Third, the aggravating truth is that happiness is always relative. This is because it is generally not objective events or circumstances but our appraisals of them that determine which emotion we experience. And our appraisals are usually based on some comparison, whether to our own past, to some ideal, or to others' lives. How happy we are following a positive event depends on what we use as a standard for comparison. Earning $35,000 a year might seem terrific to a new college graduate used to getting by on a small allowance or part-time salary, but it is likely to be a comedown for someone who has been making $50,000 a year.

Appraisals That Elicit Happiness

In one study, people from England, Canada, and the United States strongly agreed about the kinds of appraisals that lead to joy or happiness (Shaver et al., 1987). One type of appraisal concerns achievement: completing a task successfully, attaining or possessing something you wanted, or receiving respect or praise. The second type of appraisal involves delightful surprises: reality exceeds your expectations or you experience some highly pleasurable sensations or stimuli. The third type of appraisal involves the satisfaction of interpersonal concerns: being accepted, feeling that you belong, or receiving love or affection.

The Relativity of Happiness

Perhaps more than any other basic emotion, happiness depends on our appraisal of events in relation to some standard. The most common standards are our own past experience—how we have fared before in this particular domain—and other people's experience—how others are currently doing in this domain.

Comparisons with Past Experience

Since it takes a change in circumstances to trigger happiness, we are happy only when we think things are better than they used to be or might be. An ironic consequence of this principle of happiness is that extremely positive events can spoil our hopes of future happiness because they raise our expectations. This observation has given rise to the *adaptation-level theory* of happiness, which is based on the notion that just as our senses adapt to a given level of stimulation, we adapt or adjust to a certain level of happiness, which then becomes our standard of comparison (Brickman, Coates, and Janoff-Bulman, 1978).

The adaptation-level theory was demonstrated by Philip Brickman and his colleagues (1978) when they studied a group of people who had won between $50,000 and $1 million in the Illinois lottery. These winners had hit the jackpot anywhere from one month to a year before the researchers got in touch with them. Winning the lottery, they all agreed, had been a highly positive event in their lives. Yet these lucky people were no more (or less) happy than other Illinois citizens. Winning the lottery had also, oddly, cast a shadow over their chances for future happiness: the positive aspects of daily life had lost some of their ability to produce happiness. Such everyday activities as talking with a friend, watching television, hearing a good joke, getting a compliment, or buying new clothes seemed significantly *less* pleasurable to the lottery winners than to people who had not won any money. It seemed as if winning the lottery had changed the winners' standards of happiness.

Comparisons with Others

We may be reluctant to admit it, but we feel better when other people are worse off than ourselves. Sharing a small dormitory room with two roommates may seem a completely unsatisfactory housing arrangement, until we consider the plight of the homeless. Thomas Wills (1981) calls this the *downward-comparison principle* of happiness. A downward comparison makes us feel better because it lowers the standard against which we evaluate our own circumstances.

The downward-comparison principle explains why income is not as strongly related to happiness as we might at first expect. People who make good incomes are of course somewhat happier than people with low incomes, but this is more the case when one makes the comparison *within* a single country than when one compares income groups *between* two countries. For example, people in the United States who make a great deal of money are generally happier than people at or below the poverty level; but overall, Americans are not much happier than people in poorer countries (see Diener, 1984). The relative strength or weakness of the happiness–income correlation may also have to do with the social and economic context of a given time period. Between 1946 and 1978, for example, when real income (adjusted for inflation) rose dramatically in the United States, measured happiness did not increase at all. It even began to drift downward (Diener, 1984). Why? People tend to evaluate their own income by comparing it with what others make. Because incomes were rising across the United States during the postwar period, few people really felt better off than before relative to others. Thus, how much you make relative to other people in your own society is a more important predictor of happiness than how much you make compared to people in India or Zaïre or Spain.

Consistent with the idea that we have some cognitive control over our emotions is the fact that people can deliberately select standards of comparison that either increase or decrease their happiness. People choose to compare themselves with those who are worse off, primarily because using that standard improves their own sense of well-being. In a study of breast cancer patients, researchers found that nearly all of the women with breast cancer felt lucky, in comparison to others (Wood, Taylor, and Lichtman, 1985). Women who had been treated by the less disfiguring surgical procedure known as lumpectomy considered themselves better off than women who had had a breast removed. And women who had had a single breast removed considered themselves better off than women who had lost both breasts. Virtually no woman spontaneously compared her condition with people who had less severe cancer, with women who did not have breast cancer, or with her own past condition. As we will see in the next chapter, most people have a remarkable capacity to maintain an optimistic outlook. This ability may well be adaptive. Many studies have shown that attitude affects health (see Chapter 20). The optimistic, "Every cloud has a silver lining" view may help people continue coping, even as they go through a crisis like breast cancer.

Perhaps the ability to remain optimistic balances our seemingly endless quest for true happiness—again, helping us cope with our particular circumstances. The relativity of happiness, its transitory nature, and our fairly constant reevaluations and reappraisals of our situation and goals may well be adaptive, at least up to a point. Dissatisfaction or unhappiness may keep us striving toward new goals and ideals, refueling our motivation to achieve something more (or at least to achieve something different).

CULTURAL ASPECTS OF EMOTION

No matter what aspect of emotion we examine, we find order and regularity. Clearly, anger, fear, sadness, joy, surprise, and love (our list of basic emotions) follow a set of predictable patterns. These patterns seem to be universal. Despite enormous differences in cultures, whether we look at tribal cultures in the South Pacific or technological societies in Europe and North America, we find a striking degree of consistency in the triggers of basic emotions, the action tendencies associated with them, and their expression (Scherer, Walbott, and Summerfield, 1986; Shaver and Schwartz, in press). This agreement across cultures is, as we noted earlier, consistent with the idea that the basic emotions are biologically determined and have an evolutionary basis.

In considering the cultural consistencies in emotion, it helps to think of emotion as a three-level hierarchy (Shaver and Schwartz, in press; also see Rosch et al., 1976, as discussed in Chapter 9). The broadest categories into which emotions can be divided—the *superordinate categories*—are positive emotions and negative emotions. The basic emotions, the six on our list, are in the *midlevel category* of emotions that people tend to think of when they hear the word "emotion." (Just as you think of "robin" before you think of "avian" when you hear the word "bird," so you think of "anger" before you think of "irritation" when you hear the word "emotion.") Then, any emotions that are further subdivisions of the basic emotions can be considered in a *subordinate category*. Subordinate emotions reflect subtle variations of the basic emotions, usually variations in intensity or in the situations that give rise to the emotion.

Anger can be experienced as irritation or rage (a difference in intensity) or as envy or exasperation (a difference in the situation)—these are all subordinate emotions of anger. In the same way, love can be experienced as fondness or lust or infatuation. Some subordinate emotions combine elements of two or more basic emotions; jealousy, for example, often contains elements of anger, sadness, and fear—but it is always tied to particular people in particular situations. Subordinate emotions tend to vary from culture to culture and indeed are not widely agreed on in scientific theory.

According to Phillip Shaver and Judith Schwartz (in press), it is the difference between the basic and the subordinate emotions that reconciles the apparent universality of emotion, on the one hand, with the cultural diversity of emotion, on the other. We have seen that evidence supports the view that the basic emotions are biologically determined. Shaver and Schwartz have proposed that subordinate emotions are culturally or cognitively determined.

Again, subordinate emotions tend to be evoked in response to specific situations, which in turn tend to be culturally determined and affected by values, beliefs, and social scripts (Scherer, Walbott, and Summerfield, 1983; Scherer, 1986). That is, events that initiate emotional experiences reflect what a given culture considers dangerous, what it sees as worth having, and what it considers to be grave losses (Lutz and White, 1986; Lutz, 1987). Some subordinate emotions— like loneliness, a particular kind of sadness—may be felt in many cultures but be triggered, expressed, felt more or less intensely, and discussed (or perhaps not even admitted) in different ways depending on the social context. Specific forms of fear, such as guilt or anxiety about authority, vary from culture to culture because the specific events that elicit the fears vary. Within the United States, for example, people in a middle-class conservative community may tend to fear differences in opinion or lifestyle; in a poor black ghetto, the overriding fear may center on the presence of an all-white police force. In a strongly religious society, people may fear any hint of blasphemy: women in a strict Moslem culture may fear the consequences of their own rebellious feelings or acts. In Micronesia, walking on a tribal chief's property may arouse fear and guilt (Lutz, 1982). Nevertheless, although the specific triggering events differ, they have something in common: they are all events that signal danger (see Scherer, 1986; Shaver and Schwartz, in press). Thus, we come full circle to certain elements that underlie all the differences, that are cross cultural and universal.

There is much evidence, particularly research with infants and young children, to support the view that the basic emotions are biologically determined and subordinate emotions are culturally or cognitively determined. It seems, as was mentioned earlier, that in very young infants basic emotions are triggered directly by specific events, probably with no cognitive appraisal. However, within a few months, the patterns of a baby's emotional responses begin to resemble those of adults and depend upon similar "readings" of the meaning of events (Sroufe, 1984). A baby may laugh when her mother playfully puts on a mask at home, but wail when a stranger dons a mask in a psychology lab. The baby clearly understands the difference. Also, as children learn to talk, they learn the terms for basic emotions quite early (Bretherton and Beeghly, 1982) and can understand and label basic emotions in other people long before they can understand and discuss subordinate emotions (Reichenbach and Masters, 1983). Finally, in contrast to findings with basic emotions, no research has yet found any physiological differences among any subordinate emotions.

A few other cultural aspects of emotion should be noted. There are universal expressions for basic emotions, but individual cultures, each with its own social code, tend to regulate when and where emotion can be expressed (Shaver and Schwartz, in press). For example, in one study, researchers observed the emotional expressions of Japanese and American subjects watching films in two different situations (Ekman and Oster, 1979). When each subject watched the films alone, all subjects displayed the same facial expressions. However, differences showed up when subjects watched films in the presence of an authority figure. The Japanese smiled more and controlled their emotions more than the Americans. Thus, it seems that each culture has its own display rules, which specify who can show what emotion to whom, and when (Ekman, 1980).

In addition, cultures can invent both specific, subordinate emotions and new terms for them. Culturally important but nonuniversal situations can easily lead to the creation of new, culture-specific emotion words. And cultures differ widely in the language used to describe and discuss emotions. For example, Tahitian culture has many words for anger but few for sadness and guilt (Levy, 1984). In situations in which Americans would say they were "sad," Tahitians would be more likely to say they were "troubled" or "tired." Do such language differences reflect cultural differences in the emotions actually experienced or differences in the amount of attention or emphasis that different cultures give to various emotions? Psychologists and anthropologists have reached no consensus on the answer. If the question sounds familiar to you, however, that is because it can be seen as a form of the general question about linguistic relativity discussed at the end of Chapter 10, on language: Do linguistic differences reflect differences in perception, cognition, and experience? Does language determine thought, or does it simply reflect cultural differences in values and priorities? As we saw in Chapter 10, it seems fairly clear that language does *not* directly determine thought, though language and thought are intimately related. In the case of emotions and language, we can again apply the distinction between basic and subordinate, between the universal and the cultural. Universality underlies emotion and its expression—including the language used to label and describe it; but culture and experience and cognition—including cultural uses of language—predominate when it comes to subtleties of emotion (that is, when it comes to the subordinate emotions). Once again, nature and nurture are clearly working together in the emotional life of each of us.

SUMMARY

What Is Emotion?

▪ A useful working definition states that emotion is a pattern of responses, involving arousal and impulses to action, thoughts, and behavioral expression (including actions, facial expressions, and vocal qualities), to an event relevant to our needs, desires, and goals.

Arousal

▪ The physiological changes that constitute arousal are controlled by the autonomic nervous system. The sympathetic division prepares us for action under stress; the parasympathetic division returns us to a more relaxed state.
▪ The James-Lange theory disagreed with the late nineteenth-century popular view that arousal was a consequence of emotion. According to James and Lange, arousal, or the perception of it, *is* the emotion.
▪ Cannon proposed that there must also be a subjective experience of emotion, probably controlled by the cortex, simultaneous to the triggering of arousal, in order to account for the swiftness with which emotion can descend.

▪ Schachter proposed in his two-factor theory that emotion is composed of both physiological arousal *and* a content-based cognitive interpretation of that arousal. His experiments with injections of adrenaline supported his ideas.
▪ Ekman's studies found important differences among emotional states, including physiological differences and clear distinctions between positive and negative emotions.
▪ As it is now understood, arousal serves to intensify the emotional state.
▪ The impulse to act seems to be a central element of emotion and may account for arousal. This impulse also may illustrate that emotion is functional and adaptive: it motivates us to fight or flee, for instance.

Expressive Behavior

▪ Facial expressions, body language, and vocal qualities convey emotions in human communication.
▪ Darwin believed that much of human emotional expression has an evolutionary basis. Evidence for this theory comes from striking similarities in the expression and interpretation of basic emotions around the world and from the presence of emotional expression in very young infants.

■ The facial feedback hypothesis holds that the subjective experience of emotion results from an awareness of our facial expressions. There is some evidence to support this.

■ The vascular theory attempts to explain how facial feedback works. This theory proposes that changes in facial muscles alter patterns of blood flow to the brain, which then dictates the specific emotion.

Appraisal

■ Whatever the biological basis or component of emotion may be, it is clear that cognitive interpretation (appraisal) of events with respect to personal needs and goals plays a large role in human emotion.

■ Negative and positive appraisals are probably the most basic type made.

■ Certain specific appraisals trigger certain emotions, and people around the world agree on what appraisals elicit which basic emotions.

■ Appraisal often takes place unconsciously.

■ Cognitive control of emotion can be achieved through religious training or therapy. Other ways to control emotion include altering our goals and desires, altering our appraisals by reevaluating events or situations, and suppressing unwanted emotions. Cognition and emotion are closely intertwined.

■ We compare our current situation with our own past experience and feel happy if we think things have improved. According to the adaptation-level theory, we are constantly readjusting our standards of comparison, usually upward.

■ We also tend to compare ourselves with others who are worse off than we are, which usually results in some feelings of happiness. Humans have an amazing capacity to remain optimistic.

■ The likelihood that we will grow dissatisfied with a steady state of affairs may keep us striving; our ability to remain optimistic may also be adaptive, by helping us cope.

Happiness: An In-depth Look at One Emotion

■ Happiness is not usually determined by objective circumstances; it is transitory and relative.

■ Agreed-upon appraisals that elicit happiness include those that involve achievement, positive surprises bringing a high degree of pleasure, and satisfaction of interpersonal concerns.

Cultural Aspects of Emotion

■ Basic emotions are consistent cross-culturally; other emotions vary from culture to culture.

■ Emotions, like most concepts, can be organized into a hierarchy, consisting of (1) positive and negative (superordinate) emotions; (2) basic (midlevel) emotions; and (3) subordinate emotions, which are subcategories of basic ones.

■ Basic emotions are probably biologically determined; subordinate emotions tend to be those that vary across cultures and so are probably learned.

■ Each culture has its own social code as to how and where emotions are to be expressed.

■ Some cultural differences in emotion are reflected in language differences—for example, in vocabulary used to describe and discuss emotion.

KEY TERMS

appraisal
arousal
emotion

facial feedback hypothesis
galvanic skin response (GSR)

James-Lange theory
two-factor theory
vascular theory

CONCEPT REVIEW

1. Define *emotion*. Distinguish between basic emotions and subordinate emotions.

2. Describe the James-Lange theory. How do the James-Lange theory and Cannon's critique differ regarding the role of arousal in emotion? How does Schachter's two-factor theory resolve the difference?

3. What five problems, identified by Ekman, have prevented the development of a theory of emotions in the past? What significant change in Schachter's theory does Ekman's view require?

4. How does arousal relate to the "impulse to act"? What is the adaptive value of this relationship?

5. What contemporary evidence supports Darwin's view that emotions have a genetic basis and have survival value for our species?

6. Describe the facial feedback hypothesis and the experimental evidence supporting it. How does the facial feedback hypothesis support the vascular theory of emotions?

7. Explain the relationship between appraisal and emotions. Does appraisal imply cognitive control over emotions?

8. What is the difference between unconscious appraisal and cognitive appraisal in emotions? Is the difference merely a matter of awareness, or is there a qualitative difference as well?

9. How would James account for happiness? How would Schachter account for happiness? Use information from the chapter's in-depth examination of happiness to evaluate the James-Lange view and Schachter's view.

10. What cultural differences have been identified in emotions? Are there any universals? What evidence supports the differences and the universals?

CRITICAL THINKING

1. In light of the chapter's discussion of the role of cognitive appraisals in emotion, analyze the effects of emotions on cognitive processes like problem solving, decision making, and concept formation.

2. Does the argument that we have cognitive control over our emotions suggest that we can make intentional use of our emotions? If this is true, then do we use our emotions to manipulate others, especially when the manipulation leads toward a goal or satisfies a need? In other words, are emotions, as defined, always responses to situations, or are they also intentional acts?

...*Motivation*

Until recently, forty-two-year-old Walter Hudson was regarded as the fattest man in the world. Hudson lives in upstate New York with his brother and sister, and until 1987 he had not been out of the house in seventeen years because he had gotten too large to fit through the doors. Since then he has lost about 900 pounds, and now weighs about 500. Walter admits that overeating caused his weight problem—for breakfast, he might have two boxes of frozen sausage, one pound of bacon, one dozen eggs, and a loaf of bread. For lunch, he could eat four Big Macs, four double cheeseburgers, and eight large fries. A typical dinner would be three large ham steaks or two chickens, four baked potatoes, four sweet potatoes, and four heads of broccoli. Each meal was accompanied with six quart-size bottles of soda and most of a large cake. To get through the interval between meals, he also snacked.

All of us eat, and most of us enjoy it. What made Hudson so unusual was that he ate so much more than the rest of us. His enormous intake was driven by a motivation we share with him: hunger. In Hudson's case, the motivation seems to have gone haywire and taken over his life. Why, you might wonder, would a person eat so much? What motivates such behavior? To psychologists, the term **motivation** refers to the processes that energize, maintain, and direct behavior toward goals. These processes *regulate* behavior by initiating it when it is needed or appropriate and terminating it when the goal is reached. The case of Walter Hudson exemplifies the importance of regulation in motivation, because his eating behavior was clearly not well-controlled. He ate far more than he needed for survival, and in fact ate so much that he endangered his health.

In this chapter, we explore motivation that stems from biological needs (such as thirst and hunger) as well as acquired physiological motivations (such as drug addiction and sensation seeking) and social motives (such as self-esteem and striving to achieve). Because researchers have studied these varying motivations at different times during the history of psychology, the language they use to describe motivational processes differs. We begin by briefly considering the development of motivational theories and concepts in psychology.

MOTIVATION the processes that, taken together, energize, maintain, and direct behavior toward goals

OVERVIEW OF MOTIVATIONAL CONCEPTS

Instinct Theories

Darwin's theory of evolution, which emphasized the continuity between people and other species, had a powerful impact on early theorizing about motivation. Much of the behavior of lower animals, such as web spinning by spiders, seems to be the result of **instincts**—innate, fixed responses characteristic of a species that propel it toward some end state. Instinctive behavior is fixed, rather than flexible, because it does not depend on the state of the organism at the time of the behavior. Instincts are also irrational in that they are not under the conscious control of the individual. If instincts are the primary motivational force initiating the behavior of so-called lower animals, then, ran Darwin's argument, instincts may also motivate human behavior. Researchers began to propose instinct explanations for a wide variety of human behavior, including conformity (the "herd instinct"), isolation (the "antisocial instinct"), and many others. The proliferation of instincts (at one point more than 2500 instincts had been proposed) made it clear that the term was not particularly useful for explaining human behavior, because any behavior could be "explained" by proposing an instinct for that behavior. Psychologists have replaced the term "instinct" with "fixed action pattern," which has a more precise meaning. A **fixed action pattern** is a stereotyped and often-repeated *pattern* of movement, which is not altered by experience. Most human behavior is too flexible to be caused by fixed action patterns.

INSTINCTS the innate, fixed responses characteristic of a species that propel it toward some end state

FIXED ACTION PATTERN a stereotyped and often-repeated pattern of movement characteristic of a species and evoked by specific stimuli; not altered by experience

Walter Hudson at the beginning of his weight-loss program, when he weighed about 1400 pounds.

Drive-Reduction Theories

In contrast to instinct theories, drive-reduction theories, the origins of which are largely credited to Clark Hull, propose that the behavior of the individual depends on its physical state. In particular, **drives** are motivational states that result from physiological deficits or needs and instigate behaviors to reduce those needs. For example, an organism in a state of food deprivation is motivated by the hunger drive, and an organism in a state of water deprivation is motivated by the drive of thirst. Drive-reduction theories allow greater flexibility in behavior than theories of instincts or fixed action patterns because many different behaviors might satisfy the same drive. For example, a person who is hungry might go grocery shopping and cook dinner, reheat leftovers, order a pizza, or go out to a restaurant, all of which would result in a reduction of the hunger drive.

Biologically, the goal of drive reduction is **homeostasis**—maintaining a balanced or constant physiological state. For example, drinking to reduce thirst has the goal of maintaining a constant fluid concentration in the body's cells. The human body achieves homeostasis in much the same way a thermostat maintains a constant temperature. When the room temperature drops below the "set" or desired temperature, the furnace is turned on, and when the temperature reaches the desired level, the furnace is turned off.

Of course, with a moment's reflection it becomes obvious that much human behavior is not motivated by physiological drives such as hunger and thirst. There are no known biological needs that impel us to go to the movies, write novels, or study psychology. To accommodate such behaviors into their analysis, drive-reduction theorists proposed two types of drives—primary and secondary. *Primary drives* are based on physiological need states, and *secondary drives* are acquired or learned through their association with primary drives. For example, wanting money when you are short of cash might become a secondary drive; the need for money is not a physiological need, but it is associated with the reduction of hunger: money buys food.

Drive-reduction theories have evolved to acknowledge that behavior is controlled not only by internal states but also by external conditions, or stimuli. You might continue to study even if you were getting hungry, but if a friend set a

DRIVE a motivating state resulting from physiological deficits or a need that instigates behaviors to reduce that need

HOMEOSTASIS a constant, balanced physical state; also, the process of maintaining this state

According to drive-reduction theory, behavior is motivated by the urge to satisfy bodily needs, such as the need to get warm.

milkshake on your desk, you would probably stop studying and drink the shake; the milkshake would reduce your hunger drive if you drank it. Such external stimuli that serve as anticipated rewards for certain behaviors are called **incentives**.

Drive-reduction theories have had a major impact on psychological theorizing about motivation, and they continue to explain some types of behavior quite well. However, drive-reduction theory has been criticized on several grounds. First, the theory assumes that all motivated behavior has the goal of decreasing tension or discomfort. Yet humans engage in some behavior that seems to have the goal of *increasing* tension. For example, people watch horror films, ride on roller coasters, and consume stimulants such as caffeine and nicotine. To account for these behaviors, researchers have proposed *optimal-level theories,* which assume that we seek to maintain our level of arousal or tension at an optimal or comfortable level, much as we seek to maintain physiological homeostasis. When our level of arousal becomes too great, we engage in behaviors to reduce it, and when it drops too low, we engage in behaviors to increase it (Hebb, 1955; Berlyne, 1960). We discuss optimal-level theories in greater detail later in this chapter.

Probably because drive-reduction theories began with the assumption of continuity between humans and other species, they allow no role for higher mental processes, or cognitions, in motivated behavior. Yet as we saw in Chapter 12, the cognitive abilities of humans influence nearly all of our responses. A second criticism of drive-reduction theory, then, has concerned its mechanistic or noncognitive nature.

INCENTIVE   an external stimuli that serves as anticipated reward for a certain behavior

Cognitive Theories

EXPECTANCY-VALUE THEORY   a theory that ascribes behavior to expectations for success in relation to the value placed on that success

Expectancy-value theories are one type of theory that includes cognitive activity in motivational processes. These theories propose that behavior is the result of two types of cognitions—the individual's expectation that a behavior will result in achieving some goal, plus the value of that goal to the individual (Lewin, 1951; Tolman, 1959). For example, if you have a low expectation that studying will improve your performance in class, you will not study, according to expectancy-value theories, even if you value good performance very highly. Similarly, if you do not value good performance at tennis, you will be unlikely to practice, even if you have a strong expectation that practice improves performance. One of the many behaviors to which expectancy-value theory has been applied is achievement behavior, as we will see later on, in the section on social motivation.

Expectancy-value theories represent a significant shift in motivational theories because they place importance on cognitive determinants of behavior. The types of cognitions these theories stress, however, are limited to just two—expectancies and values, and some researchers have argued that this is too limited a role. For example, as we shall see, Bernard Weiner has developed a theory of achievement motivation that emphasizes how we explain our own successes and failures to ourselves.

Nevertheless, this transition in motivation research from mechanistic and physiologically based theories to more cognitive theories is a significant one. Indeed, it parallels the development of theoretical approaches to the study of emotion, as we saw in Chapter 12. This means that from the primary early focus on animal behaviors, motivation research has shifted to a primary concern with what we think of as uniquely human behaviors, such as achievement striving and seeking self-esteem. In the next sections of this chapter, we will consider in detail several examples of motivated behavior, ranging from the biological motivators like hunger and thirst to the search for self-esteem.

BASIC BIOLOGICAL MOTIVATION: THIRST AND HUNGER

In some basic motivational processes, internal drive states are the crucial factor. In others, external incentives play a much more important role. This difference is apparent in the contrast between the way the body regulates water balance and the way it regulates weight.

Thirst and Water Balance

Water is the principal constituent of all living cells and is essential to all physiological processes. Since water continually leaves the body in sweat, urine, and exhaled air, we must take in fluids to maintain our water balance. How do we know when the body needs water? What mechanisms regulate our desire to drink? Thirst provides a good example of a basic motive that is guided primarily by internal stimuli. Certain stimuli produce sensations of thirst, creating the desire to drink, and other stimuli reduce that desire.

Internal stimuli control the thirst drive, maintaining the body's water balance.

Inducing Thirst

The stimuli that induce drinking come from three different sources. The first is an increased salt concentration in the fluid compartments of the body—inside cells, around cells, and in the blood. Specialized cells in the hypothalamus (see Chapter 3) are sensitive to this change in salt concentration, and their activation results in the sensation of thirst. The location of these cells was discovered by implanting small tubes into various areas of an animal's brain and then stimulating the areas with very small amounts of salt solutions injected through tubes (Andersson, 1953). When cells in specific areas are stimulated—but only in these areas—an animal is driven to drink.

Another source of the urge to drink is a decrease in the volume of fluid in the circulatory system (Fitzsimons, 1961). This stimulus is not related to specific changes in chemical concentration, only to the amount of fluid. That is why severe bleeding causes intense thirst. How does the brain recognize changes in blood volume? All blood is filtered through the kidneys. If the kidneys sense a drop in blood supply or blood pressure, they release an enzyme, *renin*, that alters the structure of a substance in the blood—renin converts one substance into another substance called *angiotensin*. When angiotensin reaches the hypothalamus, it acts directly to induce drinking (Fitzsimons, 1969).

The third major stimulus for drinking is produced by the expenditure of energy or by an increase in body temperature. The mechanism involved is probably identical to that involved when the hypothalamus reacts to changes in salt concentration. Energy expenditure and increased body temperature both are followed by sweating, which takes water from the blood as it cools the body. As water is drawn from the blood, its salt concentration rises, stimulating the "salt-sensing" cells and resulting in the drive to drink.

Satiating Thirst

After a hard run, we feel thirsty and gulp down a glass of water. Long before the body has absorbed this water from the stomach and before the salt concentration of our blood has returned to normal, our thirst is quenched and the urge to drink disappears. Our system's homeostasis is still out of balance, but we cease drinking

The hunger drive is controlled by both internal and external stimuli. Thus, the amount we eat is not just a physiological reaction to hunger. At a banquet such as this—where food is attractive, plentiful, and free—we are likely to eat more than we would at an ordinary meal.

because other stimuli tell us that it is time to stop. One of these stimuli is stomach distention, which gives us the feeling of fullness. It has been suggested that cold water satisfies thirst more quickly than warm water because cold water moves out of the stomach much more slowly and so sends clearer stomach-distention signals to the brain (Deaux, 1973).

Stomach-distention signals are not the only stimuli that tell us we are sated. If a dog is allowed to drink freely but the water it drinks is prevented from reaching its stomach (diverted through an incision made in the neck for experimental purposes), the dog does not drink indefinitely. It laps up some water, then stops drinking. A little later it begins to drink again, but once more it stops. There appears to be a "mouth-metering" mechanism that gauges the amount of fluid that has been ingested, comparing it with the amount needed to restore the water balance. If the internal need is not fulfilled, internal stimuli (from one of the three sources described above) override the messages sent by the mouth, and the animal again begins to drink (Bellows, 1939).

Animals can maintain a correct water balance even when the mouth-meter is bypassed. They can learn to press a bar that sends spurts of water directly into their stomachs, and they stop pressing the bar when they are sated, even though no water passes through their mouths (A. Epstein, 1960).

We can see that several physiological mechanisms monitor and control thirst. By providing several ways to sense the need for water, these mechanisms increase the likelihood that the proper homeostatic condition will be maintained.

Hunger and Weight Regulation

With drinking, a variety of internal stimuli dominate in the regulation of a basic drive. With eating, internal and external stimuli interact to produce the desire to eat. If you have ever eaten a hot fudge sundae after a large meal, you know that internal hunger signals (such as stomach contractions) had little to do with your action. The sundae looked and tasted delicious, and these external and perceptual factors were enough to persuade you to eat it. Researchers are still working at teasing apart the interaction of external and internal factors involved in the control of eating.

Regulation of Eating

Exactly what mechanisms regulate our eating patterns? The internal mechanism we are most conscious of is the message sent by the stomach. Stomach contractions, commonly known as hunger pangs, signal that it is time to eat; stomach fullness, the distention that occurs when we have eaten enough food, signals that it is time to stop eating.

Physiological mechanisms that primarily operate outside of awareness also help regulate eating. One of these mechanisms involves levels of glucose and insulin in the blood. High glucose levels, which result from absorption of nutrients into the bloodstream, make us feel less hungry, while high insulin levels increase our hunger (Rodin, 1985). The levels of these substances in our blood seems to be monitored by the hypothalamus, a fingertip-sized brain structure whose role in eating is evidently quite complex. Damage to various parts of the hypothalamus has pronounced effects on food consumption. After damage to the lateral hypothalamus, an animal loses interest in food, suggesting that cells in this area are crucial to the onset of eating. Damage to the ventromedial hypothalamus is followed by massive weight gain, sometimes a tripling of body weight—evidence that cells in this area are crucial to sensations of satiety and to halting food intake. In addition, some neurons within the hypothalamus fire at the taste and sight of food (Rolls, Burton, and Mora, 1976).

Eating is also affected by external stimuli. Even when we have recently eaten a full meal, the sight or smell of food can trigger eating. Not everyone responds with equal strength to external food cues; those who are particularly susceptible to

EXTERNAL　a person who is especially responsive to food cues

food cues are known as **externals**. Externals are far more responsive than other people to the sight or aroma of food—as well as to other environmental cues that have nothing to do with eating. In one study, for example, people who were identified as externals ate more M&Ms after a full meal than other people did (Rodin and Slochower, 1976).

Other research has shown both the general power of external food cues over physiological hunger indicators and their power over externals in particular. For example, in one study, subjects who had fasted for 18 hours were served a juicy steak while their blood chemistry was monitored (Rodin, 1984). Even before they begin to eat, the sight and smell of the meat and the sound of it sizzling in the pan increased their feelings of hunger; their blood levels of insulin also increased dramatically. Insulin levels of those subjects identified as externals rose even higher than those of the other subjects. Such results indicate clearly that external food cues *can* affect internal physiological regulators of hunger.

Regulation of Body Weight

Mechanisms that regulate when and for how long we eat operate in the context of the body's long-term goal: the regulation of body weight. The body has a remarkable ability to maintain a steady weight. Even people who do not continually monitor their weight manage to keep it within a range of a few pounds, despite great variations in physical activity and the caloric value of the foods they eat (Keesey and Powley, 1975). This is not a uniquely human ability; laboratory animals with unrestricted access to food also regulate their body weights within a narrow range.

Maintaining a constant body weight requires a balance between calories expended and calories consumed. Most of the calories we consume in food are burned to keep our physical systems going. Some of us require more food to keep our bodies functioning than others, because people differ in their **basal metabolism rate,** the rate at which they expend calories when resting.

BASAL METABOLISM RATE　the rate at which calories are burned during rest

SET POINT　the constant weight a body seeks (seems "set") to maintain

Each person's body seems to have a **set point,** a weight that the body seems "set" to maintain. Researchers have observed that rats who have been deprived of food or have been force-fed manage to return to their set point. When semistarved rats are allowed to eat freely, they eat just enough to regain their former weight over a period of some days. Rats that have been force-fed to the point of obesity begin losing weight as soon as they are allowed to eat freely, and they keep losing until they return to their normal weight. Such studies indicate that the regulation of body weight is a matter of maintaining a balance between calories consumed and expended over a period of weeks or months, not simply day by day (Keesey and Corbett, 1983).

It has been proposed that each person's set point may be related to the number and size of fat cells in the body. Fat cells remain fairly constant in number, but increase or decrease in size as weight is gained or lost (Sjostrom, 1980). According to one theory, the fat cells secrete glycerol into the bloodstream; the increased level of glycerol informs the hypothalamus about the body's energy stores. When fat cells are relatively depleted, they secrete less glycerol, signaling that a person should increase food consumption over a period of time. When the fat cells are full, they secrete more glycerol, signaling that food consumption should be cut back. Support for the theory comes from the finding that rats injected with extra glycerol virtually stop eating (Bennett and Gurin, 1982). Thus, fat cells are apparently the source of the relatively long-term mechanism for control of eating and body weight (Kolata, 1985).

What can we hypothesize at this point about the 1000-pound-plus weight that Walter Hudson, in this chapter's opening, seems "set" to maintain, with his gargantuan appetite and eating habits? What could be askew internally? What might be said about his responsiveness to food cues? For all the knowledge that scientists have gained about hunger and eating-regulating mechanisms, it is still not absolutely clear, as you will see in the next section, why some people grow grossly—or perhaps just somewhat—overweight.

Obesity

If we have all of these mechanisms for regulating eating and body weight, why do so many people become overweight? Approximately 30 million Americans have enough excess body fat to be considered *obese* (20 percent or more over ideal body weight), and another 35 million are *overweight* (less than 20 percent over ideal body weight). Researchers have uncovered several possible explanations for excess weight gain.

Most people assume that individuals who become obese simply eat too much. But research reveals that obese people may consume no more calories than people of normal weight (Garrow, 1978; Wooley, Wooley, and Dyrenforth, 1979; Spitzer and Rodin, 1981; Thompson et al., 1982). Most obese people seem to have "energy-efficient" metabolisms: they require fewer calories to maintain a given weight level. Obese people also have higher levels of insulin, which enhances the conversion of sugar to fat, making it easier for the body to deposit fat in its fat cells. High insulin levels also contribute to psychological reasons for eating: extra insulin in the blood makes people hungrier, makes sweet foods taste better, and encourages people to eat more (Rodin, 1985). Finally, obese people may simply have more fat cells in their bodies. Once existing fat cells are filled, continued consumption of more calories than the body burns stimulates the body to make more fat cells. Sad to say, these extra fat cells do not disappear during weight loss; they simply shrink. These "starved" fat cells increase the urge to eat and regain the lost weight.

Obese people's slow, efficient metabolism, together with their large number of fat cells, have led Judith Rodin and Janice Marcus (1982) to suggest that obesity is highly adaptive in an environment where food supplies are scarce or the availability of food fluctuates. But in a food-abundant culture, such people—who are primed to overeat—find that their fuel-efficient physiology leads to obesity. In other words, obesity may no longer be adaptive.

Self-Control of Body Weight: Dieting and Exercise

"You can never be too rich or too thin," said the American-born Duchess of Windsor, and her remark reflects the high value our culture places on being slim and willowy. Americans go to great lengths, suffer extreme torment, and spend huge amounts of money in the quest to be thin. The President's Council on Fitness and Sports has estimated that in 1984 we spent $31 billion on diet and fitness. The weight-control industry is booming; since 1968, Weight Watchers alone has served about 25 million people; it is a business so profitable that Weight Watchers grossed $189 million in a single year (Thresher, 1986).

Most weight-control programs focus on dieting—restricting caloric intake as a means of reducing body weight. Since maintaining body weight depends on a balance of caloric intake and expenditure, this method of peeling off pounds seems sensible. Yet recent evidence suggests that dieting to lose weight is a strategy of limited value—and may even be counterproductive.

One consequence of a severely reduced caloric intake is increased metabolic efficiency, resulting in a lower metabolic rate—the body learns to maintain itself on fewer calories. When restricted caloric intake is the result of a natural food shortage, this is a highly adaptive response, but to a person on a diet it is enormously frustrating. The decrease in energy output caused by a lowered metabolic rate may even equal the decrease in caloric intake. Almost everyone who has tried to lose weight is familiar with the dieter's plateau, when weight stabilizes despite continued restriction of caloric intake (see Thompson et al., 1982).

Another consequence of dieting is that fat cells shrink but, as noted, do not disappear (Kolata, 1985). A person with a large number of tiny fat cells could be overweight by medical and social standards, yet be biologically starving because of the fat cells' demand to be filled. If caloric intake increases only slightly, the body uses the extra calories to fill up these starving cells. Even worse, dieting can result in the loss of lean body tissue, including muscle. The net result of a diet can be a body that is thinner but less fit.

Successful control of body weight requires regular exercise as well as a sensible diet.

Attempts to regulate weight through self-control also seem to foster binge eating. Many people try to control their weight by monitoring every mouthful of food they eat, worrying about their calorie consumption, and resisting their impulses to eat heartily. Others are unrestrained eaters, who sail through life paying little attention to the caloric consequences of their food intake. The connection between self-restraint and binge eating became clear when researchers asked students to drink milkshakes as part of an experiment (Herman and Mack, 1975). Students classified as "restrained" and "unrestrained" eaters drank either one or two milkshakes, and those in a control group drank none. Afterward, the students were asked to taste three flavors of ice cream. The more milkshakes the "unrestrained" eaters had drunk, the less ice cream they ate; but the "restrained" eaters ate *more* ice cream after drinking milkshakes than when they began the tasting with empty stomachs. The researchers concluded that restrained eaters must regard dieting as an "all or nothing" endeavor. When these people break their restraint, they seem to think, "Well, I've blown my diet, so I might as well pig out." Later research has supported the idea that a slight breakdown in control by restrained eaters is often followed by binge eating (Ruderman, 1986).

Taken together, these studies help explain why most people who successfully diet away extra pounds eventually regain the weight (Wing and Jeffrey, 1979). What we know about the effects of dieting and self-restraint certainly supports a highly pessimistic view of dieting.

Does this mean that we are doomed to live with excess weight? Recent research suggests that exercise is an effective alternative to dieting as a means of weight control. Dieting reduces our metabolic rate, but exercise increases it—not only during the exercise itself, but for up to 7 hours after we stop exercising. This means that our bodies burn more energy even when we are resting. Regular exercise also increases lean body mass (including muscle) and reduces body fat. Lean body mass is heavier for its volume than body fat, so if we exercise regularly, we may lose inches even though our weight stays the same. Replacing fat with lean tissue provides an extra benefit: compared with body fat, lean body mass burns about three times as many calories at rest (Thompson et al., 1982).

These findings offer a clear lesson for those of us who wish to lose weight: stay away from stringent diets; instead, eat well-balanced, moderate meals, and exercise regularly.

ACQUIRED MOTIVATION: STIMULUS SEEKING AND AROUSAL

Activities directed toward satisfying thirst and hunger are obviously related to basic biological needs for water and food. In contrast, many of our activities—and those of other animals as well—involve acquired or learned motivation and seem unrelated to specific biological needs. Some of our actions, things we may do for "fun" or "thrills," such as skydiving and mountain climbing, actually endanger our lives. The concept of basic biological needs also cannot adequately describe or explain self-destructive behaviors like substance abuse or drug addiction any more than they can explain human urges to explore the unknown, from the infant's curiosity about a closed box to the exploration of outer space.

We are not the only species that becomes absorbed in "unnecessary" activities. Rhesus monkeys who were given a series of mechanical puzzles (such as undoing a chain, lifting a hook, or opening a clasp) kept working at the devices until they were highly competent, despite the fact that they received no reward for solving the puzzles (Harlow, Harlow, and Meyer, 1950). To explain this unrewarded activity, researchers proposed that the monkeys were displaying a "manipulative drive." Similar studies have produced hypotheses about a "curiosity drive" (Butler, 1954) and an "exploratory drive" (Montgomery, 1954), in which activity seemed to be its own reward. Human infants and children also manipulate, explore, and learn about new things in the environment, apparently just for the fun of it.

The internal conditions that give rise to these activities are not apparent, as they are in physiological drives (Bolles, 1967). Yet these activities do have adaptive significance, because investigating and manipulating the environment generate knowledge that can be used in times of stress or danger.

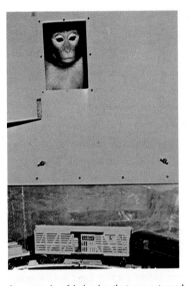

An example of behavior that cannot readily be explained by a drive-reduction model of motivation. A monkey will work hard for the privilege of viewing an electric train, but it would be difficult to say what drive is reduced as a result.

Optimal-Level Theories

One way of explaining these activities is to attribute them to a built-in tendency of organisms to seek a certain optimal level of stimulation and activity. Theories stressing this idea are called, logically, **optimal-level theories,** and resemble the homeostatic model of physiological drive reduction (Arkes and Garske, 1977). Instead of maintaining an optimal level of blood sugar or water balance, however, the organism attempts to maintain an optimal level of arousal in the brain. Maintaining this optimal level may require continually seeking out new and challenging situations. Suppose, for example, that you took up skiing in part for the excitement of it. At first, traversing the bunny slope feels exciting. As you become competent at the task, however, the bunny slope does not create the same level of arousal, and you begin to ski more challenging trails to regain the thrill.

Individuals seem to differ in the amount of stimulation they need to reach an optimum level of arousal. Psychologist Hans Eysenck (1967) has proposed that some people have a naturally high level of arousal in the brain's cortex and therefore need little additional stimulation to reach their optimal level. Eysenck believes that *introverts* belong to this group—they avoid social situations because the stimulation they bring would put them over their optimum level. Others, according to Eysenck, have a naturally low level of cortical arousal and seek stimulating experiences to bring their arousal to its optimum level. *Extroverts* belong to this group—they seek companionship, noise, and excitement to increase their naturally low level of arousal to an optimum level.

OPTIMAL-LEVEL THEORY a theory that stresses the organism's tendency to seek a certain optimal level of stimulation and arousal in the brain

Some people seem to need more stimulation than others in order to reach an optimal state of cortical arousal.

OPPONENT-PROCESS THEORY
the theory that ties motivation to two components—a primary reaction (say, fear) to a stimulus and an opposing response (say, relief) that eventually becomes the real motivating force

Research by psychologist Marvin Zuckerman supports Eysenck's theory that people differ in their general preference for stimulation. Zuckerman has studied people he calls "sensation seekers"—those who seem to need a high level of stimulation to reach their optimum level. In a survey of over 10,000 people, Zuckerman (1978) found that sensation seekers seem to have a general preference for risky activities—people who like risky sports also tend to like other intense experiences, including spicy food, hallucinogenic drugs, and a variety of sexual partners.

Opponent-Process Theory

An alternative explanation of risk-taking and self-destructive behaviors is provided by viewing them in terms of what Richard Solomon (1980) has called opponent processes. In **opponent-process theory,** two forces are involved in acquired or learned motivation: a primary process that is an intense positive or negative response to a stimulus, and a secondary process that opposes the first. If the primary process is positive, the opposing or secondary process is negative, and vice versa. The secondary process is an opposite reaction of the central nervous system that is automatically triggered by the primary process. The secondary process helps the body recover equilibrium or homeostasis after the primary process. This theory, too, resembles the physiological drive-reduction model.

According to opponent-process theory, the primary reaction starts and stops sharply; it begins with the onset of the stimulus and ends with its termination. The secondary process is more sluggish: it starts some time after the stimulus is perceived and builds slowly; then it takes time to dissipate. After several experiences with the stimulus, the pattern changes: the primary process (1) remains unaltered, but the opponent process (2) is strengthened. Figure 13.1 shows what happens when these primary and secondary processes combine: over time, the primary process becomes weak, and the secondary process has a relatively powerful effect. According to opponent-process theory, then, over time it is the secondary or opposing process that has the more powerful motivational effect on behavior.

Opponent-process theory can explain why some people habitually court danger in sports like hang gliding, auto racing, and skydiving. To put it simply, they

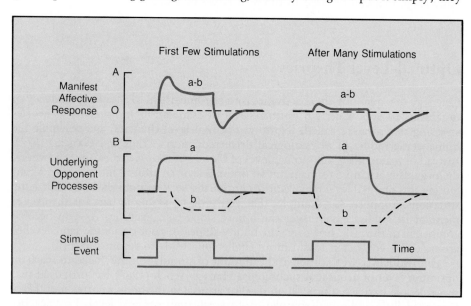

Figure 13.1 The comparison of the combined effects of the primary process (a) and the secondary process (b). The bottom panel shows the stimulus duration; the middle panel shows the component processes separately; the upper panel shows the difference between the primary (a) and the secondary (b) opponent processes. Note that the change which results from several repetitions of a given experience (good or bad) is entirely due to the changes which occur in the opponent process. The primary process remains unchanged with repeated experiences. (Adapted from Solomon, 1980.)

do it because it feels so good when they stop. During a parachutists's first jump, the predominant feeling is terror. On landing, terror is replaced by a stunned, exhilarated feeling, which lasts for several minutes, followed by normal composure. With experience, the negative emotion of fear diminishes as the person adapts to the situation, although even experienced skydivers are often anxious before a jump. On landing safely, parachutists are exhilarated; this positive emotion may last for hours and does not diminish with experience. When asked why they continue to jump, skydivers give this exhilaration as an explanation (S. Epstein, 1967).

Opponent-process theory may also explain drug addiction. A novice reacts to an opiate with a potent rush, which is succeeded by a less intense but still pleasurable state. When the effects of the drug wear off, the opponent process may leave the new user with a runny nose and eyes, sweaty hands, abdominal pressure, and muscle pains. The discomfort is interpreted as a "craving," and it disappears with another dose of the drug. This time, however, the drug produces a diminished rush and a less euphoric state, and the aftereffects may be even more uncomfortable. Abstinence from the drug may eventually result in agony. The rush represents a positive primary process; the aversive state that grows with experience represents a negative opponent process. To escape from the aversive state, the person takes more of the drug in a higher dosage and becomes increasingly fearful of allowing its effects to wear off. Whereas the skydiver jumps to experience the opponent process (it feels so good when it's over), the addict takes more drugs to avoid the opponent process (it feels so bad when it stops).

Opponent-process theory has its critics. One problem is that the theory is primarily descriptive, rather than predictive: although certain behaviors seem to fit opponent-process theory after the fact, it is difficult to specify in advance what behaviors will follow the patterns of opponent-process theory, or which motivational processes even have opponents. In addition, the physiological mechanisms that underlie opponent processes have not been specified. The opponent-process theory's explanation of drug addiction has also been challenged (see the accompanying box).

SOCIAL MOTIVATION: ACHIEVEMENT AND SELF-ESTEEM

Once we move beyond the needs that human beings share with other animals for the necessities of life, and beyond our drive-impelled behavior to obtain these necessities, human motivation becomes extremely complex. One reason for this complexity is the tremendous variation in human behavior, goals, and preferences. For one person, jogging is the road to physical health; for another, it means only aching muscles and sore feet. One person becomes absorbed in reading books and deciphering ancient manuscripts; another likes nothing better than a game of touch football. Psychologists have approached the problem of accounting for individual differences in motivation from several directions.

One approach is based on work done by Henry Murray and his colleagues in the late 1930s. Murray emphasized the role of "psychogenic," or nonphysiological, needs in determining human behavior. He accepted Sigmund Freud's idea that people express their motives more clearly when they are free-associating, saying whatever comes to mind, than when giving direct reports (see Chapter 17). Guided by clinical evidence, Murray devised the Thematic Apperception Test (TAT), in which people write or tell brief stories about pictures that show ambiguous situations. The stories are then analyzed for signs of particular motives. Using the TAT, Murray (1938) identified a lengthy list of human motives, of which achievement, affiliation, and power have been studied intensively. These motives are all *social motives*, in the sense that their satisfaction involves other people, either directly or indirectly.

PSYCHOLOGY TODAY AND TOMORROW

Why Are Some Drugs Addictive?

Opponent-process theory, along with most other theories of addiction, assumes that some drugs are addictive because repeated administration of the drug creates physiological dependence. When the drug is withheld, the person experiences the distress associated with withdrawal. To alleviate this distress, the addict takes more of the drug. Thus, dependence theories argue that people take drugs to avoid the distress of withdrawal.

This common-sense view of addiction has recently been challenged by two physiological psychologists, Roy Wise and Michael Bozarth (1987). They point out that there are several aspects of addictive behavior that *cannot* be explained by dependence theory. First, many addicts return to the drug even after they have been detoxified, or taken off the drug long enough for full physical withdrawal from it. Second, some people voluntarily abstain from taking a drug they are addicted to, even when this means they must go through withdrawal, indicating that withdrawal alone does not compel people to take drugs. Third, recent evidence suggests that the distress associated with withdrawal has been greatly exaggerated (Zinberg, Harding, and Apsler, 1978). Withdrawal from heroin is now known to cause distress comparable to a case of the flu—unpleasant, but certainly bearable. Finally, dependence theories cannot explain why people take these drugs *before* they become addicted to them.

If people don't take drugs simply to avoid withdrawal, then why do they take them? Wise and Bozarth argue that people take drugs for the reinforcing effects—because the drugs make them feel good. This idea is not new. Various addictive drugs—heroin, cocaine, amphetamines, alcohol, and nicotine—have different physiological effects that are considered pleasurable, at least by some people. But Wise and Bozarth hypothesize that there is a single reinforcing effect common to all addictive drugs, and that the physiological mechanisms associated with addiction can be located in the brain. This hypothesis is dramatically new, providing a single underlying explanation for all addictions.

Wise and Bozarth argue that *all* addictive drugs, whether they are classified as stimulants or not, act as *psychomotor stimulants*. That is, even addictive drugs that are known to depress the central nervous system, such as heroin and alcohol, also have the independent effect of stimulating mental processes that produce physical motion. The behavioral evidence of this stimulation may be overwhelmed by the depressant effects of the drugs, especially at high doses. The psychomotor stimulation appears to be the result of activation of the motor pathways of the brain. Evidence now suggests that these neural pathways may be the same ones that are sensitive to the neurotransmitter dopamine (see Chapter 3).

Why are the psychomotor effects addictive? Wise and Bozarth propose that the dopamine pathways involved in psychomotor stimulation are also the pathways involved in operant reinforcement, or reward. This means, they say, that the brain pathways that are stimulated by addictive drugs are the very same ones that are stimulated by reward seeking. The anticipation of a reward in operant conditioning produces pleasurable sensations and motivates the organism to approach the reward. What Wise and Bozarth are theorizing is that addictive drugs produce those same pleasurable sensations. Thus, the drug taker, wishing to feel that pleasure, conditions himself or herself to go through the action (drug taking) that is associated with the feeling—much as a rat in a Skinner box may learn to go through actions like approaching and pressing a lever in order to obtain a food reward.

This theory has not yet been thoroughly tested. But it is an exciting proposal that could have very important implications for the treatment of addictions.

Achievement Motivation

ACHIEVEMENT MOTIVE   the need to attain some standard of excellence

The **achievement motive** refers to the need to attain some standard of excellence; that standard is usually defined in social or societal terms. By focusing on the study of the achievement motive, we can see how human social motives are measured and analyzed and how their study can produce practical benefits.

Individual Differences in Achievement Motivation

Achievement motivation was explored intensively by David McClelland and John Atkinson (McClelland et al., 1953; Atkinson, 1958a). Their subjects looked at several pictures from the TAT, then spent several minutes writing a story that told what was happening in each picture, what led up to it, what the characters were thinking, and what would happen next. TAT stories are supposed to reflect the individual's needs, fears, and wants—feelings that may not be conscious and that normally would not be expressed. The stories are scored for achievement imagery (J. Atkinson, 1958b). In stories that score high on achievement, the main character is concerned with standards of excellence and a consistently high level of performance, with unique accomplishments (such as inventions or awards), and with the tenacious pursuit of a long-term goal or career. Stories that show fear of failure indicate low achievement motive, and the greater the fear, the lower the achievement motive. Although these types of *projective tests,* on which subjects respond to ambiguous stories in ways that reflect their own motivations and concerns, have been criticized as being unreliable, researchers have achieved acceptable levels of agreement among those who score the tests, which indicates that the tests are, indeed, reliable. A large number of studies have shown that the test is a valid and useful measure of the achievement motive.

McClelland's and Atkinson's studies found that people who showed high achievement motivation in TAT stories performed better on such tasks as anagram puzzles and addition problems than did people who made low scores. The high scorers also persisted longer at difficult tasks, were more likely than low scorers to recall interrupted tasks (the uncompleted tasks stayed on their minds), and chose "experts" as work partners in preference to "friendly" partners (because experts were more likely to contribute to success).

In one study that followed from Atkinson's work, people were given a choice of where to stand when throwing rings at a target in a ring-toss game (Weiner, 1972). Those who scored high in achievement motivation and also showed little anxiety in taking the test generally stood at an intermediate distance from the target. This position made the game challenging but not impossible. Subjects with low achievement motivation and high test anxiety stood either so close to the target that success was guaranteed or so far away that no one could blame them for missing. In daily life, people with high achievement motivation tend to pursue careers that are difficult enough to be challenging but not so difficult as to end inevitably in failure. People with low achievement motivation are less realistic. They tend to choose very easy jobs, in which success is certain, or very difficult jobs, at which they are unlikely to succeed but cannot be blamed for failing.

John Atkinson (1964) developed a general theory to explain these individual differences in achievement motivation. He argued that previous findings on individual differences in achievement motivation are consistent with an expectancy-value theory of achievement motivation, in which achievement behavior is the result of one's expectation for success coupled with the value that one places on that success.

An Attributional Theory of Achievement Motivation

Bernard Weiner (1985; 1986a; 1986b) has argued persuasively that other cognitions in addition to expectancies and values are involved in achievement behavior. Weiner maintains that the perceived causes of events related to achievement determine our motivation to succeed. In Weiner's theory, these causal attributions can be analyzed in terms of their locus, stability, and controllability (see Figure 13.2). *Locus* (from the Latin for "place") refers to where one locates the cause: Is the cause internal (within the person) or external (in the environment)? *Stability* refers to the possibility of change over time: Can the cause change, or is it stable and relatively permanent? *Controllability* refers, obviously, to degree of control: How much power, if any, does one have over the cause?

People high in achievement motivation usually attribute their performance to internal factors—their successes to high ability and intense effort, their failures to

PSYCHOLOGY TODAY AND TOMORROW

Achieving Intimacy: What Are Friends For?

One of the social motivations common to human beings is the need for intimacy—close, warm, personal interaction with others. Rare is the person who can endure life without friends to talk to, share experiences with, and lean on occasionally for support and sympathy. People do differ, however, in how much of this kind of contact with others they need. They also differ in the amount they actually seek: one problem often seen by psychotherapists in recent years is what might be called *intimacy inhibition*. In this situation, people want closeness but their need to maintain a "safe" emotional distance inhibits them from communicating freely and openly with others. The aim of therapy in such cases is to help the person feel more comfortable with the emotional demands of an intimate relationship.

One study found that people who are strongly motivated to achieve intimacy with others have different patterns of friendship from those of people for whom intimacy is less important than power in a relationship. In this study (McAdams, Healy, and Krause, 1984), subjects were divided into two groups, depending on whether they were higher in intimacy motivation or in power motivation. (The Thematic Apperception Test was used to assign subjects to one group or the other.) The subjects then answered a questionnaire about the number and nature of their interactions with their friends and completed a "friendship log" describing five friends and characterizing their relationship—explaining why they were friends, for example.

The results revealed some important differences in friendship patterns between the two groups. Intimacy motivation seemed related to what the researchers called a "communal" pattern of friendship—one that is more "expressive, self-effacing, and disclosing" (McAdams, Healy, and Krause, 1984). In contrast, subjects who were high in power motivation seemed to have a more "agentic" friendship pattern—one that is more "assertive, expansive, and self-protective." Intimacy motivation was found to be associated with being a good listener and with being willing to reveal personal information. Power motivation seemed to involve experiencing friendship as an arena in which to play a dominant, controlling role and to have an impact on others. Moreover, subjects higher in power motivation—particularly men—reported many more "friendship episodes" involving interaction with a group rather than with just one other person. This fits in with the notion that groups both lessen the pressure on any given individual to disclose personal information and offer a better opportunity for self-display and domination of others. As we might expect, subjects high in intimacy motivation reported more one-on-one friendship episodes than group interactions.

One interesting finding of this study is that intimacy or power motivation was more important in friendship patterns than were sex differences. This disputes the common notion that being a good listener and revealing one's feelings with friends is more characteristic of women than of men. The study indicated that what matters more is how motivated a person is to achieve intimacy.

lack of effort. People low in achievement motivation are more likely to attribute success to external factors such as the ease of the task or simply good luck; they tend to attribute failure to internal factors like lack of ability. Such attributions allow us to predict how successful a person expects to be when confronted again with a particular task. A person who attributes earlier success to stable factors like ability and task difficulty will expect to succeed the next time the task is undertaken. A person who attributes earlier success to unstable factors is less certain of succeeding at the next attempt—especially if luck is emphasized.

These differences in attributions explain differences in the way people approach tasks. People who choose achievement-related activities may do so because in the past they have experienced strong positive emotion after success, which they attributed to their own ability and effort. Perhaps they tend to persist in the face of failure because they believe that failure is the result of insufficient effort and that increased effort brings success. People low in achievement motivation give up easily: since, according to them, they have failed in the past because of

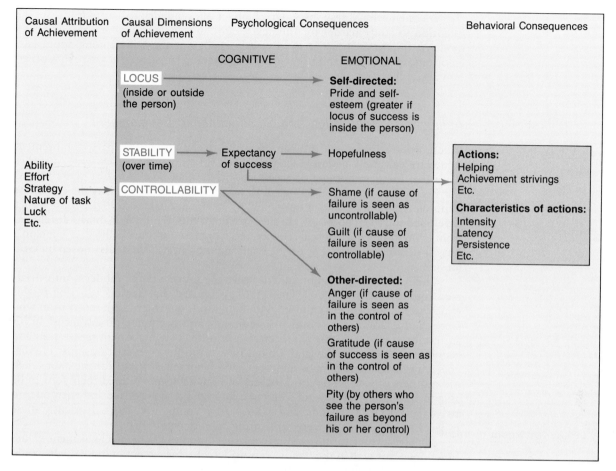

| Causal Attribution of Achievement | Causal Dimensions of Achievement | Psychological Consequences | Behavioral Consequences |

Figure 13.2 Bernard Weiner has proposed that our attributions of events relating to achievement set up a complex series of psychological and behavioral responses. The key links in this attributional chain are the causal dimensions of the achievement (whether a success or a failure)—its locus, stability, and controllability. The arrows in this diagram indicate the relationship between these dimensions and their possible psychological and behavioral consequences; each arrow may be thought of as representing the word "affects" or "influences." (Adapted from Weiner, 1985, p. 565.)

their own lack of ability, they tend to believe there is nothing they can do to bring about success—so why bother? (Brody, 1983).

As an example, imagine that you do poorly on the psychology midterm. You might attribute your performance to your lack of intelligence (an internal, stable, and uncontrollable cause), to your lack of effort (an internal, unstable, and controllable cause), to the difficulty of the test (an external, unstable, and uncontrollable cause), or to the instructor's bias (an external, stable, and uncontrollable cause). The type of attribution you make for your poor performance on the exam will affect your emotional response. If you believe that you failed because you are unintelligent, you will probably feel hopeless or discouraged. But if you believe that you failed because the test was unfair and much too difficult, you may feel anger toward your instructor. The type of attribution you make also affects your beliefs about your chances of doing better on the next midterm. If you attribute your failure to lack of intelligence, you may expect to do just as badly next time. If you attribute your failure to lack of effort, however, you may be more optimistic. Because effort is controllable, you can decide to study harder for the next exam—in other words, you will be more motivated to study. Thus, according to Weiner, the emotions you experience, combined with your expectations for future performance, determine your motivation to prepare for the next exam, which in turn will influence your actions.

Weiner's model is quite consistent with research on emotion (see Chapter 12). Like many other researchers, he views our cognitive appraisals of events as the triggers of emotional responses, which affect our tendency to act (in this case, the intention to study harder for the next exam) and our eventual actions. Weiner's model is important because it so clearly spells out the links among appraisals, emotions, motivation, and behavior. It represents a substantial advance in motivation research.

Achievement Motivation and Socioeconomic Development

Where does achievement motivation come from? At least in part, achievement values are culturally determined. Since such values may be societywide, it makes sense that the development of an entire society may be affected by these values. The notion that a society's economic development in particular may depend on its achievement values is not a new one. In 1904, German sociologist Max Weber developed such a hypothesis. He suggested that modern capitalism had developed from Protestant values of self-reliance and from the Calvinist belief that a person's success demonstrates that he or she is among the "elect," the souls chosen by God for salvation.

The so-called Protestant ethic is still very much alive in modern, industrialized countries. David McClelland (1961) proposed that parents adhering to this ethic reared independent children with high levels of achievement motivation who were then as adults responsible for economic and technological advances. In his search for evidence of this link between measures of achievement motivation and economic growth, McClelland looked first at mother–son relationships. He discovered that mothers of high achievers had higher expectations for their sons than did mothers of low achievers. Mothers of high achievers wanted their sons to be able to find their way around a city at a young age, to be active and energetic, to strive hard, to make friends, and to succeed at competitive tasks. Evidently these expectations themselves were motivating for the children.

McClelland went on to explore a larger question: if high achievement values functioned this way in the family, raising actual achievement in individuals, could these values contribute to an entire society's economic and technological development? McClelland did find correlations between achievement strivings within a society and such economic indicators as the society's consumption of electricity. McClelland used an ingenious method for measuring an entire society's achievement strivings. He analyzed and scored folk tales, stories in children's readers, speeches of leaders, poems, and plays from various societies as if they were all TAT stories. His scores enabled him to estimate societal levels of achievement motivation as far back in history as ancient Greece and found a number of striking differences among societies. Of course, such correlational studies cannot prove that differences in achievement motivation *caused* the observed economic differences, but the findings are nevertheless provocative.

One of the questions that McClelland's work raises is, if achievement motivation is in part culturally determined and essentially learned, can people be trained to be achievement-oriented? On a small scale, it seems that they can. David McClelland and David Winter (1969) found that when they trained and encouraged a group of college students to create fantasies of successful achievement, the students managed to raise their grades and improve their college performance.

Applying their model to an entire community, McClelland and Winter (1969) succeeded in raising the levels of achievement motivation among businessmen in a village in India. This program, called the Kakinada Project, consisted of encouraging businessmen to create high-achievement fantasies, to make plans that would help them realize the goals of a successful entrepreneur, and to communicate with one another about their goals and their methods of reaching them. McClelland approached the project pragmatically; his aim was to raise achievement motivation among the businessmen rather than to identify the best techniques for doing so. For that reason, he does not know exactly why his project succeeded. He does not know whether one technique worked and the others had no effect, or whether all of them helped. Nevertheless, the program was successful. The businessmen became more productive entrepreneurs, starting several industries, enlarging their business, and creating jobs for more than 5000 of their neighbors. Unlike other economic development projects, which typically have only a short-term effect, the Kakinada project seemed to have effects that lasted for over a decade (McClelland, 1978).

Intrinsic and Extrinsic Motivation

As Weiner suggested, achievements (or failures to achieve) can be attributed, among other things, to either external or internal causes. We can also analyze actions and achievement strivings by considering whether the rewards sought are internal or external. Whether we are writing a poem, studying psychology, weeding a flower bed, playing racquetball, or baking a pie, we have reasons for our actions—we expect some kind of reward, even if it is only pleasure in the action itself. Behavior undertaken for the sake of some external reward, such as money, praise, or approval, is considered to be **extrinsically** (externally) **motivated**. Behavior undertaken simply for its own sake, for the enjoyment or satisfaction it brings, is considered to be **intrinsically** (internally) **motivated** (Deci, 1975; Deci and Ryan, 1980; 1985). In some ways, extrinsically motivated behavior tends to be thought of as resembling *work*, and intrinsically motivated behavior as resembling *play*.

Extrinsically motivated behavior depends on the external conditions that support it. We persist with it only as long as the external rewards or punishments connected with it continue, and how diligently we persist depends on the magnitude of those consequences. Intrinsically motivated behavior persists despite setbacks and frustrations. Most of our daily behavior results from a mixture of both kinds of motivation. Going to college may be mostly a matter of intrinsic motivation, for the pleasure of learning. But the effort put into daily assignments may be partly motivated by extrinsic factors—high grades, praise from the instructor, admiration from peers, or approval from parents.

In some cases, extrinsic motivation can weaken intrinsic motivation, and our interest in an activity may decline. This decline in interest following extrinsic rewards for an intrinsically motivated task is known as the *overjustification effect*. There are, in other words, too many reasons for the behavior, both intrinsic and extrinsic; thus, the behavior is overjustified. In such a situation, people tend to focus on the external reason or reasons for their behavior, and the external reward itself becomes the goal, not the intrinsic reward of satisfaction or pleasure. The external cause and reward take precedence, and we persist only as long as the external reward continues. For instance, if someone who looks forward to the

EXTRINSICALLY MOTIVATED
motivated by external rewards

INTRINSICALLY MOTIVATED
motivated by pleasure in an activity for its own sake, for self-fulfillment

The same task may be regarded as work by people who are extrinsically motivated to perform it and as play by those who are intrinsically motivated.

crossword puzzle in the daily newspaper is paid several times for solving it, she is likely to do it less often once the payment has stopped. Why? Because payment has evidently made work out of play. Thus, an external incentive makes us revise our attributions for our own behavior, which then alters our intrinsic motivation (DeCharms, 1968).

Nevertheless, it is overly simplistic to suggest that rewards *always* undermine intrinsic interest in an activity. Edward Deci and Richard Ryan (1980; 1985) have suggested that rewards provide us with two kinds of information: who or what is controlling our behavior and how competent we are. If we see the rewards as reminders of external controls on our behavior, our intrinsic motivation is undermined. If, on the other hand, we see the rewards as testimony to our competence, our intrinsic motivation is reinforced. It is not the reward itself that undermines intrinsic interest, but the manner in which it is bestowed. Certainly, an artist who produces a painting and is later offered money for it will feel competent and will maintain intrinsic interest in painting. But an artist who is paid to produce a picture in a particular style may view the payment of the money as an external constraint and may indeed lose some instrinsic interest in painting (or at least in that particular style of painting—it is not yet clear to what degree the loss of intrinsic motivation generalizes to other aspects of an activity).

There are a number of other ways in which intrinsic motivation can be enhanced or undermined (Deci and Ryan, 1985). Just as it is the manner in which a monetary reward is tied to an intrinsically interesting activity that can affect that intrinsic motivation, so the specific way a supervisor at work gives feedback on performance can either enhance or undermine interest in the job (Harackiewicz and Larson, 1986). If a supervisor communicates a belief in our competence on the job, our intrinsic interest is likely to be reinforced; but if the supervisor's words or manner emphasize external justifications for working, it is likely that our intrinsic interest will be undermined. Similarly, the kinds of goals set for job performance and the way in which they are set also tend to affect intrinsic motivation (Manderlink and Harackiewicz, 1984; Harackiewicz, Manderlink, and Sansone, in press). For example, if goals are set too frequently or are too short-term, they tend to focus attention on the goal, rather than on the satisfaction of doing the work, as the reason for performing the work and can undermine intrinsic motivation. Long-term goals do not seem to interfere with intrinsic motivation in the same way (Manderlink and Harackiewicz, 1984).

The Need for Self-Esteem

Our achievement-related behavior and our intrinsically motivated behavior may both be related to a much larger, more encompassing motive—our need for self-esteem. Many psychologists have proposed that people need to feel worthwhile, competent, and positive about themselves (Maslow, 1950; Rosenberg, 1979; Greenwald, 1980; Rogers, 1980; Taylor and Brown, 1988). Within the past few years, studies have begun to illuminate the influence of this motive on what we believe about ourselves, our responses to information about our strengths and weaknesses, and our behavior in situations that might lead others to pass judgment on us. This research suggests that most people will go to great lengths to maintain a favorable view of themselves.

Beliefs about the Self

Most people have positive views of themselves; they think that they compare well with others and that they have some control over events and over their future. Indeed, these self-views are usually so unrealistically positive that researchers have described them as illusions that contribute to self-esteem (Taylor and Brown, 1988). For example, most college students see themselves as more intelligent, more competent, and more motivated than the average college student, and they

In order to maintain our self-esteem, we tend to overestimate our ability to control events. As an example, we may believe that winning a lottery is a matter of choosing the right number, not of sheer chance.

see others as less friendly and less motivated than themselves (Tabachnik, Crocker, and Alloy, 1983; Brown, 1986; Campbell, 1986). Most people see themselves in such a rosy glow that they believe their own abilities to be unique but their faults (if they think they have any) to be common and shared by others (Campbell, 1986). If they acknowledge any lack of talent or ability, they tend to dismiss the area of endeavor as unimportant.

People also overestimate the degree to which they can control events (Langer, 1975). Even when the events are entirely determined by chance, people are unrealistically positive about the extent of their influence. This *illusion of control* leads us to think that we can influence the number that comes up on a toss of dice or the winning lottery ticket. That's why people think they have a better chance in a game if they throw the dice themselves and why they go to such great lengths to pick the "right" number in state lotteries. This explanation gives us a motivational angle on the human tendency to ignore probabilities and the laws of chance. For example, the gambler's fallacy, (explained in Chapter 9), can be partially attributed to this illusion of control.

Most of us are also overly optimistic about our future (Taylor and Brown, 1988). Most people expect good things to happen to them; for example, when college students look ahead, they expect to be hired at a superior salary, to like their jobs, and, when they become parents, to have a gifted child. Yet people are more realistic about the future of others. Similarly, people expect bad fortune to strike others, not themselves. They think that others are much more likely to contract a serious illness, get mugged, have trouble finding a job, or be in an auto accident.

Our self-serving, unrealistic beliefs about ourselves and our futures seem to indicate that we are out of touch with reality. Yet these beliefs do not reflect unhealthy tendencies or mental illness of any kind. On the contrary, people who are depressed and low in self-esteem (these characteristics often go together) are the ones who seem to lack self-serving biases or distorted notions about themselves and their future, a pattern of thought called **depressive realism** (Abramson and Alloy, 1981; Tabachnik, Crocker, and Alloy, 1983; Brown, 1986). In other words, depressed people may have a more objectively realistic view of themselves and their role in the world, but this very outlook may render them *less* able to cope (see Chapter 18). Indeed, some researchers have argued forcefully that maintaining a positive view of the self is adaptive, because it helps us to persist in the face of failure (Taylor and Brown, 1988).

We noted a similar argument in our discussion of happiness in Chapter 12. Our self-esteem needs—to maintain a strong, positive, not necessarily realistic

DEPRESSIVE REALISM the pattern of thought linked to depression in which self-serving, positive biases are absent

self-image and to remain optimistic about the future despite setback—may be quite adaptive. An optimistic outlook seems to promote healing and health, to help us deal with crises, and generally to help us cope. This optimism may work in tandem with our constant reevaluations of our own happiness (including our tendencies to compare ourselves with others who are worse off and to feel dissatisfaction with a steady state of affairs) may motivate us to keep striving and to explore new options—in other words, they may spur achievement motivation.

Reactions to Information about the Self

There are a number of ways in which we manage to maintain our positive views of ourselves in the face of inevitable setbacks, failures, frustrations, and rejections. In the first place, most of the information we get about ourselves is positive. Others avoid giving us unpleasant news about ourselves and, when they are forced to do so, they tend to phrase it as gently as possible. This allows us to interpret it in the best possible light. Whenever our actions are neither clearly positive nor clearly negative, we tend to view them as positive (Taylor and Crocker, 1981).

When we do get unvarnished bad news about ourselves, we fend it off with remarkable ease (Taylor and Brown, 1988). If someone tells us we are rude or careless or inept, we tend to perceive the information as inaccurate, since it just doesn't fit the picture we have of ourselves. Faced with outright failure, most people deny responsibility—even though they are quick to take credit for their successes (Bradley, 1978). Normal people tend to attribute the good things that happen to them, such as getting a job or a good grade on an exam, or being liked by others, as due to their own positive qualities. But they see their setbacks, such as failing an exam or being fired from a job, as due to something outside themselves (Tennen and Herzberger, 1987). Whenever we fail, we seem able to come up with a variety of excuses (Snyder, Higgins, and Stuckey, 1983).

SELF-HANDICAP a deliberate self-destructive behavior that serves to protect one's favorable self-image and to avoid self-blame for failure

Behavior That Protects Self-Esteem

The motive to maintain or increase self-esteem has as many implications for the way we behave as it does for the way we think about ourselves. We go out of our way to avoid situations that could provide clear evidence of our shortcomings. Even such potentially destructive behavior as drinking alcoholic beverages and taking drugs can be used to protect our favorable views of ourselves. Some psychologists have argued that such behavior becomes a deliberate **self-handicap** in uncertain situations (Jones and Berglas, 1978). Someone who isn't sure of success, as when faced with an important job interview, may have several drinks before the appointment. If he doesn't land the job, he can use the drinking as an excuse. Being able to say, "I would have done better if I hadn't been drinking," protects his self-esteem. Should he succeed *despite* the self-imposed handicap, he can feel particularly good about himself. Self-handicapping is related to the desire to take credit for success and avoid blame for failure. A person who succeeds at a task despite drinking may feel particularly competent; but if he fails, he can always blame the alcohol.

Maintaining Self-Esteem When Outperformed

Our need to believe in our competence means we must figure out a way to handle situations in which others' performance is clearly better than our own. Abraham Tesser and his colleagues (Tesser and Campbell, 1983; Tesser, 1986; 1988) pointed out that superior performance by others can have two possible consequences for self-esteem: we may either take pride in others' accomplishments or feel upset because they clearly surpassed us.

In the first case, when someone we know displays a remarkable achievement, we bask in his or her reflected glory (Cialdini et al., 1976; Cialdini and Richard-

When "our" team wins a championship, we may boost our self-esteem by taking pride in the team's achievement—especially if our own lack of skill at the sport is not important to us.

son, 1980). For example, college students are more likely to talk about their football team in the first person ("*We* won") and to wear clothing with their school's colors on Mondays after a football victory than they are on Mondays after a loss. It is as if they want to emphasize their connection to a winning, but not to a losing, team (Cialdini et al., 1976). In the second case, another's remarkable achievement only brings us pain. For example, when a close colleague wins an award that you have coveted or a friend gets into a college that has rejected you, your self-esteem may very well suffer.

How can we predict whether someone will feel pride or chagrin at the successes of others? Tesser argues that two factors determine our reactions. One is the *relevance* of the achievement to our own self-definition; the other is the degree of *closeness* between ourselves and the achiever. When a person outperforms us in a domain that is important to us, we feel the pain of social comparison. But when the other person's achievement is in an area that we regard as irrelevant to us, we can feel pride in the achiever. For example, when a friend gets a part on a soap opera, you are likely to feel proud if you do not aspire to be an actor, or upset if you do but have not had comparable success. Closeness also determines the intensity of the pride or pain. A superior performance by your best friend, your sibling, or your spouse clearly has a greater impact on your feelings about yourself than a superior performance by someone you know only slightly (Salovey and Rodin, 1980).

In a series of experiments, Tesser has shown that people often adjust their closeness to another so as to make it easier to bask in reflected glory or to avoid painful social comparisons. That is, we try to increase either the psychological or physical distance between ourselves and someone who outperforms us in a self-relevant area. We may decide the other person is not, after all, such a good friend, or we may actually move away physically from the other person.

When there is no way to adjust closeness, people generally adjust their self-definitions in order to avoid painful comparisons. College students who had been outperformed by a close friend indicated that the skill on which they had been surpassed was not actually important to them (Tesser, 1988; Rosenberg, 1979). If your best friend always beats you at tennis, you may maintain the friendship by deciding that you don't really care much about tennis. Suddenly, being good at tennis is no longer part of your self-definition. In achievement motivation terms, you would assign a lower value to tennis and be less motivated to play and succeed at it.

What Tesser has discovered about the effects of being surpassed has implications for family life. Family members' accomplishments can affect other members' sense of self. When one sibling outperforms another, especially when they are close in age, the surpassed child may suffer intensely or glow with pride. When siblings share the same goals and aspirations, the pain of social comparison on being consistently outperformed may drive them apart. Tesser believes that such negative comparison can be avoided if parents encourage each child to develop a unique definition of self—especially when it comes to skills and activities. If one child is absorbed in baseball, the other might be steered to swimming or soccer. When activities that are important to siblings' self-definition do not overlap, none of the children are threatened by the others' successes, and all can take pride in the family's accomplishments (Tesser and Campbell, 1983).

How Social Motives Regulate Behavior

Social motives seem to be a potent influence on our interactions with others, but none of the explanations we have considered describes how this influence is actually exerted. In the case of biologically based drives, such as hunger and thirst, physiological mechanisms control behavior. But there are no physiological mechanisms connected with social motives. How do we cease our striving to achieve when it is time to eat or simply time to relax and have some fun?

Behavioral Self-Regulation

BEHAVIORAL SELF-REGULATION
monitoring and adjusting our own
behavior in relation to our goals, values, standards, and concerns

Psychologists Michael Scheier and Charles Carver (1988) believe that we engage in a form of **behavioral self-regulation**. Periodically, we monitor our behavior and compare it with our goals, values, or concerns. During the comparison process, we appraise our behavior to determine whether or not it is taking us toward our goal or meeting some standard. If it is not, we are thrown into an unpleasant emotional state, which motivates us to reduce the discrepancy between our goals and our behavior by adjusting our actions. (Of course, we can also reduce the discrepancy by reinterpreting our goals, as discussed in Chapter 12. Scheier and Carver are concerned primarily with alteration of behavior.)

Scheier and Carver suggest that this comparison occurs whenever we engage in self-reflection or suddenly pay attention to ourselves. Suppose you are walking down the street and happen to glimpse your reflection in a store window. The slumped, untidy figure you see does not at all match your self-image. If you are like most people, you adjust your clothes, smooth your hair, correct your posture, or pull in your stomach—trying to bring your appearance into line with your goals or standards. When we become self-conscious, a comparison between our behavior and our standards is triggered, which then leads to an emotional response. If our behavior is not up to standard, the emotion leads to an attempt to bring our behavior into line.

Such a model of self-regulation is compatible with the research on emotions explored in Chapter 12. In the case of self-regulation, the person—with goals, concerns, values, and standards—momentarily becomes aware of the self. This awareness serves as a trigger; the perceived self is appraised, and the appraisal is followed by some emotional response to the self (pride, if the person meets the standards; shame, guilt, or embarrassment, if not). The emotional response generates a tendency to act—to attempt to reduce or eliminate any discrepancy between behavior and the standard.

An earlier study by Carver (1974) is generally seen as lending support to Scheier and Carver's model. In this study, the researcher observed college students engaged as teachers in what they thought was a concept-formation task. Their job was to punish another student for errors in learning the concepts. Some of the students already had indicated that they believed in the effectiveness of punishment as a teaching tool; the rest believed that punishment was not effective. Among students who carried out their task in a room where a small mirror hung on the wall, those who believed in the effectiveness of punishment used a great deal more punishment than those who did not believe in it. But among students who carried out their task in a room without a mirror, there was little difference in the amount of punishment dealt out. The presence of the mirror was designed to induce self-attention or self-reflection, and its effect was in line with the model of behavioral self-regulation. Apparently, only when the mirror led students to think about their behavior did their standard of nonpunitiveness influence their behavior. (See Figure 13.3.)

Goal and Need Hierarchies

Behavioral self-regulation explains how motivation that has no biological basis can guide and regulate behavior. Thus far, we have looked at the self-regulation model in relatively simple terms and in rather straightforward situations. Most human actions, of course, are fairly complex. Consider the case of Michael, a young man who is searching for a compatible marriage partner. He has found an attractive woman and is courting her. But Sally repeatedly rebuffs him, thus creating a discrepancy between his current state and his goal of marriage. Michael will not continue indefinitely to try to win her love. Eventually, he will abandon his efforts and look for another, more receptive woman.

Scheier and Carver explain this more complicated situation by viewing human goals as ordered hierarchically. They contend that people have *superordinate* goals, which are abstract, long-term goals: becoming an engineer, getting married, having children. But people also have more specific, *subordinate* goals to help

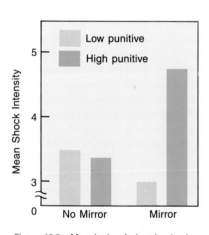

Figure 13.3 Magnitude of electric shock given by subjects to an experimental accomplice during a bogus learning task, as a function of self-directed attention and their attitudes toward the use of punishment. (Adapted from C. S. Carver, Facilitation of physical aggression through objective self-awareness. *Journal of Experimental Social Psychology,* 1974, *10,* 365–370.)

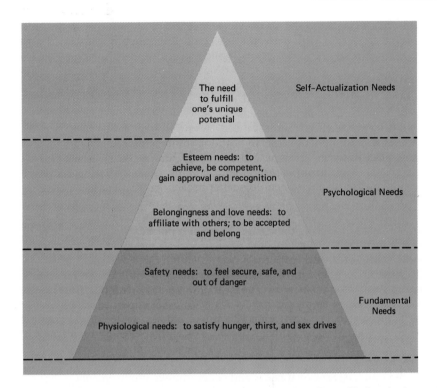

Figure 13.4 This pyramid represents Maslow's hierarchy of needs. According to Maslow, fundamental needs must be satisfied before a person is free to progress to psychological needs, and these in turn must be satisfied before a person can turn to self-actualization needs. Maslow (1970) later added a need for transcendence that is even higher than the need for self-actualization. (After Maslow, 1971.)

them in their quest for the broader superordinate goals. In the case of Michael, his superordinate goal is marriage, and his subordinate goal is to persuade Sally to marry him. In the face of repeated failure to achieve the subordinate goal, he can substitute a different subordinate goal—finding a more agreeable partner. When construed this way, the model can account for the great flexibility we show in our goal-directed behavior. Most people have several superordinate goals. These may be ordered and analyzed in terms of overall significance, or they may be ordered chronologically, according to which goal takes priority at what time.

The notion of a hierarchy of goals has been proposed by other psychologists, most significantly by Abraham Maslow (1954). Maslow suggested a way in which motives as diverse as biologically based hunger, achievement motivation, and the need for self-esteem can be organized into a single hierarchy.

Maslow believed that the hierarchy of human motives, or needs, formed a pyramid. The base of the pyramid is made up of **basic needs,** physiological motives such as thirst and hunger. The intermediate level consists of psychological motives such as love and self-esteem (see Figure 13.4). Motives at these two intermediate motivational levels are also known as **deficiency needs;** when they are not met, people seek to satisfy them in whatever way is feasible. Deficiency needs, in other words, are motivating when they are *not* met. Failure to fulfill these needs— failure to attain a feeling of security, social acceptance, or self-esteem—can produce profound pathological discomfort and maladjustment that may be almost as debilitating as physical starvation. The highest motives in Maslow's hierarchy, called **metaneeds,** include needs for intellectual accomplishments, creativity, justice, *self-actualization* (which is Maslow's term for the fulfillment of the individual's potential), and, finally, transcendence (a spiritual sense of peace, belonging, and oneness with the universe).

According to Maslow, when a lower need is not fulfilled, it takes precedence over any higher needs. Extreme hunger or thirst is so urgent that severely deficient individuals have no opportunity to worry about social acceptance or self-esteem, let alone the creative exercise of their talents. Similarly, people whose basic needs

BASIC (DEFICIENCY) NEEDS the physiological needs in Maslow's hierarchy

METANEEDS the highest needs in Maslow's hierarchy

are filled but who continually seek social acceptance are not free to create scholarly or artistic works. But once the lower need is reliably fulfilled, the person moves on to the next level of needs, which then assume priority.

Little research has been done to test Maslow's hierarchical concept of motivation. His theory predicts, for example, that altruism is impossible unless the needs for love and belonging are satisfied. If this is true, then children who are still engaged in satisfying their basic needs for safety would be less likely to help others than children who are further advanced. Using in-depth interviews, researchers have found some support for this hypothesis among children with a wide range of psychological disorders (Haymes, Green, and Quinto, 1984). Research on other aspects of Maslow's theory is scarce, although his influence has been strongly felt in the humanistic or phenomenological approach to treatment.

The theory has had its critics. The ordering of needs is somewhat arbitrary, and some behavior clearly contradicts the theory. For example, some people go on hunger strikes, starving themselves to make a political point; and the poor give a higher percentage of their income to charity than the wealthy, a finding that is difficult to reconcile with Maslow's need hierarchy.

Maslow's concept of motivation is nevertheless useful in drawing attention to the complexity of human motivation. It illuminates an important issue in the regulation of behavior: people have several different superordinate goals—to be well fed, to be satisfied with respect to thirst and sex, to feel good about themselves, and so on. Maslow's theory provides us with a set of hypotheses about the precedence of different goals when they compete to control behavior. The theory also emphasizes, and thus reminds us of, the aspects of human motivation that extend beyond basic survival needs and economic accomplishments—that extend, in other words, into the most complex areas of human behavior.

SUMMARY

Overview of Motivational Concepts

▪ Early theories of motivation focused on instincts and drive reduction and dealt primarily with biologically based behavior. More recent cognitive theories ascribe complex human behavior to expectations, values, and needs for achievement and self-esteem.

Basic Biological Motivation: Thirst and Hunger

▪ The three major stimuli inducing thirst are increased salt concentration in body fluids; decreased amount of fluid in the circulatory system; and energy expenditure or increased body temperature, both of which result in sweating.
▪ The two major stimuli that indicate thirst satiation are stomach distention and "mouth-watering" mechanisms that gauge the amount of ingested fluid.
▪ The mechanisms that regulate eating are, internally, stomach contractions and distention and, outside awareness, monitoring of glucose and insulin levels in the blood by the hypothalamus. External stimuli also affect eating; the sight and aroma of food act as cues to which some people are more vulnerable than others.
▪ Organisms tend to maintain a fairly constant body weight; this weight, or set point, may be related to the number and size of fat cells in the body.
▪ There are several possible explanations for obesity, in addition to overeating. Obese people require fewer calories to maintain a given body weight; have higher insulin levels, which encourage eating and fat deposits; and may have more fat cells than others. Obesity may be the result of a no-

longer useful adaptation to scarce food supplies.
▪ Dieting and self-restraint in terms of eating may be of limited value in losing weight. Exercise is a more effective means of keeping unneeded pounds off.

Acquired Motivation: Stimulus Seeking and Arousal

▪ Optimal-level theories relate behavior to a need for a given level of stimulation and activity. Individuals differ in their preferred arousal levels and in what kind of and how much stimulation they require.
▪ According to opponent-process theory, humans may engage in risk-taking and self-destructive behaviors, including taking addictive drugs, because a secondary, opposing process occurs to balance the initial response to a stimulus. The return to balance becomes the motivating force.

Social Motivation: Achievement and Self-Esteem

▪ Motivation to obtain some standard of excellence has been one of the most studied aspects of social motivation. Achievement motivation is measured using the Thematic Apperception Test.
▪ In contrast to people with low achievement motivation, those with high achievement motivation attempt harder tasks, persist longer, and choose goals that are challenging but not overwhelmingly difficult. They do not court failure, as those with low achievement motivation seem to do.

■ People seek to attribute their successes and failures to specific causes, which can be analyzed as internal or external and more controllable or less controllable. Attributions affect expectations for future performance.

■ Achievement strivings can be analyzed as extrinsically (for some reward) or intrinsically (for enjoyment or satisfaction) motivated. Extrinsic motivation can sometimes undermine intrinsic motivation, producing the overjustification effect.

■ The need for self-esteem may be a very powerful, encompassing need, governing both achievement and intrinsic motivation.

■ People generally strive to maintain an overall positive self-image by overestimating their control over the future and avoiding situations that reveal shortcomings.

■ People's reactions to others' accomplishments depend upon the relevance of the achievement to their own ambitions and the relative closeness they feel to others. People adjust this

degree of closeness, if possible, to increase vicarious glory or decrease painful social comparisons. If this is not possible, they adjust their own self-definition.

■ We regulate our own behavior by periodically assessing it in relation to our goals and values. A great discrepancy produces emotional discomfort, which motivates us to reduce that discrepancy and bring our behavior into line.

■ Human goals can be viewed hierarchically, divided into superordinate and subordinate goals. Our ability to alter and interchange subordinate goals accounts for some of the flexibility of human behavior.

■ Maslow's hierarchy of needs consists of basic physiological needs, intermediate deficiency needs, and metaneeds. According to Maslow, an unfulfilled lower need takes precedence over higher needs until satisfied.

KEY TERMS

achievement motive	externals	intrinsically motivated
basal metabolism rate	extrinsically motivated	metaneeds
basic needs	fixed action pattern	motivation
behavioral self-regulation	homeostasis	opponent-process theory
depressive realism	incentives	optimal-level theory
drive	instincts	self-handicap
expectancy-value theory		set point

CONCEPT REVIEW

1. Name the various processes that might be included when a psychologist refers to "motivation."

2. Distinguish between *instinct* and *drive*. What components are missing from instinct and drive theories but are crucial to a cognitive theory of motivation?

3. Describe the manner in which various physiological mechanisms are coordinated to maintain the body's water balance.

4. Identify the roles of internal and external stimuli in the recognition of hunger, the maintenance of body weight, and the development of obesity. How does activity like exercise affect these two kinds of stimuli?

5. How do behaviors like the unrewarded puzzle-solving of rhesus monkeys provide evidence in support of optimal-level theories? What is the hypothetical relationship of introvert and extrovert traits to optimal-level theories?

6. Explain the opponent-process theory of motivation. How can this theory account for addictive behaviors?

7. Distinguish social motivation from the physiologically oriented theories discussed in the first half of the chapter.

8. Outline the factors that may influence an individual's motivation to achieve. How can one alter one's achievement motivation?

9. Identify the factors that would affect intrinsically motivated behavior. Extrinsically motivated behavior?

10. Describe the ways in which our awareness of self may affect our motivation. How does self-esteem affect this relationship between self and motivation?

11. Outline the various goal and need hierarchies described in the chapter. How do these hierarchies help us account for social motivation?

CRITICAL THINKING

1. This chapter divides motivation into two distinct approaches, one proposing a biological basis for behavior and the other a social basis. Are these two views necessarily incompatible? Present several examples of behavior in which both biological and social motivation may be at work.

2. In what ways do the theories of operant and classical conditioning function as theories of motivation as well? Which of the theories presented in this chapter are most closely aligned with the behavioral approach? How does the discussion illustrate the ways in which concepts like behavioral self-regulation, intrinsic motivation, and opponent process depend on principles of conditioning?

...........Sexuality

.....*Sexuality and Love*

Love and sex, sex and love: we think of the two as so closely connected, it is difficult to talk of one without at least mentioning the other. When researchers asked college men and women the basis on which they chose their sexual partners, most gave answers that stressed love and emotional commitment (Allgeier et al., 1988). A well-known sex researcher, John Money, argues that the inability to form romantic love attachments is one of the roots of aberrant sexual behavior (Holden, 1988): when people never learn to associate sex with love, they may come to derive their sexual pleasure in abnormal ways. This is not to say that sex never occurs outside of love. Certainly it does. But the capacity to combine love and erotic pleasure, at least on some occasions, is a sign of healthy psychological adjustment.

SEXUALITY   all the factors that contribute to a person's ability to give and receive erotic pleasure

In this chapter we discuss both sexuality and love. **Sexuality** is all the factors that contribute to a person's ability to give and receive erotic pleasure. We begin with a look at the development of sexual identity. We then turn to a discussion of human sexual responses: the extent to which these responses are influenced by hormones, the stimuli that people find sexually arousing, the four phases of the sexual response cycle, and some of the sexual problems that people can experience. Next we examine the range of sexual behavior in our society, including the impact of the AIDS crisis. We conclude the chapter with a look at sex, intimacy, and love.

THE DEVELOPMENT OF SEXUAL IDENTITY

[When I was a little girl,] I always felt like a little boy, and used to dress up in boys' clothing. Mom called me a tomboy but I knew I wasn't a tomboy. I was a boy. (Fleming and Feinbloom, 1984, p. 731.)

SEXUAL IDENTITY   a person's sense of being male or female

An important part of a person's sexuality is his or her sense of being male or female—that is, a sense of **sexual identity.** Sexual identity refers to the patterns of *sexual* behavior associated with being either male or female; in contrast, a person's *gender identity* reflects the *social* behavior associated with masculinity or femininity. We discuss gender identity in Chapter 15; in this section we look at how the development of sexual identity is influenced by genetic and hormonal factors, as well as social ones.

Prenatal Sexual Development

A person's genetic sex is determined at conception by one of the chromosomes in the father's sperm, which may be either an X (female) or a Y (male). Since all the mother's eggs contain one X chromosome, an egg that is fertilized by an X-bearing sperm will have two X chromosomes and develop into a girl. An egg that is fertilized by a Y-bearing sperm will have one X and one Y chromosome and develop into a boy.

In the first few weeks after conception, the sexual development of males and females is the same. Sexual differentiation begins around the sixth week, when testes start to form in male embryos. The testes produce male hormones, which, in turn, trigger the development of male external genitals. If male hormones are absent or insufficient, the embryo (regardless of its chromosomal makeup) will develop female-looking genitals. The same is true of brain development. Without male hormones, the hypothalamus will be set to maintain the female-style, cyclical production of sex hormones. With male hormones, in contrast, the hypothalamus will be set to maintain continual production of sex hormones.

There are times, however, when this developmental pattern goes awry and an embryo with the chromosomes of one sex is exposed to the hormonal influences of the other. For example, because of malfunctioning adrenal glands or drugs the mother is taking, a female embryo may be exposed to high levels of male sex

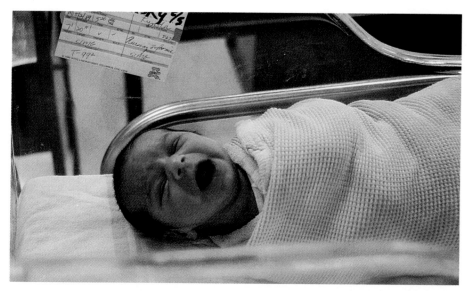

Powerful social influences on our sexual identity begin the moment we are born.

hormones. The result is a genetic female with male-looking genitals. Conversely, the body cells of a male embryo sometimes fail to respond to male hormones, a condition called *androgen insensitivity syndrome*. In this case, the baby is born genetically male but with a female external anatomy. These children may be raised as boys or girls, depending on what their appearance dictates. Often their abnormal condition is not discovered until adolescence, when they fail to develop the "appropriate" signs of sexual maturation. These unusual cases of children assigned to the wrong sex as babies provide a way of assessing the relative importance of social and biological influences on sexual identity.

Assessing Social and Biological Influences on Sexual Identity

The social influences on sexual identity begin at the moment of birth when the doctor announces "It's a boy" or "It's a girl." From that time on, people help shape the child's sense of being male or female. They encourage the child to behave in "appropriate" ways and to develop an image of the self as either masculine or feminine. Are these social forces powerful enough to overcome biological influences? Can a genetic male be successfully encouraged to think of himself as a girl, or a genetic female to think of herself as a boy?

Studies of children assigned to the opposite sex as babies have helped provide some answers. In one study, for instance, nine out of ten genetic males who had androgen insensitivity syndrome and were raised as girls developed a secure female identity (Green, 1981). This suggests that the social influences on sexual identity are indeed very strong.

Not all such sexual reassignments are successful, however. Consider the case of a baby boy whose genitals were accidentally mutilated to the point where he would never be able to function as a normal male (Money and Ehrhardt, 1972). When he was seventeen months old, doctors performed surgery to change his anatomical sex to female. From then on the parents raised the child as a girl. At age four, the youngster was unmistakably feminine. She played with dolls, was proud of her ruffled dresses, and otherwise behaved like a "typical" girl. She seemed to be developing a female sexual identity, while her twin brother was developing into a "typical" boy. It seemed at this point that social influences had overcome the effects of genes and prenatal hormones. By age thirteen, however, despite treatments with female hormones, this child had developed a masculine gait and was called "cave woman" by other youngsters. She wanted to become a mechanic, and her fantasies showed some discomfort with her female role. Psychiatrists reported that she was not a happy child. At the age of sixteen she was having considerable trouble adjusting to life as a young woman (Diamond, 1982). As this case indicates, we cannot say that the social influences on sexual identity are always able to eradicate the combined influences of genes and prenatal hormones. In many instances the biological factors continue to have some effect.

Another piece of evidence in support of this view comes from a condition called Guervodoces syndrome, which has been observed in several dozen males in the Dominican Republic. An enzyme deficiency prevents genetically normal boys from having normal male genitals at birth. As babies and young children, they look like girls and are raised as such. At puberty, their genitals suddenly masculinize, and their gender identities seem to make a corresponding switch. Exactly how this phenomenon occurs is not yet known, but the role of male hormones is strongly implicated (Bancroft, 1984).

The influence of hormones on sexual identity must be complex, however. Simply being exposed to the hormones of one sex or the other is not usually enough to cause identification with it. For example, a study of girls who were accidentally exposed prenatally to abnormal levels of male hormones showed that most grew up to think of themselves as women. Yet these children were born with masculinized features that required corrective surgery, including a greatly enlarged clitoris that resembled a penis. As children, none of them was "ultra-feminine." All preferred boys as playmates, dressing in jeans to wearing dresses, outdoor games and sports to playing with dolls, and fantasizing about future careers instead of marriage. But the girls' behavior was within acceptable "tomboy" limits, and most expected to fall in love with and marry a man. In short, they appeared to have developed female sexual identities (Ehrhardt and Meyer-Bahlburg, 1981). This finding suggests that sex hormones may incline us toward behaviors sometimes considered masculine or feminine. But whether we come to see ourselves as a man or a woman is also strongly influenced by what we are taught to think.

Inconsistent Sexual Identity: The Case of Transsexualism

TRANSSEXUALISM a condition in which people develop a sexual identity that is inconsistent with their genetic and anatomical sex

Transsexualism is a rare condition in which people develop a sexual identity that is inconsistent with their genetic and anatomical sex. The young woman we quoted at the beginning of our discussion of sexual identity is one example. Despite the fact that physically she was a female, she thought of herself as a boy. Transsexuals often say they feel trapped in the body of the wrong sex. Male transsexuals think of themselves as women and want heterosexual (not homosexual) relations with men, while female transsexuals think of themselves as men and want heterosexual (again, not homosexual) relations with women.

Transsexuals, most of whom are male, sometimes request surgery to "correct" their anatomies. For men, this involves removing the testes and most of the penis and constructing a vagina from the remaining tissue. A series of hormone treatments reduces body hair and encourages the development of breasts, which can be further enlarged by silicone implants. For female transsexuals, surgery involves removal of the breasts and uterus and construction of an artificial penis, accompanied by male hormone treatments to encourage muscle development, the growth of facial hair, and a lower pitch to the voice. Although male-to-female transsexual surgery produces fairly normal-looking and -functioning female genitals, the female-to-male operation has been less successful. The surgically created penis rarely looks or functions like that of a genetic male.

The advisability of sex-change surgery has recently been called into question. Some psychiatrists argue that transsexuals who receive these operations are no better adjusted than those who do not; for this reason Johns Hopkins University, which once had a major program for transsexual surgery, has now stopped the practice. Others contend that when candidates for sex-change operations are carefully screened beforehand and adequately counseled afterward, they adjust well to their new anatomies.

Renée Richards, ex-tennis pro and former coach of Martina Navratilova, is a well-known and successful transsexual. However, many transsexuals continue to have adjustment problems after their gender change.

Richard Green (1982a), who has studied transsexuals extensively, believes that both prenatal hormones and early social influences are probably involved in the development of the condition. But exactly what social influences foster transsexualism is not yet certain. It is not simply a matter of children mimicking adults around them, because the children of transsexuals develop gender identities just like those of children with conventional parents (Green, 1978). We are still quite a long way from explaining this unusual condition.

HUMAN SEXUAL RESPONSES

It's funny because all your life all that stuff is wrong and you're not supposed to let a boy touch you, and then the priest says something and all of a sudden everything is supposed to be all right. But my wedding night was terrible and I cried and cried because I didn't know what I was supposed to do and it did not seem right. (DeLora and Warren, 1977, p. 197)

The so-called sexual revolution of the 1960s and 1970s brought more openness about sex into our society. Books on sexual techniques became best sellers, mainstream publications allowed more explicit references to sex, and TV and radio talk shows explored sexual topics. Despite this new frankness about sexual matters, many Americans remain poorly informed about sex and reproduction. One recent survey showed that the majority of adults do not know the answers to such basic questions as when during the monthly cycle a woman is most likely to become pregnant and what ovulation is (*Psychology Today*, April 1989). This lack of knowledge exists even among many college-educated people. In this section we outline some fundamental facts about human sexual responses.

The Bases of Sexual Responses

Human reproductive physiology is similar to that of other mammals, but human sexual responses are markedly different. In most other species, sexual activity is tied to the female reproductive cycle. The hormones that induce ovulation (the release of a mature egg, ready to be fertilized) also cause changes in the female's behavior, known as **estrus** or, colloquially "heat." The female rat, for example, goes into estrus about every fifteen days, during which she will mate with any and every available male. When not in estrus, however, she will kick and scratch any male that attempts to mount or nuzzle her. (McClintock and Adler, 1978)

And so it is with most animal species. Throughout the animal kingdom, hormone cycles usually determine when sexual activity will occur, and instincts guide the positions and techniques that are used. Among the apes and monkeys, our closest relatives, hormonal control of sexual behavior is less powerful than in rats. Females of these species occasionally mate when they are not in estrus, perhaps to appease a dominant male or to maintain a relationship with a male companion. But such mating out of season is relatively rare.

The human female is sexually unique. Unlike the females of other species, she may invite or refuse sex any day of the month, any month of the year. Some women report that during the middle of the menstrual cycle, when they are ovulating and most likely to be fertile (that is, to become pregnant), they are more easily aroused, more likely to initiate intercourse, and more apt to experience orgasm. Many others say they feel more interested in sex just before or after menstruation, when conception is very unlikely (McCauley and Ehrhardt, 1976). Still others report no relationship between their interest in sex and their phase in the menstrual cycle. Looking for a connection between ovulation and sexual responsiveness, researchers asked women to listen to erotic tapes at different points in their menstrual cycles while their levels of arousal were assessed (Hoon, Bruce, and Kinchloe, 1982). There was no mid-cycle peak in arousal. Indeed, there was no pattern of any kind.

This finding suggests that female hormones are unrelated to a woman's sexual interest, and other evidence supports this conclusion. Removal of the ovaries, or female sex glands (the source of **estrogen,** the principal female hormone), does not diminish sexual interest or satisfaction (Waxenberg, 1969). Similarly, women who take estrogen for medical reasons experience no increase in sexual arousal (Sopchak and Sutherland, 1960). Female hormones, in other words, serve reproductive functions, not sexual ones.

This is not true of the principal male hormone, **testosterone.** A minimum level of testosterone seems to be needed for normal male arousal. Men with a genetic predisposition for very low testosterone levels tend to be infertile and to lack interest in sex. When these men are given testosterone, they often have sexual fantasies, show sexual interest, and become sexually active (Rubin, Reinisch, and Haskett, 1981). Many men whose testes (the major source of testosterone) have been removed suffer a gradual decline and disappearance of sexual responsiveness. However, some men who lack testes remain sexually active for years (Heim, 1981). Perhaps in them the adrenal cortex, a secondary source of male sex hormones, produces enough testosterone to maintain sexual functioning.

What about men with high testosterone levels? Do they have stronger than normal sex drives? Very often they do. Moreover, high levels of sexual activity are associated with high levels of testosterone in women as well as in men (Offir, 1982). (In women this testosterone is produced by the adrenal cortex.) But it is not clear whether this relationship means that greater amounts of testosterone *cause* higher levels of sexual arousal and activity. It is just as likely (as some studies have shown) that sexual arousal and activity stimulate the production of testosterone (Rosen and Hall, 1984).

Although testosterone seems to be involved in the male sexual response, many other factors are too. In fact, among men as well as women, biology is far less important than cultural norms, social experiences, and psychological factors in determining the who, where, when, and why of sexual behavior. This explains the diversity of sexual practices among human beings, despite their shared biology. In some societies, for instance, unlike our own, homosexual relationships are en-

ESTRUS ("heat") a set of behavioral changes and a readiness to mate that occur in the females of most species of mammals at the time of ovulation

ESTROGEN the principal female hormone

TESTOSTERONE the principal male hormone

Original
flacon
signed
LALIQUE

A PERFUME MUST BE A WORK OF ART

Nina
NINA RICCI
PARIS

Many people believe that perfume enhances sexual attractiveness.

couraged as a sexual outlet before marriage (Davenport, 1965). The members of one New Guinea tribe believe that a boy must have his mother's milk to thrive as a child, but later he needs a "man's milk" (semen) to become a virile warrior (Holden, 1988). Similarly, in the Siwan society of Africa, virtually all males have homosexual experiences, which they talk about openly. Male friends even share their sons with one another for sexual pleasure (Crooks and Baur, 1987). Masturbation, or self-stimulation, is likewise affected by cultural norms and values. Some societies permit or even encourage it among children, alone or in groups, in the belief that this early sexual experimentation heightens adult sexual response. In other cultures (especially those in which a man may be married to several women at once), masturbation is considered a normal way of supplementing marital relations. In short, human sexual behavior is not just biologically driven. It is also a product of how we learn to think and feel about sexual activities.

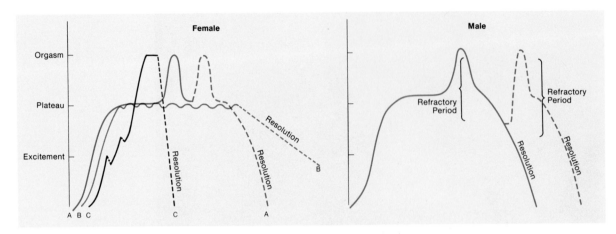

Figure 14.1 Graphs summarizing Masters and Johnson's description of coitus in the human male and female. The four phases are defined in terms of measurable physiological changes. In both sexes excitement leads to a plateau phase that may be maintained for considerable periods without orgasm. The male has only one pattern of response after this: he ejaculates quickly in orgasm, and his arousal decreases rapidly. There is a period after his ejaculation, the refractory period, in which he is incapable of another ejaculation. He may repeat the orgasmic phase several times before returning to an unaroused state. The female may variously have one orgasm or several orgasms in succession (line A), not achieve orgasm at all and return relatively slowly to an unaroused state (line B), or, rarely, have a single prolonged orgasm followed by rapid resolution (line C).

Sexually Arousing Stimuli

EROGENOUS ZONES areas of the body that are particularly sensitive to erotic touch

Touch is the most obvious source of sexual stimulation. Certain areas of the body, called **erogenous zones,** are particularly sensitive to erotic touch (the glans of the penis, the clitoris, the mouth, the nipples, the inside of the thighs). The degree of sensitivity in different areas depends on the person. A touch that is highly arousing to one person may have no effect on another or be disagreeable to a third.

Odors exert a powerful influence on mating activity in most animals. If urine from a female mouse in estrus is placed on the back of a male mouse, other male mice will sexually assault him (Connor, 1972). In humans, however, it is not clear whether odors emitted by the opposite sex are sexually arousing. To the extent that they are, women seem more sensitive to them than men, but in neither sex do odors seem to play the important role they do in other species (Rogel, 1978). Despite this fact, many people continue to believe that certain odors have an aphrodisiac (sexually arousing) effect, as perfume advertisements indicate.

The popularity of erotic films, books, and magazines testifies to the effectiveness of visual sexual stimulation. Both men and women are aroused by these materials (Heiman, 1975), and both men and women create their own erotic images through sexual fantasies. Interestingly, such fantasies may be the most powerful of all sexual stimulants. When adults were instructed to fantasize about sexually exciting situations, they became more aroused than did others who looked at sexually explicit slides or read sexually explicit stories (Byrne and Lambreth, 1971). Sexual fantasies frequently accompany sexual intercourse, even among people who are sexually well-adjusted and find their partners attractive. In one study, 65 percent of suburban housewives said that they sometimes had erotic fantasies during intercourse with their husbands, and 37 percent said they had these fantasies most of the time. These women reported that sexual fantasies enhanced their sexual responsiveness (Hariton and Singer, 1974).

Phases of the Sexual Response Cycle

All healthy men and women are physiologically equipped to respond to sexual stimulation—both physical stimulation (touching and being touched) and psychological stimulation (erotic or romantic sights, sounds, and fantasies). Although

Figure 14.2 Male reproductive organs and external genital structures.

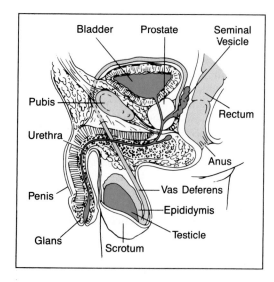

no two people react to stimulation in exactly the same way, there is a general pattern of sexual response that both men and women of all ages share. The pioneering sex researchers William Masters and Virginia Johnson (1966) found that this pattern is the same regardless of whether sexual arousal is caused by masturbation, intercourse, or oral-genital contact. According to Masters and Johnson, the human sexual response can be divided into four phases—excitement, plateau, orgasm, and resolution (see Figure 14.1).

During the **excitement phase,** the heart begins to beat faster and the breathing rate increases. Blood flow to the genital organs also increases, causing the penis to become erect and the clitoris to swell. (The male and female genitals are diagrammed in Figures 14.2 and 14.3.) Drops of moisture form on the walls of the vagina. Women's (and some men's) nipples may become erect, and women may develop a "sex flush" (a reddening of the skin, usually beginning on the chest, caused by dilation of small blood vessels).

In the **plateau phase,** the genitals become fully engorged with blood. The clitoris retracts into its hood, though it remains highly sensitive. The entrance to the vagina contracts by as much as 50 percent, and the uterus rises slightly, causing the inside of the vagina to balloon. The glans of the penis enlarges and deepens in color, and some fluid (which can contain live sperm) may seep out of the penis's opening. The testes swell and pull up higher within the scrotum. As excitement reaches a peak, the feeling that orgasm is inevitable sweeps over the person.

EXCITEMENT PHASE the first phase in the human sexual response cycle, during which the body begins to show physiological signs of arousal

PLATEAU PHASE the second phase in the human sexual response cycle, during which the body reaches its peak of sexual arousal

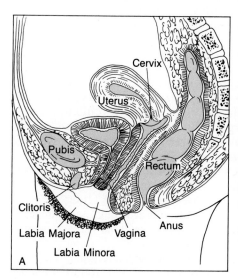

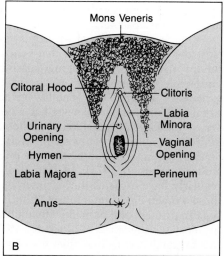

Figure 14.3 Female reproductive organs (A) and external genital structures (B).

ORGASM the third phase in the human sexual response cycle, during which waves of muscular contractions sweep over the body, accompanied by feelings of intense pleasure

EJACULATION the discharge of semen during male orgasm

SEMEN the fluid containing live sperm that is released during ejaculation

RESOLUTION PHASE the fourth and final phase of the human sexual response cycle, during which the body gradually returns to its normal state

REFRACTORY PERIOD the time following orgasm during which a man cannot become sexually aroused again

SEXUAL DISORDER any problem that persistently prevents a person from engaging in sexual relations or from reaching orgasm during sex

MALE ERECTILE DISORDER the inability to achieve or maintain an erection; when an erection has never been achieved, the condition is called *primary erectile disorder;* when the problem occurs only in certain situations, the condition is called secondary erectile disorder

PREMATURE EJACULATION ejaculation before the male or his sex partner would like

INHIBITED MALE ORGASM the inability to ejaculate during sexual activity

VAGINISMUS involuntary muscle spasms that close the vaginal entrance so that penetration by a penis is extremely painful

During **orgasm,** muscular contractions force the blood that has been collecting in the genitals back into the bloodstream. The muscles around the vagina push the vaginal walls in and out and the uterus pulsates. The muscles in and around the penis contract rhythmically, causing **ejaculation**—the discharge of **semen,** a fluid that contains sperm. For both men and women, the first five or six orgasmic contractions are the strongest and most pleasurable. In both sexes, the anus also contracts during orgasm, and some people experience intense muscle spasms in their faces and limbs. The subjective experience of orgasm is much the same in men and women. When a group of gynecologists, psychologists, and medical students were given descriptions of orgasms written by males and females, they correctly identified the writer's sex no more often than would occur by guessing (Vance and Wagner, 1976).

The body gradually returns to its normal state during the **resolution phase.** Muscle tension dissipates and the genitals return to their usual size, color, and shape. Men now experience a **refractory period,** ranging from minutes to hours, during which they cannot become sexually aroused again. Women, in contrast, may have *multiple orgasms,* one after another, before going through the resolution phase.

Sexual Disorders

Sometimes a person cannot be sexually aroused or, if aroused, cannot be sexually satisfied. The person may be tired, preoccupied with something else, drunk, angry at the partner, anxious about "performing" well, or simply uninterested in sex at the time. This happens to everyone on occasion. For some people, it is a recurring experience that can be very upsetting. Any problem that persistently prevents a person from engaging in sexual relations or from reaching orgasm during sex is known as a **sexual disorder** (American Psychiatric Association, 1987).

Types and Causes of Sexual Disorders

Men and women differ in the sexual disorders they may experience. In men, a common disorder is **male erectile disorder,** the inability to achieve or maintain an erection. When a man has never been able to have an erection (a rare condition), the problem is called *primary erectile disorder.* When he has had effective erections in the past but now has problems in certain situations, the condition is known as *secondary erectile disorder.* Other men have no difficulty getting an erection, but ejaculate before they or their partners would like. Such **premature ejaculation** is a common sexual complaint among male college students (Werner, 1975). The opposite problem is called **inhibited male orgasm,** the inability to ejaculate during sex with a partner.

One sexual disorder of women is **vaginismus,** involuntary muscle spasms that close the vaginal entrance, so that penetration by a man's penis is extremely painful. In many cases, the vaginal spasms are so severe that sexual intercourse is impossible. Other women engage in and enjoy sexual intercourse but do not experience orgasm. This inability to achieve orgasm is called **inhibited female orgasm.** Those who have never had an orgasm through any means are said to have *primary inhibited orgasm.* Those who can no longer achieve orgasm through the kinds of stimulation that were once effective are said to have *secondary inhibited orgasm.* Secondary inhibited orgasm is a common complaint among female college students (Werner, 1975). In fact, probably a third or more of women do not regularly have orgasms during intercourse (Kinsey et al., 1953; Hunt, 1974). If these women enjoy intercourse, find it pleasurable and arousing, and can reach orgasm through oral or manual manipulation, they are considered sexually normal by most sex therapists (LoPiccolo, 1978).

Research reveals that most sexual problems have no physiological basis (Masters and Johnson, 1970). Instead, for psychological reasons, certain people are unable to respond freely to sexual stimulation. Some of these reasons may be related to conflicts between the partners, others to personal conflicts. Sex therapists find that many of their clients were brought up with rigid moral standards about sex. Intellectually they may have rejected the belief that sex is wrong, but emotionally they have not. Other psychological sources of sexual problems range from having one's body ridiculed during childhood to having suffered outright sexual abuse. Fear of failure may also cause sexual disorders. A person may have one disappointing sexual experience and begin to wonder about his or her sexual adequacy. This anxiety can inhibit the next sexual encounter, confirming the person's self-doubts and virtually guaranteeing continued difficulty.

At times, however, physiological factors are responsible for sexual disorders. In perhaps 5 to 10 percent of men with erectile disorder, hormonal abnormalities may be responsible (Bancroft, 1983). These cases may be identified by monitoring the men during sleep. Those whose erectile failure is due to psychological causes will usually have erections during REM sleep (described in Chapter 6); those whose erectile failure is due to physiological causes will not. Other factors, such as severe diabetes or the taking of certain prescription drugs, may also be related to sexual disorders in men.

Sex Therapy

In the approach to treatment of sexual disorders developed by Masters and Johnson (1970), the couple is always treated as a unit by a pair of sex therapists, one male and one female. The focus is on the couple's sexual relationship. The therapists seek to educate the couple about human sexual responses, to reduce any sexual anxiety they are experiencing, and to help them change their sexual behavior to be more satisfying. Usually, to lessen the fear of failure, the couple is told not to engage in sexual intercourse for the time being and is assigned "nondemanding" sexual exercises, such as massaging one another. More sexual activities are gradually introduced, until at last the couple is permitted to engage in intercourse.

Although many of the techniques that Masters and Johnson developed are still used, both the philosophy and the methods of sex therapy have broadened during the past decade. Today sex therapists believe that sexual problems are seldom isolated. To solve them, the couple's entire relationship must usually be looked at and any conflicts in it resolved. Thus, issues as seemingly mundane as the division of household chores can come within the scope of modern-day sex therapy (Helman, LoPiccolo, and LoPiccolo, 1980).

The conditions of sex therapy have also changed. There may be only a single therapist, and the clients may be treated individually or in groups. Educational films and books may be used, and self-help techniques are sometimes prescribed in the treatment of premature ejaculation or orgasmic dysfunction. Training in directed masturbation is often a part of the treatment for primary orgasmic dysfunction (Helman, LoPiccolo, and LoPiccolo, 1980).

The fact that the clients are given "permission" to try out new activities by an authority figure (the therapist) may be therapeutic in itself. In most cases, sex therapy is brief (ten to fifteen sessions), but intensive. When therapy is successful, the clients find increased pleasure and satisfaction in their sexual relations. Sexual partners also develop a greater acceptance of themselves and of their individual differences.

Sexual Responsiveness and Aging

Most of us think of sexual responsiveness as something that emerges at puberty, reaches full strength in a person's twenties, and gradually fades with advancing age. We resist the idea that children and the elderly also have sexual urges. To Americans, sex is the province of those in the age range from adolescence to middle adulthood.

INHIBITED FEMALE ORGASM a woman's inability to achieve orgasm; women who have never had an orgasm through any means are said to have primary inhibited orgasm; those who can longer achieve orgasm through the kinds of stimulation that were once effective are said to have secondary inhibited orgasm

Contrary to the popular belief that the elderly lose interest in sex, most people remain sexually active throughout their adult lives.

Yet there is overwhelming evidence that sexual activity takes place throughout the life span. Pioneering sex researcher Alfred Kinsey and his associates (1948, 1953) found that, on the average, men age sixty-five and older reported having sex about four times a month, usually with their wives. In addition, 25 to 30 percent said that they supplemented intercourse with masturbation. Subsequent studies have found much the same thing: most older people maintain relatively active sex lives. Table 14.1 contains data from a survey conducted in the 1980s (Brecher, 1984). It shows that the vast majority of men and women over age fifty stay sexually active, having sex at least once a week. In other cultures, especially those that highly value their elderly, the sex lives of older people are even more vigorous (Crooks and Baur, 1987). For example, the elderly of Abkhazia in the Caucasus Mountains of Russia have been known to continue having sex even after age 100 (Beach, 1978).

Some physiological decline in sexual functioning does occur with aging, however (Brecher, 1984). Hormone production generally decreases in both sexes. It also takes more intense physical stimulation for a longer period of time to produce penile erection and vaginal lubrication. Elderly men find that they may not ejaculate on every occasion and that less semen is emitted with each ejaculation. In old

TABLE 14.1 Sexual Activity in a Sample of Elderly Persons

	IN THEIR 50s	*IN THEIR 60s*	*70 AND OVER*
Women			
Orgasms when asleep or while waking up	26%	24%	17%
Women who masturbate	47%	37%	33%
Frequency of masturbation among women who masturbate	0.7/week	0.6/week	0.7/week
Wives having sex with their husbands	88%	76%	65%
Frequency of sex with their husbands	1.3/week	1.0/week	0.7/week
Men			
Orgasms when asleep or while waking up	25%	21%	17%
Men who masturbate	66%	50%	43%
Frequency of masturbation among men who masturbate	1.2/week	0.8/week	0.7/week
Husbands having sex with their wives	87%	78%	59%
Frequency of sex with their wives	1.3/week	1.0/week	0.6/week

Source: Edward M. Brecher and the Editors of Consumer Reports Books (1984), *Love, sex and aging.* Mount Vernon, NY: Consumers Union, p. 316.

PSYCHOLOGY TODAY AND TOMORROW

Methods of Studying Sexual Behavior

How do psychologists study something as private as sexual behavior? They do so using the same methods (described in Chapter 2) that they use for research in other areas.

SURVEYS

One of these methods is the survey. The first large-scale survey of sexual behavior was conducted by Alfred Kinsey and his colleagues. They spent eighteen years talking to people of different ages, backgrounds, and marital statuses about their sex lives. Interviews with nearly 12,000 men and women in the United States resulted in the books *Sexual Behavior in the Human Male* (1948) and *Sexual Behavior in the Human Female* (1953).

Some aspects of Kinsey's approach have been criticized. His sample underrepresented blacks, farmers, the uneducated, and the poor, and his reliance on volunteers as subjects may have biased the results (people who volunteer to answer questions about their sex lives may differ in important ways from people who do not). Yet for years Kinsey's research furnished the only comprehensive data on sexual practices in America. It made public discussion of sexual behavior acceptable in our society, and it laid the foundation for a change in our views on homosexuality (Gagnon, 1975). It remains the standard against which all other surveys of sexual behavior are assessed.

OBSERVATIONAL STUDIES

Sexual behavior is also studied through direct observation—watching men and women in the act of being sexually stimulated. William Masters and Virginia Johnson (1966) conducted the first studies of this kind. Volunteers masturbated and had intercourse in a laboratory where their physiological responses could be closely observed. Women, for example, masturbated with an artificial penis equipped with a light and camera. Over twelve years, nearly 700 men and women between the ages of eighteen and eighty-nine, most of them married couples, took part in Masters and Johnson's research. In all, the research team observed some 10,000 sexual episodes.

Masters and Johnson's work has been criticized for many of the same reasons as Kinsey's research was. Their sample, like Kinsey's, underrepresented the poor and the uneducated, and they, too, relied on volunteer subjects who may well have been atypical of the population as a whole. In addition, sexual responses in a laboratory may differ from those experienced at home, in private. The presence of observers in itself probably influenced some aspects of subjects' sexual behavior. Nevertheless, Master and Johnson's research was extremely important. It provided objective information about human sexual activity, thereby dispelling many myths about what goes on during intercourse, and it led to a fuller understanding of human sexual problems.

EXPERIMENTS

Surveys and observational studies are descriptive methods. They can tell us *what* occurs during sex, but not *why*. If we are to discover how various factors influence sexual behavior, we need controlled experiments in which specific hypotheses can be tested. In one such study, Julia Heiman (1975) examined the kinds of things that men and women find sexually arousing. Her subjects listened to various tapes while their physiological responses were recorded. Group 1 listened to an *erotic* tape with explicit sexual material; group 2 listened to a *romantic* tape that involved a tender, affectionate exchange, but no sexual contact; group 3 listened to an *erotic-romantic* tape that had both romantic conversation and explicit sex; and group 4 listened to a *control* tape with neither sexual or romantic content. The results refuted the stereotyped notion that women find romance more arousing than erotic material. Women and men alike showed high levels of arousal to tapes depicting explicit sex, and both sexes showed equally weak responses to the romantic tape and to the control one. Adding romance to explicit sex did nothing to heighten women's arousal.

Of course, controlled experiments on sexual behavior have limitations. A laboratory is a very artificial setting for assessing sexual arousal. It is hard to say if the responses observed there adequately mirror those that occur in everyday environments. In addition, certain experiments on sexual behavior cannot be conducted for ethical reasons. For example, it would clearly be unethical to expose children to pornography in order to assess the effects on their subsequent sexual behavior. Because of these limitations, sex researchers do not often conduct experiments on human subjects. Experimental studies with animals are more common and are quite useful, but they cannot reflect the full complexity and variety of human sexual responses.

age, too, the intensity of orgasmic contractions generally decreases, and the refractory period is usually longer. But none of these changes really diminishes the pleasure of sexual activity. Sex can remain highly satisfying regardless of the aging process.

SEXUAL BEHAVIOR IN AMERICA

So far we have looked mainly at heterosexual intercourse between consenting adults and ignored many other varieties of sexual behavior. To present a more nearly complete picture of sex in our society, we now broaden our focus and consider the diversity of sexual practices in which Americans engage. In addition to heterosexual relationships, our discussion includes masturbation, homosexuality, and various forms of sexual abuse. (Psychologists study these and other sexual practices using the methods described in the accompanying box.)

Some Sexual Practices

Masturbation

Attitudes toward masturbation have changed during the past few decades. Fifty years ago physicians regularly warned youngsters that self-stimulation (or "self-abuse," as masturbation was then called) could cause acne, fever, blindness, and even insanity. Today most people know that this is nonsense. By the mid-1970s, only about 15 percent of young adults surveyed believed that masturbation was wrong, less than half the proportion of adults over fifty-five who condemned the practice (Hunt, 1974). No matter what they tell researchers, however, most Americans are somewhat ashamed of and secretive about masturbating. Few admit to their mates or friends that they stimulate themselves. Apparently, the idea lingers that "playing with yourself" is immature behavior, symptomatic of personal inadequacies, or dissatisfaction with one's sexual partner.

Yet surveys indicate that masturbation is common. In his extensive survey of nearly 12,000 American men and women, Kinsey and his associates (1948, 1953) discovered that 93 percent of men and 62 percent of women had masturbated at some time during their lives. Twenty years later, in a survey by Morton Hunt (1974), that figure remained much the same, but other statistics about masturbation were significantly different. People were beginning to masturbate at a much younger age. The percentage of girls who reported having masturbated by the age of thirteen increased from 15 percent in 1953 to 33 percent in 1974. Similarly, the percentage of boys who masturbated by age 13 climbed from 45 to 63 percent. The frequency of masturbation also rose dramatically. For example, among young women in 1974, the average rate was about once every ten days—twice as often as Kinsey had reported.

Was the Hunt survey representative of the population as a whole? Although it was sponsored by the Playboy Foundation, it was not a survey of the readers of *Playboy* magazine. A private research organization collected the data from 2000 subjects, making an effort to match the sample to the wider population regarding race, marital status, level of education, and place of residence. It was not a truly random sample because it underrepresented the very poor, but it was more representative than most sex surveys (Offir, 1982). Like most sex surveys, it was probably skewed by volunteer bias. Those who agreed to tell researchers about their sex lives were probably different in some respects from those who refused. In addition, respondents first took part in extensive group discussions, so their answers on the survey may have been influenced by ideas they heard expressed there.

Heterosexuality

HETEROSEXUALITY sexual attraction to members of the opposite sex

Heterosexual refers to sexual attraction to members of the opposite sex. Heterosexual activity usually involves sexual intercourse (penis in vagina) in a variety of positions. In addition, many heterosexual couples enjoy petting to orgasm, oral-genital stimulation, anal intercourse, intercourse between the thighs, dressing in fantasy costumes, or other forms of sex play. The marital status of heterosexual couples also varies. The partners may be unmarried (premarital sex), married to each other (conjugal sex), or married to other people (extramarital sex). In the following sections we will discuss premarital and extramarital sex.

PREMARITAL SEX   In Kinsey's day, most Americans claimed that they strongly disapproved of premarital sex. Yet 98 percent of men with a grade-school education, 85 percent of male high-school graduates, and 68 percent of male college graduates told researchers that they had had sexual intercourse before getting married (Kinsey et al., 1948). Nearly 50 percent of the married women in Kinsey's sample had also had premarital sexual experience, most of them with their future husbands.

Today, few Americans remain virgins until marriage. One reason is that people are marrying at an older age. Most do not wish to spend a decade or more of adulthood without experiencing intercourse. Thus, among women in their twenties who have never married, 82 percent have had sex (Tanfer and Horn, 1985). But delayed marriage is not the only reason for an increased rate of premarital sex. Even by the age of twenty, more than 70 percent of women and 80 percent of men have had intercourse (Hayes, 1987). Apparently, American attitudes toward premarital sex are changing. Premarital sex is now considered more acceptable than it used to be.

Also slowly changing is the traditional "double standard," the belief that premarital sex is more acceptable for men than it is for women. When the Hunt survey (1974) asked people about their attitudes toward sex without marriage, 83 percent of the women and 84 percent of the men said that they felt the same way regardless of whether the question applied to males or females. Of course, this alone is not proof that the double standard has eroded. In some cases it still strongly affects people's sexual behavior. Gradually, however, many Americans are coming to believe that, at least in theory, men and women should have equal freedom of sexual expression.

Changing attitudes toward premarital sex extend to the adolescent population. Most teenagers believe that marriage is not a prerequisite for sex. They feel that as long as two people are really fond of each other, sex between them is permissible (Sorensen, 1973; Hass, 1979). These attitudes are echoed in adolescent behavior. A little over 50 percent of teenage girls, and probably a larger percentage of boys, have had more than one sexual partner (Hofferth, 1987). However, their desire for committed, caring relationships leads most adolescents to reject casual, indiscriminate sex. In particular, most teenage girls restrict their sexual activity to partners they love and hope to marry someday (Zelnick, Kanter, and Ford, 1981).

Our society is increasingly coming to see sexual experimentation among adolescents as normal. Many parents and school officials no longer lecture youngsters on the "immorality" of premarital sex. Instead, they focus on preventing teenage pregnancy and sexually transmitted diseases. In one survey, 83 percent of Americans urged that twelve-year-olds be taught about AIDS and other sexually transmitted diseases, and 84 percent said that school health clinics should make birth control information available (*Time*, 1986).

EXTRAMARITAL SEX   People have extramarital sex for a number of reasons. Some are dissatisfied with their marriages; some are under pressure at home; some are seeking status; some are asserting their independence; some are trying to punish their spouse; and some are attracted by the lure of the forbidden (Gould, 1980). Men are less likely than women to become emotionally involved in their extramarital relationships; they seem to find it easier to separate sex from love. Women are more likely to romanticize an extramarital encounter and become involved in a full-blown love affair (Blumstein and Schwartz, 1983).

About half of all husbands and a quarter of all wives in the Kinsey sample had had extramarital sex (Kinsey et al., 1948; Kinsey et al., 1953). In the young-adult age group (the early twenties), the rate among women was especially low—only 8 percent. This generally lower rate for women than men may be changing, however. By 1980, the rate of extramarital sex among young, middle-class, well-educated women was about 25 percent, while among men from similar backgrounds it was not much higher, just slightly under 33 percent (Macklin, 1980). Do these figures reflect a genuine increase in the incidence of extramarital affairs among young women? Researchers are not certain. It may simply be that women today are more willing to admit to marital infidelity (Hyde, 1982; Offir, 1982).

It is important to realize, too, that the way people behave does not always represent the values they hold. The majority of Americans today still believe that extramarital sex is wrong, and those who accept it in principle say that they wouldn't want their own spouse to have sex with someone else. In Hunt's (1974) sample, for example, more than 80 percent of men and women reported that they would object if their own husband or wife became involved in an extramarital affair.

Homosexuality

HOMOSEXUALITY   sexual attraction to members of one's own sex

BISEXUAL   sexual attraction to members of both sexes

Many discussions of love and sex sound as if everyone is attracted only to people of the opposite sex. This is far from true, of course. A good many people are either **homosexual** (attracted to members of their own sex) or **bisexual** (attracted to members of both sexes). To classify people according to their sexual preferences, Kinsey and his associates (1953) developed a seven-point scale that runs from 0 (exclusively heterosexual) to 6 (exclusively homosexual) (see Table 14.2). People who are predominantly heterosexual but also have some homosexual experience are assigned to categories 1 or 2, depending on the frequency of their homosexual encounters. In the same manner, categories 4 and 5 are for predominantly homosexual people who have varying degrees of experience with heterosexual relationships. Finally, category 3 is for bisexuals who engage in heterosexual and homosexual activity with equal frequency.

Kinsey's data suggested that homosexual experiences are not rare among American adults of all ages. In his survey, 37 percent of men and 13 percent of women had engaged in homosexual activity sometime during their lives. Higher percentages admitted to feeling at least some sexual interest toward a member of their own sex, even though they had never acted on that interest.

Critics charge that Kinsey's findings probably overrepresent the degree of homosexuality in the male population. Among those Kinsey interviewed were many men who had been in the army or in prison (environments unusually conducive to homosexual contact), as well as men from various homosexual groups. Hunt (1974) estimates that probably closer to 23 percent of men have had at least some overt homosexual experience, and about 3 to 4 percent are exclusively homosexual.

Judeo-Christian religious traditions, which prevail in the United States, are strongly antihomosexual (Rosen and Hall, 1984). In the Massachusetts Bay colony, settled by the Pilgrims, homosexual activity was considered a "crime against

TABLE 14.2   Heterosexual-Homosexual Ratings (Ages 20–35)

CATEGORY		IN FEMALES	IN MALES
	Entirely heterosexual experience:		
0	Single	61–72%	48–81%
0	Married	89–90	80–96
9	Previously married	75–80	
1	At least some homosexual experience	4–9	2–4
2	More than incidental homosexual experience	1–4	3–7
3	As much homosexual experience as heterosexual experience, or more	0–3	2–4
4	Mostly homosexual experience	1–3	2–3
5	Almost exclusively homosexual experience	1–3	1–3
6	Exclusively homosexual experience	1–3	2–5

Source: From data in Kinsey et al, (1953), *Sexual behavior in the human female.* Philadelphia: W. B. Saunders, p. 488. Reprinted by permission of The Kinsey Institute, Bloomington, IN.

Homosexuality is a sexual preference for members of one's own sex. No longer classified as a disorder by the American Psychiatric Association, its causes—like the origins of heterosexuality and bisexuality—remain unclear despite extensive research.

nature," punishable by death. Homosexuality continued to be dealt with as a crime for many generations. Gradually, however, during the twentieth century, it began to be thought of more as a mental disorder. Then research was conducted which showed that homosexuals were just as psychologically healthy as heterosexuals (Hooker and Chance, 1975). There was virtually no evidence that homosexuality should be labeled a "sickness" to be "treated" and "cured." The gay liberation movement, which arose in the late 1960s, pressed for an end to the age-old discrimination against homosexual men and women. Taking a fresh look at homosexuality, the American Psychiatric Association decided to drop the category "homosexuality" from its diagnostic manual of mental disorders (American Psychiatric Association, 1973, 1987).

We are still left with the question of why this variation in sexual preference occurs. Why are some people sexually attracted to members of their own sex, others predominantly to the opposite sex, and still others to both sexes? Several theories have been proposed. Among traditional psychoanalysts, heterosexuality is one of the outcomes of learning to identify with the parent of your own sex, which involves adopting that parent's attitudes and values, including sexual preference (see Chapter 17). Homosexuality, in contrast, is said to have its roots in family situations that keep a child from developing a strong sex-appropriate identity. For instance, if a boy has a harsh, rejecting father, with whom he cannot identify, or a passive father and an overprotective mother who will not "let go" of the child, he may, according to Freudian theorists, become homosexual (Bieber et al., 1962; Saghir and Robins, 1973). Yet in a study of nearly 1000 homosexuals and nearly 500 heterosexuals, this theory was not borne out. No consistent differences in family background were found between the two groups (Bell, Weinberg, and Hammersmith, 1981).

Other psychologists have proposed different theories. One is that sexual preference is at least partly determined by sex hormones, with homosexual (gay) men presumably having low testosterone levels. But research does not consistently support this theory, either. In fact, some studies have found higher than average testosterone levels in gay men (e.g., Meyer-Bahlburg, 1977) and that when gay men with low testosterone levels are given testosterone supplements, their *homosexual* desires and behaviors intensify (Bancroft, 1981). Among lesbians (female homosexuals), about one-third have elevated levels of male hormones (Meyer-Bahlburg, 1979). However, this finding is not enough to demonstrate that female homosexuality has a hormonal basis.

Another possibility is that sexual preference is simply learned early in life, as many other attitudes and behaviors are. Suppose a young adolescent boy has a sexual experience with one of his friends. Later, he fantasizes about the incident while masturbating. The pleasure of orgasm reinforces the homosexual thoughts and makes them more likely to recur. Continued reinforcement increases the chances that this boy will begin to seek out more homosexual encounters, until a learned pattern of homosexuality has been established (McGuire, Carlise, and Young, 1965). Youngsters may also learn sexual preferences through imitation of their friends. Homosexuals of both sexes usually say that they preferred the company and activities of the opposite sex during childhood (Gadpaille, 1981). Perhaps girls who associated mostly with boys and boys who associated mostly with girls come to adopt their playmates' sexual preferences, along with other attitudes and interests.

Biological factors and social learning might also combine with one another to steer a person toward a certain sexual preference. For instance, Richard Green (1980) suggests that inborn temperament and behavioral predispositions (perhaps linked to prenatal hormones) encourage a child to gravitate to a peer group of one sex or the other. If parents don't object to a son who plays only with girls or a daughter who plays only with boys, learning from friends may eventually cause a homosexual orientation. This theory, of course, is only speculative. No explanation of how sexual preference develops has yet been confirmed.

Consistent with the idea of homosexuality as a normal variation in sexual preference, the love relationships of homosexuals are in many ways the same as those of heterosexuals. In a study of several hundred gay men and women, as well as a control group of heterosexuals, Letitia Anne Peplau (1981) found that 61 percent of the homosexual women and 41 percent of the homosexual men had committed, loving relationships, just as heterosexuals do. Most of these relationships were not patterned after traditional, role-based heterosexual marriages. Instead, they resembled relationships among "best friends" of the same sex with the addition of erotic pleasure. There was no "husband" and no "wife," but rather a pair of partners who took equal responsibility for breadwinning and household chores, and who were equally likely to initiate sex.

Another difference between heterosexual and homosexual couples is that the homosexual ones are more likely to break up. In Peplau's study, most partners stayed together for less than two years. One reason for this pattern is that homosexual relationships do not involve legal marriage and so are easier to dissolve. Often, too, there are no outside factors—such as children, family pressures, or financial dependence—encouraging the partners to stay together and try to resolve their conflicts. As a result, the social cement is often weaker for homosexual couples than it is for heterosexuals.

Sexual Abuse

Some forms of sexual behavior violate community norms to such an extreme that they are regarded with abhorrence, considered abusive, and punished with imprisonment. In many societies, including our own, rape and incest fall into the category of sexual abuse. Both can cause physical and emotional harm to the victims.

RAPE sexual intercourse that is the result of physical force, threat, or intimidation

RAPE When sexual intercourse is the result of physical force, threat, or intimidation, it is called **rape.** Rape is far more common in our society than most people think. Studies reveal that as many as 44 percent of women have been subjected to rape or attempted rape at least once (Russell, 1984). There are also many male rape victims, who generally suffer even greater physical injury than female rape victims do. Males are also more likely than women to be subjected to gang rapes (Kaufman et al., 1980).

Most psychologists feel that the primary motive for rape is not sexual desire, but either anger or the need to assert power. Anger against women was the cause a third of the time in a study of over 100 convicted rapists. These rapes, which were unpremeditated, were particularly violent, and the rapist deliberately tried to de-

In her Oscar-winning performance in *The Accused,* Jodie Foster helped to dispel the myth that women who dress and behave provocatively are "asking" to be raped.

grade his victim (Groth and Burgess, 1977). Rapes that result from a desire to assert power are generally planned and fantasized about beforehand. The rapist stalks his victim and threatens physical harm, but he uses no more force than is needed to carry out the rape. Either type of rape can reward the rapist in many ways. It can relieve his frustrations, compensate for helpless feelings, reassure him of his sexual prowess, help him assert his identity, defend him against homosexual urges, and bolster his status among peers, in addition to giving him sexual gratification (Groth and Burgess, 1977).

Note that sexual gratification is low in importance on this list. This is suggested by the fact that most rapists have other sexual outlets available to them. The majority are young men who are married to or dating women with whom they have sex on a voluntary basis. For some reason, however, they lack the ability to establish a satisfying, loving relationship with their wives or other women.

Rapists differ from normal men in other ways as well. In one study, for instance, both rapists and a control group of normal men became sexually aroused when they listened to audiotaped descriptions of mutually enjoyable sex; but only the rapists became aroused by descriptions of rape (Abel, Blanchard, and Becker, 1978). In addition, a small group of rapists because aroused when listening to tapes of aggression that had no sexual content. Interestingly, too, the rapists (but not the normal men) consistently *under*estimated their own level of arousal as objectively measured by their physical responses. (The accompanying box discusses research into the relationship between violent pornography and sex crimes.)

What, psychologically, happens to the victims of rape? Typically, they are in shock at first and show acute anxiety, fear, and disbelief. As this initial reaction subsides, other symptoms appear. Rape victims may lose their appetites, startle at minor noises, and develop headaches, insomnia, or fatigue. Some are plagued by frightening dreams or have irrational fears (Burgess and Holstrom, 1974). Many are no longer able to lead normal sex lives. They become afraid of sex or they are unable to become sexually aroused and to have an orgasm. These sexual dysfunctions sometimes persist for years after the assault (Becker et al., 1982; Gilbert and Cunningham, 1986).

When we think of rape, we usually think of a man attacking a stranger in a dark alley or an isolated parking lot. However, this stereotype does not fit a large proportion of rapes. Many victims know the men who rape them. In one form of acquaintance rape, called *date rape,* a woman is assaulted when on a date with a man she has recently met. One survey found that 10 percent of the women attending a large university had experienced some type of forced sexual encounter, half of which involved penetration (Yegidis, 1986). Nearly 6 percent of the male students who responded to this survey admitted that during the past year they had forced a date to engage in some form of sexual activity. Earlier surveys have

PSYCHOLOGY TODAY AND TOMORROW

Does Violent Pornography Cause Sex Crimes?

Nearly 80 percent of Americans have been exposed to pornography—written, photographic, or video material portraying explicit sexual activity (Abelson et al., 1970). Although critics have claimed that pornography in and of itself is harmful, exhaustive studies have failed to support this blanket condemnation (Commission on Obscenity and Pornography, 1970). In the past few years, however, a new case has been made against it. The focus is now on pornography that involves violence against women. Critics charge that this violent material makes sex crimes against women more likely. Depictions of rapes, beatings, mutilations, and murders, the opponents say, encourage men to devalue women and weaken men's inhibitions against sexual assault.

As evidence in support of these charges, critics cite several studies that suggest that violent pornography has a powerful effect on sexual attitudes and behavior. In one such study, college men watched movies that featured sexual violence against women and afterward their attitudes toward the subject were assessed (Malamuth and Check, 1981). Compared with men who watched neutral films, these men were more likely to accept violence directed against women. To a lesser extent, they were also more likely to accept myths about rape, such as the belief that "many women have an unconscious wish to be raped." Psychologists suggest some possible reasons for these effects (Malamuth and Donnerstein, 1982). First, by being exposed to images of sex linked with aggression, viewers may come to see this as a "proper" pairing. Second, by presenting women as somehow wanting to be assaulted, the films implant or reinforce a dangerous myth. Third, the men on the screen, even if murderers and rapists, still act as models for antisocial behavior.

Opponents of violent pornography are quick to point out that the films in this study were not hard-core pornographic. Instead, they were two mainstream feature films: *Swept Away* and *The Getaway*. If these relatively mild portrayals of rape and sexual coercion can influence men's atti-

tudes, people ask, how much more powerful an effect would bloody scenes of torture and mutilation have? Research has not yet answered this question unequivocally. It may be that extremely violent attacks on women would be so disturbing to normal men that they would "turn off" to the idea of even milder forms of this behavior. But if no such reverse effect occurs in many cases, the possibilities are alarming.

On the basis of such research, the federal Commission on Pornography recently issued a report (1986) in which it urged new restrictions on violent pornography. The report's conclusions have been criticized by some of the very researchers whose work it cites (Donnerstein and Linz, 1986; Donnerstein, Linz, and Penrod, 1987). These researchers argue that when the commission focused on violent *pornography* alone, it missed the point of many of the studies that have been conducted. Taken together, these studies suggest that any negative effects on attitudes and behavior that pornography may have come not from their sexually explicit or pornographic content, but rather from their violence: "The most well documented finding in the social science literature is that *all* sexually violent material in our society, whether sexually *explicit* or not, tends to promote violence against women" (Donnerstein, Linz, and Penrod, 1987, p. 179).

suggested an even higher incidence of this practice. Over the last 30 years, between 20 and 25 percent of college women have reported that a date has used physical force in an attempt at sexual intercourse (Kanin, 1957; Kanin and Parcell, 1977; Wilson and Durrenberger, 1982; Shotland and Goodstein, 1983).

Many psychologists think that the high incidence of date rape may stem partly from a lingering double standard, coupled with differences in how men and women interpret sexual signals (Goleman, 1989). The double standard may lead some women to believe they will be considered "loose" if they have sex without making a token protest. Men, aware of this pattern, may assume that all protest is a sham, that women who say "no" really mean "yes." So they persevere when a date resists their advances, and the end result can be rape.

Experts suggest that women can protect themselves from date rape by avoiding situations in which they feel vulnerable; by making it clear early in the encounter that they do not wish to have sex; and, if the situation starts to get out of hand, stating flatly "This is rape, and I'm calling the police." Men, for their part, should assume that "no" always means "no," and halt their advances as soon as the woman protests. They should also realize that a women who flirts or dresses in "sexy" clothing is not necessarily inviting sex (Goleman, 1989).

INCEST Sexual activity between close relatives is called **incest.** Although some authorities limit the definition of incest to genital intercourse, most also include oral-genital contact, fondling of the genitals, and coerced masturbation. This broader definition allows the term "incest" to be applied when a close relative sexually molests a very young girl (with whom genital intercourse is difficult) or engages in homosexual activity with a child (Meiselman, 1978).

INCEST sexual activity between close relatives

Until a decade or so ago, it was assumed that incest was extremely rare. But then a number of books written by women who had been victims of incest were published and widely read. In addition, many cases of sexual abuse of children by their parents were reported in the media. As a result, authorities and the general public became aware that incest is not rare, and that it is not limited to poor, uneducated, socially isolated families. Some middle-class suburban families that appear normal and respectable are in fact incestuous.

Most cases of incest are not reported. Young children are seldom in a position to go to authorities with complaints about a parent or some other relative. Often the guilty adult has deliberately made the child fearful of divulging their "secret" to anyone else. And even when children do muster the courage to seek help, the person in whom they confide may not believe them. Notifying authorities also brings children into the legal system, which can add more stress and can intensify emotional damage (Rosen and Hall, 1984).

Most incest involves an older male molesting a child. Father–daughter incest has been intensively studied. It is one of the most destructive forms of incest, particularly if it begins when the girl is very young. It is not unusual for an incestuous father to molest all his daughters, starting with the oldest and proceeding down the line. Fathers in such cases often have a history of emotional deprivation and other psychological problems. The family is often deeply troubled, with much hostility between husband and wife and between parents and children. The mother may fail to intervene, often through fear of her husband's violence (Mrazek, 1981).

Although father–daughter incest is the most prevalent kind in court records and the files of therapists, brother–sister incest may actually be more common (Mrazek, 1981). We know little about the long-term consequences of other, less common types of incest, nor are we certain about how frequently they occur.

Generally, the younger the child and the closer the relationship with the molester, the more damaging the emotional consequences. Very young children are small, naive, and dependent, so they cannot usually repel an incestuous advance. Yet they are not mature enough to cope with the strong conflicting feelings stirred up by sexual relations with an adult—particularly a parent. When therapists treat people who were incest victims as children, they find that these clients often suffer from depression, self-abusive behavior, and a variety of sexual problems. Lingering effects on the personality may include feelings of inferiority, the inability to trust others, repressed anger, and profound difficulties in establishing and maintaining warm relationships (Steele and Alexander, 1981). Incest, in short, can have negative repercussions throughout the victim's life.

Sexual Behavior and the AIDS Crisis

Researchers are investigating the extent to which the AIDS crisis is changing people's sexual attitudes and behavior. The term AIDS is short for Acquired Immune Deficiency Syndrome, a condition that results when a virus attacks the body's natural defenses against infection and disease. The person becomes vulnerable to all sorts of illnesses that the immune system would normally fight off. The AIDS virus also enters the brain and causes neurological damage, resulting in symptoms that range from mild confusion and poor coordination to severe senility similar to that seen in Alzheimer's disease (Barnes, 1987). In more than 70 percent of the cases, a person found to have AIDS dies within two years of the diagnosis (Allgeier and Allgeier, 1988).

AIDS cannot be transmitted by casual social contact, such as shaking hands, kissing, or touching objects previously touched by an infected one. It can be passed on only when blood, semen, or breast milk from an infected person enters the bloodstream of another person. This makes sexual intercourse with an infected male a very high-risk behavior. The virus in his semen can enter the blood of his partner through microscopic ruptures in vessels of the vagina, mouth, or anus. Anal intercourse is especially dangerous, for this practice tends to cause small tears in the rectal tissue, allowing the AIDS virus ready access to the bloodstream of a new host. This is why homosexual men are at particularly high risk for contracting AIDS. Sharing needles when injecting drugs intravenously is another high-risk behavior. If one of the users carries the AIDS virus, tiny traces of his or her blood can be left on the needle and transmitted to the next person who uses the needle. Pregnancy, birth, and breast-feeding also place the babies of women with AIDS at high risk.

AIDS has become an epidemic of frightening proportions. The first cases were identified in 1980, and by the end of 1981, 225 cases had been reported in the United States. By the spring of 1983, the number had risen to 1400, and by 1987 there were 40,000 known cases (D'Emilio and Freedman, 1988). That figure had doubled to 80,000 by 1989 (*AIDS Weekly Surveillance Reports*, 1989). Thousands more people are carrying the AIDS virus, many of whom do not yet know it. The disease has a long latency period, meaning that people can be infected with the virus for many years before having any symptoms. Some authorities estimated that 1.5 million Americans were harboring the AIDS virus by the end of the 1980s.

Since there is no cure for AIDS, and no vaccine that prevents infection, the only hope for halting the spread of AIDS is to stop high-risk behaviors. In terms of sexual activity, this means avoiding sexual contact with known carriers of the virus, with people who engage in behavior that places them at risk, and with those whose exposure to possible infection is in any way in doubt. If such avoidance is impossible in some cases, careful and consistent use of condoms can reduce (but not eliminate) the risk of contracting AIDS.

Studies indicate that people are increasingly adopting these "safer sex" practices. Homosexual men report that they have become more cautious in their choice of partners and more likely to take precautions, including the use of condoms (Joseph et al., 1987; Becker and Joseph, 1988). These efforts seem to be paying off, for the rate of infection with AIDS among gay men is no longer rising.

Nevertheless, there are still many people who continue to put themselves at risk of getting AIDS. One group that has shown little change in its high-risk behavior is the adolescent population (Becker and Joseph, 1988). Although nearly half of all teenagers say that they are "very worried" about AIDS, few of them take precautions against it (Hayes, 1987). Only one-third of sexually active adolescents regularly use contraceptives at all, and less than one-quarter of these use condoms (National Center for Health Statistics, 1984). It is true that adolescents make up less than 1 percent of diagnosed AIDS cases, but there is little doubt that many of them are being exposed to the AIDS virus. Twenty-one percent of AIDS cases are diagnosed among people in their twenties, most of whom were probably infected as teenagers (Kegeles, Adler, and Irwin, 1988). The risk for adolescents is especially high in inner cities, where teenagers are more likely to abuse intravenous drugs and to become sexually active at an early age. Since the incidence of

Condoms, if they are used consistently and correctly, can prevent transmission of the AIDS virus.

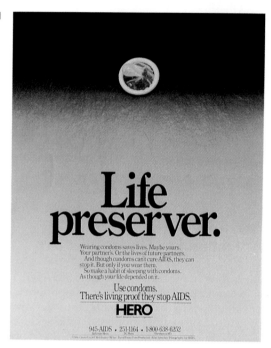

AIDS is also relatively high in inner cities, teenagers there are more likely to be exposed (DiClemente, Boyer, and Morales, 1988).

One reason adolescents are not more careful is that they often feel invulnerable. Physically, they are approaching the peak of their strength, and in their short lives they have probably had little experience with serious illness. Cognitively, they find it hard to plan far ahead or to consider the long-term consequences of their behavior. This may make them foolishly optimistic about their chances of escaping death and disease, including AIDS (Becker and Joseph, 1988).

Second, contraceptive use requires planning and forethought, which may make sex seem too calculated to some adolescents. Teenage girls who have had sex only a few times are especially likely to resist seeing themselves as sexually active. They may prefer to think of themselves as swept away by passion, and people who are swept away by passion do not plan ahead by stocking up on condoms.

Third, people are more likely to follow rules for safer sex when social norms support these practices (Joseph et al., 1987). Because adolescents do not perceive themselves to be at any great risk, their peer group as a whole has not developed norms that encourage—or demand—safer sex. Consequently, the impetus for developing such norms probably has to come from adults. However, many parents and teachers are reluctant to discuss sexual matters openly with adolescents, which means that they are unlikely to make a clear and convincing argument about the dangers of AIDS (D'Emilio and Freedman, 1988).

SEX, INTIMACY, AND LOVE

Intimacy is the process by which people try to get emotionally close to each other by exploring similarities and differences in the ways they think, feel, and behave. People in an intimate relationship display their intimacy by being physically close to each other. When they are talking, walking, or working on a shared task, their bodies often brush. They may hold hands, embrace, or kiss. Sex is the ultimate form of physical closeness, but the connection between sex and intimacy is complex. Intimacy is not an act, but a quality, and many people who are intimate in other ways do not express their bond sexually. Yet sex helps to establish intimacy, because it involves intimate touching and forces us to lower some of our social barriers. Thus, most people consider sex an important part of intimacy—but not

INTIMACY the process by which people try to get emotionally close to each other by exploring similarities and differences in the ways they think, feel and behave nearly as important as sharing thoughts, feelings, and dreams (Waring et al., 1980). Through such sharing, partners develop a deep knowledge of each other. They believe that they know the other person's innermost self, the self that is sometimes hidden from public view.

LOVE a feeling of deep affection for and attachment to another person

The emotion of love usually accompanies intimate relationships. **Love** is a feeling of deep affection for and attachment to another person. It is a kind of emotional glue that binds two people together. When we love someone, we want to be physically close, to spend time together, to get to know the other person completely, and to do things to please the other person (Shaver et al., 1987). Although this is a satisfactory description of love in general, the specific experience of love differs from one person to another. How can we explain these differences in the emotion? Some psychologists have tried to answer this question. Let's look at two provocative views.

A Triangular Theory of Love

According to psychologist Robert Sternberg (1986), love varies from one relationship to another because its mix of components differ. Sternberg suggests that love has three possible components: intimacy, passion, and commitment. In his theory, intimacy is the emotional component of love. It refers to feeling close and bound together by mutual affection. Passion is love's motivational component. It is the drive that leads to romance, physical attraction, and sexual consummation. Finally, there is commitment, the cognitive component of love. It refers to the decision to label a certain relationship "love" and to seek to maintain that relationship over time.

Different types of love, Sternberg claims, have different amounts of these three components. *Liking* consists of intimacy without passion or commitment. *Infatuation*, or love at first sight, is passion alone, in the absence of commitment or intimacy. When a person is committed to a relationship that lacks both intimacy and passion, the result is *empty love*, to use Sternberg's term. *Romantic love* is intimacy and passion combined, without much commitment (though commitment may come later). When passion is absent but intimacy and commitment are present, we have what is called *companionate love*, the kind of love that sometimes occurs after many years of marriage. Passion and commitment without intimacy

Children's secure bonding with parents is reflected in secure attachments in their adult sexual relationships.

produces *fatuous love,* the type that is found in a marriage that follows a whirl-wind courtship. The partners have a strong sexual attraction and have decided to share their lives, but they have not yet developed much knowledge of each other or deep feelings of emotional closeness. What Sternberg refers to as *consummate love* is the richest of all; it consists of all three components—intimacy, passion, and commitment.

One strength of Sternberg's theory is that, in identifying love's structure (its components), it can account for love's many variations. Another strength is that the theory can deal with love as a process, as something that changes over time. It allows us to describe change in terms of shifts in the mix of love's three components. In a marriage, for instance, the passion component may fade over the years, while intimacy and commitment remain strong. Fatuous love, characterized by passion and commitment, may gradually acquire intimacy and become consummate love.

Sternberg's theory also has some limitations, the most basic of which is the fact that it is primarily descriptive. While it defines different types of love in terms of three components, it gives us no framework for understanding why these different types occur and who is most likely to experience each one.

A Developmental Perspective

A developmental perspective recently proposed by Cindy Hazan and Philip Shaver attempts to overcome this limitation (Hazan and Shaver, 1987; Shaver, Hazan, and Bradshaw, 1988; Shaver and Hazan, 1988). According to this view, love relationships differ because people have learned different things about love during early childhood. More specifically, Hazan and Shaver assert that adults show three major styles of love relationship, which mirror the types of attachments that develop between infants and their parents—especially the mother, who is usually a baby's primary caregiver (see Chapter 15).

People with a *secure* style of attachment find it easy to get close to a partner and feel comfortable relying on that person. They rarely worry about being abandoned or having someone demand too much intimacy of them. Peers find them confident, likeable, and open (Kobak and Sceery, 1988). In contrast, people with an *anxious/avoidant* style of attachment say that when someone tries to get close they feel uncomfortable. They find it hard to trust another person completely and do not like to be dependent. Others often describe them as relatively defensive. Finally, people with an *anxious/ambivalent* style of attachment say that their partners are reluctant to get as emotionally close as they would like. They often worry that their partners do not really love them and will not stay with them for long. Their desire to get extremely close sometimes scares other people away. Peers describe them as self-conscious, insecure, and preoccupied with relationship issues.

Hazan and Shaver (1987) are convinced that these three adult styles of attachment have their roots in the child's relationship with the parents during infancy. They found that adults' descriptions of their parents' behavior toward them in early childhood could be used to predict the nature of their most important adult love relationship. People with a secure style of loving described their parents as generally warm and supportive; those with an anxious/avoidant style said their parents were demanding, critical, and uncaring; those with an anxious/ambivalent style said their parents were unpredictable—sometimes responsive, sometimes not. Significantly, the same parental characteristics can also be used to predict secure, avoidant, or ambivalent forms of attachment by infants to parents. Interestingly, too, these three styles of attachment occur in roughly the same proportions in adults as in babies. In Hazan and Shaver's research, close to 60 percent of adults were categorized as secure, and the rest were fairly equally divided between anxious/avoidant and anxious/ambivalent styles of loving.

On the basis of Hazan and Shaver's findings, some psychologists speculate that the nature of a baby's attachment to parents shapes the *schemas,* or mental models (see Chapter 8), that the child develops about close relationships and the self. These early schemas are used to organize and guide relationships with others throughout life (Bretherton and Waters, 1985). It is as if we learn a role in a certain kind of movie and tend to keep playing it all our lives. New experiences can change our views of what is possible in a love relationship, thus encouraging us to rewrite our role. According to this theory, however, complete change in a person's style of loving is unlikely. We tend to stick with the role we learned during infancy because it feels familiar and "comfortable" to us, even in the midst of considerable emotional pain.

The theory that adult styles of loving evolve from infants' styles of attachment to their parents has several appealing features. First, it is consistent with the observation that love can take many forms. Second, it explains how at least some of these forms of love come into existence. Third, it allows both healthy and unhealthy forms of love to fit into a single framework. Fourth, it offers a possible explanation as to why the adult quest for love is so widespread. Just as babies need secure attachment to their parent to provide a sound emotional base from which to explore the world, so adults need love relationships to gain the sense of confidence and self-worth that enables them to use their creative talents to the fullest (Heard and Lake, 1986). This new perspective on love points the way to an exciting direction for future research into intimate human relationships (Clark and Reiss, 1988; Sternberg, 1986).

SUMMARY

The Development of Sexual Identity

- Sexual identity, the sense of being male or female, is influenced by both biological factors (genes and hormones) and social ones (how a person is taught to behave and to view the self).
- Transsexualism, in which sexual identity is inconsistent with a person's anatomical sex, is an unusual condition that is still not fully understood.

Human Sexual Responses

- Human sexual behavior is not under the rigid hormonal control found in other animal species. In humans, social, cultural, and psychological factors are far more important than biological ones in determining the who, where, when, and why of sexual activity.
- People are sexually aroused by various kinds of stimuli, including tactile, auditory, and visual ones. But sexual fantasies are often the most powerful forms of sexual stimulation.
- According to Masters and Johnson, the human sexual response can be divided into four phases: excitement, plateau, orgasm, and resolution. These four phases occur in both men and women regardless of their age or their form of sexual activity.
- Any problem that persistently prevents a person from engaging in sexual relations or from reaching orgasm during sex is known as a sexual disorder. Today there are various forms of sex therapy to treat these sexual problems.
- Most people stay sexually active into old age. Although, physiologically, there are some declines in sexual functioning with advancing years, these are usually not enough to diminish the pleasure of sexual activity.

Sexual Behavior in America

- There is a wide variety of sexual practices in our society. Masturbation, for instance, is extremely common, and Americans may be masturbating much earlier in life than they once did. Premarital sex appears to have increased among women. As has generally been the case with men, only a minority of American women remain virgins until marriage. The incidence of extramarital sex appears to have stayed relatively constant except among young women, whose rate is now approaching that of men. Homosexual experience is fairly common during adolescence, but only a small proportion of our population is exclusively homosexual.
- The primary motive for rape is not sexual gratification, but anger or the assertion of power. Victims of rape may have trouble maintaining a normal family or work life, and they often suffer sexual problems that can last for years. Incest occurs in families of all social classes. The victims almost always suffer psychological damage, and the younger the child the worse that damage is.
- Sexual behavior may be gradually changing as a result of the AIDS crisis. Homosexual men report that they are now being more cautious about their sexual partners and are more likely to take precautions, including the use of condoms. One group that does not yet seem to be practicing "safer sex" is the adolescent population. One reason is that, due to a number of factors, teenagers often feel invulnerable to risks.

Sex, Intimacy, and Love

- The emotion of love often accompanies intimate relationships in which the partners express their closeness through sexual activity. But why can the experience of love be so different from one relationship to another? One theory is that different instances of love have different mixes of three components: intimacy, passion, and commitment. Another theory is that different styles of loving in adulthood evolve from different styles of attachment (secure, anxious/avoidant, and anxious/ambivalent) that develop between infants and their parents.

KEY TERMS

bisexual
ejaculation
erogenous zones
estrogen
estrus
excitement phase
homosexual
heterosexual
incest

inhibited female orgasm
inhibited male orgasm
male erectile disorder
orgasm
orgasmic dysfunction
plateau phase
premature ejaculation
rape

refractory period
resolution phase
semen
sexual disorder
sexual identity
sexuality
testosterone
transsexualism
vaginismus

CONCEPT REVIEW

1. Describe the evidence in support of the views that strongly emphasize social influences on sexual identity. What kind of evidence supports an emphasis on biological influences?

2. Define *transsexualism*. How is this condition treated? What are the suggested causes?

3. What are the phases of the human sexual response cycle? Who originally identified these phases? What makes human females sexually unique?

4. Describe the major sexual dysfunctions. How do Masters and Johnson account for these problems? Describe the various approaches to treatment of these problems.

5. In general, how does aging affect sexual performance and satisfaction?

6. How have attitudes toward masturbation changed during the past few decades?

7. Describe current trends in attitudes and behavior regarding premarital and extramarital heterosexual activity.

8. Distinguish between *homosexuality* and *bisexuality*. What factors are thought to be involved in the development of a homosexual orientation?

9. Define *rape* and *incest*. How prevalent is incest in our society? What are some of the psychological consequences of rape and incest for the victims?

10. In general, how has the AIDS epidemic affected sexual behavior? Why are many adolescents still at high risk for getting AIDS?

11. Describe the basic components of Sternberg's triangular theory of love. In what ways does Hazan and Shaver's developmental perspective disagree with Sternberg's theory? What are advantages of each of these two theories?

CRITICAL THINKING

1. Considering that sexual behavior involves intimate and private acts, describe the special problems that sex researchers face, and discuss how these problems may influence their findings. How might research of this nature affect the behavior of individual subjects and couples who agree to participate?

2. What special contributions can psychology make to our understanding of love? Are there aspects of love that may remain beyond the scope of scientific investigation?

PART FIVE

The Developing Person

..Infancy and Childhood

The fetus began its struggle to be born on a freezing night in January. The struggle was long and hard, prompting the attending physician to give the mother a dose of chloroform. In 1882, this was a risky process, and both mother and fetus lapsed into unconsciousness. With forceps, the physician pulled the limp infant into the world. He was a big baby, weighing at least 10 pounds, and his skin was blue. Slaps on the buttocks had no effect; the baby refused to breathe. The physician began mouth-to-mouth resuscitation, desperately forcing air into the unconscious body. Minutes went by. At last the blue skin took on a rosy tint, the tiny chest heaved, and a loud cry broke the silence. Franklin Delano Roosevelt had entered the world (Davis, 1972).

In the years that followed his difficult birth, this infant became the only man who would be elected to four terms as president of the United States. But Franklin Roosevelt became the unique person that he was through the same process of change by which you became—and are still becoming—the unique person that you are. This universal process of age-related change over the life span is known as **development.** It's a familiar word, but psychologists who study the life span use it in a specific way; they apply it to *any* age-related change in body or behavior, whether the change is positive, negative, or neutral.

DEVELOPMENT   any age-related change in body or behavior, whether positive, negative, or neutral

Developmental change is influenced by more than the normal factors we all experience at about the same point in our life spans—beginning to walk, starting school, becoming parents, and so on. Our development is also influenced by the particular cultural circumstances of our times, such as wars, depressions, and inventions, as well as by physical or social circumstances unique to each of us— illness, divorce, winning a lottery, going to prison. All these factors feed into the complex interaction of heredity and environment, which influence each other in a never-ending spiral. In this chapter, as we trace the child's path from womb to the brink of puberty, and in the next chapter, as we follow the course of development from adolescence through old age, we observe development in the context of its major themes.

THEMES AND ISSUES IN DEVELOPMENT

As the story of development unfolds, several enduring themes appear. The first theme concerns the respective roles of nature (our heredity) and nurture (our environment). The second theme has to do with whether people change radically as they pass through life, or whether personality and cognitive capabilities tend to remain fairly stable from infancy through old age. The third theme concerns the nature of development: whether our skills and abilities develop in a smooth, continuous manner or go through a series of separate, distinct stages.

Nature and Nurture

As we indicated in Chapter 1, all psychologists emphasize the interaction of heredity and environment in development, but they may disagree about the relative importance of each in specific areas. Some developmental psychologists, for example, believe that our personality is heavily influenced by our inborn temperament (nature). Others believe that our experiences while growing up (nurture) are the primary influence.

MATURATION   the changes in body or behavior that result from physical processes and not from learning

Our heritage as members of the human species ensures that each of us has a genetically programmed timetable for **maturation,** which refers to changes in body or behavior that result from physical processes and not from learning. Puberty—the onset of sexual maturity—is a clear example of such a genetically timed event. It appears that genes also affect longevity and the rate at which a person ages (Kirkwood, 1985). Besides affecting the rate of physical maturation, genes influence our physical form and our behavioral capacities.

This aspect of "nature" ensures that development is neither accidental nor random. As children grow, we see an orderly, predictable development in every

Development in every area is affected by both heredity and environment.

area of functioning. Babies raise their heads before they sit up; they sit up before they stand; and they stand before they walk. They babble before they talk, and they speak single words before they put them together into sentences. Similar patterns of development continue throughout life.

Each of us has our own genetic makeup. But that makeup finds unique expression—in both physical and behavioral ways—through our environmental encounters. If identical twins were fed different diets—one well nourished, one malnourished—the twin who ate well would grow taller than the other twin. Genes, then, do not specify a particular height, but a *pattern* of growth that varies depending on environmental factors. The amount by which growth can vary is known as a **reaction range,** which refers to the unique span of possible responses to environmental influences that a person encounters, including the physical context of development, social relationships, and cultural factors (see Figure 15.1).

When we look at any aspect of development, whether physical, cognitive, or social, nature and nurture are so closely intertwined that it is virtually impossible to separate them. According to Sandra Scarr (1982; Scarr and McCartney, 1983), this interaction probably affects development in three ways. First, the home may provide a passive genetic influence. Children share their parents' genes. They also live in an environment provided by their parents, in which the available experiences are partly determined by their parents' own genes and experiences. A child whose parents are musicians will grow up surrounded by music, will learn to sing and play instruments at an early age, and will have musicians as role models. Second, a child's genetically influenced appearance and behavior evoke particular responses from others, which, in turn, will affect the way the child behaves. Third, a child actively seeks out some kinds of experiences and ignores others. Because children cannot pay attention to everything that goes on, they select experiences that are pleasant, interesting, or challenging. They avoid things that are boring, too easy, or too hard. These nature-nurture interactions continue throughout life, with passive influences waning as children leave home and active influences increasing in strength as children become more independent.

REACTION RANGE a genetic trait's span of possible responses to the environmental influences that a person encounters

Stability and Change

If we know a child's characteristics, can we predict what kind of adult that child will become? Are abilities and personality stable, or do they change over the life span? These are important questions, because if the course of development is set

SENSITIVE PERIOD a sharply restricted span of time during which an animal is extremely susceptible to specific environmental influences

IMPRINTING an immediate attachment formed by some species of birds to the first moving object they see upon hatching

by experiences in early childhood, then the chances of recovery from deprivation must be slim.

Researchers became especially concerned about early experience when they discovered the existence of **sensitive periods** (or "critical periods") in animals. A sensitive period is a sharply restricted span of time during which an animal is extremely susceptible to certain kinds of environmental influences. The same experiences encountered before or after this period may have little influence. The most spectacular example of a sensitive period occurs in some species of birds, which develop a strong, long-lasting attachment to another object through a process called **imprinting**. It develops when the newly hatched bird sees and follows the first moving object it encounters—usually its mother. But a bird can become imprinted on a human being, a bouncing rubber ball, a box on wheels, or a bird of another species. Although imprinting occurs only during a sensitive period shortly after birth, its effects can be modified by later experience (Columbio, 1982). Sharply defined sensitive periods have not been identified for human babies, but some developmentalists believe that unless children form a close, emotional bond to another person during their first two years, their social development will suffer (MacDonald, 1985).

No matter which side of the argument they come down on, developmentalists generally agree that there is some stability to development and that change is possible. The disagreement is over how much of either is probable.

Take the matter of intellectual functioning. In Chapter 11 we cited several longitudinal studies in which researchers found no way to predict a child's IQ score from tests given in infancy (Wohlwill, 1980). Yet, as we noted in Chapter 7, other researchers have found that the rapidity with which a five-month-old habituates to an object and then pays attention to some new object is a fairly good predictor of the child's scores at age six (Rose and Wallace, 1985). Similar discrepancies have been found concerning personality. Some researchers have found little connection between early temperament and later personality; others have found that the way fifteen-month-old babies behave when reunited with their mothers after a brief separation foretells their social and cognitive competence at the age of four (Waters, Wippman, and Sroufe, 1979).

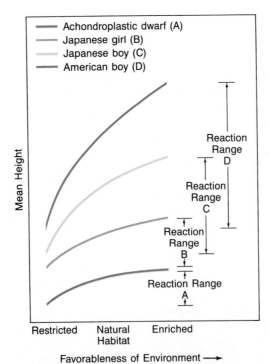

Figure 15.1 When the heights of adolescents with four different genetic makeups are compared, it becomes clear that environment and genes combine to produce development. The Japanese boy (genetic makeup C) who had grown up in an optimum environment would be taller than the American boy (genetic makeup D) who had grown up in a severely restricted environment. But if both environments were natural, severely restricted or optimum, the American boy would be taller. Under no circumstances could the dwarf (genetic makeup A) be as tall as any of the other three. (From Gottesman, 1974.)

Continuity and Discontinuity

A final theme in the study of human development is the issue of continuity versus discontinuity. Do we human beings develop our skills and abilities in a smooth, continuous manner, as a daisy grows from a seedling to a mature, blooming plant? Or do we develop by going through a series of clearly differentiated stages, as a butterfly goes from caterpillar to pupa to winged insect?

Psychologists who see development as continuous trace the gradual emergence of skills and behavior. For example, they see the seeds of later language development in the "turn-taking" dialogues of early infancy, when parents supply both sides of the conversation, and in social games like peekaboo, where the baby gets specific lessons in nonverbal conversational skills. In the field of cognitive development, many developmental psychologists who view development as continuous take information processing as their model and see the child's increasingly complicated thought and behavior as the faster and more experienced use of just a few primitive mental processes (Siegler, 1983).

Those who assume that development progresses through stages look for distinctive milestones that mark the onset of the various stages. For example, they see the ability to use words to stand for objects as signaling a clear step from one stage to another. In **stage theories,** like those of Jean Piaget and Erik Erikson, development proceeds in discrete steps that always occur in a given sequence. Within each stage, abilities, motives, and skills are linked together in some cohesive pattern. When new ways of functioning emerge, they are not simply recombinations of earlier patterns but a radical restructuring. The step from one stage to the next is fairly abrupt, and all the abilities and behavior that typify the stage should appear at about the same time (Flavell, 1985).

After dominating the field of cognitive development for several decades, the concept of distinct stages fell into disrepute when research failed to support it consistently (Fischer, 1983). It was found that a closer look at an earlier stage often revealed some aspects of a behavior that supposedly emerges, full-blown, in a later stage. For example, according to stage theory, two-year-olds are supposed to believe that other people see everything just as they do; when sharing a picture, however, they carefully turn it toward the other person. In addition, the transition between stages is usually lengthy, and the various abilities within a stage may develop at staggered intervals and sometimes in different orders (Flavell, 1985).

Despite these problems, the notion of stages is still very useful in describing development. As we will see, Piaget's cognitive theory has had an enormous influence on our understanding of children's thought. So has Erikson's theory of psychosocial development, which incorporates eight stages corresponding to the way our culture commonly divides the life span. In this chapter we look at the infancy and childhood stages; the stages of adolescence and adulthood will be considered in the next chapter.

Before we consider the various stages of development during the life span, however, let's take a brief look at how human beings develop before and immediately after birth.

STAGE THEORIES theories in which abilities, motives, or skills emerge in a predictable, patterned sequence, producing fairly abrupt changes in behavior

PRENATAL DEVELOPMENT

Your own birth was as unlikely as winning the grand prize in a state lottery. Of the 350 million sperm released in a single ejaculation, each with a different genetic makeup, only one in a thousand finds its way to the fallopian tube that contains the mother's egg, or ovum. And of those sperm, only one has a chance to fertilize the ovum. These basic mechanisms ensure genetic variability for our species and within your own family.

At the moment of conception, a predictable sequence of development begins, transforming the fertilized egg, or **zygote,** into a baby. During this transformation, which takes thirty-eight weeks to complete, the genetic instructions within the zygote interact with the uterine environment to determine physical appearance, the tendency toward certain personality characteristics, and intellectual potential. Nature and nurture are at work long before the baby draws its first breath.

ZYGOTE the fertilized ovum during the first two weeks of development

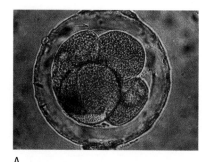

A

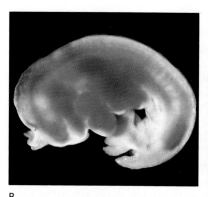

B

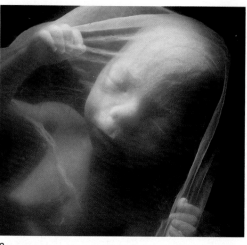

C

(A) A human zygote (fertilized egg) at the four-cell stage of the germinal period; it would still be traveling down the mother's fallopian tube and would not yet be implanted in her uterus. (B) A four- to five-week-old embryo. (C) A fetus at sixteen weeks.

Stages of Prenatal Development

The course of prenatal development falls into three basic periods: germinal, embryonic, and fetal. During the **germinal period** (from fertilization to two weeks), the zygote begins the process of rapid cell division that eventually produces a human body. At first the cells are all identical, but within two weeks they begin to differentiate into three primary layers that will form various tissues and organs. How do cells know whether they are destined to be part of the nervous system, the skeleton, or the organs? What triggers the process is still a mystery, but some scientists believe that gene-regulating chemicals within the zygote reprogram all embryonic cells, sending them to particular locations and assigning their functions. Some aspects of this mystery are beginning to yield to research: molecules that seem to direct the nature and growth of nerve cells have recently been identified (Thoenen and Edgar, 1985).

Soon after the start of the **embryonic period** (from two to eight weeks), the organism, now called an **embryo,** is connected to the mother's body by a flexible structure called the **placenta,** which delivers nutrients and oxygen and carries away wastes. During this period, the embryo grows until it measures more than an inch in length. Its heart beats, and the beginnings of kidneys, liver, and a digestive tract have appeared. There is a spinal cord and a recognizable brain, and bone cells have begun to form. During this period of development the organism is most vulnerable to prenatal environmental influences and may be spontaneously aborted (miscarried) if it is seriously defective.

Once the major organs and physical features have taken shape, the developing organism is known as a **fetus.** During the **fetal period** (from eight weeks to birth), development shifts from forming organs to organizing their structures and establishing their functions. During the fetal period, the organism's activity level rises steadily. At nine weeks, the fetus bends its fingers; it also curls or straightens its toes in response to touch. Gradually, responses change. Instead of moving the entire body, the fetus moves only muscles in the stimulated area. Spontaneous movements are frequent and strong, and by sixteen weeks the mother begins to notice them. At this time, the fetus is 6 or 7 inches long and weighs 4 ounces. The face looks human. Although the major internal organs are present and working, they could not keep the fetus alive outside the uterus.

By twenty-four weeks, rhythmic activity cycles develop; the fetus appears to sleep and wake. The fetus can cry, open and close its eyes, and look up, down, and sideways. If born at this time, it may survive, though only with intensive medical care. During the last six weeks before birth the fetus seems much like a full-term infant; it sucks its thumb, yawns, and grunts, just like the newborn it will soon become.

GERMINAL PERIOD   the prenatal developmental phase from fertilization to two weeks when the zygote begins the process of rapid cell development

EMBRYONIC PERIOD   the prenatal developmental phase from two weeks to eight weeks, when major organ systems form

EMBRYO   the prenatal developing organism from two weeks to eight weeks

PLACENTA   the flexible structure of tissue that delivers nutrients and oxygen to a developing organism and carries away wastes

FETUS   the prenatal developing organism from eight weeks until birth

FETAL PERIOD   the prenatal developmental phase from eight weeks until birth, when organs organize their structures and establish their functions

Threats in the Prenatal Environment

The uterus may seem to be a safe environment, but external factors can threaten the health—and even the survival—of the growing fetus. A malnourished mother may be unable to supply the nutrients that are necessary for healthy growth. In addition, **teratogens,** which are agents that can alter or kill the developing organism, can reach the fetus through the placenta. Teratogens include diseases such as rubella (German measles) and AIDS, toxins such as drugs and alcohol, and radiation and other environmental pollutants.

Drugs, whether legitimate medicines or illegal street drugs like heroin and cocaine, are a major hazard for the developing fetus. In the 1960s many European women who took the sedative thalidomide early in pregnancy (while fetal limbs were forming) gave birth to babies without arms or legs. Recently, researchers have discovered that the acne medication Accutane, if used by pregnant women, may cause fetal death or serious malformation of the baby's face, skull, brain, heart, and thymus gland (Schmeck, 1985).

Widely used legal drugs—such as cigarettes, caffeine drinks (coffee and cola), and especially alcohol—may pose threats to the fetus. Alcoholic mothers have three times as many stillbirths as other mothers, and their babies often have **fetal alcohol syndrome,** which is characterized by mental retardation, slowed growth, and physical malformation. Even social drinking by the mother may have lingering effects on the child, causing slowed reaction time and trouble concentrating during the preschool years (Streissguth et al., 1984). Recently, researchers have found that children whose mothers took more than three drinks a day during pregnancy had IQ scores five points below the overall average at age four (Streissguth et al., 1989). If mothers stop social drinking as soon as they learn they are pregnant, they can reduce the lingering effects of alcohol exposure (Coles et al., 1987). (Since most women don't find out they are pregnant until four to six weeks into the pregnancy, the wisest course seems to be to avoid alcohol entirely if there is any possibility of pregnancy.) Cigarette smoking has different effects: mothers who smoke are more likely to miscarry and to have babies who die early in infancy, and are twice as likely as nonsmokers to have babies with low birth

TERATOGEN an agent, such as disease, toxin, or environmental pollutant, that can alter or kill the developing organism during the prenatal period

FETAL ALCOHOL SYNDROME a condition afflicting babies of alcoholic mothers, characterized by mental retardation, slowed growth, and physical malformation

Pregnancy and smoking are a bad combination. Women who smoke while pregnant run a higher risk of miscarrying or of delivering babies with low birth weight.

weights. Caffeine, too, has come under scrutiny as potentially harmful (Jacobsen et al., 1984). Many physicians now advise prospective mothers to give up caffeine before becoming pregnant.

As environmental pollution spreads, its effects on the fetus have come under increasing study. Pollutants in the air or food, such as lead, mercury, and PCBs (synthetic hydrocarbons that are part of many industrial products), may build up in the bodies of mother and fetus—with insidious effects. In one study, women who regularly ate fish contaminated with PCBs showed a high level of premature births and low-birth-weight babies (Jacobsen et al., 1985).

Whether or not teratogens produce an abnormality in a developing fetus depends on the dosage, the genetic susceptibility of the fetus, the mother's physical condition, and the timing of the exposure (Johnson and Kochlar, 1983). Timing is extremely important: organs that are forming are especially vulnerable to teratogens. On organs that have already formed or on those that have not yet begun to develop, however, the same agents have less serious effects—or no effects at all.

DEVELOPMENT OF THE NEWBORN

Human newborns are the most helpless and immature of all primate species. They cannot sit or stand, let alone walk or run. If we were to be born at the same stage of development as other primates, we would have to spend twenty-one months in the uterus, not nine (Gould, 1977). A human newborn still resembles a fetus; it seems that the evolution of our large brain has made it necessary for us to be born "too soon." If the human brain were any larger at birth, the fetus could not pass through the birth canal; but if the birth canal were much wider, a woman could not walk upright (Leakey and Lewin, 1977).

Some babies are premature even by human standards. Those who are born so early (before thirty-three weeks in the uterus) or tiny (less than 2000 grams) that they need medical assistance to survive have the best chance if they go home to an upper- or middle-class environment. Babies who would probably have developed normally in a middle-class home are likely to show intellectual impairment when they grow up in a disadvantaged home (Kopp, 1986). The interaction of nature and nurture is as important in the case of prematurity as it is in any other aspect of development.

Reflexes and Sensory Abilities

Human newborns may be weak and helpless, but in some ways they are surprisingly capable. Evolution has sent them into the world equipped with more than a dozen *reflexes*—unlearned responses to specific stimuli—that enable young babies to master essential motor skills. A gentle touch on the cheek or corner of the mouth causes a baby to turn its head (and mouth) in that direction; this *rooting reflex* helps the baby find the nipple. Within a few days, newborns are eating smoothly, which means that they have coordinated three separate reflexes: sucking, swallowing, and breathing. Other reflexes that may help babies adapt to their new surroundings include closing the eyes to bright lights and jerking away from sources of pain.

Some of their responses make newborns seem more capable than they actually are. When an object passes near them, they reach out, opening their hands as if to grab it. But the newborn's reach seems to be an involuntary motion of the arm and shoulder that is controlled by the brain stem. It simply indicates that the infant is paying attention to the object. This primitive response disappears after a month or so. When it reappears at about four months, control has shifted to the cortex, and a more mature pattern has been established in which the eye guides hand and fingers (Hofsten, 1984).

Babies come into the world with their senses functioning: they can see, hear, smell, feel, and taste. But some of the newborn's sensory systems are developed

Sucking and grasping are two of the reflexes with which babies are born.

further than others. The newborn's senses of touch, taste and smell are more acute that the senses of sight and hearing. This staggered development of the sensory systems probably minimizes the chaotic jumble of sensations a newborn would otherwise have to deal with (Turkewitz and Kenny, 1982).

Sight, though functional, is probably the least developed sense in newborns (Gottlieb, 1983). Their vision is blurry and lacks depth perception. Although hearing is not yet acute, newborns can distinguish their mother's voice from that of another woman (DeCaspar and Fifer, 1980). Babies are very sensitive to taste: bitter liquids produce a rudimentary gag reflex; sour liquids cause them to purse their lips; sweet liquids relax them (Rosenstein and Oster, 1988). They also seem to distinguish between "pleasant" and "unpleasant" odors (Steiner, 1979). At ten days old, breast-fed babies can recognize the scent of their own mother (Cernoch and Porter, 1985). (Sensation and perception in babies are discussed in detail in Chapters 4 and 5.)

Babies come into the world ready to use their sensory abilities. They can learn, as long as the connections between events involve responses that help them survive—such as head turning and sucking, which are associated with feeding. This ability to connect one event with another is vital to their development, because such simple connections provide the basis for all later behavior.

A Basis for Social Interaction

The newborn's capacities seem designed to ensure the baby's survival, because they mesh naturally with the ways adults tend to behave with babies. Most adults respond quickly to a baby's cries in order to stop the inherently arousing and aversive sounds (Frodi et al., 1978). Newborns see objects most clearly at a distance from 6 to 12 inches from the eye—approximately the range of eye contact with an adult who is cradling or nursing an infant. Newborns prefer sounds in the frequency range of the human voice, especially high-pitched voices; in a seemingly automatic adjustment, most adults, even those who have no experience with babies, tend to talk to infants in a high-pitched, exaggerated voice (Newport, Gleitman, and Gleitman, 1977; Papousek, Papousek, and Bornstein, 1985). Thus the behavioral "tools" for survival seem built into newborn behavior, and the caregiving context promotes the sort of interchange between adult and baby that is necessary if the baby is to flourish.

Temperament and Social Interaction

TEMPERAMENT observable differences in emotional behavior, responsiveness to stimulation, and motor activity

Any parent with more than one child will tell you that no two babies are alike. Some are fussy, some are easy-going; some are tremendously curious, some seem indifferent. In other words, each baby has his or her own **temperament,** which consists of early, observable differences in emotional behavior, responsiveness to stimulation, and motor activity (Goldsmith et al., 1987). In temperament are the seeds of a baby's developing personality.

Many researchers believe that a newborn's temperament is primarily determined by heredity (Scarr and McCartney, 1983; Buss and Plomin, 1984). In this view, genes influence a baby's level of activity and the way he or she responds to the environment. Together, these factors determine the way a baby interacts with others, the way others interact with a baby, and what sort of experiences a baby seeks out or avoids. As a baby interacts with people and objects in the environment, aspects of temperament may remain stable, may change, or may even disappear.

Social relations—and thus environmental influences on temperament—begin almost immediately. Baby and parents carry on intricate nonverbal communication from the first days. Parents catch their baby's gaze, smile, blow on the skin or touch it lightly, and jiggle the baby. The baby responds, either returning the gaze or smiling reflexively. Before the baby is a month old, the smile is accompanied by brightened eyes and becomes almost a grin (Field, 1981).

From the very beginning, parents imitate their newborns' sounds and facial expressions. They interpret their newborns' smiles, noises, and changes in expression as meaningful answers to their own questions (Papousek and Papousek, 1984). These early "conversations," in which the parent takes both sides of the dialogue, establish the basis for social interaction, and eventually language.

Through individual differences in temperament, heredity affects the way early social relationships develop. Babies who return a parental gaze steadily or who smile early encourage their parents' attempts to establish a social relationship. Babies who are rarely alert and quiet, who seem instead to spend all their time either sleeping or crying, can frustrate a parent's attempts to communicate (Osofsky and Connors, 1979).

In a major longitudinal study, Alexander Thomas and Stella Chess (1977) found four major categories of temperament in infants: easy (40 percent), difficult (10 percent), slow to warm up (15 percent), and average (35 percent, who did not fit into any distinctive category). But they concluded that the key to personality development was not the child's temperamental category but the "goodness of fit" between the infant's temperament and the parents' style. For example, parents who are upset by a "difficult" baby's impulsiveness and react to their twelve-month-old's escapades with repeated prohibitions and hand slaps may wind up with a two-year-old who is always in trouble. But parents who simply keep tempting objects out of a "difficult" baby's reach may have no more than average trouble with their two-year-old (Lee and Bates, 1985).

Regardless of temperament, all babies grow and become more independent. They seek out certain kinds of experiences more and more actively. In doing so, they are helping shape their own development, which is traditionally divided into three broad areas—physical, cognitive (including language development), and social development.

PHYSICAL DEVELOPMENT IN INFANCY AND CHILDHOOD

Physically helpless newborns soon become competent toddlers, deftly manipulating objects and exploring every corner of their world. This transformation takes place gradually and systematically. Establishing body stability and learning to coordinate the joints and muscles precedes sitting, standing, walking, manipulating objects, and responding rapidly to environmental change (Shumway-Cook and Woollacott, 1985). Babies must master all these different tasks within a constantly changing environment that keeps altering the nature of each task. Walking up stairs, for example, requires different actions of muscles and joints than does walking on level ground.

Brain Development

As we saw in Chapter 3, many physical responses depend on the maturation of the brain. At birth the cortex is exceedingly immature, and most newborn behavior is probably reflexive or controlled by lower parts of the brain. PET scans (an imaging technique described in Chapter 3) of infants between the ages of five days and eighteen months support this view (Chugani and Phelps, 1986). In newborns, the most active areas of the brain are the primary motor and sensory areas, the basal ganglia (which integrate information from various parts of the brain), the brain stem (which controls such automatic activities as breathing and circulation), and the cerebellum (which is involved in movement). By eleven weeks, activity begins to spread through the cortex. By seven and one-half months, the pattern of activity in a baby's brain resembles that seen in adult brains. Neurons have matured, and synaptic connections between neurons are multiplying.

Areas of the cortex that control particular sensory and motor functions develop at different rates, with each controlled skill appearing as the corresponding cortical area develops. Hearing improves rapidly as the sensory areas mature. Deficiencies in vision also disappear. By six months, an infant's vision and hearing are as acute as an adult's (Banks and Salapatek, 1983; Olsho, 1984).

Maturation and experience *both* seem to be necessary for the development of true depth perception. This was made clear in a classic series of experiments involving the "visual cliff" (Gibson and Walk, 1960; Scarr and Salapatek, 1970; Campos et al., 1978). The visual-cliff apparatus consists of a sheet of clear plexiglass over a patterned surface that gives the illusion of having a deep and a shallow side, as shown in the photograph below. Very young babies who are placed on the plexiglass seem to notice the apparent drop but are not frightened. Their hearts slow, an indication of interest. Older babies who can crawl seem frightened by the drop: their hearts speed up, and they will not cross the plexiglass over the "deep" side, even to reach their mothers, who beckon and hold out toys.

The visual-cliff apparatus. An infant who can crawl may cross the glass surface over the "shallow" side but is unlikely to venture out over an edge that appears to be a sudden drop or to cross the surface over the "deep" side.

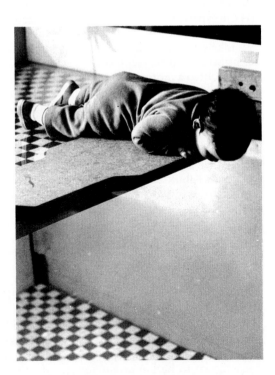

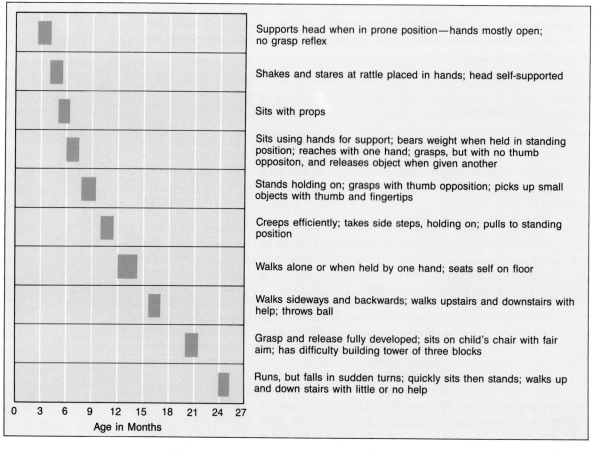

Figure 15.2 Some of the milestones in motor development that occur over the first two years of life. Each bar indicates the approximate average age of occurrence. Individual infants may demonstrate these skills somewhat earlier or later than the average indicated. (After Lenneberg, 1967, and Bayley, 1969.)

This fear of heights, which protects babies from serious falls, develops only after development in the visual cortex makes depth perception possible *and* the baby has the experience with crawling that is needed to transfer the perception of depth into a warning of danger.

Like sensory skills, motor skills cannot develop until the corresponding areas of the brain mature. Yet motor development is not simply a matter of brain maturation. Often a motor skill also depends on development in the sensory receptors, in other parts of the brain, in the spinal cord, or on the growth of joints and muscles (Parmelee and Sigman, 1983; Thelen, 1987). Some researchers believe that a baby's use of the body and nervous system leads to growth in corresponding brain areas, rather than the other way around (Rose, 1973). The processes are probably interdependent. The important point is that no skill develops in isolation from other aspects of development.

Once babies begin to walk, their world expands. They can approach other people (fostering social interaction) or leave them (fostering independence). Walking also brings changes in the way they are treated. ʟ cause walking makes a youngster seem less like a baby, parents are likely to begin to expect their toddler to adapt to family routines. Figure 15.2 charts the progress during a baby's first two years.

Stimulation and Physical Development

Environmental factors influence how fast and how well children develop physical, perceptual, and motor skills. Nutrition, illness, and stress are obvious influences, but sensory stimulation, physical handling, and motor-skill training have also been shown to be important for an infant's development.

Normally, babies receive a wide variety of sensory stimulation from their environment. Their parents pick them up, talk to them, play games with them, give them toys, and take them on outings. Babies who have little social or intellectual stimulation and who lack opportunities for physical activity are profoundly retarded. In one particularly dramatic example, babies in a foundling home in Lebanon spent most of their first year lying on their backs in bare cribs, virtually ignored by adults. No one played with them or answered their cries. At meal times they ate from a bottle that was supported by a pillow. As a result, infants more than a year old could not even sit up (Dennis and Sayegh, 1965). But when these infants were propped into sitting positions and allowed to play for as little as an hour each day with such ordinary objects as fresh flowers, pieces of colored sponge, and colored plastic disks, their rate of motor development accelerated immediately.

Similarly, gentle touching and physical handling seem to benefit premature infants. In one study, researchers went to a hospital nursery every day for ten days and spent 15 minutes, three times a day, stroking the heads, shoulders, backs, arms, hands, legs, and feet of premature babies (Scafidi et al., 1986). They also gently flexed and then extended each infant's arms and legs. These "preemies" spent more time awake, gained weight more rapidly, and left the hospital about six days earlier than those in a control group.

Differences in cultural practices also point to the effects of stimulation. In a number of African tribes, infants sit, stand, walk, or crawl about a month earlier than American infants. Their faster development is not the result of genetic differences but of routine child-care practices (Super, 1976). African mothers tend to spend more time training their babies in basic motor skills; one tribe's instruction in walking starts when babies are about seven months old.

There are limits to the accelerating effects of stimulation and training, however. No matter how much exercise infants are given, none will walk at six months; the physical and neural components of the skill must mature first. African babies' acceleration remains within the normal range of human differences, and the babies show accelerated development only in the specific skill in which they are trained. The important point is that, within limits, genetically controlled developmental sequences respond to environmental stimulation. As we will see, this applies to cognitive development as well as to motor skills.

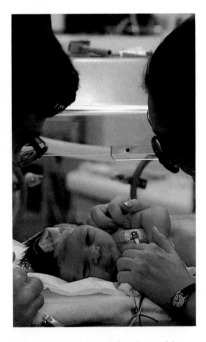

This prematurely born infant is receiving medical care from her doctors and emotional care from her parents. Such stimulation helps to foster healthy development in at-risk babies, especially if parents continue to provide special attention at home.

Although cultural practices can accelerate or retard the development of motor skills, Hopi babies, who spend much of their time bound to cradleboards, walk only a month or so later than babies who have extensive practice in crawling and standing.

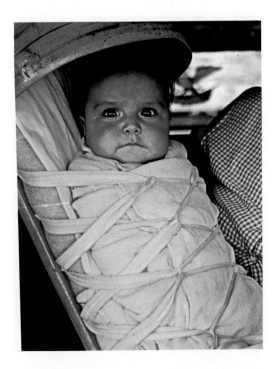

COGNITIVE DEVELOPMENT

Instead of buying their three-year-old another teddy bear, some parents choose "toys" designed to educate their child. Some researchers believe that such active efforts to promote learning are beneficial, others think they are unnecessary, and some believe they are downright harmful. But even those who favor early education warn parents not to push their children and to keep "educational" sessions from becoming too serious. As psychologist Edward Zigler has pointed out, children learn for the same reason that birds fly—they're programmed to do it (see Collings, 1984).

The new impetus to bring the classroom into the nursery has been fueled in part by researchers' discovery that babies, like newborns, are more capable creatures than psychologists once believed (see Chapter 7). Stage theorists tell us that children go through progressive restructurings of the mind, in which what children can learn is sharply limited by their level of maturation (nature). But psychologists who see development as more continuous tell us that children accumulate information gradually and learn to process it more and more swiftly, efficiently, and completely. If so, what children can learn is limited by how much they already know (nurture). In this section, we look at both the classic stage theory of Jean Piaget and the continuous-development approach of information processing.

A Stage Approach: Piaget's Theory

For nearly sixty years, Swiss psychologist Jean Piaget (1896–1980) devoted himself to understanding the development of children's intelligence. His careful observations of infants and children have provided a comprehensive account of mental development, and his ideas have served as the basis for much of our knowledge about how a child's mind grows. Piaget (1952; 1954) produced a strict stage theory of development, in which a child actively constructs his or her knowledge of the world. As a child develops, the mind undergoes a series of reorganizations. With each reorganization, the child moves into a higher level of psychological functioning. The stages are the outgrowth of human evolutionary history: children are born with a set of specifically human systems (called sensorimotor sys-

By touching and mouthing everything they can get hold of, babies learn about their world. They also learn that their actions can affect the objects around them.

tems) that allow them to interact with the environment and to incorporate experience and stimulation. Three psychological processes are vital to intellectual growth: the use of schemes, assimilation, and accommodation.

Schemes

Newborns know nothing about the objects and people that makeup their world or how their own actions affect those objects. But they begin almost immediately to acquire this knowledge by acting on objects around them, using recurrent action patterns, which Piaget called **schemes.** Grasping, throwing, and rolling are examples of an infant's schemes, which are the infant's form of thought. They seem to be related to the procedural memory schemas that we explored in Chapter 8.

Older children and adults still think in action schemes when they drive a car or play a piano, but they have also developed internalized, abstract schemes. These internalized schemes allow them to manipulate objects mentally, classify them, and understand their relationships. Adding numbers in the head replaces counting on the fingers; logical reasoning replaces trial-and-error experimentation. A ten-month-old baby, for example, may explore gravity by dropping peas from her high chair and watching intently as each one hits the floor. But an older child has internalized the notion that dropped items fall to the floor and no longer has any interest in testing it.

SCHEME a recurrent action pattern or mental structure involved in the acquisition and structuring of knowledge

Assimilation and Accommodation

The separate action schemes in a baby's mind slowly become organized, so that related behavior or thought is clustered into systems. Once babies coordinate grasping and looking, for example, they can do both at the same time. According to Piaget, this process reflects two other basic processes: *assimilation* and *accommodation.* In **assimilation,** a child adapts new information so that it fits into the framework of existing schemes. In **accommodation,** a child modifies existing schemes to make sense of new information. The two processes work together as the child interacts with the world.

ASSIMILATION the incorporation of new knowledge into existing schemes

ACCOMMODATION the modification of existing schemes to incorporate new knowledge

This child possesses a scheme for grasping objects and pulling them to her that does not adequately match the features of the environment that she is now trying to assimilate. Her scheme will not get the toy through the bars of the playpen. An accommodation to her scheme—the addition of turning to grasping and pulling—achieves a state of equilibrium.

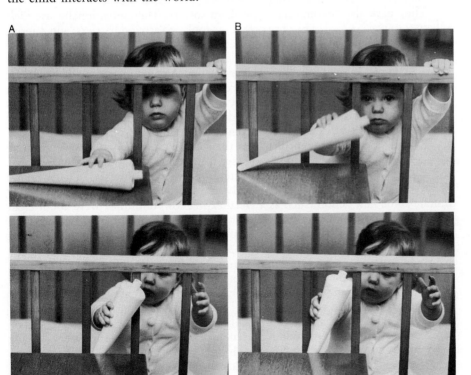

We can see how assimilation and accommodation work at a simple level by watching a baby boy's first encounter with milk in a cup. The baby already sucks competently on a nipple, so at first he sucks on the cup the way he has always sucked on his bottle (assimilation). Doing it this way makes more milk run down his chin than enter his mouth. So he adjusts his mouth-using skills until they are as effective with the hard rim of the cup as they were with the soft rubber nipple (accommodation). Through this sort of activity, children increase their knowledge of the world and their competence in it.

Stages of Cognitive Development

At each of Piaget's stages, thought is organized in a different manner. He proposed four progressively complex stages that all children go through in the same order. Although maturation is important in the emergence of each stage, neither heredity nor environment by itself can explain the emergence of each succeeding stage. Whatever labels are attached to them, Piaget's stages closely correspond to infancy, the preschool years, later childhood, and adolescence.

SENSORIMOTOR STAGE (BIRTH TO TWO YEARS)   Through most of the **sensorimotor stage,** a period when knowledge is based on the infant's sensations and physical actions, infants use their action schemes to work on the world, repeating behavior that gives them pleasure. In the process they learn about relationships among objects and relationships between their own behavior and those objects.

Babies have a lot to learn about objects. According to Piaget, newborns lack any notion of **object permanence,** the awareness that objects continue to exist when out of sight. If you drop a napkin over a stuffed animal in the hand of a baby less than eight months old, the child seems suddenly to forget about the toy and may let it drop (Gratch, 1972). But by the latter part of their first year, babies are aware that their rattles, high chairs, and parents continue to exist even when they are out of sight. When they watch you place a pillow over a toy, they will burrow beneath the pillow to retrieve it. For the first time, babies show that they have *internalized* concepts of the objects and people in their world.

They have also become active problem solvers. They intentionally use their schemes to reach a goal. They use objects as tools, go around barriers, and remove obstacles—all without any apparent forethought or planning. After the first birthday, babies begin to act like little scientists. Faced with a problem, they set about solving it through the process of trial and error. And by the second half of their second year, trial and error no longer are necessary; babies can solve problems in their heads. This is possible because they can now represent objects in their minds with symbols, an advance that allows them to "think about" their actions. Fittingly, Piaget called this ability **representational thought** (or *symbolic thought*).

Representational thought provides the foundation for another key cognitive process, known as **deferred imitation** (see the accompanying box). This is simply the ability to mimic, after a delay, actions previously observed. Piaget (1951) believed that imitation developed slowly and that babies could not immediately imitate some new action (such as a facial expression) until they were about eight months old. Deferred imitation, he contended, could come only with representational thought—when babies were about a year and a half old. This advance not only allows youngsters to imitate actions they have witnessed an hour or a day before but also opens the world of make-believe. Now they can scold a doll just as their mother scolded them or stir a "pretend" cup of tea with a spoon. For Piaget (1951), creativity, language use, mathematics, and the sciences all stem from our capacity for symbolic thought.

Piaget's timetables are not universally accepted. How soon babies can imitate facial expressions and how soon representational thought is possible are still being debated. Andrew Meltzoff and Keith Moore (1983) have reported that newborns will stick out their tongues, protrude their lips, or open their mouths in imitation of an adult, revealing, in their view, a capacity for sensory coordination and representational thought. Other researchers contend that early imitation is an

SENSORIMOTOR STAGE   in Piaget's theory, the period from birth to about age two when knowledge is based on sensations and physical actions

OBJECT PERMANENCE   understanding that objects continue to exist when out of sight

REPRESENTATIONAL THOUGHT   the ability to mentally symbolize objects that are not directly visible

DEFERRED IMITATION   the ability to mimic observed actions after a lapse of time

PSYCHOLOGY TODAY AND TOMORROW

Piaget Observes His Children

Piaget's theory of cognitive development grew out of endless hours of meticulous observation of his three children, Jacqueline, Lucienne, and Laurent. In the following passage, he describes the emergence of deferred imitation in sixteen-month-old Jacqueline:

"At 1; 4 (3) [one year, four months, three days], J[acqueline] had a visit from a little boy of 1; 6, whom she used to see from time to time, and who, in the course of the afternoon got into a terrible temper. He screamed as he tried to get out of a play-pen and pushed it backwards, stamping his feet. J. stood watching him in amazement, never having witnessed such a scene before. The next day, she herself screamed in her play-pen and tried to move it, stamping her foot lightly several times in succession. The imitation of the whole scene was most striking. Had it been immediate, it would naturally not have involved representation, but coming as it did after an interval of more than twelve hours, it must have involved some representative or pre-representative element.

At 1; 4 (7), after a visit from the same boy, she again gave a clear imitation of him, but in another position. She was standing up, and drew herself up with her head and shoulders thrown back, and laughed loudly (like the model).

. . . With regard to her deferred imitations of the behaviours of her little friend . . . it is useful to note that at the same period J. began to reproduce certain words, not at the time they were uttered, but in similar situations, and without having previously imitated them.

Thus, at 1; 4 (8) J. said "in step" as she was walking, although she had never uttered these words and they had not been said in her presence immediately before. It was thus a case of virtual imitation becoming real imitation in an active context.

At 1; 4 (10) she pointed to her mother's nose, and said "nose," again without having uttered the word before and without hearing it immediately before.

. . . Subsequently, this phenomenon naturally becomes more and more frequent. The child tends less and less to use for the first time a word or a group of words when he has just heard them. What was important from our point of view was to note the beginning of this type of vocal imitation and to relate it to the preceding observations (1962, p. 63)

unconditioned, inborn response, possibly one with an adaptive function related to feeding or to the fostering of social interaction (Björklund, 1987). According to this view, as the baby's cortex matures, intentional gazes, smiles, and head movements replace the earlier reflexive "imitations." This view meshes nicely with other patterns in which reflexes disappear as control passes to the cortex; it also supports Piaget's belief in the gradual emergence of imitation.

PREOPERATIONAL STAGE (TWO TO SEVEN YEARS) Once children can internalize schemes and think symbolically, they enter the **preoperational stage,** when their thought is intuitive, inflexible, and focused on individual events. Although they have been using words for some time, children are now able to translate their experiences into symbols and combine the symbols according to specific rules. In short, they acquire language—the most obvious example of symbolic thought.

Although preoperational children cannot reason about numbers, they are beginning to count. Two-year-olds can count in a limited manner—they may invent their own sequence of number words, but they often use them in a consistent manner. Before long, they are compulsive counters: they count raisins in the cereal bowl, cracks in the sidewalk, and flies on the windowsill. By the time they start kindergarten, they can add and subtract by counting if the number of objects is small (Gelman and Gallistel, 1978).

PREOPERATIONAL STAGE in Piaget's theory, the period from about age two to age seven, when thought is intuitive, inflexible, and focused on individual events

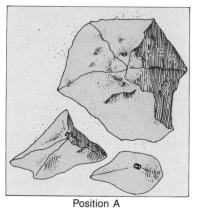

Position A

Figure 15.3 A model used to demonstrate egocentrism. Piaget and Inhelder first had children walk all around the model and look at it from all sides. Then they seated children of various ages at position A and asked them how the scene would appear to observers at other positions. Preoperational children regularly indicated that the scene would appear as it did from position A, no matter where the observer was located. Their thinking did not allow them to mentally reconstruct the scene from a point of view other than their own. (After Piaget and Inhelder, 1956.)

EGOCENTRISM the belief that everyone sees the world and responds to it exactly as you do

OPERATIONS Piaget's term for flexible, rigorous, and logical thought

CONCRETE OPERATIONAL STAGE in Piaget's theory, the period from about seven to eleven years, when thought is flexible, rigorous, and logical, but only in regard to concrete symbols

CONSERVATION Piaget's term for understanding that changes in the physical appearance of objects do not alter their weight, length, mass, or volume

Despite these new abilities, preoperational children's thought is still immature in many ways. They cannot comprehend another person's point of view; they believe that other people see things exactly as they see them and respond to them in exactly the same way, a situation that Piaget called **egocentrism** (see Figure 15.3). Research over the past decade, however, indicates that young children are not as egocentric as Piaget assumed. They clearly understand that others do not always see exactly what they see. In experiments, two-year-olds had no problem hiding a Snoopy doll behind a tabletop screen so that the experimenter could not see the doll from where she sat (Flavell, Shipstead, and Croft, 1978). John Flavell (1985) has concluded that preoperational children know *whether* another person can see what they see, but they still do not understand *how* the object looks from the other person's position.

By labeling this stage *pre*operational, Piaget was describing the limitations rather than the capacities of the preschool child. He maintained that children of this age were not yet capable of mental **operations,** his term for flexible, rigorous, and logical thought. Their attention is caught by the most immediate and highly visible features of objects or events. For these youngsters, appearances are everything. They may believe, for instance, that a change of clothes and hairstyle can transform a girl into a boy or that putting on a gorilla mask transforms a person into a real gorilla. They also have trouble integrating information over time in order to solve problems.

CONCRETE OPERATIONAL STAGE (SEVEN TO ELEVEN YEARS) At about the time children start school, they enter what Piaget called the **concrete operational stage,** in which thought is flexible, rigorous, and logical—but only in regard to concrete objects. They can manipulate symbols for objects as easily as they can manipulate the objects themselves (Siegler, 1986). As Piaget might say, they can perform mental operations on objects. This means that they can grasp the basic principles of the physical world.

One important principle that schoolchildren understand is **conservation,** Piaget's term for the recognition that changes in an object's appearance have no effect on its weight, length, mass, or volume (Figure 15.4). The classic test of conservation is to have a child watch as an experimenter fills two identical squat containers to the same level with water, as shown in the accompanying photographs. After the child agrees that the amounts are the same, the experimenter pours the liquid from one container into a tall, narrow container and asks the child whether the tall and the squat containers now hold the same amount of water. A concrete-operational child says that they indeed hold an equal amount; a preoperational child says that there is more water in the tall container.

According to John Flavell (1985), three cognitive advances enable children to grasp conservation. First, older children are not fooled by appearances. Although the tall container may *appear* to hold more water, schoolchildren can infer from the available evidence that the two quantities are still the same. Second, their attention is not overpowered by the dominant feature of the situation—the height of the liquid. They can see that the narrow width of the slender container compensates for its height. Finally, their thought has become *reversible*. They can mentally reverse the transformation and understand that if the water were poured back into its original container, the amounts would be the same.

Although children at the concrete-operational stage have made major cognitive progress, some types of thought are still beyond their grasp. They will be adolescents before their thought reaches the level of abstraction that Piaget described as *formal operational thought,* the basis of his fourth and final stage. (We trace the development of formal operations in Chapter 16.)

A Continuous-Development Approach: Information Processing

When researchers began studying a broader range of thinking than Piaget had probed and applied newly developed techniques to their experiments, they discovered that he had underestimated the baby's ability to extract information about the world and the young child's grasp of various concepts (Harris, 1983). Babies as young as two months have learned to control mobiles by kicking one leg; when the mobile is returned after a two-week absence, they recognize it and show that they can recall how to operate it, at a time when Piaget proposed that only reflexive schemes were possible (Linde, Morrongiello, and Rovee-Collier, 1985). Other studies indicate that the apparent lack of object permanence in older babies may not be caused by the belief that objects cease to exist when out of sight but by a memory so fragile that the sight of the hidden toy slips away before they start to look for it (Kagan, 1984). Preoperational children can reason more systematically and understand more about the nature of physical causality than Piaget believed (Shultz, 1982). In addition, researchers have been able to train preoperational children to pass tests of conservation, which Piaget said could not be done (Gelman, 1982).

A number of modern psychologists now view cognitive development in an information-processing framework. They see no major change in mental structures as children grow; rather, thought and behavior continuously build on a small set of primitive processes that are present early in life. These processes include recognition, visual scanning of the environment, learning, and the integration of the senses (Siegler, 1983).

Notice how well this approach fits in with the increased attention in recent years to the capacities of the newborn. It has been shown, for example, that newborns can remember an object they have seen for 5 to 10 seconds and can detect a difference between that memory and another object. But they also begin forgetting almost immediately. With experience, babies' basic capacities expand (but do not alter radically), a store of knowledge is built up, memory is sharpened, and their information processing becomes faster and more efficient.

One of the cognitive processes that is in operation from our first days is *selective attention*. In the first month of life, babies may take less than a minute to forget an object they have been gazing at, yet remember from one day to the next a response they have learned, such as sucking after a tone in order to hear the sound of their mother's voice (Olson and Sherman, 1983). These differences indicate that babies appear to process events selectively; they are more likely to remember a response that has had some effect on the world than an object that they have simply looked at (Rovee-Collier, 1984).

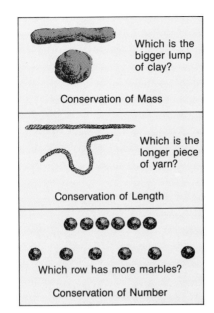

Figure 15.4 Examples of problems for which a child must acquire the concept of conservation. Concrete-operational children interiorize the possibility of making and unmaking the transformations for each task shown here. Thus, they come to see the lengths and quantities as unchanged in each case. Preoperational children, whose thinking is more static, are not able to imagine the transformations required and respond to perceptually striking but irrelevant aspects of the objects in attempting to answer the questions. For example, preoperational children will answer that there are more marbles in the bottom row than in the top one.

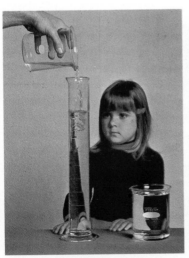

The girl taking part in this demonstration has not yet acquired the ability to understand the concept of conservation of quantity of liquid. She agrees that there is an equal amount of water in the two shorter beakers on the right, but when the water from one of them is poured into the taller beaker on the left, she incorrectly asserts that there is more water in the taller beaker than in the shorter. To develop an understanding of the principle of conservation, the child must be able to coordinate her thoughts about the length and width of the first container, the length and width of the second container, and the change or transformation brought about by pouring the liquid from the shorter beaker into the taller. Preoperational children cannot do this: they consider the state of each container separately, and consequently point to the beaker that "looks like more" as the one that actually "is more."

Babies also exhibit facility in recall, which indicates representational thought. In one study, parents of seven- to eleven-month-olds reported that their babies seemed surprised when a household object was not in its customary place (Ashmead and Perlmutter, 1980). The babies searched for people who "should" have been there and objects they were accustomed to seeing; they remembered the routine of games like peekaboo. Apparently, these babies had developed some way of representing familiar objects and people and could retrieve the images without specific clues from the outside.

As children grow, their recall blossoms—as long as what they are to remember is familiar and matters to them. Anyone who is around three-year-olds for very long can testify to their flawless recall when it comes to singing advertising jingles, chanting nursery rhymes, and reminding their parents about promised treats. Like young babies, three-year-olds can recall their own activities more readily than objects they have seen (Jones, Swift, and Johnson, 1988).

As children develop, their knowledge base broadens and they become more skilled at integrating new information with what they already know about the world. It is difficult to overstate the importance of a knowledge base. When they are interested in a topic, young children may acquire an enormous and active store of knowledge. In one study, researchers found a four-year-old with an immense store of knowledge about dinosaurs (Chi and Koeske, 1983). Given new information about dinosaurs, this four-year-old would probably remember more of it than would the average adult. Like the experts we described in Chapter 9, his large knowledge base allowed him to plug in new knowledge to already existing schemas. But much of what four- and five-year-olds encounter has little connection to their relatively small store of knowledge. Without any related concepts to connect it with in memory, they find it difficult to store or retrieve the new information (Flavell, 1985).

As they grow older, children gradually use strategies to increase the efficiency of their memory. Preschoolers use certain strategies, such as touching objects they want to remember and sometimes repeating words aloud, but they use far fewer of them than older children do, and their strategies are less sophisticated. Among schoolchildren, most of the youngest use rehearsal as a memory aid—but in an inefficient manner. Only older schoolchildren vary their rehearsal technique, making it more efficient and indicating some sort of planning toward a goal (Ornstein and Naus, 1978).

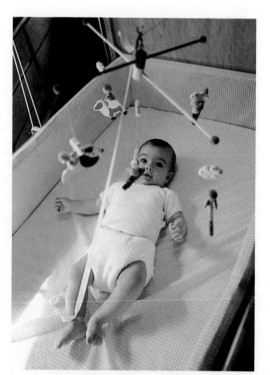

Babies can make their own fun. Several investigators have found that if a mobile is attached to an infant in such a way that the infant's own movements activate the mobile, the infant soon discovers this relationship and coos, smiles, and seems to delight in making the appropriate kick to set the mobile in motion.

Part of the reason children increasingly make use of memory is that their understanding of metacognition is growing. (Flavell, 1985). As was noted in Chapter 9, *metacognition* refers to knowledge of one's own cognitive processes, including the way memory works. Young children, who are lacking in metacognitive knowledge, frequently run into trouble because they don't realize they have not understood a problem, and they don't understand why they can't succeed in solving it (Paris and Lindauer, 1982; Robinson and Robinson, 1984). As in every other area of development, maturation and experience both contribute to children's increasing expertise in managing their own cognitive skills. It has also been found that an extra boost from parents and teachers can speed their development (Brown, 1980; Paris, Cross, and Lipson, 1984).

Finally, improved memory, according to some researchers, may also depend on increased processing efficiency. The younger the child, the more attention he or she must devote to basic processing tasks, such as identifying and retrieving information (Case, Kurland, and Goldberg, 1982). With maturation and experience, children need to pay less and less attention to these mental search processes; their thinking becomes faster, more automatic, and more efficient (Case, 1978; 1985). This in turn frees space in short-term memory for other data a child might want to think about and for manipulating the data in sophisticated ways. In this view the basic capacity of short-term memory is not itself changed or expanded; rather, increasingly efficient processing takes up less mental "room."

Vygotsky's Theory of Cognitive Development

Soviet psychologist Lev Vygotsky (1896–1934) emphasized the importance of social interaction in the child's cognitive development. His ideas serve as a kind of bridge between theories of cognitive development (including language development) and theories of social development. In Vygotsky's view, everything that makes us human—concepts, language, voluntary attention, and logical memory—grows out of social interaction. Children are active organizers who use the tools and language of their culture in continual interaction with the social world, affecting both the world and themselves in the process.

Vygotsky also suggested that children's cognitive abilities blossom more readily in a social context. That is, when children cannot yet master a skill by themselves, they may very well be able to do so with appropriate guidance from adults or more capable peers. A five-year-old, for example, may not be able to make a batch of cookies alone, but with an adult giving advice and helping out in difficult spots, the child can measure the ingredients, mix the dough, form the cookies, and bake them. Later, the child will be able to bake without assistance. Vygotsky's ideas have obvious implications for parenting and teaching, because they emphasize cooperation, support, and awareness of the individual child's potential for specific skills.

Language held a special place in Vygotsky's view of development. He believed that once children developed inner speech—his term for symbolic thought—the nature of development itself changed. Many researchers who have studied the way language seems to grow out of the interaction between infant and caregiver have been influenced by Vygotsky's ideas (Bruner, 1983).

Language Acquisition

Young babies are physically incapable of speech. Their vocal tract is shaped more like that of an adult chimpanzee than like that of an adult human (Stark, 1986). Before a baby can say "ma-ma," the size and shape of the mouth and throat must change, and both the motor cortex and the brain's left hemisphere, where most people process speech, must mature.

But language is not simply a matter of maturation; cognitive advances are equally important. It is no accident that the first words do not appear until babies are halfway through Piaget's sensorimotor stage and that a true grasp of language awaits their emergence from that stage. Until babies develop object permanence, they cannot label objects with any consistency. Until they develop a rich store of concepts, they cannot learn words, because adding a new word is actually a process of learning which concept the word refers to. Like other aspects of development, language acquisition proceeds in an orderly sequence—a sequence that is the same in all human cultures (Brown, 1973).

Prespeech Communication

A baby's first cries are simply signals of distress, not attempts to communicate. At about two months, babies respond to smiles and words with sounds of joy, called cooing. By six months, babies babble, chanting sequences of sounds that resemble syllables. Toward the end of the first year, babbling changes again: strings of syllables take on the stresses and intonational patterns of adult sentences. The meaningless sounds are so close to the cadence of speech that babies sound as if they have mastered a foreign language or invented a new one.

At about nine or ten months, before children actually talk, they begin to understand the basis of communication. Parents usually become aware of this when their baby actively seeks help in getting at an out-of-reach object (Bates, 1979). The baby looks at the adult and the object, while opening and shutting an outstretched hand and fussing loudly. This conscious attempt to communicate marks the shift from noises to the beginnings of speech.

First Words and Sentences

By the time their first birthday approaches, many children have produced their first words. Generally, these are the names of things and people, and babies use the names primarily to remark that someone or something has appeared or disappeared. Instead of simply playing with sound, the baby is now planning and controlling speech (de Villiers and de Villiers, 1978). Children understand more words than they can produce, but production of words comes quickly. In one study, three toddlers acquired their first fifty words within four to six months (Stoel-Gammon and Cooper, 1984).

OVEREXTENSION stretching the meaning of a word so that it refers to events or objects that resemble it

At first young children's speech is marked by **overextension,** the stretching of the meaning of a word for an object to cover other objects or actions that resemble it in some way. Up to a third of children's early words are extended in this fashion (Nelson et al., 1978). A small girl who has learned "bow-wow," for example, may extend it from dogs to all four-footed animals. But as new words enter her vocabulary and new experiences refine her concepts, overextensions disappear. Eventually, she will have separate names for all animals (E. Clark, 1983).

At first, children produce a single word at a time, because their limited processing ability does not leave enough "space" in short-term memory for them to plan and produce a longer utterance. But sometime between eighteen and thirty months, available space expands enough for them to process two words at a time. Now they can form rudimentary sentences—but with no more than two words. These first sentences are stripped to essentials and small function words are omitted: "Mommy book," "Daddy play," "Drink milk." Because these "bare-bones" sentences resemble a telegram, psychologists call them **telegraphic speech** (Brown, 1973). Although brief, these sentences show the rudiments of grammar. Children will say "eat cake" but not "cake eat."

TELEGRAPHIC SPEECH speech in the two-word stage, in which utterances are stripped to content words and omit function words

By the time children are three or four, they have begun to discern grammatical patterns in adult speech. Once they learn a rule of grammar, they apply it with rigid consistency. As a result, children who once unconsciously used the proper irregular forms produce sentences like "Daddy goed to work" and plurals like "foots" and "mouses." This phenomenon is known as **overregularization.** Although a child's command of language may suddenly seem to slip backward, such errors actually signal progress. Children are learning rules that reflect the regularities they notice in the speech of others.

OVERREGULARIZATION rigidly applying grammatical rules, which produces speech errors

It takes children much longer to understand and produce complex sentences, which often require the application of several rules simultaneously. Sometimes they are tripped up by their assumptions. Children tend to assume that speech order directly reflects reality—that people talk about things in the order in which they occur. So, for example, when parents say, "Eat your pie after you eat your broccoli," children may think they have been told to eat their dessert first (C. Chomsky, 1969).

The process of language acquisition is helped enormously by the special ways in which adults speak to small children. They talk slowly, substitute nouns for pronouns, and use short sentences with carefully placed pauses and inflections. This speech has been called **motherese,** but because almost all adults (even child-less men) use it consistently when speaking to small children, some researchers refer to it as *child-directed speech* (Snow, 1986).

MOTHERESE the altered, simplified speech used by adults with small children

Theories of Language Development

Our overview of language acquisition has largely been limited to description (see Figure 15.5); we have said little about *how* this enormous task is accomplished. The problem is that no one has yet provided a satisfactory explanation. Some psychologists are convinced that language is primarily a matter of maturation (nature); others are just as certain that learning (nurture) explains all we need to know. And a third group maintains that the key is social and cognitive interaction.

The chief spokesman for nature's role in language acquisition has been linguist Noam Chomsky (1975; 1979). He attributes language acquisition to brain maturation and a child's exposure to adult speech. Chomsky believes that all children have an innate capacity that allows them to speak, just as wings allow birds to fly. As children acquire their native language, they are aided by an *inborn* knowledge of universal principles of language structure.

Behaviorists have a very different view of how language develops. They explain language acquisition as the learned result of reinforced vocalization. When babies begin to label objects with words, they are showered with praise and approval (Bijou and Baer, 1965). Older children are reinforced when their use of words achieves their purposes. Social cognitive theorists say that imitation plays a major role in the process (Bandura, 1977). In their view, children imitate words and general rules they observe in the speech of others.

Both views have been criticized. The biological maturation view cannot explain how a child grasps meaning (Bohannon and Warren-Leubecker, 1985); the behavioral view ignores evidence that parents rarely praise children's grasp of grammar or correct their syntactical errors (Brown and Hanlon, 1968). In the past decade a third view has been proposed, one that emphasizes social and cognitive interaction. Maturation is still vital: until children reach a certain cognitive level, they cannot acquire language. But active learning in social situations—inferring a speaker's intent from context—is equally important. We have seen that the parent at first supplies both sides of a conversation with a baby. From these early exchanges children learn to take turns, to make eye contact, and to indicate that they are paying attention (Siegler, 1983). Through such interaction, infants also learn *scripts*, or general understandings of the routine elements in a procedure, which—as we saw in Chapter 8—allow us to behave appropriately when a given situation recurs (Schanle and Abelson, 1977). In these ways, the social interactions of infancy lay the foundations on which language is built, and language, in turn, becomes an essential aspect of social existence.

SOCIAL DEVELOPMENT

The discovery, from time to time, of children who have been shut away in attics or closets forcefully demonstrates our need for other people. Recall from Chapter 2 the case of Genie, who was nearly fourteen when she was rescued from a life of almost total isolation. When Genie was discovered, she could neither talk nor

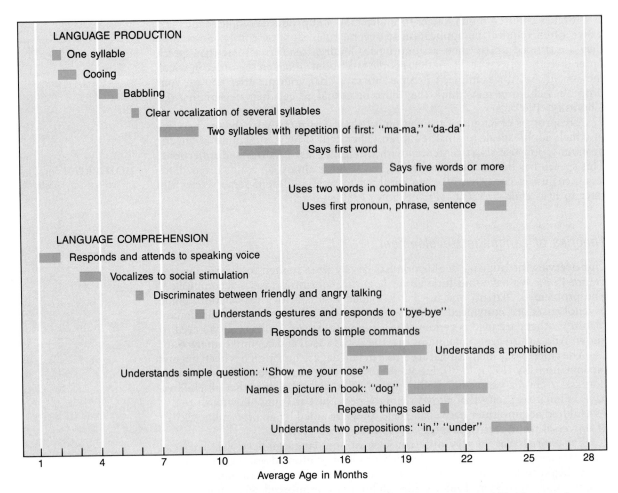

Figure 15.5 Highlights of language development during the first two years of life. The ages shown are approximate, and the length of the bars reflects the age range that researchers have reported for the appearance of a particular linguistic advance. (Adapted from Lenneberg, 1967; McCarthy, 1954; Bayley, 1969.)

stand, and a researcher described her as "unsocialized, primitive, hardly human" (Curtiss, 1977, p. 9). But in the care of a loving foster family, Genie responded to other people and eagerly entered into social interaction. Social interaction seems to be necessary for us to become human (Mead, 1934).

Attachment

> **ATTACHMENT** the emotional bond that develops between infant and caregiver, providing the infant with emotional security

Genie was deprived of the most basic form of social interaction, the physical and social contact between parent and child that leads to a close emotional relationship. This close relationship between caregiver and infant is called **attachment.** Emotional security based on close physical contact is the key aspect of attachment in humans. Attachment also occurs in animals; earlier we saw that newly hatched birds imprint on their mothers. A similar sort of rapid bonding occurs among herd animals, where mothers bond to their newborn infants immediately after birth; if mother and newborn are kept apart for 24 hours, the mother will reject her baby and drive it away when it attempts to nurse. Human bonding, however, instead of occurring immediately, seems to be a long-term process, with affectional ties being established over weeks or months (Myers, 1990).

Until fairly recently, it was assumed that attachment served an adaptive function: attachments formed because parents fulfilled the baby's immediate physical needs, such as hunger and thirst (Bowlby, 1969). But an ingenious and now classic study altered this view. Young rhesus monkeys were taken from their mothers and raised with two surrogate "mothers," one made of bare wire mesh and the other covered with soft terry cloth (Harlow and Harlow, 1966; 1969). Although the bare wire "mother" was equipped with a mechanism from which the baby monkeys could obtain food, they showed little affection for it. Instead they became attached to the soft, cuddly, terry cloth "mother." They clung to it, ran to it when frightened, and used it as a base from which to explore the world (see Figure 15.6). Attachment theorists assume that babies react in a similar fashion; they become attached to their parents in good part because of the emotional security that comes from being cuddled by someone they can depend on.

The Development of Attachment

Attachment appears to develop through four predictable phases (Bowlby, 1969; Ainsworth et al., 1978). At first, babies respond to anyone; they do not seem to care who diapers or cuddles them. During the second phase, which lasts from about two months to seven months, they begin to respond to their parents in special ways; but they will not protest if they are left alone with a stranger. At about seven months, true attachment to the parents begins. Before it can emerge, babies must take a giant cognitive step: they must develop some notion that people continue to exist after they disappear from view. This "person permanence" develops about the same time as babies show object permanence, and often even earlier (Levitt, Antonucci, and Clark, 1984).

Babies who have become attached to their parents stay close to them, clinging to them or crawling after them. Now babies show **separation distress:** they protest when they are parted from their mothers and express joy at the mother's return. A month or two after this stage of attachment develops, babies also show wariness of strangers. Especially when the parent is absent, they may respond to strangers with fear or withdrawal, looking away, frowning, or even crying at a stranger's approach.

SEPARATION DISTRESS an infant's discomfort when parted from an attachment figure

Figure 15.6 In Harlow's experiments, infant monkeys were presented with a new and frightening object (the mechanical bear) and were given a choice of two surrogate mothers to flee to. Infant monkeys of all ages greatly preferred the terrycloth mother to the wire mother, even though some of the infant monkeys received food only from the wire mother. (After Harlow, 1959.)

When children are between two and three years old, they enter the final stage of attachment, which lasts throughout life. The emotional bond remains strong, but give-and-take enters the relationship. The child gradually begins to understand the parent's feelings and motives. When the parent leaves, the child continues to feel secure, confident that the parent will return.

Not all babies become attached in the same way, however. About two-thirds develop *secure attachments:* when their mothers return after a separation, the babies actively seek them out and their distress disappears (Ainsworth et al., 1978). Other babies develop insecure attachments. Some have *avoidant attachments:* when reunited after a separation, they shun contact with their mothers. Others have *ambivalent attachments:* when reunited, they alternate between seeking contact and angrily squirming to get away. These variations in attachment mean different things in different cultures (Lamb et al., 1984). German mothers, for example, promote early independence in their children and so regard avoidant attachments positively; they consider "secure" babies to be spoiled (Grossmann et al., 1985). (See the accompanying box for a discussion of attachment in a day care setting.)

The sort of attachment that develops between mother and child seems related to the mother's style of interaction. Mothers of securely attached babies generally are warm, responsive, not intrusive, and not abusive (Lamb et al., 1988). Some researchers suspect that American mothers of avoidant babies tend to be overstimulating and intrusive, while those of ambivalent infants tend to be less involved with their babies and often not emotionally available to them (Isabella, Belsky, and von Eye, 1989). In fact, simply by rating mothers on the sensitivity of their responses, researchers were able to predict the quality of their babies' attachment with an accuracy rate of 94 percent (Smith and Pederson, 1988). The quality of the bond is also related to the baby's style of interaction. Babies who are especially irritable and fussy tend to develop either avoidant or ambivalent attachments (Belsky, Rovine, and Taylor, 1984).

Stability and Attachment: Basic Trust

If a secure attachment has important effects on a baby's social development, we might expect to find these effects persisting past infancy. Such a connection has turned up in several studies, providing evidence of stability in these developmental effects. The contrast between children who as infants were securely attached and those who were insecurely attached has been found to be striking. Securely attached infants generally become competent, confident, friendly, independent preschoolers, who are good at solving problems (Sroufe, Fox, and Pancake, 1983; Sroufe et al., 1984; Lütkenhaus, Grossman, and Grossman, 1985). Insecurely attached infants tend to become preschoolers who crave attention, seek constant approval, and cling to caregiving adults so closely that interaction with other children suffers. It would seem that the quality of a baby's attachment somehow "causes" such outcomes in preschoolers.

This assumption has been criticized by researchers who believe that these outcome studies are not measuring the long-term effects of attachment, but instead reflect a continuous pattern of parent–child interaction (Lamb et al., 1984; Lamb and Bornstein, 1986). In this view, the way children behave at any point in their development simply reflects their current relationship. If the relationship remains stable from infancy, it affects the child's development in a similar fashion over the early years. But if the relationship changes—say, a working mother returns to full-time mothering or a mother returns to work—then a child's behavior begins to reflect the quality of that change.

Erik Erikson (1950; 1963) proposed his influential stage theory of development before the major studies in attachment were done, but his view of infancy supports the idea that early experience does have a powerful impact on development. Erikson regarded each stage as dominated by a particular developmental task reflecting a conflict between a person's needs and society's demands. That conflict must be resolved before a person can proceed to the next stage (see Figure 15.7). For infants, who are in the first stage, the conflict is *basic trust versus mistrust.* Erikson's concept of trust closely resembles that of secure attachment:

PSYCHOLOGY TODAY AND TOMORROW

The Changing American Family and Day Care

In the past, the traditional nuclear family consisted of father as breadwinner, mother as full-time homemaker, and baby. Such families are no longer the American norm. Today's typical mother is employed outside the home, and more than a quarter of all homes are headed by only one parent. How do these sweeping social changes affect children's development?

The lack of a single, central caregiver seems to produce no ill effects on children who are at least one year old when they start receiving good day care (Clarke-Stewart and Fein, 1983; Lamb et al., 1988). But there is some argument about the effects of all-day care for younger infants. Some studies find that these babies are as securely attached to their mothers as babies whose mothers are with them all day (Doyle and Somers, 1978; Chase-Lansdale and Owen, in press; Gottfried and Gottfried, 1988). However, other studies find that the proportion of insecure attachments rises sharply when babies spend more than twenty hours a week in day care (Belsky and Rovine, 1988).

There may be some methodological problems in these day care studies (Weinraub, Jaeger, and L. Hoffman, in press). The experimental situation (placing the baby in a strange room and arranging a series of encounters in which a stranger enters and the mother leaves, then returns) may not seem so "strange" to babies who are accustomed to attending day care centers. Thus, the situation may not be a true test of the baby's attachment behavior—distress at the mother's departure and obvious joy at her return. In such studies, the additional *insecure attachments* are primarily avoidant in nature: the toddlers seem "almost too independent" and pay little attention to the mother's return.

In any case, when an already attached infant or toddler enters day care, the transition may be bumpy. The youngsters are clearly distressed when their mothers leave, but most adjust quickly and before long have no objection to being dropped off at the center. The quality of the bond may shift temporarily during the transition, but in most cases it again becomes secure (Thompson, Lamb, and Estes, 1982).

Mothers who are absent from their young children during working hours seem to make up for it after work and on weekends (Easterbrooks and Goldberg, 1985). Employed mothers engage in more social and verbal play with their children and handle them more vigorously than home-bound mothers do.

Long-term studies have found that babies who go to a sitter's home or stay with a sitter in their own home for the first two years do just as well, socially and intellectually, as babies who stay with their mothers. But babies who go to a day care center before they are two seem less attentive, less socially responsive, and more apathetic, and they have more behavioral problems (Scarr, 1983; McCartney et al., 1985). The researchers point out, however, that the negative effects of early day care were probably the result of lack of attention from a caring adult. In these centers, each adult was responsible for eight babies; overworked caregivers had little time to interact with their charges after attending to their immediate needs. Older children seem to thrive in good day care (McCartney et al., 1985; Scarr, 1983). Children who entered day care after their second birthday were more advanced cognitively and socially than children who stayed home with their mothers all day.

The quality of care seems all-important. Among a group of eight-year-olds, those who had attended high-quality day care centers (spacious, well-equipped, low adult–child ratios, well-trained teachers) were happier, friendlier, and more socially competent than those who had attended poor-quality centers (crowded, poorly equipped, high adult–child ratios, untrained teachers) (Vandell et al., 1988).

As employment outside the home becomes the norm the need for day care will increase. The problem is finding *good* day care: care that provides children with attention, affection, and stimulation. The key to good day care is a well-trained staff with little turnover and enough caregivers to ensure individual attention for each child. Because there are as yet no federal standards for day care, parents who plan to use day care centers should carefully observe the center in operation and ask lots of questions before they enroll their child (Scarr, 1984).

Stage	1	2	3	4	5	6	7	8
Maturity								Ego Integrity vs. Despair
Adulthood							Gener-ativity vs. Stagnation	
Young Adulthood						Intimacy vs. Isolation		
Puberty and Adolescence					Identity vs. Role Confusion			
Latency				Industry vs. Inferiority				
Locomotor-Genital			Initiative vs. Guilt					
Muscular-Anal		Autonomy vs. Shame, Doubt						
Oral Sensory	Basic Trust vs. Mistrust							

Figure 15.7 Erikson views life as a succession of biological stages, each having its own developmental conflict, whose resolution has lasting effects on personality. Erikson's psychosocial stages represent an extension and expansion of Freud's psychosexual stages, with parallels between the first four stages of each theory. (After Erikson, 1950.)

constant, reliable care enables babies to feel that their needs will be met and that their parents can be counted on. This basic trust colors their later social relations, so that they enter them with positive expectations, warmth, and trust. Mistrustful—or insecurely attached—infants may grow into suspicious, impatient, frustrated, even fearful individuals who have difficulty forming close relationships.

What happens when children do not develop an attachment of any kind? Studies have consistently shown that institutionalized infants who form no attachments during the first two years of life become children who demand attention, cling to adults, and show shallow, indiscriminate friendliness (MacDonald, 1985). As eight-year-olds, they are often restless and disobedient, and they are unpopular with other children.

But perhaps the picture is not so bleak. In institutions that have a staff large enough so that each child has at least one warm, responsive relationship, infants become attached to that person much as they would to a parent (Dontas et al., 1985). Other researchers have found that youngsters who were adopted between the ages of four and six did develop warm relationships with their adoptive parents (Tizard and Hodges, 1978). Good environments can often make up for early deprivation, and many children have surmounted devastating early experiences. The outcome rests on such factors as the child's age, temperament, and genetic susceptibility to adverse environmental conditions; the severity of the deprivation; and the material and emotional quality of the new environment (MacDonald, 1985; Rutter, 1979).

A Sense of Self: Autonomy, Initiative, and Industry

Attachment also seems to be a factor in the development of children's sense of self—their awareness of themselves as separate individuals. Before we trace the connection, however, we need to establish just when the self emerges. Some sort of crude awareness of "me" and "not me" may be present from birth. Day-old babies cry when they hear the recorded wails of another newborn but fall silent and turn their heads to listen when they hear their own recorded cries (Martin and Clark, 1982). Yet not until a month or so after their first birthday do they develop a sense of themselves as active, independent agents who can cause their own movements through space (Harter, 1983). Toward the end of the second year cognitive advances allow toddlers to view themselves as an object, a "thing" that has unique features. This can be observed when children begin to recognize themselves in a mirror.

The role of attachment in the development of a sense of self was shown by a study in which toddlers with their noses daubed with rouge were placed in front of a mirror (Lewis, Brooks-Gunn, and Jaskir, 1985). Seventy-five percent of insecurely attached toddlers responded by reaching for their nose, indicating that they realized that the smudged nose in the mirror was their own. But only 26 percent of securely attached toddlers reached for their nose. Apparently, insecurely attached youngsters develop a sense of self early because they rely less on their mothers for security and more on themselves than securely attached children do.

Attachment continues to affect self-concept among six-year-olds. Researchers have found that securely attached children tend to describe themselves positively, yet admit their imperfections (Cassidy, 1988). Those with avoidant attachments tend to describe themselves as perfect, as if admitting imperfections would reawaken the feeling of rejection by their parents. Finally, those with ambivalent attachments seem to feel unworthy and have little confidence that they can control their aggressive impulses.

These effects are consistent with attachment studies and with Erikson's view of early attachment. Basic trust, Erikson proposed, is necessary if infants are to learn to tolerate frustration and to wait for gratification. The way children resolve this first developmental task affects the resolution of each subsequent stage and the way that their self is forged—either positively or negatively.

In Erikson's second stage or early childhood, the basic conflict is between shame (or doubt) and **autonomy,** the feeling of self-control and self-determination. It arises as children begin to run about and to exercise some control over their actions, a development that inevitably leads to a collision with social restraints. If parents grant them autonomy in matters the children can handle, but protect them from their excesses, children will develop self-control and self-esteem. But if children are shamed into feeling incompetent, their self-doubt undermines their budding autonomy.

By the time they enter the preschool years, a stage that Erickson called the *play age,* children must deal with the conflict between *initiative and guilt.* They are ready for positive, constructive activities that they undertake simply for the sake of being active. This gives them a sense of purpose, but when their initiatives

AUTONOMY the feeling of self-control and self-determination

This baby believes the reflection is a potential playmate because its concept of self as object has not yet developed.

encounter negative responses from parents, they may develop a nagging sense of guilt.

In Erikson's final psychosocial stage of childhood, the school age, children must resolve the issue of *industry versus inferiority.* Erikson saw this as a decisive stage, because children now want to learn adult skills and gain recognition for their endeavors. When they are successful, they become competent, productive individuals, but when they continually meet criticism instead of praise, they begin to doubt their own abilities and develop a deep sense of inferiority. In Chapter 16, we will explore the remaining stages in Erikson's theory, which cover the rest of the life span.

Social Relationships and Social Development

As children grow, their relationships with others change. During children's infancy, parents are primarily nurturing, loving caregivers. Once children begin to walk and talk, parents shift their emphasis from physically caring for the child to teaching the child to act in ways that society considers good or acceptable. Their aim, although they may not be conscious of it, is to help the child absorb society's attitudes, values, and customs. This process, called **socialization,** is an interactive one. The parents instruct, but the child's temperament and capabilities influence the methods used by parents and their effectiveness. We might look at each aspect of socialization as being something parents do *with* their children, not *to* or *for* them (Maccoby and Martin, 1983).

SOCIALIZATION the process of acquiring the attitudes, values, and customs expected from members of society

INTERNALIZATION the incorporation of values, attitudes, and beliefs so that they become one's own

The goal of socialization is **internalization.** If the process is successful, children will incorporate society's values to such an extent that they feel guilty whenever they violate these standards. Parents are not the only socialization agents the child encounters. Peers, teachers, other community members, and the media all play important roles in the process.

Relationships with Parents

The parent–child relationship both reflects and sets the tone for the home. How the parents perceive their own child and children in general determines the disciplinary methods they use. Diana Baumrind (1986) has identified four major patterns of parenting: authoritarian, permissive, rejecting-neglecting, and authoritative.

Authoritarian parents place their own needs first and expect children to accept their word on matters of right and wrong without question. They punish their children by asserting their own power through threats, commands, spankings, and the withdrawal of privileges.

Permissive parents are just the opposite. They place childrens' needs first and consult their children about matters of policy, allowing them to regulate their own activities and set their own standards. When discipline seems necessary, permissive parents rely on reason.

Rejecting-neglecting parents seem indifferent to their children. Like authoritarian parents, they place their own needs first, but they make no attempt to have their children meet any standards. They rarely discipline their children, but when they do, they are likely to use physical punishment or drastic withdrawal of privileges.

Authoritative parents exert firm but reasonable control over their children, often setting high standards. They encourage a verbal give-and-take that an authoritarian parent would not tolerate. Discipline relies primarily on reason, so that the child will realize the consequences of a forbidden action and understand the punishment.

Perhaps it is not surprising that during the preschool and early school years, children of authoritative parents seem to do best on every count (Baumrind, 1986). Compared with other children, they are more cooperative and comfortable in social situations, tend to be leaders in social groups, and enjoy intellectual challenges. Children of rejecting-neglecting parents seem to fare the worst, probably because their parents take no real interest in them and discipline them in an erratic fashion. As we will see in Chapter 16, adolescents in trouble tend to be from rejecting-neglecting homes.

Parents' style of discipline has other long-term implications. Parents who rely primarily on their power, whether they yell, threaten, take away privileges, or spank, tend to have self-centered children whose aim in resolving moral problems is to avoid punishment (Brody and Shaffer, 1982). In contrast, parents who rely primarily on reason tend to have children who have successfully internalized their parents' moral values (M. Hoffman, 1984).

Relationships with Peers

Children's relationships with their peers are important for several reasons. First, children have to earn their membership in the peer group. At home, no matter what they do, they cannot lose their relationships with parents and siblings, but when children enter the peer group, they run the risk of being excluded. Second, relationships with peers provide interaction with equals, rather than with powerful adults or less powerful younger siblings. Finally, the peer group gives children their first opportunity to compare themselves with others their own age.

The importance of peers has been confirmed by research findings that children who are disliked and rejected by their peers are more likely than other children to drop out of school, to develop emotional problems, and to become juvenile delinquents. They are usually unhappy, lonely children. Children who lack friends but are not actively disliked by others are no more likely than the average child to be unhappy or to have later academic, personal, or social problems (Asher and Dodge, 1986).

Most children have special relationships with one or more of their peers. These friendships change in meaning, depth, and complexity as children grow. The changes are linked to cognitive development; as children come to understand what other people are like, their view of what friendship means evolves. As childhood progresses, friendships change in three major ways: from a purely behavioral relationship to an emotional one; from a self-centered relationship to a mutual one; and from a smooth, brief relationship to a sometimes bumpy, enduring one (Shantz, 1983).

By the time they reach school age, children have a clear idea of the behavior that society considers appropriate for males and for females.

Gender and Identity

GENDER IDENTITY the inner experience of gender; the unchanging sense of self as male or female

GENDER ROLE a socially prescribed pattern of behavior and attitudes for males and females

A central aspect of identity, one that profoundly affects both our social relationships and our feelings about ourselves, has to do with gender. Our **gender identity** is our unchanging sense that we are either male or female. Our **gender role** consists of the attitudes and patterns of behavior that society considers acceptable for our gender. Sex differences in behavior appear at a very early age, and these differences become magnified during childhood. As children grow, they adopt and internalize their gender roles. Once again the nature/nurture theme emerges. Biology sets the stage by providing minute differences, and socialization exaggerates those differences.

Researchers believe that biology affects behavior through the action of male and female hormones on the fetal brain. Prenatal exposure to higher than normal levels of male hormones has been linked to increased feelings of aggression in both boys and girls (Reinisch, 1981). Boys who were exposed to additional male hormones before birth had significantly higher scores than their brothers on tests designed to measure potential for aggressive behavior. Girls who were similarly exposed had much higher scores than their unexposed sisters.

Many aspects of gender roles have *no* biological basis. The lessons begin in parents' perceptions of their newborns. Parents of newborns rated daughters as softer, more vulnerable, and less alert than sons, even though researchers could detect no differences between them (Huston, 1983). Fathers seem especially conscious of gender differences. They play more roughly with their sons than with their daughters, tumbling them about and using toys less than they do with their daughters (Parke and Suomi, 1980).

Parents, siblings, peers, and other adults respond to a child's predispositions. For example, baby boys are generally more active than baby girls (Phillips, King, and Dubois, 1978). Parents may respond to this higher level of activity by playing more physically with boys; as a result, girls and boys tend to get different kinds of care and to experience different kinds of social interaction. Parents' responses to the same activity also differ with their child's sex. In one study, parents *never* encouraged girls when they played with building blocks, and *only* girls were discouraged when they manipulated objects (Fagot, 1978). Such treatment permits boys to explore the physical world more freely. When working together on a task, parents tend to let a son resolve his own problems but step in to help a daughter as soon as she gets into trouble (Huston, 1983). But boys are more likely than girls to be punished for violating their gender role, a practice that may make them more responsive throughout life to sex-typed labels.

By the time they have developed gender identity, at about the age of three, children also understand what behavior is appropriate for girls and boys. In fact, they possess informal theories about gender that encompass suitable behavior, clothes, toys, dress, and adult occupations for males and females. These "theories" are known as **gender schemas;** like other cognitive schemas, they can be considered a kind of stereotype. Once these schemas develop, preschoolers organize new information around them (Bem, 1983; 1985). If new information does not fit their schemas, preschoolers ignore it or distort it until it does fit. For example, a male nurse seen on a hospital soap opera is likely to be recalled as female (Huston, 1983; Carter and Levy, 1988).

GENDER SCHEMA a self-constructed pattern of associations for each gender, which determines the way new information is organized

Gender roles are probably reinforced when children imitate the behavior of their same-sex parent (see Chapter 7). Other models include peers, teachers, familiar adults, and TV characters. Peers also apply gender roles to one another. In nursery school, boys who play with dolls or play dress-up are loudly criticized and mocked as "sissies" by other children (Fagot, 1977). Boys and girls who are punished in this way for "inappropriate" cross-gender play usually stop it at once, apparently because the punishment reminds them of their gender schemas. But children punished for play *appropriate* to their sex are not so easily swayed. They tend to keep right on with their game (Lamb, Easterbrooks, and Holden, 1980).

Teachers reinforce gender roles by encouraging independence in boys and dependence in girls. In one study (Serbin et al., 1973), children made paper party baskets. When it came time for the handle to be stapled onto the basket, boys were handed the stapler and told how to use it. But teachers took the girls' baskets and stapled the handles for them. Many aspects of school life steer boys and girls into traditional gender roles. Until recently, for example, girls had few opportunities to participate in organized sports. As a result, they missed the lessons in such social skills as competitiveness, confidence, teamwork, leadership, and persistence that most boys pick up on the athletic field (Eccles and Hoffman, 1984).

Finally, the media—newspapers, magazines, books, movies, and television—provide children with many stereotypical gender models. Children unquestioningly accept the information they get from television as accurate (Greenberg, 1982). Stereotypes are common in commercial TV programming for children: female characters—except for special characters like Wonder Woman or She-Ra—are passive and deferential, while male characters are aggressive and constructive (Sternglanz and Serbin, 1974). As for adult programming, the competent, assertive women who can now be seen on prime-time television are vastly outnumbered by the passive women who appear in reruns. In fact, one researcher found that children in grades one through six who watched television after school (when reruns dominate the schedule) and on Saturday mornings had much more stereotypical views of gender roles than children who watched prime-time TV (Greer, 1980).

Some researchers have voiced concern that gender-role socialization has lagged behind social changes (Eccles and Hoffman, 1984). Traditional gender-role training, they say, no longer prepares girls to fit into their greatly expanded adult roles in today's world. Motherhood no longer occupies the major portion of a woman's adult years; employment outside the home is now the female norm. But as we will see in the next chapter, the physical, cognitive, emotional, and social forces with which adolescents must contend may make teenagers cling even more tenaciously to traditional roles.

SUMMARY

Themes and Issues in Development

■ The influences of heredity and environment (nature and nurture) on development are so closely intertwined that it is almost impossible to separate them.
■ Developmentalists disagree as to whether the course of development is stable and set early in development or whether abilities and personality change over the life span.
■ Another area of disagreement is whether development is continuous, with skills and behavior emerging gradually, or whether it progresses through sharply demarcated stages.

Prenatal Development

■ The thirty-eight weeks of prenatal development are divided into the germinal, embryonic, and fetal periods.
■ Organs form during the embryonic period, when the developing embryo is most susceptible to the influence of teratogens.

Development of the Newborn

■ Babies come into the world equipped with more than a dozen reflexes that enable them to adapt to their new environment.
■ Vision and hearing are not fully developed in newborns, but their other sensory abilities are acute.
■ The behavioral "tools" for survival seem built into newborn behavior.
■ The interaction of the baby's temperament and the parents' responses determines not only the quality of the infant-caregiver relationship but also the development of the baby's personality.

Physical Development in Infancy and Childhood

■ As the cortex matures, control of behavior passes from the lower parts of the brain to the cortex.
■ Motor skills emerge as body and brain mature, but sensory stimulation may hasten the required brain growth and speed the development of physical, perceptual, and motor skills. Such acceleration is limited to the normal range of human differences.

Cognitive Development

■ In Piaget's stage theory of cognitive development, cognition develops as the child applies assimilation and accommodation to existing schemes.
■ During the sensorimotor stage, children develop object permanence, representational thought, and deferred imitation.
■ During the preoperational stage, children acquire language; they are still egocentric and their thought is intuitive, inflexible, and focused on individual events.
■ During the concrete operational stage, children's thought is flexible, rigorous, and logical, but only in regard to concrete objects.
■ According to information-processing views of development, cognition develops gradually as primitive mental processes become faster and more efficient and as the child amasses a store of knowledge about the world.
■ Memory and thought also improve as children develop strategies to increase memory and as their grasp of metacognition improves.

- Physical maturation and cognitive development are equally important in the emergence of language.
- The shift from babbling to words becomes possible only after the older baby begins to understand the possibilities of communication.
- Theories of language acquisition focus on maturation, on learning, or on a combination of cognitive maturation and social interaction.

Social Development

- Attachment goes through four predictable phases, from indiscriminate social responsiveness, to discriminate social responsiveness, to specific attachments, to a mutual partnership.
- Secure attachments are associated with social competence, independence, and persistence in problem-solving among preschoolers, indicating stability in development.

- In Erikson's theory of psychosocial development, children move through four major stages, each marked by a conflict whose solution affects the course of future development. For infants the conflict is between basic trust and mistrust; for toddlers, between autonomy and shame or doubt; for preschoolers, between initiative and guilt; and for school-age children, between industry and inferiority.
- When socialization is successful, children internalize the values and attitudes of their culture.
- The major parenting styles are authoritarian, permissive, rejecting-neglecting, and authoritative. Children of authoritative parents seem to do best; children of rejecting-neglecting parents seem to do worst.
- Biological differences between the genders emerge in behavior and capabilities, and socialization exaggerates the differences as soon as babies are born.
- Once children form gender schemas, they begin to develop gender roles, which are reinforced by parents, peers, teachers, and the media.

KEY TERMS

accommodation
assimilation
attachment
autonomy
concrete operational stage
conservation
deferred imitation
development
egocentrism
embryo
embryonic period
fetal alcohol syndrome
fetal period
fetus

gender identity
gender role
gender schema
germinal period
imprinting
internalization
maturation
motherese
object permanence
operations
overextension
overregularization
placenta

preoperational stage
reaction range
reflex
scheme
sensitive period
sensorimotor stage
separation distress
socialization
stage theories
telegraphic speech
temperament
teratogens
zygote

CONCEPT REVIEW

1. Define the term *development* as it is used in psychology.

2. Describe the three "enduring themes" relating to development that are presented at the beginning of the chapter. How is each theme manifested in the process of development?

3. Name the stages of prenatal development. Why do teratogens create the most damage during the embryonic period?

4. Describe the general abilities of a newborn. Which appear to be the most developed and which are the least developed at birth?

5. Describe how both heredity and environment influence a baby's temperament.

6. What is the evidence that physical stimulation is important for the healthy physical development of infants?

7. Define Jean Piaget's basic concepts of *scheme, assimilation,* and *accommodation.* Illustrate each concept with an example.

8. Outline Piaget's stages of cognitive development. Define

the important concepts at each stage—egocentrism, object permanence, and so on.

9. Identify the distinguishing features of the information-processing approach to cognitive development. What makes this framework more "continuous" than the stage approach of Piaget?

10. Describe the stages of language acquisition and development. What are the roles of overextension and overregulation in the acquisition of language rules? How does Chomsky believe that humans acquire language?

11. Outline the developmental stages of attachment. Describe different types of attachment. How do the two first stages of Erikson's psychosocial theory account for the development of attachment?

12. Identify examples of different parenting styles and how these parenting styles affect the parent–child relationship?

13. Summarize the various explanations of the development of gender identity.

CRITICAL THINKING

1. How does each of the basic theories and concepts presented in the chapter reflect one or more of the basic themes presented at the beginning of the chapter?

2. Human development is one of the most interdisciplinary fields of psychology. Review the major ideas of the chapter and judge the importance of the topics of Chapters 4 to 14 for each of these ideas.

...Adolescence and Adulthood

Harry Lieberman died at the age of 106. Seven months earlier, just before his birthday, Lieberman, who had begun a second career as a painter when he was in his seventies, talked about his life:

> One hundred and five years is not old. It's not young, but it's not old. I call myself 105 years mature. The maturity comes with age.
>
> Look who I am. I walk straight. You could do the same thing. People ask me, "How do you feel?" Mostly I tell them I have no complaints. I don't mean to say I have no complaints; I have plenty complaints! But what is the use? Could you help me? The age is there. The body—105 years, you're bound to have something wrong. When you buy an old building, even if you put in new plumbing, the age comes with it.
>
> . . . In my life, what I got, I collected like a bee flying from one flower to the other. It picks up the essence and it makes honey. And this is what I collected in these 105 years, and I am willing to pay it back to the public. I belong to the world. I don't live for myself; I live to create. You live in a community, you have to be one of the community, and see what you can do to help.
>
> I, myself, I am not so sure there is a life Upstairs. So I feel the life I got now is paradise. My heaven is right down here because if I am not around tomorrow, a hundred years from now my paintings will still be here and people will enjoy my work. They can put you six feet down, but the spiritual work you leave lives forever. I don't ask for more. (Quoted in Barash and Aguilera-Hellweg, 1983, p. 62)

Lieberman, who emigrated from Poland to the United States at the age of twenty-nine, ran a confectionery business until he was seventy-four. To relieve the boredom of retirement, he turned to painting and developed a highly successful second career in primitive-style oils and watercolors. Shortly before his death, he was still painting. Much of Lieberman's story is unique, but in his life he dealt with universal tasks and concerns: the physical, cognitive, and social changes that all of us face as we grow from adolescent to elder.

ADOLESCENCE

Adolescence is the period during which young people move out of childhood and get ready to take up their adult lives. It is a period of profound change in every aspect of life: physical, psychological, and social. During adolescence, girls and boys take on the physical characteristic of adults, they begin to think more like adults, and they begin assuming adult privileges and responsibilities. So many kinds of changes take place within adolescence that psychologists no longer regard it as a uniform phase of life. Consider the vast differences between the interests, needs, and capabilities of a thirteen-year-old eighth-grader and a nineteen-year-old college student; both are adolescents, yet studies of the first are unlikely to help us understand the second. Today, researchers divide adolescence into three subphases: early adolescence, from eleven through fourteen, roughly corresponding to the junior high school years; middle adolescence, from fifteen through eighteen, roughly corresponding to the high school years; and late adolescence (or youth), from nineteen through twenty-one, roughly corresponding to the college years (Steinberg, 1985).

Although psychologists have staked out this ten-year period as the stage of adolescence, setting clear-cut limits has proved difficult. At the lower end of adolescence, at the age of eleven, girls' bodies are obviously changing, yet the hormonal preliminaries to adolescence have been working silently within their bodies for at least two years and most have been growing rapidly for one year (Faust, 1977: Bogin, 1988). At the other end of adolescence, some young people have assumed their adult roles as worker, spouse, and parent by the age of eighteen, effectively placing themselves in adulthood, while others may not assume these responsibilities until their mid-twenties or later. In short, the changes of adolescence do not all happen at the same time or at the same rate, so that as young people advance into adulthood, they may be mature in one area but immature in another.

All this variation is testimony to the fact that adolescence as a distinct phase of life is culturally determined. Many traditional societies do not recognize the existence of adolescence as such; instead, the passage from childhood to adulthood is abrupt, consisting of ceremonial rites that may be preceded by several weeks or months of intensive training (Steinberg, 1985). In industrial societies, we regard adolescence as a separate period of human development, but that cultural definition is less than 100 years old. Before that time, most young people were part of the work force by the time they were fifteen or sixteen. Their incomes were essential to their families' survival. It was only when jobs began to require extensive education and families became affluent enough to keep their children in school that societies like ours came to think of adolescence as a distinct phase of life.

Since then the time span of adolescence has been extended in both directions, by biology and by society. Biology has pushed adolescence back into childhood at least two years. Since the beginning of this century, improved nutrition and the conquest of disease have led to earlier physical maturation (Roche, 1979). Social changes have lengthened adolescence on the other end. With increased schooling and delayed entry into the labor market, adult responsibilities are put off much longer. Together, these trends have widened the gap between biological and social maturation.

Physical Changes in Adolescence

Girls and boys enter adolescence with the physical appearance of a child but, within a few years, they have adult bodies and the capacity to reproduce. The term for this dramatic transformation of early adolescence is puberty. **Puberty** is actually a series of interrelated biological processes that change the immature child into a sexually mature person. The events that mark puberty follow a well-defined sequence, although youngsters progress through them at different rates (Brooks-Gunn and Warren, 1985). During childhood, both boys and girls produce low, steady levels of **androgens** (male hormones) and **estrogens** (female hormones) in roughly equal amounts. Then, in response to some as yet unexplained biological signal, the hypothalamus begins pouring large amounts of hormones into the child's bloodstream each night. This nightly surge of hormones sets off similar surges from the pituitary gland, and these pituitary hormones stimulate a girl's

PUBERTY   a series of interrelated biological processes that transform a child into a sexually mature individual

ANDROGENS   male hormones

ESTROGENS   female hormones

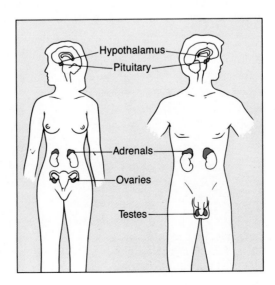

Figure 16.1 The endocrine system, showing only the major glands involved in pubertal changes. The hypothalamus (a part of the brain with neural and endocrine functions) signals the pituitary gland, which in turn stimulates hormonal secretions from other endocrine glands. This process produces many of the changes typifying adolescent physical and pubertal development.

ADOLESCENT GROWTH SPURT
a rapid increase in height and weight that accompanies puberty

PRIMARY SEX CHARACTERISTICS
the sexual organs that are directly responsible for reproduction

SECONDARY SEX CHARACTERISTICS the sexual characteristics that appear at puberty but that have no direct reproductive function

MENARCHE the first menstrual period

ovaries to produce estrogens and a boy's testes to produce androgens (Bogin, 1988). Puberty has begun (see Figure 16.1).

First, an **adolescent growth spurt** brings children toward their adult height and weight. While this growth is occurring, bodily proportions change. The **primary sex characteristics,** the sexual organs that are directly responsible for reproduction, reach maturity, and the **secondary sex characteristics,** such as breasts and body hair, which are not directly involved in reproduction, appear.

Girls enter the growth spurt at around age ten, with growth peaking at the age of twelve and continuing until they are about fifteen (Faust, 1977). Parents and adolescents often regard **menarche,** or the first menstrual period, as the true indicator of puberty in girls. But this event, which generally occurs when a girl is about twelve, actually appears relatively late in puberty. Even at that, most girls do not ovulate (and therefore become fertile) for another year or two after menarche.

Boys generally begin their growth spurt about two years later than girls, with growth peaking at the age of fourteen. The penis and scrotum usually begin their accelerated growth at age twelve, and about a year and a half later a boy ejaculates for the first time (Tanner, 1978). By about age fifteen, a boy's semen contains mature sperm.

Experts once assumed that much typical adolescent behavior—such as interest in the other sex and in challenging parental authority—could be traced directly to a heightened sex drive associated with increased hormone production. Yet researchers have discovered that social, not biological, factors seem to have the strongest influence on such behavior. Once about half the boys and girls in a classroom have reached puberty, the entire class begins behaving like the typical adolescent, even though close to half have not yet reached puberty (Petersen, 1985). It seems that whatever contribution hormones make to adolescent behavior is heavily influenced by peer standards.

Adolescents are acutely aware of their maturing bodies and their physical appearance, and this awareness has a psychological impact, whether they regard their new bodies with pride, pleasure, embarrassment, or shame. The way they react depends largely on nonbiological factors, including childhood thoughts and feelings about sexuality, cultural standards, and the reactions of parents and peers (Petersen, 1985).

These reactions are based in part on the culturally defined body ideal for each sex. In our society, a "real man" is broad-shouldered and muscular. The "perfect woman" is long-legged, small-breasted and slim—far thinner than the natural female figure. Little wonder that in a large survey of adolescents, most of the boys, but just over one-half of the girls, were proud of their bodies (Offer,

Adolescents of about the same age show a wide range of physical development. The "ideal" height and weight for boys as well as girls is culturally—not biologically—determined.

Ostrow, and Howard, 1981). The rest said they frequently felt ugly and unattractive. Some girls are so dissatisfied with their bodies that they become clinically depressed (Rodin, Silberstein, and Striegel-Moore, 1985). Our culture's unnaturally slim body ideal for women probably contributes to the fact that far more teenaged girls than boys experience eating disorders such as anorexia nervosa and bulimia nervosa, which are discussed in a box in Chapter 18.

Girls and boys also respond differently to the timing of puberty. Early sexual maturation seems to be an advantage for boys, but not for girls. Boys who develop early are usually confident, have high self-esteem, are popular with their peers, and stand out in athletics (Livson and Peskin, 1980). But early-maturing girls tower over their classmates and frequently become the object of teasing and unwanted sexual attention (Petersen, 1985). Late-maturing boys are rarely popular; late-maturing girls are usually popular, outgoing, and carefree, although they lose this advantage to early-maturing girls during high school (Simmons, Blyth, and McKinney, 1983). It seems that standing out from peers in a positive manner improves self-esteem (as in the case of early-maturing boys), but standing out in ways that are considered embarrassing (as early-maturing girls and late-maturing boys do) harms self-esteem.

Cognitive Development in Adolescence

Adolescence also ushers in new ways of thinking about oneself and the world. Separate skills developed earlier in childhood can now be combined and coordinated, so that they can be applied generally and with increasing sophistication (Neimark, 1982). Because young people are now able to deal with the possible and the hypothetical, they can think scientifically, understand their relation to society, and apply abstract principles to their moral judgments.

Formal Operations

Jean Piaget (1952) described the ability to deal with abstractions and logical possibilities as the stage of **formal operations,** which he regarded as the culmination of cognitive development. Individuals at this stage can isolate elements of a problem and systematically explore all possible solutions. By contrast, a concrete-operational child randomly tests solutions, forgetting some possibilities and repeating failed attempts.

The difference between these problem-solving approaches becomes clear when we look at a typical experiment conducted by Piaget and Barbel Inhelder (1969). The two investigators gave children and adolescents four beakers of colorless, odorless liquids, labeled 1, 2, 3, and 4. Using empty glasses, the subjects were to find the liquid or combination of liquids that turned yellow when a few drops from a bottle labeled *g* were added (see Figure 16.2). The yellow color was produced when *g* (potassium iodide) was added to a mixture of 1 (diluted sulfuric acid) and 3 (oxygenated water). The liquid in beaker 2 was plain water and had no effect on the reaction. The liquid in 4 (thiosulfate) prevented the yellow from appearing. Among those tested by Piaget and Inhelder, only adolescents were able to solve the problem by themselves. Younger children, who were apparently in the concrete-operational stage, often began in a systematic manner and tried all the single possibilities. But they tested *combinations* of liquids only after hints from the experimenter, and then in a random and incomplete manner.

Most tests of formal operational thought have been drawn from Piaget's work and focus on scientific and mathematical reasoning, which are not very relevant to adolescent life outside the classroom. To test whether the shift from concrete to abstract thinking is evident in other areas, several researchers have compared the ways in which children and adolescents think about social and political principles. They have found a similar progression in problem-solving and abstract thought. Their studies have shown, for example, that children younger than thirteen cannot describe the purpose of government or law; in fact, they have no concept of

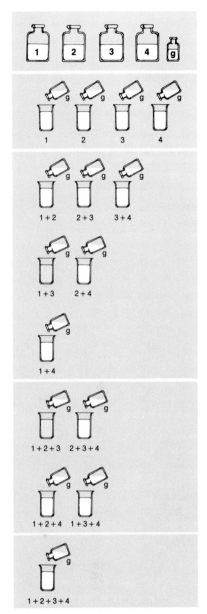

Figure 16.2 A problem that requires the systematic examination of hypotheses for its solution. The chemicals selected by Piaget and Inhelder for this problem have unexpected interactions. It is virtually impossible to determine how the color yellow is produced without trying every possible combination of the liquids, as shown here, and keeping track of the results. Not until children reach the formal-operational period can they conceive of such a procedure. (After Piaget and Inhelder, 1969.)

FORMAL OPERATIONS in Piaget's theory, logical, abstract thought that develops during puberty and is the culmination of cognitive development

TABLE 16.1	Percentages of Adolescents at Various Levels of Abstraction in Concept of Government			
	Age			
	11	*13*	*15*	*18*
Concrete	57%	25%	7%	0%
Low-level abstraction	28	64	51	18
High-level abstraction	0	7	42	71
Don't know or not ascertained	15	5	0	13

Source: J. Adelson, The growth of thought in adolescence, *Educational Horizons* (Summer 1983), 158.

society or community. Focusing on the concrete, they think only in terms of specific people, events, and objects: "teachers" instead of "education," and "judges" or "police" instead of "law." As a result, they evaluate all actions without regard to communal needs. As their ability to think abstractly increases, adolescents begin to understand the invisible network of rules and obligations that bind citizens together. Nearly three-quarters of eighteen-year-olds are thinking at a high level of abstraction (see Table 16.1) (Adelson, 1983; Adelson and Hall, 1987).

Moral Judgment

According to Lawrence Kohlberg (1976; Colby et al., 1983), moral reasoning develops along the same lines—from the concrete and specific to the abstract, from the immediate and personal to the global. Influenced by Piaget, Kohlberg proposed that moral reasoning develops in an unvarying progression of six stages. In the first two stages, the *premoral level,* values simply reflect external pressure. The dominant motives are to avoid punishment (stage 1) and to serve one's own needs and interests (stage 2). In the next two stages, the *conventional level,* value is placed in maintaining the conventional social order and the expectations of others. The dominant motives are to be a good person in one's own and others' eyes (stage 3) and to avoid breakdowns in the social system (stage 4). In the final two stages, the *principled level,* value resides in adhering to universal principles and standards. The dominant motives are a sense of obligation to the social contract (stage 5) and a belief in the validity of universal moral principles (stage 6).

Kohlberg based his stage theory on the responses of boys between the ages of ten and sixteen to a series of moral dilemmas, in which individual human needs or welfare conflicted with the demands of authority or law. For example, subjects were presented with a story about a poor man who broke into a store and stole medicine for his dying wife after the store owner had refused to let him pay for the medicine later. Subjects were asked whether the man's action was right or wrong, and why. It made no difference to Kohlberg whether the subjects believed the man had been right or wrong; he was concerned with the reasons they gave for their decision.

After following the boys in the original study for twenty years, Kohlberg and his associates (Colby et al., 1983) concluded that, first, the level of response was related to age: the use of premoral reasoning declined steadily after the age of ten, and stage 3 reasoning began declining in adolescence. Principled reasoning first appeared in young adulthood. Second, socioeconomic status was related to progression through the stages: each stage appeared earlier among middle-class subjects. Third, formal education was an important factor: every man who reasoned on the principled level had completed college. (See Figure 16.3.)

Kohlberg's theory has been controversial. Critics argue that people may use different types of moral reasoning in different situations (Hoffman, 1984); that personal needs and context affect moral reasoning more than broad moral principles do (Saltzstein, 1983); and that individuals do not always progress through the stages, but may actually regress (Rest, 1983). Other critics have noted that while

A sense of membership in a community or society emerges during adolescence.

the stages may fit educated people in Western individualistic cultures, they ignore values in other societies, such as the communal values of the Israeli kibbutzim (Snarey, 1987).

Because no females were included in Kohlberg's research, Carol Gilligan (1982) argues that his theory contains a built-in male bias. It equates moral development with the acceptance of justice, so that moral problems arise from conflicting rights. Women, however, are socialized to be concerned with nurturance and the needs of others. They base their moral reasoning on the values of compassion, responsibility, and obligation, which leads them to see moral problems as the result of conflicting needs and responsibilities. Gilligan believes that a theory of moral development that applies to both sexes must incorporate an ethic of caring as well as an ethic of justice.

Gilligan contends that these differing ethics place women's moral judgments at a lower level than men's on Kohlberg's scale of moral development. Yet other researchers have been unable to substantiate this claim (Braebeck, 1982). For example, after reviewing more than 100 studies that applied Kohlberg's scale to 8000 subjects, Lawrence Walker (1984) found no significant difference between the sexes in moral development.

Social Development in Adolescence

As teenagers develop the cognitive skills that make deeper analysis of their world possible, they begin to turn these skills on the subject closest at hand—themselves. They begin to ask questions such as "Who am I?" "What should I do with my life?" "What does it mean to be an adult?" "What do I believe in?" Physical maturity, increasing independence from parents and family, and new capabilities for intimacy with others, as well as social norms and parental expectations, focus the adolescent's attention on these difficult questions. Add to this the adolescent's uncertainty about the future and anxiety over all the choices that must be made, and it seems obvious that adolescence is a time of inner and outer turmoil.

For a long time, many experts thought that adolescence was indeed a period of storm and stress. Many psychiatrists, psychologists, and social workers viewed teenagers as moody, unhappy, confused creatures with low self-esteem (Offer, Ostrov, and Howard, 1981b). Most articles in the popular press are still based on the assumption that adolescents live on the brink of chaos and that most go through a period of emotional disturbance. However, an inspection of the objective evidence shows that the idea of adolescence as a time of turmoil is simply a persistent myth. In every study that has been conducted, the rate of emotional

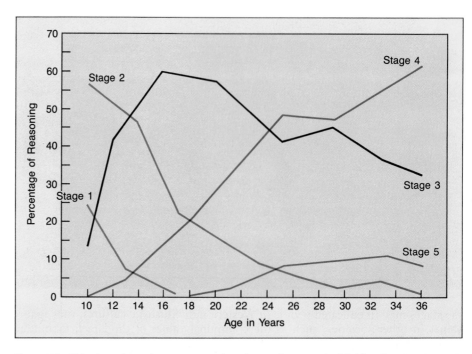

Figure 16.3 This chart shows the mean proportion of reasoning at each of Kohlberg's stages for each age group. As the boys in the study matured, premoral reasoning (stages 1 and 2) gradually disappeared, and advanced conventional reasoning (stage 4) became more prevalent than early conventional reasoning (stage 3). Postconventional reasoning (stage 5) first appeared toward the end of adolescence but never accounted for more than 10 percent of moral thought. (From Colby et al., 1983.)

disturbance among adolescents has been found to be exactly what it is among adults—somewhere between 10 and 20 percent (Hathaway and Monachesi, 1963; Douvan and Adelson, 1966; Rutter, 1980; Weiner, 1982; Offer, Ostrov, and Howard, 1984).

Most adolescents, then, are capable of dealing with the stresses they encounter and the changes they are living through. As they do this, adolescents test their feelings about themselves. This may lead them to consolidate the self-concepts they have already formed, to find new self-concepts, or perhaps to integrate the old and the new—in short, to grapple with what Erik Erikson (1980) saw as the major developmental task of adolescence: forming an identity.

Forming an Identity

IDENTITY a coherent sense of individuality; in Erikson's theory, its development is the major task of adolescence

Children enter adolescence already possessing an **identity**—a sense of their own individuality that encompasses thoughts and feelings about the self and provides a sense of personal continuity. But the one they have lacks coherence and integration. Adolescents' new bodies, responsibilities, and cognitive powers make the restructuring and reorganization of identity almost inevitable.

In the process of forming their identity, adolescents explore interests and possible occupations and work out their personal belief systems. They may "try on" a number of roles and experiment with various beliefs. Society makes this exploration possible by providing what Erikson called a "psychosocial moratorium"—the period of high school and college, when most young people are still free from adult roles and responsibilities. For some, this comes as an exciting opportunity, especially when they discover that their choices seem exactly right for them. For others, it is a period of intense distress, either because nothing seems "right" for them or because choosing one option means giving up another that is just as attractive (Waterman, 1988). Indeed, Erikson (1980) characterized the central struggle of adolescence as one of identity versus role confusion.

Erikson's concept of identity is so complicated and all-encompassing that it is difficult to test. For that reason, researchers usually assess adolescents' progress toward identity in terms of three of its major components: the tasks of selecting an occupation, forging religious beliefs, and determining political beliefs. Building on Erikson's theory, James Marcia (1980) proposed that adolescent identity took one of four forms: foreclosure, moratorium, diffusion, or achievement. In *foreclosure*, adolescents uncritically accept the goals and expectations of others, either parents or peers. In *moratorium*, they struggle with issues of identity, but put off making any final decisions. In *diffusion*, adolescents decline to make any decisions, even tentative ones, about what they will do or believe. In *achievement*, adolescents pursue goals of their own choice.

In contemporary Western cultures, the preferred path is to move from moratorium to achievement. Young people who take this route are generally more independent, self-confident, flexible, and intellectually creative than their peers. But this path was unavailable to most young people in earlier centuries. In our own past and in all traditional societies, foreclosure is the typical—even preferred—course of development (Baumeister, 1986; Cote and Levine, 1988). This path produces young people who tend to be conforming, respectful of authority, and religious. Adolescents in the diffusion form create problems for all cultures. Such young people may be disturbed, relate poorly to others, lack a sense of direction, and show a low level of moral reasoning.

Adolescent Sexuality

Sexual identity is an important part of the adolescent self. The physical changes of puberty bring an intensified feeling of gender. Boys begin to swagger and value muscles, and girls suddenly become super-feminine. These heightened sex-role displays are probably less the result of "raging hormones" than of social factors. First, youngsters whose bodies are blatantly announcing their sexual maturation to the world feel an inner uncertainty about their new situation. Adhering to a prescribed sex role is safer than experimenting with unconventional behavior. Second, the peer group often demands conformity to sex roles, and straying too far from the group's standards carries certain social costs. But this does not mean that pressure for adolescent sex-role conformity is highly restrictive. No one tells young people what they *must* do, only what they must *not* do.

In the middle years of adolescence, most teenagers begin to form beliefs about both the physical and the emotional aspects of sexuality.

As adolescents come to terms with their bodies and their feelings, they also must deal with the task of incorporating sexuality into their social relationships. Aware that they are sexual beings, able to reproduce, they find that sexuality takes on a new and important meaning. The traditional view holds that sexuality is primarily "body-centered" for boys and "person-centered" for girls (Reiss, 1973). That is, boys are basically interested in the physical expression of sexuality and only later develop the capacity for tender and loving sexual relationships; girls, however, are concerned with tender, loving relationships from the beginning. During early adolescence, boys do seem more preoccupied with sex; in a national sample, 80 percent of the boys but only 50 percent of the girls said that they often thought about sex (Offer, Ostrov, and Howard, 1981).

However, studies of middle-class adolescents indicate that boys are as "person-centered" as girls when it comes to sexuality within a dating relationship (McCabe and Collins, 1979). Although boys believe that sexual intimacies should progress much further and faster than girls do, boys are just as insistent as girls that their dating relationships be marked by sincerity, compatibility, understanding, affection, concern, tenderness, trust, security, mutual respect, and companionship. Girls become more interested in physical intimacy as they reach young adulthood; by the time they reach their mid-twenties, 90 percent of both sexes approve of sexual intercourse within a steady relationship.

Relationships with Family and Peers

As adolescents move toward a more nearly equal relationship with their parents, they begin to assert their rights and question their parents' wisdom, making some tension inevitable. Yet the image of rebellious teenagers and wounded parents turns out to be another myth of adolescence. In three out of four families, a child's transition into adolescence, with its accompanying change in family roles, causes only minor and sporadic conflict (Hill, 1985). Between 85 and 90 percent of adolescents say that "most of the time my parents are satisfied with me," and between 75 and 85 percent say that "my parents are usually patient with me" (Offer, Ostrov, and Howard, 1981).

Family relationships seem to change at the expense of the mother's authority—at least when the teenager is a boy. Among boys studied by Laurence Steinberg (1981), most became much less deferential to their mothers when they entered puberty. Gradually, they became more dominant in family discussions until, by the time they had reached late adolescence, they had more family authority than

Despite occasional minor conflicts, parents and adolescent children get along well in the majority of families.

their mothers. In all these families, the father remained the most powerful family member. Both boys and girls distance themselves from their parents during adolescence, although relationships rarely turn hostile and the change is not large enough to be considered a sign of family turmoil (Steinberg, 1988).

Minor parent–child conflict seems to peak in early adolescence, just before a youngster enters high school. Then disagreements wane and relationships steadily become more harmonious. Conflict may fade because parents, as well as adolescents, have come to accept a shift in some areas of authority. In one study (Smetana, 1988), parents and adolescents (aged thirteen to eighteen) generally agreed that parental authority was always appropriate in areas related to moral transgressions (stealing, not sharing, lying, hitting) and violations of convention (not doing chores, calling parents by their first names, not keeping parents informed of activities). But as adolescents grew older, parents gradually ceded authority to them on such matters as sleeping late, watching MTV, wearing punk clothes, and hanging out with a friend of whom parents disapproved.

Adolescents in the United States typically go through a period when they temporarily substitute peer group norms for parental authority (Steinberg and Silverberg, 1986). This often causes direct conflict with parents, both in minor areas (styles of dress or tastes in music) and in antisocial behavior (cheating, stealing, or trespassing). Conformity to peers tends to peak in the ninth grade, then declines during the high school years (Berndt, 1979; Krosnick and Judd, 1982). But the waning of peer pressure does not necessarily signify an increase in parental influence. By the age of sixteen or seventeen, adolescents are beginning to control their own lives and to determine which adult standards they will adopt for themselves.

Problems of Adolescence

Most adolescents successfully resolve conflicts between their own needs and social demands. But a small percentage, who still have unresolved conflicts from earlier stages of development, may find old problems resurfacing and the accompanying stress intolerable. For nearly twenty years, adolescent drug use, suicide, juvenile delinquency, and births to mothers in their teens rose at alarming rates. In recent years, however, the proportion of adolescents with these problems has begun to decline.

What has caused this change? According to the **birth-cohort theory**, the more "crowded" a generation is, the higher the level of disturbance among its members (Easterlin, 1980; Fuchs, 1983). That is, members of a crowded "baby boom" generation face more competition for limited resources—good grades, admission to the best colleges, jobs, promotions, and even dates and mates. Some of those who sense themselves failing may react with rage and commit delinquent acts; others may react with feelings of worthlessness and commit suicide. The theory is that in a crowded generation, both the number and the rate (percentage) of individuals who commit destructive or self-destructive acts will increase.

The theory's predictions do hold up. The years 1947 to 1964 were baby-boom years, followed by a "baby bust." Statistics show that the rate of various disturbances began to fall in 1980, as the baby boomers moved out of adolescence and very young adulthood. Daily marijuana use, which had peaked in 1978 at 10.7 percent of high school seniors, declined to 4.9 percent by 1985 (Kozel and Adams, 1986). Rates of suicide, burglary, auto theft, robbery, and homicide began to drop (Offer and Holinger, 1983). The birth rate among adolescents has also been dropping, and the pregnancy rate among girls who are fifteen or older has declined, although the pregnancy rate among the youngest adolescents is still climbing (Kantrowitz, 1987).

If the birth-cohort theory is correct, we might expect youthful disorders to continue their decline, at least until the end of the century. But other factors may prevent the expected drop—or at least slow it. For example, the cheapness and availability of drugs, as well as adolescents' beliefs about the dangers of drugs, will influence the rate of substance abuse. Even with the declines mentioned above, however, a sizable number of adolescents still have problems.

BIRTH-COHORT THEORY the theory that crowded birth groups increase the social and economic stress on their members, leading to an increase in stress-related disorders

Drug and Alcohol Abuse

Drugs and alcohol are available to all adolescents, but some never use them, and others use them infrequently. About half of junior high school students and three-fourths of high school students have tried alcohol, which is the most popular drug among adolescents. More than 15 percent of thirteen-year-olds and 54 percent of high school seniors have tried marijuana, although, as we have seen, heavy marijuana usage is declining. In 1985, only 13 percent of high school seniors had tried cocaine (Kozel and Adams, 1986); but with the wide availability of cheap forms of cocaine (such as "crack"), its use among adolescents has increased.

Abuse of alcohol or drugs by adolescents is associated with poor school performance, disrupted family life, and antisocial behavior. A study of Philadelphia high school students, for instance, showed that those who used drugs at least once a week were more likely than nonusers to have repeated a grade, to have been suspended from school, and to have had conflicts with their teachers (Kovach and Glickman, 1986). They had more crises in their families, had more conflicts with their parents, and were more likely to have had trouble with the law. Heavy substance use of any kind is often a warning of future trouble, usually of an antisocial or self-destructive nature. In fact, most adult alcoholics were problem drinkers as adolescents (Zucker, 1987).

Psychologists have looked for factors that predict adolescent abuse of drugs and alcohol. Researchers have discovered that certain personality factors in childhood are associated with later heavy drug use (Brook et al., 1986a; Block, Block, and Keyes, 1988). Youngsters who were low achievers, lost their temper easily, were often depressed, or seemed unable to postpone gratification were most likely to abuse drugs as adolescents. But the high-risk children who learned to control their temper and who became high achievers with high educational aspirations did not succumb to substance abuse. Some researchers have speculated that youngsters at risk who go on to abuse drugs are those who seek out peers similar to themselves (Block, Block, and Keyes, 1988). Their mutual influence draws them into a social environment that fosters drug abuse.

Family factors also seem important. In one study (Barnes, 1984), adolescents who were problem drinkers tended to have parents who gave them little love or attention (see Table 16.2). The parents seemed uninterested in their children and often had little contact with them. These parents apparently had adopted the neglecting-rejecting parenting pattern described in Chapter 15. Similar family backgrounds seem related to the use of hard drugs. Other researchers (Brook et

Most adolescents experiment with alcohol, but relatively few develop problems with substance abuse.

al., 1986b) have found that adolescents who abuse hard drugs tended to have mothers who spent little time with them and exerted little control over their activities.

Juvenile Delinquency

Crime is primarily a problem of the young and the male. Arrests for violent crime and crimes against property peak among fifteen- to nineteen-year-olds (Wilson and Herrnstein, 1985), while eight out of ten people arrested for serious crimes are males (U.S. Bureau of Justice Statistics, 1983). Researchers are not certain why crime is so heavily concentrated among the young, but some have speculated that it may be related to the nature of adolescence. During these years, parental control is weakening, but adolescents have not yet accepted adult standards and responsibilities.

Much juvenile delinquency is what authorities call *social delinquency:* lawbreaking that is the result of peer pressure (Miller, 1958). More difficult to handle is *unsocialized delinquency:* law-breaking that is the result of adolescents' inability to control their behavior (Glueck and Glueck, 1950). Besides lacking self-control, these adolescent law-breakers tend to be aggressive, impulsive risk takers who seek excitement. Most have not accepted the values of their families or society.

In one study, the major difference between delinquent and nondelinquent boys was the marked lack of attachment that delinquents felt for their families (Offer, Strov, and Howard, 1981). Other researchers have found delinquency associated with homes in which discipline was lax or erratic and parents displayed little love for their children (McCord and McCord, 1959)—again, the neglecting-rejecting pattern of parenting.

Teenage Pregnancy

Despite increased sex education and the greater availability of contraceptives and abortion, each year nearly 500,000 babies are born to adolescent girls in the United States (Lewin, 1988). The incidence of teenage pregnancy is much higher in this country than in more sexually permissive Western European nations—three times higher than in Sweden and seven times higher than in the Netherlands (Leavitt, 1986). One reason is the failure to use birth control. Only one-third of sexually active teenagers say they always use contraceptives (Hevesi, 1986).

Most adolescents who become pregnant do not do so intentionally, but they seem to have no motivation to avoid it (Moore, 1985). Most have little interest in academic matters and are doing poorly in school (Furstenberg, Brooks-Gunn, and Morgan, 1987). Eighty percent of adolescent mothers who become pregnant between the ages of fifteen and seventeen never complete high school (*New York Times*, 1985). These young women find themselves trapped in economic insecurity—without the skills that enable them to get a job and burdened with the emotional and economic responsibilities of caring for an infant. Within two years,

TABLE 16.2 Parental Nurturance and Adolescent Problem Drinkers (Percent)

	Mother Nurturance			Father Nurturance		
	LOW (N = 35)	MEDIUM (N = 50)	HIGH (N = 37)	LOW (N = 51)	MEDIUM (N = 40)	HIGH (N = 37)
Problem drinkers	26	24	8	26	18	5
Nonproblem drinkers and abstainers	74	76	92	74	83	95

Source: G. M. Barnes, (1984), Adolescent alcohol abuse and other problem behaviors: Their relationships and common parental influences, *Journal of Youth and Adolescence*, 13, 344.

Teenage mothers who choose to keep their babies face many difficulties, especially if they try to raise their babies alone. Those who do best live at home with their parents, while continuing their education.

65 percent are pregnant again (Bolton, 1980). Girls who "solve" their problems by getting married seem to do better initially, but they usually drop out of school and later find themselves divorced and without job skills (Moore, 1985). Teenage mothers who stay home with their parents and complete their education do best in the long run (Furstenberg, 1976).

ADULTHOOD

Adulthood, the longest period in the life span, used to be considered the end of "growing up" and the start of "growing old." People became adults, remained in their physical prime for a decade or so, and then began to decline. The truth about human development is quite different. Decay begins much earlier—during the fetal period, in fact, when extra neurons die without making connections within the brain. Moreover, not all changes after maturity involve deterioration. With age, people generally come to understand themselves and others better. Most continue to improve in some aspects of intellectual functioning until they are about sixty-five years old (Horn, 1982). And many are still making important contributions to society when they are seventy, eighty, or even ninety years old.

Traditionally, adulthood has been divided into three periods: young adulthood (the years from eighteen or twenty until about forty), middle adulthood (from forty until about sixty-five), and late adulthood (from sixty-five on). But the distinctions between these periods are blurring—their sharp edges rubbed away by changes in society and the extension of good health far into old age. Because of such changes, the majority of today's older adults may be thought of as "young-old." Whether they are sixty-five or eighty-five, they are nearly as vigorous and active as middle-aged adults. The number of frail and ill, "old-old" people is relatively small (Neugarten and Neugarten, 1987).

People have "social clocks" in their heads to help them judge their own and other people's behavior as being early, late, or on time. Over the past twenty years, the influence of these social clocks has weakened. We seem to be moving toward an **age-irrelevant society,** in which major life events, such as marriage, parenthood, and retirement, are not closely tied to specific chronological ages.

This new fluidity in adult tasks, roles, and capabilities affects attitudes and behavior at all ages. In the 1960s, for example, nearly 90 percent of adults agreed that the best age for a woman to marry was between nineteen and twenty-four.

AGE-IRRELEVANT SOCIETY a society in which major life events, such as marriage, parenthood, and retirement, are not closely tied to specific chronological ages

Two decades later, only 40 percent agreed on that age (Neugarten and Neugarten, 1987). Today, a company chief executive may be thirty, sixty, or eighty; a new mother may be eighteen or thirty-eight; a seventy-five-year-old may start a business; and a fifty-five-year-old may decide to retire. As we examine the biological, cognitive, and social aspects of adulthood, we will see that stereotypical views of what it means to be young, middle-aged, or old may not apply to the majority of people.

Physical Changes in Adulthood

During the young adult years, most people are at the peak of their physical agility, speed, and strength. Yet, silently and almost imperceptibly, physiological aging has already begun. Although people still think of themselves as being in prime condition, the efficiency of their heart and lungs and their muscle tone and strength have begun to decline. Even if their weight remains constant, the proportion of fatty tissue to muscle increases. The first tiny wrinkles appear beside the eyes, and the skin begins to age. The acuity of vision and hearing also declines (see Chapter 5).

By middle adulthood most of these physical changes have become apparent. Many people are upset by them because society places a high value on youthful appearance. Men and women often try to reverse, slow down, or conceal the unmistakable signs of age. However, not all these physical changes result from the normal processes of aging. Some are due to poor health. Some are due to bad habits or chronic abuse: improper nutrition, smoking, the abuse of alcohol, and overexposure to direct sunlight. Some changes are due to simple disuse: lack of exercise, for instance, accelerates the loss of muscle mass, strength, and tone; decreases joint mobility; speeds aging in the cardiovascular and respiratory systems; encourages obesity; and hastens the bone loss of osteoporosis (de Vries, 1983).

The clearest biological marker of middle age among women is **menopause,** or the end of menstruation, which occurs gradually around the age of fifty when the ovaries cease producing estrogen. According to the popular wisdom, a menopausal woman is irritable, nervous, and depressed, suffers from headaches or backaches, and is always tired. Yet the only symptoms consistently reported are hot

MENOPAUSE   the end of menstruation

Some of the health problems that adults experience result, not from the aging process itself, but from unhealthy habits such as poor diet, smoking, and lack of exercise.

PSYCHOLOGY TODAY AND TOMORROW

Living with Alzheimer's Disease

Alzheimer's disease develops very slowly. As we saw in Chapter 3, memory loss is frequently the first sign of the disease. The loss becomes severe and soon bears little relation to the memory lapses that are typical of normal aging. A person who is aging normally misplaces the car keys; a person with Alzheimer's disease forgets that he or she ever owned a car.

Recall is the first cognitive process to decline in Alzheimer's disease (Vitaliano et al., 1986). When those with mild Alzheimer's disease are compared with normal individuals, scores on recall tests differ, but scores on tests of attention and recognition memory are similar in both groups. Within two years, however, the groups can be distinguished on all three tests.

As patients become aware that their mental abilities are deteriorating, many become terrified or depressed. At first, they may try to conceal their difficulties by writing notes to themselves, listing simple work routines, names, and phone numbers. One woman with Alzheimer's disease keep rehearsing possible conversations, trying to anticipate what might be said. By applying intense effort, she managed to keep working at her job as telephone supervisor for nearly six months after her condition was diagnosed (Clark, 1984).

The terror eventually disappears, but by then the disease has progressed so far that patients are disoriented. They may dress for a snowstorm in midsummer, forget the names of their children, fail to recognize a spouse, or, while sitting in their living room, ask when they will be going home. Later they become unable to feed or dress themselves. In the disease's final stages, those

with Alzheimer's cannot speak or walk. Eventually, they die, often from pneumonia, urinary tract infections, or other complications common among the bedridden.

Nothing can halt the progression of the disease, but the period during which people with Alzheimer's disease can continue to function independently may be prolonged. Treating the early depression often enables patients to apply their waning attention to the tasks of daily living. Simple memory aids, such as a prominent calendar, a telephone with memory dialing and labels on frequently used items help patients continue to function. These memory crutches act as permanent recall cues. Behavior therapy, which we explore in Chapter 19, may also be helpful.

flashes and sweating (Harman and Talbert, 1985). Most women experience only minor discomforts and emerge from menopause with increased happiness and health (Neugarten et al., 1963). Although decreased hormone levels may reduce the intensity and duration of their sexual response, the majority of postmenopausal women continue to be both interested in sex and sexually active (Weg, 1983).

Unlike women, men at midlife do not lose their ability to reproduce. They do tend to need more direct stimulation to become sexually aroused and the intensity of their orgasms decreases; after a climax they require more time before they can become aroused again. But these changes in sexual response may enhance the pleasure of sexual activity by making sexual intercourse last longer than it once did.

Most of the physical changes of later adulthood, as in middle adulthood, are caused by disease, disuse, and abuse—not by the aging process itself. Older adults who keep exercising, never smoke, never abuse alcohol or other drugs, and watch their diets are likely to remain vigorous and active until shortly before their deaths. Nevertheless, most older people find that their ability to adapt to stress and change is less efficient. For example, in healthy, active older adults, the heart works as well as it ever did while resting. But when they are exposed to the stress of exercise or emotional upset, the heart does not react as quickly as it once did, and afterward it takes longer to return to normal (Lakatta, 1985).

For many people, the thought of an aging brain may be more worrisome than the prospect of an aging body. Some loss of brain cells does occur in old age, but many individuals show little or no effect from it. Although brain cells cannot replace themselves, the growth of new connections among other cells seems to compensate for part of the loss (Bondareff, 1985). Cognitive decline traceable to the disruption of brain-cell circuits or the loss of neurons primarily affects older adults who are in poor health. Serious mental deterioration, as in Alzheimer's disease, is not a part of normal aging (see the accompanying box).

Cognitive Development in Adulthood

For decades, there was almost no research into cognitive development during adulthood. It was simply taken for granted that cognitive changes in adulthood took the form of a steady decline, as cross-sectional IQ testing seemed to indicate. Then researchers took another look at adult cognition and found evidence for the emergence of new, and perhaps improved, ways of thinking.

Postformal Thought

Piaget assumed that formal operations was the highest form of thought. In this stage, thought is abstract, logical, and stripped of any emotional bias, which makes it superb for solving problems in mathematics and physics; but it may not be the most practical mode for resolving the messy dilemmas of life. Many people in middle and later adulthood may not use formal operations, yet their thought is highly adaptive because it incorporates social responsibility and an awareness of emotional and interpersonal factors. Researchers like Gisela Labouvie-Vief (1982; 1985) see this further reorganization of thought in middle adulthood as evidence of a stage of cognitive development beyond formal operations.

This additional stage, known as **postformal thought** (Kramer, 1983), emerges as adults learn through experience that their assumptions and ways of thinking influence the knowledge they glean from the world. They are able to accept contradiction in their thought and development. The ability to integrate conflicting viewpoints into a larger framework makes postformal thought adaptive, problem-oriented, and more flexible than formal thought. This sort of skill tends to make middle-aged adults better jurors, for example, than young adults, who tend to base their conclusions on fragmentary information (Labouvie-Vief, 1985; Blanchard-Fields, 1986).

For example, in one study, when presented with a series of social dilemmas, adults in their thirties and forties displayed a form of postformal thought that was virtually absent from the reasoning of adolescents in their teens and college students in their early twenties (Blanchard-Fields, 1986). In judging emotionally laden problems of everyday life—such as a clash between an adolescent boy and his parents over a visit to grandparents—only the oldest group was able to focus on the facts, weigh the issues involved, and come up with a judgment that acknowledged the validity of each point of view. Adolescents tended to take one side or the other, without dealing with the opposing view; college students recognized both viewpoints but believed that it was possible for a neutral party to determine which side was "right" and which was "wrong." Apparently, it takes years of experience to foster the sort of interpretive thought that we associate with wisdom—thought that goes beyond the knowledge of facts to an understanding of their significance.

POSTFORMAL THOUGHT the problem-oriented, flexible thought characteristic of middle adulthood, involving social responsibility, an ability to integrate conflicting information, and an awareness of emotional and interpersonal influences on knowledge

Studying Adult Cognition

The study of adult cognition is complicated. First, it is almost impossible to separate the effects of aging from the effects of social change (Neugarten, 1977). Each *cohort,* or group of people born at a particular time, grows up under different social, economic, and technological conditions from the cohorts that precede and follow it. The consequences of these conditions, known as "cohort effects," heavily influence the performance of different age groups on the same test. The knowledge base of each cohort is different—sometimes radically so. Today's young adults, for example, are likely to have much more education than their grandparents did.

Second, disease often affects cognitive function. Researchers have found that undiagnosed hypertension and cardiovascular disease are responsible for much of the age-related decline that experimental studies reveal (Barrett and Watkins, 1986). In addition, most studies of older adults probably include individuals with mild brain disorders, such as those in the early stages of Alzheimer's disease. For these reasons, cognitive tests may reflect impairment due to disease instead of the normal cognitive processes of late adulthood. An awareness of these problems helps us understand why studies of older adults' cognition may lead us to underestimate their mental abilities.

Young adults usually perform better on any learning or memory task than people in middle or late adulthood (Poon, 1985). They are also faster in completing tests involving speed or eye–hand coordination (Perlmutter and Hall, 1985; Salthouse, 1985). But during middle adulthood, verbal and reasoning skills tend to improve, provided individuals remain healthy. So does the ability to organize and process visual information, such as finding a simple figure embedded in a complex one. Middle-aged adults also tend to be more knowledgeable than they have ever been, and their ability to think flexibly—a valuable problem-solving skill, as we saw in Chapter 9—is likely to be as good as it had been earlier in life.

Among older adults, the ability to process sensory information slows noticeably. It takes them longer than it once would have to dial a telephone, zip up a jacket, or cut with a knife. What causes the slowdown? Some researchers believe that activity in the entire central nervous system slows with age (Salthouse, 1985). The only motor activities that escape this general slowdown are those that have become automatic, such as the highly practiced skill of a typist. The slowdown is relative, however: when healthy, physically fit older adults are matched with unhealthy, sedentary young adults, the old do as well on motor tasks as the young (Salthouse, 1985).

The cognitive change that most people associate with aging is memory loss. Many older adults complain about being unable to recall words or forgetting where they have put things. Researchers have found that in most cases such complaints are related not to scores on objective tests of memory, but to measures of depression (O'Hara et al., 1986). Depression may cause older people to focus on their own shortcomings and make them especially sensitive to each apparent sign of failing memory (Zarit, 1980).

Some memory decline is characteristic of late adulthood, but researchers are not certain just what aspects of the memory system are involved (Howe and Hunter, 1986). Research indicates that the capacity of short-term memory seems unaffected by aging, and the speed with which information is lost from short-term memory does not change (Kausler, 1982; Poon, 1985). Yet when older people must retrieve, manipulate, or reorganize information in short-term memory, age differences become apparent (Walsh, 1983).

Older adults also show a decline in some aspects of long-term memory, such as recall. In one study, older adults recognized pictures as accurately as college students did (Park, Puglisi, and Smith, 1986). Yet they did worse than young and middle-aged adults at recalling verbal material they recently learned. Yet older adults can use efficient memory strategies (such as reorganization, elaboration, and rehearsal) to encode information in long-term storage (see Chapter 8). When laboratory tests are designed to require the use of these strategies, the recall of older adults is as good as that of younger adults (Mitchell and Perlmutter, 1986). Some researchers believe that older people may fail to use memory strategies

Older adults show no decline in their ability to perform familiar activities. Longtime bridge players, for example, know from experience how best to channel their mental energy in paying attention to various aspects of the game.

because they have less mental energy to spend on focusing their attention. This may be one reason that practiced activities, which require little attention, show no decline with age (Craik and Byrd, 1982). Another factor that keeps performance levels high in such practiced activities as typing, bridge, and chess is the older person's ability to compensate for age-related losses by developing other skills. For example, older typists compensate for their slowed reaction times by looking farther ahead in their copy than younger typists do (Salthouse, 1984).

Does IQ Decline with Age?

Although people in their seventies, eighties, and nineties make important contributions to society, studies consistently show that scores on IQ tests decline with age. The gradual drop begins sometime between the ages of forty and seventy.

Not all aspects of intelligence decline equally, and some people show no decline until quite late in life (Horn, 1982; Schaie and Herzog, 1983). Scores on the WAIS verbal scale (see Chapter 11) decline very little; some of the subscores even increase with age. This shows an increase in *crystallized intelligence,* which includes verbal skills and the ability to solve problems by drawing on stored knowledge. The decline seems concentrated on the performance, or nonverbal, scale, which taps *fluid intelligence,* that includes spatial orientation and inductive reasoning. Until adults are about sixty-five, increases in crystallized intelligence generally offset declines in fluid intelligence (Horn, 1982). This pattern of decline, known as the "classic aging pattern," is found in men and women, in whites and blacks, and in middle-class and working-class individuals (Botwinick, 1977).

Several factors may be responsible for this comparative decline. One is the timed nature of the WAIS performance scale; the older person's slowed processing ability and tendency to deliberate over answers probably contribute to the drop in scores (Willis, 1985). Cohort differences are another factor. Older adults' lower levels of education and lack of experience in taking academic tests help widen age differences in scores. In one study, educational differences among cohorts *did* magnify IQ declines (Schaie and Herzog, 1983). Researchers who compared groups of adults with the same educational level found almost no IQ decline until the age of 65 (Botwinick, 1977). A third factor contributing to the decline is older adults' failure to organize new information and the difficulty they have in keeping their attention focused (Horn, 1982).

Longitudinal studies give us a fairly optimistic picture of intelligence. In a study that followed adults of all ages over a fourteen-year period, Warner Schaie found that between the ages of forty-six and sixty, the average IQ decline amounted to only 3 points (Schaie and Herzog, 1983; Schaie, 1984). Those who retained their intellectual abilities into later adulthood led lives that were high in environmental stimulation and kept up their interest in education.

Training programs aimed at getting older people to use memory strategies and to test possible solutions to problems in a systematic manner have improved their performance on learning and memory tasks (Hoffman et al., 1988). One training program has actually reversed long-term declines in IQ test scores (Schaie and Willis, 1986). Such research suggests that the cognitive decline that appears in most IQ tests may be the result of mental disuse—not deterioration. Once again, we find that stimulation and practice can maintain intellectual flexibility far into old age.

Social Development in Adulthood

As people move through adulthood, they focus their energies and motivations on different emotional and social tasks. Young adults must deal with the completion of education, entry into the work force, marriage, and parenthood. Being middle-aged means being a member of the age group that runs society and therefore involves coming to terms with issues of power and responsibility. The developmental tasks of older adults tend to be personal: understanding and accepting their lives, adjusting to retirement, and facing their own mortality. Erik Erikson's theory, the only one that deals comprehensively with the entire life span, remains the classic approach to the psychosocial development of adults as well as of children. (We described the tasks of infancy and childhood in Chapter 15; for a quick review of all the stages in Erikson's theory, look back at Figure 15.7.)

Erikson's Central Tasks of Adulthood

In Erikson's (1963; 1982) view, the major task facing young adults is the development of **intimacy,** in which they commit themselves to a close relationship that demands sacrifice and compromise. This advance comes out of the inner struggle between intimacy and isolation. When intimacy gains the upper hand, the adult is

INTIMACY the ability to commit the self to a close relationship that demands sacrifice and compromise; in Erikson's theory, the development of intimacy is the major task of young adulthood

In Erikson's view, developing a sense of generativity—a concern for the well-being of future generations—is a central task of adulthood.

able to love another without fearing loss of the self. Intimacy can come only if individuals first develop identity during adolescence, so that they are no longer emotionally dependent on their parents. When isolation predominates, young adults' emotional relationships are routine and cold.

When people move into middle adulthood, the major conflict as described by Erikson is between generativity and stagnation. **Generativity** involves a concern for future generations. Many people express this concern directly, by nurturing children—their own or other people's. But generativity can also be expressed through creativity or productivity. When stagnation predominates, people lack concern for future generations or for society. They tend to be self-absorbed and bored with life. Eventually, they find their lives empty, and they feel a vague but nagging sense of loss.

During the eighth and final stage of life, the central conflict is between **ego integrity,** which is a sense of the wholeness and meaningfulness of one's life, and despair. Those who resolve this conflict accept themselves as they are and believe in the dignity of their efforts and choices. They have achieved wisdom, which Erikson sees as the strength of late adulthood. Those who do not resolve the conflict sink into despair; they live in fear of death and yearn for a chance to live their lives over again.

Although little research has been done on Erikson's theory, some longitudinal studies have supported its broad outlines. In two studies that followed men into middle adulthood, both lower-class and middle-class men seemed to develop the strengths of each stage in order, and those who had not resolved one of the earlier stages seemed to stall at that stage (Vaillant and Milofsky, 1980). For example, almost none of the men who had failed to develop an intimate relationship with another person forged a commitment to his occupation as an outlet for the creative and productive potential of generativity. Social class and education had no effect on a man's progression through the stages.

Some psychologists have contended that Erikson's theory may not describe the development of women as accurately as it seems to predict the development of men. Carol Gilligan (1982) believes that the developmental tasks of each stage are very different for men and women because the genders are socialized so differently. Throughout childhood, women meet their developmental tasks within a context of relationships, so that achieving intimacy in young adulthood does not present a great departure from their earlier development. For them, the relationships involved in intimacy must be tempered by the need for personal integrity. This is not true for men, because their upbringing does not emphasize relationships. Intimacy ends their isolation and prepares them to move into the generativity of middle adulthood. The experience of generativity thus seems quite different for men and for women. Erikson interprets it as "man's relationship to his production as well as to his progeny" (1950, p. 268) and so makes it the central task of middle adulthood. But women, who take primary responsibility for nurturing children, are often deeply concerned with tasks related to generativity much earlier, during young adulthood.

Levinson's Transitional Phases

Building on Erikson's psychosocial theory, Daniel Levinson and his colleagues (Levinson et al., 1978) have looked at the way individuals develop in relation to society. Levinson's original study was limited to men, but he and others have begun to test it with young adult women (Brown, 1987; Roberts and Newton, 1987).

Levinson sees development as an orderly sequence that alternates between stable and transitional stages (see Figure 16.4). During stable phases, people pursue their goals fairly tranquilly, since pertinent developmental tasks have been solved. Transitional phases can lead to major changes, because individuals are questioning the pattern of their lives and exploring new possibilities.

During the transition to early adulthood (which occurs between the ages of eighteen and twenty), men and women both work at becoming psychologically independent from their parents (see the accompanying box). Then they enter a

GENERATIVITY a concern for future generations, consisting of procreativity, productivity, and creativity; in Erikson's theory, the development of generativity is the major task of middle adulthood

EGO INTEGRITY a sense of the wholeness and meaningfulness of one's life; in Erikson's theory, the development of ego integrity is the major task of later adulthood

Figure 16.4 A model of the developmental sequence of a man's life developed by Daniel Levinson. The major life eras are childhood and adolescence, early adulthood, middle adulthood, and later adulthood; within each era there are distinctive stages, and between eras a major transition occurs. (Levinson et al., 1978.)

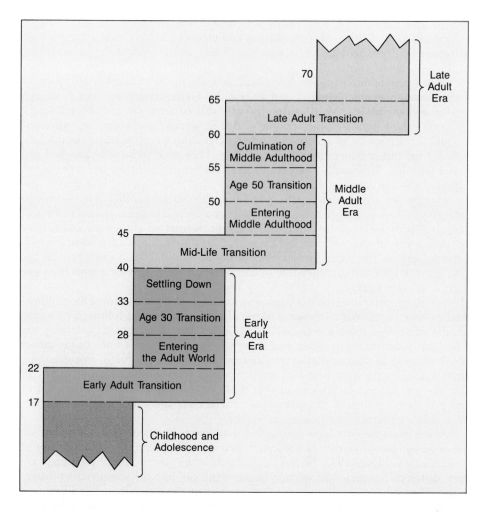

MIDLIFE CRISIS Levinson's term for the state of physical and psychological distress that a man experiences when the developmental tasks he faces during the transition to middle adulthood threaten to overwhelm his internal resources and social supports

stable phase, during which they begin to establish themselves in the adult world and set up a home and family.

Another transitional phase occurs during the late twenties. At this time adults evaluate the pattern of their lives and, if they find it flawed, are likely to make changes. Men are likely to settle down and concentrate on consolidating their careers. Many women reverse their priorities: those who had stressed marriage and motherhood develop personal goals for the future, and those who had focused on their careers become more concerned with marriage and family. Many women do not commit themselves to an occupation until near the end of this period (Roberts and Newton, 1987).

Researchers have not yet established how the rest of Levinson's phases apply to women. For men, the next shift comes during the transition to middle adulthood (between age forty and forty-five). They reevaluate their lives once again, and most conclude that their youthful dreams will never come true. Levinson found that this transition is almost invariably accompanied by a **midlife crisis**— the state of physical and psychological distress that a man experiences when the developmental tasks threaten to overwhelm his internal resources and social supports (Cytrynbaum et al., 1980). Among the men Levinson studied, 80 percent went through such an upheaval in their early forties. The idea of a midlife crisis has so permeated popular writing on middle age that most people probably accept such a crisis as an inevitable part of life. Yet not a single other longitudinal study has uncovered a general crisis in midlife, as illustrated in Figure 16.5 (Hoffman et al., 1988).

Once into their forties, men may make further changes and try to rebuild their lives. By the mid-fifties, they resettle into their lives and most find the rest of the decade a time of fulfillment. The additional choices that men make at sixty, when they begin the transition into late adulthood, define the shape of their re-

PSYCHOLOGY TODAY AND TOMORROW

Prolonged Adolescence in Young Adulthood

When people assume adult roles, they are presumed to have emerged from adolescence. However, recent research indicates that psychological adolescence, as manifested by emotional dependence on parents, may linger long into young adulthood. Most young adults are nearly thirty years old by the time they have established mature relationships with their parents.

After studying 150 men and women between the ages of twenty-two and thirty-two, Susan Frank and her associates (Frank, Avery, and Laman, 1988) concluded that until they are into their mid-twenties, the majority of young adults are still so emotionally tied to their parents that they have little confidence in their ability to live on their own and to make decisions based on their own values. During their early twenties, only about 20 percent of these adults felt that they could cope with most aspects of their lives without their parents' assistance; among those in their late twenties, 80 percent felt that they could make it on their own. Other researchers have described the early twenties as a time when young adults are unable to see their parents as separate individuals with their own needs and strengths and weaknesses. Instead, they see their parents in terms of their own needs: "Were they good or bad parents, did they love me or not, were they too restrictive or demanding?" (Goleman, 1988).

Among those in Frank's study who had developed mature relationships, women usually felt closer to both parents than men did, and they were more likely than men to see their parents as separate individuals. Men with mature relationships were more likely to feel prepared to meet life's challenges, and to feel that they had their parents' respect, but their relationships often lacked intensity and depth.

Among those with immature relationships, women tended to remain dependent on their parents but to see them as judgmental or self-preoccupied, or both ("When I fail he says 'I told you so'"). Men with immature relationships were more likely to be emotionally distant from their parents and to resent their parents' offers of assistance ("She wants control and wants someone to be dependent on her"). Their often contemptuous attitudes toward their parents were likely to conceal feelings of inferiority and anger at what they saw as their parents' inability to accept their sons as they were.

One unexpected finding was the ineffectiveness of marriage in helping young adults achieve a more mature relationship with their parents. Married adults were as likely to be mired in immature relationships with their parents as were unmarried adults of the same age. Other researchers believe that people tend to have more mature relationships with their spouses than with their parents, because they can walk away from conflicts with their parents but feel compelled to work out their marital conflicts (Goleman, 1988).

---

maining years. Five years later, when retirement arrives for most men, the task is to find a new balance of involvement between self and society—both in the world and in the family. For a growing number of men, a final transition occurs at about age eighty, when they come to terms with dying.

Changes in Social Roles

Adulthood is marked by the assumption of many new social roles, including spouse, parent, and worker.

MARRIAGE AND PARENTHOOD Newly married couples undergo a period of adjustment during which they sort out issues of power, authority, and control. A study of childless couples (Kurdek and Schmitt, 1986) found that the first year of marriage was spent in learning to live together and realizing that one's actions have consequences for one's partner. During the next two years, the couples began exploring their compatibility. This was often a time of stress and disillusionment, and many weak marriages broke down at this time. By the fourth

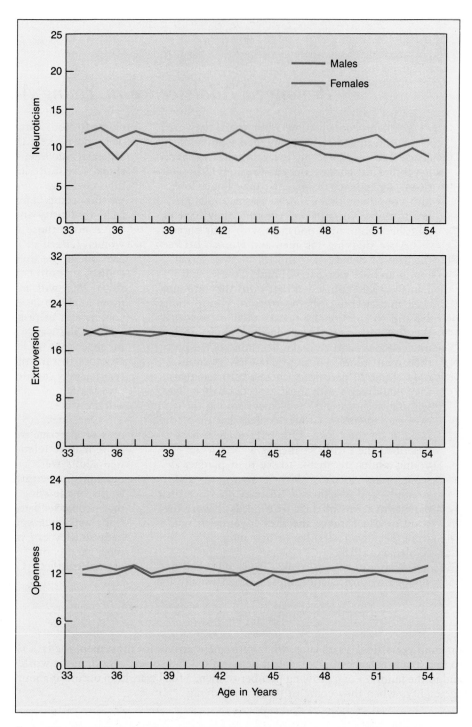

Figure 16.5 Personality ratings from a large national sample provide no evidence of a midlife crisis. Mean levels of neuroticism, extroversion, and openness to experience show remarkable stability between the ages of thirty-three and fifty-four. (From Costa et al., 1986.)

year of marriage, marital stress declined and each partner's individuality reappeared. Family traditions had been established and most couples' relationships had improved.

It appears that the level of marital satisfaction may be related to the personality characteristics of the partners. In the happiest marriages, both partners are usually emotionally mature, considerate of others, adaptable, and high in self-esteem (Cole, Cole, and Dean, 1980). Emotionally immature adults tend to expect too much of marriage and are unprepared to deal with the normal crises of married life (Spanier and Lewis, 1980).

The role of parent brings about even more dramatic shifts. Assuming the responsibility for a tiny, helpless, but immensely appealing human being leads to radical changes in the way people live. Some researchers go even farther: they believe that personality development in adulthood revolves around parenthood, and they call this shaping force the **parental imperative.** According to David Gutmann (1988), the parental imperative is a part of our evolutionary inheritance and heightens gender roles during the parenting years. That is, when a man becomes a father, he becomes more traditionally masculine, suppressing any urges of dependency or sympathy that might interfere with his ability to provide for and protect his child. A new mother becomes more traditionally feminine, suppressing any assertive, masterful, or aggressive urges that might harm her baby or drive off her mate.

Once the children are grown, parents are free to indulge their individual desires. Now, says Gutmann, both sexes become more **androgynous,** embracing characteristics typical of both gender roles. Women become more aggressive, more managerial or political, and less dependent on their husbands. Men become less interested in their occupations, more interested in companionship, and more dependent on their wives.

Some research has supported Gutmann's views. Mothers of young children generally rate themselves higher on measures of tenderness than other women do, and fathers of young children rate themselves higher on autonomy than do other men (Abrahams, Feldman, and Nash, 1978). Researchers have also found that, regardless of social class, many older men see themselves as cooperative and nurturing and as less dominant than they once were. But other studies have not found the kinds of personality shifts that Gutmann describes. In a longitudinal study of middle-class parents, only women showed the expected personality changes (Feldman and Aschenbrenner, 1983). Fathers of six-month-old babies were no more masculine than they had been two months before their babies were born; in fact, they had become more nurturing, warm, sensitive, responsive, and tolerant of others' shortcomings. In a study of middle-aged men and women, increased androgyny came only with the arrival of grandchildren (Feldman, Birigen, and Nash, 1981).

It may be that when mothers and fathers share in providing their child's material support, care, and emotional security (as a majority now do), parenthood may demand less dramatic changes in gender roles and personality. With today's young adults freer to express their androgyny than in years past, the tendency toward a *reversal* of sex roles in middle adulthood may also diminish.

PARENTAL IMPERATIVE
Gutmann's theory that parenthood controls personality in adulthood by heightening gender roles in the protection and nurturance of children

ANDROGYNOUS having a self-concept that incorporates both masculine and feminine characteristics

In middle adulthood, many women shift their priorities from raising a family to developing a career.

WORK AND RETIREMENT Work occupies a considerable portion of most adults' lives. Our jobs define our position in society, and often our identity. If we are fortunate, our jobs give meaning to our lives, provide satisfying activity, offer an outlet for creativity, and give us opportunities for social interaction (Perlmutter and Hall, 1985). People whose jobs require thought, judgment, and analysis generally continue to develop intellectually. Mental exercise on the job seems to keep the mind in shape, just as physical exercise tones the body. Researchers have shown that when workers participate in solving work-related problems and decision making, their interpersonal skills increase (Crouter, 1984).

Personality influences a person's occupational choice, but the job also affects the worker's personality. In a ten-year longitudinal study, Melvin Kohn (1980) discovered that workers who did complex, self-directed work became more open-minded and flexible. In contrast, those who did routine work tended to be intolerant and obedient (Kohn, 1980). Such findings hold true for women as well as men (Miller et al., 1979).

The emotional tone of the workplace carries over into a worker's daily life. Social relations at work set a prevailing mood that affects employees' psychological well-being (Hoffman et al., 1988). The quality of social relations with fellow employees is related to self-esteem, levels of anxiety, and tendencies toward depression.

At the same time, social roles and relationships outside the workplace can sometimes offset a negative work environment. When work-related stress leads to depression, it tends to be most disturbing for those who have few social roles. In a study of more than 400 women and men whose jobs ranged from waitress and truck driver to physician and lawyer, Rena Repetti and Faye Crosby (1984) found that single people were most likely to be depressed and married parents were least likely to be depressed. The researchers attributed the difference to the number of major social roles (worker, spouse, parent) a person fills.

Social roles can also increase a worker's chances of success at work. Marriage is strongly associated with occupational success in men, perhaps because of the strong support married men get from their wives (Mortimer, Lorence, and Kumka, 1982). Women probably do not get a similar career boost from marriage, but that may change as families adjust to the fact that more and more women are developing career commitments.

Because many couples now share the tasks of child rearing, they may feel less pressure to change their personalities upon becoming parents in order to fulfill the gender roles traditionally prescribed for mothers and fathers.

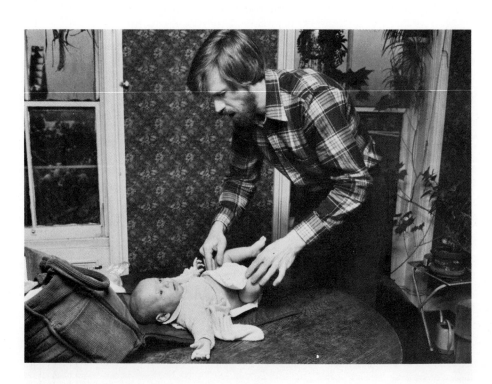

At retirement, people relinquish their social role as worker, yet most mentally hold on to that role. Retired people continue to think of themselves as plumbers, accountants, teachers, or physicians. Maintaining their former self-concepts allows them to keep up their self-esteem (Atchley, 1980).

When they retire, most people adjust in a predictable pattern (Atchley, 1976). Once they know the date of their retirement, workers begin to distance themselves from their jobs. Most also fantasize about their future, often creating an unrealistically rosy picture of retired life. After they retire, they tend to go through a "honeymoon," in which they dash from one leisure pursuit to another, like a child in a room full of toys. The honeymoon may last for years, although among 2000 men in a longitudinal study, it began to wane after six months (Ekerdt, Bosse, and Levkoff, 1985). For those with unrealistic fantasies, a period of disenchantment is usually inevitable. In fact, most retired men are at their lowest ebb, in terms of life satisfaction and physical activity, at the end of the first year. Slowly, they begin to search for a new life pattern. By the end of the second year, their satisfaction and activities begin to increase. Eventually, most settle down into a satisfying way of life. For the lucky ones who enter retirement with a realistic picture of its possibilities, this stable phase comes much more quickly.

Development in Late Adulthood

Different cohorts age in different ways, and changes in life patterns are the result of historical events during the cohort's life span (Hagestad and Neugarten, 1985). Today's older adults are finding that old age has changed dramatically since the time of their grandparents. For one thing, there are more old people. In 1900, about 4 percent of the population had reached their sixty-fifth birthdays. Today 12 percent of the population is older than sixty-five, and by 2020 the figure will rise to 20 percent (Holden, 1987). This growing group of older people is healthier, more vigorous, better educated, and more likely to be economically self-sufficient than older adults of past generations. Acording to some psychologists, the attitudes and activities of today's seventy-year-olds resemble those of fifty-year-olds a decade or two ago (Horn and Meer, 1987).

Older adults' increased affluence has also led to a revolution in their living arrangements. At the turn of the century, few older adults had their own households; most lived with a grown child or other relative (usually a sibling). Today, the overwhelming majority of older adults live independently: 84 percent of married couples and 67 percent of unmarried adults have their own households. Only about 5 percent live in nursing homes and similar institutions.

What happens to personality as people age? At one time, researchers believed that the typical pattern of adjustment to old age was **disengagement** (Cumming and Henry, 1961). As people aged, they gradually and voluntarily withdrew from social roles and decreased their involvement with others. At the same time, society gradually withdrew from the old, handing over to the young the roles and responsibilities once held by their elders. Disengagement was supposedly a universal, biologically based process, welcomed by the old and highly satisfactory both to older adults and to society in general.

But longitudinal studies found little evidence of disengagement and no sign that disengagement necessarily made later life satisfying (Palmore, 1970). Although older adults did lose some social roles, most did not become completely disengaged. In fact, these studies found that it was the highly active older adults, not the disengaged, who were most satisfied with their lives.

Today, most psychologists agree that either disengagement or activity—or something in between—may be appropriate, depending on the individual (Maddox and Campbell, 1985). Although socially involved adults are more likely than others to say they are satisfied, some disengaged adults are just as content. Researchers have found that people age according to patterns they established early in life: disengaged older adults were disengaged as young adults and in midlife (Neugarten, Havighurst, and Tobin, 1968; Neugarten, 1971).

DISENGAGEMENT a gradual, voluntary withdrawal from society and decreasing involvement with other people, once believed to be the typical pattern of adjustment to old age

DEATH AND DYING

As losses mount and the body becomes frailer, the "old-old" begin their psychological preparation for death. The onset of this period is not determined by chronological age, but by a person's social, physical, and mental situation. An eighty-five-year-old who is married and in good health, who has friends and an interest in the world, may not yet have begun his or her preparation, while a sixty-five-year-old who is widowed, friendless, and in poor health may have completed it.

In several studies, older adults who were highly anxious about death were extremely sensitive to the pace of time and uneasy about its passage (Kastenbaum, 1985). Once preparations for death have been successfully completed, the aging person feels differently about time's passage and its uses (Marshall, 1980). There is a new kind of freedom, in which the person can anticipate the future without any anxiety about impending death. Instead, he or she feels grateful for whatever time remains.

As part of their preparation for death, many old people turn inward. They may try to make sense of their lives through a process known as **life review.** According to Robert Butler (1975), life review is a universal developmental process that is part of Erikson's final stage, the struggle between integrity and despair. As the old reflect on their past and try to come to terms with it, they may feel anxiety, guilt, depression, or despair. But if the conflicts can be resolved, they may emerge with a sense of life's integrity or wholeness and a feeling of having lived a meaningful life. If conflicts are not resolved, the person is left in turmoil.

Not all researchers accept Butler's theory. Studies indicate that not all older people review their past. Even those who do may not try to come to terms with their past (Lieberman and Tobin, 1983; Kastenbaum, 1985). Some use the life review to construct a personal myth about their lives that enables them to retain a sense of self without having to resolve old conflicts.

In addition to preparing themselves for impending death on the psychological level, individuals also deal with death at an interpersonal level, preparing loved ones to live on without them (Shneidman, 1980). The way people face death seems to reflect their total personalities—their "philosophy of life." Most of us will meet death in the same way in which we have met life's other challenges.

LIFE REVIEW the process of reflecting on the past in order to come to terms with it before death

An elderly person who is in good health and is involved with life is likely to find it easier to deal with the prospect of death than is a person who is ill and isolated.

SUMMARY

Adolescence

■ Adolescence is the period of transition from childhood to adulthood that has been lengthening because of biological and social influences.

■ During puberty, a well-defined series of interrelated biological processes transforms a child into a sexually mature person.

■ Adolescents generally enter Piaget's stage of formal operations, in which their thought is reorganized and they become able to deal with abstractions and logical possibilities. In Kohlberg's view, their moral reasoning also becomes increasingly abstract as they develop universal moral principles.

■ Erikson saw adolescence as a time of conflict between identity and role confusion, during which identity grows out of choices, commitments, and the consolidation of self-concept.

■ Adolescents must incorporate their emerging sexuality into their social relationships. Among middle-class adolescents, boys are as likely as girls to believe that dating relationships should involve emotional as well as physical intimacy.

■ Conflicts between adolescents and their parents peak in early adolescence, then wane as family relationships change and parents gradually hand over more authority.

■ According to the birth-cohort theory, the competition for limited resources among members of a "crowded" generation contributes to an increase in such problems of adolescence as drug and alcohol abuse, juvenile delinquency, and teenage pregnancy.

Adulthood

■ Adulthood is traditionally divided into early, middle, and late periods. The distinctions between periods are blurring as we move closer to being an age-irrelevant society.

■ Many of the physical changes associated with aging are the result of poor health, bad habits or chronic abuse of the body, and disuse; they are not the result of normal aging processes.

■ During adulthood, thought may undergo a further reorganization into the stage of postformal thought, in which context and conflicting viewpoints are incorporated into the solution of problems.

■ Cohort effects, undiagnosed hypertension or cardiovascular disease, and early stages of brain disorder have made it virtually impossible to establish the existence of "normal" cognitive decline with age.

■ Tested declines in memory may be the result of slowed activity in the central nervous system, the failure of older adults to use memory strategies, or a reduced store of mental energy.

■ In Erikson's theory, the major conflict for young adults is between intimacy and isolation; for those in middle adulthood, the struggle is between generativity and stagnation; and for those in late adulthood, the conflict is between ego integrity and despair. Levinson finds alternating stable and transitional phases in adult development.

■ The major social roles of adulthood are those of spouse, parent, and worker.

■ Adjusting to marriage means dealing with issues of power, authority and control; the level of marital satisfaction seems to depend on the maturity and personality characteristics of the partners.

■ Gutmann has proposed that adult personality development is heavily influenced by the parental imperative, with parenthood heightening gender roles and the departure of adult children allowing adults to become more androgynous.

■ The nature of a person's occupation affects cognitive skills, personality, and social relations, but social roles and relationships outside the workplace affect job satisfaction and contribute to success at work.

■ People react to old age in a manner consistent with their earlier personality, with some choosing disengagement and others continuing to remain highly active.

Death and Dying

■ As death approaches, older adults begin to prepare for the end of life, with many turning inward to undertake a life review.

■ Most people meet death in the same way in which they have met life's other challenges.

KEY TERMS

adolescent growth spurt	estrogens	menopause
age-irrelevant society	formal operations	midlife crisis
androgens	generativity	parental imperative
androgynous	identity	postformal thought
birth-cohort theory	intimacy	primary sex characteristics
disengagement	life review	puberty
ego integrity	menarche	secondary sex characteristics

CONCEPT REVIEW

1. Describe the major physical changes that mark adolescence. Why do psychologists have difficulty in creating a uniform definition of adolescence?

2. Identify the kinds of formal operations that become possible during adolescence. What does Piaget mean by "formal"?

3. Outline the stages of Kolhberg's theory of moral development. Why has the applicability of this theory to females been challenged?

4. What was meant by the view of adolescence as a period of "storm and stress"? Describe the basic reasons that this view has been rejected. In what way might Erikson's recognition of adolescence as a time for developing one's identity play a role in the storm-and-stress view?

5. Describe the kinds of conflicts that a typical adolescent may have with his or her parents. Is sexual development and expression part of this conflict?

6. Name some of the common problems of adolescence and identify their possible causes. How does the birth-cohort theory account for some of these problems?

7. What physical characteristics mark the stages of adulthood? What are the most dramatic changes that are experienced during this time of life?

8. How does postformal thought differ from Piaget's stage of formal operations? How might postformal thought be useful in coping with the changes in cognitive ability that occur during adulthood? What areas of cognitive activity appear to be most affected by progress through adulthood?

9. Does IQ decline with age? Explain your answer.

10. Describe Erikson's three psychosocial stages of adulthood.

11. Describe Levinson's basic transitional stages of male adulthood. How do these transition stages and other life events shape important roles in the family and work?

12. What is meant by "old-old" and "young-old"? How do these concepts relate to an understanding of the behavior of the elderly?

CRITICAL THINKING

1. Review Chapters 15 and 16 and identify the essential elements of each era of life according to their uniqueness to that period and to their commonality across all periods.

2. What are the most prevalent forms of research presented in the chapter? Which is the most appropriate method for studying newborns? Can the same techniques be used to study the elderly?

PART SIX

Personality, Abnormality, and Adjustment

.. *Personality*

Sigmund Freud, the father of pyscho-analysis, startled the Viennese medical community with his theories about the causes of hysteria. His writings on child-hood sexuality and personality develop-ment remain astute and controversial to this day.

PERSONALITY an individual's characteristic and distinctive patterns of thinking, feeling, and behaving

One of the puzzles of personality is why people who grow up in similar situations develop in such different ways. For instance, researchers studied one family consisting of both parents, two daughters, and a son. The mother was a paranoid schizophrenic, convinced that a family member was trying to poison her, she would eat only in restaurants. One daughter developed similar fears, also refusing to eat except in restaurants; she too developed paranoid schizophrenia. Another daughter ate at restaurants unless her father was present; then she ate at home without fear. She graduated from college and led a normal life. The son scoffed at the family fears. From the age of seven, he always ate at home and showed no traces of anxiety. He later graduated from college with highest honors and embarked on a brilliant career (see Goleman, 1987).

Research shows that some children who experience traumatic events while growing up may become delinquent or abuse drugs; others may become depressed or develop eating disorders; and still others, exposed to similar hardships, remain resilient and well-adjusted (Rutter, 1979). The existence of such invulnerable children, who thrive in the midst of chaos, abuse, or abject poverty, has led a number of psychologists to conclude that some aspects of personality may be inborn (Farber and Egeland, 1987), a topic we explored in Chapter 15.

Whether or not experts can explain the basis of personality, each of us has amassed a store of knowledge about individual characteristics. You have discovered, for example, that if you tell two friends a joke, one usually finds it hilarious, while the other misses the point. Such diverse reactions are common in other social situations. Introduced to a young woman, one young man will smile politely and go back to what he was doing; another will shuffle his feet and lower his eyes; and a third will ask for her phone number. Everyday experience and psychological research agree on the uniqueness of each person and his or her responses to the world. Moreover, these unique characteristics appear to be stable and enduring aspects of personality.

Such differences among people and the stability of any person's behavior over long periods are the essence of personality. Although there is no single definition that is accepted by all theorists, most would agree that **personality** consists of an individual's characteristic and distinctive patterns of thinking, feeling, and behaving. Regardless of their approach, all personality theorists address two key questions. First, when several people confront the same situation, why don't they all behave the same way? Second, what accounts for the relative consistency of a person's behavior from one situation to the next? These questions inevitably lead to others. Do we inherit personality traits from our parents? How do outside forces—our experiences, relationships, culture, and the times in which we live—shape us? Are we motivated by unconscious forces, or do we act as we do from either conscious choice or habit? Can we—do we—change over time?

Faced with the extraordinary complexity of human behavior and the wide range of individual differences in personality, theorists have developed a variety of explanations in their attempts to answer these questions. The resulting theories of human diversity often seem contradictory, but in some ways they complement one another. Each of the five theories discussed in this chapter—psychoanalytic, trait, behavioral, humanistic, and biological—sheds light on certain aspects of personality, but none can satisfactorily account for all aspects.

Whenever personality theorists attempt to test their theories or to apply them in counseling, therapy, or the world of work, they try to measure key features of personality. Personality assessment is similar to intelligence testing in that researchers measure individual differences; in the case of personality, however, the differences are not cognitive abilities but emotions, motives, behavior, interests, attitudes, and values. The particular personality tests selected by theorists depend on their theoretical orientation, but several principles of assessment are common to all approaches. As we saw in the discussion of intelligence testing in Chapter 11, no matter what measures are used, the issues of reliability and validity are central. Thus, the questions to be asked about personality tests center on whether they are reliable (that is, do they measure specific aspects of personality consistently?) and whether they are valid (that is, do they measure what we think they do?)

FREUD AND PSYCHOANALYTIC THEORIES

The most influential theorist in the field of personality has been Sigmund Freud (1856–1939), who conceived the first comprehensive theory of personality. As a physician in nineteenth-century Vienna, Freud became interested in personality when he tried to account for certain strange physical problems manifested by some of his patients. Many of them suffered from what seemed to be a neurological defect: paralysis of an arm, loss of sensation in a hand, deteriorated hearing or vision. But Freud, trained as a neurologist, knew that in many cases the defect had no physical origin. A patient who complained of no feeling in a hand, for instance, said that the affected region was confined to the area that is covered when wearing a glove. Yet this pattern is physically impossible, because it does not correspond to any known grouping of nerves.

Freud speculated that the symptoms of such "hysterical disorders" could be caused by emotional stress, and he began treating them with hypnosis. Working with Josef Breuer (1842–1925), he had discovered that symptoms sometimes disappeared if, while hypnotized, the patient recalled critical events connected with the symptoms (Breuer and Freud, 1937/1957). After a time, however, Freud gave up the use of hypnosis and simply asked patients to lie down on a couch and say whatever came to mind—a technique he called **free association.** In the course of their apparently aimless statements, themes often emerged that centered on the patient's important emotional conflicts. As these conflicts were explored, the patient could begin to understand and to resolve them.

Freud became convinced that "hysterical disorders" were rooted in forbidden childhood wishes and fears. He found that these feelings were invariably related to aggression or to sexuality, and the childhood experiences connected with them had been forgotten until hypnosis or free association brought back the memories. From such evidence, Freud theorized the existence of an aspect of personality, unknown to the conscious mind, that he called the unconscious.

In his view, the contents of the conscious mind are only a small part of personality. The mind is like an iceberg, with our conscious thoughts resembling the iceberg's small tip; beneath the surface—out of awareness—lies the massive unconscious. The **unconscious** includes instinctual drives and infantile goals, hopes, wishes, and needs, and all memories that are not available to the conscious mind. These impulses have been repressed, or concealed from conscious awareness, because they are unacceptable and cause internal conflict. For example, a young woman who felt sexually attracted to her father would remove the thought from consciousness and be completely unaware of her sexual impulses. The process devised by Freud to retrieve repressed memories and feelings, allowing them to be examined and understood, is known as **psychoanalysis.**

Free association turned out to be only one method of reaching the unconscious. The "royal road to the unconscious," as Freud saw it, was provided by the analysis of dreams, because in his view dreams are disguised or censored expressions of unconscious desires and conflicts (Freud, 1900/1955). All dreams, according to Freud, have both a manifest content and a latent content. The **manifest content,** or the events the dreamer relates, is a kind of coded message from the dreamer's unconscious. The **latent content** is the underlying meaning of the dream, which can be decoded only through the process of analysis. If properly analyzed and interpreted, the dream should lead to important discoveries about the patient's personality.

According to Freud, unconscious conflicts express themselves in several other ways: slips of the tongue, accidents, and even jokes may express our most deeply hidden feelings. A young man away at college who misses his family may type "the weather here has been lonely" (instead of "lovely") in a letter home, or he may miss the plane that is to take him back to school after the holidays. In the Freudian view, these events, like dreams, are disguised expressions of unconscious conflict. Jokes also allow us to express forbidden feelings (Freud, 1905/1962). When we laugh at a joke, we are often indulging sexual, aggressive, or destructive feelings that we must conceal from others and often from ourselves.

FREE ASSOCIATION   a way of tapping unconscious thought by having a person say anything that comes to mind, with no attempt to produce logical, coherent explanations

UNCONSCIOUS   the level of consciousness that contains instinctual drives, infantile goals, hopes, wishes, and needs, and all memories that are not available to the conscious mind

PSYCHOANALYSIS   Freud's therapeutic method, a process that aims at retrieving repressed memories and feelings from the unconscious

MANIFEST CONTENT   the events from a dream that are remembered by the dreamer

LATENT CONTENT   the underlying meaning of a dream

Basic Structural Concepts

Although Freud's view of unconscious conflicts emerged from his work with troubled patients, the idea was based on a coherent theory of personality that he believed could explain the behavior of everyone. Freud divided personality into three separate but interacting systems or structures: the *id,* the *ego,* and the *super-ego.* Each of these systems has its own highly specific role in maintaining normal personality functioning.

Freud sometimes referred to the three systems almost as if they had wills of their own—as if the ego were a rational, self-controlled person at war with an irrational and impulsive person (the id) and a harshly moralistic person (the super-ego). Psychoanalytic views of personality will be less confusing if we take the terms in the sense intended by Freud, as metaphorical names for the functional (not physical) divisions of personality. The id, ego, and superego are not persons, places, or physical things; they are names given to hypothetical mental systems.

The Id

ID the primitive, instinctual, animal-like part of the personality that is present at birth

The **id** is the primitive, instinctual, animal-like part of the personality. Because it is the only aspect of personality that exists at birth, it can be thought of as the "infant" within us that persists throughout life. The id is demanding and hedonistic. It operates according to what Freud called the *pleasure principle:* the id wants to obtain pleasure immediately and at all times, and it wants to avoid pain at all costs. This aspect of personality follows no rules or logic, harbors no doubts, knows no time, and has no moral code.

The Ego

EGO the rational part of the personality that develops to mediate between the id and reality

As infants begin to experience the world, they soon discover that it is not always a gratifying place. The id's demands, no matter how urgent, are not automatically met, but the id can do nothing about it; it has no way to operate on the world. Sometime during the first year of life, the **ego,** the rational part of the personality that has the task of mediating between the id and reality, begins to emerge. This aspect of personality uses memory, reason, and judgment to satisfy the id's demands. In the process, it anticipates the consequences of particular means of gratification, sometimes even delaying gratification in order to achieve long-range goals. Because the ego's major task is to cope with reality, it operates under what Freud called the *reality principle.*

In Freud's view, a baby's personality consists only of the id, which operates according to the pleasure principle: regardless of the possible consequences, it wants what it wants when it wants it. The ego and the superego begin to develop later in childhood.

The ego's functioning contrasts sharply with that of the id. The unconscious, amoral, illogical id directs crude and primitive thought patterns that Freud called *primary process thinking*. Dreams, which break rules of space, time, and logic, and which often contain bizarre, irrational images, are manifestations of the id at work. The ego functions in an entirely different fashion. Part of the ego is conscious; it obeys the rules of logic and reason and learns from experience. It functions in a fashion that Freud called *secondary process thinking* (Erdelyi, 1985). We can see the ego at work if we consider what happens when a child observes a candle flame. When she reaches out to touch the pretty yellow flame, she is burned. From this experience she learns not to touch the flame (an ego function) even though she still feels the desire to do so (an id impulse).

The ego's activities are vital to health and safety. The ego does much more than act as a brake on the id's ceaseless demands for gratification. Through its attempts to satisfy the id, the ego develops the mind's higher functions: perception, learning, discrimination, memory, judgment, and planning. Sometimes the ego does its job so thoroughly that it distorts or avoids reality instead of coping with it. This ironic overperformance develops when the ego resorts to defense mechanisms, as we will see in a later section.

The Superego

The third aspect of personality, the **superego,** is concerned with meeting the demands of morality and social convention. Where the id demands gratification, the superego seeks perfection. The superego begins to develop around the age of two or three, the period during which children are toilet-trained and become aware that they must conform to social rules that govern "good" and "bad" behavior. Its development is more or less complete by the age of six. Like the ego, the superego enables the individual to cope with reality—but a particular kind of *social* reality. (The ego is concerned with consequences, with reward and punishment: "If I hit my little brother, Mother will be angry and punish me." The superego is concerned with social rules, that is, with doing the right thing: "It is wrong to hit my little brother.") From the promptings of parents and other family members, the child begins to develop a set of social rules, all of which repose in the superego, which is roughly equivalent to the child's conscience.

These three distinct aspects of personality have to work together. The ego must find a way to satisfy the id, which seeks pleasure, without clashing with the superego, which demands socially and morally acceptable behavior. Sometimes the ego is seen as a kind of referee that must find a way of arranging compromises between the demands of the id and the superego. This interplay of pulls and pushes—inner conflict and its resolution—was seen by Freud as the primary determinant of human behavior and personality; he called it **psychodynamics.**

Basic Psychodynamics

The idea that opposing forces are continually at play within every person is basic to Freud's theory. The ego's task of managing this conflict is not easy. When the demands of physical reality (conflict with the external world), of morality (conflict with the superego), or of the passions (conflict with the id) become too insistent, the person is filled with anxiety. **Anxiety** is a state of psychic pain that alerts the ego to danger; it is akin to fear. Anxiety is such an unpleasant emotion that the ego goes to great lengths to avoid it. It may do something as simple and obvious as withdrawing from the anxiety-provoking situation. Or, if the anxiety is overwhelming and inescapable, the entire personality may collapse so completely that the person cannot meet life's ordinary demands. Between these two extremes are several strategies—defense mechanisms—that the ego can use to defend itself.

SUPEREGO the part of the personality that is concerned with meeting the demands of morality and social convention; similar to the conscience

PSYCHODYNAMICS the interplay of inner conflicts and their resolution that is the primary determinant of human behavior and personality

ANXIETY in Freud's theory, the fear or apprehension that alerts the ego to danger

Anxiety is such an unpleasant state that the ego frequently employs defense mechanisms to avoid it.

DEFENSE MECHANISMS irrational techniques used by the ego to reduce anxiety—excluding the source from consciousness or distorting it

REPRESSION the fundamental defense mechanism that keeps threatening thoughts and memories buried in the unconscious

TRAUMATIC psychologically damaging

RATIONALIZATION a defense mechanism that provides plausible—socially acceptable—explanations for behavior that is motivated by unconscious or unacceptable reasons

SUBLIMATION a positive defense mechanism in which erotic energy is channeled into a socially constructive activity

Defense Mechanisms

When inner conflict is acute and anxiety threatens, the ego often tries to reduce the anxiety by means of irrational techniques known as **defense mechanisms.** The ego either tries to exclude the source of anxiety from consciousness (which requires vast quantities of emotional energy) or distorts it, reducing the threat (which requires less energy). Although we may at times notice our use of defense mechanisms, they operate most powerfully when they are unconscious.

The fundamental defense mechanism, one that keeps threatening thoughts and memories from penetrating consciousness and pushes them back into the unconscious, is called **repression.** As we have seen, one of Freud's earliest hypotheses concerned repression. He observed that his patients were unable to recall **traumatic,** or psychologically damaging, childhood events without considerable probing. These traumatic memories, he said, are concealed from conscious awareness and kept in the unconscious by strong forces. According to Freud, the threats from these unpleasant memories, the expenditures of energy needed to conceal them, and the anxiety generated in the process are responsible for many emotional disorders (as we will see in Chapter 18). Freud also believed that repression is a part of all other defense mechanisms; before these defensive strategies can be used, the anxiety-producing impulse must be repressed.

A familiar, extremely common defense mechanism is **rationalization,** in which we give ourselves a plausible explanation for doing (or not doing) something that we are in fact doing (or not doing) for quite different reasons. We may not be conscious of the real reason for our behavior, or the real reason may be unacceptable to us. For example, we may justify ignoring the homeless man on the street who asks us for money by telling ourselves that he would only spend it on liquor. This allows us to avoid the guilt we might experience if we thought we had refused to help a deserving person. Other defense mechanisms are described in Table 17.1.

Defense mechanisms at times may serve a useful purpose, because they relieve minor anxieties and allow us to meet the demands of daily life. Yet they all distort reality and so may impair our ability to cope with things as they are in the world. For example, parents of a retarded child who persuade themselves that the youngster's failure to talk is due to shyness may deprive their child of months or even years of programs that might have increased the child's ability to function.

Not all defense mechanisms have negative effects. Freud identified one "positive" defense mechanism, which he called sublimation. **Sublimation** is the diversion of erotic energy away from its original source and toward a socially constructive activity. Many of the achievements of civilization, said Freud, were fueled by sublimation. He suggested, for example, that Leonardo da Vinci's urge to paint Madonnas was a sublimated expression of his longing to be reunited with his mother, from whom he had been separated at an early age (Freud, 1930/1962). In fact, Freud thought that civilization itself rested on the sublimation of our sexual and aggressive urges.

The Psychosexual Stages of Development

Freud was the first psychological theorist to emphasize the developmental aspects of personality and to stress the decisive role of infancy and childhood in establishing a person's basic character. Indeed, Freud believed that personality is formed by the time a child enters school and that later growth merely elaborates this basic structure. According to his theory, the child passes through a series of five "psychosexual" stages, so named because the stages originate in the sexual instincts and within each stage a different part of the body becomes the focus of sensual pleasure.

During the **oral stage** (from birth to about 18 months), the baby's mouth is the primary source of pleasure. In their active search for oral stimulation, babies suck, mouth, and chew on whatever they can find. During the **anal stage** (from about 18 months to three years), the child's attention shifts to the anus and the pleasures of holding in and pushing out feces. These pleasures are barely established, however, before the child encounters the social demands of toilet training. Freud regarded toilet training as a crucial event, a systematic attempt to impose social requirements on the child's natural impulses just as the youngster had begun to gain some bodily control.

ORAL STAGE (from birth to about 18 months) psychosexual stage when the mouth is the primary source of sensual pleasure

ANAL STAGE (from about 18 months to three years) psychosexual stage when the anus is the primary source of sensual pleasure

TABLE 17.1 Defense Mechanisms

THE DEFENSE	THE REALITY	EXAMPLE
Repression	See the text.	
Rationalization	See the text.	
Sublimation	See the text.	
Denial	Refusal to recognize a threatening source of anxiety.	A high school boy with a failing academic record wants to become a doctor, denying the importance of good grades and asserting that "somehow" it will all work out.
Regression	Return to an earlier, less threatening stage of development in response to some perceived threat.	People often distract themselves from their anxieties by eating too much—a return to comforting behavior that gave them pleasure in childhood. A frightened child on the first day of school may begin sucking his or her thumb, a habit given up years before.
Projection	Turning an inward threat into a threat from the external world.	A woman who feels an impulse to shoplift may begin to fear that her purse will be stolen or that salesclerks will shortchange her. A man who frets about the sexual promiscuity of the younger generation may be projecting onto young people his fear about his own sexual impulses.
Displacement	Transferring emotions that a person is afraid to feel or express to a nonthreatening situation.	A woman who has been angry at her boss may come home and yell at the babysitter.
Reaction formation	Replacement of an anxiety-producing impulse or feeling by its opposite.	A mother who resents her child may shower him or her with expressions of love. A man who wants to start fires may become a firefighter and spend his time putting them out.

Carl Gustav Jung.

PHALLIC STAGE (from about three to six years) the psychosexual stage when sensual pleasure centers on fondling the genitals

LATENCY STAGE (six to eleven years) psychosexual stage when children repress their sexual feelings

GENITAL STAGE (from puberty onward) the final stage of psychosexual development, when sensual pleasure focuses on sexual intercourse

ARCHETYPES Jung's term for myths, dreams, symbols, and other ideas and images that are common to all human beings and that form the collective unconscious

BASIC ANXIETY Horney's term for the anxiety that arises out of a child's sense of helplessness and isolation

During the **phallic stage** (from about three to six years), the child's attention focuses on the genitals and the pleasure of fondling them. It is at this stage that children find out about genital differences between the sexes, a discovery that precipitates the *Oedipal conflict*, which Freud saw as critical in a child's psychological development. Until they reach the phallic stage, all children feel close to their mother, but now youngsters develop a particularly strong attachment to the parent of the other sex and a corresponding resentment and hatred of the same-sex parent, who seems a sexual rival. Freud believed that the young boy, with his intense love for his mother and the resentment of his father, would come to fear that his father would punish him for his forbidden love by castrating him. To avoid punishment, the boy would then repress his erotic feelings for his mother and identify with his father, adopting his father's values. A young girl, discovering that she lacks a penis, would blame her mother for the lack and develop what Freud called "penis envy." Winning her father would give her vicarious possession of a penis. When she realizes that her father is unattainable, the girl would repress her feelings for him and identify with her mother, adopting the mother's values. When the child identifies with the values of the same-sex parent, the superego emerges.

Once the Oedipal conflict has been resolved, the child enters a period of **latency** (from about six years to puberty). Throughout this period, children repress their sexual feelings, making their sexuality "latent." They busy themselves with exploring the world and learning new things. The surge of hormones that accompanies puberty encourages the reappearance of sexuality, and the adolescent enters the final stage of sexuality, the **genital stage,** (from puberty onward) when sexual intercourse becomes the focus of sensual pleasure. These stages of personality growth are distinct, but Freud never proposed that children shift abruptly from one stage to another; he believed that the transitions are gradual and the ages only approximate.

Post-Freudian Psychoanalytic Theory

After Freud's death in 1939, some of his followers expanded on his ideas and extended his work into new areas. Others, notably Carl Jung (1875–1961), had broken with Freud before his death. Jung had a different concept of the unconscious, arguing that it contains far more than repressed instinctual urges. He distinguished the *personal unconscious* from the *collective unconscious*. In his analytic psychology, the collective unconscious is a vast storehouse of **archetypes**— myths, dreams, symbols, and other ideas and images shared by all humanity. He believed that human beings of all eras and in all parts of the world are molded by these archetypes.

One group of psychoanalytic thinkers, known as neo-Freudians, softened the biological emphasis that Freud had placed on the instinctual forces that drive behavior, focusing instead on social and interpersonal drives and instincts. Where Freud emphasized conflicts between society and the instinctual sexual and aggressive drives, these thinkers—notably Karen Horney (1885–1952), Alfred Adler (1870–1937), and Erich Fromm (b. 1900)—emphasized conflicts between people. They agreed with Freud that early childhood experiences were important to personality development, but they defined those experiences in terms of interpersonal issues. Adler, for example, stressed a basic need to overcome feelings of inferiority relative to others.

Horney (1945) believed that childhood conflicts grow out of feelings of helplessness. Her theory revolved around what she called "basic anxiety" and "basic hostility." **Basic anxiety** develops because the child feels isolated and helpless in a potentially hostile world. Young children, discovering that they are weak and small in a land of giants, soon learn that they are utterly dependent on parents for all their needs and safety. Warm, loving, and dependable parents create a sense of security that reassures the child and produces normal development. Parents who severely disturb a child's sense of security—by their indifference, erratic behavior, or disparaging attitudes—increase the child's feelings of helplessness, which, in turn, foster basic anxiety.

In Horney's view, basic anxiety is generally accompanied by **basic hostility,** which arises from the child's resentment over parents' indifference, inconsistency, and interference. Children cannot express this hostility directly, because they need and fear their parents and must have their love. But repressing the hostility increases feelings of unworthiness and anxiety, and children are torn between hostility toward the parents and dependence on them. This conflict between anxiety and dependence can lead to neurosis. The neurotic behavior described by Horney (1937) is often identical to that observed by Freud: rigid, obsessional actions, unconscious hostility toward parents, and jealousy of siblings. But Horney's explanation of this behavior was radically different from Freud's; in her view, it was a product of social relationships rather than an expression of innate sexuality and aggressive instincts.

The difference between neo-Freudians and Freud is perhaps most obvious in Erik Erikson's (1980) reformulation of Freud's psychosexual stages of development in "psychosocial" terms: trust, autonomy, identity, and other aspects of interpersonal relations (which were discussed in Chapter 15). Erikson also saw psychological development as continuing throughout adulthood—even into old age—and his ideas, rather than Freud's, underlie much modern work in the area of life-span developmental psychology.

Another group of post-Freudians moved away from the emphasis on the id and its instinctual urges; they began exploring the adaptive functions of the ego. This group of psychoanalytic theorists, including Heinz Hartmann, David Rapaport, and Robert White, are known as *ego analysts*. They argue that the ego has functions above and beyond satisfying the id, such as learning to process information and to cope with the environment. This position led to a concern with the basic cognitive processes of perception, memory, and thought (Kohut, 1977; Erdelyi, 1985). In fact, the work of these modern theorists may provide a way to integrate basic experimental research in cognitive psychology with psychoanalytic thought (Kihlstrom, 1988).

Alfred Adler.

BASIC HOSTILITY Horney's term for a child's hostility that arises in response to parental indifference, inconsistency, and interference

Karen Horney argued that social factors rather than instinctual drives are the crucial determinants of personality. The young child, weak and dependent, needs to have a steady, loving relationship with his or her parents.

PSYCHOLOGY TODAY AND TOMORROW

"It Looks Like a Monster with Big Feet"

Rorschach inkblots are the basis of a widely used projective test of personality. In interpreting a person's response to the ten inkblots in the series, examiners pay at least as much attention to the style of the responses as to their content. For example, a person's tendency to see white or shaded areas as meaningful, or to see the blot as a whole rather than as a collection of parts, is deemed significant in scoring and interpretation.

When presented with the inkblot shown here, a young female outpatient said that "it sort of looks like a monster with big feet. A cute little thing. Really a dashing monster. Such a friendly little guy." Further probing by the examiner showed that the woman was responding to the blot as a whole instead of to the various portions of it, and was concerned primarily with its shape or form, which, while humanlike, was not distinctly human. Interpreting the meaning of Rorschach responses is a complicated task and requires a skilled and experienced examiner. Despite the fact that researchers have been unable to establish its reliability and validity, the test remains widely used.

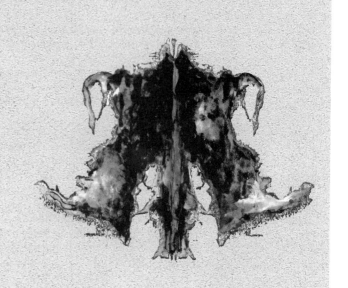

(From R. I. Lanyon and L. D. Goodstein, *Personality assessment,* © 1971, p. 50. Reprinted by permission of John Wiley and Sons, Inc., New York.)

Assessing Personality from the Psychoanalytic Perspective

PROJECTIVE TEST a test that draws out unconscious conflicts and motives through free-association responses to ambiguous stimuli

Freud drew on free associations, slips of the tongue, and, most of all, dreams to assess the personalities of his patients. This means, of course, that he relied on what his patients told him. Other clinicians and psychologists have tried to standardize various techniques that tap the unconscious. They use **projective tests,** in which subjects look at vague or ambiguous stimuli, then respond with free association, either by describing what they see or by telling a story about the stimulus. Since the subjects must provide the meaning themselves, their responses reflect the *projections* of their own unconscious motives, thoughts, and feelings onto the test stimulus. The way subjects interpret ambiguous material is supposed to reveal their personality characteristics. Some of the ambiguous materials are highly abstract images such as inkblots; others are concrete images, such as pictures of social situations. Two of the most widely used projective tests are the Rorschach Inkblot Test and the Thematic Apperception Test.

RORSCHACH INKBLOT TEST a projective test in which people respond by free association to a series of ten symmetrical inkblots

The **Rorschach Inkblot Test** was developed by Swiss psychiatrist Hermann Rorschach (1921). When taking the test, a person looks at a series of ten symmetrical inkblots that increase in color and complexity and then reports what he or she sees, using free association. The examiner asks certain general questions in an attempt to discover what quality or pattern in the inkblots prompted the person's responses (S. Beck, 1961; Exner, 1974). An inkblot like those used in the Rorschach Test and a sample response are presented in the accompanying box.

Another widely used projective test is the **Thematic Apperception Test (TAT),** which also requires the person to describe what is shown on cards. In the TAT, the person responds to a series of ambiguous scenes that involve one, two, or three people. As many as thirty black-and-white scenes may be shown, with the choice of specific cards determined by the person's age and sex. Each card is the stimulus for a story: the person is asked to describe the situation, tell what led up to it and what each character is thinking, then provide an ending.

The stories are usually analyzed on an individual basis; one person's stories are not compared with those of others, although researchers are aware of the responses most frequently evoked by the cards. Henry Murray, who developed the test nearly sixty years ago, recommended interpreting TAT stories in terms of his own theory of personality (Murray et al., 1938), but a variety of other systems, including some based on psychoanalytic theory, are also used. No matter what methods are used, examiners assume that the test taps particular kinds of fantasy. Common assumptions are that the subject will identify with the hero or heroine of the story, that the stories will reveal the subject's motives, and that unusual responses are more likely than typical ones to reveal important aspects of personality.

Projective tests tend to have problems of reliability and validity. The reliability of the Rorschach and the TAT is undermined by clinicians' and researchers' failure to agree on a single scoring system for either test. For example, clinical psychologists agree only moderately well about interpretations of responses to the TAT and predictions based on them. Once the answers to a projective test are scored, the examiner must interpret the responses, which makes the overall assessment of personality highly subjective. Examiners may find what they expect to find, or they may project their own theories and personality into their interpretations (Anastasi, 1982).

The validity of projective tests is also low, because they are not very effective in predicting behavior (Chapman and Chapman, 1969; Peterson, 1978). There is

In the Thematic Apperception Test, the subject's descriptions of the ambiguous situations shown in a series of pictures are analyzed for clues to his or her personality.

some evidence, for example, that some types of Rorschach responses that are supposed to reveal personality traits actually reflect verbal ability. Projective tests seem most useful when regarded not as *assessments* of personality, but as clinical *tools* that assist clinicians in opening discussions with patients and in suggesting topics that might be explored in therapy (Anastasi, 1988).

Criticisms and Contributions of Psychoanalytic Theories

Psychoanalytic theories have been controversial since they were first proposed. They have been attacked by philosophers of science, by psychologists, and by feminists. Some critics have attacked specific psychoanalytic concepts, while others have framed their assault in more general terms.

One consistent criticism has been the difficulty of testing the basic concepts of psychoanalytic theory. Many of Freud's ideas are phrased in such vague and metaphorical terms that they are difficult to formulate in a way that can be tested empirically. For example, a six-year-old boy could reveal an Oedipal conflict by displaying great love for his mother, by ignoring her, or by showing hostility. If he uses the defense mechanism of repression, his forbidden love has been pushed into his unconscious, but if he uses reaction formation, he transforms the love into hostility.

Even when Freudian concepts can be distilled into testable hypotheses, they have not fared well in empirical studies. For example, Freud's description of the female personality simply has not held up. He contended that women suffered from penis envy and were culturally and morally inferior to men. The rejection of these claims by feminists has been supported by research; studies consistently indicate a much smaller difference between male and female personality development than Freud supposed (Fisher and Greenberg, 1985). His view of female personality development was bound to the culture of his time.

Psychoanalytic theory is much better at hindsight than at foresight, and in Chapter 9 we explored the kinds of biases produced by hindsight. The theory can provide logical explanations of behavior that has already occurred but cannot predict how an individual's personality will develop or how any person will behave in the future. Such prediction was not Freud's intent, however; for him, the theory's importance lay in its ability to find systematic meaning in the thoughts, feelings, words, and actions of people with emotional problems (Rieff, 1979).

Psychoanalytic theory has also been criticized for the small size of the sample on which the theory is based. The subjects of most of Freud's published case studies were upper-middle-class Viennese women. On the statements of these adult women with emotional problems, Freud built a universal theory of personality. Yet he never worked directly with children. Some investigators are uncomfortable with a theory of normal personality that is based on retrospective childhood accounts of people with emotional problems.

Despite these criticisms, Freud has made a lasting contribution to our understanding of human beings. Few would dispute that his thoughts about human personality have had a profound influence. Some aspects of psychoanalytic theory have withstood a number of tests. When thousands of studies of psychoanalytic concepts were evaluated, many of Freud's ideas were supported (Fisher and Greenberg, 1985). As Freud proposed, children do seem to have an early erotic interest in the parent of the other sex. Dreams do seem to provide a release for emotional tensions. People who focus on oral activities do tend to be dependent and passive, while those who are preoccupied with anal functions do tend to be stingy, compulsive, and orderly—just as Freud had proposed (Masling, Johnson, and Saturansky, 1974; Masling et al., 1981). However, these characteristics do not seem to be connected with critical events in the oral or anal stages of development, as Freud maintained.

Freud's description of the unconscious and its influence on behavior was one of his greatest contributions to psychology. It enabled us to see impulses, conflicts, or experiences that have slipped from awareness as motives for behavior.

Even psychologists who do not accept the concept of an "unconscious" agree that we have stored much more information about the past than we are aware of (see Kihlstrom, 1988). Acceptance of the notion that much of our thought is unconscious has changed the way we look at art, at literature, and at life itself.

Finally, Freud's psychoanalytic methods revolutionized the treatment of emotional problems. He provided method in a field that had lacked any consistent approach. His view of psychological disorders respected the humanity of patients by casting abnormality as one end of a continuum of adjustment, not as a qualitatively different state of being. To Freud we owe the idea that individual psychotherapy (the "talking cure") can help patients gain knowledge about the self and thus increase their control over their own actions. Even forms of therapy that reject much or all of Freud's basic theory rely on variations of his therapeutic technique.

Psychoanalysis has had an enormous influence on the thought of psychologists, psychiatrists, and ordinary citizens. Our tendency to see behavior as powerfully influenced by our past experiences and as reflecting irrational inner forces is largely the result of Freud's emphasis on both factors.

TRAIT THEORIES OF PERSONALITY

Psychologists who rely on trait theories of personality believe that the search for unconscious motives is not necessary for an understanding of personality. Their view of personality probably has a lot in common with your own. For instance, suppose you are looking for someone to sell your company's products. You would most likely select your new employee on the basis of the candidate's personality: you would probably choose an outgoing, sociable person over someone who was shy and withdrawn. The characteristics you are looking for—outgoing personality and sociability—are the everyday equivalent of what psychologists call traits. A **trait** is a predisposition to respond to situations in a consistent way. We can only infer that such predispositions exist; we cannot see, hear, or touch them. But trait theorists believe that if we can specify an individual's traits, we can understand that person and predict his or her behavior in the future. Trait theorists' view of the inner forces of personality are very different from Freud's; instead of emphasizing inner conflict and change, they focus on the stability and consistency of inner forces that are expressed in behavior.

TRAIT a predisposition to respond to situations in a consistent way

Trait theories rest on two key assumptions. First, they assume that most traits exist in all people to some degree. Looking at the trait of dependency, for example, trait theories assume that everyone can be classified as more or less dependent. Second, they assume that we can measure the degree to which a trait exists in

Trait theorists believe that an individual's personality is organized around characteristics, such as shyness, that everyone possesses to a greater or lesser degree.

a person. For example, we could establish a scale on which an extremely dependent person would score 10 while a very independent person would score 1. People can be classified on such a continuum for virtually any trait. Thus, a few people are aggressive in many situations, others rarely show a trace of aggression, and most of us fall somewhere in the middle.

Although some psychologists regard traits as real entities that exist within the mind, most others consider traits to be no more than metaphors that they can use to describe the uniqueness and consistency of human behavior. When trait theorists search for this underlying consistency, they look for the best way to describe the common features of a person's behavior. Take the case of Roland, a doorman in an apartment building who handles his job with great dignity and always greets people courteously. A trait theorist would assume that Roland's behavior as a doorman is typical of his behavior in other situations. Reviewing these other situations, the trait theorist might try to discover whether Roland is proud, friendly, interested in people, self-confident, or something else. In other words, the theorist would ask, "What is the underlying structure that organizes Roland's behavior?"

Allport and the Classification of Traits

For nearly four decades, trait theory was dominated by Gordon Allport (1897–1967), a researcher who had a lifelong interest in the uniqueness of each individual. Over the years, Allport (1937, 1961, 1966) developed and refined his theory, but he remained firm in his conclusion that traits accounted for the consistency of human behavior. In his view, the presence of a trait could lead a person to interpret a broad array of situations as calling for a similar, if not identical, response. For example, an aggressive person would see aggression as an appropriate response to a variety of situations.

The English language provides a vast array of specific descriptions for a countless number of behavioral responses. In 1936, Allport (Allport and Odbert, 1936) searched an unabridged dictionary and found about 18,000 different words that could be used to describe people. Even after he omitted clearly evaluative terms (like "disgusting") and terms that described transient states (like "abashed"), more than 4,000 words remained. Surely, Allport thought, this multitude of descriptions could be reduced to a few essentials.

CARDINAL TRAIT Allport's term for a single trait that dominates most of a person's acts

In his attempt to clarify and simplify these descriptions, Allport described behavior as characterized by three kinds of traits: cardinal, central, and secondary. A **cardinal trait** is a single trait that so pervades a person's disposition that most of his or her acts seem dominated by it. A person whose "ruling passion" is greed or ambition could be characterized by this cardinal trait. Famous historical and mythical figures have given their names to cardinal traits. The term "Machiavellian," after the sixteenth-century Italian political theorist Machiavelli, describes a person who persistently manipulates others. The term "narcissistic," after the mythical Greek youth Narcissus who fell in love with his own reflection, describes a person who is inordinately preoccupied with himself or herself.

CENTRAL TRAITS Allport's term for habitual ways of dealing with the world that, together, dominate a person's personality

Allport believed that cardinal traits are rare and that most individuals do not have one predominant trait. Instead, on the basis of their life experience, people develop a few **central traits,** habitual ways of responding that can be summed up in trait names like "honest," "sociable," or "affectionate." Less influential are **secondary traits,** characteristic modes of behavior that are less prominent than central traits and are expressed in fewer situations. Secondary traits are subject to fluctuation and change. We can see them as generalized tastes and preferences that people display, such as preferences for certain foods or styles of music.

SECONDARY TRAITS Allport's term for minor, often changing traits, that often appear as tastes or preferences

In addition to his classification of traits as cardinal, central, or secondary, Allport made another key distinction. He was careful to distinguish between traits he considered common and those he considered individual. **Common traits,** such as aggression, are basic modes of adjustment seen to some degree in all individuals. Because we must all live in a competitive world, each of us develops a unique level of aggression and each of us can be placed somewhere on a scale of aggressiveness. But since each person is unique, Allport argued, each person also has

COMMON TRAITS Allport's term for basic ways of dealing with the world that are seen to some degree in every person

individual traits, which are unique ways of responding to the world. Allport (1961) later renamed individual traits **personal dispositions,** since he believed that the uniqueness of individual experience led each person to develop a unique set of dispositions to behave in certain ways. A personal disposition cannot be measured by a standardized test; it can be discerned only by carefully studying an individual.

INDIVIDUAL TRAITS/PERSONAL DISPOSITIONS Allport's term for unique, individual ways of responding to the world that cannot be measured by tests but only discerned by studying the person

Factor Analysis

More recent theorists have concentrated on what Allport called common traits, trying to quantify them in a precise, scientific manner. Their primary tool in this task has been **factor analysis,** a statistical method that can be used to identify underlying factors, or traits, that account for consistency in behavior. For example, people may describe themselves as enjoying parties, spending large amounts of time on the telephone with friends, and choosing jobs that allow them to interact with other people. This range of behavior can be explained by the underlying factor of sociability.

FACTOR ANALYSIS a statistical method that identifies underlying factors, or traits, that account for consistency in behavior

Factor analysis isolates underlying traits by making statistical analyses of large collections of behavioral descriptions or test items. It identifies which groups of "descriptors" go together, or co-occur statistically, and so allows researchers to reduce a large number of descriptors to a smaller number of underlying dimensions of personality. Raymond Cattell (1965) used factor analysis to identify sixteen basic personality factors, including emotional stability, outgoingness, assertiveness, self-assurance, and self-discipline. Using the same technique, Hans Eysenck (1970) arrived at a smaller core of three basic personality dimensions: extraversion (vs. introversion), neuroticism (vs. emotional stability), and psychoticism (vs. self-control). More recently, many personality researchers have agreed on the five personality factors identified by Warren Norman (1963): extraversion, agreeableness, conscientiousness, emotional stability, and openness to experience (McCrae and Costa, 1985).

Eysenck proposes that these basic traits have a biological basis. He suggests, for example, that people who are extraverted have a low level of cortical arousal. That is, the extravert's cerebral cortex is naturally rather quiet, and so she or he seeks stimulating environments—such as loud parties, intense social interactions, and risky situations—to increase arousal. By contrast, the introvert has a naturally high level of cortical arousal, so she or he seeks situations that minimize stimulation, such as sitting quietly alone. This basic difference has been consistently supported by research. Extraverts fall asleep more quickly than introverts and are less sensitive to pain, suggesting that extraverts operate at a lower level of arousal. Studies have also found that arousal seems to be related to performance: moderate levels of arousal lead to optimal performance, and performance deteriorates when arousal is too low or too high (Yerkes and Dodson, 1908; Broadhurst, 1959; Duffy, 1962). This difference may explain why extraverts do better on ability tests if they feel time pressure of if they have had caffeine, both of which increase arousal. The opposite is true for introverts, who appear to be more highly aroused: they do better with no time pressure and without caffeine (Revelle, Amaral, and Turriff, 1976).

Much of the latest work in the trait tradition concentrates on particular traits, with researchers developing a theoretical network to explain how a given trait predicts behavior in a variety of settings (see Buss and Cantor, 1989). For example, Mark Snyder (1987) has identified the trait of *self-monitoring,* which describes how closely we watch our own actions and adapt our behavior to the present situation. Some people are "social chameleons." They are so adaptable that they seem to have no stable personality of their own: their words, their actions, their style of dress, even their emotional expressions change radically as the situation shifts. They behave like actors who throw themselves wholeheartedly into each new role—grave and dignified in church, subservient with their employers, friendly and talkative at parties. They seem to spend their lives playing to the people around them. Low self-monitors, in contrast, pay little attention to the situation, making few concessions to social demands. No matter where they are, they are the same. Thus, friendly low self-monitors are gregarious whether they are in the boss's office or socializing with friends. Their style of dress and the way they present themselves show little change across situations. They seem to be playing to an inner audience of one. (In Chapter 21 we explore the impact of self-monitoring on the consistency of attitudes and behavior.)

Measuring Personality Traits

A major strength of the trait approach to personality is that traits can be measured objectively. Trait researchers have developed self-report inventories, which share the assumption and method of intelligence tests (discussed in Chapter 11). Personality inventories assume that people possess varying amounts of the trait being measured and that the trait can be measured directly. Because no single item is applicable to everyone, a reliable assessment requires many items.

Researchers have used three different procedures in their development of personality inventories. Some inventories are developed primarily by *factor analysis*. As we have seen, this method allows researchers to determine which groups of items go together and measure the same underlying traits. For example, Cattell (1972) developed a standardized test called the Sixteen Personality Factor Questionnaire (16PF) to measure the sixteen basic traits in his theory. More recently, many researchers have found that the NEO Personality Inventory (Costa and McCrae, 1985)—a 144-item questionnaire designed to measure neuroticism, extraversion, and openness to experience (NEO)—is also a convenient way to measure agreeableness and conscientiousness.

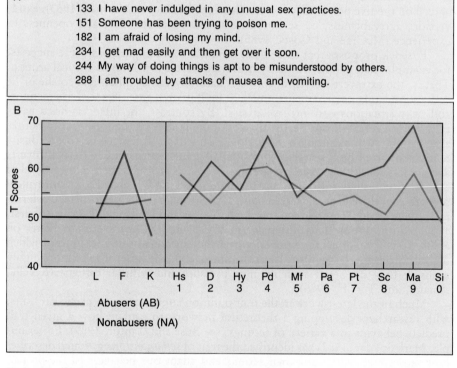

Figure 17.1 (A) Sample MMPI items. (B) MMPI profiles for abusive and nonabusive fathers. The letters along the bottom of the graph correspond to the scales described in Table 17.2. Note that the two groups obtained different profiles: Fathers who abused their children scored much higher than nonabusive fathers on the depression (D), psychopathic deviate (Pd), and mania (Ma) scales. Although it appears that the MMPI can differentiate between abusive and nonabusive parents, further study would be necessary before a more conclusive profile of an abusive parent could be drawn. [Minnesota Multiphasic Personality Inventory (MMPI™). Copyright © The University of Minnesota, 1943, renewed 1970. Profile form 1948, 1976, 1982.]

Another type of personality test is constructed by the *empirical method*. Items are first selected without regard to their possible relationship to a certain trait such as depression. These items are then administered to an experimental group of people who are already known to be high in this trait (or whatever traits the test developer wants to measure), as well as to another group of people in which the trait is already known to be low or absent. Those items that are consistently answered one way by most subjects high in the trait and a different way by most subjects low in the trait are kept as a part of the test; they successfully differentiate the groups. All other items are discarded. For example, the Minnesota Multiphasic Personality Inventory (MMPI), originally designed to help diagnose psychiatric patients, was developed in this way. By giving the same test items to psychologically healthy people and people suffering from various psychological disorders, researchers constructed a true-or-false test that discriminated between

TABLE 17.2   Scales of the MMPI

Clinical Scales

Hypochondriasis (Hs)	Items selected to discriminate people who persist in worrying about their bodily functions despite strong evidence that they have no physical illness.
Depression (D)	Items selected to discriminate people who are pessimistic about the future, feel hopeless or worthless, are slow in thought and action, and think a lot about death and suicide.
Hysteria (H)	Items selected to discriminate people who use physical symptoms to solve difficult problems or to avoid mature responsibilities, particularly under severe psychological stress.
Psychopathic deviate (Pd)	Items selected to discriminate people who show a pronounced disregard for social customs and mores, an inability to profit from punishing experiences, and emotional shallowness with others, particularly in sex and love.
Masculinity-femininity (Mf)	Items selected to discriminate men who prefer homosexual relations to heterosexual ones, either overtly or covertly (because of inhibitions or conflicts). Women tend to score low on the scale, but the scale cannot be interpreted simply "upside down" for women.
Paranoia (Pa)	Items selected to discriminate people who have delusions about how influential and how victimized they are or how much attention is paid them by other people.
Psychasthenia (Pt)	Items selected to discriminate people with obsessive thoughts, compulsive actions, extreme fear or guilt feelings, insecurity, and high anxiety.
Schizophrenia (Sc)	Items selected to discriminate people who are constrained, cold, aloof, apathetic, and inaccessible to others and who may have delusions or hallucinations.
Mania (Ma)	Items selected to discriminate people who are physically overactive and emotionally excited and have rapid flights to disconnected, fragmentary ideas; the activities may lead to accomplishment but more frequently are inefficient and unproductive.
Social introversion (Si)	Items selected to discriminate people who are withdrawn from social contacts and responsibilities and display little real interest in other people.

Validity Scales

Lie Scale (L)	Items that reflect socially desirable but unlikely behavior and are therefore likely to be marked *true* by a naive faker.
Infrequency Scale (F)	Items that are rarely marked *true* except by people who either are deliberately trying to give an exaggerated impression of their problems or are in fact highly deviant.
Correction Scale (K)	Items that reflect how defensive or how frank the person is being. The scale is sensitive to attitudes more subtle than those that affect the Lie Scale.

Source: Based on W. G. Dahlstrom, G. S. Welsh, and L. E. Dahlstrom (1972). *An MMPI handbook,* Vol. 1. Minneapolis: University of Minnesota Press.

the groups. The separate scales on the MMPI have proved to be valid tools for diagnosing various psychiatric problems, including depression, paranoia, hypochondria, and so forth (Dahlstrom et al., 1975; Winters et al., 1985) (see Figure 17.1). The MMPI even includes an L (for "lie") scale to detect people who are faking their responses in order to appear psychologically healthy and an F (or infrequency) score that detects people who are deliberately lying to make themselves appear more disturbed or who are simply answering questions at random (see Table 17.2). Although it is useful in detecting psychiatric problems, the MMPI is not an efficient tool for assessing personality differences in people without psychological disorders. An updated version, called MMPI-2, was published in 1989.

A third type of personality test is the *rational,* or *deductive, scale.* In building a rational scale, the testmaker first defines the various constructs (depression, sociability, and so on) that the test is supposed to measure, then writes items that appear to fit the definitions. Naturally, when this method of construction is used, the test reflects the framework of a particular theory of personality. For example, D. N. Jackson (1974) developed the Personality Research Form (PRF) to assess the psychological needs identified by Murray's theory of needs. The PRF provides an *objective* measure of the same traits that Murray attempted to measure with the *projective* TAT.

Evaluating the Trait Approach: The Person–Situation Debate

Trait theories have been criticized as shedding little light on human behavior. Traits merely describe behavior, but labeling the behavior does not provide an explanation for it. Worse, it may lure us into circular reasoning. If smiling is identified as one of the characteristics of friendliness, we learn nothing when we are told that John smiles because he is friendly. There is another danger: once a trait has been labeled, it may take on an existence of its own. We may begin to think of the trait as a "thing" instead of simply a shorthand description of a behavioral tendency. This effect can have ominous implications: a person who has been labeled as "shy" may give up making any effort in social situations and become even more withdrawn.

Finally, critics say that there is little evidence that traits persist across situations. We know intuitively that there must be some interaction between personality and situation, but exactly what it is has baffled researchers. Consider the following situation. Last night you observed Karen at a party. She stood quietly in a corner of the room, seemingly more interested in the books on the wall beside her than in the other guests. She spoke in response to direct questions, but her replies were brief, and when the person talking to her wandered away, she made no attempt to seek out anyone else. What kind of statement can you make about Karen's personality? That depends on how you explain her behavior. If you think her behavior is due primarily to her underlying disposition, you might say that she is basically either shy or aloof. But if you think her behavior is due primarily to the situation in which she finds herself, you might guess that none of Karen's friends is at the party, or that it is very late and she is tired, or that her past experiences with large parties have led her to expect few guests to share her interests. Among friends or at a smaller party, she might appear sociable and outgoing. Of course, as Mark Snyder (1987) points out, we must wonder how people choose their situations. Why did Karen come to this party in the first place?

In the past trait theorists have emphasized the influence of disposition, but this emphasis was challenged more than twenty years ago, when Walter Mischel's (1968) intensive review of trait research showed that correlations between traits and behavior rarely exceeded +.30. (Recall from Chapter 2 that correlation coefficients range from −1 to +1.) Mischel concluded that broad trait measures of personality are of little value in predicting behavior outside of test situations. His argument generated a heated debate that has led psychologists to look more closely at the way person and situation interact.

Trait theory is useful in describing predispositions to behave in a certain way in similar situations. This approach is helpful in the analysis of the specific conditions in a situation that cause, say, aggressive people to behave aggressively.

In most cases, the inconsistency of behavior probably indicates healthy, competent functioning (Mischel, 1973). It means that we are adapting appropriately to the demands of the situation. The greatest consistency may be shown by people who are immature or who cannot cope with challenging situations. In fact, traits seem to predict behavior best in stressful situations (Wright and Mischel, 1987). This first became clear in a study of emotionally disturbed children at a summer camp, who showed the most consistent behavior when they were placed in situations that exceeded their competencies (Mischel, 1984). When under stress, children who had been rated as aggressive consistently became aggressive and children who had been rated as withdrawn consistently withdrew. When situations were less demanding and the children could deal adequately with them, however, there was little cross-situational consistency in their behavior.

Despite its shortcomings, the trait approach is useful in two ways. First, the names of traits give us a way to describe individual differences in behavior. They allow us to summarize a person's typical behavior and, when there is a reasonable degree of stability, to forecast future behavior in similar situations (Buss and Craik, 1983). Second, traits can be regarded as predispositions to respond *in similar situations* (Revelle, 1983). For example, a person who is high in anxiety may not always be more anxious than other people. But when placed in a situation that gives rise to anxiety, the anxious person may respond more rapidly and more intensely. When psychologists use the concept of traits in this way, they are taking into account the interaction of person and situation. A goal that has become increasingly important to personality researchers is the identification of the specific conditions in a situation that are connected with trait-related behavior. Their aim is to establish stronger correlations between traits and behavior (Buss and Cantor, 1989; Wright and Mischel, 1987). This approach provides a richer, more complex picture of personality, one in which both consistencies and variations in behavior are recognized.

Another problem for personality theorists is how variability and consistency come about. Behaviorists believe that they can explain this relationship; their interpretation focuses on learning.

BEHAVIORAL THEORIES OF PERSONALITY

As the behavioral perspective advanced in psychology in the United States (see Chapter 1), many researchers became convinced that personality could be explained by the way people learned and responded to the demands of the environment. Many learning theorists rejected Freud's ideas as too subjective, but some tried to assimilate his work into their own theories of personality development.

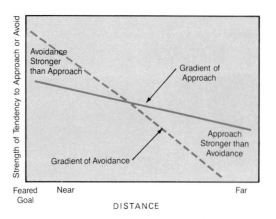

Figure 17.2 Simple graphic representation of an approach–avoidance conflict. The tendency to approach is the stronger of the two tendencies far from the goal, while the tendency to avoid is the stronger of the two near to the goal. Therefore, when far from the goal, the subject should tend to approach part way and then stop; when near to it, he should tend to retreat part way and then stop. In other words, he should tend to remain in the region where the two gradients intersect. (Adapted from Dollard and Miller, 1950.)

APPROACH-AVOIDANCE CONFLICT   a situation in which two motives clash, so that satisfying one frustrates the other

The most ambitious attempt to translate psychodynamic phenomena into behavioral learning concepts was made in the 1940s at Yale University by John Dollard and Neal Miller (1950). Dollard and Miller viewed personality as composed of habits, which are made up of learned associations between stimuli and responses. Neurotic behavior is learned in the same way as any other behavior and is simply an extreme example of ordinary conflict, in which two motives clash in such a way that satisfying one motive frustrates the other. Such a situation is called an **approach-avoidance conflict.** In their analysis of these conflicts, Dollard and Miller made several assumptions. First, the nearer an organism comes to a goal, the stronger the tendency to approach it becomes. Second, the nearer an organism comes to a feared object, the stronger is the tendency to avoid it. Third, as an organism nears an object, the tendency to avoid the feared object increases more rapidly than does the tendency to approach the goal. Fourth, the stronger the drive behind the tendency to approach or avoid something, the stronger the tendency will be.

Conflict occurs when avoidance and approach tendencies have equal strength (where the gradients cross in Figure 17.2). People caught in an approach-avoidance conflict vacillate and can be trapped in a situation that both attracts and repels them. A child just learning to walk is often caught at the point of conflict. A little girl who is still unsteady on her feet wants to approach her mother's outstretched hands, yet refuses to cross the distance between her and her mother because she is afraid of falling. Adults can also be caught in an approach-avoidance conflict. For example, married couples who separate often try to patch up their differences. While they are living apart, the tendency to approach is strong, and they reunite. But once they are living together again, all the negative aspects of their relationship resurface and again they break up, retreating because the tendency to avoid unpleasantness is now stronger than the tendency to approach.

Dollard and Miller's analysis was important for two reasons. First, it showed that psychoanalytic observations could be translated into a more testable learning framework. Second, it helped pave the way for behavior therapy—a set of procedures, based on behavioral learning principles, for changing neurotic and psychotic behavior. (In Chapter 19 we will see how behavior therapy is used to help people cope with their problems.)

Radical Behavioral Approaches

Even though B. F. Skinner's radical behaviorism is not a theory of personality, he has had a great impact on personality theory. Unlike Dollard and Miller, Skinner (1975) rejects such concepts as "drive," which cannot be directly observed and must be inferred. Moreover, Skinner sees no need for a general concept of personality structure. He focuses instead on a *functional* analysis of behavior—that is, he analyzes the relationships between environmental events and specific responses. This exclusive focus on the environment is known as *radical behaviorism,* because it makes no allowance for cognitive or symbolic processes. For example, a radical behaviorist's analysis of Karen's behavior at the party would focus on the situation, discussing Karen's various actions purely in terms of past reinforcements that she had received in similar situations. In this approach, anyone whose history of reinforcement was identical to Karen's would respond exactly as she did in each situation. To behaviorists, describing Karen as "shy" only sums up her previous history of reinforcement; it says nothing about her "nature." Skinner believes that because any behavior can be explained by reinforcing events in the past, internal events (feeling and thinking) are unnecessary for understanding behavior and can be ignored.

Skinnerian principles have produced a good deal of systematic research on the effects of reinforcement and its role in human behavior. They have also led to the development of effective ways of changing behavior, as we will see in Chapter 19. But the picture of personality drawn by Skinner's original views has been adapted by the majority of today's behaviorists to accommodate the effect of internal events.

Social Cognitive Approaches

Social cognitive theorists, while firmly linked to the behavioral tradition, emphasize the role of cognition as intervening between stimulus and response (Bandura, 1986), as we saw in Chapter 7. Views of personality based on social cognitive theory differ most sharply from Skinner's radical behaviorism in their belief that the cognitive capabilities of human beings—reason, memory, and thought—play an important role in determining human action. This suggests images of human existence very different from those of radical behaviorists. In the radical behaviorist view, which restricts itself to the two components of environment and behavior, behavior is a relatively passive response to the environment. In the social cognitive view, it is equally important to include the person who is performing the behavior. In fact, Albert Bandura (1977, 1978, 1986) has proposed a model of **reciprocal determinism,** in which each of these factors (environment, behavior, and person) influences and is influenced by the others. Not only do the person *and* the environment influence behavior, but the behavior also feeds back on its determinants to influence both the situation and the person. For example, a child who reacts aggressively, either in response to a particular situation or because of underlying disposition, may, by his or her actions, cause parents or other children to respond angrily. This angry environment may in turn lead to even more aggressive behavior from the child.

According to social cognitive theorists, our behavior is indeed partly determined by events in the environment, but it is also determined by cognitive events that are unique for each person. First, we perceive each situation in the light of our own memories, competencies, expectations, personal standards, rules, and values. Second, we can alter the situation to suit our desires. Instead of simply reacting passively, we actively transform the environment. Thus, social cognitive theorists emphasize cognitive processes where radical behaviorists emphasize reinforcement; they emphasize observation where radical behaviorists emphasize direct experience; and they emphasize self-regulation where radical behaviorists emphasize the control exerted by the environment (Kihlstrom, 1988).

Social cognitive theory is faced with the same demands as other personality theories: accounting for each person's unique reaction to a situation as well as each person's relatively consistent behavior. According to Walter Mischel (1973, 1979), five overlapping and interlocking concepts, drawn from the basic principles of observational learning, can explain both.

RECIPROCAL DETERMINISM the interaction of environment, behavior, and person that determines behavior

1. *Competencies:* Through learning and experience, each person has acquired a unique set of skills for dealing with various situations.
2. *Encodings:* Each person has a unique way of perceiving and categorizing experience. One person may see a situation as threatening while another sees it as challenging, and the way it is encoded determines the response.

3. *Expectancies:* Through learning, each person has acquired different expectations of being rewarded or punished for various kinds of behavior.
4. *Values:* The value a person places on various rewards—such as money, social approval, or good grades—influences the person's behavior.
5. *Plans:* Through learning, each person formulates plans and rules that guide behavior. One person may plan to lose five pounds and then pass up delicious desserts; another may plan to enter politics and so avoids any actions that could later become an embarrassment in a political campaign.

These cognitive aspects of personality are seen by Mischel simultaneously as products of past learning and as guides for future learning. As individuals confront new situations, the interaction continues, leading to new learning and further development of the personality.

In the view of Nancy Cantor and John Kihlstrom (1987), social behavior is intelligent behavior, which means that personality is a demonstration of social intelligence. When people react differently to similar life situations, it is because each person's intellectual resources are unique. Each of us has a different store of information about ourselves, other people, and the situations we may encounter. We each have different rules, skills, and strategies that guide our impressions and plans. These unique intellectual resources not only allow each of us to react differently in various situations but also make behavior difficult to predict.

When assessing personality, social cognitive theorists do not look for global traits, nor do they rely on simple self-descriptions. Instead they examine people's approaches to specific kinds of situations, looking at the way individuals interpret a situation, what they think about their own capabilities, and the strategies they use to manage the situation. The accompanying box describes how researchers use this approach to investigate the way people's intellectual resources affect their approach to major life tasks.

SELF-EFFICACY a personal judgment of one's own competence in a specific situation

When personality is examined this way, **self-efficacy,** which refers to our judgment of our own competence in a particular situation, becomes an important aspect of personality. Such judgments require us to weigh personal and situational factors, then infer our capacity for effective action. Bandura (1982) has assessed self-efficacy by asking people to rate their own probable performance on a series of tasks that vary in difficulty, designating which tasks they can do and their degree of certainty. Their performance is then compared with their perceptions of self-efficacy. The two are highly correlated; in fact, perceptions of self-efficacy are better predictors of future behavior than a person's previous performance on the same task. Apparently, the way we interpret our successful actions has a larger impact on our future behavior than the success itself.

The power of self-efficacy was evident in a study of people who had just stopped smoking (Condiotte and Lichtenstein, 1981). At the end of treatment, the ex-smokers indicated how confident they were that they could resist the urge to smoke in a series of situations. By looking at the self-efficacy ratings, researchers could accurately predict which ex-smokers would smoke again, how soon they would slip, and the specific situation in which they would smoke their first cigarette. The same ratings also predicted how the ex-smokers would react in the event that they yielded to temptation and smoked a single cigarette. Those with high self-efficacy ratings usually regained control over their urge to smoke; their slip was not repeated. But those with low ratings found that their perceived self-efficacy had plummeted even further and they had a total relapse.

Self-efficacy is built on several kinds of information: our own successes and failures, our observations of the successes and failures of others, the encouragement of others, and our physiological state (whether we are tired, in pain, or under stress). Perceived self-efficacy helps account for many aspects of life, including physiological reactions to stress, response to failure, strivings to reach a goal, choice of occupation—even the speed of recovery from a heart attack (Bandura, 1982).

PSYCHOLOGY TODAY AND TOMORROW

Studying Cognitive Strategies for Managing a Situation

When students make the transition from high school to college, they face imposing and perhaps threatening tasks. For most, academic success is both important and anxiety-provoking, and so it offers an opportunity to see how personality affects the way individuals meet this challenge. In addressing this question, Nancy Cantor and her colleagues (1987) studied students in the Honors College at the University of Michigan and discovered that successful students did not all follow the same path to academic success.

Each student filled out two lengthy questionnaires during freshman year, the first in early October and the second in January, after the new semester had started. They were also interviewed in depth and took part in an "experience-sampling" study. At random times during the day, a pager would beep, and they would jot a description of whatever they were doing on an activity report sheet.

The students adopted two distinctly different cognitive strategies for tackling their academic requirements, each reflecting different aspects of personality. Although the strategies had little in common, both groups of students did equally well during their first semester.

Some students adopted a defensive, almost pessimistic, strategy. Desite their history of academic success, they began college with low expectations. Just before they began a task—a term paper, a new assignment, a mid-term exam—they felt anxious and out of control. Yet their uneasiness motivated them to plan their actions so comprehensively that instead of failing, they succeeded. Their approach could be summed up as "I go into academic situations expecting the worst, even though I know I'll probably do OK." So, despite their low expectations, their self-efficacy was actually not low.

Other students adopted an optimistic strategy. They began college with high expectations. When they approached a task, they felt positive, calm, and in control. They made few plans, but their confidence motivated them to work hard and, like the defensive pessimists, they succeeded. Their approach was sunny: "I generally go into academic situations with positive expectations about how I will do."

The "pessimists" found the prospect of getting good grades more important, difficult, stressful, challenging, and time-consuming than the "optimists." Yet the experience-sampling reports indicated that both groups spent the same amount of time working on academic tasks. The pessimists were as involved in their studies as the optimists and found their successes just as rewarding. In fact, pessimism was a successful strategy *only* for students who found academic tasks intrinsically motivating.

Students who were successful optimists succeeded as long as their approach remained optimistic. Those who, despite expectations of success, engaged in the sort of detailed planning that enabled pessimists to succeed wound up with lower grade-point averages than the rest.

For students in this study, personality expressed itself in consistent differences in strategies for academic achievement and in the way reflective planning affected their ability to handle threatening academic situations. But, as cognitive theorists maintain, the effect was an interaction of person and situation. Yet the pessimists' apprehension was domain-specific; the researchers noted that the self-concept of pessimists was not negative in other areas and that their pessimism did not extend to their expectations of success in social interaction.

Evaluating the Behavioral Approach

Behavioral theories have been widely criticized. The quarrels of other theorists with radical behaviorism are concerned in part with charges that it *oversimplifies* life. Because it reduces human action to small, measurable units of behavior and ignores thought and feeling, radical behaviorism has been criticized as a naive oversimplification of human existence that distorts whatever it measures (London, 1969). The exclusion of thought and feeling by radical behaviorists, critics assert,

Treatments based on the behavioral approach to personality have proved effective in helping people stop such unwanted behaviors as cigarette smoking.

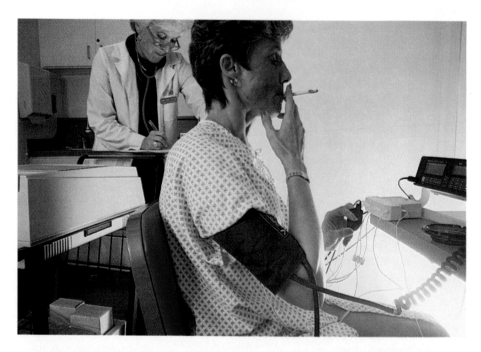

means that behaviorists refuse to study anything that distinguishes humans from other animals; hence, their principles do not reflect the uniqueness and abilities of human beings.

Behavioral theories are also criticized because they are *deterministic,* a charge that arises because behaviorists see most human behavior as the product of conditioning. Not free will, they say, but the stimuli that surround us determine what we will do. Most such criticism is a response to the position taken by radical behaviorists: that a person's behavior is primarily a response to stimuli and—in theory—would be completely predictable if only that individual's history of reinforcement were known (Overton and Reese, 1973).

Despite these criticisms, behavioral theories have made major contributions to the study of personality. When applied to personal problems, behavioral theories have produced treatments that are faster, cheaper, and often more effective than treatments that have come from other theoretical approaches to personality. Behavior therapy has been used to end smoking and bed-wetting, to help mentally retarded people become more nearly self-sufficient, to end phobias such as intense fear of snakes, and to draw children out of the isolation of autism (Kazdin and Wilson, 1978). Such treatment programs are explored in Chapter 19.

The objectivity of behavioral theories of personality also stands in sharp contrast to the vague, inferential statements that have come from some other theories of personality. Because behaviorists and social cognitive theorists use clearly defined language and study behavior that can be measured, their claims can be tested and retested.

By giving a major role to cognitive processes, social cognitive theory appears to avoid most of the criticisms that beset radical behaviorism. But some critics argue that this "new behaviorism" is still oversimplified. They maintain that a person's personality is determined by more than the easily accessible self-statements upon which many social cognitive theorists have focused. Although social cognitive theory takes cognitive processes into account and sees the individual as initiating actions, it is still deterministic. It continues to regard our expectations, our perceptions, and even our self-reinforcement as heavily influenced by learning.

Social cognitive approaches may provide the most promising way of studying its intricacies. By taking into account the power of the situation as well as the characteristics of the individual, the cognitive perspective allows researchers to study how individuals perceive and interpret social situations. Its reciprocal determinism, stressing the mutual influence of person, environment, and behavior, opens the way for an understanding of the uniqueness and complexity of the individual.

For a rounded picture of the range of opinion about behavioral approaches, we need to gain some familiarity with a group of psychologists who have been among behaviorism's sharpest critics. These humanistic psychologists believe that our inner drives toward growth, happiness, and creative expression play a more decisive role in shaping our behavior patterns than do the pressures of our surroundings.

THE HUMANISTIC PERSPECTIVE

Humanistic psychologists emphasize the potential of human beings for growth, creativity, and spontaneity. Rejecting the determinism of Freud and the behaviorists, they stress the uniqueness of the individual and the human freedom to make choices. The most influential humanistic psychologists have been Abraham Maslow and Carl Rogers.

Maslow's Humanistic Psychology

The guiding spirit behind humanistic psychology has generally been identified as American psychologist Abraham Maslow (1908–1970). Maslow deliberately set out to create what he called a "third force" in psychology as an alternative to psychoanalysis and behaviorism. He based his theory of personality on the characteristics of healthy, creative people who used all their talents, potential, and capabilities, rather than on studies of disturbed individuals as Freud had done. Maslow (1971a, 1971b) proposed that these healthy people strive for and achieve *self-actualization* (see Chapter 13). By this he meant that they develop their own potential to its fullest; yet instead of competing with others, each strives to be "the

---

TABLE 17.3   Characteristics of Self-Actualized Persons

They are realistically oriented.

They accept themselves, other people, and the natural world for what they are.

They have a great deal of spontaneity.

They are problem-centered rather than self-centered.

They have an air of detachment and a need for privacy.

They are autonomous and independent.

Their appreciation of people and things is fresh rather than stereotyped.

Most of them have had profound mystical or spiritual experiences although not necessarily religious in character.

They identify with mankind.

Their intimate relationships with a few specially loved people tend to be profound and deeply emotional rather than superficial.

Their values and attitudes are democratic.

They do not confuse means with ends.

Their sense of humor is philosophical rather than hostile.

They have a great fund of creativeness.

They resist conformity to the culture.

They transcend the environment rather than just coping with it.

Source: A. Maslow (1954). *Motivation and personality.* New York: Harper & Row.

In Carl Rogers's view, a child may engage in an activity not only to enjoy it for its own sake but also to meet the conditions of worth set by the parents.

best me I can be." Maslow (1966, 1968) believed that most psychologists were pessimistic, dwelling too heavily on the misery, conflict, and hostility that kept people from fulfilling their potential. Instead, he took an optimistic view, stressing people's possibilities and their capacities for love, joy, and artistic expression. This reflected his belief that within every person, there is an active drive toward health—an impulse toward the actualization of one's potentialities. But a person's impulses toward self-actualization can be distorted by society, habit, or faulty education.

In Maslow's humanistic psychology, as we saw in Chapter 13, there are two groups of human needs: *basic needs* and *metaneeds*. Some basic needs are physiological (for food, water, sleep, and so on) or psychological (for affection, security, self-esteem, and the like). These basic needs are also called *deficiency needs*, because if they are not met, a person seeks to make up for their absence. *Metaneeds*— or growth needs—include the need for justice, goodness, beauty, order, and unity. In most instances, deficiency needs take priority over growth needs. People who lack food or water cannot attend to justice or beauty. Nor can those who lack basic security and self-esteem feel free to consider fairness, feel deep and reciprocal love, be democratic, or resist restrictive conformity. The metaneeds are real, and when they are not met, a person may develop such **metapathologies** as alienation, anguish, apathy, and cynicism.

METAPATHOLOGY   the alienation, anguish, apathy, or cynicism that arises when metaneeds are not filled

By studying a group of historical figures whom he considered to be self-actualized, Maslow (1954) developed a portrait of the self-actualized person, who shows the personality characteristics listed in Table 17.3. In deriving this description of the self-actualized personality, Maslow went beyond such famous figures as Abraham Lincoln, Henry David Thoreau, Ludwig van Beethoven, Thomas Jefferson, William James, Eleanor Roosevelt, and Albert Einstein, to include college students and some of his own friends.

The Self Theory of Rogers

Like Maslow, American clinical psychologist Carl Rogers (1902–1987) believed that people are governed by an innate impulse toward positive growth. But instead of developing his theory from studies of self-actualized people, Rogers based his view of personality on observations made while practicing psychotherapy. Most of Rogers's clients seemed unable to accept their own feelings and experiences. In their youth they had apparently come to believe that unless they acted in dishonest or distorted ways, others would neither like nor love them. So in order to be accepted, they had begun to deny their own feelings.

Figure 17.3 Carl Rogers believed that the fundamental problem of personality is how to make the self more congruent with the total experience of the organism. It is through the therapeutic relationship, in which the therapist creates an atmosphere of total acceptance, or "unconditional positive regard," that the client may achieve closer—or even complete—congruence. (From Rogers, 1971.)

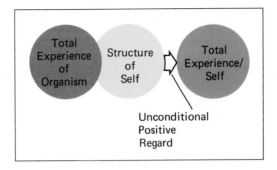

Most children encounter this problem to some extent, because they discover that they are objects of **conditional positive regard.** By this term, Rogers (1971) meant the withholding of love and praise by parents and other powerful people when children do not conform to family standards or to the standards of society. A boy who comes to dinner with dirty hands may be told that he is "disgusting" and be sent away from the table. If he prefers to stay home and read instead of going out to play, he may be told that he is a bookworm who should get out more. But if he keeps his hands clean and decides to join the local soccer team, he is likely to be rewarded with smiles and compliments. Because conditions are placed on positive regard, a process begins in which the child learns to act and feel in ways that earn approval from others rather than in ways that he or she may find more intrinsically satisfying.

The process continues into adulthood. To maintain positive regard, adults suppress actions and feelings that are unacceptable to important people in their lives. As a result, what Rogers called **conditions of worth** are established: extraneous standards whose attainment ensures positive regard. If conditions of worth are rigid, so that behavior can no longer be flexible, emotional problems can arise. For example, one young woman was persuaded while still in high school to give up the idea of a career devoted to helping others. Because docility and mildness were conditions of worth for her, she accepted her parents' values and rejected her own wishes. Within a few years, she was engaged to a young man who defined her life for her. But before they were married, she discovered that she was "everything that *he* wanted to be and nothing that *I* was" (Rogers, 1980, p. 209). Realizing that she was ignoring her own perceptions and emotions, she broke the engagement and entered therapy.

The discomfort that can accompany the denial and distortion of our own experiences highlights the distinction that Rogers makes between the organism and the self. The **organism** encompasses the total range of a person's possible experiences; the **self,** by contrast, consists of only those parts of experience that the individual recognizes and accepts. Ideally, the organism and the self should be identical, because, in principle, a person should be able to recognize and accept all experience. In practice, however, the organism and the self often oppose each other (see Figure 17.3). According to Rogers, a person may deny feelings or experiences if they are incompatible with the self-concept. Even an action can be disowned by saying, "I don't know why I did that" or "I must have been carried away." This idea is similar to the psychoanalytic concept of repression and to its neo-Freudian reformulations.

People who are psychologically adjusted, or in Rogers's term **fully functioning,** are able to assimilate all their experiences into their self-concept (Rogers, 1971). Such people are open to experience, aware, and not defensive; they have harmonious relations with others, and they have unconditional positive self-regard.

If the breach between the self and the organism grows too wide, a person may become defensive, tense, conflicted, and unable to relate well to others. Such people are often argumentative and hostile, and they may project their denied feelings onto others. In Chapter 19, we will see how Rogers developed a therapy that attempts to heal the split between self and organism so that the person can learn to accept all experiences as genuine.

CONDITIONAL POSITIVE RE-GARD Rogers's term for the withholding of love and praise when a child fails to meet parental or social standards

CONDITIONS OF WORTH Rogers's term for extraneous standards whose attainment ensures positive regard

ORGANISM the total range of a person's possible experiences

SELF those parts of experience that a person recognizes and accepts

FULLY FUNCTIONING the psychological adjustment that results when people assimilate all their experiences into their self-concept

UNCONDITIONAL POSITIVE REGARD Rogers's terms for continued support no matter what a person says or does

Although nearly all people are subjected to conditional positive regard, most do not become so hostile, defensive, or unable to relate to others that they require therapy. But what about people who grow up receiving **unconditional positive regard**—those who always reaped approval and acceptance no matter what they did? It might seem that such people would become selfish, cruel, and destructive. Freud had asserted that all human beings have aggressive and destructive instincts, and it is to prevent such antisocial tendencies that children are punished and police forces are maintained. However, Rogers maintained that in his years of therapeutic experience he had seen little evidence for this pessimistic view. He was convinced that the human organism naturally seeks growth, self-actualization, and pleasant, productive relations with others. When not restricted by social forces, a person wants to become what most of us would recognize as healthier and happier.

Criticisms and Contributions of Humanistic Theory

Humanistic theorists of personality are not research oriented, and as such they are seen as unscientific and subjective by some critics. The charge is that their theories are based on inferences stated in such a vague and imprecise manner that they cannot be verified scientifically. For example, how can metaneeds be shown to be essential to full human development? And how do we know when a basic need has been gratified? How do we determine the "conditions of worth" that Rogers asserts we develop as a standard of conduct?

In contrast to most humanistic psychologists, Rogers did gather data on his theory. By recording therapy sessions and analyzing their content, he systematically tested inferences drawn from his theory. For example, he compared self-concept before and after therapy and discovered the conditions required for constructive personality change as well as evidence of such changes (Rogers, 1989). However, his theory of personality is less open to test. Giving unconditional positive regard to children from birth, for instance, might have very different—and less beneficial—effects than providing unconditional positive regard to people who have become unable to accept many of their feelings and actions.

A second charge against humanistic approaches is that they lack neutrality. Maslow's claim that human nature is "good," for example, has been called an intrusion of subjective values into what should be a neutral science. His study of self-actualized people has been criticized because the sample was chosen on the basis of Maslow's own subjective criteria. How can self-actualized people be identified without knowing the characteristics of such people? And if their characteristics are already known, how can they be listed as if they were the result of an empirical study?

However "unscientific" researchers may find humanistic theories, this approach to personality is nevertheless rooted in basic human concerns, and its optimistic focus on human growth and insistence on "higher" needs may serve to remind us of them. Maslow's influence, for example, has inspired many researchers to pay attention to healthy, productive people. The focus of humanistic theories on integration and wholeness of the self may be a valuable corrective to research that tends to fragment the self in order to study it.

In fact, the work of Maslow and Rogers has had a significant impact on research, therapy, and counseling. It has led many psychologists to concentrate on their patients' or clients' personal growth and to let clients know that they are still accepted even if they behave in self-destructive ways. The group therapy movement can trace its strength and impetus to humanistic psychology. Group therapy is generally characterized by a focus on growth and on personal interaction freed from conventional restraints. The humanistic approach has also been responsible for the establishment of personal growth centers throughout the United States. Perhaps the most famous of these is the Esalen Institute in California, where Maslow worked until his death in 1970. The Center for the Study of the Person in La Jolla, California, where Carl Rogers was a fellow until his death in 1987 is also widely known for its humanistic emphasis.

THE BIOLOGICAL PERSPECTIVE

A biological basis for personality has not been as firmly established as has the biological basis for other human capacities. Yet some aspects of personality show clear traces of biological influence. How do researchers detect the presence of biological influences on personality? A favorite method is the study of twins, in which researchers compare identical twins with fraternal twins. Identical twins have the same genetic background, whereas fraternal twins are no more alike genetically than any pair of siblings. Therefore, if identical twins are significantly more alike on some aspect of behavior than fraternal twins are, researchers assume they have found evidence of biological influence. Similarly, in adoption studies, researchers compare adopted children's personality with the personality of their adoptive and their biological parents.

One aspect of personality that is influenced by biology is **temperament,** the individual's pattern of activity, response to stimuli, susceptibility to emotional stimulation, and general mood (Buss, Plomin, and Willerman, 1973). Differences in temperament are apparent among newborn infants, and twin studies have shown biological influences as early as two months—the youngest twins studied (Torgersen and Kringlen, 1978). Heredity seems to have its strongest influence on physiological functions—such as sleep and feeding patterns and the infant's level of excitability. Some babies sleep and eat more readily than others, and some babies respond to a very slight stimulus—a light, a sound, a touch—but others respond only if the stimulus is intense. Some babies are more physically active than others—they are restless and wave their arms and legs about—while other babies seem placid and move more slowly. Some babies fuss and cry a lot; they are irritable and hard to soothe once they begin to fret.

By the time babies are eight or nine months old, genetic influences on sociability appear. Some babies are especially "cuddly" and sociable; others do not like to be held closely. Within another year or so, these differences in sociability are expressed in different ways and in response to different events. Differences in the way babies respond to cuddling become differences in the way toddlers cooperate with other people, how upset they become when left with a stranger, and whether they are likely to strike up a conversation (Goldsmith and Gottesman, 1981).

Another area in which twin studies have found biological influences is called *task-oriented behavior.* In babies, this difference shows up primarily in the length of time an infant pays attention to some object. During the preschool period, biologically influenced differences appear in how long children persist at a task, how hard they will work toward some goal, and even how well they do on tests of intellectual competence (Matheny, 1980).

By following babies through their first eight years of life, psychologist Jerome Kagan (1989) has found one personality trait—shyness—that appears to be linked to biological differences. About one infant in ten seems subdued and restrained in new situations, and three-quarters of these infants go on to become shy and inhibited children. Their shyness seems related to physiology; extremely shy children have an abnormally low stress threshold, so that during the mildest stress, their heart rate, muscle tension, and hormonal levels differ from those of other children. A genetic basis to shyness has also appeared in twin studies and studies of adopted children.

In a study of older Swedish twins, most of whom had been separated at birth, researchers found that, whether twins grew up together or apart, their tendencies toward fearfulness as adults were similar (the correlations were +.49 for identical twins reared together and +.37 for identical twins reared apart) (Plomin et al., 1988). The genetic influences on other aspects of personality—anger, distress, activity level, and sociability—were also clear but not as strong. No matter which trait was examined, its strength generally dwindled during the last half of the life span, indicating the role of individual experiences on personality.

As we saw in Chapter 15, human beings never develop in a particular way because of heredity alone; environment—family, peers, social setting, and unique experiences—always acts on our inherited nature. Sometimes an inherited tendency will not even appear unless the child encounters specific conditions, and sometimes a biologically based aspect of personality will disappear unless environ-

TEMPERAMENT the individual's pattern of activity, response to stimuli, susceptibility to emotional stimulation, and general mood

mental conditions sustain it (Gottlieb, 1983). Kagan (1989) found that one-quarter of the extremely shy toddlers were sociable youngsters by the age of eight, presumably because their parents had consistently encouraged the development of sociability in their shy children and discouraged their shyness.

We now turn from theories of personality and their explanation of human behavior to an examination of abnormal behavior. In the next chapter, we will see how the theories examined in this chapter affect the way psychologists explain psychological disorders.

SUMMARY

Freud and Psychoanalytic Theories

- According to Freud's psychoanalytic theory, personality resides largely in the unconscious. Memories and feelings that have been repressed to avoid anxiety can be retrieved through psychoanalysis, in which techniques such as free association and dream analysis are used.
- Personality structure is based on the interaction of three systems: the id, the ego, and the superego.
- The ego uses defense mechanisms to reduce anxiety.
- By the time the child has passed through the oral, anal, and phallic psychosexual stages, personality is largely formed.
- Post-Freudian psychoanalytic theorists have deemphasized instinctual forces, instead emphasizing social and interpersonal drives as the determinants of personality.
- Projective tests have low reliability and low validity and are best regarded as tools for the clinician.
- Psychoanalytic concepts have been difficult to test, and many have not held up; yet Freud has made a lasting contribution to the understanding of human personality.

Trait Theories of Personality

- Trait theorists assume that all traits exist in all people to a degree that can be measured.
- Allport believed that central traits are the major influence on personality, but that each person's personality includes both common traits and personal dispositions.
- Factor analysis is the primary tool for the identification and measurement of common traits.
- The five major personality factors now accepted by many personality researchers are extraversion, agreeableness, conscientiousness, emotional stability, and openness to experience.
- Trait theorists measure personality with self-report inventories.
- The interaction of person and situation determines whether a trait will be expressed.

Behavioral Theories of Personality

- Radical behavior theorists see behavior as relatively passive responses to situations.

- When behavior can be explained solely in terms of past reinforcements, there is no need for the concept of personality structure.
- Social cognitive theories have added cognitive processes to the behavioral view; they talk in terms of reciprocal determinism, in which environment, behavior, and person interact.
- Radical behavioral theories have been criticized for being deterministic and for oversimplifying personality.
- Social cognitive theory, while still deterministic, incorporates human complexity and individual initiative into the explanation of personality.

The Humanistic Perspective

- Humanistic personality theories emphasize the human potential for growth, creativity, and spontaneity.
- Maslow saw personality as determined by a hierarchy of needs and their satisfactions; only after deficiency needs are satisfied can people become self-actualized through the satisfaction of metaneeds.
- Rogers believed that few people become fully functioning because as children their parents gave them conditional positive regard—that is, offered them love and praise only when they conformed to parental or social standards.
- The resulting denial and distortion of experience led to splits between organism and self.
- Humanistic theories have been criticized as being unscientific, vague, and highly subjective, yet they may act as a corrective to other theories that tend to fragment the self.

The Biological Perspective

- According to the biological perspective, some aspects of personality are biologically determined.
- Differences in temperament exist from birth, and these biologically determined characteristics interact with experience.

KEY TERMS

anal stage
anxiety
approach-avoidance conflict
archetypes
basic anxiety
basic hostility
cardinal trait
central traits
common traits
conditional positive regard
conditions of worth
defense mechanism
ego
factor analysis
free association

fully functioning
genital stage
id
individual traits/personal dispositions
latency stage
latent content
manifest content
metapathology
oral stage
organism
personality
phallic stage
projective test
psychoanalysis
psychodynamics

rationalization
reciprocal determinism
repression
Rorschach Inkblot Test
secondary traits
self
self-efficacy
sublimation
superego
temperament
Thematic Apperception Test (TAT)
trait
traumatic
unconditional positive regard
unconscious

CONCEPT REVIEW

1. Define and describe the basic components of Freud's model of the personality.

2. Define *anxiety.* How do defense mechanisms work?

3. Describe the five psychosexual stages that Freud believed were crucial in the development of the personality.

4. Distinguish Freud's concept of the unconscious from Jung's. How does Horney's view of anxiety differ from Freud's?

5. How do projective assessments work? Given the difficulty of establishing the validity of these tests, why are they still considered useful?

6. What is Allport's definition of *trait?* What are the three kinds of traits that he proposed?

7. How is factor analysis used to develop a set of traits? Is this the same as the empirical method? Outline the several sets of traits recently developed by trait theorists.

8. Describe the essential components of social cognitive theory, and distinguish this perspective from Skinner's radical behaviorism. What important component has been denied by Skinner but is of central concern for social cognitive theory?

9. What are the characteristics of self-efficacy, in the social cognitive approach to studying personality? Which of the criticisms of other behavioral theories does social cognitive theory avoid? Which criticisms still apply to it?

10. What processes do Abraham Maslow and Carl Rogers identify as contributing to the development of the unique individual? Define these processes and concepts used in humanistic psychology.

11. Which areas of personality appear to be genetically influenced? What evidence supports the biological perspective on personality?

CRITICAL THINKING

1. The chapter suggests that personality psychologists are concerned with, on the one hand, accounting for the differences in people's responses to the same situation and, on the other hand, accounting for the consistency of individuals' responses in different situations. How would Freud explain these two patterns of response? What about Allport and the other trait theorists? Skinner? Bandura? Rogers and Maslow?

2. In trait theory, current research by Mark Snyder focuses on self-monitoring. How does this differ from Bandura's concept of self-efficacy? Have any principles been introduced in earlier chapters that would help to differentiate these two approaches?

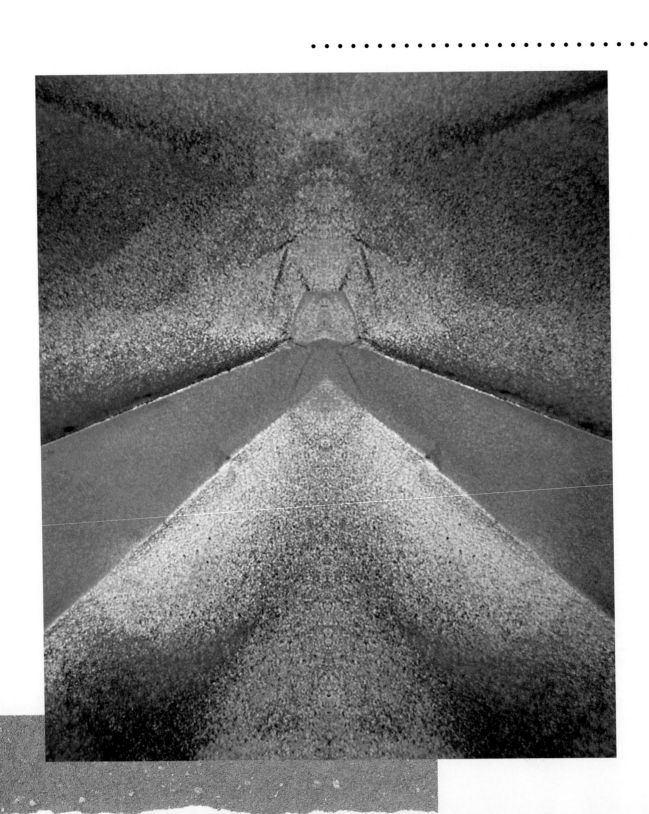

Psychological Disorders

A thirty-two-year-old man complained that his thoughts were being repeated in public and that he was being tortured by invisible rays. He claimed that people who lived on the other floors of his apartment building transmitted abusive messages to him through the central heating system. At times he stared into the mirror, grimacing at his reflection. Or, in the midst of an apparently sensible conversation, he suddenly broke into song or interjected words that bore no relation to the situation, such as "Emperor Napoleon!" He often laughed boisterously and for no apparent reason. Sometimes he screamed at passers-by from his balcony. He complained about odd sensations in his hair and scalp, saying that both felt "as if they were congealed." At last, he began to pound on the walls in the middle of the night, waking his family and people in the neighboring apartments (Bleuler, 1978).

Psychologists would have no trouble deciding that this man's behavior is clearly abnormal and would diagnose him as "schizophrenic." You probably came to the same conclusion. How are such judgments made? What standards do any of us use to decide whether someone is simply a nonconformist, a little eccentric, or seriously disturbed? As we will see, that question is extremely difficult to answer, and the problem of tracing psychological disorders back to their source is even more complex.

UNDERSTANDING ABNORMALITY

Most kinds of abnormal behavior are far less dramatic than the symptoms of the wall-pounding schizophrenic; in fact, most people with psychological disorders seem "normal" most of the time. Attempts to define abnormality make it clear that the standards that separate normal and abnormal behavior are not as clear-cut as we might assume.

Definitions of Abnormality

To establish the line between normal and abnormal behavior, we must first divide thought patterns and behavior that the community considers acceptable from those that are considered unacceptable. These standards may change from one society to another and from time to time within the same society.

The simplest way to define abnormal behavior is in terms of *norm violation*. Each society has a set of **social norms**—rules that prescribe "right" and "wrong" behavior—by which its members live. Social norms cover every aspect of life, from the person one may marry to the food one may eat. Since these rules are absorbed in childhood during the process of socialization, we take them so much for granted that we notice them only when they are broken.

Norms can change, as they have in American society during the past few decades. Not many years ago, for example, a divorced parent who engaged in sexual activity might lose custody of his or her children, but today this behavior has become acceptable. By contrast, behavior that once would have been considered normal—beating an unruly child so severely as to cause injury—is now seen as child abuse. This shifting nature of norms makes them inappropriate as guides to normality. In addition, using norms as a standard tends to enforce conformity and to mark the nonconformist as "abnormal." In spite of these problems, norms remain the dominant standard of our culture because they have been so deeply engrained.

Another way to define abnormal behavior is in terms of its statistical rarity. Using *statistical abnormality* as the standard, we consider people abnormal when their behavior differs greatly from that of the majority (the "average"). This is a simple way of making a diagnosis, and this approach is used in some areas of psychological functioning—for instance, people who score below a certain level on intelligence tests are considered retarded, as we saw in Chapter 11. The use of statistical definition of abnormality, however, does present problems. One prob-

SOCIAL NORMS society's rules for appropriate behavior in every aspect of life

lem is that we have no way to distinguish between the two extremes above and below the "average": according to this definition, both geniuses and retardates are considered "abnormal." An even greater problem is the fact that, from a statistical standpoint, some abnormality must exist. Even if we could improve general intelligence so that no one scored below what is now considered "normal," some people would score lower than others. These people, whose level of functioning would once have been normal, would then be classified as abnormal.

Less restrictive than norm violation or statistical rarity is the standard of *personal discomfort*, which is based on an individual's self-assessment. According to this definition, only those who are distressed by their own thoughts or behavior are abnormal. This standard is also faulty, primarily because the same behavior patterns can make one person miserable but bother another only a little. In fact, some people (schizophrenics, rapists, and murderers, for example) may be violent or dangerous and not feel any distress at all. Limiting the definition to personal discomfort, then, gives us no yardstick for evaluating any specific behavior.

A fourth definition is the standard of *maladaptive behavior*. If a physically healthy person cannot hold a job, deal with family and friends, or get out of bed in the morning, most of us would agree that he or she is psychologically disturbed. In many cases, severe personal distress accompanies such behavior patterns. The advantage of maladaptive behavior as a standard is that it focuses on a person's behavior in relation to the behavior of others. The major disadvantage is that "adaptive behavior," like normality, is subjectively defined and difficult to apply as a consistent standard. Germans who cooperated in the genocidal programs of the Nazi regime had adapted to the demands of their society; their behavior would be considered "adaptive", despite being morally objectionable.

Finally, we can define abnormality in terms of its *deviation from an ideal*. The trouble with this definition is that it immediately labels most of us as abnormal, because ideal adjustment is beyond the grasp of most people. The pursuit of such an ideal can make people feel disturbed or seriously inadequate when in fact they are only imperfect human beings. In addition, the definition of the ideal personality can change as quickly and as often as social norms do.

These ways of defining abnormal behavior do not exhaust the possibilities. We might define any behavior that makes observers uncomfortable as "abnor-

Social deviance can be mistaken for mental illness. Is the sign-carrier emotionally ill? A mental health professional would have to evaluate his overall ability to function before a proper diagnosis could be made.

Unable to cope with the demands of a job and the tasks of life, severely disturbed people may live in the streets, as this "bag lady" does.

mal," or any behavior that is unpredictable, incomprehensible, or simply unconventional. None of the definitions is perfect. In practice, the judgment of abnormality, whether made by diagnosticians or by family and friends, is usually based on a combination of standards. The person's happiness, relation to social norms, and ability to cope—as well as society's ability to cope with the person—are all taken into account.

Perspectives on Abnormality

When confronted with what they considered abnormal behavior, people have always sought some explanation for it, whether supernatural (possession by demons) or natural (a blow to the head). Modern explanations have tended to concentrate either on the **biogenic theory,** which takes the position that abnormal behavior has a physical cause, or on the **psychogenic theory,** which regards emotional stress or maladaptive behavior patterns as the primary cause.

    The biogenic view goes back nearly 2500 years to ancient Greece, although it was not firmly established until the nineteenth century, when German physician Emil Kraepelin (1883) argued that brain pathology has a central role in mental disturbances. He applied the same scientific standards of observation and classification to mental disturbances that physicians used with physical diseases. The result was the first comprehensive classification system of psychological disorders. Kraepelin's system became the basis for the diagnostic manual used by today's clinicians, the *DSM-III-R* (American Psychiatric Association, 1987).

    By the turn of the century, one mysterious psychological disorder after another yielded to biogenic explanation. The success of the biogenic approach led to the **medical model** of abnormal behavior, in which each kind of abnormal behavior is seen as having specific organic causes and a specific set of symptoms. The medical model still influences the terms we apply to psychological disorders and to those who suffer from them: "mental illness," "therapy," "pathology," "cure," "patient," "symptom," and "syndrome" (Price, 1978).

    In the past few decades, many psychiatrists have criticized the influence of the medical model. Perhaps the most relentless of the critics has been Thomas Szasz

BIOGENIC THEORY   the theory that all abnormal behavior has a physical cause

PSYCHOGENIC THEORY   the theory that abnormal behavior can be traced to emotional stress or maladaptive behavior patterns

MEDICAL MODEL   the view that all abnormal behavior has specific organic causes and a specific set of symptoms

(1961), and American psychiatrist who asserted that most "mental illnesses" are actually "problems in living." Szasz contended that when we label abnormal behavior an "illness," we deprive people of responsibility for their own behavior. Although such arguments have had some influence, the biogenic approach to understanding and treating abnormal behavior still thrives.

The rise of biogenic theory did not mean that physicians ignored the role of psychological, as opposed to biological, factors in abnormal behavior. It seemed clear, for example, that a serious depression sometimes could be traced to lingering grief over a death. Yet specifically psychological theories were not advanced until after Franz Anton Mesmer, an eighteenth-century Austrian physician, identified the power of suggestion in curing mental disorders. In treating his patients, Mesmer used "mesmerism," an early form of hypnosis described in Chapter 6. Later, in the nineteenth century, the famous Parisian neurologist Jean Martin Charcot found hypnosis to be highly successful in treating hysteria, a disorder in which physical symptoms appear without any corresponding organic causes. It was Charcot's example that influenced Josef Breuer and Sigmund Freud to use hypnosis in the treatment of psychological disorders.

From his experience with hypnosis, Freud developed the techniques of psychoanalysis, as we saw in Chapter 17. Although his psychoanalytic theory is a general theory of personality, it is also a detailed theory of abnormal behavior. Since Freud developed his theory, other psychogenic theories have focused on the role played by society in the development of disorders. Behavioral and humanistic-existential perspectives also view abnormal behavior as psychogenic, while the neuroscientific perspective takes a biogenic view.

The Neuroscientific Perspective

Ever since the Greek physician Hippocrates (c. 460–c. 360 B.C.) suggested that abnormal behavior is a result of too much phlegm or bile circulating through the body, scientists have attempted to find biogenic explanations for psychological disorder. Today the neuroscientific perspective focuses on genes, biochemistry, and neurological impairments, but it does not rely on the medical model or suggest that most abnormal behavior is the result of biological abnormality. In many cases, the organic cause of a disorder is undeniable, as when impairment is traced to brain injury, infection, tumor, alcoholism, or untreated syphilis. Researchers have also been establishing some organic basis for severe psychological disorders, in which a person's perception of reality is highly distorted. In the case of schizophrenia, for example, research has focused on genetic defects, abnormalities in brain structure, and biochemical abnormalities. But the discovery that a biochemical abnormality is associated with a particular disorder does not prove that the abnormality caused the disorder. Both may have been caused by some other, unknown factor, or the abnormality may have left the person vulnerable to psychogenic factors.

The Psychoanalytic Perspective

Psychoanalytic theorists hold that mental disorders have their roots in childhood, when the structure of personality is formed. If the child fails to resolve life's early conflicts between pleasure and discipline, the balance among id, ego, and superego is disturbed. Early conflicts and unresolved problems (which often center on the child's relationships with his or her parents) are buried in the unconscious. When the person later encounters additional stress or conflict, the problems resurface in various ways, and mental disorder may develop. As we saw in Chapter 17, conflicts among the id, the ego, and the superego may produce anxiety, but the adult is unaware that the reason for his or her anxiety can be traced to childhood experiences. Sometimes the anxiety is directly expressed in abnormal behavior. In the psychoanalytic view, a woman's snake phobia may have its roots in a conflict between her libido and her parents' prohibition of sex; for her, snakes may be symbols of penises. At other times the anxiety is indirect: the repression of painful memories may result in amnesia.

The Behavioral Perspective

Although behavioral theorists also see a psychogenic basis for emotional disorders, most adherents of this approach reject Freudian concepts. They believe that the learning principles of classical and instrumental conditioning can explain the development of abnormal behavior. Behavioral theorists assume that abnormal behavior is learned in the same way as any other behavior. The person with a psychological disorder has simply learned *inappropriate* behavior or has failed to learn the adaptive behavior that most people acquire. For example, a behaviorist would see a snake phobia as a classically conditioned response: during childhood, snakes have been paired with some fear-provoking stimulus, such as an unrelated injury.

The Social-Cognitive Perspective

Today, many behavioral theorists view abnormal behavior in terms of learning theory and human thought processes. They believe that the way we interpret events may be even more important than the events themselves (Bandura, 1986). A poor grade on an essay might produce self-blame and a feeling of failure in one person, the determination to try harder in another, and the conviction that the instructor misgraded the essay in a third. The precise interpretation determines the way a person feels about the event and how he or she will behave in the future. For example, Aaron Beck (Beck et al., 1979) has suggested that depression may develop when a person comes to see life as hopeless because he or she consistently exaggerates disappointments, overgeneralizes criticisms, and recalls only the unpleasant aspects of events.

The Humanistic-Existential Perspective

Another psychogenic approach to psychological disorder is the humanistic-existential perspective, a global category consisting of humanistic and existential theories. We saw in Chapter 17 that humanistic personality theorists, among them Abraham Maslow and Carl Rogers, emphasize the potential of human beings for growth and self-actualization. Existential theorists such as Rollo May and R.D. Laing focus on *being-in-the-world* (unity between human consciousness and the world), *authenticity* (acceptance of the full range of one's mental experience), and *becoming* (the dynamic process of day-to-day self-creation). Humanistic and existential theorists share four basic assumptions. First, both approaches stress the uniqueness of each individual. Second, both place great emphasis on human potential. Third, both stress the individual's own perception of events, as opposed to a therapist's interpretation of hidden causes. Finally, both stress the individual's freedom to make choices, a freedom that makes each person responsible for his or her own behavior.

However, the two approaches differ in their views of the roots of abnormal behavior. Humanistic theorists interpret psychological disorders as the result of an incongruence between the self and its goals that people have produced in order to gain the acceptance of others; existential theorists view disorders as the result of the anxiety that arises when people are unable to find meaning in their lives.

Classification of Abnormal Behavior

In their attempts to understand and treat psychopathology, psychologists and psychiatrists have classified abnormality into various categories. The most widely accepted classification is found in the third revised edition of *Diagnostic and Statistic Manual of Mental Disorders*, commonly called *DSM-III-R* (American Psychiatric Association, 1987), which consists of highly detailed descriptions of virtually all known forms of psychological disorders. When diagnosing patients in

Admission to a psychiatric hospital automatically labels one as "mentally ill." A middle-class person with the same symptoms as a lower-class person may avoid both the hospital and the label.

terms of the *DSM-III-R*, clinicians evaluate them on five axes: the problem for which the patient is being diagnosed; any accompanying long-term psychological disorder; any relevant physical problem; current sources of stress; and an overall rating of the patient's current functioning in the areas of work, social relationships, and leisure activities. Although *DSM-III-R* is tied to the medical model, it does not assume that all disorders have a biological cause. Instead, it merely describes the disorders as fully as possible without speculating about causes. Yet despite the widespread acceptance of *DSM-III-R*, disagreement persists over the idea that abnormal behavior can be assessed and categorized.

Advantages of Classification

To treat a disorder, we first must be able to talk about it. The *DSM-III-R* sorts abnormal behavior into various categories, describing each in detail and giving it a label, such as "schizophrenia, paranoid type" or "bipolar disorder." A psychologist or psychiatrist names the patient's problem by attaching the label that most closely describes his or her behavior. If we can describe a person's problem accurately, we have a better chance of predicting the future course of his or her behavior and selecting the appropriate treatment.

A classification system also enables us to advance our knowledge about various disorders. Without it, researchers would have no way of sorting out the vast array of disordered behavior, and any sort of systematic research would be impossible. Agreed-upon labels allow researchers and clinicians to exchange information about research findings and clinical experience.

Criticisms of Psychiatric Classification

Some theorists believe that the use of terminology based on the medical model is a serious error because it labels people as "sick." As we have seen, some critics contend that abnormal behavior is not illness, but a "problem in living" (Szasz, 1961). Yet if we call people "sick" and treat them accordingly, say some social scientists, they are likely to act out that role (Scheff, 1975).

Other critics argue that labeling disordered behavior gives us a false sense of having explained it. If we say that a man is highly suspicious because he is "paranoid," we tend to believe that we understand the cause of his actions. Yet all the label does is to describe a behavior pattern; it says nothing about the cause.

Finally, some critics say that labels stigmatize people. Once the label is attached, personal problems increase: relationships are disrupted, jobs are lost, civil rights are taken away. Someone who accepts the label of "mental patient" may readily adopt the role that goes with it. The label even affects treatment, because it influences the perceptions and expectations of both the patient and the mental health professional.

A provocative experiment in the early 1970s brought the issue of labeling to a head (Rosenhan, 1973). Eight people with no history of psychiatric problems arranged to have themselves admitted to mental hospitals by reporting a single bizarre symptom. They said they heard voices saying things like "empty," "hollow," and "thud." Once admitted, the pseudopatients never again referred to these hallucinated voices. Some of the real patients soon realized that these people were impostors, but members of the hospital staff did not. Indeed, staffers viewed even normal behavior, such as note taking, as symptoms of the pseudopatients' disorder. Within a few weeks, the pseudopatients were released with the diagnosis "schizophrenia in remission." The author of this study concluded that once a person is diagnosed as mentally ill, any subsequent behavior tends to be reinterpreted in that light. Some researchers, however, argued that the hospital staffers *had* acted responsibly (Spitzer, 1976); they knew that except when induced by drugs, hallucinations are a symptom of serious mental disorder. Moreover, the pseudopatients had committed themselves voluntarily, and staff members would assume that "sane" people would not want to be hospitalized. Finally, the extremely short hospital stays testify to staff members' rapid response when the "patients" failed to manifest further symptoms.

Labeling is not the only problem connected with the classification of abnormal behavior. Diagnosis based on the *DSM*—that is, on the medical model—has often proved unreliable, a fact that has led to continual revision of the manual. For example, if the same patient is examined by two different professionals, one may diagnosis the person's behavior as schizophrenic while the other calls it depressive. The third revision of the manual, *DSM-III*, tried to solve this problem by providing a highly specific set of criteria for each disorder—something that had been missing from earlier editions. Some studies (e.g., Helzer et al., 1981) indicated that the revision was fairly successful, but others (e.g., Zimmerman et al., 1986) indicated that substantial inadequacies remained. Diagnostic reliability still seemed especially poor in the area of personality disorders, which involve long-standing habits of maladaptive thought and behavior (Drake and Valliant, 1985). *DSM-III-R*, the latest revision, corrected many of the diagnostic criteria in light of this critical research. As the process of revision continues, the reliability and validity of psychiatric diagnosis should also continue to improve.

DSM-III-R is the most practical system of classification yet devised. It reflects patterns of psychopathology that are found around the world, in extremely isolated cultures as well as in highly industrialized societies (J. Murphy, 1976;

Figure 18.1 An artist's representation of three phobias: (A) fear of heights, called acrophobia; (B) fear of enclosed spaces, called claustrophobia; and (C) fear of dirt, called mysophobia. (After Vassos, 1931.)

Draguns, 1980). As we investigate the various forms of psychological disorder in this chapter, we use the terminology of *DSM-III-R*. This means we eliminate some of the older, widely known diagnostic labels, such as "neurosis." Such terms were dropped from the *DSM* because they implied a psychoanalytic view of causation, and so they were inappropriate for a system that avoided any speculation about the causes of abnormal behavior. Yet many—perhaps most—mental health professionals, no matter what their theoretical background, continue to use the term *neurosis* to indicate milder psychological disorders and *psychosis* (a term retained in *DSM-III-R*) to indicate incapacitating disorders.

DSM-III-R describes hundreds of psychological disorders that afflict humanity—too many to explore in an introductory psychology text. In the rest of this chapter, we describe the major forms of disorder—anxiety disorders, mood disorders, and schizophrenia—plus a few of the less common disorders. The others you will encounter in your abnormal psychology course.

ANXIETY DISORDERS

Almost all of us experience anxiety at one time or another. **Anxiety** is a feeling of dread, apprehension, or fear that is often accompanied by increased heart rate, perspiration, muscle tension, and rapid breathing. Anxiety also affects cognition, throwing us into a state of confusion and making it difficult to think clearly or solve problems.

Mild anxiety is part of life. It motivates us to pay bills, write term papers, drive slowly on foggy mornings, and get medical checkups. We may even become anxious when we are thrust into social situations, make decisions about money, or worry about our cholesterol levels. But such anxieties generally do not interfere with our lives.

For some people, however, anxiety over some situation takes up more and more of their time and attention. It becomes so severe or so persistent that it interferes with family life, social activities, and work. This condition is called an **anxiety disorder**. Anxiety disorders may take the form of a phobia, a panic attack, a generalized anxiety, obsessions, or compulsions. (See the accompanying box regarding two eating disorders that involve anxiety.)

Phobic Disorder

Phobic disorders develop when anxiety is concentrated in the intense, irrational fear of some object or situation (see Figure 18.1). A phobic person goes to great lengths to avoid the feared stimulus. The focus of anxiety may be slightly dangerous (snakes, dogs, elevators, or high places), or it may involve no real danger at all (walking across a footbridge). The difference between a phobic reaction and normal avoidance is one of severity. A normal person may feel apprehensive at the sight of a snake; a person with a snake phobia suffers intense anxiety (pounding heart, sweating, and so on) and rearranges his or her life to avoid snakes. One woman, for example, refused to go into her backyard or basement for fear that she might encounter a snake. Phobias constrict people's behavior and erode self-esteem. Yet they are relatively common: up to 13 percent of the general population has some sort of phobia (Myers et al., 1984).

Panic Disorder

Some people suffer from **panic disorder**, a disorder characterized by panic attacks, which strike from time to time and for no apparent reason. A **panic attack** is a brief period in which the anxiety becomes almost unbearable. In addition to experiencing physical symptoms of intense anxiety, the person feels a sense of

ANXIETY a feeling of dread, apprehension, or fear, accompanied by heightened physiological arousal

ANXIETY DISORDER any disorder in which anxiety becomes so severe that it interferes with daily life

PHOBIC DISORDER an anxiety disorder in which anxiety centers on an intense, irrational fear of some object or situation

PANIC DISORDER a disorder characterized by panic attacks

PANIC ATTACK a brief period of intense, debilitating anxiety

impending, inescapable disaster—that he or she will die, go insane, or commit some horrible act. Because the attacks are unpredictable, many people with panic disorder also develop a phobia called **agoraphobia:** they refuse to leave their homes for fear that an attack will strike while they are "in the open." However, agoraphobia is more often contracted without panic disorder, as when a person so fears some specific occurrence in public, such as loss of bladder control, that he or she cannot bear to leave the house. One percent of the population has both agoraphobia and panic disorder; from 3 to 6 percent have only agoraphobia (Myers et al., 1984).

AGORAPHOBIA   an intense irrational fear of open places

Generalized Anxiety Disorder

When people live under chronic anxiety, worrying unrealistically about two or more unrelated aspects of their lives, they are suffering from **generalized anxiety disorder.** They worry excessively about something dreadful that is about to happen to themselves or to people they care about. For example, they may fear that their child will be injured, their spouse will abandon them, their financial problems will overwhelm them, or they will fail at such simple tasks as shopping and doing the laundry. They may even become anxious about their anxiety, worrying that it will cause them to lose friends, leave school, or go crazy. People with generalized anxiety disorder may also have panic attacks, although the sources of these attacks are different from those of their generalized anxiety.

GENERALIZED ANXIETY DISORDER   a chronic state of diffuse, unfocused anxiety

Obsessive-Compulsive Disorder

A woman spent up to thirteen hours each day washing her hands and scrubbing her house. Before she used a bar of soap, she had to pour bleach over it to make certain it was clean. But she could not pick up the bottle of bleach until she had scrubbed it with cleanser. If she happened to bump the edge of the sink during this

People with a generalized anxiety disorder may feel threatened by environmental stimuli that would not bother other people. Being surrounded by mirrors, for example, may prove so disorienting that a panic attack results.

PSYCHOLOGY TODAY AND TOMORROW

Eating Disorders

The *DSM-III-R* (American Psychiatric Association, 1987) includes a category of disorders that usually first become evident in infancy, childhood, or adolescence. Among the disturbances that commonly afflict young people are the eating disorders known as anorexia nervosa and bulimia nervosa.

The number of American girls who develop eating disorders is increasing, which some psychologists attribute to conflicting cultural demands. At a time when young women are coming to grips with their new bodies and their sexuality, society bombards them on the one hand with advertisements and other inducements to enjoy rich foods and on the other hand with warnings to adhere to an unnaturally slim body ideal (Sorosky, 1986). Girls' self-concepts are so strongly related to their attractiveness (Lerner, Orlos, and Knapp, 1976) that most adolescent girls are dissatisfied with their weight and preoccupied with efforts to reduce it. Such a situation makes girls vulnerable to anorexia nervosa or bulimia.

Anorexia nervosa is a pattern of self-starvation brought about by fanatical dieting. It is most common among affluent, well-educated adolescent girls in developed countries, where the pressure to be slender is especially intense. (Up to 95 percent of anorexics are female.) To be diagnosed as anorexic, a girl must weigh at least 15 percent less than original body weight expected for her age and height; must show an intense fear of gaining weight; must show a disturbance in the way she experiences her body's weight, shape, or size; and must have missed at least three consecutive menstrual periods (the body responds to starvation by halting menstruation) (American Psychiatric Association, 1987, p. 67).

The anorexic girl resembles a skeleton, with protruding ribs, a skull-like head, and clawlike hands. In most cases, she seems to enjoy the loss of each additional pound and denies that she is skinny. Yet she often is so malnourished that she must be hospitalized and forced to eat. Left untreated, anorexia nervosa is an extremely dangerous disorder. The victim may starve herself to death or die from the medical complications of malnutrition.

The anorexic girl exerts rigid control over her eating. By contrast, in *bulimia nervosa* (sometimes called the "binge-purge syndrome") a girl goes through repeated episodes in which her eating is totally out of control. During her periodic food binges, she consumes large quantities of high-calorie foods—several pounds of chocolate, perhaps, or several large pizzas—in the course of an hour or two. In an attempt to manage her weight, the girl may either induce vomiting after each binge or train herself to throw up after each meal. Instead of vomiting, some bulimics use heavy doses of laxatives to induce diarrhea. The dangers of both kinds of purges include damage to the digestive tract and disruption of the body's chemical balance.

Unlike anorexics, bulimics are aware that their binges are abnormal. They are afraid that someday they will be unable to stop their bingeing, and they feel ashamed and depressed after each episode. Like anorexics, most bulimics are well-educated, affluent girls who are terrified of becoming fat. Bulimia is much more prevalent than anorexia and is especially common among college women. Among women under the age of thirty, only one or two out of a hundred are affected, but in special groups, such as women students at private colleges, the rate may rise as high as 10 or even 25 percent (Pyle and Mitchell, 1986).

Social pressure is not the only factor in the development of eating disorders. Some psychodynamic theorists see anorexia nervosa as deliberate starvation in a struggle for identity (Bruch, 1977). In starving herself, the girl is attempting to escape from parents who have never seen her as an individual and so have failed to transmit any notion of competence or self-worth. Other theorists believe that the chain of events that sets off anorexia nervosa is so tangled that it must be seen as the result of a complex interaction of biological, psychological, and social causes, both within the family and in the society at large (Hsu, 1983).

In the case of bulimia, Craig Johnson and Karen Maddi (1986) believe, a somewhat different mix of genes, personality, and family background seems to be involved. Bulimics may have a genetic predisposition toward mood disorders. This vulnerability is heightened by life in a conflicted and disorganized family. The combination leads bulimic girls and women to tend to have high expectations for themselves that are accompanied by low self-esteem and a feeling that they lack control over their lives. The attainment of society's ideal thin body becomes a way to exert control, but the binge-and-purge aspects of bulimia may intensify their emotional instability and further reduce their self-esteem. One out of five bulimics may meet the *DSM-III-R* criteria for major depression.

The irrational urge to wash one's hands repeatedly is a common obsessive-compulsive disorder.

OBSESSIVE-COMPULSIVE DISORDER an anxiety disorder characterized by rituals of orderliness or cleanliness, such as continual handwashing

OBSESSION an involuntary, irrational thought that occurs repeatedly

COMPULSION an action that a person feels compelled to do, even though it is irrational

process, she had to start all over again. Simply washing her hands could turn into a two-hour ritual (Gelman, 1989). Her compulsions were symptoms of an obsessive-compulsive disorder.

People with an **obsessive-compulsive disorder** may suffer from an obsession or a compulsion—or, in most cases, from both. An **obsession** is an involuntary, irrational thought that occurs repeatedly, while a **compulsion** is an action that a person performs uncontrollably again and again, although he or she has no conscious desire to do so. A pathological obsession is so persistent that it interferes markedly with daily life. Severe obsessions often have a violent or sexual quality, such as a desire to burn down the house or to rape a neighbor. Compulsions are generally either checking rituals, such as looking under the bed, or contamination compulsions, such as repeated handwashing (Rachman and Hodgson, 1980). While carrying out the compulsion, a person rarely seems anxious, but if prevented from carrying it out, he or she becomes extremely anxious. Compulsive rituals are often obsessive, as when continual handwashing is caused by a preoccupation with germs. The majority of patients realize that their compulsions are "silly" or "absurd," even as they repeat them (Stern and Cobb, 1978).

Explanations of Anxiety Disorders

Each theoretical perspective has its own explanation of the development of anxiety disorders. Neuroscientific interpretations focus on genes and biochemistry; psychoanalytic interpretations on unacceptable impulses; behavioral interpretations on faulty learning; social cognitive interpretations on perceptions of experience; and humanistic-existential interpretations on a frustrated search for personal meaning.

In the neuroscientific view, panic disorders seem clearly linked to heredity. When one identical twin develops a panic disorder, in 30 percent of the cases the other twin shares the disorder. Yet when one fraternal twin develops a panic disorder, the other twin shows no increased chances of developing it (Torgersen, 1983). On the biochemical level, panic disorders seem related to depression. Both respond to antidepressant drugs, which affect the availability of two neurotransmitters: norephinephrine and serotonin (Hoehn-Saric, 1982). A different abnormality in brain chemistry seems related to the development of generalized anxiety disorders, which may be related to overactivity among some neurons. Generalized anxiety disorders are often relieved by tranquilizers, such as Valium and Librium, which affect the brain by increasing the availability of GABA—a transmitter that keeps neurons from firing (see Chapter 6). Obsessive-compulsive disorders seem linked to low levels of another transmitter, serotonin. Clomipramine, a drug that increases serotonin levels, often relieves obsessions and compulsions (Gelman, 1989).

In the psychoanalytic view, anxiety disorders arise when unacceptable impulses generated by the id threaten to overwhelm the ego and interfere with its functioning. These impulses evoke anxiety because they are usually shameful (such as inappropriate sexual urges) or dangerous (such as murderous urge). In an attempt to push the impulses back into the unconscious, the ego uses defense mechanisms in an increasingly rigid manner. A phobic disorder develops when the ego displaces the fear and hostility onto some "safe" object (snakes, elevators). As long as the person avoids the phobic object, he or she feels no anxiety. A panic disorder results when the threatening impulses move so close to the conscious mind that the ego's desperate attempts to repress them lead to a panic attack; once the ego pushes the impulse back into the unconscious, the attack passes. A generalized anxiety disorder develops when the impulse is repressed, but the anxiety is not. An obsessive-compulsive disorder occurs when the ego defends itself by going to the opposite extreme. If the unacceptable impulse is the urge to play with feces or be generally messy, for example, a person may develop cleanliness rituals.

In the behavioral view, people learn to be anxious. The process is one of avoidance learning, which we explored in Chapter 7. Through conditioning, a person connects the avoidance of some object or situation with the relief of anxiety. For instance, a man might be badly frightened by a ferocious looking dog. The next time he sees a dog, he feels anxious, crosses the street to avoid the animal, and experiences a sense of relief. He begins to avoid dogs, and each time he does so, his feeling of relief reinforces his avoidance. Eventually his fear of dogs develops into a phobia. Obsessive-compulsive rituals may develop in a similar way. Some action (checking under beds or handwashing) reduces a person's anxiety so successfully that it develops into a habit. Even though the ritual consumes several hours each day, its inconvenience is overshadowed by the relief the person feels after completing it.

In the social cognitive view, anxiety disorders are based less on people's past experiences than on their perception of them. Anxiety is caused by the images people conjure up, what they focus on, and what they tell themselves. They may see a vicious pit bull terrier in every playful puppy, a mugging in every stroll down a city street, and a fatal fall each time their child climbs the playground slide. The chances of disaster are blown out of all proportion. In addition, some people develop anxiety disorders through observational learning (see Chapter 7): watching other people react with pain or fear to some object or situation lays the foundation for a phobia or some other anxiety. Many children have picked up irrational fears from watching their parents' reactions to snakes, spiders, mice, or insects. In addition, simply reading or hearing about some distasteful or dangerous situation can initiate a phobia. Air travel phobia, for example, may develop after a person reads newspaper coverage of an airline disaster or watches its aftermath on TV. Here, too, each time the person must travel and decides to drive or take a bus or train, the phobia is strengthened. Many social cognitive theorists believe that memory and expectations play an important role in this development and may be especially potent in engendering panic attacks (Barlow, in press). The racing heart, sweating, and other physiological symptoms of a panic attack become conditioned stimuli for further attacks, so that "fear of fear" can trigger panic. For example, a woman subject to panic attacks, may notice that her heart is pounding or that she has suddenly begun to sweat; this causes her to fear that an attack is beginning, which intensifies her symptoms, which increase her fear, and the spiral reaction leads to a genuine panic attack.

In the humanistic-existential view, anxiety disorders are caused by a kind of frustration—caused by the distance between one's self-concept and one's ideal self. As we saw in Chapter 15, this gap often develops when a hostile, rejecting family and society teach the growing child that he or she falls short of their expectations. According to Carl Rogers and other humanistic clinicians, the anxiety is based on conflict between a negative self-concept and continual efforts to reach the self's potential. In the view of existential clinicians, anxiety arises out of conflict between the true self and the "inauthentic," conforming self adopted to please society. The person who feels guilty for not having fulfilled his or her personal values can develop phobias, panic disorders, or generalized anxiety, while people who see a wide gap between their ideal values and their actual way of life can develop obsessive-compulsive disorders (Frankl, 1962).

SOMATOFORM DISORDERS

Somatoform disorders are characterized by persistent physical (somatic) symptoms that have no physiological cause. Most people think of bodily ailments that are "all in your head" as psychosomatic, but, as we will see in Chapter 20, psychosomatic disorders are psychological problems that manifest themselves in real bodily ailments. Somatoform disorders, on the other hand, involve no actual physiological symptoms. Typical somatoform disorders include hypochondriasis and conversion disorders.

SOMATOFORM DISORDER a disorder that shows physiological (somatic) symptoms without any underlying physiological malfunction

Hypochondriasis

A person with **hypochondriasis** is preoccupied with bodily symptoms that might indicate serious illness. Although hypochondriacs are actually in good health, they live with the conviction that they harbor cancer, heart disease, diabetes, or some other life-threatening ailment. Hypochondriacs do not imagine their symptoms; rather, they exaggerate minor symptoms and report them as meaningful. Each vagrant twinge or cramp, each headache, each skipped heartbeat is taken as a sign that major disease has struck. Most hypochondriacs change physicians often, searching for someone who will confirm their dire self-diagnoses.

Conversion Disorders

Conversion disorders are more dramatic than hypochondriasis because they involve physical disability: the person becomes paralyzed, blind, or deaf, or loses sensation in some part of the body. Yet there is no known organic basis for the disorder; instead, it seems to express psychological conflict. Although no medical evidence supports these afflictions, the person is not faking. Many "miraculous cures" in which paralyzed patients walk or blind people suddenly see may come about because the original dysfunction was the result of conversion disorder.

Diagnosing conversion disorders is difficult. They tend to be either *under*diagnosed (when physicians do not recognize that the motor or sensory loss they see has no organic basis) or *over*diagnosed (when patients in the early stages of some neurological disorders seem to be suffering from conversion disorder).

Explanations of Somatoform Disorders

Psychoanalytic and behavioral explanations of somatoform disorders differ sharply. In the psychoanalytic view, people with hypochondriasis relieve their anxiety by regressing to the state of a sick child. This not only frees them from unacceptable impulses but also gets them extra attention, support, and "babying" from family, friends, and medical personnel. Those with conversion disorder manage to block out both the awareness and the expression of a forbidden impulse by incapacitating some critical part of their body. A person who fears expressing a murderous anger, for example, might become paralyzed. Or a person who feels guilt about urges to masturbate might develop "glove anesthesia," in which the hand becomes completely numb below the wrist (see Figure 18.2).

Behavioral theorists would interpret any somatoform disorder as the result of a person's adopting some social role ("diabetic," "paraplegic") that brings them some sort of reinforcement, such as the attention and support described in the psychoanalytic account. A concert violinist who doubts his skill might develop a cramp in his bowing arm, which ends the possibility of performing but keeps his self-esteem intact and spares him the negative consequence of a poor performance.

DISSOCIATIVE DISORDERS

Dissociative disorders involve the dissociation, or splitting off, of personality components that are normally integrated. Amnesia, fugue, and multiple personality are varieties of dissociative disorders.

Amnesia, Fugue, and Multiple Personality

Amnesia is the partial or total loss of memory due to psychological or organic factors, as we saw in Chapter 8. Psychogenic amnesia differs from organic amne-

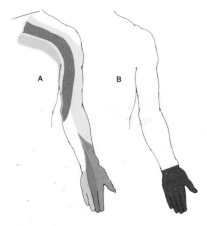

Figure 18.2 A patient who complained to a doctor that his right hand had become numb might be diagnosed either as suffering from damage to the nervous system or as a neurotic suffering from hysteria, depending on the exact pattern of his numbness. The skin areas served by different nerves in the arm are shown in A. The "glove anesthesia" shown in B could not result from damage to these nerves.

HYPOCHONDRIASIS a preoccupation with bodily symptoms that might involve physical illness

CONVERSION DISORDER a physical dysfunction with no organic basis

DISSOCIATIVE DISORDER the dissociation, or splitting off, of aspects of memory and identity, which are usually integrated

AMNESIA the partial or total loss of memory of past experiences

sia in several ways. It appears suddenly, often following severe stress, and disappears just as suddenly. It is selective, meaning that the person forgets everything connected with the particular theme or stressful event. In many cases, the forgotten material can be recovered under hypnosis.

Related to amnesia is another dissociative disorder called **fugue** (from the Latin for "flight"). People in a fugue state forget their identities and flee from their homes and families. They may be absent for days, months, or years; and they often take up a totally new life. If they later regain their memory, they remember nothing of what happened while they were in the fugue state.

A rare and extreme form of dissociation is **multiple personality,** a division of the person's identity into two or more distinct personalities, each clearly defined and different from the others. Two actual cases of multiple personality, *The Three Faces of Eve* (Thigpen and Cleckley, 1957) and *Sybil* (Schreiber, 1974), have been widely publicized in films and books. In most instances, the personalities take extreme forms: one may be an inhibited conformist, while the other is rebellious and outgoing, even sexually promiscuous or violent.

The contrast between personalities is apparent in the case of Sue Ellen Wade, age thirty-seven, who said "another self" called Ellen had forced her to attempt suicide on several occasions. Ellen periodically "took over" and spent afternoons in motel rooms with strangers, even flaunting her promiscuity in front of her husband. Sue, the "real self," was a conscientious mother, homemaker, and part-time secretary. Sue was physically abused at the orphanage where she grew up, and she created Ellen, an imaginary friend who could resist the abuse but who soon became an alternative personality (Spitzer et al., 1983). Like Sue Ellen, the majority of people who have multiple personalities recall a childhood marred by severe physical abuse and sexual molestation (Greaves, 1980).

Since multiple personality is sometimes called "split personality," it is often erroneously confused with schizophrenia. The confusion arises because the word "schizophrenia" comes from the Greek for "to split" and "mind." As we will see, schizophrenia refers to a separation of ideas, emotions, and perceptions from reality—not to the development of separate personalities.

FUGUE a dissociative disorder that involves flight from the home as well as flight from the self

MULTIPLE PERSONALITY a rare dissociative disorder in which a person's identity splits into two or more distinct personalities

Explanations of Dissociative Disorders

In the case of dissociative disorders, the psychoanalytic, behavioral, and humanistic-existential explanations are somewhat compatible. In the psychoanalytic interpretation, dissociative disorders develop when unacceptable impulses are repressed. People with amnesia protect their fragile egos by wiping all awareness of the forbidden impulse from memory. People in fugue or with multiple personalities act out the unconscious episode (directly or symbolically) while in the dissociated state. In the behavioral interpretation, dissociative disorders develop in the same way as somatoform disorders: the person adopts a social role that has reinforcing consequences. In the humanistic-existential interpretation, dissociative disorders are a defense against anxiety arising from the conflict between aspirations and a negative self-concept.

MOOD DISORDERS

All of us experience changes in mood from time to time, but for some people the fluctuations become so exaggerated that they interrupt normal functioning and cause severe and prolonged distress. Such intense mood swings are known as **mood disorders,** but because they involve disturbances of emotion, or affect, they are sometimes called *affective disorders.*

MOOD DISORDER a mood swing so intense that it disrupts normal functioning and causes severe and prolonged distress

Major depression leaves a person feeling unable to do tasks as simple as washing dishes or clearing a table.

MAJOR DEPRESSION   one or more intense episodes of depression without any intervening episode of joy

Major Depression

Sometimes we feel sad, disappointed, or guilty, and lose interest in food or sex. Such feelings are common after an unpleasant event: the loss of a job, an argument with a friend, or a poor mark on an exam. Occasionally the upset comes for no apparent reason, as if we just got up on the wrong side of the bed. Although these symptoms of normal depression are simply intensified in the sort of depression found among college students, the depression that brings most adults to a therapist is quite different, for it goes far beyond mood to involve most aspects of functioning (Gotlib, 1984). In most cases, the course of abnormal depression, known as **major depression,** involves a gradual onset over weeks or months, lasts for several months, then ends as it began—slowly and gradually. While in a major depressive episode, a person's mood, motivation, thought, and physical and motor functioning show radical changes (see Table 18.1).

Many of the typical symptoms of depression were apparent in Paula Stansky, a fifty-seven-year-old widow. Stansky, a cheerful, energetic woman who was meticulous about her housework, gradually found herself becoming easily fatigued. She lost her cheerfulness and no longer cared how her house looked. Within a few weeks, she had stopped going to church and canceled her usual social activities. When she stopped bathing, changing her clothes, and eating, her grown children took her to a hospital. During the admission procedures, she cried periodically and was agitated, wringing her hands, rolling her head toward the ceiling, and rocking in her chair. Yet she could only shake her head when the interviewer asked what she was feeling or thinking about (Spitzer et al., 1983).

Severe depression is a major problem in the United States, with from 1 to 2 percent of men and from 3 to 4.6 percent of women diagnosed as having major depression (Myers et al., 1984). At some time in their lives, between 8 and 12 percent of men and between 20 and 26 percent of women will have at least one major depressive episode (Boyd and Weissman, 1981). Depression is the most frequent problem in outpatient psychiatric clinics, where it accounts for one-third of all patients (Woodruff et al., 1975).

BIPOLAR DISORDER   a mood disorder characterized by extreme moods of alternating depression and euphoria

Bipolar Disorder

Some patients who have periodic depressive episodes also have periods of intense, unrealistic elation, a combination that characterizes **bipolar disorder,** commonly called *manic-depressive illness*. The first sign of bipolar disorder is almost always a manic episode of intense euphoria, excitement, and activity (see Table 18.2), which is followed by a depressive episode. The manic episode tends to begin suddenly, to last from several days to several months, and then to end as abruptly as it began. The addition of manic episodes is not the only characteristic that differentiates bipolar disorder from major depression; the two syndromes differ in many respects (Depue and Monroe, 1978; Hirschfeld and Cross, 1982). For example, bipolar disorder is much less common than depression and more likely to occur in someone who has an intimate relationship, and the episodes tend to be briefer.

DYSTHYMIA   a mood disorder characterized by mild, persistent depression

Dysthymia and Cyclothymia

Not everyone who has depressed periods suffers from major depression, and not everyone who experiences mood swings has bipolar disorder. Some people have chronic mild mood disturbances that affect functioning but lead to only moderate impairment. There are two types of this impairment. Mild, persistent depression is known as **dysthymia.** A person with dysthymia tends to be morose, introverted, overly conscientious, and incapable of having fun (Akiskal, 1983). Although dysthymics are troubled by some of the same symptoms found in major depression, their symptoms are much less severe and fewer in number. People

TABLE 18.1 Symptoms of Major Depression

SYMPTOM	DESCRIPTION
Depressed mood	Utter despair, loneliness, or boredom
Feelings of worthlessness or guilt	Belief in lack of valued attributes: intelligence, attractiveness, health, social skills; exaggerated self-blame or guilt
Reduced motivation	No pleasure or interest in usual activities (work, family, friends, leisure activities, sex)
Disturbed appetite and sleep	Cannot sleep, shows no interest in food—or sleeps and eats to excess
Psychomotor retardation or agitation	Low energy, with slow, deliberate movements; or agitation (pacing, fidgeting, and moaning)
Reduced energy	Feels exhausted all the time
Thought difficulties	Indecisive; has trouble thinking, concentrating, remembering
Recurrent thoughts of death or suicide	May attempt suicide

who never go longer than a few months without a phase of moderately manic or depressive behavior have **cyclothymia.** Like dysthymia, cyclothymia is more persistent and less severe than bipolar disorder. Both patterns are likely to persist unchanged over a lifetime, but in a few cases, dysthymia becomes major depression and cyclothymia becomes bipolar disorder (Depue et al., 1981; Akiskal et al., 1983).

CYCLOTHYMIA a mood disorder characterized by moderate moods of alternating depression and euphoria

Explanations of Mood Disorders

Most modern psychoanalytic therapists believe that depression arises in people who have experienced some very early loss, disappointment, or inadequacy. When they later suffer another loss (death, divorce, or being passed over for promotion), they are plunged back into this early trauma. They also feel abandoned by their loved ones and incapable of controlling their lives. Helpless and hopeless, they withdraw.

Social cognitive therapists believe that the key to depression may be learned helplessness: the conviction, which develops after repeated failure, that one lacks any control over the environment. When people find that their actions never seem to bring them pleasure or to end their pain, they cease trying to make any adaptive responses—even when the situation makes it relatively easy for them to do so (Seligman, 1975). As we will see in Chapter 20, learned helplessness has also been connected with the inability to adjust to stressful events. It fosters major depression when people give up all hope and decide that their ineffectiveness is permanent, a basic aspect of their own personality, affecting most or all areas of their lives (Peterson and Seligman, 1984; Abramson, Metalsky, and Alloy, 1989). This view stresses the cognitive aspects of depression—not what happens to people, but how they *interpret* what happens to them. Research indicates that depressed patients do tend to explain unpleasant events as a result of their own weaknesses or inabilities (Raps et al., 1982). Those who explain events in this way also tend to become depressed when exposed to stress (Alloy et al., 1990).

Some researchers are convinced that cognition is even more central in the development of depression than learned helplessness studies would indicate. Aaron Beck (1967; 1976) believes that the fundamental cause of depression is the tendency to see oneself as a loser. Depressed people see the self, the world, and the future as unpromising and bleak. No matter what the situation, they interpret it negatively. Yet their pessimism may sometimes be realistic. When evaluating social interactions, depressed people are more accurate than nondepressed people in assessing the impressions they make on others (Lewinsohn et al., 1980). Apparently, depressed people see themselves more or less as other people see them, whereas people who are not depressed exaggerate their own good qualities. Per-

TABLE 18.2 Symptoms of Manic Episodes	
SYMPTOM	**DESCRIPTION**
Elevated, expansive, or irritable mood	Agitation mixed with irritability
Hyperactivity	Restlessness and increased physical activity
Sleeplessness	Sleeps only 2 or 3 hours a night, yet has high energy levels
Talkativeness	Loud, rapid, and continual speech
Flight of ideas	Racing thoughts
Distractibility	Abrupt switches of attention from one topic to another
Inflated self-esteem	Images of self as attractive, important, and powerful
Reckless behavior	Shopping sprees, reckless driving, careless business investments, sexual adventures, and the like

haps optimism is adaptive. As we saw in Chapter 13, our self-esteem may depend on an unrealistically positive self-image and an unwarranted optimism about the future (Taylor and Brown, 1988).

In the neuroscientific view, genes are implicated in some mood disorders, especially in bipolar disorder. When one identical twin develops bipolar disorder, the other twin has an 80 percent chance of developing the disturbance; among fraternal twins, the chance of the second twin having bipolar disorder drops to 20 percent (Kolata, 1986). Researchers have even discovered the segment on chromosome 11 where a critical gene is located (Egeland et al., 1987).

The genetic linkage is not as clear in the case of major depression: a second identical twin has a 40 percent chance of developing the disorder, and a fraternal twin has only an 11 percent chance (Allen, 1976). Yet heredity does play some role in major depression. Among the biological and adoptive parents and siblings of people with major depression, eight times as many biological relatives as adoptive relatives suffered from major depression—and fifteen times as many biological relatives had committed suicide (Wender et al., 1986). (The accompanying box discusses the role of depression and other factors in suicide among adolescents.)

Researchers have found two possible ways in which heredity might influence depression. The disorder seems linked to hormonal imbalance or neurotransmitter imbalance or both, probably as a result of an inherited biochemical malfunctioning. Depressed patients often have abnormal levels of certain hormones; in fact, depression in some patients can be relieved by reducing thyroid activity and in others by giving estrogen, a sex hormone (Prange et al., 1977). And neurotransmitters apparently play a critical role in depression. According to the **catecholamine hypothesis,** when brain levels of the neurotransmitter norepinephrine (one of the catecholamines) climb, a person becomes manic; when they fall, the person becomes depressed (Schildkraut, 1965). Yet the neurotransmitter connection is more complicated than this hypothesis suggests. Later research indicates that a deficiency of another transmitter, serotonin, must exist before norepinephrine levels affect mood so drastically, and that thyroid hormones are also involved (Whybrow and Prange, 1981). Despite this complex interaction, depression can often be treated with tricyclic antidepressants, which increase norepinephrine levels and seem gradually to recalibrate the complicated cycle involving serotonin, norepinephrine, and thyroid activity (Whybrow et al., 1984).

Convincing as the neuroscientific evidence is, other researchers have found that cognitive therapy, which aims at changing people's thoughts about themselves, is just as effective as tricyclics in lifting depression (Hollon and Beck, 1986), and that a combination of the two is the most effective treatment. In fact, other forms of psychotherapy are also effective with depression. Depression is probably the result of a complex interaction among many factors, including biology, thoughts, stress, and interpersonal support.

CATECHOLAMINE HYPOTHESIS the view that depression is caused by low brain levels of norepinephrine and mania by high levels

PSYCHOLOGY TODAY AND TOMORROW

Why Do Adolescents Kill Themselves?

Suicide, once an uncommon cause of death among the young, is now the second leading cause of death among adolescents—exceeded only by accidents. Most adolescents who kill themselves are boys. Girls make three times as many attempts at suicide as boys, but boys are three times as likely to succeed in their attempts (Weiner, 1980). There are several reasons for this difference. First, boys use more lethal means. The overwhelming majority shoot themselves, while girls are most likely to use poison. Second, girls usually want to be rescued; their attempt is meant as a message. In contrast, boys who try suicide are truly determined to destroy themselves. Third, girls have better social support systems than boys. Girls tend to have more intimate friendships and to exchange confidences, while boys regard their friends as companions in fun. So boys often have no one to turn to when they are troubled.

Adolescents who are likely to make a suicide attempt tend to have similar family backgrounds. Often they come from broken homes (Garfinkel, Froeser, and Hood, 1982). Even when the family is intact, either it is filled with strife or the youngster feels rejected by one or both parents (Corder, Page, and Corder, 1974). Those who try to kill themselves are more likely than controls to have both a personal and family history of alcohol and drug abuse (Garfinkel et al., 1982). A family history of suicide is especially ominous. In one study, one-third of the adolescents who killed themselves had a relative who had committed or attempted suicide (Holden, 1986). Perhaps when a family member has broken the taboo against suicide, it makes suicide appear to be a reasonable option in time of trouble.

Sometimes a wave of suicides seems to sweep through the young people in a community. For example, in Omaha, Nebraska, three adolescents committed suicide within five days, and another four made unsuccessful attempts (Leo, 1986). The dead youths knew one another only casually. The first suicide probably broke the community taboo against such acts, making it possible for other adolescents to consider suicide as a possible solution to their problems.

The adolescent who solves his or her problems with a gun, a rope, or an overdose of barbiturates is not a "normal" child who comes home one day and decides to commit suicide. After matching successful suicide victims to controls, psychiatrist Mohammad Shafii and his colleagues (1985) interviewed the adolescents' families, friends, and teachers. They found that most of the suicides recently had undergone some sort of stress, tended to abuse alcohol or drugs (70 percent), had trouble with the law or had shown some other antisocial behavior (70 percent), were depressed (76 percent), and were rigid perfectionists who tended to isolate themselves from others (65 percent).

Many researchers have noted a link between depression and suicide (Barraclough et al., 1969; Weiner, 1980). Both depressed adolescents and those who kill themselves are low in self-esteem; they have failed to live up to their own impossibly high standards; they have turned the anger they feel toward others against themselves; they feel alone, helpless, and vulnerable; and they are afraid of being alone and abandoned. The particular events that destroy self-esteem or signify failure vary from one youth to the next. Often the triggering incident is the breakup of a relationship. However, any experience that produces shame, guilt, and humiliation can precipitate a suicide attempt. Being arrested, beaten up, or raped often precedes suicide. The incident does not have to be violent, however. An adolescent may feel that life is not worth living after being refused admission to a college.

SCHIZOPHRENIA

Schizophrenia is a group of disorders characterized by thought disturbance and often accompanied by delusions, hallucinations, attention deficits, and bizarre motor activity. In the example that opened this chapter, we met a man with schizophrenia whose contact with reality was radically impaired. His inability to meet even the ordinary demands of life demonstrates that schizophrenia is a **psychotic disorder,** one that is characterized by a generalized failure to function adaptively.

SCHIZOPHRENIA a group of disorders characterized by disorganized thought, perception, and emotion, and by bizarre behavior

PSYCHOTIC DISORDER a disorder characterized by a generalized failure to function in all areas of life

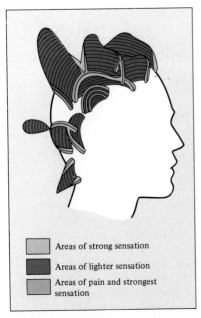

▨	Areas of strong sensation
▨	Areas of lighter sensation
▨	Areas of pain and strongest sensation

Figure 18.3 A schizophrenic woman's drawing of her own tactile hallucinations, showing the areas of sensation and their associated strengths. (After Pfeifer, 1970.)

Schizophrenia is more common than most of us realize. Between 1 and 2 percent of people in the United States have had or will have at least one schizophrenic episode (Robins et al., 1984).

During a lucid interval, a young woman tried to describe what it is like to be schizophrenic:

The most wearing aspect of schizophrenia is the fierce battle that goes on inside my head in which conflicts become irresolvable. I am so ambivalent that my mind can divide on a subject and those parts subdivide over and over until my mind feels like it is in pieces, and I am totally disorganized. At other times, I feel like I am trapped inside my head, banging against its walls, trying desperately to escape while my lips can utter only nonsense. . . .

Recently, my mind has played tricks on me, creating The People inside my head who sometimes come out to haunt me and torment me. They surround me in rooms, hide behind trees and under the snow outside. They taunt me and scream at me and devise plans to break my spirit. The voices come and go, but The People are always there, always real.

. . . My fears are so intense that before I do most things I must pass through a "wall of terror" that stands between myself and my goal. Leaving the house, talking to someone, or taking a walk can create panic, simply because I do not feel like part of the world. It is a foreign place to me. Since my childhood I have felt like an outsider looking in. (The New York Times, 1986)

Types of Schizophrenia

Schizophrenia manifests itself in different ways. Since no one person shows all the symptoms described in the following section, clinicians have sorted the disorder into five major subtypes described in Table 18.3. The divisions, which are based on the predominant symptoms displayed, make it possible for researchers to study groups of patients with similar symptoms. Only this approach offers hope of discovering whether and how the causes of different symptoms differ, and whether different kinds of schizophrenia respond best to different treatments. Researchers have suggested that patients' dominant symptoms may identify those with a good chance of recovery (Strauss, Carpenter, and Bartko, 1974; Andreasen and Olsen, 1982). Generally, patients with predominantly positive symptoms (those involving the presence of something—delusions or hallucinations, for example) are more likely to improve than are those with predominantly negative symptoms (those involving the absence of something—lack of affect, speech, or emotional response). Patients with the latter pattern of symptoms are likely to have experienced a long, slow slide into schizophrenia over several years, and they often develop the disorder in its most severe form. Researchers have also discovered that men are more likely to develop this pattern than are women (Lewine, 1981). Not only are men more likely to be seriously affected, but they also tend to develop the disorder earlier—before the age of twenty-five. This distinction has led some researchers to speculate that there may be only two kinds of schizophrenia, with the variety marked by positive symptoms more closely linked with biochemical abnormalities and thus more responsive to medication than the kind marked by negative symptoms (Haracz, 1982).

The catatonic stupor, in which the person remains immobile and unresponsive for long periods, is a common symptom of schizophrenia.

Symptoms of Schizophrenia

No schizophrenic displays all the symptoms of schizophrenia at all times, and some schizophrenics may display only some of the symptoms on occasion (see Figure 18.3). Although the schizophrenic person generally displays a variety of abnormalities, thought disorders are often the most apparent symptom.

TABLE 18.3   Five Types of Schizophrenia

TYPE	DESCRIPTION
Disorganized (hebephrenic) schizophrenia	Individuals live in private worlds dominated by hallucination, delusions, and fantasy. Behavior is almost completely unpredictable, and speech may be unintelligible. Most severe disintegration of personality.
Catatonic schizophrenia	Individuals show either excessive, sometimes violent, motor activity or a mute, unmoving, stuporous state. Some catatonic schizophrenics alternate between these two extremes, but often one or the other behavior pattern predominates.
Paranoid schizophrenia	Individuals have delusions of persecution, grandeur, or both. Paranoid schizophrenics trust no one and are constantly watchful, convinced that others are plotting against them. May seek to retaliate against supposed tormentors.
Undifferentiated schizophrenia	Individuals are schizophrenic but do not meet the above criteria, or else they show symptoms of several subtypes.
Residual schizophrenia	Individuals are not in an active phase of schizophrenia, but show residual symptoms.

Disorders of Thought

A schizophrenic's thought may be disordered in form or in content.

PROBLEMS WITH THE FORM OF THOUGHT   In some schizophrenics, particularly those labeled "disorganized," there is a split among various ideas or between ideas and emotions. Instead of linking concepts and symbols to establish logical connections between ideas, they jump from one mental track to another, so that their speech often becomes incoherent. Concepts, ideas, and symbols may be thrown together merely because of their sounds. Such a series of rhyming or similar-sounding words is called a **clang association.** Besides disrupting logical connections between their words, schizophrenic patients sometimes repeat the same word or phrase over and over, seemingly unable to move their thoughts onward—a symptom known as **perseveration.** More often, their speech shows **loosening of associations,** in which each sentence is generated from some mental stimulus in the previous sentence and wanders further from the central idea. At times there is no logical link between successive words or phrases:

> It's all over for a squab true tray and there ain't no music, there ain't no nothing besides my mother and my father who stand alone upon on the Isle of Capri where there is no ice, there is no nothing but changers, changers, changers. That comes like in first and last names, so that thing does. Well, it's my suitcase, sir. I've got to travel all the time to keep my energy alive (Hagen, unpublished case example).

PROBLEMS WITH THE CONTENT OF THOUGHT   The dissociation of concepts frequently produces **delusions,** irrational beliefs that are maintained despite overwhelming evidence that they have no basis in reality. Delusions take several forms. Some are delusions of grandeur, in which a person believes that she or he is some famous person like Martha Washington or Jesus Christ. Some are delusions of persecution, in which a person believes that others, perhaps extraterrestrial beings or secret agents, are plotting against her or him. Some are delusions of sin and guilt, in which the person believes that he or she has committed some terrible deed or brought evil into the world. Some are delusions of control, in which the person either exaggerates his or her control over events and people or else feels under the power of other people or mysterious forces. Finally, one of the most common delusions among schizophrenics is the delusion that their thoughts are being tampered with. They may feel that their thoughts are broadcast (heard by others), withdrawn (stolen by others), or inserted in their minds by others.

CLANG ASSOCIATION   an illogical speech pattern characteristic of schizophrenics, in which words are used together simply because they rhyme or sound similar

PERSEVERATION   the tendency for schizophrenic speech to dwell on the primary association to a given stimulus

LOOSENING OF ASSOCIATIONS the tendency for schizophrenic speech to lose the logical thread so that each sentence is generated by associations to some word in the previous sentence

DELUSION   an irrational belief that is maintained despite overwhelming evidence that it has no basis in reality

Figure 18.4   These paintings were done by a male schizophrenic with paranoid tendencies. Both illustrations are characterized by the consistent symbolism of watchful eyes, grasping hands, and the self as subject matter. In the first painting, which reflects a subdued emotional state, there is a strong emphasis on the eyes, with a figure watching over the shoulder. The torso of the central figure is surrounded by hands, and the figure in the background is reaching out. The second painting, elaborate in composition and vivid in color, reflects a more active emotional state. Again there is an emphasis on the eyes and on the hands, represented by tentacles and claws.

Disorders of Perception

HALLUCINATION a distortion of sensory perceptions

Schizophrenics seem to perceive the world in a distorted fashion. They often report **hallucinations,** or distortions of sensory perception. Auditory hallucinations are most common, and they often take the form of insulting comments or running commentaries on the schizophrenic's behavior. Less common are hallucinations of touch, taste, vision, or odors. These hallucinations differ from the imagery of normal people in two ways: they are spontaneous and apparently uncontrollable, and the schizophrenic perceives them as real.

Disordered perception affects the schizophrenic's world in other ways. Laboratory tests show that schizophrenics have difficulty estimating the size of objects (Strauss, Foureman, and Parwatikar, 1974), time, and the positioning of their own hands and feet. According to one current theory (Maher, 1977; Maher and Maher, 1979), perceptual abnormalities are fundamental in schizophrenia, and they arise because the schizophrenic has lost the ability to direct his or her attention. Flooded with information from all the senses and unable to screen out any part of it, the schizophrenic's mental organization short-circuits. The sensory overload leads to altered perceptions, peculiar thought associations, bizarre speech, inappropriate emotions, and strange behavior patterns.

Other Symptoms

Disordered functioning extends to all aspects of the schizophrenic's behavior. Thus, schizophrenics show disorders of mood. Their emotional responses are often inappropriate to the situation (they may weep at a joke) or completely absent. When emotional responses disappear (a condition called *blunted* or *flattened affect*), the schizophrenic's face remains immobile and the voice becomes a monotone.

Disorders of motor behavior are also common. Schizophrenics may perform repetitive, inappropriate acts, such as slapping their leg for several hours, or they may cease all physical activity. When this happens, the patient is said to be in a *catatonic stupor*, remaining in one position for hours at a time and responding to nothing.

Finally, although many schizophrenics function relatively well much of the time, others often withdraw from all involvement in the world's activity, becoming preoccupied with their own thoughts (see Figure 18.4). They may act as if other people did not exist. These schizophrenics seem to live in a world of their own.

Explanations of Schizophrenia

Over the past decade, psychoanalytic, behavioral, and humanistic-existential views of schizophrenia have received much less attention than neuroscientific views. Although some elements of these views may well be incorporated into the development of the disorder, it has become increasingly clear that unless a person has a genetic or biochemical predisposition, there is little chance that he or she will become schizophrenic.

In the traditional psychoanalytic view, the schizophrenic's ego is so weak that it cannot defend itself against the impulses of the id. Overwhelmed by anxiety, the patient regresses to the stage of infancy, before the ego emerged. Later psychoanalysts traced schizophrenia to a damaging mother–child relationship, in which hostile, stressful, or contradictory early interactions led the child to withdraw gradually from other people (Sullivan, 1962). For example, children who are continually involved in contradictory exchanges, as when the child says, "I'm scared," and the mother replies, "No, you're not. You're just surprised," may have difficulty in testing reality (Sullivan, 1953). In this view, the disorder finally appears when challenging social demand lead to overwhelming anxiety, and the patient withdraws completely.

In the traditional behavioral view, schizophrenics are people who have never learned to respond to social stimuli (Ullmann and Krasner, 1975). Paying no attention to such stimuli, they respond in a bizarre fashion to other stimuli, which leads to rejection by other people. This heightens their feelings of alienation and the strangeness of their behavior. If their odd behavior is then consistently rewarded with attention, sympathy, and release from responsibility, their idiosyncratic responses become habitual, and the disorder is established.

In the traditional humanistic-existential view, schizophrenics are people who have rejected the alienated, false mind set regarded as normal in industrial societies and have ceased to suppress their feelings (Laing, 1967). Schizophrenia is a retreat into the self that represents a search for an authentic identity.

Some nonpsychoanalytic theorists have also proposed that the origin of schizophrenia can be found in the family. In this view, a hostile, aggressive family atmosphere and garbled patterns of communication between parents and child foster the disorder. In one study, incoherent communication by parents predicted whether their adolescent children would be diagnosed as schizophrenic five years later (Doane et al., 1981). Communication patterns within the families of schizophrenics do seem to be blurred, muddled, vague, confused, fragmented, or incomplete (Hassan, 1974; Wynne et al., 1975; Lewis et al., 1981). In an example of contradictory communication, a young man who was nearly ready for release from the hospital was visited by his mother:

> He was glad to see her and impulsively put his arms around her shoulders, whereupon she stiffened. He withdrew his arm and she asked, "Don't you love me anymore?" He then blushed, and she said, "Dear, you must not be so easily embarrassed and afraid of your feelings." The patient was able to stay with her only a few minutes more and following her departure he assaulted an aide. (Bateson et al., 1956, p. 251)

Note, however, that instead of being the cause of schizophrenia, deviant communication may be the parents' attempts to make themselves understood by a severely disturbed child (Liem, 1974).

Yet other studies have linked an emotionally charged family atmosphere to relapses among formerly hospitalized schizophrenics. The best predictor of whether patients will be rehospitalized in less than a year is the prevalence of highly critical remarks by family members and verbal indications that the relatives are emotionally overinvolved with the patient (Vaughan et al., 1984).

Schizophrenia also appears to be linked to social class. Several factors may contribute to the fact that schizophrenia is most prevalent among people in lower socioeconomic classes (Hollingshead and Redlich, 1958). First, life in lower socioeconomic classes is full of hardships and stresses that people in the middle and upper classes never encounter. Second, as people develop serious mental dis-

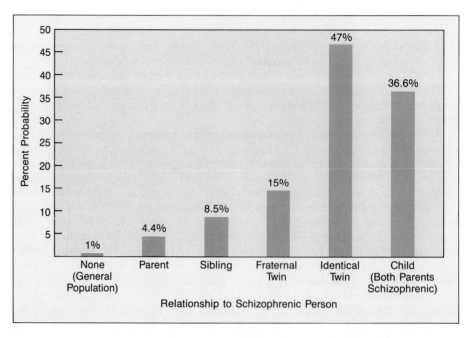

Figure 18.5 The probability that a relative of a schizophrenic will also be schizophrenic varies with the degree of relationship. Note that if a fraternal twin is schizophrenic, the probability is significantly higher than that for any other sibling, but much higher for an identical twin. (After Gottesman, 1978.)

orders, their work performance is impaired, and they drift downward in society. By the time they are diagnosed, they have reached the lower classes. Finally, different socioeconomic classes have different attitudes toward psychological disturbance. People in the lower socioeconomic classes are more resistant to the idea that they are psychologically disturbed, so they are likely to go much longer without treatment and to be diagnosed only after they are unable to function (Gove, 1982).

Neuroscientific studies of schizophrenia have produced mounting evidence that schizophrenia is at least in part genetically transmitted. As Figure 18.5 indicates, when one identical twin has schizophrenia, the other twin has a 47 percent chance of developing the disorder; among fraternal twins, the second twin runs a 15 percent risk of schizophrenia (Gottesman, 1978). A person who has no schizophrenic relatives has only a 1 percent chance of becoming schizophrenic. As we saw in Chapter 2, adoption studies give us the clearest picture of genetic influences. Among forty-seven children who were given up for adoption at birth by their schizophrenic mothers, 16.6 percent developed schizophrenia, but no adopted children in a control group showed signs of the disorder. About half of the high-risk children showed signs of some major psychosocial disability (Heston, 1966). Studies in Denmark, where the central government keeps extensive records on citizens, also have produced impressive evidence of schizophrenia's genetic connection. When researchers compared adopted children of Danish schizophrenics with adoptees whose parents had no psychiatric history, they discovered that 21.9 percent of the schizophrenics' children showed characteristics of schizophrenia, compared with only 6.3 percent of children in the control group (Haier, Rosenthal, and Wender, 1978).

Researchers are not certain how a genetic predisposition to schizophrenia affects the central nervous system. Abnormal brain structure and biochemical abnormalities have been related to the disorder, but no researcher has linked either to genes. Earlier we saw that there may be two major kinds of schizophrenics: those with positive symptoms and those with negative symptoms. CT scans, which produce cross-sectional x-rays of the living brain, show that many schizophrenics with negative symptoms have abnormal brain structures. The ventricles (fluid-filled cavities within the brain) tend to be larger than in normal brains, and schizophrenics' cognitive functioning seems to be impaired (Golden, Rosen, and

Zelazowski, 1980; Reveley, 1985). Magnetic resonance imaging (MRI) indicates that these schizophrenics have extremely small frontal lobes, small cerebrums, and small skulls, indicating retarded growth (Andreasen et al., 1986).

As for biochemical abnormalities, schizophrenics with positive symptoms may have abnormal levels of dopamine, a neurotransmitter. According to the **dopamine hypothesis,** schizophrenia is associated with excess activity in those parts of the brain that use dopamine to transmit neural impulses. The major evidence for this hypothesis comes from research on antipsychotic drugs (phenothiazines and butyrophenones), which effectively reduce the positive symptoms of schizophrenia (Haracz, 1982). The drugs work by blocking the brain's receptor sites for dopamine, which effectively reduces dopamine activity. As we saw in Chapter 6, massive doses of amphetamines (which promote dopamine release and prevent its reuptake) produce a form of psychosis that is superficially similar to schizophrenia. When schizophrenics are given small doses of amphetamines, their symptoms are heightened dramatically (Van Kammen, 1977). Other evidence indicates that the dopamine hypothesis needs modification. Antipsychotic drugs block dopamine activity within a few hours, but schizophrenics who take them improve only gradually over a period of several weeks (Davis, 1978). Excess dopamine activity is apparently involved in schizophrenia, but the relationship is far from simple and not as clear as it first seemed.

If genes, brain structure, and biochemistry are not the whole story, how do we explain the development of schizophrenia? Most researchers have adopted the **diathesis-stress model.** In this view, a person inherits a genetic predisposition, or diathesis (from the Greek for *arrangement* or *disposition*), to schizophrenia, but unless it is combined with severe environmental stress, the disorder will not develop. Given the biological predisposition, a person's vulnerability to schizophrenia depends on the accumulation of stress and on his or her coping skills.

Studies with schizophrenics have produced six major stresses that have been associated with the development of schizophrenia (Mirsky and Duncan, 1986). First, the person at risk has feelings of clumsiness and being "different," which appear to result from impaired attention. Second, because of this impairment, the person becomes increasingly dependent on his or her parents. Third, because of the basic organic impairment, the person does poorly in school and develops inadequate coping skills. Fourth, family interactions are stressful, with high levels of criticism and emotional overinvolvement. Fifth, garbled family communications produce a person who has trouble communicating outside the family and so becomes increasingly isolated. Finally, a parent or other family member is frequently hospitalized.

Whether schizophrenics actually have undergone more stress than other people is uncertain. Perhaps the critical element is their reaction or vulnerability to stress. Some researchers have found that schizophrenics become highly anxious

DOPAMINE HYPOTHESIS the view that schizophrenia is connected to excess activity in brain areas that use the neurotransmitter dopamine to transmit neural impulses

DIATHESIS-STRESS MODEL the view that schizophrenia is caused by a genetic predisposition combined with severe environmental stress

In exploring biological factors in schizophrenia, researchers have found structural differences in the brains of normal and schizophrenic people.

when faced with problems that only annoy other people (Cohen, Nachmani, and Rosenberg, 1974; Serban, 1975).

SOCIAL DISORDERS

In addition to the major mental disorders we have explored so far, several other classes of disturbance warrant a brief mention. Because they often create social complications and involve longstanding habits of thought and behavior, we have grouped personality disorders, sexual disorders, and substance abuse disorders together as social disorders.

Personality Disorders

PERSONALITY DISORDER a social disorder involving inflexible and maladaptive personality traits that impair social or occupational functioning

SOCIOPATH a person who is indifferent to the rights of others, feels no guilt, and does not learn from experience or punishment

ANTISOCIAL PERSONALITY DISORDER see sociopath

When personality traits become so inflexible and maladaptive that they impair a person's social or occupational functioning, they are considered **personality disorders.** Someone with a personality disorder often does not recognize that his or her behavior is at all unusual or disturbed. The person seems unable to grasp the existence of the problem because it pervades the personality and colors all thought and behavior. Because the disturbed behavior began in childhood or adolescence, it is difficult to change. Moreover, since their actions generally cause more discomfort to others than to themselves, most people with personality disorders have little motivation to change. Although *DSM-III-R* describes eleven different personality disorders and proposes two additional categories, only one—the antisocial personality—is included here. There are two reasons for focusing on this particular disorder: it has been the most intensively researched, and clinicians generally agree on its diagnosis.

The **sociopath,** or person with **antisocial personality disorder,** is indifferent to the rights of others. Such people seem to be blind to moral considerations, to lack a conscience, and to be untouched by the wide range of emotions shared by other people. Yet their ability to reason and to perform tasks is unimpaired. In the *DSM-III-R* classification, a sociopath displays at least four of the following qualities: aggressiveness, impulsiveness, recklessness, deceptiveness, involvement in criminal activities, inability to hold down a job, inability to maintain a lasting sexual attachment, failure to act as a responsible parent, and failure to honor financial obligations (American Psychiatric Association, 1987).

Beyond these verifiable kinds of behavior are more subjective characteristics that are emphasized by experienced researchers (e.g., Cleckley, 1976). Most striking is the sociopath's total lack of emotion in social relationships. The sociopath is simply indifferent to others, showing no guilt over a callous murder and no sadness at the death of a parent or friend. When one young sociopath killed a neighborhood child by shooting her in the head, his shallowness of emotions showed clearly:

> He spoke of the incident . . . in a nonchalant, unfeeling way, and was very suave and unnaturally composed in explaining why he was on the ward. He said, "I was showing her the gun. I didn't know it was loaded. She turned her head and it got her in the temple. I told the police I was very sorry. You're to find out if there is anything mentally wrong with me. I thought I'd have to go to reform school. . . . " (Zax and Stricker, 1963, p. 240)

Despite this lack of emotion, sociopaths may be impulsive. They may buy presents for a friend or give money to charity, but there is little feeling in these acts. Although usually intelligent, cunning, clever, and even charming, sociopaths seem to have little insight into their disorder and are slow to learn from experience. No matter how often they face prison terms, social sanctions, expulsion from school, and loss of jobs, they tend to repeat the very behavior patterns that have brought punishment down on them.

TABLE 18.4 Common Sexual Disorders

DISORDER	DESCRIPTION
Fetishism	Sexual gratification that depends on some inanimate object or particular part of a partner's body other than the genitals (such as a foot). Almost entirely a male disorder.
Transvestism	Sexual gratification that depends on dressing in clothing of the other sex. Almost entirely a male disorder.
Transsexualism	A discordant gender identity, in which the person feels he or she is trapped in the body of the other sex.
Exhibitionism	Sexual gratification obtained from the deliberate exposure of the genitals in a public place. Almost entirely a male disorder.
Voyeurism	Sexual gratification obtained through secret observation of another person's sexual activity or genitals. Almost entirely a male disorder.
Pedophilia	Sexual gratification obtained through sexual contacts with children. Almost entirely a male disorder.
Sadism	Sexual gratification obtained by dominating another person or by inflicting physical or psychological pain on him or her.
Masochism	Sexual gratification obtained from pain or from being humiliated by or submitting to another person.

Sexual Disorders

Social attitudes toward sex, as well as common sexual practices, vary across cultures and from one period to another in the same culture. In our own society, standards for defining sexual disorders have changed. But even with today's widespread tolerance of alternative ways of sexual expression, some behavior is still considered "abnormal" by psychologists and psychiatrists. The dividing line between normal and abnormal sexual behavior is not as sharp as most people suppose. Mild forms of many of the common sexual disorders listed in Table 18.4 are not considered abnormal. For example, many people become sexually aroused by the sight of lacy underwear without being labeled fetishists, or by swimming in the nude without being labeled exhibitionists. But someone who is aroused *only* by the sight of underwear or by nude swimming would be considered sexually abnormal. According to *DSM-III-R*, any of the kinds of sexual behavior described in the table becomes abnormal when it is a person's primary means of sexual arousal, when it harms the person or others, when it distresses the person, or when it impairs social or occupational functioning.

Substance Abuse

As long as a person's use of a drug—whether alcohol, marijuana, cocaine, or any other consciousness-altering substance—does not interfere with his social or occupational functioning, the practice does not fall into the category of psychological disorders. But when a person's life becomes devoted to getting and using the drug, the condition fits all the definitions of abnormality discussed at the beginning of this chapter. The accompanying box summarizes the *DSM-III-R*, criteria for the disorder known as **psychoactive substance dependence.**

There are as many varieties of substance abuse as there are drugs; in Chapter 6, we looked at the major substances involved in abuse, but in this chapter we focus on only one—alcohol. The long-term abuse of almost all psychoactive substances can produce psychological disorder.

Alcoholism is a major subcategory of mental disorder and, with nearly 18 million alcoholics and alcohol abusers, it has become the most serious drug problem in the United States (National Institute on Alcohol Abuse, 1987). Alcohol abuse involves many social and personal costs. The social damage of alcohol takes many forms: decreased job productivity due to inefficiency, accidents, absence, and low morale; death, injury, and property damage from alcohol-related auto-

PSYCHOACTIVE SUBSTANCE DEPENDENCE a social disorder whose essential features are impaired control of substance use and continued use of the substance in spite of negative consequences

PSYCHOLOGY TODAY AND TOMORROW

Criteria for Drug Dependence

According to *DSM-III-R* (American Psychiatric Association, 1987, pp.167–168), a person has gone beyond casual drug use and developed the disorder called *psychoactive substance dependence* when he or she displays any three of the following nine behavior patterns.

1. *Preoccupation with the drug:* The person keeps thinking about the moment when he or she can have a drink, smoke a joint, or snort a line of cocaine.

2. *Unintentional overuse:* The person repeatedly finds that he or she has taken more of the drug than intended.

3. *Tolerance:* The person has to take increasingly large doses of the drug to get the desired effect.

4. *Withdrawal:* When the drug level drops, the person shows psychological and physical withdrawal symptoms, which may be as mild as slight anxiety and tremors or as serious as psychosis or death.

5. *Relief substance abuse:* When withdrawal symptoms begin, the person usually takes more of the drug to relieve them.

6. *Persistent desire or efforts to control drug use:* The person tries repeatedly to quit and just as repeatedly relapses.

7. *A pattern of drug-impaired performance in social or occupational circumstances, or when drug use is dangerous:* The person drives after several drinks or smokes marijuana on the job.

8. *The abandonment of important social, occupational, or recreational activities for the sake of drug use:* A person quits a job, breaks off a friendship, or neglects a child when the duties conflict with drug use.

9. *Continued drug use despite serious drug-related problems:* A person who has been fired for drug use or repeatedly arrested for possession continues to use the drug; a person with emphysema continues to smoke.

mobile accidents; and increased medical care for alcoholics. People with ailments linked to alcohol consumption fill approximately half of the occupied hospital beds in the United States (United States Department of Health and Human Services, 1981). The economic costs for these alcohol-related problems was more than $116 billion in 1983 (National Council on Alcoholism, 1986). The personal costs of alcoholism are severe psychological and physiological deterioration; as we saw in Chapter 15, an alcoholic woman's baby may pay a price for her addiction by developing fetal alcohol syndrome.

Alcohol is a depressant, suppressing inhibitions and allowing people to do or say things they ordinarily would not. Its effects on social behavior are apparently due more to expectations than to changes in brain chemistry, a phenomenon we discussed in Chapter 6. Alcoholics build up a physical tolerance for alcohol. To experience the original feeling of well-being or freedom from anxiety, they must increase their intake of alcohol. Often drinkers develop such a physical and psychological dependence on alcohol that they feel normal only when they have been drinking and experience severe, painful withdrawal symptoms if they stop.

Because of alcohol's toxic effects on the body and the malnutrition that often accompanies chronic alcoholism, alcoholics are likely to develop diseases affecting the liver, brain, and nervous system. Prolonged alcoholism leads to degenerative brain disease. A chronic alcoholic whose blood alcohol level drops suddenly may experience delirium tremens, better known as DTs. This infrequent but terrifying reaction is actually a withdrawal symptom. For a period of three to six days, patients with DTs tremble, perspire heavily, become disoriented, and suffer nightmarish hallucinations.

Whether a person develops alcoholism is not simply a matter of heavy drinking; alcoholics also seem to have an inherited sensitivity to alcohol. For example, men whose family history includes alcoholics in more than one generation show stronger cardiac reactions to stress than other men (Finn and Pihl, 1987). Perhaps

Alcoholism is the most widespread drug problem, affecting about one in nine American adults.

such overreactions to stress lead people to use alcohol as a way of reducing the effects of stress. Although studies indicate that alcoholics inherit a tendency to metabolize alcohol rapidly (Schuckit and Rayses, 1979), a Danish study indicates that other factors may be involved (Schulsinger et al., 1986). This study followed the sons of alcoholic fathers from early childhood and found that the boys were restless, impulsive children with a high incidence of reading problems and poor verbal skills. Although none of these men (now in their late twenties) has yet become an alcoholic, it appears that a genetic susceptibility to alcohol may work in a complicated manner, with their way of metabolizing alcohol forming only one strand in the causal web.

Explanations of Social Disorders

Any social disorder makes dealing with the world more difficult, but social disorders differ from other psychological disorders in that they may not cause the afflicted person any special distress. From the neuroscientific point of view, genetic and physiological factors may play a subtle role in fostering the antisocial personality. Danish adoption studies show that sociopaths adopted in infancy are four to five times more likely to have other sociopaths among their biological relatives than among their adoptive relatives (Schulsinger, 1972). What does the sociopath inherit that leads to aggressive, antisocial behavior? Research indicates that people with antisocial personality disorders may be in a permanent state of underarousal (Hare, 1970). This lack of arousal could explain their unshakable poise (they are never anxious), their seeming inability to learn how to avoid punishment (the prospect of punishment arouses no anxiety), and their impulsiveness (a form of thrill-seeking to compensate for underarousal) (Quay, 1965). In fact, when sociopaths are injected with adrenaline, which promotes arousal, their ability improves in experiments involving the avoidance of electric shock. Perhaps such nervous system deficits produce a predisposition toward antisocial personality.

In the psychoanalytic view, personality disorders grow out of a disturbed relationship between mother and infant. As a result, the sociopath, for example, has a disordered ego and a weak superego. Unable to withstand the demands of the id, he or she simply cannot delay gratification. Because of a distorted view of reality, the sociopath fails to respond to the actual demands of a situation.

Behavioral theorists agree that the family is the place to look for the origins of the sociopath's aggressive, antisocial behavior, but they see the disorder as the result of modeling and reinforcement (Bandura, 1977). The growing child imitates the aggressive, antisocial behavior observed in parents, peers, or on the TV screen. Many children may do this, but the child who develops an antisocial personality receives an unusual pattern of reinforcement. The parents pay little attention to their child, except to punish him or her. And when they do reinforce the child, the rewards are arbitrary: there is no apparent connection between the child's behavior and its consequences (Snyder, 1977).

In explaining sexual disorders, the psychoanalytic perspective holds that the major source of difficulty is the Oedipal conflict, which, as we saw in Chapter 17, involves the child's sexual attraction to the parent of the other sex. The castration anxiety or penis envy that attends this conflict may carry over into adulthood and give rise to abnormal sexual behavior. Thus, for example, Freud theorized that fetishism is a displacement of sexual interest to a safer object than a person, who represents the other-sex parent. The behaviorist perspective interprets sexual disorders as resulting from a conditioning process in which early sexual experiences become paired with an unconventional stimulus, which then becomes the source of sexual arousal. Thus, transvestites and transsexuals may have been reinforced in childhood by being given attention and being told that they were "cute" when they dressed up in their mothers' or sisters' clothes (Rekers and Lovaas, 1974). The neuroscientific perspective takes into account the possibility that sexual disorders may be related to neurological problems, since sexual arousal is controlled in part by the central nervous system. However, research on this possibility has been inconclusive (Blumer and Walker, 1975; Rada, 1978).

In explaining alcoholism, the psychoanalytic view holds that alcoholics are seeking oral gratification and want to be cared for by others. They repress their anxiety by drinking to intoxication. Behavioral theorists see alcoholism as a habit maintained by such reinforcement as social approval, enhanced ability to engage in relaxed social activities, and the reduction of tension. At first, alcohol is associated with the reduction of psychological pain; later, when excessive drinking makes the alcoholic feel guilty, alcohol may also be associated with the reduction of guilt. In the humanistic-existential view, the alcoholic drinks to escape the drudgery of a meaningless life. In the neuroscientific view, as we have seen, a genetic predisposition is responsible.

INTEGRATING PERSPECTIVES ON ABNORMALITY

Abnormal psychology is a multifaceted field, in terms of both the wide span of disorders it deals with and the theories about their causes. As we will see in the next chapter, the theory of abnormal behavior adopted by clinicians has a profound effect on the therapy a patient may receive. Some theories focus on biogenic causes and others on psychogenic factors, but physical and mental functioning cannot realistically be separated. Since the mind is a function of the nervous system, psychogenic and biogenic theories of abnormal behavior should be seen as complementary. Abnormal behavior is determined by the interaction of so many factors that it requires multiple approaches.

The diathesis-stress model of schizophrenia, because it focuses on the interaction of factors, may be the most helpful framework for understanding many forms of abnormality. Some people are more vulnerable to a particular disorder because of genetic predisposition, physiological deficits, events in their early development, an unusual learning history, or family and interpersonal circumstances. But not all vulnerable people develop the disorder. Whether the disorder actually develops depends on the level of stress in the person's environment and on his or her social and personal resources.

SUMMARY

Understanding Abnormality

■ Abnormality can be defined as norm violation, as deviation from a statistical average, as personal discomfort, as maladaptive behavior, or as deviation from an ideal personality.

■ Explanations of abnormality are primarily either biogenic—based on physical causes—or psychogenic—based on maladaptive behavior causes.

■ Major perspectives of mental disorders are neuroscientific, psychoanalytic, behavioral, social cognitive, and humanistic-existential.

■ Classifying abnormal behavior allows researchers and clinicians to exchange information about disordered behavior and to describe a person's problems in a way that increases the chances of selecting proper treatment and predicting the course of behavior.

■ Classification can be a disadvantage if it labels people as "sick," makes us think we have explained the behavior, or stigmatizes people and inappropriately influences treatment.

■ *DSM-III-R* is being continually revised, so that the reliability and validity of psychiatric diagnosis should also continue to improve.

Anxiety Disorders

■ Anxiety disorders include phobic disorder, panic disorder, generalized anxiety disorder, and obsessive-compulsive disorder.

■ Neuroscientific interpretations focus on genes in the case of panic disorder and abnormal brain chemistry in the case of generalized anxiety disorder.

■ Psychoanalytic interpretations of anxiety disorders focus on unacceptable impulses.

■ Behavioral interpretations of anxiety disorders focus on faulty learning.

■ Social cognitive interpretations focus on people's perceptions of their past experiences.

■ Humanistic-existential interpretations focus on a frustrated search for personal meaning.

Somatoform Disorders

■ Somatoform disorders include hypochondriasis and conversion disorders.

■ Psychoanalytic interpretations of somatoform disorders see a regression to the state of a sick child in hypochondriacs and an incapacitation that blocks awareness of forbidden impulses in conversion disorder.

■ Behavioral interpretations see both as the result of adopting a reinforcing social role.

Dissociative Disorders

■ Dissociative disorders include amnesia, fugue, and multiple personality.

■ Psychoanalytic, behavioral, and humanistic-existential interpretations of dissociative disorders all focus on repression of unacceptable impulses and the various ways of coping with it.

Mood Disorders

■ Mood disorders include major depression, bipolar depression, dysthymia, and cyclothymia.

■ Depression is the most frequent problem in outpatient psychiatric clinics.

■ In the psychoanalytic interpretation, depression arises from a return to an early trauma after a later painful loss.

■ In the social cognitive interpretation, depression is the result of the lack of hope that follows learned helplessness or a bleakly pessimistic view of self and world.

■ In the neuroscientific interpretation, bipolar disorders are probably caused by an inherited biochemical malfunctioning.

Schizophrenia

■ There are five major subtypes of schizophrenia (a psychotic disorder), although some researchers believe that there are actually only two major varieties of the disorder.

■ Patients with one major variety (predominantly positive symptoms) are more likely to improve than patients with the second variety (predominantly negative symptoms).

■ Schizophrenia is characterized by disordered thought (including delusions), disordered perception (including hallucinations), and bizarre behavior.

■ In the psychoanalytic view, schizophrenics withdraw from the world because of a damaging mother–child relationship.

■ In the behavioral view, schizophrenics ignore social stimuli and have been rewarded for bizarre responses to other stimuli.

■ In the humanistic-existentialist view, schizophrenics have rejected the false "normal" mindset and have retreated into the self.

■ In the neuroscientific view, schizophrenics have inherited a disposition that produces abnormal biochemistry or else have abnormal brain structures.

Social Disorders

■ Social disorders include personality disorders (such as antisocial personality disorder), sexual disorders, and substance abuse.

■ In the neuroscientific view, personality disorders and alcoholism arise from a combination of genetic and physiological factors.

■ In the psychoanalytic view, personality disorders grow out of a disturbed mother–infant relationship, while substance abusers (e.g., alcoholics) want to be cared for by others and drink to repress anxiety.

■ In the behavioral view, personality disorders are the result of modeling and reinforcement, while substance abuse is a habit maintained by reinforcements.

■ In the humanistic-existential view, alcoholics drink to escape the drudgery of a meaningless life.

Integrating Perspectives on Abnormality

■ Psychogenic and biogenic theories of abnormal behavior should be seen as complementary.

KEY TERMS

agoraphobia
amnesia
antisocial personality disorder
anxiety
anxiety disorder
biogenic theory
bipolar disorder
catecholamine hypothesis
clang association
compulsion
conversion disorder
cyclothymia
delusion
diathesis-stress model

dissociative disorder
dopamine hypothesis
dysthymia
fugue
generalized anxiety disorder
hallucination
hypochondriasis
loosening of associations
medical model
major depression
mood disorder
multiple personality
obsession

obsessive-compulsive disorder
panic attack
panic disorder
perseveration
personality disorder
phobic disorder
psychoactive substance dependence
psychogenic theory
psychotic disorder
schizophrenia
social norms
sociopath
somatoform disorder

CONCEPT REVIEW

1. Name and describe the five ways of defining abnormal behavior given in the chapter. What are the advantages and disadvantages of each approach?

2. Summarize the five perspectives on abnormal behavior discussed in the chapter. What kind of research or evidence does each viewpoint accept as support for its explanation?

3. Why has the term "neurosis" been dropped in *DSM-III-R*? What are the criticisms of the classification scheme used in *DSM-III-R*?

4. Define *anxiety* and describe the anxiety disorders presented in the chapter. What distinguishes normal anxiety from anxiety disorder?

5. How would proponents of each of the five perspectives explain a phobia? How would each group explain obsession and compulsion?

6. Describe hypochondriasis and conversion disorders, the two types of somatoform disorders presented in the chapter.

What are the behavioral and psychoanalytic explanations of each disorder?

7. The text indicates that a large number of those suffering from multiple personality experienced severe physical and sexual abuse in childhood. How does this information fit with the various explanations of dissociative disorders?

8. Name and describe each of the major mood disorders. How is depression different from bipolar disorder? Describe the proposed role of neurotransmitters in depression.

9. Describe the types of schizophrenia and their associated symptoms. What forms may be taken by the disorders of thought and perception that are symptoms of schizophrenia?

10. Each perspective on abnormal behavior includes an explanation of the causes of schizophrenia. Describe each of these views.

11. What distinguishes a social disorder from the disorders discussed in the rest of the chapter? Describe these disorders and how they are explained by the various perspectives.

CRITICAL THINKING

1. The *diathesis-stress model* of schizophrenia as emerging from the interaction of disposition and environmental stress offers a way to integrate several views on that disorder. Apply this concept to other psychological disorders. Could this model help to integrate the various perspectives on abnormal behavior?

2. What research methods (see Chapter 2) would be most appropriate in studying psychological disorders? What are the ethical issues that must concern researchers who investigate individual suffering for the purposes of science?

....*Approaches to Treatment*

■ A college sophomore has become obsessed with her weight. She has been losing weight steadily and, although she is of average height, she weighs less than 90 pounds. But she is convinced that she looks fat and eats no more than 500 calories a day.

■ A high school senior seems listless and withdrawn; his grades are slipping and he refuses to take part in family or school activities. He says no one understands or appreciates him and that no one ever will. Lately, he has thought about committing suicide.

■ At the prospect of air travel, a woman becomes apprehensive; she tries to make a required business flight, but her heart pounds and her palms start to sweat as she walks through the boarding gate and down the corridor. As the open plane door comes into view, she hesitates, turns, and flees.

■ A businessman has been abusing alcohol. He drinks during lunch and in the evening and even in the office from a bottle he keeps in his desk. Clients have started complaining about his failure to follow through on requests, and his business has been slipping.

■ A woman sits on a park bench in a large city; although it is a warm day, she wears several layers of clothing. Beside her is a shopping cart filled with her jumbled belongings. She keeps up a rude, running commentary on the passing pedestrians.

Where can these troubled people turn if they want help? Most people with problems talk to acquaintances—a friend, a neighbor, a hairdresser, or a bartender. Some seek out a therapist on their own. Often the decision to ask for professional help is not made by the person in trouble; instead a family member or close friend realizes the problems have gotten out of hand and approaches a therapist or mental health clinic. No matter who makes the initial contact, the decision to consult a therapist is only the first step. Psychotherapy comes in many forms, from formal sessions between therapist and client to assistance from a lay volunteer on a telephone hot line. And psychotherapy is not the only form of treatment for psychological disorders; drugs and psychosurgery are also available.

The sometimes bewildering variety of therapeutic choices raises another question. Should the anorexic college student, the severely depressed high school student, the phobic woman, the alcoholic man, and the homeless woman receive the same kind of therapy, or do different disorders respond best to different treatments? Does the homeless woman actually need therapy, or would a job and a place to live help her more? These are the sorts of issues we deal with in this chapter.

THE NATURE OF PSYCHOTHERAPY

PSYCHOTHERAPY a systematic series of interactions between a person trained to treat psychological problems and another person who is to be helped

PSYCHIATRIST a physician (an M.D.) who specializes in the diagnosis and treatment of psychological disorders

CLINICAL PSYCHOLOGIST a mental health professional who has completed a doctorate (Ph.D. or Psy.D.) in clinical psychology and a one-year clinical internship

PSYCHIATRIC SOCIAL WORKER a mental health professional with a master's degree in social work and specialized training in the treatment of psychological disorders

PSYCHIATRIC NURSE a registered nurse with special training in the treatment of psychological disorders

Psychotherapy refers to a systematic series of interactions between a person trained to treat psychological problems and another person who is to be helped. In contrast to the lay advice given by family and friends, psychotherapy is a relatively formal arrangement with a paid professional. The therapist's professional training varies. A **psychiatrist** is a physician (an M.D.) who specializes in the diagnosis and treatment of mental illness. In most cases, she or he has completed a three-year residency in psychiatry after finishing medical school. A **clinical psychologist** has earned a doctorate (Ph.D. or Psy.D.) in clinical psychology and has completed a one-year clinical internship. A **psychiatric social worker** has earned a master's degree in social work, with specialized training in the form of courses or an internship in psychiatric social work. A **psychiatric nurse** is a registered nurse with special training in the treatment of psychological disorders. A **psychoanalyst** has had special training in the techniques of psychoanalysis and has been psychoanalyzed as part of the training. Most psychoanalysts are psychiatrists, but other professional therapists may also take such training.

The approach adopted by psychotherapists depends on their training, their view of the therapist's role, and their own style. Most adopt one of two basic goals: the first is to help the patient understand his or her motive for behaving in a particular way; the second is to change the patient's behavior directly, paying little or no attention to underlying motives. There are numerous varieties of psychotherapy, each with its own program. In fact, more than 1000 distinct forms have been cataloged (Prochaska, 1984). Some therapists still adhere closely to their particular theoretical perspective, but there has been a growing trend toward eclecticism, with therapists drawing on the insights of a variety of perspectives (Garfield, 1980; 1982). Later we will investigate therapists' increasing inclination to learn from one another.

Some therapists refer to the people they treat as "patients," while others call them "clients." Psychologists disagree as to which is more appropriate. *Patient* comes from the medical model of abnormality, as we saw in Chapter 17; as the analysis of psychological disorders moved away from this model, many clinicians became uncomfortable with the term, seeing it as inextricably linked with the notion that people with psychological disorders were sick. *Client* escapes such connotations, but some clinicians feel that it demeans the therapeutic relationship. It strips the relationship of intimacy and reeks of the purchase of services. After all, stockbrokers and insurance agents have "clients." In recent years, as researchers have discovered the role of genes, biochemistry, and neurological impairment in some disorders and as the neuroscientific perspective has become more influential, the medical model has come to seem more attractive and the term "patient" less offensive.

Whatever therapists call the people who seek their help and whatever the theory behind any particular school of therapy, most varieties of psychotherapy share certain features. All therapists offer support along with a willingness to listen to the client's problems and take them seriously. This support and interest are so important that many clients report some relief from their distress after a single interview with a therapist (Howard et al., 1986). Another important ingredient in most psychotherapies is hope: a person often comes to therapy feeling demoralized; by providing hope, therapists combat such feelings (Frank, 1961; 1983; Bootzin, 1985). As we explore basic therapeutic perspectives, our emphasis will be on their differences. Keep in mind, however, that their similarities are equally important.

PSYCHODYNAMIC THERAPIES

All therapies that focus on a dynamic interplay of conscious and unconscious elements are known as **psychodynamic therapies**. As developed by Freud, psychoanalysis is at once a general theory of personality, a theory of psychopathology, and a form of psychotherapy. But few therapists today adhere to standard Freudian psychoanalysis, so our discussion of the psychoanalytic approach to psychological disorders must be expanded to encompass therapists who follow the broader, psychodynamic tradition.

Freudian Psychoanalysis

Freud's clinical experience led him to conclude that the source of "neurosis" is anxiety that develops when shameful or forbidden impulses threaten to break into consciousness (see Chapter 17). By resorting to defense mechanisms—especially repression—a person can "blot out" unacceptable thoughts or impulses for a while. But these impulses remain buried in the unconscious, provoking anxiety and draining strength from the ego, which expends its energy to keep them subdued. In Freud's view, the proper treatment for anxiety-based disorders is to allow the unacceptable thoughts to emerge into consciousness, where they can be confronted and "worked through." By this means, anxiety is eliminated and psychic energy is liberated for more worthwhile endeavors.

The aim of psychoanalysis is to uncover these long-buried impulses, putting

PSYCHOANALYST a mental health professional with special training in the techniques of psychoanalysis

PSYCHODYNAMIC THERAPY an approach to psychotherapy that focuses on the dynamic interplay of conscious and unconscious elements

the patient in touch with his or her unconscious, where past traumas and child-hood conflicts still reside. Psychoanalysts use many techniques to unlock the doors of memory, but the major tool is *free association*. The patient lies on a couch, or sits in a chair in a relaxing position, to help loosen the restraints on the unconscious. Once relaxed, she or he free-associates, putting into words whatever thoughts come to mind in whatever order, without imposing self-censorship or logical structure and without interruption from the therapist, whose remarks are kept to a minimum and who sits out of the patient's view. This image of couch and analyst has so pervaded the culture that it immediately comes to mind when we think of psychiatry or therapy of any kind. Actually, few therapists today use a couch, and most sit facing the patient.

Therapist and patient also look for clues to the troubling anxiety in dreams, because when a person dreams, the usual restraints on the unconscious are loosened. Because the unconscious is censored even in sleep, forbidden material appears only in symbolic form. Unconscious conflicts (the dream's *latent content*) are disguised by the obvious story line of the dream (its *manifest content*) (see Chapter 17). For instance, if a patient who has just had a baby dreams that she has given birth to two boys and that one has died, she may be symbolically expressing her ambivalent feelings toward her son, whom she both wants and does not want.

RESISTANCE a patient's attempt to block treatment during psychodynamic therapy

The conscious recognition of forbidden thoughts is not pleasant. At this stage in therapy, patients often begin to show signs of **resistance,** or attempts to block treatment. They may pick an argument with the therapist, make jokes, even miss appointments rather than face the unpleasant material. Many discontinue therapy at this point. The therapist's ability to recognize and interpret resistance is crucial to treatment, because it enables the patient to learn to confront and analyze painful conflicts that would otherwise be avoided.

TRANSFERENCE a patient's transfer to the therapist of childhood feelings toward important people in his or her life, particularly the parents

As analysis progresses, the patient may respond to the analyst with strong feelings—sometimes love and at other times hostility. Freud interpreted these emotions as evidence of **transference,** the transfer to him of his patients' childhood feelings toward important people in their lives, particularly their parents. Freud believed that unless this stage, called *transfer neurosis*, developed, therapy would not be effective. Transference is vital to the analytic process because it allows patients to relive their childhood conflicts, with the analyst in the parental role. The process allows a patient to bring out repressed emotions, unsatisfied needs, and misconceptions; with the analyst's help, the patient learns to deal with these feelings realistically.

Psychoanalysis can be effective, but it is a long, expensive process. In a typical therapy, the patient undergoes three to five 1-hour psychoanalytic sessions each week for several years. When treatment is successful, the patient eventually breaks through resistance, confronts unconscious conflicts, and resolves the transference neurosis, thereby eliminating anxiety and self-defeating responses to it.

Other Psychodynamic Therapies

Freud's ideas were challenged almost as soon as he published them. His students Carl Jung and Alfred Adler developed their own theories, as we saw in Chapter 17. Later psychoanalysts also made important revisions in both theory and therapy. One group, whose members included Erik Erikson, formed a loosely knit band called *ego psychologists*. Although they accept a major portion of Freudian theory, ego psychologists reject Freud's assertion that the ego is primarily engaged in finding acceptable ways to satisfy the id's demands. To them, the ego has important functions of its own, such as memory, judgment, perception, and planning. Instead of concentrating therapy on conflicts produced by unacceptable impulses of the id, ego psychologists tend to focus on how the person can use the ego's constructive functions and on how they learn to cope with anxiety. Ego psychologists do work primarily within the Freudian tradition, leading patients to insight through the same techniques of free association, dream interpretation, and analysis of resistance and transference. This adherence to Freudian tradition is not found among neo-Freudians, a group of psychodynamic theorists whose ranks include Erich Fromm, Karen Horney, and Harry Stack Sullivan. Neo-Freudians emphasize social influences and interpersonal relationships.

Although most psychodynamic therapists believe that training in psychoanalytic theory and technique enhances their effectiveness, only a small percentage of them rigorously follow Freud's techniques. Many retain the general psychoanalytic framework, uncovering unconscious motivation, breaking down defenses, and dealing with resistance, but they practice a greatly modified form of psychoanalysis. Instead of merely listening and providing unobtrusive guidance, the therapist takes an active role, offering interpretation and advice. Instead of emphasizing events in the distant past, the therapist focuses on current personal relationships and specific problems. This emphasis makes therapy less intensive and more accommodating to people's lives. In traditional psychoanalysis, the patient was forbidden to make any major life changes during the course of analysis—which meant postponing marriage, divorce, job changes, and the like for two, three, four, or more years. Today's psychodynamic therapy is not only less restrictive but also briefer—a matter of a year or sometimes less.

Until recently, little research was done on the effectiveness of psychodynamic methods, in good part because of the complexity of psychoanalytic theory. Recent intensive study of tapes of therapy sessions, however, indicates that psychodynamic methods enable patients to identify the central conflicts in their relationships with others (Lubrosky, Crits-Cristoph, and Mellon, 1986). Once these conflicts are identified, patients become more involved and expressive during therapy sessions (Silberschatz, Fretter, and Curtis, 1986); the more positive the patient's immediate response to the identification of a conflict, the more likely it is that improvement will follow and therapy will be successful (Lubrosky, Crits-Cristoph, and Mellon, 1986).

BEHAVIOR THERAPIES

In **behavior therapy,** psychological problems are regarded as learned responses and the primary target of therapy is the problem behavior itself. Because the same principles govern all behavior, the therapist applies the principles of learning (discussed in Chapter 7) to the client's troubling behavior. Thoughts and emotions are seen as hidden responses, not clues to deep-seated conflict; thus they are subject to the same laws of learning as observable acts and are equally open to change (e.g., Wolpe, 1978). The focus on learning leads behavior therapists to regard the environment as playing a crucial role in determining behavior and to see problem behavior as specific to particular situations.

BEHAVIOR THERAPY an approach to psychotherapy in which psychological problems are regarded as learned responses and the primary target of therapy is the problem behavior itself

Therapies Based on Classical Conditioning and Extinction

Behavior therapists believe that *unlearning* may be the key to resolving some psychological disorders. Often the client's task is to unlearn the connection between particular stimuli and her or his maladaptive responses. This is accomplished by using classical conditioning and extinction to change the emotions evoked by certain stimuli—be it joy, fear, pleasure, or disgust. Sometimes the unlearning uses extinction to relieve the client of anxiety (as in the case of a student who is debilitated by anxiety during every exam), and sometimes the unlearning involves destroying the excessive pleasure that the client finds in stimuli by creating aversions to them (as in the case of a person who is trying to give up alcohol). Among the many classical conditioning techniques that use these principles are *systematic desensitization, flooding, aversion therapy,* and *covert sensitization.*

Through systematic desensitization, this man is gradually being cured of his abnormal fear of heights.

Systematic Desensitization

Perhaps the earliest example of the therapeutic use of classical conditioning was an experiment in which a little boy named Peter was cured of his fear of rabbits by being given candy and other snacks as a rabbit was gradually brought closer and closer (Jones, 1924). **Systematic desensitization,** which was developed by Joseph Wolpe (1958), is a similar procedure in which the client relaxes and then is gradually exposed to anxiety-producing stimuli.

In systematic desensitization, clients unlearn anxiety through extinction. Systematic desensitization involves three steps. First, the therapist trains the client in deep-muscle relaxation, generally using Edmund Jacobson's technique of progressive relaxation (which is described in Chapter 20). Second, therapist and client construct a hierarchy of fears—that is, a list of anxiety-producing situations ranked from the least to the most feared, as shown in Table 19.1. Third, in the actual desensitization, the therapist describes the least anxiety-provoking scene on the list and asks the client to imagine it. Once the client can imagine the scene without any anxiety, the therapist asks the client to imagine the next scene in the hierarchy. This procedure is repeated over a series of sessions until the client can remain relaxed and anxiety-free while imagining the scene that was once the most frightening.

Systematic desensitization is not confined to imaginary stimuli; it can be used with actual feared objects or situations as well (as it was with young Peter). The technique has been effective in the treatment of phobias, recurrent nightmares, complex interpersonal problems, and other anxiety-related problems (Kazdin and Wilson, 1978; Masters et al., 1987). A person who has been crippled by the fear of rejection can become less timid and more spontaneous, especially when desensitization is used in tandem with assertiveness training, in which people learn how to assert themselves without becoming aggressive.

SYSTEMATIC DESENSITIZATION a behavioral therapy technique that involves an extinction procedure in which the client is gradually exposed to anxiety-producing stimuli

Flooding

Flooding might be described as cold-turkey extinction therapy. It has been used to treat many of the same anxieties as systematic desensitization, but **flooding** involves continuous, intense exposure to the anxiety-provoking situation. The technique has been particularly useful in the elimination of obsessive-compulsive rituals (Rachman and Hodgson, 1980). For example, if a man's handwashing ritual is based on the fear of contamination, flooding would require him to touch

FLOODING a behavioral therapy technique that involves extinction of a conditioned response through continuous, intense exposure to the anxiety-provoking situation

and handle dirt or whatever substance he is trying to avoid; he would then be prevented from carrying out his cleansing ritual. Over repeated trials, the intense anxiety elicited by "contamination" would gradually be extinguished. This treatment is intensive and requires that someone be with the client 24 hours a day to prevent the ritual. For that reason, it is primarily used with patients who have been admitted to a hospital, where they are under constant supervision.

Aversion Therapy

Instead of using extinction, **aversion therapy** changes emotional responses by pairing the maladaptive response with an aversive stimulus, such as electric shock or nausea-producing drugs. Through classical conditioning, the formerly attractive stimulus becomes repellent. Aversion therapy has been effective in the treatment of alcoholism and abnormal sexual behavior (Rachman and Wilson, 1980). For example, a child molester is given electric shocks or a whiff of ammonia while being shown slides of children. Because it gradually becomes paired with the shocks or offensive odor, the sight of children no longer arouses him. Such harsh therapy, particularly when it involves electric shock, has been controversial, even among behavior therapists.

AVERSION THERAPY a behavioral therapy technique that relies on punishment and negative reinforcement

Covert Sensitization

An alternative to the use of painful shock is a technique called **covert sensitization,** in which clients visualize the behavior they are trying to eliminate and then conjure up the image of an extremely painful or revolting stimulus (Cautela, 1966; Cautela and Kearney, 1986). For example, a therapist may instruct an alcoholic to close her eyes, relax, and picture herself picking up a drink. As she imagines tasting the alcohol and swallowing, she is told to imagine that she feels nauseated, starts gagging, and vomits all over the floor, the drink, the bartender, and finally herself. The client imagines the scene in vivid detail, again and again, until the mere thought of drinking turns her stomach. She also practices visualizing an alternative, "relief" scene, in which the decision not to drink results in pleasurable sensations.

COVERT SENSITIZATION a behavioral therapy technique in which clients visualize unwanted behavior, then imagine a painful or revolting stimulus

Covert sensitization and aversion therapy are most successful when combined with techniques aimed at teaching the client adaptive responses to replace the maladaptive responses that brought them into therapy. A problem drinker, for example, may need to learn not only how to avoid alcohol but also how to control stress more effectively (see Chapter 20) and how to be more effective in relationships with other people.

TABLE 19.1 One Client's Hierarchy of Death-Related Fears

RATINGS	ITEMS
5	Seeing an ambulance
10	Seeing a hospital
20	Being inside a hospital
25	Reading the obituary notice of an old person
30–40	Passing a funeral home (the nearer, the worse)
40–55	Seeing a funeral home (the nearer, the worse)
55–65	Driving past a cemetery (the nearer, the worse)
70	Reading the obituary notice of a young person who died of a heart attack
80	Seeing a burial assemblage from a distance
90	Being at a burial
100	Seeing a dead man in a coffin

Note: The items listed elicited increasing amounts of anxiety from a client being systematically desensitized to the fear of death. A rating of 100 means "as tense as you ever are"; a rating of zero means "totally relaxed."
Source: Wolpe, J., and D. Wolpe (1981). *Our useless fears.* Boston: Houghton Mifflin.

Instrumental conditioning techniques can be effective in teaching autistic children.

Therapies Based on Instrumental Conditioning

Behavior therapists also believe that instead of being burdened with maladaptive emotional responses (that need to be unlearned), some people have never learned the appropriate response in the first place or else they have been reinforced for it so seldom that they rarely produce it. When a client's behavior is deficient or missing altogether, therapists can use instrumental conditioning techniques to reinforce desirable behavior and to extinguish undesirable behavior. Instrumental conditioning has been effective in teaching retarded children to care for themselves, teaching language to autistic children, increasing the adaptive behavior of schizophrenics, increasing hyperactive children's ability to attend to schoolwork, and helping people who overeat, cannot sleep, or have difficulty studying.

Often therapists find it helpful to write a contract that specifies exactly what behavior will earn reinforcement. This is particularly useful in the solution of marital and family conflicts. All parties agree on exactly what behavior each desires from the others. That behavior, along with rewards and sanctions, is spelled out in the contract, which all parties sign.

Since reinforcement can so effectively change behavior, what would happen if the environment were structured so that appropriate behavior in all areas of life is reinforced and inappropriate behavior is extinguished? Psychologists have developed such a situation in the **token economy,** in which a wide range of appropriate behavior is rewarded with tangible conditioned reinforcers (tokens) that can be used to "buy" secondary—or even primary—reinforcers. Token economies are used primarily in institutions. In the typical token economy ward, various kinds of desirable behavior and the token reward for each are listed on a board. Within the institution is a canteen where patients can exchange their tokens for reinforcers, such as candy, toiletries, or cigarettes. In many cases, tokens can also be spent on privileges—television time, access to the telephone, overnight passes, and so forth.

The effectiveness of token economies in establishing desirable behavior was studied in a classic experiment. Severely disturbed patients were placed on a strict token economy (Paul and Lentz, 1977). The move drastically changed the patients' lives. Instead of being medicated and left to their own devices, the patients had to behave appropriately in order to get tokens (always accompanied by praise). Their maladaptive behavior (muteness, screaming, incontinence, or violence) was ignored in an attempt to extinguish it. Patients got tokens for appropri-

TOKEN ECONOMY   a behavioral therapy technique, used primarily in institutions, in which appropriate behavior is rewarded with tokens that can be exchanged for reinforcers

ate behavior in almost every aspect of hospital life: personal care, bed making, bathing, behavior at meals, classroom participation, and social interaction.

Patients had to have tokens to "buy" necessities (such as food) as well as luxuries and privileges. Patients without tokens were shut out of the dining hall, but when lack of tokens posed a health problem, the patients got a free "medical meal" (an unappetizing mush made up of the regular food thrown into a blender and dyed purple-gray). The program was so effective that 98 percent of the patients improved enough to be discharged from the hospital. In comparison, only 71 percent of the patients in another innovative therapy program and only 45 percent of patients in the regular hospital program improved enough to be released. Token economies apparently are more effective than traditional forms of treatment with severely disturbed patients.

Cognitive Behavior Therapy

Not all behavior therapists rely on the techniques of conditioning. In recent years, behavior therapists have placed an increasing emphasis on the role of cognition in changing maladaptive behavior, and many now regard themselves as practicing **cognitive behavior therapy.** All varieties of cognitive behavior therapy attempt to change the way people think about themselves and the world, although they vary in the techniques used to accomplish this. The major types of cognitive behavior therapy are known as *modeling* and *cognitive restructuring.*

Therapists who specialize in **modeling,** in which people learn new behavior by watching another person, depend on the fact that in such observational learning the model's actions act as information (see Chapter 7). Modeling has been particularly effective in the treatment of phobias (Rosenthal and Bandura, 1978). For example, young children have been able to overcome an intense fear of dogs by watching movies of a five-year-old boy (called "Fearless Peer") playing with a cocker spaniel, grooming it, feeding it, lying down on the grass with it, and even hugging it, with his face close to the dog's open mouth (Bandura and Menlove, 1968). After observing Fearless Peer over a number of sessions, many of the children had overcome their fear of dogs to such an extent that they could climb into a playpen with a dog, pet it, and remain alone with it. When children watch movies of several children playing with a variety of dogs, modeling is even more effective.

When modeling is combined with practice sessions, it is known as *participant modeling;* in this version, the therapist models the feared activity—whether it is handling snakes, climbing to a high place, or driving on an expressway—and then helps the client confront and master a graduated series of threatening activities (Bandura, 1986). This procedure is a basic part of observational learning (as we saw in Chapter 7) and one we all use to learn many skills in daily life—imitating the behavior of a model until we have mastered the activity. When applied to social skills, a similar procedure is called *behavioral rehearsal.* This version of modeling has been especially effective in assertiveness training (Bellack et al., 1983).

These methods of changing behavior are successful because they change the way people think about themselves and others. According to Albert Bandura (1977; 1982), the key to successful behavior therapy is the client's belief that he or she can successfully execute whatever behavior is required to produce a desired outcome. This sense of mastery, which Bandura calls *self-efficacy,* affects all aspects of life, determining how hard people will try, how long they will persist, and whether they will attempt an act at all. Since success raises expectations and failure lowers them, expectations can be raised in two ways: by experiencing the sense of mastery that follows a person's own successful performance or by observing the success of another. Participant modeling and behavioral rehearsal are effective therapy techniques because they are powerful means of changing efficacy expectations.

Instead of working on behavior, some behavior therapists focus on the way clients perceive the world and how their false assumptions lead to self-defeating

COGNITIVE BEHAVIOR THERAPY an approach to behavioral therapy that places emphasis on the role of cognition in changing maladaptive behavior; an attempt to change the way people think about themselves and the world

MODELING a cognitive behavioral technique in which a person learns new behavior by watching another person

Albert Ellis.

COGNITIVE RESTRUCTURING
a cognitive behavioral technique that focuses on changing a person's perceptions and irrational assumptions of self and world

RATIONAL-EMOTIVE THERAPY (RET) a method of cognitive restructuring that directly confronts clients with their irrational beliefs

SELF-INSTRUCTIONAL TRAINING a method of cognitive restructuring that gives people new ways of thinking and talking to themselves about their problems

COGNITIVE THERAPY a method of cognitive restructuring that helps people discover for themselves how inappropriate their thoughts have been

behavior. In **cognitive restructuring,** the aim is to identify irrational assumptions and to subject them to the cold light of reason.

Several treatments can be considered as variations of cognitive restructuring. Perhaps the oldest is **rational-emotive therapy (RET),** which was developed by Albert Ellis (1962; Ellis and Grieger, 1977). Ellis argues that thousands of people lead unhappy lives because of their irrational beliefs. They may believe that everyone they meet must love them and approve of their actions. Or they may believe that they must be competent at everything they do, whether it's playing tennis, baking a cake, filling out tax returns, learning a computer program, making love, growing gardenias, or writing a poem. Or they may believe that the world should be arranged so that they experience only pleasure and never feel pain. It is not what happens to people that causes anxiety or depression, according to Ellis; instead, people's debilitating responses occur when their experiences are filtered through their irrational beliefs. During therapy, clients are confronted with the irrationality of their beliefs. For example, Ellis might say, "So what if your mother didn't love you. That's *her* problem!" Clients are instructed to monitor and correct their thoughts and to rehearse making realistic appraisals of situations. In the process they are helped to establish a more realistic cognitive framework that allows them to interpret their experiences differently.

Another effective way of changing people's thought patterns has been developed by Donald Meichenbaum (1977; Meichenbaum and Jerenko, 1982), whose **self-instructional training** focuses on what he calls "self-talk." Instead of changing people's beliefs, Meichenbaum gives them new ways of thinking about their problems and new ways of talking to themselves before, while, and after they act. By changing negative self-talk ("I always foul things up") to positive self-talk ("One step at a time; I can handle the situation"), clients eliminate their old self-defeating ways of thought that have become self-fulfilling prophecies. Thus, Meichenbaum's therapy changes efficacy expectations, working with thoughts instead of behavior.

The third method of cognitive restructuring is Aaron Beck's **cognitive therapy.** Beck (1976) agrees that irrational thoughts and faulty assumptions can lead to emotional disorders, and his therapy uses a questioning method that helps people discover for themselves how inappropriate their thoughts have been. Cognitive therapy has been especially successful in treating depression, and Beck and his colleagues (1979) have developed a detailed manual for its use. The therapist's questions are designed to make clients examine the connection between their own interpretation of events and their subsequent feelings. Once they discover that their destructive thoughts are not based on fact, the therapist can help them correct their assumptions and develop realistic interpretations of events. This enables them to shake off their view of themselves as losers. A careful analysis of twenty-eight studies showed that cognitive therapy is more effective than other therapies, including drug therapy, in treating acute depression (Dobson, 1989). Cognitive therapy is also more effective than drug treatment in reducing the chances that a person will have a subsequent depressive episode (Hollon and Beck, 1986).

Interest in cognitive techniques is growing, primarily because they seem to work. Nearly fifty studies have demonstrated the usefulness of cognitive behavior therapy, finding it to be as effective as behavioral therapies that emphasize conditioning techniques (Miller and Berman, 1983; Berman, Miller, and Massman, 1985).

The Trend toward Synthesis and Integration

In the past few decades, many therapists have become aware that relying on a single technique was causing them to overlook some aspects of a client's problems. This realization has led them to broaden their methods of treatment. Most behavior therapists now assess the multiple causes of the person's disorder and devise a comprehensive treatment. The central component of the treatment varies, depending on whether the goal of therapy is to change behavior, emotion, or cognition. For example, in the treatment of depression, the therapist might use cognitive restructuring supplemented by training in relaxation, time management, parenting, coping skills, and social skills (Lewinsohn et al., 1985). This trend toward multicomponent treatment "packages" has been the result of behavior therapists' growing tendency to specialize in a single type of disorder, such as anxiety disorders, depression, alcoholism, or schizophrenia.

HUMANISTIC THERAPIES

In **humanistic therapies,** the goal is growth, not cure. Instead of curing "patients," therapists help clients fulfill their individual human potential. Most of these therapies grew out of humanistic theories of personality, which (as we saw in Chapter 17) were developed as a "third force" in psychology to provide an alternative to the major forces of psychoanalysis and behaviorism. Humanistic therapists emphasize clients' sense of freedom and their ability to choose their own future. A close client–therapist relationship is encouraged, and the therapist tries to share the client's experience while providing an uncritical atmosphere that fosters the emergence of the client's inner strength.

HUMANISTIC THERAPY an approach to psychotherapy in which the goal is to help clients fulfill their individual human potential

Client-Centered Therapy

The best known variety of humanistic therapy is Carl Rogers' system of **client-centered therapy,** which is sometimes called *nondirective counseling.* [Toward the end of his life, Rogers (1980) began to call it *person-centered therapy,* in order to suggest that his principles extend beyond the client–therapist relationship to encompass all human interaction.] Client-centered therapy is based on the belief that all people are motivated to fulfill their own individual potentials, so that the therapist's job is to help clients clarify their feelings and value their experiences (Rogers, 1951; 1989). If the therapist is successful, the split between self and organism will heal (see our discussion of Rogers' self theory in Chapter 17).

CLIENT-CENTERED THERAPY a nondirective humanistic therapy that encourages people to clarify their feelings and value their experience

If therapists are to accomplish this task, they must have three qualities. In Rogers' words, the therapist must have *congruence* (or genuineness)—the ability to realize what the client is experiencing at any moment and then put it into words. The therapist must also have *empathic understanding*—the ability to "hear" the client at all levels of communication: words, thoughts, feelings, and unspoken cries for help. Rogers described his own empathic understanding of an adolescent boy who came to him for help:

> *Like many an adolescent today he was saying . . . that he had no goals. When I questioned him on this, he insisted even more strongly that he had no goals whatsoever, not even one. I said, "There isn't anything you want to do?" "Nothing . . . Well, yeah, I want to keep on living." . . . I resonated very deeply to that phrase. He might simply be telling me that, like everyone else, he wanted to live. On the other hand, he might be telling me—and this seemed to be a definite possibility—that at some point the question of whether or not to live had been a real issue with him. . . . I didn't know for certain what the message was. I simply wanted to be open to any of the meanings that this statement might have, including the possibility that he might at one time have considered suicide. My being willing and able to listen to him at all levels is perhaps one of the things that made it possible for him to tell me, before the end of the interview, that not long before he had been on the point of blowing his brains out. (Rogers, 1980, pp. 8–9)*

Finally, the therapist offers the client *unconditional positive regard*—manifesting total acceptance no matter what the client says or does. Instead of interpreting or instructing, the therapist clarifies the client's feelings by restating what he or she has said. Empathy and intuition, then, are the hallmarks of client-centered therapy.

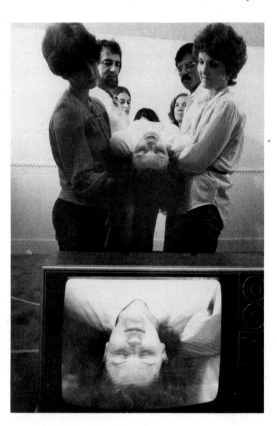

Using Fritz Perls's approach to therapy, this group is performing an exercise in trust (and videotaping it for later discussion).

Gestalt Therapy

GESTALT THERAPY a humanistic therapy that blends humanistic philosophy and Freudian concepts, using therapeutic techniques that are radically different from those of psychoanalysis

Gestalt therapy is a blend of Freudian concepts and humanistic philosophy developed by Frederick (Fritz) Perls (1970), who was trained as a Freudian psychoanalyst. Perls's use of the word "Gestalt" is not directly related to the theory of perception discussed in Chapter 5, although Gestalt therapists see themselves as applying to all aspects of life the idea that Gestalt psychologists applied to visual experience (Resnick, 1974). The goal of Gestalt therapy is self-awareness and self-responsibility. Gestalt therapy emphasizes the *now* (the present rather than the past), focuses on the *spatial* (what is present rather than what is absent), and concentrates on the *substantial* (on action rather than on fantasy) (Korchin, 1976).

The techniques of Gestalt therapy are radically different from those of psychoanalysis. Specific rules of communication help the client focus on the present. Clients are not allowed to speak impersonally or to say "you" but must say "I" ("I am," "I do," "I feel") to show that they take responsibility for their actions and feelings. They act out their past conflicts, shifting roles as they slip from one aspect of their personality to another. Other exercises develop clients' awareness of their own movements, tone of voice, and feelings. All these exercises lead to acceptance of feelings and unification of various aspects of the self.

GROUP AND FAMILY APPROACHES

During the past twenty years, an increasing number of therapists have been treating people in couples, families, or groups. Many therapists have moved away from individual therapy because it is both expensive and time-consuming. Group and family therapy provides a cheaper, quicker way of helping clients. Individual therapy may also obscure the causes of the client's problem, because the therapist sees the client alone, separated from his or her normal environment and stripped of all human relationships. Since interpersonal conflicts are at the root of many psychological disorders—or at least exacerbate them (Horowitz and Vitkus, 1986)—group and family therapy allow issues between people to be faced directly. As the divorce rate has increased, the demand for marital therapy has grown. Troubled marriages are easier to help when both partners are in therapy together than when only one partner sees a therapist (Gurman, Kniskern, and Pinsof, 1986).

Group Therapy

The concept of group therapy can be traced to Joseph Hershey Pratt, a Boston internist who worked with tuberculosis patients at the turn of the century. In an attempt to relieve their debilitating depression and isolation, he began to arrange regular group sessions for severely ill patients (Korchin, 1976). Although group methods based on psychological principles were developed in the 1930s and 1940s, it was not until midcentury that group therapy began to grow. The movement gained impetus when it became necessary to treat large numbers of people, both veterans and civilians, who had suffered from the social, political, and economic upheavals that accompanied World War II.

Therapy groups are conducted by almost every kind of therapist, including psychodynamic, behavioral, and humanistic. Groups lower the cost of therapy by allowing more patients to be treated at once, each at lower fees, but there are other advantages to the group setting. Within the group, people discover that their own problems are not "unacceptable" as they had feared, but relatively common (Yalom, 1975). The sense of belonging to the group and the intimacy that develops among its members often gives clients comfort and courage. In fact, many clients who are extremely resistant to individual therapy seem to respond to the emotional support of the group. This is particularly true when all members of the group have a common problem, such as drug addiction, alcoholism, or obesity.

Family and Marital Therapy

In family and marital therapy, the group is a natural one, formed by the bonds of kinship. Although the symptoms of one member (the "identified patient") may have brought the couple or family into therapy, the family is viewed as the treatment unit, and the assumption is that the family as a whole is disturbed (Kerr and Bowen, 1988).

There are several types of family therapy. In the *family systems approach*, therapists see people as members of a family social system that consists of interlocking roles (Ackerman, 1958; Minuchin and Fishman, 1981; Kerr and Bowen, 1988). In the course of living together, each couple or family, consciously or unconsciously, creates roles for each member to fill. There may be a "weak" member, a "strong" member, a "caretaker," a "scapegoat," a "disciplinarian," and so on. When roles are inappropriate or unduly restrictive, the most fragile member of the unit may show symptoms of mental disorder, but all members apparently contribute to the disturbance. Some therapists contend that when one person develops a disorder, it is because the family role system requires a "sick" member; if the "sick" person becomes "normal," the family unit itself will begin to show problems (Minuchin, 1974).

In the *communications approach* (also known as the strategic approach), therapists assume that psychological disorder develops in a family whose members' subtle nonverbal signals directly contradict their verbal signals (Watzlawick, Weakland, and Fisch, 1974).

Behavioral family therapy, too, emphasizes family interactions. During therapy, members are made aware of the way their actions reinforce one another's

In family therapy, the roles and behavior patterns of all family members are assessed and may be restructured.

behavior. Some therapists see family distress as the result of "coercion," in which each member uses aversive acts or words to influence the others' behavior (Patterson, 1982). In marital behavior therapy, the therapist assumes that wife and husband have been locked into frustrating behavior for so long that each has lost sight of the effect of their words and acts on the other and that they are unaware of the sources of their unhappiness. The aim of therapy is to shift the couple's behavior toward positive, mutually reinforcing interactions, to improve communication between them, and to improve their skills for solving problems and settling conflicts (Jacobson and Margolin, 1979).

Family therapy has also been used to prevent relapses in schizophrenic patients. As we saw in Chapter 18, an emotionally charged family atmosphere has been linked to rapid relapses (within a year) among schizophrenics (Vaughan et al., 1984). One study described an attempt to reduce the level of expressed emotion within families (Falloon et al., 1982; 1985). Therapists worked with all members of schizophrenics' families, teaching them about the nature and course of the disorder, discussing what level of functioning they could reasonably expect from the patient, and reducing stress within the family by teaching problem-solving and crisis-management strategies and calmer ways of expressing emotion. At nine months and again at two years after the schizophrenics had been released, those whose families were in the therapeutic program showed fewer schizophrenic symptoms, needed less medication, and were less likely to relapse than other released schizophrenics who were in individual therapy. Other research in which family therapists have trained the families of schizophrenics has shown similar positive results (Gurman, Kniskern, and Pinsof, 1986).

THE EFFECTIVENESS OF PSYCHOTHERAPY

Does psychotherapy work? Is time, not therapy, responsible for the improvement that most patients show? Does it make any difference what kind of therapy a person has? With such a bewildering array of therapies available, it would be helpful to know whether human problems respond best to systematic desensitization, psychoanalysis, or some other form of treatment. Answering these questions is more difficult than you might think, and psychologists have been wrestling with them for years.

One reason the evaluation of therapy is such a complex and perplexing task is that precise criteria for "improvement" are difficult to define and apply. The assessment of the therapist and client may be valuable, but both are subjective perceptions and give us no objective standard for measuring the outcome of therapy. The person who seems recovered in the therapist's office may still be having problems on the job or at home. The client who says "therapy saved my life" may be exaggerating the amount of improvement in order to justify spending all that money and to keep from letting the therapist down.

Another problem comes from the assessment of the patient's original status; diagnoses are as subjective as assessments of outcome. Both the label and the degree of disturbance are difficult to measure objectively. A person considered "seriously depressed" by one therapist may be diagnosed as "moderately depressed" by another.

A final problem arises from the fact that many people seem to get better with the passage of time, even when they have had no therapy of any kind. Such instances of *spontaneous remission,* or the sudden disappearance of symptoms in people who have not received formal psychotherapy, may also be misleading, because these people may have received help from unacknowledged sources—friends, relatives, religious advisers, family physicians, or even a sympathetic bartender.

Over thirty-five years ago, Hans Eysenck (1952) shook the therapeutic world by questioning the value of therapy. He reviewed twenty-four studies of the outcome of therapy and reported that 41 percent of patients in psychoanalysis had improved, as had 64 percent of those who received eclectic treatment (combining several therapeutic approaches), but he also reported that other sources showed that 72 percent of hospitalized patients had improved without any treatment at all. If patients do as well or better *without* treatment than with it, then there is little point in seeking professional help.

Other psychologists reanalyzed the studies Eysenck had reviewed and came up with conflicting conclusions. When Allen Bergin (1971; Bergin and Lambert, 1978) made different but equally defensible assumptions about the patients' classification, he showed that as many as 83 percent of the patients in psychoanalysis had improved or recovered. As outcome studies mounted, it became possible to take another look at the situation. In an attempt to get around the problems of classification, a team of researchers made a statistical analysis of 475 controlled

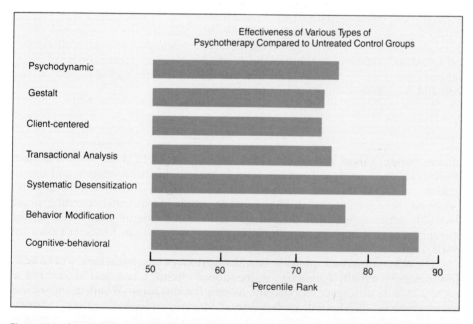

Figure 19.1 Is psychotherapy effective? Researchers who reviewed 475 studies think the answer is yes. Clients receiving each of the types of psychotherapy shown in this graph were compared with untreated control groups. The bars indicate the percentile rank that the average treated client attained on outcome measures when compared with control subjects for each type of therapy. Thus, the average client receiving psychodynamic therapy scored more favorably on outcome measures than 75 percent of the untreated controls. (Adapted from Smith, Glass, and Miller, 1980.)

PSYCHOLOGY TODAY AND TOMORROW

How To Choose a Therapist

If your moods become extreme, recurrent, and difficult to shake off or if you find yourself repeatedly engaging in destructive or restrictive behavior, you may decide to see a therapist. But how do you decide which therapist is best for you?

One way is to ask someone you know who has been in therapy and who has changed in ways that seem good to you. Another way is to check with local consumer groups or, if you are female, with women's centers. Other places to call are departments of psychology, counseling, education, nursing, or social work at a nearby college or university. If none of these sources is available and the yellow pages is your only guide, keep in mind the fact that the size of the ad and the flashiness of the layout has little to do with the skill of the therapist (Task Force on Consumer Issues in Psychology).

Once you have made an initial selection, ask for a consultation. This commits you to nothing but a single office visit that allows you to decide whether therapy would be useful and whether you feel this particular therapist would be able to help you. During the consultation, find out whether the therapist is licensed or certified by the state. Ask about the therapist's educational background and therapeutic orientation, and think about whether you would feel comfortable in such a treatment program. Note the therapist's style and what seem to be his or her values. Are they compatible with yours? Find out how often the therapist will expect to see you and how long the treatment is expected to last. Ask about fees (Linehan and Ivanoff, 1987).

After the consultation, ask yourself this series of questions, prepared by the Task Force on Consumer Issues in Psychotherapy of the American Psychological Association:

- Did I have positive feelings toward the therapist? Could I trust this person?
- Was I treated as a sick person or as a human being?
- Was I satisfied with the therapist's answers to my questions? Were they direct or evasive?
- Was I taken seriously? Was I treated with respect?
- Was I comfortable with the office atmosphere?
- Am I comfortable with the therapist's suggested plan of treatment?

If your impression of the therapist is negative, do not continue the relationship. If you are uncertain, think about the meeting, perhaps even scheduling a second session before making a decision. You are not committed to enter treatment with this particular therapist. Remember that you are purchasing services from a professional, that the choice about whether to enter treatment is yours, and that you have the right to leave therapy at any time.

---

studies (Smith, Glass, and Miller, 1980) (see Figure 19.1). They looked at such measures as the client's self-esteem, level of anxiety, job achievement, and school grades and found that the average client who had received psychotherapy did better on these measures than 80 percent of people in untreated control groups. The only problem was that the ratings of the client's status were based on the therapist's overall impression, which, in turn, was based on the client's own reports.

The other important question is which variety of psychotherapy works best. In the massive statistical analysis just mentioned (Smith, Glass, and Miller, 1980), there was little difference in outcome among the therapies. Whether clients had psychodynamic, behavioral, or humanistic therapy, and whether they had individual therapy or group therapy, the outcome was about the same. But in studies with typical outpatients, rather than college students (whose problems tend to be much less severe), behavioral therapies were more successful than psychodynamic therapies (Andrews and Harvey, 1981). And when researchers looked at the treatment of addiction, the institutional management (but not cure) of psychotic disorders, and the treatment of childhood disorders such as bed-wetting and hyperactivity, behavioral therapy again was more effective (Kazdin and Wilson, 1978). Earlier we saw that particular kinds of therapy seem well-suited for specific disorders: systematic desensitization and participant modeling for phobias; flooding for obsessive-compulsive rituals; aversion therapy for sexual deviations and alcoholism; token economies for the management of hospital wards; cognitive therapy for depression; and family therapy for the families of schizophrenics.

Yet the question is not settled. In recent years, research evaluating the methods of psychotherapy has improved. Detailed treatment manuals for many different types of psychotherapy have been written and evaluated. Many of the recent studies indicate that therapies from different perspectives can be equally effective.

The latest research on effectiveness has shifted its focus. In addition to looking at the *outcome* of therapy, researchers are looking at the *process* of therapy, asking how clients' lives, thoughts, and feelings are affected by what happens during therapeutic sessions. Perhaps such an approach will enable us to discover the effects of the specific techniques that therapists (of any variety) use, and the outcome of completed treatments no longer will be the central issue.

Although definitive answers still elude researchers, the issue of which therapy to choose is less hotly contested than it once was. As the trend toward integration continues and fewer and fewer therapists adhere to a single form of therapy, the rigid lines between therapeutic schools are becoming increasingly blurred.

INTEGRATION AND ECLECTICISM IN PSYCHOTHERAPY

As therapists have seen evidence of the effectiveness of competing treatments, they have tended to trade ideas and borrow techniques from one another. When discussing therapies, clinicians are more likely to focus on similarities between different therapies than on their differences. Earlier we saw that all therapies provide troubled people with support and hope. Another important aspect shared by all therapies is the relationship between therapist and client, known as the **therapeutic alliance** or the **therapeutic bond.** An important feature of this alliance is the client's perception of the therapist as an ally in the process of therapy. When the client perceives the therapist as helpful and sympathetic, the chances of substantial improvement or recovery increase—no matter what kind of therapy is involved (Beutler, Crago, and Arizmendi, 1986; Orlinsky and Howard, 1986).

The sharing of ideas and techniques has taken several forms. Earlier we saw that many behavior therapists have expanded their concern from what the client *does* to how he or she *thinks* and *feels* about self, behavior, and others. Some cognitive behavior therapists have gone even further, suggesting that another appropriate area of concern is to bring hidden matters into awareness—a goal that psychodynamic therapists have always had (Mahoney, 1980). Like cognitive behavior therapists, psychodynamic therapists have become as concerned with cognitive function as with emotions; they have also begun to promote direct behavior change—the traditional concern of behavior therapists. Some clinicians have suggested that an appropriate blend of therapy might involve using psychodynamic techniques to identify the client's central conflicts and behavioral techniques to help the person cope effectively with those conflicts (Wachtel, 1984).

THERAPEUTIC ALLIANCE/ THERAPEUTIC BOND the relationship between client and therapist, in which client perceives therapist as a helpful ally

BIOMEDICAL APPROACHES TO THERAPY

Psychodynamic, behavioral, and humanistic therapies, whether individual or group, are based on psychogenic approaches to mental disorders, as we saw in Chapter 18. These therapies work directly at changing behavior, emotions, or cognition. Therapies based on biogenic theories, on the other hand, use drugs, electroconvulsive therapy, or psychosurgery to intervene directly in the workings of the central nervous system. Drugs are the most common form of intervention:

Antipsychotic drugs such as Thorazine and Stelazine help to ease the symptoms of psychotic patients.

each year about 12 percent of adult Americans take at least one dose of some psychoactive drug. The drug is usually an antianxiety drug; about one in ten adults uses an antianxiety drug, while only 3 percent take an antidepressant drug, and only 1 percent an antipsychotic drug (Uhlenhuth et al., 1983).

Antianxiety Drugs

The commonly prescribed antianxiety drugs are depressants; as we saw in Chapter 6, depressants reduce pain, tension, and anxiety by depressing activity in the central nervous system. Antianxiety drugs are called "minor" tranquilizers, and the most popular are Tranxene (chemical name: clorazepate dipotassium), Librium (chlordiazepoxide) and Valium (diazepam). Tranquilizers are so popular that Valium is one of the most frequently prescribed (and abused) drugs in the world.

This popularity is due to tranquilizers' ability to help us cope with difficult periods in our lives; half of all prescriptions are written for people with physical illnesses who need assistance in controlling their emotional reactions to the illness (Uhlenhuth et al., 1983). As their name indicates, antianxiety drugs are widely used to treat anxiety disorders as well as stress-related physical disorders and symptoms of alcohol withdrawal. Antianxiety drugs have an important use in therapy, but they also have side effects. Because they act on the central nervous system, they can cause fatigue, drowsiness, and impaired motor control. People who take them probably should not drive, and their synergistic effect rules out even social drinking. The combination of tranquilizers and alcohol can be fatal—especially if a person has taken a heavy dose of tranquilizers. Such a situation is likely to arise if a person has been taking the drug for a lengthy period, because the body develops a tolerance for antianxiety drugs, so that larger and larger doses are required to produce the same effect. Considering their side effects, these drugs are better for short-term crises than for long-term chronic conditions.

Antipsychotic Drugs

Antipsychotic drugs, known as "major" tranquilizers or *neuroleptics*, dramatically affect the positive symptoms of psychosis—agitation, thought disorder, hallucinations, and delusions. They do not affect anxiety or the negative symptoms—social withdrawal and blunted affect. The most commonly prescribed antipsychotic drugs are the phenothiazines, including Thorazine (chlorpromazine), Prolixin (fluphenazine), Stelazine (trifluoperazine), and Mellaril (thioridazine).

Phenothiazines caused a revolution in the treatment of schizophrenia. Thorazine was introduced in the United States in the mid-1950s, and within eight months it had been used by approximately 2 million patients. Because patients improved so dramatically, Thorazine opened up the mental hospitals. Patients who had been confined to locked wards could wander freely about the hospital grounds; many chronic patients improved enough to be discharged. This release of patients spurred the community mental health movement, which we will investigate later in this chapter. Phenothiazines also advanced our knowledge of schizophrenia, because the effort to discover how these drugs worked led researchers backward to the dopamine hypothesis, which we discussed in Chapter 18.

Antipsychotic drugs seemed like the success story of the century. But psychiatrists soon discovered that their power is limited. Phenothiazines do not cure schizophrenia, and if released patients stop taking the drug, their symptoms generally return. Consequently, many patients have traded chronic hospitalization for a "revolving-door" existence: release, followed by relapse, hospitalization, and another release after the drug again enables them to function outside. Nor does the drug make people "normal"; once they leave the hospital, patients who take phenothiazines usually make only a marginal adjustment to society.

The glittering hopes raised by phenothiazines have also been tarnished by a serious side effect known as *tardive dyskinesia*. Tardive dyskinesia is a muscle disorder in which patients grimace and smack their lips uncontrollably. It appears after at least six months of continuous treatment with the drug, usually in patients who are more than forty years old. The disorder does not disappear when the drug is discontinued, and it is difficult to treat. Since the vast majority of psychotic patients in the United States take phenothiazines on a daily basis, tardive dyskinesia presents a serious problem.

Antidepressant Drugs

The antidepressant drugs, which lift the mood of depressed patients, were discovered by accident in 1952 when Irving Selikof and his colleagues noticed that patients with tuberculosis who took a drug called Iproniazid became cheerful and optimistic. Iproniazid blocks the action of monoamine oxidase (MAO), an enzyme that degrades neurotransmitters, including norepinephrine and serotonin. (As we saw in Chapter 3, norepinephrine levels have a strong effect on our moods.) Because Iproniazid causes liver damage, it is no longer prescribed, but other MAO inhibitors are still used occasionally. When taking an MAO inhibitor, a person must follow a highly restricted diet because the drugs can be fatal if they combine with tyramine—a component of many foods, including aromatic cheese, yogurt, avocado, chicken liver, cream, pickles, red wine, and beer.

Less dangerous than MAO inhibitors and even more effective in lifting depression are the tricyclics, named after their three-ringed molecular structure. The major tricyclics are Tofranil (imipramine), Elavil (amitriptyline), and Sinequan (doxepin). Tricyclics increase the availability of serotonin and norepinephrine at receptor sites in the brain, and MAO inhibitors decrease the destruction of these neurotransmitters, so both classes of drugs support the norepinephrine hypothesis of depression discussed in Chapter 18 (Berger, 1978).

The drug most often used to treat bipolar mood disorder is lithium, which is administered as a simple mineral salt, lithium chloride. Lithium quickly ends manic episodes, and, when taken regularly, it seems to eliminate the radical mood swings of bipolar patients (Bassuk and Schoonover, 1977). Because of its effect on mood, it is sometimes effective in cases of major depression. Yet lithium is a risky drug. It can cause kidney and liver damage, stomach upset, and weight gain, but the major problem is that it can be fatal. A dose that effectively controls mood swings is extremely close to a dose that is toxic, causing convulsion, delirium, or death (Lydiard and Gelenberg, 1982). When patients take the drug, their blood levels of lithium must be closely monitored.

Electroconvulsive Therapy

Anyone who saw the movie *One Flew Over the Cuckoo's Nest* has only unpleasant feelings about **electroconvulsive therapy (ECT)**, even if they do not know this technical term for "shock treatment." That picture of ECT greatly exaggerates its typical side effects, but the treatment is drastic and must be used with great caution. ECT is primarily used to treat severe depression, and it works swiftly—in most cases faster than antidepressant drugs (Greenblatt, 1977; Scovern and Kilmann, 1980). Before antipsychotic and antidepressant drugs were available, ECT was used widely for a variety of disorders including schizophrenia and depression. Today it is considered a treatment of last resort; in 1980, nearly 34,000 patients received ECT—or about 2.4 percent of all patients admitted to psychiatric hospitals (National Institute of Mental Health, 1985).

In ECT the patient receives a series of brief electrical shocks of approximately 70 to 130 volts, spaced over a period of several weeks. The shock induces a convulsion similar to an epileptic seizure. Although no one understands exactly how ECT works, it is the convulsion that seems to produce the therapeutic effect; when the shock is too weak to produce convulsions, there is no effect on mood (Greenblatt, 1977). Because the patient is anesthetized before the shock is administered, the treatment involves little discomfort. Sedatives and muscle relaxants prevent involuntary muscular contractions and physical injury. Afterward, patients do not remember the treatment itself.

Yet most patients fear ECT, primarily because in rare cases debilitating memory loss occurs (Roueché, 1974). Some temporary memory loss is common—both the ability to learn new material and the ability to recall old events. After treatment, the ability to learn new material gradually returns; memory of the past is severely impaired during the first week after treatment, but within seven months, nearly all memories have returned for most patients (Squire and Slater, 1978; Squire, Slater, and Miller, 1981). Yet even this degree of memory loss may not be necessary. Researchers have discovered that when ECT is limited to the nondominant brain hemisphere (in most people, the right hemisphere), there is no memory loss and it is just as effective at lifting depression (Horne et al., 1985).

ECT is a controversial treatment, and many people regard it as a form of torture. In 1982, the voters of Berkeley, California, passed a referendum making the administration of ECT a misdemeanor punishable by a fine of up to $500 and six months in jail. This ban was later reversed by the courts, but the fact that it was passed by the voters reveals the widespread public opposition to the treatment. Yet research indicates that ECT is extremely effective for severe depression that has not responded to antidepressant drugs, especially when the depression is unrelated to any precipitating event or is a psychotic depression that involves delusions and hallucinations (National Institute of Mental Health, 1985).

Psychosurgery

Psychosurgery is the most extreme of all biomedical treatments. It involves serious risk for the patient, and its effects are irreversible. Modern psychosurgery began in 1935, when Egas Moniz and Almeida Lima developed the procedure known as **prefrontal lobotomy.** In this procedure, a surgeon inserts an instrument into the brain and rotates it, severing the nerve fibers that connect the frontal lobe (thought center) with the thalamus (emotional center). Its purpose was to interrupt communication within the brain and so reduce the impact of disturbing stimuli on mood and behavior.

During the next twenty years, other methods of psychosurgery evolved and operations were performed on thousands of patients. Some extremely disturbed patients seem to have benefited from the procedure, but others were left in a permanent vegetative state. A few even died. Most psychosurgery ended abruptly in the 1950s, when the discovery of antipsychotic drugs provided a safer way to treat severely disturbed patients.

Today the crude lobotomies of the 1940s and 1950s are never performed. They have been replaced by "fractional operations," which destroy very small amounts of brain tissue in precise locations—the site varying depending on whether the patient is severely depressed or highly aggressive (Valenstein, 1986). Such operations do not have the side effects and risks associated with lobotomy. Nevertheless, they are considered treatments of last resort, to be used only with severely disturbed patients who have responded to none of the other available treatments.

COMMUNITY MENTAL HEALTH SERVICES

After a lengthy stay in a mental hospital, people seldom find it easy to reenter society. Released patients often find themselves too far from the hospital for any supplementary care and too fragile to cope independently with the pressures of the outside world. Without community support, these patients may not be able to make a successful return to society. Community mental health centers, halfway houses, hot lines, paraprofessionals, and other support groups offer some assistance, both to discharged patients and to patients whose problems are not severe enough to require hospitalization; but the ultimate goal of such community services is to prevent disorder from arising in the first place.

Community Mental Health Centers

For a quarter of a century, community mental health centers have been helping discharged patients reenter society. The centers were established for this purpose in 1963, when the Community Mental Health Centers Act mandated the establishment of one mental health center for every 50,000 people. Besides helping former patients, the centers were supposed to provide psychological services that had not been available within the community, to educate community workers (police, teachers, and clergy, for example) in the principles of preventive mental health, to train paraprofessionals, and to carry out research. Because of cutbacks in funding, the goals have not been met, but centers that are in operation supply important support to troubled people.

Many centers provide outpatient services. People can walk into a clinic and receive therapy once, twice, or several times a week without leaving home or giving up a job and without feeling stigmatized as institutionalized mental patients. These outpatient services also bridge the gap between hospitalization and complete independence by providing therapy and counseling for patients released from hospitals. The need for outpatient services is obvious; between 1955 and 1975, the number of visits to outpatient clinics increased from 379,000 to 4.6 million (Kiesler, 1982), as illustrated in Figure 19.2.

Mental health centers also provide specialized inpatient care within general hospitals, a service that permits severely disturbed people to be hospitalized within the community. Friends and family can visit, and the patient feels less isolated and more accepted. Many centers also run day hospital arrangements, in which patients spend the day inside the hospital and go home each night. The first day hospital was established at the Menninger Clinic in 1949; within thirty years, more than 1000 day hospitals had been set up across the country. Such an arrangement has been both practical and productive: it enables people to stay with their families; it reduces hospitalization costs; and it prevents relapses in discharged patients (Greene, 1981; Straw, 1981). Night hospitals provide the flip side of the day-hospital arrangement. Patients can work or go to school during the day and spend their nights in the hospital. Both arrangements give patients a more nearly normal life than does full-time hospital care.

Mental health centers also provide emergency services. Such services often take the form of storefront clinics that are open around the clock to deal with crises—a suicide attempt, a drug overdose, or a panic attack. Other centers may

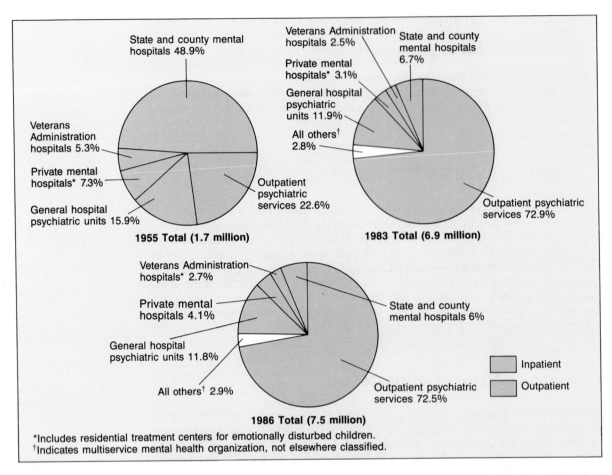

Figure 19.2 The percentage of cases treated by inpatient and outpatient facilities in 1955, 1983, and 1986. The three circles illustrate the dramatic increase in outpatient treatment, especially between 1955 and 1983. (*Sources:* 1955—The National Institute of Mental Health, Provisional data on patient care episodes in mental health facilities, Statistical Note 139, August 1977. 1983 and 1986—Unpublished provisional estimates from the Survey and Reports Branch, Division of Biometry and Applied Sciences, National Institute of Mental Health, Washington, D.C.)

have teams of psychologically trained personnel on call, ready to go to general hospital emergency rooms and deal with psychological traumas.

Not all general hospitals are affiliated with mental health centers. In areas without mental health centers, some community services may be unavailable. Many patients whose abuse of drugs or alcohol brings them to the emergency room are cared for by the general hospital, which has neither a specialized staff nor separate inpatient facilities for psychiatric patients (Hendryx and Bootzin, 1986).

Halfway Houses

Halfway houses, which provide an intermediate step between hospital and community, are residences for people with common problems. The residents provide support for one another and can draw on whatever supplementary services they need until they are able to function entirely on their own. The scope of available services ranges from simple custodial care, where no therapy or skills training is provided, to a wide array of services that cover all facets of a patient's reentry. In most halfway houses, a graduate psychology student provides supervision and counseling, but a psychiatrist or psychologist sometimes is available on a regular basis. Halfway houses have helped many people move from custodial care to community life, including drug addicts, newly released mental patients, paroled convicts, and alcoholics. Reports indicate that residents of halfway houses are less likely to be rehospitalized than are patients who return to the community without any supplementary support (Cannon, 1975).

The demand for halfway houses far exceeds the supply. Where halfway houses are not available, former mental patients often go to nursing homes, board-and-care facilities, or large, converted SRO (single room occupancy) hotels. Some of these arrangements are little more than "back wards" located within the community. But at least these former inpatients have a roof over their heads. Many discharged patients and people in need of therapy are homeless (see the accompanying box). Without adequate financing, community-based care too often degenerates into a wholesale dumping of discharged patients into run-down hotels, to survive as best they can.

Crisis Intervention: The Hot Line

Clinics, hospitals, and halfway houses are costly and complicated ways of meeting the needs of troubled people. An immediate, economical, and effective way to deal with emergency situations is the crisis hot line. People in the midst of a crisis can phone at any time and receive counseling, sympathy, comfort, and referrals to clinics and hospitals. The best known hot-line system is the Los Angeles Suicide Prevention Center, established more than thirty years ago. Similar hot lines have been set up for crime victims, alcoholics, rape victims, drug addicts, child-abusing parents, runaway children, and people under stress of all kinds. Since 1960, more than 180 suicide-prevention hot lines and 600 youth and/or drug hot lines have been established in the United States (Trowell, 1979).

A Friend in Need: Nonprofessional Helpers

Although most people with psychological problems do not seek help from a professional psychotherapist, this does not mean that they go without any sort of comfort or counseling. People who lack the funds, who think their problems are not serious enough to need professional help, or who fear or distrust psychotherapy are likely to ask family or friends for support and guidance. Some turn to

Social workers provide counseling in the informal atmosphere of a shelter for battered women.

These young men have broken their addiction to drugs, but before returning to their communities, they are living in a halfway house. There, with support from each other and from trained counselors, they are preparing to resume life "on the outside."

self-help books (see the accompanying box on page 593). Others go one step further and join a self-help group.

Peer self-help groups, which are groups of people who share a certain problem, meet regularly to discuss that problem without the help of mental health professionals. Self-help groups have been organized to deal with hundreds of problems: there are groups for dieters, stutterers, rape victims, drug addicts, former mental patients, compulsive gamblers, widows, women who have had mastectomies, patients on dialysis, cancer patients, families of cancer patients, alcoholics, spouses of alcoholics, children of alcoholics, parents of hyperactive children, single parents, child abusers, and so forth. It has been estimated that 3.7 percent of American adults—or more than 6 million people—are currently attending self-help group meetings (Jacobs and Goodman, 1989). Some groups, like Alcoholics Anonymous and Weight Watchers, use social support, along with other techniques, to help members overcome a specific problem. In other groups, social support itself is the primary goal. No matter what the specific aim of the group, its underlying assumption is that people who have the same problem are able to provide one another with a special kind of help that is not available from more formal services.

Community workers provide another source of help. Teachers, police officers, and members of the clergy often are asked for advice and comfort by troubled people, and they frequently find themselves in situations where knowledge is essential. They may have to intervene in a potentially violent family quarrel, talk a suicidal person out of jumping off a bridge, or persuade a truant youngster not to drop out of school. Many community workers have been equipped to handle such situations through workshops conducted by community health centers, whose staffs include qualified personnel to advise them on the handling of psychological problems in the classroom and community.

Help is also offered by paraprofessionals, people who have some training in counseling. Many paraprofessionals work alongside mental health professionals in a clinic or volunteer settings. Others run hot lines. When paraprofessionals are well-trained and experienced, they may provide extremely effective counseling (Hattie, Sharpley, and Rogers, 1984).

PSYCHOLOGY TODAY AND TOMORROW

The Homeless: Victims of Good Intentions

A blind woman lives on the sidewalk in front of a New York City drugstore, swearing, waving her metal cane, and muttering threats at passers-by. A man lives in a large plastic bag atop a rock in Central Park, surrounded by rats, which he feeds. Another man lives on the street near the twin towers of the World Trade Center because, he says, it is a good place from which to take off for outer space. A woman lives on the sidewalk in front of an uptown restaurant; she defecates in the street, burns dollar bills she is given, and alternately sings, yells, and curses (Barbanel, 1987b, 1987c).

These people are some of the thousands who have become familiar sights in the nation's cities, large and small. Officials estimate that New York has about 45,000 homeless people who live in bus and train stations, in parks, in doorways, and on sidewalks. In the nation as a whole, their numbers are estimated at anywhere from 350,000 to 3 million (Mathews, 1988). Some of the homeless are mentally ill; in Chicago, one in four of the homeless has previously been in a mental hospital (Rossi et al., 1987). In a southwestern city, half of the homeless men waiting in line at a soup kitchen were either severe alcoholics or profoundly disturbed (Kahn et al., 1987). But the rest are not disordered; rather, they cannot find work, they have slipped through the "safety net" when government programs and services were cut back, or they simply cannot afford to pay for shelter in cities like New York, where a housing shortage has driven up rents.

After accounting for those who have been pushed into the streets by poverty, we are left with at least 15,000 mentally disordered homeless people in New York City alone. In the days before antipsychotic medication was available, these people would have been confined to mental hospitals. Today they are medicated and released—often to be caught up in the revolving-door situation described in the text. Unless these ex-patients request hospitalization, they are unlikely to get it. The presence of a thought disorder is not by itself sufficient grounds to pick up a person who wants to be free. According to New York State law (which resembles civil rights legislation in many other states), people cannot be hospitalized involuntarily unless they are likely to harm themselves or others—that is, unless they are suicidal or violent.

Concerned by the plight of mentally ill people who seemed unable to care for themselves, New York City officials recently reinterpreted the involuntary commitment law to permit involuntary hospitalization of anyone who is at risk of physical harm "within the reasonably foreseeable future." This broader definition permitted them to pick up people who were in no immediate danger, but whose self-neglect might put them there. In sweeps by teams consisting of a psychiatrist, a social worker, and a nurse, all the people described in the first paragraph above were picked up, taken to a psychiatric hospital, bathed, deloused, told of their civil rights, interviewed, and given appropriate medication (Barbanel, 1987a). Such a program clearly benefits people who are unable to care for themselves, but the policy's problems took less than 24 hours to appear.

Joyce Brown, the woman who burns money, yells at passersby, and has even physically assaulted some would-be benefactors, immediately asked the courts to set her free. "I like the streets and I am entitled to live the way I want to live," she told a reporter (Barbanel, 1987c). Brown, who is in her early forties, is intelligent and articulate; she has no serious health problems, has kept warm, and has been properly clothed. She said that she destroyed money because she regarded money tossed at her as an insult and because she believed accepting paper money from men was a mark of prostitution. Her habit of using the street as a toilet may result not from disturbance, but from the realization that nearby restaurants and shops would not let her use their facilities. Within a few months, Brown was released because the courts, while allowing the city to keep her in a hospital, forbade forced medication (James, 1988). She moved to a women's shelter and started practicing her typing skills in the hope of getting a secretarial job. But before many months had passed, she was back on the sidewalk in front of the restaurant.

The case of Joyce Brown reminds us of the problems of defining disorder that we explored in Chapter 18. Society still grapples with the problems of forced treatment for mental disorders and whether it will allow people whose behavior offends or embarrasses others to live as they please.

Suicide-prevention hot lines are available in all areas of the United States.

PREVENTION
OF PSYCHOLOGICAL DISORDER

The basic goals of psychologists are to prevent the development of disorder, to detect and treat minor disorders and keep them from becoming major, and to minimize the effects of major disorders on the victim and on society. No one is more aware than psychologists that success in reaching the first goal would make concern about the other goals unnecessary. But the enormous effort involved in treating minor disorders and minimizing the effects of major disorders occupies all the time and energy of most therapists and community psychologists.

In this chapter, we have explored the ways in which psychologists work toward the last two goals. Some critics have charged that psychology as a field and community efforts in particular have become too occupied with helping the individual in trouble. The major thrust, these critics maintain, should be toward prevention, especially through improvement of the social conditions that underlie so many psychological problems—in both the individual and in the community.

Some forms of psychological disturbance, including schizophrenia, are linked with social class, as we saw in Chapter 18. Poverty, discrimination, and the lack of valued roles for certain groups (such as the elderly) often increase stress to unmanageable levels, fostering emotional disorder. The effects of economic recessions provide some support for this view. Each time unemployment in the United States rises sharply, it is accompanied by increases in admissions to mental hospitals, suicides, and death from stress-related illnesses such as heart disease and cirrhosis of the liver (Pines, 1982).

Such evidence indicates that if psychologists are to work on their primary goal—preventing the development of psychological disorders—they will have to turn their attention to the design of social systems that foster health and growth. Recently, the National Mental Health Association Commission on the Prevention of Mental-Emotional Disabilities suggested four immediate targets for action (Long, 1986):

1. Make sure that all babies are wanted and healthy. To reach this target, society would have to provide family planning services, comprehensive prenatal care, and continuing information about health, nutrition, and the skills of parenting.

PSYCHOLOGY TODAY AND TOMORROW

Self-Help Books: Do They Help?

The shelves in bookstores are crowded with hundreds of self-help books. Every month new titles are published, and some become best sellers. Is the money spent for these books wasted, or do they actually help people solve their problems?

Studies by Forest Scogin (Scogin, Jamison, and Gochneaur, 1989) indicate that self-help books can work about as well as psychotherapy. Scogin used two self-help books with forty-five men and women who were either mildly or moderately depressed. One of the books, *Feeling Good: The New Mood Therapy,* showed how to use the techniques of cognitive therapy to combat depression, while the other, *Control Your Depression,* used more traditional behavioral techniques. Four weeks after they had been given the books, two-thirds of the men and women were significantly less depressed. Among a control group of people who got no treatment of any kind, only 20 percent showed similar improvement. In more than forty studies that have compared self-help books with actual psychotherapy, people who read the books still do well, improving significantly—although not as much as those who are treated by therapists (Goleman, 1989).

Self-help books seem to work best for those who read easily and have had some college education. People for whom reading is a struggle tend to give up before finishing the book (Goleman, 1989). Some self-help books work better than others, and those that do are often recommended to patients by their therapists. In a national sur-vey, the following books were most often recommended to clients by clinical psychologists:

- *The Relaxation Response,* by Herbert Benson and Miriam Klipper
- *On Death and Dying,* by Elisabeth Kübler-Ross
- *Parent Effectiveness Training,* by Thomas Gordon
- *Between Parent and Child,* by Chaim Ginott
- *Your Perfect Right: A Guide to Assertive Living,* by Robert Alberti and Michael Emmons
- *What Color Is Your Parachute?* by Richard Bolles
- *When I Say No I Feel Guilty,* by Manuel Smith
- *The Boys and Girls Book About Divorce,* by Richard Gardner
- *Feeling Good: The New Mood Therapy,* by David D. Burns
- *How To Survive the Loss of a Love,* by Melba Colgrove, Harold Bloomfield, and Peter McWilliams

The survey was conducted in 1986, and while most of these books are still available, other, newer books may provide similar help. Therapists suggest that people who want to rely on self-help books may do best if their progress is monitored by mental health professionals (Goleman, 1989).

2. **Prevent adolescent pregnancy.** This target would require health and sex education programs in high schools, counseling about contraception and health services, and programs to develop responsible decision making.

3. **Promote academic mastery and psychosocial skills** in the early school years. Reaching this target would involve the incorporation of competence-building and mental health strategies into existing school programs.

4. **Provide social support for families in stressful situations.** This target would require information, training, and services for high-risk individuals, especially single parents and those with infants. It would involve home visits, training in coping skills, and mutual-support groups.

Meeting these aims would significantly reduce the incidence of psychological disorder in U.S. society. But society cannot be changed quickly. In the meantime, we can keep working at psychology's other goal: providing every individual affected by psychological disorder, whether major or minor, with access to the best treatment available.

SUMMARY

The Nature of Psychotherapy

- The goal of psychotherapy is to alleviate problems, either by helping patients to understand their motives or by directly changing their behavior.
- Professionals who treat psychological disorders may be psychiatrists, clinical psychologists, psychiatric social workers, psychiatric nurses, or psychoanalysts.

Psychodynamic Therapies

- The aim of Freudian psychoanalysis is to uncover repressed impulses, primarily through free association and dreams and through understanding resistance and transference.
- Ego psychologists and neo-Freudians emphasize coping with present situations, including stress, social influence, and interpersonal relationships.

Behavior Therapies

- Techniques in classical conditioning focus on learned responses and are based on extinction. They include systematic desensitization, flooding, aversion therapy, and covert sensitization.
- Techniques in instrumental conditioning generally reinforce desirable behavior and extinguish undesirable behavior. These include token economy.
- Cognitive behavior therapy uses modeling and cognitive restructuring to increase a person's self-efficacy. These methods help people change the way they think about themselves and the world.

Humanistic Therapies

- Humanistic therapies aim to help clients grow and fulfill their potential.
- In client-centered therapy, the aim is to clarify feelings and value personal experiences.
- Client-centered therapists must have congruence and empathic understanding and must offer unconditional positive regard.
- Gestalt therapy aims at self-awareness and self-responsibility.

Group and Family Approaches

- Group therapy, an inexpensive, rapid form of therapy that places the client's problems in the context of social relationships, may be psychodynamic, behavioral, or humanistic.
- In family and marital therapy, the entire family is viewed as being in treatment.
- In the family systems approach, the role each family member plays in the family social system is emphasized.
- In the communications approach, therapists assume that family members' nonverbal signals contradict their spoken words.
- In behavioral family therapy, the stress is on family interaction and how members reinforce one another's behavior.

The Effectiveness of Psychotherapy

- Assessing the effectiveness of therapy has been difficult because assessments of outcome are subjective; assessments of the client's original status are difficult to measure objectively; and spontaneous remission can cloud the appraisal.
- Some studies have shown that all varieties of therapy work equally well; others have shown that behavioral therapies seem to be more effective. Particular kinds of therapy seem well-suited for specific disorders.

Integration and Eclecticism

- The current trend is toward the exchange of ideas and techniques among different schools of psychotherapy.
- All therapies provide support to troubled people, offer them hope, and establish a therapeutic alliance between client and therapist.

Biomedical Approaches to Therapy

- Biomedical approaches treat psychological disorders by using drugs, electroconvulsive therapy, or psychosurgery to alter the workings of the central nervous system.
- Drugs are the most common intervention, whether antianxiety, antipsychotic, or antidepressant.
- Antianxiety drugs are common, but are better for short-term crises than for long-term chronic conditions.
- Although the antipsychotic phenothiazines eliminate schizophrenic symptoms and allow patients to return to society, they may cause tardive dyskinesia, a muscle disorder.
- Antidepressant drugs regulate moods and have been effective with depression and bipolar mood disorder, although most have serious side effects.
- Electroconvulsive therapy is effective in treating major depression, although it may affect later memory loss unless it is applied only to the nondominant hemisphere.
- Psychosurgery is used only as a last resort when other treatments have failed.

Community Mental Health Services

- Community mental health centers may provide outpatient services, inpatient services, emergency services, and training for community workers.
- Halfway houses can ease the discharged patient's transition into community life.
- The crisis hot line provides an inexpensive, immediate, effective way to deal with emergencies by telephone.
- Nonprofessional interpersonal support for people with problems comes from family, friends, self-help groups, community workers, and paraprofessionals.

Prevention of Psychological Disorders

- Psychologists try to prevent the development of disorder, to detect and treat minor disorders and keep them from becoming major, and to minimize the effects of major disorders on the patient and on society.
- Four immediate targets for action toward prevention include wanted and healthy babies, prevention of adolescent pregnancy, promotion of academic and interpersonal skills, and social support for people in stressful situations.

KEY TERMS

aversion therapy
behavior therapy
client-centered therapy
clinical psychologist
cognitive restructuring
cognitive behavior therapy
cognitive therapy
covert sensitization
electroconvulsive therapy (ECT)
flooding

Gestalt therapy
humanistic therapy
modeling
prefrontal lobotomy
psychiatric nurse
psychiatric social worker
psychiatrist
psychoanalyst
psychodynamic therapy

psychotherapy
rational-emotive therapy
resistance
self-instructional training
systematic desensitization
therapeutic alliance (or therapeutic
    bond)
token economy
transference

CONCEPT REVIEW

1. The chapter lists a number of types of training for people who may practice various forms of psychotherapy. What is the essential feature that distinguishes each type? What are the differences among a clinical psychologist, a psychiatrist, and a psychoanalyst?

2. What are the major concepts used by a psychodynamically oriented psychotherapist? How do these concepts aid the psychoanalyst in achieving the basic goal of analysis?

3. Identify the basic goal of behavioral therapy. How are the various techniques based on classical conditioning used to reach this goal? How are the concepts of instrumental conditioning used to achieve this goal?

4. What components of classical and instrumental conditioning can be identified in the therapeutic techniques of modeling, cognitive restructuring, and cognitive therapy? What components of these treatment approaches are *not* typical of classical and instrumental conditioning? What realization by therapists is contributing to the trend toward integrating these various approaches?

5. Outline the basic therapeutic goals of client-centered therapy. How are this approach and Gestalt therapy similar? How are they different?

6. What makes group therapy attractive to clients? To therapists?

7. Describe the various types of family therapy. What basic assumption is made about the family in therapy? Under what circumstances is family therapy useful in the treatment of schizophrenia?

8. Describe the difficulties researchers face in attempting to discover the effectiveness of psychotherapy. Which therapies are more effective for specific disorders? What components are shared by all therapeutic approaches?

9. Name and describe the major classes of psychoactive drugs. How does each of the most commonly used drugs work?

10. Under what circumstances are electroconvulsive therapy and psychosurgery used today? How do they work?

11. Describe the community mental health movement. How successful has it been? What are its advantages and disadvantages? What alternatives exist for an individual in need of psychological support?

CRITICAL THINKING

1. Recall Chapter 2's discussion of ethical considerations in the treatment of research subjects, and consider the fragile nature of individuals suffering from mental illness or even mild psychological problems. What are the important ethical issues for the practitioners of psychotherapy?

2. In the area of psychotherapy, many psychotherapists consider themselves "eclectic." In contrast, the research-oriented areas of psychology tend to be more strictly governed by theoretical or research-based arguments. What is it about psychotherapy that makes it more open to a wide range of approaches?

... *Health Psychology and Adjustment to Stress*

The !Kung people of southern Africa believe that their health is at the mercy of spirits and ghosts. Accidents, illness, and death occur when these spirits shoot invisible arrows into people. Until the embedded arrows are removed from their flesh, victims cannot recover. Only !Kung healers, who have a special power, can remove the arrows. In the curing ceremony, the healer enters a trance, with his soul leaving his body to battle the spirits for the sick person's soul. The ceremony begins when the family and friends of the victim gather around a fire. As the women clap and sing, the healer dances himself into a trance state, at last breaking into a heavy sweat. Trembling, he lays his hands on the sick person and draws the "badness" into himself. Then, with a soul-wrenching cry, he hurls the arrows of sickness out of his body into the air.

The !Kung believe that diseases are caused by gods, spirits, departed relatives or friends, or living enemies—not by bacteria, viruses, parasites, or physical deterioration. In every disease, they see some form of human hatred, jealousy, or misdeed that has brought down the intervention of gods or ghosts (Lambo, 1978). Such beliefs reflect the !Kung conviction that psychological factors play a role in disease—although the !Kung do not use this term. Anthropologist Marjorie Shostak (1981) described a case in which a !Kung woman became ill with malaria shortly after her father died. The healer's soul journeyed to the world of the dead and found the father cradling his daughter's spirit in his arms. The father held her closely, saying that he could not bear to be without his daughter. This was wrong, the healer argued; the woman had a right—even an obligation—to live: "Your daughter has so much work to do in life—having children, providing for family and relatives, helping with grandchildren" (p. 293). When the father reluctantly agreed to free his daughter, her spirit returned to her body and she recovered.

HEALTH PSYCHOLOGY: MIND AND BODY

Until recently, people in Western societies would have dismissed as "ignorant" the notion that a case of malaria might be linked to the death of a loved one. Everyone "knew" that malaria is caused by a parasite injected into the human bloodstream by the bite of a mosquito. The medical model of disease, which we explored in Chapter 18, did not consider how the mind could affect the body. But our attitudes toward illness and health are changing. Just as psychotherapists are becoming more aware of the role of biological factors in psychological disorders, so physicians are taking psychological factors into account when treating physical disease. The mind, they have discovered, affects both our chances of developing a disease and the course of our recovery—even in cases like malaria, where psychological factors are not the direct cause of illness.

HEALTH PSYCHOLOGY the branch of psychology that aims at understanding the relationship between the mind and the individual's physical condition

The view that mind and body are both involved in health and illness has led to the emergence of **health psychology,** the branch of psychology that deals with how people stay healthy, why they become ill, and how they react when illness develops. The primary aim of health psychologists is the prevention of illness, a goal similar to the community psychologist's aim of preventing psychological disorders (see Chapter 19).

Health psychology's rapid growth reflects changes in patterns of illness and health. At the turn of the century, the leading causes of illness and death in the United States were acute infectious diseases such as tuberculosis, influenza, polio, gastrointestinal disorders, and measles. Today none of these diseases poses a major threat, because their incidence and severity have been sharply reduced by vaccines, antibiotics, and improved nutrition and sanitation. The only infectious diseases that have become more serious in the past few decades are sexually transmitted diseases (STDs), most notably AIDS. But other than STDs, the major causes of disability and death in the United States today are chronic, noninfectious illnesses—particularly heart diseases, cancer, and diabetes.

This changing profile of health and illness made the growth of health psychology all but inevitable, because many chronic illnesses are associated with problems of behavior. Smoking, overeating or poor nutrition, abuse of alcohol and drugs, and reactions to stress have been implicated in the development of modern dis-

Most societies recognize the interaction of mind and body in producing both good health and illness. Here a healer treats a fellow member of Mexico's Huichole people.

eases. By adopting healthier habits early in life, we can prevent some of these diseases. And even if we should contract one of them, we can continue to live normal lives for many years by changing our behavior in appropriate ways. The implication of lifestyle in chronic disease means that treatment is not a one-shot, win-or-lose effort, as with infectious diseases. We can't take tetracycline for two weeks and go back to our old habits. It also means that we cannot wait passively for a physician to cure us; we must become active participants in regaining and maintaining our own health. Dealing with chronic illness raises a set of psychological issues that few families or physicians faced in past generations.

These psychological issues are at the heart of health psychology, which is based on a biopsychosocial model. Health psychologists assume that biological, psychological, and social processes are all important influences on health and illness. A disease cannot be understood apart from the person and the social context in which it developed. How we think and feel and the settings in which we live and work have medical consequences. Because context is so important, health psychology focuses on the way higher-level processes (such as cultural values and practices, social institutions, interpersonal relationships, and personal beliefs and habits) interact with lower-level processes like body chemistry. Because of this interaction, health psychologists assume that health and illness have multiple causes and multiple effects. In this model, health is not the normal "steady state" of the organism, but a condition that must be achieved and maintained. Accordingly, research and practice in health psychology focus on promoting health and preventing disease and injury—an approach that makes people's attitudes, behavior, and environmental conditions matters of primary concern. Although health psychologists are also interested in how people deal with pain, discomfort, and chronic illness, in the structure and functioning of the health care system, and in public health policies, this chapter concentrates on efforts aimed at promoting health and understanding stress.

KEEPING HEALTHY

Establishing and maintaining health, known as **primary prevention,** has several aspects: encouraging people to adopt healthy lifestyles, persuading them to take precautions against health risks, and identifying and counseling those whose health is at risk. Most primary prevention efforts aim at discovering why people develop unhealthy habits and how they can be helped to change them—a goal that is often easier than persuading people to adopt healthy behavior. Most health habits are developed during childhood and adolescence, when we give little

PRIMARY PREVENTION establishing and maintaining health by reducing risky behavioral practices and environmental conditions

Since chronic diseases are more prevalent than infectious illnesses in modern societies, changes in lifestyle have become necessary to regain and maintain good health.

thought to the possibility of future disease. During adulthood, we may see little need to change habits that might be hazardous to our health. Efforts to encourage good health habits are complicated by the fact that most physicians are not trained to prescribe lifestyle changes until they detect symptoms of disease. Such challenges obstruct health psychologists' efforts to examine the psychological, social, and behavioral factors that affect health.

Influences on Health Habits

Many of us gamble with our health simply because we have never established healthy habits and find it very hard to change our ways (Hunt et al., 1979). Most adults with good nutritional habits grew up eating three balanced meals a day and limiting their consumption of sweets and snacks. Most physically active adults grew up playing ball, hiking, swimming, and engaging in other sports. As long as the environment provides opportunities to exercise, they continue to do so. In fact, the best predictors of regular exercise in adults are a history of athletic participation and access to exercise facilities (Dishman, 1982).

Once established, health habits resist change—whether the habits are good or poor. Even when we are convinced that we should give up poor habits, we find it difficult to change. Our old ways, such as overeating or smoking or drinking too much, bring us immediate pleasure; the new, more healthful lifestyle may be inconvenient or even painful if the old habit has to do with an addiction like smoking. The rewards of good health are so far in the future that they may not seem worth the effort.

Social Influences

Whether we develop healthy or unhealthy habits depends in part on social factors. Socioeconomic factors are important, because they influence the sort of medical care we get and thus our tendency to take preventive health measures. In middle-class families, most children have regular check-ups with a family physician, are immunized against infectious diseases, and learn that preventive health measures are important. But in low-income families, children generally have no regular source of medical care and rely on outpatient clinics and hospital emergency rooms, where little preventive medicine is practiced (Butler, Starfield, and Stenmark, 1984).

Cultural values also influence our health habits. Before World War I, it was considered improper for women to smoke, and for a woman to light a cigarette in public was an act of social defiance. As values changed, the proportion of girls and women who smoked gradually increased and continued to climb, even after findings about the health risks of smoking began to send the proportion of male smokers down. Although signs indicate that women are now beginning to heed these warnings, lung cancer has overtaken breast cancer as the major cause of cancer deaths among women (*The New York Times*, 1987).

Many of our health habits are the result of socialization within the family. The effects of parental models can last a lifetime—whether the habits displayed are healthy or unhealthy. When their parents overeat, drink heavily, use recreational drugs, or smoke, young people are far more likely to do so, too (Stunkard, 1979; Leventhal and Cleary, 1980; Moos, Cronkite, and Finney, 1982).

Emotional Influences

Although it is tempting to say that certain personality traits predispose us to bad habits, attempts to unequivocally link personality and unhealthy habits generally have failed (Rodin, 1981). We know, however, that our emotional state does affect health practices. Some people react to stress and emotional upset by overeating (Polivy and Herman, 1976); others overeat in response to boredom or loneliness. In each case, they have learned to handle unpleasant emotions with the solace of food. Smoking, drinking, and drugs are other habits that may be used to cope with the tension that accompanies stress.

Cognitive Influences

We tend to overlook the role that our thoughts, beliefs, and attitudes play in establishing and maintaining healthy or unhealthy habits, but researchers have found that they are often major influences (Hochbaum, 1958; Rosenstock, 1974). According to the **health belief model,** good health practices depend on whether we believe that we are vulnerable to illness and injury and whether we are convinced that changing our behavior will affect our health (Rosenstock, 1974).

HEALTH BELIEF MODEL a model that assumes good health practices depend on attitudes, beliefs, and thoughts about vulnerability to illness and the value of changed behavior

Proper nutrition and other good health habits begin early in life.

Many people simply do not believe that they will ever get sick or be hurt, so they see no reason to change their habits (Taylor and Brown, 1988). Young people's feelings go beyond an unrealistic optimism; they often believe that they are indestructible and that nothing they do could actually harm them (Elkind, 1970). They see heart attacks, cancer, and diabetes as diseases of old age; at sixteen, old age can seem as remote as ancient Greece. Adults who have never had a serious illness may also feel invulnerable; they are convinced that their constitution is exceptionally strong or that doctors can fix anything. Becoming convinced of our own vulnerability is actually the first step toward establishing good health habits or breaking bad ones. Sometimes the knowledge that our actions affect others helps us change. When they are pregnant, for instance, women are more likely to follow a physician's advice to stop smoking than at any other time in their lives (Barec, MacArthur, and Sherwood, 1976).

The health belief model also predicts that we are less likely to develop good health habits if we do not believe that changing our behavior will reduce the threat to our health. A man whose father has diabetes may be concerned about developing the disease himself, but he may make no attempt to lose weight because he does not believe that his actions will lessen his own risk. A woman who fears breast cancer may fail to examine her breasts regularly because she has a fatalistic belief that early detection through self-examination will not improve her chances of complete recovery.

Programs for Developing Good Health Habits

On the assumption that the basic way to prevent illness is to persuade people to develop good health habits, psychologists use a range of intervention strategies, drawing heavily on the principles of learning discussed in Chapter 7. Some of the strategies are aimed at changing attitudes (which we will explore in Chapter 21), some at changing behavior, and some at changing the way people think about themselves, their situation, and their ability to alter it.

Direct Treatment

Many direct approaches use the techniques developed by behavior therapists, which we examined in Chapter 19. Treatment programs are used to help people give up smoking, stop drinking, lose weight, or stop abusing drugs. Some focus primarily on the habit itself; others aim at cognitive restructuring. In most cases the programs are remarkably successful; but with the passage of time, the old habits often reassert themselves. No matter what the original problem, from 15 to 60 percent of the people who take part in programs aimed at changing health-related behavior relapse (Leventhal and Cleary, 1980; Kaplan, 1984). In the hope of reducing the relapse rate, some psychologists have turned to a relapse-prevention program based on training in behavioral and cognitive skills (Marlatt and Gordon, 1985). People who enter the program learn how to identify and avoid, or deal with, situations that are likely to lead to a relapse. They also learn to expect an occasional lapse and how to minimize their guilt, frustration, or anxiety on such occasions. Along with these skills goes training in relaxation and other ways of handling stress.

Participating in a program—any program—motivates people to change, but launching new habits seems to be easier than maintaining them. For this reason, many health psychologists have turned their attention to children, hoping to prevent them from developing unhealthy habits in the first place.

Media Campaigns

Most of us are familiar with attempts to use the mass media to inform the public of health risks. Ads in newspapers, in magazines, and on TV warn us about AIDS, about drug abuse, and about smoking, for instance. Each year the American

These messages are part of public-service advertising campaigns aimed at changing people's behavior, but they may be more effective in altering opinions than behavior.

Cancer Society sponsors a "smokeout," a publicity campaign that urges smokers to stop for one day and combines warnings about the dangers of smoking with information on how to break the habit. Such campaigns can change public opinion. Thirty years ago, many people either did not know that smoking posed a serious health risk or disbelieved the warnings they heard. Today, almost everyone is aware of smoking's harmful effects, and most smokers say they want to quit. Yet little evidence exists to show that media campaigns cause widespread changes in smoking or other health behavior (Meyer et al., 1980). One reason for this limited success may be the fact that the media are also widely used to *promote* unhealthy habits like smoking; see the accompanying box.

Although "public health messages" in the media may have limited effect, programs that provide specific information can convince people to change their habits or take immediate steps to improve their health. For instance, Chicago TV stations once used the nightly news program to help people quit smoking: hundreds of smokers participated in a seventeen-part program designed by psychologists (Gruder et al., 1986). The nightly news was also used by a New York TV station to educate people about colon cancer. The station provided detection kits to viewers who asked for them, and several cases of cancer were detected before any symptoms had appeared.

Media campaigns may be most effective when combined with direct treatment. In the Stanford Heart Disease Prevention Project (Farquhar, Maccoby, and Solomon, 1984), researchers studied three similar communities; one served as a control, one was subjected to an intense media campaign focused on risk factors connected with heart disease, and the third received the same media campaign along with behavioral therapy for people in high-risk groups. The media campaign by itself produced moderate changes in health habits, but the combination of treatment and information was much more effective.

Numerous media campaigns have been used to slow the spread of AIDS, which is transmitted primarily through the exchange of bodily fluids, especially during sex, and through sharing needles by intravenous drug users. Posters, pamphlets, newspaper ads, and placards on buses and subways as well as radio and TV commercials have been part of media campaigns aimed at providing information about risks and behavioral changes that reduce those risks. Yet increasing knowledge among high-risk groups does not always lead to changes in risky behavior. Among members of gay and bisexual groups in San Francisco, New York, and London (Temoshok, Sweet, and Zich, 1987), increased knowledge about AIDS and the perception of high risk were not associated with changes in sexual behavior. As the Stanford project indicated, media campaigns, while essential, do not change behavior by themselves. For successful behavioral change, they need to be combined with other means of supporting changes in health habits.

PSYCHOLOGY TODAY AND TOMORROW

Promoting a Poor Health Habit: The Example of Cigarette Advertising

Media campaigns over the past twenty years have succeeded in alerting the public to the health risks of smoking. Ironically, however, the media have also been used to try to persuade certain segments of the population to take up this unhealthy habit.

Although tobacco companies assert that they are only trying to influence people who already smoke to switch to another brand, it is hard to discount the power of advertisements in persuading people to start smoking. Cigarettes are one of the most heavily advertised products in the United States. More than $2 billion a year is spent on cigarette ads (Albright et al., 1988). This advertising reaches nonsmokers and smokers alike, and it seems unlikely that such a powerful and pervasive message would not convince some nonsmokers that smoking offers some advantages.

What does the potential smoker think he or she will gain from smoking? To answer that question, we must examine the cigarette advertisements themselves and consider the audience at which they are directed. Since cigarette advertising was banned from television in 1971, tobacco companies have relied largely on magazine ads. Besides the appeals typical of such advertising (glamour, sex appeal, affluence, and fun), a number of new themes emerged in the 1980s that seemed to be intended to undermine the association between cigarette smoking and illness. One theme was the absence of the physical reality of smoking, such as full ashtrays and visible smoke from the lighted cigarettes the models were holding. A second theme was the "healthy" cigarette—one that was low in tar and nicotine. Most tobacco companies introduced "light" versions of their existing brands, and some brought out entirely new "low tar" brands. A third theme was vitality: the models used were young and vigorous and were often shown engaging in sports or social activities (Altman et al., 1987).

In a related trend, more advertisements were placed in magazines aimed at young people (such as *Rolling Stone* and *Cycle World*) and women (such as *Ladies Home Journal* and *Mademoiselle*) and fewer in general-interest magazines. In cigarette ads aimed at women, prominent themes are fashion, glamour, "liberation," romantic success, and slimness. For youth, the emphasis is on images of adventure and risk, in ads that seek to exploit young people's desire to identify with strong, adventurous, rebellious figures like the "Marlboro man" (Altman et al., 1987).

Advertising, then, promotes a poor health habit by linking smoking to images of health, adventure, fun, and glamour. These images are likely to seem more immediately motivating to many people than the possibility of avoiding illness at some vague point in the distant future.

Workplace and School Campaigns

Newscasts have only a short time to catch our interest and persuade us to change our ways, but at school or work we are open to persuasion for hours on end. Campaigns mounted in these locations may improve psychologists' chances of changing our health habits. Nearly two-thirds of organizations with fifty or more employees have at least one program promoting the health of their employees (Roberts and Harris, 1989). For example, AT&T's Total Life Concept program provides free blood-pressure and cholesterol screenings, then allows employees to choose among courses that help them change their lifestyles in ways that affect blood pressure, cholesterol levels, or stress. Follow-up support groups help employees who have completed the programs to maintain their new lifestyle. Year-long followups indicate that the program improves participants' health and morale (Roberts and Harris, 1989).

Many school districts have incorporated into their curricula a set of specific programs to prevent the use of drugs, to reduce adolescent pregnancies, and to combat the spread of such STDs as genital herpes and AIDS. Others have allowed psychologists to set up auxiliary programs on school grounds. In Houston, for example, psychologist Richard Evans and his colleagues (1978) designed a pro-

Many corporations offer their employees screening procedures, such as blood pressure checks, along with follow-up programs to help them improve their health habits.

gram aimed at reducing children's motivation to smoke. Teenagers already know that smoking is risky, but, as we have seen, their belief in their own invulnerability makes an appeal based on future illness ineffective. Instead, Evans concentrated on the current disadvantages of smoking (the cost of cigarettes, the bad breath of smokers, and so on). By showing the students films that explained the techniques used by advertisers to sell cigarettes, Evans created an image of the smoker as someone who was easily duped. This combated the adolescent image of smokers as sophisticated and rebellious figures. Posters with the message "You can decide for yourself" appealed to adolescents' need for independence. These techniques were backed up by older, high-status, nonsmoking peer leaders who modeled ways of resisting social pressure to smoke. The goal was "behavioral inoculation," a social version of immunization. In the case of infectious disease, when exposed to a weak version of a germ, we develop antibodies that fight off stronger attacks. By analogy, if adolescents are exposed to weak pressures to smoke, they develop counterarguments that protect them in the face of stronger social pressure.

After comparing smoking rates among teenagers who have been exposed to such programs with rates among other teenagers, researchers have concluded that the campaign is worth the effort (Leventhal and Cleary, 1980). It appears that some teenagers who might otherwise have smoked never begin and that others take up the habit much later than they otherwise would have.

Schools are also the location for programs aimed at developing problem-solving and social skills that will enable youngsters to cope with stressful situations (Danish, Galambos, and Laquatra, 1985). The better equipped we are to deal with stressful events in our lives, the less likely we are to develop health problems during stressful periods.

Community Campaigns

When entire communities focus on a health problem, change becomes more probable. Community-wide programs have succeeded in developing healthy lifestyles and in reducing deaths among large numbers of people. Among the 180,000 residents of North Karelia, Finland, for example, a ten-year campaign directed at smoking, diet, and hypertension sharply reduced the death rate from cardiovascular disease. The campaign was backed by extensive media appeals and the active participation of local groups within the community. At a time when deaths from cardiovascular disease among Finland's general population were declining by 11 percent, deaths in North Karelia dropped by 24 percent (Puska et al., 1983a; 1983b).

In Lycoming County, Pennsylvania, researchers instituted a program aimed at increasing physical activity among the 118,000 residents while reducing smoking, hypertension, serum cholesterol levels, and obesity (Stunkard, Felix, and Cohen, 1985). The program used five channels to reach the public—the mass media, the workplace, health agencies (physicians, hospitals, etc.), schools, and voluntary community agencies. The first results indicated a doubling of health-promoting activities at a time when similar activities declined by 42 percent in a neighboring county.

Social Engineering

All the programs we have examined so far deal with health problems by focusing on the individual. Their premise is that when people establish healthy habits, they can cope more effectively with their environment. Another way to promote good health is to change the environment (Wandersman et al., 1985). This is the most controversial approach to modifying behavior because it involves social engineering—taking action that affects an entire society. Social engineering to promote healthy behavior can be directed at individuals, at changes in laws, or at the environment itself.

Laws to change individual behavior throughout a society include lowering the highway speed limit, raising the legal age for drinking, and banning smoking on airplanes and in other public facilities. Often this method is effective. When speed limits were lowered in 1973, primarily to conserve energy, the number of deaths and injuries on the highways dropped significantly (Fielding, 1978). But social engineering sometimes backfires. During the Prohibition era (1919–1933), the outlawing of alcoholic beverages led to a rise in organized crime and widespread flouting of the law by the general public.

An example of current efforts at social engineering is the international attempt to curtail production of chlorofluorocarbons, with the aim of slowing the destruction of the world's ozone layer, a natural shield against harmful ultraviolet rays. Scientists have predicted sharp rises in skin cancers and radical changes in the world's climate unless such measures are successful (Dickson and Marshall, 1989).

Some health risks are preventable, but no matter how carefully we arrange our lives or how rigorously we adhere to healthy habits, there is one health risk we cannot avoid—stress.

STRESS AND HEALTH

The symptoms of stress are all too familiar. You may have felt them during a job interview; although you wanted to appear confident and self-assured, your heart raced and your mouth felt dry. Or perhaps you have felt them as your responsibilities mounted—schoolwork, job, your role in the community theater play—until you were overwhelmed by small problems, you skipped meals without realizing it, and at night you were too tired to sleep. Or perhaps the health of a family member has produced the symptoms: your mother had to go into the hospital for tests; although there was "nothing to worry about," you found yourself unable to study.

STRESS   a pattern of disruptive physiological and psychological reactions to events that threaten the ability to cope

Stress is a pattern of disruptive physiological and psychological reactions to events that threaten our ability to cope. The physiological symptoms are those of arousal: increases in pulse rate, blood pressure, respiration, and the level of certain hormones. The cognitive symptoms include obsessive thoughts and an inability to concentrate. The emotional symptoms include fear, anxiety, and excitement, anger, embarrassment, and depression. A certain amount of stress is an inevitable part of life; as stress researcher Hans Selye (1974) put it, "Complete freedom from stress is death." But acute stress can interfere with functioning in every area of our

TABLE 20.1 Social Readjustment Rating Scale
The amount of life stress a person has experienced in a given period of time, say one year, is measured by the total number of life change units (LCUs). These units result from the addition of the values (shown in the right column) associated with events that the person has experienced during the target time period.

RANK		MEAN VALUE
1	Death of spouse	100
2	Divorce	73
3	Marital separation	65
4	Jail term	63
5	Death of close family member	63
6	Personal injury or illness	53
7	Marriage	50
8	Fired at work	47
9	Marital reconciliation	45
10	Retirement	45
11	Change in health of family member	44
12	Pregnancy	40
13	Sex difficulties	39
14	Gain of new family member	39
15	Business readjustment	39
16	Change in financial state	38
17	Death of close friend	37
18	Change to different line of work	36
19	Change in number of arguments with spouse	35
20	Mortgage over $10,000	31
21	Foreclosure of mortgage or loan	30
22	Change in responsibilities at work	29
23	Son or daughter leaving home	29
24	Trouble with in-laws	29
25	Outstanding personal achievement	28
26	Spouse begin or stop work	26
27	Begin or end school	26
28	Change in living conditions	25
29	Revision of personal habits	24
30	Trouble with boss	23
31	Change in work hours or conditions	20
32	Change in residence	20
33	Change in schools	20
34	Change in recreation	19
35	Change in church activities	19
36	Change in social activities	18
37	Mortgage or loan less than $10,000	17
38	Change in sleeping habits	16
39	Change in number of family get-togethers	15
40	Change in eating habits	15
41	Vacation	13
42	Christmas	12
43	Minor violations of the law	11

Source: Holmes, T. H., and R. H. Rahe (1967). The Social Readjustment Rating Scale. *Journal of Psychosomatic Research, 11,* 213–218.

lives, and chronic stress has been linked to the degeneration of general health, colds and flu, allergies, high blood pressure, increased risk of heart disease, and fatal heart attacks (Jemmott and Locke, 1984).

There are three basic approaches to the study of stress. One is to identify the events in our lives that cause stress. The second is to analyze the personal factors that shape our response to those events. And the third is to trace the physiological consequences of stress.

Causes of Stress

At some time, most of us find our lives disrupted by extremely upsetting events—death of a loved one, work overload on the job, or perhaps surviving a disaster. And all of us must deal with minor annoyances on a daily basis—traffic jams, noisy neighbors, computer malfunctions, romantic breakups, too little money, too much work, too little sleep. Is it possible to assess the impact of such events on our psychological and physical well-being?

Measuring the Impact of Stressful Events

The first attempt to measure the consequences of stressful events on our lives was made by Thomas Holmes and Richard Rahe (1967), who devised the Social Readjustment Rating Scale based on the stressful events that medical patients had experienced in the months before they became ill (see Table 20.1). From their research, Holmes and Rahe concluded that change itself was the major factor in stress. Winning $10,000 was as stressful as losing that amount—what mattered was the change in a person's financial condition. Any event that forced people to make adjustments in their lives caused psychological wear and tear.

Problems with the scale soon appeared. It made no distinction between pleasant and unpleasant events, and later research indicated that only stress resulting from unpleasant events contributes to illness (Chiriboga, 1977). In addition, the scale had no place for chronic stress—those daily hassles that arise on the job and in intimate relationships—yet a tense, discordant marital relationship may be more stressful than getting a divorce (House and Robbins, 1983). Finally, the scale made no provision for individual differences in reactions, although the same event (for example, a thirty-day jail term) may affect one person as a disaster and another as a minor annoyance. A second scale, known as the Bedford College Life Event Instrument, provides a more accurate measure of the actual impact of stressful events (Brown and Harris, 1978). In place of a checklist, the Bedford College scale uses in-depth interviews to determine just how the subject perceived various events. No matter which scale is used, however, stressful events do seem to correlate with ill health.

The death of a spouse is one of life's most stressful events. It puts the widow or widower at greater risk of illness and premature death.

Illness and injury are more common among people whose jobs involve high levels of stress.

Major Sources of Stress

LOSS OF A LOVED ONE According to Holmes and Rahe (1967), life's three most stressful events are the death of a spouse, divorce, and marital separation. Premature death rates are consistently higher among people who are widowed, divorced, or single than among people who are married. This correlation holds true for men as well as for women, for whites as well as for nonwhites, and for almost every cause of death, including heart attack, cancer, stroke, cirrhosis, hypertension, pneumonia, suicide, and even automobile accidents (Lynch, 1977). A study of 4500 British widowers, for instance, found that the mortality rate during the first six months after their wives died was 40 percent higher than among other men of the same age (Parkes, Benjamin, and Fitzgerald, 1969). Children, too, are not immune to the disruption of relationships. Many children who develop cancer have recently lost someone who was very close to them (Jacobs and Charles, 1980).

Can people actually die of grief? From time to time the media carry reports of people who seem to have died of sorrow. In one example of this phenomenon, a sixty-nine-year-old man died suddenly the day after his wife's funeral. His car nudged the rear bumper of the car in front of him. He got out of his car, walked around, got back in the car, and slumped over the steering wheel, dead (Engel, 1971). In another case, thirty-nine-year-old twins, who had been described as "inseparable," died within a week of each other—cause of death, unknown. A twenty-seven-year-old army captain suddenly died of "cardiac irregularity and acute congestion"; ten days earlier he had commanded the ceremonial troops at President John F. Kennedy's funeral (Taylor, 1986).

Healthy people do not die in this manner. Sudden and rapid death seems to strike when a person with a preexisting physiological weakness (such as undetected heart disease or infection) suffers a severe shock (Cottington et al., 1980). Most of us survive the death of a loved one, although we may be psychologically and physiologically vulnerable for a time.

STRESS ON THE JOB Stress in the workplace is associated with high rates of illness and injury (Taylor, 1986). Occupational stress may take many forms, from a disagreement with the boss to a change in working hours or responsibilities, but the major source of stress is work overload. When we are expected to work long hours, meet high standards, and perform more tasks than we feel we can handle, we feel the stress. Other factors that contribute to stress on the job are responsibility for others, lack of clear-cut job requirements or standards, contradictory

PSYCHOLOGY TODAY AND TOMORROW

Post-traumatic Stress Disorder among Vietnam Veterans

Man-made disasters—especially wars—may provoke more severe stress reactions than natural disasters do (Glesser, Green, and Einget, 1981). A soldier may break down after a close brush with death, especially if several of his buddies were killed. But the incident usually comes after months of fear, deprivation, extreme cold or heat, lack of sleep, and narrow escapes. Often the stress of combat does not surface until the soldier returns to civilian life.

During World War I post-traumatic stress disorder was called "shell shock"; in World War II it was called "combat fatigue." No matter what name it goes by, the incidence of post-traumatic stress disorder is much higher among Vietnam veterans than among veterans of the two world wars. As many as 400,000 Vietnam vets still suffer mild to severe forms of the disorder (Lyons, 1984). Their symptoms include nightmares, vivid flashbacks to scenes of horror, chronic startle reactions, and a sense of irritation and distractibility that interferes with their ability to work.

Four factors helped to increase the stress on men who fought in Vietnam (Walker and Cavenar, 1982). First, they were unable to develop the group ties and social supports that generally protect soldiers from stress. Most had been shipped to Vietnam alone and then transferred from place to place before they could establish bonds with other soldiers. Second, Vietnam veterans did not receive the public support given to veterans of other wars. Public opposition to the war and the lack of an all-out campaign to win it fostered an atmosphere of purposelessness. When veterans came home, there were no cheering crowds and victory parades because there was no victory. Third, high rates of drug use among the troops tended to hide psychological problems from military psychiatrists. Soldiers "treated themselves" with drugs and got no counseling for their problems. Finally, many soldiers were shipped home suddenly, with little or no time to ease the transition from combat to civilian life. Yet society expected them to pick up their lives as if nothing had happened.

These factors were aggravated by the youth of the Vietnam soldier. The average age of soldiers in Vietnam was 19.2 years, compared to 26 years for soldiers in World War II (Lyons, 1984). Youths went to Vietnam at a time when most young people are still building their identity, working out commitments to occupations and political beliefs (see Chapter 16). Vietnam veterans spent this period of their lives on the battlefield. For many, the result was identity diffusion. On their return, many felt that "I'm changed," "I don't fit in," "I'm twenty and I came back fifty." As these men approached midlife, unresolved identity issues began to resurface.

The special problems of Vietnam veterans went unrecognized for years. The federal government, the press, the medical profession, and the public saw these veterans as no different from other members of their generation who "turned on" to drugs in the 1960s and "turned off" to traditional occupations. It was 1980 before the American Psychiatric Association recognized post-traumatic stress disorder as a specific psychological diagnosis. In the past few years, the Veterans Administration and the general public have become more sympathetic to the special situation of Vietnam veterans. Tangible evidence of the change is the memorial in Washington, D.C., dedicated in 1982 to Americans who died in Vietnam.

demands by supervisors or coworkers, lack of any opportunity to develop social relationships, premature or delayed promotion, and lack of control over our work.

People who work in high-stress occupations may pay a high price. Air traffic controllers, who spend their days juggling the flights of giant airliners while aware that a minor mistake may kill hundreds of people, are four times as likely as the pilots who fly the planes to suffer from hypertension and more than twice as likely to develop diabetes or peptic ulcers (Cobb, 1976). Not all workers in stressful jobs become ill, however. Many workers develop their own way of handling the stress. Some may show up late, leave early, do as little work as possible, or sabotage management's efforts to increase productivity. Others simply quit and move to a

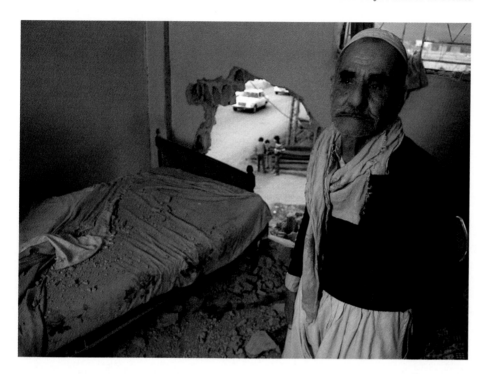

Traumatic events, like this bombing in Lebanon, leave survivors with predictable patterns of stress. They may be "emotionally anesthetized" for a long time afterward.

less stressful job. Still others, taking a more positive approach, learn to deal with the stress, perhaps with the aid of the coping techniques discussed later in this chapter.

DISASTERS Traumatic events—earthquakes, floods, fires, airplane crashes, rapes, assaults, or wars—produce distinctive patterns of stress. For days, weeks, even years after such an event, victims may relive it in painful memories and nightmares. Many suffer from extreme fatigue, hypersensitivity to noise, loss of appetite, and diminished sexual desire. They feel "emotionally anesthetized"—unable to respond to affection or to take an interest in daily life (Brody, 1982). Wars, which may place participants under uninterrupted stress for months, seem to produce a unique response; as the accompanying box indicates, hundreds of thousands of Vietnam veterans have not yet been able to shake the effects of that war.

Natural or man-made disasters, such as earthquakes or nuclear plant accidents, are most likely to cause severe stress when a high percentage of the community is affected and many lives are lost (Glesser, Green, and Einget, 1981). Survivors often feel numb and unable to act. One of the first disasters to be studied for their effects on survivors was a flood in the mining town of Buffalo Creek, West Virginia, in 1972. One man who lived through the flood, which left 125 dead and hundreds homeless, described his immediate reaction:

I just didn't—I really didn't feel anything. Things just wasn't connected. Like I couldn't remember my own telephone number . . . I couldn't remember where I lived . . . I was just standing there and it seemed like I really didn't have anything on my mind at the time. Just everything disappeared. (Erikson, 1976, p. 162)

Survivors may feel guilty, as if their own survival had caused others to die. Such reactions seemed common among the people who survived the collapse of two skywalks over the lobby of a Kansas City hotel in 1981. In the weeks and months after that disaster, which killed 113 people and injured 200, those who had been injured showed fewer emotional problems than people who had not. It was as if the injured had "paid their debt" with cuts, fractures, and concussions and escaped the burden of guilt carried by uninjured survivors (Brody, 1982).

Daily hassles may be more stressful than major crises.

Minor Sources of Stress

We noted earlier that daily hassles may be more stressful than major unpleasant events. Researchers have devised a "hassles scale" (see Figure 20.1) in order to explore the effects on health of continual mild stress—traffic jams, waiting in lines, misplacing the keys, running out of money before payday, and the like (Lazarus, 1980). The link clearly exists; in one study, everyday hassles were a better predictor of declines in physical health, the onset of depression, and the development of anxiety than were major life events (Delongis et al., 1982). Whether daily hassles have a cumulative effect, simply wearing us down, or whether they make us more vulnerable when a big event (getting fired or divorced) comes along is uncertain. Perhaps both are involved.

Since only unpleasant stress has been connected with illness, Richard Lazarus and his colleagues (Lazarus, Kanner, and Folkman, 1980; Kanner et al., 1981) have been exploring the possibility that pleasant events have positive effects. They have developed an "uplift" scale that allows them to trace the connection between everyday pleasures, such as listening to music, walking in the country, having a pleasant dinner with friends, or playing with one's child, and health. Perhaps "uplifts" like these act as buffers against stress.

Responses to Stress

One person thrives on deadlines; another is immobilized by them. One person is thrilled by an invitation to speak at a political rally; a second is terrified; a third is bored. One woman views the discovery of a malignant breast tumor as a death

SAMPLE ITEMS FROM THE "HASSLES" SCALE	SAMPLE ITEMS FROM THE "UPLIFTS" SCALE
Directions: Hassles are irritants that can range from minor annoyances to fairly major pressures, problems, or difficulties. They can occur few or many times.	*Directions:* Uplifts are events that make you feel good. They can be sources of peace, satisfaction, or joy. Some occur often, others are relatively rare.
Listed below are a number of ways in which a person can feel hassled. First, circle the hassles that have happened to you in the past month. Then look at the numbers on the right of the items you circled. Indicate by circling a 1, 2, or 3 how *severe* each of the circled hassles has been for you in the past month. If a hassle did not occur in the last month *do not* circle it.	On the list below, circle the events that have made you feel good in the past month. Then look at the numbers on the right of the items you circled. Indicate by circling a 1, 2, or 3 how *often* each of the circled uplifts has occurred in the last month. If an uplift did not occur in the last month, *do not* circle it.

Severity	*How Often*
1—Somewhat severe	1—Somewhat often
2—Moderately severe	2—Moderately often
3—Extremely severe	3—Extremely often

1. Misplacing or losing things	1 2 3	
2. Troublesome neighbors	1 2 3	
3. Social obligations	1 2 3	
4. Inconsiderate smokers	1 2 3	
5. Thoughts about death	1 2 3	
6. Health of a family member	1 2 3	
7. Not enough money for clothing	1 2 3	
8. Concerns about owing money	1 2 3	

1. Practicing your hobby	1 2 3
2. Being lucky	1 2 3
3. Saving money	1 2 3
4. Liking fellow workers	1 2 3
5. Gossiping; "shooting the bull"	1 2 3
6. Successful financial dealings	1 2 3
7. Being rested	1 2 3
8. Feeling healthy	1 2 3
9. Finding something presumed lost	1 2 3

Figure 20.1 Measuring hassles and uplifts. Scales like those shown here have been developed to examine the link between minor sources of stress and physical illness, and to explore whether life's little pleasures can serve as buffers between ourselves and stress. (Kanner et al., 1981.)

sentence and loses interest in daily events; another views coping with her cancer as a challenge and finds that daily events take on new meaning. Individual differences in response to potentially stressful events are so varied that many psychologists have concluded that the key aspects of stress are psychological and cognitive.

How We Appraise the Situation

Some researchers have become convinced that the impact of stress bears little relationship to the event itself; the critical factors are our appraisals of the event and of our ability to cope with the situation (Lazarus, 1968; Lazarus and Folkman, 1984) (see Figure 20.2). In this view, when we face new or changing circumstances, we first determine what these events mean—a process known as **primary appraisal.** The result of our primary appraisal depends on our situation, motives, and goals, as we saw in Chapter 12. One student who gets a C on a chemistry exam may see the event as beneficial ("I never thought I'd pass"), a second may see it as neutral ("I'm only taking chemistry because it's required"), and a third may see it as ominous ("I need at least a B in this course to get into medical school"). Once we have made our primary appraisal, we analyze an event we have labeled as "negative" to see just how much danger it represents. A student might see the effect of the grade as irreparable harm ("I'm automatically excluded from the premed program"), a threat ("My chances of getting the B that I need for med school are slim"), or a challenge ("I'll just have to work twice as hard and try for an A on the final").

The next step is **secondary appraisal,** the process of assessing whether we have the ability and resources to cope with the situation. The level of stress we feel depends on the balance between the primary and secondary appraisals. If the degree of perceived harm or threat is high and the self-appraisal is low, we will feel considerable stress. Suppose the premed student with a C is struggling with a full load of difficult courses and a part-time job; he is likely to feel severe stress. But another premed student who has no outside employment but does have a roommate willing to help her study is likely to handle the situation with much less strain. When the threat or harm seems small and our coping ability is high, stress is slight.

The Importance of Control

No matter what sort of event we encounter, whether we experience stress depends in part on whether we believe that events are predictable and that we have some control over what happens to us. This became clear during World War II, when researchers noted that Londoners, who were bombed regularly, showed few signs of anxiety. But residents of surrounding villages, where bombing was infrequent and unpredictable, showed high levels of anxiety and apprehension (Vernon, 1941). Predictable events are less stressful because we can prepare for them. If we know when an unpleasant or painful event will occur, we also know when it will

PRIMARY APPRAISAL the initial determination of the meaning of new or changing circumstances

SECONDARY APPRAISAL the assessment of one's coping ability and resources for dealing with new or changing circumstances

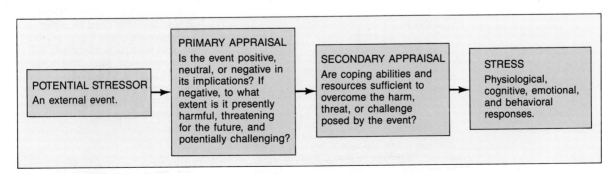

Figure 20.2 The role of appraisal in the experience of stress. (From Taylor, 1986, p. 149.)

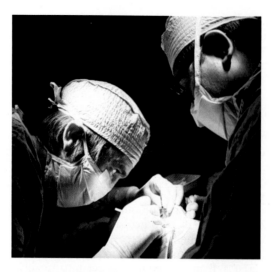

Surgeons may suffer somewhat less anxiety and stress than might be thought. Their high level of training and skill provides a sense of control over life-or-death situations.

not occur. This knowledge lets us know when it is safe to resume normal activities. But when aversive events are unpredictable, anticipatory stress remains constantly high.

Animals and people share a preference for predictable stress. Given a choice between a severe electric shock at predictable intervals and a weak shock that may occur at any moment, a rat will choose the more unpleasant shock whose arrival it can predict (Badia, Culbertson, and Harsh, 1973). Researchers asked college women to perform simple verbal and math tasks while being subjected to bursts of loud, unpleasant noise comparable to the noise of a motorcycle engine (Glass and Singer, 1972). One group heard the noise at random intervals; the other group heard the same noise at regular intervals. After the noise was turned off, both group's worked at complex proofreading tasks and two unsolvable puzzles. Women who had been exposed to unpredictable noise gave up sooner and made many more mistakes than women who had been able to predict just when the noise would burst out. Apparently, the women who devoted their energy to overcoming the distraction and irritation of random noise had little left to apply toward the new task.

The feeling of being in control may be even more important than the ability to predict events (Thompson, 1981). In another experiment (Glass, Reim, and Singer, 1971), college men worked on a series of simple tasks against a background of random noise like that used in the study of college women. Half the students were told that they could stop the noise at any time by signaling their partners, although the researcher preferred that they not interrupt the sound. The other students had no way of controlling the noise. Students in the first group did not use their power to stop the noise, yet when given another task they performed much better and showed significantly less tension than the students who had no control over the noise (see Figure 20.3).

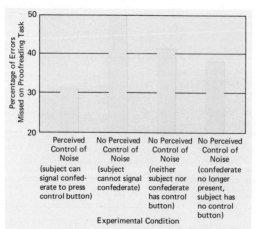

Figure 20.3 Coping with a stressful environment. In two experiments David Glass and colleagues have shown that exposure to uncontrollable and unpredictable noise has a much greater effect on performance of a subsequent task in a quiet environment than exposure to controllable and unpredictable noise. More effort is required to adapt to the unpredictable and uncontrollable noise, which leaves the person less able to deal effectively with future tasks.

Apparently, the inability to control or avoid danger can be more stressful than danger itself. During World War II, fighter pilots had the highest casualty rates among flight crews, yet they reported less fear than either bomber pilots or their gun crews, who stood a much better chance of surviving (Rachman, 1978). What made the fighter pilots so fearless? They had control over their flight paths and could take evasive action, while the bomber pilots had to fly in formation. Members of the bomber gun crews, who had no control of any kind over the plane's flight, were the most fearful of all. It seems that our perceptions of control, not our actual degree of control, determine our level of anxiety.

Feelings of helplessness impaired performance in the noise experiment and were associated with anxiety among flight crews. These results suggest that learned helplessness, which we explored in Chapter 18 as a possible factor in the development of depression, may give us a way of understanding the effects of uncontrollable stress. In fact, the failure to adjust to stressful events seems to be closely associated with the development of learned helplessness. In one experiment, college students were subjected to an inescapable loud tone. On a later occasion they made few attempts to get away from the noise and performed poorly on a new task (Hiroto and Seligman, 1975). Another group of students, who could press a button to shut off the tone during the first task, promptly switched off the sound and were much more efficient when asked to complete a new second task. Unpredictable failure can induce learned helplessness as proficiently as inescapable noise. Students who faced a series of unpredictable failures on a series of problems also learned to feel helpless. The danger of learned helplessness is that it carries over from one situation to another. Students who could not escape the loud tone were also helpless in the problem-solving task.

Learned helplessness helps to explain why some people feel overwhelmed by stressful events, but it does not tell us why other people, placed in situations that they cannot control, do not become helpless. Nor does it account for the fact that many people feel sad or guilty after enduring aversive events that could not have been avoided. The development of learned helplessness apparently depends on how people interpret their lack of control (Abrahamson, Seligman, and Teasdale, 1978). People are in danger of becoming helpless only when they see their lack of control as due to causes that are permanent (so that no change can be expected), internal (the result of deficiencies within themselves), and global (applicable to many areas of their lives).

Physiological Consequences of Stress

If people under severe stress often contract flu or develop heart disease or diabetes, stress must affect the functioning of the body in some way. But how are psychological experiences translated into physiological symptoms?

The Stress Syndrome

The first researcher to link physiological processes with stress was Hans Selye (1956; 1976). As a medical student, Selye was taught the medical model: each disease has its own particular cause and its own unique symptoms. In practice, however, he noticed that patients suffering from a wide variety of diseases often had similar symptoms, including loss of appetite, apathy, and weakness. He suspected that these symptoms were a generalized response to a stressful attack on the body. Years later, he tested this hypothesis in the laboratory by exposing mice to extreme cold, prolonged hunger, fatigue, and a variety of toxic substances. He found that all of these stressors produced the same physiological response: enlarged adrenal glands, shrunken thymus and lymph nodes, and stomach ulcers.

This common reaction led Selye to propose the existence of a *general adaptation syndrome*. He applied this theory to humans as well as to laboratory animals. The syndrome has three stages: alarm, resistance, and exhaustion (see Figure 20.4). In the alarm stage, an initial shock causes the autonomic nervous system to

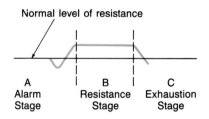

Figure 20.4 Selye's general adaptation syndrome. (A) In the alarm phase, the body first reacts to a stressor. At this time, resistance is diminished. (B) The resistance state occurs with continued exposure to a stressor. (C) The exhaustion stage results from long-term exposure to the same stressor. At this point resistance may again fall below normal. (Based on Selye, 1974.)

send adrenal hormones through the body, preparing the glands and organs for action, and the brain releases catecholamines, alerting us to danger. In the resistance stage, local defenses take over. If the stressor is a virus, the immune system is called into play: antibodies rush to the scene. If the stressor is a psychological threat, the sympathetic nervous system prepares for "fight or flight." The body has been mobilized. In most cases, the stressor is defeated and the body returns to normal. But sometimes the stress continues. When this happens, the prolonged resistance exhausts the body's resources, and the organism succumbs to exhaustion. Exhaustion causes physiological damage and sometimes death. If a man falls into icy water, for example, he goes numb (the alarm stage). Then his autonomic nervous system takes over, enabling him to adapt to the cold (the resistance phase). If he stays in the icy water too long, however, he becomes exhausted and may not recover, even if he is rescued.

Selye's research was a milestone, but he may have underestimated the role that psychological factors play in illness (Mason, 1974). In addition, Selye's concept of exhaustion is too broad to explain exactly how particular diseases develop in people under stress. Later research suggests that specific stressors, personality traits, or socioeconomic conditions are implicated in specific disorders. Researchers have discovered such factors in hypertension, coronary heart disease, and cancer, three of the leading causes of chronic illness and death.

Hypertension

Hypertension, or high blood pressure, is a common disease; an estimated 30 million Americans suffer from it. Even people who do not have hypertension generally respond to severe stress with a rise in blood pressure (Shapiro and Goldstein, 1982). The reaction can become chronic and dangerous in individuals whose blood pressure already is elevated (Galton, 1973).

Studies have linked high blood pressure with general environmental stress. Among men in Detroit, hypertension was more common among those who lived in areas characterized by poverty, crime, crowding, and high divorce rates than among men who lived in areas where these kinds of stress were low (Harburg et al., 1973; Gentry et al., 1982). The connection between environmental stress and hypertension appeared in both white and black men, but was more pronounced among black men. Apparently, genetic makeup and minority status (an additional form of stress) combine with other stressors to increase rates of hypertension among black people.

In these studies, black men who displayed "suppressed rage" (the tendency to direct anger inward) on psychological measures were also more likely to be hypertensive than those who directed their anger at the world. How does rage become a physiological disability? Hypertensive men and women are particularly sensitive to the physiological effects of stress (Steptoe, 1984). Their blood pressure rises rapidly in response to minor stress, or even the anticipation of it. Once their blood pressure rises, it takes longer to return to normal levels than it does in most people. This pattern is probably hereditary, because twin studies have shown that both identical twins show such exaggerated blood pressure responses much more often than both fraternal twins (Rose and Chesney, 1986). Longitudinal studies indicate that people whose blood pressure shows this exaggerated reaction to stress are more likely than others to become hypertensive (Falkner, et al., 1981). Such findings provide hope in the fight against hypertension, because identifying such people early in life could enable physicians to intervene early with measures to prevent the disease.

Coronary Heart Disease

Coronary heart disease (CHD) is the leading cause of chronic illness and death in the United States. CHD develops when the blood vessels that bring oxygen and nutrients into the heart are narrowed or closed, so that the heart muscle begins to starve. CHD has been linked to hypertension, diabetes, smoking, obesity, high levels of cholesterol, and low levels of physical activity (American Heart Association, 1984). Taken together, however, these risk factors account for less than half the known cases of CHD.

Some years ago, two physicians, Meyer Friedman and Ray Rosenman (1974) identified a behavioral and emotional pattern that they believed greatly increased the risk of CHD. They called this pattern the **Type A personality.** Such people are impatient, highly competitive, and hostile when thwarted. They continually struggle to achieve more in less time, regardless of the social and psychological consequences, and are nagged by the feeling that they could achieve still more if they tried a little harder. Type A's tend to blame themselves for failures that are beyond their control (Brunson and Matthews, 1981). Type B's, in contrast, are more patient, more relaxed, and better able to roll with the punches. Only about 10 percent of the people studied by Friedman and Rosenman met all the criteria for classification as pure Type A's and another 10 percent were pure Type B's.

Early research showed a powerful connection between Type A personality and CHD. When more than 2000 male executives were followed for eight and one-half years, Type A's were twice as likely as Type B's to develop CHD or to have a heart attack, and among men who survived the first heart attack, Type A's were five times as likely to have a second (Rosenman et al., 1975). Then apparently conflicting research began to appear. In one study of people who had survived a heart attack (Ragland and Brand, 1988), Type A's lived longer than Type B's. This puzzling finding may mean that the high-achieving Type A's were more successful at changing their lifestyle in accordance with their physicians' instructions, but researchers are not certain. Other research indicates that workaholic Type A's are not in as much danger as was once feared (Booth-Kewley and Friedman, 1987). There seemed to be no association between the impatient struggle to accomplish ever more work and coronary heart disease. Instead, both depression and CHD seemed to develop in Type A's who often give vent to their anger, hostility, and aggression. Other researchers have confirmed the link between CHD and the negative emotions of hostility and anger (Matthews, 1988; Blakeslee, 1989).

In exploring why the hostility and anger of Type A's sometimes lead to CHD, some researchers have found that Type A's have an extremely responsive physiology. When exposed to stress, their bodies respond with exceptionally high levels of sympathetic nervous system activity, which causes wear and tear on the heart (Williams et al., 1982; Blakeslee, 1989). And once their sympathetic nervous system is aroused, it stays that way because their parasympathetic nervous system seems so weak that it fails to calm them down. Type A's are also less responsive to their body's warning signals than other people; they do not feel the symptoms of fatigue or stress that tell other people to slow down (Carver, DeGregorio, and Gillis, 1981).

The vulnerability of Type A's is not limited to coronary heart disease. People whose personalities place them at risk for one illness are also at risk for other diseases. Instead of particular personality patterns leading to specific diseases, it appears that the same personality patterns are associated with many different diseases (Friedman and Booth-Kewley, 1987). This relationship may mean that any behavior that increases stress makes a person more vulnerable to a host of disorders.

Research indicates that by changing their behavior, Type A's can greatly reduce their risk. When Friedman and his colleagues (1984) showed survivors of a first heart attack how to change their behavior, their rate of heart attacks dropped sharply compared with other survivors who had only the customary medical supervision. Over a three-year period, just over 7 percent of survivors who were trained in relaxation, self-control, and goal-setting had a second heart attack, compared with 13 percent of the survivors in the control group.

TYPE A PERSONALITY a pattern of behavior marked by impatience, competitiveness, and hostility

Cancer

The link between stress and cancer is only beginning to be traced. The term "cancer" refers to more than 100 different diseases, but all involve a malfunction in the mechanisms that control cell reproduction. The normal duplication of cells—a slow, regular process—is replaced by a rapid production of abnormal cells that invade the body's organs and tissues. Some cancers develop quickly; others take decades to become detectable; still others have an irregular and unpredictable course.

The origin of some cancers has a genetic component, but in many cases what the person inherits may be a defect in genes related to cell regulation or to the differentiation of tissue (Chang et al., 1987). The defect apparently does not produce cancer itself, but a vulnerability to it, so that a cancer develops with a smaller exposure to carcinogens than would be required in people without the defect. Other researchers have located what appears to be an inherited loss of "tumor suppressor genes" in patients with cancer of the colon (Fearon, Hamilton, and Vogelstein, 1987). Certain cancers run in families and ethnic groups, but whatever genetic involvement exists may be compounded by a shared lifestyle. For example, although breast cancer is common among North American women and rare among Asian women, the longer Japanese-American women live in the United States and the more Americanized they become, the more likely they are to develop breast cancer (Wynder et al., 1963).

Many cancers are *not* hereditary. Diet and exposure to carcinogens are suspected of playing an important role in their development, but psychological factors may also be involved. Stressful life events, especially the loss or disruption of social supports, have been linked to cancer (Sklar and Anisman, 1981). A lack of social support may explain why single people are somewhat more likely to develop cancer than married people.

How can stress be involved in the development of cancer? Animal and human research both indicate that uncontrollable stress directly affects the immune system (Laudenslager et al., 1983; Rodin, 1986). Such discoveries have focused research on interaction among psychological factors, the central nervous system, and the immune system and led to the establishment of a rapidly developing field called *psychoneuroimmunology*. It appears that stress may depress the functioning of the immune system, making it possible for cancer cells to establish themselves and spurring the growth of established tumors (Sklar and Anisman, 1979; Visintainer, Volpicelli, and Seligman, 1982). Other studies have suggested that depression also reduces immune functioning (Jemmott and Locke, 1984). (Researchers in this area are beginning to uncover a link between relatively minor stress and vulnerability to infectious disease; see the accompanying box.)

Some psychologists have investigated the possibility that certain personality traits are involved in this interaction. One line of research has investigated the notion that people who learn to cope with stress through the defense mechanisms of repression and denial (which were discussed in Chapter 17) are more vulnerable to cancer than those who deal with stress more directly (Dattore, Shontz, and Coyne, 1980; Bahnson, 1981). Another line of research has explored the proposal that once cancer has appeared, particular personality factors may influence its course (Levy, 1983). In this view, combative people who are angry about having developed cancer and hostile toward medical personnel live longer than cancer patients who are passive and accepting. None of this research has yet produced firm evidence linking personality types to cancer; indeed, there may be no "cancer-prone" personality; instead, as we saw in the discussion of CHD, certain personality characteristics may increase our vulnerability to many disorders.

COPING WITH STRESS

One woman has a full-time job and two children, teaches Sunday school, serves as den mother to a group of Cub Scouts, and works in her local Democratic club—yet she always seems full of energy and ready for new experiences. Another can barely manage to handle her one child and a part-time job; she always feels tired and complains of allergies, colds, and headaches. The second woman is overwhelmed by the pressures in her life. The first woman is **coping:** she has worked out a way of handling the external and internal pressures that might otherwise lead

COPING   the process of managing external and internal pressures in a way that diminishes stress

PSYCHOLOGY TODAY AND TOMORROW

Exam Stress and Immune Functioning

The new field of psychoneuroimmunology is making interesting discoveries about the effects that stress has on our immune systems. Although the mechanisms involved are still not clear, we do know from recent research that stressful events depress our normal immune functioning and thus make us more vulnerable to infectious diseases.

Initial research measured the effects of major sources of stress, like bereavement and prolonged sleep deprivation. More recently, investigators have found that even relatively minor stressors, like final exams, can cause declines in immune functioning. In one study (Kiecolt-Glaser et al., 1986) blood samples were taken from a group of first-year medical students a month before their examinations and again on the last day of their exam period. Analysis showed a significant decline in "killer" cells that help the body fight off disease microbes. (A statistical procedure was used to filter out possible effects of other variables, such as poor nutrition, lack of sleep, and caffeine intake.) This meant that these students' ability to resist infection was somewhat compromised simply because of exam stress. The subjects did not necessarily become ill, however, since their immune responses were still functioning—merely at a lower level than normal.

The investigators also sought to determine whether an antistress intervention, in the form of relaxation training, might moderate the effects of stress. One group of subjects was given ten sessions of instruction in various relaxation techniques, which they were encouraged to practice on their own as well as in the class. The researchers found that subjects who received this training had a significantly smaller drop in immune functioning than those who did not.

The medical students in this experiment were comparatively healthy, symptom-free people with considerable experience in examination taking. Thus, this decline in immune functioning during exam week—a stressful period, certainly, but one for which students could prepare and which they had been through before—suggests that our immune systems are quite sensitive even to commonplace, predictable sources of stress.

Another implication of this study is that any activity that moderates the affects of stress seems to help the immune system continue functioning normally. Students who want to get through exam week—or any other stressful period—in good health might want to schedule breaks for exercise, meditation, or going out with friends.

to stress. Successful coping depends on a combination of problem-solving ability and emotional self-regulation (Cohen and Lazarus, 1979). People who cope well solve problems by changing aspects of their environment that are harmful or threatening; they regulate their emotions by maintaining a positive self-image and satisfactory relationships with others.

The importance of family and friends to our health stems from the social support they provide in stressful times. This support can take the form of tangible assistance (meals when we are sick or money when we run short), information (practical advice on our problems or feedback on our ideas), and emotional support (the knowledge that we are loved and cared for) when our self-esteem is threatened (Schaefer, Coyne, and Lazarus, 1981). Social support seems to soften the effects of stressful events, so that we are less likely to become ill and tend to recover faster when illness does strike (Berkman and Syme, 1979).

Researchers have studied successful coping in action. In one study, S. C. Kobasa (1979) singled out a group of executives who had encountered a large number of potentially stressful events in the preceding three years. Some of these executives had also had health problems during the period; others had not. When Kobasa compared the two groups, she found that the healthy, but highly stressed, executives had a strong sense of commitment and became deeply involved with people and activities. They felt in control of their lives, taking credit for their successes and blame for their failures. They welcomed challenge and tended to see new activities and changes in routine as opportunities for growth.

Kobasa concluded that the combination of commitment, control, and challenge makes a person "hardy." Such people are able to defuse potentially stressful situations. They tend to appraise each new situation and their own ability to cope with it in positive terms. As a result, they take direct action and learn about the people and events involved—a process that makes them even better prepared to deal with future situations. Some psychologists (Ganellen and Blaney, 1984) have criticized Kobasa's study on the grounds that she identified the characteristics of hardiness only *after* the executives had been sorted into healthy and unhealthy categories. Before we can say that hardiness predicts health, we would first have to identify the hardy and then see whether they developed health problems. Nevertheless, Kobasa's work provides a useful description of positive coping styles.

Many people lack the qualities of Kobasa's hardy executives. They tend to avoid grappling with stressful situations, even denying that a problem exists. Their stress mounts and they may become ill. What can be done to equip such people with techniques that enable them to cope with stressful events? Some programs aim at altering people's physiological responses to stress; others focus on their cognitive and behavioral responses.

Controlling Physiological Arousal

PROGRESSIVE RELAXATION a technique that induces relaxation by tensing and releasing different muscle groups in sequence

If we could control our bodily responses to stressful events, perhaps we could prevent many stress-related illnesses. The most common approach to reducing physiological arousal is some form of relaxation training. In **progressive relaxation,** which was developed by Edmund Jacobson (1938; 1964), a person learns to relax various muscles at will. Control comes through tensing and then releasing different muscle groups in sequence. The first step in training might be to bend the left hand as far back as possible and to notice the pattern of strain in the back of the hand and up the arm. After maintaining that position for about 10 seconds, the person lets the hand relax completely and notices the difference in sensation. The object of this training program is to teach people how each muscle group feels when relaxed and to provide practice in achieving further relaxation. Once a person can distinguish patterns of muscle tension from those of relaxation, there is no need to tense the muscles before relaxing them. Instead the person relaxes the muscles from whatever level of tension they have reached.

Progressive relaxation is an effective treatment for a variety of stress-related disorders. Studies have shown that progressive relaxation effectively reduces general tension and anxiety (Borkovec, Grayson, and Cooper, 1978), relieves insomnia (Borkovec et al., 1979), and reduces high blood pressure (Jacob, Kraemer, and Agras, 1977). In an abbreviated form, progressive relaxation is also an important part of systematic desensitization, as we saw in the discussion of behavior therapy in Chapter 19.

AUTOGENIC TRAINING technique that induces relaxation by self-suggestion and imagery

A second relaxation procedure, called **autogenic training,** depends on self-suggestion and imagery. This technique was developed by Johannes Schultz and Wolfgang Luthe (1969) after they noted that people under hypnosis seemed able to induce physiological changes in themselves. When a hypnotized person hears the suggestion that an arm is getting heavy, measurable changes often occur in the arm's muscle potential—an indication that the muscle is relaxing. Schultz and Luthe speculated that people could achieve the same effects through suggestive language, without having to be hypnotized. In autogenic training, the person repeats suggestions, such as "My arm is heavy. I am at peace. My arm is heavy." Each attempt to relax lasts from 30 to 60 seconds. After a person has learned to make the whole body "heavy," she or he follows similar procedures to induce warmth, control heart rate and respiration, and cool the forehead. Progressive relaxation and autogenic training are both effective treatments for insomnia (Nicassio and Bootzin, 1974).

BIOFEEDBACK a technique for gaining control over physiological function by monitoring a continuous flow of information about the function

A third technique for reducing physiological arousal is **biofeedback,** a form of instrumental conditioning designed to make us aware of an unconscious physiological process so that we can learn to control it. Electronic devices monitor

In the progressive-relaxation approach to coping with stress, tension and anxiety are reduced by exercises that relax the muscles.

whatever physiological function is to be controlled (such as heart rate or blood pressure) and provide a continuous flow of information about it. The person being monitored receives the information in the form of lights, clicks, changes in sound volume, or displays on an oscilloscope screen. Given this constant feedback, some people can learn, through trial and error, to influence the normally involuntary functioning of some body systems (Yates, 1980).

By helping people learn to regulate various body processes, biofeedback has been effective in the treatment of stress-related ailments. It has been especially useful in reducing the incidence and severity of tension headaches and migraines (Blanchard et al., 1985). A patient who suffers from headaches caused by muscle tension in his neck and forehead sits in a comfortable chair in a dim room. Electrodes pasted onto his forehead connect him to a machine that monitors muscle tension. When muscles in the forehead are relaxed, he hears a low tone through the earphones. As muscles become tense, the tone rises in pitch; the tenser the muscles, the shriller the tone. The patient's task is to keep the pitch of the tone low. By attending to slight body cues connected with muscle relaxation, the patient slowly learns to maintain a low tone, in the process developing some ability to keep forehead muscles relaxed.

The same general procedure—using biofeedback to learn to control a specific physiological response, then controlling it without biofeedback—has been successful in retraining muscles following strokes and injuries to the spinal cord, in lowering blood pressure, and in treating Raynaud's disease (in which a reduced flow of blood to the extremities produces cold, pain, and in extreme cases gangrene) (Sterman, 1978; B. Brown, 1980; Olton and Noonberg, 1980; Yates, 1980).

Control through biofeedback is not easy, and some of the early claims about it—that people could learn to control brain waves, for example—have been questioned. In situations where it does work, biofeedback seems no more effective—and much more expensive—than simple relaxation techniques. Indeed, some critics believe that changes in arousal attributed to biofeedback are actually the result of relaxation, an enhanced sense of control, suggestion, or even a placebo effect (Turk et al., 1979).

Meditation, which we explored in Chapter 6, is another method of controlling physiological function. During meditation, metabolism slows, oxygen consumption drops, breathing and heart rate slow, blood pressure falls, and the skin becomes more resistant to electrical conduction. The body's state during meditation resembles that of relaxation, and some researchers have found no physiological measures that distinguish between the states (Holmes, 1984). Some people use meditation as a way of controlling stress.

Stress Management

Relaxation and biofeedback attempt to control our physical responses to stress; stress management programs attempt to change our cognitive and behavioral responses (Meichenbaum and Jaremko, 1983). The object of these programs is to change our appraisal of potentially stressful situations and provide us with the skills that enable us to cope with them.

In the first phase of a stress management program, people learn that the way they interpret a situation helps to create and maintain stress. They also learn how to identify the sources of stress in their lives and their customary patterns of dealing with it. In the program's second phase, people are introduced to an array of new techniques for coping with stress. These are usually drawn from the strategies used by social-cognitive therapists, such as the positive self-talk of self-instructional training (see Chapter 19). Most programs also include relaxation techniques and training in specific skills. A man who feels that he is being pushed around at work is given assertiveness training; a woman who feels overwhelmed by demands on her time is given help in time management. All participants are encouraged to "inoculate" themselves against stress by planning ahead and developing specific strategies for dealing with situations they find especially difficult (Meichenbaum and Turk, 1982). In the program's final phase, participants practice their new coping skills in their daily life. They describe their experiences to the trainer and the group, who provide feedback and suggestions.

Stress management programs have been used successfully to treat stress-related physical problems (like headaches and high blood pressure), to change behavioral responses that induce stress (for example, by training Type A individuals to use Type B coping skills), and to reduce health risks that have developed as responses to stress (such as problem drinking and obesity).

Environmental Intervention

Some environments are inherently stressful. For example, nursing homes that insist that residents follow established routines inevitably deprive older adults of personal freedom. Research shows that such loss of control can destroy hope and lead to helplessness, aggravating the stresses of illness. Restructuring the environment to restore control seems to increase coping skills and improve health. This point was demonstrated when Ellen Langer and Judith Rodin (1976) gave nursing-home residents an opportunity to take responsibility and make small decisions. They were allowed to choose which night they would see a movie. They also chose a plant, which they were expected to care for themselves. Other residents were told which night they would see the movie and were each given a plant, which the staff cared for. Within three weeks, residents who had been encouraged to take a modest degree of control over their environment were more active and happier than residents who had been encouraged to depend on the staff. The restoration of control had lasting effects. Eighteen months later, the residents who had been encouraged to take responsibility were still more vigorous and active, and they were more likely to be alive (Rodin and Langer, 1977). Only 15 percent of the "responsible" residents had died, compared with 30 percent of the "dependent" residents.

Other research has shown that when nursing-home residents learn effective skills for coping with daily stress, their sense of control also improves. When residents were trained in specific ways of handling stressful situations, they saw themselves as having freedom to change their environment and a say in determining the outcome of events (Rodin, 1986). Afterward they spent more of their time in energetic activity and felt better than residents who had no skill training. Eighteen months later their health had also improved.

The importance of these findings extends beyond the nursing home. Hospitals, schools, and the workplace can be structured so as to increase people's sense of control and responsibility among patients, students, and workers. Such restructuring has the potential for far-reaching influences on health and capabilities.

SUMMARY

Health Psychology: Mind and Body

- Health psychology focuses on how people stay healthy, why they become ill, and how they react when illness develops.
- Health psychology assumes that biological, psychological, and social processes all play important roles in health and illness.

Keeping Healthy

- Research in primary prevention indicates that health habits are influenced by social, emotional, and cognitive factors.
- According to the health belief model, health habits depend on perceived vulnerability and the belief that behavioral changes will affect health.
- Intervention strategies by health psychologists include direct treatment, media campaigns, campaigns in schools and at work, community-wide campaigns, and social engineering.

Stress and Health

- Stressful events appear to affect our health if they involve unpleasant change.
- The impact of stress seems to depend on a person's primary (degree of perceived harm) and secondary (degree of coping ability perceived) appraisals of events.
- Hans Selye held that the body responds to stress in three stages: alarm, resistance, and, with continued stress, exhaustion.
- A connection has been found between general environmental stress and hypertension.
- Studies indicate that people with Type A personalities are vulnerable to coronary heart disease, but the same personality pattern may be associated with many different diseases.
- Intense stress appears to increase susceptibility to cancer by reducing the immune system's ability to function.

Coping with Stress

- Successful coping depends on the ability to solve problems and to regulate one's own emotions—by changing harmful aspects of the environment and by maintaining a positive self-image and satisfying interpersonal relationships.
- Techniques for reducing the body's physiological responses to stress include progressive relaxation, autogenic training, and biofeedback.
- People can learn to manage stress through programs that change their cognitive and behavioral responses.
- The inherent stress in some controlled environments can be reduced by restoring people's control over events.

KEY TERMS

autogenic training
biofeedback
coping
health belief model

health psychology
meditation
primary appraisal
primary prevention

progressive relaxation
secondary appraisal
stress
Type A personality

CONCEPT REVIEW

1. Define *health psychology* and list the types of activities in which health psychologists may be involved.

2. Outline the social, emotional, and cognitive influences on health. What is the *health belief model*?

3. Give several examples of programs designed to promote good health habits. Review the research on the effectiveness of each type of program.

4. Define *stress*. What are the causes of stress? Why would winning $10,000 be as stressful as losing the same amount?

5. Describe the patterns of stress produced by disasters. Are man-made disasters, such as the Vietnam War, more stressful than natural disasters? Why or why not? What major sources of stress is everyone likely to encounter at some point?

6. How do primary and secondary appraisal relate to the problem of control over events? Why is predictability such an important factor in our experience of stress? How is learned helplessness affected by control and predictability?

7. Describe the physiological changes that occur in response to stress, according to Selye's general adaptation syndrome.

8. What specific factors relate hypertension, heart disease, and cancer to stress? What are the characteristics of the Type A personality that make one prone to these diseases?

9. Summarize the various methods of coping with stress. What kinds of research evidence support the effectiveness of each of these methods?

10. Which aspects of stress do stress management and environmental intervention attempt to control? How effective are these methods?

CRITICAL THINKING

1. Chapter 18 introduced the *diathesis-stress model*, which proposes the interaction of disposition and environmental stress to account for the onset of schizophrenia. Does this model apply to the kinds of stress presented in this chapter?

2. The prevention of stress-related disease is a new and growing role for psychology. Other areas of psychology besides health psychology have the potential to guide society in the elimination of risks to health and well-being. Identify these areas and speculate about how psychology might help to shape public health policy and personal health habits.

PART SEVEN

Social Psychology

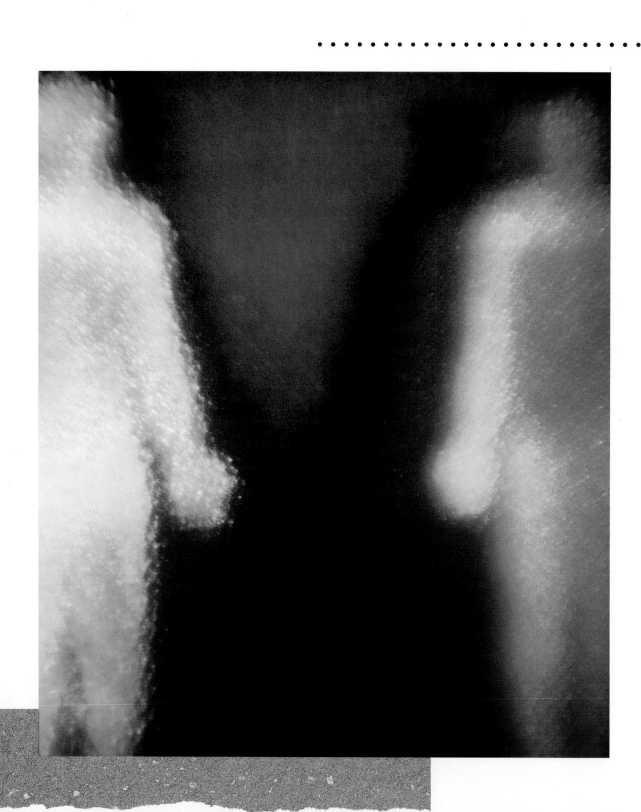

CHAPTER 21

Attitudes, Social Cognition, and Interpersonal Attraction

On December 22, 1984, Bernard H. Goetz, a white, 37-year-old electrical engineer, boarded a subway train in New York City. Four black teenagers gathered
around him and asked him for five dollars. Goetz shot all four youths, then fled
through the subway tunnel. Nine days later he surrendered to the police. None of
the teenagers was killed, but one, Darrel Cabey, suffered brain damage and was
paralyzed.

This "subway vigilante" case was the focus of heated nationwide debate and
for good reason. Because it was full of ambiguities, subjective responses were
inevitable. Some observers thought that racism was at the heart of the case; others
thought that introducing the issue of race obscured the facts or read too much into
them. Some believed that Goetz's action was justified by the menacing behavior of
the four youths and by the fact that Goetz had been mugged a few years before;
others were convinced that Goetz had overreacted in trigger-happy fashion to
what was essentially a prank. To some, Goetz's behavior reflected a psychological
abnormality; to others, it was the four young men, roaming the subway to prey
on passengers, whose behavior was abnormal.

One point *was* made clear by this controversial case: there is no way to
separate the facts—the actions of Goetz and of the four youths—from the beliefs
and perceptions that produced Goetz's shooting response, as well as the public's
responses to the situation. Put more simply, attitudes and the ways in which both
individuals and groups think about one another in social situations played an
important role. The topic of attitudes has been a central and distinct one in social
psychology, the area of psychology we turn to now.

ATTITUDES

ATTITUDE   an evaluative response to
a particular object, idea, person, or
group of people

In psychological terms, an **attitude** is an evaluative response to a particular object,
idea, person, or group of people. This response reflects an *individual* preference
or aversion, but attitudes are often measured *collectively,* as in polls and surveys:
individual preferences are grouped together to give a broad picture of the views
held by, say, a region, a town, a nation, or a group of voters. Of course, these
collective measures are extremely influential in both business and politics. Surveys
of consumer attitudes influence the stock market, investments, interest rates, unemployment, and plans for industrial and commercial expansion. Most businesses
are built upon market research, another name for the measurement and prediction
of attitudes. For large corporations, a proper reading of consumer attitudes can
mean millions of dollars in profits, and an incorrect reading, a loss of millions. In
preparing to launch its "new Coke" in April 1985, for example, the Coca-Cola
Company researched consumer taste preferences, but failed to take into account
the public's attitude toward the original Coca-Cola as a part, even a symbol, of
the traditional American lifestyle. A public outcry, coupled with a significant loss
of market share, prompted the company to revive the old formula in July and
market it as "classic Coke."

The Three-Component Model of Attitudes

Traditionally, attitudes are considered to have three components: an affective, or
emotional, component (how we feel about the attitude object); a behavioral component (how we act toward the object); and a cognitive component (our knowledge, beliefs, and thoughts about the object) (Smith, 1947; Krech and Crutchfield,
1948; Kramer, 1949; Chein, 1951; Allport, 1954).

A 1984 study provides a good illustration of the three-component model in
action (Breckler, 1984). First, emotional reactions of college students to a live
snake were assessed in terms of heart rate and the students' verbal descriptions of
their feelings. Second, behavioral responses were judged according to the students' descriptions of their behavior when or if they saw a snake; their answers to
the questions of exactly how close to a live snake they'd be willing to go; and their

readiness to pet and hold a live snake. Cognitive responses, the third component, were judged according to students' level of agreement with statements like "Snakes are soft and smooth" or "Snakes attack anything that moves"; students' ratings of snakes on dimensions like clean/dirty and beautiful/ugly; and the subjects' own descriptions of their thoughts about snakes. The study's results supported the three-component model. Each component, the study found, was distinct in itself but was correlated with the other two. We saw in Chapter 12 that appraisal (the cognitive component) produces an emotional reaction, which in turn generates a behavioral tendency. In addition to influencing one another, the three components may each be influenced by other factors (Insko and Schopler, 1967; Greenwald, 1968; Triandis, 1971).

Formation of the Affective Component

Emotional responses—whether to a person's physical appearance, an animal, a landscape, or even a word—may simply be the product of classical conditioning (discussed in Chapter 7). That is, at least a portion of our attitudes may be formed by learned associations to emotion-arousing circumstances. For example, a man who spent a particularly unhappy year living in the Southwest may never want to see another cactus—an attitude toward the desert has been formed. A woman may hate shellfish after associating it with an upset stomach. If a person loved an actress's most recent film, he or she might be a little more susceptible to an advertising message she delivers on TV.

A concise illustration of classical conditioning's role in attitude formation can be found in an experiment in which a series of mild electric shocks changed women's attitudes toward specific words, which then became "attitude objects" (Zanna, Kiesler, and Pilkonis, 1970). The women received an electric shock just after they saw the word "light"; when they saw the word "dark," the shock ended. Although all the women had previously preferred the word "light," they found the word "dark" more attractive after the experiment.

A negative emotional response acquired through classical conditioning is not necessarily neutralized by positive information: telling the women in the just-described experiment that the word "light" has no inherent emotional content would not alter their response, at least at first. Someone who acknowledges that snakes have many positive qualities, such as controlling rodents, might still feel an aversion to snakes. The best way to alter negative emotional responses acquired through conditioning is probably by extinction through some type of behavioral therapy.

An affective response to an attitude object may also be the result of the **exposure effect,** in which repeated neutral encounters produce positive feelings toward the object. (Negative responses cannot be produced merely by repeated neutral encounters; the encounters must be aversive to produce negative responses.) No one has been able to explain why the exposure effect works. We might guess that the very recognition of familiar things is pleasant; when we listen to a familiar piece of music, we tend to enjoy it partly because of its familiarity. Yet this explanation, though plausible, has not been supported by research evidence. It has been shown conclusively (e.g., Kunst-Wilson and Zajonc, 1980) that people come to like things they have seen even when they do not recognize the objects, and even when they are unaware of having seen the objects before (as when images are flashed very briefly on a screen).

Formation of the Behavioral Component

Behavioral responses to attitude objects are often learned through instrumental conditioning (discussed in Chapter 7). A classic example comes from a study at the University of Hawaii (Insko, 1965). During interviews, students were repeatedly complimented for expressing a favorable attitude toward Aloha Week, a traditional autumn celebration. A week later, the students filled out a questionnaire that included a question about the possibility of adding an Aloha Week to

Bernard Goetz, known as "the subway vigilante."

EXPOSURE EFFECT the phenomenon whereby repeated neutral encounters with an object produce positive feelings toward that object

the university's spring schedule. Students who had been verbally reinforced for praising the autumn festival were more likely to favor the addition of a spring celebration than were students in a control group.

The Goetz case described at the beginning of the chapter offers a somewhat more complicated example. Some observers feared that an acquittal for Goetz would serve as a symbolic reinforcement for vigilante behavior, which would then increase. (Goetz was eventually acquitted on the shooting charges but served a six-month prison sentence for carrying an unlicensed handgun. No increase in vigilante behavior was recorded.)

Formation of the Cognitive Component

Education through information is the most clear-cut way in which cognitive responses to attitude objects are formed. As Chapter 20 indicated, public service educational campaigns that present the effects of smoking or diet, explain the benefits of exercise, or warn about the ways in which AIDS can be transmitted are all aimed at the cognitive component of broad attitudes toward these health issues. Again, the link between the cognitive component (understanding, say, that smoking causes cancer and other diseases) and the behavioral or emotional components (continuing to enjoy smoking) does not seem to be very direct, since this type of campaign has been found to be effective in forming beliefs and thoughts but less effective in altering or forming new behaviors and emotional responses (Taylor, 1986).

Attitude Consistency, Dissonance, and Change

How do attitudes change once they are formed? Can they be manipulated by advertisers or propagandists, and if so, under what conditions? How concerned are we that our attitudes be consistent with one another and with our behavior?

Cognitive Dissonance Theory

Cognitive dissonance theory is one of the most important in social psychology, both in terms of the volume of research it has generated and in terms of its ability to withstand challenges. Its basic tenet is a human need for consistency and self-justification.

According to this theory, people want their beliefs to be consistent with one another and want their behaviors to be consistent with their beliefs. Social psychologist Leon Festinger (1957) proposed that when people become aware of inconsistency among their beliefs or between their attitudes and their behavior, they experience **cognitive dissonance,** an unpleasant state of arousal that motivates them to reestablish consistency by changing one of their attitudes or by changing their behavior. Thus, if a person behaves in a way that runs counter to his or her attitude, cognitive dissonance is created in that person; he or she then attempts to reduce the dissonance by changing either the attitude or the behavior.

These principles were revealed when Festinger and his colleague J. Merrill Carlsmith conducted what is now considered a classic experiment in 1959. Subjects spent 2 hours performing an exceedingly dull task: putting round pegs in round holes and square pegs in square holes. Each person was then asked, as a favor to the experimenter, to lie to the next subject, telling that person that the task was interesting and enjoyable. Some subjects were offered $1 for doing this; others were offered $20. Almost all the subjects agreed to do this. In subsequent interviews with the researchers, subjects were asked how much they had *actually* enjoyed the task. Contrary to our common-sense assumption, and to principles of operant conditioning, those who had been given $1 were *more* likely to say that they really enjoyed the task than were subjects who had received $20 (see Figure 21.1). According to the researchers' interpretation, those who had received

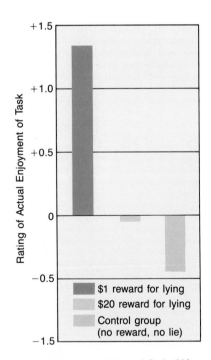

Figure 21.1 In Festinger and Carlsmith's experiment, subjects who had been paid only $1 for lying about having enjoyed a boring task were much more likely to report later that they really *had* enjoyed the task than were subjects who had received $20. (Data from Festinger and Carlsmith, 1959.)

Information can influence our attitudes toward health issues by changing our cognitive understanding of them.

only $1 for lying experienced cognitive dissonance, which they reduced by changing their attitude to make it consistent with their behavior. The other subjects were less likely to change their attitudes and say that they really had enjoyed the task, presumably because $20 (a sizable amount of money thirty years ago) provided sufficient external justification for lying; they did not need any internal justification because they experienced no cognitive dissonance.

Challenges to Cognitive Dissonance Theory

Other psychologists have disputed Festinger and Carlsmith's explanation. Some have argued that subjects in cognitive dissonance experiments have not truly changed their attitudes but merely *report* that their attitudes have changed because they do not want to look inconsistent or foolish to the experimenters (Tedeschi, Schlenker, and Bonoma, 1971). This interpretation is based on the concept of *self-presentation*, the way a person consciously presents herself or himself to others. However, the self-presentation analysis has not been supported by research. Attitude change seems to occur even when only the subjects themselves know about any inconsistency—when, say, one researcher induces the behavior and another measures subsequent attitudes (Hoyt, Henley, and Collins, 1972).

An alternative explanation for the Festinger and Carlsmith results was proposed by Daryl Bem, who interpreted the results of dissonance experiments in terms of *self-perception theory.* According to Bem (1965), we must often infer our attitudes by observing our own behavior, just as we observe and make inferences about others. Subjects in the Festinger and Carlsmith study, when asked their true attitude toward the boring task, would think to themselves either, "I told the next subject it was interesting for only $1, so I must have really thought it was interesting," or "I told the next subject it was interesting in order to get $20, not because I really thought it was interesting."

Both the self-perception and the cognitive dissonance explanations seem to account for the results of the dissonance studies. The primary distinction between the two theories is that cognitive dissonance theory posits an unpleasant state of arousal as crucial to a change in attitudes. Self-perception theory, in contrast, does not require any unpleasant state to explain attitude change.

Because the original cognitive dissonance experiments never actually measured arousal, it was impossible to determine which theory was correct. Later studies have shown that behavior inconsistent with attitudes *does* produce arousal,

COGNITIVE DISSONANCE an unpleasant state of arousal created when a person becomes aware of inconsistency among his or her beliefs or between his or her attitudes and behavior; motivates person to reestablish consistency by changing either attitude or behavior provided there is no clear external justification or reward for the behavior (Cooper and Fazio, 1984). In one study (Cooper, Zanna, and Taves, 1978), subjects wrote an essay that contradicted their true attitudes. Some subjects were assigned their essay position by the experimenter, and others were requested to write on a given position as a favor to the experimenter. In addition, half the subjects were given phenobarbital, a tranquilizer that would prevent arousal, and half were given a placebo (an inert "sugar pill"). As predicted by cognitive dissonance theory, among the subjects who took a placebo, those who had a greater degree of choice—those who wrote as a "favor"—were more likely to change their attitudes to match their essay positions than were those who had been assigned their essay positions and so had less choice in the matter. But subjects who took the tranquilizer showed little or no attitude change, whether or not they had much choice about their essay positions, presumably because the drug had prevented any dissonance-induced arousal.

The results of this study clearly support the predictions of cognitive dissonance theory, and not those of self-perception theory, at least under certain conditions. It seems that the *degree* of inconsistency between attitudes and behavior may be the relevant factor in determining whether cognitive dissonance or self-perception has been at work. This would make sense, since the greater the inconsistency, the more likely we would be to feel unpleasant arousal. Indeed, researchers have shown that when our behavior is only slightly inconsistent with our attitudes, attitudes are more likely to change by self-perception processes; but when our behavior is very different from our attitudes, then attitude change is more likely to occur through a resolution of dissonance (Fazio, Zanna, and Cooper, 1977).

Conditions for Attitude Change

A high degree of inconsistency between behavior and attitudes is a major condition necessary for dissonance-induced attitude change, but it is not the only one. A number of other conditions have been summarized by Joel Cooper and Russell Fazio (1984) (see Figure 21.2). One is that the inconsistent behavior must be seen as having negative consequences. For example, in a replication of the Festinger and Carlsmith research, attitude change was experienced only by those subjects who believed that their false claim of enjoying the boring task actually deceived others (Cooper and Worchel, 1970). In addition, as we have said, dissonance depends on the subjects' belief that inconsistent behavior was freely chosen. People who experience dissonance and change their attitudes because of it seem to go one step further: they believe that since they choose to behave in a certain way, they are responsible for any negative consequences. In addition, they must believe that no external factor like a drug could cause their arousal (Linder et al., 1967; Cooper and Brehm, 1971; Collins and Hoyt, 1972; Goethals and Cooper, 1972). For instance, in Chapter 12's discussion of a study by Schachter and Singer (1962), subjects were given adrenaline and were led to interpret their subsequent arousal as either euphoria or anger. The arousal produced by behavior inconsistent with an attitude can also be misinterpreted, however. When subjects were given a placebo and told that the pill caused arousal, the arousal did *not* lead to attitude change (Zanna and Cooper, 1974). Apparently, subjects attribute their arousal to the drug instead of to their inconsistent behavior, and thus do not feel motivated to reduce the inconsistency.

Cognitive Dissonance and Self-Affirmation

Recently, cognitive dissonance theory has faced another challenge. Social psychologist Claude Steele has questioned whether the need to see oneself as consistent is really what motivates the attitude change found in cognitive dissonance studies. According to Steele, attitude change is motivated not simply by the need for consistency, but by the need to maintain the integrity of our entire *self-system*, a complex set of beliefs about ourselves. For most of us the self-system includes a

Figure 21.2 Cognitive dissonance can induce a change in attitudes through a series of steps, beginning with our perception that a behavior inconsistent with our attitudes has negative consequences. (Based on Cooper and Fazio, 1984.)

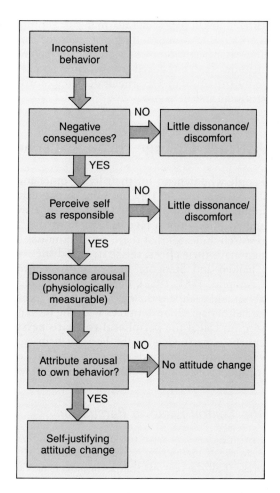

Figure 21.2 Cognitive dissonance can induce a change in attitudes through a series of steps, beginning with our perception that a behavior inconsistent with our attitudes has negative consequences. (Based on Cooper and Fazio, 1984.)

view of ourselves as good, competent, adhering to a particular set of values, capable of free choice, and capable of controlling important outcomes. When we behave in ways that violate our views of ourself, we are motivated to do something to restore the integrity of our self-system. In most cognitive dissonance studies, once the subject has written an essay that contradicts his or her attitudes, the only available means of restoring the integrity of the self-system is to change attitudes. However, according to Steele, the self-system is more flexible than this. If, as Steele claims, the goal is to reinforce one's self-system, rather than simply to maintain consistency between attitudes and behaviors, then a variety of behaviors that affirm any aspect of the self-system might satisfy this goal. For example, after hurting a friend's feelings, we might find the act of donating blood sufficient to affirm the self and thus to reduce the motivation associated with behaving counter to our attitudes.

In a study to test this hypothesis, Steele identified a set of subjects who were strong on esthetic values—that is, who appreciated and valued beauty in the arts, architecture, literature, and so on (Steele and Liu, 1983). All subjects were asked to write essays that expressed opposition to high funding priorities for research and treatment of chronic diseases and handicaps (a position that ran counter to the attitudes of all subjects in the study), under conditions of high or low perceived choice. Next, some of the "high choice" subjects were given a chance to affirm their esthetic values by completing a "values survey." All subjects then indicated their final opinion about funding priorities for research and treatment of chronic diseases. As predicted, subjects in the high-choice condition who had not been given a chance to affirm their esthetic values changed their attitudes to conform to the essay they had written, whereas subjects in the low-choice condition did not. More interestingly, subjects with esthetic values who had been given a chance to affirm those values did not reduce dissonance by changing their attitudes. A comparison group of subjects who were low in esthetic values and were exposed to the same high-choice, value-affirmation condition did reduce dissonance by changing their attitude about funding priorities for chronic diseases. Thus, it seems that the unpleasant state of arousal created by behaving in ways that run counter to our attitudes can be reduced by affirming an unrelated aspect of the self-system. This self-affirmation may be the underlying motive for reducing discrepancies between attitudes and behavior.

Attitude Change through Persuasion

People who depend for their living on changing attitudes, such as politicians and advertisers, usually rely on more direct techniques than cognitive dissonance for inducing attitude change. Through some message, they hope to convince their audience to adopt a favorable view of their product, candidate, or idea. Recent research indicates that there are two modes by which persuasive communications may have their effect: the first, called the *systematic mode* (Chaiken, 1980, 1986; Chaiken and Stangor, 1987), or the **central route to persuasion** (Petty and Cacioppo, 1981, 1986), occurs when the recipient of a persuasive message thinks about and evaluates the quality of the arguments presented in the communication, and either agrees or disagrees with the message on the basis of this evaluation. The second, called the **peripheral route to persuasion,** occurs when the message recipient is persuaded on the basis of heuristic thinking, previous learning experiences, or other methods that do not require evaluation of quality of the arguments in the message. Let's consider each of these routes to persuasion in more detail.

The Central Route to Persuasion

Imagine that you wish to persuade people to buy a particular car—a Camaro, for example. One strategy you might use is to buy advertising space in which you present all the reasons that a Camaro is an excellent car and a good value. In using this approach, you would be trying to persuade people via the central route to persuasion—by getting them to think about and evaluate the quality of your arguments and, you hope, to agree with your position.

But persuasion via the central route is not simply a matter of having some good arguments to place in your ad. It is a complex process, which can be broken down into five stages: attention, comprehension, yielding, retention, and action (McGuire, 1972, 1985). First, the target audience of your ad must notice it and pay *attention* to it long enough to be exposed to your persuasive communication. If your ad is uninteresting or your target consumer is distracted, your arguments will have no effect. Second, *comprehension* of the message is necessary—if your arguments are so complex and technical that they go beyond the expertise of your audience, even very good arguments will go right over the target's head. Third, *yielding* to the persuasive message results when the target's cognitive responses to the message or the product are generally favorable (Petty and Cacioppo, 1986) (such as "That's a good reason to buy a Camaro" or "This woman seems to know what she's talking about"). Next, *retention* is necessary: after yielding, the target must remember the message until he or she is in a position to do something about it. If your Camaro ad is convincing for a few minutes but is forgotten before your target is prepared to buy a new car, the ad will not increase your sales. Finally, the target must take *action* based on your message. Even a well-remembered persuasive ad won't increase sales if it doesn't convince your target to act on his or her new attitude toward Camaros.

The Peripheral Route to Persuasion

The peripheral route to persuasion includes any method of persuasion other than via convincing arguments (Petty and Cacioppo, 1986; Chaiken and Stangor, 1987). Many techniques of persuasion take the peripheral route, including those based on learning principles such as classical conditioning. By pairing your prod-

CENTRAL ROUTE TO PERSUASION a message recipient's evaluation of the quality of the arguments presented in a persuasive communication

PERIPHERAL ROUTE TO PERSUASION a message recipient's use of heuristic thinking, previous learning experiences, or other methods that do not require evaluation of the quality of the arguments in the message

uct or issue with a stimulus that is known to produce a positive emotional response, you may induce in your target a conditioned positive response to the product. That is why sexual and romantic images are so frequently used in advertisements for products ranging from beer to breath mints to shampoo.

The effectiveness of the central and the peripheral routes to persuasion varies with the circumstances. The central route is more effective when the target's motivation to think about the issue is high, and the peripheral route is better used when motivation or ability to think about the arguments is low (Chaiken, 1980, 1986a, 1986b; Petty et al., 1981, 1983; Cacioppo and Petty, 1984; Petty and Cacioppo, 1984; Wood et al., 1985; Axsom et al., 1987).

In the latter case, targets often respond to characteristics of communications that *seem* related to the quality of the arguments but are actually independent of message quality. Such surface characteristics include the number of arguments presented; the length of the message; the physical attractiveness, likability, or credibility of the communicator; and the level of agreement among different communicators. Targets behave as if they were using heuristics (rules of thumb, discussed in Chapter 9) to decide whether or not to agree with the message (Chaiken, 1980, 1986). For example, a person using a heuristic mode of message evaluation might be more convinced by an ad with six arguments than an ad with two arguments, even if the two arguments are excellent and the six are all poor.

In one study (Petty and Cacioppo, 1984), students at the University of Missouri were exposed to arguments in favor of instituting comprehensive examinations that each student would have to pass before being allowed to graduate. Some students were exposed to strong arguments—for example, "Prestigious universities have comprehensives to maintain academic excellence; institution of the exams has led to a reversal in the declining scores on standardized achievement tests; and average starting salaries are higher for graduates of schools with the exams." Other students were exposed to weak arguments—such as, "Adopting the exams would allow the university to be at the forefront of a national trend; graduate students have complained that since they have to take comprehensives, undergraduates should have to take them also; and by not administering the exams, the university is violating a tradition dating back to the ancient Greeks." The number of arguments, as well as the quality, varied: half of each group of subjects was presented with three arguments, and the other half was exposed to nine arguments. The level of motivation to think about the message was varied by telling some subjects that the comprehensive exams, if accepted, would begin the next year (and therefore would affect the students in the study); others were told that

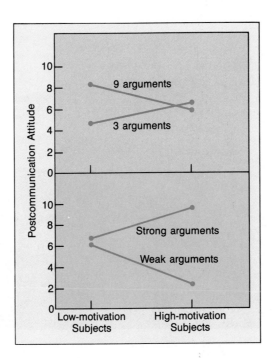

Figure 21.3 In a study of persuasion, subjects who were highly motivated to think about the message were more likely to be persuaded to change their attitudes by strong arguments (bottom right); the sheer number of arguments did not significantly influence their attitudes (top right). In contrast, subjects whose motivation was low (because they would not be affected by the change proposed in the message) responded more strongly to the number of arguments (top left) than to their quality (bottom left). (Petty and Cacioppo, 1984, p. 76.)

the exams would not begin for ten years (and therefore would not affect the subjects).

The results of the study are displayed in Figure 21.3. Highly motivated students—those who would be directly affected by the exams—found strong arguments more persuasive than weak arguments, and found nine arguments no more persuasive than three. Low-motivation students—those who would not be affected by the new policy—responded more heuristically, finding nine arguments more persuasive than three, and they were not more responsive to strong arguments than to weak ones. Students' cognitive responses—their thoughts in response to the message—revealed that highly motivated students thought more critically about the arguments being presented.

Influences on Consistency between Attitudes and Behavior

More than fifty years ago, psychologist Richard LaPiere (1934) traveled around the United States with a Chinese couple. He expected to encounter anti-Oriental attitudes that would make it difficult for the party to find places to sleep and eat. But he was wrong. "In something like 10,000 miles of motor travel," wrote LaPiere, "twice across the United States, up and down the Pacific coast, we met definite rejection from those asked to serve us just once" (p. 232).

Judging by the friendly behavior of the innkeepers and tradespeople these travelers encountered, we might conclude that Americans in the 1930s were almost entirely free of prejudice against Orientals. However, this conclusion would also be wrong. LaPiere followed up his travels by writing a letter to each of the 251 establishments that he and his friends had visited, asking whether they would provide food or lodging to Chinese individuals. Of the 128 who responded, more than 90 percent answered with a flat no. One said yes, and the rest said their decision would depend on the circumstances. People's attitudes toward serving Chinese, then, seemed to be extremely inconsistent with the behavior they had already shown.

As this study illustrates, research has frequently shown only a weak correlation between attitudes and behavior. Some of this weakness can be explained by the way attitudes and behaviors are measured. Most attitude measures are cast in general terms: "What are your feelings about religion?" "Do you oppose abor-

A person's attitude—say, toward legal speed limits—may be inconsistent with his or her behavior. Such inconsistency makes it difficult to predict behavior on the basis of attitudes.

tion?" When behavior is measured, however, very specific behaviors in specific situations are studied: "Did you go to church last Sunday?" "Did you attend the anti-abortion demonstration on Saturday?" Such specific instances do not provide a sample of behavior that would be representative of the general attitude (Fishbein and Ajzen, 1980). The closer the match between the attitude measured and the behavior observed, the higher the correlation between attitudes and behavior (Ajzen, 1987). Moreover, a specific behavior may relate closely only to a very specific attitude. A family's record of attending church tells us something (obviously) about their future church attendance, but (not so obviously) it may or may not tell us anything substantive about their religious attitudes. The match between measured attitude and behavior is really a question of validity for the researcher: Will a study measure what it really intends to measure? What kind of behavior does one want to be able to predict? A person may believe strongly in "law and order" but may consistently exceed the legal speed limit on the highway; here, the specific attitude about driving is more informative than the general one about law and order.

By ensuring a careful match between attitude and behavior, we can of course greatly increase the usefulness of attitudes in predicting behavior. But it is also possible, however, that attitudes and behavior are more strongly related for some people in some circumstances and for some attitudes than others. Researchers have searched for *moderating variables*—that is, variables that affect the strength of the attitude–behavior relationship. Indeed, the pertinent question is not so much "Do attitudes predict behavior?" as "When, for whom, and for which attitudes are attitudes and behavior consistent?"

Direct versus Indirect Experience

Some attitudes are more consistent with behavior than others. Attitudes based on rational arguments (the result of the central route) tend to be more strongly related to behavior than those based on other influences (via the peripheral route) (Petty and Cacioppo, 1986). And attitudes based on direct, repeated experience, and thus on strong associations with an attitude object—a person, book, sport, or store, for instance—are more likely to predict behavior than are attitudes based on indirect or secondhand experience (Fazio, 1986). A positive attitude toward another race, for example, would probably be more closely consistent with behavior toward a member of that race if there had been direct previous experience with members of that race. In contrast, a positive racial attitude based on indirect experience (such as hearsay or knowledge of other people's experiences) might not predict behavior in a specific encounter very accurately.

Social Norms and Self-Consciousness

Attitudes are not the only influence on behavior, and when other influences are strong, the attitude–behavior link may be weak. One important influence on behavior is the set of social norms that govern appropriate behavior in specific situations (Fishbein and Ajzen, 1980; Ajzen, 1987). When you see someone you intensely dislike at a party, you may hide your true feelings and behave properly and politely. Your behavior in this case is consistent with social norms of politeness and with cultural scripts for parties, but it is inconsistent with your attitudes.

People also behave more consistently with their attitudes when they are made self-aware or self-conscious—that is, when their attention is focused on themselves rather than on the situation or on other people (Scheier and Carver, 1988). When they are aware of being watched or listened to, or when watching or listening to themselves, people may become aware of the discrepancy between their attitudes and their behavior and adjust their behavior accordingly (see the discussion of behavioral self-regulation in Chapter 13).

PSYCHOLOGY TODAY AND TOMORROW

The Functions of Attitudes

That people's attitudes differ on a multitude of subjects is obvious enough from the behavioral choices they make. One person has a closetful of the latest fashions; another, with the same income, lives in jeans and T-shirts. One person drives a sports car, another a station wagon. These choices, like many others, express contrasting attitudes about clothing and automobiles. What may be less obvious is that these attitudes serve functions for the people who hold them.

What do attitudes "do" for people? Social psychologists have noted two important functions. First, attitudes may serve a social-adjustive function. That is, they may help people fit into social groups and behave in ways acceptable to others. For example, the attitude "An elaborate wardrobe is important" will be extremely useful for a person who works in the fashion industry. Likewise, the attitude "A high-performance car is great to drive and to be seen driving" will help a young person fit in with a group of friends who dote on sports cars.

But attitudes do not necessarily fulfill a social-adjustive function. They may instead serve to express a person's underlying values. In this case, an individual's jeans-only wardrobe may express the value that clothing is of less importance in life than the inner person. And the station wagon in the driveway may be a statement that the owner thinks of a car as just a means of getting from one place to another.

Social scientists have found that they can distinguish between these two types of people, which they call *high self-monitoring* and *low self-monitoring* (Snyder, 1987); we discussed these two social orientations in Chapter 17. High self-monitoring people strive to hold the attitudes that help them fit into important social situations. In contrast, low self-monitors choose attitudes that allow them to express their underlying values and dispositions.

Advertisers, whose business is persuading people to change their attitudes, have perceived these differences, too, and they accordingly produce two very different kinds of ads. The "soft sell," or image-oriented advertising, invites the potential customer to identify with an attractive idea of the product. Thus, the customer is led to think "I too can be a Marlboro man" or "I too can be one of the unforgettable women who wear Revlon." In this kind of advertising, little or nothing is said about the nature or quality of the product itself. In the "hard sell," by contrast, the emphasis is on the quality, value, and/or price of the product. A certain breakfast cereal has all the vitamins and fiber you need, *and* it tastes good; a car gets great gas mileage, has lots of leg room, and has the best owner satisfaction rating in its class.

Studies of high- and low-self-monitoring people have found that high self-monitors are more likely to be persuaded by messages that appeal to feelings and images, and low self-monitors are more likely to be persuaded by messages that stress underlying values (DeBono, 1987). Moreover, the context of the message—whether it is delivered in an image-oriented, adjustment-oriented format or a value-oriented format—affects the way it is received. High-self-monitoring people actually seem to pay closer attention to messages couched in "image" terms, and low self-monitors are more likely to attend to messages delivered in "values" terms (DeBono and Harnish, 1988). These findings suggest that communicators who want to change people's attitudes should consider carefully what functions the attitudes serve and design their messages accordingly.

Personality Type

Another approach to the attitude–behavior issue involves identifying types of people who typically show strong correlations between their attitudes and their behavior and types of people who do not. This personality approach has revealed one trait in particular that moderates the attitude–behavior relationship: self-monitoring.

We saw in our discussion of personality traits in Chapter 17 that high self-monitors are people who typically try to behave in a manner appropriate to the situation in which they find themselves, whereas low self-monitors typically do not attempt to mold their behavior to fit their situation (Snyder, 1987). (Studies of the self-monitoring trait have helped to illuminate the functions that attitudes serve for people; see the accompanying box.) One might expect, then, that high self-monitors would tend to show a higher discrepancy between their attitudes and behavior and low self-monitors a lower one.

These expectations were borne out by an experiment in which students served as jurors in a mock court case involving allegations of sex discrimination in employment (Snyder and Swann, 1976). The students read résumés of two biologists, Ms. C. A. Harrison and Mr. G. C. Sullivan. Both had applied for the position of assistant professor of biology at a university, and Mr. Sullivan had been hired. Ms. Harrison filed suit, claiming sex discrimination. The jurors considered the arguments presented by both sides, and each juror stated which verdict he or she would support. The relationship between general attitudes toward affirmative action and the various jurors' verdicts was considered separately for high and low self-monitors. Among low self-monitors, verdicts were strongly related to attitudes: those who favored affirmative action gave verdicts favorable to Ms. Harrison, and those who opposed affirmative action gave unfavorable verdicts. Among high self-monitors, however, verdicts could not be predicted from their attitudes toward affirmative action.

What all this tells us about attitudes and behavior is that the relationship between them is complex. Today, as you have just seen, researchers in this area focus more on the cognitive processes that moderate the relationship between attitudes and behavior.

SOCIAL COGNITION

Social cognition refers to the way we think and reason about ourselves, about other people, about relations between people, and about the various groups to which we and other people belong. When we deal directly with other individuals, we try to discover their intentions, attitudes, beliefs, abilities, preferences, personality characteristics, and the like. When we deal with social events and situations—with larger groups, with communities, or with national and international relations—we try to understand the conflicts, alliances, commitments, loyalties, values, rules, norms, expectations, and indeed all the social and cultural forces that may control behavior. These broad concerns are the province of psychologists who study social cognition.

SOCIAL COGNITION the way we think and reason about ourselves, about other people, about relations between people, and about the various groups to which we and other people belong

Perceiving Others: The Naive-Scientist Model

One of the early investigations of our attempts to understand our social relations was made by Fritz Heider (1958), who proposed that we do this in much the same way that scientists try to understand the causes of events in the natural world. This has been called the "naive scientist" model: we can all be considered "naive" in this respect because we receive no rigorous training but come to this approach "naturally." According to Heider, we seek to attribute social behavior either to external forces (circumstances) or to internal influences (emotions, traits, and so on).

Heider's idea was further developed by Harold Kelley (1967), who theorized that in inferring the causes of another person's behavior, we seek three types of information:

1. Is the behavior *distinctive*—that is, does the person behave this way only in response to a single stimulus?

2. Is the behavior *consistent*—that is, does the person usually respond in this way to this stimulus?

3. Is there a *consensus* of behavior—that is, do others respond in the same way to the same stimulus?

The way we perceive other people may be quite different from the way they perceive themselves.

An instructor seeking the causes of a student's failure to turn in an important assignment would want to know (1) whether the student also fails to turn in work for other instructors and does not complete tasks outside of school; (2) whether the student has done this before in this particular class; and (3) whether other students have also regularly failed to turn in assignments. After answering these questions, the instructor may infer that the student is not interested in this particular course, cannot cope well with pressure, is preoccupied with something else, stayed up late the previous night, or did not understand the instructions.

To state the point another way, we attempt to infer others' motives for behaving as they do, and the inferred motives help us form an image of others' personalities (Jones and Davis, 1965). However, much of the behavior we observe has many possible motives, and not all behavior is equally informative. Observing an employee being considerate toward the boss could mean that the employee is genuinely polite and kind, but it could also mean that she or he is angling for a raise. The useful clues to a person's nature are the distinctive, unexpected, unusual ones. Thus, if an employee is rude to everyone but the boss, we feel quite safe in concluding that she or he is an inconsiderate person who has an ulterior motive for behaving politely toward the boss.

Behind the naive-scientist perspective lay a dissatisfaction with the implication of cognitive dissonance theory that our attitudes and behavior toward ourselves and others are governed by face-saving, self-justifying, irrational processes. The naive-scientist view, in contrast, held that people are, or try to be, rational processors of social information.

The contemporary view in social psychology falls somewhere in between. According to this view, we try to make the best possible and most intuitively logical judgments we can about ourselves and others, given a number of constraints. Not surprisingly, our social perceptions are subject to the same sorts of cognitive and attributional biases as our other thought processes. In trying to understand social relations, we apply the same heuristics that we use in more abstract problem solving and thinking. Our dependence on the cognitive frameworks known as *schemas* (see Chapters 3 and 9) has particular consequences in the social domain, playing a role in stereotyping and prejudice.

Causal Attribution Biases

Cognitive biases should be familiar to you from Chapter 9. Research has revealed that the same types of biases operate in the inferences we make about the causes of other people's behavior.

One of the first attribution biases to be identified came from the finding that of the three types of information thought by Kelley to be important in causal attributions—distinctiveness, consistency, and consensus—consensus information has the least impact on inferences about the causes of behavior (McArthur, 1972; see Kassin, 1979). Imagine, for example, that you are feeling blue because the editor of your campus newspaper has just rejected your first article. Would it make you feel better to know that many other writers experience the same frustration? Would that knowledge make the difference in whether or not you would continue to submit articles? Probably not, according to research on the use of consensus information (Nisbett, et al., 1976). Consensus information has little effect for a number of reasons. It tends to be presented in terms of statistics, and thus is less interesting and immediate than other types of information. In addition, the way other people behave does not intuitively seem *causally* relevant to your own behavior. Similarly, you may have your own knowledge or intuitions about consensus information, based on how you have behaved in the past (Fiske and Taylor, 1984).

A second bias discovered early by research on causal attribution is the tendency to attribute another person's behavior to the person, rather than to the situation—a tendency called the **fundamental attribution error** (Ross, 1977). For example, in one study (Jones and Harris, 1967) subjects were told that another student had written an essay either supporting or condemning Fidel Castro, Cuba's Communist leader. The subjects were told either that the student had freely chosen the position advocated in the essay or that the student had been assigned to the pro- or anti-Castro position. Subjects were then asked what the essay-writing student's true attitude toward Castro was. One would expect that subjects would make strong inferences about the student's true attitude if they thought the student had freely chosen the position advocated in the essay, but would be unable to judge the student's real attitude if the position had been assigned. Yet even when the subjects believed that the student had had no choice about which position to advocate, they inferred that a student who wrote a pro-Castro essay really did favor Castro and that a student who wrote an anti-Castro essay really did oppose Castro. In other words, the subjects attributed the behavior of the student to something about the student, rather than to the situation the student was in.

Closely related to the fundamental attribution error is the *actor-observer bias*, which refers to our tendency to see other people's behavior as reflecting their true dispositions but to see our own behavior as caused more by the situation (Jones and Nisbett, 1972). When you are late for work, you probably explain your behavior in terms of the situation—heavy traffic, the need to run an errand, and the like. In contrast, your fellow workers are likely to attribute your behavior to something about *you*—perhaps that you are habitually late and inconsiderate. The actor-observer bias may explain many disagreements and conflicts in relationships, because two parties in a relationship may have very different understandings about why they each behave as they do: each may blame problems on the other's personality defects, yet excuse his or her own behavior as a response to the situation.

The actor-observer bias may arise for two reasons. First, the actor and the observer may have different sets of information available to them. You may know very well why you are late, but your observers may have little or none of this information, so their conclusion that you are to blame, and not the situation, may be for them a logical inference. Second, the visual perspectives of actors and observers are quite different. Actors' visual attention is quite literally focused outward, on the situation, whereas observers' visual attention is focused on the actors' behavior. This difference in visual perspective alone may contribute to the tendency of actors to explain their behavior in terms of the situation and of ob-

FUNDAMENTAL ATTRIBUTION ERROR the tendency to attribute another person's behavior to the person, rather than to the situation

The actor-observer bias can produce considerable tension between people. The "actor" who has a very good reason for being late is likely to get little sympathy from the "observer" who has been kept waiting.

servers to explain an actor's behavior in terms of the actor herself (Nisbett et al., 1973; Storms, 1973; Taylor and Fiske, 1975).

Heuristics in Social Perception

Does this growing list of attribution biases mean that we are poor processors of social information? Sometimes, yes; but overall, not necessarily. Given the overwhelming amount of information that we must process in every social situation, there is no way for us to be careful and completely logical all the time. Furthermore, our lives are full of uncertainties large and small. Getting through even an uneventful day involves making myriad decisions about ourselves, others, and the likelihood of various outcomes. Detailed analysis of every situation is impractical and sometimes unwarranted.

In the face of these difficulties, we behave more like "cognitive misers" than like naive scientists. Our goal is to process information quickly and reasonably accurately, and we do this by using heuristics to assess the probable correctness of our judgments. The use of heuristics is a very practical, if not strictly scientific, solution—although scientists, too, must often make practical decisions, follow hunches, and rely on intuition. Heuristics streamline the decision-making process and lighten the mental work load.

One frequently used heuristic, introduced in Chapter 9, is *availability*. We make judgments on the basis of the most readily available information or evidence—usually the associations that spring to mind right away (Taylor, 1982). This heuristic depends on how easy it is to retrieve from memory instances of a given category. We use the availability heuristic when we want to figure out how likely an event will be—whether an earthquake, a heart attack, a hijacking, a friend's response to an invitation, or a rejection of proferred love—or when we seek to make a general statement about prevalent conditions, whether political, personal, or social. How do you respond, for example, when an irate executive claims that foreign cars have taken over the United States market? If you can think of lots of friends and neighbors who own foreign cars, you may agree with the executive; but if most people in your community drive American cars, you may disagree. Availability often yields a fairly accurate reading, since the more we see of any phenomenon, the more pervasive it probably is. However, the availability heuristic is subject to bias. Each of us is more attentive to certain things than to others, and what we attend to is what comes to mind first when we are making a judgment on the basis of availability. What we are most easily able to imagine also influences our judgments; the more vividly we can imagine a war or a terrorist attack, the more likely we may expect such an attack to be (Tversky and Kahneman, 1974).

Another heuristic, which we apply to the social world as well as to other sorts of judgments, is *anchoring and adjustment*. Our most readily accessible tool for judging another's actions is ourselves: our beliefs about what we would do in the same situation. We tend to anchor our judgments in ourselves—that is, to use ourselves as a standard for comparison—and we are likely to fail to adjust our inferences to take individual differences into account. For example, when asked how creatively another person handled a difficult situation, you are likely to refer to the way *you* would have handled it, to assess your own behavior as creative or uncreative, and to judge the other's action accordingly (see Fong and Markus, 1982; Fiske and Taylor, 1984). Some psychologists maintain that the fundamental attribution error is the result of anchoring and adjustment. For example, in the study discussed above, subjects may have anchored their judgments in the *content* of the pro- and anti-Castro essays rather than in the situation under which the essays were written (Quattrone, Finkel, and Andrus, 1982).

Yet another heuristic often used to make inferences about probability is *representativeness*, first discussed in Chapter 9 (Kahneman and Tversky, 1973; Tversky and Kahneman, 1982; Fiske and Taylor, 1984). Suppose you are given the following description: "Steve is very shy and withdrawn, invariably helpful, but with little interest in people, or in the world of reality. A meek and tidy soul, he has a need for order and structure and a passion for detail" (Tversky and Kahneman, 1974). Using only this information, you must guess what Steve does for a living: Is he a farmer, a trapeze artist, a librarian, a salvage diver, or a surgeon? If you had enough information about the personality traits of people in each of these occupations, you might be able to calculate the probability that someone like Steve would be found in each one of them. Lacking such data, you would estimate how representative Steve is of the typical person in each occupation and would probably guess that because of his shyness, meekness, love of order, and so forth, Steve must be a librarian, because these attributes are associated with our stereotype of a librarian. The actual probability that Steve is representative of librarians depends on factors other than the stereotype. For instance, what are the base rates of these various occupations in the population? Are there more farmers than librarians? The representativeness heuristic can lead us to ignore statistically relevant information such as base rates.

Schemas and Stereotypes

Each person we meet is a unique individual, a fact that makes our social world extremely varied and complex. However, if we were actually to treat each person as unique, our cognitive abilities to attend to and think about others would quickly be overwhelmed. Consequently, we simplify matters by forming mental representations of *types* of people on the basis of important or noticeable similarities and differences between them. In other words, we categorize people, just as we categorize objects and events (see Chapter 9). There are many ways to categorize others—for example, by their dominant personality traits (extroverts, approval seekers), by their occupations or roles (mothers, lawyers), or by their membership in large social categories defined by physical attributes (race, gender, age) (Taylor and Crocker, 1981).

Although these categorizations are initially based on perceptible differences among types of people, such as skin color or number of wrinkles on the face, we quickly make additional generalizations about what members of a category are

This woman's inability to walk limits her mobility, but the human tendency to stereotype may limit her in other ways as well. She may be unfairly judged as being unable to do simple tasks, such as shopping, because others think that handicapped people are incompetent.

A girl's talent in mathematics is likely to be attributed to hard work or luck rather than innate ability because many people hold the stereotype that girls are not naturally "good" at math.

STEREOTYPES complex mental representations of different types of people, containing all the information that we know or believe to be generally true of them

like. Women, we might decide, are more emotional, whereas men are more reliable in a crisis. Eventually, we develop complex mental representations of different types of people, containing all the information that we know or believe to be generally true of them. These mental representations, which are similar to the schemas for objects and events that were discussed in Chapter 9, are called **stereotypes.** A stereotype may be either an accurate or an inaccurate generalization about what members of a category are like.

Stereotypes are useful in social situations because knowing a person's category membership suggests what we should look for (or look out for) in them, enables us to predict what they will be like and how they will behave, and helps us to remember their characteristics (Crocker and Park, 1988; Hamilton and Trolier, 1986). Stereotypes also affect our interpretations of others' behavior. In one study, white schoolchildren were shown stick-figure drawings of children while the experimenter read stories about the characters in the drawings (Sagar and Schofield, 1980). The stories were ambiguous, or open to interpretation. For example, one story read, "Mark was sitting at his desk, working on his social studies assignment, when David started poking him in the back with the eraser end of his pencil. Mark just kept on working. David kept poking him for awhile, then he stopped." Some subjects were told that David was black, others that he was white. Subjects tended to rate David's behavior as mean and threatening when he was described as black and as playful and friendly when he was described as white. Thus, subjects' stereotypes about blacks and whites led them to interpret exactly the same behavior differently.

Stereotypes also affect our causal attributions of other people's behavior. We tend to attribute behavior that fits our stereotypes to stable characteristics or personality traits and to attribute behavior that violates our stereotypes to temporary influences on behavior. For example, in one study, subjects learned that a person had been successful at a stereotypically masculine task. When the person was described as male, subjects tended to attribute his success to ability, whereas when the target was described as female, they attributed her success to luck or effort (Deaux and Emswiller, 1974).

Moreover, simply believing that a group of people are in the same category leads us to perceive a set of people as similar to one another and different from members of other categories (Tajfel, Sheikh, and Gardner, 1964; Wilder, 1981).

Finally, we tend to organize and remember information about people according to their category membership. In one study, subjects listened to a tape recording of a discussion among six male teachers, three black and three white. As each of the teachers spoke, subjects saw a slide of the speaker. Subjects were then given a list of all the statements made during the discussion and a set of photographs of the speakers, and were asked to match each speaker with the statements he had made. Subjects were more likely to make within-race errors (that is, to attribute a statement made by a black to the wrong black) than across-race errors (that is, to attribute a statement made by a black to a white, or vice versa), indicating that they had organized information in memory according to the race of the speaker. Similar within-group errors have been found when the speakers were male and female rather than black and white (Taylor et al., 1978).

Ingroups and Outgroups

> Father, Mother, and Me,
>   Sister and Auntie say
> All the people like us are We,
>   and everyone else is They.
> And They live over the sea,
>   While we live over the way,
> But—would you believe it?—They look upon We
>   As only a sort of They!

Rudyard Kipling

This poem describes the pervasive human tendency to categorize people into ingroups (us) and outgroups (them)—in other words, into the broadest possible stereotypes or schemas. Note that those two stereotypes are set up in opposition to each other, with positive emotions linked to the ingroup and negative emotions to the outgroup.

Even when group boundaries are determined by some arbitrary criterion—such as people who draw the letter "A" out of a hat versus people who draw the letter "B"—people will accept those group boundaries and favor the ingroup over the outgroup (Brewer, 1979). This **ingroup bias** is expressed in *prejudice* (negative evaluations of the outgroup) and in *discrimination* (the allocation of more rewards or resources to ingroup members than to outgroup members). Ingroup bias persists even when randomly selected members do not know the other members of their ingroup, and even when they personally have nothing to gain by favoring the ingroup (Brewer, 1979; Tajfel and Turner, 1986; Wilder, 1986).

The mere fact of categorization into "us" and "them" is sufficient to produce discrimination against outgroups. In one study, eight adolescents in the Netherlands were randomly divided into two teams of four (Rabbie and Horowitz, 1969). After both groups completed a few simple tasks, the researcher announced that members of one group would get transistor radios. The lucky group would be determined by the flip of a coin. Once the radios had been distributed, the adolescents rated the members of each group. Hostility was already apparent. The adolescents in each group saw the other group—the outgroup—as less open, less responsible, and less desirable as friends.

This ingroup/outgroup division has a number of cognitive effects, which can reinforce negative stereotypes and make discrimination and prejudice more likely (Hamilton and Trolier, 1986). First, members of the ingroup tend to assume that outgroup members are similar to one another and different from the ingroup. When researchers divided people into two groups on the basis of artistic preferences, the members of each group assumed that fellow members held opinions and beliefs similar to their own, even on matters that had nothing to do with art (Allen and Wilder, 1979). Thus, differences between groups are exaggerated and differences within groups are minimized. Second, and paradoxically, people see their ingroup as more diverse than the outgroup members (Quattrone and Jones, 1980; Park and Rothbart, 1982; Quattrone, 1986). Third, appraisals of outgroup members are polarized: for example, competent outgroup members may be evaluated very positively, but incompetent outgroup members will be strongly rejected (Linville and Jones, 1980; Linville, 1982).

INGROUP BIAS the tendency to favor an ingroup over an outgroup, expressed in prejudice and discrimination

Given these tendencies, it is not surprising that information about ingroup and outgroup members seems to be processed differently. Negative acts of outgroup members tend to be remembered, but negative acts of fellow ingroup members are easily forgotten. Attributions of causes for ingroup and outgroup behavior are also made very differently. In a variation of the fundamental attribution error, we attribute ingroup members' successes to their personal qualities and ascribe their failures to situational factors beyond their control. We do the opposite for outgroup members, attributing their successes to the situation and their failures to their personal weaknesses (Pettigrew, 1979). Thus, ingroup and outgroup divisions lead to a number of cognitive biases that can create further divisions between the groups and practically guarantee that such rifts will persist.

The Self-Fulfilling Prophecy

SELF-FULFILLING PROPHECY an initially false expectation about another person's behavior that actually causes the person to behave in such a way that the expectation is confirmed

Stereotypes can have negative consequences because they can actually affect the self-perceptions and behavior of outgroup members. A **self-fulfilling prophecy** is an initially false expectation about another's behavior that actually causes the other person to behave in such a way that the expectation is confirmed. The teacher–student relationship has been the focus of much research on the self-fulfilling prophecy. These studies (reviewed in Brophy and Good, 1974) have generally confirmed that teachers who expect certain students to do poorly in school behave toward those students in ways that cause their performance to conform to the teachers' expectations. Self-fulfilling prophecies that are based on teachers' racial or sexual stereotypes are most likely to occur in overcrowded classrooms and similar situations that prevent teachers from getting to know students well; it fades as a teacher gets more familiar with individual students. Moreover, some students will be more vulnerable than others to an adult's expectations of them (see Crocker and Park, 1988).

An illustration of how the self-fulfilling prophecy operates outside the classroom comes from a study of the effects of stereotypes about physical attractiveness by social psychologists Mark Snyder, Elizabeth Tanke, and Ellen Berscheid (1977). They based their work on previous research showing a widespread belief that those who are physically attractive are also warm and smart and have a host of other desirable attributes. If the self-fulfilling prophecy was at work, the researchers reasoned, this belief should affect behavior. Male subjects were each given a photograph of an attractive or an unattractive woman, which they believed was a picture of the woman to whom they then talked by telephone for ten minutes. The conversation between each pair was tape recorded, with the male and female voices on separate tracks. Independent scorers rated the sound of each voice for warmth and friendliness. The results showed that male subjects who thought they were speaking to an attractive woman were friendlier than males who thought they were speaking to an unattractive woman. The women, in turn, responded more warmly to men who had been given attractive pictures than to men who had been given unattractive pictures. Apparently, the male subjects' expectations that attractive women are warmer than unattractive women were indeed self-fulfilling prophecies.

Changing Social Stereotypes

We have seen that stereotypes and categorization into groups may affect the way we process information about outgroups, so that ambiguous information is interpreted as consistent with the stereotype, behavior that is inconsistent with the stereotype is attributed to temporary or unstable causes, and outgroup members tend to be confused with one another and seen as similar to one another. All these information-processing effects of stereotypes make stereotypes resistant to change, for even if an outgroup member behaves in ways that do not fit our stereotype, we may persist in perceiving him or her as fitting the stereotype. In addition, research on the self-fulfilling prophecy suggests that even if a person otherwise does not fit our stereotype, our own behavior toward the person may induce him or her to behave consistently with our stereotype. Consequently, even erroneous stereotypes may be difficult to change.

Stereotypes can change under some circumstances. In one study (Weber and Crocker, 1983), subjects' stereotypes about various occupations were assessed (for example, subjects believed that lawyers are generally well-dressed, intelligent, and wealthy). They then learned about characteristics of several lawyers, some of which fit their stereotype, and some of which contradicted it. Although all subjects learned about the same number of contradictory behaviors, the way the information was presented was varied. For some subjects, a few of the lawyers showed several characteristics that contradicted the stereotype, whereas for other subjects, each lawyer had one characteristic that contradicted the stereotype. The researchers measured how much subjects' stereotypes had changed as a result of this new information. When a few lawyers had several contradictory characteristics, they were seen as "exceptions to the rule," and subjects were less likely to change their overall view of lawyers. However, when each lawyer had one characteristic that contradicted the stereotype, subjects were more likely to adjust their view of lawyers in response. Thus, it seems that a few dramatic instances in which the stereotype is clearly wrong may be less effective at changing stereotypes than several individuals who each have one attribute that violates the stereotype.

In short, then, stereotypes are difficult to change. However, some research indicates that change is possible. One of the most promising new directions involves studies in which members of different racial or ethnic groups are encouraged to work with one another cooperatively, rather than competitively (Aronson et al., 1978; Cook, 1984; Slavin, 1985). Cooperation entails and fosters close contact in which individuals help one another solve problems, and in doing so obtain the sort of information about outgroup members that can change stereotypes. When a white student works in a cooperative problem-solving setting with a Hispanic student, for example, the individual contributions of each become important. As a result, students are encouraged to view each other as individuals, not as members of outgroups or ingroups. This decreased focus on social categories in turn leads to increased perceptions that ingroup and outgroup members are similar to each other, increased acceptance of outgroup members, and decreased stereotyping of outgroup members (Miller and Brewer, 1986).

Entire classrooms have been structured to encourage such cooperation across racial and ethnic boundaries, and these programs have had notable success at improving intergroup relations in the classroom (Slavin, 1985). Unfortunately, as

Contact and cooperation can help to change the stereotypes that members of different racial and ethnic groups hold about each other.

yet there is little evidence that these new attitudes are extended to interactions that occur outside the classroom walls (Miller and Brewer, 1986). (Recent research on changes in white Americans' racial attitudes is discussed in the accompanying box.)

INTERPERSONAL ATTRACTION AND FRIENDSHIP

We have discussed a number of explanations for tension and hostility between individuals and between groups. What about positive relations between or among people? What determines whom we are attracted to? What is the basis for friendship, on any of its levels of intimacy?

The Effects of Similarity

Similarity, especially similarity in attitudes, appears to play an important role in interpersonal attraction.

Similarity in Attitudes

The most consistent finding in social psychology literature and research on friendship and attraction is that people like others whose attitudes resemble their own. Attitude similarity or dissimilarity is one of the first types of information we seek in an interaction. We are very sensitive to subtle cues about another person's attitudes, picking up such cues within a few minutes of meeting a stranger. In one illustrative study (Lloyd, Paulse, and Brockner, 1983), subjects were asked, after a brief interaction with a stranger of the opposite sex, to rate the stranger's attractiveness. Each subject was also asked to respond to measures that rated her or his own self-esteem and self-consciousness. Although none of the subjects knew the other person's self-esteem and self-consciousness rating, they consistently judged the people who were most like themselves on these measures to be most attractive.

This study makes clear that when we find strangers attractive, they often turn out to resemble us in some way. How do we decide so readily whether or not a stranger resembles us? We seem to attribute our own qualities to any attractive stranger, as another study revealed (Marks, Miller, and Maruyama, 1981). College students who judged both themselves and strangers on a number of personality traits assumed that physically attractive strangers were more like themselves than were unattractive strangers. The assumption was so strong that the students declared that they were similar to attractive strangers even on such undesirable traits as greed, conceit, phoniness, selfishness, and hostility (see Figure 21.4). In contrast, the students denied their close resemblance to unattractive strangers, even on such positive traits as thoughtfulness, intelligence, open-mindedness, dependability, and honesty.

People also tend to believe that attractive people have attitudes and tastes like their own. In another study, subjects assumed that attractive peers were likely to endorse their own attitudes and beliefs on an array of topics, ranging from issues that were deeply important to them, such as politics, to trivial matters, such as their preferences among cigarette brands (Marks and Miller, 1982). Subjects again distanced themselves from unattractive peers, assuming that their attitudes on important issues differed, although indicating that on trivial matters their attitudes were probably similar.

There even seems to be a general tendency to assume that *any* stranger, not just an attractive one, will have similar attitudes (although we still expect attractive strangers to be more like us than unattractive ones are) (Byrne, Clore, and Smeaton, 1986). We may also overestimate attitude similarity in our friends and romantic partners (Byrne and Blaylock, 1963).

PSYCHOLOGY TODAY AND TOMORROW

Are White Americans' Racial Attitudes Really Changing?

In the two and a half decades since the modern civil rights movement in the United States was at its peak, survey researchers have documented a steady decrease in anti-black prejudice among whites. For example, in 1942, only 2 percent of white southerners agreed that blacks and whites should go to the same schools, whereas in 1970, 45 percent of white southern respondents supported integrated schools. A Harris poll conducted from the years 1963 to 1978 showed gradual but consistent changes in racial attitudes; in 1978 whites had become less likely to ascribe negative traits such as violent, inferior, criminal, and unintelligent to blacks than at any previous time. These results suggest that white Americans are substantially less anti-black than they were a few decades ago.

Other research, however, suggests that these changes may be more superficial than real. What may have changed is not the racist attitudes themselves, but the acceptability of *expressing* such attitudes. Many items in traditional measures of prejudice are highly susceptible to such social desirability concerns (McConahay, Hardee, and Batts, 1981; McConahay, 1986). Studies that avoid social desirability biases by using unobtrusive measures of anti-black attitudes, such as willingness to help a black person in need, still reveal a substantial degree of anti-black prejudice (Crosby, Bromley, and Saxe, 1980).

Psychologists Samuel Gaertner and John Dovidio (1986) have proposed that a new form of racism has developed in the U.S., which they call *aversive racism*. In contrast to traditional racists, aversive racists sympathize with the victims of past injustice; identify more generally with a liberal political agenda; and regard themselves as nonprejudiced and nondiscriminatory. However, because of the prevalence of anti-black attitudes in the culture, aversive racists almost unavoidably possess negative feelings and beliefs about blacks, including discomfort, disgust, or fear. Because the self-schemas of aversive racists include being unprejudiced, when a situation or event threatens to reveal the negative aspects of their attitudes, aversive racists try to deny these feelings and avoid acting in a prejudiced manner. In some situations, then, aversive racists will behave in very positive ways toward blacks. In other situations, however, when the racist nature of their behavior is more ambiguous, their anti-black affect will be expressed in subtle, and rationalizable, ways.

In one study that tested the aversive racism perspective, white subjects who were either high or low in prejudice as measured by traditional surveys heard an unambiguous emergency involving either a black or a white victim (Gaertner and Dovidio, 1977). Subjects were led to believe that they were participating in an extrasensory perception experiment, in which they would try to receive telepathic messages from a sender who was located in a cubicle across the hallway, and whom they could hear through an intercom system. Subjects learned the race of the sender, who was either black or white, when they saw her picture on an ID card. Some subjects believed that other receivers were participating in the experiment at the same time, whereas others believed that they were the only receiver. Midway through the experiment, subjects heard a terrible crash from across the hall, accompanied by screams for help from the sender. The researchers observed whether the subjects tried to help the sender.

When the subjects believed they were alone with the sender, they were more likely to help the black sender (94 percent) than the white sender (81 percent). However, when they thought other receivers were present, they helped the black sender much less frequently (38 percent) than the white sender (75 percent). This pattern was similar for subjects who were high and low in traditional prejudice. When they could explain their lack of helpfulness by reasoning that someone else could help instead, subjects' anti-black feelings influenced their behavior. However, when there was no such excuse for not helping, almost all subjects helped the black victim.

The similarity–attraction link has recently been called into question, however, by Milton Rosenbaum's (1986) *repulsion hypothesis*, which asserts that it is dissimilar attitudes that lead to disliking, rather than similar attitudes that lead to liking. According to Rosenbaum, similarity of attitudes is often irrelevant and has few effects; it is dissimilarity that in most cases motivates us. The repulsion hypothesis is based on evidence that people are no more attracted to another when

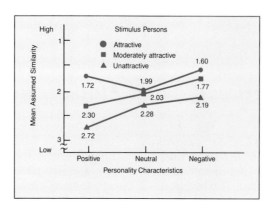

Figure 21.4 Mean assumed trait similarity between self and target persons. The numbers beside each data point are mean responses. Lower numbers reflect greater assumed trait similarity. (Adapted from Marks, Miller, and Maruyama, 1981.)

they have information on attitude similarity than they are when they do not have such information.

Donn Byrne and his colleagues (Byrne, Clore, and Smeaton, 1986) have attacked the repulsion hypothesis, arguing that in the absence of information, we tend to assume that a stranger's attitudes are similar to our own. Recent evidence indicates that increased attitude similarity *does* increase attraction (Byrne, Smeaton, and Nurnen, 1989). These conclusions were drawn from two experiments. In one, subjects evaluated a stranger's attractiveness on the basis of sets of attitude-survey responses; the greater the number of responses that were similar to the subjects' own, the higher the attractiveness rating. In the other experiment, statements of attitudes similar to the subjects' own proved to be successful reinforcers in a visual discrimination task.

Attitude similarity probably has such a powerful effect because it bolsters our self-worth by making us feel competent and correct (Byrne and Clore, 1970). When other people validate our attitudes by sharing them, we are likely to find them attractive.

It might be expected, then, that showering someone with praise would be the surest path to friendship. Yet research has shown that unquestioning approval does not necessarily produce the most favorable attitudes toward the approving person. In one study (Aronson and Linder, 1965), subjects responded more to an *increase* in approval than to consistent, unchanging approval. In this experiment, women overheard a series of remarks about themselves made by a confederate of the researchers. Women in one group heard only complimentary remarks, and those in a second group heard very derogatory remarks. A third group heard very derogatory remarks, which gradually became positive and at last were highly complimentary (this was called the *gain* condition). A fourth group heard comments that were at first very positive but became less favorable and finally very disparaging (this was called the *loss* condition). When each woman was asked how much she liked the confederate, the confederate who had begun by saying negative things and ended by being laudatory was liked the best. The confederate who had been uniformly positive was liked—but not as much as the one who had switched from criticism to approval. The confederate who had said consistently negative things was also preferred to the one who had begun with compliments and ended with disapproval. Thus, a shift from disapproval to approval proved especially rewarding, and loss of approval was especially discouraging or even aversive.

In a recent reinterpretation of the similarity–attraction link, John Condon and William Crano (1988), using earlier formulations (Aronson and Worchel, 1966; McWhirter and Jecker, 1967), found evidence that attraction may have its source in one person's inference of another's liking, which, in turn, is based on agreement (attitude similarity). Condon and Crano claim that we all learn to associate agreement with mutual affection or liking. Because in the past we have learned to associate agreement with liking and have been reinforced for liking those who cared for us (parents, friends, and lovers), we assume, first, that if someone agrees with us, she or he will also like us, and second, that we will like her or him. These assumptions serve as the stimulus for attraction: we are attracted because we expect to be liked, and we expect to like in return.

Other types of similarity have also been studied, though less extensively than attitude similarity has been. These other similarities seem to come into play primarily—though not exclusively—in romantic relationships, along with the factors in sexual attraction that we discussed in Chapter 14.

Similarity in Appearance

In romantic novels and movies, the handsome hero almost always ends up with the beautiful heroine. Life apparently follows fiction in this sense, since beauty attracts beauty. Studies of dating relationships indicate that people of similar physical attractiveness tend to pair off (Murstein, 1972). For example, a study of clients of a Los Angeles dating service showed that couples tended to sort themselves out on the basis of physical similarity (Folkes, 1982). Selection was made on the basis of information available to all subscribers; this information consisted of a questionnaire about the subscriber's occupation, age, attitudes, interests, and background, as well as a photograph and a five-minute videotape. From this information a member could express interest in meeting another member; the second member could then decide to initiate the relationship by releasing his or her surname and phone number, by initiating contact, or by actually dating. The subscribers who were studied had an average age of thirty-six years. As it turned out, the physical attractiveness of subscribers they chose to contact or date was similar to their own.

One possible explanation for this pattern is that when choosing a date, people consider not only the attractiveness of the other person but also the probability of being rejected by that person. Dating, in other words, follows the rules of the marketplace: a man calculates risks and rewards before he approaches a woman for a date. If a man considers himself to be fairly unattractive, he considers it probable that an attractive woman will reject him, so he lowers his sights to a somewhat less attractive date. Some evidence of this "matching process" has been supplied by research in which it was found that when there was no possibility of refusal, men tended to choose more attractive women for dates than they would have chosen under ordinary conditions (Berscheid et al., 1971).

Other studies have produced more contradictory results. In one experiment (Huston, 1973), men who rated themselves low in physical attractiveness seemed to select dates who were as attractive as those selected by men who rated themselves high in physical attractiveness. This held true even though men who gave themselves low ratings also believed they had a poorer than average chance of being accepted by the most attractive females. It is possible that the men with a low evaluation of themselves were less sensitive to rejection than those who considered themselves to be attractive. Unattractive men may become accustomed to

Generally, among couples, like attracts like. Men and women tend to be drawn toward people of similar backgrounds and levels of physical attractiveness.

being turned down, and the chance of a highly rewarding partner may encourage them to risk refusal.

Another possible interpretation is that people will try to develop dating relationships with the most attractive partner available, regardless of the probability of rejection. But since they are rejected by those who think they can find more attractive dates, people of similar attractiveness end up paired. According to this explanation, such a "sorting process" can explain the finding that dating couples tend to be similar in physical attractiveness.

Similarity in Social Background

Not only do most couples tend to be similar in physical attractiveness, they also tend to share the same race, religion, economic status, and educational level. Young people often encounter strong social pressures, especially from parents, to marry someone with a similar social history. Such a sorting process is encouraged, as you will see shortly, by our tendency to live near and encounter daily those who resemble us on a number of counts.

The Effects of Complementary and Compatible Needs

Another factor that helps explain interpersonal attraction and friendship is the meshing of one person's needs with those of another (Winch, 1958). Thus, a person with the need to dominate is attracted to one with the need to be dominated; a person with a need to care for others is drawn to one with a need to be cared for. In describing a friendship between two teenage boys, psychologist Robert White (1972) provided a good example of how two personalities can complement each other:

> Ben, whose school experience had been so unstimulating that he never read a book beyond those assigned, discovered in Jamie a lively spirit of intellectual inquiry and an exciting knowledge of politics and history: Here was a whole world to which his friend opened the door and provided guidance. Jamie discovered in Ben a world previously closed to him, that of confident interaction with other people. Each admired the other, each copied the other, each used the other for practice.

Later research, however, suggests that friendships may depend more on a compatibility of needs than on a simple complementarity. An example of compatible needs in a pair of friends is a high level of dominance in one person and a low need for autonomy (independence) in the other. A high need for dominance in one partner and a low need for dominance in the other would be complementary but would not necessarily be compatible. The importance of compatibility appeared in an assessment of camp counselors who had worked together for at least one month and had formed friendships. There was strong evidence that counselors with compatible need structures tended to become friends (Wagner, 1975).

Compatibility of needs may be important for a harmonious marriage. When the need structures of married couples were studied, there was no evidence of any relationship between marital adjustment and simple complementarity. But couples who scored high on a scale of marriage adjustment had similar needs for affiliation, aggression, autonomy, and nurturance. Apparently, similarity in these needs makes for a harmonious marriage. A couple with similarly high needs for affiliation, for example, can socialize a great deal, while a couple who are both low in the need for affiliation can be stay-at-homes. Sharply different levels of need for affiliation would be expected to produce tension between marriage partners.

It seems that in addition to individual needs, the social context of a relationship must also be taken into account, since it also affects the compatibility of need structures (Wagner, 1975). Knowledge of needs may be a reliable guide to friendship patterns and marital adjustment, but the principles for determining need compatibility are quite complex and subtle.

The Effects of Proximity

All the factors in interpersonal attraction that we have discussed thus far—similarity, approval, inferred liking, complementarity and compatibility of needs—necessarily take effect *after* we have had the opportunity to meet and get to know a little bit about another person. Such opportunities are provided by **proximity,** or physical nearness, which therefore plays a central role in determining whom we choose as friends.

The powerful effects of proximity were demonstrated in a study (Segal, 1974) of a police academy in which male cadets were alphabetically assigned to dormitory rooms and classroom seats. Upon entry, a cadet whose name began with A was likely to room with another cadet whose name also began with A, or with B or C, and sit near him in class. After six weeks, the researcher asked cadets about their choices of friends among their classmates. There was a remarkable tendency for cadets to choose as friends classmates whose names began with letters near their own in the alphabet. Among the sixty-five friendships formed among the cadets, twenty-nine (45 percent) were between men next to each other in alphabetical order, and such choices were more likely to be reciprocated than were choices made out of alphabetical order. Just the accident of names predisposed Smith to become friends with Simmons rather than with Adkins and predisposed Adkins to become friends with Abelson.

One reason that proximity is a powerful factor in friendship is that proximity presupposes a certain amount of similarity. People who live close to each other tend to be similar in many ways: socioeconomic status, school background, educational attainment, ethnic background, political leanings, clothing style, family structure, and so forth. People who work together tend to have a certain level of education and training in common, and often have similar values (Crocker, 1981). And romantic partners, as you have seen, tend to have similar backgrounds. Thus,

PROXIMITY physical nearness, which plays a central role in interpersonal attraction and friendship

Proximity—as in sharing a dorm room—has a major influence on the friendships we form.

geographic proximity promotes a host of processes that combine to generate and maintain friendships as well as romantic relationships. It would be no accident if you married the girl or boy next door.

There is a rich interplay among friendship, proximity, and similarity. Proximity not only promotes the formation of friendships but also predisposes people to *become* more similar to each other—in language, in culture, in dress, in likes and dislikes, in political opinions, and in income. At the same time, a reciprocal influence exists between friendship and proximity. Proximity determines the range of people with whom it is possible to make friends, and it ensures repeated exposure. But once friendships are formed, friends tend to remain close to each other and to maintain contact. Thus, friendship promotes proximity.

Similarity, too, affects the development of friendships. Like the relationship between friendship and proximity, the relationship between similarity and friendship is reciprocal: we want our friends to share our views and tastes, and we want them to be like us in many ways. Similarity may also promote proximity. For example, people tend to move into neighborhoods that are occupied by others more or less like themselves. They seek out ethnic and religious affinity, and similarity of socioeconomic level. No one likes to be among people who are "different" and to risk being considered an "outsider." Thus, proximity, similarity, and friendship all enhance and reinforce one another.

SUMMARY

Attitudes

- An attitude is an evaluative response to a particular object, idea, person, or group of people. Attitudes may be thought of as having three components: affective (how we feel), behavioral (how we act), and cognitive (what we think and believe).
- The affective component of an attitude is typically formed through classical conditioning, as we learn particular associations to emotion-arousing circumstances. The exposure effect also plays a role, with repeated neutral encounters producing positive (but not negative) feelings about an attitude object. The behavioral component of an attitude is probably the result of instrumental conditioning. The cognitive component of an attitude usually results from the acquisition of information about the attitude object.
- Cognitive dissonance theory holds that an inconsistency between two of our attitudes or between our attitudes and our behavior produces an unpleasant state of arousal that motivates us to reestablish consistency by changing either an attitude or a behavior.
- Self-perception theory holds that we change our attitudes when we perceive them to be inconsistent with our behavior, without necessarily experiencing unpleasant arousal.
- Some researchers argue that attitude change is motivated primarily by people's need for self-affirmation as good and worthwhile.
- Attitudes may be changed through persuasion, via either the central route (in which the message recipient evaluates the quality of the arguments presented) or the peripheral route (in which the recipient uses heuristic thinking, previous experiences, or some method other than evaluation of the quality of the persuasive arguments).
- The degree of consistency between attitudes and behavior is influenced by the amount of direct experience a person has

with the attitude object; by social norms and the person's self-consciousness; and by personality type (especially the extent to which the person is self-monitoring, trying to match his or her behavior to the situation regardless of his or her attitude).

Social Cognition

- Social cognition refers to the way we think and reason about ourselves as social beings, about other people, about relations between people, and about the various groups to which we and other people belong.
- According to the "naive scientist" model of social cognition, people are rational processors of information, trying to make the best possible and most intuitively logical social judgments about ourselves and others by analyzing behavior for distinctiveness, consistency, and consensus.
- In making inferences about social relations, we apply heuristics (rules of thumb) that result in social schemas. These cognitive frameworks are subject to causal attribution biases. First, we may reject consensus information (a general agreement about the appropriate response to a social stimulus) because we perceive it as irrelevant to our own situation. Second, we may commit the fundamental attribution error, ascribing another person's behavior to the person rather than to the situation. Third, the actor-observer bias may cause us to see other people's behavior as revealing what they are really like but to see our own behavior as resulting from the situation.
- We often act like "cognitive misers" rather than naive scientists, using heuristics to assess the likelihood that our perceptions of others are accurate. Frequently used heuristics are availability of information, anchoring and adjustment, and representativeness.
- A stereotype is a kind of schema, a mental representa-

tion containing all the information that we know or believe to be generally true about different types, or categories, of people.

■ We tend to categorize people into ingroups and outgroups and to maintain an ingroup bias, favoring ingroups through prejudice and discrimination against outgroups.

■ Prejudice and discrimination can generate a self-fulfilling prophecy, whereby an outgroup member behaves in a way that confirms the initially false expectations of an ingroup member.

■ Stereotypes are difficult, but not impossible, to change.

Interpersonal Attraction and Friendship

■ Attraction between people is partially determined by similarity in attitudes, appearance, and social background.

■ Interpersonal attraction and friendship are also influenced by complementary and compatible needs in the two people involved.

■ Proximity, or physical nearness, provides the opportunity for people to meet and get to know one another.

KEY TERMS

attitude
central route to persuasion
cognitive dissonance
contact hypothesis
discrimination

exposure effect
fundamental attribution error
ingroup bias
peripheral route to persuasion

prejudice
proximity
self-fulfilling prophecy
social cognition
stereotypes

CONCEPT REVIEW

1. Define *attitude* and distinguish its three traditional components. Outline the development of each of these components.

2. Explain how cognitive dissonance theory accounts for attitude change. Give an account of at least one of the classic experiments supporting dissonance theory.

3. What are the basic points of difference between self-perception theory and cognitive dissonance theory? What is the relationship between self-perception and self-affirmation?

4. Use an example from advertising to distinguish the central route and the peripheral route to persuasion.

5. Outline the various factors that may affect the consistency between our attitudes and our behavior.

6. Describe the naive-scientist model developed by Fritz Heider. How does this model account for the fundamental attribution error and other cognitive biases?

7. Identify the heuristics most frequently used in social perception.

8. How do stereotypes give rise to discrimination and ingroup bias?

9. Identify the aspects of similarity between individuals and explain how each contributes to attraction and friendship. What is the repulsion hypothesis?

10. Describe the bases of attraction and friendship other than similarity. Do these factors contradict or complement the role of similarity?

CRITICAL THINKING

1. Consistency versus change is an important theme in social psychology, and it has been discussed in other chapters in this unit as well as in Chapter 21. Identify the other discussions of this theme and determine whether, on the whole, they form a fundamental issue or question for psychology regarding the consistency of human behavior.

2. In reviewing this chapter, which of the major theoretical perspectives in psychology appears to be the most frequently used by social psychologists? Explain why this is the case.

...*Social Influence and Group Processes*

On May 25, 1989, in a prosperous New Jersey suburb, five members of the high school football team were arrested and charged with sexually assaulting a mentally retarded seventeen-year-old girl. The assault allegedly took place in the basement of the family home of the team's co-captains: twin brothers, aged eighteen. All the boys came from middle-class families. One boy's father was a physician; the remaining fathers were business executives. Watching the assault were eight other boys—one of them the son of a police lieutenant. According to police reports, three of the arrested boys actually had sexual contact with the girl, one of the others participated but did not have sexual contact himself, and the fifth egged the others on. There was no indication that either drugs or alcohol was involved (*The New York Times*, 1989a; 1989b).

News of the assault stunned community residents, who, though they were aware that the boys had discipline problems in school, could not understand how these advantaged boys could participate in such an act. They were just as shocked by the tacit acceptance of the assault by the boys who stood by and did not intervene. We are especially disturbed by such events when nothing in the backgrounds of the people involved seems to explain their actions. But the influence of situations can often overpower the effects of disposition or background—whether we are talking about gang rape such as the one in New Jersey, a "celebrating riot" such as the melees that occasionally erupt after sports victories, or popular political uprisings such as the "democracy movement" that swept China and Eastern Europe in 1989.

Such events are less puzzling when viewed in terms of the second major theme of social psychology: the influence of a situation on social behavior—especially the influence of other people. As we saw when we explored the other major theme, the cognitive construction of social reality, in Chapter 21, we tend to explain the behavior of other people in terms of their attitudes and personality, which leads us to underestimate the effects of the situation on their actions. But as many of the classic studies in social psychology have shown, situations and social influence have a powerful influence on behavior—an influence that often violates our intuitive grasp of social cause and effect. In this chapter we will consider some of these classic findings, as well as some recent developments in the area of social influence and such group processes as cooperation and competition.

SOCIAL INFLUENCE

Our behavior is affected by internal states such as our needs, memories, and beliefs, but it is also affected by external stimuli and how we interpret them. The impact of social influence can be seen in many types of behavior—not only when people join a riot but also when they obey authority, cooperate with each other, or aid a person in distress. Its effects range from the influence exerted by the mere presence of others to the complex effects of brainwashing.

Social Facilitation

The simplest form of social influence—the mere presence of others—was studied by the earliest social psychologists at the turn of the century. For example, an early researcher, Norman Triplett (1897), noted that bicycle racers do much better in competitive races than when racing alone against the clock. He decided that the presence of others performing the same task increases a person's motivation and thus improves performance. At first it appeared that Triplett's explanation was correct. **Social facilitation,** or enhanced performance in the presence of others, was supported by a number of subsequent studies in human beings as well as in many animal species (Travis, 1925; Dashiell, 1930).

Some conflicting evidence appeared, however. Researchers discovered that people actually took longer to solve complex problems and made more mistakes when they worked on a task in the presence of others (Allport, 1920). They also

SOCIAL FACILITATION enhanced performance in the presence of others

Performance of a well-practiced activity tends to improve in the presence of others.

took longer to learn a complex maze when other people were around (Pessin and Husband, 1933). Experiments with animals were also ambiguous. Social facilitation appeared among animals that ate or drank in the presence of others: for example, a chicken allowed to eat grain until it would eat no more began eating again when it was joined by a hungry chicken (Bayer, 1929). But when placed in groups, animals became slower at learning mazes. A solitary cockroach found its way through a maze much more rapidly than did pairs or groups of three cockroaches (Gates and Allee, 1933).

These findings turned out to be less inconsistent than they had seemed at first. Social facilitation occurred when people or other animals worked on simple tasks or on tasks they had already mastered, but their performance worsened on complex tasks or on tasks that required them to learn new skills. In other human and animal studies, as discussed in the following sections, researchers had already found that motivation in itself also affected performance, sometimes helping it and sometimes hindering it.

The Concept of Dominant Response

Significantly, behaviorist Kenneth Spence (1958) had discovered that the differences in performance that emerge when motivation, drive, or arousal is varied are not random but quite systematic. He noted that when an individual's motivation increases, performance on simple tasks improves but performance on complex tasks deteriorates. He explained these results by invoking the concept of dominant response. **Dominant responses** are those that have been extremely well learned and are therefore most likely to be made by an organism in a given situation. For example, eating may be the dominant response when food is placed before a hungry or greedy animal, and escape may be the dominant response when an animal is threatened. In well-learned tasks, such as walking, the dominant responses are mainly correct; but when the individual is learning a new skill, such as riding a bicycle, the dominant responses are mainly wrong. For example, if we encounter an overhanging tree branch while we are walking, our dominant response is to duck under it; if we are just learning to ride a bike, however, ducking is likely to upset our balance and cause a spill.

Robert Zajonc (1965) made a connection between these findings and the results of social facilitation experiments. Zajonc asked: What happens when we are learning in the presence of another person? He concluded that the presence of someone else has an arousing effect, and when we are aroused, our dominant responses are enhanced.

DOMINANT RESPONSE an extremely well learned response that is most likely to be made in a given situation

Most research on social facilitation has supported Zajonc's view (Geen and Hange, 1977; Bond and Titus, 1983). As one example, when people work at tasks in the presence of observers, their palms sweat, which is a sign of arousal (Martens, 1969). Another example involves learning to trace the path through a maze with a finger. The presence of others interferes with performance when a person is just beginning to learn the path, but once the individual has mastered the maze, the presence of others improves speed and efficiency (Hunt and Hillery, 1973). The presence of others leads to many learning errors when the maze is complex, but fewer errors when the maze is simple.

Arousal in Social Facilitation

What is the nature of the arousal underlying social facilitation? One possibility is that the presence of spectators or other individuals working on the same task makes the person apprehensive about being evaluated (Cottrell, 1972). This seemed to be the case in a field study at the University of California in Santa Barbara, where researchers timed male and female runners as they covered two 45-yard segments of a footpath (Worringham and Messick, 1983). Twelve of the runners ran both segments with no observers present. Another twelve ran the first segment with no observers, but in the second segment they were watched by a woman seated on the grass near the path. A third set of twelve ran the first segment with no observers, but in the second segment they passed a woman who, engrossed in a book, sat facing away from them. Running speed during the second segment increased only in the group that had been observed by the woman who watched them as she sat near the path. Since all groups were unaware that they were being timed, only the group watched by the woman could have been concerned that they were being evaluated.

Arousal is also affected by the characteristics of the spectators. Both the size of the audience and its status affected the amount of anxiety that college students said that they felt while performing a simple learning task or said that they would feel while reading a paper they had written (Seta et al., 1989). In this study, the size of the audience varied from two to thirty-two; its status was high (faculty members), low (high school students), or mixed. In most cases, the larger the audience, the greater the students' anxiety and the more errors they made on the learning task. But the composition of the audience was also important: students were more anxious when performing before a small high-status audience than before a much larger low-status group. In addition, the variables of size and status interacted. Adding members to a low-status audience increased a student's anxiety more than did adding members to a high-status audience. Presumably, when the audience is high in status, people are already so anxious that increasing its size makes little difference. Moreover, adding low-status members to a small, high-status audience may even cause a decrease in anxiety because, overall, the audience seems less threatening (Seta et al., 1989).

Social facilitation is the simplest form of social influence because it merely inhibits or encourages existing behavior. In social facilitation the *direction* of behavior does not change, and the mere presence of others does not lead to the formation of new habits or to the extinction of old ones. In contrast, other forms of social influence that we hardly notice can induce people to act against their beliefs or moral standards: (1) social pressure to conform to a prevailing attitude or perception and (2) the process that leads people to obey authority. Let us look at each of these in some detail—first conformity, then obedience. We'll conclude the section by briefly considering some subtle forms of hidden influence.

Conformity to Social Norms

SOCIAL NORM a shared standard of behavior used as a guideline in relations with others

The norms of a culture are social forces that exert a powerful, although often unrecognized, pressure on individuals to conform. A **social norm** is a shared standard of behavior, a guideline people follow in their relations with others. It is

Appropriate dress is a social norm that varies from place to place. This runner's outfit will probably slow him down, but he can still run his race. If he tried to dine at an elegant French restaurant, however, he would be turned away.

difficult to imagine much behavior that is not affected by social norms: the food we eat, the clothes we wear, the books we read, the movies we see, the music we listen to, the religious and political beliefs we hold, are all affected to a great degree. For example, cultural influences determine how we eat—whether with forks, chopsticks, or fingers—and even the situations in which we shift from one method to another. At a banquet, for instance, we use a knife and fork to eat chicken, but at a picnic we pick it up with our fingers. In Morocco, people eat from a common dish with their fingers; at a Moroccan restaurant, Americans do the same thing.

Conformity can be defined as the tendency to shift one's views or behavior closer to the norms expressed by other people. It is the result of implicit or explicit social pressure. When you conform, it is not necessarily because you are convinced that what you are doing or saying is right. You may simply take a particular public stance because you believe that others prefer, or even demand, that you do so.

In some cultures (for example, in China or Japan), conformity has a relatively positive connotation; in the United States, conformity to the less important social norms tends to be regarded as slavish imitation. Yet despite the negative connotation conformity has in this culture, norms often serve important social functions. They protect weaker members of the community and promote social integration. They ensure that vital social processes, such as procreation, mating, distribution of goods, succession of authority, and preservation of property, are carried out in an orderly way, without conflict or strife.

Behavior that is most important to the community is generally regulated by law. Of course, law forbids us to kill, rob, or pillage, but it also ensures conformity in other areas of life. The law forces us to go to school until we are sixteen, to drive on the right side of the road, to pay taxes on our income, and to limit ourselves to one spouse at a time. Less important norms are backed by custom. Custom says that we should not break into a line of people who are waiting to buy movie tickets; we should not come to a funeral dressed as a clown; we should not smoke in a house of worship.

CONFORMITY   the tendency to shift one's views or behavior closer to social norms

Conformity in an Ambiguous Case: Sherif's Experiments

There are situations in which individual conformity goes beyond matters of law and custom. Social influence can even lead people to question information received by their senses. In a classic experiment that marked the beginning of con-

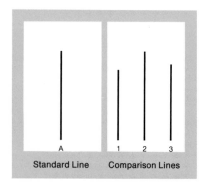

Figure 22.1 The stimuli in a single trait in Asch's experiment. The subject must state which of the comparison lines he judges to be the same length as the standard. The discrimination is an easy one to make: control subjects (those who made the judgments without any group pressure) chose line 2 as correct over 99 percent of the time.

formity research, Muzafer Sherif (1936) used a visual illusion to demonstrate the way people conform to norms even in making judgments about perceptual phenomena. He used the *autokinetic effect*, in which a stationary pinpoint of light, when viewed in total darkness, appears to move. People viewed such lights by themselves, and over the course of many judgments, each arrived at a stable—but different—range of judgments about the distance the light "moved." Afterward, several individuals, each with a different pattern of judgment, viewed the light together and judged aloud how far the light moved. In the course of making these judgments, their widely divergent estimates converged until they closely resembled one another.

The situation in this experiment differs substantially from that found in social facilitation. In social facilitation, the effect is caused by the mere presence of others—their behavior provides no reinforcement and furnishes no cues as to appropriate responses. In the conformity experiment, however, the person does receive information from others. Although the use of this information is not required as a guide to behavior, it is available. If the person feels any compulsions to follow it, then social influence has exerted an effect.

In Sherif's experiments, people who viewed the light from the beginning made similar judgments during the first session together. And people who started by making their judgments in groups, but then watched the light by themselves, were found to have adopted the social norm as their own. They persisted in giving approximately the same estimates that had been developed within the group.

Conformity in an Unambiguous Case: Asch's Experiments

Some psychologists wondered whether Sherif's findings would also apply to situations in which *unambiguous* information was available. Solomon Asch thought that if people could judge unambiguous stimuli under optimal conditions, the sort of convergence that Sherif had found would not appear. But when Asch (1951) tested his idea with fifty male college students, the results surprised him.

Each student was told that he was participating in an experiment on visual judgment in which he would compare the length of two lines. He was shown two white cards: one card with a single vertical line (the standard) and another with three vertical lines of different lengths (see Figure 22.1). The subject's task was to determine which of the three lines on the second card was the same length as the standard.

The student sat in a room with six other apparent subjects, who were actually Asch's confederates. After unanimous judgments on two sets of cards, a third set was shown. This time, although the correct response was obviously line 2, each confederate in turn declared with great certainty that line 1 matched the standard. Now the true subject was faced with a dilemma. His eyes told him that line 2 was the correct choice, but six other people had unanimously and confidently selected line 1. Thirty-two percent of the time, subjects bowed to social influence and conformed with the obviously incorrect choice; about 74 percent of the subjects conformed on at least one trial.

Factors Influencing Conformity

What could make a subject go against the evidence of his senses to agree with others?

SITUATIONAL VARIABLES For one thing, the judgments of the confederates were unanimous; not one of them hinted that another answer might be possible. By varying the basic experiment, Asch found that the extent of agreement was an important influence. When just one confederate gave the correct answer, thus confirming the test subject's "unpopular" view, the proportion of subjects who conformed dropped dramatically—from 32 percent to 5 percent. It appears that a single voice raised in opposition to an otherwise unanimous judgment can have a remarkable effect on other people who have been hesitating to express their own dissenting view (see Figure 22.2).

Another situational factor that influenced conformity in Asch's experiments was the requirement that his subjects interact face to face with the confederates. Later research showed that when people can respond anonymously, they conform less often (Deutsch and Gerard, 1965).

However, the Asch experiments included some situational factors that might have actually lowered the pressure to conform. The confederates were complete strangers to the subjects, with no special claim on their loyalty or affection. Consequently, subjects had little reason to fear that nonconformity would have social repercussions. The existence of this situational factor, which would logically reduce the pressure to conform, has led some psychologists to conclude that Asch's work revealed only the tip of the iceberg—that if the pressure to conform among strangers is so strong, it seems likely that the pressure to conform among friends may be far stronger.

Other situational variables have also been shown to affect the extent of conformity. Our degree of self-doubt is important. People who are not certain of their ability to make the judgment conform more than others (e.g., Campbell, Tesser, and Fairy, 1986). Group pressure is important. The larger the number of people who express an incorrect opinion, the more likely we are to conform. The extremity of the norm is equally important. The more extreme the group norm, the larger the proportion who depart from the correct answer. Finally, differences in conformity between men and women are discussed in the accompanying box.

NORMATIVE INFLUENCE AND INFORMATIONAL INFLUENCE

People are pushed to conform to the unanimous opinion of others by two forces: normative influence and informational influence (Deutsch and Gerard, 1955; Jones and Gerard, 1967; Ross, Bierbrauer and Hoffman, 1976). When **normative influence** prevails, we agree with the expressed judgments of others even though we know they are wrong. We go along either to reap the rewards of conformity or to avoid any punishment associated with bucking the crowd. The subjects in Asch's experiments may have accepted clearly erroneous judgments because they feared that failing to do so would lead to their ridicule or rejection.

At times, however, conformity is the result of **informational influence**, in which we rely on the responses of others as a source of information about reality. In such cases, we conform because we believe the others may be correct. Informational influence may be especially powerful in ambiguous situations, such as Sherif's study involving the autokinetic effect, but it may also play a role in seem-

NORMATIVE INFLUENCE
yielding to group pressure as a result of a desire to comply even when one disagrees with the others

INFORMATIONAL INFLUENCE
yielding to group pressure as a result of the knowledge gained from the others' behavior

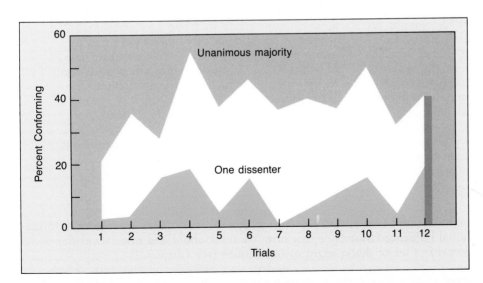

Figure 22.2 Solomon Asch found that when just one confederate refused to conform to the erroneous majority view, the proportion of subjects who conformed fell from an average of 32 percent to an average of 5 percent over twelve trials. (Asch, 1955.)

PSYCHOLOGY TODAY AND TOMORROW

Do Women Conform More Than Men?

Popular stereotypes suggest that women conform more readily to group opinion than men do and that women are more easily influenced by others (e.g., Broverman et al., 1972). Social psychologist Alice Eagly noticed that although many textbooks presented the sex difference in conformity and persuasibility as fact—even calling it "large, strong and clear," "well-established," and "consistent"—the books cited only a few studies in support of the claim. She decided to take a fresh look at the issue.

Eagly (1978) examined all published studies on persuasion and conformity that included both men and women as subjects. Her work revealed that some researchers draw the wrong conclusions on the basis of inadequate evidence. In addition, when researchers are predominantly male, subtle factors may influence their findings, such as the topic they choose for their persuasion or conformity study. Indeed, it may be that male-oriented topics have traditionally been used in persuasion studies simply because before 1970, most researchers were males. Few studies conducted after 1970 have found that women are more persuadable than men.

Eagly found that of sixty-two studies that measured sex differences in persuasibility, fifty-one—more than 80 percent—found no difference. Men and women were equally likely to accept or reject arguments meant to change their views on specific issues. Ten of the studies found that women were more persuasible than men, and one study found that men were more persuasible than women. In the eleven studies that did show a sex difference, the topic used may have played an important role. Eagly found that studies in which women were more persuasible generally centered on stereotypical male concerns, such as power tools, while the study in which men were more easily persuaded used nutrition as the topic. These findings suggest that all of us—whether male or female—are more easily persuaded when we have less interest or expertise in the topic.

Sex differences also narrowed when Eagly

reviewed studies of conformity. Of sixty-one conformity studies that involved group pressure, thirty-eight reported no difference between the sexes, twenty-one found females to be more conforming, and two found males to be more conforming. Of twenty-two studies that did not involve group pressure, nineteen reported no sex difference, one reported more conformity among males, and two reported more conformity among females.

The fact that twenty-one group-pressure studies showed women conforming more than men raises an important question: Under group pressure, do women express public agreement with others even though they privately disagree? To find out, Eagly and her students (Eagly, Wood, and Fishbaugh, 1981) conducted an experiment in which subjects first privately expressed their opinion on a topic, then learned that others in the group disagreed with them, and then were asked to state their position publicly. A sex difference appeared, but it was not what most social psychologists would have expected. In general, women reported the same opinion in public and in private—they did not change their opinion to conform to the group's consensus. Men who had privately agreed with the group changed their opinion in public *away from* the opinion expressed by the group. Thus, when there was no social pressure, both sexes responded similarly; but when group pressure existed, men changed their opinion so as to disagree with the group.

Eagly's experiment shows that the greater apparent conformity to group pressure among women is not a result of women's caving in to group pressure; they stoutly maintain their own opinions. Instead, the difference arises when men express a public opinion that is at variance with their private view—perhaps to show the group that they are not easily influenced. Clearly, in interpreting observed sex differences, we must be careful not to draw premature conclusions about their source.

ingly unambiguous situations, such as Asch's study. Our reliance on informational influence reminds us that how we think about and understand our social world is a major determinant of our actions (see Chapter 21).

THE INFLUENCE OF THE MINORITY　The results of conformity research bring to mind the words of John Stuart Mill, who spoke of the "tyranny of the majority," which necessarily imposes its will on the dissenting minority. Yet history provides plentiful evidence that over time minorities can change majority views. If this were not so, environmental issues—to cite just one example—would not be the subjects of publicity and concern that they have become.

Majority and minority influences show themselves in different ways. French social psychologist Serge Moscovici (1980) noted that when individuals find themselves in situations that demand conformity, their private reactions are often changed more by minority influence than by the influence of the majority. The majority is powerful in producing public compliance, in which the individual's *behavior*—whether word or deed—changes to meet pressures to conform. But, at the same time, the minority often induces the individual to accept its views privately, so that people's *attitudes* shift away from the majority opinion.

In a study of opinion concerning gay rights (Maas and Clark, 1983), researchers found that people's private attitudes moved toward the minority position at the same time that their public expression of attitudes followed the usual pattern of conformity to the majority view. In another study (Nemeth and Wachtler, 1983), the presence of a dissenting minority in a group problem-solving situation had a delayed effect on an individual's private efforts to solve the problem. Individuals who had been exposed to a minority opinion were more likely to find new solutions on a subsequent occasion and to look at the problem differently than were those who had worked on their own throughout the experiment or were aware only of the majority view.

The moderating influence of the minority on later behavior has been demonstrated in a study of jury decisions (Nemeth and Wachtler, 1983). People who served on a mock jury, charged with deciding personal injury cases, seemed unmoved by a confederate who consistently advocated lower compensation for the victim than the majority believed was warranted. But on later personal injury cases, the influence of the minority confederate became clear. Subjects who had been exposed to the minority opinion in the first case—even though they had conformed to the majority judgment—tended to award significantly lower compensation on later cases than did subjects who had not been exposed to a minority confederate.

Presumably, the influence of the minority is effective because the minority's dissenting position makes them stand out from the crowd, attracting attention, and because the minority's willingness to go against the majority testifies to their conviction and consistency. Faced with the minority position, observers may experience cognitive dissonance (see Chapter 21) and rethink their beliefs.

Bibb Latané and Sharon Wolf (1981) proposed that what seems to give minorities their strength is their conviction and consistency, which make them appear stronger and more immediate in the eyes of others. In this view, all social influ-

People demonstrating against a majority position gain influence when members of the majority begin to question their own beliefs. These women were part of an ongoing demonstration at a Cruise missile site in Greenham, England.

ence operates through the same factors: the strength, immediacy, and size of the group (see Tanford and Penrod, 1984).

As we saw in the discussion of attribution theory (Chapter 21), when someone behaves in a manner that is inconsistent with our expectation of that person's role or personality, we may assume that the "deviant" behavior reflects strong conviction. The action emphasizes the strength of the person's belief, and we infer that the grounds for the unexpected behavior are valid. When this happens, we may take the minority view more seriously. It may appear to us as a carefully considered opinion that deserves further analysis—and even adoption.

Conformity to Social Roles: Zimbardo's Experiment

Social conformity of a more ominous sort was studied when Philip Zimbardo and his colleagues (Aimbardo, Haney, and Banks, 1973) advertised in newspapers for volunteers to take part in a mock prison experiment. The volunteers were randomly assigned roles as prisoners and guards. Both groups were placed in the basement of the Stanford University psychology building and given minimal instructions: they were told to assume their assigned roles and that the guards' job was to "maintain law and order."

In only a few hours the behavior of the two groups had become sharply differentiated, as each group conformed to what was considered the "appropriate" social role. The "guards" had adopted behavior patterns and attitudes that are typical of guards in maximum security prisons, with most of them becoming abusive and aggressive. Most of the "prisoners" had become passive, dependent, and depressed, although some became enraged at the guards. The suffering among the "prisoners" was so great that one had to be released in less than 36 hours; several other "prisoners" also had to be released before the experiment, intended to run for two weeks, was ended after six days.

Obedience to Authority

OBEDIENCE behavior that complies with the explicit commands of an authority figure

"When you think of the long and gloomy history of man," wrote C. P. Snow (1961), "you will find more hideous crimes have been committed in the name of obedience than have been committed in the name of rebellion." **Obedience** refers to any behavior that complies with the explicit commands of a person in authority. The Spanish Inquisition, the Nazis' extermination of Jews, and the massacre of Vietnamese civilians by American soldiers at My Lai are historical examples of inhumane behavior resulting from obedience to authority.

Obedience does not always have such destructive results. Compliance with the demands of parents and teachers, for example, is an important part of developing into a mature, responsible adult. And compliance with the law is essential if any society is to function successfully, although most of the research on obedience has focused on the negative consequences of unquestioning compliance.

Milgram's Experiments

The most dramatic and extensive investigation of obedience was conducted by Stanley Milgram (1963), who studied men of all ages and from a wide range of occupations. Each subject was paid to take part in what he was told was a study of the effects of punishment on learning. The experimenter, dressed in a white laboratory coat, instructed each subject to read a list of word pairs to a "learner" (really a confederate of the experimenter) whose task it was to memorize them. The learner was taken into an adjacent room, out of the subject's sight, for the duration of the experiment. Every time the learner made a mistake, the subject was told to punish him by administering a shock from an impressive-looking shock generator (which was not connected to any source of electricity). The generator had thirty clearly marked voltage levels, with switches ranging from 15 to

Blind obedience to authority reached the level of fanaticism in Hitler's Germany, with devastating results.

450 volts and labels ranging from "Slight Shock" to "Danger: Severe Shock." Whenever the learner made a mistake, the subject was to increase the voltage by one level and administer the shock.

Acting under instructions, the learners made many errors, necessitating increasingly severe shocks. When the shock level reached 300 volts, the learner pounded on the wall in protest and then fell silent. At this point, the experimenter instructed the subject to treat the silence as a wrong answer and to raise the voltage. If the subject asked to stop the experiment, the researcher sternly told him to go on.

When told about this study, most people underestimate the power of the situation to influence behavior, an outcome that is consistent with the research on causal attribution that we explored in Chapter 21. Psychiatrists, college students, and middle-class adults consulted by Milgram believed that virtually all subjects would break off the experiment before dangerous shock levels were reached. Yet among forty subjects, twenty-six, or 65 percent, continued to obey the experimenter to the very end (see Figure 22.3). These subjects were not sadists. Many of them showed signs of extreme anxiety during the session, and they frequently wanted to stop. But despite their distress, most of them obeyed the experimenter's commands that they continue (Milgram, 1974). (At the time these experiments were conducted, the present strict guidelines for the protection of human subjects, discussed in Chapter 2, did not exist.) Clearly, our willingness to obey authority is greater than most people believe.

Factors Influencing Obedience

Many factors influence the extent to which people will obey authority, especially when obedience means acting against their own moral standards. Of first importance is whether the person giving the instructions is viewed as a legitimate authority. From the time we are children, we are taught that certain people can, by virtue of their social position, legitimately expect compliance with their wishes. When a police officer orders a driver to pull over to the side of the road or a physician requests that a patient undress, people usually do as they are told. Indeed, the sight of a person in uniform is often enough to prompt compliance. In one experiment (Bickman, 1974), researchers approached people on the streets of New York City and ordered them either to pick up a paper bag or to give a dime to a stranger. Half the researchers were dressed in neat street clothes and half were in guard uniforms. Less than 40 percent of the subjects obeyed the "civilian," but

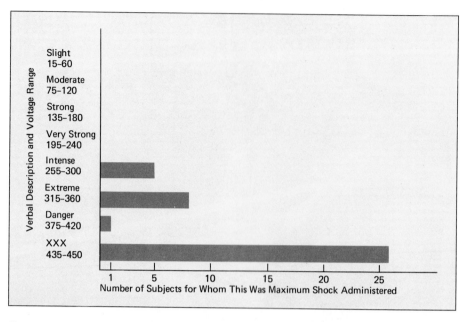

Figure 22.3 Results of Stanley Milgram's classic experiment on obedience. Subjects were told to administer increasing amounts of shock to a "learner" on the pretext that scientists were studying the effects of punishment on learning. Of forty experimental subjects, all administered shocks scaled "intense" or higher, and only fourteen refused to go all the way to the most severe, "XXX" shock level. (After Milgram, 1963.)

more than 80 percent obeyed the "guard," even when he walked away after delivering the order and could not see whether they complied.

Another situational factor that affects obedience is the degree of face-to-face contact. In Milgram's original experiment (1963), the experimenter's presence encouraged compliance. Obedience dropped sharply (from 65 percent to 22 percent) in an experimental variation (1965) in which the experimenter did not remain in the room with the subject, but left the laboratory after issuing instructions and gave subsequent orders by phone. As in the defiance of group norms, disobedience to authority seems easier when people do not have to confront authority directly.

Milgram also found that increasing the proximity of the subject to the victim increased the likelihood that the subject would defy authority. In his original study, Milgram's subjects could not see their victim, and the only audible protest was the pounding on the wall. When subjects were placed closer to the victim, however, compliance dropped. In one condition, although the victim was in another room, the subject could hear the groans escalate to screams as the shocks were increased. In another arrangement, the victim and subject were in the same room—seated only 18 inches apart. In the final condition, the subject was required to force the victim's hand onto a shock plate to administer punishment. The maximum shock that subjects would deliver decreased steadily as contact with the victim increased. When the victim was remote, subjects apparently found it easier to deny the pain they were inflicting. As such denial became less possible, the victim's suffering exerted greater influence in the struggle between individual conscience and authority.

Social support for defiance is another factor that increases people's resistance to authority. In a test of this factor (Milgram, 1965), the subject was teamed with two other "subjects" who were actually the experimenter's confederates. After the shock level had reached 150 volts, one of the confederates announced that he would not continue and took a seat in another part of the room. After 210 volts, the second confederate refused to go any further. Although the experimenter ordered the true subjects to continue, only 10 percent of them did so.

In this last condition, people were forced to choose between obedience and resistance to authority. The fact that 90 percent chose to disobey orders should not lead us to be complacent about resistance to authority. Some one person must always be first to resist, and in real life no confederates will lead the way. In addition, the real world may inflict far more severe penalties for disobedience than the disapproval of an unknown experimenter.

The tendency toward conformity and obedience so dramatically demonstrated in the laboratory and in natural settings may strike some people as alarming. But conformity and obedience are neither good nor bad in and of themselves. They are facts of social behavior and can lead to either desirable or undesirable outcomes. Milgram believed that as we come to understand such submission better, we may learn to avoid it when necessary.

Hidden Influence

Demands for obedience and pressure for conformity to social norms are not the only ways people can be made to comply. People can be influenced to behave in specific ways through a variety of more subtle and insidious means.

One such means is by doing someone a favor. In American society we have an unwritten "rule of reciprocity," which demands that when someone does us a favor we repay it in kind (Cialdini, 1984). This rule was explored in a study at Cornell University (Regan, 1971). Two situations were set up. In one, while a subject waited between two phases of a psychological experiment, another waiting subject (who was a confederate of the researcher) left the room for a couple of minutes and came back with two bottles of Coca-Cola. The confederate said that he had asked the researcher if it was all right to have a cold drink and added, "He said it was okay, so I bought one for you, too." In the other condition, the confederate did not buy Cokes, either for himself or for the other waiting subject. After the experiment was apparently completed, the confederate asked subjects to buy some raffle tickets on a new car. The subjects who had been given a Coca-Cola bought twice as many tickets as subjects who had not been given a Coke.

Another subtle way of securing compliance is the "foot-in-the-door" technique, by which agreement to a trivial request opens the door to agreement to a much larger request. In one study (Freedman and Fraser, 1966), people agreed to display on their houses a 3-inch sign reading "Be a Safe Driver." A few weeks later, researchers asked these people to display a large, ugly sign saying "Drive Carefully" on their front lawns. Only 24 percent refused; yet among people who had never been approached to display the small sign (and so had not allowed the researchers to "get a foot in the door"), 83 percent refused to comply.

HELPING AND HURTING: PROSOCIAL AND ANTISOCIAL BEHAVIOR

An individual's actions can help or harm others. When we promote the benefit of another person or group, psychologists describe our actions as *prosocial behavior*. When we act in ways that are harmful to another person or group, we have shown *antisocial behavior*.

Helping

Imagine that you are driving along a deserted lane in the country. As you round a bend in the road, you see that a car has gone off the road and smashed into a tree. As you get closer, you see that the driver, who is alone, is slumped over the steering wheel. Would you stop to help? Why or why not?

Now imagine that you are on a weekend excursion in a big city. The sidewalks are crowded with pedestrians, and the streets are jammed with cars creeping along in the rush-hour traffic. You notice that the crowd parts at one spot on the sidewalk. As you approach, you see a poorly dressed middle-aged man slumped on the sidewalk. He seems to be unconscious. The passing crowd ignores him, stepping around or even over his body. Would you stop to help? Why or why not?

If you are like most people, these two situations strike you as quite different, and your impulse to help is not the same. Yet in both cases a human being is apparently in trouble. The question of when and why people help others has been a major topic in research by social psychologists.

Is Helping Ever Truly Altruistic?

Altruistic acts are helping acts that offer no obvious rewards: making an anonymous donation to charity may be altruistic, but making the same donation to secure a tax deduction is not. Risking one's life to rescue a child from a burning building may be altruistic, but risking one's life to earn applause from the crowd on the street is not. Acting to relieve one's own distress at the sight of another's pain is also not considered altruism (Batson, 1987). Although the altruistic person may experience internal satisfaction, the motive is to help someone else in need. In addition, to be considered altruistic, an act must be intentional: accidentally frightening a mugger away from a victim is not altruistic behavior.

Robert Trivers (1971) introduced the notion of another kind of false altruism, which he called **reciprocal altruism**. He suggested that when a person helps another, he or she increases the chances that the person who is helped will reciprocate and may one day help either the helper or the helper's kin. Thus, reciprocal altruism is not truly altruistic, because the person may expect the good deed to be returned at some later date.

These restrictions on the definition of altruism lead us to ask whether helping another person is ever truly altruistic. If you stop to help the woman whose car has crashed, is your primary motivation to relieve that suffering or to ease your own distress and anxiety at the sight of someone who has been hurt? This question has been difficult to answer, in part because our feelings of sympathy and concern for another are often accompanied by feelings of personal distress. However,

RECIPROCAL ALTRUISM the performance of an altruistic act on the chance that it may be reciprocated at a later date

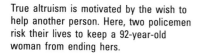

True altruism is motivated by the wish to help another person. Here, two policemen risk their lives to keep a 92-year-old woman from ending hers.

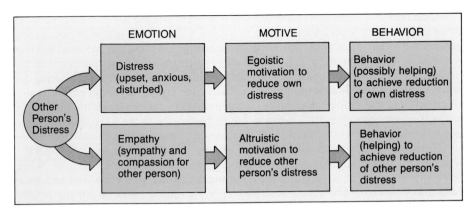

Figure 22.4   Helping behavior may be motivated by altruism (a desire to reduce another person's distress) as well as by egoistic concerns (a desire to reduce our own distress at seeing another person in need). (Adapted from Batson, Fultz, and Schoenrade, 1987.)

social psychologist Daniel Batson (1987) has concluded that some helping is motivated by altruistic concerns. His research has shown that empathic feelings (sympathy, compassion, tenderness, and warmth) can be separated from the personal distress (feeling disturbed, worried, and upset) that is often associated with the sight of someone in need (see Figure 22.4).

According to Batson, if our motivation for helping is primarily to reduce our own distress, then we will be less likely to help if we can relieve our distress by escaping from the situation. But if the motivation is empathy for another's suffering, then the possibility of an easy escape will not reduce our desire to help. This view has been supported by several studies (Coke, Batson, and McDavis, 1978; Batson et al., 1981; Toi and Batson, 1982). In one study (Coke, Batson, and McDavis, 1978), people heard a radio broadcast describing a graduate student's need for research participants; then they each received a written appeal for help. Escape was easy—all they had to do was toss the request in the nearest wastebasket. The researchers used a questionnaire to measure the subjects' personal distress, as well as their empathy for the graduate student in need. Feelings of personal distress were only modestly related to offers of assistance, but feelings of empathy were highly related: almost every subject who reported feelings of sympathy or compassion for the graduate student offered their aid in her research. Under some circumstances, it appears, helping is truly altruistic.

Bystander Intervention in Emergencies

Whether a rescuer is motivated by personal distress or empathy makes little difference to the person in trouble, of course. If the situation affects behavior as strongly as research seems to indicate, what circumstances make people more likely—or less likely—to help? One notorious example of *failure* to help occurred in New York City twenty-five years ago. A young woman named Kitty Genovese was savagely attacked outside her apartment building in Queens at 3:00 A.M. She screamed for help, and although thirty-eight neighbors came to their windows, not one offered assistance. No one even called the police. The attack lasted more than 30 minutes while Kitty Genovese was sexually assaulted, stabbed, and finally killed. The murder caused a sensation, and press accounts wondered how people could be so indifferent to the fate of another human being. Many saw it as an example of the city dweller's reluctance to "get involved." Yet investigation revealed that the witnesses had been far from indifferent. Genovese's neighbors watched her ordeal transfixed, "unable to act but unwilling to turn away" (Latané and Darley, 1976, pp. 309–310).

After this tragic incident, social psychologists Bibb Latané and John Darley (1976) staged a number of "emergencies" and recorded the responses of bystanders. They concluded that the presence of others inhibits would-be altruistic bystanders from helping. Latané and Darley offer three situational factors that may explain the failure of bystanders to respond.

AUDIENCE INHIBITION
normative influence of bystanders that
inhibits response in an emergency

SOCIAL INFLUENCE the informational influence of bystanders that
inhibits response in an emergency

DIFFUSION OF RESPONSIBILITY
the diminishment of personal responsibility caused by the presence of others,
which inhibits response in an
emergency

One factor is **audience inhibition**. When other people are present, we think twice because we are concerned about how they will evaluate our behavior. Emergencies are often ambiguous. Smoke pouring from a building might signal a fire or it might be normal incinerator fumes; cries of help from the next apartment might be genuine or might be coming from the neighbor's television set. Offering aid when none is wanted or needed places the altruistic bystander in an embarrassing situation, and the embarrassment is compounded by the presence of others who act as if no emergency exists. We may fail to help because we have succumbed to normative influences conveyed by the presence of bystanders.

A second factor is **social influence**. When others are present, each person waits for the others to define the situation as an emergency by their actions. While searching for a clue as to whether the situation is serious, everyone tries to appear calm and collected. The result is that each bystander is taken in by the others' nonchalance and led—or misled—to define the situation as a nonemergency. We may fail to help because of informational influence; the information provided by the actions of others has determined our interpretation of the situation.

A third factor is **diffusion of responsibility**. The presence of other people seems to reduce the need for any one individual to act. An onlooker assumes that someone who is qualified to give aid—a doctor or police officer, or a friend or relative of the victim—may be among the bystanders. This diminishes the sense of personal responsibility and allows the onlooker to leave the scene without feeling guilty.

At the beginning of this section, you were asked to consider how you would respond in two cases of need. If you said you would probably help the accident victim on the deserted lane but not the unconscious man on the city sidewalk, were you influenced by the behavior of other pedestrians in the second instance? Was their influence normative or informational? Darley and Latané's findings suggest that bystanders are least likely to intervene if all three forces—audience inhibition, social influence, and diffusion of responsibility—are operating (see Figure 22.5).

One of their experiments supports this belief. Men who thought they were participating in a study of repression sat in cubicles equipped with television monitors and cameras. While the experimenter ostensibly went to check some equipment, the subjects filled out a questionnaire. As the men worked on their questionnaires, the experimenter staged an elaborate performance. He entered the room with the equipment and innocently picked up two wires. Immediately, he

Before helping a stranger in an emergency, bystanders must overcome audience inhibition, social influence in defining the situation, and diffusion of responsibility.

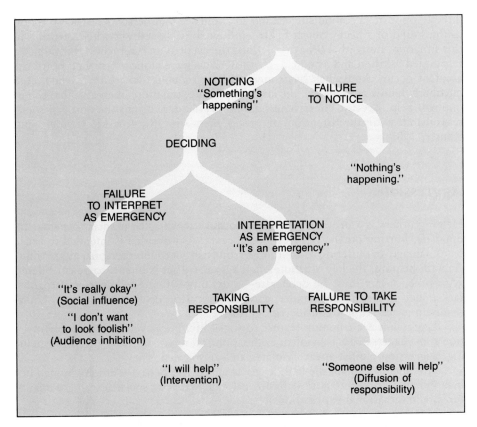

Figure 22.5   As this "decision tree" indicates, in an emergency a bystander must first notice that something is happening, then interpret it as an emergency, and finally decide that he or she has a personal responsibility to intervene. But the presence of others complicates this process: the presence of strangers may prevent us from concluding that the situation is an emergency (social influence); group behavior may lead us to define the situation as one that does not require action (audience inhibition); and when other people are there to share the burden of responsibility, we may not feel obligated to help (diffusion of responsibility). Thus, the more witnesses to an emergency, the less likely the victim is to receive aid. This combination of factors was what inhibited Kitty Genovese's neighbors from helping her. (After Latané and Darley, 1976.)

screamed, threw himself in the air, hit a wall, and crashed to the floor. A few seconds later he began to moan softly. As Latané and Darley predicted, the willingness of the subjects to help the experimenter seemed to depend on the number of social forces at work.

Among subjects who believed they were alone in the situation, 95 percent almost immediately came to his assistance, but among those who thought that an unseen person in another cubicle had also witnessed the accident, altruism dropped to 84 percent. In this case, the difference can be attributed to diffusion of responsibility. When other factors were added to the situation, the rate of intervention decreased further. If subjects could see another person (a confederate of the experimenter) whose lack of response indicated that an emergency might not exist (social influence), or if they thought that someone was watching them (audience inhibition), 73 percent offered to help. When the subject could see the confederate and believed that the confederate could also see the subject, so that all three factors were at work, only 50 percent of the subjects tried to assist the experimenter.

Studies such as this are persuasive, but under certain conditions the presence of others does not prevent bystanders from offering assistance. When bystanders have clear evidence that an emergency exists, the inhibiting effect of others is weakened. For example, if bystanders can gauge one another's reactions through nonverbal cues, they are likely to come to the aid of an apparent accident victim. In one experiment (Darley, Teger, and Lewis, 1973), half the subjects were seated directly opposite a second subject and so could see that person's startled reaction to the sound of a heavy object falling, followed by a nearby worker's groans. In this situation, nonverbal behavior defined the event as an emergency, and subjects responded as often and as quickly as those who were alone when they heard the accident occur. And when bystanders make up a cohesive group (friends, club members, fellow employees), the larger the group, the more likely it is that someone will help, because cohesiveness among bystanders brings the norm of social responsibility to the attention of group members (Rutkowski, Gruder, and Romer, 1983).

Aggression

AGGRESSION any act intended to cause pain, damage, or suffering to another person

Helping others is a prosocial act of conformity that has clear social benefits. Its opposite, hurting others, has clear social costs. Any act that is intended to cause pain, damage, or suffering to another person is an act of interpersonal **aggression**. As with helping, the key attribute of an aggressive act is intent: to be considered aggressive, an act must be deliberate—a definition that encompasses verbal attacks, such as insults and slander, as well as physical or material injuries. Unintended injuries are not considered aggressive.

Aggression is a common feature of social life. News reports invariably mention some aggressive act—violent crime, political terrorism, or war. Unlike helping, aggression almost always violates a clear social norm.

Attempts to explain the high levels of aggressive behavior among human beings fall into three categories: biological explanations, social learning explanations, and situational explanations.

Biological Influences on Aggression

The idea that human aggression has a biological basis has a long history and many champions. One of them, Sigmund Freud, proposed that we are driven to self-destructive and aggressive behavior by a death instinct (*Thanatos*) that is at least as powerful as the life instinct (*Eros*) that impels us toward growth and fulfillment. Today, psychologists generally consider Freud's concept of a death instinct highly speculative. But the underlying idea—that human aggression has a biological basis—lives on. As yet no evidence for a genetic basis of human aggression has been found. However, such evidence does exist for several animal species, including the mouse, on whose chromosomes specific gene locations for aggression have been isolated (Eleftheriou, Bailley, and Denenberg, 1974).

In specific cases, violent behavior in humans has been linked to various types of brain damage, such as strokes, injuries to the frontal or temporal lobes from falls or blows to the head, and brain tumors (Mark and Ervin, 1970). As we saw in Chapter 3, some research has linked certain parts of the brain, shown in Figure 22.6, with human aggression. But brain damage cannot explain the incidence of

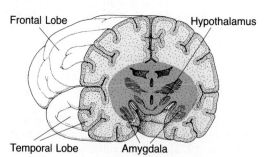

Frontal Lobe

Hypothalamus

Temporal Lobe   Amygdala

Figure 22.6 Some researchers suggest that there is a biological origin of aggression in the oldest and most primitive parts of the human brain. Evidence from animal and human studies suggests that the hypothalamus and other structures in the temporal lobe (shown in blue) play an important role in mediating aggressive behavior. In some cases, surgical removal of the hypothalamus and amygdala has resulted in complete loss of emotional reactivity. (After Scherer, Abeles, and Fischer, 1975.)

human aggression. An estimated 10 to 15 million Americans suffer from some form of brain injury, but the majority of these people are no more aggressive than anyone else. Of greater importance is the fact that the majority of people with a history of violent behavior have no brain injury at all.

Social Learning Mechanisms

Most aggressive behavior requires intricate, learned skills (Bandura, 1976). According to social learning theory (discussed in Chapter 7), exposure to models of violent behavior and reinforcement for aggressive acts explain why people attack one another.

THE IMPORTANCE OF MODELS   By observing others, we learn how and when to perform specific aggressive acts (such as how to fire a gun) as well as general strategies of aggression ("Get them before they get you"). In American culture, two of the most influential models are family members and the characters portrayed on television and in films.

Parents frequently provide powerful models of aggression for their children. Every year several hundred thousand American children are abused by adults, and a significant proportion of them later commit violent acts themselves (Widom, 1989). But such modeling is not necessary for aggression to occur: most aggressive adults did not have criminally violent parents, and most aggressive children have not been abused. In subtle ways, law-abiding parents who resort to "acceptable" forms of aggression to solve problems, favor coercive methods of child-rearing, and are hostile toward the world in general promote aggressive behavior in their children. Such parents serve as models of aggression through their words and attitudes (Bandura, 1976).

The example of parents may be particularly important in fostering aggression, because children see parents in action on a daily basis and their behavior is immediate—not viewed through a distancing medium such as television or film (Bandura, 1973). Studies have shown that children are more likely to imitate the aggressive acts of live models (whether parent or stranger) than of filmed models or cartoon characters (see Figure 22.7).

Although parents may be the most important models for children's aggressive behavior, television also provides a potentially important source of aggressive models. Research indicates that children who watch a great deal of televised violence are more likely to become aggressive adults, but it is not clear whether viewing violence causes aggressive behavior or whether aggressive people are drawn to violent TV programs (Freedman, 1984).

Controlled experiments in the psych lab indicate that filmed violence is often followed by aggressive acts (Freedman, 1984). In typical studies, college students watch clips from violent films and then have the opportunity of punishing or harming someone. Sometimes they are allowed to administer electric shocks to a stranger (usually a confederate of the researcher) for making errors in a learning task. The filmed violence clearly increases the frequency and severity of the shocks (which subjects believe are real) (Roberts and Maccoby, 1985). In the laboratory subjects see *only* violent films, whereas in real life a viewer sees a

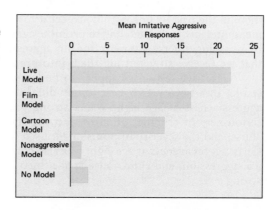

Figure 22.7   Bandura and his colleagues found that live models were more effective than either film models or cartoon characters in eliciting imitative aggressive behavior in children. (After Bandura, 1973.)

There is some evidence that watching televised violence in childhood is associated with aggressive behavior in adulthood.

variety of TV programs, some violent, some not. In addition, aggressive acts committed in the laboratory are sanctioned by the experimenter, which is quite different from punishable violent criminal activity in the real world.

A study that monitored children's natural behavior (Josephson, 1987) indicated that TV violence may have an effect, but its nature depends on the characteristics of the child. In this study, second- and third-grade boys' level of aggressiveness was rated by their teachers. Then the boys watched either a violent or a nonviolent segment of a TV show, after which they played a game of hockey. The boys who had been rated as aggressive and who had seen the violent segment showed increased aggressiveness during the game. The nonaggressive boys who had watched the violent segment were even less aggressive than usual during the hockey game. However, if the boys were later reminded of the segment by being shown objects that had figured prominently in the violence, even the nonaggressive boys became more aggressive. The accompanying box describes other studies of the immediate effects of media violence.

Such studies tell us something about the short-term effect of TV violence, but little about the cumulative effect of years of TV watching. Researchers (Eron et al., 1972; Huesmann, Lagerspetz, and Eron, 1984) have conducted longitudinal field studies of the relationship between TV viewing and aggression, but these studies are correlational in nature, which means that they cannot establish causality (see Chapter 2).

THE IMPORTANCE OF REINFORCEMENT According to social learning theory, people do not behave aggressively unless aggression has "paid off" for them in the past or unless they expect it to pay off in the future. Such reinforcement interacts with modeling to promote aggression. We learn aggressive behavior by watching others, and we refine our aggressive skills through the reinforcements that we receive after putting them into practice (Bandura, 1976).

Aggressive responses appear to be learned early in life and to remain fairly stable. In a twenty-two-year longitudinal study (Heusmann et al., 1984), boys' aggressiveness at age eight was a strong predictor of criminal convictions, the seriousness of criminal offenses, moving traffic violations, drunk driving, wife abuse, and the severity of punishment used with their own children at age thirty. Girls' aggressiveness at age eight was also correlated with criminal behavior, physical aggression, and child abuse at age thirty, although the connection was not as strong.

PSYCHOLOGY TODAY AND TOMORROW

Media Reports of Prize Fights and Executions: The Impact on the Murder Rate

Although laboratory research has clearly demonstrated that viewing violence can cause aggression, researchers disagree sharply about whether these findings can be generalized to daily life. In an attempt to settle the question, sociologist David Phillips (1986) used natural experiments in which he investigated the effects of media reports of sanctioned violence—prize fights and legal executions—on the murder rate.

PRIZE FIGHTS AND MURDER

Prize fights are a form of violence that is rewarded with fame, championship titles, and money—exactly the sort of situation in which publicity might encourage others to engage in some form of violence, including murder (Comstock, 1977). This led Phillips (1983) to investigate the murder rate in the days immediately before and after well-publicized heavyweight championship boxing matches between 1973 and 1978. Phillips found that the nationwide murder rate peaked three days after the fights, with an average of 7.47 more murders than would be expected on the third day following the fight and 4.15 more than expected on the fourth day. The fights did not merely hasten murders that would have occurred anyway, because the murder rate did not drop *below* normal in the days after these "extra" murders were committed.

The type of person killed just after a prize fight was significantly similar to the type of person beaten in the ring. After a young white man was defeated, murders of young white men increased; after a young black man was defeated, murders of young black men increased. When a fight was heavily publicized, the subsequent increase in the murder rate was especially pro-

nounced. Although researchers are still debating the meaning of these findings (Freedman, 1984; Baron and Reiss, 1985; Phillips, 1986), it is difficult to find any explanation other than the publicity conferred by the media on the organized violence of prize fighting.

CAPITAL PUNISHMENT AND MURDER

If rewarded violence increases aggression, then it seems that media portrayals of punished violence should lead to a decrease in aggression. Yet most studies of capital punishment find that it has no deterrent effect; laws that permit or require capital punishment do not seem to lower the murder rate (Blumstein, Cohen, and Nagin, 1978). However, studies that examine the long-term effect of the death penalty on murder rates may miss the temporary effects of media reports of actual executions.

Between the years 1858 and 1921, capital punishment was in effect in England, and weekly homicide statistics were available for the city of London. When Phillips examined the murder rate in London during this period, he found that the number of homicides dropped below the expected rate during the week of a well-publicized execution. However, homicides rose by almost the same number two weeks later, canceling the deterrent effect. The executions seemed merely to have postponed the murders.

Although they rely on a correlational method, Phillips' findings are interesting because they point to a connection between media coverage of violence and the incidence of actual violence. Further research is needed on the causality involved in this connection.

Situational Factors

The social learning explanation of aggression makes good sense. But certain situations seem so unbearable, so frustrating, that we would expect anyone to explode in anger, regardless of the consequences.

According to the **frustration-aggression hypothesis** put forward by John Dollard and his colleagues, "aggression is always a consequence of frustration," and, conversely, "frustration always leads to some form of aggression" (1939, p. 1). Dollard defined **frustration** as interference with any form of goal-directed

FRUSTRATION-AGGRESSION HYPOTHESIS the proposal that aggression is always a consequence of frustration and that frustration always leads to aggression

FRUSTRATION interference with any goal-directed activity

behavior. When people are thwarted in their attempts to obtain food or water, sex or sleep, love or recognition, he and his colleagues argued, they are likely to become aggressive.

To test this hypothesis, a team of researchers (Barker, Dembo, and Lewin, 1941) created a frustrating situation for a group of children. The children were taken to a room, shown a collection of attractive toys, and told that they could look but not touch. Later, when the children were allowed to play with the toys, they were extremely hostile—smashing the toys against the walls and floor. Another group of children who had not been frustrated in advance played happily and peacefully with identical toys.

One possible consequence of frustration is displaced aggression, which can take many forms. Since aggressive responses often bring punishment to the aggressor, a frustrated person can express aggression safely by displacing it. Thus, the angry employee who has been reprimanded by his boss might kick his dog when he returns home or insult his golf partner.

Aggression is only one of many possible responses to frustration, however. Some people withdraw when frustrated, and others intensify their nonaggressive efforts to reach a goal. According to some psychologists (e.g., Berkowitz, 1962), the key to predicting aggression is not the frustration but the level of anger it arouses. In this view, frustration is neither necessary nor sufficient to provoke aggression. Anger, which may be sparked by such experiences as verbal attacks as well as by frustration, is the crucial factor (Rule and Nesdale, 1976). As we saw in Chapter 12, anger is an emotion that results from specific appraisals of events and the way they relate to our concerns. Anger is likely to follow the appraisal that a goal has been unjustifiably or deliberately blocked by another person. If anger is one cause of aggression, then such appraisals should contribute to aggression. Indeed, studies have shown that people's tendency to respond to frustration with anger and aggression increases if they perceive that the other person frustrated them intentionally and without justification (Zillman and Cantor, 1976; Kulik and Brown, 1979).

GROUP PROCESSES: COOPERATION AND PERFORMANCE

Each day brings choices between fulfilling only our own needs and considering the needs of others. Such choices range from the trivial (whether to grab a seat on a crowded bus) to the vital (deciding how the earth's limited resources will be distributed). Because so many of life's prizes—and even necessities—are scarce, people cannot always act in ways that maximize both their own immediate goals and those of others. As social beings, we must try to strike a balance between self-interest and cooperation.

Cooperation versus Competition

Suppose that you and a friend are arrested for a petty theft. The district attorney believes that the two of you have also committed an armed robbery, but does not have enough evidence to take you to court. In an attempt to get a confession for armed robbery, she has you and your friend questioned in separate rooms. If neither you nor your friend confesses, the court will send both of you to prison for one year on the petty theft charge. If both of you confess to armed robbery, the DA will recommend leniency—eight years instead of ten. If only one of you confesses, that person will be sentenced to only three months for turning state's evidence, but the other will go to prison for the full ten years. The dilemma is obvious. The best strategy for both of you is to stick to your alibis and refuse to confess; you will both get one year in prison, but no more. However, if you follow this strategy but your friend does not, you will go to prison for ten years.

The Prisoner's Dilemma Game

		Prisoner II	
		Don't Confess	Confess
Prisoner I			
Don't Confess		Penalty for lesser charge for I—1 year	"Book" thrown at I— 10 years
		Penalty for lesser charge for II—1 year	Leniency for II— 3 months
Confess		Leniency for I— 3 months	Leniency for I— 8 years
		"Book" thrown at II—10 years	Leniency for II— 8 years

Figure 22.8 The prisoner's dilemma can be diagrammed as a 2 × 2 matrix. Each person must choose one of two options, prisoner I controlling the horizontal rows and prisoner II the vertical columns: the outcomes of a joint decision are given by the intersection between the row and column chosen. The best outcome is obtained by both partners cooperating with each other—in this case, by cooperating *not* to confess—but studies show that a selfish strategy is chosen more often than a cooperative one.

And if you confess but your friend does not, you will get off with a three-month sentence.

This situation is called the prisoner's dilemma (see Figure 22.8). It has proved a valuable tool for discovering the conditions under which people are most likely to cooperate with each other. The experimenters explain the rules of the game, or some variation of it, to pairs of subjects. Then the game begins. Typically, the experiment runs fifteen to twenty trials. Cooperation promises the most favorable outcome in every case, yet blind self-interest is the most commonly chosen strategy. In most studies, between 60 and 70 percent of the subjects behave selfishly despite the costs involved in that strategy (Oskamp and Kleinke, 1970).

Among all the possible strategies that can be used in the prisoner's dilemma game, only one will produce long-term stability in a social system. This fact was discovered when researchers asked game theorists in economics, sociology, political science, and mathematics to submit the best strategy for a continuing prisoner's dilemma game—as opposed to the one-shot version in which only a single decision is made and the individuals ostensibly never meet again (Axelrod and Hamilton, 1981). The strategies were then programmed on a computer and played out in a tournament, in which each game required 200 moves. The winning strategy was a tit-for-tat approach in which the person's first move is cooperative but each subsequent move is identical to the other player's last move. Thus, the tit-for-tat strategy begins with cooperation. Whenever the opponent makes a noncooperative move, the tit-for-tat strategy involves retaliation. But the strategy is a forgiving one: cooperation resumes as soon as the other player makes a cooperative move.

Whether these theoretical results can be generalized to life in the real world, where stakes are often high and the consequences serious, is uncertain (Pruitt and Kimmel, 1977). For example, some argue that the fact that the United States and the Soviet Union are capable of destroying each other serves to deter each from the use of force against the other. Because of the consequences, both nations are reluctant to issue a direct threat, much less to launch an attack.

Promoting Social Cooperation

So far we have focused on choices between cooperation and competition faced by two individuals and the personal consequences of those decisions. But many individual choices between cooperation and self-interest have consequences for communities, societies, and ultimately for all humanity.

The Tragedy of the Commons

Consider what Garrett Hardin (1968) called "the tragedy of the commons." A commons is an open pasture where any member of the community can graze cattle. People naturally take advantage of the free grazing by adding more animals to their herds whenever they can. Disease, poaching, and war may keep the animal and human populations low, so that the system works for a time. But eventually the day of reckoning comes: the population grows beyond the capacity of the commons to sustain it, and the overgrazed grass becomes sparse. It is only a matter of time before the once-lush pasture is barren.

Each individual herder may have some sense of this outcome. But when she or he weighs the personal benefits of acquiring another animal against the cost of damage to the common pasture, the answer is clear. When the extra animal is sold, the herder gets all the money, but the cost of overgrazing is shared by all herders, in the form of a slight decrease in the weight (and thus the value) of each animal. The logical course for the herder to pursue in order to maximize personal gain is to add another animal—and another, and another. This is the "tragedy of the commons": in persuing individual interest, people move steadily toward eventual ruin for all.

The tragedy of the commons is an example of a **social trap**: personal decisions start people, organizations, or societies moving in some direction or cause relationships to form that later prove to be unpleasant or lethal, yet seem virtually impossible to stop (Platt, 1970). Today the world sees the jaws of another social trap closing upon it: the earth's ozone layer, the natural shield that protects plant and animal life from the sun's intense ultraviolet radiation, is being depleted by emissions of chlorofluorocarbons into the atmosphere. It is in the best interest of individuals to continue using spray cans, air conditioners, and refrigerators, and the industrialization of developing nations probably requires the processes that release chlorofluorocarbons, but the cumulative, long-term effect may be disastrous (Dickson and Marshall, 1989).

It is easy to see how social traps develop. Behaviorists have demonstrated over and over that the immediate consequences of an action have more impact on behavior than do long-term outcomes. Short-term rewards are seductive. The herder is quickly rewarded for buying and selling another animal. And because punishment for overgrazing lies years in the future, it has little effect on the herder's daily behavior. Thus, in the commons and in a world full of similarly structured situations, powerful psychological and social forces steadily work against cooperation.

Breaking out of Social Traps

According to Hardin (1968), the tragedy of the commons cannot usually be avoided by appeals to conscience, because such appeals leave participants free to choose between behaving as responsible citizens or nations and behaving according to immediate self-interest. Mutually agreed-upon coercion is the surest way to

SOCIAL TRAP an unpleasant or lethal situation for a group caused by consistent choice of self-interest over cooperation by its members

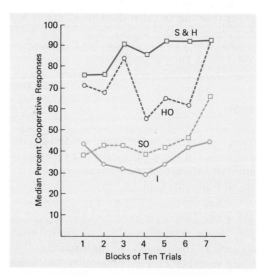

Figure 22.9 The standard prisoner's dilemma game does not permit communication between partners, but when the game is altered so that communication is allowed, strategies change. For example, Wichman varied the amount of communication possible in four ways: in one condition (I), isolated subjects could neither see nor hear each other; in a second condition they could hear each other (HO); in a third they could see each other (SO); and in a fourth they could both see and hear each other (S&H). As this graph shows, the more extensive the communication, the higher the rate of cooperation. (After Wichman, 1970.)

Individual effort tends to decline as the size of the work group increases.

get people out of social traps. By coercion, Hardin does not mean depriving people of all freedom, but simply making it so difficult or expensive to exploit the commons that few will choose to do so.

Research suggests that there may be other ways to break out of social traps. Improving communication seems to be a promising approach. It has been shown to be effective in the prisoner's dilemma game (see Figure 22.9). Communication may increase cooperation for three reasons. First, communication allows individuals to become acquainted, thus increasing their concern for one another. Second, communication permits people to exchange information relevant to a cooperative decision. And third, communication allows people to state their intentions and to assure others that those intentions are honest (Dawes, McTarish, and Shaklee, 1977). In fact, communication at a meeting of the European Community led member nations, which had planned to support a goal of 85 percent reduction in chlorofluorocarbon use by the end of the century, to agree on a complete ban by that date (Dickson and Marshall, 1989).

Group Performance

When members of a group are working cooperatively, they can clearly accomplish more than a single individual can. Indeed, some human achievements are possible only when several people participate through a group process that integrates their contributions. The economic, technological, and political complexity of contemporary society demands such diverse skills that no one can ever hope to master them all. Most industrial, scientific, and governmental enterprises now require many specialists, each contributing expertise in a different field.

However, researchers studying group processes have discovered that as groups increase in size, each group member's contribution tends to decline. In an early study (Moede, 1927), researchers found that when people pull together on a rope, each exerts less force than if he or she were pulling on the rope alone. Working alone, one person pulled nearly 63 kg, but two people working together pulled, not 126 kg (2 × 63), but 118 kg. And three people pulled 160 kg, which is only about two and one half times what a single individual pulls. This and other studies led to the conclusion that people work less hard when they are part of a group than when they work alone. Apparently, individuals slacken their efforts when there are many contributors to a common task. In short, they loaf.

The **social impact theory** holds that the larger the group, the less pressure there is on any one member to produce (Latané, 1973). The theory suggests that it is diffusion of responsibility for the group's work that leads each individual to reduce his or her effort. Social psychologist Stephen Harkins (1987) suggests that

SOCIAL IMPACT THEORY the hypothesis that the larger the group, the less pressure there is on any one member to produce; that diffusion of responsibility leads to diminished individual effort

Environmental psychologists have found that the distress of crowding results from increased physiological arousal and lack of perceived control in a situation of high density.

it is specifically the anonymity of performance that encourages loafing. When each individual believes that no one can detect how much he or she is contributing, all tend to produce less. When individual contributions can be identified, as when the experimenter measures how much each has contributed, loafing is reduced (Williams, Harkins, and Latané, 1981).

Researchers have discovered that being evaluated by others is not the only thing that keeps people working. When people can evaluate their own performance by comparing it to the previous performance of others on the same task, they work hard—even though the experimenter cannot calculate how much they have contributed (Szymanski and Harkins, 1987). Self-evaluation apparently produces an incentive: it gives people information about their own abilities and provides them with the satisfaction of matching or surpassing the "standard" performance on the task. It seems that social loafing develops when there is no way for people to tell how well they are doing.

ENVIRONMENTAL PSYCHOLOGY

The focus of this chapter has been on the effects of social situations, including the effects of other people, on social behavior. However, it is important to note that the physical environment can also have a powerful influence on the way people interact. As we saw in Chapter 1, psychologists who study the relationship between people and their physical settings practice *environmental psychology*.

Environmental psychology developed during the 1970s, inspired, in part, by increasing concern about the environment and its effect on people (Stokols, 1972). Among the topics studied by environmental psychologists are cognitive mapping, which we investigated in Chapter 7, the effects of crowding and noise on physical and mental health, and personal space—the area surrounding each of us into which other people may not enter uninvited (Holohan, 1986). We can get an idea of the methods and scope of environmental psychology by exploring a single area: the important topic of density and crowding.

Have you ever gone to the supermarket on a Saturday and felt so overwhelmed by the crowded aisles that you couldn't remember what you were there to buy? Have you ever felt that life in a big city is impersonal and unfriendly? or felt anxious when trying to negotiate the crowded sidewalks on a busy shopping day? Many people find that being in crowds or living in crowded environments is unpleasant—even stressful.

Research on crowding among animals has demonstrated that packing organisms too closely together has a number of negative effects. For example, rats raised in overpopulated colonies behave abnormally (Calhoun, 1962). They tend to neglect their young and to fight among themselves; they may even become cannibals. Yet crowding among humans is not always negative. At times, crowds are stimulating and enjoyable. Sitting among 80,000 people in a crowded football stadium may be an exciting, even exhilarating, experience.

When studying the effect of crowds, researchers distinguish between **physical density**, which refers to the number of people in a given amount of space, and **crowding**, which is the psychological experience of distress that arises from the perception of restricted space. Density and crowding often go together, but not always. At the football stadium you may be in a situation of high density without feeling crowded, while on a romantic picnic you may feel crowded in a situation of low density, with only a few other people nearby.

Psychologists have tried to explain why high density sometimes, but not always, leads to the unpleasant feeling of crowding. They have come up with two explanations: increased arousal and lack of perceived control. Social psychologist Jonathan Freedman (1975) proposed that physical density increases a person's level of physiological arousal, and further research supported his proposal (Epstein et al., 1981). As we saw in Chapter 12, increased arousal intensifies emotional reactions to events and situations. Heightened arousal explains why increased density in an unpleasant situation (as many people find supermarkets to be) amplifies our negative reaction to the packed store. It also explains why increased density in a pleasant situation (such as football games or rock concerts) intensifies the positive aspects of the experience.

If the distress of crowding develops when the arousal associated with high density exaggerates our negative emotional reactions, then perhaps people who know *why* they are reacting so strongly are better equipped to handle their negative reactions. A study conducted in a Manhattan supermarket supports this prediction. Researchers (Langer and Saegert, 1977) sent eighty women with identical shopping lists into a crowded supermarket. The task was to find the most economical brand and size of each item on the list. Half the women were told beforehand about the physiological and psychological consequences of crowding; the others were not. The women who had been warned that crowding might cause increased arousal and stress found items on their grocery list more readily, felt more comfortable, and even perceived the market as less crowded than did the women who had not been forewarned.

Although Freedman's analysis of crowding may explain situations in which high density is experienced as pleasant, it does not explain why low density is sometimes perceived as crowded. According to the second explanation of density's effects, our feeling of control—or lack of it—determines the level of density that leads to the distress of crowding. As we saw in Chapter 20, stress is reduced when people feel in control of a situation, while the loss of perceived control often creates stress (Glass and Singer, 1972; Cohen, 1981). Being in a crowded environment can reduce the control we have over social contact—whom we see, when we see them, and for how long. In a small town, contact with other people is likely to be by choice, while in a large city we may see hundreds of people in less than a block, whether we want to or not.

The importance of control has been supported by studies of life in college dormitories. Students who lived in dormitories with rooms opening off long corridors, in which many people shared the bathrooms and lounges, tended to complain of crowding and had low expectations of being able to control their social interactions. But students who lived in dormitories designed as suites, with short corridors and fewer people sharing the bathrooms and lounges, were less likely to complain of crowding, even though the number of residents in each dormitory was identical. Students in suites also felt more in control of their social interactions. When given mental tasks, students in the long-corridor dormitory performed more poorly than did students in the short-corridor dormitory (Baum and Valins, 1977; Baum and Gatchel, 1981).

Characteristics of streets and neighborhoods can affect the degree of control we feel over our contacts with other people. In a recent study (Fleming, Baum,

PHYSICAL DENSITY   the number of people in a given amount of space

CROWDING   the psychological experience of distress that arises from the perception of restricted space

and Weiss, 1987), researchers compared residents of an urban neighborhood who lived on streets lined with stores (which increased foot traffic and brought strangers onto the street) with residents of the same neighborhood who lived on purely residential streets. People who lived on streets with stores felt their neighborhood was more crowded and persisted less on a task than did people who lived on streets without stores. People on the store-lined streets also showed elevated levels of the hormones epinephrine and norepinephrine, suggesting stress-related physiological arousal, and they had higher levels of stress, including depression, anxiety, and general distress. These negative effects were related to feelings of helplessness and of an inability to control their social contacts or their lives in general.

In the preceding chapter we described the fundamental attribution error, in which we tend to see other people's behavior as caused by personal factors and to underestimate the impact of situations. The research we have discussed in this chapter shows that our social and physical environment has powerful effects—which are often very different from what our common sense would have led us to expect. In the next chapter we turn to behavior in wider social environments—the domain of industrial and organizational psychology.

SUMMARY

Social Influence

- Social facilitation, the simplest form of social influence, improves performance, but only when people are working on simple tasks or on tasks they already have mastered.
- Social influence improves performance on these tasks because arousal evokes dominant responses and leads to increased motivation.
- Conformity is the result of social pressure in the form of normative or informational influence; it is easiest to resist when people can remain anonymous or when someone else already has objected to the majority view.
- Obedience to authority can lead to destructive behavior, but such obedience can be overridden by absence of the authority figure, proximity to the victim, or conformity to peers.
- Subtle form of hidden influence include the rule of reciprocity and the foot-in-the-door technique.

Helping and Hurting: Prosocial and Antisocial Behavior

- To be altruistic, an act must be intentional and the dominant motive must be empathic: the relief of another's distress or suffering.
- Reciprocal altruism is not truly altruistic, because the person may expect a later return of the good deed.
- In emergencies, the presence of bystanders seems to inhibit the giving of aid because of audience inhibition, social influence, and the diffusion of responsibility.
- Biological explanations of aggression, whether they invoke genetic abnormalities or brain damage, fall short of explaining its wide occurrence.

- Social learning explanations of aggression point to exposure to violent models and reinforcement for aggression.
- Situational explanations of aggression draw on the frustration-aggression hypothesis and on the level of anger provoked.

Group Processes: Cooperation and Performance

- Although a strategy of cooperation helps both players in the Prisoner's Dilemma game, most people choose self-interest.
- The only strategy that leads to long-term stability is the tit-for-tat strategy, in which the player begins with a cooperative move, then echoes the other player's subsequent moves.
- The individual choice of self-interest over cooperation can lead to such social traps as the tragedy of the commons.
- Societies can break out of social traps through mutually agreed-upon coercion or enhanced communication.
- Although social impact theory assumes that social loafing is the result of the diffusion of responsibility for the group's work, the opportunity for self-evaluation can reduce social loafing as effectively as evaluation by others.

Environmental Psychology

- The physical environment has a powerful influence on social behavior.
- The distress that is associated with crowds depends not on physical density, but on the psychological experience of crowding.
- The distress of crowding depends on increased arousal, combined with the lack of perceived control.

KEY TERMS

aggression	frustration	reciprocal altruism
audience inhibition	frustration-aggression hypothesis	social facilitation
conformity	informational influence	social impact theory
crowding	normative influence	social influence
diffusion of responsibility	obedience	social norm
dominant response	physical density	social trap

CONCEPT REVIEW

1. How does social facilitation account for improved performance by groups? Are there physiological aspects to social facilitation? Is their effect always positive?

2. Describe Muzafer Sherif's experiment and give an account of how it explains conformity.

3. What was Solomon Asch actually attempting to prove with his classic experiment? What was so surprising about his results? As a consequence of this research, what factors can be identified in conformity?

4. Distinguish between normative and informational influences on conformity. How is minority influence a kind of informational influence?

5. Identify the factors that contribute to obedience. Which of these factors were present in Milgram's experiment involving the administration of "shocks"? Which were evident in Zimbardo's experiment with "prisoners" and "guards"?

6. Define *altruistic behavior*. Present the evidence for its existence in humans. If altruistic behavior exists, how does one explain situations in which people fail to offer aid?

7. Distinguish between the biological and the social learning explanations of aggression. In which category of explanation does the frustration-aggression hypothesis belong?

8. Explain how the tragedy of the commons develops. What solution appears to be the most effective in preventing the tragedy or reversing its effects? How is the prisoner's dilemma game related to the tragedy of the commons?

9. Describe the mechanisms that can be used to enhance group performance. How does participation in a group weaken individual performance?

10. What is the difference between crowding and physical density? How does physiological arousal affect the individual's perception of crowding?

CRITICAL THINKING

1. Develop a critique of the ethical aspects of the experiments conducted by Asch, Zimbardo, and Milgram. What kinds of harm can come to the subjects in these experiments? Discuss other ways in which experiments could have been conducted.

2. Social psychology (discussed in Chapters 21 and 22) and personality (discussed in Chapter 17) are often treated as combined fields. What common ground or special focus is shared by these two areas? Do both areas attempt to answer the same questions or solve the same problems?

... *Industrial/ Organizational Psychology*

Pick up any issue of *The Wall Street Journal* or *Forbes* magazine and you will probably find an economist worrying about declines in the ability of the United States to compete in world markets. Articles point to such problems in the workplace as stagnant productivity, increased competition from abroad, and the harmful effects of government regulations. Other articles express concern about the health, safety, and general well-being of employees, or about problems in the public sector, where inefficient bureaucracies seem to impede rather than implement society's attempts to provide services. All these problems grow out of the nature of modern society. We live in a society of organizations, all of which profoundly affect our lives as employees or employers, as consumers or manufacturers of products and services, and as citizens. Organizations are essential, but they do not always work efficiently. Their inefficiencies have created a need for industrial and organizational psychologists, who work at identifying and explaining organizational malfunctions and work-related problems encountered by employees.

Industrial/organizational psychology—or *I/O psychology*, as it is often called— is concerned with human behavior in the workplace. Although I/O psychology is a product of the twentieth century, its roots go back to the way people thought about humanity and machines a century earlier. Industry had concentrated on building new and better equipment but had paid little attention to the human beings who ran the machines. Gradually, it became clear that industry needed to consider the interaction of workers and machines. If the right conditions could be found, if human motivation and energy could be tapped, everyone would profit.

THE BIRTH AND DEVELOPMENT OF INDUSTRIAL/ORGANIZATIONAL PSYCHOLOGY

Industrial psychology was born one day in 1900, when an American industrial engineer named Frederick Taylor watched a group of men load 92-pound "pigs" of iron at the Bethlehem Steel Company. The crew of seventy-five men picked up the pigs and carried each one several yards away from the furnace, where they dropped it onto a pile waiting to be loaded onto railroad cars. Taylor noted their movements and decided that if a few simple principles were applied to their labor, their productivity might be quadrupled. Taylor was right. One worker who followed Taylor's instructions for handling the pigs more efficiently was able to increase his day's output from 12½ to 47½ tons.

SCIENTIFIC MANAGEMENT the system that uses the methods of experimental psychology to redesign the workplace

Taylor believed that it was possible to create more efficient factories, which would provide ample profits for management and higher salaries for labor. Taylor's system, known as **scientific management,** used the methods of experimental psychology to redesign the workplace. Under this system, management was enabled not only to change work methods to make them more efficient but also to choose the best workers for each job, train them in new methods, develop cooperation between managers and workers, and involve workers in the design and conduct of work (Murchinsky, 1983).

Taylor's application of experimental psychology to the workplace was one of three separate movements that combined to produce the field of industrial/organizational psychology. The second movement involved testing and assessment by personnel psychologists, who relied on the research that we discussed in Chapters 11 and 17. The third was the human relations movement, which emphasized job motivation and work satisfaction (Landy, 1985).

Hugo Münsterberg (1913/1973), a pioneer in personnel psychology, was as concerned with efficiency as Taylor was, but he took a different approach. Where Taylor had stressed the need to change people's behavior, Münsterberg emphasized matching people to the jobs for which they were best suited. He tried to discover just what individual qualities—intelligence, personality traits, and experience—contributed to people's performance in various jobs. Following Münsterberg's example, personnel experts began to investigate what qualities each job

Before Frederick Taylor applied his principles of scientific management to the iron and steel industry, workdays were long and hard, but productivity was low.

required, to assess each applicant's capabilities by using various measurement techniques, and then to fill each job with a qualified worker.

Meanwhile, the human relations approach was developing. In 1927, industrial psychologists conducted a series of experiments at Western Electric's plant in Hawthorne, Illinois, to discover which working conditions would increase or decrease productivity. But they came up with something entirely different from their hypothesis: no matter how they manipulated working conditions, after each intervention the workers' productivity increased. This response came to be known as "the Hawthorne effect." It led researchers to conclude that workers' feelings affect their job performance, and that the way workers *perceive* their situation may have more influence on their performance than their actual, objective working conditions (Landy, 1985). Although some aspects of this experiment have been questioned (Rice, 1982), the Hawthorne studies caused many industrial psychologists to shift their attention from job efficiency to increasing workers' satisfaction. They concluded that feelings and motivations were as important as efficient assembly lines. They also discovered that social relations among workers had a powerful influence on workers' motivation and performance.

As the field of industrial psychology grew, it became apparent that its name was too narrow to convey its scope. Instead of working with individual behavior in isolation, industrial psychologists examined *organized* behavior: individual behavior that depended on that of other people and on the organization of a number of tasks into a given job's responsibilities. The focus expanded to include not only the single individual within an organization but also the entire organization itself (Landy, 1985). Accordingly, since 1970 industrial psychology has been known as **industrial/organizational psychology,** which may be defined as the application of psychological principles to the performance of organizations and of the people who work in them.

I/O psychologists work in a wide variety of settings, as we saw when we discussed areas of specialization for psychologists in Chapter 1. No matter where I/O psychologists work, they are likely to focus on a general problem area. Those who specialize in *personnel and human resources management* deal with such matters as decisions about and practices for the selection, placement, and training of employees; the appraisal of work performance; and systems of wages and compensation. I/O psychologists who specialize in organizational behavior concentrate on such topics as worker motivation, employee attitudes, leadership, and managerial psychology. I/O psychologists who specialize in *organizational development* focus on planned organizational change and intervention. I/O psycholo-

INDUSTRIAL/ORGANIZATIONAL PSYCHOLOGY the application of psychological principles to the performance of organizations and of the people who work in them

These men were members of a cable crew at Western Electric's Hawthorne plant, where industrial psychologists conducted pioneering studies on worker productivity.

gists who specialize in *industrial relations* study the psychological aspects of labor, management, and their relationship, including collective bargaining and the settlement of disputes. Finally, some I/O psychologists specialize in *engineering psychology*, which focuses on the interface between human beings and machines (Murchinsky, 1983). In the sections that follow we will explore some of these major concerns, beginning with employee selection—the problem of matching the worker to the job.

MATCHING WORKERS TO JOBS

When you apply for a job, you try to appear intelligent, capable, and highly motivated. You smile brightly and subject yourself to the selection process, all the while conscious of your sweaty palms, the slight tug in the middle of your stomach, and perhaps a feeling of resentment at the probing questions—some of which may seem completely unrelated to the job you seek. But your potential employer also has problems. First, he or she must choose a new employee who has the abilities and inclinations that fit the demands of the job. Second, there is the possibility that the person under consideration might quit shortly after training or have to be fired for obvious incompetence. To help avoid these problems, many employers rely on psychological tests or on interviews, or on a combination of the two, as predictors of job performance.

Psychological Tests as Predictors of Job Performance

People differ in their traits, aptitudes, and abilities, and these differences may affect how well an individual performs in a particular job. Employers use a variety of tests to identify such individual differences, with varying degrees of success. Most employers believe that intelligence is a good predictor of job performance: intelligent employees are expected to learn a job more quickly, to perform it more efficiently, and to be less likely to quit without notice. Because individual intelligence tests, like those discussed in Chapter 11, are too expensive to be used in screening job applicants, employers use group intelligence tests that have been developed for use in personnel selection. One of these tests is the Otis Self-Administering Test of Mental Ability, which has been widely used to fill clerical and supervisory positions.

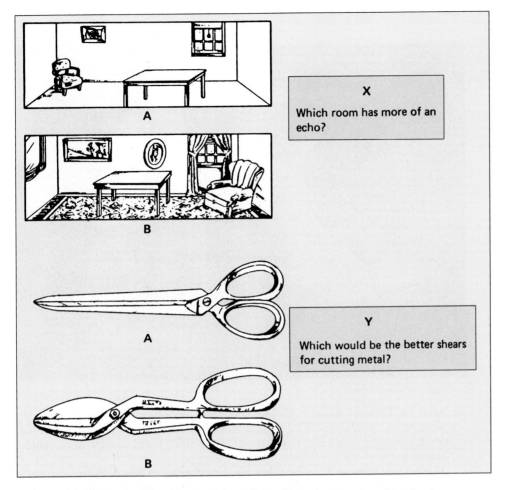

Figure 23.1 The Bennett Mechanical Comprehension Test is used to assess job applicants' understanding of mechanical principles and spatial relations. The applicant answers short questions about pictures such as the ones shown here. (Adapted from Ghiselli, 1966. Reproduced by permission from the *Bennett Mechanical Comprehension Test.* Copyright © 1942, 1967 by The Psychological Corporation. All rights reserved.)

For some kinds of jobs, assessing a person's ability to handle words and numbers by means of an intelligence test is less important than determining his or her ability to understand mechanical principles and spatial relations (see Figure 23.1); for other jobs, such as industrial worker, truck driver, or heavy-equipment operator, motor ability is the key trait that must be tested. In addition, some employers attempt to assess an applicant's personality. They may rely on self-report inventories like the ones discussed in Chapter 17, or they may use interest inventories, which are somewhat similar but explore the person's degree of interest in various activities. Other kinds of tests that may be used include handwriting analysis; honesty tests, such as polygraph (lie detector) examinations; and assessment centers.

Predictive Validity: Test Scores and Job Performance

As we saw in Chapter 11, if a test is to be useful, it must be both reliable and valid—that is, it must measure something consistently and it must measure what it purports to measure. Furthermore, if a test is to be useful in screening job applicants, it should have predictive validity: a person's scores on the test should have some relation to his or her subsequent job performance. In a test that correlated perfectly with success on the job (+1), the highest-scoring applicant would do best on the job and the lowest-scoring applicant would do worst.

Few tests have such high validity. Most are only "moderate" predictors of job success, with a correlation of about +.30. Tests of perceptual accuracy, for exam-

The value of a test in predicting job performance depends on its relevance to the tasks actually involved in the job. Manual dexterity is important in some jobs, but not in others.

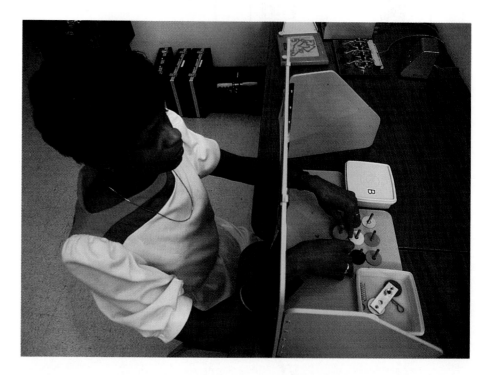

ple, seem to correlate about +.30 with success in clerical occupations. Some tests are worthless as predictors. The same tests of perceptual accuracy correlate only +.05 with success as a sales clerk, which may make them useless in screening applicants for such jobs (Ghiselli, 1973).

Intelligence tests seem to be fairly good predictors of job performance: they correlate about +.55 across all job categories, but they are better predictors for some occupations than for others. Correlations run as high as +.61 for cognitively complex jobs and as low as +.27 for jobs with few cognitive demands (Hunter and Hunter, 1984). These correlations are not any higher because the abilities measured by a given test are often necessary, but not sufficient, for job success. A dentist must have manual dexterity, so a person who fails such a test could not succeed at dentistry; however, dentistry also requires academic intelligence, diagnostic skills, and personality characteristics that keep patients coming back. In other cases, a test that has validity in one employment situation is not valid for the same type of job in another workplace. This problem arises because working conditions, the tasks involved in the job, and the characteristics of the workforce all vary from one company or industry to another.

Regardless of these limitations, a number of I/O psychologists still advocate the use of intelligence tests by personnel departments. It has been estimated that if the federal government used tests of cognitive aptitude for hiring, it could save $16 billion each year in labor costs, and that smaller employers, such as the Philadelphia police department, could save $18 million each year (Schmidt and Hunter, 1981).

Handwriting analysis, which is widely used in Europe and by at least 3000 companies in the United States, seems worthless as a predictor of job performance (Hunter and Hunter, 1984).

Since the 1980s, honesty tests have been used in some organizations, not only to select employees but also to promote or fire them. The most popular test initially was the polygraph, or lie detector, which essentially measures autonomic arousal associated with emotion. Yet as a test of an employee's honesty, the lie detector has serious limitations. For one thing, there is no distinctive, involuntary physiological response that generally accompanies a lie (Lykken, 1981). Conversely, changes in the measured physiological responses do not necessarily mean that a person is lying; he or she may only be anxious. In addition, people who know how the polygraph works can sometimes thwart it; for example, they can think of some anxiety-arousing situation when answering simple questions such as their address. A lie would then produce the same polygraph reading as a truthful answer. In 1988, controversy over the polygraph led Congress to outlaw its use by private companies unless they were in the business of providing security personnel or were investigating theft, embezzlement, or industrial espionage (*Congressional & Administrative News*, 1988).

With these restrictions on use of the polygraph, most employers must rely on paper-and-pencil honesty tests. These tests ask direct questions about employee theft ("Have you ever taken company merchandise?") and indirect questions about attitudes toward theft ("Do you think it would be easy for a dishonest person to steal from an employer?"). Such tests have problems with validity. Subjects may not answer truthfully, and those who do so and fit a "dishonest" profile may not actually steal (Sackett, 1985). Current employees may be falsely labeled dishonest, come under suspicion, or even be fired because of these tests, so their use has many pitfalls.

Special programs known as *assessment centers* are used to determine whether people have managerial potential. An assessment center is an organization's standardized set of situational exercises and sometimes psychological tests that are administered to produce a profile of each candidate. The situational exercises involve an array of job-related tasks, such as presenting a business plan, writing a business letter, and participating in a mock committee discussion. Assessors rate the participants on personality dimensions—decisiveness, career ambition, sensitivity, integrity, and the like—that have been determined to be important in the position for which they are being considered (Miner, 1988). Assessment-center ratings are quite accurate in predicting job performance and success, especially for people in management positions (Thornton and Byham, 1982).

Legal Aspects of Test Validity

The use of personality, intelligence, and aptitude tests to select or promote employees has often been seen as discriminatory. Such tests can be used to keep people of a particular race, color, religion, sex, or nationality out of jobs or to deny them promotion. If tests are used to discriminate against any of these groups, they are in violation of the Civil Rights Act of 1964.

Discrimination need not be intentional. The courts may determine that the use of a test violates the Civil Rights Act if the plaintiff can show statistically that such use has an **adverse impact** on members of a minority group, regardless of the employer's intentions. By applying the "four-fifths rule," that is, if the number of minority applicants hired is less than four-fifths of the number of majority applicants hired, the courts consider that the test has an adverse impact on minorities. To be without adverse impact, a test that leads, for example, to the hiring of 5 percent of majority applicants for a job must also lead to the hiring of at least 4 percent of minority applicants.

Proof of adverse impact is not enough to get a ruling of discrimination, however. If it can be shown that the test has predictive validity, the employer can continue to use it—unless the plaintiff can show that an alternate, but nondiscriminatory, test exists (Griffin, 1980). The test need not always predict performance on the job; predicting performance in a training program fulfills the requirement (*Washington* v. *Davis*, 1976). In fact, in some instances, content validity is enough to prove that a test is related to the job (*National Education Association* v. *State of South Carolina*, 1978). Recently, the U.S. Supreme Court has ruled that the plaintiff, not the employer, must prove that a discriminatory practice does not serve legitimate business goals (Greenhouse, 1989). This would have the effect of forcing the plaintiff to show that a test does *not* have predictive validity.

Although the courts have relied on predictive or content validity in their rulings, some psychologists have suggested that these types of validity are useful only in filling simple, repetitive jobs. For jobs involving complex tasks, they believe that *construct validity*, in which the test measures whatever trait or capability it claims to measure, is enough to warrant a test's use (Lerner, 1977). Yet the courts are not interested in the issue of validity unless its absence leads to discrimination. Presumably, a test based on the casting of horoscopes would be accepted

ADVERSE IMPACT the discriminatory effect on minorities that occurs when a test results in the hiring of less than four-fifths of the number of majority applicants hired

by the courts as long as it did not discriminate against any group specified in the Civil Rights Act.

Interviews As Predictors of Job Performance

The majority of employers report that the most important aspect of their employee-selection procedure is the interview (Eder and Buckley, 1988), which goes far beyond the scope of the psychological test. An interviewer attempts to assess the applicant's attitude, motivation, and behavior (Landy, 1985). Although the purpose of the interview is to gather information about the applicant, it is not a simple fact-finding process.

First impressions often have a strong impact on an interviewer. Before the applicant has said more than a few words, the interviewer may already have categorized him or her, relying on appearance, behavior, and information already available on the application. This pre-interview judgment may become a self-fulfilling prophecy, determining how the interviewer interprets the applicant's answers (Eder and Buckley, 1988). Most job applicants are aware of this tendency, so they dress to create a good impression and try to present what they think the interviewer wants to see.

An interview is actually a complex, dynamic process, in which the characteristics of the interviewer, the applicant, and the situation interact (Eder and Buckley, 1988). Subjective factors play such an important role that some I/O psychologists believe the typical interview does not validly predict an applicant's potential (Thayer, 1983). Consider some of the factors that enter into the interview:

■ Most interviewers give more weight to unfavorable information than to favorable information.

■ Most interviewers have an image of the "ideal" applicant, against which they evaluate the people they interview.

■ Interviewers differ widely in the cues (words, appearance, behavior) they use to evaluate an applicant, yet they are unable to state just what cues they do use.

■ Most interviewers rely more heavily on the applicant's posture, gestures, and facial expressions than on his or her words.

■ Interviewers tend to rate more highly those applicants who are of the same gender or ethnic background as themselves or who share the interviewer's attitudes—although this higher rating does not seem to affect job offers (Schmitt, 1976; Eder and Buckley, 1988).

The invalidity of the interview stems not just from the biases and backgrounds of interviewer and applicant, but from the structure of the interview as well. Because most interviews are conducted without a standardized interview guide, applicants are compared on dissimilar data. For example, if you ask one student the sum of 2 plus 2 and another the square root of 3.763, you cannot fairly conclude that the second student is worse in arithmetic—yet this is essentially what many interviewers do.

Worse, an interview can be discriminatory, especially when the interviewer delves deeply into aspects of the applicant's life that have no bearing on job performance. To help guard against such irrelevant probing, the Washington State Human Relations Commission ruled that certain questions may not be a normal part of job interviews. The commission has forbidden interviewers to ask applicants about arrests, citizenship, personal information (such as marital status, spouse's salary, pregnancies, children, child-care arrangements, and whether the applicant owns or rents a house), or military discharge information (Arvey, 1979). Interviewers are also instructed to avoid questions so broad that their answers are likely to provide information (such as a health condition) that is unrelated to job performance.

As presently conducted, interviews correlate only +.14 with job performance (Hunter and Hunter, 1984). (See the accompanying box for a discussion of inter-

Employers rely heavily on interviews in deciding whom to hire, and applicants know that the first impression is very important.

views from the applicant's point of view.) But interviews can be a useful part of the job selection process if an employer sticks to questions that reveal information pertinent to job duties, uses a structured interview format with well-trained interviewers, and gives interviewers feedback on the later success or failure of the applicants they hire (Landy, 1985).

For decades, I/O psychologists have been trying to improve the job selection process. After sifting through all these studies, John and Ronda Hunter (1984) concluded that the predictive validity of interviews is so low that an employer would do better to fill jobs on the basis of information from biographical data forms (see Figure 23.2). No matter what study the researchers looked at, however, they found that applicants' scores on ability tests have the highest predictive validity for performance in entry-level jobs,—that is, for which training will occur after hiring.

WORK MOTIVATION

Work motivation affects how long employees stay with a company, how dependably they perform their duties, and how innovative they are on the job. Because so many aspects of behavior at work are affected by motivation, no single theory has been able to explain them all. Instead, I/O psychologists have drawn on a variety of theories to help them understand the conditions that underlie work motivation. The theories fall into three broad categories: need theories, cognitive theories, and reinforcement theory.

Need Theories of Work Motivation

Much of our behavior is motivated by needs, as we saw in Chapter 13. Several theories of work motivation have related performance on the job to the strength of various needs that are unrelated to basic drives.

One need theory of work motivation is based on Abraham Maslow's hierarchy of needs, which we explored in Chapters 13 and 17. In Maslow's view, lower needs take precedence, and only after they are met will a person be motivated by those higher in the hierarchy. When applied to work motivation, this theory assumes that workers first concentrate on pay and job security. With adequate pay and assured jobs, their concerns turn to relationships with their coworkers and

PSYCHOLOGY TODAY AND TOMORROW

The Realistic Job Preview

The usefulness of job interviews in predicting job performance seems so slight as to make us wonder whether there is any point in continuing to use them as part of the hiring process. But we must bear in mind that interviews do more than provide information to employers; they also provide information to the applicant about the job. Many interviewers paint such a positive picture of job openings that applicants see life in the organization through a rosy haze. Applicants develop unrealistically high expectations, which are toppled once they report for work. The dissatisfaction and job turnover that often follow cost companies money and make workers unhappy. Perhaps these high expectations help explain the low validity of interviews.

In an attempt to reduce the proportion of "revolving-door" employees, some companies have begun to use the *realistic job preview (RJP)*, in which a conscious effort is made to create realistic expectations about the job, primarily by providing information about the job's disadvantages.

Realistic job previews come in an assortment of forms, and some have been fairly effective. One team of I/O psychologists (Meglino et al., 1988) studied the effect of RJPs on more than 500 U.S. Army recruits. They discovered that RJPs cut turnover when trainees saw videotaped previews that not only dispelled commonly held negative impressions of Army life but also described difficulties that new recruits probably would not have anticipated. Trainees who saw this kind of RJP not only had significantly lower turnover (2.47 percent) than other recruits, but they were also more committed to the Army, were more satisfied with their jobs, and saw the Army as more caring, trustworthy, and honest. However, recruits who saw RJPs that focused entirely on problems of Army life had higher turnover (13.19 percent) than those who saw no preview at all (7.81 percent).

Although not all RJPs have been successful in reducing turnover, some have managed to change the date of departure. Among prospective bank tellers in one study (Wanous and Dean, 1984), the dropout rate after one year remained the same. However, among tellers who dropped out, those who had had an RJP tended to leave during the training period, whereas those without an RJP waited nearly six months before they left. In this case, the RJP did not cut down the mismatches, but it did save the bank $1400 on each employee who left during the training period.

After reviewing RJPs in various companies, Steven Premack and John Wanous (1985) found that realistic job previews do reduce turnover, especially in companies where turnover has been unusually high. RJPs seem to persuade some applicants to pass up the job; among those who are hired, RJPs lower expectations but raise initial levels of job commitment and job satisfaction and increase performance levels. The effect on turnover is modest, ranging from 6 percent in companies with low turnover to 24 percent in companies with extremely high turnover.

supervisors. Only after the work environment is satisfying can workers then become motivated by the "metaneed" to fulfill themselves through work (Muchinsky, 1987).

Maslow's views become important when we are considering the match between people and jobs. In the view of Richard Hackman and Greg Oldham (1976), people who are primarily motivated by lower psychological needs (so that their metaneeds are weak) will not perform well in complex, challenging jobs that allow discretion and independence. But people who are motivated by metaneeds, such as the need for personal growth or self-actualization, will respond to the requirements of such jobs and apply themselves with enthusiasm. Thus, an employee's performance and job satisfaction become a function of how well job requirements match the strength of metaneeds.

Although Maslow's theory has had broad influence, attempts to test it in the workplace have had disappointing results. In a longitudinal study of workers, researchers found that satisfying psychological needs such as job security or friendship did *not* diminish the importance of these needs in the workers' eyes. Nor did changes in the satisfaction of needs in one category affect the importance of needs in any of the other categories (Lawler and Suttle, 1972). These research-

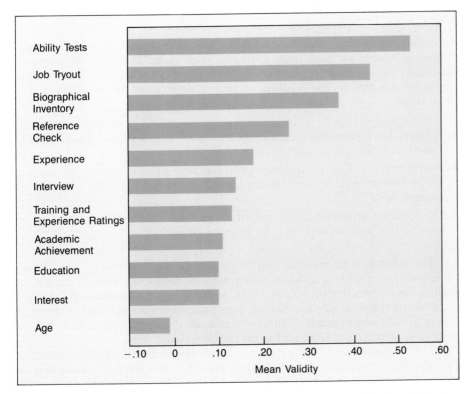

Figure 23.2 Mean validities of various predictors of performance in entry-level jobs. An analysis of a number of studies revealed that applicants' scores on tests of cognitive and psychomotor ability are the best single predictor of their performance (as rated by supervisors) in entry-level jobs. The mean validities found by these studies are shown here for ability tests and ten other predictors. (Adapted from Hunter and Hunter, 1984, p. 90.)

ers also found that needs seem to be divided into only two categories: the basic biological needs and all the rest of Maslow's needs—combining psychological and metaneeds in a single group. Other psychologists have found that most research either rejects the propositions of Maslow's theory or at best gives them weak support (Wahba and Bridwell, 1976). They have concluded, however, that the theory's vagueness makes it virtually impossible to derive any testable hypotheses from it.

Another application of need theory to work motivation is that of David McClelland (1976; McClelland and Boyatzis, 1982) and his students, whose studies of the need for achievement were discussed in Chapter 13. McClelland believes that a strong need for power is probably a necessity for managers in large, hierarchical organizations. His research suggests that among effective managers the need takes the form of a concern for *socialized power;* such people tend to be emotionally mature, to exercise their power for the benefit of others, and to listen to the advice of experts. They channel their need for power into building up the organization and making it successful. Managers with a concern for *personalized power,* in contrast, have little self-control and tend to exercise their power impulsively. They develop loyalty to themselves instead of to the organization, and when they leave, their subordinates fall into disarray and group morale suffers.

Cognitive Theories of Work Motivation

Several theories of work motivation are based on the effects of various factors on the way we think about our jobs. Some of these cognitive theories focus on our expectations, some on our attempts to maintain cognitive consistency, and others on our intentions.

Expectancy Theory

According to **expectancy theory**, we are motivated not only by our goals but also by how attainable we think those goals are. Since Victor Vroom (1964) proposed expectancy theory, it has become one of the major ways of explaining work motivation. In this theory, our work motivation is determined by the interaction of three factors:

- *Valence:* The satisfaction we anticipate from a job outcome (such as a transfer to a more desirable location)
- *Instrumentality:* Our perception of that outcome's relationship to our current job performance (Does the transfer depend on the quality of the work we are doing now?)
- *Expectancy:* Our expectations that effort will affect our performance (Can we increase our performance level by working harder?)

The valence of an outcome can be positive (a word of praise, a raise, or a promotion) or negative (criticism, being fired, or demoted). Valence can also be high or low, depending on how strongly we feel about the outcome. If Dennis, a beginning worker, is given a boring, low-paid, repetitive job and if there are plenty of such jobs available, Dennis may not care if he gets fired. In this case, the valence is negative but low: he has no reason to work hard.

The instrumentality of the outcome is also important. If Maria believes that the raises her company gives out each July are automatic, she will assume that her job performance has no effect on her annual raise. Again, there is no reason for Maria to work hard.

Expectancy is perhaps the most important factor of all. If Mario works in a factory, tending the machinery that places caps on soft-drink bottles, he cannot increase the number of cases that come off the line, no matter how hard he works. He can see no relationship between how much effort he puts in and his ultimate job performance. There is no reason for Mario to put out extra effort. In contrast, if Mario were delivering soft drinks to supermarkets and received a commission on any deliveries he made over a certain level, he would see a close relationship between effort and performance, and his motivation would be much higher.

When valence is high, instrumentality is clear, and expectancy is strong, workers should be highly motivated. In fact, the programs recommended by I/O psychologists to motivate employees rely on these elements. Companies are urged to provide attractive incentives (valence) and clear descriptions of how to attain them (instrumentality); they are also urged to make certain employees know their wages will depend on performance (expectancy).

Expectancy theory is behind the "cafeteria compensation" programs that some major companies have begun to introduce during the past few years. Under these plans, employees choose a customized packet of wages and benefits that suit their circumstances and desires. The first such plan was put into effect at TRW's Defense and Space Systems Group (Curry, 1982). TRW's plan focused on medical and life insurance benefits. All employees received minimum medical and life insurance, but each individual could select from an array of additional benefits those that had the highest valence for them. Some employees chose life insurance for their dependents, some chose additional accident coverage for themselves, some simply took a salary increase funded by the money that the company would have spent on the extra benefits. Since TRW instituted its plan, the scope of such cafeteria programs has widened. In many programs, for example, a working mother or father may choose company-paid day-care services while a childless employee may choose extra paid vacation. No matter how the plan is set up, the organization's goal is to make it clear that outcomes with high valence for individual employees depend on their willingness to exert effort in ways that will improve their job performance.

Expectancy theory is popular among managers for two reasons. First, it predicts effort, performance, and satisfaction for many employees. Second, its principles are clear and relatively easy to apply in day-to-day management. But expectancy theory does a good job of predicting work-related behavior only when

PSYCHOLOGY TODAY AND TOMORROW

Equity Theory: A Window Office May Be as Rewarding as a Raise

Everyone who works in a large organization knows that work space is as closely linked to job importance as is salary. A private office, its size, a door that closes, a window, the size of a desk, and the style of a chair are clear signals of an employee's status in the company. This common-sense observation led I/O psychologist Jerald Greenberg (1988) to test equity theory as it applied to office status.

While the offices of a large insurance company were being redecorated, employees had to be shifted around. Greenberg seized the opportunity to reassign them in a carefully controlled manner. He arranged for all of the office moves to last for two work weeks and assigned people to temporary offices in a way that explored equity theory. Employees were shifted to offices that were two staff levels above their own, one staff level above, the same staff level, one staff level lower, or two staff levels lower.

The employees responded just as equity theory predicts. The performance of those in offices usually occupied by people who outranked them improved sharply; the performance of those in offices usually occupied by people beneath them dropped sharply; the performance of those who remained at their customary level showed no change. Those who were moved two levels showed larger changes than those who were moved only a single level up or down. When employees returned to their own offices, their performance returned to its customary level.

It appears that employees see the characteristics of their work space as part of their job outcomes and respond to the "rewards" of office environment in the same way that they respond to the rewards of salaries, bonuses, raises, or job titles.

people's efforts are consciously directed toward a goal. Among people whose behavior is beyond their conscious awareness, expectancy theory fails as a predictor (Miner, 1980). A personal sense of control also seems to be a factor. People who believe they have control over events in their lives generally behave in accordance with expectancy theory, but people who believe that they are pawns of fate, or that their lives are controlled by powerful others, do not (Miner, 1988).

Equity Theory

When the information we pick up from the world is inconsistent, we experience *cognitive dissonance*, the unpleasant state of cognitive imbalance that we discussed in Chapter 21. Our attempts to restore cognitive equilibrium may affect our attitudes as well as our behavior. This reasoning, which underlies the various theories of cognitive consistency described in Chapter 21, is the basis for equity theory.

Equity theory looks at whether we believe we are being treated fairly on the job. As proposed by J. S. Adams (1965), **equity theory** says that we are motivated to eliminate perceived inequities. How do we know that inequities exist? First we make a rough determination of the ratio between inputs (such as effort) and our

EQUITY THEORY the cognitive theory that sees employees as motivated to remove perceived inequities—either by action or by rethinking the situation

rewards (such as salary). Then we compare that ratio with the ratio we perceive as existing for others. If the two ratios are not equal, we perceive an inequity and experience cognitive dissonance. If we are underrewarded, we feel resentful; if we are overrewarded, we feel guilty. We are motivated to reduce this tension, and the greater the tension, the greater our motivation to do something about it.

We can restore equity in two ways: we can change our behavior or we can change our thoughts (Muchinsky, 1987). Suppose you discover that Joan, who works at the desk next to yours, is being paid $2000 a year more than you. You and Joan joined the company at about the same time and have similar duties. If you decide to restore equity by changing your behavior, you may reduce your inputs: you stop working so hard, you stretch your coffee break, you are out the door on the stroke of five. Or you may try to change your outcomes: you can ask for a raise. Or you may change Joan's inputs: you may manipulate the situation so that she has to work harder, perhaps by seeing that reports you would normally handle land on her desk. Or you may quit your job and go to work for a company whose salary schedule you believe is more equitable.

Instead of changing your behavior, you may just change the way you think about the inequity. You can distort your own inputs or outcomes: you may tell yourself that you do not really work as hard as Joan and thus do not deserve the same salary. Or you can distort Joan's inputs or outcomes: you may convince yourself that she handles a number of difficult accounts and so deserves extra money. Or you can stop comparing yourself with Joan: you can begin to compare yourself with Carlos, who started work a few months after you did and is paid a little less than you are.

Until recently, I/O psychologists applied equity theory primarily to the way feelings about fairness in salaries, bonuses, and raises affected work motivation. But it has become clear that our perceptions of fairness or unfairness in other work outcomes may also affect work motivation. Researchers have found, for example, that job titles are included in equity assessments (Greenberg and Ornstein, 1983). Employees who were underpaid but given a lofty job title responded by working harder. (See the accompanying box for another application of equity theory to the workplace.)

Like expectancy theory, equity theory does not predict the performance of all employees. It appears that there is a link between personality and perceptions of equity: people react differently to both fairness and unfairness, because they have different levels of *equity sensitivity* (Huseman, Hatfield, and Miles, 1987). That is, when they compare themselves to other people, they prefer different outcome/input ratios. Those known as "equity sensitives" want the same proportion of input and outcome, and so their work motivation and job satisfaction are affected just as equity theory predicts. "Benevolents" behave like altruists; they are content with proportionately smaller outcomes. It is not known whether their altruism is truly unselfish or a response to the need for social approval or an enhanced self-image (a distinction we discussed in Chapter 22), but in any case, they are distressed both by equity and by overreward. "Entitleds" want more than their share; they are satisfied only when they are overrewarded and are almost as distressed by fairness as by inequity.

Goal-Setting Theory

Goal-setting theory holds that instead of being motivated by our needs or our feelings of inequity, we are motivated by our conscious intentions to attain a specific goal. As we saw in Chapter 13, motivated behavior requires a goal, and the conscious setting of goals apparently heightens motivation. According to Edwin Locke (1968), who developed the theory, once a goal is accepted and a conscious commitment is made to work toward it, the person's heightened motivation will be reflected in increased effort and persistence.

Several factors can affect the intensity of motivation (Locke et al., 1981): the specificity of the goal, its difficulty, the individual's ability, the concrete awards attached to the goal, and the accuracy of feedback. We are more motivated to work for a 10 percent increase in sales (a specific goal) than for increased produc-

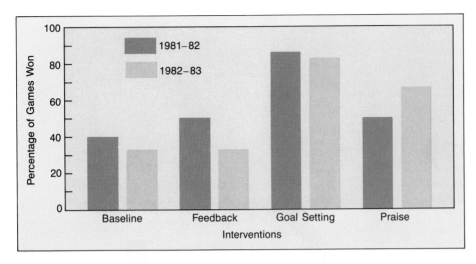

Figure 23.3 Percentage of hockey games won in response to three interventions. In two successive seasons, a university hockey team increased the percentage of games it won after each of three interventions: feedback regarding players' performance, goal setting by each player, and praise from the coach. (Anderson et al., 1988, p. 92.)

tivity (a general goal). We commit ourselves more deeply when the goal is difficult than when it is easy or when we are urged to "just do your best." We will not be motivated unless we have the ability required to meet the goal. We will become more committed to a goal when we know that its attainment will bring money, promotion, or other concrete rewards. Unless we get feedback on our performance, our motivation will decline. But when we are given accurate feedback, we can effectively adjust our strategies, our persistence, or the intensity of our efforts toward the goal (Landy, 1985).

Researchers have been testing goal setting for twenty years, and the vast majority of studies support it (Latham and Yukl, 1975; Locke et al., 1981). In one interesting experiment, I/O psychologists used goal setting combined with feedback to turn around a university hockey team (Anderson et al., 1988). Over the past three seasons, the team's record had declined until they were winning fewer than 40 percent of their games. Goal setting took the form of increasing the number of "hits"—legal body blocks on an opponent who has control of the puck or has just passed it. A successful hit momentarily knocks the opponent out of play, thus usually increasing the team's chances of retrieving the puck—and of winning the game. Each player set his own goal for hits and received feedback in the form of a mark on a graph posted in the locker room. During the two-year study, the mean hit rate more than doubled and the team had winning seasons, qualifying for the playoffs (see Figure 23.3).

Most I/O psychologists are convinced that goal setting is an effective way to increase job performance, although they are not certain exactly how it works. In fact, goal setting is the basic concept behind management by objectives (MBO), a popular technique used to improve performance in corporations (see Figure 23.4).

Reinforcement Theory

Some I/O psychologists have applied instrumental conditioning to the workplace, where it is called **reinforcement theory.** As we saw in Chapter 7, reinforcement can change our behavior because it changes our expectancies. A wide variety of companies—fast-food chains, hospitals, and the armed forces—have tried to increase employee motivation with schedules of positive reinforcement.

The effectiveness of reinforcement has been shown again and again. Yet there are problems with using it as a motivational technique. One kind of problem emerges when a company changes the reinforcement schedule. An hourly wage is

REINFORCEMENT THEORY the theory of work motivation that applies the techniques of instrumental conditioning to change workers' expectancies

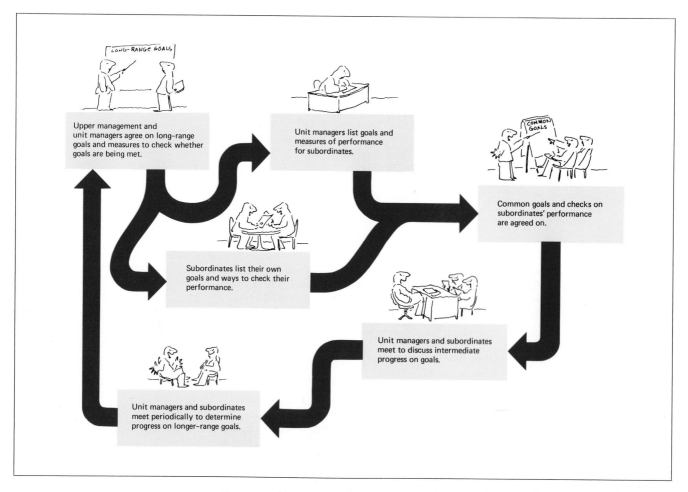

Figure 23.4 Management by objectives. In the MBO system, managers state their goals clearly and involve the appropriate workers in them from the start. The workers state their own goals too, and both workers and managers go through a cycle of discussion, review, and evaluation.

not reinforcing because workers receive the same reward no matter how hard they work. But paying them by the piece (on either a variable or a fixed-ratio schedule) may lead employees to overwork, in a reminder of the "sweatshop" conditions that were once common in the garment industry. Is it ethical for an employer to set unrealistically high quotas and to induce employees to work to the point of exhaustion (Muchinsky, 1987)?

Another problem arises because of individual differences; what reinforces one person will not reinforce another, so that a uniform program of rewards is unlikely to be effective with all employees. A third problem is linked with the phenomenon of extinction: organizations sometimes institute programs and then withdraw them. If employees have been receiving special rewards, as when department store clerks get time off with pay for meeting sales standards, their motivation plummets when the rewards are discontinued. Many workers become less productive than they had been before the program was introduced.

WORK-RELATED ATTITUDES

No matter what method is used to motivate employees, its success will depend on the employees' attitudes. Little wonder, then, that I/O psychologists pay close attention to work-related attitudes. Two of the most extensively investigated attitudes are job satisfaction and organizational commitment.

Job Satisfaction

The question of what makes workers happy is of great interest to both employers and workers. One reason is basically humanitarian: since most of us spend a substantial part of our adult lives at work, it obviously matters to us whether we spend that time in satisfying and fulfilling situations. A second reason is practical: people's feelings about their work presumably affect job performance, turnover, absenteeism, tardiness, and the like.

What Is Job Satisfaction?

Job satisfaction is an expression of people's emotional attitudes toward their work. It can be measured in terms of overall satisfaction with the job or in terms of satisfaction with specific aspects of the job.

The major sources of dissatisfaction with a job are ambiguous or conflicting roles—or both. Dissatisfied workers are those who do not know what they are expected to accomplish or who feel that they are subjected to contradictory demands. Thus **job satisfaction** may be defined as a reflection of the match between what workers want from a job and what they actually receive (McCormick and Ilgan, 1980).

JOB SATISFACTION the result of the match between what workers want from a job and what they actually get

Job Satisfaction and Performance

Does job satisfaction cause a worker to perform well, or does the feeling that he or she is doing a good job make a satisfied worker? I/O psychologists can cite studies that support either proposal, but close analysis of the research indicates that while overall job satisfaction does have a moderate, consistent connection with performance, the connection appears to be heavily influenced by the level of a person's job. One research team found that among professionals, supervisors, and managers, the correlation is about +.41, but among workers in nonsupervisory or nonmanagerial positions the correlation falls to +.20 (Petty, McGee, and Cavender, 1984). After reviewing the research, this team concluded that the relationship between job satisfaction and performance is circular, but that the cycle probably begins with performance. Once individual workers perceive that they are doing a good job, they become more satisfied, and their satisfaction may further enhance their performance.

Research generally supports the conclusion that job satisfaction lowers absenteeism and turnover rates. Unhappy workers take more days off than do workers who like their jobs. But once again, the correlation between attendance and job satisfaction is modest: −.35 (Muchinsky, 1987).

The more people dislike their jobs, the more likely they are to quit; this much seems obvious. But here again, the correlation is smaller than we might expect—about −.40 (Muchinsky, 1987). Unhappy workers do not add up their dissatisfactions one day and walk out the door. The decision to quit, as distinct from thinking about quitting, depends on a series of variables: the economic climate (which affects the availability of other jobs), the worker's opportunities (whether he or she has another job offer or feels confident about finding other employment), and the cost-benefit analysis the worker performs. An unhappy worker who decides that the costs of quitting are too high may engage in cognitive restructuring, reevaluating the job in more positive terms. Or the worker may turn to indirect forms of withdrawal, such as absenteeism (Mobley, Horner, and Hollingsworth, 1978).

Most studies of job satisfaction focus on the work situation—wages, hours, working conditions, management, status. But a longitudinal study of 5000 middle-aged men indicates that personality may be as important as the situation in determining job satisfaction (Staw and Ross, 1985). Over a five-year period, men tended to report similar levels of satisfaction despite changes in employer, occupation, status, salary, or redesign of their jobs. It seems that some people are chronically disposed to be happy or unhappy, and that one predictor of satisfaction in the present job is the person's level of satisfaction with previous jobs.

Organizational Commitment

Job satisfaction, which refers to workers' feelings about their specific jobs, may fluctuate, but organizational commitment, which refers to workers' attitudes toward the organization as a whole, remains fairly stable. **Organizational commitment** has been defined as the strength of the individual worker's identification with, and involvement in, a particular organization (Saal and Knight, 1988). Workers who are committed to their organization accept its goals and values, are willing to expend extra effort for the organization, and want to maintain their connection with it. A highly committed employee expresses extreme devotion to the company, perhaps foregoing an attractive offer from a competitor, and defends the company when others make disparaging remarks about it.

Employees who are committed to their organization display helpful and cooperative behaviors that go above and beyond the call of duty. Such *organizational citizenship behavior* includes assisting a coworker with a problem, volunteering for difficult tasks, working late—all the helpful activities that might not be listed in a job description but that are nevertheless important if organizations are to function smoothly. In a study of two large banks, researchers (Smith, Organ, and Near, 1983) found that direct assistance, which they call altruism, was strongly influenced by job satisfaction. It appeared whenever another employee had a problem, needed assistance, or requested some service. Indirect assistance, which they describe as generalized compliance, consisted of acts that served the interests of the organization, such as punctuality or not wasting time. Job satisfaction did not predict compliance; instead this form of organizational citizenship behavior was influenced by the need for social approval and by a high level of support from supervisors. Another study of the effect of workers' attitudes on their behavior is described in the accompanying box.

Trends in Research on Work-Related Attitudes

In recent years the study of work-related attitudes has gone far beyond job satisfaction and organizational commitment. One area now being explored is that of employee attitudes toward the introduction of computers and robotics into the workplace. Studies have found, for example, that low-skill workers react negatively to robotics, seeing them as threats to job security, whereas highly skilled workers see robotics as an opportunity to expand their own skills (Chao and Kozlowski, 1986).

Realizing that attitudes and behavior in the workplace affect family matters and other aspects of nonwork life (Rice et al., 1985), I/O psychologists began to encourage the implementation of *quality of work life (QWL) programs,* which attempt to integrate a variety of managerial policies aimed at improving the general health and well-being of employees. For example, Bonne Bell, a cosmetics company, instituted a fitness program and built tennis and volleyball courts, a track, and shower and locker facilities for employees (Roberts and Harris, 1989). Employees get an extra half-hour at lunch if they use the facilities, and those who exercise four days a week during a six-month period get a $250 bonus. Employees also get bonuses if they lose excess weight or stop smoking for six months—but if they return to their old habits, they must donate twice the sum of the bonus to the corporation's charitable foundation. Company representatives say that employees enjoy the new regime and that absenteeism and sick days have dropped. Such programs have given I/O psychologists new opportunities to have a positive impact on work organizations.

SOCIAL INFLUENCES AT WORK

When increased competition cut into the sales of its chain of retail stores, a parent company closed many of them and laid off a number of workers in each of the

PSYCHOLOGY TODAY AND TOMORROW

Workers' Attitudes and Absenteeism after a Blizzard

When a crippling snowstorm brought Chicago to a virtual standstill, I/O psychologist Frank Smith (1977) got a chance to find out how work-related attitudes affect employees' behavior. The blizzard, which had not been forecast, was so severe that the city's transportation system ground to a halt. None of the 3000 managerial employees at the headquarters of a large merchandising corporation would have been penalized for staying home on the day after the storm, but many, with considerable effort, did make their way to work. Attendance in the various departments ranged from 39 to 97 percent.

Several months before the storm, as it happened, these employees had filled out attitude surveys. When Smith examined the responses, he found that job-related attitudes were an excellent predictor of which employees had braved the snow in Chicago and which ones had taken the day off. Attendance on the day after the storm correlated strongly with six measures of job satisfaction among the managerial employees. The strongest correlation was for an employee's satisfaction with his or her career prospects (+.60), followed by satisfaction with supervision (+.54), financial rewards (+.46), organizational commitment (+.42), kind of work (+.37), and amount of work (+.36). None of the measures correlated strongly with attendance among managerial employees who showed up for work on the same day at the company's New York office (where there had been no storm), and some had essentially *no* correlation.

This study is important because it represents a rare opportunity to examine the effects of work-related attitudes on specific behavior. During the average day, many factors affect an employee's likelihood of attendance, which means that the effects of attitudes are obscured. But the snowstorm made other factors less relevant and let the effects of job-related attitudes among these managerial employees come through clearly.

remaining stores. Among the remaining managers and sales clerks, the firing of coworkers had a noticeable impact: their commitment to the parent company declined, which affected the workers' effectiveness and productivity (Brockner et al., 1987).

Frequently, workers who survive a layoff feel guilty about their own relative good fortune and sorry for their fired coworkers (Brockner et al., 1986). This response to the misfortune of fellow workers demonstrates a basic truth about work groups and organizations. Organizations are social systems (Katz and Kahn, 1978), and social processes have a profound influence on work-related attitudes and behavior. The social contexts that surround us in the workplace largely determine even basic estimates about what might otherwise be considered factual or objective properties of our jobs (Salancik and Pfeffer, 1978). In fact, contemporary managers are learning to make their organizations more effective by viewing them as miniature cultures (Peters and Waterman, 1982), paying particular attention to the kinds of social influences in the workplace that I/O psychologists have been studying for years. Among the survivors in the retail stores, for example, the drop in organizational commitment was in line with the predictions of equity theory. Commitment declined most among workers who identified closely with their fired coworkers and believed that the company had poorly compensated their colleagues with severance pay, help in finding new jobs, and other services. When workers believed that the company's compensation had been generous, commitment declined only slightly (Brockner et al., 1987). This means that by taking adequate care of dismissed employees, the organization can soften the impact of layoffs on the commitment, motivation, and performance of survivors.

Many corporations have established quality of work life programs, which encourage employees to stay healthy and physically fit.

Leadership

The effect of layoffs on work groups is only one example of how social processes affect the work group. Another social process that I/O psychologists have explored extensively is leadership. The impact of leadership on an organization may be somewhat exaggerated in the public mind (Meindl, Ehrlich, and Dukerich, 1985). Yet managers do play a major role in shaping employees' attitudes and behavior, as well as in planning and directing work.

Approaches to the Study of Leadership

I/O psychologists have long been interested in the question of what makes a leader effective. There are four basic approaches to this question. The first emphasizes personal traits; the second, behavior; the third, situations. The fourth and newest approach considers various combinations of these factors.

THE TRAIT APPROACH The trait approach to studying leadership is based on the assumption that effective leadership depends on certain stable, enduring personal characteristics. This view reflects the common-sense notion that leaders are born, not made: "Some people can lead and some can't—regardless of how hard they try, how smart they are, or how many Dale Carnegie courses they have taken" (Howell and Dipboye, 1982, p. 128). Trait theory implies that the key to running a successful organization is *selection:* find the right managers and everything else will fall into place.

After a period of great popularity among I/O psychologists during the 1930s and 1940s, trait approaches fell out of favor. As researchers tried to identify the physical characteristics, personality traits, and abilities of "natural leaders," study after study found no strong and consistent correlation between individual traits and leadership effectiveness.

Once I/O psychologists realized that the search for individual traits was too simplistic, they began to find the connection they sought. The key was to look at the way specific traits interact and at how various situations can enhance or diminish the effectiveness of a leader's traits. Research now indicates that effective leaders are likely to be self-confident, emotionally stable, and able to tolerate stress, to have high energy levels and high initiative, and to display a lack of defensiveness (Yukl, 1989).

THE BEHAVIORAL APPROACH The behavioral approach to the study of leadership focuses on what managers do, not on who they are. This view is similar to the belief that leadership is a set of techniques for managing people that anyone can learn, and its adherents emphasize leadership *training.* Research on the behavioral approach has centered on styles of leadership.

Early studies distinguished between *democratic* and *autocratic* leadership. A democratic leader invites participation, sharing decisions with subordinates. An autocratic leader wants no input: the boss's word is law. When it was first described, democratic leadership was hailed as the modern, enlightened approach to management. However, it has not lived up to these promises (Howell and Dipboye, 1982).

John Hemphill, Ralph Stogdill, and their colleagues (1963) have proposed a somewhat different view of leadership styles. According to these psychologists, the most significant difference is between *task-oriented* leadership and *people-oriented* leadership. Task-oriented managers are concerned with production, so they devote most of their time and energy to planning, assigning tasks, and supervising production. Achieving organizational goals comes first; people come second. People-oriented managers give priority to establishing mutual trust, respect, and rapport with subordinates. Later research indicates that the best leaders rank high on both aspects: they place high priority on organizational goals *and* on the people who carry them out.

Task-oriented leaders emphasize production goals, focusing on the tasks performed by their subordinates rather than on the subordinates themselves.

THE SITUATIONAL VIEW According to a third view, the identity of the leader (personality traits) and what he or she does (behavior) have less impact on the effectiveness of a leader than does the *situation:* the nature of the task, the organization, and the work group. The success of a business depends on economic trends, not on who occupies executive positions or how the executives run the company (Lieberson and O'Connor, 1972). The record of a major-league baseball team reflects the skill of the players, not the effectiveness of the manager (Allen, Panian, and Lotz, 1979). This approach echoes the saying, "Anyone can win with a winner; no one can win with a loser" (Howell and Dipboye, 1982, p. 128).

The situational view is a useful antidote to the popular view that everything depends on the individual in charge. It balances trait and behavior approaches, which may overemphasize the effects of leadership. But the majority of I/O psychologists think that developing a "leaderless" theory is equivalent to throwing out the baby with the bathwater. Today, the theories that attract the most interest are those that consider the interaction of several factors.

CONTINGENCY THEORIES Contingency theories are based on the view that effective leadership is contingent on (depends on) particular combinations of leadership traits, behavior, and situations. Fred Fiedler's **cognitive resource theory** examines the interaction of situation, traits, and leadership style in producing effective group performance (Fiedler and Garcia, 1987). According to Fiedler, the situation determines how leadership style and such traits as intelligence, expertise, and experience are related to the performance of work groups. Situational variables include stress, group support, and complexity of the task. When stress is low, intelligence is important and leads to good decisions, while experience plays only a minor role. When stress is high, experience is important and leads to good decisions, while intelligence contributes nothing or leads to serious errors. When leaders are intelligent, a directive leadership style (in which leaders give top priority to completing a task) increases group performance, but when leaders' ability is low, participative leadership (in which leaders are nondirective and focus on good interpersonal relationships) becomes more effective. Fiedler's model is fairly new and has not been tested by research.

Other contingency theories emphasize factors that come from the group rather than situational factors. In **life-cycle theory**, proposed by Paul Hersey and Kenneth Blanchard (1988), the major factor becomes the ability to foster maturity and responsibility in group members. Over time, people develop and change, and with the proper experiences they become more competent and experienced, acquiring the capacity to handle discretion and responsibility. The key to good leadership is knowing the maturity level of subordinates and becoming aware of

COGNITIVE RESOURCE THEORY
a contingency theory of leadership that examines the interaction of situation, traits, and leadership style

LIFE-CYCLE THEORY a contingency theory of leadership that emphasizes leaders' ability to foster maturity and responsibility in group members

TABLE 23.1   Possible Leader Responses to a Problem: The Vroom-Yetton-Yago Leadership Model

AI	Autocratic: You make the decision alone.
AII	Autocratic: You obtain information from your subordinates, often without telling the subordinates about the problem. Then you make your own decision.
CI	Collective: You share the problem with subordinates individually, getting ideas and suggestions without bringing them together as a group. Then you make your own decision.
CII	Collective: You share the problem with your subordinates as a group, obtaining their collective ideas and suggestions. Then you make your own decision.
GII	Group: You share the problem with your subordinates as a group, generating and evaluating alternatives. Then the group makes the decision.

Source: Victor H. Vroom and Arthur G. Yago (1988), *The New Leadership*, Englewood Cliffs, NJ: Prentice-Hall.

VROOM-YETTON-YAGO MODEL a theory proposing that effective leadership depends on the selection of the appropriate approach—ranging from autocratic to collective to participatory—to a particular decision-making problem

their readiness for less task-oriented and directive leadership. Good leaders attempt to move their subordinates up the readiness scale by leading them in ways that allow them to develop such maturity. Many organizations subscribe to the life-cycle theory of leadership, although its scientific merits are not yet known.

Another leadership model, proposed by Victor Vroom and Philip Yetton (1973), assumes that the characteristics of effective leadership vary from one situation to the next. But unlike Fiedler, these researchers assume that leaders alter their style according to the problem at hand. The basic model has evolved into the **Vroom-Yetton-Yago model,** which provides managers with a practical procedure that helps them understand and resolve decision-making problems (Vroom and Yago, 1988). The procedure leads to one of five possible responses to a problem, as shown in Table 23.1. These responses range from unilateral, or autocratic, decisions (AI and AII), through collective decisions (CI and CII), to participatory decisions involving group members (GII). To identify the style of response that is most effective for a particular problem, the manager answers a series of questions that lead through the decision-making tree shown in Figure 23.5. One strength of this model is its specificity: the precise definitions embodied in it allow researchers to measure responses and outcomes in actual work settings. Research has generally supported the basic model; managers whose decisions are consistent with the model's recommendations generally have more success than managers whose decisions violate the model (Field, 1982; Heilman et al., 1984).

PATH-GOAL THEORY a contingency theory of leadership, based on expectancy theory, that proposes the leader's role is to influence the expectations of group members; clarifies the paths (members' behavior) that lead to desired goals (high-valance outcomes)

The **path-goal theory** of leadership, which was developed by Martin Evans and Robert House (Evans, 1970; House, 1971), also assumes that leaders can change their style to match the situation. The path-goal theory is based on expectancy theory, which we discussed earlier, and proposes that the leader's role is to influence the expectations of group members. By clarifying the paths (members' behavior) that lead to desired goals (high-valence outcomes), the leader can affect expectations and increase employees' motivation. The most appropriate leadership style depends on the situation (the structure of the task, the type of authority system, and the nature of the work group) and on the personal characteristics of the group members. Workers with a strong sense of personal control (see Chapter 20) can be motivated by a *participative leader,* one who consults them and considers their opinions. Workers who lack a sense of control and feel that outside forces determine outcomes are more likely to be motivated by a *directive leader,* one who lets them know what they are expected to do, as well as how and when to do it. When group members feel little support from their coworkers, a *supportive leader,* who shows a friendly concern for their well-being, is most effective. In some situations an *achievement-oriented leader,* who conveys confidence that the workers will perform at their peak level, can motivate the group.

Transformational Leadership

As researchers looked at modern organizations, it gradually became clear that existing views of leadership could not explain the radical changes and strong emo-

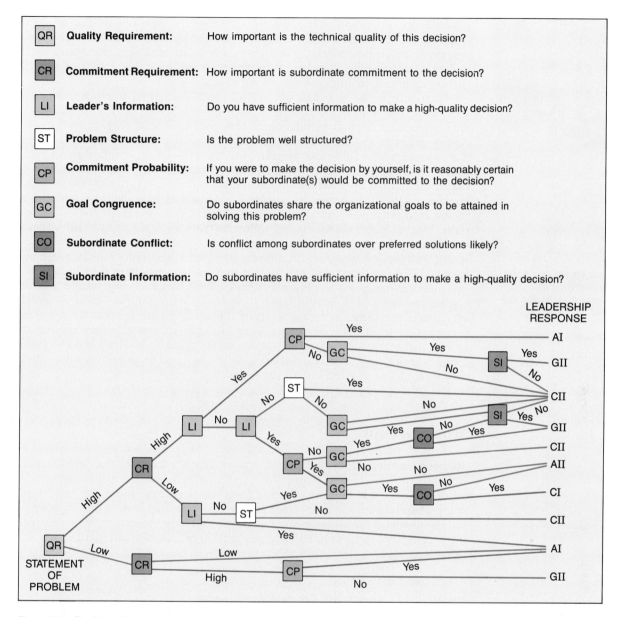

Figure 23.5 The Vroom-Yetton decision-making tree. Once a problem has been identified, a group leader can follow the various paths through this decision-making tree to arrive at the level of subordinate participation that is likely to be most effective (see Table 23.1). The model shown here is for group-level problems when time is important. Other models have been devised for use with group problems when time is less crucial and with individual problems when time is and is not important. (Reprinted from *The New Leadership* by Victor H. Vroom and Arthur G. Jago. Englewood Cliffs, NJ: Prentice-Hall, 1988. Used by permission of the authors.)

tions that some leaders induced in group members. When Chrysler Corporation was on the verge of bankruptcy in 1979, Lee Iacocca not only persuaded the federal government to guarantee $1.5 billion in loans to the company but also enlisted the enthusiastic support of Chrysler employees, convincing them to give back increases in wages and fringe benefits that they had won over years of collective bargaining. Iacocca thus provided **transformational leadership,** leadership that produces large-scale organizational change by changing the goals of group members and deepening their commitment. According to Bernard Bass (1985), transformational leaders (1) are charismatic, (2) provide individualized attention to subordinates, and (3) stimulate subordinates intellectually. Through their charisma, they arouse enthusiasm, trust, loyalty, and pride in group members and convey a sense of confidence that members can do more than they ever thought

TRANSFORMATIONAL LEADERSHIP leadership that produces large-scale organization change by changing the goals of group members and deepening their commitment; works through the leader's charisma, individualized attention to subordinates, and ability to stimulate them intellectually

Participative leaders are people-oriented, placing priority on consulting their subordinates and maintaining solid, trusting relationships with them.

possible. By providing individualized attention through one-on-one contact, transformational leaders discover what motivates each group member and how best to use his or her abilities. Through intellectual stimulation, transformational leaders arouse members' awareness of problems and how they might be solved, stirring their imagination and generating insights.

Charisma (from the Greek for "gift of grace") is central to transformational leadership, but it must be combined with the other two factors of individual attention and intellectual stimulation. Sociologist Max Weber (1947) gave the concept of charisma its present meaning, which refers to a leader's persuasive power that is based on the followers' *perceptions* of his or her extraordinary gifts (Yukl, 1989). Over the past twenty years, I/O psychologists have been systematically examining charisma—what it is and how it affects followers. In the view of Robert House (1977), a *charismatic leader* is a deeply self-confident person with a strong need for power and a conviction that his or her own ideals and beliefs are right. When a leader is charismatic, followers trust the correctness of the leader's beliefs, obey the leader willingly, feel affection for the leader (whose word they accept without question), are emotionally involved in the leader's goals, adopt the leader's beliefs as their own, believe that they can contribute to the group's success, and are motivated to perform at peak levels. Charisma is generally used to explain the accomplishment of leaders who head organizations—chief executive officers and presidents in the top strata of public and private sectors. A number of U.S. presidents—Roosevelt, Kennedy, and Reagan, for example—are considered to have had charismatic appeal. However, some researchers (Tichy and Devanna, 1986) believe that charismatic leaders are not restricted to the top echelon; they may be found at any level of an organization.

Work Groups

Without question, leadership affects a work group's attitudes and performance. But the group also exerts a strong influence on each member's behavior.

The workers in any organization form social groups, and as we saw in the study of layoffs among chain-store employees, what happens to one member of the group affects the attitudes and behavior of the other members. When analyzing the effects of the group, I/O psychologists have looked at internal and external influences.

Internal Influences on Group Effectiveness

If the members find that belonging to the group helps them achieve their goals, and if group members like one another, the group will be *cohesive;* that is, it will stay together. High cohesiveness stems from a number of factors, including the group's success in achieving its goals, the smallness of the group, group solidarity in response to external threats, and members' perceptions that they share similar beliefs, backgrounds, and other characteristics (Howell and Dipboye, 1982).

Members of highly cohesive groups help one another and credit the group for successes. But cohesive groups are not always productive. Members of highly cohesive groups share norms. If productivity is one of the group's strong norms, then the group will be productive; if the group rejects productivity as a norm, members' productivity will suffer.

External Influences on Group Effectiveness

As Americans, we assume that rewarding individual effort encourages even greater achievement. That may be true for individuals, but the opposite can happen for groups. If the group's task requires cooperation and interdependence, then a system that rewards individual effort will be counterproductive. Instead of working together, group members will compete with one another, spurred on by the promise of the biggest raise or bonus.

Stress is another powerful external influence on group effectiveness. In organizations, stress can come from within the company, as when one group competes with another for rewards or recognition. In this case, the external stress may increase cooperation among group members. If the group's task requires cooperation, such stress can lead to improved performance. But sometimes external stress causes too much cooperation within the group—with disastrous results. Members' strong wish to preserve the harmony of the group in the face of external stress leads them to avoid any kind of disagreement; as a result, they go along uncritically with whatever view they sense is emerging. This tendency, known as *groupthink*, says Irving Janis (1989), describes the conditions surrounding President John F. Kennedy's decision in 1961 to help anti-Castro rebels invade Cuba by way of the Bay of Pigs. The invasion was a disaster, both for the United States and for Kennedy personally. How could such an intelligent president have approved a plan, put forth by a group of his top advisers, that in retrospect seemed doomed to failure?

Janis's research into the decision-making processes behind the Bay of Pigs and other international foreign-policy fiascos suggests that groupthink contributes heavily to such miscalculations. Groupthink helps a highly cohesive group—such as Kennedy's advisers—maintain its cohesiveness under the pressure of external threats. Janis (1989) believes that groupthink arises when members become dependent on the group for maintaining their self-esteem and for coping with the stresses of policymaking. They are so intent on preserving the group's harmonious atmosphere that they avoid raising controversial issues, questioning weak arguments, or voicing their doubts. Members generally share the illusion that their own organization is invulnerable and that the group's goals are always morally justified. Their views of outside groups are stereotyped, and they use their intelligence to rationalize the group's consensus instead of examining its costs and risks.

Although Janis's theory has been criticized (Etheredge, 1985), it does suggest that when group members suspend their ability to think critically and independently, the group's decision-making ability is compromised.

Lee Iacocca, a prominent example of transformational leadership.

Other Aspects of Group Effectiveness

Group effectiveness may also depend on a number of other factors, such as its size and its homogeneity. One additional aspect of group influence that has been investigated by I/O psychologists is the *quality circle*, which has been a strong feature of Japanese organizations since the early 1960s. A quality circle consists of a small group of employees who meet regularly to identify problems in their sector of the company, to suggest solutions, and to present them to management. Many U.S. companies, including Control Data, Honeywell, Hughes Aircraft, Lockheed, Martin Marietta, and Motorola, have used quality circles with some success (Miner, 1988). The companies report savings through greater efficiency, reduced overtime, and less absenteeism. For example, Hughes Aircraft reports that quality circles have led to improvement in product quality, service, job performance, safety, working conditions, company morale, and productivity (Sasaki and Hutchins, 1984). Yet some quality circles have been failures and others only qualified successes. Research indicates that they can improve performance, but that getting the circles started is a lengthy and expensive process (Miner, 1988).

A second way in which I/O psychologists have attempted to use group processes to enhance productivity is with the *self-managing work group*. The degree of autonomy granted a self-managing work group varies from one organization to another. Within these small groups, members may set group goals for productivity and quality, decide what methods they will use, distribute tasks within the group, and set their own working hours. Self-managing groups reduce costs, because fewer managers are required. In some organizations, the groups have increased productivity, quality, or job satisfaction and have reduced employee turnover, absenteeism, or accidents. These improvements have been attributed to increased industrial democracy, but since the degree of self-management varies so widely, its effects are still unclear (Miner, 1988).

Workers at an American plant owned by Nissan, a Japanese automobile manufacturer, meet in a "quality circle."

A third feature that has attracted the interest of I/O psychologists is the *two-tiered wage structure,* in which new employees earn salaries that are substantially lower than those of employees who were hired under the terms of an earlier union contract. This means that two employees with the same job title and the same responsibilities receive different salaries for similar work. Some studies (Martin and Peterson, 1987) indicate that group members respond to the two-tiered structure just as equity theory would predict. Among employees at a chain of supermarkets, those hired at the new, lower wage saw the system as unfair, while longtime employees saw themselves as slightly advantaged. Their perception of unfairness made new employees less committed to the organization than longtime employees.

These new areas of study have given I/O psychologists opportunities to extend and apply their knowledge in real-life settings. As research into factors contributing to group effectiveness continues, we will learn more about how to organize more efficient and productive workplaces.

SUMMARY

The Birth and Development of Industrial/Organizational Psychology

■ Industrial psychology has its roots in three separate movements: industrial engineering, personnel psychology, and the human relations movement.

■ As the field of industrial psychology broadened to include the entire organizations as well as the individuals within them, its name was changed to industrial/organizational (I/O) psychology.

Matching Workers to Jobs

■ On the whole, intelligence tests that measure various job-related abilities are fairly good predictors of job performance.

■ Unless tests have predictive validity, their use in hiring may be considered discriminatory if they have an adverse impact on minorities.

■ Interviews are generally poor predictors of performance because of the way the characteristics of interviewer, applicant, and situation interact.

Work Motivation

■ Work motivation affects how long employees stay with a company, how dependably they perform their duties, and how innovative they are on the job.

■ Need theories of work motivation relate job performance to the strength of various psychological needs.

■ Expectancy theory is a cognitive theory that sees work motivation as determined by the interaction of valence, instrumentality, and expectancy.

■ Equity theory is a cognitive theory that sees workers as experiencing cognitive dissonance when they feel overrewarded or underrewarded and as motivated to reduce the resulting tension.

■ Goal-setting theory is a cognitive theory that sees workers as motivated by conscious intentions to reach specific goals.

- Reinforcement theory applies instrumental conditioning in the workplace to increase workers' productivity.

Work-Related Attitudes

- Job satisfaction reflects the match between what workers want from a job and what they get.
- The relationship between job satisfaction and performance is apparently circular, with the perception of good performance initiating the cycle.
- Employees who are committed to their organization display helpful and cooperative behaviors at work.

Social Influences at Work

- The trait approach to leadership assumes that effective leadership depends on stable, enduring personal characteristics, such as self-confidence, high energy and initiative, and a lack of defensiveness.
- The behavioral approach to leadership sees leadership as a set of techniques for managing people that can be learned.
- The situational approach to leadership sees the leader's traits and behavior as less important to his or her effectiveness than the nature of the work situation.

- Among contingency theories, Fiedler's cognitive resource theory sees the situation as determining what traits and leadership style will be effective.
- Life-cycle theory sees effective leadership as knowing how to help subordinates develop maturity and assume responsibility.
- The Vroom-Yetton-Yago leadership model assumes that effective leaders must be able to change their decision-making style to meet the demands of the situation.
- The path-goal theory assumes that effective leaders are able to influence the expectancies of group members, and that the most effective leadership style is a function of the situation and the personal characteristics of group members.
- Transformational leadership can be accomplished by leaders with charisma who give subordinates individualized attention and stimulate them intellectually.
- Cohesiveness, an internal influence on groups, affects productivity through group norms.
- Individualized rewards, an external influence on groups, can disrupt a group's cooperative efforts.
- Stress, an external influence on groups, can enhance cooperation but it can also lead to groupthink, compromising the group's ability to make critical decisions.

KEY TERMS

adverse impact	industrial/organizational psychology	path-goal theory
cognitive resource theory	job satisfaction	reinforcement theory
equity theory	life-cycle theory	scientific management
expectancy theory	organizational commitment	transformational leadership
goal-setting theory		Vroom-Yetton-Yago model

CONCEPT REVIEW

1. Describe the kinds of research and applications involved in the field of industrial/organizational psychology.

2. Which type of psychological test appears to have the greatest value in predicting worker performance? Which tests have the lowest predictive validity? Name and describe the various kinds of job-performance tests discussed in the chapter.

3. Describe the value of an interview in the employee-selection process. What difficulties may an interview cause?

4. How are Maslow's and McClelland's need theories of motivation applied specifically to work motivation?

5. Describe the expectancy, equity, and goal-setting theories of work motivation. What value does each of these cognitive theories have in predicting worker performance?

6. How successfully has reinforcement theory been applied to the workplace?

7. What are some determinants of job satisfaction? How do these relate to job performance?

8. What is organizational commitment, and what kinds of steps might an I/O psychologist recommend to increase it?

9. Describe the various theoretical approaches to understanding leadership.

10. How does a quality circle improve the productivity of an organization? What other means of improving productivity have been studied?

CRITICAL THINKING

1. Quite a few areas of psychology contribute to I/O psychology. Identify these areas and the kinds of contributions they make. If a company wanted to improve worker productivity, what kinds of recommendations could a physiological or perceptual psychologist make? What recommendations could psychologists in other areas make?

2. Operant and classical conditioning theories seem to be very important in I/O psychology. Why is this the case?

... *Using Statistics in Research*

When researchers test a hypothesis, whether by experimental or nonexperimental methods (see Chapter 2), they may end up with masses of observations that mean little in themselves. How do researchers deal with a stack of unanalyzed findings? And how do they figure out whether their experiment has confirmed or refuted their hypothesis? They must tackle the task of reducing their observations to manageable and intelligible form. To do so, they employ analytical procedures drawn from the field of statistics.

One basic statistical procedure involves assembling, classifying, tabulating, and summarizing facts or data to present relevant information about a specific subject in an unambiguous and precise fashion. Using this approach, researchers can reduce large accumulations of data to numbers that are simpler and more informative.

STATISTICS: THE BASICS

The first step may be simply to summarize data collected for a sample or a population, to come up with a number known as a descriptive statistic. Your grade point average (GPA) is one example: it is a descriptive statistic that summarizes the results of your past academic efforts. Similarly, the results of the latest Gallup poll summarize public attitudes toward the president's policies. Using these statistics, investigators can say something meaningful about their findings with a few words and figures.

Psychologists often use statistics to describe the behavior of a group in which a single variable is being studied. Suppose you are studying memory, and you want to test the hypothesis that the more time that elapses after a person commits a series of items to memory, the more items that person will forget. Your hypothesis, in other words, is that delay increases forgetting.

Let's say that you design an experiment in which subjects will memorize a list. Your independent variable is the time interval (number of minutes) between the time when your subjects originally learn the list and the time when you ask them to recall it; you suspect that if you change this time interval, your subjects' behavior will change. You recruit 120 students, bring them into the psychology lab, and give them a list of a dozen words to learn. After they have learned the list, you test half of them immediately and the other half 1 hour later.

Your impression is that the students in your second group, which you have called the Delayed Recall group, have forgotten more words than the first group, which you have called the Immediate Recall group. But your impressions or "hunches" are not enough: saying that one group seems to have done better than another is just a beginning. Without greater precision, you will not be able to

Number of Errors	IMMEDIATE RECALL GROUP Frequency	DELAYED RECALL GROUP Frequency
0	2	0
1	7	0
2	15	0
3	27 Mode	1
4	5	3
5	2	2
6	1	6
7	0	11
8	1	23 Mode
9	0	9
10	0	4
11	0	1
12	0	0

Figure A.1 Memory experiment: frequency distribution table.

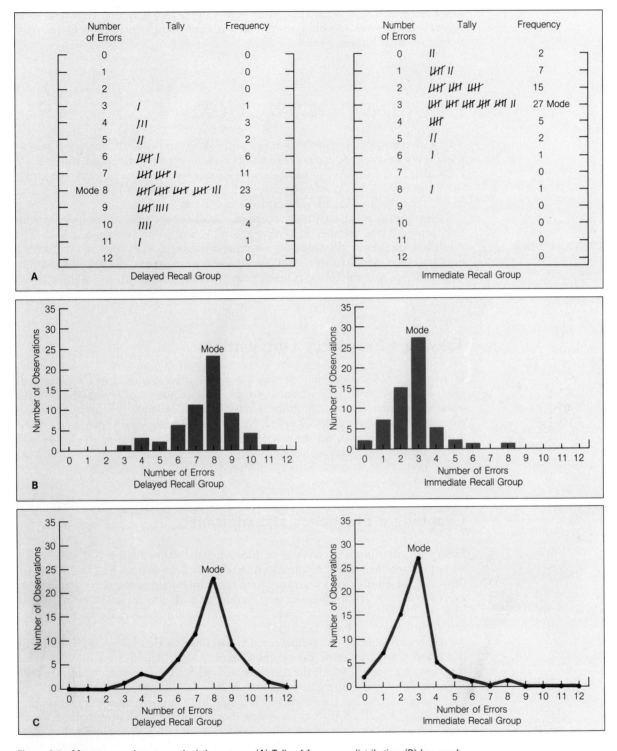

Figure A.2 Memory experiment: graphed three ways. (A) Tally of frequency distribution, (B) bar graph of frequency distribution, and (C) frequency polygon.

compare your results with those of other experimenters on a similar problem, with results from a related study that has been done in the past, or with results you may get in the future.

You want to know whether delay really does increase forgetting or, conversely, whether the lower recall in the delayed condition was simply due to chance, as when you flip a coin five times and happen to obtain heads all five times. How can you summarize your observations in a way that tells you—and others—the answer to this question at a glance? You may decide to set up a frequency distribution.

FREQUENCY DISTRIBUTION

To create a frequency distribution for your observations in the memory experiment, your first step is to count the number of subjects in each group whose score is 0—that is, the number of subjects who have forgotten 0 items. You then count the number of subjects whose score is 1 (the number who have forgotten one item), then the number of subjects whose score is 2, and so on.

Next you draw up a table to record the number of subjects in each group who have scored 0, the number who have scored 1, and so on (see Figure A.1). The result is a **frequency distribution**—a representation that shows the relationship between the scores themselves and the *frequency* you have observed (the number or percentage of subjects who make each score).

FREQUENCY DISTRIBUTION a representation that shows the relationship between responses and the observed frequency of those responses

Tallying a Frequency Distribution

Figure A.2 shows a number of ways in which your results can be described. Figure A.2A shows a tally of both groups. The frequency distribution you have made shows that most of the Immediate Recall group made fewer than four errors, whereas most of the Delayed Recall group made more than five errors. Already it is clear that, on the whole, there were fewer errors in the Immediate Recall than in the Delayed Recall group.

Graphing a Frequency Distribution

Frequency distributions can also be plotted graphically. Figure A.2 shows two ways to graph the frequency distribution table we have just set up. The scores (in this case, the number of words forgotten) are plotted along the horizontal, or X, axis (also known as the *abscissa*). The frequency with which each score was made (the number of students who made each score) is plotted along the vertical, or Y, axis (also known as the *ordinate*).

One way to graph the frequency distribution is with a *histogram*, in which a bar graph is used to show the scores (Figure A.2B). Another method is with a *frequency polygon*, in which the distribution is plotted with points, which are then connected to form a line graph (Figure A.2C).

The histogram and the frequency polygon both confirm your impression that the Delayed Recall group has forgotten more words than the Immediate Recall group. And these graphs allow you to see the results a bit more clearly than your table or the tally did: unlike the table, they show the shape of the distribution.

One characteristic of a distribution is its degree of symmetry. When the results form a *symmetrical distribution*, the polygon or graph does not "lean" or "hang out" to one side or the other. Instead, each side is close to being a mirror image of the other. What causes this symmetry? It may result from the action of some variable—or it may be the result of chance. When, however, the polygon does "hang out" markedly in one direction or the other, a statistician would say you had a *skewed distribution*. One "tail" of the distribution is considerably longer than the other: more subjects have obtained scores at the extreme end of one side of the graph than at the extreme end of the other side.

MEAN

DELAYED RECALL GROUP

IMMEDIATE RECALL GROUP

3 + 4 + 4 + 4 + 5 + 5 + 6 + 6

+ 6 + 6 + 6 + 6 + 7 + 7 + 7 + 7 +

7 + 7 + 7 + 7 + 7 + 7 + 7 + 7

+ 8 + 8 + 8 + 8 + 8 + 8 + 8 +

8 + 8 + 8 + 8 + 8 + 8 + 8 + 8

+ 8 + 8 + 8 + 8 + 8 + 8 + 8 +

8 + 9 + 9 + 9 + 9 + 9 + 9 + 9

+ 9 + 9 + 10 + 10 + 10 + 10 +

11 = 454

0 + 0 + 1 + 1 + 1 + 1 + 1 + 1

+ 1 + 2 + 2 + 2 + 2 + 2 + 2 +

2 + 2 + 2 + 2 + 2 + 2 + 2 + 2

+ 2 + 3 + 3 + 3 + 3 + 3 + 3 +

3 + 3 + 3 + 3 + 3 + 3 + 3 + 3

+ 3 + 3 + 3 + 3 + 3 + 3 + 3 +

3 + 3 + 3 + 3 + 3 + 3 + 4 + 4

+ 4 + 4 + 4 + 5 + 5 + 6 + 8 =

162

$$\text{Mean} = \frac{\text{Sum of scores}}{\text{Number of scores}} = \frac{454}{60}$$

$$\text{Mean} = \frac{\text{Sum of scores}}{\text{Number of scores}} = \frac{162}{60}$$

Mean = 7.566 = 7.6

Mean = 2.7

MEDIAN AND MODE

DELAYED RECALL GROUP

IMMEDIATE RECALL GROUP

3, 4, 4, 4, 5, 5, 6, 6, 6, 6, 0, 0, 1, 1, 1, 1, 1, 1, 1, 2,

6, 6, 7, 7, 7, 7, 7, 7, 7, 7, 2, 2, 2, 2, 2, 2, 2, 2, 2, 2,

7, 7, 7, 8, 8, 8, 8, 8, 8, 8, 2, 2, 2, 2, 3, 3, 3, 3, 3, 3,

8, 8, 8, 8, 8, 8, 8, 8, 8, 8, 3, 3, 3, 3, 3, 3, 3, 3, 3, 3,

8, 8, 8, 8, 8, 8, 9, 9, 9, 9, 3, 3, 3, 3, 3, 3, 3, 3, 3, 3,

9, 9, 9, 9, 9, 10, 10, 10, 10, 3, 4, 4, 4, 4, 4, 5, 5, 6, 8

11

Median = Exact center score = 8   Median = Exact center score = 3

(Because there are an even number of subjects in each group, the median falls halfway between the two circled central scores)

Mode = Most frequent score. In the Delayed Recall group, 23 subjects made 8 errors, and in the Immediate Recall group, 27 subjects made 3 errors.

Mode = 8   Mode = 3

Figure A.3 Measures of central tendency.

MEASURES OF CENTRAL TENDENCY

Psychologists also want to know about the group's overall performance: the performance, scores, or characteristics of *many* or *most* of the subjects in an investigation. How many words, *on the average*, does a person forget when immediately recalling a list? What is the income of the *typical* college graduate? How many children does the *average* woman plan to have? Here we loosely use the terms "typical" and "average," but we need a way to be more precise about such statements. We need a mathematical way to describe the distribution—a single number that will characterize or sum up the distribution.

There are several ways to summarize a frequency distribution. One way is to obtain a **measure of central tendency**—a number that represents the middle of the distribution—and use this measure to characterize the group as a whole. (When we talk about the "middle," we are speaking in terms of averages.)

The psychologist may choose one of three different measures of central tendency—the *mode,* the *mean,* or the *median*—depending partly on how the scores are distributed (see Figure A.3).

MEASURE OF CENTRAL TENDENCY   a descriptive statistic that represents the middle of a distribution of responses—the mode, mean, or median

The Mode

MODE   the score that most frequently appears in a distribution

The **mode** is the highest point of a distribution on a polygon: it is the score that the largest number of subjects have made, or the value that is most frequently obtained. In your Delayed Recall group, the mode, or number of errors most frequently made, was 8; in the Immediate Recall group the mode was 3. Thus, when you use this measure of central tendency to look for "middle" scores in both of your experimental groups, you find some support for your hypothesis: the Delayed Recall group seems to have made more errors.

The mode is useful when we are studying qualitative variables, such as mood state, marital status, and psychopathological diagnosis. The mode of a frequency distribution can also give us a rough idea of whether the shape of the distribution is symmetrical or lopsided. If the mode is very much closer to the extreme of a distribution than to the center, then the distribution is lopsided, or skewed.

But the mode is rarely used as a statistical measure. It is only a rough estimate of the distribution's center: it merely tells us which score or category is most frequent—and little else.

The Mean

MEAN   the arithmetic average of a distribution of scores

A more precise measure of central tendency is the **mean,** which is the arithmetic average of the distribution of scores. The mean, in contrast to the mode, can be expressed in fractions or percentages if necessary.

The mean is found by adding all the scores and then dividing the sum by the number of people who took the test (see the accompanying box). In your study of forgetting, the mean of the Delayed Recall group was 7.6 and the mean of the Immediate Recall group was 2.7; these results again support your hypothesis. Note that the *mean* of the Delayed Recall group happens to be 7.6 errors, quite close to the *mode* of 8 errors. And the same is true of the Immediate Recall group—their *mean* of 2.7 errors also happens to be close to their *mode* of 3 errors. But the mean, as we have noted, is usually a more precise measure than the mode.

The mean is the measure of central tendency most used by psychologists. But it is inappropriate in some instances: it is sensitive to extreme scores, so it can be misleading when the distribution is highly skewed. If one score is extremely high (or extremely low), this unusual score can "pull" the mean away from representing the more truly typical scores.

WORKING WITH STATISTICS

Calculating the Mean

The mean is equal to the sum of the scores divided by the number of observations. Conventionally, we abbreviate "sum of the scores" by ΣX, where Σ is the Greek capital letter sigma, meaning "sum," and X is a given score, such as 3 errors, a heart rate of 65 beats per second, or an IQ of 118. The number of observations that are being summed is designated by N. Thus,

$$\text{Mean} = \frac{\Sigma X}{N}$$

The Median

One way to eliminate the problem of skewing is to find the median. The **median** divides the entire distribution into halves: when all the scores of a distribution are arranged from highest to lowest, the median falls in the exact center. The median is a useful measure of central tendency in a distribution where a few extreme scores cause the mean to be "pulled away" from the center.

Medians are often used in reporting average incomes: a few large incomes can inflate the estimate for the mean, but they will have no effect on the median. In your study, the median of the Delayed Recall group was 8, while that of the Immediate Recall group was 3.

All three measures of central tendency told you something about the performance of both groups in your experiment—and in an efficient way. Among the subjects in your Delayed Recall group, there was a considerable amount of forgetting (7.6 words, on the average), as compared with the Immediate Recall group (2.7 words, on the average). You can consider these two means as representative of the performance of the two groups.

But how well does the mean of each group represent the performance of the "typical" subject in that group? Are most subjects in each group fairly close to that group's mean, or are many of them relatively far from it? To answer that question, you will have to consider the dispersal, or variability, of scores in each group.

MEDIAN the score that falls in the exact middle of a distribution, when all scores are arranged from highest to lowest

MEASURES OF VARIABILITY

Variability refers to the way in which an entire set of scores spreads out from the mean or median. Sometimes scores are clustered closely around the center; if so, the distribution is said to have a *low variability*. At other times they are widely spread out—in which case the distribution is said to have a *high variability*.

Suppose you give your list of words to a third group of sixty subjects, and in this group the scores turn out to be tightly clustered: twenty-five people have forgotten seven words and thirty-five have forgotten eight words. When you add these scores and divide by 60, you will find that this group has a mean that is identical to the mean of your original Delayed Recall group (7.6). But in this third group, the mean predicts the performance of the average subject much better than it does in your Delayed Recall group. The prediction is more accurate because the variability of the new group is much smaller.

VARIABILITY the degree to which a group of responses spreads out from the mean or median

The Range

RANGE   the difference between the smallest and the largest scores in a statistical distribution

Psychologists use several different measures of variability. The simplest is the **range** of scores, which is calculated by subtracting the lowest score from the highest. In your original study, the Delayed Recall group had a range of 8 points (from 3 to 11). In your new group, in which twenty-five subjects forgot seven words and thirty-five forgot eight words, the range is much narrower—only 1 (from 7 to 8). If you know the mean and the range of scores, you have some idea of how representative the mean is in describing individual scores, and that is what measures of variability provide for the psychologist.

However, the range is not always an accurate measure of variability because it reflects only two scores from the entire group. Suppose two businesses each have ten employees. In the first business, eight employees each make $50,000 annually; the ninth employee makes $20,000 and the tenth makes $80,000. In the second business, the mean salary is the same: one employee makes $20,000, one makes $80,000, two make $30,000, two make $40,000, two make $60,000, and two make $70,000. The range of salaries in both businesses is the same, $60,000. Yet it is clear that there is less variability in the first business, where all but two of the salaries fall close to the mean, so the range does not tell us enough to give us a clear picture of the distribution.

The Standard Deviation

STANDARD DEVIATION (S.D.) the preferred measure of variability; it shows how much figures in a given set of data vary from the mean

To deal with problems like the one we have just described, psychologists and other scientists often use another measure that takes into account every score in the distribution: the **standard deviation (S.D.).** To find the standard deviation, we take each score's distance from the mean and square that distance—so that we have a positive number that will not cancel out any of the other scores. After adding the squared differences, we divide that sum by the number of scores, and then take the square root of the answer (see the accompanying box). We now have a precise mathematical way of describing the degree to which the scores cluster around the mean. For the Delayed Recall group, the standard deviation calculated in this manner is 1.57 words forgotten, and for the Immediate Recall group, the standard deviation is .96 word forgotten.

NORMAL CURVES

NORMAL CURVE OF DISTRIBUTION a bell-shaped, symmetrical distribution, in which mean, median, and mode are the same

The standard deviation is an important determinant of the shape of the famous "bell-shaped curve"—a distribution you have probably seen in graphs of such data as the heights of American people, their incomes, or their educational levels. The "bell-shaped curve," more scientifically known as the **normal curve of distribution,** is a curve that often results when large amounts of data are plotted. For example, imagine that instead of recruiting 120 subjects for your experiment in memory, you recruited thousands. Then imagine that you repeated the experiment on these thousands of subjects hundreds of times, using hundreds of different twelve-word lists. After averaging each subject's performance on all the lists, you would have several thousand scores in your frequency distribution. With so many scores, there would be many more distinctive points to plot on the horizontal axis. For example, you would have some subjects who forgot, on the average, 0.34 item; others who forgot 11.58 items; and still others who obtained many other scores. You would have a much smoother curve than either of the frequency polygons in Figure A.2C. Large numbers of observations are more reliable and more systematic than small numbers. For example, 1000 tosses of a coin are more likely to generate a 50–50 split between heads and tails than 10 tosses.

When all the data from your new experiment are entered on a frequency polygon, the distribution would form a smooth, symmetrical bell-shaped curve,

WORKING WITH STATISTICS

How To Find the Standard Deviation

Ascertaining the standard deviation is not difficult, although it is tedious to compute without the aid of a calculator. To find the standard deviation:

1. Determine the mean of the scores.
2. From each score, subtract the mean and square the difference. (Scores are squared to eliminate the negative signs that result when dealing with scores that fall below the mean.)
3. Add the squares together.
4. Divide the sum by the number of scores.
5. Take the square root of the value you have obtained. This figure is the standard deviation.

A more succinct way to put it is to translate the formula for finding the standard deviation into words:

Standard deviation =

$$\sqrt{\frac{\text{sum of } (\text{score} - \text{mean})^2}{\text{number of scores}}}$$

This translates into the equation for the standard deviation:

$$\text{SD} = \sqrt{\Sigma(X - M)^2/N}$$

where (as previously) X is any score, N is the total number of observations, M is the mean, and Σ is the symbol that indicates that we should sum the quantities in the parentheses (that is, we take each score, subtract the mean, square the obtained difference, and add them all up).

The standard deviation for the Delayed Recall group, calculated according to the procedure we have described, is 1.57 items forgotten. In the Immediate Recall group it is .96 item.

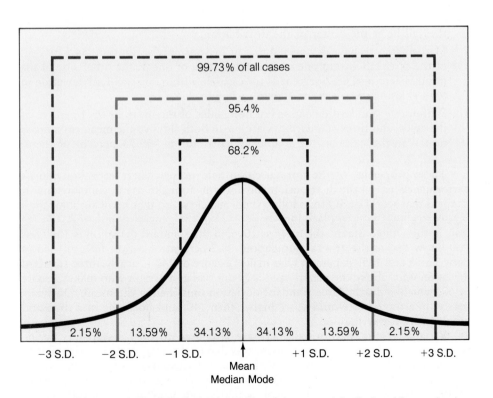

Figure A.4 The curve of normal distribution (normal curve). In a normal distribution of frequencies the mean, the median, and the mode all fall at the middle of the distribution. Do not be deceived into thinking that every standard deviation comprises 34.1 percent of the cases. As we count deviations away from the mean they comprise fewer and fewer cases. The second standard deviation comprises only 13.6 percent of the observations.

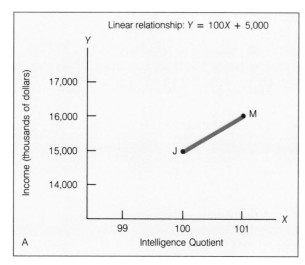
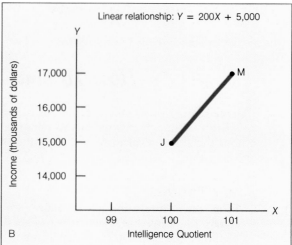

Figure A.5   Linear relationships.

the normal curve of distribution (see Figure A.4). The normal curve is a theoretical curve that represents an infinite number of cases, and it is important because it reliably reflects the distribution of many characteristics of life. If we plotted the IQs, vocabulary, or running speed of the American people, in each case our data would form a normal curve.

Every normal curve reflects certain unvarying relationships among the mean of the distribution, its standard deviation, and the number of observations, cases, or scores in the distribution.

1.   The mean, median, and mode are all at the same point on a normal curve, and they all lie at the center of the distribution.

2.   Mathematicians have discovered that in any normal distribution, 34.1 percent of the cases fall within one standard deviation of one *or* the other side of the mean. Therefore, 68.2 percent of the cases lie within one standard deviation of *both* sides of the mean, as shown in Figure A.4.

3.   Within *two* standard deviations of both sides of the mean lie 95.4 percent of the cases, and three standard deviations on both sides of the mean encompass nearly all the cases in the frequency distribution—99.73 percent of them.

These properties of the normal curve help us see where each individual's performance lies on the distribution and allow us to make useful comparisons. It happens that scores on IQ tests follow a normal curve, so that knowing someone's IQ score allows you to place him or her within the general population. On IQ tests in the United States, the mean is 100 and the standard deviation is 15. Thus you know that in the general population, 68.2 percent of people have IQ scores between 85 and 115. A person who makes a score of 140 is nearly three standard deviation units above the mean—and is as unusual as a person who makes a score of 60, which is nearly three standard deviation units below the mean. Only one person in a thousand would score higher than 140, and only one in a thousand would score lower than 60.

Variability and the normal curve are also used to help researchers decide whether the outcome of an experiment was due to the independent variable or to chance. For example, in the experiment we have discussed comparing delayed and immediate recall, are the differences we observed due to random variability (chance) or to the real effect of time of recall (the independent variable)? Researchers use the normal curve to calculate the probability of getting an obtained result by chance alone, using the assumption that there has been no effect of the independent variable. The assumption that the independent variable has had no effect is called the *null hypothesis*. If the probability is small of getting the observed results by chance alone (less than 5 times out of 100, or .05), the results are said to be "statistically significant." We would then reject the null hypothesis, and conclude instead that the independent variable did have an effect.

GRAPHING A LINEAR RELATIONSHIP AMONG VARIABLES

When we spoke in Chapter 2 about the independent and dependent variables, we noted that in most investigations, psychologists are interested in discovering how these two variables are related to each other. The relationship can usually be expressed mathematically.

Suppose you discover that for every 1 point increase in people's IQ scores, the income they earn is $1000 higher per year. You could draw this relationship in a graph (see Figure A.5A). Algebraically, you could express this relationship as follows.

- Each person's IQ score can be represented by a distance on the X axis of the graph: the higher a person's IQ is, the farther out to the right on the X axis the point representing that person will lie.
- Each person's income can be represented by a distance on the Y axis of the graph: the more income a person makes, the higher up on the right on the Y axis will be the point representing that person.

So let us say that Jane Doe has an IQ of 100 and an income of $15,000 a year. We represent Jane Doe with point J on the graph. Mary Roe has an IQ of 101 and an income of $16,000 a year. We represent Mary Roe with point M on the graph. If we connect the two points with a line, we see that it is at a 45-degree angle, and its equation will be

$$Y = 100X + 5000$$

What if we find that for every added IQ point, a person's income increases $2000 a year instead of $1000? In this case, for every unit increase in Y, we will have two increases in X, so the equation will be

$$Y = 200X + 5000$$

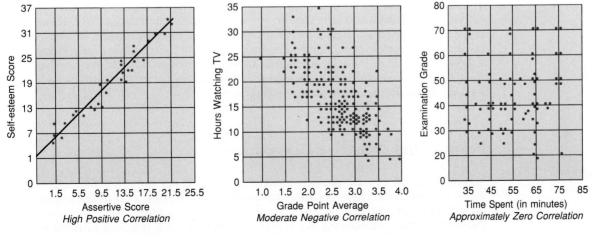

Figure A.6 Scatter plots showing three types of correlation. (From Spence et al., 1976.)

and the graph will look like Figure A.5B. This type of relationship is called a **linear relationship** (or **linear function**), because it can be represented graphically as a straight line.

Note, though, that not all relationships are this simple. There are some relationships in which, for every unit increase in one variable (such as IQ scores), there is no constant and predictable increase in the other variable. For example, if we measured a person's problem-solving performance on a test, we would find that as the person became more aroused (as his or her nervous system became more excited), his or her performance would improve—but only up to a point. When the person's arousal level rose higher than a certain point, his or her performance would deteriorate. As the person became excessively aroused, in other words, performance would suffer.

MEASURING CORRELATIONS

Setting Up a Scatter Plot

When researchers are studying a large number of observations, they sometimes use a scatter plot to organize the data (see Figure A.6). When using a **scatter plot**, the psychologist measures one variable on the horizontal axis and the other variable on the vertical axis; then, using a single point for each observation, he or she plots ratings on the two variables. The resulting figures are called "scatter plots" because they show how the points scatter over the range of possible relationships (Spence et al., 1976).

The Correlation Coefficient

The more closely the pattern of dots in a scatter plot approaches a straight line, the more we can detect a correlation, or linear relationship, between the two variables. The most common measure of correlation is the **correlation coefficient**, symbolized by the letter r. The correlation coefficient is a statistic that helps us estimate how well we can predict scores on the dependent variable on the basis of the independent variable—that is, how closely the two are related.

Suppose we want to know whether there is a relationship between intelligence and creativity. Let's say that we have found some highly intelligent people and have taken some measurements of their creativity. If all our highly intelligent people are also highly creative, there is the highest possible correlation, that is, a perfect correlation: r equals 1. If the two characteristics (intelligence and creativity) tend to appear together in most cases but by no means all, the correlation is not perfect, although it is still very high: r may be somewhere around .95. If the association is less close, there is a lower correlation and r will be smaller. If there is no discernible pattern of relationship between the two characteristics, r will equal 0. Some of our highly intelligent people are highly creative, some are somewhat creative, and some are totally uncreative, but there is no way of predicting a person's creativity from his or her intelligence.

Positive and Negative Correlation

When two variables (say, physical punishment by a parent and aggressive behavior by the child) change in the same direction, we say there is a **positive correlation** between them (indicated by a plus sign). The more physical punishment a parent uses, for instance, the more aggressive the child is. It is also possible to have a **negative correlation** between two variables: as one variable increases, the other decreases. Television watching and grade point average are an example: the *more* hours a student spends watching television, the *lower* his or her grade point average is likely to be.

The scatter plots in Figure A.6 illustrate three classes of correlation.

NEGATIVE CORRELATION a relationship between two variables in which a high rank on one measure is accompanied by a low rank on the other

- In the first scatter plot the points come close to forming a straight line that relates a person's self-esteem to his or her degree of assertiveness. The scatter plot shows a high positive correlation: we can see that a person's degree of self-esteem is highly correlated with his or her assertiveness—that is, there is a strong relationship between the two variables, so that the higher the self-esteem, the higher the assertiveness.

- In the second scatter plot, the points show a negative correlation, indicating that students who spend a lot of time watching TV tend to get low grades and those who watch little TV tend to get high grades. But notice that the points are much less perfectly aligned than in the first scatter plot: the correlation is only moderate.

- The third scatter plot shows the correlation between the length of time required to complete a test in introductory psychology and the student's grade on that test. In this case, the points wander all over the diagram, showing no relationship at all.

The Strength of a Correlation

The correlation coefficient has a possible range that stretches from -1, which indicates a perfect negative correlation between two variables; through 0, which indicates no correlation; to $+1$, which indicates a perfect positive correlation. The closer the correlation coefficient is to $+1$ or to -1, the greater the linear association between the two variables, so the more reliable our predictions will be from one variable to the other.

As we have noted, a perfect correlation (either $+1$ or -1) indicates that knowing one variable always allows you to predict the other with certainty. For example, if scores on a math test varied directly with IQ, in such a way that a test score of 125 would be gotten by people with an IQ of 125 and a test score of 105 would be gotten by people with an IQ of 105, there would be a perfect positive correlation (a correlation of $+1$) between test scores and IQ. In real life, of course, people with an IQ of 125 often do poorly and people with an IQ of 105 often do well; so the correlation—although positive—is not $+1$. A perfect correlation is not likely to exist between IQ scores and math test scores: you cannot predict with certainty what score a person will get on a math test by knowing his or her IQ.

Correlations come in all sizes, and few ever attain a perfect $+1$ or -1. For example, the correlation between the height of a parent and the height of the parent's child of the same sex is about $+.50$, which indicates a moderately strong relationship. The correlation between IQ scores and school grades is about $+.45$, also moderately strong. The correlation between physical punishment by a parent and physical aggression by the child is about $+.20$—positive but weak. When a correlation is 0, there is no relationship at all between two variables. For example, the correlation between shoe size and political beliefs is essentially 0.

Although some of the material in this appendix may have seemed esoteric, it lies at the heart of any progress in understanding human behavior. Even a general knowledge of the statistical methods psychologists use will deepen your understanding of the research presented in this book and will enable you to analyze it with a more critical eye.

SUMMARY

Statistics: The Basics

■ Researchers generally analyze data by means of statistics. Statistics reduce masses of data to simpler and more informative numbers.

Frequency Distribution

■ When the behavior of a group on a single variable is studied, a frequency distribution, or a representation showing the number of subjects who obtain each given score, is often used.
■ Frequency distributions may take the form of tables, histograms (bar graphs), or frequency polygons (line graphs).
■ A frequency distribution may be *symmetrical* or *skewed*.

Measures of Central Tendency

■ One way of summarizing a frequency distribution is by obtaining a measure of central tendency, which may be the mode, or most frequently obtained score; the mean or arithmetical average; or the median, or the score that falls in the exact middle of the distribution.

Measures of Variability

■ Measures of variability indicate how closely clustered the distribution of scores is.
■ The simplest measure of variability is the *range*, which is the difference between the highest and lowest scores.
■ More reliable is the standard deviation (S.D.), a value that indicates the extent to which figures in a given set of data "cluster" around the mean.

Normal Curves

■ In a normal curve of distribution, the mean, the median, and the mode fall at the same point, and the curve has a smooth bell shape.

Graphing Relationships among Variables

■ Most relationships between variables can be expressed mathematically.
■ A linear relationship can be represented graphically as a straight line.
■ A scatter plot shows how the points representing the researcher's observations scatter over the range of possible relationships between variables.

Measuring Correlations

■ Correlation coefficients show the extent to which a relationship between two variables can be predicted.
■ When two variables change in the same direction, there is a positive correlation between them; when one variable increases and the other decreases, there is a negative correlation.
■ A correlation coefficient is expressed as a number ranging from -1 (a perfect negative correlation) through 0 (no correlation at all) to $+1$ (a perfect positive correlation).

KEY TERMS

correlation coefficient
frequency distribution
linear relationship/linear function
mean
measure of central tendency

median
mode
negative correlation
normal curve of distribution

positive correlation
range
scatter plot
standard deviation (S.D.)
variability

Absolute Threshold the weakest stimulus a person can detect half the time

Accommodation (1) a reflexive change in the lens of the eye to bring into sharp focus objects at different distances; (2) the modification of existing schemes to incorporate new knowledge

Acetylcholine (ACh) a neurotransmitter that plays important roles in both the peripheral and central nervous systems, conveying messages to muscles and affecting learning and memory

Achievement Motive the need to attain some standard of excellence

Achievement Tests tests measuring learning in a given field

Acquisition (1) the process by which an association is learned in classical, or operant, conditioning; (2) attending to a stimulus and encoding it into memory

Action Potential a sudden positive change in electric charges inside a neuron that leads to the discharge of a neural impulse

Acuity sharpness of eyesight; the eye's ability to resolve (distinguish) lines and shapes

Adaptation a change in sensitivity in response to a constant, unchanging level of stimulation

Adolescent Growth Spurt a rapid increase in height and weight that accompanies puberty

Adverse Impact the discriminatory effect on minorities that occurs when a test results in the hiring of less than four-fifths of the number of majority applicants hired

Afterimage a sensory impression that persists after removal of a stimulus

Age-Irrelevant Society a society in which major life events, such as marriage, parenthood, and retirement, are not closely tied to specific chronological ages

Aggression any act intended to cause pain, damage, or suffering to another person

Agoraphobia an intense irrational fear of open places

All-or-Nothing Law the rule that a neuron either fires in response to stimulation or it does not

Ambiguity unclearness in meaning that occurs when two or more plausible interpretations of a sentence exist

Ambiguous Figure a figure that can be interpreted in at least two ways, because there is just as much information for one perception as for the other

Amnesia the partial or total loss of memory serious enough to be considered abnormal

Amplitude the intensity of a sound wave as determined by wave height; usually expressed in decibels (dB)

Amygdala a part of the limbic system that is involved in regulating fear, anger, and aggression as well as memory

Anal Stage (from about 18 months to three years) psychosexual stage when the anus is the primary source of sensual pleasure

Analogy a parallel or correspondence between two different systems whose parts are similar in some way

Anchoring making a judgment that is biased by the effect of the starting point from which a decision is made

Androgens male hormones

Androgynous having a self-concept that incorporates both masculine and feminine characteristics

Anterograde Amnesia the loss of the ability to lay down new long-term memories just after a brain injury or trauma

Anticipation a slip that inserts a later phoneme earlier than planned

Antisocial Personality Disorder see **sociopath**

Anvil one of the ossicles in the middle ear

Anxiety (1) in Freud's theory, the fear or apprehension that alerts the ego to danger; (2) a feeling of dread, apprehension, or fear, accompanied by heightened physiological arousal

Anxiety Disorder any disorder in which anxiety becomes so severe that it interferes with daily life

Aphasia a disruption in the ability to produce or understand language

Apparent Motion the perception of motion from a rapid succession of motionless images

Appraisal the cognitive interpretation of an event in terms of an individual's needs and desires; a central aspect of emotion

Approach-Avoidance Conflict a situation in which two motives clash, so that satisfying one frustrates the other

Aptitude Tests tests measuring stable abilities for reaching specific goals; tests for predicting future performance

Archetypes Jung's term for myths, dreams, symbols, and other ideas and images that are common to all human beings and that form the collective unconscious

Arousal physical excitement; the physiological changes that are part of emotion

Artificial Intelligence (AI) the science that develops computer programs that behave intelligently

Assimilation the incorporation of new knowledge into existing schemes

Association Areas parts of the brain that are responsible for the higher psychological functions, such as learning, remembering, planning, reasoning, and perceiving meaning

Associative Learning learning a correlation between two events

Atmosphere Effect in deductive reasoning, an error in which the presence of "some versus all" words in the premises suggests accepting invalid conclusions containing the same words

Attachment the emotional bond that develops between infant and caregiver, providing the infant with emotional security

Attitude an evaluative response to a particular object, idea, person, or group of people

Audience Inhibition normative influence of bystanders that inhibits response in an emergency

Auditory Cortex the area in the upper part of the temporal lobes that is responsible for receiving and analyzing sounds

Autistic Fantasy daydreams that lack any connection with reality; they occur in a state of consciousness removed from the normal waking state

Autogenic Training technique that induces relaxation by self-suggestion and imagery

Autonomic System the subdivision of the peripheral nervous system that affects heart rate, certain glandular secretions, and the activities of smooth muscles

Autonomy the feeling of self-control and self-determination

Availability a heuristic that relies on how easily relevant events are remembered

Aversion Therapy a behavioral therapy technique that relies on punishment and negative reinforcement

Aversive Conditioning the form of learning based on aversive stimuli, including escape learning, avoidance learning, and punishment learning

Avoidance Learning by responding in time to a warning signal, the learner avoids an unpleasant stimulus

Axon the nerve fiber between the dendrites and the terminal buttons that conducts nerve impulses away from the cell body to other neurons

Basal Metabolism Rate the rate at which calories are burned during rest

Basic Anxiety Horney's term for the anxiety that arises out of a child's sense of helplessness and isolation

Basic Hostility Horney's term for a child's hostility that arises in response to parental indifference, inconsistency, and interference

Basic Level Terms terms at the middle level of a concept hierarchy that provide the most information and are most efficient

Basic Needs the physiological needs in Maslow's hierarchy

Basilar Membrane the thin sheet of tissue in the cochlea to which are attached hair cells that are sensory receptors for sound

Behavior Therapy an approach to psychotherapy in which psychological problems are regarded as learned responses and the primary target of therapy is the problem behavior itself

Behavioral Self-Regulation monitoring and adjusting our own behavior in relation to our goals, values, standards, and concerns

Behaviorism a psychological school that focuses on observable, measurable behavior and asserts that learning is the key factor in human psychology

Biofeedback a technique for gaining control over physiological function by monitoring a continuous flow of information about the function

Biogenic Theory the theory that all abnormal behavior has a physical cause

Bipolar Disorder a mood disorder characterized by extreme moods of alternating depression and euphoria

Birth-Cohort Theory the theory that crowded birth groups increase the social and economic stress on their members, leading to an increase in stress-related disorders

Bisexual sexual attraction to members of both sexes

Blocking the process by which an organism fails to become conditioned to a second redundant stimulus presented simultaneously with an initially, more valid conditioned stimulus

Brain the master control center for all human activities

Brain Lateralization different capabilities developed in the right versus left hemispheres of the brain

Brain Stem the oldest part of the brain, located at the base of the skull, which regulates the basic bodily functions

Brainstorming a creative technique in which a group of people suggest unusual products or novel solutions in a situation free from criticism or ridicule

Cardinal Trait Allport's term for a single trait that dominates most of a person's acts

Case Study a method of collecting data in which researchers conduct an intensive investigation of an individual or small group, sometimes over a period of time

Catecholamine Hypothesis the view that depression is caused by low brain levels of norepinephrine and mania by high levels

Cell Body the part of a neuron that produces the energy needed to carry on its work

Central Nervous System the brain and the spinal cord

Central Route to Persuasion a message recipient's evaluation of the quality of the arguments presented in a persuasive communication

Central Traits Allport's term for habitual ways of dealing with the world that, together, dominate a person's personality

Cerebellum the part of the brain that is involved with posture, movement, balance, and fine motor control

Cerebral Hemispheres the two halves, right and left, of the cerebrum

Cerebrum the cerebral cortex and the tissue beneath it (divided into left and right cerebral hemispheres); the part of the brain that allows us to plan, learn, and reason

Chunk the larger clusters of information that we can recognize as a familiar pattern

Chunking the process by which the brain organizes incoming data into chunks

Circadian Rhythm a behavioral and physiological cycle that occurs over a roughly 24-hour period

Clang Association an illogical speech pattern characteristic of schizophrenics, in which words are used together simply because they rhyme or sound similar

Classical Conditioning the form of learning in which two stimuli are associated so that the first evokes the response that normally follows the second; also called Pavlovian conditioning

"Clever Hans" Phenomenon attributing more understanding to an animal than is warranted; Clever Hans was a horse who responded to his trainer's subtle cues, not to the sense of linguistic requests

Client-Centered Therapy a nondirective humanistic therapy that encourages people to clarify their feelings and value their experience

Clinical Psychologist a mental health professional who has completed a doctorate (Ph.D. or Psy.D.) in clinical psychology and a one-year clinical internship

Clinical Psychology the branch of psychology involving the study, diagnosis, and treatment of mental and behavior disorders

Cochlea a spiral, fluid-filled chamber in the inner ear

Cognition all the ways of using one's store of knowledge in order to plan something in the imagination, usually in the hope of solving a problem

Cognitive Behavioral Therapy an approach to behavioral therapy that places emphasis on the role of cognition in changing maladaptive behavior; an attempt to change the way people think about themselves and the world

Cognitive Dissonance an unpleasant state of arousal created when a person becomes aware of inconsistency among his or her beliefs or between his or her attitudes and behavior; motivates person to reestablish consistency by changing either attitude or behavior

Cognitive Map an integrated internal representation of the way objects and landmarks are arranged in the environment

Cognitive Perspective a psychological school that focuses on the process of thinking and knowing—cognition

Cognitive Resource Theory a contingency theory of leadership that examines the interaction of situation, traits, and leadership style

Cognitive Restructuring a cognitive behavioral technique that focuses on changing a person's perceptions and irrational assumptions of self and world

Cognitive Therapy a method of cognitive restructuring that helps people discover for themselves how inappropriate their thoughts have been

Common Ground the knowledge and context shared by discourse participants

Common Traits Allport's term for basic ways of dealing with the world that are seen to some degree in every person

Complementary Colors pairs of colors that can be mixed to produce gray or white (in the case of lights) or gray or black (in the case of paints)

Componential Intelligence in Sternberg's theory, the ability to process information

Compulsion an action that a person feels compelled to do, even though it is irrational

Concepts the ideas underlying categories for grouping items according to their shared properties

Concrete Operational Stage in Piaget's theory, the period from about seven to eleven years, when thought is flexible, rigorous, and logical, but only in regard to concrete symbols

Concurrent Validity a positive correlation between test scores and other measures

Conditional Positive Regard Roger's term for the withholding of love and praise when a child fails to meet parental or social standards

Conditioned Response (CR) a response that, through association, is evoked by the conditioned stimulus in anticipation of the unconditioned stimulus in classical conditioning

Conditioned Stimulus (CS) a formerly neutral stimulus that, through association, evokes a response normally evoked by the unconditioned stimulus in classical conditioning

Conditions of Worth Roger's term for extraneous standards whose attainment ensures positive regard

Cones photoreceptors (receptor cells) in the eye that are specialized for vision in bright light; convey information about color and fine details

Confirmation Bias in inductive reasoning, an error in which a generalization is tested by using only examples that can confirm it rather than seeking those that might disprove it

Conformity the tendency to shift one's views or behavior closer to social norms

Confounding Variable a factor that is one possible cause of a phenomenon and that interferes with the accurate measurement of the causal factor under study in an experiment

Conjunction Fallacy judging the joint probability of two events to be greater than the probability of the less-likely one

Consciousness all mental experiences, whether or not we are aware of them

Conservation Piaget's term for understanding that changes in the physical appearance of objects do not alter their weight, length, mass, or volume

Construct Validity measuring aspects of the theoretical construct that a test focuses on

Consulting the providing of expert advice, usually for a fee

Consumer Psychology the branch of psychology that studies consumers' preferences, buying habits, and responses to advertising

Content Validity covering a representative sample of whatever is being measured

Contextual Intelligence in Sternberg's theory, the ability to adapt to the world; practical intelligence

Continuous Reinforcement Schedule the pattern of reinforcement in which a reward follows each response

Contralateral Control the pattern of brain organization whereby the left side of the cortex controls the right side of the body, and vice versa

Control Condition the condition in an experiment that remains unchanged (is not manipulated) and that serves as a point of comparison for the experimental condition

Control Group the group of subjects in an experiment who are exposed to all the same factors as the experimental subjects *except* the experimental condition

Convergence the eyes' movement inward as they focus on objects close to the viewer

Conversion Disorder a physical dysfunction with no organic basis

Conversion Error in deductive reasoning, an error in which people believe that a premise and its converse are true; believing that "all A's are B's" implies that "all B's are A's"

Cooperative Principle assumptions regarding cooperation in language use implicitly agreed upon by speaker and listener

Coping the process of managing external and internal pressures in a way that diminishes stress

Cornea the curved, transparent surface at the front of the eye that helps focus light rays

Corpus Callosum a wide band of nerve fibers connecting the cerebral hemispheres

Correlation Coefficient a statistical calculation stating the degree of relationship between two variables; a perfect positive correlation is indicated by the coefficient $+1$; a perfect negative correlation is indicated by -1

Correlational Research studies that investigate the relationships between variables to determine whether they occur together at a rate significantly higher than would be expected to happen by chance

Cortex the outer layer of the cerebrum; the part of the brain most vital to our ability to think and reason

Counseling Psychology the subfield of clinical psychology that deals with less severe behavioral disorders and emotional problems

Counterbalancing a procedure for eliminating the effect of confounding variables by making sure that they are evenly distributed across the experimental and control conditions

Covariation of Events a state in which two events vary together so that as one changes, the other also changes (a condition for causality)

Covert Sensitization a behavioral therapy technique in which clients visualize unwanted behavior, then imagine a painful or revolting stimulus

Cross-sectional Study a study in which subjects are divided into subgroups on the basis of some variable, then each subgroup is assessed regarding one or more other variables

Crowding the psychological experience of distress that arises from the perception of restricted space

Crystallized Intelligence acquired knowledge, which does not decline with age

CT Scan (Computerized Tomography) a technique in which an x-ray is moved around the head, resulting in a cross-sectional look at the brain

Cyclothymia a mood disorder characterized by moderate moods of alternating depression and euphoria

Decay the degeneration of short-term memory traces due to the passage of time

Decoding pattern recognition for written words

Deductive Reasoning a form of logical reasoning in which we draw out the implications of some assumptions

Deep Structure a representation that exhibits the basic grammatical relations between subjects, verbs, and direct and indirect objects

Defense Mechanisms irrational techniques used by the ego to reduce anxiety—excluding the source from consciousness or distorting it

Deferred Imitation the ability to mimic observed actions after a lapse of time

Delusion an irrational belief that is maintained despite overwhelming evidence that it has no basis in reality

Demand Characteristics bias in the research setting that seems to suggest or "demand" a particular response from subjects

Dendrites short fibers branching out from the cell body, which form the "input zone" of a neuron

Dependent Variable the factor expected to change when the independent variable changes

Depressant any drug that retards the action of the central nervous system by changing brain chemistry to slow physiological and mental activity

Depressive Realism the pattern of thought linked to depression in which self-serving, positive biases are absent

Depth Perception the ability to recognize distances between objects (relative distance) and from the observer to objects (absolute distance)

Development any age-related change in body or behavior, whether positive, negative, or neutral

Developmental Psychology the study of psychological change throughout life

Diathesis-Stress Model the view that schizophrenia is caused by a genetic predisposition combined with severe environmental stress

Dichotic Listening a process of selective attention, exemplified by a person hearing two simultaneous, but different, messages, one in each ear, and attending to only one, remaining unaware of the other

Difference Threshold the smallest change in a stimulus that produces a change in sensation

Diffusion of Responsibility the diminishment of personal responsibility caused by the presence of others, which inhibits response in an emergency

Discourse any connected series of statements, either written or spoken

Discrimination the process by which an organism learns to distinguish among stimuli and to respond differently to each

Disengagement a gradual, voluntary withdrawal from society and decreasing involvement with other people, once believed to be the typical pattern of adjustment to old age

Displacement (1) newly arriving information displaces or bumps out of short-term memory traces of previous information; (2) the ability to refer to anything not actually present, like past and future

Dissociation Theory the view that during hypnosis, consciousness splits into independent systems, each unaware of what the others think or feel

Dissociative Disorder the dissociation, or splitting off, of aspects of memory and identity, which are usually integrated

Distance Senses vision and hearing; senses that can pick up information from objects too far away to touch

Dominant Response an extremely well learned response that is most likely to be made in a given situation

Dopamine a catecholamine neurotransmitter that is involved with fine control of the skeletal muscles

Dopamine Hypothesis the view that schizophrenia is connected to excess activity in brain areas that use the neurotransmitter dopamine to transmit neural impulses

Double-Blind Procedure method of avoiding bias in an experiment in which neither the experimenter nor the subjects know who is in the experimental group and who is in the control group

Down Syndrome a disorder caused by the presence of an extra chromosome and characterized by retardation

Drive a motivating state resulting from physiological deficits or needs that instigate behaviors to reduce those needs

Dysthymia a mood disorder characterized by mild, persistent depression

Eardrum the oval membrane that separates the outer and middle ear; it vibrates when struck by a sound wave

Echoic Memory storage of auditory sensory information

Ecological Validity a characteristic possessed by studies in which the subjects behave as they would in real-life environments

Educational Psychology the study of all psychological aspects of the learning process

Ego the rational part of the personality that develops to mediate between the id and reality

Ego Integrity a sense of the wholeness and meaningfulness of one's life; in Erikson's theory, the development of ego integrity is the major task of later adulthood

Egocentrism the belief that everyone sees the world and responds to it exactly as you do

Ejaculation the discharge of semen during male orgasm

Elaborative Rehearsal reviewing material by expanding on its meaning, drawing inferences about it, and relating it to other things

Electroconvulsive Therapy (ECT) "shock treatment"; a series of brief electrical shocks that induce convulsions

Electroencephalograph an instrument that records fluctuations in electric voltage in the brain

Embryo the prenatal developing organism from two weeks to eight weeks

Embryonic Period the prenatal developmental phase from two weeks to eight weeks, when major organ systems form

Emotion the pattern of responses to an event relevant to needs or goals, including bodily changes, impulses to act, thoughts, and expression

Empiricist scientist who believes in verifying phenomena by experiment and experience

Encoding Specificity the principle that a memory is easiest to retrieve if the retrieval situation is the same as or similar to the one in which we originally learned

Endocrine System the collection of glands that release hormones

Endogenous Opioids neuropeptide chemicals: opium-like substances that occur naturally in the body, reducing pain

Environmental Psychology the study of the relationship between people and their physical settings

Epinephrine a catecholamine neurotransmitter that boosts alertness, arousal, and readiness to act

Equity Theory the cognitive theory that sees employees as motivated to remove perceived inequities—either by action or by rethinking the situation

Erogenous Zones areas of the body that are particularly sensitive to erotic touch

Escape Learning learning of a response which produces relief, or escape, from an aversive situation

Estrogen the principal female hormone

Estrus ("heat") a set of behavioral changes and a readiness to mate that occur in the females of most species of mammals at the time of ovulation

Eugenics the selective breeding of humans

Excitement Phase the first phase in the human sexual response cycle, during which the body begins to show physiological signs of arousal

Expectancy Theory the cognitive theory that sees work motivation as the result of how attainable workers believe their goals are

Expectancy-Value Theory the theory that ascribes behavior to expectations for success in relation to the value placed on that success

Experiential Intelligence in Sternberg's theory, the ability to learn from experience and carry out familiar tasks efficiently

Experiment a method of collecting data in which researchers actively control the factors that may affect the variable under study

Experimental Condition the condition in an experiment in which the independent variable is manipulated in order to test its effects

Experimental Psychology the laboratory study of sensation, perception, learning, memory, problem solving, communication, emotion, and motivation

Experimenter Effect a bias that the experimenter unwittingly introduces into a study

Exposure Effect the phenomenon whereby repeated neutral encounters with an object produce positive feelings toward that object

Expressive Aphasia a condition in which the ability to produce coherent speech is impaired

Expressive Power a language's ability to communicate virtually anything

Externals people who are especially responsive to food cues

Extinction the gradual decline and disappearance of a conditioned response when it no longer is reinforced

Extrinsically Motivated motivated by external rewards

Facial Feedback Hypothesis the proposal that our subjective emotional experience is the result of facial expressions—that is, that the expression creates the emotion

Factor Analysis a statistical technique for formulating correlations between assorted variables and one common factor; often used in personality theory to identify underlying factors, or traits, that account for consistency in behavior

Feature Analysis the theory that we perceive a form on the basis of a relatively small collection of features, which can be combined, rotated, and expanded

Feedback information about the most recent performance that is used to adjust succeeding performances

Fetal Alcohol Syndrome a condition afflicting babies of alcoholic mothers, characterized by mental retardation, slowed growth, and physical malformation

Fetal Period the prenatal developmental phase from eight weeks until birth, when organs organize their structures and establish their functions

Fetus the prenatal developing organism from eight weeks until birth

Figure–Ground Distinction the tendency to perceive a scene as a solid, well-defined object (figure) standing out from a less distinct background (ground)

Fixation the tendency to apply automatically an inappropriate strategy to a new problem, then rigidly cling to that approach

Fixed Action Pattern a stereotyped and often-repeated pattern of movement characteristic of a species and evoked by specific stimuli; not altered by experience

Fixed-Interval Schedule a pattern of reinforcement in which a reward comes for the first response that is made after a specified time has elapsed

Fixed-Ratio Schedule the pattern of reinforcement in which a reward comes after a specific number of responses

Flooding a behavioral therapy technique that involves extinction of a conditioned response through continuous, intense exposure to the anxiety-provoking situation

Fluid Intelligence the ability to learn and perform, which declines with age

Focal Color the basic colors, like red, blue, or brown; the ideal or best-example color within the range of a given color term

Forensic Psychology the application of psychological principles to law enforcement and court procedures

Formal Operations in Piaget's theory, logical, abstract thought that develops during puberty and is the culmination of cognitive development

Fovea the center of the retina that lies almost directly opposite the pupil; contains only cones

Fractionation a creative technique in which an idea is broken down into parts and the parts are examined for new possibilities or properties

Framing presenting a problem so that we focus on describing the outcomes as gains or losses from a presumed reference point

Free Association a psychodynamic technique of tapping unconscious thought by having a person say anything that comes to mind, with no attempt to produce logical, coherent explanations

Frequency the number of sound waves, or compression and expansion cycles, that occur within 1 second; expressed in a unit known as a hertz (Hz); the basis of pitch

Frequency Distribution a representation that shows the relationship between responses and the observed frequency of those responses

Frequency Theory the theory that pitch is signaled to the brain by the frequency of the basilar membrane's vibration as a unit

Frustration interference with any goal-directed activity

Frustration-Aggression Hypothesis the proposal that aggression is always a consequence of frustration and that frustration always leads to aggression

Fugue a dissociative disorder that involves flight from the home as well as flight from the self

Fully Functioning the psychological adjustment that results when people assimilate all their experiences into their self-concept

Functional Fixedness the inability to use a familiar object for an unfamiliar function

Functionalism a school of thought associated with William James that emphasizes the adaptiveness of human thought and behavior

Fundamental Attribution Error the tendency to attribute another person's behavior to the person, rather than to the situation

GABA (Gamma Amino-Butyric Acid) a neurotransmitter that seems to be the central nervous system's main inhibitory transmitter

Galvanic Skin Response (GSR) the measure of the skin's resistance to electrical conduction; a measure of arousal

Ganglia collections of nerve-cell bodies

Ganglion Cells neurons in the retina that do the final processing of signals within the eye

Gender Identity the inner experience of gender; the unchanging sense of self as male or female

Gender Role a socially prescribed pattern of behavior and attitudes for males and females

Gender Schema a self-constructed pattern of associations for each gender, which determines the way new information is organized

General Intelligence Factor (g Factor) a basic component underlying all types of intellectual abilities and explaining correlations among all kinds of intelligence measures

Generalized Anxiety Disorder a chronic state of diffuse, unfocused anxiety

Generativity a concern for future generations, consisting of procreativity, productivity, and creativity; in Erikson's theory, the development of generativity is the major task of middle adulthood

Genital Stage (from puberty onward) the final stage of psychosexual development, when sensual pleasure focuses on sexual intercourse

Germinal Period the prenatal developmental phase from fertilization to two weeks when the zygote begins the process of rapid cell development

Gestalt School psychologists who believe that a meaningful overall pattern (*gestalt*) is perceived before its parts are recognized

Gestalt Therapy a humanistic therapy that blends humanistic philosophy and Freudian concepts, using therapeutic techniques that are radically different from those of psychoanalysis

Given-New Contract an implicit agreement between speaker and listener to represent new information so it can be efficiently linked with old

Glial Cells cells that keep neurons functioning by supplying them with nutrients, clearing away their wastes, helping to separate them from other neurons, and giving them a structural and chemical foundation in which to grow and organize themselves

Goal-Setting Theory the cognitive theory that sees workers as motivated by conscious intentions to attain specific goals

Grammar the rules governing sentence formation

Habituation a simple form of learning in which the response to a stimulus decreases after lengthy or repeated presentation; similar to "boredom"

Hair Cells sensory receptors attached to the basilar membrane, the semicircular canals, and the olfactory epithelium

Hallucination a distortion of sensory perceptions

Hallucinogen any drug with the ability to produce hallucinations

Hammer one of the ossicles in the middle ear

Health Belief Model a model that assumes good health practices depend on attitudes, beliefs, and thoughts about vulnerability to illness and the value of changed behavior

Health Psychology the branch of psychology that aims at understanding the relationship between the mind and the individual's physical condition

Hemispheric Specialization see **brain lateralization**

Heritability a numerical estimate of the relative influence of heredity on differences in a single trait among individuals in a single group

Heterosexual sexual attraction to members of the opposite sex

Heuristics quick and intuitively sensible mental rules-of-thumb that allow us to reason and make judgments

Hindsight a bias in judgment, based on availability, in which a possible outcome is afterward seen as having been very probable

Hippocampus a part of the limbic system that is involved in memory and emotion

Homeostasis a constant, balanced physical state; also, the process of maintaining this state

Homosexual sexual attraction to members of one's own sex

Hormones chemical substances released from glands that control a wide range of physiological activities

Human Factors Psychology the branch of psychology that helps create designs for machinery and work environments that are comfortable, efficient, and appropriate for people

Humanistic Perspective a psychological school that emphasizes subjective experience and the total human being, the individual's freedom of choice, and an inherent potential for growth

Humanistic Therapy an approach to psychotherapy in which the goal is to help clients fulfill their individual human potential

Hypnogogic Image an image produced in the state of consciousness that exists as a person is falling asleep

Hypnopompic Image an image produced in the state of consciousness that exists as a person is waking up

Hypnosis a social interaction in which a person's responses to the suggestions of another result in altered perceptions, memories, and voluntary actions

Hypnotic any depressant drug that induces sleep

Hypochondriasis a preoccupation with bodily symptoms that might involve physical illness

Hypothalamus a structure in the center of the brain that controls hunger, thirst, and sexual desire; regulates body temperature; controls circadian rhythms; and is involved in emotion

Hypothesis a testable prediction or proposition that attempts to explain some observed phenomenon

Iconic Memory storage of visual sensory information

Id the primitive, instinctual, animal-like part of the personality that is present at birth

Identity a coherent sense of individuality; in Erikson's theory, its development is the major task of adolescence

Ill-Defined Problem a problem with no agreed-on rules or form for solution

Implicit Memory a memory that results from unattended stimulation; it influences performance even though it cannot be consciously recalled

Imprinting an immediate attachment formed by some species of birds to the first object they see upon hatching

Incentives external stimuli that serve as anticipated rewards for certain behaviors

Incest sexual activity between close relatives

Independent Variable the factor in a research study that is manipulated by the experimenter to determine its effects

Individual Traits Allport's term for unique, individual ways of responding to the world that cannot be measured by tests but only discerned by studying the person

Induced Motion the illusion that a stationary object is moving, created when objects near it move

Inductive Reasoning a form of logical reasoning in which we infer a general rule from specific cases; it can produce probabilities, but not certainty

Industrial Psychology the application of psychological principles to the performance of organizations and of the people who work in them

Informational Influence yielding to group pressure as a result of the knowledge gained from the others' behavior

Ingroup Bias the tendency to favor an ingroup over an outgroup, expressed in prejudice and discrimination

Inhibited Ejaculation the inability to ejaculate during sexual activity

Inhibited Female Orgasm a woman's inability to achieve orgasm. Women who have never had an orgasm through any means are said to have *primary inhibited orgasm*. Those who can no longer achieve orgasm through the kinds of stimulation that were once effective are said to have *secondary inhibited orgasm*.

Insomnia the inability to sleep; chronic sleeplessness

Instincts the innate, fixed responses characteristic of a species that propel it toward some end state

Instrumental Conditioning the form of learning in which a voluntary response is strengthened or diminished by its consequences; also called operant conditioning

Intelligence general abilities that help people achieve their goals

Intelligence (Ability) Tests tests measuring stable, general abilities

Intelligence Quotient (IQ) the ratio of mental age to chronological age multiplied by 100

Interference the blurring of one memory by others that are similar to it and which compete with its retrieval

Interjudge Reliability the extent to which a test produces the same results when scored by different judges

Internal Consistency Reliability the extent to which different parts of a test produce the same results

Internalization the incorporation of values, attitudes, and beliefs so that they become one's own

Interneurons neurons that connect one neuron to another, thus integrating brain activities and other bodily processes

Intimacy the ability to commit the self to a close relationship that demands sacrifice and compromise; in Erikson's theory, the development of intimacy is the major task of young adulthood

Intrinsically Motivated motivated by pleasure in an activity for its own sake, for self-fulfillment

Introspection a technique in which subjects report their own conscious experience in response to various stimuli

Ions tiny, electrically charged particles inside the membrane of neurons, which supply the electric charge

Iris the ring of muscle around the pupil that controls the amount of light reaching the receptors; the pigmented portion of the eye

James-Lange Theory the theory that emotion is the perception of bodily changes

Job Satisfaction the result of the match between what workers want from a job and what they actually get

Just Noticeable Difference (jnd) see **difference threshold**

Key-Word System a mnemonic system based on associating an unfamiliar item to its translation by using a similar-sounding keyword in a visual image

Kinesthesis the sense that provides information about body movement and position

Language Competence grammatical knowledge that forms the basis of our ability to make linguistic judgments

Latency Stage (six to eleven years) psychosexual stage when children repress their sexual feelings

Latent Content a dreamer's unconscious wishes, which influence the content of a dream, where they appear in symbolic form; the underlying meaning of a dream

Lateral Geniculate Nucleus (LGN) a six-layered grouping of cell bodies in the thalamus that accept signals from ganglion cells and send them on to the visual cortex

Law of Effect the proposal that a response that produces an annoying or a satisfying outcome will weaken or strengthen, respectively, that response's connection to the situation

Learning a long-lasting change in an organism's disposition to behave in certain ways as a result of experience

Lens the transparent structure behind the iris that focuses light waves on to the retina

Life-Cycle Theory a contingency theory of leadership that emphasizes leaders' ability to foster maturity and responsibility in group members

Life Review the process of reflecting on the past in order to come to terms with it before death

Limbic System a part of the brain that helps control emotions and species-typical behaviors such as mating and fighting

Linear Relationship/Linear Function a relationship between variables that can be represented graphically as a straight line

Linguistic Determinism the theory that language determines how we perceive and understand the world

Linguistics the study of language knowledge and structure

Lobes regions of the cerebral cortex: frontal, parietal, temporal, and occipital

Longitudinal Study a study that follows the same group of subjects over a period of time

Long-Term Memory a system of unlimited capacity holding our knowledge and long-retained memories that are forgotten only very slowly

Loosening of Associations the tendency for schizophrenic speech to lose the logical thread so that each sentence is generated by associations to some word in the previous sentence

Love a feeling of deep affection for and attachment to another person

Lucid Dream a dream in which a person is aware that he or she is dreaming

Maintenance Rehearsal the unthinking, rote repetition of material to be remembered

Major Depression one or more intense episodes of depression without any intervening episode of joy

Male Erectile Disorder the inability to achieve or maintain an erection. When an erection has never been achieved, the condition is called *primary erectile disorder.* When the problem occurs only in certain situations, the condition is called *secondary erectile disorder.*

Manifest Content the surface meaning of dreams, consisting of interwoven daily events, memories, and sensations during sleep; the events from a dream that are remembered by the dreamer

Maturation the changes in body or behavior that result from physical processes and not from learning

Mean the arithmetic average of a distribution of scores

Means–End Analysis breaking a problem into subgoals that can be reached by solving smaller problems

Measure of Central Tendency a descriptive statistic that represents the middle of a distribution of responses—the mode, mean, or median

Median the score that falls in the exact middle of a distribution, when all scores are arranged from highest to lowest

Medical Model the view that all abnormal behavior has specific organic causes and a specific set of symptoms

Meditation a method of refocusing attention through "concentration" or "mindfulness" to produce relaxation or a heightened state of spirituality

Medulla the part of the brain stem that helps regulate many autonomic activities, such as circulation and breathing

Memory the cognitive process of preserving current information for later use

Memory Trace the physiological changes assumed to occur in the brain when recording information about an event; as time passes, the trace decays

Menarche the first menstrual period

Menopause the end of menstruation

Mental Age a measurement of intelligence based on average abilities for a given age group

Mental Model the use of abstract symbols or imagery to represent and reason about a problem

Mental Retardation significantly below-average intellectual functioning combined with impaired ability to function in the world

Mental Set the tendency to repeat a representation of an object and its function that worked in other situations

Metacognition the knowledge about and ability to monitor our own cognitive processes

Metamemory the knowledge of what our memories contain and how our own memory works in different situations

Metaneeds the highest needs in Maslow's hierarchy

Metapathology the alienation, anguish, apathy, or cynicism that arises when metaneeds are not filled

Method of Loci a mnemonic system based on visual imagery involving a series of loci (places) that are firmly fixed in memory

Midlife Crisis Levinson's term for the state of physical and psychological distress that a man experiences when the developmental tasks he faces during the transition to middle adulthood threaten to overwhelm his internal resources and social supports

Mild Retardation retardation within an IQ range of 50–69

Mnemonic System strategy deliberately designed to help people remember particular kinds of material

Mode the score that most frequently appears in a distribution

Model a person from whom behavior is learned by observation

Modeling a cognitive behavioral technique in which a person learns new behavior by watching another person

Moderate Retardation retardation within an IQ range of 35–49

Mood Disorder a mood swing so intense that it disrupts normal functioning and causes severe and prolonged distress

Morphemes the basic units of meaning in a language—words; suffixes and prefixes

Motherese the altered, simplified speech used by adults with small children

Motion Aftereffect the illusion that a stationary object is moving, created by prolonged viewing of motion in the opposite direction

Motivation the processes that, taken together, energize, maintain, and direct behavior toward goals

Motor and Sensory Areas parts of the brain that are responsible, respectively, for movement and the detection of stimuli

Motor Neurons neurons that connect to the body's skeletal muscles and carry signals that cause those muscles to contract, producing movement

MRI (Magnetic Resonance Imaging) a technique involving measurement of the effects of magnetic fields on brain molecules, producing a detailed cross-sectional image of the brain

Multiple Personality a rare dissociative disorder in which a person's identity splits into two or more distinct personalities

Myelin Sheath a fatty covering made of glial cells around part of some neurons, which helps increase the speed of electrical signals

Myopia nearsightedness; a condition in which light waves are focused in front of the retina, blurring vision for distant objects

Naturalistic Observation a method of collecting data in which researchers carefully observe and record behavior in natural settings without causing any interference

Negative Correlation a relationship between two variables in which a high rank on one measure is accompanied by a low rank on the other

Negative Reinforcement strengthening a response that leads to removal of an aversive stimulus

Neodissociation Theory a variation of dissociation theory that maintains the dissociated systems continue to pass information back and forth, even though the information does not register in awareness

Nerve Impulse a spreading action potential along a neuron

Nerves pathways containing bundles of fibers that transmit sensations and other kinds of information to the central nervous system, as well as commands to muscles and glands

Neurons specialized nerve cells that connect motor and receptor cells and transmit information throughout the body

Neuropeptides a class of brain chemicals that seem to function as neurotransmitters

Neurotransmitter chemical messenger that travels across the synaptic cleft from one neuron to another

Norepinephrine a catecholamine neurotransmitter that is involved with learning, memory, and emotion

Normal Curve of Distribution a bell-shaped, symmetrical distribution, in which mean, median, and mode are the same

Normative Influence yielding to group pressure as a result of a desire to comply even when one disagrees with the others

Norms frequencies with which particular scores are made and which serve as standards of comparison for test takers

NREM (or Non-REM) Sleep the state of sleep, divided into four stages, in which there is no rapid eye movement

Obedience behavior that complies with the explicit commands of an authority figure

Object Permanence understanding that objects continue to exist when out of sight

Observational Learning the form of learning by watching others and noting the consequences of their behavior

Obsession an involuntary, irrational, recurring thought

Obsessive-Compulsive Disorder an anxiety disorder characterized by rituals of orderliness or cleanliness, such as continual handwashing

Olfaction the sense of smell

Olfactory Epithelium the patch of tissue in the nose that contains receptor cells for odors

Operant Conditioning see **instrumental conditioning**

Operationalizing a Hypothesis restating a hypothesis so as to specifically suggest a way of testing it

Operations Piaget's term for flexible, rigorous, and logical thought

Opponent-Process Theory (1) the theory of color vision that proposes the antagonistic pairing of complementary colors (red with green and blue with yellow) and the same photopigment working in opposing directions with each color of the pair, so that stimulation of one color cancels out the other; (2) the theory that ties motivation to two components—a primary reaction (say, fear) to a stimulus and an opposing response (say, relief) that eventually becomes the real motivating force

Optic Chiasm the junction within the brain where the optic nerves converge and axons are rerouted so that signals from each half of the visual field are carried to the opposite side of the visual cortex

Optic Disk the area in the retina where the optic nerve leaves the eye, causing a blind spot in vision

Optic Nerve the nerve, formed by the axons of the ganglion cells, that carries visual signals from the retina to the brain

Optimal-Level Theories theories that stress the organism's tendency to seek a certain optimal level of stimulation and arousal in the brain

Oral Stage (from birth to about 18 months) psychosexual stage when the mouth is the primary source of sensual pleasure

Organism Carl Rogers's term for the total range of a person's possible experiences

Organizational Psychology the branch of psychology that studies the principles of organizational performance

Organizational Commitment the strength of a worker's identification with and involvement in an organization

Orgasm the third phase in the human sexual response cycle, during which waves of muscular contractions sweep over the body, accompanied by feelings of intense pleasure

Orienting Reflex a physiological reaction of "surprise" or arousal to a novel stimulus

Ossicles a series of bones in the middle ear which convert changes in sound pressure into mechanical movement

Oval Window the flexible membrane that divides the middle ear from the inner ear

Overextension stretching the meaning of a word so that it refers to events or objects that resemble it

Overregularization rigidly applying grammatical rules, which produces speech errors

Panic Attack a brief period of intense, debilitating anxiety

Panic Disorder a disorder characterized by panic attacks

Parasympathetic Division the part of the autonomic system that exerts control in relaxed situations, enhancing digestion and conserving energy by slowing down the heart rate and the blood flow to the skeletal muscles

Parental Imperative Gutmann's theory that parenthood controls personality in adulthood by heightening gender roles in the protection and nurturance of children

Partial Reinforcement Schedule the pattern of reinforcement in which only some responses are rewarded

Path-Goal Theory a contingency theory of leadership, based on expectency theory, that proposes the leaders role is to influence the expectations of group members; clarifies the paths (members' behavior) that lead to desired goals (high-valance outcomes)

Peg-Word System a mnemonic system involving the memorization of a list of simple words to use as memory pegs

Percentile System a method for comparing test scores to norms by dividing scores into 100 equal parts (or percentiles); shows the proportion of norms above and below any individual score

Perception the organization and interpretation of sensory signals by the brain to produce a mental representation of the original stimuli

Perceptual Constancy the tendency for an object's size, shape, color, and brightness to remain constant despite changes in the retinal image

Perceptual Memory storage of sensory information

Perceptual Set a readiness to interpret stimuli in a specific way on the basis of expectations, experience, or psychological state

Performance System language processes, including memory, engaged when we design and use spoken and written language

Performance Test an intelligence subtest that measures nonverbal abilities

Peripheral Nervous System the relay system of nerve cells outside the skull and backbone connecting the central nervous system and all parts of the body; contains ganglia and nerves

Peripheral Route to Persuasion a message recipient's use of heuristic thinking, previous learning experiences, or other methods that do not require evaluation of the quality of the arguments in the message

Perseveration (1) a slip in which a sound is repeated; (2) the tendency for schizophrenic speech to dwell on the primary association to a given stimulus

Personal Dispositions see **individual traits**

Personality an individual's characteristic and distinctive patterns of thinking, feeling, and behaving

Personality Disorder a social disorder involving inflexible and maladaptive personality traits that impair social or occupational functioning

Personality Psychology the study of individual differences in behavior, the sources and consequences of such differences, and the degree of consistency of characteristics within the individual across situations and over time

Personnel Psychology the branch of psychology that involves plans for screening job applicants and evaluating job performance

PET Scan (Positron Emission Tomogram) a technique involving injection of radioactive substances into the brain, yielding a vivid computerized picture of the metabolic activity of the living brain

Phallic Stage (from about three to six years) the psychosexual stage when sensual pleasure centers on fondling the genitals

Pheromone a chemical whose odor, on emission by an animal, triggers a behavioral reaction in other animals of the same species

Phi Phenomenon the apparent motion caused by still lights flashing rapidly in sequence

Phobic Disorder an anxiety disorder in which anxiety centers on an intense, irrational fear of some object or situation

Phonemes speech sounds; the basic unit of sound in a language

Phonological Rules rules governing the combination of phonemes to make words

Photopigment a light-sensitive chemical within photoreceptors whose response transduces light to a neural signal

Phrase-Structure Rules rules governing the hierarchical organization of words in a sentence

Phrase-Structure Tree the graphic representation of phrases and their interdependencies in a sentence

Physical Density the number of people in a given amount of space

Physiological Perspective a psychological school that is concerned with the biological processes that underlie behavior

Physiological Psychology/Neuropsychology the branch of psychology that studies the connection between the nervous and endocrine systems and behavior

Pitch the subjective interpretation of a sound's frequency as high or low

Pituitary Gland a structure located at the base of the brain that regulates the actions of other endocrine glands

Place Theory the theory that pitch is signaled to the brain by the vibration of particular areas of the basilar membrane

Placenta the flexible structure of tissue that delivers nutrients and oxygen to a developing organism and carries away wastes

Plateau Phase the second phase in the human sexual response cycle, during which the body reaches its peak of sexual arousal

Polysomnography recordings of physiological activity (brain waves, eye movements, muscle tension) during sleep

Pons the part of the brain stem that integrates the movements of the body's right and left sides

Positive Correlation a relationship between two variables in which a high rank on one measure is accompanied by a high rank on the other

Positive Reinforcement strengthening a response by rewarding it

Postformal Thought the problem-oriented, flexible thought characteristic of middle adulthood, involving social responsibility, an ability to integrate conflicting information, and an awareness of emotional and interpersonal influences on knowledge

Posthypnotic Amnesia a hypnotized person's inability to remember events after hypnosis in response to hypnotic suggestion

Posthypnotic Suggestion suggestion of the hypnotist that a hypnotized person carries out after hypnosis

Postsynaptic Potential an electrical reaction, either excitatory or inhibitory, in a receiving dendrite, which follows chemical stimulation

Preconscious the area of mental processes that is not in alert awareness but that may be recalled at will; all personal knowledge

Predictive Validity a positive correlation between test scores and future performance

Prefrontal Lobotomy a surgical procedure in which nerve fibers connecting the frontal lobe (thought center) with the thalamus (emotional center) are severed

Premack Principle more preferred activities can be used to reinforce less preferred ones

Premature Ejaculation ejaculation before the male or his sex partner would like

Preoperational Stage in Piaget's theory, the period from about age two to age seven, when thought is intuitive, inflexible, and focused on individual events

Primary Appraisal the initial determination of the meaning of new or changing circumstances

Primary Colors the three basic colors whose mixing can produce the entire color spectrum

Primary Prevention establishing and maintaining health by reducing risky behavioral practices and environmental conditions

Primary Reinforcer a stimulus that reduces some basic drive or need

Primary Sex Characteristics the sexual organs that are directly responsible for reproduction

Priming the facilitation in processing a given item caused by presenting it, or a related item, in an earlier series

Proactive Interference the blurring of newly learned information by previously learned, competing information

Productivity the ability to produce an infinite number of sentences

Profound Retardation retardation based on a below-20 IQ

Program Evaluation the cooperation of psychologists, economists, political scientists, and sociologists to evaluate the effectiveness and cost of government social programs

Progressive Relaxation a technique that induces relaxation by tensing and releasing different muscle groups in sequence

Projective Test a test that draws out unconscious conflicts and motives through free-association responses to ambiguous stimuli

Propositions basic conceptual units that make up a sentence and that can be either true or false

Prototype the most typical example—a best instance or most representative member—of a category

Proximity physical nearness, which plays a central role in interpersonal attraction and friendship

Psychiatric Nurse a registered nurse with special training in the treatment of psychological disorders

Psychiatric Social Worker a mental health professional with a master's degree in social work and specialized training in the treatment of psychological disorders

Psychiatrist a physician (an M.D.) who specializes in the diagnosis and treatment of mental, emotional, or behavioral disorders

Psychoactive Drug any drug that interacts with the central nervous system by changing brain chemistry to affect mood, perception, or behavior, thus altering consciousness

Psychoactive Substance Dependence a social disorder whose essential features are impaired control of substance use and continued use of the substance in spite of negative consequences

Psychoanalysis Freud's therapeutic method, a process that aims at retrieving repressed memories and feelings from the unconscious

Psychoanalyst a mental health professional with special training in the techniques of psychoanalysis

Psychodynamic Perspective a psychological school that is concerned with unconscious inner forces, impulses, and conflicts that are believed to influence behavior

Psychodynamic Therapy an approach to psychotherapy that focuses on the dynamic interplay of conscious and unconscious elements

Psychodynamics the interplay of inner conflicts and their resolution that is the primary determinant of human behavior and personality

Psychogenic Theory the theory that abnormal behavior can be traced to emotional stress or maladaptive behavior patterns

Psycholinguistics the study of the mental processes involved in how we use and understand language

Psychology the scientific study of mental processes and behavior

Psychopharmacology the study of the relationship between drugs and behavior

Psychotherapy a systematic series of interactions between a person trained to treat psychological problems and another person who is to be helped

Psychotic Disorder a disorder characterized by a generalized failure to function in all areas of life

Puberty a series of interrelated biological processes that transform a child into a sexually mature individual

Punishment weakening or suppressing a response by producing an aversive consequence

Pupil the opening in the center of the eye through which light waves enter the eye chamber

Randomization a method of assigning people to a group in such a way that each person has an equal chance of being chosen

Range the difference between the smallest and the largest scores in a statistical distribution

Rape sexual intercourse that is the result of physical force, threat, or intimidation

Rational-Emotive Therapy (RET) a method of cognitive restructuring that directly confronts clients with their irrational beliefs

Rationalization a defense mechanism that provides plausible—socially acceptable—explanations for behavior that is motivated by unconscious or unacceptable reasons

Reaction Range a genetic trait's span of possible responses to the environmental influences that a person encounters

Realistic Fantasy daydreams that resemble waking thought; they occur in a state of consciousness in which awareness is removed from the outer world

Reasoning logical thought; the ability to think logically

Recall the process of retrieving stored information from memory without having that information present

Receptive Aphasia a condition in which the ability to comprehend speech and to generate coherent speech is impaired

Receptive Field the area in the retina from which a neuron gathers sensory information

Reciprocal Altruism the performance of an altruistic act on the chance that it may be reciprocated at a later date

Reciprocal Determinism the interaction of environment, behavior, and person that determines behavior

Recognition the process of identifying a piece of information as familiar

Reconditioning the relearning of a conditioned then extinguished response

Recursion embedding sentences within sentences and phrases within phrases

Reference an indication of the external object or thing a word points to or represents

Reflex Response an immediate, involuntary action by the nervous system

Refractory Period the time following orgasm during which a man cannot become sexually aroused again

Rehearsal the silent repetition or reviewing of material in order to remember it

Reinforcement Schedule pattern of reward that maintains conditioned response

Reinforcement Theory the theory of work motivation that applies the techniques of instrumental conditioning to change workers' expectancies

Reliability measuring consistently

REM (Rapid Eye Movement) sleep the state of sleep that is characterized by rapid eye movements and contradictory physiological characteristics; most dreams occur in this state

Replication repetition of a scientific study; if its findings are accurate, any study should be able to be replicated

Representational Thought the ability to mentally symbolize objects that are not directly visible

Representativeness a heuristic that judges probability according to the resemblance of a predicted event to a prototype

Repression the fundamental defense mechanism that keeps threatening thoughts and memories buried in the unconscious

Resistance a patient's attempt to block treatment during psychodynamic therapy

Resolution Phase the fourth and final phase of the human sexual response cycle, during which the body gradually returns to its normal state

Resting Potential a negative charge within a neuron's membrane that prevents the neuron from firing

Retention the preservation of stored information over an interval

Reticular Activating System a latticework of neurons through the center of the brain stem that plays a critical role in keeping us alert and aroused and enabling us to focus our attention

Retina the surface at the back of the eye where rods and cones are located

Retrieval the process by which information is taken out of storage for use

Retrieval Cue stimulus that triggers the retrieval of memories

Retroactive Interference the blurring of previously learned information by competing information learned subsequently

Retrograde Amnesia the loss of memory for experiences leading up to a brain injury or trauma

Reverie the state of consciousness filled with unrelated images that are not under the conscious control of the fantasizer

Reversal a slip in which sounds are exchanged between words

Rods the photoreceptors (receptor cells) in the eye that are specialized for vision in dim light; convey information about brightness but not about color

Role Enactment Theory the view that hypnosis is not an altered state, but an extreme example of role playing

Rorschach Inkblot Test a projective test in which people respond by free association to a series of ten symmetrical inkblots

Round Window the membrane at the base of the cochlea

Sample a representative selection of members of a defined population

Scatter Plot a graph on which a large number of data are plotted; used to show the range of possible relationships

Schema large cluster of interrelated concepts that encodes general knowledge of people, objects, events, and procedures

Scheme a recurrent action pattern or mental structure involved in the acquisition and structuring of knowledge

Schizophrenia a group of disorders characterized by disorganized thought, perception, and emotion, and by bizarre behavior

School Psychology the approach to psychology concerned with testing children in elementary and secondary schools and devising programs to train teachers and parents to help students with emotional or learning problems

Scientific Management the system that uses the methods of experimental psychology to redesign the workplace

Scientific Method a set of procedures that scientists follow in conducting their research, consisting of (1) observing a phenomenon of scientific interest, (2) formulating a hypothesis about it, and (3) collecting data for or against what the hypothesis proposes

Script procedural schema, or general understandings of the various elements that a routine entails

Secondary Appraisal the assessment of one's coping ability and resources for dealing with new or changing circumstances

Secondary Reinforcer a formerly neutral stimulus that does not reduce any primary need and that has acquired reinforcing power by becoming associated with a primary reinforcer

Secondary Sex Characteristics the sexual characteristics that appear at puberty but that have no direct reproductive function

Secondary Traits Allport's term for minor, often changing traits, that often appear as tastes or preferences

Second-Order Conditioning the form of learning in which a conditioned stimulus becomes associated with a second neutral stimulus that precedes it, which then evokes the conditioned response itself

Segmentation Problem the problem of identifying words within a stream of speech sounds

Self those parts of experience that a person recognizes and accepts

Self-Efficacy a personal judgment of one's own competence in a specific situation

Self-Fulfilling Prophecy an initially false expectation about another person's behavior that actually causes the person to behave in such a way that the expectation is confirmed

Self-Handicap a deliberate self-destructive behavior that serves to protect one's favorable self-image and to avoid self-blame for failure

Self-Instructional Training a method of cognitive restructuring that gives people new ways of thinking and talking to themselves about their problems

Semantic having to do with meaning

Semantic Memory the collection of knowledge about words, concepts, and meanings we hold in long-term memory

Semen the fluid containing live sperm that is released during ejaculation

Semicircular Canals three fluid-filled canals in the inner ear that make up the vestibular organ

Sensation the activation of sensory receptors and the processing and transmission of these signals to higher centers in the brain

Sense a definition of a word

Sensitive Period a sharply restricted span of time during which an animal is extremely susceptible to specific environmental influences

Sensorimotor Stage in Piaget's theory, the period from birth to about age two when knowledge is based on sensations and physical actions

Sensory Memory the momentary lingering of sensory data after stimulation has ceased

Sensory Neurons neurons that receive and transmit information about the outside world, initiating the process of sensations

Separation Distress an infant's discomfort when parted from an attachment figure

Septum a part of the limbic system that is involved in pleasure and the restraint of aggression

Serotonin a neurotransmitter that is involved in mood and emotion

Set Point the constant weight a body seeks (seems "set") to maintain

Severe Retardation retardation within an IQ range of 20–34

Sexual Disorder any problem that persistently prevents a person from engaging in sexual relations or from reaching orgasm during sex

Sexual Identity a person's sense of being male or female

Sexuality all the factors that contribute to a person's ability to give and receive erotic pleasure

Shaping the process by which an organism is reinforced for ever-closer approximations of a desired behavior

Short-Term Memory the holding bin for information that a person has actively in mind; also called working memory

Slip of the Tongue a speech error in which we say something we did not intend to say

Social Cognition the way we think and reason about ourselves, about other people, about relations between people, and about the various groups to which we and other people belong

Social Cognitive Theory the view that learning involves the application of cognitive processes, including observational learning, expectancies, and self-regulating processes

Social Facilitation enhanced performance in the presence of others

Social Impact Theory the hypothesis that the larger the group, the less pressure there is on any one member to produce; that diffusion of responsibility leads to diminished individual effort

Social Influence the informational influence of bystanders that inhibits response in an emergency

Socialization the process of acquiring the attitudes, values, and customs expected from members of society

Social Norms society's rules for appropriate behavior in every aspect of life

Social Psychology the branch of psychology concerned with the ways in which our thoughts, feelings, and behavior are influenced by other people and by society as a whole

Social Trap an unpleasant or lethal situation for a group caused by consistent choice of self-interest over cooperation by its members

Sociopath a person who is indifferent to the rights of others, feels no guilt, and does not learn from experience or punishment

Somatic System the subdivision of the peripheral nervous system that transmits sensations from the outside world to the spinal cord and/or brain and relays the central nervous system's orders to contract the body's skeletal muscles

Somatoform Disorder a disorder that shows physiological (somatic) symptoms without any underlying physiological malfunction

Somatosensory Cortex the area along the forward edges of the parietal lobes that is the major area for receiving skin sensations

Spatial Learning the form of learning where things are located in the environment

Speech Act utterance designed to have some effect—such as a promise, a bet, a request

Speech Plan the entire plan of utterance, including syntactic choices, insertion of morphemes, and translation of morphemes into sound segments

Spinal Cord the column of neurons that serves as a link between the brain and the peripheral nervous system and as an information-processing system for reflex responses

Spontaneous Recovery the reappearance of an extinguished response upon returning to the familiar situation and the conditioned stimulus

Stage Theories theories in which abilities, motives, or skills emerge in a predictable, patterned sequence, producing fairly abrupt changes in behavior

Standard Deviation (S.D.) the preferred measure of variability; it shows how much figures in a given set of data vary from the mean

Standard Score System a method for comparing test scores to norms by converting scores using the standard deviation and plotting them around the mean

Standardization Group a representative sample of test takers whose scores become norms

Stanford-Binet Test the modified, widely used version of Binet's original test

State-Dependent Memory storage of information that is more easily retrieved when a person is in the same physiological state as when he or she learned the information

Stereopsis the perception of depth based on binocular disparity

Stereotypes complex mental representations of different types of people, containing all the information that we know or believe to be generally true of them

Stimulant any drug that stimulates the central nervous system by changing brain chemistry to speed physiological and mental activity

Stimulus Generalization the tendency for a conditioned response to be evoked by similar stimuli or situations

Stirrup one of the ossicles in the middle ear

Stress a pattern of disruptive physiological and psychological reactions to events that threaten the ability to cope

Structuralism an attempt to analyze the structure of the conscious mind by breaking it down into its component elements

Subconscious the area of mental processes in which stimuli are monitored but are not registered in subjective awareness

Sublimation a positive defense mechanism in which erotic energy is channeled into a socially constructive activity

Superego the part of the personality that is concerned with meeting the demands of morality and social convention; similar to the conscience

Suprachiasmatic Nucleus a region of the hypothalamus that is one of the master pacemakers for regulating circadian rhythms

Surface Structure the actual sequence of words in a sentence

Survey a method of collecting data in which researchers obtain information about people's characteristics, attitudes, opinions, or behavior by asking them questions

Syllogism one method of deductive reasoning, in which two premises (if true) lead to a correct conclusion

Sympathetic Division the part of the autonomic system that prepares the body for stressful situations by increasing heart rate, blood pressure, and blood-sugar level and by slowing down digestion

Synapse the area between neurons where communication occurs, including the first neuron's terminal button, the synaptic cleft, and the second neuron's receptor sites

Synaptic Cleft a tiny gap between the terminal buttons of one neuron and those of another

Synaptic Vesicle small spherical container that stores neurotransmitters; located inside terminal buttons

Synergistic combined action of drugs, in which the effect of two together is greater than the sum of the two drugs

Syntax the rules governing the combination of words and roots into phrases and sentences

Systematic Desensitization a behavioral therapy technique that involves an extinction procedure in which the client is gradually exposed to anxiety-producing stimuli

Taste Buds sensory receptors for taste stimuli

Telegraphic Speech speech in the two-word stage, in which utterances are stripped to content words and omit function words

Temperament the individual's pattern of activity, response to stimuli, susceptibility to emotional stimulation, and general mood

Teratogens agents, such as diseases, toxins, and environmental pollutants, that can alter or kill the developing organism during the prenatal period

Terminal Button small structure at the end of a branch of the axon, part of the "output zone" of a neuron

Testosterone the principal male hormone

Test-Retest Reliability the extent to which repeated administrations of a test to the same people produces the same results

Thalamus a pair of egg-shaped structures that link the higher brain regions with the other parts of the nervous system and help integrate the brain's activities

Thematic Apperception Test (TAT) a projective test in which people respond to a series of ambiguous scenes involving one, two, or three persons by telling a story about it

Theory an attempt to fit all the currently known facts about a subject into an integrated and logical whole

Therapeutic Alliance (or Therapeutic Bond) the relationship between client and therapist, in which client perceives therapist as a helpful ally

Time-Order Relationship a relationship in which one factor precedes a second one in time and therefore may possibly have caused the second

Tip-of-the-Tongue Phenomenon the experience of knowing that we know something, being able to retrieve part of it, but experiencing difficulty retrieving the complete memory

Token Economy a system in which desired behaviors are rewarded with symbolic tokens exchangeable for primary rewards and/or privileges; often used as a therapeutic technique by institutions

Trait a predisposition to respond to situations in a consistent way

Transduction the conversion of sensory stimuli into neural activity

Transference a patient's transfer to the therapist of childhood feelings toward important people in his or her life, particularly the parents

Transformational Leadership leadership that produces large-scale organization change by changing the goals of group members and deepening their commitment; works through the leader's charisma, individualized attention to subordinates, and ability to stimulate them intellectually

Transformation Rules rules governing the changing of deep structures into surface structures

Transsexualism a condition in which people develop a sexual identity that is inconsistent with their genetic and anatomical sex

Traumatic psychologically or physically damaging

Two-Factor Theory the theory that emotion consists of arousal and cognitive interpretation of the arousal

Type A Personality a pattern of behavior marked by impatience, competitiveness, and hostility

Ultradian Rhythm any cycle that occurs more frequently than once each day (ultradian = "faster than a day")

Unconditional Positive Regard Rogers' terms for continued support no matter what a person says or does

Unconditioned Response (UCR) an unlearned or innate response to a stimulus

Unconditioned Stimulus (UCS) a stimulus that evokes a response innately, not dependent upon prior learning

Unconscious the area of mental processes that is not available to the conscious mind, but whose contents may slip out in disguised form

Vaginismus involuntary muscle spasms that close the vaginal entrance so that penetration by a penis is extremely painful

Validity measuring what a test purports to measure

Variability the degree to which a group of responses spreads out from the mean or median

Variable any measurable or observable factor that can differ in either amount or form from one instance of it to another

Variable-Interval Schedule the pattern of reinforcement in which rewards come for the first response after a random period of time since the last reward

Variable-Ratio Schedule the pattern of reinforcement in which rewards come for the first response after a random number of responses since the last reward

Vascular Theory the theory that facial expressions cause emotions because facial muscles alter patterns of blood flow to the brain

Vestibular Sense the sense of balance

Visual Cortex the area in the occipital lobes that is the primary region for receiving and analyzing visual information

Volley Theory a revision of the frequency theory that assumes that neurons vibrate in volleys instead of in unison to send signals about pitch to the brain

Weber's Law the law stating that the increase in stimulus intensity needed to produce a second stimulus that is a just noticeably different is proportional to the intensity of the first stimulus

Wechsler Adult Intelligence Scale (WAIS) an individual IQ test for adults

Wechsler Intelligence Scale for Children (WISC) an individual IQ test for children aged 6 to 16

Wechsler Preschool and Primary Scale of Intelligence (WPPSI) an individual IQ test for children aged 4 to 6½

Well-Defined Problem a problem with a clear structure and accepted rules for solution

Working Backward solving a problem by working backward from the goal

Young-Helmholtz Trichromatic Theory the theory that color vision depends on the combined responses of three types of cones, each most sensitive to light waves of different frequencies

Zygote the fertilized ovum during the first two weeks of development

REFERENCES

Note: The number in brackets after each entry refers to the chapter in this book in which that work is cited.

Abel, G. G., E. B. Blanchard, and **J. V. Becker.** An integrated treatment program for rapists. In R. T. Rada (Ed.), *Clinical aspects of the rapist.* New York: Grune & Stratton, 1978. [14]

Abelson, H., R. Cohen, E. Heaton, and **C. Suder.** Public attitudes toward and experience with erotic materials. In Commission on Obscenity and Pornography, *Technical reports of the Commission on Obscenity and Pornography* (Vol. 6). Washington, D.C.: U.S. Government Printing Office, 1970. [14]

Abelson, R. P. Script processing in attitude formation and decision making. In J. Carroll and J. W. Payne (Eds.), *Cognition and social behavior.* Hillsdale, N.J.: Erlbaum, 1976, pp. 33–46. [1]

Abrahams, B., S. S. Feldman, and **S. C. Nash.** Sex role self-concept and sex role attitudes. *Developmental Psychology,* 1978, *14,* 393–400. [16]

Abramson, L. Y., and **L. B. Alloy.** Depression, non-depression, and cognitive illusions: A reply to Schwartz. *Journal of Experimental Psychology,* 1981, *110,* 436–447. [13]

Abramson, L. Y., G. I. Metalsky, and **L. B. Alloy.** The hopelessness theory of depression: A metatheoretical analysis with implications for psychopathology research. *Psychological Review,* 1989. [18]

Abramson, L. Y., M. E. P. Seligman, and **J. Teasdale.** Learned helplessness in humans: Critique and reformulation. *Journal of Abnormal Psychology,* 1978, *87,* 49–74. [20]

Ackerman, N. *The psychodynamics of family life.* New York: Basic Books, 1958. [19]

Adams, J. S. Inequity in social exchange. In L. Berkowitz (Ed.), *Advances in experimental social psychology* (Vol. 2). New York: Academic Press, 1965. [23]

Adams, M. J. Aristotle's logic. In G. H. Bower (Ed.), *The psychology of learning and motivation* (Vol. 18). New York: Academic Press, 1984. [9]

Adams, M. J. (Coordinator). *Odyssey: A curriculum for thinking.* Watertown, Mass.: Mastery Education Corporation, 1986. [11]

Adelman, P. K., and **R. B. Zajonc.** Facial efference and the experience of emotion. *Annual Review of Psychology,* 1989, *40,* 249–280. [12]

Adelson, J. The growth of thought in adolescence. *Educational Horizons.* Summer 1983, 156–162. [16]

Adelson, J., and **E. Hall.** Children and other political naïfs. In E. Hall (Ed.), *Growing and changing.* New York: Random House, 1987. [16]

Ader, R., and **N. Cohen.** Conditioned immunopharmacological responses. In R. Ader (Ed.), *Psychoneuroimmunology.* New York: Academic Press, 1981, pp. 281–319. [7]

Adler, N. E., H. P. David, B. N. Major, S. H. Roth, N. F. Russo, and **G. E. Wyatt.** Psychological responses to abortion. Unpublished manuscript, 1989. [1]

Ainsworth, M. D. S., M. C. Blehar, E. Waters, and **S. Wall.** *Patterns of attachment.* Hillsdale, N.J.: Lawrence Erlbaum, 1978. [16]

Aitchison, J. *The articulate mammal: An introduction to psycholinguistics.* New York: McGraw-Hill, 1976. [10]

Ajzen, I. Attitudes, traits and actions: Dispositional prediction of behavior in personality and social psychology. In L. Berkowitz (Ed.), *Advances in experimental social psychology* (Vol. 20), New York: Academic Press, 1987, pp. 1–63. [21]

Akiskal, H. S. Dysthymic disorder: Psychopathology of proposed chronic depressive subtype. *American Journal of Psychiatry,* 1983, *140,* 11–20. [18]

Akiskal, H. S., R. M. A. Hirschfeld, and **B. I. Yerevanian.** The relationship of personality to affective disorders. *Archives of General Psychiatry,* 1983, *40,* 801–810. [18]

Akmajian, A., R. A. Demers, and **R. M. Harnish.** *Linguistics: An introduction to language and communication* (2nd ed.). Cambridge, Mass.: MIT Press, 1984. [10]

Albright, C. L., D. G. Altman, M. D. Slater, and **N. Maccoby.** Cigarette advertising in magazines: Evidence for a differential focus on women's and youth magazines. *Health Education Quarterly,* Summer 1988, *15,* 225–234. [20]

Allen, M. G. Twin studies of affective illness. *Archives of General Psychiatry,* 1976, *33,* 1476–1478. [18]

Allen, M. P., S. K. Panian, and **R. E. Lotz.** Managerial succession and organizational performance: A recalcitrant problem revisited. *Administrative Science Quarterly,* 1979, *24,* 167–180. [23]

Allen, V. L., and **D. A. Wilder.** Group categorization and attribution of belief similarity. *Small Group Behavior,* 1979, *10,* 73–80. [21]

Allgeier, B., and **R. Allgeier.** *Sexual interactions* (2nd ed.). Lexington, Mass.: Heath, 1988. [14]

Allman, J., F. Miezin, and **D. McGuinness.** Direction- and velocity-specific responses from beyond the classical receptive field in the middle temporal visual area (MT). *Perception,* 1985, *14,* 105–126. [5]

Alloy et al. see Kayne et al., p. R-20.

Allport, F. H. The influence of the group upon association and thought. *Journal of Experimental Psychology,* 1920, *3,* 159–182. [22]

Allport, G. W. *Personality: A psychological interpretation.* New York: Holt, Rinehart & Winston, 1937. [17]

Allport, G. W. *The nature of prejudice.* Reading, Mass.: Addison-Wesley, 1954. [21]

Allport, G. W. *Pattern and growth in personality.* New York: Holt, Rinehart & Winston, 1961. [17]

Allport, G. W. Traits revisited. *American Psychologist,* 1966, *21,* 1–10. [17]

Allport, G. W., and **H. S. Odbert.** Trait-names: A psycho-lexical study. *Psychological Monographs,* 1936, *47,* Whole No. 211. [17]

Altman, D. G., M. D. Slater, C. L. Albright, and **N. Maccoby.** How an unhealthy product is sold: Cigarette advertising in magazines, 1960–1985. *Journal of Communication,* Autumn 1987, *37,* 95–106. [20]

Altmann, S. A. Primate communication. In G. A. Miller (Ed.), *Communication, language, and meaning.* New York: Basic Books, 1973. [10]

American Association on Mental Deficiency. *Manual on terminology and classification in mental retardation* (1977 revision). Washington, D.C.: American Association on Mental Deficiency, 1977. [11]

American Heart Association. *Heart facts.* Dallas: American Heart Association, 1984. [20]

American Psychiatric Association. *Diagnostic and statistical manual of mental disorders (DSM-I)* (1st ed.). Washington, D.C.: American Psychiatric Association, 1973. [14]

American Psychiatric Association. *Diagnostic and statistical manual of mental disorders (DSM-III)* (3rd ed., rev.). Washington, D.C.: American Psychiatric Association, 1987. [13, 14, 18]

American Psychological Association. *Ethical principles of psychologists.* Washington, D.C.: American Psychological Association, 1981. [2]

Ames, A., Jr. Visual perception and the rotating trapezoidal window. *Psychological Monographs,* 1951, *65* (7, Whole No. 234). [5]

Anastasi, A. *Psychological testing.* New York: Macmillan, (5th ed.) 1982 and (7th ed.) 1988. [11, 17]

Anders, T. F., and **H. P. Roffwarg.** The effects of selective interruption and deprivation of sleep in the human newborn. *Developmental Psychobiology*, 1973, *6* (1), 77–89. [6]

Anderson, D. C., C. R. Crowell, M. Doman, and G. S. Howard. Performance posting, goal setting, and activity-contingent praise as applied to a university hockey team. *Journal of Applied Psychology*, 1988, *73*, 87–95. [23]

Anderson, J. R. *Cognitive psychology and its implications.* San Francisco: W. H. Freeman, 1980. [7, 10, 16]

Anderson, J. R. Interference: The relationship between response latency and response accuracy. *Journal of Experimental Psychology: Human Learning and Memory*, 1981, *7*, 311–325. [8]

Anderson, J. R. Acquisition of cognitive skill. *Psychological Review*, 1982, *89*, 369–406. [7]

Anderson, J. R. A spreading activation theory of memory. *Journal of Verbal Learning and Verbal Behavior*, 1983, *22*, 261–295. [8]

Anderson, J. R. *Cognitive psychology and its implications* (2nd ed.). New York: W. H. Freeman, 1985. [7, 9]

Anderson, J. R., and G. H. Bower. A propositional theory of recognition memory. *Memory and Cognition*, 1974, *2*, 406–412. [8]

Anderson, J. R., C. F. Boyle, R. Farrell, and B. Reiser. Cognitive principles in the design of computer tutors. *Proceedings of the Sixth Annual Conference of the Cognitive Science Society*, 1984, pp. 2–9. [7]

Andersson, B. The effect of injections of hypertonic NaCl solutions into different parts of the hypothalamus of goats. *Acta Physiologica Scandinavica*, 1953, *28*, 188–201. [13]

Andreasen, N. C., and S. Olsen. Negative v. positive schizophrenia: Definition and validation. *Archives of General Psychiatry*, 1982, *39*, 789–794. [18]

Andreasen, N. C., H. A. Nasrallah, V. Dunn, S. C. Olson, W. M. Grove, J. C. Ehrhardt, J. A. Coffman, and J. H. W. Crossett. Structural abnormalities in the frontal system in schizophrenia: A magnetic resonance imagining study. *Archives of General Psychiatry*, 1986, *43*, 136–144. [18]

Andrews, G., and R. Harvey. Does psychotherapy benefit neurotic patients? A reanalysis of the Smith, Glass, and Miller data. *Archives of General Psychiatry*, 1981, *38*, 1203–1208. [19]

Arkes, H. R., and J. P. Garske. *Psychological theories of motivation.* Monterey, Calif.: Brooks/Cole, 1977. [13]

Arnold, M. B. *Emotion and personality.* New York: Columbia University Press, 1960. [12]

Aronson, E., N. Blaney, C. Stephan, J. Sikes, and M. Snapp. *The jigsaw classroom.* Beverly Hills, Calif.: Sage, 1978. [21]

Aronson, E., and D. E. Linder. Gain and loss of esteem as determinants of interpersonal attractiveness. *Journal of Experimental Social Psychology*, 1965, *1*, 156–172. [21]

Aronson, E., and S. Worchel. Similarity versus liking as determinants of interpersonal attractiveness. *Psychonomic Science*, 1966, *5*, 157–158. [21]

Arvey, R. Unfair discrimination in the employment interview: Legal and psychological aspects. *Psychological Bulletin*, 1979, *86*, 736–765. [23]

Asch, S. E. Effects of group pressure upon the modification and distortion of judgments. In H. Guertzkow (Ed.), *Groups, leadership, and men.* Pittsburgh: Carnegie Press, 1951. [22]

Asch, S. E. Opinions and social pressure. *Scientific American*, 1955, *193*, 31–35. [22]

Asher, S. R., and K. A. Dodge. Identifying children who are rejected by their peers. *Developmental Psychology*, 1986, *22*, 444–449. [15]

Ashmead, D. H., and M. Perlmutter. Infant memory in everyday life. In M. Perlmutter (Ed.), *New directions in child development*, No. 10. *Children's memory.* San Francisco: Jossey-Bass, 1980. [15]

Aslin, R. N., D. B. Pisoni, and P. W. Jusczyk. Auditory development and speech perception in infancy. In P. H. Mussen (Ed.), *Handbook of child psychology* (4th ed.). Vol. 2. *Infancy and developmental psychobiology.* (M. M. Haith and J. J. Campos, Eds.). New York: Wiley, 1983. [5]

Atchley, R. C. *The sociology of retirement.* New York: Halstead Press, 1976. [16]

Atchley, R. C. *The social forces in later life* (3rd ed.). Belmont, Calif.: Wadsworth, 1980. [16]

Atkinson, J. W. (Ed.). *Motives in fantasy, action, and society.* New York: Van Nostrand Reinhold, 1958a. [13]

Atkinson, J. W. Thematic apperceptive measurement of motives within a context of motivation. In J. W. Atkinson (Ed.), *Motives in fantasy, action, and society.* New York: Van Nostrand Reinhold, 1958b. [13]

Atkinson, J. W. *An introduction to motivation.* Princeton, N.J.: Van Nostrand, 1964. [13]

Atkinson, C., and R. M. Shiffrin. The control of short-term memory. *Scientific American*, 1971, *225*, 82–90. [8]

Atkinson, R. C. Mnemotechnics in second-language learning. *American Psychologist*, 1975, *30*, 821–828. [8]

Au, T. K. Language and cognition. In R. L. Schiefelbusch and L. L. Lloyd (Eds.), *Language perspectives*, Austin, Tex.: Pro-Ed, Inc., 1988. [10]

Averill, J. R. A semantic atlas of emotional concepts. *JSAS Catalogue of Selected Documents in Psychology*, 1975, *5*, 330 (Ms. No. 421). [12]

Axelrod, R., and W. D. Hamilton. The evolution of cooperation. *Science*, 1981, *211*, 1390–1396. [22]

Axsom, D., S. Yates, and S. Chaiken. Audience response as a heuristic cue in persuasion. *Journal of Personality and Social Psychology*, 1987, *53*, 30–40. [21]

Ayllon, T., and N. H. Azrin. *The token economy: A motivational system for therapy and rehabilitation.* New York: Appleton-Century-Crofts, 1968. [7]

Azrin, N. H., and R. B. Foxx. *Toilet training in less than a day.* New York: Simon & Schuster, 1974. [7]

Baddeley, A. D. *The psychology of human memory.* London: Harper & Row, 1976. [8]

Baddeley, Alan. *Working memory.* Oxford University Press, 1984. [8]

Baddeley, A. D., N. Thomson, and M. Buchanan. Word-length and time structure of short-term memory. *Journal of Verbal Learning and Verbal Behavior*, 1975, *14*, 575–589. [8]

Badia, P., S. Culbertson, and J. Harsh. Choice of longer or stronger signalled shock over shorter or weaker unsignalled shock. *Journal of Experimental Analysis of Behavior*, 1973, *19*, 25–32. [20]

Bahnson, C. B. Stress and cancer: The state of the art. *Psychosomatics*, 1981, *22*, 207–220. [20]

Bahrick, H. P. Memory and people. In J. Harris (Ed.), *Everyday memory, actions, and absentmindedness.* New York: Academic Press, 1983. [8]

Bahrick, H. P., and D. Karis. Long-term ecological memory. In C. R. Puff (Ed.), *Handbook of research methods in human memory and cognition.* New York: Academic Press, 1982. [8]

Bailey, J. M., and J. M. Horn. A source of variance in IQ unique to the lowest-scoring monozygotic (MZ) cotwin. *Behavior Genetics*, 1986, *16*, 509–519. [11]

Baldwin, W. R. A review of statistical studies of relations between myopia and ethnic, behavioral, and physiological characteristics. *American Journal of Optometry and Physiological Optics*, 1981, *58*, 516–527. [4]

Balota, D. A. Automatic semantic activation and episodic memory encoding. *Journal of Verbal Learning and Verbal Behavior*, 1983, *22*, 88–104. [5]

Bancroft, J. Hormones and human sexual behavior. *Journal of Sex and Marital Therapy*, 1984, *10*, 3–21. [14]

Bandura, A. Influence of models' reinforcement contingencies on the acquisition of imitative responses. *Journal of Personality and Social Psychology*, 1965, *1*, 589–595. [7]

Bandura, A. Social-learning theory of identificatory processes. In D. A. Goslin (Ed.), *Handbook of socialization theory and research*. Chicago: Rand-McNally, 1969. [7]

Bandura, A. *Aggression: A social learning analysis*. Englewood Cliffs, N.J.: Prentice-Hall, 1973. [22]

Bandura, A. Social learning analysis of aggression. In E. Ribes-Inesta and A. Bandura (Eds.), *Analysis of delinquency and aggression*. Hillsdale, N.J.: Lawrence Erlbaum, 1976. [22]

Bandura, A. *Social learning theory*. Englewood Cliffs, N.J.: Prentice-Hall, 1977. [7, 15, 17, 18]

Bandura, A. Self-efficacy: Toward a unifying theory of behavioral change. *Psychological Review*, 1977, *84*, 191–215. [19]

Bandura, A. The self system in reciprocal determinism. *American Psychologist*, 1978, *33*, 344–358. [19]

Bandura, A. Self-efficacy mechanisms in human agency. *American Psychologist*, 1982, *37*, 122–147. [17, 19]

Bandura, A. *Social foundations of thought and action*. Englewood Cliffs, N.J.: Prentice-Hall, 1986. [7, 9, 16, 17, 19]

Bandura, A., and **F. L. Menlove.** Factors determining vicarious extinction of avoidance behavior through symbolic modeling. *Journal of Personality and Social Psychology*, 1968, *8*, 99–108. [19]

Bandura, A., D. Ross, and **S. A. Ross.** Imitation of film-mediated aggressive models. *Journal of Abnormal and Social Psychology*, 1963, *66*, 3–11. [7]

Banks, M. S., R. N. Aslin, and **R. D. Letson.** Sensitive period for the development of human binocular vision. *Science*, 1975, *190*, 675–677. [5]

Banks, M. S., and **P. Salapatek.** Infant visual perception. In P. H. Mussen (Ed.), *Handbook of child psychology* (4th ed.) (Vol. 2). M. M. Haith and J. J. Campos (Eds.), *Infancy and developmental psychobiology*. New York: Wiley, 1983. [5, 15]

Barasch, M., and **M. Aguilera-Hellweg.** *Breaking 100: Americans who have lived over a century*. New York: Quill, 1983. [16]

Barbanel, J. Mentally ill homeless taken off New York streets. *The New York Times*, October 29, 1987*a*, A1, B9. [19]

Barbanel, J. 10 homeless people held at Bellevue Mental Unit. *The New York Times*, October 30, 1987*b*, B3. [19]

Barbanel, J. Woman battles Koch's program for mentally ill. *The New York Times*, November 2, 1987*c*, B3. [19]

Barber, T. X. *Hypnosis: A scientific approach*. New York: Psychological Dimensions, 1976. [6]

Barber, T. X., N. P. Spanos, and **J. F. Chaves.** *Hypnotism: Imagination and human potentialities*. New York: Pergamon Press, 1974. [6]

Barec, L., C. MacArthur, and **M. Sherwood.** A study of health education aspects of smoking in pregnancy. *International Journal of Health Education*, 1976, *19* (suppl. 1), 1–17. [20]

Barker, R. G., T. Dembo, and **K. Lewin.** *Frustration and regression: An experiment with young children*. University of Iowa Studies in Child Welfare, 1941, *18*, 386. [22]

Barnes, D. M. Brain damage by AIDS under active study. *Science*, 1987, *235*, 1574–1577. [14]

Barnes, G. M. Adolescent alcohol abuse and other problem behaviors. *Journal of Youth and Adolescence*, 1984, *13*, 329–348. [16]

Baron, J. *Rationality and intelligence*. New York: Cambridge University Press, 1985. [11]

Baron, J. *Thinking and deciding*. New York: Cambridge University Press, 1988. [11]

Baron, J. N., and **P. C. Reiss.** Same time next year: Aggregate analyses of the mass media and violent behavior. *American Sociological Review*, 1985, *50*, 347–363. [22]

Barraclough, B. M., B. Nelson, J. Bunch, and **P. Sainsbury.** The diagnostic classification and psychiatric treatment of 100 suicides. *Proceedings of the Fifth International Conference for Suicide Prevention*. London, 1969. [18]

Barrett, T. R., and **S. K. Watkins.** Word familiarity and cardiovascular health as determinants of age-related recall differences. *Journal of Gerontology*, 1986, *41*, 222–224. [16]

Bartoshuk, L. M. Bitter taste of saccharin related to the genetic ability to taste the bitter substance 6-*n*-propylthiouracil. *Science*, 1979, *205*, 934–935. [1979]

Bartoshuk, L. M. Separate worlds of taste. *Psychology Today*, 1980, *14*, 48–63. [4]

Bass, B. M. *Leadership and performance beyond expectations*. New York: Free Press, 1985. [23]

Bassuk, E. L., and **S. C. Schoonover.** *The practitioner's guide to psychoactive drugs*. New York: Plenum, 1977. [19]

Bates, E. *The emergence of symbols*. New York: Academic Press, 1979. [15]

Bateson, G., D. Jackson, J. Hayley, and **J. Weakland.** Toward a theory of schizophrenia. *Behavioral Science*, 1956, *1*, 251–264. [18]

Batson, C. D. Prosocial motivation: Is it ever truly altruistic? In L. Berkowitz (Ed.), *Advances in experimental social psychology* (Vol. 20). New York: Academic Press, 1987. [22]

Batson, C. D., B. Duncan, P. Ackerman, T. Buckley, and **K. Birch.** Is empathic emotion a source of altruistic emotion? *Journal of Personality and Social Psychology*, 1981, *40*, 290–302. [22]

Batson, C. D., J. Fultz, and **P. A. Schoenrade.** Distress and empathy: Two qualitatively distinct vicarious emotions with different motivational consequences. *Journal of Personality*, 1987, *55*, 19–40. [22]

Battig, W. F., and **W. E. Montague.** Category norms for verbal items in 56 categories: A replication and extension of the Connecticut category norms. *Journal of Experimental Psychology Monograph*, June 1969. [9]

Baum, A., and **R. J. Gatchel.** Cognitive determinants of reaction to uncontrollable events: Development of reactance and learned helplessness. *Journal of Personality and Social Psychology*, 1981, *40*, 1078–1089. [22]

Baum, A., and **S. Valins.** *Architecture and social behavior: Psychological studies of social density*. Hillsdale, N.J.: Lawrence Erlbaum, 1977. [22]

Baumeister, R. F. *Identity*. New York: Oxford University Press, 1986. [16]

Baumrind, D. Familial antecedents of social competence in middle childhood. Unpublished monograph, Institute of Human Development, University of California, Berkeley, 1986. [15]

Bayer, E. Beitrage zur Zweikomponententheorie des Hungers. *Zeitschrift für Psychologie*, 1929, *112*, 1–54. [22]

Bayley, N. Mental growth during the first three years. *Genetic Psychology Monographs*, 1933, *14*, 1–93. [11]

Bayley, N. Consistency and variability in the growth of intelligence from birth to eighteen years. *Journal of Genetic Psychology*, 1949, *75*, 165–196. [11]

Bayley, N. On the growth of intelligence. *American Psychologist*, 1955, *10*, 805–818. [11]

Bayley, N. *Manual for the Bayley Scales of Infant Development*. New York: Psychological Corp. 1969. [15]

Beck, A. T. *Depression: Clinical, experimental, and theoretical aspects*. New York: Harper & Row, 1967. [12, 18]

Beck, A. T. *Cognitive therapy and the emotional disorders*. New York: International Universities Press, 1976.

Beck, A. T., A. J. Rush, B. F. Shaw, and **G. Emery.** *Cognitive theory of depression*. New York: Guilford Press, 1979. [18, 19]

Beck, S. J. *Rorschach's test*. Vol. 1, *Basic processes* (3rd ed.). New York: Grune & Stratton, 1961. [17]

Becker, J. V., L. J. Skinner, G. G. Abel, and **E. C. Treacy.** Incidence and types of sexual dysfunctions in rape and incest victims. *Journal of Sex and Marital Therapy*, 1982, *8*, (1), 65–74. [14]

Becker, M. H., and J. G. Joseph. AIDS and behavioral change to reduce risk: A review. *American Journal of Public Health*, 1988, *78*, 394–410. [14]

Bekesy, G. von. Current status of theories of hearing. *Science*, 1956, *123*, 779–783. [4]

Bell, A., M. S. Weinberg, and S. K. Hammersmith. *Sexual preference: Its development in men and women.* Bloomington: Indiana University Press, 1981. [14]

Bellack, A. S., M. Hersen, and J. M. Himmelbach. A comparison of social skills training, pharmacotherapy and psychotherapy for depression. *Behavior Research and Therapy*, 1983, *21*, 101–108. [19]

Bellezza, F. S. Updating memory using mnemonic devices. *Cognitive Psychology*, 1982, *14*, 301–327. [8]

Bellows, R. T. Time factors in water drinking in dogs. *American Journal of Physiology*, 1939, *125*, 87–97. [13]

Belsky, J., and M. J. Rovine. Nonmaternal care in the first year of life and the security of infant-parent attachment. *Child Development*, 1988, *59*, 157–167. [15]

Belsky, J., M. Rovine, and D. G. Taylor. The Pennsylvania infant and family project. *Child Development*, 1984, *55*, 718–728. [15]

Bem, D. J. An experimental analysis of self-persuasion. *Journal of Experimental Social Psychology*, 1965, *1*, 199–218. [21]

Bem, S. L. Gender schema theory and its implications for child development: Raising gender-aschematic children in a gender-schematic society. *Signs*, 1983, *8*, 598–616. [15]

Bem, S. L. Androgyny and gender schema theory: A conceptual and empirical integration. In T. B. Sonderegger (Ed.), *Nebraska symposium on motivation* (Vol. 32). Lincoln: University of Nebraska Press, 1985. [15]

Bennett, W., and J. Gurin. *The dieter's dilemma.* New York: Basic Books, 1982. [13]

Berger, P. A. Medical treatment of mental illness. *Science*, 1978, *200*, 974–981. [19]

Bergin, A. E. The evaluation of therapeutic outcomes. In A. E. Bergin and S. L. Garfield (Eds.), *Handbook of psychotherapy and behavior change: An empirical analysis.* New York: Wiley, 1971. [19]

Bergin, A. E., and M. J. Lambert. The evaluation of therapeutic outcomes. In S. L. Barfield and A. E. Bergin (Eds.), *Handbook of psychotherapy and behavior change: An empirical analysis* (2nd ed.). New York: Wiley, 1978. [19]

Berko, J. The child's learning of English morphology. *Word*, 1958, *14*, 150–177. [10]

Berkowitz, L. *Aggression: A social psycho-*

logical analysis. New York: McGraw-Hill, 1962. [22]

Berlin, B., and P. Kaye. *Basic color terms: Their universality and evolution.* Berkeley: University of California Press, 1969. [10]

Berlyne, D. E. *Conflict, arousal and curiosity.* New York: McGraw-Hill, 1960. [13]

Berman, J. S., C. Miller, and P. J. Massman. Cognitive therapy versus systematic desensitization: Is one treatment superior? *Psychological Bulletin*, 1985, *97*, 451–461. [19]

Berndt, T. J. Developmental changes in conformity of peers and parents. *Developmental Psychology*, 1979, *15*, 608–616. [16]

Bernstein, I. Learned taste aversion in children receiving chemotherapy. *Science*, 1978, *200*, 1302–1303. [7]

Bernstein, I. L., and M. M. Webster. Learned taste aversions in humans. *Physiology and Behavior*, 1980, *25*, 363–366. [7]

Berscheid, E., K. Dion, E. Walster, and G. M. Walster. Physical attractiveness and dating choice: A test of the matching hypothesis. *Journal of Experimental Social Psychology*, 1971, *7*, 173–189. [21]

Beutler, L. E., M. Crago, and T. G. Arizmendi. Research on therapist variables in psychotherapy. In S. L. Garfield and A. E. Bergin (Eds.), *Handbook of psychotherapy and behavior change: An evaluative analysis* (3rd ed.). New York: Wiley, 1986. [19]

Bickman, L. The social power of a uniform. *Journal of Applied Social Psychology*, 1974, *4*, 47–61. [22]

Bieber, L., et al. *Homosexuality: A psychoanalytic study.* New York: Basic Books, 1962. [14]

Bijou, S. W., and D. M. Baer. *Child development.* Vol. 2. *Universal stage of infancy.* Englewood Cliffs, N.J.: Prentice-Hall, 1965. [15]

Binet, A., and T. Simon. Methodes nouvelles pour le diagnostic du niveau intellectuel des anormaux. *L'Année Psychologique*, 1905, *11*, 191–244. [11]

Birch, H. G., C. Piniero, E. Alcade, T. Toca, and J. Craviota. Relation of kwashiokor in early childhood and intelligence at school age. *Pediatric Research*, 1971, *5*, 579–592. [11]

Bisiach, E. The (haunted) brain and consciousness. In A. J. Marcel and E. Bisiach (Eds.), *Consciousness in contemporary science.* Oxford: Clarendon Press, 1988. [6]

Björklund, D. F. A note on neonatal imitation. *Developmental Review*, 1987, *7*, 86–92. [15]

Blakeslee, S. Cynicism and mistrust tied to early death. *The New York Times*, January 17, 1989. [20]

Blamey, P. J. Psychophysical and speech studies with an electrotactile speech processor. *Annals of Otology, Rhinology and Laryngology*, 1987, *96* (1), 87–89. [4]

Blanchard, E. B., F. Andrasik, D. D. Evans, D. F. Neff, K. A. Appelbaum, and L. D. Rodichok. Behavioral treatment of 250 chronic headache patients: A clinical replication series. *Behavior Therapy*, 1985, *16*, 308–327. [20]

Blanchard-Fields, F. Reasoning on social dilemmas varying in emotional saliency. *Psychology and Aging*, 1986, *1*, 325–333. [16]

Bleuler, M. *The schizophrenic disorders.* New Haven, Conn.: Yale University Press, 1978. [18]

Block, J. Studies in the phenomenology of emotions. *Journal of Abnormal and Social Psychology*, 1957, *54*, 358–363. [12]

Block, J., J. H. Block, and S. Keyes. Longitudinally foretelling drug usage in adolescence: Early childhood personality and environmental precursors. *Child Development*, 1988, *59*, 336–355. [16]

Block, N. J. and G. Dworkin. *The IQ controversy: Critical readings.* New York: Pantheon, 1976. [11]

Bloom, B. L., S. J. Asher, and S. W. White. Marital disruption as a stressor: A review and analysis. *Psychological Bulletin*, 1978, *7*, 488–498. [2]

Bloom, F. E., A. Lazerson, and L. Hofstadter. *Brain, mind, and behavior.* New York: Freeman, 1985. [3]

Bloom, S. G. For a few scents more. *San Jose Mercury News*, March 21, 1984, pp. C1–2. [4]

Blumer, D., and A. E. Walker. The neural basis of sexual behavior. In D. F. Benson and D. Blumer (Eds.), *Psychiatric aspects of neurological disease.* New York: Grune & Stratton, 1975. [18]

Blumstein, P., D. Cohen, and D. Nagin (Eds.). *Deterence and incapacitation: Estimating the effects of criminal sanctions on crime rates.* Washington, D.C.: U.S. Government Printing Office, 1978. [22]

Blumstein, P., and P. Schwartz. *American couples.* New York: William Morrow, 1983. [14]

Bogin, B. *Patterns of human growth.* New York: Cambridge University Press, 1988. [16]

Bohannon, J. H. III, and A. Warren-Leubecker. Theoretical approaches to language acquisition. In J. B. Gleason (Ed.), *The development of language.* Columbus, Ohio: Charles E. Merrill, 1985. [15]

Bolles, R. C. *Theory of motivation.* New York: Harper & Row, 1967. [13]

Bolles, R. C. Species-specific defense reactions and avoidance learning. *Psychological Review*, 1970, *77*, 32–48. [7]

Bolton, F. G., Jr. *The pregnant adolescent: Problems of premature parenthood.* Beverly Hills, Calif.: Sage, 1980. [16]

Bondareff, W. The neural basis of aging. In J. E. Birren and K. W. Schale (Eds.), *Handbook of the psychology of aging* (2nd ed.). New York: Van Nostrand Reinhold, 1985. [16]

Booth-Kewley, S., and H. S. Friedman. Psychological predictors of heart disease: A quantitative review. *Psychological Bulletin,* 1987, *101,* 343–362. [20]

Bootzin, R. R. The role of expectancy in behavior change. In L. White, B. Tursky, and G. Schwartz (Eds.), *Placebo: Clinical phenomena and new insights.* New York: Gilford Press, 1985. [19]

Bootzin, R. R., and M. Engle-Friedman. Sleep disturbances. In L. L. Carstensen and B. A. Edelstein (Eds.), *Handbook of clinical gerontology.* Elmsford, N.Y.: Pergamon Press, 1987.

Boring, E. G. *Sensation and perception in the history of experimental psychology.* New York: Appleton-Century-Crofts, 1942. [5]

Boring, E. G. Size constancy in a picture. *American Journal of Psychology,* 1964, *77,* 494–498. [5]

Borkovec, T. D., J. B. Grayson, and K. M. Cooper. Treatment of general tension: Subjective and physiological effects of progressive relaxation. *Journal of Consulting and Clinical Psychology,* 1978, *46,* 518–528. [20]

Borkovec, T. D., J. B. Grayson, G. T. O'Brien, and T. C. Weerts. Relaxation treatment of pseudoinsomnia and ideiopathic insomnia: An electroencephalographic evaluation. *Journal of Applied Behavior Analysis,* 1979, *12,* 37–54. [20]

Borkovec, T. D., T. W. Lane, and P. H. VanOot. Phenomenology of sleep among insomniacs and good sleepers: Wakefulness experience when cortically asleep. *Journal of Abnormal Psychology,* 1981, *90,* 607–609. [6]

Bornstein, M. H. Perceptual development. In M. H. Bornstein and M. E. Lamb (Eds.), *Developmental psychology.* Hillsdale, N.J.: Lawrence Erlbaum, 1984. [5]

Bornstein, M. H., and M. D. Sigman. Continuity in mental development from infancy. *Child Development,* 1986, *57,* 251–274. [11]

Botwinick, J. Intellectual abilities. In J. E. Birren and K. W. Schaie (Eds.), *Handbook of the psychology of aging.* New York: Van Nostrand Reinhold, 1977. [16]

Bouchard, T. J. *Separated identical twins: Preliminary findings.* Invited address, annual meeting of the American Psycho-logical Association. Los Angeles, August 1981. [11]

Bower, G. H. Mental imagery and associative learning. In L. W. Gregg (Ed.), *Cognition in learning and memory.* New York: Wiley, 1972. [8]

Bower, G. H. Improving memory. *Human Nature,* 1978, *1,* 64–72. [8]

Bower, G. H. Mood and memory. *American Psychologist,* 1981, *36,* 129–148. [8]

Bower, G. H. Affect and cognition. *Philosophical Transactions of the Royal Society of London (Series B).* 1983, *302,* 387–402. [9]

Bower, G. H., M. Clark, D. Winzenz, and A. Lesgold. Hierarchical retrieval schemes in recall of categorized word lists. *Journal of Verbal Learning and Verbal Behavior,* 1969, *8,* 323–343. [8]

Bower, G. H., and E. R. Hilgard. *Theories of learning* (5th ed.). Englewood Cliffs, N.J.: Prentice-Hall, 1981. [7]

Bower, G. H., M. B. Karlin, and A. Dueck. Comprehension and memory for pictures. *Memory and Cognition,* 1975, *3,* 216–229. [8]

Bower, G. H., and D. Winzenz. Comparison of associative learning strategies. *Psychonomic Science,* 1970, *20,* 119–120. [8]

Bowlby, J. *Attachment and loss.* Vol. 1. *Attachment.* New York: Basic Books, 1969. [15]

Bowmaker, J. K., and H. M. A. Dartnell. Visual pigments of rods and cones in a human retina. *Journal of Physiology,* 1980, *298,* 501–511. [4]

Boyd, J. H., and M. M. Weissman. Epidemiology of affective disorders: A reexamination and future directions. *Archives of General Psychiatry,* 1981, *38,* 1039–1045. [18]

Boynton, R. M. *Human color vision.* New York: Holt, Rinehart & Winston, 1979. [4]

Bradley, G. W. Self-serving biases in the attribution process: A reexamination of the fact or fiction question. *Journal of Personality and Social Psychology,* 1978, *36,* 56–61. [13]

Bradley, R. H., and B. M. Caldwell. The relation of infants' home environments to achievement test performance in first grade: A follow-up study. *Child Development,* 1984, *55,* 803–809. [11]

Braebeck, M. Moral judgment: Theory and research on differences between males and females. *Developmental Review,* 1982, *3,* 274–291. [16]

Braine, M. D. S., B. J. Reiser, and B. Rumain. Some empirical justification for a theory of natural propositional logic. In G. H. Bower (Ed.), *The psychology of learning and motivation* (Vol. 18). New York: Academic Press, 1984, pp. 313–372. [9]

Bransford, J. D. *Human cognition. Learn-ing, understanding and remembering.* Belmont, Calif.: Wadsworth, 1979. [8]

Bransford, J. D., and M. K. Johnson. Considerations of some problems of comprehension. In W. G. Chase (Ed.), *Visual information processing.* New York: Academic Press, 1973. [8, 10]

Bransford, J. D., R. Sherwood, N. Vye, and J. Rieser. Teaching thinking and problem solving. *American Psychologist,* 1986, *41,* 1078–1089. [9]

Bransford, J. D., and B. S. Stein. *The ideal problem-solver.* New York: W. H. Freeman, 1984. [9]

Bravo, M., R. Blake, and S. Morrison. Cats see subjective contours. *Vision Research,* 1988, *28,* 861–865. [5]

Brecher, Edward M. Love, sex, and aging. Boston: Little, Brown, 1984. [14]

Breckler, S. J. Empirical validation of affect, behavior and cognition as distinct components of attitude. *Journal of Personality and Social Psychology,* 1984, *47,* 1191–1205. [21]

Bretherton, I., and M. Beeghly. Talking about internal states: The acquisition of an explicit theory of mind. *Developmental Psychology,* 1982, *18,* 906–912. [12]

Bretherton, I., and E. Waters. Growing points of attachment theory and research. *Monographs of the Society for Research in Child Development,* 1985, *50,* Serial 209. [14]

Brewer, M. B. Ingroup bias in the minimal intergroup situation: A cognitive-motivational approach. *Psychological Bulletin,* 1979, *86,* 307–324. [21]

Brickman, P., D. Coates, and R. Janoff-Bulman. Lottery winners and accident victims: Is happiness relative? *Journal of Personality and Social Psychology,* 1978, *36,* 917–927. [12]

Brines, M. L., and J. L. Gould. Bees have rules. *Science,* 1979, *202,* 571–573. [10]

Broadhurst, P. L. The interaction of task difficulty and motivation: The Yerkes-Dodson law revived. *Acta Psychologica,* 1959, *16,* 321–338. [17]

Brockner, J., J. Greenberg, A. Brockner, J. Bortz, J. Davy, and C. Carter. Layoffs, equity theory, and work performance: Further evidence of the impact of survivor guilt. *Academy of Management Journal,* 1986, *29,* 373–384. [23]

Brockner, J., S. Grover, T. Reed, R. DeWitt, and M. O'Malley. Survivors' reactions to layoffs: We get by with a little help for our friends. *Administrative Science Quarterly,* 1987, *32,* 526–541. [23]

Brody, G. H., and D. R. Shaffer. Contributions of parents and peers to children's moral socialization. *Developmental Review,* 1982, *2,* 31–75. [15]

Brody, J. E. Remembering the Hyatt disaster: Emotional scars persist a year later.

The New York Times, July 6, 1982, pp. C1, C4. [20]

Brody, N. *Human motivation: Commentary on goal-directed action.* New York: Academic Press, 1983. [13]

Breuer, J., and Freud, S. *Studies of hysteria.* New York: Basic Books, 1957. (Originally published, 1937). [17]

Brook, J. S., M. Whiteman, A. S. Gordon, and P. Cohen. Dynamics of childhood and adolescent personality traits and adolescent drug use. *Developmental Psychology*, 1986a, 22, 403–414. [16]

Brook, J. S., M. Whiteman, A. S. Gordon, and P. Cohen. Some models and mechanisms for explaining the impact of maternal and adolescent characteristics on adolescent state of drug use. *Developmental Psychology*, 1986b, 22, 460–467. [16]

Brooks-Gunn, J., and F. F. Furstenberg, Jr. The children of adolescent mothers. *Developmental Review*, 1986c, 6, 224–251. [16]

Brophy, J. E., and T. Good. *Teacher–student relationships: Causes and consequences.* New York: Holt, Rinehart and Winston, 1974. [21]

Broverman, I. K., S. R. Vogen, D. M. Broverman, F. E. Clarkson, and P. S. Rosenkrantz. Sex-role stereotypes: A current appraisal. *Journal of Social Issues*, 1972, 28, 59–78. [22]

Brown, A. L. Metacognitive development and reading. In R. Spiro, B. Bruce, and W. Brewer (Eds.), *Theoretical issues in reading comprehension*, Hillsdale, N.J.: Erlbaum, 1980. [15]

Brown, A. M., R. C. Dowell, and G. M. Clark. Clinical results for postlingually deaf patients implanted with multichannel cochlear prostheses. In G. Clark and P. A. Busby (Eds.), International Cochlear Implant Symposium and Workshop. *Annals of Otology Rhinology, and Laryngology*, 1987, 96 (1) 127–128. [4]

Brown, B. B. *Super mind: The ultimate energy.* New York: Harper & Row, 1980. [20]

Brown, G. W., and T. Harris. *Social origins of depression.* New York: Free Press, 1978. [20]

Brown, J. J. Evaluations of self and others: Self-enhancement biases in social judgments. *Social Cognition*, 1986, 4, 353–376. [13]

Brown, P. K., and G. Wald. Visual pigments in single rods and cones of the human retina. *Science*, 1964, 144, 45–52. [4]

Brown, P. L. Studying seasons of a woman's life. *The New York Times*, September 14, 1987, C23. [16]

Brown, R. *A first language: The early stages.* Cambridge, Mass.: Harvard University Press, 1973. [15]

Brown, R., and C. Hanlon. Derivational complexity and order of acquisition in child speech. In J. R. Hayes (Ed.), *Cognition and the development of language.* New York: Wiley, 1970. [15]

Brown, R., and E. H. Lenneberg. A study in language and cognition. *Journal of Abnormal and Social Psychology*, 1954, 49, 454–462. [10]

Brown, R., and D. McNeill. The "tip-of-the-tongue" phenomenon. *Journal of Verbal Learning and Verbal Behavior*, 1966, 5, 325–337. [8]

Bruch, H. Psychological antecedents of anorexia nervosa. In R. A. Vigersky (Ed.), *Anorexia nervosa.* New York: Raven Press, 1977. [18]

Brundin, P., and A. Björklund. Survival, growth and function of dopamineric neurons grafted to the brain. In F. J. Seil, E. Herbet, and B. M. Carlson (Eds.), *Neural regeneration: Progress in brain research.* Vol. 71. Amsterdam: Elsevier, 1987, pp. 293–308. [3]

Brunson, B. I., and K. A. Matthews. The Type A coronary-prone behavior pattern and reactions to uncontrollable stress: An analysis of performance strategies, affect, and attributions, during failure. *Journal of Personality and Social Psychology*, 1981, 40, 906–918. [20]

Bruner, J. S. *In search of mind.* New York: Harper & Row, 1983. [15]

Burgess, A. W., and C. L. Holstrom. *Rape: Victims of crisis.* Bowie, Md.: R. J. Brady, 1974. [14]

Burt, C. The genetic determination of differences in intelligence: A study of monozygotic twins reared together and apart. *British Journal of Psychology*, 1966, 57, 137–153. [11]

Buss, A. H., and R. Plomin. *Temperament.* Hillsdale, N.J.: Erlbaum, 1984. [15]

Buss, A. H., R. Plomin, and L. Willerman. The inheritance of temperament. *Journal of Personality*, 1973, 41, 513–524. [17]

Buss, D. M., and N. Cantor. *Personality research for the 1990's.* New York: Springer-Verlag, 1989. [17]

Buss, D. M., and K. H. Craik. The act frequency approach to personality. *Psychological Review*, 1983, 90, 105–126. [17]

Butler, J. A., B. Starfield, and S. Stenmark. Child health policy. In H. W. Stevenson and A. E. Siegel (Eds.), *Child development research and social policy.* Chicago: University of Chicago Press, 1984. [20]

Butler, R. A. Curiosity in monkeys. *Scientific American*, 1954, 190, 70–75. [13]

Butler, R. N. *Why survive?* New York: Harper & Row, 1975. [16]

Bykov, K. *The cerebral cortex and the internal organs.* Moscow: Foreign Languages Publishing House, 1927/1959. [7]

Byrne, D., and B. Blaylock. Similarity and assumed similarity of attitudes between husbands and wives. *Journal of Abnormal and Social Psychology*, 1963, 67, 636–640. [21]

Byrne, D., and G. L. Clore. A reinforcement model of evaluative responses. *Personality: An International Journal*, 1970, 1, 103–128. [21]

Byrne, D., G. L. Clore, and G. Smeaton. The attraction hypothesis: Do similar attitudes affect anything? *Journal of Personality and Social Psychology*, 1986, 51, 1167–1170. [21]

Byrne, D., and J. Lambreth. The effects of erotic stimuli on sex arousal, evaluative responses, and subsequent behavior. Technical report of the commission on obscenity and pornography (Vol. 8). Washington, D.C.: U.S. Government Printing Office, 1971. [14]

Cain, W. S. Odor identification by males and females: Predictions versus performance. *Chemical Senses*, 1982, 7, 129–142. [4]

Calhoun, J. Population density and pathology. *Scientific American*, 1962, 206, 139–148. [22]

Campbell, J., A. Tesser, and P. Fairy. Conformity and attention to the stimulus: Some temporal and contextual dynamics. *Journal of Personality and Social Psychology*, 1986, 51, 315–324. [22]

Campbell, J. D. Similarity and uniqueness: The effects of attribute type, relevance, and individual differences in self-esteem and depression. *Journal of Personality and Social Psychology*, 1986, 50, 281–294. [13]

Campos, J. J., K. Barrett, M. Lamb, H. Goldsmith, and C. Sternberg. Socioemotional development. In P. Mussen (Ed.), *Handbook of child psychology* (4th ed., vol. 2): M. M. Haith and J. Campos (Eds.), *Infancy and developmental psychology*, New York: Wiley, 1983. [12]

Campos, J. J., S. Hiatt, D. Ramsay, C. Henderson, and M. Svejda. The emergence of fear on the visual cliff. In M. Lewis and L. Rosenblum (Eds.), *The origin of affect.* New York: Plenum, 1978. [15]

Cannon, M. S. The halfway house as an alternative to hospitalization. In Zusman and E. Bertsch (Eds.), *The future role of the state hospital.* Lexington, Mass.: Lexington Books, 1975. [19]

Cantor, N., and J. F. Kihlstrom. *Personality and social intelligence.* Englewood Cliffs, N.J.: Prentice-Hall, 1987. [17]

Cantor, N., J. K. Norem, P. M. Niedenthal, C. A. Langston, and A. M. Brower. Life tasks, self-concept ideals, and cognitive strategies in a life transition. *Journal of Personality and Social Psychology*, 1987, 53, 1178–1191. [17]

Caramazza, A., and E. B. Zurif. Dissociation of algorithmic and heuristic processes in language comprehension: Evidence from aphasia. *Brain and Language*, 1976, *3*, 572–582. [10]

Carlson, N. R. *Physiology of behavior* (3rd ed.). Boston: Allyn & Bacon, 1986. [4]

Carmichael, L., H. P. Hogan, and A. A. Walter. An experimental study of the effect of language on the reproduction of visually perceived form. *Journal of Experimental Psychology*, 1932, *15*, 73–86. [8, 10]

Carr, C. E., and M. Konishi. Axonal delay lines for time measurement in the owl's brainstem. *Proceedings of the National Academy of Science*, 1988, *85*, 8311–8315. [5]

Carter, D. B., and G. D. Levy. Cognitive aspects of early sex-role development: The influence of gender schemas on preschoolers' memories and preference for sex-typed toys and activities. *Child Development*, 1988, *59*, 531–543. [15]

Cartwright, R. A network model of stress and dreams. Paper presented at the Arizona Conference on Sleep and Dreams, Tucson, 1989. [6]

Cartwright, R. D. *Night life: Explorations in dreaming.* Englewood Cliffs, N.J.: Prentice-Hall, 1977. [6]

Carver, C. S. Facilitation of physical aggression through objective self-awareness. *Journal of Experimental Social Psychology*, 1974, *10*, 365–370. [13]

Carver, C. S. Physical aggression as a function of objective self-awareness and attitudes toward punishment. *Journal of Experimental Social Psychology*, 1975, *37*, 1251–1281. [13]

Carver, C. S., E. DeGregorio, and R. Gillis. Challenge and type A behavior among intercollegiate football players. *Journal of Sport Psychology*, 1981, *3*, 140–148. [20]

Carver, R. P. *Sense and nonsense in speed reading.* Silver Springs, Md.: Revrac Publications, 1971. [10]

Case, R. Intellectual development from birth to adulthood. A neo-Piagetian interpretation. In R. Siegler (Ed.), *Children's thinking: What develops?* Hillsdale, N.J.: Erlbaum, 1978. [15]

Case, R. *Intellectual development: Birth to adulthood.* New York: Academic Press, 1985. [15]

Case, R., D. M. Kurland, and J. Goldberg. Operational efficiency and the growth of short-term memory span. *Journal of Experimental Child Psychology*, 1982, *33*, 386–404. [15]

Caspi, A., G. H. Elder, Jr., and D. J. Bem. Moving against the world: Life-course patterns of explosive children. *Developmental Psychology*, 1987, *23*, 308–313. [2]

Cassidy, J. Child–mother attachment and the self in six-year-olds. *Child Development*, 1988, *59*, 121–124. [15]

Catania, A. C., and D. Cutts. Experimental control of superstitious responding in humans. *Journal of the Experimental Analysis of Behavior*, 1963, *6*, 203–208. [7]

Cattell, R. B. Theory of fluid and crystallized intelligence: A critical experiment. *Journal of Educational Psychology*, 1963, *54*, 1–22. [11]

Cattell, R. B. *The scientific analysis of personality.* Baltimore: Penguin, 1965. [17]

Cattell, R. B. The 16PF and basic personality structure: A reply to Eysenck. *Journal of Behavioral Science*, 1972, *1*, 169–187. [17]

Cautela, J. R. Treatment of compulsive behavior by covert sensitization. *Psychological Record*, 1966, *16*, 33–41. [19]

Cautela, J. R., and A. J. Kearney. *The covert conditioning handbook.* New York: Springer, 1986. [19]

Ceci, S. J., and J. K. Liker. A day at the races: A study of IQ, expertise, and cognitive complexity. *Journal of Experimental Psychology: General*, 1986a, *115*, 255–266. [11]

Ceci, S. J., and J. K. Liker. Academic and nonacademic intelligence: An experimental separation. In R. J. Sternberg and R. K. Wagner (Eds.), *Practical intelligence: Nature and origins of competence in the everyday world* (pp. 119–142). New York: Cambridge University Press, 1986b. [11]

Ceci, S. J., and J. K. Liker. Stalking the IQ-expertise relation: When the critics go fishing. *Journal of Experimental Psychology: General*, 1988, *117*, 96–100. [11]

Cernock, J. M., and R. H. Porter. Recognition of maternal axiliary odors by infants. *Child Development*, 1985, *56*, 1593–1598. [5, 15]

Cialdini, R. B., and K. D. Richardson. Two indirect tactics of image management: Basking and blasting. *Journal of Personality and Social Psychology*, 1980, *39*, 406–415. [13]

Chaikin, A. After 15 years, still no cure for astronauts' space sickness. *San Jose Mercury News,* June 26, 1984, pp. C1+. [4]

Chaiken, S. Heuristic versus systematic information processing and the use of source versus message cues in persuasion. *Journal of Personality and Social Psychology*, 1980, *39*, 752–766. [21]

Chaiken, S. Physical appearance and social influence. In C. P. Herman, M. P. Zanna, and E. T. Higgins (Eds.), *Physical appearance, stigma, and social behavior: The Ontario symposium* (Vol. 3). Hillsdale, N.J.: Erlbaum, 1986, pp. 143–177. [21]

Chaiken, S. The heuristic model of persuasion. In M. P. Zanna, J. M. Olson, and C. P. Herman (Eds.), *Consistency in social behavior: The Ontario symposium* (Vol. 5). Hillsdale, N.J.: Erlbaum, 1986. [21]

Chaiken, S., and C. Stangor. Attitudes and attitude change. *Annual Review of Psychology*, 1987, *38*, 575–630. [21]

Chang, E. H., K. F. Pirollo, Z. Q. Zou, H.-Y. Cheung, E. L. Lawler, R. Garner, E. White, W. B. Bernstein, J. W. Fraumeni, Jr., and W. A. Blattner. Oncogenes in radioresistant noncancerous skin fibroblasts from a cancer-prone family. *Science*, 1987, *237*, 1036–1039. [20]

Chao, G. T., and S. W. J. Kozlowski. Employee perceptions on the implementation of robotic manufacturing technology. *Journal of Applied Psychology*, 1986, *71*, 70–76. [23]

Chapman, L. J., and J. P. Chapman. Illusory correlation as an obstacle to the use of valid psychodiagnostic signs. *Journal of Abnormal Psychology*, 1969, *74*, 271–287. [17]

Chase, W. G., and K. A. Ericsson. Skill and Working Memory, in G. H. Bower, ed., *The psychology of learning and motivation* (Vol. 16). New York: Academic Press, 1982. [8]

Chase-Lansdale, P. L., and M. T. Owen. Maternal employment in a family context: Effects on infant–mother and infant–father attachments. *Child Development.* (in press) [15]

Cheesman, J., and P. M. Merikle. Distinguishing conscious from unconscious perceptual processes. *Canadian Journal of Psychology*, 1986, *40*, 343–367. [5]

Chein, I. Notes on a framework for the measurement of discrimination and prejudice. In M. Jahoda, M. Deutsch, and S. W. Cook (Eds.), *Research in methods in social relations.* New York: Dryden Press, 1951, pp. 381–390. [21]

Cherry, E. C. Some experiments on the recognition of speech with one and two ears. *Journal of the Acoustical Society of America*, 1953, *25*, 975–979. [6]

Chi, M. T. H., and D. R. Koeske. Network representation of a child's dinosaur knowledge. *Developmental Psychology*, 1983, *19*, 29–39. [15]

Chiriboga, D. A. Life event weighting systems: A comparative analysis. *Journal of Psychosomatic Research*, 1977, *25*, 309–320. [20]

Chomsky, C. Acquisition of syntax in children from 5 to 10. Cambridge, Mass.: MIT Press, 1969. [15]

Chomsky, N. *Syntactic structures.* The Hague: Mouton, 1957. [10]

Chomsky, N. *Aspects of a theory of syntax.* Cambridge, Mass.: MIT Press, 1965. [10]

Chomsky, N. *Reflections on language.* New York: Pantheon, 1975. [10, 15]

Chomsky, N. *Language and responsibility.* New York: Pantheon, 1979. [15]

Chugani, H. T., and **M. E. Phelps.** Maturational changes in cerebral function in infants determined by ^{18}FDG positron emission tomography. *Science,* 1986, *231,* 840–843. [15]

Cialdini, R. B. *Influence: How and why people agree to things.* New York: William Morrow, 1984. [22]

Cialdini, R. B., R. J. Borden, A. Thorne, M. R. Walker, S. Freeman, and **L. R. Sloan.** Basking in reflected glory: Three (football) field studies. *Journal of Personality and Social Psychology,* 1976, *34,* 366–375. [13]

Clancey, W. J. The epistemology of a rule-based expert system: A framework for exploration. *Artificial Intelligence,* 1983, *20,* 215–251. [9]

Clapper, J. P., and **G. H. Bower.** The impact of category knowledge on representing instances. Paper presented at the Western Psychological Association Convention, Burlingame, Calif., 1988. [9]

Clark, E. V. Meanings and concepts. In P. H. Mussen (Ed.), *Handbook of child psychology* (4th ed.) Vol. 3. J. H. Flavell and E. M. Markman (Eds.), *Cognitive development.* New York: Wiley, 1983. [15]

Clark, H. H. Language use and language users. In G. Lindzey and E. Aronson (Eds.), *Handbook of social psychology* (3rd ed.). Reading, Mass.: Addison-Wesley, 1984. [10]

Clark, H. H., and **E. V. Clark.** *Psychology and language.* New York: Harcourt Brace Jovanovich, 1977. [10]

Clark, M. A slow death of the mind. *Newsweek,* Dec. 3, 1984, 56–62. [16]

Clark, M. S., and **H. T. Reis.** Interpersonal processes in close relationships. *Annual Review of Psychology,* 1988, *39,* 609–672. [14]

Clarke-Stewart, K. A., and **G. G. Fein.** Early childhood programs. In P. H. Mussen (Ed.), *Handbook of child psychology* (4th ed.) (Vol. 2). M. M. Haith and J. J. Campos (Eds.), *Infancy and developmental psychobiology.* New York: Wiley, 1983. [15]

Cleckley, H. M. *The mask of sanity.* St. Louis: Mosby, 1976. [18]

Coan, R. W. *Human consciousness and its evolution: A multidimensional view.* Westport, Conn.: Greenwood, 1987. [6]

Cobb, S. Social support as a moderator of life stress. *Psychosomatic Medicine,* 1976, *38,* 300–314. [20]

Cohen, B. D., G. Nachmani, and **S. Rosenberg.** Referent communication disturbances in acute schizophrenia. *Journal of Abnormal Psychology,* 1974, *83,* 1–13. [18]

Cohen, F., and **R. Lazarus.** Coping with the stresses of illness. In G. C. Stone, F. Cohen, and N. E. Adler (Eds.), *Health psychology—A handbook.* San Francisco: Jossey-Bass, 1979. [20]

Cohen, S. Aftereffects of stress on human performance and social behavior: A review of research and theory. *Psychological Bulletin,* 1981, *88,* 82–108. [22]

Coke, J. S., C. D. Batson, and **K. McDavis.** Empathic mediation of helping: A two-stage model. *Journal of Personality and Social Psychology,* 1978, *36,* 752–766. [22]

Colby, A., L. Kohlberg, J. Gibbs, and **M. Liberman.** A longitudinal study of moral judgment. *Monographs of the Society for Research in Child Development,* 1983, *48* (Whole No. 200). [16]

Cole, C. L., A. L. Cole, and **D. G. Dean.** Emotional maturity and marital adjustment. *Journal of Marriage and the Family,* 1980, *42,* 533–539. [16]

Cole, R. A., and **J. Jakimik.** A model of speech perception. In R. A. Cole (Ed.), *Perception and production of fluent speech.* Hillsdale, N.J.: Erlbaum, 1980. [10]

Coles, C. D., I. E. Smith, J. S. Lancaster, and **A. Falek.** Persistence over the first month of neurobehavioral differences in infants exposed to alcohol prenatally. *Infant Behavior & Development,* 1987, *10,* 23–38. [15]

Collins, B. E., and **M. G. Hoyt.** Personal responsibility for consequences: An integration and extension of the "forced compliance" literature. *Journal of Experimental Social Psychology,* 1972, *8,* 558–593. [21]

Collins, G. Does early teaching of infants have merit? *The New York Times,* February 1, 1984, C1+. [15]

Coltheart, M. Reading, phonological recoding, and deep dyslexia. In M. Coltheart, K. Patterson, and J. Marshall (Eds.), *Deep dyslexia.* Boston, Mass.: Routledge and Kegan Paul, 1980. [10]

Coltheart, Max. Iconic memory and visible persistence, *Perception and Psychophysics,* 1980, *27* (3), 183–228. [8]

Columbio, J. The critical period concept. *Psychological Bulletin,* 1982, *91,* 260–275. [15]

Colwill, R. M., and **R. A. Rescoria.** Postconditioning devaluation of a reinforcer affects instrumental responding. *Journal of Experimental Psychology: Animal Behavior Processes,* 1985, *11,* 120–132. [7]

Combs, B. J., D. R. Hales, and **B. K. Williams.** *An invitation to health: Your personal responsibility.* Menlo Park, Calif.: Benjamin/Cummings, 1980. [6]

Commission on Obscenity and Pornography. *Report.* Washington, D.C.: U.S. Government Printing Office, 1970. [14]

Comstock, G. Types of portrayal and aggressive behavior. *Journal of Communication,* 1977, *27,* 189–198. [22]

Condon, J. W., and **W. D. Crano.** Inferred evaluation and the relation between attitude similarity and interpersonal attraction. *Journal of Personality and Social Psychology,* 1988, *54,* 789–797. [21]

Congressional & Administrative News, Employee Polygraph Protection Act of 1988, 1988, no. 5, 102 STAT 646–653. [23]

Connor, J. Olfactory control of aggressive and sexual behavior in the mouse (Mus musclus L.). *Psychonomic Science,* 1972, *27,* 1–3. [14]

Cook, S. W. The 1954 social science statement and school desegregation: A reply to Gerard. *American Psychologist,* 1984, *39,* 819–832. [21]

Cooper, J., and **J. W. Brehm.** Prechoice awareness of relative deprivation as a determinant of cognitive dissonance. *Journal of Experimental Social Psychology,* 1971, *7,* 571–581. [21]

Cooper, J., and **R. H. Fazio.** A new look at dissonance theory. In L. Berkowitz (Ed.), *Advances in experimental social psychology* Vol. 17. New York: Academic Press, 1984, pp. 229–266. [21]

Cooper, J., and **S. Worchel.** Role of undesired consequences in arousing cognitive dissonance. *Journal of Personality and Social Psychology,* 1970, *16,* 199–206. [21]

Cooper, J., M. P. Zanna, and **P. A. Taves.** Arousal as a necessary condition for attitude change following induced compliance. *Journal of Personality and Social Psychology,* 1978, *36,* 1101–1106. [21]

Corder, B. F., P. V. Page, and **R. F. Corder.** Parental history, family communication, and interaction patterns in adolescent suicide. *Family Therapy,* 1974, *1,* 285–290. [18]

Coren, S., C. Porac, and **L. M. Ward.** *Sensation and perception.* San Diego, Calif.: Academic Press, 1984. [4]

Costa, P. T., Jr., et al. Cross-sectional studies of personality in a national sample. *Psychology and Aging,* 1986, *1,* 144–149. [16]

Costello, C. G. Fears and phobias in women: A community study. *Journal of Abnormal Psychology,* 1982, *91,* 280–286. [2]

Cote, J. E., and **C. Levine.** A critical examination of the ego identity status paradigm. *Developmental Review,* 1988, *8,* 147–184. [16]

Cottingham, E. M., K. A. Matthews, E. Talbott, and **L. H. Kuller.** Environmental events preceding sudden death in women. *Psychosomatic Medicine,* 1980, *42,* 567–574. [20]

Cottrell, N. B. Social facilitation. In C. G. McClintock (Ed.), *Experimental social psychology.* New York: Holt, Rinehart & Winston, 1972. [22]

Cowan, Nelson. Evolving conceptions of memory storage, selective attention, and their mutual constraints within the human information-processing system. *Psychological Bulletin*, 1988, *104* (2), 163–191. [8]

Coyle, J. T., D. L. Price, and M. R. DeLong. Alzheimer's disease: A disorder of cortical cholinergic innervation. *Science*, 1983, *219*, 1184–1190. [3, 15]

Craik, F. I. M., and M. Byrd. Aging and cognitive deficits: The role of attentional resources. In F. I. M. Craik and S. Trehub (Eds.), *Advances in the study of communication and affect*. Vol. 8. *Aging and cognitive processes*. New York: Plenum, 1982. [16]

Craik, F. I. M., and R. S. Lockhart. Levels of processing: A framework for memory research. *Journal of Verbal Learning and Verbal Behavior*, 1972, *11*, 671–684. [8]

Crick, F., and G. Mitchison. The function of dream sleep. *Nature*, 1983, *304*, 111–114. [6]

Critchlow, B. The powers of John Barleycorn: Beliefs about the effects of alcohol on social behavior. *American Psychologist*, 1986, *41*, 751–764. [6]

Crocker, J. Judgment of covariation by social perceivers. *Psychological Bulletin*, 1981, *90*, 272–292. [21]

Crocker, J., and B. Park. The consequences of social stereotypes. In L. S. Sproull (Ed.), *Advances in information processing in organizations* (Vol. 3). Greenwich, Conn.: Jai Press, 1988, pp. 39–80. [21]

Crooks, R., and K. Baur. *Our sexuality* (3rd ed.). Menlo Park, Calif.: Benjamin/Cummings, 1987. [14]

Crosby, F., S. Bromley, and L. Saxe. Recent unobtrusive studies of black and white discrimination and prejudice: A literature review. *Psychological Bulletin*, 1980, *87*, 546–563. [21]

Crouse, J. H. Retroactive interference in reading prose materials. *Journal of Educational Psychology*, 1971, *62*, 39–44. [8]

Crouse, J., and D. Trusheim. *The case against the SAT*. Chicago: University of Chicago Press, 1988. [11]

Crowe, S. J., S. R. Guild, and L. M. Polvogt. Observations on the pathology of high-tone deafness. *Bulletin of Johns Hopkins Hospital*, 1934, *54*, 315–379. [4]

Cumming, E., and W. E. Henry. *Growing old*. New York, Basic Books, 1961. [16]

Curry, S. A. A corporate response: The TRW experience. In D. L. Salisbury (Ed.), *America in transition: Implications for employee benefits*. Washington, D.C.: Employee Benefits Research Institute, 1982. [23]

Curtis, H., and N. S. Barnes. *Biology* (5th ed). New York: Worth, 1989. [3]

Curtiss, S. *Genie: A psycholinguistic study of a modern-day "wild child."* New York: Academic Press, 1977. [2, 15]

Cytrynbaum, S., et al. Midlife development. In L. W. Poon (Ed.), *Aging in the 1980s*. Washington, D.C.: American Psychological Association, 1980. [16]

Dahlstrom, W. A., G. S. Welsh, and L. E. Dahlstrom. *An MMPI handbook*. Vol. 2. *Research applications* (rev. ed.). Minneapolis: University of Minnesota Press, 1975. [17]

Daly, E. M., J. W. Lancee, and J. Polivy. A conical model for the taxonomy of emotional experience. *Journal of Personality and Social Psychology*, 1983, *45*, 443–457. [12]

Daneman, M., and P. A. Carpenter. Individual differences in working memory and reading. *Journal of Verbal Learning and Verbal Behavior*, 1980, *19*, 450–466. [10]

Danish, S. J., H. L. Galambos, and N. L. Laquatra. Life development intervention: Skill training for personal competence. In R. D. Felner, L. A. Jason, J. N. Moritsugu, and S. S. Farber (Eds.), *Preventive psychology: Theory, research, and practice*. New York: Pergamon Press, 1985. [20]

Darley, J. M., A. I. Teger, and L. D. Lewis. Do groups always inhibit individuals' responses to potential emergencies? *Journal of Personality and Social Psychology*, 1973, *26*, 295–399. [22]

Darwin, C. *The expression of emotions in man and animals*. Chicago: University of Chicago Press, 1967. (Originally published, 1872.) [12, 14]

Darwin, C. T., M. T. Turvey, and R. G. Crowder. An auditory analogue of the Sperling partial report procedure: Evidence for brief auditory storage. *Cognitive Psychology*, 1972, *3*, 255–267. [8]

Dashiell, J. F. An experimental analysis of some group effects. *Journal of Abnormal and Social Psychology*, 1930, *25*, 190–199. [22]

Dattore, P. J., F. C. Shontz, and L. Coyne. Premorbid personality differentiation of cancer and noncancer groups: A test of the hypothesis of cancer proneness. *Journal of Consulting and Clinical Psychology*, 1980, *48*, 388–394. [20]

Davenport, W. Sexual patterns and their regulation in a society of the southwest Pacific. In F. A. Beach (Ed.), *Sex and behavior*. New York: Wiley, 1965. [14]

Davies, G., H. Ellis, and J. Shepherd (Eds.). *Perceiving and remembering faces*. London: Academic Press, 1981. [8]

Davis, J. M. Dopamine theory of schizophrenia: A two-factor theory. In L. C. Wynne, R. L. Cromwell, and S. Matthysse (Eds.). *The nature of schizophrenia: New approaches to research and treatment*. New York: Wiley, 1978. [18]

Davis, K. L., R. C. Mohs, B. M. Davis, M. I. Levy, T. B. Horvath, G. S. Rosenberg, A. Ross, A. Rothpearl, and N. Rosen. Cholinergic treatment in Alzheimer's disease. In S. Corkin, K. L. Davis, J. H. Growdon, E. Usdin, and R. J. Wurtman (Eds.), *Aging*. Vol 19. *Alzheimer's disease: a report of progress in research*. New York: Raven Press, 1982. [8]

Davis, K. S. *FDR: The beckoning of destiny*. New York: Putnam, 1972. [15]

Dawes, R. M., J. McTavish, and H. Shaklee. Behavior, communication, and assumptions about other people's behavior in a common dilemma situation. *Journal of Personality and Social Psychology*, 1977, *35*, 1–11. [22]

Day, R. S. Alternative Representations. In G. H. Bower, (Ed.), *The psychology of learning and motivation: Vol. 22.. Advances in Research and Theory*. New York: Academic Press, 1988. [8]

Deaux, E. Thirst satiation and the temperature of ingested water. *Science*, 1973, *181*, 1166–1167. [13]

Deaux, K. Sex and gender. In M. Rosenzweig and L. Porter (Eds.), *Annual Review of Psychology* (Vol. 36). Palo Alto, Calif.: Annual Reviews, Inc., 1985. [12]

Deaux, K., and T. Emswiller. Explanations of successful performance on sex-linked tasks: What is skill for the male is luck for the female. *Journal and Personality and Social Psychology*, 1974, *29*, 80–85. [21]

de Bono, E. *The five day course in thinking*. New York: Basic Books, 1967.

DeBono, K. G. Investigating the social-adjustive and value-expressive functions of attitudes: Implications for persuasion processes. *Journal of Personality and Social Psychology*, 1987, *52*, 279–287. [21]

DeBono, K. G., and R. J. Harnish. Expertise, source attractiveness, and the processing of persuasive information: A functional approach. *Journal of Personality and Social Psychology*, 1988, *55*, 541–546. [21]

DeCasper, A. J. and W. P. Fifer. Of human bonding: Newborns prefer their mothers' voices. *Science*, 1980, *208*, 1174–1176. [5, 15]

Deci, E. L., and R. M. Ryan. The empirical exploration of intrinsic motivational processes. In L. Berkowitz (Ed.), *Advances in experimental social psychology* (Vol. 13). New York: Academic Press, 1980. [13]

Deci, E. L., and R. M. Ryan. *Intrinsic motivation and self-determination in human behavior*. New York: Plenum, 1985. [13]

DeLongis, A., J. C. Coyne, G. Dakof, S. Folkman, and **R. S. Lazarus.** Relationship of daily hassles, uplifts, and major life events to health status. *Health Psychology,* 1982, *1,* 119–136. [20]

DeLora, J. S., and **C. A. Warren.** *Understanding sexual interaction.* Boston: Houghton Mifflin, 1977. [14]

Dement, W. C. *Some must watch while some must sleep.* San Francisco: Freeman, 1974. [6]

Dement, W. C., and **E. A. Wolpert.** The relation of eye movements, body mobility, and external stimuli to dream content. *Journal of Experimental Psychology,* 1958, *55,* 543–553. [6]

D'Emilio, J., and **E. B. Freedman.** *Intimate matters: A history of sexuality in America.* New York: Harper & Row, 1988. [14]

DeMonasterio, F. M. Center and surround mechanisms of opponent-color X and Y ganglion cells of retina of macaques. *Journal of Neurophysiology,* 1978, *41,* 1418–1434. [4]

Dengrove, E., and **R. S. Dengrove.** Hypnotic susceptibility and cognitive-behavior therapy. *International Journal of Psychosomatics,* 1987, *34,* 35–37. [6]

Dennett, D. C. Quining qualia. In A. J. Marcel and E. Bisiach (Eds.), *Consciousness in contemporary science.* Oxford: Clarendon Press, 1988. [6]

Dennis, M. Syntax in brain-injured children. In M. Studdert-Kennedy (Ed.), *Psychobiology of language.* Cambridge, Mass.: MIT Press, 1983. [10]

Dennis, M., and **H. A. Whitaker.** Language acquisition following hemidecortication: Linguistic superiority of the left over the right hemisphere. *Brain and Language,* 1976, *3,* 404–433. [10]

Dennis, W., and **J. Sayegh.** The effect of supplementary experiences upon the behavioral development of infants in institutions. *Child Development,* 1965, *36,* 81–90. [15]

Depaulo, B., J. I. Stone, and **G. D. Lassiter.** Telling ingratiating lies: Effects of target sex and target attractiveness on verbal and nonverbal deceptive success. *Journal of Personality and Social Psychology,* 1985, *48,* 1191–1203. [12]

Depue, R. A., and **S. M. Monroe.** The unipolar-bipolar distinction in the depressive disorders. *Psychological Bulletin,* 1978, *85,* 1001–1029. [18]

Depue, R. A., J. F. Slater, H. Wolfstetter-Kausch, D. Klein, E. Goplerud, and **D. Farr.** A behavioral paradigm for identifying persons at risk for bipolar depressive disorder: A conceptual framework and five validation studies. *Journal of Abnormal Psychology,* 1981, *90,* 381–438. [18]

deRivera, J. The structure of anger. In J. deRivera (Ed.), *Conceptual encounter:*

A method for the exploration of human experience. Washington, D.C.: University Press of America, 1981, pp. 35–81. [12]

Deutsch, M., and **H. B. Gerard.** A study of normative and informational influences on social judgment. *Journal of Abnormal and Social Psychology,* 1965, *51,* 629–636. [22]

DeValois, R. L., and **K. K. DeValois.** Neural coding of color. In E. C. Carterette and M. P. Friedman (Eds.), *Handbook of perception,* Vol. V. *Seeing.* New York: Academic Press, 1975. [4]

deVilliers, J. G., and **P. A. deVilliers.** *Language acquisition.* Cambridge, Mass.: Harvard University Press, 1978. [15]

Devitt, M., and **K. Sterelny.** *Language and reality.* Cambridge, Mass.: MIT Press, 1987. [10]

de Vries, H. A. Physiology of exercise and aging. In D. S. Woodruff and J. E. Birren (Eds.), *Aging* (2nd ed.). Monterey, Calif.: Brooks/Cole, 1983. [16]

Diamond, M. Sexual identity: Monozygotic twins reared in discordant sex roles and a BBC follow-up. *Archives of Sexual Behavior,* 1982, *11* (2), 181–185. [14]

Diamond, M. *Enriching heredity: The impact of the environment on the anatomy of the brain.* New York: Free Press, 1988. [3]

Dickinson, A. *Contemporary animal learning theory.* Cambridge: Cambridge University Press, 1980. [7]

Dickson, D., and **E. Marshall.** Europe recognizes the ozone threat. *Science,* 1989, *243,* 1279. [20, 22]

DiClemente, R. J., C. B. Boyer, and **E. S. Morales.** Minorities and AIDS: Knowledge, attitudes, and misconceptions among black and Latino adolescents. *American Journal of Public Health,* 1988, *78,* 55–57. [14]

Diener, E. Subjective well-being. *Psychological Bulletin,* 1984, *95,* 542–575. [12]

Dinges, D. Cognitive performance during the hypnopompic state: Effects of sleep depth. Paper presented at the Arizona Conference on Sleep and Dreams, Tucson, 1989. [6]

Dishman, R. K. Compliance/adherence in health-related exercise. *Health Psychology,* 1982, *1,* 237–267. [20]

Doane, J., K. West, M. J. Goldstein, E. Rodnick, and **J. Jones.** Parental communication deviance and affective style as predictors of subsequent schizophrenia spectrum disorders in vulnerable adolescents. *Archives of General Psychiatry,* 1981, *38,* 679–685. [18]

Dobson, K. S. A meta-analysis of the efficacy of cognitive therapy for depression. *Journal of consulting and clinical psychology,* 1989, *37,* 414–419. [19]

Dodd, D. H., and **J. M. Bradshaw.** Leading

questions and memory: Pragmatic constraints. *Journal of verbal learning and verbal behavior,* 1980, *19,* 695–704. [10]

Dollard, J., L. W. Doob, N. E. Miller, O. H. Mowrer, and **R. R. Sears.** *Frustration and aggression.* New Haven, Conn.: Yale University Press, 1939. [22]

Dollard, J., and **N. E. Miller.** *Personality and psychotherapy: An Analysis in terms of learning, thinking, and culture.* New York: McGraw-Hill, 1950. [17]

Donnerstein, E. I., and **D. G. Linz.** The question of pornography. *Psychology Today,* 1986, *20,* 56–59. [14]

Donnerstein, E. I., D. G. Linz, and **S. Penrod.** *The question of pornography: Research findings and policy implications.* New York: Basic Books, 1987. [14]

Dontas, C., O. Maratos, M. Fafoutis, and **A. Karangelis.** Early social development in institutionally reared Greek infants. *Monographs of the Society for Child Development,* 1985, *50* (209), 136–146. [15]

Doty, R. L., S. Applebaum, H. Zusho, and **R. G. Settle.** Sex differences in odor identification ability: A cross-cultural analysis. *Neuropsychologia,* 1985, *23,* 667–672. [4]

Douvan, E., and **J. Adelson.** *The adolescent experience.* New York: Wiley, 1966. [16]

Doyle, A., and **K. Somers.** The effects of group and family day care on infant attachment behaviors. *Canadian Journal of Behavioral Sciences,* 1978, *10,* 38–45. [15]

Draguns, J. G. Psychological disorders of clinical severity. In H. C. Triandis and J. G. Draguns (Eds.), *Handbook of cross-cultural psychology* (Vol. 6). *Psychopathology.* Boston: Allyn & Bacon, 1980. [18]

Drake, R. E., and **G. E. Valliant.** A validity study of axis II of *DSM III. American Journal of Psychiatry,* 1985, *142,* 553–558. [18]

Dreyfus, H. L., and **S. E. Dreyfus.** Putting computers in their place. *Social Research,* 1986, *53,* 57–76. [9]

Duffy, E. *Activation and behavior.* New York: Wiley, 1962. [17]

Dulany, D. E., R. A. Carlson, and **G. I. Dewey.** A case of syntactical learning and judgment: How conscious and how abstract? *Journal of Experimental Psychology: General,* 1984, *113,* 541–555. [7]

Duncker, K. On problem solving (L. S. Lees, Trans.). *Psychological Monographs,* 1945, *58* (Whole No. 270). [9]

Dutton, D., and **A. Aron.** Some evidence for heightened sexual attraction under conditions of high anxiety. *Journal of Personality and Social Psychology,* 1974, *30,* 510–517. [12]

Eagly, A. H. Sex differences in influenceability. _Psychological Bulletin,_ 1978, _85,_ 86–116. [22]

Eagly, A. H., W. Wood, and L. Fishbaugh. Sex differences in conformity: Surveillance by the group as a determinant of male nonconformity. _Journal of Personality and Social Psychology,_ 1981, _40,_ 384–394. [22]

Easterbrooks, M. A., and W. A. Goldberg. Effects of early maternal employment on mothers, toddlers, and fathers. _Developmental Psychology,_ 1985, _21,_ 774–783. [15]

Easterlin, R. _Birth and fortune._ New York: Basic Books, 1980. [16]

Eccles, J. S., and L. W. Hoffman. Sex roles, socialization, and occupational behavior. In H. W. Stevenson and A. E. Siegel (Eds.), _Child development research and social policy._ Chicago: University of Chicago Press, 1984. [15]

Edelman, M., W. E. Gall, and W. Cowan. _Synaptic function._ New York: Wiley, 1987. [3]

Eder, R. W., and M. R. Buckley. The employment interview: An interactionist perspective. _Research in Personnel and Human Resources Management,_ 1988, _6,_ 75–107. [23]

Egeland, J. A., et al. Bipolar affective disorders linked to DNA markers on chromosome 11. _Nature,_ 1987, _325,_ 783–787. [18]

Ehrhardt, A. A., and H. F. L. Meyer-Bahlburg. Effects of prenatal sex hormones on gender-related behavior. _Science,_ 1981, _211,_ 1312–1318. [14]

Ekerdt, D. J., R. Bosse, and S. Levkoff. An empirical test for phases of retirement. _Journal of Gerontology,_ 1985, _40,_ 95–101. [16]

Ekman, P. Universals and cultural differences in facial expression of emotion. In J. K. Cole (Ed.), _Nebraska Symposium on Motivation._ Lincoln: University of Nebraska Press, 1972. [12]

Ekman, P. _The face of man: Expressions of universal emotions in a New Guinea village._ New York: Garland STPM Press, 1980. [12]

Ekman, P. Methods for measuring facial action. In K. Scherer and P. Ekman (Eds.), _Handbook on methods of nonverbal communications research._ New York: Cambridge University Press, 1981. [12]

Ekman, P. Expression and the nature of emotion. In K. Scherer and P. Ekman (Eds.), _Approaches to emotion._ Hillsdale, N.J.: Erlbaum, 1984. [12]

Ekman, P., and W. V. Friesen. Constants across culture in the face and emotion. _Journal of Personality and Social Psychology,_ 1971, _17,_ 124–129. [12]

Ekman, P., and W. V. Friesen. _Unmasking the face: A guide to recognizing emotions from facial expressions._ Englewood Cliffs, N.J.: Prentice-Hall/Spectrum, 1975. [12]

Ekman, P., W. V. Friesen, and P. Ellsworth. _Emotion in the human face: Guidelines for research and an integration of findings._ Elmsford, N.Y.: Pergamon, 1972. [12]

Ekman, P., R. W. Levenson, and W. V. Friesen. Autonomic nervous system activity distinguishes among emotions. _Science,_ 1983, _221,_ 1208–1210. [12]

Ekman, P., and H. Oster. Facial expressions of emotion. _Annual Review of Psychology,_ 1979, _30,_ 527–554. [12]

Eleftheriou, B. E., D. V. Bailley, and V. H. Denenberg. Genetic analysis of fighting behavior in mice. _Physiology and Behavior,_ 1974, _13,_ 773–777. [22]

Elkind, D. _Children and adolescents._ New York: Oxford University Press, 1970. [20]

Ellis, A. _Reason and emotion in psychotherapy._ New York: Lyle Stewart, 1962. [19]

Ellis, A., and R. Grieger. _Handbook of rational emotive therapy._ New York: Springer Verlag, 1977. [19]

Ellis, A. W. On the Freudian theory of speech errors. In V. A. Fromkin (Ed.), _Errors in linquistic performance._ New York: Academic Press, 1980. [10]

Ellis, A. W., and A. W. Young (Eds.) _Human cognitive neuropsychology._ Hillsdale, N.J.: Erlbaum, 1988. [3]

Engel, G. L. Sudden and rapid death during psychological stress. _Annals of Internal Medicine,_ 1971, _74,_ 771–782. [20]

Engen, T. Remembering odors and their names. _American Scientist,_ 1987, _75,_ 497–503. [4, 8]

Engen, T., and B. M. Ross. Long term memory of odors with and without verbal description. _Journal of Experimental Psychology,_ 1973, _100,_ 221–227. [8]

Engle-Friedman, M., E. A. Baker, and R. R. Bootzin. Reports of wakefulness during EEG identified stages of sleep. _Sleep Research,_ 1985, _14,_ 152. [6]

Epstein, A. N. Water intake without the act of drinking. _Science,_ 1960, _131,_ 497–498. [13]

Epstein, S. M. Toward a unified theory of anxiety. In B. A. Maher (Ed.), _Progress in experimental personality research_ (Vol. 4). New York: Academic Press, 1967. [13]

Epstein, Y. M., R. L. Woolfolk, and P. M. Lehrer. Physiological, cognitive, and nonverbal responses to repeated exposure to crowding. _Journal of Applied Social Psychology,_ 1981, _11,_ 1–13. [22]

Erdelyi, M. _Psychoanalysis: Freud's cognitive psychology._ New York: W. H. Freeman, 1985. [17]

Erdelyi, M. H., and B. Goldberg. Let's not sweep repression under the rug: Toward a cognitive psychology of repression. In J. F. Kihlstrom and F. J. Evans (Eds.), _Functional disorders of memory._ Hillsdale, N.J.: Erlbaum, 1979. [8]

Erickson, R. P. On the neural basis of behavior. _American Scientist,_ 1984, _72,_ 233–241. [4]

Ericsson, K. A., W. G. Chase, and S. Faloon. Acquisition of a memory skill. _Science,_ 1980, _208,_ 1181–1182. [8]

Erikson, E. H. _Childhood and society._ New York: Norton, 1950. [15, 16]

Erikson, E. H. _Childhood and society_ (2nd ed.). New York: Norton, 1963. [15, 16]

Erikson, E. H. _Identity and the life cycle._ New York: Norton, 1980. [16, 17]

Erikson, E. H. _The life cycle completed._ New York: Norton, 1982. [16]

Erikson, K. _Everything in its path: Destruction of community in the Buffalo Creek flood._ New York: Simon & Schuster, 1976. [20]

Eron, L. D., L. R. Huesmann, M. M. Lefkowitz, and L. O. Walder. Does television cause aggression? _American Psychologist,_ 1972, _27,_ 253–263. [22]

Estes, W. K. Array models for category learning. _Cognitive Psychology,_ 1986, _18,_ 500–549. [9]

Etheredge, L. S. _Can governments learn?: American foreign policy and Central American revolutions._ New York: Pergamon, 1985. [23]

Evans, M. G. The effects of supervisory behavior on the path–goal relationship. _Organizational Behavior and Human Performance,_ May 1970, 277–298. [23]

Evans, R. I., R. M. Rozelle, M. B. Mittelmark, W. B. Hansen, A. L. Bane, and J. Havis. Deterring the onset of smoking in children: Knowledge of immediate psychological effects and coping with peer pressure, media pressure, and parent modeling. _Journal of Applied Social Psychology,_ 1978, _8,_ 126–135. [20]

Exner, J. E. _The Rorschach: A comprehensive system._ New York: Wiley, 1974. [17]

Eyferth, K. Leistungen verschiedener Gruppen von Besatzungskindern in Hamburg-Wechsler Intelligenz Test für Kinder (HAWIK). _Archiv für die gesamte Psychologie,_ 1961, _113,_ 222–241. [11]

Eysenck, H. _The biological basis of personality._ Springfield, Ill.: Charles C. Thomas, 1967. [13]

Eysenck, H. J. The effects of psychotherapy: An evaluation. _Journal of Consulting Psychology,_ 1952, _16,_ 319–324. [19]

Eysenck, H. J. _The structure of human personality._ London: Methuen, 1970. [17]

Fabian, W.D., Jr., and S. M. Fishkin. A replicated study of self-reported changes in psychological absorption with marijuana intoxication. *Journal of Abnormal Psychology*, 1981, *90*, 546–553. [6]

Fagan, J. F. III. A new look at infant intelligence. In D. K. Detterman (Ed.), *Current topics in human intelligence* (Vol. 1). Norwood, N.J.: Ablex, 1985, pp. 223–246. [11]

Fagot, B. I. Consequences of moderate cross-gender behavior in children. *Child Development*, 1977, *48*, 902–907. [15]

Fagot, B. I. The influence of sex of child on parental reactions to toddler children. *Child Development*, 1978, *49*, 459–465. [15]

Falkner, B., H. Kushner, G. Onesti, and E. T. Angelakos. Cardiovascular characteristics in adolescents who develop essential hypertension. *Hypertension*, 1981, *3*, 521–527. [20]

Falloon, I. R., J. L. Boyd, C. W. McGill, et al. Family management in prevention of exacerbation of schizophrenia: A controlled study. *New England Journal of Medicine*, 1982, *306* (24), 1437–1440. [19]

Falloon, I. R., J. L. Boyd, C. W. McGill, M. Williamson, J. Razani, H. B. Moss, A. M. Gilderman, and G. M. Simpson. Family management in the prevention of morbidity of schizophrenia. *Archives of General Psychiatry*, 1985, *42*, 887–896. [19]

Fancher, R. E. *The intelligence men: Makers of the IQ controversy*. New York: Norton, 1986. [11]

Fantz, R. L. Pattern vision in newborn infants. *Science*, 1963, *140*, 296–297. [5]

Farah, M. J. Psychophysical evidence for a shared representational medium for mental images and percepts. *Journal of Experimental Psychology: General*, 1985, *114*, 91–103. [9]

Farah, M. J., D. N. Levine, and R. Calvanio. A case study of mental imagery deficit. *Brain and Cognition*, 1987. [9]

Farber, E., and B. Egelund. *The invulnerable child*. New York: Guilford Press, 1987. [17]

Farquhar, J. W., N. Maccoby, and D. S. Solomon. Community applications of behavioral medicine. In W. D. Gentry (Ed.), *Handbook of behavioral medicine*. New York: Guilford Press, 1984. [20]

Faust, M. S. Somatic development of adolescent girls. *Monographs of the Society for Research in Child Development*, 1977, *42*, Serial no. 169. [16]

Fazio, R. H. How do attitudes guide behavior? In R. M. Sorrentino and E. T. Higgins (Eds.), *Handbook of motivation and cognition: Foundations of social behavior*. New York: Guilford, 1986. [21]

Fazio, R. H., M. P. Zanna, and J. Cooper. Dissonance and self-perception: An integrative view of each theory's proper domain of application. *Journal of Exper-*

imental Social Psychology, 1977, *13*, 464–479. [21]

Fearon, E. R., S. R. Hamilton, and B. Vogelstein. Clonal analysis of human colorectal tumors. *Science*, 1987, *238*, 193–197. [20]

Fehr, B. and J. A. Russell. Concept of emotion viewed from a prototype perspective. *Journal of Experimental Psychology: General*, 1984, *113*, 464–486. [12]

Feigenbaum, E. Cochlear implant devices for the profoundly hearing impaired. *IEEE Engineering in Medicine and Biology Magazine*, June 1987, 10–21. [4]

Feigenbaum, E. A. The art of artificial intelligence: Themes and case studies in knowledge engineering. *International Joint Conferences on Artificial Intelligence*, 1977, *5*, 1014–1029. [9]

Feigenbaum, E. A., P. McCorduck, and H. P. Nii. *The rise of the expert company*. New York: Random House, 1988. [9]

Feingold, A. Cognitive gender differences are disappearing. *American Psychologist*, 1988, *43*, 95–103. [11]

Feldman, D. H. *Nature's gambit*. New York: Basic Books, 1986. [11]

Feldman, S. S., and B. Aschenbrenner. Impact of parenthood on various aspects of masculinity and femininity. *Developmental Psychology*, 1983, *19*, 278–289. [16]

Feldman, S. S., Z. C. Beringen, and S. C. Nash. Fluctuations of sex-related self-attributions as a function of the state of family life cycle. *Developmental Psychology*, 1981, *17*, 24–35. [16]

Feltz, D. L., and D. M. Landers. Effects of mental practice on motor skill learning and performance: A meta-analysis. *Journal of Sport Psychology*, 1983, *5*, 25–57. [7]

Ferster, C. B., and B. F. Skinner. *Schedules of reinforcement*. Englewood Cliffs, N.J.: Prentice-Hall, 1957. [7]

Festinger, L. *A theory of cognitive dissonance*. Stanford, Calif.: Stanford University Press, 1957. [21]

Festinger, L., and J. M. Carlsmith. Cognitive consequences of forced compliance. *Journal of Abnormal and Social Psychology*, 1959, *58*, 203–211. [21]

Fiedler, F. E., and J. E. Garcia. *New approaches to leadership: Cognitive resources and organizational performance*. New York: Wiley, 1987. [23]

Field, G. A test of the Vroom-Yetton normative model of leadership. *Journal of Applied Psychology*, 1982, *67*, 523–532. [23]

Field, J., D. Muir, R. Pilon, M. Sinclair, and P. Dodwell. Infants' orientation to lateral sounds from birth to three months. *Child Development*, 1980, *51*, 295–298. [5, 14]

Field, T. M. Infant arousal, attention, and

affect during early interaction. In L. P. Lipsitt (Ed.), *Advances in infancy research* (Vol. 1). Norwood, N.J.: Ablex, 1981, pp. 57–100. [15]

Fielding, J. Successes of prevention. *Milbank Memorial Fund Quarterly*, 1978, *56*, 274–302. [20]

Fields, H. L. Neural mechanisms of opiate analgesia. In H. L. Fields (Ed.), *Advances in pain research and therapy*. Vol. 9. New York: Raven Press, 1985, pp. 479–484. [3]

Finke, R. A., and K. Slayton. Explorations of creative visual synthesis in mental imagery. *Memory and Cognition*, 1988, *16*, 252–257. [9]

Finn, P. R., and R. O. Pihl. Men at high risk for alcoholism: The effect of alcohol on cardiovascular response to unavoidable shock. *Journal of Abnormal Psychology*, 1987, *96*, 230–236. [18]

Fischer, K. W. Illuminating the Processes of Moral Development, in A. Colby, L. Kohlberg, J. Gibbs, and M. Lieberman (Eds.), A longitudinal study of moral judgment, *Monographs of the Society for Research in Child Development*, 1983, *48*, 97–107. [23]

Fischer, R. A cartography of the ecstatic and meditative states. *Science*, 1971, *174*, 898. [6]

Fischhoff, B. Hindsight ≠ foresight: The effect of outcome knowledge on judgment under uncertainty. *Journal of Experimental Psychology: Human Perception and Performance*, 1975, *1*, 288–299. [9]

Fishbein, M., and I. Ajzen. *Understanding attitudes and predicting social behavior*. Englewood Cliffs, N.J.: Prentice-Hall, 1980. [21]

Fisher, S., and R. P. Greenberg. *The scientific credibility of Freud's theories and therapy*. New York: Columbia University Press, 1985. [17]

Fiske, S. T., and S. E. Taylor. *Social cognition*. Reading, Mass.: Addison-Wesley, 1984. [21]

Fitzsimons, J. T. Drinking by rats depleted of body fluid without increase in osmotic pressure. *Journal of Physiology*, 1961, *159*, 297–309. [13]

Fitzsimons, J. T. The role of renal thirst in drinking induced by extracellular stimuli. *Journal of Physiology*, 1969, *201*, 349–368. [13]

Flavell, J. H. *Cognitive development* (2d ed.). Englewood Cliffs, N.J.: Prentice-Hall, 1985. [8, 15]

Flavell, J. H., S. G. Shipstead, and K. Croft. Young children's knowledge about visual perception: Hiding objects from others. *Child Development*, 1978, *49*, 1208–1211. [15]

Fleming, I., A. Baum, and L. Weiss. Social density and perceived control as mediators of crowding stress in high-density residential neighborhoods. *Journal of Personality and Social Psychology*, 1987, *52*, 899–906. [22]

Fleming, M., and **D. Feinbloom.** Similarities in becoming transsexuals and adolescents. *Adolescence*, 1984, *19*, 729–748. [14]

Flynn, J. R. Massive IQ gains in 14 nations: What IQ tests really measure. *Psychological Bulletin*, 1987, *101*, 171–191. [11]

Folkes, V. S. Forming relationships and the matching hypothesis. *Personality and Social Psychology Bulletin*, 1982, *8*, 631–636. [21]

Folkman, S. Personal control and stress and coping processes: A theoretical analysis. *Journal of Personality and Social Psychology*, 1984, *46*, 839–852. [12]

Fong, G. T., and **H. Markus.** Self-schemas and judgments about others. *Social Cognition*, 1982, *1*, 191–205. [21]

Fowler, C. A., G. Wolford, R. Slade, and **L. Tassinary.** Lexical access with and without awareness. *Journal of Experimental Psychology: General*, 1981, *110*, 341–362. [5]

Fraiberg, S. *Insights from the blind.* New York: Basic Books, 1977. [4]

Franck, G., E. Salmon, R. Poirrier, B. Sadzot, G. Franco, and **P. Maquet.** Evaluation of human cerebral glucose uptake during wakefulness, slow wave sleep and paradoxical sleep by positron emission tomography. *Sleep Research*, 1987, *16*, 46. [6]

Frank, J. D. *Persuasion and healing: A comparative study of psychotherapy.* Baltimore: Johns Hopkins University Press, 1961. [19]

Frank, J. D. The placebo in psychotherapy. *Behavioral and Brain Sciences*, 1983, *6*, 291–292. [19]

Frank, R. G., H. C. Shulberg, and **W. P. Welsh.** Research selection bias and the prevalence of depressive disorders in psychiatric facilities. *Journal of Consulting and Clinical Psychology*, 1985, *53*, 370–376. [2]

Frank, S. J., C. B. Avery, and **M. S. Laman.** Young adults' perceptions of their relationships with their parents: Individual differences in connectedness, competence, and emotional autonomy. *Developmental Psychology*, 1988, *24*, 729–737. [16]

Frankl, V. E. *Man's search for meaning.* Boston: Beacon Press, 1962. [18]

Frazier, L., and **J. D. Fodor.** The sausage machine: A new two-stage parsing model. *Cognition*, 1978, *6*, 291–325. [10]

Freedman, J. *Crowding and behavior.* San Francisco: W. H. Freeman, 1975. [22]

Freedman, J. L. Effect of television violence on aggression. *Psychological Bulletin*, 1984, *96*, 227–246. [22]

Freedman, J. L., and **S. C. Fraser.** Compliance without pressure: The foot-in-the-door technique. *Journal of Personality and Social Psychology*, 1966, *4*, 195–202. [22]

Freud, S. *The interpretation of dreams.* New York: Basic Books, 1955; Avon, 1965. (Originally published 1900). [1, 6, 17, CT2]

Freud, S. Introductory lectures on psychoanalysis. In J. Strachey (Ed. and Trans.), *The standard edition of the complete psychological works of Sigmund Freud* (Vols. 15 and 16). London: Hogarth Press, 1961 and 1963. (Originally published, 1917.) [17]

Freud, S. *Civilization and its discontents* J. Strachey (Ed. and Trans.). New York: Norton, 1962. (Originally published, 1930). [17]

Freud, S. *Jokes and their relation to the unconscious.* In J. Strachey (Ed.), *The standard edition of the complete psychological works of Sigmund Freud* (Vol. 6). London: Hogarth Press, 1962. (Originally published, 1905). [17]

Friedman, H. S., and **S. Booth-Kewley.** The "disease-prone personality." *American Psychologist*, 1987, *42*, 539–555. [20]

Friedman, M., and **R. H. Rosenman.** *Type A behavior and your heart.* New York: Knopf, 1974. [20]

Friedman, M., C. E. Thoresen, J. J. Gill, L. H. Powell, D. Ulmer, L. Thompson, V. A. Price, D. D. Rabin, W. S. Breall, T. Dixon, R. Levy, and **E. Bourg.** Alteration of Type A behavior and reduction in cardiac recurrences in postmyocardial infarction patients. *American Heart Journal*, 1984, *108*, 237–248. [20]

Frijda, N. The laws of emotion. *American Psychologist*, 43, 1986, 349–358. [12]

Frisby, J. P. *Seeing: Illusion, brain and mind.* New York: Oxford University Press, 1980. [4, 5]

Frodi, A. M., M. E. Lamb, L. A. Leavitt, and **W. L. Donovan.** Fathers' and mothers' responses to infant smiles and cries. *Infant Behavior and Development*, 1978, *1*, 187–198. [15]

Fromkin, V. (Ed.), *Speech errors as linguistic evidence.* The Hague: Mouton Publishers, 1973. [10]

Fuchs, V. R. *How we live.* Cambridge, Mass.: Harvard University Press, 1983. [16]

Funnell, E. Phonological processes in reading: New evidence in acquired dyslexia. *The British Journal of Psychology*, 74, 1983, 159–180. [10]

Furstenberg, F. F., Jr., J. Brooks-Gunn, and **S. P. Morgan.** *Adolescent mothers in later life.* New York: Cambridge University Press, 1987. [16]

Gadpaille, W. J. Homosexuality. In R. C. Simons and H. Pardes (Eds.), *Understanding human behavior in health and illness* (2nd ed.). Baltimore: Williams & Wilkins, 1981. [14]

Gaertner, S. L., and **J. F. Dovidio.** The subtlety of white racism, arousal, and helping behavior. *Journal of Personality and Social Psychology*, 1977, *35*, 691–707. [21]

Gaertner, S. L., and **J. F. Dovidio.** The aversive form of racism. In J. F. Dovidio and S. L. Gaertner (Eds.), *Prejudice, discrimination and racism.* New York: Academic Press, 1986. [21]

Gagnon, J. H. Sex research and social change. *Archives of Sexual Behavior*, 1975, *4*, 111–141. [14]

Galanter, E. Contemporary psychophysics. In R. Brown, E. Galanter, E. H. Hess, and G. Mandler, *New directions in psychology.* New York: Holt, Rinehart & Winston, 1962. [4]

Galton, L. *The silent disease: Hypertension.* New York: Crown, 1973. [20]

Ganellen, D. C., and **P. H. Blaney.** Hardiness and social support as moderators of the effects of life stress. *Journal of Personality and Social Psychology*, 1984, *47*, 156–173. [20]

Garcia, J., F. R. Ervin, and **R. A. Koelling.** Learning with prolonged delay of reinforcement. *Psychonomic Science*, 1966, *5*, 121–122. [7]

Garcia, J., and **R. A. Koelling.** Relation of cue to consequence in avoidance learning. *Psychonomic Science*, 1966, *4*, 123–124. [7]

Garcia, J., K. W. Rusiniak, and **L. P. Brett.** Conditioning food-illness aversions in wild animals: *Caveant canonici.* In H. Davis and H. M. B. Hurwitz (Eds.), *Operant-Pavlovian interactions.* Hillsdale, N.J.: Erlbaum, 1977. [7]

Gardner, B. T. Project Nim: Who taught whom? *Contemporary Psychology*, 26, 1981, 425–427. [10]

Gardner, B. T., and **R. A. Gardner.** Teaching sign language to a chimpanzee. *Science*, 1969, *165*, 644–672. [10]

Gardner, B. T., and **R. A. Gardner.** Evidence for sentence constituents in the early utterances of child and chimpanzee. *Journal of Experimental Psychology: General*, 1975, *104*, 244–267. [10]

Gardner, H. *The shattered mind.* New York: Basic Books, 1974. [10]

Gardner, H. *Frames of mind: The theory of multiple intelligence.* New York: Basic Books, 1984. [11]

Garfield, S. L. *Psychotherapy: An elective approach.* New York: Wiley, 1980. [19]

Garfinkel, B. D., A. Froese, and **J. Hood.** Suicide attempts in children and adolescents. *American Journal of Psychiatry*, 1982, *139*, 1257–1261. [18]

Garrow, J. S. *Energy balance and obesity in man.* New York: American Elsevier, 1978. [13]

Gates, A. I. Recitation as a factor in memorizing. *Archives of Psychology,* 1917, No. 40. [8]

Gates, M., and **W. C. Allee.** Conditioned behavior of isolated and grouped cockroaches on a simple maze. *Journal of Comparative Psychology,* 1933, *13,* 331–358. [22]

Gazzaniga, M. S. The split brain in man. *Scientific American,* August 1967, *217,* 24–29. [6]

Gazzaniga, M. S. *The social brain: Discovering the networks of the mind.* New York: Basic Books, 1985. [6]

Gazzaniga, M. *Mind matters, brain states.* Boston: Houghton Mifflin, 1988. [5]

Gellhorn, E. Motion and emotion: The role of proprioception in the physiology and pathology of the emotions. *Psychological Review,* 1964, *71,* 457–472. [12]

Gelman, D. Haunted by their habits. *Newsweek,* March 27, 1989, 71–75. [18]

Gelman, R. Accessing one-to-one correspondence: Still another paper on conservation. *British Journal of Psychology,* 1982, *73,* 209–220. [15]

Gelman, R., and **C. R. Gallistel.** *The child's understanding of number.* Cambridge, Mass.: Harvard University Press, 1978. [15]

Gentry, W. D., A. P. Chesney, H. E. Gary, R. P. Hall, and **E. Harburg.** Habitual anger-coping styles: I. Effect on mean blood pressure and risk for essential hypertension. *Psychosomatic Medicine,* 1982, *44,* 195–202. [20]

Ghiselli, E. E. *The validity of occupational aptitude tests.* New York: Wiley, 1966. [23]

Ghiselli, E. E. The validity of aptitude tests in personnel selection. *Personnel Psychology,* 1973, *26,* 461–477. [23]

Gibson, E. J., and **E. S. Spelke.** The development of perception. In P. H. Mussen (Ed.), *Handbook of child psychology* (4th ed.). Vol. 3, J. H. Flavell and E. M. Markman (Eds.), New York: Wiley, *Cognitive development.* 1983. [5]

Gibson, E. J., and **R. D. Walk.** The visual cliff. *Scientific American,* April 1960, 64–71. [15]

Gibson, J. J. *The perception of the visual world.* Boston: Houghton Mifflin, 1950. [5]

Gibson, J. J. Observations on active touch. *Psychological Review,* 1962, *69,* 477–491. [5]

Gibson, J. J. *The senses considered as perceptual systems.* Boston: Houghton Mifflin, 1966. [5]

Gilbert, B., and **J. Cunningham.** Women's postrape sexual functioning: Review and implications for counseling. *Journal of Counseling and Development,* 1986, *65,* 69–71. [14]

Gilligan, C. *In a different voice.* Cambridge: Harvard University Press, 1982. [16]

Glass, A. L., and **K. J. Holyoak.** *Cognition* (2nd ed.). New York: Random House, 1986. [9]

Glass, D. C., and **J. E. Singer.** *Urban stress.* New York: Academic Press, 1972. [20, 22]

Glass, D. C., B. Reim, and **J. R. Singer.** Behavioral consequences of adaptation to controllable and uncontrollable noise. *Journal of Experimental Social Psychology,* 1971, *7,* 244–257. [20]

Glenberg, A. M., and **M. M. Bradley.** Mental contiguity. *Journal of Experimental Psychology: Human Learning and Memory,* 1979, *5,* 88–97. [8]

Glesser, G. C., B. L. Green, and **C. Einget.** *Prolonged psychological effects of disaster: A study of the Buffalo Creek Flood.* New York: Academic Press, 1981. [20]

Glick, M. L., and **K. J. Holyoak.** Analogical problem solving. *Cognitive Psychology,* 1980, *12,* 306–355. [9]

Glueck, S., and **E. Glueck.** *Unraveling juvenile delinquency.* New York: Commonwealth Fund, 1950. [16]

Godden, D. R., and **A. D. Baddeley.** Context-dependent memory in two natural environments: On land and under water. *British Journal of Psychology,* 1975, *66,* 325–332. [8]

Goethals, G. R., and **J. Cooper.** The role of intention and postbehavioral consequences in the arousal of cognitive dissonance. *Journal of Personality and Social Psychology,* 1972, *3,* 293–301. [21]

Gold, P. E. Glucose modulation of memory storage processing. *Behavioral Neural Biology,* 1986a, *45:*342–349. [8]

Gold, P. E., J. Vogt, and **J. L. Hall.** Posttraining glucose effects on memory: Behavioral and pharmacological characteristics. *Behavioral Neural Biology,* 1986b, *46:*145–155. [8]

Gold, P. E. Sweet memories, *American Scientist,* March–April 1987, *75,* 151–155. [8]

Goldgaber, D., M. I. Lerman, O. W. McBride, U. Saffiotti, and **D. C. Gajdusek.** Characterization and chromosomal localization of a cDNA encoding brain amyloid of Alzheimer's disease. *Science,* 1987, *235,* 877–880. [3]

Golden, C. J., J. A. Moses, Jr., and **R. Zelazowski.** Cerebral ventricular site and neuropsychological impairment in young chronic schizophrenics. *Archives of General Psychiatry,* 1980, *37,* 618–626. [18]

Goldsmith, H. H., A. H. Buss, R. Plomin, M. K. Rothbart, A. Thomas, S. Chess, R. A. Hinde, and **R. B. McCall.** Roundtable: What is temperament? Four approaches. *Child Development,* 1987, *58,* 505–529. [15]

Goldsmith, H. H., and **I. I. Gottesman.**

Origins of variation in behavioral style: A longitudinal study of temperament in young twins. *Child Development,* 1981, *52,* 91–103. [17]

Goleman, D. *The varieties of the meditative experience.* New York: Dutton, 1977. [6]

Goleman, D. Thriving despite hardship: Key childhood traits identified. *The New York Times,* October 13, 1987, pp. C1, C11. [17]

Goleman, D. Therapists find last outpost of adolescence in adulthood. *The New York Times,* November 8, 1988, pp. C1, C13. [16]

Goleman, D. Subtle but intriguing differences found in the brain anatomy of men and women. *The New York Times,* Tuesday, April 11, 1989, pp. C1, C6. [3]

Goleman, D. Feeling gloomy? A good self-help book may actually help. *The New York Times,* July 6, 1989. [19]

Goleman, D. When the rapist is not a stranger: Studies seek new understanding. *The New York Times,* August 29, 1989, pp. C1, C6. [14]

Goodall, J. *The chimpanzees of Gombe.* Cambridge, Mass.: Harvard University Press, 1986. [2]

Gotlib, I. H. Depression and general psychopathology in university students. *Journal of Abnormal Psychology,* 1984, *93,* 19–31. [18]

Gottesman, I. I. Developmental genetics and ontogenetic psychology. In A. D. Pick (Ed.), *Minnesota Symposia on Child Psychology.* Vol. 8. Minneapolis: University of Minnesota Press, 1974, pp. 55–80. [15]

Gottesman, I. I. Schizophrenia and genetics: Where are we? Are you sure? In L. C. Wynne, R. L. Cromwell, and S. Matthysse (Eds.), *The nature of schizophrenia: New approaches to research and treatment.* New York: Wiley, 1978. [18]

Gottfried, A. E., and **A. W. Gottfried** (Eds.). *Maternal employment and children's development: Longitudinal research.* New York: Plenum Press, 1988. [15]

Gottlieb, G. The psychobiological approach to developmental issues. In P. H. Mussen (Ed.), *Handbook of child psychology* (4th ed.). Vol. 2, J. J. Campos and M. M. Haith (Eds.), *Infancy and developmental psychobiology.* New York: Wiley, 1983. [5, 15, 17]

Gould, J. L. Processing of sun-azimuth information by honey bees. *Animal Behavior,* 1984, *32,* 149–152. [7]

Gould, R. E. Sexual problems. In W. H. Norman and T. J. Scaramella (Eds.), *Midlife.* New York: Brunner/Mazel, 1980. [14]

Gould, S. J. *Ontogeny and phylogeny.* Cambridge, Mass.: Belknap Press of Harvard University Press, 1977. [15]

Gove, W. R. The current status of the labelling theory of mental illness. In W. R. Gove (Ed.), *Deviance and mental illness.* Beverly Hills, Calif.: Sage, 1982. [18]

Graham, K. R. Explaining "virtuoso" hypnotic performance: Social psychology or experiential skill? *Behavioral and Brain Sciences,* 1986, *9,* 473–474. [6]

Grantham, D. W. Motion aftereffects with horizontally moving sound sources in the free field. *Perception & Psychophysics,* 1989, *45,* 129–136. [5]

Grantham, D. W., and **F. L. Wightman.** Auditory motion aftereffects. *Perception & Psychophysics,* 1979, *26,* 403–408. [5]

Gratch, G. A study of the relative dominance of vision and touch in six-month-old infants. *Child Development,* 1972, *43,* 615–623. [15]

Greaves, G. B. Multiple personality: 165 years after Mary Reynolds. *Journal of Nervous and Mental Disease,* 1980, *168,* 577–596. [18]

Green, D. M., and **J. A. Swets.** *Signal detection theory and psychophysics.* New York: Wiley, 1966. [4]

Green, R. Sexual identity of 37 children raised by homosexual or transsexual parents. *American Journal of Psychiatry,* 1978, *135,* 692–697. [14]

Green, R. Patterns of sexual identity in childhood: Relationship to subsequent sexual partner preference. In J. Marmor (Ed.). *Homosexual behavior.* New York: Basic Books, 1980. [14]

Green, R. Environmental determinants of human sexuality. In D. Gilmore and B. Cook (Eds.), *Factors in mammal reproduction.* London: Macmillan, 1981. [14]

Green, R. Gender identity disorders and transvestism. In J. Greist, J. Jefferson, and R. Spitzer (Eds.), *Treatment of mental disorders.* New York: Oxford University Press, 1982. [14]

Greenberg, B. S. Television and role socialization. In D. Pearl, L. Bouthilet, and J. Lazer (Eds.), *Television and behavior.* Washington, D.C.: National Institute of Mental Health, 1982. [15]

Greenberg, J. Equity and workplace status: A field experiment. *Journal of Applied Psychology,* 1988, *73,* 606–613. [23]

Greenberg, J., and **S. Ornstein.** High status job title as compensation for underpayment: A test of equity theory. *Journal of Applied Psychology,* 1983, *68,* 285–297. [23]

Greenblatt, M. Efficacy of ECT in affective and schizophrenic illness. *American Journal of Psychiatry,* 1977, *134,* 1001–1005. [19]

Greene, L. R. Psychiatric day treatment as alternative to and transition from full time hospitalization. *Community Mental Health Journal,* 1981, *17,* 191–202. [19]

Greene, R. L. Sources of recency effects in free recall. *Psychological Bulletin,* 1986, *99,* 221–228. [5]

Greenhouse, L. Court, ruling 5 to 4, eases burden on employers in some bias suits. *The New York Times,* June 6, 1989, pp. A1, A24. [23]

Greenwald, A. G. On defining attitudes and attitude theory. In A. G. Greenwald, T. C. Brock and T. M. Ostrom (Eds.), *Psychological foundations of attitudes.* New York: Academic Press, 1968, pp. 361–388. [21]

Greenwald, A. G., and **D. L. Ronis.** Twenty years of cognitive dissonance: Case study of the evolution of a theory. *Psychological Review,* 1978, *85,* 53–57. [21]

Greenwald, A. G. The totalitarian ego: Fabrication and revision of personal history. *American Psychologist,* 1980, *35,* 603–618. [13]

Greenwald, A. G. Self and memory. In G. H. Bower (Ed.), *The psychology of learning and motivation.* New York: Academic Press, 1981. [8]

Greer, L. D. Children's comprehension of formal features with masculine and feminine connotations. Unpublished master's thesis. Department of Human Development, University of Kansas, 1980 (cited in A. C. Huston, 1983). [15]

Gregory, R. L. *The intelligent eye.* New York: McGraw-Hill, 1970. [5]

Gregory, R. L. *Eye and brain* (3rd ed.). New York: McGraw-Hill 1977. [5]

Gregory, R. L., and **J. G. Wallace.** Recovery from early blindness: A case study. *Experimental Psychology Society Monograph,* 1963, No. 2. [5]

Grice, H. P. Logic and conversation. In P. Cole and J. L. Morgan (Eds.), *Syntax and semantics.* Vol. 3: *Speech acts.* New York: Seminar Press, 1975. [10]

Griffin, G. Legal views of test validity. Unpublished paper, Northwestern University, November 1980. [23]

Grinspoon, L. *Marihuana reconsidered* (2nd ed.). Cambridge, Mass.: Harvard University Press, 1977. [6]

Grossmann, K., K. E. Grossmann, G. Spangler, G. Suess, and **L. Unzer.** Maternal sensitivity and newborns' orientation responses as related to quality of attachment in Northern Germany. *Monographs of the Society for Child Development,* 1985, *50,* Serial No. 209, 232–256. [15]

Groth, A. N., and **A. W. Burgess.** Rape: A sexual deviation. *American Journal of Orthopsychiatry,* 1977, *47,* 400–406. [14]

Gupta, B. S. Dextroamphetamine and measures of intelligence. *Intelligence,* 1977, *1,* 274–280. [11]

Gurman, A. S., D. P. Kniskern, and **W. M. Pinsof.** Research on the process and outcome of marital and family therapy. In S. L. Garfield and A. E. Bergin (Eds.), *Handbook of psychotherapy and behavior change: An evaluative analysis* (3rd ed.). New York: Wiley, 1978. [19]

Gustavson, C. R., J. Garcia, W. G. Hankins, and **K. W. Rusiniak.** Coyote predation control by aversive conditioning. *Science,* 1974, *184,* 581–583. [7]

Guthrie, E. R. *The psychology of learning.* New York: Harper & Row. 1935. [7]

Gutmann, D. *Reclaimed powers.* New York: Basic Books, 1988. [16]

Haber, R. N., and **L. G. Standing.** Direct measures of short-term visual storage. *Quarterly Journal of Experimental Psychology,* 1969, *21,* 43–45. [8]

Hackman, R. J., and **G. R. Oldham.** Motivation through the design of work. *Organizational Behavior and Human Performance,* 1976, *3,* 417–426. [23]

Hadley, M. E. *Endocrinology,* Englewood Cliffs, N.J.: Prentice-Hall, 1984. [3]

Hagestad, G. O., and **B. L. Neugarten.** Age and the life course. In R. H. Binstock and E. Shanas (Eds.), *Handbook of aging and the social sciences* (2nd ed.). New York: Van Nostrand Reinhold, 1985. [16]

Haier, R., D. Rosenthal, and **P. H. Wender.** MMPI assessment of psychopathology in the adopted-away offspring of schizophrenics. *Archives of General Psychiatry,* 1978, *35,* 171–175. [18]

Hainline, L., and **E. Lemerise.** Infants' scanning of geometric forms varying in size. *Journal of Experimental Child Psychology,* 1982, *33,* 235–256. [5]

Halgren, E. Mental phenomena induced by stimulation of the limbic system. *Human Neurobiology,* 1982, 1:251–260. [3]

Hall, J. F. Recall versus recognition: A methodological note. *Journal of Experimental Psychology, Learning, Memory, and Cognition,* 1983, *9,* 346–349. [7]

Hall, J. F. *Learning and Memory* (2nd ed.). Boston: Allyn & Bacon, 1989. [8]

Hall, J. L., J. Vogt, L. Gonder-Frederick, and **P. E. Gold.** Glucose effects on memory in college-age and elderly subjects. Unpublished. [8]

Halliday, G. Lucid dreaming: Using nightmares and sleep-wake confusion. In J. Gackenbach and S. La Berge (Eds.), *Conscious mind, sleeping brain: Perspectives on lucid dreaming.* New York: Plenum Press, 1988. [6]

Halpern, B. P. Tasting and smelling as active, exploratory sensory processes. *American Journal of Otolaryngology,* 1983, *4,* 246–249. [4]

Halpern, D. F. *Thought and knowledge: An introduction to critical thinking.* Hillsdale, N.J.: Erlbaum, 1984. [9]

Hamilton, D. L., and **T. K. Trolier.** Stereotypes and stereotyping: An overview of the cognitive approach. In J. F. Dovidio and S. L. Gaertner (Eds.), *Prejudice, discrimination, and racism.* Orlando, Fla.: Academic Press, 1986, pp. 127–163. [21]

Hammond, P., G. S. V. Mouat, and **A. T. Smith.** Motion aftereffects in cat striate cortex elicited by moving gratings. *Experimental Brain Research,* 1985, *60,* 411–416. [5]

Harackiewicz, J. M., and **J. R. Larson, Jr.** Managing motivation: The impact of supervisor feedback on subordinate task interest. *Journal of Personality and Social Psychology,* 1986, *51,* 547–556. [13]

Harackiewicz, J. M., G. Manderlink, and **C. Sansone.** Competence processes and achievement orientation: Implications for intrinsic motivation. In A. Boggiano and T. S. Pittman (Eds.), *Motivation and achievement: A social-developmental analysis.* New York: Cambridge University Press, in press. [13]

Haracz, J. L. The dopamine hypothesis: An overview of studies with schizophrenic patients. *Schizophrenia Bulletin,* 1982, *8,* 438–469. [18]

Harburg, E., J. C. Erfurt, L. S. Havenstein, C. Chape, W. J. Schull, and **M. A. Schork.** Socio-ecological stress, suppressed hostility, skin color, and black-white male blood pressure: Detroit. *Psychosomatic Medicine,* 1973, *35,* 276–296. [20]

Hardin, G. The tragedy of the commons. *Science,* 1968, *162,* 1243–1248. [22]

Hare, R. D. *Psychopathy: Theory and research.* New York: Wiley, 1970. [18]

Hare-Mustin, R. T., and **J. E. Hall.** Procedures for responding to ethics complaints against psychologists. *American Psychologist,* 1981, *36,* 1494–1505. [2]

Hariton, E. B., and **J. L. Singer.** Women's fantasies during sexual intercourse: Normative and theoretical implications. *Journal of Consulting and Clinical Psychology,* 1974, *42,* 313–322. [14]

Harkins, S. G. Social loafing and social facilitation. *Journal of Experimental Social Psychology,* 1987, *23,* 1–18. [22]

Harlow, H. F. Love in infant monkeys. *Scientific American,* 1959, *200* (6), 68–74. [15]

Harlow, H. F., and **M. K. Harlow.** Learning to love. *American Scientist,* 1966, *54,* 244–272. [15]

Harlow, H. F., and **M. K. Harlow.** Effects of various mother-infant relationships on rhesus monkey behaviors. In B. M. Foss (Ed.). *Determinants of infant behavior* (Vol. 4). London: Methuen, 1969. [16]

Harlow, H. F., M. K. Harlow, and **D. K. Meyer.** Learning motivated by a manipulation drive. *Journal of Experimental Psychology,* 1950, *40,* 228–234. [13]

Harman, S. M., and **G. B. Talbert.** Repro-

ductive aging. In C. E. Finch and E. L. Schneider (Eds.), *Handbook of the biology of aging* (2nd ed.). New York: Van Nostrand Reinhold, 1985, pp. 457–510. [16]

Harre, R. *Great scientific experiments.* New York: Oxford University Press, 1983. [5]

Harris, P. L. Infant cognition. In P. H. Mussen (Ed.), *Handbook of child psychology* (4th ed.). Vol. 2. M. M. Haith and J. J. Campos (Eds.), *Infancy and developmental psychobiology.* New York: Wiley, 1983. [15]

Harris, R. J. Inferences in information processing. In G. H. Bower (Ed.), *The psychology of learning and motivation: Advances in theory and research* (Vol. 15). New York: Academic Press, 1982. [8]

Harter, S. Developmental perspectives on the self-system. In P. H. Mussen (Ed.), *Handbook of child psychology* (4th ed.). Vol. 4. E. M. Hetherington (Ed.), *Socialization, personality, and social development.* New York: Wiley, 1983. [15]

Hass, A. *Teenage sexuality.* New York: Macmillan, 1979. [14]

Hassan, S. A. Transactional and contextual invalidation between the parents of disturbed families: A comparative study. *Family Process,* 1974, *13,* 53–76. [18]

Hastie, R. Memory for information that confirms or contradicts a personality impression. R. Hastie et al. (Eds.), In Person memory: *The cognitive basis of social perception,* Hillsdale, N.J.: Erlbaum, 1980.

Hathaway, S., and **E. Monachesi.** *Adolescent personality and behavior.* Minneapolis: University of Minnesota Press, 1963. [16]

Hattie, J. A., C. F. Sharpley, and **H. J. Rogers.** Comparative effectiveness of professional and paraprofessional helpers. *Psychological Bulletin,* 1984, *95,* 534–541. [19]

Haviland, J. M., and **M. Lelwica.** The induced affect response: 10-week-old infants' responses to three emotion expressions. *Developmental Psychology,* 1987, *23,* 97–104. [12]

Haviland, S. E., and **H. H. Clark.** What's new? Acquiring new information as a process in comprehension. *Journal of Verbal Learning and Verbal Behavior,* 1974, *13,* 512–521. [10]

Hawkins, R. D., and **G. H. Bower** (Eds.). *Computational models of learning in simple neural systems.* Vol. 23. *The psychology of learning and motivation.* New York: Academic Press, in press. [7]

Hawkins, R. D., and **E. R. Kandel.** Is there a cell biological alphabet for simple forms of learning? *Psychological Review,* 1984. [7]

Hayes, C.D. (Ed.). *Risking the future.* Vol.

1. *Adolescent sexuality, pregnancy, and childbearing.* Washington, D.C.: National Academy Press, 1987. [14]

Hayes, J. R. Three problems in teaching general skills. In S. F. Chipman, J. W. Segal, and R. Glaser (Eds.). *Thinking and learning skills.* Vol. 2. *Research and open questions.* Hillsdale, N.J.: Erlbaum, 1985, pp. 391–405. [11]

Haymes, M., L. Green, and **R. Quinto.** Maslow's hierarchy, moral development, and prosocial behavioral skills within a child psychiatric population. *Motivation and Emotion* 1984, *8,* 23–31. [13]

Hazan, C., and **P. Shaver.** Romantic love conceptualized as an attachment process. *Journal of Personality and Social Psychology,* 1987, *52,* 511–524. [14]

Healy, A. F. Detection errors in the word *The:* Evidence for reading units larger than letters. *Journal of Experimental Psychology: Human Perception and Performance,* 1976, *2,* 235–242. [1976]

Heath, R. G. Pleasure and brain activity in man. *Journal of Nervous and Mental Diseases,* 1972, *154,* 3–18. [3]

Hebb, D. Drives and the CNS. *Psychological Review,* 1955, *62,* 243–253. [13]

Hebb, D. O. *The organization of behavior.* New York: Wiley, 1949. [7, 14]

Hebb, D. O. What psychology is about. *American Psychologist,* 1974, *29,* 71–79. [2]

Hecaen, H., and **M. L. Albert.** *Human neuropsychology.* New York: Wiley, 1978. [3]

Hefner, R. S., and **H. E. Hefner.** Hearing in large and small dogs: Absolute thresholds and size of the tympanic membrane. *Behavioral Neuroscience,* 1983, *97,* 310–318. [4]

Heider, E. R. Universals in color naming and memory. *Journal of Experimental Psychology,* 1972, *93,* 10–20. [10]

Heider, E. R., and **D. C. Olivier.** The structure of color space and memory for two languages. *Cognitive Psychology,* 1972b, *3,* 337–354. [10]

Heider, F. *The psychology of interpersonal relations: A theory of interdependence.* New York: Wiley, 1958. [21]

Heilman, M. E., H. A. Hornstein, J. H. Cage, and **J. K. Herschlag.** Reactions to prescribed leader behavior as a function of role perspective: The case of the Vroom-Yetton model. *Journal of Applied Psychology,* February 1984, *69,* 50–60. [23]

Heim, N. Sexual behavior of castrated sex offenders. *Archives of Sexual Behavior,* 1981, *10,* 11–19. [14]

Heiman, J. R. The physiology of erotica: Women's sexual arousal. *Psychology Today,* 1975, *8,* 90–94. [14]

Heiman, J. R., L. LoPiccolo, and **J. LoPiccolo.** The treatment of sexual dysfunction. In A. Gurman and D. Kniskern (Eds.), *Handbook of family therapy.* New York: Brunner/Mazel, 1980. [14]

Helmholtz, H. V. *Handbook of physiological optics* (Vol. III). New York: Optical Society of America, 1925. [5]

Helzer, J. E., I. F. Brockington, and **R. E. Kendell.** Predictive validity of *DSM III* and Feigner definitions of schizophrenia. *Archives of General Psychiatry,* 1981, *38,* 791–797. [18]

Hemphill, J. K. (Ed.). *The engineering study.* Princeton, N.J.: Educational Testing Service, 1963. [23]

Henderson, L. Issues in the modelling of pronunciation assembly in normal reading. In K. Patterson, J. Marshall, and M. Coltheart (Eds.), *Surface in dyslexia: Neuropsychological and cognitive analyses of phonological reading.* Hillsdale, N.J.: Erlbaum, 1986. [10]

Hendryx, M., and **R. R. Bootzin.** Psychiatric episodes in general hospitals without psychiatric units. *Hospital and Community Psychiatry,* 1986, *37,* 1025–1029. [19]

Hering, E. *Zur Lehre vom Lichtsinne.* Vinenna: Gerold, 1878. [4]

Herman, C. P., and **D. Mack.** Restrained and unrestrained eating. *Journal of Personality,* 1975, *43,* 647–660. [13]

Herman, L. M. Receptive competencies of language-trained animals. In S. Kaufman (Ed.), *Advances in the study of behavior* (Vol. 17). New York: Academic Press, 1987. [10]

Herman, L. M., D. G. Richards, and **J. P. Wolz.** Comprehension of sentences by bottlenosed dolphins. *Cognition,* 1984, *16,* 129–219. [10]

Herrnstein, R. J., R. S. Nickerson, M. de Sánchez, and **J. A. Swets.** Teaching thinking skills. *American Psychologist,* 1986, *41,* 1279–1289. [11]

Hersey, P., and **K. H. Blanchard.** *Management of organizational behavior.* Englewood Cliffs, N.J.: Prentice-Hall, 1988. [23]

Hess, R. D., and **T. M. McDevitt.** Some cognitive consequences of maternal intervention techniques: A longitudinal study. *Child Development,* 1984, *55,* 2017–2030. [11]

Heston, L. L. Psychiatric disorders in foster home reared children of schizophrenic mothers. *British Journal of Psychiatry,* 1966, *112,* 819–825. [18]

Hevesi, D. Harris Poll reports teenagers favor contraceptives at clinics. *The New York Times,* December 17, 1986, p. B12. [16]

Higbee, K. L. *Your memory.* Englewood Cliffs, N.J.: Prentice-Hall, 1977. [8]

Hilgard, E. R. *Hypnotic susceptibility.* New York: Harcourt Brace Jovanovich, 1965. [6]

Hilgard, E. R. *Divided consciousness: Mul-*

tiple controls in human thought and action. New York: Wiley-Interscience, 1977. [6]

Hilgard, E. R. Hypnosis and consciousness. *Human Nature,* 1978, *1,* 42–49. [6]

Hilgard, E. R., and **G. H. Bower.** *Theories of learning* (4th ed.). Englewood Cliffs: N.J.: Prentice-Hall, 1975. [8]

Hilgard, E. R., and **J. R. Hilgard.** *Hypnosis in the relief of pain.* Los Altos, Calif.: Kaufmann, 1983. [6]

Hilgard, J. R. *Personality and hypnosis: A study of imaginative involvement* (2nd ed.). Chicago: University of Chicago Press, 1979. [6]

Hill, A. L. Savants: Mentally retarded individuals with specific skills. In N. R. Ellis (Ed.), *International review of research in mental retardation* (Vol. 9). New York: Academic Press, 1978. [11]

Hill, J. P. Family relations in adolescence, *Genetic, Social, and General Psychology Monographs,* 1985, *111,* 233–248. [16]

Hillyard, S. A., and **J. C. Hansen.** Attention: Electrophysiological approaches. In M. G. H. Coles, E. Donchin, and S. W. Porges (Eds.), *Psychophysiology Systems, processes, and applications.* New York: Guilford, 1986. [4]

Hintzman, D. L. "Schema abstraction" in a multiple trace memory model. *Psychological Review,* 1986, *93,* 411–428. [9]

Hiroto, D. S., and **M. E. P. Seligman.** Generality of learned helplessness in man. *Journal of Personality and Social Psychology,* 1975, *31,* 311–327. [20]

Hirshfeld, R. M. A., and **C. K. Cross.** Epidemiology of affective disorders: Psychosocial risk factors. *Archives of General Psychiatry,* 1982, *39,* 35–46. [18]

Hitch, G. J., and **M. S. Halliday.** Working memory in children. In D. E. Broadbent (Ed.), *Functional aspects of human memory.* London: The Royal Society, 1983. [8]

Hobson, J. A. *The dreaming brain.* New York: Basic Books, 1988. [6]

Hobson, J. A., and **R. W. McCarley.** The brain as a dream state generator: An activation-synthesis hypothesis of the dream process. *American Journal of Psychiatry,* 1977, *134,* 1335–1348.

Hochbaum, G. *Public participation in medical screening programs.* (DHEW Publication 572, Public Health Service). Washington, D.C.: U.S. Government Printing Office, 1958. [20]

Hochberg, J. *Perception* (2nd ed.). Englewood Cliffs, N.J.: Prentice-Hall, 1978. [4]

Hoehn-Saric, R. Neurotransmitters in anxiety. *Archives of General Psychiatry,* 1982, *39,* 735–742. [18]

Hofferth, S. L. Influences on early sexual and fertility behavior: Factors affecting the initiation of sexual intercourse. In S. L. Hofferth and C. D. Hayes (Eds.),

Risking the future. Vol. 2. *Adolescent sexuality, pregnancy, and childbearing.* Washington, D.C.: National Academy Press, 1987. [14]

Hoffman, L., S. Paris, E. Hall, and **R. Schell.** *Developmental psychology today* (5th ed). New York: Random House, 1988. [16]

Hoffman, M. L. Moral development. In M. H. Bornstein and M. E. Lamb (Eds.), *Developmental psychology.* Hillsdale, N.J.: Erlbaum, 1984. [15, 16]

Hohmann, A., and **O. D. Creutzfeldt.** Squint and the development of binocularity in humans. *Nature,* 1975, *254,* 613–614. [5]

Holden, C. Identical twins reared apart. *Science,* 1980, *207,* 1323–1328. [11]

Holden, C. Youth suicide. *Science,* 1986, *233,* 839–841. [18]

Holden, C. Adjusting to an aging population. *Science,* 1987, *236,* 772. [16]

Holden, C. Doctor of sexology. *Psychology Today,* May 1988, 45–48. [14]

Holender, D. Semantic activation without conscious identification in dichotic listening, parafoveal vision, and visual masking: A survey and appraisal. *The Behavioral and Brain Sciences,* 1986, *9,* 1–66. [5]

Holing, D. Dolphin defense. *Discover,* October 1988, *9,* 68–73. [7]

Hollingshead, A., and **F. Redlich.** *Social class and mental illness.* New York: Wiley, 1958. [18]

Hollon, S. D., and **A. T. Beck.** Cognitive and cognitive-behavioral therapies. In S. L. Garfield and A. E. Bergin (Eds.), *Handbook of psychotherapy and behavior change: An evaluative analysis* (3rd ed.). New York: Wiley, 1986. [18, 19]

Holmes, D. S. Meditation and somatic arousal reduction: A review of the experimental evidence. *American Psychologist,* 1984, *39,* 1–10. [20]

Holmes, T. H., and **R. H. Rahe.** The social readjustment rating scale. *Journal of Psychosomatic Research,* 1967, *11,* 213–218. [20]

Holohan, C. J. Environmental psychology. *Annual Review of Psychology,* 1986, *37,* 381–407. [22]

Hooker, E., interviewed by P. Chance. Facts that liberated the gay community. *Psychology Today,* 1975, *9,* December, 52–55. [14]

Hoon, P. W., K. Bruce, and **B. Kinchloe.** Does the menstrual cycle play a role in sexual arousal? *Psychophysiology,* 1982, *19,* 21–26. [14]

Horn, J. Intellectual ability concepts. In R. J. Sternberg (Ed.), *Advances in the psychology of human intelligence* (Vol. 3). Hillsdale, N.J.: Erlbaum, 1986, pp. 35–77. [11]

Horn, J. C., and **J. Meer.** The vintage years. *Psychology Today,* May 1987, *21,* 76–90. [16]

Horn, J. L. The theory of fluid and crystalized intelligence in relation to concepts of cognitive psychology and aging in adulthood. In F. I. M. Craik and S. Trehub (Eds.), *Aging and cognitive processes.* New York: Plenum, 1982. [16]

Horne, R. L., M. M. Pettinati, A. Sugarman, and **E. Varga.** Comparing bilateral to unilateral electroconvulsive therapy in a randomized study of EEG monitoring. *Archives of General Psychiatry,* 1985, *42,* 1087–1092. [19]

Horney, K. *Our inner conflicts.* New York: Norton, 1945. [17]

Horney, K. *The neurotic personality of our times.* New York: Norton, 1965. (Originally published, 1937). [17]

Horowitz, L. M., and **Vitkus, J.** The interpersonal basis of psychiatric symptoms. *Clinical Psychology Review,* 1986, *6,* 443–469. [19]

Hostetler, A. J. Alzheimer's trials hinge on early diagnosis. *APA Monitor,* October 1987, *18,* 14–15. [8]

House, J. S., and **C. Robbins.** Age, psychosocial stress, and health. In M. W. Riley, B. B. Hess, and K. Bond (Eds.), *Aging in society.* Hillsdale, N.J.: Erlbaum, 1983. [20]

House, R. J. A path–goal theory of leader effectiveness. *Administrative Science Quarterly,* 1971, *16,* 321–338. [23]

House, R. J. A 1976 theory of charismatic leadership. In J. G. Hunt and L. L. Larson (Eds.), *Leadership: The cutting edge.* Carbondale, Ill.: Southern Illinois University Press, 1977. [23]

Howard, K. I., S. M. Kopta, M. S. Krause, and **D. E. Orlinsky.** The dose-effect relationship in psychotherapy. *American Psychologist,* 1986, *41,* 159–164. [19]

Howell, W. C., and **R. L. Dipboye.** *Essentials of industrial and organizational psychology.* Homewood, Ill.: Dorsey, 1982. [23]

Hoyt, M. F., M. D. Henley, and **B. E. Collins.** Studies in forced compliance: The confluence of choice and consequences of attitude change. *Journal of Personality and Social Psychology,* 1972, *23,* 205–210. [21]

Hsu, L. K. G. The aetiology of anorexia nervosa. *Psychological Medicine,* 1983, *13,* 231–237. [18]

Hubel, D. H., and **M. S. Livingstone.** Segregation of form, color, and stereopsis in primate area 18. *Journal of Neuroscience,* 1988, *7,* 3378–3415. [4]

Hubel, D. H., and **T. N. Wiesel.** Receptive fields, binocular interaction and functional architecture in the cat's visual cortex. *Journal of Physiology,* 1962, *160,* 106–154. [4]

Hubel, D. H., and **T. N. Wiesel.** Brain mechanisms of vision. *Scientific American,* 1979, *241,* 150–163. [4]

Huesmann, L. R., K. Lagerspetz, and **L. D. Eron.** Intervening variables in the TV violence–aggression relationship. *Developmental Psychology,* 1984, *20,* 746–775. [22]

Hull, C. L. *Principles of behavior.* New York: Appleton-Century-Crofts, 1943. [7]

Hull, J. G., and **C. F. Bond, Jr.** Social and behavioral consequences of alcohol consumption and expectancy: A meta-analysis. *Psychological Bulletin,* 1986, *99,* 347–360. [6]

Hunt, M. *Sexual behavior in the 1970s.* New York: Dell, 1974. [14]

Hunt, P. J., and **J. M. Hillery.** Social facilitation in a coaction setting: An examination of the effects over learning trials. *Journal of Experimental Social Psychology,* 1973, *2,* 563–571. [22]

Hunt, W. A., J. D. Matarazzo, S. M. Weiss, and **W. D. Gentry.** Associative learning, habit, and health behavior. *Journal of Behavioral Medicine,* 1979, *2,* 111–124. [20]

Hunter, J. E., and **R. F. Hunter.** Validity and utility of alternative predictors of job performance. *Psychological Bulletin,* 1984, *96,* 72–98. [11, 23]

Hurvich, L. M., and **D. Jameson.** An opponent-process theory of color vision. *Psychological Review,* 1957, *64,* 384–404. [4]

Huseman, R. C., J. D. Hatfield, and **E. W. Miles.** A new perspective on equity theory: The equity sensitivity construct. *Academy of Management Review,* 1987, *12,* 222–234. [23]

Huston, A. C. Sex-typing. In P. H. Mussen (Ed.), *Handbook of child psychology* (4th ed.). Vol. 4, E. M. Hetherington (Ed.), *Socialization, personality, and social development.* New York: Wiley, 1983. [15]

Huston, T. L. Ambiguity of acceptance, social desirability, and dating choice. *Journal of Experimental Social Psychology,* 1973, *9,* 32–42. [21]

Huxley, A. The doors of perception. In D. Goleman and R. J. Davidson (Eds.), *Consciousness: Brain, states of awareness, and mysticism.* New York: Harper & Row, 1979. [6]

Hyde, J. S. *Human sexuality.* New York: McGraw-Hill, 1982. [14]

Hyde, J. S., and **M. C. Linn.** Gender differences in verbal ability: A meta-analysis. *Psychological Bulletin,* 1988, *104,* 53–69. [11]

Hyman, B. T., G. N. Van Hoesen, A. R. Domasio, and **C. L. Barnes.** Alzheimer's disease: Cell-specific pathology isolates the hippocampal formation. *Science,* 1984, *225,* 1168–1170. [3]

Insko, C. A. Verbal reinforcement of attitude. *Journal of Personality and Social Psychology,* 1965, *2,* 621–623. [21]

Insko, C. A., and **J. Schopler.** Triadic consistency: A statement of affective-cognitive-conative consistency. *Psychological Review,* 1967, *74,* 361–376. [21]

Institute of Medicine. *Marijuana and health.* Washington, D.C.: National Academy Press, 1982. [6]

Isabella, R. A., J. Belsky, and **A. von Eye.** Origins of infant-mother attachment: An examination of interactional psychology during the infant's first year. *Developmental Psychology,* 1989, *25,* 12–21. [15]

Izard, C. E. *The face of emotion.* New York: Appleton-Century-Crofts, 1971. [12]

Izard, C. E., E. A. Hembree, L. M. Dougherty, and **C. C. Spizzari.** Changes in facial expressions of 2- to 19-month-old infants following acute pain. *Developmental Psychology,* 1983, *19,* 418–426. [12]

Jackson, D. D. Reunion of identical twins, raised apart, reveals some astonishing similarities. *Smithsonian,* October 1980, 48–56. [11]

Jackson, D. N. *Personality research form manual.* Goshen, N.Y.: Research Psychologists Press, 1974. [17]

Jacob, R. G., H. C. Kraemer, and **S. Agras.** Relaxation therapy in the treatment of hypertension. *Archives of General Psychiatry,* 1977, *34,* 1417–1427. [20]

Jacobs, M. K., and **G. Goodman.** Psychology and self-help groups: Predictions on a partnership. *American Psychologist,* 1989, *44,* 536–545. [19]

Jacobs, T. J., and **E. Charles.** Life events and the occurrence of cancer in children. *Psychosomatic Medicine,* 1980, *42,* 11–24. [20]

Jacobson, E. *Progressive relaxation* (2nd ed.). Chicago: University of Chicago Press, 1938. [20]

Jacobson, E. *Anxiety and tension control.* Philadelphia: Lippincott, 1964. [20]

Jacobson, J. L., S. W. Jacobson, G. G. Fein, P. M. Schwartz, and **J. K. Dowler.** Prenatal exposure to an environmental toxin: A test of the multiple effects model. *Developmental psychology,* 1984, *20,* 523–532. [15]

Jacobson, N. S., and **G. Margolin.** *Marital therapy: Strategies based on social learning and behavior exchange principles.* New York: Brunner/Mazel, 1979. [19]

Jacobson, S. W., G. G. Fein, J. L. Jacobson, P. M. Schwartz, and **J. K. Dowler.** The effect of intrauterine PCB exposure on visual recognition memory. *Child Development,* 1985, *56,* 853–860. [15]

Jacoby, L. L. Perceptual enhancement: Persistent effects of an experience. *Journal of Experimental Psychology: Learning, Memory, and Cognition,* 1983, *9,* 21–38. [8]

Jacoby, L. L., and **L. R. Brooks.** Nonanalytic cognition: Memory, perception, and concept learning. In G. H. Bower (Ed.), *The psychology of learning and motivation: Advances in research and theory* (Vol. 18). New York: Academic Press, 1984, pp. 1–47. [9]

Jacoby, L. L., and **M. Dallas.** On the relationship between autobiographical memory and perceptual learning. *Journal of Experimental Psychology: General,* 1981, *110,* 306–340. [8]

James, G. A forced hospital stay ends for Joyce Brown. *The New York Times,* January 20, 1988, p. B2. [19]

James, W. *The principles of psychology.* New York: Holt, 1890. [5, 11]

James, W. *Psychology: The briefer course.* New York: Harper & Row, 1892. [6]

James, W. What is an emotion? In K. Dunlap (Ed.), *The emotions.* Baltimore: Williams & Wilkins, 1884/1922, pp. 11–30. [12]

Janis, I. L. *Crucial decisions: Leadership in policymaking and crisis management.* New York: Free Press, 1989. [23]

Janis, I. L., and **L. Mann.** *Decision making: A psychological analysis of conflict, choice, and commitment.* New York: Free Press, 1977. [9]

Jarvik, M. E. Probability learning and a negative recency effect in the serial anticipation of alternative symbols. *Journal of Experimental Psychology,* 1951, *41,* 291–297. [9]

Jemmott, J. B. III, and **S. E. Locke.** Psychosocial factors, immunologic mediation, and human susceptibility to infectious diseases: How much do we know? *Psychological Bulletin,* 1984, *95,* 78–108. [20]

Jencks, C., **J. Smith, H. Ackland, M. J. Bane, D. Cohen, H. Gintis, P. Heyns,** and **S. Michelson.** *Inequality: A reassessment of the effects of family and schooling in America.* New York: Basic Books, 1972. [11]

Jensen, A. R. How much can we boost I.Q. and scholastic achievement? *Harvard Educational Review,* 1969, *39,* 1–123. [11]

Jensen, A. R. Sir Cyril Burt in perspective. *American Psychologist,* 1978, *33,* 499–503. [11]

Jensen, A. R. Raising the IQ: The Ramey and Haskins study. *Intelligence,* 1981, *5,* 29–40. [11]

Johnson, C., and **K. L. Maddi.** The etiology of bulimia: Biopsychosocial perspectives. *Adolescent Psychiatry,* 1986, *13,* 253–288. [18]

Johnson, D. M., **G. R. Parrott,** and **R. P. Stratton.** Production and judgment of solutions to five problems. *Journal of Educational Psychology Monograph Supplement,* 1968, *59* (6, Pt. 2). [9]

Johnson, E. J., and **A. Tversky.** Affect, generalization and the perception of risk. *Journal of Personality and Social Psychology,* 1983, *45,* 20–31. [9]

Johnson, E. M., and **D. M. Kochlar** (Eds.). *Teratogenesis and reproductive toxicology.* New York: Springer, 1983. [15]

Johnson, G. *Machinery of the mind: Inside the new science of artificial intelligence.* New York: Time Books, 1986. [9]

Johnson-Laird, P. N., and **M. Steedman.** The psychology of syllogisms. *Cognitive Psychology,* 1978, *10,* 64–99. [9]

Johnson-Laird, P. N. *Mental models.* Cambridge, Mass.: Harvard University Press, 1983. [8, 9, 10]

Jones, D. C., **D. J. Swift,** and **M. A. Johnson.** Nondeliberate memory for a novel event among preschoolers. *Developmental Psychology,* 1988, *24,* 641–645. [15]

Jones, E. E., and **S. C. Berglas.** Control of attributions about the self through self-handicapping strategies: The appeal of alcohol and the role of underachievement. *Personality and Social Psychology Bulletin,* 1978, *4,* 200–206. [13]

Jones, E. E., and **K. E. Davis.** From acts to dispositions: The attribution process in person perception. In L. Berkowitz (Ed.), *Advances in experimental social psychology* (Vol. 2). New York: Academic Press, 1965. [21]

Jones, E. E., and **H. G. Gerard.** *Foundations of social psychology.* New York: Wiley, 1967. [22]

Jones, E. E., and **V. A. Harris.** The attribution of attitudes. *Journal of Experimental Social Psychology,* 1967, *3,* 1–24. [21]

Jones, E. E., and **R. E. Nisbett.** The actor and the observer: Divergent perceptions of the causes of behavior. In E. E. Jones et al. (Eds.), *Attribution: Perceiving the causes of behavior.* Morristown, N.J.: General Learning Press, 1972. [21]

Jones, M. C. A laboratory study of fear: The case of Peter. *Pedagogical Seminary,* 1924, *31,* 308–315. [19]

Joseph, J. G., **S. B. Montgomery, C. Emmons, R. C. Kessler, D. G. Ostrow, C. B. Wortman, M. E. O'Brien,** and **S. Eshleman.** Magnitude and determinants of behavioral risk reduction: Longitudinal analysis of a cohort at risk for AIDS. *Psychology and Health,* 1987, *1,* 73–96. [14]

Josephson, W. L. Television violence and children's aggression: Testing the priming, social script, and disinhibition predictions. *Journal of Personality and Social Psychology,* 1987, *53,* 882–890. [22]

Jouvet, M. The function of dreaming: A neurophysiologist's point of view. In M. S. Gazzaniga and C. Blakemore (Eds.), *Handbook of psychobiology.* New York: Academic Press, 1975. [6]

Just, M. A., and **P. A. Carpenter.** *The psychology of reading and language comprehension.* Boston: Allyn & Bacon, 1987. [9, 10]

Justice, B. *Who gets sick: How thoughts, moods, and beliefs can affect your health.* Los Angeles: J. P. Tarcher, 1988. [7]

Kagan, J. *The nature of the child.* New York: Basic Books, 1984. [15]

Kagan, J. *Unstable ideas: Temperament, cognition, and self.* Cambridge, Mass.: Harvard University Press, 1989. [17]

Kahn, M. W., **M. Hannah, C. Hinkin, C. Montgomery,** and **D. Pitz.** Psychopathology on the streets: Psychological assessment of the homeless. *Professional Psychology,* 1987. [19]

Kahneman, D. *Attention and effort,* Englewood Cliffs, N.J.: Prentice-Hall, 1973. [8]

Kahneman, D., and **A. Tversky.** On the psychology of prediction. *Psychological Review,* 1973, *80,* 237–251. [9, 21]

Kamin, L. G. *The science and politics of IQ.* New York: Wiley, 1974. [11]

Kamin, L. J. Predictability, surprise, attention, and conditioning. In B. A. Campbell and R. M. Church (Eds.), *Punishment and aversive behavior.* New York: Appleton-Century-Crofts, 1969. [7]

Kandel, E. R. Small systems of neurons. *Scientific American,* 1979, *241,* 66–87. [7]

Kanin, E. Male aggression in dating-courtship relations. *American Journal of Sociology,* 1957, *63,* 197–204. [14]

Kanin, E., and **S. Parcell.** Sexual aggression: A second look at the offended female. *Archives of Sexual Behavior,* 1977, *6,* 1. [14]

Kanisza, G. Subjective contours. *Scientific American,* 1976, *234,* 48–52. [5]

Kanner, A. D., **J. C. Coyne, C. Schaeffer,** and **R. S. Lazarus.** Comparison of two modes of stress measurement: Daily hassles and uplifts versus major life events. *Journal of Behavioral Medicine,* 1981, *4,* 1–39. [20]

Kantrowitz, B. Kids and contraceptives. *Newsweek,* February 16, 1987, 54–65. [16]

Kaplan, R. M. The connection between clinical health promotion and health status: A critical overview. *American Psychologist,* 1984, *39,* 755–765. [20]

Kassin, S. M. Consensus information, prediction, and causal attribution: A review of the literature and issues. *Journal of Personality and Social Psychology,* 1979, *37,* 1966–1981. [21]

Kastenbaum, R. Dying and death. In J. E. Birren and K. W. Schaie, *Handbook of the psychology of aging* (2nd ed.). New York: Van Nostrand Reinhold, 1985. [16]

Katz, D., and **R. L. Kahn.** *The social psy-*

chology of organizations (2nd ed.). New York: Wiley, 1978. [23]

Kaufman, A., P. Divasto, R. Jackson, D. Voorhees, and J. Christy. Male rape victims: Noninstitutionalized assault. *American Journal of Psychiatry*, 1980, *137*, 221–223. [14]

Kavanaugh, D. J., and G. H. Bower. Mood and self-efficacy: Impact of joy and sadness on perceived capabilities. *Cognitive Therapy and Research*, 1985. [9]

Kayne, N. T., L. B. Alloy, D. Romer, and J. Crocker. Predicting depression and elation reactions in the classroom: A test of an attributional diathesis-stress theory of depression. *Journal of Abnormal Psychology*. In press. [18]

Kazdin, A. E. *Behavior modification in applied settings*. Homewood, Ill.: Dorsey Press, 1975. [7]

Kazdin, A. E., and G. T. Wilson. *Evaluation of behavior therapy: Issues, evidence and research strategies*. Cambridge, Mass.: Ballinger, 1978. [17, 19]

Keesey, R. E., and S. W. Corbett. Metabolic defense of the body weight set-point. In A. J. Stunkard and E. Stellar (Eds.), *Eating and its disorders*. New York: Raven Press, 1983. [13]

Keesey, R. E., and T. L. Powley. Hypothalamic regulation of body weight. *American Scientist*, 1975, *63*, 558–565. [13]

Kegeles, S. M., N. E. Adler, and C. E. Irwin, Jr. Sexually active adolescents and condoms: Changes of one year in knowledge, attitudes, and use. *American Journal of Public Health*, 1988, *78*, 460–461. [14]

Kegeles, S., et al. *American Journal of Public Health*, 1988, *78*, 460–461. [14]

Kelley, H. H. Attribution theory in social psychology. In D. Levine (Ed.), *Nebraska symposium on motivation* (Vol. 15). Lincoln, Neb.: University of Nebraska Press, 1967. [21]

Kerr, M. E., and M. Bowen. *Family evaluation*. New York: Norton, 1988. [19]

Kiecott-Glaser, J. K., et al. Modulation of cellular immunity in medical students. *Journal of Behavioral Medicine*, 1986, *9*, 5–21. [20]

Kiesler, C. A. Mental hospitals and alternative care. *American Psychologist*, 1982, *37*, 349–360. [19]

Kihlstrom, J. F. Hypnosis. *Annual Review of Psychology*, 1985, *36*, 385–418. [6]

Kihlstrom, J. F. The cognitive unconscious. *Science*, 1987, *237*, 1445–1452. [6]

Kihlstrom, J. F. Personality. In E. R. Hilgard (Ed.), *Fifty years of psychology: Essays in honor of Floyd Ruch*. Glenview, Ill.: Scott, Foresman, 1988. [17]

Kimura, D. Functional asymmetry of the brain in dichotic listening. *Cortex*, 1967, *3*, 163–178. [10]

Kinsbourne, M., and M. Hiscock. The normal and deviant development of func-

tional lateralization of the brain. In M. M. Haith and J. J. Campos (Eds.), *Handbook of child psychology*. Vol. 2. *Infancy and developmental psychobiology* (4th ed.). New York: Wiley, 1983, pp. 157–280. [3]

Kinsbourne, M., and F. Wood. Short-term memory processes and the amnesic syndrome. In D. Deutsch and J. A. Deutsch (Eds.), *Short-term memory*. New York: Academic Press, 1975. [8]

Kinsey, A. C., W. B. Pomeroy, and C. E. Martin. *Sexual behavior in the human male*. Philadelphia: Saunders, 1948. [14]

Kinsey, A. C., W. B. Pomeroy, C. E. Martin, and P. H. Gebhard. *Sexual behavior in the human female*. Philadelphia: Saunders, 1953. [14]

Kintsch, W., and T. A. Van Dijk. Toward a model of text comprehension and production. *Psychological Review*, 1978, *85*, 363–394. [10]

Kirkwood, T. B. L. Comparative and evolutionary aspects of longevity. In C. E. Finch and E. L. Schneider (Eds.), *Handbook of the biology of aging* (2nd ed.). New York: Van Nostrand Reinhold, 1985. [15]

Klawans, H. *Toscanini's fumble and other tales of clinical neurology*. Chicago: Contemporary Books, 1988. [3]

Klein, S. B. *Learning: Principles and applications*. New York: McGraw-Hill, 1987. [7]

Klima, E. S., and U. Bellugi. Teaching apes to communicate. In G. A. Miller (Ed.), *Communication, language, and meaning: Psychological perspectives*. New York: Basic Books, 1973. [10]

Klima, E. S., and U. Bellugi. *The signs of language*. Cambridge, Mass.: Harvard University Press, 1979. [10]

Kobak, R. R., and A. Sceery. Attachment in late adolescence: Working models, affect regulation, and perception of self and others. *Child Development*, 1988, *59*, 135–146. [14]

Kobasa, S. C. Stressful life events and health: An inquiry into hardiness. *Journal of Personality and Social Psychology*, 1979, *37*, 1–11. [20]

Koch, C. The action of the corticofugal pathway on sensory thalamic nuclei: A hypothesis. *Neuroscience*, 1987, *23*, 399–406. [4]

Kohlberg, L. Moral stages and moralization: A cognitive-developmental approach. In T. Lickona (Ed.), *Moral development and behavior: Theory, research, and social issues*. Chicago: Rand McNally, 1976, pp. 31–53. [16]

Kohn, M. Job complexity and adult personality. In N. J. Smelser and E. H. Erikson (Eds.), *Themes of work and love in adulthood*. Cambridge, Mass.: Harvard University Press, 1980. [16]

Kohut, H. *The restoring of the self*. New

York: International Universities Press, 1977. [17]

Kolata, G. Math genius may have hormonal basis. *Science*, 1983, *222*, 1312. [3]

Kolata, G. Why do people get fat? *Science*, 1985, *227*, 1327–1328. [13]

Kolata, G. Manic depression: Is it inherited? *Science*, 1986, *232*, 575–576. [18]

Kolb, B., and B. Milner. Performance of complex arm and leg movements after focal brain lesions. *Neuropsychologia*, 1981, *19*, 491–503. [3]

Kolb, B., and I. Q. Whishaw. *Fundamentals of human neuropsychology*. San Francisco: Freeman, 1980. [3]

Kopp, C. B. Risk factors in development. In P. H. Mussen (Ed.), *Handbook of child psychology* (4th ed.) (Vol. 2). New York: Wiley, 1983. [15]

Korchin, S. J. *Modern clinical psychology*. New York: Basic Books, 1976. [19]

Kosslyn, S. M. *Image and mind*. Cambridge, Mass.: Harvard University Press, 1980. [8, 9]

Kosslyn, S. M. *Ghosts in the mind's machine*. New York: Norton, 1983. [9]

Kosslyn, S. M. Seeing and imagining in the cerebral hemispheres: A computational approach. *Psychological Review*, 1987, *94*, 148–175. [9]

Kosslyn, S. M., J. D. Holtzman, M. J. Farah, and M. S. Gazzaniga. A computational analysis of mental image generation: Evidence from functional dissociations in split-brain patients. *Journal of Experimental Psychology: General*, 1985, *114*, 311–341. [9]

Kovach, J. A., and N. W. Glickman. Levels and psychosocial correlates of adolescent drug use. *Journal of Youth and Adolescence*, 1986, *15*, 61–78. [16]

Kozel, N. J., and E. H. Adams. Epidemiology of drug abuse: An overview. *Science*, 1986, *234*, 970–974. [6, 16]

Kraepelin, E. *Textbook of psychiatry* (8th ed.). New York: Macmillan, 1923. (Originally published 1883.) [18]

Kramer, B. M. Dimensions of prejudice. *Journal of Psychology*, 1949, *27*, 389–451. [21]

Kramer, D. A. Post-formal operations? *Human Development*, 1983, *26*, 91–105. [16]

Krech, D., and R. S. Crutchfield. *Theory and problems of social psychology*. New York: McGraw-Hill, 1948. [21]

Kripke, D. F., and D. Sonnenschein. A biological rhythm in waking fantasy. In K. S. Pope and J. L. Singer (Eds.), *The stream of consciousness*. New York: Plenum Press, 1978. [6]

Kroll, N. E. A., T. E. Parks, S. R. Parkinson, S. L. Bieber, and A. L. Johnson. Short-term memory while shadowing: Recall of visually and aurally presented letters. *Journal of Experimental Psychology*, 1970, *85*, 220–224. [8]

Krosnick, J., and C. Judd. Transitions in social influence at adolescence: Who induces cigarette smoking? *Developmental Psychology*, 1982, *18*, 359–368. [16]

Kulik, J. A., R. L. Bangert-Drowns, and C.-L. C. Kulik. Effectiveness of coaching for aptitude tests. *Psychological Bulletin*, 1984, *95*, 179–188. [11]

Kulik, J. A., and R. Brown. Frustration, attribution of blame, and aggression. *Journal of Experimental Social Psychology*, 1979, *15*, 183–194. [22]

Kunst-Wilson, W. R., and R. B. Zajonc. Affective discrimination of stimuli that cannot be recognized. *Science*, 1980, *207*, 557–558. [21]

Kurdek, L. A., and J. P. Schmitt. Early development of relationship quality in heterosexual married, heterosexual cohabiting, gay, and lesbian couples. *Developmental Psychology*, 1986, *22*, 305–309. [16]

LaBerge, S. P., L. E. Nagel, W. C. Dement, and V. P. Zarcone. Lucid dreaming verified by volitional communication during REM sleep. *Perceptual and Motor Skills*, 1981, *52*, 727–732. [6]

Labouvie-Vief, G. Discontinuities in development from childhood to adulthood: A cognitive-developmental view. In T. M. Field, A. Huston, H. C. Quay, L. Troll, and G. E. Finley (Eds.), *Review of human development*. New York: Wiley, 1982. [16]

Labouvie-Vief, G. Intelligence and cognition. In J. E. Birren and K. W. Schaie (Eds.), *Handbook of the psychology of aging* (2nd ed.). New York: Van Nostrand Reinhold, 1985. [16]

Laing, R. D. *The politics of experience*. New York: Pantheon, 1967. [18]

Laird, J. D. Self-attribution of emotion: The effects of expressive behavior on the quality of emotional experience. *Journal of Personality and Social Psychology*, 1974, *24*, 475–486. [12]

Laird, J. D., and M. Crosby. Individual differences in the self-attribution of emotion. In H. London and R. Nisbett (Eds.), *Thinking and feeling: The cognitive alteration of feeling states*. Chicago,: Aldine, 1974. [12]

Lakatta, E. G. Heart and circulation. In C. E. Finch and E. L. Schneider, *Handbook of the biology of aging* (2nd ed.). New York: Van Nostrand Reinhold, 1985. [16]

Lamb, M. E., and M. H. Bornstein. *Development in infancy* (2nd ed.). New York: Random House, 1986. [15]

Lamb, M. E., M. A. Easterbrooks, and G. W. Holden. Reinforcement and punishment among preschoolers: Characteristics, effects, and correlates. *Child Development*, 1980, *51*, 1230–1236. [15]

Lamb, M. E., C.-P. Hwang, F. L. Bookstein, A. Broberg, G. Hult, and M. Frodi. Determinants of social competence in Swedish preschoolers. *Developmental Psychology*, 1988, *24*, 58–70. [15]

Lamb, M. E., R. A. Thompson, W. P. Gardner, E. L. Charnov, and D. Estes. Security of infantile attachment as assessed in the "strange situation": Its study and biological interpretation. *The Behavioral and Brain Sciences*, 1984, *7*, 127–171. [15]

Lambo, T. A. Psychotherapy in Africa. *Human Nature*, 1978, *1*, March, 32–39. [20]

Landman, J. T., and R. M. Dawes. Psychotherapy outcome: Smith and Glass' conclusions stand up under scrutiny. *American Psychologist*, 1982, *37*, 504–516. [2]

Landy, F. J. *Psychology of work behavior* (3rd ed.). Homewood, Ill.: Dorsey Press, 1985. [23]

Lang, P. J., D. G. Rice, and R. A. Sternbach. The psychophysiology of emotion. In N. S. Greenfield and R. A. Sternbach (Eds.), *Handbook of psychophysiology*. New York: Holt, Rinehart & Winston, 1972. [12]

Lange, C. G., and W. James. *The emotions*. Baltimore: Williams & Wilkins, 1922. [12]

Langer, E. J. The illusion of control. *Journal of Personality and Social Psychology*, 1975, *32*, 311–328. [13]

Langer, E. J., and J. Rodin. The effects of choice and enhanced personal responsibility for the aged: A field experiment in an institutional setting. *Journal of Personality and Social Psychology*, 1976, *34*, 191–198. [20]

Langer, E. J., and S. Saegert. Crowding and cognitive control. *Journal of Personality and Social Psychology*, 1977, *35*, 175–182. [22]

Lanyon, R. I., and L. D. Goodstein. *Personality assessment*. New York: Wiley, 1971. [17]

LaPiere, T. R. Attitudes vs. actions. *Social Forces*, 1934, *13*, 230–237. [21]

Lashley, K. S., and J. T. Russell. The mechanism of vision: XI. A preliminary test of innate organization. *Journal of Genetic Psychology*, 1934, *45*, 136–144. [5]

Latané, B. *A Theory of social impact*. St. Louis: Psychonomic Society, 1973. [22]

Latané, B., and J. M. Darley. Help in a crisis: Bystander rsponse to an emergency. In J. W. Thibaut, J. T. Spence, and R. C. Carson (Eds.), *Contemporary topics in social psychology*. Morristown, N.J.: General Learning Press, 1976. [22]

Latané, B., and S. Wolf. The social impact of majorities and minorities. *Psychological Review*, 1981, *88*, 438–453. [22]

Latham, G. P., and G. A. Yukl. A review of research on the application of goal setting in organizations. *Academy of Management Journal*, 1975, *18*, 824–845. [23]

Laudenslager, M. L., S. M. Ryan, R. C. Drugan, R. L. Hyson, and S. F. Maier. Coping and immunosuppression: Inescapable but not escapable shock suppresses lymphocyte proliferation. *Science*, 1983, *221*, 568–570. [20]

Lawler, E. E., and J. L. Suttle. A causal correlational test of the need hierarchy concept. *Organizational Behavior and Human Performance*, 1972, *7*, 265–287. [23]

Lazarus, R. S. Emotions and adaptation: Conceptual and empirical relations. In W. Arnold (Ed.), *Nebraska symposium on motivation*. Lincoln: University of Nebraska Press, 1968. [20]

Lazarus, R. S. The stress and coping paradigm. In C. Eisdorfer, D. Cohen, and A. Kleinman (Eds.), *Conceptual models for psychopathology*. New York: Spectrum, 1980. [20]

Lazarus, R. S. Thoughts on the relations between emotion and cognition. *American Psychologist*, 1982, *37*, 1019–1024. [12]

Lazarus, R. S., and E. Alfert. The short-circuiting of threat by experimentally altering cognitive appraisal. *Journal of Abnormal and Social Psychology*, 1964, *69*, 195–205. [12]

Lazarus, R. S., and S. Folkman. *Stress, appraisal, and coping*. New York: Springer, 1984. [20]

Lazarus, R. S., A. Kanner, and S. Folkman. Emotions: A cognitive-phenomenological approach. In R. Plutchik and H. Kellerman (Eds.), *Theories of emotion*. New York: Academic Press, 1980. [12, 20]

Leakey, R. E., and R. Lewin. *Origins*. New York: Dutton, 1977. [15]

Leavitt, H. School clinics vs. teen pregnancies. *Insight*, Dec. 22, 1986, 26. [16]

Lee, C. L., and J. E. Bates. Mother–child interaction at age 2 years and perceived difficult temperament. *Child Development*, 1985, *56*, 1314–1325. [15]

Lenneberg, E. H. *Biological foundations of language*. New York: Wiley, 1967. [15]

Leo, J. Could suicide be contagious? *Time*, February 24, 1986, 59. [18]

Lerner, B. *Washington v. Davis*: Quantity, quality, and equality in employment testing. In P. Kurland (Ed.), *The Supreme Court Review* (1976 vol.). Chicago: University of Chicago Press, 1977. [23]

Lerner, R. M., J. B. Orlos, and J. R. Knapp. Physical attractiveness, body attitudes, and self-concept in late adolescence. *Adolescence*, 1976, *11*, 313–326. [18]

Leventhal, H., and P. D. Cleary. The smoking problem: A review of the research and theory in behavioral risk modification. *Psychological Bulletin*, 1980, *88*, 370–405. [20]

Levine, M., I. N. Jankovic, and M. Palij. Principles of spatial problem solving. *Journal of Experimental Psychology: General*, 1982, *111*, 157–175. [7]

Levinson, D. J., C. N. Darrow, E. B. Klein, M. H. Levinson, and B. McKee. *The seasons of a man's life.* New York: Knopf, 1978. [16]

Levinson, S. C. *Pragmatics.* New York: Cambridge University Press, 1983. [10]

Levitt, M. J., T. G. Antonucci, and M. C. Clark. Object–person permanence and attachment. *Merrill-Palmer Quarterly*, 1984, *30*, 1–10. [15]

Levy, R. I. The emotions in comparative perspective. In K. R. Scherer and P. Ekman (Eds.), *Approaches to emotion.* Hillsdale, N.J.: Erlbaum, 1984. [12]

Levy, S. M. Host differences in neoplastic risk: Behavioral and social contributors to disease. *Health Psychology*, 1983, *2*, 21–44. [20]

Lewicki, P. Processing information about covariations that cannot be articulated. *Journal of Experimental Psychology: Learning, Memory, and Cognition*, 1986a, *12*, 135–146. [7]

Lewicki, P. *Nonconscious social information processing.* Orlando, Fla.: Academic Press, 1986b. [7]

Lewin, K. *Field theory in the social sciences.* New York: Harper, 1951. [13]

Lewin, T. Fewer teen mothers, but more are unmarried. *The New York Times*, March 20, 1988, p. E6. [16]

Lewine, R. R. J. Sex differences in schizophrenia: Timing or subtype? *Psychological Bulletin*, 1981, *90*, 432–444. [18]

Lewis, J. M., E. H. Rodnick, and M.J. Goldstein. Intrafamilial interactive behavior, parental communication deviance, and risk for schizophrenia. *Journal of Abnormal Psychology*, 1981, *90*, 448–457. [18]

Lewis, M., J. Brooks-Gunn, and J. Jaskir. Individual differences in self-recognition as a function of the mother–infant attachment relationship. *Developmental Psychology*, 1985, *21*, 1181–1187. [15]

Lewisohn, P. M., H. Hobermen, L. Teri, and M. Hautzinger. An integrative theory of depression. In S. Reiss and R. Bootzin (Eds.), *Theoretical issues in behavior therapy.* New York: Academic Press, 1985. [19]

Lewinsohn, P. M., J. M. Sullivan, and S. J. Grosscup. Changing reinforcing events: An approach to the treatment of depression. *Psychotherapy: Theory, Research, and Practice*, 1980, *17*, 322–334. [18]

Liberman, M. C. Single-neuron labeling in the cat auditory cortex. *Science*, 1982, *216*, 1239–1241. [4]

Lichtenstein, S., P. Slovik, B. Fischhoff, M. Layman, and J. Combs. Judged frequency of lethal events. *Journal of Experimental Psychology: Human Learning and Memory*, 1978, *4*, 551–578. [9]

Lieberman, M. A., and S. Tobin. *The experience of old age.* New York: Basic Books, 1983. [16]

Lieberson, S., and J. F. O'Connor. Leadership and organizational performance: A study of large corporations. *American Sociological Review*, 1972, *37*, 117–130. [23]

Liem, J. H. Effects of verbal communications of parents and children: A comparison of normal and schizophrenic families. *Journal of Consulting and Clinical Psychology*, 1974, *42*, 438–450. [18]

Linde, E. V., B. A. Morrongiello, and C. K. Rovee-Collier. Determinants of retention in 8-week-old infants. *Developmental Psychology*, 1985, *21*, 602–613. [15]

Linder, D. E., J. Cooper, and E. E. Jones. Decision freedom as a determinant of the role of incentive magnitude in attitude change. *Journal of Personality and Social Psychology*, 1967, *6*, 245–254. [21]

Lindsay, P. H., and D. A. Norman. *Human information processing.* New York: Academic Press, 1972. [5]

Linehan, M. M., and A. M. Ivanoff. *Guidelines for getting help with problems in living.* University of Washington Suicidal Behaviors Research Clinic, 1987. [19]

Linville, P. W. The complexity–extremity effect and age-based stereotyping. *Journal of Personality and Social Psychology*, 1982, *42*, 193–211. [21]

Linville, P. W., and E. E. Jones. Polarized appraisals of outgroup members. *Journal of Personality and Social Psychology*, 1980, *38*, 689–703. [21]

Livingstone, M. S. Art, illusion, and the visual system. *Scientific American*, 1988, pp. 79–85. [4]

Livingstone, M. S., and D. Hubel. Separation of form, color, movement, and depth: Anatomy, physiology, and perception. *Science*, 1988, *240*, 740–749. [4, 5]

Livson, N., and H. Peskin. Perspectives on adolescence from longitudinal research. In J. Adelson (Ed.), *Handbook of adolescent psychology.* New York: Wiley, 1980. [16]

Lloyd, K., J. Paulse, and J. Brockner. The effect of self-esteem and self-consciousness on interpersonal attraction. *Personality and Social Psychology Bulletin*, 1983, *9*, 397–403. [23]

Locke, E. A. Toward a theory of task motivation and incentives. *Organizational Behavior and Human Performance*, 1968, *3*, 157–189. [23]

Locke, E. A., K. N. Shaw, L. M. Saari, and G. P. Latham. Goal setting and task performance, 1969–1980. *Psychological Bulletin*, 1981, *90*, 125–152. [23]

Loehlin, J. C., G. Lindzey, and J. N. Spuhler. *Racial differences in intelligence.* San Francisco: W. H. Freeman Co. 1975. [11]

Loftus, E. F. *Memory.* Reading, Mass.: Addison-Wesley, 1980. [6,8]

Loftus, E. F., and G. R. Loftus. On the permanence of stored information in the human brain. *American Psychologist*, 1980, *35*, 409–420. [6]

Loftus, E. F., D. G. Miller, and H. J. Burns. Semantic integration of verbal information into a visual memory. *Journal of Experimental Psychology: Human Learning and Memory*, 1978, *4*, 19–31. [8, 10]

Loftus, E. F., and J. C. Palmer. Reconstruction of automobile destruction: An example of the interaction between language and memory. *Journal of Verbal Learning and Verbal Behavior*, 1974, *13*, 585–589. [10]

Loftus, E. F., J. Schooler, and W. A. Wagenaar. The fate of memory: Comment on McCloskey and Zaragoza. *Journal of Experimental Psychology: General*, 1985, *114*, 375–380. [8]

Loftus, G. R. Eye fixations and recognition memory for pictures. *Cognitive Psychology*, 1972, 525–551. [8]

London, M., and D. W. Bray. Ethical issues in testing and evaluation for personnel decisions. *American Psychologist*, 1980, *35*, 890–901. [11]

London, P. *Behavior control.* New York: Harper & Row, 1969. [17]

Long, B. B. The prevention of mental-emotional disabilities: A report from a National Health Association Commission. *American Psychologist*, 1986, *41*, 825–829. [19]

Lopez-Lozano, J. J., B. Brera, J. Abascal, and G. Bravo. Preparation of adrenal-medullary tissue for transplantation in Parkinson's disease: A new procedure. *Journal of Neurosurgery*, 1989, *71*, 452–454. [3]

LoPiccolo, J. Direct treatment of sexual dysfunction in the couple. In J. Money and H. Musaph (Eds.), *Handbook of sexology.* New York: Elsevier-North Holland Press, 1978. [14]

Luborsky, L., B. Singer, and J. Mellon. Advent of objective measures of the transference concept. *Journal of Consulting and Clinical Psychology*, 1986, *54*, 39–47. [19]

Luce, R. D., and C. L. Krumhansl. Measurement, scaling, and psychophysics. In R. C. Atkinson, R. J. Herrnstein, G. Lindzey, and R. D. Luce (Eds.), *Stevens' handbook of experimental psychol-*

ogy (2nd ed.). New York: Wiley, 1988, pp. 3–74. [4]

Luchins, A. S. Classroom experiments on mental set. *American Journal of Psychology*, 1946, *59*, 295–298. [9]

Luria, A. *The man with a shattered world*. Chicago: Regnery, 1976. [3]

Luria, A. R. *The mind of a mnemonist*. New York: Basic Books, 1968. [8]

Luria, A. R. *Traumatic aphasia*. The Hague: Mouton, 1970. [3]

Lütkenhaus, P., K. E. Grossmann, and K. Grossmann. Infant–mother attachment at 12 months and style of interaction with a stranger at the age of 3 years. *Child Development*, 1985, *56*, 1538–1542. [15]

Lutz, C. The domain of emotion words on Ifaluk. *American Ethnologist*, 1982, *9*, 113–128. [12]

Lutz, C., and G. M. White. The anthropology of emotions. *Annual Review of Anthropology*, 1986, *15*, 405–436. [12]

Lutz, C. Goals, events, and understanding in Ifaluk emotion theory. In D. Holland and N. Quinn (Eds.), *Cultural models in language and thought*. Cambridge, Eng.: Cambridge University Press, 1987, pp. 290–312. [12]

Lydiard, R. B., and A. J. Gelenberg. Hazards and adverse effects of lithium. *Annual Review of Medicine*, 1982, *33*, 327–344. [19]

Lykken, D. T. *A tremor in the blood: Uses and abuses of the lie detector*. New York: McGraw-Hill, 1981. [23]

Lynch, J. J. *The broken heart: The medical consequences of loneliness*. New York: Basic Books, 1977. [20]

Lynn, R. IQ in Japan and the United States shows a growing disparity, *Nature*, 1982, *297*, 222–223. [11]

Lyons, R. D. Vietnam veterans turn to therapy. *The New York Times*, Nov. 13, 1984, pp. C1, C6. [20]

Maass, A., and R. D. Clark III. Internationalization versus compliance: Differential processes underlying minority influence and conformity. *European Journal of Social Psychology*, 1983, *13*, 197–215. [22]

Maccoby, E. E., and J. A. Martin. Socialization in the context of the family. In P. H. Mussen (Ed.), *Handbook of child psychology* (Vol. 4). New York: Wiley, 1983, pp. 1–101. [15]

MacDonald, K. Early experience, relative plasticity, and social development. *Developmental Review*, 1985, *5*, 99–121. [15]

Machado, L. A. *The right to be intelligent*. (M. C. Wheeler, Trans.). Oxford: Pergamon, 1980. [11]

Mackintosh, N. J. *Conditioning and associative learning*. Oxford: Clarendon Press, 1983. [7]

Macklin, E. Nontraditional family forms: A decade of research. *Journal of Marriage and the Family*, 1980, *42*, 905–922. [14]

MacNichol, E. F., Jr. Three-pigment color vision. *Scientific American*, 1964, *211*, 48–56. [4]

Maddox, G. L., and R. T. Campbell. Scope, concepts, and methods in the study of aging. In R. H. Binstock and E. Shana, *Handbook of aging and the social sciences* (2nd ed.). New York: Van Nostrand Reinhold, 1985. [16]

Maher, B. A., and W. B. Maher. Psychopathology. In E. Hearst (Ed.), *The first century of experimental psychology*. Hillsdale, N.J.: Erlbaum, 1979. [18]

Maher, E. A. (Ed.). *Contributions to the psychopathology of schizophrenia*. New York: Academic Press, 1977. [18]

Mahoney, M. J. Psychotherapy and the structure of personal revolutions. In M. J. Mahoney (Ed.), *Psychotherapy process: Current issues and future directions*. New York: Plenum, 1980. [19]

Main, M., and C. George. Responses of abused and disadvantaged toddlers to distress in agemates. *Developmental Psychology*, 1985, *21*, 407–412. [2]

Malamuth, N. M., and J. V. P. Check. The effects of mass media exposure on acceptance of violence against women: A field experiment. *Journal of Research in Personality*, 1981, *15*, 436–446. [14]

Malamuth, N. M., and E. Donnerstein. The effects of aggressive-pornographic mass media stimuli. In L. Berkowitz (Ed.), *Experimental social psychology*. New York, Academic Press, 1982. [14]

Manderlink, G., and J. Harackiewicz. Proximal versus distal goal setting and intrinsic motivation. *Journal of Personality and Social Psychology*, 1984, *47*, 918–928. [13]

Mandler, G. *Mind and body*. New York, Norton, 1984. [12]

Manley, G. A., C. Koppl, and M. Konishi. A neural map of interaural intensity differences in the brainstem of the barn owl. *Journal of Neuroscience*, 1988, *8*, 2665–2676. [5]

Mann, L. Use of a "balance sheet" procedure to improve the quality of personal decision making: A field experiment with college applicants. *Journal of Vocational Behavior*, 1972, *2*, 291–300. [9]

Marcel, A. Conscious and unconscious perception: Experiments on visual masking and word perception. *Cognitive Psychology*, 1983, *15*, 197–238. [5, 6]

Marcel, A. J. Conscious and unconscious perception: An approach to the relations between phenomenal experience and perceptual processes. *Cognitive Psychology*, 1983, *15*, 238–300. [6]

Marcel, A. J. Phenomenal experience and functionalism. In A. J. Marcel and E. Bisiach (Eds.), *Consciousness in contemporary science*. Oxford: Clarendon, 1988. [6]

Marcia, J. E. Identity in adolescence. In J. Adelson (Ed.), *Handbook of adolescent psychology*. New York: Wiley-Interscience, 1980. [16]

Mark, V. H., and F. R. Ervin. *Violence and the brain*. New York: Harper & Row, 1970. [22]

Marks, G., and N. Miller. Target attractiveness as a mediator of assumed attitude similarity. *Personality and Social Psychology Bulletin*, 1982, *8*, 728–735. [2]

Marks, G., N. Miller, and G. Maruyama. Effect of targets' physical attractiveness on assumption of similarity. *Journal of Personality and Social Psychology*, 1981, *41*, 198–206. [2]

Marlatt, G. A., and J. R. Gordon (Eds.). *Relapse prevention*. New York: Guilford Press, 1985. [20]

Marr, D. *Vision*. New York: W. H. Freeman, 1982. [5]

Marshall, G., and P. Zimbardo. The affective consequences of "inadequately explained" physiological arousal. *Journal of Personality and Social Psychology*, 1979, *37*, 970–988. [12]

Marshall, V. W. *Last chapters*. Monterey, Calif.: Brooks/Cole, 1980. [16]

Marslen-Wilson, W. D. Functional parallelism in spoken word recognition. *Cognition*, 1987, *25*, 71–102. [10]

Marslen-Wilson, W. D., and A. Welsh. Processing interactions and lexical access during word recognition in continuous speech. *Cognitive Psychology*, 1978, *10*, 29–63. [10]

Martens, R. Palmar sweating and the presence of an audience. *Journal of Experimental Social Psychology*, 1969, *5*, 371–374. [22]

Martin, G., and J. Pear. *Behavior modification: What it is and how to do it*. Englewood Cliffs, N.J.: Prentice-Hall, 1978. [7]

Martin, G. B., and R. D. Clark. Distress crying in neonates: Species and peer specificity. *Developmental Psychology*, 1982, *18*, 3–9. [15]

Martin, J. E., and M. M. Peterson. Two-tier wage structures: Implications for equity theory. *Academy of Management Journal*, 1987, *30*, 297–315. [23]

Martindale, C. *Cognition and consciousness*. Homewood, Ill.: Dorsey, 1981. [6]

Maslach, C. Negative emotional biasing of unexplained arousal. *Journal of Personality and Social Psychology*, 1979, *37*, 953–969. [12]

Masling, J., C. Johnson, and C. Saturansky. Oral imagery, accuracy of perceiving others, and performance in Peace Corps training. *Journal of Personality and Social Psychology*, 1974, *30*, 414–419. [17]

Masling, J., J. Price, S. Goldband, and E. S. Katkin. Oral imagery and autonomic arousal in social isolation. *Journal of Personality and Social Psychology*, 1981, *40*, 395–400. [17]

Maslow, A. H. Self-actualizing people: A study of psychological health. *Personality*, 1950, Symposium No. 1, 11–34. [13]

Maslow, A. H. *Motivation and personality*. New York: Harper & Row, 1954. [13, 17]

Maslow, A. H. *The psychology of science; A reconnaissance*. New York: Harper & Row, 1966. [17]

Maslow, A. H. *Toward a psychology of being* (2nd ed.). New York: Van Nostrand Reinhold, 1968. [17]

Maslow, A. H. *The farther reaches of the human mind*. New York: Viking, 1971*a*. [17]

Maslow, A. H. Some basic propositions of a growth and self-actualizing psychology. In S. Maddi (Ed.), *Perspectives on personality*. Boston: Little, Brown, 1971*b*. [17]

Mason, J. W. Specificity in the organization of neuroendocrine response profiles. In P. Seeman and G. M. Brown (Eds.), *Frontiers in neurology and neuroscience research*. First International Symposium of the Neuroscience Institute. Toronto: University of Toronto, 1974. [20]

Masters, J. C., T. G. Burish, S. D. Hollon, and D. C. Rimm. *Behavior therapy: Techniques and empirical findings* (3rd ed.). San Diego, Calif.: Harcourt Brace Jovanovich, 1987. [19]

Masters, W. H., and V. E. Johnson. *Human sexual response*. Boston: Little, Brown, 1966. [14]

Masters, W. H., and V. E. Johnson. *Human sexual inadequacy*. Boston, Little, Brown, 1970. [14]

Masters, W. H., and V. E. Johnson. *Homosexuality in perspective*. Boston: Little, Brown, 1979. [14]

Masur, J. E. *Learning and behavior*. Englewood Cliffs, N.J.: Prentice-Hall, 1986. [7]

Matheny, A. P. Bayley's infant behavior record: Behavioral components and twin analyses. *Child Development*, 1980, *51*, 466–475. [17]

Mathews, T. Homeless in America: What can be done? *Newsweek*, March 21, 1988, 57–58. [19]

Matthews, K. A. Coronary heart disease and type A behaviors: Update on and alternative to the Booth-Kewley and Friedman (1987) quantitative review. *Psychological Bulletin*, 1988, *104*, 373–380. [20]

Maugh, T. H. Marijuana justifies "serious concern." *Science*, 1982, *215*, 1488–1489. [6]

Mayer, R. E. *Educational psychology: A cognitive approach*. Boston: Little, Brown, 1987. [9]

McAdams, D. P., S. Healy, and S. Krause. Social motives and patterns of friendship. *Journal of Personality and Social Psychology*, 1984, *47* (4), 828–838. [13]

McArthur, L. A., M. R. Solomon, and R. H. Jaffe. Weight and sex differences in emotional responsiveness to proprioceptive and pictorial stimuli. *Journal of Personality and Social Psychology*, 1980, *39*, 308–319. [12]

McArthur, L. Z. The how and what of why: Some determinants and consequences of causal attribution. *Journal of Personality and Social Psychology*, 1972, *22*, 171–193. [21]

McBain, W. N., and R. C. Johnson. *The science of ourselves*. New York: Harper & Row, 1962. [4]

McCabe, M. P., and J. K. Collins. Sex roles and dating orientations. *Journal of Youth and Adolescence*, 1979, *8*, 407–424. [16]

McCarthy, D. Language development in children. In *Manual of Child Psychology* (2nd ed.). L. Carmichael (Ed.), New York: Wiley, 1954. [15]

McCartney, K., S. Scarr, D. Phillips, and S. Grajek. Day care as intervention. *Journal of Applied Developmental Psychology*, 1985, *6*, 247–260. [15]

McCauley, E., and A. A. Ehrhardt. Female sexual response: Hormonal and behavioral interactions. *Primary Care*, 1976, *3*, 455–476. [14]

McClelland, D. C. *The achieving society*. Princeton, N.J.: Van Nostrand-Reinhold, 1961. [13]

McClelland, D. C. Power is the great motivation. *Harvard Business Review*, 1976, *54*, 100–110. [23]

McClelland, D. C. Managing motivation to expand human freedom. *American Psychologist*, 1978, *33*, 201–210. [13]

McClelland, D. C., and R. E. Boyatzis. Leadership motive pattern and long-term success in management. *Journal of Applied Psychology*, 1982, *67*, 737–743. [23]

McClelland, D. C., and D. G. Winter. *Motivating economic achievement*. New York: Free Press, 1969. [13]

McClelland, D. C., et al. *The achievement motive*. New York: Appleton-Century-Crofts, 1953. [13]

McClelland, J. L., and D. E. Rumelhart. An interactive model of context effects in letter perception, Part I: An account of basic findings. *Psychological Review*, 1981, *88*, 375–407. [5]

McClintock, M. K., and N. T. Adler. The role of the female during copulation in wild and domestic Norway rats (*Rattus Norvegicus*). *Behavior*, 1978, *67*, 67–96. [14]

McCloskey, M., and M. Zaragoza. Misleading postevent information and memory for events: Arguments and evidence against memory impairment hypotheses, *Journal of Experimental Psychology: General*, 1985, *114* (1), 1–16. [8, 10]

McConahay, J. B. Modern racism, ambivalence, and the modern racism scale. In J. F. Dovidio and S. L. Gaertner (Eds.), *Prejudice, discrimination, and racism*. New York: Academic Press, 1986, pp. 91–125. [21]

McConahay, J. B., B. B. Hardee, and V. Batts. *Has racism declined in America? It depends upon who's asking and what is asked*. Working paper No. 8012. Durham, N.C.: Duke University Institute of Policy Sciences and Public Affairs, 1981.

McCord, W., and J. McCord. *Origins of crime*. New York: Columbia University Press, 1959. [16]

McCormick, E. J., and D. R. Ilgan. *Industrial psychology*. Englewood Cliffs, N.J.: Prentice-Hall, 1980. [23]

McCrae, R. B., and P. T. Costa, Jr. Updating Norman's "adequate taxonomy": Intelligence and personality dimensions in natural language and in questionnaires. *Journal of Personality and Social Psychology*, 1985, *49*, 710–721. [17]

McCutcheon, N. B., and J. Saunders. Human taste papilla stimulation: Stability of quality judgments over time. *Science*, 1972, *175*, 214–216. [4]

McGaugh, J. L. Preserving the presence of the past. Hormonal influence on memory storage. *American Psychologist*, 1983, *38*, 161–174. [8]

McGeer, Patrick L., Sir J. C. Eccles, and Edith G. McGeer. *Molecular neurobiology of the mammalian brain* (2nd ed.). New York: Plenum Press, 1987. [3]

McGeoch, J. A. *The psychology of human learning*. New York: Longmans, Green, 1942. [8]

McGlone, J. Sex differences in functional brain asymmetry. *Cortex*, 1978, *14*, 122–128. [3]

McGuire, R. J., J. M. Carlisle, and B. G. Young. Sexual deviations as conditioned behavior: A hypothesis. *Behaviour Research and Therapy*, 1965, *2*, 185–190. [14]

McGuire, W. J. Attitude change: The information processing paradigm. In C. G. McClintock (Ed.), *Experimental social psychology*. New York: Holt, Rinehart & Winston, 1972, pp. 108–141. [21]

McGuire, W. J. Attitudes and attitude change. In G. Lindzey and E. Aronson (Eds.), *Handbook of social psychology* (3rd ed.). New York, Random House, 1985. [21]

McWhirter, R. M., and J. D. Jecker. Attitude similarity and inferred attraction. *Psychonomic Science*, 1967, *7*, 225–226. [21]

Mead, G. H. *Mind, self and society: From the standpoint of a social behaviorist.* Chicago: University of Chicago Press, 1934. [15]

Mebert, C., and G. Michel. Handedness in artists. In J. Herron (Ed.), *Neuropsychology of left handedness.* New York: Academic, 1980. [3]

Meddis, R. *The sleep instinct.* London: Routledge & Kegan Paul, 1977. [6]

Meichenbaum, D., and R. Cameron. The clinical potential of modifying what clients say to themselves. In M. J. Mahoney and C. E. Thoresen (Eds.), *Self-control: Power to the person.* Monterey, Calif.: Brooks/Cole, 1974. [9]

Meichenbaum, D. H. (Ed.). *Cognitive behavior modification: An integrative approach.* New York: Plenum Press, 1977. [19]

Meichenbaum, D. H., and M. E. Jaremko (Eds.). *Stress prevention and management: A cognitive-behavioral approach.* New York: Plenum Press, 1982. [19]

Meichenbaum, D. H., and M. E. Jaremko (Eds.). *Stress reduction and prevention.* New York: Plenum Press, 1983. [20]

Meichenbaum, D. H., and D. Turk. Stress, coping, and disease: A cognitive-behavioral perspective. In R. W. J. Neufield (Ed.), *Psychological stress and psychopathology.* New York: McGraw-Hill, 1982. [20]

Meindl, J. R., S. B. Ehrlich, and J. M. Dukerich. The romance of leadership. *Administrative Science Quarterly,* 1985, *30,* 78–102. [23]

Meiselman, K. C. *Incest.* San Francisco: Jossey-Bass, 1978. [14]

Meltzoff, A. N., and M. K. Moore. The origins of imitation in infancy: Paradigm, phenomena, and theories. In L. P. Lipsitt and C. K. Rovee-Collier (Eds.), *Advances in infancy research* (Vol. 2). Norwood, N.J.: Ablex, 1983. [15]

Meltzoff, A. N., and M. K. Moore. Newborn infants imitate adult facial gestures. *Child Development,* 1983, *54,* 702–709. [12]

Menzel, E. M. Cognitive mapping in chimpanzees. In S. H. Hulse, H. Fowler, and W. K. Honig (Eds.), *Cognitive processes in animal behavior.* Hillsdale, N.J.: Erlbaum, 1973. [7]

Mercer, J. *Labelling the mentally retarded.* Berkeley: University of California Press, 1973. [11]

Messick, S., and A. Jungeblut. Time and method in coaching for the SAT. *Psychological Bulletin,* 1981, *89,* 191–216. [11]

Metcalfe, J. Feelings of knowing in memory and problem solving. *Journal of Experimental Psychology: Learning, Memory & Cognition,* 1986, *12,* 288–294. [9]

Meyer, A. J., J. D. Nash, A. McAlister, N.

Maccoby, and J. W. Farquhar. Skills training in a cardiovascular health education campaign. *Journal of Consulting and Clinical Psychology,* 1980, *48,* 129–142. [20]

Meyer-Bahlburg, H. F. L. Sex hormones and male homosexuality in comparative perspective. *Archives of Sexual Behavior,* 1977, *6,* 297–325. [14]

Meyer-Bahlburg, H. F. L. Sex hormones and female homosexuality: A critical examination. *Archives of Sexual Behavior,* 1979, *8,* 101–119. [14]

Milgram, S. Behavioral study of obedience. *Journal of Abnormal and Social Psychology,* 1963, *67,* 371–378. [22]

Milgram, S. Some conditions of obedience and disobedience to authority. In I. D. Steiner and M. Fishbein (Eds.), *Current studies in social psychology.* New York: Holt, Rinehart & Winston, 1965. [22]

Milgram, S. *Obedience to authority.* New York: Harper & Row, 1974. [22]

Miller, G. A. The magical number seven, plus or minus two: Some limits on our capacity for processing information. *Psychology Review,* 1956, *63,* 81–97. [8]

Miller, I. J., Jr. Human taste bud density across adult age groups. *Journal of Gerontology,* 1988, *43,* B26–30. [5]

Miller, J., C. Schooler, M. L. Kohn, and K. A. Miller. Women and work: The psychological effects of occupational conditions. *American Journal of Sociology,* 1979, *85* (1). [16]

Miller, N., and M. B. Brewer. Categorization effects on ingroup and outgroup perception. In J. F. Dovidio and S. L. Gaertner (Eds.), *Prejudice, discrimination, and racism.* New York: Academic Press, 1986, pp. 209–230. [21]

Miller, N. E. Learnable drives and rewards. In S. S. Stevens (Ed.), *Handbook of experimental psychology.* New York: Wiley, 1951. [7]

Miller, R. C., and J. S. Berman. The efficacy of cognitive behavior therapies: A quantitative review of the research evidence. *Psychological Bulletin,* 1983, *94,* 39–53. [19]

Miller, W. Lower-class culture as a generating milieu of gang delinquency. *Journal of Social Issues,* 1958, *14,* 5–19. [16]

Milner, B., S. Corkin, and H. L. Teuber. Further analysis of the hippocampal amnesic syndrome: 14-year follow-up study of H. M. *Neuropsychologia,* 1968, *6,* 215–234. [3]

Miner, J. B. *Theories of organizational behavior.* Hinsdale, Ill.: Dryden Press, 1980. [23]

Miner, J. B. *Organizational behavior: Performance and productivity.* New York: Random House, 1988. [23]

Minsky, M. *The society of mind.* New York: Simon and Schuster, 1986. [6]

Minuchin, S. *Families and family therapy.* Cambridge, Mass.: Harvard University Press, 1974. [19]

Minuchin, S., and H. C. Fishman. *Family therapy techniques.* Cambridge, Mass.: Harvard University Press, 1981. [19]

Mirsky, A. F., and C. C. Duncan. Etiology and expression of schizophrenia: Neurobiological and psychosocial factors. *Annual Review of Psychology,* 1986, *37,* 291–319. [18]

Mischel, W. *Personality and assessment.* New York: Wiley, 1968. [17]

Mischel, W. Toward a cognitive social learning reconceptualization of personality. *Psychological Review,* 1973, *80,* 252–283. [17]

Mischel, W. On the interface of cognition and personality: Beyond the person-situation debate. *American Psychologist,* 1979, *34,* 740–754. [17]

Mischel, W. Convergences and challenges in the search for consistency. *American Psychologist,* 1984, *39,* 351–364. [17]

Mitchell, D. B., and M. Perlmutter. Semantic activation and episodic memory. *Developmental Psychology,* 1986, *22,* 86–94. [16]

Moar, I. Grid schemata in memory for large-scale environments. *Proceedings of the Fifth Annual Conference of the Cognitive Science Society,* Rochester, N. Y., 1983. [7]

Mobley, W. H., S. O. Horner, and A. T. Hollingsworth. An evaluation of precursors of hospital employee turnover. *Journal of Applied Psychology,* 1978, *63,* 408–414. [23]

Moede, W. Die Richtlinien der Leistungs-Psychologie. *Industrielle Psychotechnik,* 1927, *4,* 193–207. [22]

Molfese, D. L., and V. J. Molfese. Hemisphere and stimulus differences as reflected in the cortical responses of newborn infants to speech stimuli. *Developmental Psychology,* 1979, *15,* 505–511. [10]

Molfese, D. L., and V. J. Molfese. Cortical responses of preterm infants to phonetic and nonphonetic speech stimuli. *Developmental Psychology,* 1980, *16,* 574–581. [10]

Monagan, D. Crosscurrents: CIA seals. *Science '82,* 1983, *3,* 80. [7]

Money, J., and A. A. Ehrhardt. *Man and woman, boy and girl.* Baltimore: Johns Hopkins University Press, 1972. [14]

Montgomery, K. C. The role of the exploratory drive in learning. *Journal of Comparative and Physiological Psychology,* 1954, *47,* 60–64. [13]

Montour, K. William James Sidis, the broken twig. *American Psychologist,* 1977, *32,* 265–279. [11]

Mood, D. G. In defense of external invalidity. *American Psychologist,* 1983, *38,* 379–387. [2]

Moore, E. G. Family socialization and the

IQ test performance of traditionally and transracially adopted black children. *Developmental Psychology*, 1986, *22*, 317–326. [11]

Moore, K. A. Teenage pregnancy. *New Perspectives*, Summer 1985, 11–15. [16]

Moore, R. Y., and V. B. Eichler. Loss of circadian adrenal corticosterone rhythm following suprachiasmatic lesions in the rat. *Brain Research*, 1972, *42*, 201–206. [3]

Moore-Ede, M. C., F. M. Sulzman, and C. R. Fuller. *The clocks that time us.* Cambridge, Mass.: Harvard University Press, 1982. [6]

Moos, R. H., R. C. Cronkite, and J. W. Finney. A conceptual framework for alcoholism treatment evaluation. In E. M. Pattison and E. Kaufman (Eds.), *Encyclopedic handbook of alcoholism.* New York: Gardner, 1982. [20]

Moscovici, S. Toward a theory of conversion behavior. In L. Berkowitz (Ed.), *Advances in experimental social psychology* (Vol. 13). New York: Academic Press, 1980. [22]

Motley, M. T. Verification of "Freudian slips" and semantic prearticulatory editing via laboratory-induced spoonerisms. In V. A. Fromkin (Ed.), *Errors in linguistic performance.* New York: Academic Press, 1980. [10]

Motley, M. T. What I meant to say. *Psychology Today*, 1987, *21*, 24–28. [10]

Mowrer, O., and W. Mowrer. Enuresis: A method for its study and treatment. *American Journal of Orthopsychiatry*, 1938, *8*, 436–459. [7]

Mowrer, O. H. *Learning theory and behavior.* New York: Wiley, 1960. [7]

Mozel, M. M., B. Smith, P. Smith, R. Sullivan, and P. Swender. Nasal chemoreception in flavor identification. *Archives of Otolaryngology*, 1969, *90*, 367–373. [4]

Mrazek, P. B. The nature of incest: A review of contributing factors. In P. B. Mrazek and C. H. Kempe, *Sexually abused children and their families.* New York: Pergamon, 1981. [14]

Muchinsky, P. M. *Psychology applied to work* (2nd ed.). Monterey, Calif.: Brooks/Cole, 1987. [23]

Münsterberg, H. *Psychology and industrial efficiency.* Management History Series (19). Easton, Pa.: Hive, 1973. (Originally published, 1913). [23]

Murphy, J. M. Psychiatric labeling in cross-cultural perspective. *Science*, 1976, *191*, 1019–1028. [18]

Murray, D. J. Vocalization at presentation and immediate recall, with varying recall methods. *Quarterly Journal of Experimental Psychology*, 1967, *21*, 263–276. [8]

Murray, H. A., et al. *Explorations in person-*

ality. New York: Oxford University Press, 1938. [13, 17]

Murstein, B. I. Physical attractiveness and marital choice. *Journal of Personality and Social Psychology*, 1972, *22*, 8–12. [21]

Myers, D. G. *Social psychology* (3rd ed.). New York: McGraw-Hill, 1990. [15]

Myers, J. K., M. M. Weissman, G. L. Tischler, C. E. Hozer III, P. J. Leaf, H. Orvaschel, J. C. Anthony, J. H. Boyd, J. D. Burke, M. Kramer, and R. Stoltzman. Six-month prevalence of psychiatric disorders in three communities. *Archives of General Psychiatry*, 1984, *41*, 959–967. [18]

Naranjo, C. Drug-induced states. In B. B. Wolman and M. Ullman (Eds.), *Handbook of states of consciousness.* New York: Van Nostrand Reinhold, 1986. [6]

Nathan, P. E. Alcoholism. In H. Leitenberg (Ed.), *Handbook of behavior modification and behavior therapy.* Englewood Cliffs, N.J.: Prentice-Hall, 1976. [7]

National Council on Alcoholism. *Facts on alcoholism.* New York: 1986. [18]

National Education Association v. State of South Carolina. 434 U.S. 1026 (1978). [23]

National Institute of Mental Health. *Electroconvulsive therapy: Consensus development conference statement.* Bethesda, Md.: Office of Medical Applications of Research, 1985. [19]

Natsoulas, T. Consciousness. *American Psychologist*, 1978, *33*, 906–914. [6]

Needleman, H. L., A. S. Schell, D. Bellinger, A. Leviton, and E. N. Aldred. The long-term effects of exposure to low doses of lead in childhood: An eleven-year follow-up report. *New England Journal of Medicine*, 1990, *322*, 83. [11]

Neimark, E. D. Adolescent thought. In B. B. Wolman (Ed.), *Handbook of developmental psychology.* Englewood Cliffs, N.J.: Prentice-Hall, 1982. [16]

Nelson, K., L. Rescorla, J. Gruendel, and H. Benedict. Early lexicons: What do they mean? *Child Development*, 1978, *49*, 960–968. [15]

Nemeth, C. J., and J. Wachtler. Creative problem solving as a result of majority vs. minority influence. *European Journal of Social Psychology*, 1983, *13*, 45–55. [22]

Neugarten, B. L. Grow old along with me! The best is yet to be. *Psychology Today*, December 1971, *5*, 45–48ff. [16]

Neugarten, B. L. Personality and aging. In J. E. Birren and K. W. Schaie (Eds.), *Handbook of the psychology of aging.* New York: Van Nostrand Reinhold, 1977. [16]

Neugarten, B. L., R. J. Havighurst, and S. S. Tobin. Personality and patterns of

aging. In B. L. Neugarten (Ed.), *Middle age and aging.* Chicago: University of Chicago Press, 1968. [16]

Neugarten, B. L., and D. A. Neugarten. The changing meanings of age. *Psychology Today*, May 1987, *21*, 29–33. [16]

Neugarten, B. L., V. Wood, R. J. Kraines, and B. Loomis. Women's attitudes toward the menopause. *Vita Humana*, 1963, *6*, 140–151. [16]

The New York Times. Alarming rise in breast cancer indicated by data. November 15, 1987, p. 34. [20]

Newell, A., and P. S. Rosenbloom. Mechanisms of skill acquisitions and the law of practice. In J. R. Anderson (Ed.). *Cognitive skills and their acquisition.* Hillsdale, N.J.: Erlbaum, 1981. [7]

Newell, A., and H. A. Simon. *Human problem solving.* Englewood Cliffs, N.J.: Prentice-Hall, 1972. [9]

Newport, E. H., H. Gleitman, and L. R. Gleitman. Mother, I'd rather do it myself: Some effects and noneffects of maternal speech style. In C. E. Snow and C. A. Furguson (Eds.), *Talking to children: Language input and acquisition.* Cambridge, Eng.: Cambridge University Press, 1977. [15]

Nicassio, P., and R. Bootzin. A comparison of progressive relaxation and autogenic training as treatments for insomnia. *Journal of Abnormal Psychology*, 1974, *83*, 253–260. [20]

Nickerson, R. A., and M. J. Adams. Long-term memory for a common object. *Cognitive Psychology*, 1979, *11*, 287–307. [8]

Nickerson, R. S. On improving thinking through instruction. *Review of Research in Education*, 1989, *15*, 3–57. [11]

Nicolson, R. The relationship between memory span and processing speed. In M. P. Friedman, J. P. Das, and N. O'Connor (Eds.), *Intelligence and learning.* New York: Plenum Press, 1981, pp. 179–183. [8]

Nisbett, R. E., E. Borgida, R. Crandall, and H. Reed. Popular induction: Information is not necessarily informative. In J. S. Carroll and J. W. Payne (Eds.), *Cognition and social behavior.* Hillsdale, N.J.: Erlbaum, 1976. [21]

Norman, D. A. *The psychology of everyday things.* New York: Basic Books, 1988. [8]

Norman, W. T. Toward an adequate taxonomy of personality attributes: Replicated factor structure in peer nomination personality ratings. *Journal of Abnormal and Social Psychology*, 1963, *66*, 574–583. [17]

Nosofsky, R. M. Attention and learning processes in the identification and categorization of integral stimuli. *Journal of Experimental Psychology: Learning,*

Memory, and Cognition, 1987, *13,* 87–108. [9]

Oatley, K. On changing one's mind. In A. J. Marcel and E. Bisiach (Eds.), *Consciousness in contemporary science.* Oxford: Clarendon Press, 1988. [6]

Oden, M. H. The fulfillment of promise: 40-year follow-up of the Terman gifted group. *Genetic Psychology Monographs,* 1968, *77,* 3–93. [11]

Offer, D., and **P. C. Hollinger.** Toward the prediction of violent deaths among the young. Paper presented at the meeting of the American Association for the Advancement of Science, Detroit, 1983. [16]

Offer, D., E. Ostrov, and **K. I. Howard.** *The adolescent.* New York: Basic Books, 1981*a.* [16]

Offer, D., E. Ostrov, and **K. I. Howard.** The mental health professional's concept of the normal adolescent. *Archives of General Psychiatry,* 1981*b, 38,* 149. [16]

Offer, D., E. Ostrov, and **K. I. Howard.** Epidemiology of mental health and mental illness among adolescents. In J. Call (Ed.), *Significant advances in child psychiatry.* New York: Basic Books, 1984. [16]

Offir, C. W. *Human sexuality.* New York: Harcourt Brace Jovanovich, 1982. [14]

Ogbu, J. The consequences of the American caste system. In U. Neisser (Ed.), *The school achievement of minority children: New perspectives.* Hillsdale, N.J., Erlbaum, 1986. [11]

O'Hara, M. W., J. V. Hinrichs, F. J. Kohout, R. B. Wallace, and **J. H. Lemke.** Memory complaint and memory performance in the depressed elderly. *Psychology and Aging,* 1986, *1,* 208–214. [16]

Olds, J., and **P. Milner.** Positive reinforcement produced by electrical stimulation of septal area and other regions of rat brain. *Journal of Comparative and Physiological Psychology,* 1954, *47,* 411–427. [3]

O'Leary, K. D., and **G. T. Wilson.** *Behavior therapy: Application and outcome.* Englewood Cliffs, N.J.: Prentice-Hall, 1975. [7]

O'Leary, V. E., and **R. D. Hansen.** Sex as an attributional fact. In T. Sonderegger (Ed.). *Nebraska symposium on motivation* (Vol. 32). Lincoln: University of Nebraska Press, 1985. [12]

O'Leary, V. E., and **D. Smith.** Sex makes a difference: Attributions for emotional cause. Prepared for D. Smith (chair), Two different worlds: Women, men, and emotion. American Psychological Association Convention, Atlanta, August 12–16, 1988. [12]

Olsho, L. W. Infant frequency discrimination. *Infant Behavior and Development,* 1984, *7,* 27–37. [15]

Olsho, L. W., S. W. Harkins, and **M. L. Lenhardt.** Aging and the auditory system. In J. E. Birren and K. W. Schaie (Eds.), *Handbook of the psychology of aging* (2nd ed.). New York: Van Nostrand Reinhold, 1985. [5]

Olson, G. M. Learning and memory in infants. In J. R. Anderson and S. M. Kosslyn (Eds.), *Tutorials in learning and memory: Essays in honor of Gordon Bower.* San Francisco: Freeman, 1984. [7]

Olson, G. M., and **T. Sherman.** Attention, learning and memory in infants. In P. H. Mussen (Ed.), *Handbook of child psychology,* vol. 2, 4th ed. New York, Wiley, 1983. [15]

Olton, D. S., and **A. R. Noonberg.** *Biofeedback: Clinical applications in behavioral medicine.* Englewood Cliffs, N.J.: Prentice-Hall, 1980. [20]

Orlinsky, D. E., and **K. I. Howard.** Processes and outcome in psychotherapy. In S. L. Garfield and A. E. Bergin (Eds.), *Handbook of psychotherapy and behavior change: An evaluative analysis.* New York: Wiley, 1986. [19]

Ormiston, L. H. Factors determining response to modeled hypocrisy. Unpublished doctoral dissertation, Stanford University, 1972. [7]

Orne, M. T. The use and misuse of hypnosis in court. *International Journal of Clinical and Experimental Hypnosis,* 1979, *14,* 311–341. [6]

Ornstein, P. A., and **M. J. Naus.** Rehearsal processes in children's memory. In P. A. Ornstein (Ed.), *Memory development in children.* Hillsdale, N.J.: Erlbaum, 1978. [15]

Orwell, G. *Nineteen eighty-four.* New York: Harcourt, Brace, 1949. [10]

Osborn, A. *Applied imaginations: Principles and procedures of creative problem solving* (3rd rev. ed.). New York: Scribner's, 1963. [9]

Osgood, C. E. Fidelity and reliability. In H. Quaslter (Ed.), *Information theory in psychology: Problems and methods.* Glencoe, Ill.: Free Press, 1955, pp. 374–386. [12]

Oskamp, S., and **C. Kleinke.** Amount of reward as a variable in Prisoner's Dilemma game. *Journal of Personality and Social Psychology,* 1970, *16,* 133–140. [22]

Osofsky, J. D., and **K. Connors.** Mother–infant interaction. In J. D. Osofsky (Ed.), *Handbook of infant development.* New York: Wiley-Interscience, 1979. [15]

Oswald, I. *Sleeping and waking.* Amsterdam: Elsevier, 1962. [6]

Overton, W. F., and **H. W. Reese.** Models of development: Methodological implications. In J. R. Nesselroade and H. W. Reese (Eds.), *Life-span developmental psychology: Methodological issues.* New York: Academic Press, 1973. [17]

Owsley, C. J., R. Sekuler, and **D. Siemsen.** Contrast sensitivity throughout adulthood. *Vision Research,* 1983, *23,* 689–699. [4]

Paivio, A. *Imagery and verbal processes.* New York: Holt, Rinehart and Winston, 1971. [8]

Palmore, E. B. The effects of aging on activity and attitudes. In E. Palmore (Ed.), *Normal aging.* Durham, N.C.: Duke University Press, 1970. [16]

Panskepp, J. Toward a general psychobiological theory of emotions. *Behavioral and Brain Sciences,* 1982, *5,* 407–467. [12]

Papoušek, H., and **Papoušek, M.** Learning and cognition in the everyday life of human infants. In *Advances in the study of behavior.* New York: Academic Press, 1984. [15]

Papoušek, M., H. Papoušek, and **M. H. Bornstein.** The naturalistic vocal environment of young infants. In T. M. Field and N. Fox (Eds.), *Social perception in infants.* Norwood, N.J.: Ablex, 1985. [15]

Paris, S. G., and **B. K. Lindauer.** The development of cognitive skills during childhood. In B. W. Wolman (Ed.), *Handbook of developmental psychology.* Englewood Cliffs, N.J.: Prentice-Hall, 1982. [15]

Park, B., and **M. Rothbart.** Perception of outgroup homogeneity and levels of social categorization: Memory for the subordinate attributes of ingroup and outgroup members. *Journal of Personality and Social Psychology,* 1982, *42,* 1051–1068. [21]

Park, D. C., J. T. Puglisi, and **A. D. Smith.** Memory for pictures. *Psychology and Aging,* 1986, *1,* 11–17. [16]

Parke, R. D., and **S. J. Suomi.** Adult male-infant relationships: Human and non-primate evidence. In K. Immelmann, G. Barlow, M. Main, and L. Petrinovitch (Eds.), *Behavioral development: The Bielefeld interdisciplinary project.* New York: Cambridge University Press, 1980. [15]

Parker, E. S., and **E. P. Noble.** Alcohol consumption and cognitive functioning in social drinkers. *Journal of Studies on Alcohol,* 1977, *38,* 1224–1232. [6]

Parkes, M. C., B. Benjamin, and **R. G. Fitzgerald.** Broken heart: A statistical study of increased mortality among widowers. *British Medical Journal,* 1969, *1,* 704–743. [20]

Parkinson, L., and **S. Rachman.** Intrusive thoughts: The effects of an uncontrived stress. *Advances in Behavior Research and Therapy,* 1981, *3,* 111–118. [6]

Parks, T. E. Illusory figures, illusory objects, and real objects. *Psychological Review,* 1986, *93,* 207–215. [5]

Parks, T. E., N. E. A. Kroll, P. M. Salzberg, and S. R. Parkinson. Persistence of visual memory as indicated by decision time in a matching task. *Journal of Experimental Psychology,* 1972, *92,* 437–438. [8]

Parmelee, A. H., Jr., and M. D. Sigman. Perinatal brain development and behavior. In P. H. Mussen (Ed.), *Handbook of child psychology* (4th ed.). Vol. 2. *Infancy and developmental psychobiology,* M. M. Haith and J. J. Campos (Eds.). New York: Wiley, 1983. [11, 15]

Paris, S. G., D. R. Cross, and M. Y. Lipson. Informed strategies for learning. *Journal of Educational Psychology,* 1984, *76,* 1239–1252. [9, 15]

Paris, S. G., and J. E. Jacobs. The benefits of informed instruction for children's reading awareness and comprehension skills. *Child Development,* 1984, *55,* 2083–2093. [9]

Patterson, G. R. *Coercive family processes.* Eugene, Ore.: Castilia Press, 1982. [19]

Paul, G. L., and R. J. Lentz. *Psychosocial treatment of chronic mental patients: Milieu versus social-learning programs.* Cambridge, Mass.: Harvard University Press, 1977. [19]

Pavlov, I. P. *Conditioned reflexes.* London: Oxford University Press, 1927. [1, 7]

Pearce, J. M. *An introduction to animal cognition.* Hillsdale, N.J.: Erlbaum, 1987. [7]

Penfield, W. Consciousness, memory, and man's conditioned reflexes. In K. Pribram (Ed.), *On the biology of learning.* New York: Harcourt, Brace and World, 1969. [3]

Penfield, W. The mind-brain question. In D. Goleman and R. J. Davidson (Eds.), *Consciousness: Brain, states of awareness, and mysticism.* New York: Harper & Row, 1979. [6]

Penfield, W., and T. Rasmussen. *The cerebral cortex of man.* New York: Macmillan, 1950. [2]

Peplau, L. A. What homosexuals want in relationships. *Psychology Today,* 1981, *15,* March, 28–38. [14]

Perfetto, G. A., J. D. Bransford, and A. J. Franks. Constraints on access in a problem-solving context. *Memory and Cognition,* 1983, *11,* 24–31. [9]

Perkins, D. N. *The mind's best work.* Cambridge, Mass.: Harvard University Press, 1981. [11]

Perkins, D. N., M. Faraday, and B. Bushey. Everyday reasoning and the roots of intelligence. In J. F. Voss, D. N. Perkins, and J. W. Segal (Eds.), *Informal reason-*

ing and education. Hillsdale, N.J.: Erlbaum, in press. [11]

Perlmutter, M., and E. Hall. *Adult development and aging.* New York: Wiley, 1985. [16]

Perls, F. S. Four lectures. In J. Fagan and I. L. Shepherd (Eds.), *Gestalt therapy now: Therapy, techniques, applications.* Palo Alto, Calif.: Science and Behavior Books, 1970. [19]

Perrett, D. J., A. J. Mistlin, and A. J. Chitty. Visual neurones responsive to faces. *Trends in Neurosciences,* 1987, *10,* 358–364. [4, 5]

Perrig, W., and W. Kintsch. Propositional and situational representations of text. *Journal of Memory and Language,* 1985, *24,* 503–518. [10]

Peters, T. J., and R. H. Waterman. *In search of excellence.* New York: Harper & Row, 1982. [23]

Petersen, A. C. Pubertal development as a cause of disturbance. *Genetic, Social, and General Psychology Monographs,* 1985, *3,* 205–232. [16]

Peterson, C., and M. E. P. Seligman. Causal explanations as a risk factor for depression: Theory and evidence. *Psychological Review,* 1984, *91,* 347–374. [18]

Peterson, L. R., and M. Peterson. Short-term retention of individual verbal items. *Journal of Experimental Psychology,* 1959, *58,* 193–198. [8]

Peterson, R. Review of the Rorschach. In O. K. Buros (Ed.), *The eighth mental measurements yearbook* (Vol. 1). Highland Park, N.J.: Gryphon Press, 1978. [17]

Pettigrew, T. F. The ultimate attribution error. Extending Allport's cognitive analysis of prejudice. *Personality and Social Psychology Bulletin,* 1979, *5,* 461–476. [21]

Petty, M. M., G. W. McGee, and J. W. Cavender. A meta-analysis of the relationships between individual job satisfaction and individual performance. *Academy of Management Review,* 1984, *9,* 712–721. [23]

Petty, R. E., and J. T. Cacioppo. *Attitudes and persuasion: Classic and contemporary approaches.* Dubuque, Iowa: Brown, 1981. [21]

Petty, R. E., and J. T. Cacioppo. The effects of involvement on responses to argument quality and quantity: Central and peripheral routes to persuasion. *Journal of Personality and Social Psychology,* 1984, *46,* 69–81. [21]

Petty, R. E., and J. T. Cacioppo. The elaboration likelihood model of persuasion. In L. Berkowitz (Ed.), *Advances in Experimental Social Psychology* (Vol. 19). New York: Academic Press, 1986, pp. 123–205. [21]

Petty, R. E., J. T. Cacioppo, and R. Goldman. Personal involvement as a deter-

minant of argument-based persuasion. *Journal of Personality and Social Psychology,* 1981, *41,* 847–855. [21]

Petty, R. E., J. T. Cacioppo, and D. Schumann. Central and peripheral routes to advertising effectiveness: The moderating role of involvement. *Journal of Consumer Research,* 1983, *10,* 135–146. [21]

Pfeifer, L. A subjective report of tactile hallucination in schizophrenia. *Journal of Clinical Psychology,* 1970, *26,* 57–60. [18]

Phillips, D. P. The impact of mass media violence on U.S. homicides. *American Sociological Review,* 1983, *50,* 364–371. [22]

Phillips, D. P. Natural experiments on the effects of mass media violence on fatal aggression: Strengths and weaknesses of a new approach. In L. Berkowitz (Ed.), *Advances in experimental social psychology* (Vol. 19). New York: Academic Press, 1986. [22]

Phillips, S., S. King, and L. Dubois. Spontaneous activities of female versus male newborns. *Child Development,* 1978, *49,* 590–597. [15]

Piaget, J. *Play, dreams and imitation in childhood.* New York: Norton, 1951, 1962. [15]

Piaget, J. *The child's conception of number.* Boston: Routledge & Kegan Paul, 1952. [15]

Piaget, J. *The construction of reality in the child.* New York: Basic Books, 1954. [15]

Piaget, J. *The origins of intelligence in children.* New York: International Universities Press, 1966. (Originally published, 1952). [16]

Piaget, J., and B. Inhelder. *The child's conception of space.* London: Routledge & Kegan Paul, 1956. [15]

Piaget, J., and B. Inhelder. *The psychology of the child.* New York: Basic Books, 1969. [16]

Pihl, R. O., and M. Parkes. Hair element content in learning-disabled children. *Science,* 1977, *198,* 204–206. [11]

Pines, M. Recession is linked to far-reaching psychological harm. *The New York Times,* Apr. 6, 1982. [19]

Platt, J. R. *Perception and change: Projections for survival.* Ann Arbor: University of Michigan Press, 1970. [22]

Plomin, R. Behavior genetics. In D. K. Detterman (Ed.), *Current topics in human intelligence* (Vol. 1). Norwood, N.J.: Ablex, 1985, pp. 297–320. [11]

Plomin, R., and J. C. DeFries. Genetics and intelligence: Recent data. *Intelligence,* 1980, *4,* 15–24. [11]

Plomin, R., N. L. Pedersen, G. E. McClearn, J. R. Nesselroade, and C. S. Bergeman. EAS temperaments during the last half of the life span: Twins reared apart and twins reared together. *Psychology of Aging,* 1988, *4,* 43–50. [17]

Plutchik, R. A general pyschoevolutionary theory of emotion. In R. Plutchik and H. Kellerman (Eds.), *Emotion, theory, research, and experience* (Vol. 1). New York: Academic Press, 1980. [12]

Poeppel, E., R. Held, and **D. Frost.** Residual visual function after brain wounds involving central pathways in man. *Nature,* 1973, *243,* 295–296. [6]

Polivy, J., and **C. P. Herman.** Clinical depression and weight change: A complex relation. *Journal of Abnormal Psychology,* 1976, *85,* 338–340. [20]

Poon, L. W. Differences in human memory with aging. In J. E. Birren and K. W. Schaie (Eds.), *Handbook of the psychology of aging* (2nd ed.). New York: Van Nostrand Reinhold, 1985. [16]

Posner, M. I., S. J. Boies, W. H. Eichelman, and **R. L. Taylor.** Retention of visual and name codes of single letters, *Journal of Experimental Psychology,* 1969, *79,* 1–16. [8]

Posner, M. I., and **D. E. Presti.** Selective attention and cognitive control. *Trends in Neurosciences,* 1987, *10,* 13–17. [5]

Postman, L., and **K. Stark.** Role of response availability in transfer and interference. *Journal of Experimental Psychology,* 1969, *79,* 168–177. [8]

Prange, A. J., Jr., M. A. Lipton, C. B. Nemeroff, and **I. C. Wilson.** Minireview—The role of hormones in depression. *Life Sciences,* 1977, *20,* 1305–1318. [18]

Premack, D. Toward empirical behavior laws: 1. Positive reinforcement. *Psychological Review,* 1959, *66,* 219–233. [7]

Premack, D. Reinforcement theory. In D. Levine (Ed.), *Nebraska symposium on motivation.* Lincoln: University of Nebraska Press, 1965. [7]

Premack, S. L., and **J. P. Wanous.** A metaanalysis of realistic job preview experiments. *Journal of Applied Psychology,* 1985, *70,* 706–719. [23]

Price, D. L., P. J. Whitehouse, and **R. G. Struble.** Alzheimer's disease. *Annual Review of Medicine,* 1985, *36,* 349–356. [3]

Price, R. H. *Abnormal behavior: Perspectives in conflict* (2nd ed.). New York: Holt, Rinehart & Winston, 1978. [18]

Prochaska, J. O. *Systems of psychotherapy: A transtheoretical analysis* (2nd ed.). Homewood, Ill.: Dorsey Press, 1984. [19]

Pruitt, D. G., and **M. Kimmel.** Twenty years of experimental gaming: Critique, synthesis, and suggestions for the future. In M. R. Rosenzweig and L. W. Porter (Eds.), *Annual review of psychology* (Vol. 28). Palo Alto, Calif.: Annual Reviews, 1977, pp. 363–392. [22]

Pryor, K. *Don't shoot the dog: The new art of teaching and training.* New York: Bantam, 1985. [7]

Puska, P., A. Nissinen, J. T. Salonen, and **J. Tuomilehto.** The years of the North Karelia project: Results with community based prevention of coronary heart disease. *Scandinavian Journal of Social Medicine,* 1983, *11,* 65–68. [20]

Puska, P., J. T. Salonen, A. Nissinen, J. Tuomilehto, E. Vartiainen, H. Korhonen, A. Tanskanen, P. Ronnquist, K. Koskela, and **J. Huttinen.** Change in risk factors for coronary disease during 10 years of a community intervention program (North Karelia project). *British Medical Journal,* 1983, *287,* 1840–1844. [20]

Pyle, R. L., and **J. E. Mitchell.** The prevalence of bulimia in selected samples. *Adolescent Psychiatry,* 1986, *13,* 241–252. [18]

Quattrone, G. A. On the perception of a group's variability. In S. Worchel and W. Austin (Eds.), *Psychology of intergroup relations* (2nd ed.). Chicago: Nelson Hall, 1986, pp. 25–48. [21]

Quattrone, G. A., S. E. Finkel, and **D. C. Andrus.** Anchors away! On overcoming the anchoring bias across a number of domains. Unpublished manuscript, Stanford University, 1982. [21]

Quattrone, G. A., and **A. Tversky.** Contrasting rational and psychological analyses of political choice. *American Political Science Review,* 1988, *32,* 719–736. [9]

Quay, H. C. Psychopathic personality as pathological stimulus seeking. *American Journal of Psychiatry,* 1965, *122,* 180–183. [18]

Rabbie, J. M., and **M. Horwitz.** Arousal of ingroup-outgroup bias by a chance win or loss. *Journal of Personality and Social Psychology,* 1969, *13,* 269–277. [21]

Rachman, S. J. *Fear and courage.* San Francisco: W. H. Freeman, 1978. [7, 21]

Rachman, S. J., and **R. J. Hodgson.** *Obsessions and compulsions.* Englewood Cliffs, N.J.: Prentice-Hall, 1980. [18, 19]

Rachman, S. J., and **G. T. Wilson.** *The effects of psychological therapy* (2nd ed.) Oxford: Pergamon Press, 1980. [24]

Rada, R. T. Psychological factors in rapist behavior. In R. T. Rada (Ed.). *Clinical aspects of the rapist.* New York: Grune & Stratton, 1978. [18]

Ragland, D. R., and **R. J. Brand.** Type A behavior and mortality from coronary heart disease. *New England Journal of Medicine,* 1988, *318,* 65–69. [20]

Raps, C. S., C. Peterson, K. E. Reinhard, L. Y. Abramson, and **M. E. P. Seligman.** Attributional style among depressed patients. *Journal of Abnormal Psychology,* 1982, *91,* 102–108. [18]

Ray, O. S. *Drugs, society, and human behavior* (3rd ed.). St. Louis: Mosby, 1983. [6]

Razran, G. H. S. A quantitative study of learning by conditioned salivary technique (semantic conditioning). *Science,* 1939, *90,* 89–91. [7]

Rechtschaffen, A., M. A. Gilliland, B. M. Bergmann, and **J. B. Winter.** Physiological correlates of prolonged sleep deprivation in rats. *Science,* 1983, *221,* 182–184. [6]

Reed, S. K. Pattern recognition and categorization. *Cognitive Psychology,* 1972, *3,* 383–407. [9]

Regan, D., K. Beverley, and **M. Cynader.** The visual perception of motion in depth. *Scientific American,* 1979, *241* (1), 136–151. [5]

Regan, D. T. Effects of a favor and liking on compliance. *Journal of Experimental Social Psychology,* 1971, *7,* 627–639. [22]

Reichenbach, L., and **J. C. Masters.** Children's use of expressive and contextual cues in judgments of emotion. *Child Development,* 1983, *54,* 993–1104. [12]

Reinisch, J. M. Prenatal exposure to synthetic progestins increases potential for aggression in humans. *Science,* 1981, *211,* 1171–1173. [15]

Reisenzein, R. The Schachter theory of emotion: Two decades later. *Psychological Bulletin,* 1983, *94,* 239–264. [12]

Reiss, I. L. Heterosexual relationships inside and outside marriage. Morristown, N.J.: General Learning Press, 1973. [16]

Reitman, J. S. Without surreptitious rehearsal, information in short-term memory decays. *Journal of Verbal Learning and Verbal Behavior,* 1974, *13,* 365–377. [8]

Rekers, G. A., and **O. I. Lovaas.** Behavioral treatment of deviant sex-role behaviors in a male child. *Journal of Applied Behavior Analysis,* 1974, *7,* 173–190. [18]

Repetti, R. L., and **F. Crosby.** Gender and depression. *Journal of Social and Clinical Psychology,* 1984, *2,* 57–70. [16]

Rescorla, R. A. Probability of shock in the presence and absence of CS in fear conditioning. *Journal of Comparative and Physiological Psychology,* 1968, *66,* 1–5. [7]

Rescorla, R. A., and **A. R. Wagner.** A theory of Pavlovian conditioning: Variations in the effectiveness of reinforcement and non-reinforcement. In A. H. Black and W. F. Prokasy (Eds.), *Classical conditioning II: Current research and theory.* New York: Appleton-Century-Crofts, 1972. [7]

Resnik, R. B., R. S. Kestenbaum, and **L. K. Schwartz.** Acute systemic effects of cocaine in man: A controlled study by intranasal and intravenous routes by administration. *Science,* 1977, *195,* 696–698. [6]

Resnick, S. Gestalt therapy: The hot seat of personal responsibility. *Psychology Today*, November 1974, *8*, 110–117. [19]

Rest, J. R. Morality. In P. H. Mussen (Ed.), *Handbook of child psychology* (Vol. 3). *Cognitive development*. New York: Wiley, 1983. [16]

Restak, R. *The brain*. New York: Bantam, 1984. [2]

Revelle, W. Factors are fictions, and other comments on individuality theory. *Journal of Personality*, 1983, *51*, 707–714. [17]

Reveley, M. A. CT scans in schizophrenia. *British Journal of Psychiatry*, 1985, *146*, 367–371. [18]

Revelle, W., P. Amaral, and S. Turriff. Introversion-extraversion, time stress, and caffeine: The effect on verbal performance. *Science*, 1976, *192*, 149–150. [17]

Revusky, S. H., and J. Garcia. Learned associations over long delays. In G. H. Bower (Ed.), *The psychology of learning and motivation* (Vol. 1). New York: Academic Press, 1970. [7]

Rey, G. A reason for doubting the existence of consciousness. In R. J. Davidson, G. E. Schwartz, and D. Shapiro (Eds.), *Consciousness and self-regulation: Advances in research and theory* (Vol. 3). New York: Plenum Press, 1983. [6]

Rhine, J. B. Telepathy and other untestable hypotheses. *Journal of Parapsychology*, 1974, *38*, 137–153. [2]

Rhodewalt, F., and R. Comer. Induced-compliance attitude change: Once more with feeling. *Journal of Experimental Social Psychology*, 1979, *15*, 35–47. [12]

Rice, B. The Hawthorne effect: Persistence of a flawed theory. *Psychology Today*, 1982, *16*, 71–74. [23]

Rice, R. W., D. B. McFarlin, R. G. Hunt, and J. P. Near. Organizational work and the perceived quality of life: Toward a conceptual model. *Academy of Management Review*, 1985, *10*, 296–310. [23]

Rieff, P. *Freud: The mind of a moralist* (3rd ed.). Chicago: University of Chicago Press, 1979. [17]

Rips, L. J. Cognitive processes in propositional reasoning. *Psychological Review*, 1983, *90*, 38–71. [9]

Risley, T. R. The effects and side-effects of punishing the autistic behavior of a defiant child. *Journal of Applied Behavior Analysis*, 1968, *1*, 21–34. [7]

Roberts, D. F., and N. Maccoby. Effects of mass communication. In G. Lindzey and E. Aronson (Eds.), *Handbook of social psychology* (3rd ed.) (Vol. 2). New York: Random House, 1985. [22]

Roberts, M., and T. G. Harris. Wellness at work. *Psychology Today*, May 1989, 54–58. [20, 23]

Roberts, P., and P. M. Newton. Levinsonian studies of women's adult development. *Psychology and Aging*, 1987, *2*, 154–163. [16]

Robins, L. N., J. E. Helzer, M. M. Weissman, H. Orvaschel, E. Gruenberg, J. D. Burke, and D. A. Regier. Lifetime prevalence of specific psychiatric disorders in three sites. *Archives of General Psychiatry*, 1984, *41*, 949–958. [18]

Robinson, E. J., and W. P. Robinson. Realizing you don't understand. *Journal of Child Psychology and Psychiatry*, 1984, *25*, 621–627. [15]

Robinson, R. G., K. L. Kubos, L. B. Starr, et al. Mood disorders in stroke patients: Importance of location of lesion. *Brain*, 1984, *107*, 81–93. [3]

Roche, A. F. (Ed.). Secular trends in human growth, maturation, and development. *Monographs of the Society for Research in Child Development*, 1979, *44*, Serial no. 179. [16]

Rock, I. L. *The logic of perception*. Cambridge, Mass.: MIT Press, 1984. [5]

Rock, I. L. *Perception*. New York: W. H. Freeman, 1984. [5]

Rodin, J. Current status of the internal-external hypothesis for obesity: What went wrong? *American Psychologist*, 1981, *36*, 361–372. [20]

Rodin, J. A sense of control (interview). *Psychology Today*, December 1984, pp. 38–45. [12]

Rodin, J. Insulin levels, hunger and food intake: An example of feedback loops in body weight regulation. *Health Psychology*, 1985, *4*, 1–18. [13]

Rodin, J. Aging and health: Effects of the sense of control. *Science*, 1986, *233*, 1271–1276. [20]

Rodin, J., and E. J. Langer. Long-term effects of a control-relevant intervention with the institutionalized aged. *Journal of Personality and Social Psychology*, 1977, *35*, 897–902. [20]

Rodin, J., and J. Marcus. Psychological factors in human feeding. *Pharmacotherapy*, 1982, *16*, 447–468. [13]

Rodin, J., L. Silberstein, and R. Striegel-Moore. Women and weight. In T. B. Sonderegger (Ed.), *Nebraska Symposium on Motivation*. Lincoln: University of Nebraska Press, 1985. [16]

Rodin, J., and J. Slochower. Externality in the nonobese: Effects of environmental responsiveness on weight. *Journal of Personality and Social Psychology*, 1976, *36*, 988–999. [13]

Roffwarg, H. P., J. N. Muzio, and W. C. Dement. Ontogenetic development of the human sleep–dream cycle. *Science*, 1966, *132*, 604–619. [6]

Rogel, M. J. A critical evaluation of the possibility of higher primate reproductive and sexual pheromones. *Psychological Bulletin*, 1978, *85*, 810–830. [14]

Rogers, B., and M. Graham. Similarities between motion parallax and stereopsis in human depth perception. *Vision Research*, 1982, *22*, 261–270. [5]

Rogers, C. R. *Client-centered therapy: Its current practice, implications and theory*. Boston: Houghton Mifflin, 1951. [19]

Rogers, C. R. A theory of therapy, personality, and interpersonal relationships, as developed in the client-centered framework. In S. Koch (Ed.), *Psychology: A study of a science* (Vol. 3). New York: McGraw-Hill, 1959, 184–256. [17]

Rogers, C. R. A theory of personality. In S. Maddi (Ed.), *Perspectives on personality*. Boston: Little, Brown, 1971. [17]

Rogers, C. R. *A way of being*. Boston: Houghton Mifflin, 1980. [13, 17, 19]

Rogers, C. R. *The Carl Rogers reader*. H. Kerschenbaum and V. L. Henderson (Eds.). Boston: Houghton Mifflin, 1989. [17, 19]

Roitblat, H. L. *Introduction to comparative cognition*. New York: W. H. Freeman, 1987. [7]

Rolls, E. T., M. J. Burton, and F. Mora. Hypothalamic neuronal responses associated with the sight of food. *Brain Research*, 1976, *111*, 53–56. [13]

Rorschach, H. *Psychodiagnosis: A diagnostic test based on perception*. New York: Grune & Stratton, 1942. [17]

Rosch, E. H. On the internal structure of perceptual and semantic categories. In T. E. Moore (Ed.), *Cognitive development and the acquisition of language*. New York: Academic Press, 1973. [9, 10]

Rosch, E. H., and C. B. Mervis. Family resemblances: Studies in the internal structure of categories. *Cognitive Psychology*, 1977, *7*, 573–605. [9]

Rosch, E. H., C. B. Mervis, W. Gray, D. Johnson, and P. Boyes-Braem. Basic objects in natural categories. *Cognitive Psychology*, 1976, *8*, 382–439. [9, 12]

Rose, R. J., and M. A. Chesney. Cardiovascular stress reactivity: A behavioral-genetic perspective. *Behavior Therapy*, 1986, *17*, 314–323. [20]

Rose, S. *The conscious brain*. New York: Knopf, 1973. [6, 15]

Rose, S. A., and I. F. Wallace. Visual recognition memory. *Child Development*, 1985, *56*, 843–852. [15]

Roseman, I. Cognitive determinants of emotion: A structural theory. In P. Shaver (Ed.), *Review of personality and social psychology* (Vol. 5). Beverly Hills, Calif.: Sage, 1984. [12]

Rosen, R., and E. Hall. *Sexuality*. New York: Random House, 1984. [14]

Rosenbaum, M. E. The repulsion hypothesis: On the nondevelopment of relationships. *Journal of Personality and Social Psychology*, 1986, *51*, 1156–1166. [21]

Rosenberg, M. *Conceiving the self.* New York: Basic Books, 1979. [13]

Rosenhan, D. L. On being sane in insane places. *Science,* 1973, *179,* 250–258. [18]

Rosenman, R. H., R. J. Brand, C. D. Jenkins, M. Friedman, R. Straus, and M. Wurm. Coronary heart disease in the Western Collaborative Group study: Final follow-up experience of 8½ years. *Journal of the American Medical Association,* 1975, *8,* 872–877. [20]

Rosenstein, D., and H. Oster. Differential facial response to four basic tastes in newborns. *Child Development,* 1988, *59,* 1555–1568. [5, 15]

Rosenstock, I. M. The health belief model and preventive health behavior. *Health Education Monographs,* 1974, *2,* 354–386. [20]

Rosenthal, T., and A. Bandura. Psychological modeling: Theory and practice. In S. L. Garfield and A. E. Bergin (Eds.), *Handbook of psychotherapy and behavioral change: An empirical analysis* (2nd ed.). New York: Wiley, 1978. [19]

Rosenzweig, M. R., and E. L. Bennett. Cerebral changes in rats exposed individually to an enriched environment. *Journal of Comparative and Physiological Psychology,* 1972, *80,* 304–313. [3]

Rosenzweig, M. R., and A. L. Leiman. *Physiological Psychology* (2nd ed.). New York: Random House, 1989. [7]

Ross, B. H., and G. H. Bower. Comparisons of models of associative recall. *Memory and cognition.* Belmont, Calif.: Wadsworth, 1981. [8]

Ross, J. R., and W. E. Cooper. *Like* syntax. In W. E. Cooper and E. C. T. Walker (Eds.), *Sentence processing: Psycholinguistic studies presented to Merrill Garrett.* Hillsdale, N.J.: Erlbaum, 1979. [10]

Ross, L. The intuitive psychologist and his shortcomings: Distortions in the attribution process. In L. Berkowitz (Ed.), *Advances in experimental social psychology* (Vol. 10). New York: Academic Press, 1977. [21]

Ross, L., F. Bierbrauer, and S. Hoffman. The role of attribution processes in conformity and dissent: Revisiting the Asch situation. *American Psychologist,* 1976, *31,* 148–157. [22]

Rossi, P. H., J. D. Wright, G. A. Fischer, and G. Willis. The urban homeless: Estimating composition and size. *Science,* 1987, *235,* 1336–1341. [19]

Roueché, B. Annals of medicine: As empty as Eve. *The New Yorker,* Sept. 9, 1974, pp. 84–100. [19]

Rovée-Collier, C. The ontogeny of learning and memory in human infancy. In R. Kail and N. E. Spear (Eds.), *Comparative perspectives on the development of memory.* Hillsdale, N.J.: Erlbaum, 1984. [15]

Rubin, R. T., J. M. Reinisch, and R. F. Haskett. Postnatal gonadal steroid effects on human behavior. *Science,* 1981, *211,* 1318–1324. [14]

Ruderman, A. Dietary restraint: A theoretical and empirical review. *Psychological Bulletin,* 1986, *99,* 247–262. [13]

Rule, B. G., and A. R. Nesdale. Emotional arousal and aggressive behavior. *Psychological Bulletin,* 1976, *83,* 851–863. [22]

Rumbaugh, D. M. (Ed.). *Language learning by a chimpanzee: The Lana project.* New York: Academic Press, 1977. [10]

Rumelhart, D. E., and D. A. Norman. "Representation in Memory," in R. C. Atkinson et al. (Eds.), *Stevens' handbook of experimental psychology* (2nd ed.) (Vol. 2). New York: Wiley, 1988. [8]

Russell, D. *Sexual exploitation: Rape, child sexual abuse, and sexual harassment.* Beverly Hills, Calif.: Sage, 1984. [14]

Russell, J. A. Pancultural aspects of the human conceptual organization of emotions. *Journal of Personality and Social Psychology,* 1983, *45,* 1281–1288. [12]

Russell, W. R., and P. W. Nathan. Traumatic amnesia. *Brain,* 1946, *69,* 280–300. [8]

Rutkowski, G. K., C. L. Gruder, and D. Romer. Group cohesiveness, social norms, and bystander intervention. *Journal of Personality and Social Psychology,* 1983, *44,* 545–552. [22]

Rutledge, L. L., and R. B. Hupka. The facial feedback hypothesis: Methodological concerns and new supporting evidence. *Motivation and Emotion,* 1985, *9,* 219–240. [12]

Rutter, M. Maternal deprivation, 1972–1978. New findings, new concepts, new approaches. *Child Development,* 1979, *50,* 283–305. [15, 17]

Rutter, M. *Changing youth in a changing society.* Cambridge, Mass.: Harvard University Press, 1980. [16]

Saal, F. E., and P. A. Knight. *Industrial/organizational psychology: Science and practice.* Pacific Grove, Calif.: Brooks/Cole, 1988. [23]

Sachs, J. S. Recognition memory for syntactic and semantic aspects of connected discourse. *Perception and Psychophysics,* 1967, *2,* 437–442. [10]

Sackett, Paul R. Honesty testing for personnel selection. *Personnel Administrator,* September 1985, 67–121. [23]

Sagar, H. A., and J. W. Schofield. Racial and behavioral cues in black and white children's perceptions of ambiguously aggressive acts. *Journal of Personality and Social Psychology,* 1980, *39,* 590–598. [21]

Saghir, M. T., and E. Robins. *Male and female homosexuality: A comprehensive investigation.* Baltimore: Williams & Wilkins, 1973. [14]

St. George-Hyslop, P. H., et al. The genetic defect causing familial Alzheimer's disease maps on chromosome 21. *Science,* 1987, *235,* 885–890. [3]

Salancik, G. R., and J. Pfeffer. A social information processing approach to job attitudes and task design. *Administrative Science Quarterly,* 1978, *23,* 224–253. [23]

Salovey, P., and J. Rodin. Some antecedents and consequences of social comparison jealousy. *Journal of Personality and Social Psychology,* 1980, *47,* 780–792. [13]

Salthouse, T. A. Effects of age and skill in typing. *Journal of Experimental Psychology: General,* 1984, *113,* 345–371. [16]

Saltzstein, H. D. Critical issues in Kohlberg's theory of moral reasoning. *Monographs of the Society for Research in Child Development,* 1983, *48,* 108–119. [16]

Samelson, F. World War I intelligence testing and the development of psychology. *Journal of the History of the Behavioral Sciences,* 1979, *13,* 274–282. [1]

Sarbin, T. R., and W. C. Coe. *Hypnosis: A social psychological analysis of influence communication.* New York: Holt, Rinehart & Winston, 1972. [6]

Savage-Rumbaugh, S., K. McDonald, R. A. Sevcik, W. D. Hopkins, and E. Rubert. Spontaneous symbol acquisition and communication by pygmy chimpanzees, (Pan panicus). *Journal of Experimental Psychology: General,* 1986, *115,* 211–235. [10]

Scafidi, F. A., et al. Effects of tactile/kinesthetic stimulation on the clinical course of sleep/wake behavior of preterm neonates. *Infant Behavior and Development,* 1986, *9,* 91–106. [15]

Scarr, S. *Race, social class, and individual differences in I.Q.* Hillsdale, N.J.: Erlbaum, 1981, [11]

Scarr, S. On quantifying the intended effects of interventions. In L. A. Bond and J. M. Joffe (Eds.), *Facilitating infancy and early childhood development,* Hanover, N.H.: University Press of New England, 1982. [15]

Scarr, S. Child care. Presented at Science and Public Policy Seminar, Federation of Behavioral, Psychological, and Cognitive Sciences, Oct. 21, 1983. [15]

Scarr, S. *Mother care/Other care.* New York: Basic Books, 1984. [15]

Scarr, S., and K. McCartney. How people make their own environments. *Child Development,* 1983, *54,* 425–435. [15]

Scarr, S., and P. Salapatek. Patterns of fear development during infancy. *Merrill-Palmer Quarterly of Behavior and Development,* 1970, *16,* 53–90. [15]

Scarr, S., and R. A. Weinberg. IQ test performance of black children adopted by white families. *American Psychologist*, 1976, *31*, 726–739. [11]

Schachter, S., and **J. E. Singer.** Cognitive, social, and physiological determinants of emotional state. *Psychological Review*, 1962, *69*, 379–399. [12, 21]

Schachter, S., and **L. Wheeler.** Epinephrine, chlorpromazine, and amusement. *Journal of Abnormal and Social Psychology*, 1962, *65*, 121–128. [12]

Schacter, D. L. Implicit memory: History and current status. *Journal of Experimental Psychology: Learning, Memory, and Cognition*, 1987, *13*, 501–518. [6]

Schaefer, C., J. C. Coyne, and **R. S. Lazarus.** The health-related functions of social support. *Journal of Behavioral Medicine*, 1981, *4*, 381–406. [20]

Schaeffer, J., T. Andrysiak, and **J. T. Ungerleider.** Cognition and long-term use of ganja (cannabis). *Science*, 1981, *213*, 465–466. [6]

Schaie, K. W. Midlife influences upon intellectual function in old age. *International Journal of Behavioral Development*, 1984, *7*, 463–478. [16]

Schaie, K. W., and **C. Hertzog.** Fourteen-year-cohort-sequential analyses of adult intellectual development. *Developmental Psychology*, 1983, *19*, 531–543. [16]

Schaie, K. W., and **S. L. Willis.** Can declines in adult intellectual functioning be reversed? *Developmental Psychology*, 1986, *22*, 223–232. [16]

Schank, R. C. *Dynamic memory.* Cambridge: Cambridge University Press, 1982. [6]

Schank, R. C., and **R. Abelson.** *Scripts, plans, goals, and understanding.* Hillsdale, N.J.: Erlbaum, 1977. [8, 15]

Schank, R. C., and **P. Childers.** *The cognitive computer.* Reading, Mass.: Addison-Wesley, 1984.

Scheerer, M. Problem-solving. *Scientific American*, 1963, *208*, 118–128. [9]

Scheff, T. J. *Labeling madness.* Englewood Cliffs, N.J.: Prentice-Hall, 1975. [18]

Scheier, M. F., and **C. S. Carver.** A model of behavioral self-regulation: Translating intention into action. In L. Berkowitz (Ed.), *Advances in experimental social psychology* (Vol. 21). New York: Academic Press, 1988. [13]

Schenck, C. H., S. R. Bundlie, M. G. Ettinger, and **M. W. Mahowald.** Chronic behavioral disorders of human REM sleep: A new category of parasomnia. *Sleep*, 1986, *9*, 293–308. [6]

Scherer, K. R. Emotion as process: Function, origin, and regulation. *Social Science Information*, 1982, *21*, 555–570. [12]

Scherer, K. R. Emotion as a multicomponent process: A model and some cross-cultural data. In P. Shaver (Ed.), *Review of personality and social psychology*

(Vol. 5). Beverly Hills, Calif.: Sage, 1984. [12]

Scherer, K. R. Emotion experiences across European cultures: A summary statement. In K. R. Scherer, H. G. Wallbott, and A. B. Summerfield (Eds.), *Experiencing emotion: A cross-cultural study.* Cambridge, Eng.: Cambridge University Press, 1986, pp. 173–189. [12]

Scherer, K. R., R. P. Abeles, and **C. S. Fischer.** *Human aggression and conflict.* Englewood Cliffs, N.J.: Prentice-Hall, 1975. [22]

Squire, L. R. *Memory and the brain.* New York: Oxford University Press, 1987. [8]

Scherer, K. R., R. P. Sheles, and **C. S. Kischer.** *Human aggression and conflict.* Englewood Cliffs, N.J.: Prentice-Hall, 1975. [22]

Scherer, K. R., H. G. Walbott, and **A. B. Summerfield** (Eds.). *Experiencing emotion: A cross-cultural study.* Cambridge, Eng.: Cambridge University Press, 1986. [12]

Schildkraut, J. J. The catecholamine hypothesis of affective disorders: A review of supporting evidence. *American Journal of Psychiatry*, 1965, *122*, 509–522. [18]

Schmeck, H. M., Jr. Study finds high risk from acne drug early in pregnancy. *The New York Times*, Oct. 3, 1985, p. A20. [15]

Schmidt, F. L., and **J. E. Hunter.** Employment testing: Old theories and new research findings. *American Psychologist*, 1981, *36*, 1128–1137. [23]

Schmitt, N. Social and situational determinants of interview decisions: Implications for the employment interview. *Personnel Psychology*, 1976, *29*, 79–101. [23]

Schnapf, J. L., and **D. A. Baylor.** How photoreceptor cells respond to light. *Scientific American*, 1987, *256*, 40–47. [4]

Schneider, A. M., and **B. Tarshis.** *An introduction to physiological psychology* (3rd ed.). New York: Random House, 1986. [4, 6]

Schreiber, F. *Sybil.* New York: Warner, 1974. [18]

Schuckit, M. A., and **V. Rayses.** Ethanol ingestion: Differences in blood acetaldehyde concentrations in relatives of alcoholics and controls. *Science*, 1979, *203*, 54–55. [18]

Schulsinger, F. Psychopathy: Heredity and environment. *International Journal of Mental Health*, 1972, *1*, 190–206. [18]

Schulsinger, R., J. Knop, D. W. Goodwin, T. W. Teasdale, and **U. Mikkelson.** A prospective study of young men at high risk for alcoholism: Social and psychological characteristics. *Archives of General Psychiatry*, 1986, *43*, 755–760. [18]

Schultes, R. E. *Hallucinogenic plants.* New York: Golden Press, 1976. [6]

Schultz, J. H., and **W. O. Luthe.** *Autogenic therapy.* Vol. 1. *Autogenic methods.* New York: Grune & Stratton, 1969. [20]

Schwartz, B. *Psychology of learning and behavior* (2nd ed.). New York: Norton, 1984. [7]

Scogin, R., C. Jamison, and **K. Gochneaur.** Comparative efficacy of cognitive and behavioral bibliotherapy for mildly and moderately depressed older adults. *Journal of Consulting and Clinical Psychology*, 1989, *57*, 403–407. [19]

Scovern, A. W., and **P. R. Kilmann.** Status of electroconvulsive therapy: Review of the outcome literature. *Psychological Bulletin*, 1980, *87*, 260–303. [19]

Searle, J. R. *Speech acts: An essay in the philosophy of language.* New York: Cambridge University Press, 1969. [10]

Sears, R. R. Sources of life satisfaction of the Terman gifted men. *American Psychologist*, 1977, *32*, 119–128. [11]

Sebeok, T. A., and **J. Umiker-Sebeok.** *Speaking of apes: A critical anthology of two-way communication with man.* New York: Plenum Press, 1980. [10]

Segal, B., G. Huba, and **J. L. Singer.** *Drugs, daydreaming and personality: A study of college youth.* Hillsdale, N.J.: Erlbaum, 1980. [6]

Segal, M. W. Alphabet and attraction: An unobtrusive measure of the effects of propinquity in a field setting. *Journal of Personality and Social Psychology*, 1974, *30*, 654–657. [21]

Seidenberg, M. S., M. K. Tanenhaus, J. M. Leiman, and **M. Bienkowski.** Automatic access of the meanings of ambiguous words in context: Some limitations of knowledge-based processing. *Cognitive Psychology*, 1982, *14*, 489–537. [10]

Sekuler, R., and **R. Blake.** *Perception.* New York: Knopf, 1985. [4, 5]

Sekuler, R., and **R. Blake.** Sensory underload. *Psychology Today*, December 1987, *21*, 48–51. [5]

Seligman, M. E. P. *Helplessness: On depression, development, and death.* San Francisco: Freeman, 1975. [18]

Seligman, M. E. P., and **R. Yellen.** What is a dream? *Behaviour Research and Therapy*, 1987, *25*, 1–24. [6]

Selye, H. *The stress of life.* New York: McGraw-Hill, 1956. [20]

Selye, H. *Stress without distress.* Philadelphia: Lippincott, 1974. [20]

Selye, H. *Stress in health and disease.* Woburn, Mass.: Butterworth, 1976. [20]

Serban, G. Stress in normals and schizophrenics. *British Journal of Psychiatry*, 1975, *126*, 397–407. [18]

Serbin, L. A., K. D. O'Leary, R. N. Kent, and **I. J. Tonick.** A comparison of teacher response to the pre-academic and problem behavior of boys and girls. *Child Development*, 1973, *33*, 796–804. [15]

Seta, J. J., J. E. Crisson, C. E. Seta, and M. A. Wang. Task performance and perceptions of anxiety: Averaging and summation in an evaluative setting. *Journal of Personality and Social Psychology*, 1989, *56*, 387–396. [22]

Shafii, M., et al. Psychology autopsy of completed suicide in children and adolescents. *American Journal of Psychiatry*, 1985, *142*, 1061. [18]

Shantz, C. U. Social cognition. In P. H. Mussen (Ed.), *Handbook of child psychology* (4th ed.). Vol. 3. J. H. Flavell and E. M. Markman (Eds.), *Cognitive development*. New York: Wiley, 1983. [15]

Shapiro, C. M., R. Bortz, D. Mitchell, P. Bartel, and P. Jooste. Slow-wave sleep: A recovery period after exercise. *Science*, 1981, *214*, 1253–1354. [6]

Shapiro, D., and I. B. Goldstein. Biobehavioral perspectives on hypertension. *Journal of Consulting and Clinical Psychology*, 1982, *50*, 841–858. [20]

Sharp, D., M. Cole, and C. Lave. Education and cognitive development: The evidence from experimental research. *Monographs of the Society for Research in Child Development*, 1979, *44* (1-2, Serial No. 178). [11]

Shattuck-Hufnagel, S. Speech errors as evidence for a serial-ordering mechanism in sentence production. In W. E. Cooper and E. C. T. Walker (Eds.), *Sentence processing: Psycholinguistic studies presented to Merrill Garrett*. Hillsdale, N.J.: Erlbaum, 1979. [10]

Shaver, P., and C. Hazan. A biased overview of the study of love. *Journal of Social and Personal Relationships*, 1988, *5*, 473–501. [14]

Shaver, P., C. Hazan, and D. Bradshaw. Love as attachment: The integration of three behavioral systems. In R. Sternberg and M. Barnes (Eds.), *The psychology of love*. New Haven, Conn.: Yale University Press, 1988. [14]

Shaver, P., and M. Klinnert. Schachter's theories of affiliation and emotion: Implications of developmental research. In L. Wheeler (Ed.), *Review of personality and social psychology* (Vol. 3). Beverly Hills, Calif.: Sage, 1982, pp. 37–72. [12]

Shaver, P., J. Schwartz, D. Kirson, and C. O'Connor. Emotion knowledge: Further explorations of a prototype approach. *Journal of Personality and Social Psychology*, 1987, *52*, 1061–1086. [12]

Shaver, P., and J. C. Schwartz. Cross-cultural similarities and differences in emotion and its representation: A prototype approach. In R. B. Zajonc and S. Moscovici (Eds.), *Symposium on social*

psychology and the emotions. In press. [12]

Shepard, R. N. The mental image. *American Psychologist*, 1978, *33*, 125–137. [9]

Shepard, R. N., and S. Chipman. Second order isomorphisms of internal representation: Shapes of states. *Cognitive Psychology*, 1970, *1*, 1–17. [9]

Sherif, M. *The psychology of social norms*. New York: Harper, 1936. [22]

Shiffrin, R. M. Attention, in R. C. Atkinson et al. (Eds.), *Stevens' handbook of experimental psychology* (2nd ed.). Vol. 2. New York: Wiley, 1988. [8]

Shimamura, A. P., and L. R. Squire. Memory and metamemory: A study of the feeling of knowing phenomenon in amnesic patients. *Journal of Experimental Psychology: Learning, Memory, and Cognition*, 1986, *12*, 452–460. [8]

Shneidman, E. S. Death work and stages of dying. In E. S. Shneidman (Ed.), *Death: Current perspectives* (2nd ed.). Palo Alto, Calif.: Mayfield, 1980. [16]

Shortliffe, E. H. *Computer-based medical consultations: MYCIN*. New York: American Elsevier, 1976. [9]

Shostak, M. *Nisa: The life and words of a !Kung woman*. Cambridge, Mass.: Harvard University Press, 1981. [20]

Shotland, R., and L. Goodstein. Just because she doesn't want it doesn't mean it's rape: An experimentally based causal model of the perception of rape in a dating situation. *Social Psychology Quarterly*, 1983, *46*, 220–232. [14]

Shultz, T. R. Rules of causal attribution. *Monographs of the Society for Research in Child Development*, 1982, *47*, (Serial No. 194). [15]

Shumway-Cook, A., and M. H. Woollacott. The growth of stability. *Journal of Motor Behavior*, 1985, *17*, 131–174. [15]

Siegel, R. K. Hallucinations. *Scientific American*, 1977, *237*, 132–140. [6]

Siegler, R. S. Information processing approaches to development. In P. H. Mussen (Ed.), *Handbook of child psychology* (4th ed.). Vol. 1. W. Kessen (Ed.), *History, theory, and methods*. New York: Wiley, 1983. [15]

Siegler, R. S. *Children's thinking*. Englewood Cliffs, N.J.: Prentice-Hall, 1986. [15]

Silberschatz, G., P. B. Fretter, and J. T. Curtis. How do interpretations influence the process of psychotherapy? *Journal of Consulting and Clinical Psychology*, 1986, *54*, 646–652. [19]

Simmons, R., D. Blyth, and K. McKenney. The social and psychological effects of puberty on white females. In J. Brooks-Gunn and A. Petersen (Eds.). *Girls at puberty*. New York: Plenum Press, 1983. [16]

Simon, H., and K. Gilmartin. A simulation

of memory for chess positions. *Cognitive Psychology*, 1973, *5*, 29–46. [9]

Sjostrom, L. Fat cells and bodyweight. In A. J. Stunkard (Ed.), *Obesity*. Philadelphia: Saunders, 1980. [13]

Skinner, B. F. *Behavior of organisms: An experimental analysis*. New York: Appleton-Century-Crofts, 1938. [7]

Skinner, B. F. *Walden two*. New York: Macmillan, 1948*a*. [1]

Skinner, B. F. Superstitious behavior in the pigeon. *Journal of Experimental Psychology*, 1948*b*, *38*, 168–172. [7]

Skinner, B. F. How to teach animals. *Scientific American*, 1951, *185*, 26–29. [7]

Skinner, B. F. *Science and human behavior*. New York: Macmillan, 1953. [1]

Skinner, B. F. *About behaviorism*. New York: Knopf, 1974. [7]

Skinner, B. F. The steep and thorny road to a science of behavior. *American Psychologist*, 1975, *30*, 42–49. [17]

Sklar, L. S., and H. Anisman. Stress and coping factors influence tumor growth. *Science*, 1979, *205*, 513–515. [20]

Sklar, L. S., and H. Anisman. Stress and cancer. *Psychological Bulletin*, 1981, *89*, 369–406. [20]

Sladek, J. R., Jr., T. J. Collier, S. N. Haber, A. Y. Deutsch, J. D. Elsworth, R. H. Roth, and D. E. Redmond, Jr. Reversal of Parkinsonism by fetal nerve cell transplants in primate brain. *Proceedings of the New York Academy of Science*, 1987, *495*, 641–657. [3]

Slavin, R. E. Cooperative learning: Applying contact theory in desegregated schools. *Journal of Social Issues*, 1985, *41*, 45–62. [21]

Slovic, P., and B. Fischhoff. On the psychology of experimental surprises. *Journal of Experimental Psychology: Human Perception and Performance*, 1977, *3*, 544–551. [9]

Smeaton, G., D. Byrne, and S. K. Murnen. The repulsion hypothesis revisited: Similarity irrelevance of dissimilarity bias? *Journal of Personality and Social Psychology*, 1989, *56*, 54–59. [21]

Smetana, J. G. Adolescents' and parents' conceptions of parental authority. *Child Development*, 1988, *59*, 321–335. [16]

Smith, A., and O. Sugar. Development of above-normal language and intelligence twenty-one years after hemispherectomy. *Neurology*, 1975, *25*, 813–818. [10]

Smith, C., and P. Ellsworth. Patterns of cognitive appraisal in emotion. *Journal of Personality and Social Psychology*, 1985, *48*, 813–838. [12]

Smith, C., and P. Ellsworth. Patterns of appraisal and emotion related to taking an exam. *Journal of Personality and Social Psychology*, 1987, *52*, 475–488. [12]

Smith, C. A., D. W. Organ, and J. P. Near. Organizational citizenship behavior: Its nature and antecedents. *Journal of Applied Psychology*, 1983, *68*, 653–663. [23]

Smith, E. E., and D. L. Medin. *Categories and concepts.* Cambridge, Mass.: Harvard University Press, 1981. [9]

Smith, F. J. Work attitudes as predictors of attendance on a specific day. *Journal of Applied Psychology*, 1977, *62*, 16–19. [23]

Smith, K. Test of significance: Some frequent misunderstandings. *Journal of Orthopsychiatry*, 1983, *53*, 315–321. [2]

Smith, M. B. The personal setting of public opinions: A study of attitudes toward Russia. *Public Opinion Quarterly*, 1947, *11*, 507–523. [21]

Smith, M. L., and G. V. Glass. Meta-analysis of psychotherapy outcome studies. *American Psychologist*, 1977, *32*, 752–760. [2, CT1]

Smith, M. L., G. V. Glass, and T. J. Miller. *The benefits of psychotherapy.* Baltimore: Johns Hopkins, 1980. [19]

Smith, P. B., and D. R. Pederson. Maternal sensitivity and patterns of infant-mother attachment. *Child Development*, 1988, *59*, 1097–1101. [15]

Smith, S. Language and non-verbal test performance of racial groups in Honolulu before and after a fourteen-year interval. *Journal of General Psychology*, 1942, *26*, 51–93. [11]

Smith, S. M., A. Glenberg, and R. A. Bjork. Environmental context and human memory. *Memory and Cognition*, 1978, *6*, 342–353. [8]

Smyth, M. M., P. E. Morris, P. Levy, and A. W. Ellis. *Cognition in action*, Hillsdale, N.J.: Erlbaum, 1987. [8]

Snarey, J. A question of morality. *Psychology Today*, June 1987, pp. 6–7. [16]

Snow, C. E. Conversation with children. In P. Fletcher and M. Garman, *Language acquisition.* New York: Cambridge University Press, 1986. [15]

Snow, C. P. Either-or. *Progressive*, 1961, *25* (2). 24–25. [22]

Snow, R. E., and E. Yalow. Education and intelligence. In R. J. Sternberg (Ed.), *Handbook of human intelligence.* New York: Cambridge University Press, 1982, pp 493–585. [11]

Snyder, C. R., R. L. Higgins, and R. J. Stucky. *Excuses: Masquerades in search of grace.* New York: Wiley, 1983. [13]

Snyder, M. Impression management. In L. S. Wrightsman (Ed.), *Social psychology.* Belmont, Calif.: Brooks/Cole, 1977. [18]

Snyder, M. *Public appearance, private reality.* New York: W. H. Freeman, 1987. [17, 21]

Snyder, M., and W. B. Swann, Jr. When actions reflect attitudes: The politics of impression management. *Journal of Personality and Social Psychology*, 1976, *34*, 1034–1042. [21]

Snyder, M., E. D. Tanke, and E. Berscheid. Social perception and interpersonal behavior: On the self-fulfilling nature of social stereotypes. *Journal of Personality and Social Psychology*, 1977, *35*, 656–666. [21]

Snyder, S. H. The true speed trip: Schizophrenia. In D. Goleman and R. J. Davidson (Eds.), *Consciousness: Brain, states of awareness, and mysticism.* New York: Harper & Row, 1979. [6]

Snyder, S. H. Drug and neurotransmitter receptors in the brain. *Science*, 1984, *224*, 22–31. [3]

Sokolov, E. M. Higher nervous functions: The orienting reflex. *Annual Review of Physiology*, 1963, *25*, 545–580. [7]

Solomon, R. L. The opponent-process theory of acquired motivation: The costs of pleasure and the benefits of pain. *American Psychologist*, 1980, *35*, 691–712. [13]

Sopchak, A. L., and A. M. Sutherland. Psychological impact of cancer and its treatment: VII. Exogenous sex hormones and their relation to lifelong adaptations in women with metatastic cancer of the breast. *Cancer*, 1960, *13*, 528–531. [14]

Sorenson, R. C. *Adolescent sexuality in contemporary America.* New York: World, 1973. [14]

Sorosky, A. D. Introduction: An overview of eating disorders. *Adolescent Psychiatry*, 1986, *13*, 221–229. [18]

Spanier, G. B., and R. A. Lewis. Marital quality. *Journal of Marriage and the Family*, 1980, *42*, 825–839. [16]

Spanos, N. P. Hypnotic behavior: A social-psychological interpretation of amnesia, analgesia, and "trance logic." *Behavioral and Brain Sciences*, 1986, *9*, 449–502. [6]

Spear, N. E. *The processing of memories: Forgetting and retention*, Hillsdale, N.J., Erlbaum, 1978. [8]

Spearman, C. "General intelligence" objectively determined and measured. *American Journal of Psychology*, 1904, *15*, 201–293. [11]

Spence, J. T., J. W. Cotton, B. J. Underwood, and C. P. Duncan. *Elementary statistics* (3rd ed.). Englewood Cliffs, N.J.: Prentice-Hall, 1976. [App.]

Spence, K. W. A theory of emotionality based drive (D) and its relation to performance in simple learning situations. *American Psychologist*, 1958, *13*, 131–141. [22]

Sperling, G. The information available in brief visual presentation. *Psychological Monographs*, 1960, *74* (498). [8]

Sperry, R. W. Bridging science and values: A unifying view of mind and brain. *American Psychologist*, 1977, *32*, 237–245. [6]

Spitzer, L., and J. Rodin. Human eating behavior: A critical review of studies in normal weight and overweight individuals. *Appetite: Journal for intake research*, 1981, *2*, 293–329. [13]

Spitzer, M. E. Taste acuity in institutionalized and noninstitutionalized elderly men. *Journal of Gerontology*, 1988, *43*, 71–74. [5]

Spitzer, R. L. More on pseudoscience in science and the case for psychiatric diagnosis: A critique of D. L. Rosenhan's "On being sane in insane places" and "The contextual nature of psychiatric diagnosis." *Archives of General Psychiatry*, 1976, *33*, 459–470. [18]

Spitzer, R. L., A. E. Skodol, M. Gibbon, and J. B. W. Williams. *Psychopathology: A case book.* New York: McGraw-Hill, 1983. [18]

Springer, S. P., and G. Deutsch. *Left brain, right brain* (3rd ed.). San Francisco: Freeman, 1989. [3, 7]

Squire, L. R. *Memory and the brain*, Oxford University Press, 1987. [8]

Squire, L. R., and P. C. Slater. Bilateral and unilateral ECT: Effects on verbal and nonverbal memory. *American Journal of Psychiatry*, 1978, *135*, 1316–1320. [8, 19]

Squire, L. R., P. C. Slater, and P. L. Miller. Retrograde amnesia and bilateral electroconvulsive therapy. *Archives of General Psychiatry*, 1981, *38*, 89–95. [19]

Sroufe, L. A. The organization of emotional development. In K. R. Scherer and P. Ekman (Eds.), *Approaches to emotion.* Hillsdale, N.J.: Erlbaum, 1984. [12]

Sroufe, L. A., N. E. Fox, and V. R. Pancake. Attachment and dependency in developmental perspective. *Child Development*, 1983, *54*, 1615–1627. [15]

Sroufe, L. A., E. Schork, M. Frosso, N. Lawroski, and P. LaFreniere. The role of affect in social competence. In C. Izard, J. Kagan, and R. Zajonc (Eds.), *Emotions, cognitions and behavior.* New York: Cambridge University Press, 1984. [15]

Srull, T. K., and R. S. Wyer. Person memory and judgment. *Psychological Review*, 1989, *96*, 58–83. [21]

Staats, A. W. Outline of an integrated learning theory of attitude formation and function. In M. Fishbein (Ed.), *Attitude theory and measurement.* New York: Wiley, 1967. [7]

Staats, A. W. *Learning, language, and cognition.* New York: Holt, Rinehart and Winston, 1968. [7]

Staats, A. W., and C. K. Staats. Attitudes established by classical conditioning. *Journal of Abnormal and Social Psychology*, 1958, *57*, 37–40. [7]

Staddon, J. E. R., and V. L. Simmelhag. The "superstition" experiment: A reexamination of its implications for the principles of adaptive behavior. *Psychological Review*, 1971, *78*, 3–43. [7]

Stanley, J. C. Education in the fast lane: Methodological problems of evaluating its effects. *Evaluation News*, February 1983, pp. 28–46. [11]

Stark, R. E. Prespeech segmental feature development. In P. Fletcher and M. Garman (Eds.), *Language acquisition.* New York: Cambridge University Press, 1986. [15]

Staw, B. M., and J. Ross. Stability in the midst of change: A dispositional approach to job attitudes. *Journal of Applied Psychology*, 1985, *70*, 469–480. [23]

Steele, B. F., and H. Alexander. Long-term effects of sexual abuse in childhood. In P. B. Mrazek and C. H. Kempe (Eds.), *Sexually abused children and their families.* New York: Pergamon, 1981. [14]

Steele, C. M. The psychology of self-affirmation: Sustaining the integrity of the self. In L. Berkowitz (Ed.), *Advances in experimental social psychology.* (Vol. 21). New York: Academic Press, 1988, pp. 261–302. [21]

Steele, C. M., and T. J. Liu. Dissonance processes as self-affirmation. *Journal of Personality and Social Psychology*, 1983, *45*, 5–19. [21]

Steinberg, L. Transformations in family relations at puberty. *Developmental Psychology*, 1981, *17*, 833–840. [16]

Steinberg, L. *Adolescence.* New York: Knopf, 1985. [16]

Steinberg, L. Reciprocal relation between parent–child distance and pubertal maturation. *Developmental Psychology*, 1988, *24*, 122–128. [16]

Steinberg, L. D., and S. B. Silverberg. The vicissitudes of autonomy in early adolescence. *Child Development*, 1986, *57*, 841–851. [16]

Steiner, J. E. Human facial expressions in response to taste and smell stimulation. In H. Reese and L. P. Lipsitt (Eds.), *Advances in child development and behavior* (Vol. 13). New York: Academic Press, 1979. [5, 15]

Stephan, F. K., and I. Zucker. Circadian rhythms in drinking behavior and locomotor activity in rats are eliminated by hypothalamic lesions. *Proceedings of the National Academy of Sciences (WSA)*, 1972, *69*, 1583–1586. [3]

Steptoe, A. Psychophysiological processes in disease. In A. Steptoe and A. Mathews, eds., *Health care and human behavior.* New York: Academic Press, 1984. [20]

Sterman, M. B. Biofeedback and epilepsy. *Human Nature*, May 1978, *1*, 50–57. [20]

Stern, R. S., and J. P. Cobb. Phenomenology of obsessive-compulsive reactions. *British Journal of Psychiatry*, 1978, *132*, 233–234. [18]

Stern, W. *Psychologische Methoden der Intelligenz-Prüfung.* Leipzig: Barth, 1912. [11]

Sternberg, D. B., J. Martinez, J. L. McGaugh, and P. E. Gold. Age-related memory deficits in rats and mice: Enhancement with peripheral injections of epinephrine. *Behavioral Neural Biology*, 1985, *44*, 213–220. [8]

Sternberg, R. J. *Beyond IQ: A triarchic theory of intelligence.* London: Cambridge University Press, 1985. [11]

Sternberg, R. J. A triangular theory of love. *Psychological Review*, 1986a, *93*, 119–135. [14]

Sternberg, R. J. *Intelligence applied: Understanding and increasing your intellectual skills.* San Diego, Calif.: Harcourt Brace Jovanovich, 1986b. [9]

Sternberg, R. J. The psychology of verbal comprehension. In R. Glaser (Ed.), *Advances in instructional psychology* (Vol. 3). Hillsdale, N.J.: Erlbaum, 1987, pp. 97–151. [9]

Sternberg, R. J., and J. S. Powell. Comprehending verbal comprehension. *American Psychologist*, 1983, *38*, 878–893. [9]

Sternberg, S. High-speed scanning in human memory. *Science*, 1966, *153*, 652–654. [8]

Sternglanz, S. H., and L. A. Serbin. Sex role stereotyping in children's television programs. *Developmental Psychology*, 1974, *10*, 710–715. [15]

Stevens, S. S. On the psychophysical law. *Psychological Review*, 1957, *64*, 153–181. [4]

Stevenson, H. W., T. Parker, A. Wilkinson, B. Bonnevaux, and M. Gonzalez. Schooling, environment, and cognitive development: A cross cultural study. *Monographs of the Society for Research in Child Development*, 1978, *43* (3, Serial No. 175). [11]

Stoch, M. B., P. M. Smythe, A. D. Moodie, and D. Bradshaw. Psychosocial outcome and CT findings after gross undernourishment during infancy: A 20 year developmental study. *Developmental Medicine and Child Neurology*, 1982, *24*, 419–436. [11]

Stoel-Gammon, C., and J. A. Cooper. Patterns of early lexical and phonological development. *Journal of Child Language*, 1984, *11*, 247–271. [15]

Stokols, D. On the distinction between density and crowding: Some implications for future research. *Psychological Review*, 1972, *79*, 275–277. [22]

Storms, M. D. Videotape and the attribution process: Reversing actors' and observers' points of view. *Journal of Personality and Social Psychology*, 1973, *27*, 165–175. [21]

Strack, F., L. L. Martin, and S. Stepper. Inhibiting and facilitating conditions of facial expressions. *Journal of Personality and Social Psychology*, 1988, *54*, 768–777. [12]

Strauss, J. S., W. T. Carpenter, and J. J. Bartko. The diagnosis and understanding of schizophrenia: II. Speculations on the processes that underlie schizophrenic symptoms and signs. *Schizophrenia Bulletin*, 1974, *11*, 61–76. [18]

Strauss, M. E., W. C. Foureman, and S. D. Parwatikar. Schizophrenics' size estimations of thematic stimuli. *Journal of Abnormal Psychology*, 1974, *83*, 117–123. [18]

Strauss, M. S. Abstraction of prototypical information by adults and 10-month-old infants. *Journal of Experimental Psychology: Human Learning and Memory*, 1979, *5*, 618–663. [7]

Straw, R. B. Meta-analysis of deinstitutionalization in mental health. Unpublished doctoral dissertation, Northwestern University, 1982. [19]

Streissguth, A. P., H. M. Barr, P. D. Sampson, B. L. Darby, and D. C. Martin. IQ at age 4 in relation to maternal alcohol use and smoking during pregnancy. *Developmental Psychology*, 1989, *25*, 3–11. [15]

Streissguth, A. P., D. C. Martin, H. M. Barr, B. M. Sandman, G. L. Kirchner, and B. L. Darby. Intrauterine alcohol and nicotine exposure: Attention and reaction time in 4-year-old children. *Developmental Psychology*, 1984, *20*, 533–541. [15]

Stunkard, A. J. Behavioral medicine and beyond: The example of obesity. In O. F. Pomerleau and J. P. Brady (Eds.), *Behavioral medicine: Theory and practice.* Baltimore: Williams & Wilkins, 1979. [20]

Stunkard, A. J., M. R. J. Felix, and R. Y. Cohen. Mobilizing a community to promote health: The Pennsylvania County Health Improvement Program (CHIP). In J. C. Rosen and L. J. Solomon (Eds.), *Prevention in health psychology.* Hanover, N.H.: University Press of New England, 1985. [20]

Sullivan, H. S. *Schizophrenia as a human process.* New York: Norton, 1962. [18]

Super, C. M. Environmental effects on motor development: The case of "African infant precocity." *Developmental Medicine and Child Neurology*, 1976, *18*, 561–567. [15]

Szasz, T. S. *The myth of mental illness: Foundations of a theory of personal conduct.* New York: Harper & Row, 1961. [18]

Szymanski, K., and S. G. Harkins. Social loafing and self-evaluation with a standard. *Journal of Personality and Social Psychology*, 1987, *53*, 891–897. [22]

Tabachnik, N., J. Crocker, and **L. B. Alloy.** Depression, social comparison, and the false consensus effect. *Journal of Personality and Social Psychology,* 1983, *45,* 688–699. [13]

Tajfel, H., A. A. Sheikh, and **R. C. Gardner.** Content of stereotypes and the inference of similarity between members of stereotyped groups. *Acta Psychologica,* 1964, *22,* 191–201. [21]

Tajfel, H., and **J. C. Turner.** The social identity theory of intergroup behavior. In S. Worchel and W. G. Austin (Eds.), *Psychology of intergroup relations.* (2nd ed.). Chicago: Nelson-Hall, 1986, pp. 7–24. [21]

Tanfer, K., and **M. C. Horn.** Contraceptive use, pregnancy and fertility patterns among single American women in their 20's. *Family Planning Perspectives,* 1985, *17* (1), 10–19. [14]

Tanford, S., and **S. Penrod.** Social influence model: A formal integration of research on majority and minority influence processes. *Psychological Bulletin,* 1984, *95,* 189–225. [22]

Tanner, J. M. *Fetus into man.* Cambridge, Mass.: Harvard University Press, 1978. [16]

Taraban, R., and **J. McClelland.** Conspiracy effects in word pronunciation. *Journal of Memory and Language,* 1987, *26,* 608–631. [10]

Tartter, V. C. *Language processes.* New York: Holt, Rinehart and Winston, 1986. [10]

Task Force on Consumer Issues in Psychotherapy. *Women and psychotherapy: A consumer handbook.* Washington, D.C.: Federation of Organizations for Professional Women, n.d. [19]

Taylor, S. E. A categorization approach to stereotyping. In D. L. Hamilton (Ed.), *Cognitive processes in stereotyping and intergroup behavior.* Hillsdale, N.J.: Erlbaum, 1981, pp. 83–114. [21]

Taylor, S. E. The availability bias in social perception and interaction. In D. Kahneman, P. Slovic, and A. Tversky (Eds.), *Judgment under uncertainty: Heuristics and biases.* New York: Cambridge University Press, 1982. [21]

Taylor, S. E. *Health psychology.* New York: Random House, 1986. [20, 21]

Taylor, S. E., and **J. Brown.** Illusion and well-being: A social psychological perspective on mental health. *Psychological Bulletin,* 1988, *103,* 193–210. [13, 18, 20]

Taylor, S. E., and **J. Crocker.** Schematic bases of social information processing. In E. T. Higgins, C. P. Herman, and M. P. Zanna (Eds.), *Social cognition: The Ontario Symposium* (Vol. 1). Hillsdale, N.J.: Erlbaum, 1981. [13]

Taylor, S. E., and **S. T. Fiske.** Point-of-view and perceptions of causality. *Journal of Personality and Social Psychology,* 1975, *32,* 439–445. [21]

Taylor, S. E., S. T. Fiske, N. L. Etcoff, and **A. J. Ruderman.** Categorical and contextual bases of person memory and stereotyping. *Journal of Personality and Social Psychology,* 1978, *36,* 778–793. [21]

Tedeschi, J. T., B. R. Schlenker, and **T. V. Bonoma.** Cognitive dissonance: Private ratiocination or public spectacle? *American Psychologist,* 1971, *26,* 685–695. [21]

Temoshak, L., D. M. Sweet, and **J. Zich.** A three city comparison of the public's knowledge and attitudes about AIDS. *Psychology and Health,* 1987, *1,* 43–60. [20]

Tennen, H., and **S. Herzberger.** Depression, self-esteem, and the absence of self-protective attributional biases. *Journal of Personality and Social Psychology,* 1987, *52,* 72–80. [13]

Terman, L. M. *The measurement of intelligence.* Boston: Houghton Mifflin, 1916. [11]

Terman, L. M., and **M. A. Merrill.** *Stanford-Binet Intelligence Scale: Manual for the third revision, Form L-M.* Boston: Houghton Mifflin, 1973. [11]

Terman, L. M., and **M. H. Oden.** *The gifted child grows up.* Stanford, Calif.: Stanford University Press, 1947. [11]

Terman, L. M., and **M. H. Oden.** *The gifted group at mid-life: Thirty-five years follow-up of the superior child.* Stanford, Calif.: Stanford University Press, 1959. [11]

Tesser, A. Some effects of self-evaluation maintenance on cognition and action. In R. M. Sorrentino and E. T. Higgins (Eds.), *Handbook of motivation and cognition: Foundations of social behavior.* New York: Guilford, 1986. [13]

Tesser, A. Toward a self-evaluation maintenance model of social behavior. In L. Berkowitz (Ed.), *Advances in experimental social psychology* (Vol. 21). New York: Academic Press, 1988. [13]

Tesser, A., and **J. Campbell.** Self-definition and self-evaluation maintenance. In J. Suhls and A. G. Greenwald (Eds.), *Psychological perspectives on the self* (Vol. 2). Hillsdale, N.J.: Erlbaum, 1983. [13]

Thayer, P. W. Industrial/organizational psychology: Science and applications. *G. Stanley Hall Lecture Series* (Vol. 3). Washington, D.C.: American Psychological Association, 1983, pp. 5–30. [23]

Thelen, E. The role of motor development in developmental psychology. In N. Eisenberg (Ed.), *Contemporary topics in developmental psychology.* New York: Wiley, 1987. [15]

Thigpen, C. H., and **H. Cleckley.** *The three faces of Eve.* New York: McGraw-Hill, 1957. [18]

Thoenen, H., and **D. Edgar.** Neurotrophic factors. *Science,* 1985, *229,* 238–242. [15]

Thomas, A., and **S. Chess.** *Temperament and development.* New York: Brunner/Mazel, 1977. [15]

Thomas, E. L., and **H. A. Robinson.** *Improving reading in every class: A sourcebook for teachers.* Boston: Allyn and Bacon, 1972. [8]

Thompson, J. K., G. J. Jarvie, B. B. Lahey, and **K. J. Cureton.** Exercise and obesity: Etiology, physiology, and intervention. *Psychological Bulletin,* 1982, *91,* 55–79. [13]

Thompson, L. High-tech hearing aids for the deaf. *San Jose Mercury News,* June 12, 1984, pp. C1–2. [4]

Thompson, R. A., M. E. Lamb, and **D. Estes.** Stability of infant–mother attachment and its relationship to changing life circumstances in an unselected middle-class sample. *Child Development,* 1982, *53,* 144–148. [15]

Thompson, S. C. Will it hurt less if I can control it? A complex answer to a simple question. *Psychological Bulletin,* 1981, *90,* 89–101. [20]

Thorndike, E. L. Animal intelligence. *Psychological Review Monograph,* 1898, 2. [7]

Thorndike, E. L. *Animal intelligence.* New York: Macmillan, 1911. [7]

Thorndike, E. L. *The psychology of learning.* New York: Teachers College, 1913. [7]

Thornton, G. C., and **W. C. Byham.** *Assessment centers and managerial performance.* New York: Academic Press, 1982. [23]

Thresher, A. Girth of a nation. *Nation's Business,* 1986, *74,* 50. [13]

Tichy, N., and **M. A. DeVanna.** *The transformational leader.* New York: Wiley, 1986. [23]

Time. Sex and schools: AIDS and the Surgeon General add a new urgency to an old debate. By J. Leo. November 24, 1986, 54–62. [14]

Tizard, B., and **J. Hodges.** The effect of early institutional rearing in the development of 8-year-old children. *Journal of Child Psychology and Psychiatry,* 1978, *19,* 99–118. [15]

Toi, M., and **C. D. Batson.** More evidence that empathy is a source of altruistic motivation. *Journal of Personality and Social Psychology,* 1982, *43,* 281–292. [22]

Tolman, E. C. *Purposive behavior in animals and men.* New York: Appleton-Century-Crofts, 1932. [7]

Tolman, E. C. Cognitive maps in rats and men. *Psychological Review,* 1948, *55,* 189–208. [7]

Tolman, E. C. Principles of purposive behavior. In S. Koch (Ed.), *Psychology: A* *study of science.* (Vol. 2). New York: McGraw-Hill, 1959. [13]

Tolman, E. C., and C. H. Honzik. Introduction and removal of reward and maze performance in rats. *University of California Publications in Psychology,* 1930, *4,* 257–275. [7]

Tomkins, S. S. *Affect, imagery, and consciousness,* Vol. 1. *The positive affects.* New York: Springer, 1962. [12]

Tomkins, S. S. *Affect, imagery and consciousness.* Vol. 2: *The negative affects.* New York: Springer, 1963. [12]

Torgersen, A. M., and E. Kringlen. Genetic aspects of temperament differences in twins. *Journal of American Academy of Child Psychiatry,* 1978, *17,* 433–444. [17]

Torgersen, S. Genetic factors in anxiety disorders. *Archives of General Psychiatry,* 1983, *40,* 1085–1089. [18]

Tourangeau, R., and P. C. Ellsworth. The role of facial response in the experience of emotion. *Journal of Personality and Social Psychology,* 1979, *37,* 1519–1531. [12]

Travis, L. E. The effect of a small audience upon hand-eye coordination. *Journal of Abnormal and Social Psychology,* 1925, *20,* 142–146. [22]

Triandis, H. C. *Attitude and attitude change.* New York: Wiley, 1971. [21]

Triplett, N. The dynamogenic factors in peacemaking and competition. *American Journal of Psychology,* 1897, *9,* 507–533. [22]

Trivers, R. L. The evolution of reciprocal altruism. *Quarterly Review of Biology,* 1971, *46,* 35–57. [22]

Trowell, I. Telephone services. In L. D. Hankoff and B. Einsidler (Eds.), *Suicide: Theory and clinical aspects.* Littleton, Mass.: PSG Publishing, 1979. [19]

Tucker, D. M. Lateral brain function, emotion, and conceptualization. *Psychological Bulletin,* 1981, *89,* 19–46. [3]

Tulving, E., and J. Psotka. Retroactive inhibition in free recall: Inaccessibility of information available in the memory store. *Journal of Experimental Psychology,* 1971, *87,* 1–8. [8]

Tulving, E., and D. M. Thomson. Encoding specificity and retrieval processes in episodic memory. *Psychological Review,* 1973, *80,* 352–373. [8]

Turk, D. C., D. H. Meichenbaum, and W. H. Berman. Application of biofeedback for the regulation of pain: A critical review. *Psychological Bulletin,* 1979, *86,* 1322–1338. [20]

Turkewitz, G., and P. A. Kenny. Limitations on input as a basis for neural organization and perceptual development. *Developmental Psychobiology,* 1982, *15,* 357–368. [15]

Tversky, A., and D. Kahneman. Judgment

under uncertainty: Heuristics and biases. *Science,* 1973, *185,* 1124–1131. [9]

Tversky, A., and D. Kahneman. The framing of decisions and the psychology of choice. *Science,* 1981, *211,* 453–458. [9]

Tversky, A., and D. Kahneman. Judgments of and by representativeness. In D. Kahneman, P. Slovic, and A. Tversky (Eds.), *Judgment under uncertainty: Heuristics and biases.* New York: Cambridge University Press, 1982. [9]

Tversky, A., and D. Kahneman. Extensional versus intuitive reasoning: The conjunction fallacy in probability judgment. *Psychological Review,* 1983, *90,* 293–315. [9]

Tversky, A., R. Vallone, and T. Gilovich. Misconception of chance processes in basketball. Submitted to *Science,* 1984. [9]

Tversky, B. Distortions in memory for maps. *Cognitive Psychology,* 1981, *13,* 407–433. [7]

Uhlenhuth, E. H., M. B. Balter, G. D. Mellinger, I. H. Cisin, and J. Clinthorne. Symptom checklist syndromes in the general population. *Archives of General Psychiatry,* 1983, *40,* 1167–1173. [19]

Ullmann, L. P., and L. Krasner (Eds.). *Case studies in behavior modification.* New York: Holt, Rinehart and Winston, 1965. [18]

U.S. Bureau of Justice Statistics. *Report to the nation on crime and justice.* Washington, D.C.: U.S. Government Printing Office, 1983. [16]

U.S. Department of Health and Human Services. *The fourth special report to the United States Congress on alcohol and health.* Washington, D.C.: Alcohol, Drug Abuse, and Mental Health Administration, January 1981. [18]

Vaillant, G. E., and E. Milofsky. Natural history of male psychological health. *American Journal of Psychiatry,* 1980, *137,* 1348–1359. [16]

Valenstein, E. S. *Great and desperate cures: The rise and decline of psychosurgery and other radical treatments for mental illness.* New York: Basic Books, 1986. [19]

Vance, E. B., and N. W. Wagner. Written descriptions of orgasm: A study of sex differences. *Archives of Sexual Behavior,* 1976, *5,* 87–98. [14]

Van Court, M., and F. D. Bean. Intelligence and fertility in the United States. *Intelligence,* 1985, *9,* 23–32. [11]

Vandell, D. L., V. K. Henderson, and K. S. Wilson. A longitudinal survey of children with day-care experiences of varying quality. *Child Development,* 1988, *49,* 1286–1292. [15]

Van Kammen, D. P. Y-aminobutyric acid (GABA) and the dopamine hypothesis of schizophrenia. *American Journal of Psychiatry,* 1977, *134,* 138–143. [18]

Vassos, J. *Phobia.* New York: Covici and Friede, 1931. [18]

Vaughan, C. E., K. Snyder, S. Jones, W. B. Freeman, and I. R. H. Falloon. Family factors in schizophrenic relapse: A replication in California of British research on expressed emotion. *Archives of General Psychiatry,* 1984, *41,* 1169–1177. [18, 19]

Vellotino, F. R. Dyslexia. *Scientific American,* 1987, *256,* 20–27. [10]

Vernon, P. Psychological effects of air raids. *Journal of Abnormal and Social Psychology,* 1941, *36,* 457–476. [20]

Visintainer, M. A., J. R. Volpicelli, and M. E. P. Seligman. Tumor rejection in rats after inescapable or escapable shock. *Science,* 1982, *216,* 437–439. [20]

Vitaliano, P. P., J. Russo, A. R. Bren, M. V. Vitellio, and P. N. Prinz. Functional decline in the early stages of Alzheimer's disease. *Psychology and Aging,* 1986, *1,* 41–46. [16]

von der Heydt, R., E. Peterhans, and G. Baumgartner. Illusory contours and cortical neuron responses. *Science,* 1984, *224,* 1260–1262. [5]

von Hofsten, C. Developmental changes in the organization of prereaching movements. *Developmental Psychology,* 1984, *20,* 378–388. [15]

Vroom, V. H. *Work and motivation.* New York: Wiley, 1964. [23]

Vroom, V. H., and A. G. Jago. *The new leadership.* Englewood Cliffs, N.J.: Prentice-Hall, 1988. [23]

Vroom, V. H., and P. W. Yetton. In K. N. Wexley and G. A. Yukl (Eds.), *Organizational behavior and industrial psychology.* New York: Oxford, 1975. [23]

Wachtel, P. L. On theory, practice, and the nature of integration. In H. Arkowitz and S. B. Messer (Eds.), *Psychoanalytic therapy and behavior therapy: Is integration possible?* New York: Plenum Press, 1984. [17]

Wadden, T. A., and C. H. Anderson. The clinical use of hypnosis. *Psychological Bulletin,* 1982, *91,* 215–243. [6]

Wagner, A. R. Stimulus validity and stimulus selection in associative learning. In N. J. Mackintosh and W. K. Honig (Eds.), *Fundamental issues in associative learning.* Halifax: Dalhousie University Press, 1969. [7]

Wagner, D. A. The development of short-term and incidental memory: A cross-cultural study. *Child Development,* 1974, *45,* 389–396. [11]

Wagner, D. A. Memories of Morocco: The influence of age, schooling and environment on memory. *Cognitive Psychology*, 1978, *10*, 1–28. [11]

Wagner, R. V. Complementary needs, role expectations, interpersonal attraction, and the stability of working relationships. *Journal of Personality and Social Psychology*, 1975, *32*, 116–124. [21]

Wahba, M. A., and **L. B. Bridwell.** Maslow reconsidered: A review of research on the need hierarchy theory. *Organizational Behavior and Human Performance*, 1976, *15*, 212–240. [23]

Waldrop, M. A. *Man made minds: The promise of artificial intelligence.* New York: Walker, 1987. [9]

Waldrop, M. M. Toward a unified theory of cognition. *Science*, 1988a, *241*, 27–29. [9]

Waldrop, M. M. SOAR: A unified theory of cognition. *Science*, 1988b, *241*, 296–298. [9]

Walker, J. I., and **J. O. Cavenar.** Vietnam veterans: Their problems continue. *Journal of Nervous and Mental Disease*, 1982, *170*, 174–180. [20]

Walker, J. T., R. C. Rupich, and **J. L. Powell.** The vista paradox: A natural visual illusion. *Perception and Psychophysics*, 1989, *45*, 43–48. [5]

Walker, L. K. Sex differences in the development of moral reasoning: A critical review. *Child Development*, 1984, *55*, 677–691. [16]

Wallach, M. A. Tests tell us little about talent. *American Scientist*, 1976, *64*, 57–63. [11]

Wallach, M. A. Creativity testing and giftedness. In F. D. Horowitz and M. O'Brien (Eds.), *The gifted and talented: Developmental perspectives.* Washington, D.C.: American Psychological Association, 1985, pp. 99–124. [11]

Walsh, D. A. Age differences in learning and memory. In D. S. Woodruff and J. E. Birren (Eds.), *Aging: Scientific perspectives and social issues* (2nd ed.). Monterey, Calif.: Brooks/Cole, 1983. [16]

Wandersman, A., A. Andrews, D. Riddle, and **C. Fancett.** Environmental psychology and prevention. In R. D. Feiner, L. A. Jason, J. N. Moritsugu, and S. S. Farber (Eds.), *Preventive psychology: Theory, research and practice.* New York: Pergamon Press, 1985. [20]

Wanous, J. P., and **R. A. Dean.** The effects of realistic job previews on hiring bank tellers. *Journal of Applied Psychology*, 1984, *69*. [23]

Waring, E. M., M. P. Tillman, L. Frelick, L. Russell, and **G. Weisz.** Concepts of intimacy in the general population. *Journal of Nervous and Mental Disease*, 1980, *168*, 471–474. [14]

Warren, R. M. Perceptual restoration of missing speech sounds. *Science*, 1970, *167*, 392–393. [5]

Warrington, E. K., and **L. Weiskrantz.** New method of testing long-term retention with special reference to amnesiac patients. *Nature*, 1968, *217*, 972–974. [8]

Washington v. Davis. 426 U.S. 299 (1976). [23]

Wason, P. C. Reasoning about a rule. *Quarterly Journal of Experimental Psychology*, 1968, *20*, 273–281. [2]

Waterman, A. S. Identity status theory and Erikson's theory: Communalities and differences. *Developmental Review*, 1988, *8*, 185–208. [16]

Waterman, D. A. *A guide to expert systems.* Reading, Mass.: Addison-Wesley, 1986. [9]

Waters, E., J. Wippman, and **L. A. Sroufe.** Attachment, positive effect, and competence in the peer group: Two studies in contrast. *Child Development*, 1979, *50*, 821–829. [15]

Watson, J. B., and **R. Rayner.** Conditioned emotional reactions. *Journal of Experimental Psychology*, 1920, *3*, 1–14. [7]

Watzlawick, P., J. Weakland, and **R. Fisch.** *Change: Principles of problem formation and problem resolution.* New York: Norton, 1974. [19]

Waxenberg, S. E. Psychotherapeutic and dynamic implications of recent research on female sexual functioning. In G. D. Goldman and D. S. Milman (Eds.), *Modern woman: Her psychology and sexuality.* Springfield, Ill.: Charles C Thomas, 1969. [14]

Weale, R. A. *A biography of the eye.* London: Lewis, 1982. [5]

Webb, W. B. Sleep and dream. In B. B. Wolman (Ed.), *Handbook of general psychology.* Englewood Cliffs, N.J.: Prentice-Hall, 1973. [6]

Webb, W. B. *Sleep: The gentle tyrant.* Englewood Cliffs, N.J.: Prentice-Hall, 1975. [6]

Weber, M. *Authority and legitimacy. The theory of social and economic organization* (1922). New York: Free Press, 1947, pp. 324–333, 341–345, 358–363. [23]

Weber, R., and **J. Crocker.** Cognitive processes in the revision of stereotypic beliefs. *Journal of Personality and Social Psychology*, 1983, *45*, 961–977. [21]

Weg, R. B. Changing physiology of aging. In D. S. Woodruff and J. E. Birren (Eds.), *Aging* (2nd ed.). Monterey, Calif.: Brooks/Cole, 1983. [16]

Weiner, B. *Theories of motivation: From mechanism to cognition.* Chicago: Markham, 1972. [13]

Weiner, B. An attributional theory of achievement motivation and emotion. *Psychological Review*, 1985, *92*, 548–573. [12, 13]

Weiner, B. Attribution, emotion, and action. In R. M. Sorrentino and E. T. Higgins (Eds.), *Handbook of motivation and cognition: Foundations of social behavior.* New York: Guilford, 1986a. [13]

Weiner, B. *An attribution theory of motivation and emotion.* New York: Springer-Verlag, 1986b. [13]

Weiner, I. B. Psychopathology in adolescence. In J. Adelson (Ed.), *Handbook of adolescent psychology.* New York: Wiley, 1980. [18]

Weiner, I. B. *Child and adolescent psychopathology.* New York: Wiley, 1982. [16]

Weinraub, M., E. Jaeger, and **L. W. Hoffman.** Predicting infant outcome in families of employed and non-employed mothers. *Early Childhood Research Quarterly*, in press. [15]

Weisberg, R. *Creativity: Genius and other myths.* New York: Freeman, 1986. [9]

Weiskrantz, L., E. K. Warrington, M. D. Sanders, and **J. Marshall.** Visual capacity of the hemianopic field following a restricted occipital ablation. *Brain*, 1974, *97*, 709–728. [6]

Weiss, R. S. Attachment in adult life. In C. M. Parkes and J. Stevenson-Hinde (Eds.), *The place of attachment in human behavior.* New York: Basic Books, 1982.

Weitzenhoffer, A. M., and **E. R. Hilgard.** *Stanford hypnotic susceptibility scale.* (Form A and Form B). Palo Alto, Calif.: Consulting Psychologists Press, 1959. [6]

Wender, P. H., S. S. Kety, D. Rosenthal, F. Schulsinger, J. Ortmann, and **I. Lunde.** Psychiatric disorders in the biological and adoptive families of adopted individuals with affective disorders. *Archives of General Psychiatry*, 1986, *43*, 923–929. [18]

Wendt, G. R. Vestibular functions. In S. S. Stevens (Ed.), *Handbook of experimental psychology.* New York: Wiley, 1951. [4]

Werner, A. Sexual dysfunction in college men and women. *American Journal of Psychiatry*, 1975, *132*, 164–168. [14]

Wertheimer, M. Untersuchunger zur Lehre von der Gestalt. *Psychologisches Forschung*, 1923, *4*, 301–350. [5]

White, R. W. *The enterprise of living: Growth and organization in personality.* New York: Holt, Rinehart and Winston, 1972. [21]

Whitfield, I. C. The organization of the auditory pathways. *Journal of sound and vibration research*, 1968, *8*, 108–117. [4]

Whorf, B. L. Science and linguistics. In J. B. Carroll (Ed.), *Language, thought, and reality: Selected writings of Benjamin Lee Whorf.* Cambridge, Mass.: MIT Press, 1940/1956. [10]

Whybrow, P. C., H. S. Akiskal, and **W. T. McKinney, Jr.** *Mood disorders: Toward a new psychobiology.* New York: Plenum Press, 1984. [18]

Whybrow, P. C., and **A. J. Prange, Jr.** A hypothesis of thyroid-catecholamine-receptor interaction. *Archives of General Psychiatry,* 1981, *38,* 106–113. [18]

Wichman, H. Effects of isolation and communication in a two-person game. *Journal of Personality and Social Psychology,* 1970, *16,* 114–120. [22]

Widom, C. S. Sampling biases and implications for child abuse research. *American Journal of Orthopsychiatry,* 1988, *58,* 260–270. [2]

Wilder, D. A. Perceiving persons as a group: Categorization and intergroup relations. In D. L. Hamilton (Ed.), *Cognitive processes in stereotyping and intergroup behavior.* Hillsdale, N.J.: Erlbaum, 1981. [21]

Wilder, D. A. Cognitive factors affecting the success of intergroup contact. In S. Worchel and W. G. Austin (Eds.), *Social psychology of intergroup relations,* Chicago: Nelson-Hall, 1986, pp. 49–66. [21]

Wilkes, K. W.—, yishi, duh, um, and consciousness. In A. J. Marcel and E. Bisiach (Eds.), *Consciousness in contemporary science.* Oxford: Clarendon Press, 1988. [6]

Williams, A. F., M. A. Peat, D. J. Cronch, J. K. Wells, and **B. S. Finkle.** Drugs in fatally injured young male drivers. *Public Health Reports,* 1985, *100,* 19–25. [6]

Williams, K., S. Harkins, and **B. Latané.** Identifiability as a deterrent to social loafing: Two cheering experiments. *Journal of Personality and Social Psychology,* 1981, *40,* 303–311. [6]

Williams, M. D., and **J. D. Hollan.** The process of retrieval from very long-term memory. *Cognitive Science,* 1981, *5,* 87–119. [8]

Williams, R. B., J. D. Lane, C. M. Kuh, W. Melosh, A. D. White, and **S. M. Schanberg.** Physiological and neuroendocrine response patterns during different behavioral challenges: Differential hyperresponsivity of young Type A men. *Science,* 1982, *218,* 483–485. [20]

Williams, R. L., I. Karacan, and **C. J. Hursch.** *EEG of human sleep: Clinical applications.* New York: Wiley, 1974. [6]

Willis, S. L. Educational psychology of the older adult learner. In J. E. Birren and K. W. Schaie (Eds.), *Handbook of the psychology of aging* (2nd ed.). New York: Van Nostrand Reinhold, 1985. [16]

Wills, T. A. Downward comparison principles in social psychology. *Psychological Bulletin,* 1981, *90,* 245–271. [12]

Wilson, E. O. *Sociobiology: The new synthesis.* Cambridge, Mass.: Harvard University Press, 1975. [4]

Wilson, E. O. *On human nature.* Cam-bridge, Mass.: Harvard University Press, 1978. [4]

Wilson, G. T., and **K. D. O'Leary.** *Principles of behavior therapy.* Englewood Cliffs, N.J.: Prentice-Hall, 1980. [7]

Wilson, J. Q., and **R. Herrnstein.** *Crime and human nature.* New York: Simon & Schuster, 1985. [16]

Wilson, W., and **R. Durrenberger.** Comparison of rape and attempted rape victims. *Psychological Reports,* 1982, *50,* 198. [14]

Winch, R. F. *Mate selection: A study of complementary needs.* New York: Harper & Row, 1958. [21]

Wing, R. R., and **R. J. Jeffrey.** Outpatient treatment of obesity: A comparison of methodology and results. *International Journal of Obesity,* 1979, *3,* 261–279. [13]

Winick, M., K. K. Meyer, and **R. C. Harris.** Malnutrition and environmental enrichment by early adoption. *Science,* 1975, *190,* 1173–1175. [11]

Winter, D. G. Reconstructing introductory psychology. In K. I. Spear (Ed.), *Rejuvenating introductory courses.* New Directions for Teaching and Learning (No. 20). San Francisco: Jossey-Bass, 1984. [1]

Winters, K. C., C. S. Newmark, A. E. Lumry, K. Leach, and **S. Weintraub.** MMPI codetypes characteristic of DSM-III schizophrenics, depressives, and bipolars. *Journal of Clinical Psychology,* 1985, *41,* 382–386. [17]

Wise, R., and **M. Bozarth.** A psychomotor stimulant theory of addiction. *Psychological Review,* 1987, *94,* 469–492. [13]

Wise, S. P., and **R. Desimone.** Behavioral neurophysiology: Insights into seeing and grasping. *Science,* 1988, *242,* 736–741. [5]

Wissler, C. The correlation of mental and physical traits. Contributions of the Department of Philosophy and Psychology, Columbia University (Vol. 9, No. 2). New York: Macmillan, 1901. [11]

Witty, P. A., and **M. D. Jenkins.** Intra-race testing and Negro intelligence. *Journal of Psychology,* 1936, *1,* 179–192. [11]

Wohlwill, J. F. Cognitive development in childhood. In O. G. Brim, Jr., and J. Kagan (Eds.), *Constancy and change in human development.* Cambridge, Mass.: Harvard University Press, 1980. [11, 15]

Wolkowitz, O. W., J. R. Tinklenberg, and **H. Weingartner.** A psychopharmacological perspective of cognitive function. *Neuropsychobiology,* 1985, *14,* 133–156. [8]

Wolff, S., and **H. G. Wolff.** *Human gastric function.* New York: Oxford University Press, 1947. [12]

Wolpe, J. *Psychotherapy by reciprocal inhibi-tion.* Stanford, Calif.: Stanford University Press, 1958. [7, 19, 24]

Wolpe, J. Cognition and causation in human behavior and its therapy. *American Psychologist,* 1978, *33,* 437–446. [19]

Wood, J., S. E. Taylor, and **R. Lichtman.** Social comparison in adjustment to breast cancer. *Journal of Personality and Social Psychology,* 1985, *49,* 1169–1183. [12, 21]

Woodruff, R. A., P. J. Clayton, and **S. B. Guze.** Is everyone depressed? *American Journal of Psychiatry,* 1975, *132,* 627–628. [18]

Woodward, W. R., and **M. G. Ash.** (Eds.). *The problematic science: Psychology in nineteenth-century thought.* New York: Praeger Publishers, 1982. [1]

Woodworth, R. S. *Experimental psychology.* New York: Holt, Rinehart & Winston, 1938. [12]

Woolsey, C. N. Organization of the cortical auditory system. In W. A. Rosenblith (Ed.), *Sensory communication.* New York: Wiley, 1961. [3]

Worringham, C. J., and **D. M. Messick.** Social facilitation of running: An unobtrusive study. *Journal of Social Psychology,* 1983, *121,* 23–29. [22]

Wright, J., and **W. Mischel.** A conditional approach to dispositions. *Journal of Personality and Social Psychology,* 1987, *51.* [17]

Wright, J. C. *Problem solving and search behavior under noncontingent rewards.* Unpublished Ph.D. dissertation, Stanford University, 1960. [7]

Wylie, R. *The self-concept* (Vol. 2). Lincoln: University of Nebraska Press, 1979. [21]

Wynder, E. L., T. Kajitani, J. Kuno, J. C. Lucas, Jr., A. DePalo, and **J. Farrow.** A comparison of survival rates between American and Japanese patients with breast cancer. *Surgery, Gynecology, Obstetrics,* 1963, *117,* 196–200. [20]

Wynne, L. C., M. T. Singer, J. J. Bartko, and **M. L. Toohey.** Schizophrenics and their families: Recent research on parental communication. In J. M. Tanner (Ed.), *Psychiatric research: The widening perspective.* New York: International Universities Press, 1975. [18]

Yalom, I. D. *The theory and practice of group psychotherapy* (2nd ed.). New York: Basic Books, 1975. [19]

Yamane, S., S. Kaji, and **K. Kawano.** What facial features activate face neurons in the infertemporal cortex of the monkey? *Experimental Brain Research,* 1988, *73,* 209–214. [5]

Yates, A. J. *Biofeedback and the modification of behavior.* New York: Plenum Press, 1980. [20]

Yegedis, B. L. Date rape and other forced sexual encounters among college students. *Journal of Sex Education and Therapy*, 1986, *12*, 51–54. [14]

Yeomans, James M., and David E. Irwin. Stimulus duration and partial report performance. *Perception and Psychophysics*, 1985, *37*(2), 163–169. [8]

Yerkes, R. M., and J. D. Dodson. The relation of strength of stimulus to rapidity of habit formation. *Journal of Comparative Neurology and Psychology*, 1908, *18*, 459–482. [8, 17]

Young, F. A. Primate myopia. *American Journal of Optometry and Physiological Optics*, 1981, *58*, 560–566. [4]

Younger, B. A., and L. B. Cohen. Infant perception of correlations among attributes. *Child Development*, 1983, *54*, 858–867. [7]

Younger, B. A., and L. B. Cohen. How infants form categories. In G. H. Bower (Ed.), *The psychology of learning and motivation* (Vol. 19). Orlando, Fla.: Academic Press, 1985, pp. 211–248. [7]

Yukl, G. A. *Leadership in organizations* (2nd ed.). Englewood Cliffs, N.J.: Prentice-Hall, 1989. [23]

Zajonc, R. B. Social facilitation. *Science*, 1965, *149*, 269–274. [22]

Zajonc, R. B. Validating the confluence model. *Psychological Bulletin*, 1983, *93*, 457–480. [11]

Zajonc, R. B. Emotion and facial efference: A theory reclaimed. *Science*, 1985, *228*, 15–21. [12]

Zajonc, R. B., S. Murphy, and M. Inglehart. Feeling and facial efference: Implications of the vascular theory of emotion. *Psychological Review*, 1989, *96*, 395–416. [12]

Zanna, M. P., and J. Cooper. Dissonance and the pill: An attribution approach to studying the arousal properties of dissonance. *Journal of Personality and Social Psychology*, 1974, *29*, 703–709. [21]

Zanna, M. P., C. A. Kiesler, and P. A. Pilkonis. Positive and negative attitudinal affect established by classical conditioning. *Journal of Personality and Social Psychology*, 1970, *14*, 321–328. [21]

Zarit, S. H. *Aging and mental disorders*. New York: Free Press, 1980. [16]

Zax, M., and G. Stricker. *Patterns of psychopathology: Case studies in behavioral dysfunction*. New York: Macmillan, 1963. [18]

Zelnick, M., J. F. Kantner, and K. Ford. *Sex and pregnancy in adolescence*. Beverly Hills, Calif.: Sage, 1981. [14]

Zihl, J., D. von Cramon, and N. Mai. Selective disturbance of movement vision after bilateral brain damage. *Brain*, 1983, *106*, 313–340. [5]

Zillman, D. Excitation transfer in communication-mediated aggressive behavior. *Journal of Experimental Social Psychology*, 1971, *7*, 419–434. [12]

Zillman, D., and J. R. Cantor. Effect of timing of information about mitigating circumstances on emotional responses to provocation and retaliatory behavior. *Journal of Experimental Social Psychology*, 1976, *12*, 38–55. [22]

Zimbardo, P. G., C. Haney, and W. C. Banks. *A Pirandellian prison. The New York Times Magazine*, April 8, 1973, pp. 38–60. [22]

Zimmerman, M., W. Coryell, and B. Pfohl. The validity of four definitions of endogenous depression: II. Clinical, demographic, familial, and psychosocial correlates. *Archives of General Psychiatry*, 1986, *43*, 234–244. [18]

Zinberg, N. E., W. M. Harding, and R. Apsler. What is drug-abuse? *Journal of Drug Issues*, 1978, *8*, 9–35. [13]

Zucker, R. A. The four alcoholisms. In *Nebraska Symposium on Motivation* (Vol. 14). Lincoln: University of Nebraska Press, 1987. [16]

Zuckerman, M. The search for high sensation. *Psychology Today*, 1978, *11*, 30–46. [13]

NAME INDEX

CREDITS AND ACKNOWLEDGMENTS

Photos

Chapter 1 2: Alain Choisnet/The Image Bank. 6: Culver Pictures. 8 (top and bottom): The Bettmann Archive. 9: Chris J. Johnson/Stock, Boston. 10: Renee Lynn/Photo Researchers. 16: Sepp Seitz/Woodfin Camp & Associates. 17: Nancy Pierce/Black Star. 18: Peter Menzel/Stock, Boston. 19: Billy E. Barnes. 20: Catherine Ursillo/Photo Researchers. 24: Jon Feingersh/The Stock Market.

Chapter 2 29: Geoffrey Gove. 31: Matthew Naythons/Gamma-Liaison. 32: Dr. Fred Espenak/Science Photo Library-Photo Researchers. 33: Marcia Weinstein. 34: Michael Heron/Woodfin Camp & Associates. 35: Courtesy of Dr. George Engel. 36: Andree Abecassis/The Stock Market. 40: Will & Deni McIntyre/Photo Researchers. 42: John Troha/Black Star.

Chapter 3 46: Geoffrey Gove. 53: (left) Julius Weber; (center) Lester V. Bergman & Associates; (right) UPI/Compix. 54: Martin M. Rotker/Phototake. 58: Susan Leavines/Photo Researchers. 63: Kevin Vandivier/TexaStock. 64: Michael S. Yamashita/Woodfin Camp & Associates. 71: (top) Marcia Weinstein; (bottom) Spencer Grant/The Picture Cube. 72: Dan McCoy/Rainbow. 73: NIH/Science Source-Photo Researchers. 74: Phil Matt.

Chapter 4 78: Ernst Haas/Magnum Photos. 84: Ellis Herwig/Stock, Boston. 87: Norman R. Thompson/Taurus Photos. 95: Lewis Portnoy/The Stock Market. 96: Sarah Putnam/The Picture Cube. 101: Kevin Vandivier/TexaStock. 106: Joel Baldwin/The Stock Market. 109: David Hundley/The Stock Market. 110: John Blaustein/Woodfin Camp & Associates.

Chapter 5 116: Rob Atkins/The Image Bank. 119: Elyse Rieder/Photo Researchers. 121: Virginia P. Weinland/Photo Researchers. 122: William Hogarth/The Bettmann Archive. 127: Perugino, Vatican Museum, Scala/Art Resource. 128: (left) McGraw-Hill photo by Kathy Bendo; (right) McGraw-Hill photo by Kathy Bendo. 129: Frank Siteman/Stock, Boston. 135: Phyllis Rudenjak. 140: Willie L. Hill, Jr./Stock, Boston.

Chapter 6 144: Geoffrey Gove. 147: Cary Wolinsky/Stock, Boston. 149: Gabe Palmer/The Stock Market. 153: Ted Streshinsky/Photo 20-20. 155: Allan Hobson/Photo Researchers. 157: Thelma Shumsky/The Image Works. 161: Anne Marie Rousseau/The Image Works. 162: The Bettmann Archive. 167: Roy Morsch/The Stock Market. 169: Lawrence Migdale/Photo Researchers.

Chapter 7 174: Howard Sochurek/Woodfin Camp & Associates. 178: Sally Myers/Photo Researchers. 183: Janice Sheldon/Photo 20-20. 187: Jeffry W. Myers/Stock, Boston. 189: Ken Robert Buck/The Picture Cube. 190: Pawel Lewicki/University of Tulsa. 193: Peter Miller/Photo Researchers. 197: David E. Kennedy/TexaStock. 198: Ellis Herwig/The Picture Cube. 199: Harvey Stein. 201: Suzanne Szasz/Photo Researchers. 202: Brad Bower/Picture Group.

Chapter 8 207: Roy King. 209: (left) Bettmann Newsphotos; (right) Apple Computer; (bottom) Martin M. Rotker/Taurus Photos. 210: Ann McQueen/The Picture Cube. 215: Dan Budnik/Woodfin Camp & Associates. 219: Michal Heron/Woodfin Camp & Associates. 223: Courtesy of Professor Elizabeth F. Loftus. 226: Peter Vadnai/The Stock Market. 227: Spencer Grant/Photo Researchers. 231: Tom Hannon/The Picture Cube. 233: Janice M. Sheldon/Photo 20-20.

Chapter 9 240: Ulrike Welsch/Photo Researchers. 243: Childrens Television Workshop. 249: Museum Spada, Rome/The Bettmann Archive. 250: Lester Sloan/Woodfin Camp & Associates. 252: Gabe Palmer/The StockMarket. 254: Ken Kaminsky/The Picture Cube. 255: Michael Springer/Gamma Liaison. 258: Ferry/Gamma Liaison. 264: Elizabeth Crews/Stock, Boston. 267: Hank Morgan/Photo Researchers. 269: L. L. T. Rhodes/Taurus Photos. 271: Brownie Harris/The Stock Market.

Chapter 10 274: Arthur Tress. 277: Bernheim/Woodfin Camp & Associates. 278: Kevin Vandivier/TexaStock. 285: Mike Mazzaschi/Stock, Boston. 287: Diana Walker/Gamma-Liaison. 291: Lawrence Migdale/Stock, Boston. 296: C. Bonington/Woodfin Camp & Associates. 302: Paul Fusco/Magnum. 304: James D. Wilson/Woodfin Camp & Associates.

Chapter 11 308: Bill Longcore/Photo Researchers. 314: Louis Fernandez/Black Star. 315: Jacques Chenet/Woodfin Camp & Associates. 318: Paul Meredith/Life Magazine, Time Inc. 321: Richard Hutchings/Photo Researchers. 325: George Hall/Woodfin Camp & Associates. 328: David E. Kennedy/TexaStock. 330: Greg Smith/Gamma Liaison. 333: Bob Sacha and Arnold Zann/Black Star. 335: Smiley/TexaStock. 337: H. Yamaguchi/Gamma Liaison.

Chapter 12 342: Bill Longcore/Photo Researchers. 345: Owen Franken/Sygma. 347: Harry Wilks/Stock, Boston. 348: Norman Lomax/Impact/Visions. 361: Sandy Roessler/The Stock Market. 363: Don Ploke/Las Vegas Sun. 364: Dan Budnik/Woodfin Camp & Associates. 366: Southern Living Photo Researchers.

Chapter 13 375: Geoffrey Gove. 377: UPI/Bettmann Newsphotos. 378: Kenneth Murray/Photo Researchers. 379: J. Villegier/Photo Researchers. 380: Larry Lee/Westlight. 384: John J. Krieger/The Picture Cube. 385: Courtesy of R. A. Butler. 386: A. Devaney, Inc. 393: Deborah Kahn Kalas/Stock, Boston. 395: Alan Carey/The Image Works. 396: Nancy J. Pierce/Photo Researchers.

Chapter 14 402: Geoffrey Gove. 405: Don Katchusky/The Picture Cube. 407: Jaye R. Phillips/The Picture Cube. 409: Courtesy of Nina Ricci. 414: Charles Gupton/Stock, Boston. 419: Arthur Tress. 421: AP/Wide World Photos. 422: Bettye Lane/Photo Researchers. 425: Jacques M. Chenet/Woodfin Camp & Associates. 426: Carol Lee/The Picture Cube.

Chapter 15   432: Al Hamdan/The Image Bank.   435: Ellis Herwig/Stock, Boston.   438: (left and center) Petit Format/Nestle/Science Source-Photo Researchers; (right) Lennart Nilsson, "Behold Man" (Little, Brown and Company).   439: Courtesy of American Heart Association. 441: David M. Grossman.   443: Courtesy of Dr. Richard Walk.   445: (top) Allen Green/Photo Researchers; (bottom) Marcia Keegan.   446: Elizabeth Crews.   447: George Zimbel/Monkmeyer.   451: Steve Wells.   452: Dr. Carolyn Rovel-Collier, Rutgers University.   459: Susan Lapides/ Wheeler Pictures.   461: Suzanne Szasz.   463: Alan Carey/ The Image Works.

Chapter 16   468: Alfred Gescheidt/The Image Bank. 472: John Elk III/Stock, Boston.   475: Bob Daemmrich/ The Image Works.   477: Peter Menzel/Stock, Boston. 478: Michael Heron/Woodfin Camp & Associates. 480: Larry Mulvehill/Photo Researchers.   482: Mary Ellen Mark/Archive.   483: W. Marc Bernsau/The Image Works. 484: Grey Villet/Visions.   487: Karen R. Preuss/The Image Works.   488: David H. Wells/The Image Works. 493: Raymond Depardon/Magnum.   494: Hazel Hankin. 496: Chuck O'Rear/Westlight.

Chapter 17   500: Jim Finlayson.   502: The Bettmann Archive.   504: Bill Bachman/Photo Researchers.   506: Harriet Gans/The Image Works.   508: Keystone/The Image Works.   509: (top) UPI/Bettmann Newsphotos; (bottom) Robert V. Eckert, Jr./EKM-Nepenthe.   510: R. I. Lanyon, and L. D. Goodstein. Personality Assessment, p. 50. Reprinted by permission of John Wiley & Sons, Inc., New York.   511: Sepp Seitz/Woodfin Camp & Associates.   513: Billy E. Barnes.   519: Eli Reed/Magnum.   524: Paul Fusco/Magnum.   526: Glenn Kulbako/The Picture Cube.

Chapter 18   532: Bill Longcore/Longcore Maciel Studio. 535: Dan Budnik/Woodfin Camp & Associates.   536: Barbara Alper.   539: Leonard Speier.   540: Vassos, 1931. 542: Barbara Alper.   544: Peter L. Chapman/Stock, Boston.   548: Arthur Tress.   552: David E. Kennedy/ TexaStock.   557: NIH/Science Source/PhotoResearchers. 561: Peter Menzel/Stock, Boston.

Chapter 19   566: Transcribing the Internal Horizon by Lorena Laforest Bass.   572: Jacques M. Chenet/Woodfin Camp & Associates.   574: Will and Deni McIntyre/Photo Researchers.   576: The Bettmann Archive.   578: Watriss-Baldwin/Woodfin Camp & Associates.   580: Bob Daemmrich/The Image Works.   584: Leonard Speier. 589: Mark Antman/The Image Works.   590: Joel Gordon. 592: Paul Fortin/Stock, Boston.

Chapter 20   596: Geoffrey Gove.   599: Kal Muller/Woodfin Camp & Associates.   600: Dan Chidester/The Image Works.   601: Richard Pasley/Stock, Boston.   603: (left) Dick Hanley/Photo Researchers; (right) Robert Pacheco/ EKM-Nepenthe.   605: Charles Gupton/Stock, Boston. 608: Nancy J. Pierce/Photo Researchers.   609: Topham/ The Image Works.   611: Eli Reed/Magnum.   612: Spencer Grant/Taurus Photos.   614: Ted Spiegel/Black Star. 621: Alan Carey/The Image Works.

Chapter 21   626: Geoffrey Gove.   629: UPI/Bettmann Newsphotos.   631: Spencer Grant/Photo Researchers. 636: Bob Daemmrich/The Image Works.   640: Lynne Jaeger Weinstein/Woodfin Camp & Associates. 642: David C. Binder/Stock, Boston.   643: Sybil Shelton/ Monkmeyer.   644: Michael K. Nichols/Magnum Photos. 647: Cary Wolinsky/Stock, Boston.   651: Tom Campbell/ Westlight.   653: Kenneth Jarecke/Contact Press Images/ Woodfin Camp & Associates.

Chapter 22   656: Geoffrey Gove/The Image Bank. 659: Lora E. Askinazi/The Picture Cube.   661: Peter Southwick/Stock, Boston.   665: Chris Steele-Perkins/ Magnum Photos.   667: UPI/Bettmann Newsphotos. 670: UPI/Bettmann Newsphotos.   672: Michael D. Sullivan/TexaStock.   676: Mike Greenlar/The Image Works. 680: Mark Antman/The Image Works.   682: Richard Kalvar/Magnum Photos.

Chapter 23   686: Brett Froomer/The Image Bank. 689: Culver Pictures.   690: Courtesy of AT&T Archives. 692: Billy E. Barnes.   695: David M. Grossman. 699: Ann McQueen/Stock, Boston.   706: Woodfin Camp & Associates.   707: Kevin Vandivier/TexaStock. 710: Stacy Pick/Stock, Boston.   711: Wally McNamee/ Woodfin Camp & Associates.   712: Jim Pickerell/Black Star.

Art, Text, and Tables

Chapter 3   53, Figure 3.4: (A1) Photograph by Dr. Julius Weber; (B1) Photograph from Lester V. Bergman & Assoc., Inc; and (C1) Photograph from UPI/Compix.   65, Figure 3.8: Reprinted by permission of Macmillan Publishing Company, a Division of Macmillan, Inc. from *The Cerebral Cortex of Man* by Wilder Penfield and Theodore Rasmussen. Copyright 1950 by Macmillan Publishing Company; copyright renewed © 1978 Theodore Rasmussen.

Chapter 4   86, Table 4.1: From R. Teghtsoonian, "On the Exponents of Stevens's Law and the Constant in Ekman's Law," *Psychological Review*, 1971, *78*, pp. 71–80. Copyright 1971 by the American Psychological Association. Adapted by permission   93, Figure 4.7: From J. P. Frisby, *Seeing: Illusion, Brain and Mind*, London: Roxby Press, 1979.   94, Figure 4.8: From David H. Hubel and Torsten N. Wiesel, "Brain Mechanisms of Vision," *Scientific American*, September 1979. Copyright © 1979 by Scientific American, Inc. All rights reserved.   95, Figure 4.9: Reprinted with permission from *Vision Research*, 23, C. J. Owsley, R. Sekuler, and D. Siemsen, "Contrast Sensitivity throughout Adulthood,"   97, Figure 4.11: *Ishihara* Color Blindness Test Charts. Exclusively distributed by Graham Field, Inc., Hauppauge, New York, 11788. Reprinted by permission.   100, Figure 4.13: From J. Hochberg, "An Opponent Process Theory of Color Vision," *Psychological Review*, 1957, p. 64.   102, Figure 4.15: From R. S. Hefner and H. E. Hefner, "Hearing in Large and Small Dogs: Absolute Thresholds and Size of the Tympanic Membrane," *Behavioral Neuroscience*, 1983, *97*, pp. 310–318. Copyright 1983 by the American Psychological Association. Reprinted by permission.   110, Figure 4.19: From W. N. McBain and R. C. Johnson, *The Science of Ourselves*, New York: Harper & Row, 1962. Reprinted by permission.

Chapter 5   120, Figure 5.1: From "Subjective Contours," by Gaetano Kanisza. Copyright © 1976 by Scientific American, Inc. All rights reserved.   130, Figure 5.4: From R. L. Gregory, *The Intelligent Eye*, New York: McGraw-Hill, 1970.   132, Figure 5.6: Adaptation of Figure 7-22 from

Human Information Processing, by Peter H. Lindsay and Donald A. Norman, copyright © 1972 by Harcourt Brace Jovanovich, Inc. Reprinted by permission of the publisher. 139, Schematic: From L. Hainline and E. Lemerise, "Infants' Scanning of Geometric Forms Varying in Size," *Journal of Experimental Child Psychology,* 1982, *33,* p. 241. Reprinted by permission of Academic Press.

Chapter 6 153, Table 6.1: From E. R. Hilgard, *Divided Consciousness: Multiple Controls in Human Thought and Action.* Copyright © 1977. Reprinted by permission of John Wiley & Sons, Inc. 154, Table 6.2: Reproduced by permission from Oakley Ray and Charles Ksir, *Drugs, Society, & Human Behavior,* 5th ed., St. Louis, 1990, Times Mirror/Mosby College Publishing. 158, Figure 6.3: From H. P. Roffwarg, J. N. Muzio, and W. C. Dement, "Otogenetic Development of the Human Sleep-Dream Cycle," *Science,* 1966, 132, pp. 604–619. Copyright 1966 by the American Association for the Advancement of Science. 160, Figure 6.4: From R. Fischer, "A Cartography of the Ecstatic and Meditative States," *Science,* 1971, 174, p. 898. Copyright 1971 by the American Association for the Advancement of Science. 165, Figure 6.6: From E. R. Hilgard, *Hypnotic Susceptibility,* Orlando, FL: Harcourt Brace Jovanovich, Inc., 1965. Reprinted by permission of the author.

Chapter 7 191, Figure 7.4: From R. M. Colwill and R. A. Rescorla, "Post-Conditioning Devaluation of a Reinforcer Affects Instrumental Responding," *Journal of Experimental Psychology: Animal Behavior Processes,* 1985, *11,* pp. 120–132. Copyright 1985 by the American Psychological Association. Reprinted by permission. 200, Figure 7.5: From E. M. Menzel, "Cognitive Mapping in Chimpanzees," in S. H. Hulse, H. Fowler, and W. K. Honig (Eds.), *Cognitive Processes in Animal Behavior,* Hillsdale, N.J.: Lawrence Erlbaum, 1973. Reprinted by permission.

Chapter 8 211, Figure 8.1: Adapted from R. C. Atkinson and R. M. Shiffrin, "The Control of Short-Term Memory," *Scientific American,* August 1971, p. 82. Copyright © 1971 by Scientific American, Inc. All rights reserved. 214, Figure 8.3: From R. A. Nickerson and M. J. Adams, "Long-Term Memory for a Common Object," *Cognitive Psychology,* 1979, 11, pp. 287–307. Reprinted by permission of Academic Press. 216, Figure 8.5: From G. J. Hitch and M. S. Halliday, "Working Memory in Children," in D. E. Broadbent (Ed.), *Functional Aspects of Human Memory.* Originally published in *Philosophical Transactions.* Reprinted by permission of The Royal Society, London. 220, Figure 8.7: From G. H. Bower, M. B. Karlin, and A. Dueck, "Comprehension and Memory for Pictures," *Memory and Cognition,* 1975, *3,* pp. 216–229. Reprinted by permission of the Psychosomatic Society, Inc. 221, Figure 8.8: From L. Carmichael, H. P. Hogan, and A. A. Walter, "An Experimental Study of the Effect of Language on the Reproduction of Visually Perceived Form," *Journal of Experimental Psychology,* 1932, *15,* pp. 73–86. 226, Figure 8.9: From E. K. Warrington and L. Weiskrantz, "New Method of Testing Long-Term Retention with Special Reference to Amnesiac Patients." Reprinted by permission from *Nature* Vol. 217, pp. 972–974. Copyright © 1968 Macmillan Magazines Ltd. 229, Figure 8.10: From *Memory and the Brain* by Larry R. Squire. Copyright © 1987 by Oxford University Press, Inc. Reproduced by permission. 235, Figure 8.12: From G. H. Bower, M. Clark, D. Winzenz, and A. Lesgold, "Hierarchical Retrieval Schemes in Recall of Categorized Word Lists," *Journal of*

Verbal Learning and Verbal Behavior, 1969, *8,* pp. 323–343. Reprinted by permission of Academic Press. 235, Figure 8.13: From R. S. Day, "Alternative Representations," in G. H. Bower (Ed.), *The Psychology of Learning and Motivation: Advances in Research and Theory,* 1988, 22. Reprinted by permission of Academic Press.

Chapter 9 245, Figure 9.1: From S. K. Reed, "Pattern Recognition and Categorization," *Cognitive Psychology,* 1972, *3,* pp. 383–407. Reprinted by permission of Academic Press. 247, Table 9.1: From E. H. Rosch, C. B. Mervis, W. Gray, D. Johnson, and P. Boyes-Braem, "Basic Objects in Natural Categories," *Cognitive Psychology,* 1976, *8,* pp. 382–439. Reprinted by permission of Academic Press. 247, Figure 9.2: Adapted from *Ghosts in the Mind's Machine, Creating and Using Images in the Brain,* by Stephen Michael Kosslyn, by permission of W. W. Norton & Company, Inc. Copyright © 1983 by Stephen M. Kosslyn. 248, Figure 9.3: From R. A. Finke and K. Slayton, "Explorations of Creative Visual Synthesis in Mental Imagery," *Memory and Cognition,* 1988, *16,* pp. 252–257. Reprinted by permission of the Psychosomatic Society, Inc. 257, Figure 9.4: From D. J. Kavanaugh and G. H. Bower, "Mood and Self-Efficacy: Impact of Joy and Sadness on Perceived Capabilities," *Cognitive Therapy and Research,* 1985. Reprinted by permission of Plenum Publishing Corporation. 261, Figure 9.6: From M. L. Glick and K. J. Holyoak, "Analogical Problem Solving," *Cognitive Psychology,* 1980, 12, pp. 306–355. Reprinted by permission of Academic Press. 263, Figure 9.7: From K. Duncker, "On Problem Solving," trans. L. S. Lees, *Psychological Monographs,* 1945, *58,* as it appeared in A. L. Glass and K. J. Holyoak, *Cognition,* 2d edition, New York: McGraw-Hill, Inc., 1986. 264, Figure 9.8: From D. F. Halpern, *Thought and Knowledge: An Introduction to Critical Thinking,* Hillsdale, NJ: Lawrence Erlbaum, 1984. Reprinted by permission. 268, Box: From M. M. Mitchell Waldrop, "Toward a Unified Theory of Cognition," *Science,* 1988, *241,* pp. 27–29. Copyright 1988 by the American Association for the Advancement of Science. 269, Figure 9.12: © Len Speir. 270, Figure 9.13: From *How To Solve Problems* by W. A. Wickelgren. Copyright © 1974 by W. H. Freeman and Company. Reprinted with permission.

Chapter 10 279, Figure 10.1: From J. Berko, "The Child's Learning of English Morphology," *Word,* 1958, *14,* pp. 150–177. Reprinted by permission of the International Linguistic Association. 280: Poem—The lines from "since feeling is first" are reprinted from *Is 5* poems by E. E. Cummings, Edited by George James Firmage, by permission of Liveright Publishing Corporation. Copyright © 1985 by E. E. Cummings Trust. Copyright 1926 by Horace Liveright. Copyright © 1954 by E. E. Cummings. Copyright © 1985 by George James Firmage. Figure—Reprinted by permission of the publishers from *The Signs of Language* by Edward S. Klima and Ursula Bellugi, Cambridge, Mass.: Harvard University Press, Copyright © 1979 by the President and Fellows of Harvard College. 297, Figure 10.4: From P. Ekman, W. V. Friesen, and P. Ellsworth, *Emotion in the Human Face: Guidelines for Research and an Integration of Findings,* Elmsford, NY: Pergamon Press, 1972. Reprinted by permission. 299, Figure 10.6: Figure 5.1 from *Psychology and Language,* by Herbert H. Clark and Eve V. Clark, copyright © 1977 by Harcourt Brace Jovanovich, Inc. Reprinted by permission of the publisher.

Chapter 11 312, Figure 11.1: Weschler Intelligence Scale for Children and Adults. Copyright © 1949, 1950, 1955,

Hill, 1950.   517, Table 17.2: Based on W. G. Dahlstrom, G. S. Welsch, and L. E. Dahlstrom, *An MMPI Handbook*, Vol. 1. Minneapolis: University of Minnesota Press, 1972. 525, Table 17.3: From *Motivation and Personality* by Abraham H. Maslow. Copyright 1954 by Harper & Row, Publishers, Inc. Copyright © 1970 by Abraham H. Maslow. Reprinted by permission of the publisher.   527, Figure 17.3: From *Psychology: A Study of a Science*, Volume 3 by S. Koch, ed. Copyright © 1959 by McGraw-Hill, Inc. Used by permission of McGraw-Hill Publishing Company.

Chapter 18   540, Figure 18.1: From J. Vassos, *Phobia*, New York: Dover Publications, Inc. Reprinted by permission.   552, Figure 18.3: From L. Pfeifer, "A Subjective Report of Tactile Hallucination in Schizophrenia," *Journal of Clinical Psychology*, 1970, *26*, pp. 57–60. Reprinted with permission of Clinical Psychology Publishing Co., Inc., 4 Conant Square, Brandon, VT 05733.   554, Figure 18.4: Both, courtesy of Al Vercoutere, Camarillo State Hospital. 556, Figure 18.5: From I. I. Gottesman, "Schizophrenia and Genetics: Where Are We? Are You Sure?" in L. C. Wynne, R. L. Cromwell, and S. Matthysse (Eds.), *The Nature of Schizophrenia: New Approaches to Research and Treatment*. Copyright © 1978. Reprinted by permission of John Wiley & Sons, Inc.   Figure 18.11: From M. R. Rosenzweig and A. L. Leiman, *Physiological Psychology*, 2d ed., Lexington, Mass: D. C. Heath & Company. Reprinted by permission of the author.

Chapter 19   573, Table 19.1: From J. Wolpe and D. Wolpe, *Life without Fear*, Oakland, CA: New Harbinger Publications. Reprinted by permission.   581, Figure 19.1: Adapted from M. L. Smith, G. V. Glass, and T. I. Miller, *The Benefits of Psychotherapy*, The Johns Hopkins University Press, Baltimore/London 1980.

Chapter 20   607, Table 20.1: Reprinted with permission from *Journal of Psychosomatic Research*, Vol. 11, T. H. Holmes and R. H. Rahe, "The Social Readjustment Rating Scale," Copyright 1967, Pergamon Press plc.   612, Figure 20.1: From A. D. Kanner, et al., "Comparison of Two Modes of Stress Measurement: Daily Hassles and Uplifts Versus Major Life Events," *Journal of Behavioral Medicine*, 1981, *4*, pp. 1–39. Reprinted by permission of Plenum Publishing Corporation.   613, Figure 20.2: From S. E. Taylor, *Health Psychology*, New York: McGraw-Hill, 1986. 615, Figure 20.4: From *Stress without Distress* by Hans Seyle, MD. Copyright © 1974 by Hans Seyle, MD. Reprinted by permission of Harper & Row, Publishers, Inc.; as it appeared in Taylor, *Health Psychology*, New York: McGraw-Hill.

Chapter 21   630, Figure 21.1: From L. Festinger and J. M. Carlsmith, "Cognitive Consequences of Forced Compliance," *Journal of Abnormal and Social Psychology*, 1959, *58*, pp. 203–210. Copyright 1959 by the American Psychological Association. Reprinted by permission; as it appeared in James W. Vander Zanden, *Social Psychology*, New York: McGraw-Hill.   633, Figure 21.2: From J. Cooper and R. H. Fazio, "A New Look at Dissonance Theory," in L. Berkowitz (Ed.), *Advances in Experimental Social Psychology*, Vol. 17, pp. 229–266. Reprinted by permission of Academic Press, as it appeared in Meyer, *Social Psychology*, New York: McGraw-Hill.   635, Figure 21.3: From R. E. Petty and J. T. Cacioppo, "The Effects of Involvement on Responses to Argument Quality and Quantity: Central and Peripheral Routes to Persuasion," *Journal of Personality and Social Psychology*, 1984, *46*, pp. 69–81. Copyright 1984 by the American Psychological Association. Reprinted by

permission.   645, Extract: "We and They," from *Debits and Credits* by Rudyard Kipling. Copyright 1926 by Rudyard Kipling. Reprinted by permission of Doubleday, a division of Bantam Doubleday Dell Publishing Group, Inc. 650, Figure 21.4: From G. Marks, N. Miller, and G. Maruyama, "Effect of Targets' Physical Attractiveness on Assumption of Similarity," *Journal of Personality and Social Psychology*, 1981, *41*, pp. 198–206. Copyright 1981 by the American Psychological Association. Adapted by permission.

Chapter 22   663, Figure 22.2: From S. E. Asch, "Opinions and Social Pressure," *Scientific American*, November 1955, *193*, pp. 31–35. Copyright © 1955 by Scientific American, Inc. All rights reserved.   668, Figure 22.3: From S. Milgram, "Behavioral Study of Obedience," *Journal of Abnormal and Social Psychology*, 1963, *67*, pp. 371–378. Copyright 1963 by the American Psychological Association. Adapted by permission.   671, Figure 22.4: From C. D. Batson, J. Fultz, and P. A. Schoenrade, "Distress and Empathy: Two Qualitatively Distinctive Vicarious Emotions with Different Motivational Consequences," *Journal of Personality*, 1987, *55*, pp. 19–40. Adapted by permission of Duke University Press.   673, Figure 22.5: Based on B. Latane, and J. M. Darley, "Help in a Crisis: Bystander Response to an Emergency," in J. W. Thibaut, J. T. Spence, and R. C. Carson (Eds.), *Contemporary Topics in Social Psychology*, Glenview, IL: Scott, Foresman, 1976. 674, Figure 22.6: From K. R. Scherer, R. P. Abeles, and C. S. Fischer, *Human Aggression and Conflict*, Englewood Cliffs, NJ: Prentice Hall., 1975. Adapted by permission of the authors.   675, Figure 22.7: From A. Bandura, *Aggression: A Social Learning Analysis*, © 1973. Adapted by permission of Prentice Hall, Inc., Englewood Cliffs, New Jersey.   679, Figure 22.9: From H. Wichman, "Effects of Isolation and Communication in a Two-Person Game," *Journal of Personality and Social Psychology*, 1970, *16*, pp. 114–120. Copyright 1970 by the American Psychological Association. Adapted by permission.

Chapter 23   691, Chapter 23.1: Reproduced by permission from the *Bennett Mechanical Comprehension Test*. Copyright © 1942, 1967–1970 by The Psychological Corporation. Reproduced by permission. All rights reserved. 697, Figure 23.2: From J. E. Hunter and R. F. Hunter, "Validity and Utility of Alternative Predictors of Job Performance," *Psychological Bulletin*, 1984, *96*, pp. 72–98. Copyright 1984 by the American Psychological Association. Adapted by permission.   701, Figure 23.3: From D. C. Anderson, C. R. Crowell, M. Doman, and G. S. Howard, "Performance Posting, Goal Setting, and Activity Contingent Praise as Applied to a University Hockey Team," *Journal of Applied Psychology*, 1988, *73*, pp. 87–95. Copyright 1988 by the American Psychological Association. Reprinted by permission.   708, Table 23.1: Adapted and reprinted from *Leadership and Decision-Making*, by Victor H. Vroom and Philip W. Yetton, by permission of the University of Pittsburgh Press. © 1973 by University of Pittsburgh Press.   709, Figure 23.5: Reprinted from *The New Leadership: Managing Participation in Organizations* by Victor H. Vroom and, Arthur G. Jago, 1988, Englewood Cliffs, N.J.: Prentice-Hall. Copyright 1987 by V. H. Vroom and A. G. Jago. Used with permission of the authors.

Appendix   725, Figure A.6: From J. T. Spence, J. W. Cotton, B. J. Underwood, and C. P. Duncan, *Elementary Statistics*, 3d ed., © 1976. Reprinted by permission of Prentice Hall, Inc., Englewood Cliffs, New Jersey.